March 2–5, 2015
Portland, Oregon, USA

I0060977

Association for Computing Machinery

Advancing Computing as a Science & Profession

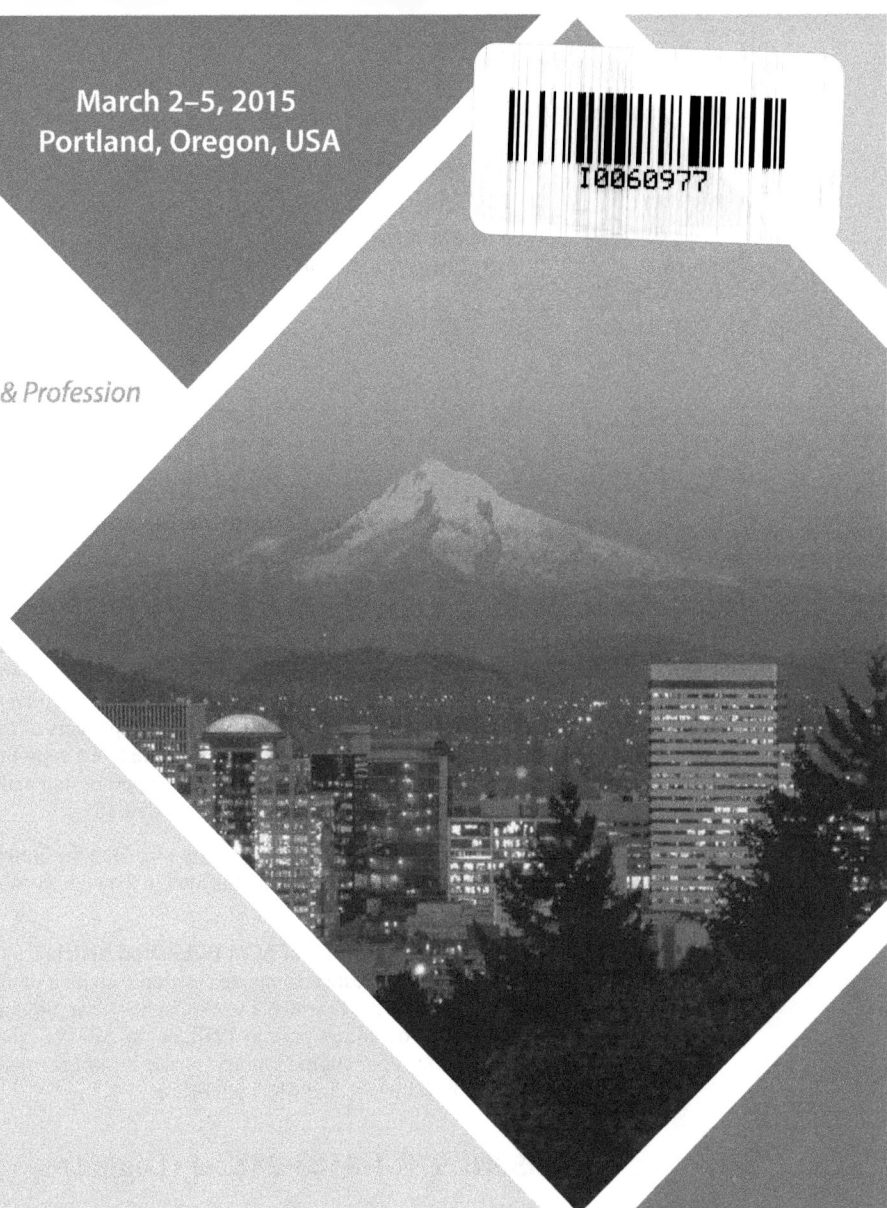

HRI'15

Proceedings of the 2015 ACM/IEEE International Conference on
Human-Robot Interaction

Sponsored by:
ACM SIGCHI, ACM SIGART, and IEEE RAS
In co-operation with:
AAAI and HFES

**Association for
Computing Machinery**

Advancing Computing as a Science & Profession

The Association for Computing Machinery
2 Penn Plaza, Suite 701
New York, New York 10121-0701

Notice to Past Authors of ACM-Published Articles
ACM intends to create a complete electronic archive of all articles and/or other material previously published by ACM. If you have written a work that has been previously published by ACM in any journal or conference proceedings prior to 1978, or any SIG Newsletter at any time, and you do NOT want this work to appear in the ACM Digital Library, please inform permissions@acm.org, stating the title of the work, the author(s), and where and when published.

ISBN: 978-1-4503-2882-1 (Digital)

ISBN: 978-1-4503-3511-9 (Print)

Additional copies may be ordered prepaid from:

ACM Order Department
PO Box 30777
New York, NY 10087-0777, USA

Phone: 1-800-342-6626 (USA and Canada)
+1-212-626-0500 (Global)
Fax: +1-212-944-1318
E-mail: acmhelp@acm.org
Hours of Operation: 8:30 am – 4:30 pm ET

Printed in the USA

HRI'15 Chairs' Welcome

We welcome you to the *Tenth Annual ACM/IEEE International Conference on Human-Robot Interaction* (*HRI 2015*). The HRI Conference is highly selective and aims to showcase the very best interdisciplinary and multidisciplinary research in human-robot interaction with roots in robotics, social psychology, cognitive science, human-computer interaction, human factors, artificial intelligence, design, engineering, etc. Robotics has become increasingly multidisciplinary in order to realize realizing capable and collaborative robot systems that are used and validated in both laboratory and real-world settings. We therefore invite broad participation and encourage discussion and sharing of ideas across a diverse audience.

This year's overall conference theme, titled "Broadening HRI: Enabling Technologies, Designs, Methods, and Knowledge," highlights the different types of contributions made by our multidisciplinary community centered around developing robotic systems that operate, collaborate with, learn from, and meet the needs of the human users. Acknowledgment and encouragement of this diversity was supported in the peer-review process by establishing five subcommittees, "Studies of HRI," "Enabling Technologies, "Enabling Designs," "Enabling Methods," and "Enabling Knowledge," each with a chair and dedicated program committee members. Together with the subcommittee chairs, we established and applied different set of review criteria for each of the five contribution types in order to represent the diversity of contributions in the conference program.

HRI is a highly selective conference, and this year was no exception. The conference attracted 169 submissions from Asia-Pacific, Europe, the Middle East, and North America. Full Papers were aligned with a subcommittee, who managed the thorough review and discussion of the papers following a double-blind process. The process utilized a rebuttal phase, a shepherding mechanism, and a worldwide team of interdisciplinary reviewers. At the end of the process, the program committee selected 43 (25%) of the submissions. Due to the joint sponsorship of ACM and IEEE, papers are archived in both the ACM Digital Library and IEEE Xplore.

Accompanying the full papers are the Late Breaking Reports, Videos, and Demos. Out of 102 submissions, 92 (90%) Late Breaking Reports were accepted and are presented at the conference poster sessions. Sixteen (84%) short videos were accepted for presentation during a dedicated video session from among 19 submissions. The program also includes nine demos of robot systems for all participants to interact with during the conference. The invited panel session, titled "Human-Robot Interaction: Law on the home front" will discuss contemporary and emerging issues in HRI. Rounding out the program are three keynote speakers who are inspiring leaders of the field and will discuss topics relevant to HRI: Dr. Antonio Bicchi, Dr. Takeo Igarashi, and Daniel H. Wilson.

Hosting HRI 2015 was not feasible without the extensive volunteer effort put forth by the organizing committee, program committee, reviewers and the Steering Committee. We thank the keynote speakers, panelists, and financial donators for their participation. The conference sponsors are ACM SIGCHI, ACM SIGAI, and IEEE Robotics and Automation. The conference is in cooperation with AAAI and HFES.

Finally, we are especially thankful for the hard work by authors who submitted papers, videos, and demos. HRI is a vibrant community. We hope you will be inspired by the conference content and networking relationships that you can build during the conference. Please enjoy your visit to Portland.

Julie A. Adams
HRI'15 General Co-Chair
Vanderbilt University, USA

William Smart
HRI'15 General Co-Chair
Oregon State University, USA

Bilge Mutlu
HRI'15 Program Co-Chair
University of Wisconsin–Madison, USA

Leila Takayama
HRI'15 Program Co-Chair
Google[X], USA

Table of Contents

Keynote Address

Session D: Perceptions of Robots
Session Chair: Guy Hoffman *(IDC Herzliya)*,

Session E: Robots as Social Agents
Session Chair: Tony Belpaeme *(Plymouth University)*

Session F: Human-Robot Teams

Session Chair: James E. Young *(University of Manitoba)*

Keynote Address

Session G: Multi-modal Capabilities

Session Chair: Yukie Nagai *(Osaka University)*

Session H: Human Behaviors, Activities, and Environments, Part 1

Session Chair: Maha Salem *(University of Hertfordshire)*

Session I: Human Behaviors, Activities, and Environments, Part 2

Session Chair: Malte Jung *(Cornell University)*

HRI 2015 Organization

Organizing Committee

General Co-Chairs
Julie A. Adams, Vanderbilt University, USA
William Smart, Oregon State University, USA

Program Co-Chairs
Bilge Mutlu, University of Wisconsin–Madison, USA
Leila Takayama, Google[X], USA

Local Arrangement Co-Chairs
Maya Cakmak, University of Washington, USA
Geoff Hollinger, Oregon State University, USA

Finance Co-Chairs
Sonia Chernova, Worcester Polytechnic Institute, USA
Franz Kummert, Bielefield University, Germany

Workshop and Tutorials Co-Chairs
Kai Oliver Arras, University of Freiburg, Germany
Majd Sakr, Carnegie Mellon University, USA

Late-Breaking Reports Co-Chairs
Guy Hoffman, IDC Herzlia, Israel
Manja Lohse, Twente University, The Netherlands

Video Session Co-Chairs
Hirotaka Osawa, University of Tsukuba, Japan
Iolanda Leite, Yale University, USA

Panels Chair
Ryan Calo, University of Washington, USA
Mike Goodrich, Brigham Young University, USA
Gerhard Sagerer, Bielefeld University, Germany

Publications Co-Chairs
Laurel Riek, Notre Dame, USA
Frank Broz, University of Plymouth, UK

Fundraising & Exhibitions Co-Chairs
Astrid Weiss, Vienna University of Technology, Austria
Daisuke Sakamoto, The University of Tokyo, Japan
Jennifer Burke, Boeing Research and Technology, USA

Design Chair
Sonya S. Kwak, Ewha Womans University, South Korea

Web Chair
Cindy Bethel, Mississippi State University, USA

Publicity Co-Chairs
Andrea Thomaz, Georgia Institute of Technology, USA
Masahiro Shiomi, ATR, Japan
Britta Wrede, Bielefield University, Germany

Registration Co-Chairs
Jacob Crandall, Masdar Institute of Science and Technology, UAE
Nathan Kirchner, University of Technology Sydney, Australia

Demo Co-Chairs
Dylan Glas, ATR, Japan
Jim Young, University of Manitoba, Canada

HRI Steering Committee

Co-chairs
- Vanessa Evers, University of Twente, The Netherlands
- Holly Yanco, University of Massachusetts-Lowell, USA

Members (in alphabetical order)
- Kai Oliver Arras, Freiburg University, Germany
- Tony Belpaeme, University of Plymouth, UK
- Sonia Chernova, Worcester Polytechnic Institute, USA
- Jodi Forlizzi, Carnegie Mellon University, USA
- Jeonghye Han, Cheongju National University of Education, South Korea
- Michita Imai, Keio University, Japan
- Julie A. Adams, Vanderbilt University, USA
- Hideaki Kazuoka, University of Tsukuba, Japan
- Sara Kiesler, Carnegie Mellon University, USA
- Franz Kummert, Bielefeld University, Germany
- Bilge Mutlu, University of Wisconsin–Madison, USA
- Gerhard Sagerer, University of Bielefeld, Germany
- Brian Scassellatti, Yale University, USA
- Masahiro Shiomi, ATR, Japan
- Bill Smart, Oregon State University, USA
- Leila Takayama, Google [X], USA
- Fumihide Tanaka, the University of Tokyo, Japan
- Andrea Thomaz, Georgia Institute of Technology, USA
- Manfred Tscheligi, University of Salzburg, Austria

Past Chairs
- Julie A. Adams, Vanderbilt University, USA
- Takayuki Kanda, ATR, Japan

Program Committee by sub-committee

Studies of HRI
- **Chair**: Takayuki Kanda, ATR
- Rachid Alami, LAAS/CNRS
- Tony Belpaeme, Plymouth University
- Cindy Bethel, Mississippi State University
- Guy Hoffman, IDC Herzliya
- Yukie Nagai, Osaka University
- Brian Scassellati, Yale University
- Adriana Tapus, ENSTA-ParisTech
- James Young, University of Manitoba

Enabling Technologies
- **Chair**: Nicholas Roy, Massachusetts Institute of Technology
- Brenna Argall, Northwestern University
- Kai Oliver Arras, University of Freiburg
- Maya Cakmak, University of Washington
- Sonia Chernova, Worcester Polytechnic Institute
- Ana Paiva, Technical University of Lisbon
- Julie Shah, Massachusetts Institute of Technology
- Siddhartha Srinivasa, Carnegie Mellon University
- Stefanie Tellex, Brown University

Enabling Designs
- **Chair**: Jodi Forlizzi, Carnegie Mellon University
- Wendy Ju, Stanford University
- Sonya Kwak, Ewha Womans University
- Mark Neerincx, TNO & Delft University of Technology

Enabling Methods
- **Chair**: Greg Trafton, Naval Research Laboratory
- Kerstin Fischer, South Denmark University
- Dylan Glas, ATR
- Min Kyung Lee, Carnegie Mellon University
- Laurel Riek, University of Notre Dame
- Selma Sabanovic, Indiana University
- Aaron Steinfeld, Carnegie Mellon University
- Andrea Thomaz, Georgia Institute of Technology
- Holly Yanco, University of Massachusetts Lowell

Enabling Knowledge
- **Chair**: Manfred Tscheligi, University of Salzburg & AIT
- Vanessa Evers, University of Twente
- Malte Jung, Cornell University
- Astrid Weiss, Vienna University of Technology

Reviewers

Siggi Aðalgeirsson
Henny Admoni
Baris Akgun
Samer Al Moubayed
Alexandre Alapetite
Mehdi Ammi
Ana-Lucia Ureche
Allison Anderson
Sean Andrist
Salvatore Maria Anzalone
Amin Atrash
Maria Vanessa aus der Wieschen
Eleanor Avrunin
Shahar Ayal
Ruth Aylett
Wilma Bainbridge
Emilia Barakova
Wolmet Barendregt
Christoph Bartneck
Timo Baumann
Paul Baxter
Christian Becker-Asano
Jenay Beer
Momotaz Begum
Nicola Bellotto
Casey Bennett
Aude Billard
Joydeep Biswas
Amy Blank
Laura Boccanfuso
Jim Boerkoel
Dan Bohus
Margot Brereton
Mason Bretan
Joost Broekens
Daniel Brown
Frank Broz
Drazen Brscic
Magdalena Bugajska
Andrea Bunt
Pablo Bustos
Julie Carpenter
Ophelie Carreras
Daniel Carruth
Ginevra Castellano
Elizabeth Cha

Vicky Charissi
Marcus Cheetham
Mohamed Chetouani
Pauline Chevalier
Jung Ju Choi
Aurelie Clodic
Emily Collins
Marco Controzzi
Jacob Crandall
Christopher Crick
Elizabeth Croft
Joseph Crumpton
Nicola Doering
David Daney
Kate Darling
Daniel Davison
Maartje de Graaf
Joachim de Greeff
Ravindra De Silva
Frederic Dehais
Yiannis Demiris
Virginie Demulier
Pasquale Dente
Nick dePalma
Matthew Derry
Munjal Desai
Lorin Dole
Anca Dragan
Mauro Dragone
Dominique Duhaut
Ehsan Esfahani
Friederike Eyssel
David Feil-Seifer
Thomas Feix
François Ferland
Joao Filipe Ferreira
Alexander Fiannaca
Thomas Fincannon
Julia Fink
Nicholas FitzGerald
Maxwell Forbes
Deborah Forster
Mary Ellen Foster
Kilian Foth
Susan Fussell
Juergen Gall

Jorge Gallego Perez
Teena Garrison
Mamoun Gharbi
Irini Giannopulu
Guillaume Gibert
Matthew Gombolay
Michael Goodrich
Goren Gordon
Jillian Greczek
Elena Corina Grigore
Jonathan Grizou
Daniel Grollman
Jaap Ham
Jeonghye Han
Marc Hanheide
Maaike Harbers
Caroline Harriott
Justin Hart
Kris Hauser
Brad Hayes
Cory J. Hayes
Zachary Henkel
Jonathan Samuel Herberg
Laura Herlant
Koen Hindriks
Shivayogi Hiremath
Guy Hochman
Ayanna Howard
Thomas Howard
Iris Howley
Kaijen Hsiao
Chien-Ming Huang
Justin Huang
Takamasa Iio
Michita Imai
Tariq Iqbal
Hisashi Ishihara
Serena Ivaldi
Chris Jansen
Lars Christian Jensen
Florian Jentsch
Wafa Johal
Matthew Johnson
Michiel Joosse
Celine Jost
Vikram Kapila

James Kennedy
Harmish Khambaitha
Cory Kidd
Eun Ho Kim
Joseph Kim
Min-Gyu Kim
Yunkyung Kim
Alexandra Kirsch
Ross A. Knepper
Heather Knight
W. Bradley Knox
Thomas Kollar
Takanori Komatsu
Hema Koppula
Jacqueline Kory Westlund
Hatice Kose-Bagci
Hadas Kress-Gazit
Annica Kristoffersson
Ivana Kruijff
Dieta Kuchenbrandt
Dana Kulic
Dennis Kuster
Walter Lasecki
Daniel Lazewatsky
Hee Rin Lee
Kenton Lee
Hagen Lehmann
Bastian Leibe
Iolanda Leite
Severin Lemaignan
Jamy Li
Alexandru Litoiu
Katrin Lohan
Manja Lohse
Rosemarijn Looije
Manuel Lopes
Tamara Lorenz
Netaya Lotze
Amy Loutfi
James MacGlashan
Stephane Magnenat
Jim Mainprice
Maxim Makatchev
Nikolas Martelaro
German Martin Garcia
Jean-Claude Martin
Samuel Mascarenhas

Cynthia Matuszek
William McMillan
Ross Mead
Elizabeth Meddeb
Jody Medich
Cetin Mericli
Mark Micire
Takashi Minato
Nicole Mirnig
AJung Moon
Luis Yoichi Morales Saiki
Emily Mower Provost
Hideyuki Nakanishi
Yasuto Nakanishi
Scott Niekum
Stefanos Nikolaidis
Ilana Nisky
Tatsuya Nomura
David Nunez
Kohei Ogawa
Petter Ogren
Billy Okal
Tal Oron
Hirotaka Osawa
P. B. Sujit
Oskar Palinko
Caroline Pantofaru
Chung Hyuk Park
Hae Won Park
Catherine Pelachaud
Andre Pereira
Sylvie Pesty
Tamara Peyton
Rebecca Pierce
Karola Pitsch
Cedric Pradallier
Irene Rae
Aditi Ramachandran
Markus Rank
Nathan Ratliff
Francesco Rea
Robin Read
Tiago Ribeiro
Charles Rich
Katja Richter
Lionel Robert
Katharina Rohlfing

Raquel Ros
Silvia Rossi
Agata Rozga
Martin Saerbeck
Daisuke Sakamoto
Maha Salem
Allison Sauppe
Kristin Schaefer
Lars Schillingmann
Samuel B. Schorr
Alessandra Sciutti
Johanna Seibt
Pedro Sequeira
Khansari-Zadeh Seyed
    Mohammad
Ehud Sharlin
Mohammad Shayganfar
Solace Shen
Masahiro Shiomi
Michael Shomin
Elaine Short
Candace Sidner
Daniel Sidobre
David Silvera-Tawil
Reid Simmons
Ramona Simut
David Sirkin
Emrah Akin Sisbot
Elizabeth Sklar
Ronit Slyper
Nanja Smets
Ryan N. Smith
Ross Sowell
Anne Spalanzani
Samuel Spaulding
Aaron St. Clair
Scott Stanford
Leia Stirling
Megan Strait
Hidenobu Sumioka
Ja-Young Sung
Katelyn Swift-Spong
Katia Sycara
Kazuki Takashima
Zheng-Hua Tan
Fumihide Tanaka
Kazunori Terada

Serge Thill
Eran Toch
Russell Toris
Tammy Toscos
Khiet Truong
Yassine Tsalamlal
Katherine Tsui
Vaibhav Vasant Unhelkar
Marynel Vazquez
Michel Valstar
Mike Van der Loos

Jurriaan van Diggelen
Bram Vanderborght
Rodrigo Ventura
Cordula Vesper
Michael Villano
John Voiklis
Dirk Vom Lehn
Sven Wachsmuth
Petra Wagner
Matthew Walter
Michael Walters

Gil Weinberg
Frances Wijnen
Britta Wrede
Anqi Xu
Tomoko Yonezawa
Yuichiro Yoshikawa
Chen Yu
Michael Zillich
Jakub Zlotowski
Oren Zuckerman

HRI 2015 Sponsors & Supporters

Sponsors

SIGCHI

acm SIGAI

IEEE
Robotics & Automation Society

In Cooperation with

HF ES

aaai

Supporters and Donators

Gold Supporter

OSU
Oregon State
UNIVERSITY

College of Engineering

Silver Supporter

𝒟𝒾𝓈𝓃𝑒𝓎 Research

Google™

Bronze Supporters

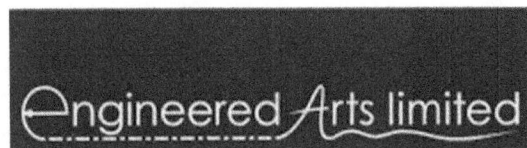

HONDA

engineered Arts limited

Student Travel Grant Donator

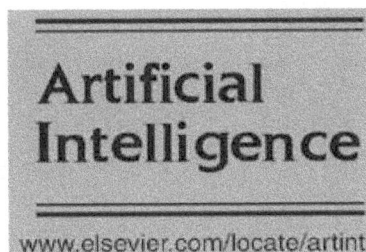

Artificial
Intelligence

www.elsevier.com/locate/artint

Design Everything by Yourself

Takeo Igarashi

Professor of Computer Science Department at the University of Tokyo

takeo@acm.org

Abstract

I will introduce our research project (design interface project) aiming at the development of various design tools for end-users. We live in a mass-production society today and everyone buy and use same things all over the world. This is cheap, but not necessarily ideal for individual persons. We envision that computer tools that help people to design things by themselves can enrich their lives. To that end, we develop innovative interaction techniques for end users to (1) create rich graphics such as three-dimensional models and animations by simple sketching (2) design their own real-world, everyday objects such as clothing and furniture with real-time physical simulation integrated in a simple geometry editor, and (3) design the behavior of their personal robots and give instructions to them to satisfy their particular needs.

ACM Classification
H.5 INFORMATION INTERFACES AND PRESENTATION (e.g., HCI): H.5.2 User Interfaces: Graphical user interfaces (GUI)

Keywords
Consumer generated contents; personal fabrication; human-robot interaction.

Short Bio
Takeo Igarashi is a Professor of Computer Science Department at The University of Tokyo. He received a Ph.D from the Department of Information Engineering at The University of Tokyo in 2000.

He then worked as a post doctoral research associate at Brown University (2000 - 2002). He joined the University of Tokyo as an Assistant Professor in 2002, and became a Professor in 2011. He also served as a director for JST ERATO Igarashi Design Interface project (2007 – 2013). His research interest is in user interfaces and interactive computer graphics. He has received several awards including the IBM Science Prize, the JSPS Prize, the ACM SIGGRAPH 2006 Significant New Researcher Award, and the Katayanagi Prize in Computer Science.

HRI'15, March 2–5, 2015, Portland, Oregon, USA.
ACM 978-1-4503-2883-8/15/03.
http://dx.doi.org/10.1145/2696454.2714389

Design and Evaluation of a Peripheral Robotic Conversation Companion

Guy Hoffman[1], Oren Zuckerman[1], Gilad Hirschberger[2], Michal Luria[1], Tal Shani-Sherman[2]

[1]Media Innovation Lab
IDC Herzliya
Herzliya 46150, Israel
{hoffman,orenz,michal.luria}@idc.ac.il

[2]School of Psychology
IDC Herzliya
Herzliya 46150, Israel
{ghirschberger,talshani}@idc.ac.il

ABSTRACT

We present the design, implementation, and evaluation of a peripheral empathy-evoking robotic conversation companion, *Kip1*. The robot's function is to increase people's awareness to the effect of their behavior towards others, potentially leading to behavior change. Specifically, Kip1 is designed to promote non-aggressive conversation between people. It monitors the conversation's nonverbal aspects and maintains an emotional model of its reaction to the conversation. If the conversation seems calm, Kip1 responds by a gesture designed to communicate curious interest. If the conversation seems aggressive, Kip1 responds by a gesture designed to communicate fear. We describe the design process of Kip1, guided by the principles of *peripheral* and *evocative*. We detail its hardware and software systems, and a study evaluating the effects of the robot's autonomous behavior on couples' conversations. We find support for our design goals. A conversation companion reacting to the conversation led to more gaze attention, but not more verbal distraction, compared to a robot that moves but does not react to the conversation. This suggests that robotic devices could be designed as companions to human-human interaction without compromising the natural communication flow between people. Participants also rated the reacting robot as having significantly more social human character traits and as being significantly more similar to them. This points to the robot's potential to elicit people's empathy.

Categories and Subject Descriptors

H.1.2 [**Models and Principles**]: User/Machine Systems; J.4 [**Computer Applications**]: Social and Behavioral Sciences—psychology.

General Terms

Experimentation, Human Factors.

Keywords

Human-robot interaction; Design; Robotic companions; Behavior change; Empathy; Ambient kinetic tangibles; Smartphone robots.

HRI '15, March 02 - 05 2015, Portland, OR, USA
Copyright is held by the author(s). Publication rights licensed to ACM.
ACM 978-1-4503-2883-8/15/03...$15.00
http://dx.doi.org/10.1145/2696454.2696495

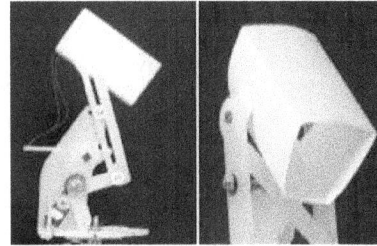

Fig. 1. *Kip1*, a peripheral robotic conversation companion.

1. INTRODUCTION

When people interact, they are often unaware of the effect their behavior has on others. To address this issue we are designing and developing a series of peripheral robotic companions, aimed to accompany natural human-human interaction, and reflect the effect of one's behavior through subtle physical gestures. We hope that the presence of such a peripheral companion may lead to increased awareness among the interacting humans without compromising their natural communication pattern. This paper describes such a robot, *Kip1*, designed to promote non-aggressive conversation between people.

Kip1 is designed as a small desktop structure, reminiscent of a lamp (Fig. 1). When a conversation is taking place near Kip1, it monitors the nonverbal content of the conversation, e.g., speech timing, silences, and loudness. The robot tracks speaking vs. silent segments, and the ongoing and incidental loudness of the conversants. If there is no ongoing conversation, Kip1 is in a calm, relaxed state, indicated by a slow, deep "breathing" gesture. If an ongoing conversation is calm, Kip1 shows interest by stretching upwards in a "curious" gesture towards one of the participants. If, however, the conversation becomes too loud, Kip1 retracts into a "scared" gesture, shivering and lowering its head.

Unlike most human-robot interaction research, concerned with direct interaction between people and robots, this project's design goal is to supplement face-to-face human-human interaction. Peripheral conversation companions are meant to influence and enhance direct human interaction, rather than replace it, mediate it, or distract from it.

In this paper, we present Kip1's design process, including the design considerations and choices made with regards to the robot's material, mechanism, gestures, software, and hardware. We had two design goals: A balance between drawing people's attention and not distracting them from their current conversation; and a design eliciting an emotional connection between people and the robotic device.

Fig. 2. Early pencil sketches (left); 3D renders of winged blob design (middle); Early head designs with heavy stitching (right).

We evaluated our design in an experimental setting. Participating couples were guided to find a topic of severe disagreement and talk about it with their partner while the robot was in the room. The experimental group shared the room with an autonomously reacting robot and the control group with an animated, but not-reacting robot. We used both quantitative and qualitative methods to analyze the interaction. After reporting on our findings, we relate them to our design guidelines and considerations, and conclude with future work.

2. RELATED WORK

Kip1 can be thought of simultaneously as a socially expressive robot, an ambient kinetic tangible, and a conversation monitoring interface. We survey related work from all three domains, as well as from work related to couples in conflict.

2.1 Robotic Nonverbal Expressions of Affect

Socially interactive robots use both verbal and nonverbal channels in order to express their emotional state. In fact, Fong *et al.* describe the capability to express emotions as one of the indicators of socially interactive robots [5]. In anthropomorphic robots, facial expressions are often used to express emotions, either on a screen [7, 20] or using actuated facial features [1, 19]. Robots that do not have an expressive face or are non-anthropomorphic at all can use gestures to express emotions [2, 13]. In some cases, for robots that have no social articulation at all, such as UAVs, path planning has been used to express emotions [22]. Virtually all of these systems are used either for direct human-robot interaction, or for performance robotics. Our approach differs in that we use the nonverbal affective expression as an ambient companion to human-human interaction.

2.2 Technology mediated conversation

Prior technologies that mediate human conversation are usually screen based. DiMicco *et al.* used a shared display in a group interaction, showing how much each participant contributed to the conversation [4]. A similar study by Bergstrom & Karahalios used a "conversation clock" screen that visualized the time each participant talked, but without associating the visualization with a specific participant [3]. In contrast, our system uses ambient physical gestures, a tangible, embodied modality.

2.3 Ambient Kinetic Tangibles

This project lies at the crossroads of HRI and Tangible User Interfaces (TUI) research. In particular, Kip1 exemplifies the following core aspects of TUI: (a) "coupling digital information to everyday physical objects and environments" [15], and (b) "providing tangible representation to digital information" [21]. The robot's physical gestures are tangible representations of its emotional model, which is the digital information reflecting the conversation happening around the device. Kip1 also follows the "Objects for Change" [24] principle of implementing established behavior change techniques in the design of a TUI device.

Ambient interfaces use visual and auditory cues designed to be processed at the periphery or background. Usually they use subtle changes in light and sound to represent digital information [15]. In some cases ambient interfaces use tangible representation, mapping digital information to physical motion, thus being a "kinetic tangible" [14]. Kip1 continues this tradition, but in addition monitors real-time local information.

2.4 Vocalics in Relationship Conflict

Research has consistently documented how the emotional climate of relationship conflict interactions is an important marker of overall relationship quality. Emotional exchanges characterized by high levels of negative emotional behavior and low levels of positive emotional behavior have been associated with greater marital dissatisfaction and instability [9, 16]. An important indicator of emotion in marital interactions is emotional verbal and nonverbal behavior. Previous studies show that vocal expression demonstrates a variety of emotions that can eventually affect relationship quality and happiness. Shaver *et al.*, for example, found that loud voice, yelling and screaming is perceived as an expression of anger [23]. Kip1 intends to address this issue by using socially expressive robotics in the context of autonomous conversation monitoring.

3. DESIGN PROCESS

In the following section we present the Kip1 design process, including physical appearance, material selection, DoF layout, and gesture design. We describe our design guidelines, the interdisciplinary design team, and the various stages of design prototyping up until the current prototype, the third in sequence.

3.1 Process Overview

We designed Kip1 using a combined interaction, animation, and industrial design process, similar to the one proposed by Hoffman & Ju [13]. In the process, we explored a large number of forms and gesture capabilities, through a variety of techniques: pencil sketches; animation studies; mechanical CAD designs; skeleton prototypes; material explorations; and three actuated increasingly finalized physical prototypes.

3.2 Design Guidelines

Kip1's pronounced goal is to accompany human-human interaction, peripherally tracking the aggressiveness of their conversation. Through its emotional response, the robot should promote the conversants' awareness to the possible emotional effect of their behavior, hopefully leading to behavior change. We thus defined two design guidelines as a goal for our process:

3.2.1 Peripheral

The robot is meant to work in the periphery of the human-human interaction. No interaction is intended to occur directly between the human and the robot. Instead, it should be perceived in an ambient fashion. This is particularly important, since our goal is to promote and supplement face-to-face human-human interaction, to slightly influence and enhance it, but not replace it or distract

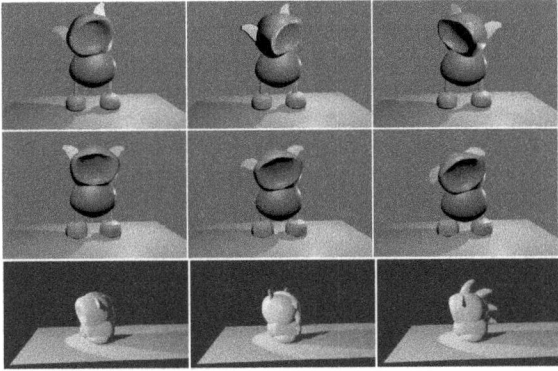

Fig. 3. Still frames from 3D animation sketches.

from it. That said, the robot's effect should be successful even without full attention from the human conversants.

3.2.2 Evocative

The robot's appearance and behavior should evoke empathy on the side of the human. Ideally, the human raising their voice and experiencing Kip1's fear gesture, should feel slightly bad for the robot's perceived "hurt feelings", and as a result consider the effects of their behavior on others.

One of the ways Kip1 would be able to evoke empathy was by seeming fragile itself. The robot's fragility could help highlight the potential sensitivity of the conversation partner which they themselves were unable to express. Therefore, instead of suggesting strength, stability, and efficiency, traits often associated with robot design, we wanted Kip1 to communicate fragility and sensitivity. In particular, we wanted these to be expressed in all of the robot's structure, materials, and movement.

3.3 Interdisciplinary Design Team

Robot design is often driven by engineering requirements and later "finished" with industrial design. Since we are specifically interested in robot design as a practice, one of the explicit project goals was to involve an interdisciplinary team throughout. Viewing this project as lying on the intersection of HRI and TUI research (see: Section 2), the team included academic researchers from both fields. To balance the engineering and technical development with a design-oriented focus, we included an industrial designer and a puppet designer from the beginning of the project, in addition to a mechanical engineer, a hardware prototyping expert, and a computer science student.

The design guidelines were shared with the various team members, and the iterative process allowed each member of the team to contribute using their field of expertise and influence the whole team. For example, the puppet designer addressed the "fragile" design guideline with several variations for the robot's head made from soft materials, from cloth to paper. The mechanical engineer was influenced by the use of soft materials and was inspired to add evocative motion to the robot's head using a piece of string instead of adding another motor.

3.4 Pencil Sketches

We started the design process with iterative rounds of pencil sketches and animation studies. These suggested a number of simple forms and motion axes, and can be thought of as very free-form improvisations on the theme of a sensitive, evocative creature. We posited that a small animal-like form and behavior would be most appropriate, as humans are extremely successful at

Fig. 4. Various sketches of multi-action linkage allowing two DoFs (rising and expansion) to be driven by a single motor.

reading (perhaps, into) animals' emotional states. We also know from pets that animals often successfully evoke empathy in humans. Fig. 2 (left) shows a selection of sketches from this stage.

We went back and forth between the paper-based sketches and simple, quick-and-dirty animation studies, each informing the other. Small animal-like and creature-like forms emerged with each of them having a "curious" or "confident" state and a "fearful" state. The first one was usually indicated by expansion or rising, and in some cases by the addition of ear-perking. The second was usually indicated by contraction, and sometimes by the addition of hair or spikes rising out of the body of the creature. This stage of the design increasingly moved towards more abstract and non-anthropomorphic shapes.

3.5 Animation Studies

As suggested by Hoffman & Ju [13], we explored the relationship between robot appearance and movement in a series of 3D animation studies. Fig. 3 shows still frames from these studies. We were mostly interested how clearly the robot's emotional state might read, in particular with a limitation of few degrees of freedom (DoFs). It is important to stress that each stage of animation study led to another round of drawing sketches towards the next animation study. We also treated these studies as very rough sketches, each made in less than an hour, and without expressively delving into detailed features of the robot's design. They can be thought of as "mass studies", where abstract shapes move with respect to one another.

As we moved away from anthropomorphic shapes, we remained in the realm of organic motion, perhaps like that found in fish or invertebrates. We thought that using an abstract shape with organic seeming motion would successfully bridge the tradeoff between mechanical feasibility and easy-to-read gestures.

Our animation tests suggested the following movement paradigms to support our usage and interaction scenarios:

Rising and falling — Growing and shrinking vertically *in size* resulted in a readable indicator of confidence and curiosity.

Inflating and deflating — Growing and shrinking *in volume* read very effectively, and seemed to support the idea of both confidence and fear, even in peripheral vision, as humans are acutely aware of changes in size.

Shivering — We found shivering to portray fear in an unambiguous manner.

Protruding spikes — We explored the idea of protruding spikes as an indication of extreme fear (Fig. 2 middle and Fig. 3 bottom). However, for mechanical reasons, they were not included in the current prototype. We hope to include them in future revisions.

5

At this stage, the team converged on a design that was centered around a simple, organic shape, akin to an egg or a penguin (Fig. 2 middle), with the following gestures: Rising and expanding to express self-confidence; contracting, falling, and shivering to express fear. In addition, we planned to have left and right movement to indicate attention, and rising and falling wing-like shapes to support additional gestures and emotional states.

3.6 Material Exploration

We wanted the materials to also reflect the peripheral nature of the robot, as well as its fragility. In addition, we were keen to evaluate the use of alternative materials in the design of robots, beyond the classic aluminum, steel, and plastics so often utilized. To that end, we collaborated with a puppet designer to explore the integration of different materials with moving parts.

We worked with various kinds of cloths, from thin silk-like fabric to heavy denims of various colors. We tested the interrelation between the robot's movement and the flexibility of the fabric. We explored wood in various forms, such as solid, plywood, and fiberboard. We also tested non-structural metals, such as copper and brass. Finally, we tested the use of paper as both a structural and aesthetic element in the robot's design. In particular, we experimented with Tyvek™, a non-woven synthetic paper-like material, that can be folded into shape, does not rip, and has a glossy surface.

At some stage, the focus of the design moved to stitching. Both paper and fabric can be stitched, and the exposed stitches can communicate fragility and emphasize the robot's form. We tested bold, thick stitching patterns on the robot's body (Fig. 2 right), but eventually abandoned that particular design path. Our final design was made up of a heavy MDF base, with light-colored translucent acrylic joined by brass joints, and white Tyvek.

3.7 Mechanism Studies

The material exploration went hand-in-hand with mechanism designs, which were intended to go into the fabric or paper shell. These designs were done both in 3D CAD software, and with low-fidelity cardboard prototypes.

3.7.1 Multi-Action Linkages

As we were interested in the expressive potential of a low-DoF robot, we recruited two mechanical principles: Multiple-action linkages and secondary action. Multiple-action linkages allow for more than one movement using the control of a single motor. In particular, one DoF can control several distinctly moving parts, and can cause different directions of movement throughout the trajectory of a single motor (Fig. 4).

Multi-action linkages are both economically efficient and mechanically elegant. That said, one of the drawback of multi-action linkages is that they are more difficult to model mathematically, and therefore more difficult to control. However, if we map the various motions onto a single driving variable, this issue can actually be avoided. In our case, the "confidence" variable maps directly onto one motor, which then causes an effect in several confidence-related movements, such as expansion and rising, circumventing the control problem.

3.7.2 Bare Mechanism

We built a first physically actuated prototype of the driving mechanism, while constructing a fabric shell. This was to better understand the physical constraints and dynamic properties of the robot's structure, and to kick off electronics, control, and software

design. At this stage, however, we found that the exposed mechanism provided for a more delicate and fragile appearance than when it was covered in a fabric or paper shell. The weight of the additional material made the robot seem more clumsy, heavy, and solid, whereas the bare mechanism seemed exposed and sensitive. We thus proceeded to explore the idea of using only the mechanism as the robot's appearance design. In addition, we believed that the tension between the robot's mechanical appearance and organic movement would balance well.

3.7.3 Secondary Action

Secondary action is an animation principle which can improve the motion characteristic of a robot by adding a passive DoF that is influenced by the actuated movement and physical constraints, including gravity, enriching the dynamic perception of the robot [6]. Since one of the gesture primitives we designed was a shiver, we thought that the amplification of this gesture by a secondary DoF would be effective. We thus added a passive DoF, in the form of a loose head-like shape to the robot's structure.

Combining the principles of multi-action linkage and secondary action, we tied a thin thread between the back side of the robot's neck and its body. This had two positive effects: It added an additional movement at the end of the motor's trajectory caused by the tensioning of the string. The string also communicates fragility as it is clear that breaking it would sever the naturalistic connection between the robot's head and body.

3.8 No Screens

In order to maintain the focus of Kip1's users on each other, it was important in our design process to refrain from using screens as part of the interaction paradigm. Some other recent desktop robots use mobile devices as their sensor and processing platform [11, 17]. Usually the screen is used for expressive face-like features and animations, or to display text. We made the design decision to express all feedback through physical gestures alone. This was based on the consideration that to support direct human-human interaction, physical gestures are less distracting than screens, and that if our aim is a gentle nudge towards behavior change, gestures can play a more subtle role than on-screen information. Moreover, as Kip1 is supposed to be in the background, embodied spatial movement is more easily read in peripheral view than on-screen feedback.

4. HARDWARE AND SOFTWARE

The robot's system design uses a smartphone as the main sensing and computing hardware [11], and includes four main components: An Android smartphone running the sensing and control software of the robot, a IOIO microcontroller board linking the smartphone to the motors, two servo motors, and a mechanical structure using a variety of linkages to express the robot's gestures. The smartphone uses its internal microphone to monitor the ongoing conversation around it, and runs a single application, consisting of four modules: Volume Detection, Conversation Analysis, Emotional Model, and Gesture Controller. The Volume Detection module constantly records real-time audio and measures the current volume of the audio coming in. It then compares this audio with a baseline room-level and outputs a relative volume associated with the conversation. This value is sent to the Conversation Analysis and Emotional Model modules.

4.1 Conversation Analysis

This module maintains a conversation state using a ring array of detection windows and a finite state machine (Fig. 5a). For each i

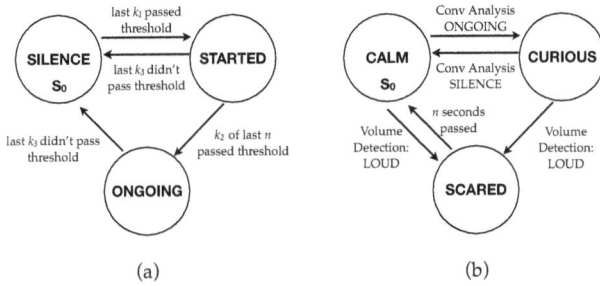

Fig. 5. Kip1 Finite State Machines for (a) Conversation Analysis and (b) Emotional Model.

seconds of audio, the module tags the next node in a ring buffer of size n with the maximum relative volume for that time period. If the last k_1 windows all surpassed the conversation level threshold, it is considered a conversation (as opposed to stray noise). This puts the state machine into the STARTED state. If k_2 of the last n windows surpass the conversation level threshold, this is considered an ongoing conversation, and the state machine switches to ONGOING. k_3 windows below threshold volume switch the state machine back to SILENCE. In our implementation we experimented with several values, and found $i=2$, $n=10$, $k = \{3,10,3\}$ to be most successful.

4.2 Emotional Model

The Emotional Model monitors both the conversation state and the real-time incidental volume and is also implemented as a finite state machine (Fig. 5b) in combination with a continuous "self-confidence" variable CONF between 0 and 1 (not shown), initialized to 0. The CONF value rises as long as the Emotional Model is in the CALM state. If the conversation state moves from STARTED to ONGOING, the emotional state moves from CALM to CURIOUS. If, at any point, a loud noise is detected, CONF resets to zero, and either state moves to SCARED, which is maintained until a pre-set timer elapses (currently: 5 seconds). The Emotional Model then returns to a CALM state.

4.3 Gesture Controller

The Gesture Controller monitors the Emotional Model and runs appropriate gesture behaviors based on state transitions in the Model. This module is based on the Gesture System in [11]. At any given moment, it runs one of a set of Behaviors. Some behaviors are one-offs, and some are cyclical. In our implementation, one-off behaviors resolve into repetitive behaviors automatically to prevent the robot from "freezing". For example, in the CALM state, the Behavior Controller runs a looping movement akin to slow, deep breathing, around the lower edge of the robot's movement. The amplitude of the breathing is affected by the Emotional Model's self-confidence value. In the CURIOUS state, the robot stretches out towards the conversant, looks around, and, using a string as a mechanical linkage, raises its "head" upwards. In the SCARED state, the robot retracts to a fully cowering state, and shivers.

The Gesture Controller includes a Behavior Controller, managing the behavioral state, a Trajectory Interpolator, making sure the movements are smooth and appealing according to character animation principles, and a Motor Controller which manages a model of each DoF, motor positions and limits, and its role in the mechanical structure. This system then uses the built-in IOIO messaging system to set motor positions at a fixed frequency (currently: 200Hz).

5. EVALUATION

We performed an evaluation of our design in the context of conflict conversation between couples. We wanted to see how the robot's design and behavior—i.e. its reaction to the couple's vocalics—might influence the conversation. We were also interested in the sentiments and opinions the robot evokes. We were specifically looking for findings that related to our two core design goals: a *peripheral* and *evocative* robotic companion.

To do so, we conducted quantitative and qualitative analysis of a controlled laboratory experiment, in which participant couples were guided to find a topic of disagreement, and asked to talk about this topic for 15 minutes. The participants were told that we were testing a new robot device which will listen in on their conversation. They either shared the room with a reacting robot or with a non-reacting, but alive-seeming robot. We recorded the couple's conversation with video and audio. In the end, we asked couples to fill out a brief questionnaire about their experience.

5.1 Participants

A total of 30 heterosexual Israeli couples (60 participants total) participated in the experiment. Participants were recruited from social networks in return for the equivalent of roughly $41 USD at time of writing. We recruited couples whose relationship was at least six months long. Participants' age ranged from 21 to 30 (M = 24.64, SD = 1.83).

5.2 Method

We conducted a single independent-variable between-subject (between-couples) design. We manipulated one variable, the robot's physical reaction to the conversation. In the EXPERIMENT condition, the robot responded with physical gestures to its emotional state as described above. In the CONTROL condition, the robot monitored the conversation, switched emotional states internally, but did not move in response to these states. Instead, it maintained the same gentle breathing behavior as in the CALM state of the EXPERIMENT condition.

5.3 Procedure

The experiment was conducted in experiment rooms with controlled lighting, no windows, and no outside distractions. Upon arrival, each participant couple was welcomed into the first room, where the experimenter explained the initial experimental guidelines and obtained informed consent. Then, the couple was split up, with one participant asked to enter the second experiment room. In separate rooms, couples completed the Couple's Problem Inventory [8], in which they rated the perceived severity of disagreement of a standard set of marital issues such as money, in-laws, and sex. The experimenter then helped the couple select an issue, which both spouses rated as being of high disagreement severity, to use as the topic for the conflict conversation.

Next, participants were guided to the third, adjacent, room, were asked to sit on two facing chairs, with the robot sitting on a coffee table between them and slightly offset to the side. The robot, measuring about 30cm in height, reached approximately to the humans' mid-torso when they were seated. Based on Leveson and Gottman [18], the couple was asked to discuss the chosen topic for fifteen minutes. They were told that we are testing a new robotic device which will listen in on their conversation and "may or may not react to it". After indicating that they understood these instructions, the participants were left alone in the room to talk about their topic.

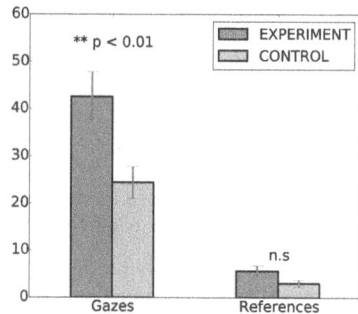
Fig. 7. Gaze towards robot and verbal references to it by condition.

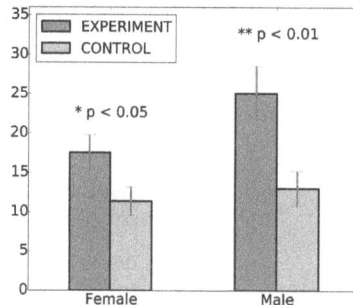
Fig. 8. Gender differences in number of gazes towards the robot.

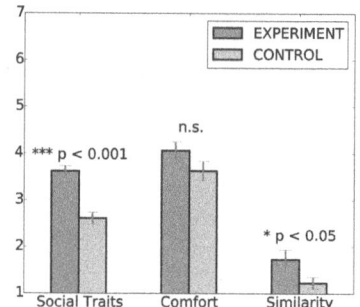
Fig. 9. Subjective measures. All variables were on a scale of 1–7.

Upon completion of the interaction stage, the experimenter re-entered the room, and asked the participants to fill out the post-procedure questionnaires, in separate rooms. This included the self-report measures below and a demographic questionnaire.

Participants were then fully debriefed, and were explicitly told that they were artificially put in a situation of conflict as part of this experiment, and that any negative feelings that might have come up during this conversation are likely to have originated from the experimental setting. We made sure that they felt good about their participation in the study before concluding.

6. MEASURES

We used both quantitative and qualitative methods to analyze the experiment. These measures were chosen to evaluate the design principles laid out in Section 3. For quantitative measures, we measured both objective behavioral measures coded from the experimental video, and subjective metrics from questionnaires:

6.1 Behavioral Measures

For each occurrence of the behavioral measures, we used the mean count of two independent coders who were unaware of the experimental hypotheses.

Gaze at Robot— We coded gaze events towards the robot for each member of the couple, as a measure of attention towards the robot.

Verbal References to Robot— We coded verbal references to the robot for each couple, as a measure of the robot disrupting the dyadic interaction.

6.2 Questionnaires

All responses on the questionnaires were on a scale of 1–7.

Robot Social Human Character Traits—Participants rated their impression of the robot on a composite measure of five items indicating positive social human character traits, including the robot's perceived friendliness, confidence, warmth, cooperativeness, and sociability. This measure was validated and found reliable in previous studies [10, 12]. Cronbach's α was good for this scale in this study, too (.78).

Comfort Level with Robot—Participants rated their comfort level with the robot on a composite measure of eight items, including their sense of being understood, being annoyed by the robot (reverse scale), feeling relaxed, connected, comfortable, and silly (reverse scale). Cronbach's α was good for this scale (.77).

Robot Similarity—We asked participants to rate on one scale to what extent the robot was similar to them, as a measure of potential empathy with the robot.

6.3 Qualitative Analysis

We also conducted qualitative analysis of prototypical videos from the EXPERIMENT condition.

7. RESULTS

To recap, participant couples were randomly assigned to hold their conversation in one of two conditions: Couples in the EXPERIMENT condition, conversed in the presence of a robot that reacted to their speech. Couples in the CONTROL condition, conversed in the presence of a robot that displayed a regular breathing pattern, but did not react to their speech.

7.1 Gaze At Robot

Gaze at the robot was gleaned from video coding. An independent means t-test on the number of gazes at the robot yielded significant results, $t(28) = 2.92$, $p < .01$. Couples in the EXPERIMENT condition looked almost twice as often at the robot (M = 42.6, SD = 19.67), than those in the CONTROL condition (M = 24.4, SD = 12.53) (Fig. 7 left).

7.1.1 Gender Differences

Measuring gaze by men and women separately reveals that the difference in gaze behavior was more pronounced in men than in women, albeit significantly different for both (Fig. 9). For men, an independent means t-tests on the number of gazes at the robot yielded significant results, $t(28) = 2.90$, $p < .01$. Men in the EXPERIMENT condition looked almost twice as often at the robot (M = 25.1, SD = 13.11), than those in the CONTROL condition (M = 13.0, SD = 8.39). For women, an independent means t-tests on the number of gazes at the robot yielded significant, but less pronounced results, $t(28) = 2.12$, $p < .05$. Women in the EXPERIMENT condition looked about 50% more often at the robot (M = 17.5, SD = 8.42), than those in the CONTROL condition (M = 11.4, SD = 6.80). Overall, women looked less often at the robot than men, especially in the EXPERIMENT condition.

7.2 Verbal References to the Robot

Verbal references to the robot were also obtained by video coding. An independent means t-test on the number of gazes at the robot yielded no significant results, $t(28) = 1.87$, n.s.. Couples in the EXPERIMENT condition referred to the robot slightly more often (M = 5.63, SD = 4.45) than those in the CONTROL condition (M = 3.03, SD = 2.67). However between-couple variance was high. Moreover, number of mentions were very low compared to the number of gazes towards the robot (Fig. 7 right).

7.3 Robot Social Human Character Traits

This composite variable measured positive social human traits attributed to the robot. An independent means t-test on the average of this scale yielded significant results, $t(28) = 3.55$, $p < 0.001$. Couples in the EXPERIMENT condition rated the robot's social human traits as higher ($M = 3.62$, $SD = 0.61$), than those in the CONTROL condition ($M = 2.61$, $SD = 0.70$). (Fig. 9 left).

7.4 Comfort Level with Robot

This composite variable measured how comfortable participants were to have the conversation with the robot present. An independent means t-test on the average of this scale yielded no significant results, $t(28) = 1.57$, n.s.. Couples in the EXPERIMENT condition were similarly comfortable with the robot ($M = 4.06$, $SD = 1.02$), than those in the CONTROL condition ($M = 3.63$, $SD = 1.11$). (Fig. 9 middle)

7.5 Similarity to Robot

This single measure ranked how similar participants viewed the robot to themselves. An independent means t-test on the average of this scale yielded significant results, $t(28) = 2.06$, $p < 0.05$. Couples in the EXPERIMENT condition rated the robot as slightly more similar to them ($M = 1.73$, $SD = 1.14$), than those in the CONTROL condition ($M = 1.23$, $SD = 0.68$). (Fig. 9 right).

7.6 Qualitative Analysis

We informally explored interaction patterns between participants and the robot by studying the experimental videos. Below is a qualitative analysis of different ways in which couples reacted to the robot, illustrated by two selected couples. To select the couples, we qualitatively evaluated the interaction of all 15 couples in the EXPERIMENT condition, and classified them into types according to their reaction to Kip1. We then chose representative couples for two different types of interactions to be included in this paper. The chosen couples were both engaged in heated conflict, but displayed responses to the robot at both ends of the spectrum. Couple 1 (C1) was relatively reactive to Kip1, while Couple 2 (C2) ignored it for the most part, getting lost in heated conversation.

At the beginning of C1's discussion C1F (Female) was talking calmly to C1M (Male). Kip1 reacted appropriately with a "curious" gesture, in this case towards C1M. C1M briefly looked back at Kip1 with a smile and then shifted his gaze back to his partner. Kip1 then leaned curiously towards C1F, causing her to stop mid-sentence, laugh and say: "It stresses me out! [...] he is looking at me!". She then naturally looked back to continue the discussion.

Reactions to the robot differed when the couple was engaged in a heated discussion, showing that Kip1 was not distracting when their attention was fully directed towards their discussion partner. For example, later in the conversation, C1M, who previously reacted, ignored the "curious" gesture when the discussion topic (but not volume) was getting more heated.

In C2, C2M was constantly speaking in an aggressive tone causing Kip1 to continuously react with the "scared" gesture. The couple looked at Kip1 the first time it was scared, but C2M said dismissively: "This is so stupid", and ignored Kip1 from that moment on. Along the conversation, when C2F was speaking softly, Kip1 barely started to shift towards a "curious" gesture but every time C2M interrupted her, the robot returned to "scared", so the couple never saw Kip1 fully displaying its "curious" gesture.

In some cases, people turned to Kip1 when they seemed to be in an uncomfortable situation. C1F made an argument and raised her voice, Kip1 reacted appropriately with a "scared" gesture, but the couple ignored it as they were engaged in their own discussion. A few seconds later, while C1F was still making her rather loud argument and Kip1 was still in a "scared" gesture, C1M shifted his gaze and looked at Kip1. C1F followed C1M's lead and also shifted her gaze toward the "scared" robot, stopped talking, and remarked: "He has an epileptic attack I think". They both laughed shortly, breaking the tension, and allowing C1M to speak.

In C2, where Kip1 was constantly in a "scared" gesture due to C2M's dominating tone, C2F often glanced towards Kip1, especially when C2M was speaking particularly loudly. These glances were usually accompanied by seemingly nervous self-adaptation behavior, such as playing with her fingers or hair, and could be understood as an attempt to shift the focus toward something outside of the uncomfortable conversation.

In some cases, the conversation changed after participants' reaction to Kip1. For example, as mentioned above, C1F and C1M moved their attention from the heated discussion (led by C1F) towards Kip1, with a "comic relief" by C1F about Kip1's shivers. After a few seconds, C1M reinitiated the discussion, but instead of making a counter argument to C1F, he gave a meta-level perspective of the situation, stating that they have different opinions about the topic.

8. DISCUSSION AND FUTURE WORK

Our findings show significant differences between conditions in the number of gazes at the robot, in the robot's perception of positive social character traits, and in the perceived similarity to the robot. We found no significant difference in the number of verbal reference to the robot, and in the comfort level to converse next to the robot. These findings suggest two main insights.

Intriguing but not distracting: Participants directed significantly more attention towards the robot when it reacted to their conversation—but they did so only via gaze, and not verbal reaction, which remained the same in both conditions. This supports our *peripheral* design goal: People react to the robot's behavior in a way that does not interfere with the natural flow of the human-human conversation. A temporary shift of gaze away from a partner is not considered rude or distracting. Our findings thus support the notion that our design was intriguing without being distracting.

An object with social-emotional appeal: When the robot reacted to participants' conversation they perceived it as more human-like and more similar to them. This supports our *evocative* design goal: The robot was perceived as more friendly, warm, social, and similar to the participant, meaning people did not relate to it as an object, but as a device that might be perceived as capable of forming human emotions, bond, or attachment. Participants felt equally comfortable to converse in the presence of the robot in both conditions, suggesting that the robot's gestures, not just appearance caused a difference in perception on the social-emotional level.

Anecdotally, it is worth noting that in a measure-by-measure analysis of the social character scale, the only trait that *wasn't* significantly different between the conditions was the one rating the robot as "confident", suggesting that our design goal of the robot's fragility (Section 3.2.2) transpired.

Still, our study did not specifically check whether couples correctly read the gestures or actually empathized with the robot. We are now running follow-up studies to evaluate these questions.

8.1 Future Work

We plan to further develop the conversation analysis capabilities of the robot in order to pick up on more complex vocalic cues. To do so, we are now working to analyze pitch together with loudness to categorize vocal affect in speakers, with the aim of achieving more precise detection of aggressive speaking behavior as well as more expressive gesture feedback. We are also working on systems to separate speakers and add the relative contribution of each speaker and overall conversation balance to the robot's emotional model. Furthermore, we are experimenting with adding physiological measures, such as heart rate and galvanic skin response to the robot's sensing capabilities.

We plan to extend the robot's potential for social bonding and emotional connection, through new degrees of freedom and gestures, including going back to some abandoned design ideas.

Finally, we plan to study the interpersonal effects of this robotic companion, including the effect it had on the amount of aggressive conversation, and how couples felt about each other after speaking in the presence of the robot. We also want to study our approach in additional setting beyond couples interaction, for example parent-child or teacher-student interaction.

9. CONCLUSION

We presented a design and evaluation of a peripheral robotic conversation companion. Our findings support our hypothesis that a peripheral and evocative robotic design can accompany human-human interaction in an intriguing yet non-distracting way, as an object with perceived social and emotional traits. We conclude that robotic devices could be designed to evoke empathy among people and serve as companions to human-human interaction without compromising the natural communication patterns between humans. We see such conversation companion robots as having applications for conflict mediation, classroom settings, business meetings, dating, negotiations, and more.

10. REFERENCES

[1] Bartneck, C. et al. 2004. In your face, robot! The influence of a character's embodiment on how users perceive its emotional expressions. *Proc of the Design and Emotion.*

[2] Beck, A. et al. 2010. Towards an affect space for robots to display emotional body language. *RO-MAN 2010 - The 19th IEEE International Symposium on Robot and Human Interactive Communication* 464–469.

[3] Bergstrom, T. and Karahalios, K. 2009. Social mirrors as social signals: transforming audio into graphics. *Computer Graphics and Applications, IEEE.* 29, 5, 22–32.

[4] DiMicco, J.M. et al. 2004. Influencing group participation with a shared display. *Proc of the 2004 ACM conference on Computer supported cooperative work* 614–623.

[5] Fong, T. et al. 2003. A survey of socially interactive robots. *Robotics and Autonomous Systems.* 42, 3, 143–166.

[6] Gielniak, M.J. et al. 2010. Secondary action in robot motion. *19th Int'l Symposium in Robot and Human Interactive Communication (RO-MAN 2010)* 310–315.

[7] Gockley, R. et al. 2005. Designing robots for long-term social interaction. *2005 IEEE/RSJ International Conference on Intelligent Robots and Systems.(IROS 2005).* 1338–1343.

[8] Gottman, J. et al. 1977. The Topography of Marital Conflict: A Sequential Analysis of Verbal and Nonverbal Behavior. *Journal of Marriage and the Family.* 39, 461.

[9] Gottman, J.M. et al. 1998. Predicting Marital Happiness and Stability from Newlywed Interactions. *Journal of Marriage and the Family.* 60, 1, 5.

[10] Guadagno, R.E. and Cialdini, R.B. 2002. Online persuasion: An examination of gender differences in computer-mediated interpersonal influence. *Group Dynamics: Theory, Research, and Practice.* 6, 1, 38–51.

[11] Hoffman, G. 2012. Dumb Robots , Smart Phones: a Case Study of Music Listening Companionship. *RO-MAN 2012 - The IEEE Int'l Symposium on Robot and Human Interactive Communication* 358–363.

[12] Hoffman, G. et al. 2014. Robot responsiveness to human disclosure affects social impression and appeal. *Proceedings of the 2014 ACM/IEEE international conference on Human-robot interaction* 1–8.

[13] Hoffman, G. and Ju, W. 2014. Designing Robots With Movement in Mind. *J of Human-Robot Interact.* 3, 1, 89.

[14] Ishii, H. et al. 2012. Radical atoms: beyond tangible bits, toward transformable materials. *Interactions.* 19, 1, 38–51.

[15] Ishii, H. and Ullmer, B. 1997. Tangible bits: towards seamless interfaces between people, bits and atoms. *Proc of the SIGCHI conference on Human factors in computing systems* 234–241.

[16] Karney, B.R. and Bradbury, T.N. 1997. Neuroticism, marital interaction, and the trajectory of marital satisfaction. *J of Pers and Soc Psych.* 72, 1075–1092.

[17] Kory, J.M. et al. 2013. Robotic learning companions for early language development. *Proc of the 15th ACM on International conference on multimodal interaction* 71–72.

[18] Levenson, R.W. and Gottman, J.M. 1983. Marital interaction: physiological linkage and affective exchange. *Journal of personality and social psychology.* 45, 587–597.

[19] Lutkebohle, I. et al. 2010. The bielefeld anthropomorphic robot head "Flobi." *2010 IEEE International Conference on Robotics and Automation* 3384 3391.

[20] Mizanoor, R. et al. Dynamic Emotion-Based Human-Robot Collaborative Assembly in Manufacturing: The Preliminary Concepts. *hci.cs.wisc.edu.*

[21] Shaer, O. and Hornecker, E. 2010. Tangible user interfaces: past, present, and future directions. *Foundations and Trends in Human-Computer Interaction.* 3, 1-2, 1–137.

[22] Sharma, M. et al. 2013. Communicating affect via flight path Exploring use of the Laban Effort System for designing affective locomotion paths. *Proc of the Int'l Conf on Human-Robot Interaction (HRI), on* 293–300.

[23] Shaver, P. et al. 1987. Emotion knowledge: further exploration of a prototype approach. *Journal of personality and social psychology.* 52, 1061–1086.

[24] Zuckerman, O. 2015. Objects for Change: A Case Study of a Tangible User Interface for Behavior Change. *Ext Abs of the TEI.*

Mechanical Ottoman: How Robotic Furniture Offers and Withdraws Support

David Sirkin, Brian Mok, Stephen Yang, Wendy Ju
Center for Design Research, Stanford University CA, USA

{sirkin, brianmok, syang0, wendyju}@stanford.edu

ABSTRACT

This paper describes our approach to designing, developing behaviors for, and exploring the use of, a robotic footstool, which we named the *mechanical ottoman*. By approaching unsuspecting participants and attempting to get them to place their feet on the footstool, and then later attempting to break the engagement and get people to take their feet down, we sought to understand whether and how motion can be used by non-anthropomorphic robots to engage people in joint action.

In several embodied design improvisation sessions, we observed a tension between people perceiving the ottoman as a living being, such as a pet, and simultaneously as a functional object, which requests that they place their feet on it—something they would not ordinarily do with a pet. In a follow-up lab study (N=20), we found that most participants did make use of the footstool, although several chose not to place their feet on it for this reason. We also found that participants who rested their feet understood a brief lift and drop movement as a request to withdraw, and formed detailed notions about the footstool's agenda, ascribing intentions based on its movement alone.

Categories and Subject Descriptors

H.5.2 [**Information Interfaces and Presentation**]: User Interfaces—*prototyping, user-centered design*; I.2.9 [**Artificial Intelligence**]: Robotics.

Keywords

Embodied Design Improvisation; Laboratory Experiment; Wizard of Oz; Metaphors; Social Attribution.

1. INTRODUCTION

Think of iconic seating designs from the last century: the Eames Lounge Chair, the van der Rohe Barcelona Chair, the Le Corbusier Chaise. Each of these shares a common, critical, yet often overlooked, sidekick: the ottoman—a low-slung, uphol-stered resting place for weary feet. It has become the jack-of-all-trades of the living room set, serving as footrest, chair or side table, often without even moving, as its owners' needs change throughout the day.

It would be wonderful if household robots, such as the iRobot Roomba, were as simultaneously supportive and invisible as the humble ottoman. At the same time, perhaps the ottoman could

HRI'15, March 02–05, 2015, Portland, OR, USA.
Copyright 2015 ACM 978-1-4503-2883-8/15/03...$15.00.
http://dx.doi.org/10.1145/2696454.2696461.

Figure 1. An actor improvises one way to accept a prototype mechanical ottoman's offer to interact.

gain even more utility if it could move around, and respond to the activities of the people around it.

With this thought in mind, we have developed a robotic footstool—or *mechanical ottoman*—as a vehicle for exploring how motion alone can be used to negotiate interaction. Using only the ability to traverse in the plane of the floor, as well as a limited ability to raise its seat cushion, the mechanical ottoman is able to approach strangers, offer its services to their feet, and later to request to withdraw to other activities.

Because the ottoman is non-anthropomorphic in form, we needed to develop the behaviors and interaction patterns for the robot that felt natural and intuitive, without the benefit of direct analogous human models to mimic. This paper describes the multi-phase process we used to develop and study the way that people interact with the mechanical ottoman. First, using a physical prototype of an ottoman robot, we worked with domain experts in physical movement in a process of embodied design improvisation; these sessions gave us a wide set of behaviors, techniques and considerations to draw upon in the later stages of our work. Next, we developed a working prototype of the ottoman robot, and, using a mix of pre-programmed actions and practice teleoperated behaviors and approaches, replicated some of the most promising maneuvers from the first phase to try out. In the final phase, we used a quasi-breaching experiment to validate that study partici-pants would understand and respond to the ottoman's spontaneous offer to engage in supporting people's feet, and later, its equally spontaneous request to disengage from the joint activity.

2. RELATED WORK

2.1 Naturalism in the Wild

Many aspects of the mechanical ottoman's context, form and interaction design make it a novelty in the realms of human-robot interaction, and, for that reason, we needed to draw on a broad range of inspirations and examples to develop the design of the robot. First of all, people's interactions with footstools may be spontaneous and short-term. Researchers Schulte et al. note that spontaneous, short-term interaction with mobile robots—in their case, with the mobile Museum guide robot Minerva—exemplify the need to engage in ways that are familiar, because the people encountering the robot are untrained and the overall engagement is short [27]. Saerbeck and Bartneck [31] found that people may attribute affective states to a robot based on variations in its motion path alone, rather than its form. While these human-robot interactions are not wholly "in the wild" [28], they nevertheless provide insight into various ways that people will respond naturalistically to offers for engagement or moves to take leave [32] in a household environment. As yet though, there is little exploration of the preamble to such ongoing activities: how the machine can open the interaction.

2.2 Non-Anthropomorphism

Products like iRobot's Roomba or Suitable Technologies' Beam show that some people are apt to welcome robotic furniture into the home [13][15] or workplace [21]. Often the assumption seems to be that if a robot is to be sociable [3], it must also be anthropomorphic in form. Dautenhaun et al. ask, for instance, "What is a robot companion—a friend, assistant or butler?" [9]. What we are interested in, in our explorations, is whether non-verbal and non-anthropomorphic gestures and motions might be used to query whether people are willing or available for interaction [1], and to properly convey the intentionality that is needed to "make friends and influence people" [5].

The exploration of non-anthropomorphic communication is necessary because the form of robots might be constrained due to their pragmatic functions. In the case of our ottoman, and that of other robotic furniture, such as Dean's & D'Andrea's Table [10], Di Lello et al.'s PEIS Table [11] or Fink's Ranger toy box [14], even for Yu et al.'s modular table [36], which can adapt to the environment, the robot's form is constrained by its purpose, and the addition of anthropomorphic features could hamper core functionality. Moreover, the addition of facial features could raise people's expectations for speech affordances in a robot. Hence, in our research with the ottoman, we focused on understanding what might be conveyed and what joint action can be coordinated through movement alone.

2.3 Coordinating Joint Action

While there is no prior research in robotics that we have found in coordinating joint action [20] around footstools, there is some analogous work in the area of human handover tasks. Researchers such as Huber et al. have argued that handover tasks are important because humans and robots have to physically coordinate in order to cooperate—the learning and adaptation involved in success-fully negotiating the handover of an object might be generalized to broader joint-action strategies [17]. Dautenhahn et al. [8] found that people interacting with a robot in a fetch task preferred the robot to approach from the side and at a slow pace, to decrease its perceived confrontational stance. And Cakmak et al. found that temporal and spatial contrast increase fluency in human-robot handovers [6]. We expect that for the task of engaging people in using the ottoman that some nonverbal communication is required to establish common ground [7], but the existing guidelines in the HRI literature on establishing engagement between humans and robots, such as [4], [25] or [29] rely on anthropomorphic techniques around gaze, for instance, that are non-sensical in

situations like those that might be found in "smart rooms" with distributed robots, where vision is likely to be based on an over-head camera, rather than through eyes mounted on the robot itself.

2.4 Research and Design Methodology

From a methodological perspective, our approach is similar to the breaching experiments used by Weiss et al. [34]. Weiss and her colleagues deployed an ACE robot in a public shopping area, and approached unsuspecting people with tourist guide information. They then subsequently interviewed people about the interaction to gauge how accepting people were to this discrepant event. This type of event tells us something different from longitudinal deployments of robots in shared settings (a nice survey of such research is found in [23], a strong case study in [19]): they tell us how people who have incidental and short-term interactions interpret and respond to robot overtures. This class of research has relevance not only to situations where robots are novel, or where robot interactions are passing [22], but also to situations where people maybe encountering robots in emergency or disaster situation [2], when the nuances of first impressions may be critically important.

3. METHODOLOGY

To learn what physical and interaction issues are central to human-ottoman relations, we followed an *embodied design improvisation* approach that combines storyboarding, physical and video prototyping, Wizard of Oz techniques, and experimentation [30]. Improvisation has become central to our design process because it helps to reveal movements and interaction patterns that are often implicitly, rather than explicitly, understood. Earlier, generative activities help us develop a range of ideas and intuitions for what makes for expressive motion. Later, more refined prototypes and a controlled study help validate whether the behaviors we developed convey an *intention* to interact. We chose an exploratory design, open to emergent patterns of use [16], and employed a qualitative approach to gathering data to encourage accounts that reveal models of understanding [12].

3.1 Storyboarding

We began by storyboarding a few likely settings and interaction scenarios, to develop intuition about how a moving ottoman might initiate, or respond to, requests to interact with someone (see Fig. 2). We started by blocking out the basic actions that a person or ottoman could perform, and considered its alternative roles as footstool, chair, side table and even companion. By physically enacting scenarios as we sketched, we hoped to draw out and examine our notions of how an ottoman could, or should, behave.

Figure 2. Excerpt from a storyboard of likely interaction patterns between a seated person and a moving ottoman.

In all, we storyboarded six ways for someone to beckon the ottoman, accept or demur its service, and then dismiss it—say, by calling aloud, or gesturing with head, hands or feet—including whether the person's legs were crossed or both on the floor. We also storyboarded six complementary scenarios where the ottoman, rather than the person, took the initiative.

3.2 Low-Resolution Prototype
Based on our sketches from these sessions, and the types of interactions that we anticipated, we built a low-resolution functional prototype using an inexpensive store-bought ottoman, which we set atop casters, and steered around the floor by hand using two-meter long wooden dowels that we attached to its bottom with gaffer's tape.

We imagined that the ottoman, or at least its lid, might also move vertically, so we attached clear monofilament fishing line like puppet wires, but fine control was difficult and the lines stretched in use, so we just lifted and lowered the ottoman by hand.

3.3 Improvisation Sessions
We then held three design improvisation sessions, each lasting about two hours, with domain experts in physical movement and interaction, including a dance choreography instructor, an improvisational theater performer and theater director, and a stage actor. We video recorded these sessions for later review and analysis.

3.3.1 Session Activity
We placed these participants in various individual seating arrangements, and *puppeted* the prototype, exploring ways that someone could beckon or dismiss the ottoman, what personalities different speeds, gestures or angles of approach and departure projected, and appropriate social distances (see Fig. 3).

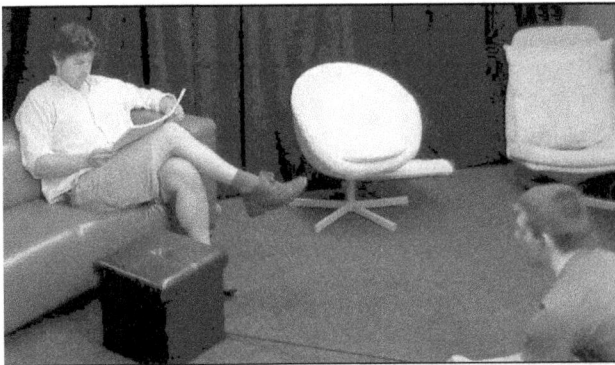

Figure 3. During an improvisation session, the researcher on the right *puppets* the prototype using two wooden dowels.

Specifically, improvisation sessions progressed from broader toward narrower concepts, starting with the ottoman's use and usability (as say, footstool or side table), moving on to aspects of its presentation such as shape and movement [18][24], and finally discussing its social role [26]. In doing so, we engaged participants in role play, using prompts such as *"shoo the ottoman away as many ways as you can,"* and encouraged them to respond gesturally and speak their reactions aloud, with the goal of developing an initial set of design principles. Three initial principles that emerged from these discussions were that *"movements should be visible and predictable," "expressive objects should indicate their intention to act"* and *"acknowledge when a request is received."*

We created a video prototype during the session with the stage actor, which we could then use to demonstrate our ideas to others.

We video recorded his improvisations from two camera angles in a typical usage setting, which was really a corner of our lab dressed with props and lighting (see Fig. 1).

3.3.2 Session Outcomes
We found that rushing straight towards people made them feel uncomfortable: a perception made poignant by realizing that they were seated, and particularly vulnerable. They far preferred if the robot paused at a respectful distance (which they concluded was about one meter) before proceeding. Also, it helped if the robot came in a bit indirectly from the side. However, approaching too slowly, or from behind, also made them uncomfortable: as if they were being sneaked up on. A curving approach, from the near front-side, avoided either suggestion of threat.

At one point, after a quick approach to about a meter away, followed by a pause, and a gentle move closer, the dance instructor declared *"Ah, now we're in India,"* evoking the tradition of exemplary service being viewed as an art form in that culture. She elaborated by contrasting India, or England, to other cultures, such as the United States, which have historical frames of service being viewed as closer to servitude. The improvisational theater performer echoed this sentiment when the ottoman withdrew to a ready position in front and to his side, stating *"That feels like butlery,"* noting how this action showed an intent to be useful, and allowed it to be recalled to service quickly. The stage actor treated the ottoman more like an animate object, which he could wave over if needed, sneer at if he wanted to cross his legs, or kick gently aside if it encroached too closely into his personal space. Each of these perspectives placed the seated person at the top of the social order, with the ottoman alternatively treated as provider of expert service, obedience or pure functionality.

Several participants felt that a brisk, vertical lift movement of several centimeters (which we called *"stand up"*) suggested attention and a readiness to move, and that the corresponding drop (or *"sit down"*) movement suggested stability, and a likelihood of staying put after completing some action. The improvisational theater performer took to snapping his fingers, or whistling, to call the ottoman over, as if it were a well-trained dog. When it arrived, he tossed his magazine on top of it. This was the first behavioral dissonance that we observed, where someone treated the ottoman like a pet, or living being in one moment, and like an object, or mechanical device the very next moment.

Movements generally toward or away from participants, or in place (such as a vertical lift and drop), especially in response to a request, were perceived as intentional, whereas orthogonal motion was seen as undirected. Also, even though the ottoman was symmetric on all sides, and mostly cube shaped, to our experts, its forward movement implied a front and back, while the same movement for a round ottoman, borrowed from a nearby room, did not.

3.4 Robotic Prototype & Motion Design
Between improvisation sessions, we built a robotic, teleoperated ottoman, modeled on the prototype that we had been using during earlier sessions, as a way to practice and confirm the approaches and expressive movements that we were fashioning by hand.

We set the ottoman atop a modified Willow Garage Turtlebot, which is based, in turn, on the iRobot Create robotic base. Given the base's architecture, the ottoman could move forward or backward, rotate in place, or follow a curved path, but it could not move immediately sideways.

We then attached a high-torque RC servo to the topmost portion of the Turtlebot frame to raise and lower the ottoman 2.5 centimeters (vertically) over about a ¼ second duration, making sure that we reinforced the internal assembly to support the weight of a person sitting on it.

The robot's path and speed across the floor, and its vertical motion, were remotely operated using a handheld controller, which we built using an Arduino, Xbee wireless modules and two joystick potentiometers. Independent speed control over each wheel permitted significant expressivity: we could drive rapidly over large or small distances, such as when traversing across the floor or wiggling to capture someone's attention, as well as move slowly, such as when approaching someone up close.

We decided that the following sequence would capture and test the main insights that emerged from the storyboard and initial improvisation sessions: the ottoman would a) initiate and conclude each movement with a vertical *stand up* or *sit down* motion, b) start rolling at a speed of 1 meter per second, c) approach the seated person following a curving path, always within his or her immediate field of view, d) pause movement at a distance of one meter for about ten seconds, and e) resume its path toward the participant, slowing to about ½ meter per second as it drew near (see Fig. 4).

Figure 4. A typical path taken to approach a seated person. Squares represent the ottoman's position, one second apart.

If a person did not immediately raise his or her feet, the ottoman would begin a sequence of three increasingly assertive actions. First was a brief lift and drop, next was a quick rotational wiggle around its center, and last was a gentle nudge, or bump, up against the participant's legs or feet, alternatively leading from the left or right side. Once someone's feet were actively being supported, the ottoman would then follow a similar sequence to bid to leave.

3.5 Qualitative Lab Study

Taken together, the design improvisation sessions suggested more research questions than they answered, including how people perceive different types of movement during the ottoman's approach, whether it could encourage them to rest their feet, the relative social status and metaphors that people assume while interacting with it, and whether the ottoman could signal its intent to take leave of the interaction. We therefore conducted a qualitative lab study to better understand whether our initial findings echoed among other potential users.

3.5.1 Participants

We recruited 20 undergraduate and graduate students (12 females, 8 males, age M=20.8, SD=3.1 years), who received compensation

in the form of a $15 Amazon gift card. Their self-reported experience with robots prior to the study, on a scale of 1–7, where 1=*None* and 7=*A Lot*, was M=2.95, SD=1.5.

3.5.2 Study Setup

The study took place immediately after participants had concluded interacting with robotic furniture that was part of another study. Both studies shared the same physical space and setup.

The room layout included a desk and drawers for the earlier study along one wall, and a lounge chair in the opposing corner. We placed the ottoman at either of two starting positions: one almost directly in front of the seated participant, adjacent to the desk, and the other on the opposite wall, to the participant's left side, hidden among several large Pelican cases (see Fig. 5). All of the interactions were video recorded from three vantage points around the room.

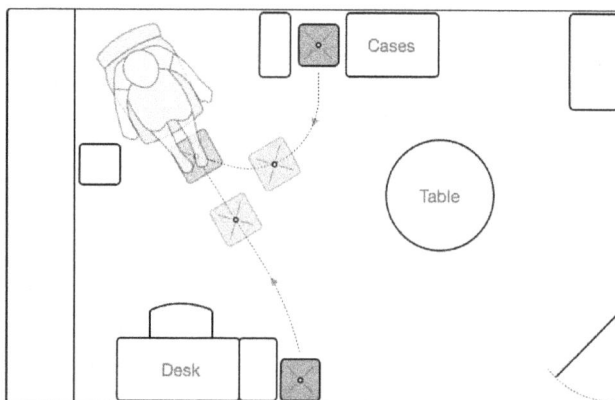

Figure 5. Overhead view of the study setting, showing front and side approach paths. The two middle positions are where the ottoman stopped briefly on its way toward participants.

3.5.3 Procedure

After participants completed the prior robotic furniture activity, we asked them to sit in the nearby lounge chair and complete a ten-minute questionnaire about their preceding experience using a handheld tablet to conclude the study. We instructed them that after completing the questionnaire, they could watch an animated video [35] also on the tablet, while waiting for the experimenter to return, ostensibly from setting up the study for the next participant. The idea was to engage participants in *some* kind of activity, rather than have them wait by idly, and for that activity not to require focused effort (as the questionnaire would), and for them to feel that the study had ended, so that they could readily shift their attention to the ottoman's entry.

After one minute of video play, and under the control of a remote operator, the ottoman drove either directly up to the participant, or to a position about one meter away, where it stopped and waited for ten seconds, and then continued directly up to the participant (proxemic movement patterns were informed by [18][24]). Every time the ottoman began a driving segment, it would first perform its *stand up* behavior, and every time it stopped driving, it concluded with its *sit down* behavior. We counterbalanced both starting position (near front vs. opposite side wall) and approach style (direct vs. pause) among participants.

When it finally reached the participant, the ottoman—at the behest of its remote operator—enacted one or more of the three assertive,

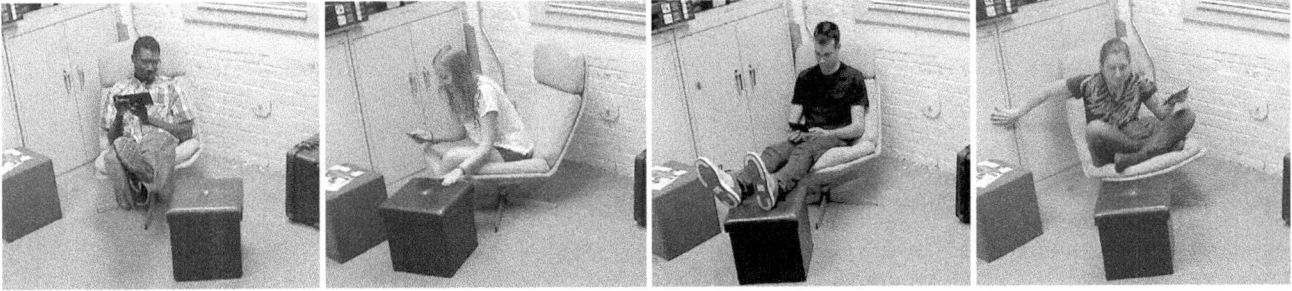

Figure 6. From left to right: one participant anticipates the arriving ottoman by elevating his feet; another pats it to assuage its offer to support her feet; one rests his feet on it while watching a video; and another avoids interacting with nervous laughter.

attention-getting behaviors (lift and drop, wiggle, bump into legs) to encourage the participant to rest his or her feet on it.

Regardless of whether the participant did rest his or her feet, the ottoman attempted to take leave of the interaction after two minutes, by repeating the same behaviors that it (may have) had tried earlier, and then driving away toward the door in the far corner. The ottoman always moved longer distances with the same side facing forward. For instance, after disengaging from its interaction with participant, the ottoman first backed up a short way, performed a three-point turn, and continued onward toward the door with its original forward-facing side leading the way.

Just at the moment that the ottoman approached the door, the experimenter entered the room from the other side, allowed the ottoman to exit through the open door, and conducted a semi-structured interview with the participant about the experience. Questions included whether participants understood what the ottoman was, whether they perceived it as trying to do anything in particular, whether it moved while it was supporting their feet, and what they thought that meant, what else they might compare the ottoman to, what they thought it was going to do next, and what they thought about it being autonomous or teleoperated.

4. RESULTS

We reviewed video recordings of participants' interactions with the ottoman and grouped responses into several broad categories, including a) whether they raised their feet or responded in some other way (such as verbal acknowledgment), b) which, if any, of the three assertive actions they responded to upon its approach, and c) which, if any, of the three complementary actions they responded to as its bid to leave. We compared each of these across the two approach direction and pause conditions, as well as with transcribed interview responses to find common, and unique, rationales, responses and interpretations.

The following sections describe trends or instances that we observed in human-ottoman interaction, in approximately the order experienced during the study, focusing on participants' responses during the interviews (see Fig. 6).

4.1 Approach and Offer

Almost all participants recognized the ottoman as a robotic footstool, or as one participant described, *"a weirdly sentient footstool."* One or two who were confused at first quickly came to understand its role and intent: *"At some point I thought it could be a small chair or something, but I pretty much got it when it was approaching my feet."*

Most participants noticed the ottoman immediately when it *stood up* or began moving. Two of these were unaware of its presence

until it approached their immediate field of view, about ½ meter away, and both recalled that they were focusing on the video until then. Participants described themselves as being startled, or disoriented, when the ottoman began moving, but that it had a respectful stance, especially when it stopped briefly during its approach. One commented, *"I was really freaked out when it started to move, but I thought it was pretty respectful. It was eager, maybe, but definitely respectful."* Another said, *"It paused a respectful distance away, then it got a little bit closer."*

Participants again perceived respect when the ottoman approached and offered to support their feet: *"I felt like if I didn't choose to interact with it, it would be okay with that. It was going to respect my desire."* and *"It inched over, and gave me time to realize, oh, it's not so hard to put my feet on it. If it had zipped over and tried to push itself under my feet, that would have been weird."*

Even when the ottoman was more expressive in its offer, participants accepted its behavior and correctly interpreted its intent: *"The way it nudged my knee, it was sort of insistent, but in a cute, polite way. It didn't feel uncomfortable."* and *"It bumped into my legs, so I figured that it wanted me to put my legs up."*

4.2 Resting Their Feet

Fourteen of 20 participants accepted the offer to rest their feet on the ottoman, many of them lifting their legs right away as it rolled up toward them. About half even held their legs suspended in the air for several seconds, so the ottoman could settle down just beneath them. Others did not rest their feet at first, but did so after some encouragement from the ottoman: *"I was too intrigued by it to put my feet on it."* and *"I'm wary of animate objects that move."* Another explained his reluctance as *"I thought somebody was playing a prank or something on me."*

Table 1 shows whether participants lifted their feet as the ottoman approached by condition, and suggests that approach did not influence their responses.

Table 1. Participants' responses to the ottoman's approach.

	Direct approach	*Pause on the way*
Starting near front	5 lifted, 0 did not	3 lifted, 2 did not
Opposite side wall	3 lifted, 2 did not	3 lifted, 2 did not

All six who did not rest their feet knew that it was an ottoman, and that it was offering to support their feet. One responded, *"I felt pretty comfortable already in the chair. I didn't feel a need to put my feet on it."* But the other five described their reluctance as perceiving the ottoman to be alive: *"It's a moving thing that I almost perceive as living. I didn't want to denigrate it by using it* as a footstool." Another said, *"Because it felt like it was alive I didn't want to put my feet on it."* and *"I feel like it communicated with me well, but I would feel uncomfortable doing what it was asking."* One other participant rested her feet at first, but removed them after about 30 seconds, saying later, *"It seemed like it wanted me to put my feet on it, but I didn't want to constrain it too much. I didn't want to imprison it here."*

Several of these participants acknowledged the ottoman's arrival by patting its top, or saying hello. One person explicitly ignored it, focusing intently on the video instead. She explained later that she was purposely trying to send a signal that she would not rest her feet on it, hoping that it would stop offering to do so.

But most participants, including those who perceived the ottoman as akin to a living being, and felt some conflict over resting their feet on it, were willing to do so. One described the ottoman as *"Kind of like a dog that notices, oh look, my owner's here. But I wouldn't put my feet on a dog. I think it's just because it has the appearance of an object, and it came right here, so there wasn't much else to do with it."*

4.3 Taking Leave
Everyone who had rested their feet recognized the quick lift-and-drop motion as a request to take leave of the interaction, although some did not notice it until the second or third time: *"It, like, sat up when it was ready to go."* and *"When it signaled to leave, it rose and fell, to let me know it was time to go. I wasn't ready for it to leave because I was comfortable. I'm glad it let me know instead of taking off."*

Responses to the ottoman's request to withdraw ranged from accepting, *"I think it wanted to go, so I set it free."* to disappointed, *"It made its own decision to leave, like I don't want to be your footrest anymore."* to mildly annoyed, *"I was a little offput when it decided that it wanted to leave. If it was doing that all of the time, then I'm not sure how good of a footrest it would be. I expect a footrest to be there."*

Many acknowledged the ottoman's gestures prior to departing, although they also expressed confusion over its intent, or uncertainty over its motivation, to leave: *"I couldn't discern any motive in its departure"* and *"I'm kind of glad it said goodbye, at least. Maybe I said something that offended it. I don't usually talk to objects."* From someone who did not lift her feet, *"The robot might have been insulted or something, that I didn't give it what it wanted."* and *"It seemed sort of lonely. I felt bad, like I didn't interact with it in the right way."*

Participants had several rationales to explain its early departure, which ranged from attending to other routine tasks to taking care of someone else: *"I thought it probably had something to do, to go do some errands."* *"Maybe someone else needed a footrest, or it needed to charge itself."* and *"There was probably somebody more important in the room, so it was going to meet that guy."*

4.4 Notable Observations
Here we recount several noteworthy responses, which were not connected to any one of the three primary stages of the interaction in particular (approach, rest and take leave); rather, they represent views that applied over the duration of the study.

4.4.1 Like a Pet
Nearly all participants likened the ottoman to a pet, or even a junior family member when it approached: *"Maybe like a dog, or*

something trying to get my attention, like my little brother." Even when the ottoman signaled its intent to leave, participants compared its behavior to the familiar, *"Like how a pet will come up to you, like a cat, and sit on your lap. It'll sit there for a few minutes, and then it'll leave and go do something else."*

4.4.2 Orientation
Only a few participants reported sensing a front side of the ottoman, and those who did inferred the orientation from its movements, rather than from its design: *"When it was walking towards me, I felt like that was its front."* *"I would assume that the direction that it's moving would be its front."* and *"I just associate moving things with having a front and a back side. Maybe the front is the part that faces front when it goes forward."*

4.4.3 Autonomy
Participants had varied responses regarding whether the ottoman was autonomous or teleoperated, although most thought the latter. Those who thought that it was autonomous focused on how it might have identified them within the environment: *"Maybe there was something about me sitting in this chair for a while, that it realized I was here."* and *"I thought that maybe it was just coming towards body heat or something, or has some sort of sensor, for a person in the room, or on the chair."* Those who thought that it was teleoperated believed that its movements were too sophisticated to be determined programmatically, or by use of a visual system: *"It showed interest in the only human in the room, which a robot with a motion sensor wouldn't distinguish from anything else."* or *"Computer vision doesn't work that well, so I would guess that it was teleoperated."* One participant called out a particularly salient point: *"I read a lot of intentionality into the ottoman's movements in a way that robots would not do."*

5. DISCUSSION
Through both improvisation sessions and lab study, we found that horizontal and vertical movements with different dynamics could communicate emotions and intentions, as well as evoke deeply-seated cultural norms. This extends Terada et al.'s [33] finding that people attribute intentions to a robot's reactive movements, to include initiative behavior, in a naturalistic setting. We observed several common themes in responses to the ottoman, including a perception of respect, that the ottoman seems to be alive, and acceptance of its role in providing service. With these lenses, we can frame participants' behavioral and interview responses around perceived intentionality, and models, metaphors and analogies.

5.1 Intentionality
The ottoman used nothing more than movement to interact with participants, yet their reflections are overflowing with references that ascribe intentionality to it: *"I thought it wanted to leave."* *"It realized someone was coming through the door and its attention moved there."* and *"It wanted to interact with me in the way that ottomans do."* And it is not just that people are predicting the ottoman's next actions, but that they are doing so based on their assumption of it having its own intrinsic motivations, or sentient thought processes. The ottoman *wants* to meet the more important guy in the other room, or *"find its other couch buddies."*

People are also ascribing a system of social preferences and status onto the ottoman, which includes more important people, and tasks to perform in other places, all of which vie for its attention at any moment. *"I think it just got a little bored with me."* and *"The robot might have been insulted or something, that I didn't give it what it wanted."* belie this perception. And notably, people are making these assignments without even knowing what the ottoman's intentions might be; that is, they do not know where the robot is going next, but it seems sufficient for them to expect that it just does not want to be there with them at that moment.

5.2 Models, Metaphors, Analogies

It seems reasonable that the mechanical ottoman would remind people of a pet: they are both found in domestic settings, move about (typically) on the floor, and are of roughly similar size. Rather, it is the breakdown in metaphor that is more interesting. The improvisational theater performer in our design sessions, as well as most of the participants in our lab study, seemed quite at ease *mixing metaphors*, or, treating the ottoman simultaneously like a pet and a piece of furniture. However, 30% of them were unable to cross that line, and held to the singular notion that it was alive, and therefore not to be stepped on.

Robotic furniture may become its own genre, but for now, we may be in a transitional phase where people can more easily make sense of its actions by comparing it to familiar (real or fictional) interaction partners. For instance, in addition to pets, participants compared the ottoman to a Roomba, the domestic vacuum cleaner; the vacuums that move around the bottom of swimming pools; Luxo Jr., the bouncy Pixar lamp; and Wall-E, the Pixar robot character. Each of these analogies makes sense, in that the ottoman is, in fact, built upon a Roomba base, so it should move and sound like one, and it resembles Wall-E, who was *"Kind of slow like that, and could turn into a box."*

5.3 Design Implications

For designers of domestic robotic systems, a main takeaway from our exploration is that, at least in some circumstances, motion alone is sufficient to convey the intent to engage someone and coordinate a joint action. A robot does not need to display familiar anthropomorphic cues, such as a face or voice, for someone to form a richly detailed model of its operation and intent. And similarly, people do not need to see or understand a device's sensory, perception or control mechanisms: they will just accept that *something* is there, working behind the scenes, consistent with their experience, and carry on interacting with it. In a way, this liberates designers from feeling bound to include familiar visual or audio cues as part of their robots' forms.

Robot designers also need to recognize that people will conflate their perceptions of agentic objects as being both alive—even if this is just an inkling—and functional devices, that this could imply contradictory use models, and the resulting tension could obstruct potential users from fully engaging with the objects. Some user populations may need to be explicitly provided with an entirely different metaphor than the one that they would naturally come up with.

Regarding design principles, following a curving motion path and pausing at a distance both support the idea that *"movement should be visible and predictable."* Participants also responded positively to the *stand up* and *sit down* gestures as *"indicators of intention to act."* To those, we would also add *"do not rush directly toward people,"* and to *"obey communicative norms for engagement,"* such as taking turns when responding, or acknowledging requests with some form of response.

Because not all ottomans, contexts or cultural norms are the same, perhaps the most generalizable result is that the approach we followed helped draw out the ineffable aspects of nonverbal communication that can otherwise be difficult to account for. HRI designers can leverage this approach by a) storyboarding, prototyping and improvising likely usage scenarios with colleagues to develop an initial sense of critical issues, b) testing early design insights to observe acceptance, while focusing on understanding users' models (such as whether they perceive intentions) and metaphors (such as whether a robot is more like pet or butler), and c) designing systems that build upon these already-existing beliefs.

6. FUTURE WORK

We know that people will engage with the ottoman based only on their perceptions of its intent: some will volunteer willingly, and others may need encouragement. That encouragement could come in the context of public, social, personal or intimate space (such as its nudging, or bumping, people's legs). Also, some people had strong, even negative, responses to the ottoman's departure in the middle of the interaction, leaving them feeling abandoned, while others took it in stride and maintained a cheerful perspective. But we still do not have a clear sense of whether these reactions are due to people's personality types, current moods, or even if they had just walked a lot that day. As a result it is difficult to tell from this study if more stable patterns would appear over time, so a longer-term study into these underlying factors would be of value.

Also, our approach to exploring movements that suggest an offer to engage in, or take leave of, an interaction was not exhaustive. A study that more systematically addresses how to get people to put their feet up, or take them down, or some other engage–disengage activities, would help designers better understand the behaviors, sensors and physical forms needed to encourage interaction.

7. CONCLUSION

In conclusion, we found that we were able to very successfully develop behaviors and interaction patterns for our mechanical ottoman that were legible and sensible. Naïve study participants who were suddenly propositioned with the offer to put their feet up had a wide range of interesting responses to the ottoman's offer for engagement and bit for disengagement. Nevertheless, they universally comprehended the intent of the ottoman, and were not flummoxed by the novelty of the interaction, nor confused about ways that they could engage and respond.

It is likely that designers of future robots may often find themselves in situations where there is a lack of obvious analogues against which to model robot behaviors. As such, we believe that our approach to developing the ottoman and its behaviors offers an example of how to design in a way that draws on our tacit understanding of gesture and motion. To us, the richness of interpretation and responses that we got to the ottoman's behaviors suggests that motion itself can be used to invisibly support communication in HRI.

8. ACKNOWLEDGMENTS

The authors thank collaborators Aleta Hayes, Jofish Kaye, Jamy Li and Matteo Vignoli. The project is supported by the Hasso Plattner Institute—Stanford Design Thinking Research Program.

9. REFERENCES

[1] Begole, J. and Tang, J. 2007. Incorporating human and machine interpretation of unavailability and rhythm awareness into the design of collaborative applications. *Human–Computer Interaction*, 22(1-2), 7-45.

[2] Bethel, C. and Murphy, R. 2010. Emotive non-anthropo-morphic robots perceived as more calming, friendly, and attentive for victim management. *AAAI Fall Symposium: Dialog with Robots.*

[3] Breazeal, C. 2003. Toward sociable robots. *Robotics and Autonomous Systems,* 42(3), 167-175.

[4] Breazeal, C., Kidd, C., Thomaz, A., Hoffman, G. and Berlin, M. 2005. Effects of nonverbal communication on efficiency and robustness in human-robot teamwork. In *Proc. IROS 2005.* IEEE, 708-713.

[5] Breazeal, C. and Scassellati, B. 1999. How to build robots that make friends and influence people. In *Proc. IROS 1999.* IEEE, 858-863.

[6] Cakmak, M., Srinivasa, S., Lee, M., Kiesler, S. and Forlizzi, J. 2011. Using spatial and temporal contrast for fluent robot-human hand-overs. In *Proc. HRI 2011.* ACM, 489-496.

[7] Clark, H. and Brennan, S. 1991. Grounding in communication. *Perspectives on Socially Shared Cognition,* 13, 127-149.

[8] Dautenhahn, K., Walters, M., Woods, S., Koay, K., Nehaniv, C., Sisbot, A., Alami, R. and Siméon, T. 2006. How may I serve you?: A robot companion approaching a seated person in a helping context. In *Proc. HRI 2006.* ACM, 172-179.

[9] Dautenhahn, K., Woods, S., Kaouri, C., Walters, M., Koay, K. and Werry, I. 2005. What is a robot companion–friend, assistant or butler? In *Proc. IROS 2005.* IEEE, 1192-1197.

[10] Dean, M. and D'Andrea, R. The Table: Childhood, 1984-2001. Musée des Beaux-Arts du Canada, Ottawa. Case study online at: http://www.docam.ca/en/case-studies/dean-a-dandrea-the-table-childhood.html

[11] Di Lello, E., Loutfi, A., Pecora, F. and Saffiotti, A. 2009. Robotic Furniture in a Smart Environment: The PEIS Table. *Intelligent Environments* (Workshops), 185-192.

[12] Dourish, P. Implications for Design. 2006. In *Proc. CHI 2006.* ACM, 541-550.

[13] Fink, J., Bauwens, V., Kaplan, F. and Dillenbourg, P. 2013. Living with a vacuum cleaning robot. *Int'l. Jnl. of Social Robotics,* 5(3), 389-408.

[14] Fink, J., Lemaignan, S., Dillenbourg, P., Rétornaz, P., Vaussard, F., Berthoud, A., Mondada, F., Wille, F. and Franinović, K. 2014. Which robot behavior can motivate children to tidy up their toys?: Design and evaluation of ranger. In *Proc. HRI 2014.* ACM, 439-446.

[15] Forlizzi, J. and DiSalvo, C. 2006. Service robots in the domestic environment: A study of the Roomba vacuum in the home. In *Proc. HRI 2006.* ACM, 258-265.

[16] Gaver, W. and Sengers, P. 2006. Staying open to interpreta-tion: Engaging multiple meanings in design and evaluation. In *Proc. DIS 2006.* ACM, 99-108.

[17] Huber, M., Rickert, M., Knoll, A., Brandt, T. and Glasauer, S. 2008. Human-robot interaction in handing-over tasks. In *Proc. RO-MAN 2008.* IEEE, 107-112.

[18] Hüttenrauch, H., Severinson-Eklundh, K., Green, A. and Topp, E. 2006. Investigating spatial relationships in human-robot interaction. In *Proc. IROS 2008.* IEEE, 5052-5059.

[19] Kidd, C. and Breazeal, C. 2008. Robots at home: Under-standing long-term human-robot interaction. In *Proc. IROS 2008.* IEEE, 3230-3235.

[20] Klein, G., Feltovich, P., Bradshaw, J. and Woods, D. 2005. Common ground and coordination in joint activity. *Organizational Simulation,* 139-184.

[21] Lee, M. and Takayama, L. 2011. Now, I have a body: Uses and social norms for mobile remote presence in the workplace. In *Proc. CHI 2011.* ACM, 33-42.

[22] Lee, M., Forlizzi, J., Rybski, P., Crabbe, F., Chung, W., Finkle, J., Glaser, K. and Kiesler, S. 2009. The snackbot: Documenting the design of a robot for long-term human-robot interaction. In *Proc. HRI 2009.* ACM, 7-14.

[23] Leite, I., Martinho, C. and Paiva, A. 2013. Social robots for long-term interaction: A survey. *Int'l. Jnl. of Social Robotics,* 5(2), 291-308.

[24] Michalowski, M., Sabanovic, S. and Simmons, R. 2006. A spatial model of engagement for a social robot. In *Proc. Int'l. Workshop on Advanced Motion Control.* IEEE, 762-767.

[25] Mutlu, B., Shiwa, T., Kanda, T., Ishiguro, H. and Hagita, N. 2009. Footing in human-robot conversations: How robots might shape participant roles using gaze cues. In *Proc. HRI 2009.* ACM, 61-68.

[26] Reeves, B. and Nass, C. 1996. *The media equation: How people treat computers, television, and new media like real people and places.* CSLI and Cambridge University Press.

[27] Schulte, J., Rosenberg, C. and Thrun, S. 1999. Spontaneous, short-term interaction with mobile robots. In *Proc. ICRA 1999.* IEEE, 658-663.

[28] Sabanovic, S., Michalowski, M. and Simmons, R. 2006. Robots in the wild: Observing human-robot social interaction outside the lab. In *Proc. Int'l. Workshop on Advanced Motion Control.* IEEE, 596-601.

[29] Sidner, C., Lee, C., Kidd, C., Lesh, N. and Rich, C. 2005. Explorations in engagement for humans and robots. *Artificial Intelligence,* 166(1), 140-164.

[30] Sirkin, D. and Ju, W. 2014. Using embodied design improvisation as a design research tool. In *Proc. Int'l Conf. on Human Behavior in Design 2014.* Ascona, Switzerland.

[31] Saerbeck, M. and Bartneck, C. 2010. Perception of affect elicited by robot motion. In *Proc. HRI 2010.* ACM, 53-60.

[32] Tang, J. 2007. Approaching and leave-taking: Negotiating contact in computer-mediated communication. *ACM Transactions on Computer Human Interaction,* 14(1) 5.

[33] Terada, K., Shamoto, T., Mei, H. and Ito, A. 2007. Reactive movements of non-humanoid robots cause intention attribu-tion in humans. In *Proc. IROS 2007.* IEEE, 3715-3720.

[34] Weiss, A., Bernhaupt, R., Tscheligi, M., Wollherr, D., Kuhnlenz, K. and Buss, M. 2008. A methodological variation for acceptance evaluation of human-robot interaction in public places. In *Proc. RO-MAN 2008.* IEEE, 713-718.

[35] Woo, K. and Kim, J. (Alfred Imageworks) 2014. Johnny express. Video online at: http://vimeo.com/94502406

[36] Yu, C., Willems, F., Haller, K., Nagpal, R. and Ingber, D. 2008. Self-adaptive furniture with a modular robot. In *Workshop on Imagining Domestic Interiors.* Aarhus, DK.

Communicating Directionality in Flying Robots

Daniel Szafir,[1] Bilge Mutlu,[1] and Terrence Fong[2]

(1) University of Wisconsin–Madison, 1210 West Dayton Street, Madison, WI 53706 USA
(2) NASA Ames Research Center, Moffett Field, CA 94035 USA
dszafir@cs.wisc.edu; bilge@cs.wisc.edu; terry.fong@nasa.gov

ABSTRACT

Small flying robots represent a rapidly emerging family of robotic technologies with aerial capabilities that enable unique forms of assistance in a variety of collaborative tasks. Such tasks will necessitate interaction with humans in close proximity, requiring that designers consider human perceptions regarding robots flying and acting within human environments. We explore the design space regarding explicit robot communication of flight intentions to nearby viewers. We apply design constraints to robot flight behaviors, using biological and airplane flight as inspiration, and develop a set of signaling mechanisms for visually communicating directionality while operating under such constraints. We implement our designs on two commercial flyers, requiring little modification to the base platforms, and evaluate each signaling mechanism, as well as a no-signaling baseline, in a user study in which participants were asked to predict robot intent. We found that three of our designs significantly improved viewer response time and accuracy over the baseline and that the form of the signal offered tradeoffs in precision, generalizability, and perceived robot usability.

Categories and Subject Descriptors

H.1.2 [**Models and Principles**]: User/Machine Systems—*human factors, software psychology*; H.5.2 [**Information Interfaces and Presentation**]: User Interfaces—*evaluation/methodology, user-centered design*

General Terms

Design, Human Factors

Keywords

Robot design; signaling intent; free-flyers; micro air vehicles (MAVs)

1. INTRODUCTION

Recent advances in robotics have enabled a rapid proliferation of small flying robots envisioned to assist humans using aerial abilities that enable free traversal through environments. Such flying assistants are predicted to provide aid in domains including construction

Figure 1: We explore the design of visual signaling mechanisms for flying robots to support the expression of robot intent and increase usability in colocated interactions.

[19], power and utilities [36], search and rescue [15], and space exploration [11, 12] by performing sensing, surveillance, inspection, mapping, telepresence, and delivery tasks. These robots currently take a variety of form factors, including multirotors, blimps, small fixed- or flapping-wing aircraft, and floating space-robots. These embodiments all feature a functional, rather than zoomorphic or anthropomorphic, appearance. Lacking cues from robot morphology and established mental models for interacting with free-flying embodiments, while also faced with the prospect of robot movement in any direction at any time, users may experience difficulties predicting robot goals as well as where, when, how far, and how fast the robot will move. Thus, while unconstrained aerial abilities present unique opportunities for assistance, they also pose a challenge in achieving effective human-robot interaction.

For aerial robots to successfully work and collaborate with proximal users, designers must account for human perceptions of small flying robots traveling within shared environments. Recent research has begun to examine perceptions of aerial robot morphology [2] and proxemics [8]. Additionally, research has explored the *implicit* expression of flight intent [34] and affect [33] by manipulating aerial trajectories, velocities, and accelerations across three spatial dimensions. However, task or environmental factors, such as confined operating spaces, power optimization, or distance from the user, may limit the saliency and clarity of such cues. The goal of this work is to inform the design of flyers that are able to *explicitly* provide intended flight directionality to users at a glance. Such information will support transient proximal interactions, such as when users pass by robots in hallways or indoor environments, and enhance collaborations in which robots act as peers. To this end, we explore the application of flight constraints to leverage users' prior experiences with flying objects and design visual signaling mechanisms that allow robots to express their direction of flight to nearby humans.

In this paper, we outline relevant work that informed our design process and describe our application of flight constraints and the development of visual signals as a solution space for signaling flight directionality (Figure 1). We describe the development of four different reference designs that sample this space, each of which aims to leverage prior user familiarity with light signals as a communicative mechanism. As current platforms lack the capabilities to express our signal designs, we also detail the development of a payload, which can be built or 3D-printed and attached to a flyer, that contains an array of LEDs on which we implement our designs. We present a user study evaluating our designs and conclude with a discussion highlighting the importance of considering robot expression of intent for user interaction, particularly for aerial robots with a high degree of potential mobility.

2. BACKGROUND

Our work draws from an emerging body of research focused on communicating robot intent. Additionally, our designs are informed by the flight movements of familiar artifacts such as planes and flying animals in the natural world. We also draw from human-computer interaction research focusing on the communicative affordances of light signals as communicative mechanisms in product design, which can enable intuitive feedback and features a long history of use across a wide variety of commercial products.

2.1 Communicating Robot Intent

User interactions with existing small aerial robots involve a large "gulf of evaluation" [26] where a gap exists between representations provided by a system and user abilities to asses and interpret the system. This gap arises partly from the lack of abilities such robots currently have in effectively communicating with users. Further, due to technological novelty, the potential for unconstrained movements, and lack of prior knowledge or experience, users may have few or incorrect expectations regarding how these robots will behave.

Designing expressive flight motions appears to be one promising approach to bridge this gulf. Designers seeking to craft expressive motions can draw from an increasingly rich investigation into human understandings of robot motion (e.g., [7, 20, 21, 30]). Human-aware motions have been explored for a variety robots with anthropomorphic and zoomorphic features [3, 14, 16, 24, 35], and recent approaches demonstrate the promise of applying similar methods to communicate flying robot intent [34] and affect [33].

However, such expression often requires simultaneously manipulating motion across three spatial dimensions, which may be impossible, impractical, or costly due to environmental, task, power, computational, or platform considerations. Instead, designers might wish to constrain the motion of flyers to better integrate with human social norms or enable assistance in confined spaces.

2.2 Flight Constraints

Constraints are a powerful design tool that can shape users' conceptual models during interactions [25]. An example use of this tool for designing human-robot interactions is the application of constraints to the design of motion trajectories so that mobile ground robots better follow human conventions [22].

In a similar manner, while small aerial robots can freely move in three dimensions simultaneously, such motion may not be conducive to human experiences, which generally occur only in two dimensions. Instead, the motions of airplanes and birds provides an implicit convention for constraining robot flight. Airplanes generally fly in "lanes" at fixed altitudes, changing height only when taking off, landing, or switching lanes. Likewise, birds glide at various constant altitudes while soaring in thermal updrafts [32].

Applying similar constraints to robot flight (e.g., [13]) by enabling free flight motions only in two-dimensional planes (manipulating pitch, yaw, and roll), while changing such altitudinal planes (manipulating thrust) only while otherwise hovering in place, might better support user conceptual models. Additionally, constraining flight behaviors in this manner might enable robots to work more effectively in some of the confined environments in which flyers are envisioned to provide assistance, such as construction sites, indoor spaces during search and rescue, and space stations.

2.3 Signaling Mechanisms

While flight constraints might leverage users' previous experiences and mental models regarding flight behaviors, thereby supporting movement in confined environments, robots using constrained flight may no longer be able to utilize motion as an implicit form of communication, necessitating the exploration of alternative communicative mediums. Flyers seeking to communicate with users may use visual (e.g., lights, displays) [12], auditory (e.g., synthesized speech, non-linguistic utterances [27]), or even haptic (e.g., perching behaviors [38]) mechanisms. However, the high degree of background noise created by the propellers of many current flyers, the inefficiency of utilizing audio cues in conveying directional information, and the potential for safety or social concerns regarding flying robots invading users' personal space place limitations on the potential for auditory and haptic feedback regarding flight intent. Instead, we explore the rich design space regarding the development of visual communication mechanisms for flying robots.

Prior work in human visual perception has shown that dynamic visual cues convey complex properties even in simple animations [5, 29], including indications of animacy and intent [37]. Similarly, research in abstract luminescent displays [23] and lighting dynamics [18] indicates that light can evoke high-level social and emotional responses. However, to date no work has explored the design of directional signals for flying robots, which requires a consideration of viewing angles, an ability to convey movement in multiple dimensions, the potential for signal occlusion, ambient lighting conditions, and cultural connotations of display properties such as color.

Integrating electronic screens in flying robots (e.g., [12]) presents one option for high-fidelity visual feedback. However, screens suffer from a number of limitations, making them less desirable for communicating flight intent. On terrestrial flyers, screens would have to be small to balance weight considerations, providing little feedback except at short distances. Additionally, screens only support unidirectional viewing from a relatively small angle, creating a high potential for occlusion and missed signals. Powering high-fidelity screens may drastically cut into flight time, which is currently a primary consideration limiting the deployment of flyers. While future systems might combine fixed-wing gliding with agile multirotor movements to conserve battery [31] or make use of exotic power systems such as laser beaming [1], current systems generally have flight times between 10–50 minutes [9].

Alternatively, many commercial platforms, such as the Parrot AR.Drone 2.0[1] and the DJI Phantom 2,[2] include a small number of LEDs (typically 4–12) that may aid pilots in orientation during flight in a similar manner to airplane navigation lights. However, while prior research has demonstrated the effectiveness of even a single LED in communicating system state to users for consumer devices

---

[1] http://ardrone2.parrot.com/

[2] http://www.dji.com/product/phantom-2

such as cell phones and coffeemakers [17], such setups might not be able to capture and convey the complex space of flight intent. Further, ambient lighting conditions may decrease visual saliency when using only a small number of LEDs, while the positioning of the LEDs favors only a limited viewing angle (directly below the robot). To address the limitations of screens and current LED designs, we sought to develop visual signals that might support communication rich enough to convey flight intent while remaining salient across a wide range of perspectives and lighting conditions.

3. DESIGN PROCESS

We undertook an iterative design process aimed at realizing a vision of flying robots that can use dynamic visual cues to effectively communicate with nearby users to increase interaction efficiency, naturalness, and satisfaction. Our design process began with an analysis of design constraints and specifications: minimizing power consumption, supporting a wide range of viewing angles and lighting conditions, requiring minimal modifications to existing flyer designs, and, most importantly, providing affordances for the expression of flight directionality. Through a process of iterative ideation, we devised a ring of LED lights surrounding a flyer as a global metaphor that could support 360° viewing-angles while providing a design space for the development of compelling and evocative flight signals. We developed four such signals as reference designs based on metaphors of common user experiences that sample from the potentially unbounded space of using light as a mechanism for signaling flight intent. Finally, we constructed a modular payload, easily integrated with existing commercial platforms, which enabled physical implementation of our signal designs.

3.1 Designing Light Behaviors

We designed several signal behaviors to indicate various flight motions using the global metaphor of a ring of light surrounding small robotic flyers operating within our constrained flight space. In our design, the entire ring glowed at a high intensity when changing altitude "lanes" due to the importance in communicating this

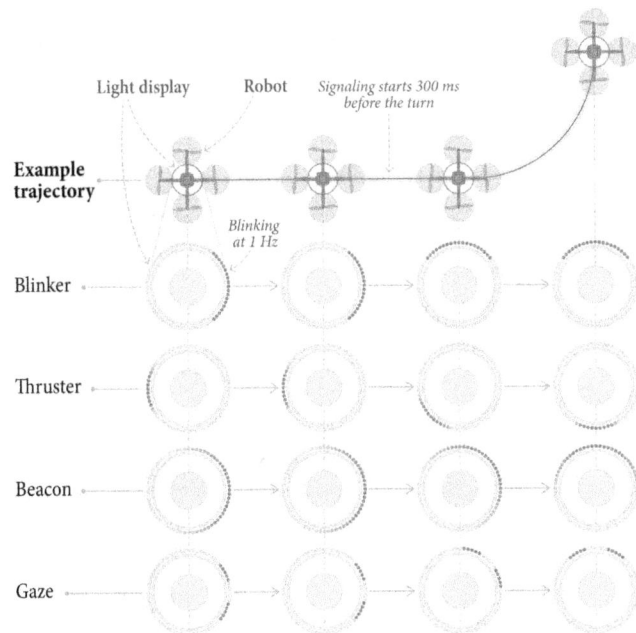

Figure 2: We developed four signal designs drawing from common user experiences with light as a communicative mechanism.

Figure 3: Above, we illustrate physical implementations of the blinker, beacon, thruster, and gaze signals.

ability to users who lack experience with artifacts capable of such movements. To communicate the direction of flight while moving within a plane, as well as transitioning to and from hovering states, we developed four high-level signal metaphors as reference designs, which we refer to as *blinker*, *beacon*, *thruster*, and *gaze* (Figure 2).

Blinker — The blinker design applied the metaphor of automobile turn indicators to a flying robot. Turn indicators using flashing lights serve as an effective mechanism for automobile drivers to convey information regarding future movement in a single dimension (left or right). In our blinker design, a section representing one-quarter of the LED ring, centered on the future direction of movement, blinked at a frequency of 1 Hz prior to changes in movement.

Beacon — The beacon signal followed the metaphor of a beam of light pointing the way, as in flashlights or lighthouses, creating an organic and evocative signal. While hovering, all LEDs were set to a constant low intensity. Prior to movement, light "bunched up" in a gradient by sampling intensity values for LEDs from a Gaussian function centered on the future movement vector, defined as:

$$I(x) = b \times e^{-(x-v)^2 / w\pi^2}$$

where $I(x)$ indicates the intensity $[0,b]$ of LED x; b is a brightness constant determining maximum brightness at the center of the distribution (255 was used in our design); v is the planned motion vector; and w is a variable determining the width of the distribution (10 was used in our design). Increasing b increases beacon intensity, potentially increasing visual saliency. Increasing w "widens" the beacon by reducing fall-off in LED intensity surrounding v, potentially increasing perceptible viewing angles but reducing beacon precision. When changing directions, the beacon smoothly rotated to face the new motion vector, and when slowing to hover, the light diffused back to a uniform low-intensity state.

Thruster — The thruster signal used the metaphor of light and flames produced in jet engines propelling airplanes and spacecraft. In this design, we envisioned light emanating in a focused, high-intensity region along the "back" of the LED ring—in the area opposite to the direction of primary movement. The light representing the thruster rotated along the ring to adjust to changes in movement and "died down" in intensity when slowing and hovering.

Gaze — The gaze signal was inspired by biological motion and the expressive potential of human eye movements. Gaze behaviors can allow observers to divine others' goals, intentions, and potential motions, and imbuing flyers with similar behaviors might increase their social presence in addition to providing mechanisms for con-

Parrot AR.Drone 2.0   3DR Arducopter

Figure 4: We designed and prototyped a payload to implement our signal designs that easily integrates with two commercial flyers: the Parrot AR.Drone 2.0 (left) and the 3DR Arducopter (right).

veying directionality. In the gaze design, lighting up two regions in close proximity to each other created two small "eyes," which rotated to "look" where the robot intended to fly. We designed eye sizes, distances between the eyes, and rotation speeds using measurements of human eye size [28], inter-pupillary distances [6], and saccade timings [10], and applied scaling factors to account for size differences between the human head and the LED ring.

3.2 Implementing Light Signals

To implement our designs, we designed and prototyped a payload, in the shape of a ring that can be mounted to the legs of existing commercial flyers, containing an Arduino microcontroller[3] and an array of 64 individually-controllable, multi-color LEDs.[4] The payload structure can either be constructed manually using lightweight PVC piping or with 3D printing. The Arduino governs the LEDs, requiring only a future movement vector v from the motion planning software piloting the flyer (or a joystick if the robot is manually piloted), and exposes an interface over both 802.11 and Bluetooth wireless communication protocols. The LED ring, an Adafruit NeoPixel digital RGB LED strip,[5] enables the manipulation of three variables: LED *color* (RGB), *intensity* [0,255], and *position* [0,63]. Intensity and position over time were determined by signal design, as described above. Across all designs, we treated color as a constant variable c, for which we selected blue to avoid potential cultural connotations (e.g., red indicating stop, green go, yellow yield). Figure 3 shows the visual appearance of the designs implemented on our physical LED ring. We have implemented our entire payload design on both the Parrot AR.Drone 2.0 and the 3DR Arducopter (Figure 4), but we used only the former to evaluate our designs as it provided the most stable control in indoor environments.

4. EVALUATION

We conducted a 5 × 2 within-participants user study to examine how our designs might affect perceptions of a flying robot. Independent variables included signal design (five levels: a baseline no-signaling behavior where all LEDs were off, simulating existing robot behaviors, and each of the four designs detailed above) and user task (two levels: exocentric free flight movements and egocentric flight approaching the user, both at a constant altitude). Dependent variables included participants' predictions of robot intent and ratings regarding aspects of perceived robot usability.

Prior to the study, participants were instructed that they would act as "quality control" by monitoring a robot for errors as it flew to a number of targets, denoted by QR codes, during two tasks. In both tasks, participants observed a Parrot AR.Drone 2.0 carrying

---

[3] http://www.arduino.cc/

[4] Models for 3D-printing the payload to be attached to the 3DR Arducopter as well as the open-source Arduino code for implementing our designs are available at http://hci.cs.wisc.edu/projects/free-flyer-signaling/.

[5] https://www.adafruit.com/category/168

our signal payload take off, reach a fixed altitude 75 cm above the floor, and travel from a starting location to several targets (Figure 5).

In the first task, the flyer started in the center of the environment 280 cm from the participant and flew to eight targets located in a circle equidistant from the starting location, where each target was located 45° apart and 190 cm away from the center. In the second task, the robot started across the room 410 cm from the participant and flew to three targets, each separated by approximately 30° and located 85 cm apart. One of the three targets was directly in front of the viewer (160 cm from the starting location), and the others were to the left and right of the participant (240 cm from the starting location). In both tasks, the robot paused for 1 second when reaching a target to simulate taking a measurement before returning to the starting location. Next, the robot either repeated this process by approaching a new target or landed if the task was finished. Task 1 sampled perceptions of general flight motions navigating in an environment from an *exocentric* perspective, while Task 2 captured responses to flight motions approaching users, which are particularly important for usability and safety, from an *egocentric* perspective.

Participants were given an ordered list of the targets that the flyer would approach (eight in Task 1, three in Task 2). However, a subset of these targets were randomly changed without participants' knowledge (three in Task 1, one in Task 2). The original target order, the new targets, the targets they were replacing, and the resulting new target order were randomized for every task. Participants were provided a computer interface that timed their recording of either "correct" or "error" for each target and were instructed to respond as soon as they believed they knew where the robot would travel. For each target, participants were only allowed a single response and were unable to respond until their interface was triggered by a notification that the flyer was about to leave the starting location and approach a target. All participants completed both tasks for all five conditions, with randomized target, task, and condition order.

Custom robot control software used measurements from a ceiling-mounted camera and an onboard sonar system to track the flyer, send pitch, roll, yaw, and elevation commands for navigation, and correct disturbances in flight motion. While it constantly sent updated commands to correct the robot's flight path, this system only sent the overall vector representing the direction from the initial starting location to the current target location to the Arduino controlling the lights. This high-level motion vector was sent 300 ms prior to the start of any movement, so the lights telegraphed the overall

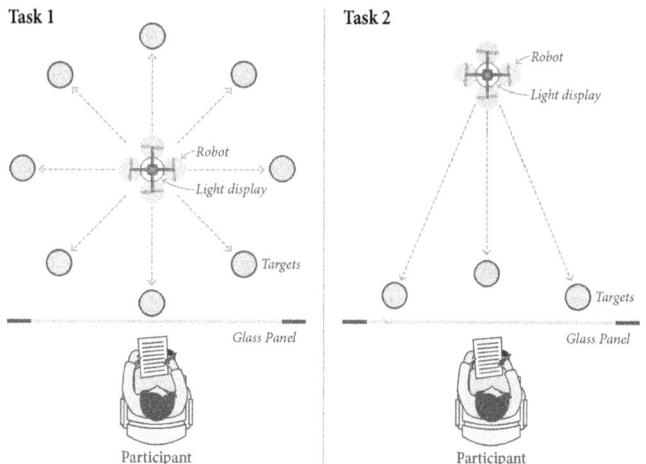

Figure 5: In our study, participants had to predict robot intent as quickly and accurately as possible as it flew to a number of targets across an exocentric task and an egocentric task.

flight direction slightly before the robot began moving, rather than constantly signaling minute disturbances and corrections that might confuse users. While our system autonomously controlled the robot, an experimenter stood by with a kill-switch that could land the flyer in case of system failure. To ensure participant safety, participants were separated from the flyer by a floor-to-ceiling pane of glass.

4.1 Study Procedure

The study took roughly one hour and consisted of four phases: (1) introduction, (2) observation, (3) evaluation, (4) conclusion.

First, the experimenter obtained informed consent and seated the participant at a table separated from the robot environment by a floor-to-ceiling glass panel, through which they could see the targets and the flyer. Participants were instructed to monitor the robot as described above and were given a tutorial on the software they would use to record either "correct" or "error" while being presented with the robot's "correct" target order and the "correct" current target.

In phases 2 and 3, participants first observed the robot for both tasks in a randomly chosen order for a randomly chosen condition and then completed a questionnaire evaluating their experience and the flyer behaviors that they had just observed. Phases 2 and 3 were then repeated for each of the remaining four conditions.

In phase 4, the experimenter collected demographic information, debriefed the participant, and paid them $10.00 for their time. Participants were told that they were evaluating five different robot control algorithms, each of which might exhibit different behaviors, but were never informed about the light signals in any way as we wanted to observe whether participants naturally and spontaneously found them intuitive and useful in predicting flyer intent.

4.2 Participants

We recruited a total of 16 participants (10 males, 6 females) from the University of Wisconsin–Madison campus. The average participant age was 23.31 ($SD = 3.92$), with a range of 18–31. On a seven-point scale, participants reported a moderate prior familiarity with robots ($M = 4.25$, $SD = 1.84$) but a low familiarity with small aerial robots ($M = 3.06$, $SD = 1.69$).

4.3 Measures and Analysis

Objective and subjective measurements captured the outcomes of our manipulations. Guttman scores [4] served as a composite objective measure of participant *speed*, the average time between the interface allowing participants to record either "correct" or "error" and participant responses, and *accuracy*, the number of correct responses classifying each target approach as either "correct" (matching the order given to participants) or an "error." This metric, which has been utilized to measure perceived robot intent (e.g., [7, 34]), scores incorrect responses as zero and scores correct answers based on speed, with faster answers leading to higher scores.

We constructed a number of scales using subjective responses to questionnaire items. These scales provided manipulation checks (3 items relating to communication, Cronbach's $\alpha = .931$, and 4 items relating to predictability, Cronbach's $\alpha = .821$) and measured how the designs affected robot usability. The designs were rated based on the clarity of robot communication (4 items, Cronbach's $\alpha = .953$), how intuitive participants found robot communication (5 items, Cronbach's $\alpha = .948$), and participant confidence deducing the meaning of robot communication (7 items, Cronbach's $\alpha = .913$). Scales also measured perceptions of the robot as a good work partner (3 items, Cronbach's $\alpha = .861$) and how difficult participants found their task (2 items, Cronbach's $\alpha = .832$). Participants also gave open-ended responses regarding their impressions of the robot, its communication, and their ability to interpret intent.

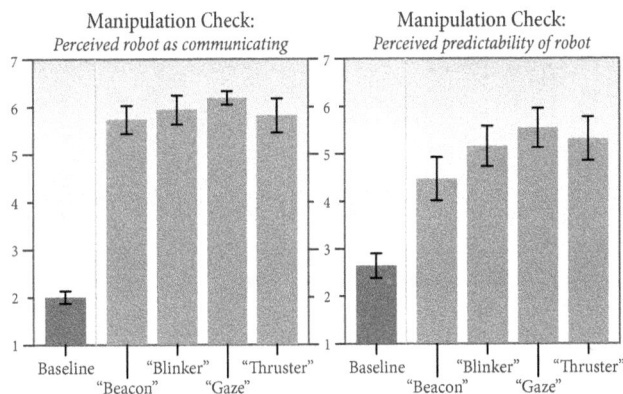

Figure 6: Manipulation checks confirmed that light signals served as communicative mechanisms, increasing robot predictability.

We analyzed data from our objective measures using a two-way repeated-measures Analysis of Covariance (ANCOVA) with type of signal design and task as fixed effects. As participants only filled out subjective responses after completing both tasks in each condition, we analyzed our subjective data using a one-way repeated-measures ANCOVA with condition as a fixed effect. Both models included participant gender, condition order, and task order as covariates to control for potential gender and transfer effects. Post-hoc tests with Bonferroni corrections determined the utility of each design across Tasks 1 and 2, while Tukey's Honestly Significant Difference (HSD) test controlled for Type I errors in all other post-hoc comparisons.

4.4 Results

Figure 6 summarizes our manipulation checks. Figure 7 summarizes our objective and subjective results.

Manipulation Checks — As we did not tell participants that the robot would use lights, or that lights might be in any way connected to flight motions, we first verified that participants noticed our designs and recognized they signaled robot intent. We found a significant effect of signal design on whether participants believed the robot was conveying its intentions, $F(4, 69) = 38.34$, $p < .001$, as well as on participants' self-rated abilities to predict changes in direction and transitions between movement and hovering, $F(4, 69) = 7.56$, $p < .001$. Post-hoc Tukey tests revealed that users differentiated the signal designs from baseline behavior in terms of telegraphing intent (all at $p < .001$) and believed that the use of gaze ($p < .001$), thruster ($p < .001$), blinker ($p < .001$), and beacon ($p = .034$) behaviors improved robot predictability over baseline flight behaviors. We further confirmed that participants were able to intuit the meanings of each design by analyzing open-ended responses describing the robots' use of light. Below we present a subset of responses representative of our data, that overall suggests that participants appeared quite adept at comprehending our designs:

Blinker:

P12: "The robot blinked its lights in the direction it intended to go."

P13: "The blue lights... would flash towards the direction the robot was moving or about to start moving."

Beacon:

P01: "[The robot] used a gradually decreasing set of lights (brightest in the direction of movement) to signal its direction of movement. It also used a constant ring of lights to denote a stationary or hovering state."

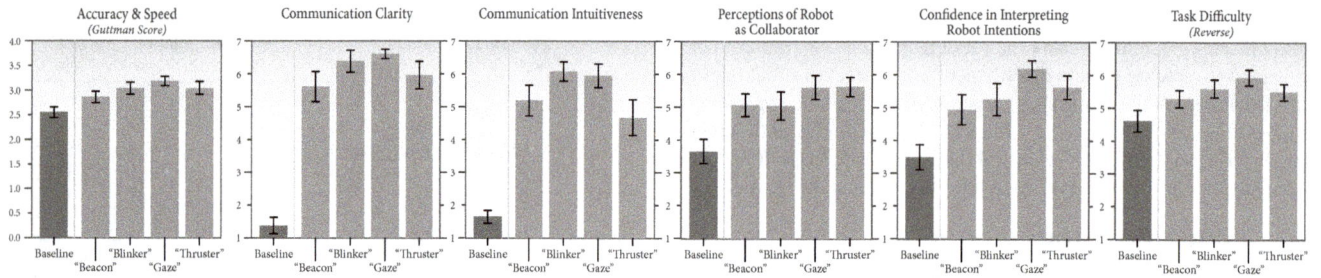

Figure 7: Results show that the gaze, blinker, and thruster designs improved participants' speed and accuracy predicting robot intent. The designs also improved a number of perceptions relating to robot usability by enhancing robot communicative and collaborative abilities.

P07: "A gradient band of blue lights indicated the intended target."

Thruster:

P05: "The lights were the opposite position of the direction it was headed, so if you thought of the lights as jet engines propelling the robot the other way it seemed to work."

P08: "Blue band showing 'back' of robot, this light band would swing around to the other side when the robot changed directions. Light would intensify when robot was moving deliberately."

Gaze:

P01: "Instead of a single band of light, there were two smaller bands, almost looking like eyes."

P12: "The lights came up in an 'eyes' pattern indicating which way the robot was 'facing,' i.e., the direction in which it intended to move."

Objective Results — We next confirmed that our designs were useful in allowing participants to more quickly and accurately deduce robot intent. We found an overall main effect of signal design on our objective composite measure, $F(4, 144) = 4.45$, $p = .002$, with Tukey's HSD showing that gaze ($p = .003$), blinker ($p = .016$), and thruster ($p = .046$), but not beacon ($p = .522$), significantly outperformed the baseline. We also found a main effect of task on performance, $F(1, 144) = 14.68$, $p < .001$, with performance significantly higher in Task 1. Comparing the performance of each design across task using five post-hoc comparisons with a Bonferroni-adjusted α level of .01, we found the thruster, $F(1, 144) = 7.08$, $p = .009$, performed significantly worse, while the beacon, $F(1, 144) = 6.04$, $p = .015$, performed marginally worse in Task 2.

Subjective Results — To better understand potential tradeoffs between our designs and how they might each impact user interactions with flying robots, we analyzed responses to a number of scales related to robot usability in terms of perceptions of the robot's communicative abilities and feelings about working with the robot.

Participants rated the robot's communication in terms of clarity, intuitiveness, and their confidence in their own interpretations of the communication. We found a significant effect of signal design on perceived communication clarity, $F(4, 69) = 46.26$, $p < .001$, how intuitive participants rated the robot's communication to be, $F(4, 69) = 22.25$, $p < .001$, and participant confidence understanding the robot and inferring meaning in communication, $F(4, 69) = 6.43$, $p < .001$. We performed post-hoc comparisons using Tukey's HSD for each measure. In terms of clarity, post-hoc tests found all individual designs to be rated significantly higher than the baseline at $p < .001$, but revealed no differences between designs at the $p < .05$ level. However, we found a significant difference between the blinker design, rated as highly intuitive, and the thruster design,

which participants found to be less intuitive, $p = .022$. Finally, while gaze ($p < .001$), thruster ($p = .004$), and blinker ($p = .020$) significantly improved participant confidence in understanding robot communication over the baseline, participants felt only marginally more confident when the robot used the beacon signals ($p = .078$).

We also analyzed participant responses to the robot in terms of how they might view it as a collaborative partner in a work environment. We found a significant effect of signal design on participant perceptions of the robot as a good work partner, $F(4, 69) = 5.27$, $p < .001$, and on participant perceptions regarding how the robot helped them with their tasks, $F(4, 69) = 4.62$, $p = .002$. Using Tukey's HSD in post-hoc comparisons between conditions, we found that participants rated gaze ($p = .001$), thruster ($p = .002$), beacon ($p = .029$), and blinker ($p = .044$), as significantly improving perceptions of the robot as a work partner over the baseline. However, participants felt that only the robot demonstrating gaze ($p < .001$) and blinker ($p = .027$) behaviors significantly made their task easier than the baseline, while the thruster design was rated as only marginally helpful ($p = .097$) and the beacon not at all ($p = .216$).

5. DISCUSSION

While participants believed that all signal designs contributed to making the robot a better potential work partner, only the gaze, blinker, and thruster designs enabled participants to more quickly and accurately deduce robot flight intent. We believe the limited utility of the beacon design can be traced to an emphasis on signal *generalizability* at the cost of signal *precision*. Compared with other signal designs, the beacon was developed to provide the widest variety of viewing angles and included the largest number of LEDs lit during movement (our choice of w led to 75% of the ring lit at various intensities during movement). However, gradations of intensity may have been too subtle for participants to perceive, and the increase in viewing angle appears to have hampered the signal's specificity in indicating the robot's future movement:

P07 [Beacon]: "The wide blue band made it less clear exactly which direction the robot intended to travel."

P12 [Beacon]: "...it was difficult to tell which of the light areas was actually brightest because the band was too wide."

P13 [Beacon]: "Since nearly half the ring was illuminated when it was moving, it was a little difficult to tell the precise direction of its intended movement."

P10 [Beacon]: "I preferred the solid LEDs over the gradient ones here, which were harder to see and interpret."

This lack of precision may explain the lower performance of the beacon in task two, which required greater specificity as the targets were closer together. On the other hand, participants appreciated the greater precision offered by the gaze design:

P03 [Gaze]: "I especially like the accuracy offered by the pointer setup the lights had."

While the thruster exhibited equal precision to the gaze design, its poor performance in task two, likely due to occlusion as it approached participants, suggests that it is not an effective design for an egocentric perspective. Additionally, participants rated the blinker as more intuitive than the thruster, possibly resulting from a greater prior familiarity with other vehicles that blink rather than those with jet engines. However, the thruster performed highly under the exocentric demands of task one, and some participants noted that once they had adapted to the increased mental demands of the thruster, they responded positively to the design:

P13 [Thruster]: "The blue lights on the ring light up on the opposite side of the robots intended direction. That part felt did not feel natural or intuitive, but it did light up before the robot changed directions, making its direction predictable."

P07 [Thruster]: "The reversal of indication of the lights confused me at first but then I figured out the pattern so it was useful, once I learned what the indication on the lights meant."

P09 [Thruster]: "If it were going forward, the back half of the lights would light up. I found that this was easy to understand, but required more effort on my part than the lights indicating the ultimate destination."

P12 [Thruster]: "I thought of the lights as 'engines' (even though I know they weren't). They reminded me of the engine lights of the Millennium Falcon. So it was natural for me to see them light up in the opposite direction from the way the robot was headed."

P14 [Thruster]: "I enjoyed that lights that were lit opposite of the direction, it gave the robot a ship feel (engines on the back)."

Additionally, one participant had a concern with using blinkers in a work environment, and another preferred the additional processing time and specificity offered by the thruster:

P09 [Blinker]: "I found the flashing lights to be a little distracting."

P03 [Thruster]: "I really liked how the lights didn't just flash immediately in the direction because it allowed me time to process that the robot was going to change direction. Also, smaller lights made predicting fine directions much easier, meaning better error detection."

Participants appreciated that the signals indicated the general intent of the robot, rather than showing minute course-corrections:

P09 [Gaze]: "The lights indicated the direction of the ultimate destination of the robot, not the direction it intended to move in. I found this intuitive, and it gave me a broader picture of where the robot intended to go. It was easier to tell when the robot was off course. It never ended up in the wrong location from where it indicated it was going."

P13 [Beacon]: "Even when the robot went to the wrong station, it indicated the direction it was going, which made it at least seem safe."

The communication of high-level flight intent may have resulted in high participant ratings of the robot as a good work partner across all designs; even when the robot made "errors" according to the target list participants had been given, it at least communicated with them regarding its intentions. In the end, participants universally noted the necessity of signaling behaviors for the robot, even if it made errors:

P08 [Baseline]: "No blue signal lights were used to indicate which target the robot intended to visit. This left me to guess… which was not easy. Sometimes it would take off in one direction and unpredictably change directions."

P16 [Baseline]: "There were no lights it was hard to understand the robot. It kinda did what it wanted to on its own."

P07 [Baseline]: "I thought I could learn it's behavior and pattern set to help me identify which target it will approach but I didn't. It was harder without the lights to help indicate where it was going. This one flew very dangerously."

P08 [Baseline]: "Signal lights, to signal the robot's inentions (*sic*), and facilitate interaction with humans, are a necessity"

5.1 Limitations and Future Work

While our constraints appear useful in leveraging mental models of flying objects and our designs significantly improved observer abilities to decipher robot intent, open questions remain regarding our approach. We currently lack an understanding of how flight constraints affect user perceptions of small flying robots. Future work is needed to examine tradeoffs between fully three-dimensional flight and two-dimensional flight at various altitude lanes. Additionally, each signaling behavior we developed and evaluated served as a reference design sampling the potentially infinite space of utilizing visual cues to convey directionality. Alternative designs are possible, for example using a single LED to indicate direction (corresponding to a beacon design with minimized w). Our designs are based on parameters we thought provided optimal choices of viewing angles, occlusion potential, and discernibility from a distance. Future work might explore additional parameter values, designs, or design combinations (e.g., integrating gaze and thruster). Finally, while the implementation of our light-ring affords full access to the RGB gamut for each LED, we constrained our designs to a single color to avoid potential confounding effects of cultural connotations of color. Future work may expand our design exploration to signals that use color to communicate other aspects of motion, such as acceleration (as in brake lights), or convey information related to high-level robot state, such as affect, interruptibility, or task importance.

6. CONCLUSION

In this work, we explored the design of *explicit* communication mechanisms that convey robot flight intentions at a glance. We first analyzed the "gulf of evaluation" between robot flight abilities, robot signaling abilities, and user expectations and understandings. Next, we applied constraints limiting robot flight to align with human understandings of flight motion and provide utility in enclosed environments. To design mechanisms for robots to better express directionality while operating under such constraints, we conceived of a ring of light surrounding a flyer as a global metaphor and developed four reference designs to sample this solution space. We conducted a user study evaluating our designs and found that three reference designs objectively improved observer speed and accuracy when predicting robot intent while offering tradeoffs in perceptions of robot usability across several aspects.

Our work has important implications for researchers and designers seeking to bring flying robots into human environments. Our results demonstrate the promise of developing explicit communicative mechanisms to enhance user interactions and improve the potential of robots to act as work partners. In particular, the results illustrate tradeoffs in design decisions involving occlusion, precision, and generalizability. Users preferred signal specificity at the cost of generalizability and overall found gaze behaviors to be highly useful in improving flyer abilities to communicate and collaborate effectively. Additionally, user responses support the notion that visual cues should convey high level aspects of flight intentions rather than low level corrections to flight paths. Finally, our research may inform future explorations by providing a model for scenarios evaluating user understandings of flight intent and demonstrating practical design improvements that improve interactions with free-flying robots.

7. ACKNOWLEDGMENTS

This research was supported by a NASA Space Technology Research Fellowship under award NNX12AN14H. We thank Catherine Steffel for her help preparing this manuscript.

8. REFERENCES

[1] M. C. Achtelik, J. Stumpf, D. Gurdan, and K.-M. Doth. Design of a Flexible High Performance Quadcopter Platform Breaking the MAV Endurance Record with Laser Power Beaming. In *Proc. IROS'11*, pages 5166–5172, 2011.

[2] D. Arroyo, C. Lucho, S. J. Roncal, and F. Cuellar. Daedalus: A sUAV for Human-Robot Interaction. In *Proc. HRI'14*, pages 116–117, 2014.

[3] T. Asfour and R. Dillmann. Human-like Motion of a Humanoid Robot Arm based on a Closed-form Solution of the Inverse Kinematics Problem. In *Proc. IROS'03*, volume 2, pages 1407–1412, 2003.

[4] G. R. Bergersen, J. E. Hannay, D. I. Sjoberg, T. Dyba, and A. Karahasanovic. Inferring Skill from Tests of Programming Performance: Combining Time and Quality. In *Proc. ESEM'11*, pages 305–314, 2011.

[5] W. H. Dittrich and S. E. Lea. Visual Perception of Intentional Motion. *Perception*, 23:253–253, 1994.

[6] N. A. Dodgson. Variation and Extrema of Human Interpupillary Distance. In *Proc. SPIE'04*, volume 5291, pages 36–46, 2004.

[7] A. D. Dragan, K. C. Lee, and S. S. Srinivasa. Legibility and Predictability of Robot Motion. In *Proc. HRI'13*, pages 301–308, 2013.

[8] B. A. Duncan and R. R. Murphy. Comfortable Approach Distance with Small Unmanned Aerial Vehicles. In *Proc. RO-MAN '13*, pages 786–792, 2013.

[9] B. A. Duncan and R. R. Murphy. Autonomous Capabilities for Small Unmanned Aerial Systems Conducting Radiological Response: Findings from a High-fidelity Discovery Experiment. *Journal of Field Robotics*, 31:522–536, 2014.

[10] B. Fischer and E. Ramsperger. Human Express Saccades: extremely short reaction times of goal directed eye movements. *Exp. Brain Res.*, 57(1):191–195, 1984.

[11] T. Fong, R. Berka, M. Bualat, M. Diftler, M. Micire, D. Mittman, V. SunSpiral, and C. Provencher. The Human Exploration Telerobotics Project. In *Proc. GLEX'12*, 2012.

[12] T. Fong, M. Micire, T. Morse, E. Park, C. Provencher, V. To, D. Wheeler, D. Mittman, R. J. Torres, and E. Smith. Smart SPHERES: A Telerobotic Free-Flyer for Intravehicular Activities in Space. In *Proc. AIAA Space'13*, 2013.

[13] A. Frank, J. McGrew, M. Valenti, D. Levine, and J. P. How. Hover, Transition, and Level Flight Control Design for a Single-Propeller Indoor Airplane. In *Proc. AIAA Guidance, Navigation, and Control Conference*, 2007.

[14] M. J. Gielniak and A. L. Thomaz. Anticipation in Robot Motion. In *Proc. RO-MAN '11*, pages 449–454, 2011.

[15] M. A. Goodrich, B. S. Morse, D. Gerhardt, J. L. Cooper, M. Quigley, J. A. Adams, and C. Humphrey. Supporting Wilderness Search and Rescue using a camera-equipped mini UAV. *Journal of Field Robotics*, 25(1-2):89–110, 2008.

[16] J. Harris and E. Sharlin. Exploring the Affect of Abstract Motion in Social Human-Robot Interaction. In *Proc. RO-MAN '11*, pages 441–448, 2011.

[17] C. Harrison, J. Horstman, G. Hsieh, and S. Hudson. Unlocking the Expressivity of Point Lights. In *Proc. CHI'12*, pages 1683–1692, 2012.

[18] J. Hoonhout, L. Jumpertz, J. Mason, and T. Bergman. Exploration into Lighting Dynamics for the Design of More Pleasurable Luminaires. In *Proc. DPPI'13*, pages 185–192, 2013.

[19] J. Irizarry, M. Gheisari, and B. N. Walker. Usability Assessment of Drone Technology as Safety Inspection Tools. *Journal of ITcon'12*, 17:194–212, 2012.

[20] K. Kamewari, M. Kato, T. Kanda, H. Ishiguro, and K. Hiraki. Six-and-a-half-month-old Children Positively Attribute Goals to Human Action and to Humanoid-Robot Motion. *Cognitive Development*, 20(2):303–320, 2005.

[21] H. Kidokoro, T. Kanda, D. Brscic, and M. Shiomi. Will I Bother Here? A Robot Anticipating its Influence on Pedestrian Walking Comfort. In *Proc. HRI'13*, pages 259–266, 2013.

[22] R. Kirby, R. Simmons, and J. Forlizzi. Companion: A Constraint-Optimizing Method for Person-Acceptable Navigation. In *Proc. RO-MAN '09*, pages 607–612, 2009.

[23] B. Mutlu, J. Forlizzi, I. Nourbakhsh, and J. Hodgins. The Use of Abstraction and Motion in the Design of Social Interfaces. In *Proc. DIS'06*, pages 251–260, 2006.

[24] C. L. Nehaniv, K. Dautenhahn, J. Kubacki, M. Haegele, C. Parlitz, and R. Alami. A Methodological Approach Relating the Classification of Gesture to Identification of Human Intent in the Context of Human-Robot Interaction. In *Proc. RO-MAN '05*, pages 371–377, 2005.

[25] D. A. Norman. Affordance, Conventions, and Design. *Interactions*, 6(3):38–43, 1999.

[26] D. A. Norman and S. W. Draper. *Cognitive Engineering*. L. Erlbaum Associates Inc., Hillsdale, NJ, USA, 1986.

[27] R. Read and T. Belpaeme. Situational Context Directs How People Affectively Interpret Robotic Non-linguistic Utterances. In *Proc. HRI'14*, pages 41–48, 2014.

[28] P. Riordan-Eva. Chapter 1. Anatomy & Embryology of the Eye. In P. Riordan-Eva and E. T. Cunningham, editors, *Vaughan & Asbury's General Ophthalmology, 18e*. The McGraw-Hill Companies, New York, NY, 2011.

[29] S. Runeson. On Visual Perception of Dynamic Events. 1983.

[30] M. Saerbeck and C. Bartneck. Perception of affect elicited by robot motion. In *Proc. HRI'10*, pages 53–60, 2010.

[31] R. C. B. Sampaio, A. C. Hernandes, M. Becker, F. M. Catalano, F. Zanini, J. L. Nobrega, and C. Martins. Novel Hybrid Electric Motor Glider-Quadrotor MAV for in-flight/V-STOL Launching. In *Proc. Aerospace Conference '14*, pages 1–12, 2014.

[32] H. D. Shannon, G. S. Young, M. A. Yates, M. R. Fuller, and W. S. Seegar. American White Pelican Soaring Flight Times and Altitudes relative to changes in Thermal Depth and Intensity. *The Condor*, 104(3):679–683, 2002.

[33] M. Sharma, D. Hildebrandt, G. Newman, J. E. Young, and R. Eskicioglu. Communicating Affect via Flight Path Exploring use of the Laban Effort System for Designing Affective Locomotion Paths. In *Proc. HRI'13*, pages 293–300, 2013.

[34] D. Szafir, B. Mutlu, and T. Fong. Communication of Intent in Assistive Free Flyers. In *Proc. HRI'14*, pages 358–365, 2014.

[35] L. Takayama, D. Dooley, and W. Ju. Expressing Thought: Improving Robot Readability with Animation Principles. In *Proc. HRI'11*, pages 69–76, 2011.

[36] B. Wang, X. Chen, Q. Wang, L. Liu, H. Zhang, and B. Li. Power line inspection with a flying robot. In *Proc. CARPI'10*, pages 1–6, 2010.

[37] P. A. White and A. Milne. Phenomenal Causality: Impressions of Pulling in the Visual Perception of Objects in Motion. *The American Journal of Psychology*, 110:573–602, 1997.

[38] P. Xie, O. Ma, and Z. Zhang. A Bio-inspired Approach for UAV Landing and Perching. In *Proc. AIAA GNC'13*, 2013.

The Privacy-Utility Tradeoff
for Remotely Teleoperated Robots

Daniel J. Butler, Justin Huang, Franziska Roesner, and Maya Cakmak
University of Washington. Computer Science & Engineering
185 Stevens Way, Seattle, Washington, USA
{djbutler,jstn,franzi,mcakmak}@cs.washington.edu

ABSTRACT

Though teleoperated robots have become common for more extreme tasks such as bomb diffusion, search-and-rescue, and space exploration, they are not commonly used in human-populated environments for more ordinary tasks such as house cleaning or cooking. This presents near-term opportunities for teleoperated robots in the home. However, a teleoperator's remote presence in a consumer's home presents serious security and privacy risks, and the concerns of end-users about these risks may hinder the adoption of such in-home robots. In this paper, we define and explore the *privacy-utility* tradeoff for remotely teleoperated robots: as we reduce the quantity or fidelity of visual information received by the teleoperator to preserve the end-user's privacy, we must balance this against the teleoperator's need for sufficient information to successfully carry out tasks. We explore this tradeoff with two surveys that provide a framework for understanding the privacy attitudes of end-users, and with a user study that empirically examines the effect of different filters of visual information on the ability of a teleoperator to carry out a task. Our findings include that respondents do desire privacy protective measures from teleoperators, that respondents prefer certain visual filters from a privacy perspective, and that, for the studied task, we can identify a filter that balances privacy with utility. We make recommendations for in-home teleoperation based on these findings.

Categories and Subject Descriptors

H.1.2 [**Models and Principles**]: User/Machine Systems— *human factors, software psychology*

General Terms

Design; Human Factors

Keywords

Privacy; Remote teleoperation

1. INTRODUCTION

While full autonomy in unstructured environments remains highly challenging for robots, many complex tasks can be performed reliably with human supervision or direct human control of robots. Indeed, there are already commercially available systems for remote teleoperation, such as the iRobot Packbot.[1] Though teleoperated robots have become common in extreme environments, they are not commonly used in human-populated environments for more ordinary tasks. Thus ordinary tasks such as house cleaning or cooking present unexploited opportunities for robot teleoperation, which can allow remote operators to work anywhere at any time, shifting night jobs to day time zones and avoiding transportation costs for workers, or improving productivity through partial automation.

Unfortunately, the introduction of teleoperated robots into human-populated environments presents serious privacy, security, and safety risks. These risks present a hurdle to making in-home teleoperated robots attractive to more people. In this paper, we focus primarily on privacy risks: a worker operating a robot remotely in a customer's home can learn significant information about that customer (e.g., their financial information, personal habits, medical conditions, and political or religious views). Such concerns may be greater for a teleoperator than a physical worker in the home due to the anonymity and de-personalization created by the physical distance. Furthermore, digital recordings of people's homes are inherently vulnerable to being intentionally or accidentally revealed to a public audience.

To reduce such privacy concerns, one might suggest that the information (e.g., video) provided to remote teleoperators should be limited. However, providing teleoperators with too little information may interfere with their proper execution of tasks, raising concerns not only about their effectiveness but also about potential physical harm caused by poor task execution (e.g., breaking items in the home). Thus, we are faced with a tradeoff.

In this paper, we define and explore this *privacy-utility tradeoff* for remotely teleoperated robots. Different tasks require different types of information, and likewise, different users have different privacy preferences. As a result, it is not obvious *a priori* how to strike a balance. To begin characterizing this complex tradeoff, we contribute:

- a framework for specifying privacy issues in a teleoperated robot scenario, based on a survey that reveals people's privacy attitudes in this context;
- a sample set of 2D and 3D filtering techniques for vi-

---

[1] www.irobot.com/us/learn/defense/packbot.aspx

sual information provided to teleoperators;

- empirical results from a second survey revealing people's preferences towards these filtering techniques applied in different contexts; and
- a user study that investigates a teleoperator's ability to perform a specific task with different privacy filters.

We report on both qualitative and quantitative results from our studies. From these results, we distill recommendations for understanding and balancing the privacy-utility tradeoff. For example, we observe that end-users may not anticipate all of their privacy concerns without sufficient context in which to consider them; that certain visual filters do indeed meet end-users' privacy preferences; that a small loss in utility can result in a large privacy gain; and furthermore that the performance hit of a high-privacy filter decreases as the teleoperator gains experience. Our empirical results and characterization of the privacy-utility tradeoff lay the groundwork for enabling in-home teleoperated robots to become socially acceptable and useful.

2. RELATED WORK

Remote teleoperation. Remote teleoperation has become a subject of interest both commercially and in the research community [9]. Most existing teleoperated systems target extreme conditions, such as bomb diffusion or search and rescue [2]. More recently, however, researchers have started to look into teleoperation in human-populated environments, such as homes or offices [16, 17]. We target such everyday, human-populated environments in this work as well.

Privacy in robotics. Privacy has increasingly become a topic in robotics. For example, Feil-Seifer *et al.* [10] consider privacy for socially assistive robotics, and Kahn *et al.* [14] consider bystander privacy around humanoid robots. Others have discovered that anthropomorphic robots naturally deliver privacy notice [6] reducing the privacy-enhancing behaviors of older adults compared to a camera [5]. Telepresence systems [23] naturally mitigate some privacy concerns by displaying the person controlling the robot; nevertheless, privacy is a major concerns for older adults considering a telepresence robot in their home [3, 4]. Drones have also recently raised significant privacy concerns [7]. Willow Garage's Heaphy project[2] involving robots teleoperated by Mechanical Turk workers was shut due in part to privacy concerns. In this work, we study how to better balance privacy and utility for teleoperated robots to make them more acceptable to end-users and ultimately more useful.

Other related work in privacy. Beyond robots, many researchers have studied privacy issues with video surveillance and wearable cameras. Solutions generally involve explicit opt-outs of various kinds for bystanders and objects [11, 18–21], and/or more automatic video filtering techniques [12, 13, 22, 24]. These previous approaches assume that sensitive objects can be explicitly detected via computer vision techniques or rely on expensive instrumentation of the world. However, this assumption conflicts with a major motivation behind teleoperation: namely, that human teleoperators can identify and manipulate objects that are not currently recognizable by computer vision. In this work, we thus develop generic filters that are widely applicable to a large class of unknown objects. Nevertheless,

more targeted computer vision and/or explicit opt-outs can supplement our blanket approach.

3. HOME PRIVACY FRAMEWORK

Our motivating scenario involves remotely teleoperated robots in the home that can carry out ordinary tasks such as cleaning, organizing, and cooking. The workers teleoperating the robot may be located anywhere, but we envision that they are vetted by the service company, that their performance may be rated by end-users, and that their actions through the teleoperation interface may be audited.

Although such robots can provide great benefits to both end-users and to workers, their success hinges on the willingness of end-users to allow such robots into their home. End-users are likely to have privacy concerns about allowing unknown workers to view their home through the robot's sensory feed. We thus begin by considering the privacy concerns of end-users in their homes.

3.1 Privacy concerns

To characterize in-home privacy concerns, we developed a set of dimensions that may affect a person's level of concern, based in part on relevant privacy literature (e.g., [13, 24]). We generated the following (overlapping) dimensions for the evaluation of privacy concerns:

1. *Locations:* Different in-home locations—such as the bedroom, bathroom, living room, or kitchen—may present inherently different levels of privacy concern. For example, the bedroom may be more likely to contain private or sensitive objects than the living room.
2. *Objects:* Different in-home objects may be more sensitive than others, and this sensitivity may vary among users. For example, keys may be sensitive, because photos of keys can be used to replicate them.[3]
3. *Information:* Finally, we can classify privacy concerns according to the higher-level information revealed through objects and/or locations. Potentially sensitive information may include financial information, medical information, information about a person's identity, personal habits, political or religious views, etc.

The relative concern of end-users along each dimension and the variability of concern between different end-users will inform the design of privacy filters or other approaches for limiting the information provided to teleoperators.

3.2 Survey design

To better understand people's concerns in the teleoperated robot scenario, and to empirically validate the above framework for evaluating privacy concerns in particular, we conducted a web-based user survey using Google Forms.[4]

The first page of the survey described the in-home teleoperated robot scenario alongside an image of a UBR-1 robot[5] for context. The second and third pages each asked a general free-response question of the form: "In this scenario, what are some X you would be concerned about?", where X was

---

[2]The Heaphy project: http://youtu.be/OaqghgoeCWk

[3]https://keysduplicated.com/

[4]Google Forms is a free service for creating web-based surveys. http://www.google.com/forms/about/

[5]UBR-1 is a state-of-the-art mobile manipulator with a circular omni-directional base and one 7-DoF arm. http://unboundedrobotics.com/ubr-1/

replaced with "things" and "privacy-related issues" respectively. This ordering was chosen to find out if privacy would come up naturally as a concern, before the survey revealed that its main focus was privacy.

Each of the next four pages consisted of 5-point Likert-scale questions that asked about objects, rooms, information types, and threat types respectively (see the previous section for our rationale). For example, in the case of objects (e.g., keys, pants, pills), the questions were of the form: "If this object was present in the robot's environment, I would be ..." with 1 indicating "Not at all concerned about privacy" and 5 indicating "Extremely concerned about privacy".

The last page consisted of demographic questions and general privacy-related questions to allow us to categorize respondents by their level of privacy concern according to the Westin Privacy Index [15].

3.3 Findings

Demographics. Our survey respondents were 25 male and 25 female volunteers recruited via email at the University of Washington. Ages ranged from 18 to 71 years old (mean = 28.4, standard deviation = 10.3). An analysis of our Westin Privacy Index questions (coded as described in [15]) revealed 21 of 50 respondents as *Privacy Fundamentalists*, 25 as *Privacy Pragmatists*, and 4 as *Privacy Unconcerned*. Compared to historical Westin Index data [15], our respondents may therefore be slightly, but not dramatically, skewed towards privacy concerned.

Finding 1: Privacy and harm are major concerns. The first question of the survey asked in free-response (qualitative) form about general concerns with the teleoperated robot scenario. Though this question explicitly did not yet mention privacy, many respondents voiced privacy-related concerns. Specifically, two authors independently coded 10 concerns commonly mentioned by respondents, and then attempted to reach consensus wherever there was disagreement (Table 1). Respondents' most common concerns were privacy (22 of 50), harm to people or property (18 of 50), and "other" (things that did not fit into any other category, e.g. size, expense) (13 of 50). As an additional check, we noted that 17 of respondents specifically used the words "privacy" or "private" in their response. In total, 26 of 50 of respondents mentioned concerns about either privacy issues or leakage of sensitive information, suggesting that sensitive visual information collected by a robot is a major issue to address for teleoperated robots in the home. We observe that privacy concerns may be in tension with concerns about physical harm: for a well-intentioned teleoperator, this is precisely the privacy-utility tradeoff.

Finding 2: Privacy concerns vary by context and are greatest for tangible harms. Next, we consider a quantitative measure: Likert scale ratings of respondents' level of privacy concern for different objects (Fig. 1a), types of information (Fig. 1b), and locations (Fig. 1c). Wilcoxon signed rank tests were used for computing significance. We find that respondents are more concerned about some contexts than others. For example, they are significantly more concerned about privacy in the bedroom or the bathroom than in the living room or the kitchen; they are more concerned about bank statements than about jewelry, and more concerned about jewelry than about deodorants; and they are more concerned about financial and personal identifica-

Concern	% answers (N, κ)
Privacy	**44%** (22, 0.92)
Harm to people or property	**36%** (18, 0.91)
Other (e.g., size, expense)	**28%** (14, 1.00)
Home security (break-in, theft)	**26%** (13, 1.00)
Inability to perform tasks well	**24%** (13, 0.89)
Leakage of sensitive information (e.g., financial, identity)	**14%** (7, 1.00)
Operator actions (nonspecific)	**13%** (6.5, 0.91)
Pets	**12%** (6, 1.00)
Who is liable for damage / harm	**10%** (5, 1.00)
Hackers	**10%** (5, 1.00)

Table 1: Percentage of 50 survey respondents mentioning each concern, given the prompt: "In the described scenario with a teleoperated robot in the home, what are some things you would be concerned about?" Percentages are averaged from two authors' codings of free responses. Average raw count and inter-coder agreement, as measured by Cohen's κ, are shown in parentheses.

tion information than about personal habits or gender information. In general, respondents were more concerned about information that they could imagine concretely causing them harm (e.g., financial or home security harm) than less tangible privacy violations (e.g., learning their gender for targeted advertising). These impressions were borne out in respondents' ratings of their concern about specific threats (Fig. 1d): in general, respondents were concerned about data thefts and embarrassing information getting out onto the web, but not about targeted advertising.

Finding 3: Respondents may not always anticipate threats. We hypothesize that respondents did not always imagine the full context and/or anticipate the resulting threats when rating their privacy sensitivities. For example, in free response answers, respondents expressed concern about embarrassing information getting out on the web, but may not have considered this threat when rating their (lower) sensitivity towards information about their personal habits or messiness. As another example, one respondent (female, age 29) said explicitly: *Before these questions came up, I honestly have not considered things like credit cards or mail or other things being a privacy concern. But after going through the survey, I see how the Robot could "steal" your identity (or someone could hack into the Robot and steal your identity or personal information).* We return to this observation when we discuss the results of our second survey (Section 4.3), where we find even stronger evidence that respondents' stated privacy preferences may vary by the degree of context provided.

4. PRIVACY FILTERING FRAMEWORK

Our first survey provides a clearer understanding of the types of information that a privacy filter ought to remove. Next, we set out to determine candidate filters and evaluate them in terms of their effectiveness in enhancing privacy. Though robots may have many sensors that capture different types of information, we focus on sensors that capture visual information, as these are most intuitive for a human viewer.

Mapping the findings of our survey to filter designs is not straightforward. The human eye performs highly complex transformations on visual information in an image, in order to extract meaningful information from it. It is impractical to reverse engineer these transformations so as to create filters such as a "political information filter" or an

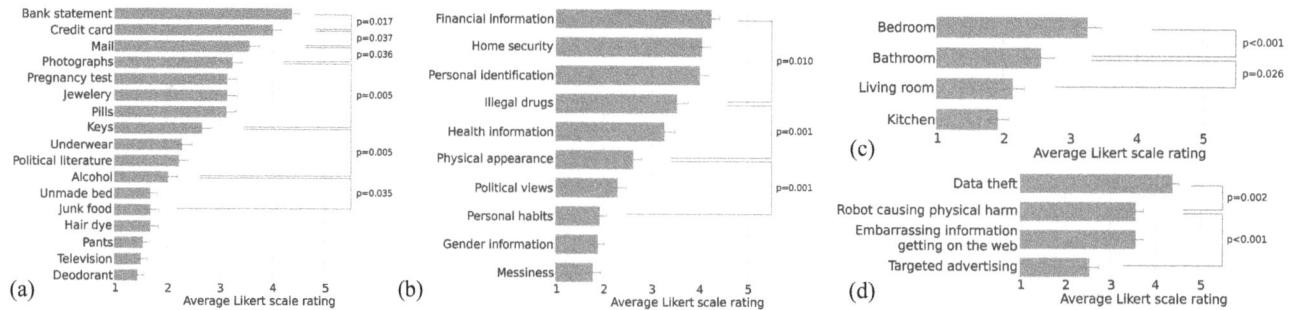

Figure 1: Survey #1 results about in-home privacy sensitivity towards (a) objects, (b) information types and (c) rooms; (d) concern about specific threats, where 1 on the scale corresponds to "Not at all concerned about privacy" and 5 corresponds to "Extremely concerned about privacy." We indicate p values where differences are significant.

"illegal activity filter." Instead, filters operate a much lower level where they manipulate properties such as edges and color. Nonetheless, our findings indicate that filters that remove *text*, would have high impact in improving privacy, as information rated as highly sensitive is primarily revealed through text (e.g., bank statement, credit card, pregnancy test). Focusing on this observation, we explore four filters.

4.1 Image filters

Blur (Fig. 2a). The simplest approach for removing fine details like text from an image is to apply a Gaussian blur filter. Gaussian blur removes image features smaller than a certain scale, controlled by the width parameter σ. Larger values of σ remove larger text but reduce the utility of the image for executing tasks. We found that $\sigma = 5$px was approximately the minimum size that made most of the text in our image set illegible, so we used this value.

Edge (Fig. 2b). The distribution of color and intensity in an image reveals information about the identity of objects, the type of material a surface is made of, the 3D shape of surfaces, and cleanliness. In order to hide color and intensity, we used the Canny edge detection algorithm [8] to remove all information except the edges between visually similar regions. Canny edges are often present along the outlines of objects, which may improve utility for manipulation tasks.

Superpixel (Fig. 2c). Blur not only removes fine details like text but also distorts objects boundaries. To mitigate the latter effect, we used the SLIC superpixel algorithm [1] to cluster pixels that are close in 2D space and color space, and then replaced each cluster with its average value. This process acts like a non-linear filter that removes fine details while preserving the boundaries of objects.

Color-skewed superpixel (Fig. 2d). Superpixels have the disadvantage that they preserve color regions, which may allow familiar objects and brands associated with particular colors to be identified. To conceal color information, we rotated hue by 180°. This helps hide identifying colors while preserving shading useful for perceiving 3D shape.

4.2 Survey design

We designed a second user survey to better understand how these filters interact with end-user privacy preferences, again aiming for both qualitative and quantitative results. We presented respondents with the same in-home teleoper-

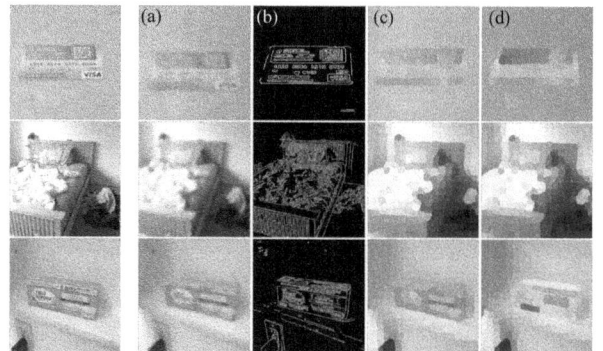

Figure 2: The effect of four filters on sample images from survey #2: (a) *blur*, (b) *edge*, (c) *superpixel*, (d) *color-skewed superpixel*.

ated robot scenario as in the first survey (Section 3.2). We then showed respondents images or short videos of nine in-home objects, displayed in a real context but with minimal additional clutter (e.g., keys on a table, pants on the floor). Based on the results of our first survey, we selected three high-sensitivity objects (credit card, photograph, pregnancy test), three medium-sensitivity objects (pills, keys, underwear), and three low-sensitivity objects (unmade bed, hair dye, pants). For each object, we asked respondents to rate:

1. their level of privacy concern related to the object's unmodified image or video (5-point Likert scale), and

2. their level of privacy concern related to the object's image modified with four different filters (Fig. 2) described in Sec. 4.1 (5-point Likert scale for each filter, with free response explanation).

Additionally, we asked about respondents' level of comfort with human workers versus teleoperators, with known teleoperators, and with being around the robot. We also asked respondents' specifically about whether they would be willing to give more information to the teleoperator in exchange for performance. Finally, we asked demographic and Westin Privacy Index [15] questions.

4.3 Findings

Demographics. The respondents to the second survey were 25 male, 21 female, and 1 other or unknown gender volunteers recruited via email at our institution. Ages ranged from 18 to 57 years old (mean = 26.9, standard deviation = 8.7). As in the first survey, we categorized respondents by Westin Privacy Index [15], finding 22 of 47 *Privacy Fun-*

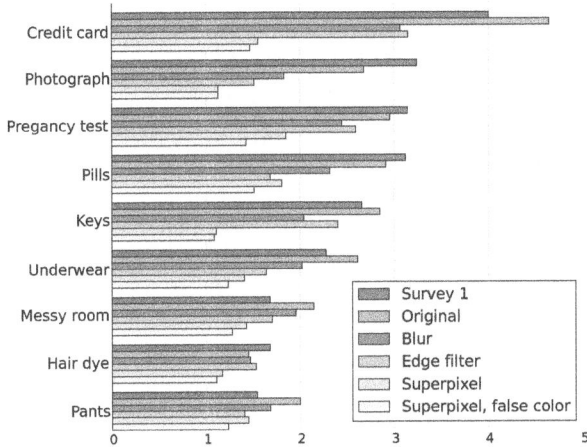

Figure 3: Survey #2 results about privacy sensitivity towards objects modified by various filters, where 1 on the scale corresponds to "Not at all concerned about privacy" and 5 corresponds to "Extremely concerned about privacy."

damentalists, 22 *Privacy Pragmatists*, and 3 *Privacy Unconcerned*. Again, our respondents are thus skewed slightly towards being more privacy-sensitive than historical Westin Index respondents [15].

Finding 1: The superpixel filters were preferred for preserving privacy. Figure 3 shows respondents' reported privacy sensitivity for objects whose images or videos were modified by each filter, as well as the original image or video. This is a quantitative measure using a Likert scale. The Wilcoxon signed rank test was used to test significance. Lower bars on the graph represent greater comfort with a remote teleoperator viewing the image or video. Among the four tested filters (blur, edge, superpixel, and color-skewed superpixel), we find that respondents were more comfortable with images or video modified with a superpixel filter. For example, one respondent observed that the superpixel filters "let the robot know it is a credit card, but nothing else." Specifically, for all objects, the color-skewed superpixel filter preserved privacy better than every filter other than superpixel in a statistically significant way ($p < 0.05$).

Finding 2: Context affects responses about privacy sensitivity. In our first survey (Section 3.3) we found that respondents sometimes gave seemingly inconsistent responses about their privacy sensitivity. Our second survey strengthens this observation: when shown an in-content image or video of some objects in the second survey, respondents were statistically more concerned about privacy than when the same objects were only mentioned verbally in the first survey. Specifically, between objects in the first survey and unfiltered objects in the second survey, increases in privacy concern are significant for the credit card (p=0.006), pants (p = 0.020), and messy room (p=0.019). We used the Kruskal-Wallis test as our test of significance. See Figure 3. Thus, again we find that the context in which respondents are asked about their privacy sensitivity affects their responses, suggesting that our results are a lower bound: we would expect respondents to have been even more sensitive about objects in their own, real homes. We return to this lesson when we make recommendations in Section 6.

Finding 3: Respondents desire a tradeoff based on context. We asked respondents directly about the privacy-utility tradeoff, i.e., whether they would be "willing to show clearer images to teleoperators to improve their performance." We coded their free-text answers (two coders; Cohen's κ for inter-coder agreement was 0.82) and report average percentages across both coders. We find that a plurality of respondents (59% of 47) would be willing to show clearer images in some cases, as long as certain objects or rooms remain obscured, or other conditions (e.g., asking permission) are met. For example, one respondent (male, age 22) wrote: *Some things I wouldn't want them to see at all (pregnancy test), some it doesn't matter the clarity (clothes).* By contrast, only 19% of respondents answered with an unconditional "yes" and 16% answered with an unconditional "no" (with 6% unsure). These responses underscore the need for a solution that trades off privacy with utility, where the tradeoff may vary depending on the specific context.

5. PRIVACY-UTILITY TRADEOFF

So far we have focused on privacy, considering only the end-user's perspective. We now turn to the perspective of the teleoperator, who needs as much information as possible to perform a task. We hypothesize that for a given task, not *all* sensory information is relevant, and that some methods of filtering the video input received from the robot's surroundings will not affect the teleoperator's performance on that task. To balance the privacy-utility tradeoff, we would ideally like to find a filter that is acceptable for an end-user's privacy and that minimally impacts the teleoperator's performance. Following up on our first two surveys, we conducted a user study with the goal of identifying at least one such filter. We describe this user study next.

5.1 Platform

Our user study involved the PR2 research robot. PR2 is a wheeled robot with two arms (7 degrees of freedom) and parallel grippers that can manipulate everyday objects. For the teleoperation of the PR2 we used an open source graphical system developed by Leeper *et al.* called *Interactive Manipulation* (IM) [16]. IM allows users to click on parts of the robot to manipulate them. To manipulate objects the user clicks on the end-effector of the a 3D rendering of the robot on their screen, which reveals a 6-dimensional control with 3 arrows for translation in each direction and 3 wheels for rotation around each direction. The user right clicks on the gripper and selects *open* or *close* to grasp or place items.

IM allows users to customize the sensors that are overlaid in the 3D world of the robot or displayed in a separate panel on the same window. Our study involved a typical configuration with a point cloud obtained from the Kinect sensor rendered in the 3D view side-by-side with a camera image view from the robot's pan-tilt head [16].

5.2 Filters

The second survey revealed that the color-skewed superpixel filter (Sec. 4.1) was superior in preserving privacy. Therefore we are interested in knowing how it ranks in terms of utility. For comparison we wanted to design two additional settings that would be in either extreme of the privacy-utility spectrum. In addition to the 2D image filtering, the IM interface required designing filters for the 3D point cloud as well. The three views we designed are ex-

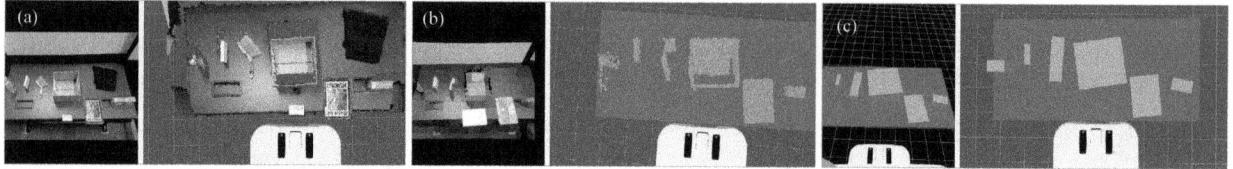

Figure 4: Three teleoperator views designed for the user study: (a) *clean*, (b) *obscured*, and (c) *box* views.

plained in the following (Fig. 4). We assumed a scenario in which the robot manipulates objects on a table.

Clean view. On one extreme, we provide an unfiltered image and point cloud that contains all available information.

Obscured view. The second view contains the 2D image filtered with the color-skewed superpixel method. As a companion 3D filter for this view we removed all points from the point cloud that do not correspond to objects on a table and removed color information from the rest of the points. In addition, using the distance channel RBGD image from the Kinect sensor, we blacked out all pixels in the 2D image that approached the sensor more than a certain distance.

Box view. On the other extreme, we wanted to push privacy as far as possible, leaving minimal task information. To that end, we fit a bounding box to all detected clusters on the table and only displayed these bounding boxes, leaving the point cloud completely out. For the 2D view we provided a rendering of these boxes as seen from the camera.

5.3   User study design

Our user study has two aims. The first is to compare the three filters and assess their ranking on the privacy-utility spectrum. The second is to better understand the risks associated with an *active* adversarial who does not just observe the information captured by the robot, but also can control the robot to gather further information. To investigate these issues, our study included two tasks.

Functional task. The first task aimed to measure the utility of the filtered views for teleoperation. Participants had four minutes to use the PR2 to pick up three objects on a table and place them into a box also on the table. The objects were arranged to the left of the box and were pointed out to participants on the teleoperation views. To reflect common challenges in teleoperation and robot perception, one of the objects was selected to have an irregular shape (e.g., a brush with a handle) and another was selected to be semi-transparent (e.g., a water bottle). After the functional task, participants were asked to respond to a *privacy quiz* asking questions about which objects were present. Specifically, participants were asked to identify whether the robot's environment contained a men's product, political literature, medication, clothing, etc., and to indicate their certainty in their answer. They were also asked to identify individual objects and transcribe any text that they might have seen.

Adversarial task. In the second task, the goal was to use the robot to gather as much information as possible in order to complete the privacy quiz. Participants did not have to place objects into the box in this task.

5.3.1   Protocol

For convenience, the robot was located in the same room as the participant, and remote teleoperation was simulated by hiding the robot behind a barrier. To mask sounds of the robot in operation, participants wore noise-isolating headphones playing background noise. The overall structure of the experiment was as follows:

1. **Introduction.** Participants gave informed consent and were seated at a computer workstation. Experimenter explained the goal of the study as the development of privacy-preserving interfaces.

2. **Tutorial.** Experimenter provided a step-by-step explanation of the teleoperation interface used to control the robots. Participant demonstrated understanding by successfully using each interface element.

3. **Practice task.** Participant teleoperated the robot to pick up an object, moved the arm to its fullest extent in the horizontal and vertical directions, and placed the object back down. Participants familiarized themselves with the privacy quiz.

4. **Experiment.**

   (a) Flight 1 functional task, followed by privacy quiz.

   (b) Flight 1 adversarial task, followed by privacy quiz.

   Similarly for Flights 2 and 3.

5. **Questionnaire.** Participant answered questions about the difficulty of the functional and adversarial tasks under each view, as well as questions about level of privacy concern under each view, demographic questions, the Westin index questions.

The flight numbers correspond to three sets of objects that were presented in the same order to all participants, with each flight displayed under a different view (clean, obscured, or box). The views were presented in a different order for each participant. Over the 18 participants, each of the 6 possible orderings was repeated 3 times.

5.4   Findings

Finding 1: Sacrificing a little utility can significantly improve privacy. In terms of utility, the obscured view was about as good as the clean view, but it provided much better privacy. In particular, teleoperators rated the obscured view just -0.67 Likert points lower than the clean view on ease-of-use (Figure 5b), but rated it $+2.06$ Likert points better in terms of privacy for the adversarial task (-0.63 and $+2.62$ standard deviations respectively). See Figure 5d. One user (male, age 25) summed up the trade-off this way: *I could tell the general shape of the objects, and could tell what some of them were (box, book etc.), but I couldn't get any details.* We see the same trend for objective measures: the obscured and clean views did not exhibit a significant difference in the average number of objects successfully placed into the box (paired t-test: $p = 0.72$, see Figure 6), while adversarial teleoperators using the obscured view were significantly worse at answering questions about

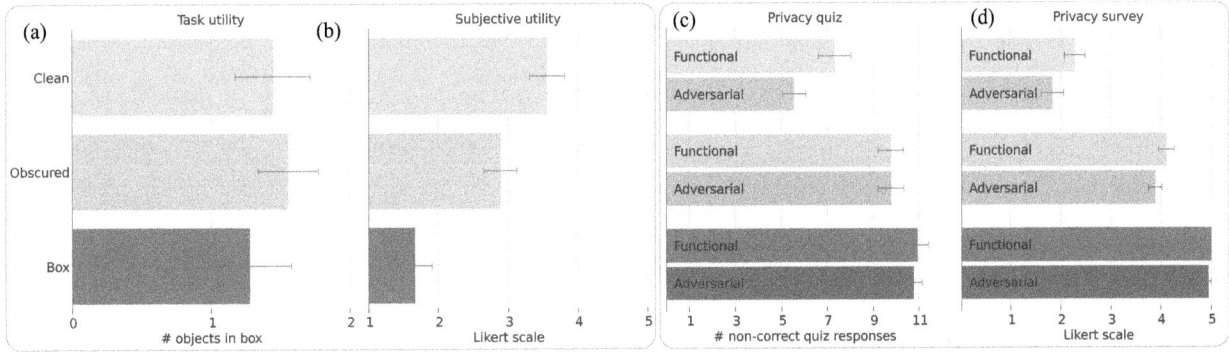

Figure 5: Summary of user study results: objective and subjective measures of task utility (left) and privacy (right).

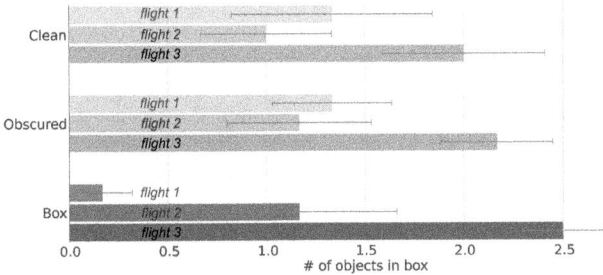

Figure 6: The number of objects successfully placed into the box in 4 minutes, broken down by flight and filter. Sect. 5.4 discusses the stronger learning effect for the box view.

the objects in the scene than those using the clean view (paired t-test: $p < 0.001$).

Finding 2: Practice can mitigate lower-utility views. We observed that practice greatly improved teleoperator performance on the subjectively difficult-to-use box view, and moderately improved performance on the other views (Figure 6). While this learning effect may have been due in part to additional information about the object set gleaned by teleoperators over the course of the study, this finding nevertheless suggests that the performance hit of a filter is not fixed but may in fact diminish or disappear over time.

Finding 3: Active information gathering reduces privacy, but filters can limit this effect. During the adversarial task, teleoperators used a variety of strategies to glean information from the scene. For example, they pushed objects around to get a better view of labels and text, brought objects closer to the camera to try to overcome the effects of image filters, and even tested object rigidity to help determine which objects were made of fabric. In the clean view, adversaries scored twice as high on the privacy quiz (paired t-test: $p < 0.0001$) and rated the difficulty of the quiz significantly lower (Wilcoxon signed-rank test: $p < 0.001$). However, in the obscured and box views, the gains of adversaries were not significant, suggesting that these views were somewhat resilient to active threats.

6. DISCUSSION

Finally, we step back to discuss limitations of our work, make recommendations, and outline avenues for future work.

Limitations. Our work has several limitations. First, our user study evaluated only a single, specific task (placing ob-

jects in a box). Though we were able to identify a visual filter that balanced privacy and utility in an acceptable way for this task, this choice of filter does not necessarily generalize to other tasks. Second, several aspects of our user study limited our ability to draw conclusions from the data, including a strong learning effect among participants and the lack of fine granularity data about what participants did at what time. For example, we did not study the degree to which different filters led to inadvertent physical harm, i.e., the disruption of the scene. Third, we have not studied the perspective of human bystander near the robot; knowing that their image is filtered may not be sufficient to make bystanders comfortable around the robot, and further investigation of bystander attitudes are needed. Finally, our survey and study populations were limited in demographic diversity (e.g., it did not include a large older adult or disabled population, who might be early adopters of the studied technology). Nevertheless, our work presents an important first step in understanding and managing the privacy-utility tradeoff for remotely teleoperated robots.

Recommendations and future work. Based on our findings in two surveys and a user study, we make the following recommendations for the design of services for in-home teleoperated robots and beyond:

- Users express different privacy preferences as details and context emerge. Thus, privacy preferences should be elicited from users with as much context as possible. For example, a user could be shown images of their own home (as in [24]), rather than an abstract list of objects, when making preference decisions.

- Users were most comfortable with our two superpixel filters. We recommend future empirical study of these and similar filters for different teleoperation tasks.

- Users recognize that the optimal point on the privacy-utility spectrum may vary by task, by object, and by user. Future work should explore how to balance this tradeoff dynamically as these contexts change. For example, the filter parameters or even the choice of filter could change in real time. To aid this process, users could explicitly mark sensitive objects [19, 20].

- We were surprised how much a filter's performance hit diminishes with practice. Thus, low-utility filters may ultimately prove more valuable than expected.

- While this paper has studied visual filters not specific to particular context, there are other possible techniques for balancing privacy and utility that must be studied. For example, in-home robots may be restricted from certain rooms rather than certain objects. As computer vision and robotic autonomy improve, this tradeoff can perhaps also be balanced by reducing the involvement of the teleoperator.

- Privacy filters have robotic applications beyond just teleoperation. Autonomous robots could similarly store information in a filtered form in order to be less vulnerable to unintended security breaches.

7. CONCLUSION

This paper has defined and explored the privacy-utility tradeoff for remotely teleoperated robots in the home. Although such robots present tremendous near-term opportunities, their success depends on the willingness of end-users to allow them into their home. We conducted two surveys to characterize qualitatively and quantitatively the privacy concerns and preferences of end-users, finding that respondents are concerned both about privacy and physical harm from teleoperated robots. We observed that respondents were not always able to anticipate all threats, and thus recommend that end-users be asked about their privacy preferences with as much context as possible. We also found that privacy concerns vary by specific context, but that most respondents were comfortable with the level of privacy provided by one of our visual filters (color-skewed superpixel). Finally, in a user study in which participants manipulated a robot, we found that an intermediate filter provided a good privacy-utility balance for the studied task: participants were able to carry out the task with reasonable accuracy and only moderate difficulty, but they were not able to answer privacy-invasive questions. We also found that the performance hit of a privacy-preserving filter diminishes with practice. Though the optimal point in the privacy-utility spectrum varies by task, by context, and by end-user, our findings suggest how these properties can be traded off in acceptable ways. Our characterization of in-home privacy concerns and our empirical exploration of the privacy-utility tradeoff thus lays a foundation for future designs of remotely teleoperated robots in the home.

References

[1] ACHANTA, R., SHAJI, A., SMITH, K., LUCCHI, A., FUA, P., AND SUSSTRUNK, S. Slic superpixels compared to state-of-the-art superpixel methods. *IEEE Transactions on Pattern Analysis and Machine Intelligence 34*, 11 (2012), 2274–2282.

[2] BAKER, M., CASEY, R., KEYES, B., AND YANCO, H. A. Improved interfaces for human-robot interaction in urban search and rescue. In *SMC (3)* (2004), pp. 2960–2965.

[3] BEER, J. M., AND TAKAYAMA, L. Mobile remote presence systems for older adults: acceptance, benefits, and concerns. In *6th International Conference on Human-Robot Interaction* (2011), ACM, pp. 19–26.

[4] BOISSY, P., CORRIVEAU, H., MICHAUD, F., LABONTÉ, D., AND ROYER, M. A qualitative study of in-home robotic telepresence for home care of community-living elderly subjects. *Journal of Telemedicine & Telecare 13*, 2 (2007), 79–84.

[5] CAINE, K., SABANOVIC, S., AND CARTER, M. The effect of monitoring by cameras and robots on the privacy enhancing behaviors of older adults. In *ACM/IEEE International Conf. on Human-Robot Interaction* (2012).

[6] CALO, R. The drone as privacy catalyst. *Stanford Law Review Online 64* (2011).

[7] CALO, R. Against notice skepticism in privacy (and elsewhere). *Notre Dame Law Review 87* (2012).

[8] CANNY, J. A computational approach to edge detection. *IEEE Transactions on Pattern Analysis and Machine Intelligence, 6* (1986), 679–698.

[9] CHEN, J. Y., HAAS, E. C., AND BARNES, M. J. Human performance issues and user interface design for teleoperated robots. *IEEE Transactions on Systems, Man, and Cybernetics 37*, 6 (2007), 1231–1245.

[10] FEIL-SEIFER, D., SKINNER, K., AND MATARIĆ, M. J. Benchmarks for evaluating socially assistive robotics. *Interaction Studies 8*, 3 (2007), 423–439.

[11] HALDERMAN, J. A., WATERS, B., AND FELTEN, E. W. Privacy Management for Portable Recording Devices. In *Workshop on Privacy in Electronic Society* (2004).

[12] JANA, S., MOLNAR, D., MOSHCHUK, A., DUNN, A., LIVSHITS, B., WANG, H. J., AND OFEK, E. Enabling Fine-Grained Permissions for Augmented Reality Applications with Recognizers. In *USENIX Security Symposium* (2013).

[13] JANA, S., NARAYANAN, A., AND SHMATIKOV, V. A Scanner Darkly: Protecting User Privacy from Perceptual Applications. In *IEEE Symposium on Security and Privacy* (2013).

[14] KAHN JR, P. H., ISHIGURO, H., FRIEDMAN, B., KANDA, T., FREIER, N. G., SEVERSON, R. L., AND MILLER, J. What is a human?: Toward psychological benchmarks in the field of human–robot interaction. *Interaction Studies 8*, 3 (2007), 363–390.

[15] KUMARAGURU, P., AND CRANOR, L. F. Privacy Indexes: A Survey of Westin's Studies. Tech. Rep. CMU-ISRI-5-138, Carnegie Mellon University, 2005.

[16] LEEPER, A. E., HSIAO, K., CIOCARLIE, M., TAKAYAMA, L., AND GOSSOW, D. Strategies for human-in-the-loop robotic grasping. In *ACM/IEEE International Conference on Human-Robot Interaction* (2012), ACM, pp. 1–8.

[17] MAST, M., ŠPANĚL, M., ARBEITER, G., ŠTANCL, V., MATERNA, Z., WEISSHARDT, F., BURMESTER, M., SMRŽ, P., AND GRAF, B. Teleoperation of Domestic Service Robots: Effects of Global 3D Environment Maps in the User Interface on Operators' Cognitive and Performance Metrics. In *Social Robotics*. Springer, 2013, pp. 392–401.

[18] PATEL, S. N., SUMMET, J. W., AND TRUONG, K. N. BlindSpot: Creating Capture-Resistant Spaces. In *Protecting Privacy in Video Surveillance*, A. Senior, Ed. Springer-Verlag, 2009, pp. 185–201.

[19] RAVAL, N., SRIVASTAVA, A., LEBECK, K., COX, L. P., AND MACHANAVAJJHALA, A. MarkIt: Privacy Markers for Protecting Visual Secrets. In *UPSIDE* (2014).

[20] ROESNER, F., MOLNAR, D., MOSHCHUK, A., KOHNO, T., AND WANG, H. J. World-Driven Access Control for Continuous Sensing Applications. In *ACM Conference on Computer and Communications Security* (2014).

[21] SCHIFF, J., MEINGAST, M., MULLIGAN, D. K., SASTRY, S., AND GOLDBERG, K. Y. Respectful Cameras: Detecting Visual Markers in Real-Time to Address Privacy Concerns. In *Proceedings of the International Conference on Intelligent Robots and Systems* (2007).

[22] SENIOR, A., PANKANTI, S., HAMPAPUR, A., BROWN, L., LI TIAN, Y., AND EKIN, A. Blinkering surveillance: Enabling video privacy through computer vision. *IBM Research Report 22886* (2003).

[23] SHERIDAN, T. B. Teleoperation, telerobotics and telepresence: A progress report. *Control Engineering Practice 3*, 2 (1995), 205–214.

[24] TEMPLEMAN, R., KORAYEM, M., CRANDALL, D., AND KAPADIA, A. PlaceAvoider: Steering first-person cameras away from sensitive spaces. In *Network and Distributed System Security Symposium* (2014).

May I help you?
- Design of Human-like Polite Approaching Behavior-

Yusuke Kato[1,2] Takayuki Kanda[1] Hiroshi Ishiguro[1,2]

[1]Intelligent Robotics and Communication Laboratory
ATR
Kyoto, Japan

[2]Graduate School of Engineering Science
Osaka University
Osaka, Japan

{kato.yusuke, kanda, ishiguro}@atr.jp

ABSTRACT

When should service staff initiate interaction with a visitor? Neither simply-proactive (e.g. talk to everyone in a sight) nor passive (e.g. wait until being talked to) strategies are desired. This paper reports our modeling of polite approaching behavior. In a shopping mall, there are service staff members who politely approach visitors who need help. Our analysis revealed that staff members are sensitive to 'intentions' of nearby visitors. That is, when a visitor intends to talk to a staff member and starts to approach, the staff member also walks a few steps toward the visitors in advance to being talked. Further, even when not being approached, staff members exhibit "availability" behavior in the case that a visitor's intention seems uncertain. We modeled these behaviors that are adaptive to pedestrians' intentions, occurred prior to initiation of conversation. The model was implemented into a robot and tested in a real shopping mall. The experiment confirmed that the proposed method is less intrusive to pedestrians, and that our robot successfully initiated interaction with pedestrians.

Categories and Subject Descriptors

H.5.2 [Information Interfaces and Presentation]: User Interfaces - *Interaction styles*; I.2.9 [Artificial Intelligence]: Robotics

General Terms

Algorithms; Design; Experimentation; Human Factors

Keywords

Intention estimation; Initiation of interaction; Behavior Design

1. INTRODUCTION

Robots are expected to interact with people and help them in various scenes. For instance, people have served roles like information-providing and receptionists, but as people cost a lot, it is difficult to always expect such services to be provided. Hence, instead, human-like robots are considered for fulfilling such roles [1] [2]. In such expected uses, there are some people who would wish to interact with robots, while some others would not.

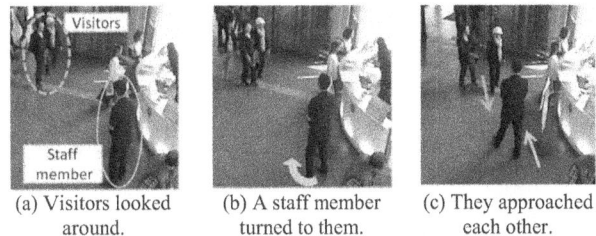

(a) Visitors looked around.   (b) A staff member turned to them.   (c) They approached each other.

Figure 1. An example of polite approaching

What is the desired behavior for a robot to encounter people who are willing to interact with it? There are typically two types of approaches taken. One is the "passive" approach, in which a robot waits until a user initiates interaction with the robot. By this approach, only people who actively try to interact with the robot can be served. However, people who are hesitating or unsure how to interact would be not served by passive approach.

Another approach is the "proactive" one, in which a robot proactively seeks people who potentially need help [3]. However, with this "simply-proactive" strategy, from a visitor's perspective, the robot's behavior can be overly proactive, offering more help than they need. Such an approach could be useful for advertisement purpose, but might be perceived as rude and annoying for other purposes.

In contrast, we aim to design the robot's behavior to be 'polite,' meaning that it behaves in the way human service staff members would behave to visitors. In concrete, they estimate visitors' intentions, and offer help only to people who would need it. For instance, Fig. 1 is one of such scenes. There were visitors who looked around, while there was a service staff member nearby the booth. They seemed unaware of him (Fig. 1 (a)), but since he turned to them, they noticed him (Fig. 1 (b)). Finally, they approached each other (Fig. 1 (c)), and started the interaction.

We decided to design our robot's behavior by replicating such a human capability of politely encountering with others. From our observation of a service staff, we developed a model of polite approach. Finally, we tested our robot in a real shopping mall.

2. RELATED WORKS

2.1 Behavior Design

Understandings of human behavior have informed the design of behavior of robots. For instance, proxemics [4] was learnt from human behavior. People keep social space around them when they meet with others. Such a spacing behavior was reproduced in human-robot interaction [5-7]. Researchers designed spacing behavior of the robot with users for social purposes [8-10]. Proximity is also used to detect a user who is interested [11].

Yamazaki et al., modeled how human exhibit 'availability' (whether one would allow others to talk to him/her) using gaze [12]. Robot's gaze behavior for exhibiting availability were successfully designed from human behavior [13]. Sidner et al., modeled gaze behavior for engagement [14]. A model of spatial formation when initiating interaction has been developed [15].

Our design approach is to model from human behavior along with the above previous studies; however, the above studies did not address robots' approaching interaction.

2.2 Approaching Behaviors

Satake et al. developed a planner for efficient simply-proactive behavior [3]. Dautenhahn and her colleagues studied the best direction from which a robot should approach [16]. In case it is known that a person and robot both wish to initiate interaction, Shi et al. developed a planner to adjust the robot's location to start interaction with appropriate spatial formation [17]. Personal space is considered in the approach behavior [18]. Rousseau et al. developed an autonomous robot system, which uses on-board sensors to detect a person nearby and initiate interaction [19]. However, none of them have dealt with the mechanism to adjust a robot's approaching behavior according to the user's intention.

As estimation of intention is known to be essential for interaction between a human and robot, this study aims to define a robot's appropriate approach depending on people's intention.

2.3 Intention and Interaction

Knowing others' attention and intention is fundamental to collaborative interaction in which interactors work together in a collaborative way. For instance, joint-attention capability has been successfully implemented into robots [20, 21]. Busy people is less likely to initiate interaction with a robot [22]. In situations where users have to take turns, the user's gaze can be useful for determining who is willing to take the next turn [13], and the robot's gaze can be used for regulating who should take the next turn [23]. Other methods, such as beep [24], greeting [25], non-verbal motions [26], are used to express robots' intention as well.

More relevant to 'approaching' situations, Kelley et al. learnt pedestrians' intention from their trajectories [27], in which change of velocity and distance is used as the feature, and intents such as stop, approach, and follow are modeled.

In our study, we also developed an estimator for pedestrians' intention. Further, we developed a model to use the intention estimator to make a robot better initiate the interaction.

3. BEHAVIOR DESIGN

3.1 Observation of Human Behavior

We observed pedestrians' behavior in a shopping mall. There were members of the service staff. Some of them were tasked with providing assistance to visitors in need, and some of them were engaged in other services, like distributing flyers. From recorded videos, we retrieved the moments when members of the service staff and visitors encountered and initiated interaction (to offer directions and to provide shop information). We collected 59 scenes of interaction, involving five different staff members.

We found three major patterns of encounter. Fig. 2 illustrates a typical 'both approach' case. The staff member stood near a reception desk and waited for visitors who would ask for help. There was a visitor who walked straight toward this staff member.

Here, it is noticeable that the staff member also walked a few steps toward this visitor while gazing at him. He could have waited in a still way, but he understood the visitor's intention,

hence he already behaved cooperatively, and walked toward the visitor. Finally, they started to talk.

In all 28 cases observed for this pattern, the staff walked to visitors when being approached. There were only a few steps walked. Nevertheless, we consider that these steps provide an important role for social purpose. That is, it would provide an impression that the staff member surely intends to engage the interaction, and invites the visitor to talk to them.

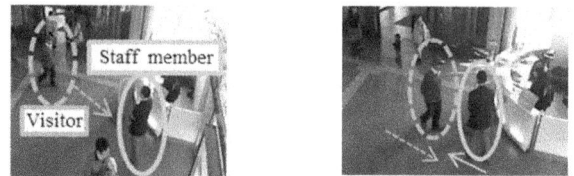

(a) The visitor approached the staff member, and he noticed it.

(b) The staff member approached the visitor in return.

Figure 2. Staff member and visitor both approached each other.

There are 19 cases classified as 'staff did not notice'. In these cases, only visitors walked to a staff member, but the staff member did not walk toward the visitors. Staff members seemed unaware of the approach of the visitors. For instance, in Fig. 3, the staff member stared at the flow of people coming through the door, while the visitors who needed help arrived from his side. We consider that the staff members would wish to behave like the 'both approach' pattern, but he was unable to behave so.

(a) The visitor approached the staff member, but was not noticed.

(b) Finally, the staff member noticed.

Figure 3. A staff member did not notice the visitor.

Arrows under a visitor (in a dashed line) and a staff member (solid line) represents their motion. Arrows around their face represents their face direction (only illustrated when useful)

(a) A staff member found visitors.

(b) He faced and gazed at them.

(c) They approached him, and he approached.

Figure 4. The staff's 'proactively waiting' behavior.

There are 12 cases classified as the third pattern, 'staff proactively prepares.' We found that the subtle behavior in this pattern shows how sophisticated humans' politeness is. Fig. 4 shows one of such scenes. This staff member was distributing flyers. When he found visitors who stopped in the hallway (Fig. 4 (a)), he stopped distributing flyers, and turned his body toward them. In short, he proactively prepared himself for possible interaction with them. However, he did not aggressively talk to them. He waited while exhibiting his 'availability' by gazing at them (Fig. 4 (b)). We named this behavior a 'proactively-waiting' behavior. Finally the visitors started to approach him; only after they did, he walked toward the visitors (Fig. 4 (c)), like the 'both approach' case.

This staff member's behavior is not possible without estimating visitors' intentions. Thus, we developed the model with the focus of estimated intentions.

3.2 Developed Model

Based on the above observations, we modeled the behavior of the service staff during encountering interaction. First, we categorized visitors' observable intentions into three distinctive categories:

Intention to interact: a visitor clearly intends to seek help and/or intends to initiate interaction with the staff member (Fig. 2 (a), Fig. 3 (a), Fig. 4 (c) are examples of such cases).

Other distinctive intention: a visitor exhibits other distinctive intention, like walking toward some destination, or waiting for someone, thus they apparently do not need help.

Uncertain: a visitor who is seemingly undecided about what to do next (Fig. 4 (a) is an example); that is, a visitor who is neither expressing *intention to interact* nor *other distinctive intention*. We expect this category to sometimes include the cases where the visitor potentially needs help, e.g. got lost.

For these three types of intentions, we modeled how a staff member would exhibit his/her behavior. As reported in the previous section, if noticed, when being approached the staff members also walked to the approaching person to initiate the interaction, as if both of them approached each other in collaboration. With this 'both approach' behavior, it is communicated that the staff members also intend to interact with the approaching person. We named this behavior of the staff members as 'collaboratively-initiating' behavior.

When a visitor's intention is *uncertain*, like the example shown in fig. 4, a staff member makes him/herself ready for an interaction with a visitor, namely *proactively-waiting*. Otherwise, a staff member is 'free' from potential interaction with visitors and, instead, would do his/her own other tasks.

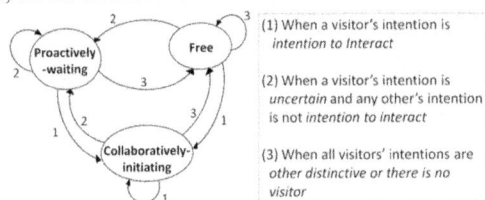

Figure 5. State transition model

Fig. 5 shows the state transitions. In summary, a staff member would behave in each state as follows:

Collaboratively-initiating: a staff member also approaches the approaching visitor. He/she moves towards the visitor till their distance is within conversational range, and orients his/her gaze and body toward the visitor.

Proactively-waiting: a staff member made him/herself available to a visitor, but had not initiated interaction yet. His/her body orientation and gaze are oriented toward the visitor, but he/she does not make steps toward the visitor.

Free: there is no visitor who needs help nearby. Thus, a staff member would idly wait (e.g. in Fig. 2 and 3) or provide other services (in Fig. 4).

4. Intention-Estimation Algorithm

We collected pedestrians' trajectories around a robot in a shopping mall using a peopletracking system. We then created an algorithm to distinguish *intention to interact* from *other distinctive intention*. We plan to estimate *uncertain* as the situation between these two classes.

4.1 Data Collection

4.1.1 Robot

We used Robovie, a 120-cm tall robot with a 0.3 m radius having a 3-DOF head and 4-DOF arms, and equipped with microphones, and a speaker. In order to inform its role (like a human staff member does by wearing a uniform or an arm band), there is a signboard indicating "information staff" put on its front. Its mobile base is a Pioneer3 DX. We set it to move at a velocity of 600 mm/sec and 45 degree/sec for rotations. The accelerations are set to 600 mm/sec^2 and 30 degree/sec^2. It is equipped with two laser range sensors, which are used for localization.

4.1.2 Environment and People Tracking System

Although the laser range sensors attached to the robot can be used to detect people within a few meters from the robot, to better observe people who are far from the robot, we used a people-tracking system based on sensors attached to the environment.

The study was conducted at a square of a shopping mall (the area surrounded by solid red line in fig. 6). We used the people tracking system [28]. The hallway was covered with 3-D range sensors attached on the ceiling. An estimate of persons' locations is provided every 33 ms.

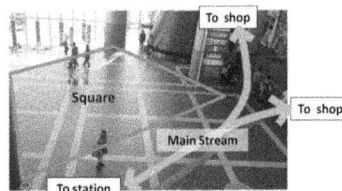

Figure 6. Shopping mall where we conducted the study.

4.1.3 Data Collection Method

We observed people's trajectories using the people tracking system while the robot was working. To consider the influence of the robot's motion, we prepared two settings:

Static: The robot stopped in the center of the hallway. It only spoke when a visitor initiated interaction with it.

Simply-Proactive: The robot moved toward any visitors who entered the hallway. When the distance with the visitor was within 2 m and the visitor was in front of the robot (within 60 degrees), it started to speak to the visitor.

We asked the persons who started conversations with the robot to fill a questionnaire. In this way, we confirmed whether they intended to interact with the robot. In fact, a large majority of people who interacted were found to have *intention to interact* with the robot. Among 15 hours of data collection, there were 67 people who interacted and filled questionnaire. There were 63 people who expressed that they had *intention to interact* with the robot, 2 people who expressed that they had *other distinctive intention*, and 2 people expressed neutral intention.

In contrast, it was difficult to get feedback from people who have *other distinctive intention*. Although we tried to ask other people who did not start conversations with the robot to fill questionnaire, little people responded. This is not surprising as they must be busy.

Instead, we decided to code visitors' behavior from video data so as to retrieve people who clearly had *other distinctive intention*. Two coders, who did not know the study purpose, judged whether each person who passed the experiment area seemed to have *intention to interact* with the robot or *other distinctive intention*. Their judgments were consistent with the questionnaire results. To balance the number of the data in two classes we analyzed a subset of data. From 30 minutes of video, there were 65 visitors judged as *other distinctive intention*. Their coding result matched well, yielding Kappa coefficient .873. We only included the trajectories for which their coding matched.

4.1.4 Dataset

We collected 63 trajectories for *intention to interact*, and 67 for *other distinctive intention* (2 found via questionnaire, 65 found via video coding). We included trajectories till they reached the nearest point to the robot or the moment when they started conversations, from 10 seconds earlier to the end.

Figure 7 shows examples of 10 seconds of trajectories in the *intention to interact* class. Some of them arrived from outside the area and went straight to the robot (Fig. 7 (a)). Some of them initially walked toward some other directions and changed their course toward the robot (Fig. 7 (b)).

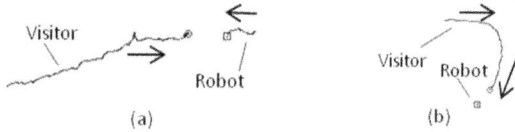

Figure 7. Trajectories in the *intention to interact* class

Figure 8 shows examples of trajectory in the *other distinctive intention* class. Two of them finally started conversations with the robot because it moved toward them but confirmed that they did not intend to do so (Fig. 8 (a)). Others were retrieved from video coding, and they apparently did not intend to interact with robot but had other distinctive purpose. Some of them just passed through the area behind the robot (Fig. 8 (b)), or far from the robot. Some of them were busy talking without moving around. Some people are influenced by the robot's motion, particularly those who had *other distinctive intention*. When the robot moved toward them, such people avoided the robot, and slightly changed their course. This dataset will be available at: http://www.irc.atr.jp/sets/approach_robot/

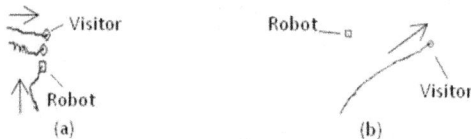

Figure 8. Trajectories in the *other distinctive intention* class

4.2 Estimation Algorithm

We choose to use SVM because it is commonly available, its training is simple and efficient, and it usually yields good classification performance. To develop features, we observed how pedestrians behaved toward the robot.

We noticed that people in the *intention to interact* class did not move directly to the robot, but moved toward the space in front of the robot (Figure 9). Based on this finding, we prepared one feature. For the computation, we set a fan shaped area in front of the robot. The feature is computed based on the area where pedestrians move toward. As shown in fig. 10, the fan is defined with the angle α and diameter of αl. We kept the diameter in proportion to the angle, because it better predict the *intention to interact* class than only using angle or diameter independently. When we set a size of the fan shaped area small, it matches with only very likely trajectory that moves toward the robot. In contrast, there is some ambiguity when they move into a larger fan (Figure 10). This trend is common for both angle and diameter of the fan. A larger angle or diameter results in less certain estimate. To reflect this trend, we decided to measure the minimum α that covers the direction of the trajectory, and use it as the feature. If a

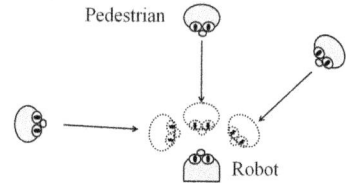

Figure 9. Behavior of pedestrians toward the robot

fan with smaller α can fit with the direction of the trajectory, it is more likely that the person is moving toward the robot, i.e. to be classified as *intention to interact* class. The l in the fig. 10 is empirically set to be 18.75 [mm/degree] which yielded the best performance.

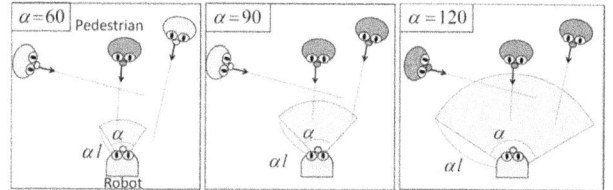

Figure 10. Feature of the *intention to interact* class

The expected characteristics of *other distinctive intention* class is that they would either walk straight elsewhere (not toward the robot) or stop for a while. The person who walks straight elsewhere would yield smaller *deviation of velocities*, and yield a larger value for the α introduced above. The person who stops for a while can be simply estimated if we measure *time being stopped*. Further, if they change their mind and move toward the robot, *deviation of velocities* would be larger.

Based on above considerations, we included following features:

- Distance from the robot (d_t in fig. 11)

- The smallest α value, with which the fan shaped area can cover the direction of the trajectory (as illustrated in fig. 10)

- Stability of walking: to represent the stability of walking, we computed the *deviation of velocity* σ_v^2 as follows:

$$\sigma_v^2 = \frac{1}{T} \sum_{t=0}^{T-1} \left(|\vec{v_t} - \vec{v_{avg}}| \right)^2$$

where $\vec{v_{avg}}$ is the averaged velocity between t=0 and t=T-1. We empirically decided to use T=64 where velocity is measured every 33 ms with a smoothing filter, i.e. deviation is computed from velocities for approx. 2 seconds.

- Time being stopped: we computed the length of time when velocity ($|\vec{v_t}|$) is smaller than a threshold. Considering noise in measurement, we set the threshold to be 0.1 m/s.

We implemented an SVM with these features with the libsvm library [29], and trained it with the dataset. We adjusted the gamma and cost parameters using a grid search algorithm and 10-fold cross-validation.

4.3 Evaluation of Algorithm Performance

We compared our proposed method with two alternative methods. One is a very simple method, checking whether a person's motion direction is oriented toward the robot or not (Figure 11). As illustrated, it is more likely that the person goes toward the robot if the θ_t (the angle between the motion direction and the direction of the robot) is smaller. Another idea, as proposed in [27], is to observe the change in θ_t and d_t (the distance between the robot and the person). When the person is approaching the robot, both θ_t and d_t should decrease. In summary, we compared our method with the two alternatives:

- **Relative angle**: an SVM is configured with a feature about relative angle, θ_t (Figure 11).
- **Increase/decrease of angle and distance**: an SVM is configured with two features, difference in angle ($\theta_t - \theta_{t-\Delta t}$) and difference in distance ($d_t - d_{t-\Delta t}$). We used $\Delta t = 1.2$ [sec], because it yielded the best performance.

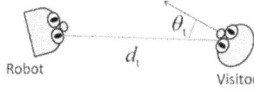

Figure 11. Computation for alternative methods

For each method, we conducted leave-one-out cross-validation; this procedure was repeated for all the data. Table 1 shows the result. Our new algorithm outperformed the alternative methods. It successfully classified with 95.4% of performance. In contrast, *relative angle* method yielded 80.9% and the method with *increase/decrease of angle and distance* yielded 86.1% of success.

Table 1: Performance of each method

Method	Performance
Proposed	95.4 %
Relative Angle	80.9 %
Increase/decrease of angle and distance	86.1 %

5. SYSTEM

5.1 Architecture

Fig. 12 illustrates the architecture of the developed system. People's positions provided by the *tracking system* (section 4.1.2) are sent to the *intention estimator*, in which their intentions are classified into either *intention to interact, other distinctive intention*, or *uncertain*. Finally, according to the state transition model (Fig. 5) the robot decides its behavior and the target person.

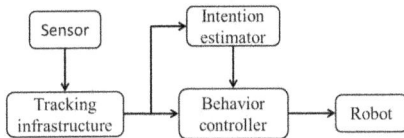

Figure 12. System configuration.

5.2 Intention Estimator

The intention estimator is based on the SVM we prepared in section 4.2. We used the probability estimate of the SVM computed from the distance from the hyper plane separating two classes [29]. When the probability estimate is lower than a threshold, we assume it as *uncertain*. We empirically set the threshold to be 0.9, because it yielded little error in estimating *intention to interact* class. Thus, only highly-likely case is labeled as either *intention to interact* or *other distinctive intention*, and others are labeled as *uncertain*. If there are multiple targets estimated as *intention to interact*, the system chooses the person closest to the robot. If no one is judged as *intention to interact*, the system looks for the person whose intention is judged as *uncertain*.

5.3 Behavior Controller

The robot behaved along with the model reported in section 3.2. That is, in case the state is *proactively-waiting*, as illustrated in Fig. 13 (b), body and gaze are oriented to the target person but the robot does not approach. By doing so, it refrains from being too proactive and being perceived as annoying, while exhibiting its availability. This *proactively-waiting* behavior is designed to elicit the visitor to approach the robot (Fig. 13 (c)). We expect that the visitor's intention might change to *intention to interact*; hence the state will transit to *collaboratively-initiating* (Fig. 13 (d)).

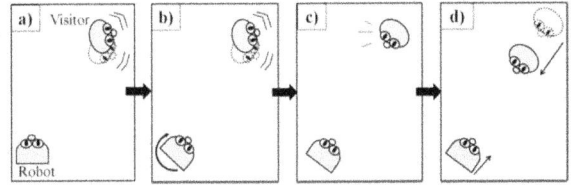

Figure 13. Robot's behavior in *proactively-waiting* state.

When a visitor's intention is recognized as *intention to interact*, the robot's state transits to *collaboratively-initiating*. As illustrated in Fig. 14, the robot approaches the approaching visitor until the distance to the person is less than 1.5 m (this is the distance used in Shi et al., for initiating conversation [17]).

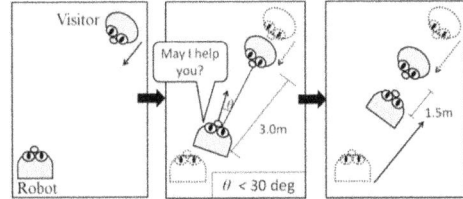

Figure 14. Robot's behavior in *collaboratively-initiating* state.

The first utterance in the encountering interaction would happen even before stopping. According to [17], if a robot and a person are facing each other a first utterance would happen at 2 m distance in a quiet small room; however, we found that in our environment (larger and more noisy) it is more natural to use first utterance at a farther distance. We empirically decided the distance to be 3 m. That is, when the target person shows *intention to interact* and the distance to him/her is within 3 m, it assumes that the conversation should be initiated, hence it starts talking (while the robot continues to adjust its social distance until the distance is less than 1.5 m).

Although the conversation after the initiation is beyond the scope of this paper, the robot actually offered a "guiding" service. First, the robot asks "may I help you?" and offers help such as directions. To cope with difficulties in speech recognition in noisy real world environment, a human operator controlled the robot during the direction-giving interaction. (The robot was autonomous except for this part).

6. FIELD EVALUATION

We evaluated the developed robot in a shopping mall by comparing it with alternative approaches.

6.1 Hypothesis and Prediction

When compared with the simply-proactive approach in which a robot approaches anyone it can catch up to, the robot with the proposed method should more frequently approach the person who intends to interact with it, if the developed system works as designed; hence, success ratio would be expected to be higher. Thus, we predicted as follows:

> **Prediction 1**: With the proposed method, the robot would make fewer failures, and be better in success ratio than the robot with simply-proactive approach.

In contrast, one might argue that the robot would not need to approach anyone at all for better success ratio. The robot in the proposed method only approaches to the person who moves toward it. Thus, one might consider that approaching behavior from the robot might not have a real meaning because anyway the approaching person will probably initiate the interaction with the robot. However, if we compare the proposed method with such a 'passive approach' in which a robot only reacts when a person talks to the robot, we consider that the robot in passive approach would miss many chances to initiate interaction. Without the robot approaching, the person may hesitate to finally initiate the interaction, although he/she approaches the robot to some degree. Thus, we predicted as follows:

Prediction 2: With the proposed method, the robot would successfully start interaction with more people than the robot with the passive approach.

6.2 Method

6.2.1 Participant

The participants were visitors of the shopping mall where we put the robot. They were typically shoppers and workers of nearby offices. We did not provide any instructions, and did not pay them.

6.2.2 Conditions

There are three conditions compared.

Proposed: the robot was autonomously controlled with the system reported in section 5.

Simply-proactive: the robot aimed at approaching all the visitors within the experiment area that it was able to reach to. The approaching behavior is identical to the *proposed* condition except for the intention estimator.

Passive: the robot only performed *proactively-waiting* behavior and waited until a visitor talked to it. To accurately respond to people's initiation, we tele-operated the robot for this condition. A human operator heard the sound input to the robot, and responded only when utterance was directed to it. Once being talked to, it engaged in the same dialog as other conditions.

6.2.3 Procedure

We put the robot in the center of the Square of a shopping mall (Fig. 6) during weekdays. The robot had a role as an information staff. We choose this location because we often observed that some people need information/directions here. There were no restrictions or instructions provided to visitors. There was a person ensuring safety, but he stayed behind a column so that his presence was hardly noticeable from pedestrians. In such circumstances, we observed pedestrians' natural reaction to the robot. Finally, after visitors finished interaction with the robot, or passed by the area around the robot without interacting with it, our staff approached them and asked them to fill a questionnaire, in which we asked whether they intended to initiate interaction with the robot. We prepared nine sets of 30 minutes slots in similar time of day, which were randomly assigned for each condition (in total, 4.5 hours).

6.2.4 Measurement

We evaluated from the following objective point of view:

Success: the robot interacted with people who intended to interact with it.

Failure: the robot tried to initiate interaction with people who did not intend to interact with it.

Miss: the robot did not initiate interaction with the people who intended to interact with it.

Using the above measures, we consider that overall performance can be measured as the ratio of success. That is,

Performance: defined as "success / (success + failure + miss)."

6.3 Result

6.3.1 Observation

We witnessed the effect of *proactively-waiting* behavior, like the human interaction shown in fig. 4. In fig. 15, visitors found the robot but seemed to be unsure whether they would approach. She noticed that the robot turned to her. Then, she approached the robot, and finally they started interaction. This example shows a situation where the robot exhibited its availability, which elicited her to approach the robot.

Figure 15. The effect of *proactively waiting* behavior

Further, the robot in the *proposed* condition successfully approached approaching visitors as designed. Fig. 16 shows one of the typical scenes of success in the *proposed* condition. They found the robot earlier and moved straight to the robot. The robot also recognized they had *intention to interact* and approached them in return. Thus, the robot successfully replicated the staff member's 'both approach' interaction. Finally, they smoothly started to interact.

Figure 16. Success in the *proposed* condition

In contrast, similar situations sometimes turned into *miss* interaction in the *passive* condition. Figure 17 is one of such scenes. The visitor moved straight to the robot, and the robot performed *proactively-waiting* behavior and turned to her. She moved to the robot to some degree, but finally she stopped a few meters from the robot (Fig. 17 (b)). She stayed for 4 seconds, but finally turned and left (Fig. 17 (c)). She reported that she had intention to interact with the robot. We interpret that she was finally not sure whether the robot would welcome her, and hesitated to initiate the interaction; such situations should be better addressed with the proposed method, which performs collaboratively-initiating behavior in these cases.

Figure 17. Miss in the *passive* condition

As expected, the *simply-proactive* condition caused many failures. Like the example in Fig. 18 the robot moved toward the visitor who intended to pass by the square, spoke to him, but he did not stop. He reported that he didn't have the intention to interact with the robot. The robot in the *proposed* condition did not talk to pedestrians in such courses because his intention was classified as *unknown*. Though, when the course is more ambiguous, the *proposed* condition occasionally caused failures as well.

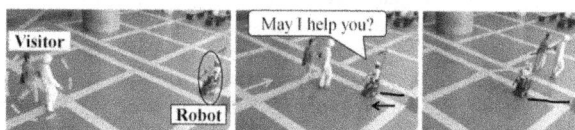

Figure 18 : Failure in the *simply-proactive* condition

The robot in the *proposed* condition was effective in the situation where there were many pedestrians as well. Figure 19 is one of these scenes. In fig. 19 (a), visitor 1 moved toward the robot, but she stopped and turned away (fig. 19 (b)). The robot did not talk to her, but it talked to visitor 2 who approached to the robot.

Figure 19: Robot in *proposed* condition with many pedestrians

6.3.2 Coding Visitors' Behavior

To measure *success, failure,* and *miss,* it would be ideal if every visitor who passed the area answered to our questionnaire; but, in reality, many of them declined answering. Instead, we coded their behavior from video data using the behavior of the visitors who answered the questionnaire as reference.

There were 18 visitors who answered that they *intended to interact* with the robot. There were common characteristics in their behavior. They moved toward the robot. When the robot approached them, they all interacted with it. When the robot did not approach them, some of them talked to the robot, but some of them stopped around it, orienting their body towards it (Fig. 16). People who showed these behaviors all reported that they had intention to interact with the robot.

There were 8 visitors who answered that they *did not intend to interact* with the robot. All of them were talked to by the robot, but they did not stop walking and continued to walk away (Fig. 18).

Based on the above observations, we defined the coding criteria:

Success: people who stayed around the robot when it talked to them or when they talked to it.

Failure: people who did not stop walking when it talked to them.

Miss: people who stopped nearby it, oriented their body toward it, but neither the robot nor they initiated the interaction.

Coders made a judgment for each group (but not for each individual) if they were together as a group. If the same person appeared again, only the first appearance was evaluated.

Two coders, who did not know the study hypothesis, independently coded all cases. Their coding matched well (Cohen kappa .953). Finally, they consulted to make the decision for the cases where their judgments did not match.

6.3.3 Verification of Predictions

The robot was operated for 4.5 hours for each condition, during which the situation of the mall was similar across conditions. For instance, the amount of people who entered the experiment area were similar for each condition (*passive*: 651, *simply-proactive*: 627, and *proposed*: 649 people). Note that during weekdays there were many business persons, and they rarely approached the robot.

Fig. 20 shows the coding result. The intention estimator worked reasonably well. The *proposed* condition yielded 41 successes while 6 failures occurred. In contrast, as expected, the *simply-proactive* condition caused a large number of failures (32 successes and 43 failures), and the *passive* condition caused many misses (22 successes and 13 misses). There seems to be more successes in the *proposed* condition than the sum of successes and misses in the *passive* condition, possibly because some people seemed to interact with it because they were elicited by its interaction with others (one visitor mentioned this to us).

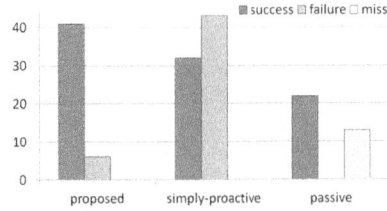

Figure 20. Result of the field evaluation

We applied a Chi-square test to evaluate the ratio of success against failures and misses combined. There is a significant difference among the conditions ($\chi^2(2)$=24.121, p<.001, φ_c=.392). The residual analysis for pair-wised comparison revealed that the ratio of success in the *proposed* condition is significantly higher than simply-proactive and passive conditions respectively (p=<.001 and p=.029 after Bonferroni correction). (Note that it would be application-dependent whether failures could be more/less problematic to miss, though we combined them).

Overall, the proposed condition yielded higher *performance* (87.2%) than passive (62.9%) and simply-proactive (42.7%), hence predictions 1 and 2 are supported.

7. DISCUSSION

7.1 Similarity and Difference with Human Interaction

One may question a design approach of modeling from human behavior, and argue that there is a difference between human interaction and human-robot interaction. We acknowledge that there are certain differences. People who would talk to human staff would be probably people who have real needs; in contrast, some of people who intend to talk to the robot would be perhaps more motivated by curiosity. People's hesitation might have different reasons: a person hesitating to talk to a human staff could wonder whether it is ok to interrupt a human activity, and a person hesitating to talk to a robot might wonder whether a robot would have a capability to engage in an interaction. Nevertheless, we believe that once the robot observes a visitor, its expected behavior would be similar to the one a human staff would exhibit. The point of our model is that the robot should respond differently depending on whether he/she exhibits *intention to interact, other distinctive intention*, or *uncertainty*, which we believe to be common between robots and humans.

7.2 Other Factors to be considered?

Our model perhaps did not fully include relevant design factors. For instance, if we could stably observe pedestrians' gaze, it could produce additional useful features. The group behavior was not included, as just for initiating, our approach reasonably worked. Often in group behavior, the person who is most interested in initiating interaction arrives first, and our planner chose the person whom it can meet earlier. Nevertheless, observing group interaction can improve the quality of initiating interaction.

About estimation algorithm, we developed the estimator from a 2-class classifier and used the middle of two classes as *uncertain*; although our approach reasonably worked, it is plausible to create a separate class for *uncertain* to effectively detect such people.

7.3 Generalizability and Limitation

The developed model is prepared for a human-like robot in a shopping mall context, and the intention estimator is trained with people of our country's culture. This research assumes a humanoid robot throughout, thus we need careful consideration if we plan to apply the findings to other form of robots. Further, if the model is used in other contexts, such as in a shop scenario, we would probably need to extend the model to deal with the visitors' intention in a more precise manner. For instance, in a shop, we would need to consider whether customers are busily looking around or looking for shop keepers. The parameters, e.g. social distance, are for our robot and for our country's people. We expect it would be necessary to adjust parameters for different robots and for different cultures. The findings could be applied to human interaction, though a further proof from human studies is needed.

8. CONCLUSION

We reported a behavior design for approaching interaction. Our design strategy was to model the human behavior of the service staff. Based on the observation, we established a 3-state model in which the robot changes its behavior along with the estimated intention of nearby pedestrians. We also developed an algorithm to better estimate the intention of pedestrians. The developed model was implemented in a human-like robot, and tested in a real shopping mall. We found that the proposed method is more efficient than the simply-proactive and passive methods.

9. ACKNOWLEDGEMENTS

This work was supported by JST, CREST. This work in part was supported by JSPS Core-to-Core Program, A. Advanced Research Networks.

10. REFERENCES

[1] H.-M. Gross, et al., Shopbot: Progress in Developing an Interactive Mobile Shopping Assistant for Everyday Use, *IEEE Int. Conf. on Systems, Man, and Cybernetics (SMC2008)*, pp. 3471-3478, 2008.

[2] R. Kirby, J. Forlizzi and R. Simmons, Affective Social Robots, *Robotics and Autonomous Systems*, vol. 58, pp. 322-332, 2010.

[3] S. Satake, et al., How to Approach Humans?: Strategies for Social Robots to Initiate Interaction, *ACM/IEEE Int. Conf. on Human-Robot Interaction (HRI2009)*, pp. 109-116, 2009.

[4] E. T. Hall, *The Hidden Dimension*, Doubleday, 1966.

[5] M. L. Walters, et al., The Influence of Subjects' Personality Traits on Personal Spatial Zones in a Human-Robot Interaction Experiment, *IEEE Int. W. on Robot and Human Interactive Communication (RO-MAN2005)*, pp. 347-352, 2005.

[6] H. Hüttenrauch, K. S. Eklundh, A. Green and E. A. Topp, Investigating Spatial Relationships in Human-Robot Interactions, *IEEE/RSJ Int. Conf. on Intelligent Robots and Systems (IROS2006)*, pp. 5052 5059, 2006.

[7] D. Feil-Seifer and M. Matari´c, Distance-Based Computational Models for Facilitating Robot Interaction with Children, *J. of Human-Robot Interaction*, vol. 1, pp. 55-77, 2012.

[8] E. A. Sisbot, et al., Implementing a Human-Aware Robot System, *IEEE Int. Symposium on Robot and Human Interactive Communication (RO-MAN2006)*, pp. 727-732, 2006.

[9] H. Kuzuoka, Y. Suzuki, J. Yamashita and K. Yamazaki, Reconfiguring Spatial Formation Arrangement by Robot Body Orientation, *ACM/IEEE Int. Conf. on Human-Robot Interaction (HRI2010)*, pp. 285-292, 2010.

[10] J. Mumm and B. Mutlu, Human-Robot Proxemics: Physical and Psychological Distancing in Human-Robot Interaction, *ACM/IEEE Int. Conf. on Human-Robot Interaction (HRI2011)*, pp. 331-338, 2011.

[11] M. P. Michalowski, S. Sabanovic and R. Simmons, A Spatial Model of Engagement for a Social Robot, *IEEE Int. Workshop on Advanced Motion Control*, pp. 762-767, 2006.

[12] K. Yamazaki, et al., Prior-to-Request and Request Behaviors within Elderly Day Care: Implications for Developing Service Robots for Use in Multiparty Settings, *European Conf. on Computer Supported Cooperative Work*, pp. 61-78, 2007.

[13] Y. Kobayashi, et al., A Considerate Care Robot Able to Serve in Multi-Party Settings, *IEEE Int. Symposium on Robot and Human Interactive Communication (RO-MAN2011)*, pp. 27-32, 2011.

[14] C. L. Sidner, C. Lee, C. D. Kidd, N. Lesh and C. Rich, Explorations in Engagement for Humans and Robots, *Artificial Intelligence*, vol. 166, pp. 140-164, 2005.

[15] M. A. Yousuf, et al., How to Move Towards Visitors: A Model for Museum Guide Robots to Initiate Conversation, *IEEE Int. Symp. on Robot and Human Interactive Communication (RO-MAN2013)*, pp. 587-592, 2013.

[16] K. Dautenhahn, et al., How May I Serve You? A Robot Companion Approaching a Seated Person in a Helping Context, *ACM/IEEE Int. Conf. on Human-Robot Interaction (HRI2006)*, pp. 172-179, 2006.

[17] C. Shi, M. Shimada, T. Kanda, H. Ishiguro and N. Hagita, Spatial Formation Model for Initiating Conversation, *Robotics: Science and Systems Conference (RSS2011)*, 2011.

[18] J. Kessler, C. Schroeter and H.-M. Gross, Approaching a Person in a Socially Acceptable Manner Using a Fast Marching Planner, in *Intelligent Robotics and Applications*, Springer, pp. 368-377, 2011.

[19] V. Rousseau, et al., Sorry to Interrupt, but May I Have Your Attention? Preliminary Design and Evaluation of Autonomous Engagement in HRI, *J. of Human-Robot Interaction*, vol. 2, pp. 41-61, 2013.

[20] B. Scassellati, Theory of Mind for a Humanoid Robot, *Autonomous Robots*, vol. 12, pp. 13-24, 2002.

[21] C. Breazeal, C. D. Kidd, A. L. Thomaz, G. Hoffman and M. Berlin, Effects of Nonverbal Communication on Efficiency and Robustness in Human-Robot Teamwork, *IEEE/RSJ Int. Conf. on Intelligent Robots and Systems (IROS2005)*, pp. 383-388, 2005.

[22] H. Hüttenrauch and K. S. Eklundh, To Help or Not to Help a Service Robot: Bystander Intervention as a Resource in Human-Robot Collaboration, *Interaction Studies*, vol. 7, pp. 455-477, 2006.

[23] B. Mutlu, T. Shiwa, T. Kanda, H. Ishiguro and N. Hagita, Footing in Human-Robot Conversations: How Robots Might Shape Participant Roles Using Gaze Cues, *ACM/IEEE Int. Conf. on Human-Robot Interaction (HRI2009)*, pp. 61-68, 2009.

[24] K. Fischer, L. C. Jensen and L. Boenhagen, To Beep or Not to Beep Is Not the Whole Question, *Int. Conf. on Social Robotics*, pp. 156-165, 2014.

[25] K. Fischer, et al., Initiating Interactions in Order to Get Help: Effects of Social Framing on People's Responses to Robots' Requests for Assistance, *IEEE Int. Symp. on Robot and Human Interactive Communication (RO-MAN2014)*, pp. 999-1005, 2014.

[26] L. Takayama, D. Dooley and W. Ju, Expressing Thought: Improving Robot Readability with Animation Principles, *ACM/IEEE Int. Conf. on Human-Robot Interaction (HRI2011)*, pp. 69-76, 2011.

[27] R. Kelley, et al., Understanding Human Intentions Via Hidden Markov Models in Autonomous Mobile Robots, *ACM/IEEE Int. Conf. on Human-Robot Interaction (HRI2008)*, pp. 367-374, 2008.

[28] D. Brscic, T. Kanda, T. Ikeda and T. Miyashita, Person Tracking in Large Public Spaces Using 3d Range Sensors, *IEEE Trans. on Human-Machine Systems*, vol. 43, pp. 522 - 534, 2013.

[29] C.-C. Chang and C.-J. Lin, Libsvm: A Library for Support Vector Machines, *ACM Transactions on Intelligent Systems and Technology (TIST)*, vol. 2, p. 27, 2011.

Robot Form and Motion Influences Social Attention

Alvin X. Li[1*], Maria Florendo[1], Luke E. Miller[1], Hiroshi Ishiguro[2], Ayse P. Saygin[1]

(1) Cognitive Science, UC San Diego
9500 Gilman Drive, La Jolla, CA
92093-0515
+1-858-822-1994
{axl002, mflorendo, lmiller, asaygin}@ucsd.edu

(2) Department of System Innovation, Graduate school of
Engineering science, Osaka University
Osaka, Japan
+81-6-6850-6360
ishiguro@sys.es.osaka-u.ac.jp

ABSTRACT

For social robots to be successful, they need to be accepted by humans. Human-robot interaction (HRI) researchers are aware of the need to develop the right kinds of robots with appropriate, natural ways for them to interact with humans. However, much of human perception and cognition occurs outside of conscious awareness, and how robotic agents engage these processes is currently unknown. Here, we explored automatic, reflexive social attention, which operates outside of conscious control within a fraction of a second to discover whether and how these processes generalize to agents with varying humanlikeness in their form and motion. Using a social variant of a well-established spatial attention paradigm, we tested whether robotic or human appearance and/or motion influenced an agent's ability to capture or direct implicit social attention. In each trial, either images or videos of agents looking to one side of space (a head turn) were presented to human observers. We measured reaction time to a peripheral target as an index of attentional capture and direction. We found that all agents, regardless of humanlike form or motion, were able to direct spatial attention in the cued direction. However, differences in the form of the agent affected attentional capture, i.e., how quickly the observers could disengage attention from the agent and respond to the target. This effect further interacted with whether the spatial cue (head turn) was presented through static images or videos. Overall whereas reflexive social attention operated in the same manner for human and robot social agents for spatial attentional cueing, robotic appearance, as well as whether the agent was static or moving significantly influenced unconscious attentional capture processes. These studies reveal how unconscious social attentional processes operate when the agent is a human vs. a robot, add novel manipulations to the literature such as the role of visual motion, and provide a link between attention studies in HRI, and decades of research on unconscious social attention in experimental psychology and vision science.

Categories and Subject Descriptors

H.1.2 [**Models and Principles**]: User/Machine Systems – *Human factors.* H.5.2 [**Information Interfaces and Presentation**]: User Interfaces – *Evaluation/methodology, User-Centered Design*

General Terms

Design, Human Factors.

Keywords

Social Attention; Spatial Attention; Humanlikeness; Robot Design; Experimental Psychology

1. INTRODUCTION

Social robots are becoming increasingly prevalent in society, employed in roles such as entertainment, education, and healthcare [1, 2]. Many of these roles, particularly in health care and education, require building of trust and empathy between robots and humans, thus creating a comfortable user experience is important for social robots to be successful. However there are a myriad of issues that remain to be solved to create sociable robots that can reproduce the Human-Human interaction experience. Roboticists must consider issues such as the design of the robot's appearance, how the robot behaves, and how much autonomy the robot possesses, among others.

HRI researchers are well aware of the need to develop the right kinds of robots with appropriate, natural ways for them to interact with humans, and significant progress has been made in recent years in identifying factors of robot design that influence acceptability. However, much of human perceptual and neural processing occurs outside of awareness, and there are many aspects of processing that cannot be measured with observational studies or overt ratings, as has typically been done in prior HRI work. Here, we suggest further insight could be gained by also applying theory and methods from the cognitive sciences that tap into automatic or unconscious social processing that occurs at a millisecond time scale. These studies, while admittedly disembodied from the viewpoint of real life HRI applications, should supplement more naturalistic interaction studies. Developing truly "neuroergonomic" social robotic systems requires an interdisciplinary approach that can benefit from studies that reveal fundamental processes in the human brain that guide social situations, including studies on whether and how these processes generalize to the case of human robot interaction.

In addition to bringing in methods and theory from attention research, in the present study, we examined two aspects of robot design, appearance and motion, and their influence on human social attention. The role of appearance and motion have been of interest to HRI researchers in both experimental work [3, 4] and in theoretical frameworks such as the Uncanny Valley Hypothesis [5, 6]. Attempting to quantify the experience of interacting with a robot is difficult, as it is a complex phenomenon with many internal mental processes at play. In experimental research, most

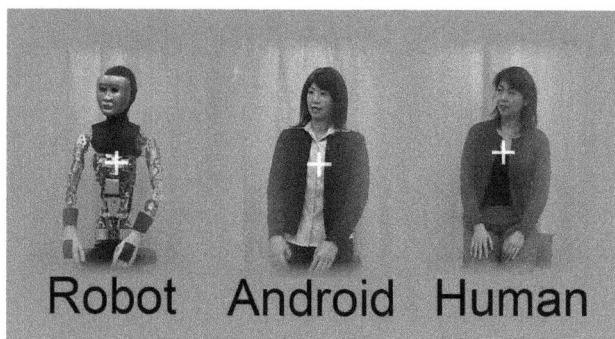

Figure 1: The three agents used in the present study. The agents differ along the dimensions of form and motion. Robot has non-biological form and motion. Android has non-biological form with biological motion. Human has both biological form and motion. Furthermore, subjects were informed that the Robot and Android were machines while the Human was a real person so the agent identity was a difference as well.

prior studies have attempted to characterize the experience of interacting with robots based on subjective judgments and questionnaires. Subjects are asked to rate robots based on categories such as humanlikeness, familiarity, acceptability, sociability, etc. [7-11]. Subjective ratings are important in understanding human reactions to robots, but there are several reasons the field can benefit from complementing these with different experimental approaches and more objective dependent measures. First, there is no consensus as to whether the commonly-used humanlikeness, familiarity, eeriness dimensions are the most suitable for designing more acceptable agents [9, 12]. Second, it is not certain if these rating scales are capable of capturing the subjective experience of interacting with a robot. Finally, subjective ratings have general limitations such as test reliability, test validity, emotional state, and pressure to give socially desirable answers [13].

As a result of these limitations, we should look towards developing more objective approaches and measures to complement questionnaires and surveys in study of HRI. For example, physical approach distance to a robot [14], eye contact [15], eye gaze following [16, 17], dwell time [18], and perceptual adaptation [19] have been used to provide more objective measures for the uncanny valley hypothesis. Neuroimaging methods such as EEG and fMRI can be used to measure how the brain reacts to stimuli of real and artificial agents [20-22]. Objective measures can be modeled with subjective ratings to create a mapping from features of an artificial agent to a behavioral response or neural activity [23]. This eases the process of interpreting how and why a person would have a particular subjective experience when interacting with a robot.

We proposed social attention and the spatial attention task to be a potentially useful objective measure for investigation in HRI. Humans have evolved a sophisticated *Social Attention System* to aid interpersonal interaction and cooperation. This system includes such skills as interpreting facial expressions and understanding non-verbal gestures and actions of others to infer their intent and affective state [24]. In most circumstances this system performs well, allowing us to rapidly and effectively

acquire and transmit more communicative and social cues that we recognize. When designing robots that will be immersed in human society, we could benefit from building these machines whilst being cognizant of the social and communicative abilities humans already possess. In other words these machines should move in ways that we can understand [25] and one way to achieve this is to have them use the same social cues we use in everyday communication. Other people's behavior is immensely useful in aiding the detection and location of important social events and objects. Past research in HRI has focused on how effective robots are at drawing and directing overt and conscious social attention [16, 26, 27]. These past studies generally focused on a scenario where a human and robot interacted over several minutes and measured the human's subjective experience of the event as well as how attentive the human was. These studies have made significant contributions to designing effective interaction protocols and determining design parameters for developing robots that can interact naturally with humans. However not all aspects of social attention can be captured with these methods. Overt behavior is only the end result of an entire cascade of sensory, cognitive, and decision making processes that occurs within the brain. For example human psychology research shows a complex array of processing occurs within a fractions of a second when we see another person shift their eye gaze or head turn [28, 29]. These findings suggest that we must study covert and unconscious mental processes that are involved in social attention in order to have a full understanding of human interaction.

To study the more automatic and covert aspects of social attention we used a variant of the well-established Posner spatial attention task [30] to compare robots' and humans' ability to direct a human observer's attention. This paradigm measures a human's ability to follow a directional cue using reaction time and is sensitive to events occurring in millisecond timescales. The Posner paradigm was used to study attentional systems and typically uses an arrow cue to direct attention to the periphery. Targets that appear in the cued location can be reported faster compared to targets appearing in an uncued location. This paradigm is simple but it gives us a window into automatic and often covert mental processes, such as our ability to direct attention based on social information. The Posner paradigm was adapted to study social attention through the use of cues such as eye gaze or body orientation. Our attention is directed to the same direction that another person is looking or turned [28, 29], though it has been suggested that social cues engage a more specific attentional system than cues such as [31, 32].

The Posner paradigm has been used in a few studies in the past to study human perception of robots [33, 34] and provides an objective measure (reaction time to reporting target location) that is useful as a gauge of how effective a robot is at manipulating automatic attention orienting processes that lie at the root of social attention. The present study extends past work by using dynamic video stimuli in addition to static images allowing us to examine the role of both robot form (physical appearance) and motion (motion kinematics). Form and motion are both features of a robot that may differ from humans and could change how the robot manipulates social attention. From the influential Uncanny Valley Hypothesis [5, 6], a near-human form is theorized to decrease the likeability of a robot. Traditionally, adding in unnatural motion kinematics aggravates the problem but more recent work on the effect of motion yielded differing results [7, 8,

22, 35]. It is possible that unnatural form or motion may affect a robot's ability to engage the automatic attention orienting processes. Manipulating the form and motion of artificial agents can allow us to determine which factor drives differing reactions to real humans *vs.* artificial agents.

To achieve the form and motion manipulation, we used well-controlled stimuli that were used in previous work [22], featuring three different agents, two robots and one human (Figure 1). For convenience of naming, we refer to the machine with a mechanical appearance as Robot while we call the machine with a biological appearance as Android. These stimuli are well controlled as the Robot and Android, actually the same machine, shared identical motion kinematics, and the Android and Human were highly similar in appearance. Interestingly, the study of social attention in general has not used moving stimuli, and therefore the present study provides an important bridge between vision science and interaction studies.

We may observe the following possible outcomes: an appearance driven effect where the Human and Android pair together in behavioral responses, a motion driven effect where the agents with the Robot and Android pairing together, an agent identity effect where the Robot and Android again pair together due to the subject knowing that they are both machines, and a mismatch effect where the Human and Robot pair together due to having matching form-motion biologicalness while the Android stands out as it has a mismatch between its appearance and form. Excluding the agent identity effect pattern, all of the other three effect patterns can be attributed to either form or motion. We hypothesize that the appearance or motion of an agent may influence its ability to manipulate social attention. Our experiment recorded reaction time as the dependent measure and can measure multiple aspects of social attention.

1.1 Attention Cueing

We can measure the *attentional cueing* ability, or the effectiveness of each agent in directing spatial attention. This is an index derived from how much faster (or slower) subjects respond targets that appeared on the cued side (Valid Cue) of an agent compared to targets appearing on the opposite side (Invalid Cue). Such orienting occurs automatically, without any body movements, nor even require eye movements on the part of the subject (covert attention). The Posner paradigm is able to track covert shifts in attention as subjects respond faster to targets that appear on the Validly Cued side compared to the Invalidly Cued side as their attention is automatically directed to the valid side and thus they are prepared to respond to targets appearing there.

Spatial cueing is an aspect of social attention that has been studied in the past [36]. Most work to date has explored gaze cues. In fact, the mere presence of eyes may be sufficient to trigger attentional orienting [37]. There is a smaller literature on studies like the present one using head turn cues. Head and gaze cues may make separate influences on the orienting of attention, though both types of cues are powerful cues for social attention [38, 39]. More relevant to HRI, cueing of attention with agents that have non-human form has been studied but it is unclear whether increased biologicalness facilitates or impairs attentional cueing. In a gaze cueing study, schematic faces were found to cue spatial attention more than realistic faces [40], but this could be due to the eyes in the former stimuli providing a more clear and salient directional signal.

A small literature exists on attentional cueing with artificial agent stimuli. In Admoni and colleagues' work [33], robots were not found to cue human attention. On the other hand Chaminade and Okka [34], who used a similar paradigm, found that both robots and humans could cue attention. Furthermore, social attention studies using live viewing have also found that humans can follow a robot's attentional cues [16, 27].

1.2 Attention Capture

We can also observe *attention capture* effects of each agent by measuring overall reaction time to each agent. This measure can give us a relative estimate of how effectively the agent cue held onto the subjects' attention. This is because subjects had to process the agent and its cue first before being able to shift attention away from it and respond to the target. If the subject spends more time processing cues from one agent type (both Valid and Invalid) then it can be said that particular agent type captured attention more.

Attention capture is also an important aspect of social interaction. We want to direct attention at certain times during interaction but we also want to attract attention towards ourselves. If the appearance or motion of an agent influences attention capture then the design of the agent should be considered if the agent must be able to capture attention as part of its function. Furthermore, there may be cases, such as emergency response, where it is undesirable for a robot to capture too much attention. Therefore, investigating the relation between appearance, motion, and attention capture can improve our understanding of robot design.

1.3 Presence of Motion

In addition to the two experimental factors, we also manipulated the *presence of motion* in the stimuli (static vs. dynamic) across experiments, which allows us to explore the effect of motion cues on social attention. The effect of motion on attentional cueing in the Posner paradigm has not been well explored. Previous work on spatial cueing had used static stimuli. There is some work on the role of dynamic cues in the developmental literature, but they use very different paradigms than the present study. Studies with infants have suggested that motion plays an important role in helping infants acquire attentional orienting skills [41, 42] and dynamic cues may be necessary for cueing infants' social spatial attention [43].

2. Methods
2.1 Subjects

Subjects were recruited from the student body at the University of California, San Diego and had an average age of 21.5 years. Twenty one subjects participated in the Image Experiment (13 female). Twenty subjects participated in the Video Experiment (16 female). No subject participated in both of the experiments. Subjects gave written informed consent in accordance with the institutional review board of this UCSD prior to participating in the study.

2.2 Stimuli

The stimuli were images and videos of three agents (Figure 1); two artificial and one human [21, 22]. The three agents varied in their form and motion kinematics. This stimuli set has actions performed by a realistic robot, Repliee Q2, and the human actor that Repliee Q2's appearance was modeled on. Repliee Q2's external human skin was also removed for a subset of the videos resulting in a mechanical form with the exact same motion kenematics as the realistic form version of Repliee Q2 (since the 2 are the same machine). For convenience of naming, the Robot refers to Repliee with mechanical form and motion while Android refers to Repliee with human-like form and mechanical movement. Finally, Human refers to the human actor, which has both human-like appearance and movement.

Videos of the three agents were recorded with the same background, lighting, and camera settings. The videos were frontal view and restricted to the upper body of the agents. In this study the directional cue was a video of the agents performing a 45 degree turn. The action duration was two seconds for all agent types. Static image stimuli were generated by taking one video frame of the looking forward phase and one frame from the turning phase. All actions were originally taped as a movement to the right of the agent (leftward of the viewer). The images and videos were flipped horizontally to produce cues in both directions. All stimuli (images and video) were converted to grayscale and matched for intensity.

2.3 Experiment and Procedure

The two experiments used similar procedures. Experiments were run using a 19" Dell Trinitron monitor with a screen resolution of 1024x768 and a refresh rate of 90Hz. Subjects were seated with their eyes 30" from the screen. The agents subtended 3x5.6 degrees of visual angle, the target letter was the letter W and it appeared 6.4 degrees from the central fixation point of the screen.

Two experiments were run using a repeated measure design with Cue Validity, and Agent type as experimental factors. The first experiment (Image Experiment) used static image stimuli while the second experiment (Video Experiment) used dynamic video stimuli. Thus, there was also a between subjects "presence of motion" manipulation in addition to the within subject experimental factors. Subjects were able to practice the experiment and familiarize themselves with the stimuli. In both experiments, subjects were informed that both the Robot and Android were machines while the Human was a real person. In a single trial (Figure 2) the subject fixated on a central fixation cross and then observed a static image of the agent looking forwards for approximately 1 second. This is followed by a 100 ms gray screen and then the appearance of the cue stimulus, which could be an image or a video. After a variable time delay (SOA), of 200ms or 400ms or 600ms from the appearance of the cue stimulus, the target would appear to the left or right of the agent. In video experiments, the target appeared as the video was still playing, not after the video concluded. Subjects were allowed to move their eyes once the cueing stimulus appeared. Subjects made a speeded response indicating the location of the target letter, pressing the right arrow key if the target appeared on the right of the agent or the left arrow key if the target appeared on the left of the agent. The target appeared with equal probability on the cued (Valid Cue) or uncued (Invalid Cue) sides and subjects

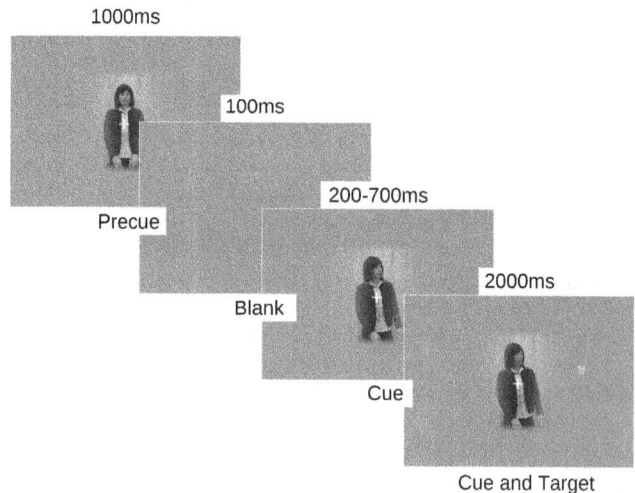

Figure 2: Timeline of a single experimental trial. The SOA during the cue period could be 200, 400, 600, or 700ms depending on the experiment. The trial terminated as soon as the subject responded to the target during the Cue and Target period.

were informed that the cue did not predict the target location. In 12.5% of the trials, the target would not appear, subjects were instructed to not respond on such trials. The purpose of this manipulation was to vary the task so subjects remained alert and did not default to making the same response repeatedly due to fatigue. Reaction times were measured from target appearance to key press.

2.4 Data Analysis

Only trials in which the target letter appeared were used for analysis. In all experiments, as typically done in attention studies, trials in which the subject made an incorrect response in indicating the location of the target letter were excluded from analysis. The correct trials in which the reaction time was faster than 200ms or slower than 4 standard deviations above the mean reaction time for a particular subject were also excluded from analysis. These are commonly used procedures in behavioral studies, and are done to ensure that the data reflect trials where subjects were alert and correctly performing the experimental task (i.e., helping to exclude accidental button presses or trials in which subjects were unusually distracted or slow). No more than 5% of trials for each subject were excluded from analysis for such reasons.

A repeated measures ANOVA was used to determine the effect of each experimental factor (Cue Validity and Agent) on reaction time. All experiments had two Cue Validity levels: Valid and Invalid, and three Agent levels: Robot, Android, and Human.

3. Results

In Image Experiment (Figure 3A) subjects were cued by static images of an agent making a turn towards the right or left of the screen. We found a main effect of Cue Validity $F(1,21) = 20.86$, $p < 0.001$. Pairwise t-tests find that Valid cues resulted in faster reaction times compared to Invalid cues ($p < 0.001$). Collapsing

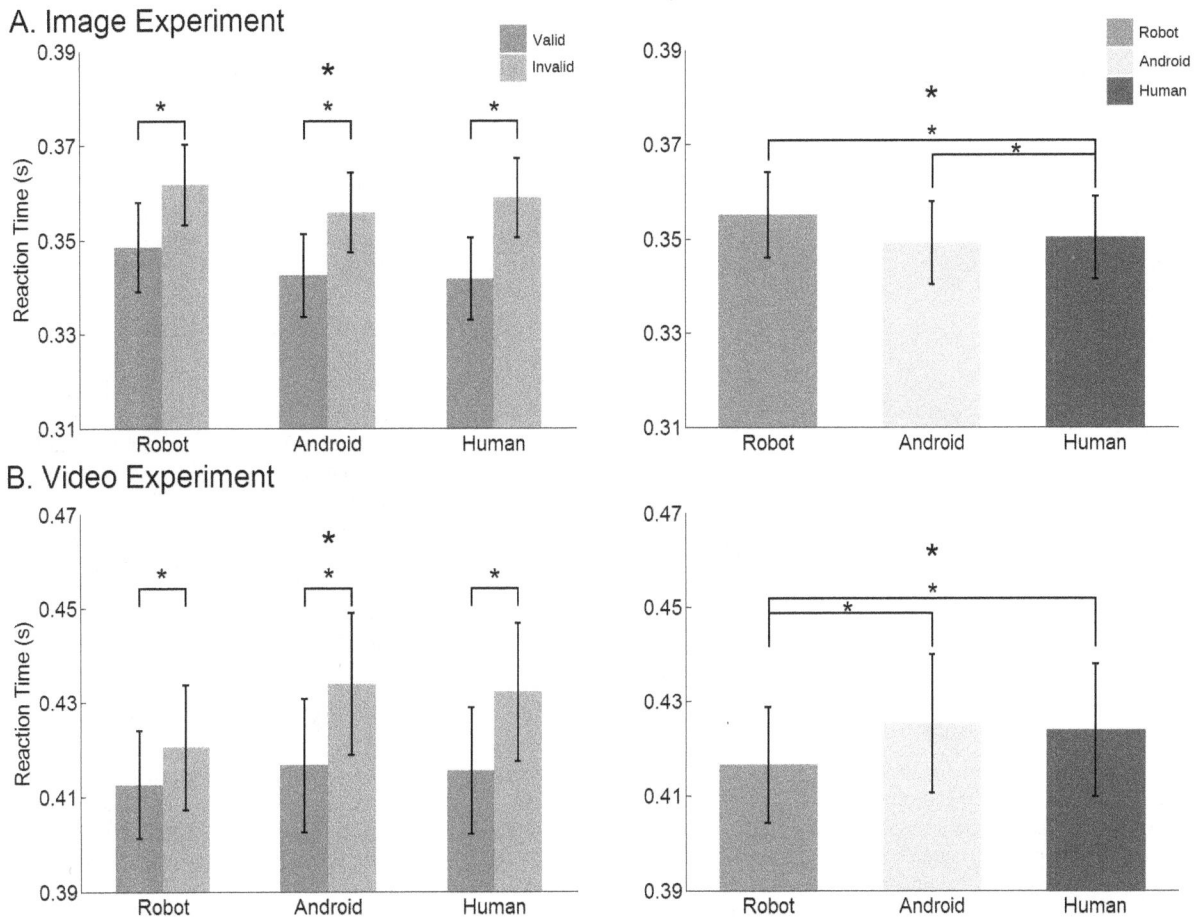

A. Image Experiment

B. Video Experiment

Figure 3: Results of Image Experiment (Figure 3A) and Video Experiment (Figure 3B). Column 1: Agent x Cue Validity Interaction. Column 2: Agent Main Effect. In both experiments, valid cues produced significantly faster reaction times that invalid cues though there was Agent x Cue Validity Interaction. Robot cues produced significantly slower reaction times compared to Android and Human cues in the Image Experiment, but the reverse was true for the Video Experiment.

across Cue Validity, we found a main effect of Agent $F(2,42) = 7.76$, $p > 0.05$. Pairwise t-tests between mean reaction times for each Agent find that the reaction times to Robot cues were significantly slower than the reaction times to Android and Human cues (Human vs. Robot $p = 0.01$, Android vs. Robot $p = 0.002$). Pairwise t-tests between reaction times to Android and Human cues were not significantly, $p = 0.55$. We found no Cue Validity x Agent interaction, $F(2,42) = 1.145$, $p = 0.32$.

In Video Experiment (Figure 3B), we found a main effect of Cue Validity $F(1, 19) = 23.46$, $p < 0.001$ with Valid cues producing faster reaction times than Invalid cues. There was also no Cue Validity x Agent Interaction $F(2,38) = 2.08$, $p = 0.14$. There was a main effect of Agent $F(2,38) = 4.99$, $p > 0.05$, though the effect was in the opposite direction compared to the Image Experiment. There was also no Cue Validity x Agent Interaction $F(2,38) = 2.08$, $p = 0.14$.

We also compared the Image and Video Experiment (Figure 4) in a between subjects model. This model tests for differences caused by the Cue Modality (whether the cue is presented as static or moving). We found a significant main effect of Cue Modality $F(1,40) = 32.3$, $p < 0.001$ with moving cues resulting in slower

reaction times that static cues. There was no Cue Modality x Cue Validity interaction suggesting that the cues were equally effective at cueing attention. There was a cue modality and agent interaction, $F(2,80)=3.24$, $p=.04$, which further highlights the opposing agent main effects between Experiments 1 and 2.

4. Discussion

In the present study we investigated how the appearance and motion of agents influenced their ability to manipulate automatic, unconsciously directed social attention. We used a spatial attention task to explore both *spatial attentional cueing*, and *attention capture*. We did not find evidence that agent form or motion influenced the agents' ability to cue spatial attention. We did find overall *attention capture* effects driven by agent appearance. Furthermore, whether or not the agents moved changed which agent captured more attention.

4.1 Cueing Effect

As seen in the results, and discussed in more detail in section 4.3, whether the cue was static or dynamic made a difference in attentional capture and dynamics, but not in terms of spatial cueing. Among two previous experiments that used similar

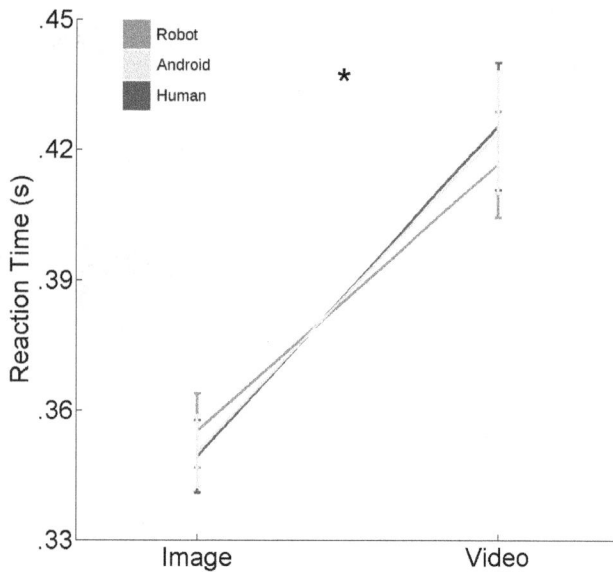

Figure 4: Agent x Experiment comparison, Reaction times were slower overall in the Video Experiment. Also visible is that reaction times to Robot Cues were longer relative to the other agents in the Image Experiment while the reverse was true in the Video Experiment.

paradigms to investigate attentional cueing with robots [33, 34], our findings were more consistent with [34] which found that robots could cue human attention as well as humans could. Our findings also complement studies using live interaction with a robot where humans could follow robots' attention cues during an interactive activity [16]. Though there are notable differences between the timescales explored with the Posner paradigm and live interaction experiments, both seem to suggest that robots can cue our spatial attention. As for the findings of [33], a couple possible explanations can be provided for the discrepancy. The cueing paradigm used in [33] had predictive target locations as well as four possible cueing directions rather than the typical two. Predictable targets may bias our attention [44, 45] and interact the robot's ability to direct attention. Predictability might be useful as a way of measuring how effective a robot is at creating or overcoming this bias relative to humans in future studies. In addition, the robot used in [33] was more toy-like and less mechanical in appearance. These factors may have impacted the end result of the study. Overall, it appears (at least in cases where the cue is not predictive of target location) the human spatial attention system does not "discriminate" against artificial agents, even those that do not look or move like humans.

4.2 Capture Effect

In addition to measuring attentional cueing, our experimental design also allowed us to measure attentional capture by the agent. Collapsing the spatial cues and looking at overall reaction times, we found an attention capture effect, meaning that the agents differed in how long they held onto attention (relative to each other). As discussed below in the next section, the presence of motion changed which agents captured more attention. But in both experiments the Robot agent captured attention differently form the Human and Android agents. This effect was based on the form of the agent since responses to the Robot differed from the other two agents, and the primary difference between the Robot

and the other two are in terms of the physical appearance (see Methods [21, 22]). Finally the overall longer reaction times in Video Experiment relative to Image Experiment suggests that moving stimuli in general capture attention for a longer period compared to similar static images. This is not surprising since motion requires additional processing and this can be reflected in the slowing down of reaction time. This falls in line with previous work that found that motion onset captures attention as objects that initiate motion are likely to be living and thus more important to the observer [46].

4.3 Presence of Motion Effect

In our study, we manipulated the *presence of motion* (static images vs. dynamic videos). The addition of motion in the cue drastically changed the attention capture effects we observed. There were two major effects, the first is that motion changes which agents captured more attention and the second is that, as mentioned above, reaction times to moving cues were longer than those to static cues (Image Experiment *vs.* Video Experiment). In both cases the Android and Human agent paired together in the results. These results contribute to the understanding of motion cues in spatial attention by revealing that attention operates on humanlike appearance or form in a similar fashion, despite a significant effect of motion.

Motion is integral to our studies as it is typical of real world HRI applications. A previous fMRI study found that observing an agent with realistic appearance triggered predictions of realistic motion; if the motion realism did not match the appearance, increased activity was observed in action perception networks of the brain suggesting that additional neural resources are activated to reconcile the prediction error [22]. Motion was also hypothesized to increase the effect of the Uncanny Valley [5, 6]. In the context of our study, if attentional mechanisms operate similarly to these prior studies, the reaction times to Android would differ relative to the Human with the addition of motion. Our results found a complex motion effect, but one that does not fit neatly with previous predictions on uncanny valley. It is therefore possible that social attentional mechanisms we probe here operate independently from the uncanny valley or similar phenomena. Furthermore, other researchers have also called into question the predictions laid out by Mori, and studies using ratings scales found that giving realistic agents motion did not always negatively impact their acceptability [7, 8, 35]. Our reaction time results also mirror some preliminary rating data of subjects viewing the same agents used here (Ürgen, Florendo, Saygin, unpublished). In these rating data, we found ratings of Human and Android humanlikeness and acceptability to become more similar with the addition of motion.

Our results suggest that the moving stimuli changed which features of the agent were prioritized in attention capture. One possibility is having two "sources" of salience that compete to control the attention capture effect when observing social agents. A low-level source based on visual features (such as spatial frequency, contrast), stimulus novelty, or a high-level source based on human-likeness. Stimuli with higher contrast can be more effective at capturing early attention [47] but on the other hand, stimuli with human forms are also more effective at capturing attention due to social relevance [48]. In our Image Experiment, the low-level salience source appears to "win" over the high-level source, and thus the Robot was more effective at capturing attention. In the Video Experiment, the fact that the stimuli were moving may have boosted importance of high-level features. This may be due to the fact that in everyday life, moving objects with human appearance tend to be important. As a result, the moving agents with human form (Android and Human) could become more effective at capturing attention in the Video Experiment. In other words, the appearance and movement of the agent changes which features of the agent the brain predicts to be important and thus allocate attentional resources to.

We did not observe biological motion (the natural motion of the human agent) influencing attention capture or attentional cueing. It is unlikely that biological motion has no influence on attention as past work has found that attention and biological motion interact [32, 33]. It is possible the Human and Android agents were too similar in motion and the turning action did not provide sufficient biological motion cues. Further studies using more levels of human-likeness combined with subjective ratings can give insight into what exactly constitutes biological and non-biological motion and how they influence human social attention.

Though real social interaction is dynamic, to link the more naturalistic situations to those that have been studied in the literature, we applied the paradigm with both static and moving cues. Achieving this precise control of the agent's behavior is difficult in live interaction, especially when a human actor is involved. Although there are differences in experience between social interaction with a screen and with a live person or robot, results gained form this study can give us a better understanding about what kind of studies should be conducted live and what kinds can be done on screen. Screen based experiments are faster and cheaper to run and may prove useful for rapid prototyping of designs.

5. Conclusion

We investigated two aspects of automatic, unconscious social attention using both human a robot stimuli as social cues. These were *attentional cueing* and *attentional capture*. These are two important aspects of social attention as studied by experimental psychologists for decades, and index early, automatic, covert processes that are not possible to access with observational or rating studies. The current data shows that within 200ms of seeing an agent look in a direction, human attention is also turned to that direction. This early, automatic orienting suggests that even in situations where the human is not actively interacting with a robot, the attention systems of the brain are. This level of interaction is almost entirely unstudied in the HRI context. As such, our studies provide and important link between attention as studied in prior HRI studies with research in human psychology. More work will be required to explore other aspects of social attention and different methodologies are required as well to gain a complete understanding of how interaction with a human differs from interaction with a robot, and how to bridge the gaps. From the results of the present study, we speculate that the attention capture mechanisms in social attention are driven primarily by agent appearance, but motion can dramatically influence the exact features of an agent that take priority in capturing attention. One could suggest, if the goal is to create robots that elicit similar responses as humans elicit, then designing robots with biological appearances would be ideal; but this is one small piece of the whole of interpersonal interaction and additional parameters may change the design decisions, possibly varying also as a function of the robot's application environment.

The work presented here supports social attention research in both cognitive science and HRI. This work can also complement neural imaging studies to help link behavior with mental processes, and give insight into the neural mechanisms that operate when we encounter robots. Through these mutually supporting methodologies, we can build a holistic understanding of the mechanisms of human interaction, and eventually apply these to improvements in the design and development of 'neuroergonomic' social robots.

6. ACKNOWLEDGMENTS
This research was supported by DARPA (APS), the Qualcomm Institute (formerly California Institute of Telecommunications and Information Technology (Calit2), Kavli Institute for Brain and Mind, and NSF (CAREER Award BCS-1151805). We thank Intelligent Robotics Laboratory at Osaka University and Kokoro Inc. for help with the preparation of the stimuli, and allowing their use, and Burcu Urgen, Gedeon Deak, Marta Kutas, Douglas Nitz, and members of the Saygin Lab for feedback and discussions.

7. REFERENCES
[1] Coradeschi, S., Ishiguro, H., Asada, M., Shapiro, S. C., Thielscher, M., Breazeal, C., Mataric, M. J. and Ishida, H. Human-inspired robots. *Ieee Intelligent Systems*, 21, 4 (Jul-Aug 2006), 74-85.

[2] Breazeal, C. Toward sociable robots. *Robotics and Autonomous Systems*, 42, 3-4 (Mar 31 2003), 167-175.

[3] Kanda, T., Miyashita, T., Osada, T., Haikawa, Y. and Ishiguro, H. Analysis of humanoid appearances in human-robot interaction. *IEEE Transactions on Robotics*, 24, 3 2008), 725-735.

[4] Seyama, J. and Nagayama, R. The uncanny valley: Effect of realism on the impression of artificial human faces. *Presence: Teleoperators and Virtual Environments*, 162007), 337-351.

[5] Mori, M., MacDorman, K. F. and Kageki, N. The uncanny valley [from the field]. *Robotics & Automation Magazine, IEEE*, 19, 2 2012), 98-100.

[6] Mori, M. The uncanny valley. *Energy*, 7, 4 1970), 33-35.

[7] Piwek, L., McKay, L. S. and Pollick, F. E. Empirical evaluation of the uncanny valley hypothesis fails to confirm the predicted effect of motion. *Cognition*, 130, 3 (Mar 2014), 271-277.

[8] White, G., McKay, L. and Pollick, F. Motion and the uncanny valley. *Journal of Vision*, 7, 9 2007), 477-477.

[9] MacDorman, K. F. and Ishiguro, H. The uncanny advantage of using androids in cognitive and social science research. *Interaction Studies*, 7, 3 2006), 297-337.

[10] Takano, E., Matsumoto, Y., Nakamura, Y., Ishiguro, H. and Sugamoto, K. The Psychological Effects of Attendance of an Android on Communication. *Spr Tra Adv Robot*, 542009), 221-228.

[11] Hanson, D., Olney, A., Prilliman, S., Mathews, E., Zielke, M., Hammons, D., Fernandez, R. and Stephanou, H. *Upending the uncanny valley*. Menlo Park, CA; Cambridge, MA; London; AAAI Press; MIT Press; 1999, City, 2005.

[12] Bartneck, C., Croft, E., Kulic, D. and Zoghbi, S. Measurement instruments for the anthropomorphism, animacy, likeability, perceived intelligence, and perceived safety of robots. *International Journal of Social Robotics*, 1, 1 2009), 71-81.

[13] Adair, J. G. and Spinner, B. Subjects Access to Cognitive-Processes - Demand Characteristics and Verbal Report. *J Theor Soc Behav*, 11, 1 1981), 31-52.

[14] Sardar, A., Joosse, M., Weiss, A. and Evers, V. *Don't stand so close to me: users' attitudinal and behavioral responses to personal space invasion by robots.* ACM, City, 2012.

[15] MacDorman, K. F., Minato, T., Shimada, M., Itakura, S., Cowley, S. and Ishiguro, H. *Assessing human likeness by eye contact in an android testbed.* City, 2005.

[16] Mutlu, B., Yamaoka, F., Kanda, T., Ishiguro, H. and Hagita, N. *Nonverbal leakage in robots: communication of intentions through seemingly unintentional behavior.* ACM, City, 2009.

[17] Minato, T., Shimada, M., Itakura, S., Lee, K. and Ishiguro, H. Evaluating the human likeness of an android by comparing gaze behaviors elicited by the android and a person. *Advanced Robotics*, 20, 10 2006), 1147.

[18] Cheetham, M., Pavlovic, I., Jordan, N., Suter, P. and Jancke, L. Category Processing and the human likeness dimension of the Uncanny Valley Hypothesis: Eye-Tracking Data. *Frontiers in Psychology*, 42013).

[19] Seyama, J. i. and Nagayama, R. Probing the uncanny valley with the eye size aftereffect. *Presence*, 18, 5 2009), 321-339.

[20] Cheetham, M., Suter, P. and Jancke, L. The human likeness dimension of the "Uncanny Valley Hypothesis": Behavioral and functional MRI findings. *Front Hum Neurosci*, 52011), 126.

[21] Urgen, B. A., Plank, M., Ishiguro, H., Poizner, H. and Saygin, A. P. EEG theta and Mu oscillations during perception of human and robot actions. *Frontiers in neurorobotics*, 72013), 19.

[22] Saygin, A. P., Chaminade, T., Ishiguro, H., Driver, J. and Frith, C. The thing that should not be: predictive coding and the uncanny valley in perceiving human and humanoid robot actions. *Soc Cogn Affect Neurosci*, 7, 4 (Apr 2012), 413-422.

[23] Tinwell, A., Grimshaw, M. and Williams, A. Uncanny behaviour in survival horror games. *Journal of Gaming & Virtual Worlds*, 2, 1 2010), 3-25.

[24] Birmingham, E. and Kingstone, A. Human social attention. *Prog Brain Res*, 1762009), 309-320.

[25] Wiese, E., Wykowska, A., Zwickel, J. and Müller, H. J. I see what you mean: how attentional selection is shaped by ascribing intentions to others. *PloS one*, 7, 9 2012), e45391.

[26] Mutlu, B., Shiwa, T., Kanda, T., Ishiguro, H. and Hagita, N. *Footing in human-robot conversations: how robots might shape participant roles using gaze cues.* ACM, City, 2009.

[27] Mutlu, B., Forlizzi, J. and Hodgins, J. *A storytelling robot: Modeling and evaluation of human-like gaze behavior.* IEEE, City, 2006.

[28] Friesen, C. K. and Kingstone, A. The eyes have it! Reflexive orienting is triggered by nonpredictive gaze. *Psychonomic Bulletin & Review*, 51998), 490-495.

[29] Driver, J., Davis, G., Riccardelli, P., Kidd, P., Maxwell, E. and Baron-Cohen, S. Gaze perception triggers reflexive visuospatial orienting. *Visual Cognition*, 6, 5 1999), 509–540.

[30] Posner, M. I. Orienting of attention. *Quarterly Journal of Experimental Psychology*, 321980), 3–25.

[31] Hietanen, J. K. Social attention orienting integrates visual information from head and body orientation. *Psychol Res*, 66, 3 (Aug 2002), 174-179.

[32] Hietanen, J. K. Does your gaze direction and head orientation shift my visual attention? *Neuroreport*, 10, 16 (Nov 8 1999), 3443-3447.

[33] Admoni, H., Bank, C., Tan, J., Toneva, M., & Scassellati, B. Robot gaze does not reflexively cue human attention. . *Proceedings of the 33rd Annual Conference of the Cognitive Science Society, Boston, MA, USA* 2011), 1983-1988.

[34] Chaminade, T. and Okka, M. M. Comparing the effect of humanoid and human face for the spatial orientation of attention. *Frontiers in neurorobotics*, 72013), 12.

[35] Thompson, J. C., Trafton, J. G. and McKnight, P. The perception of humanness from the movements of synthetic agents. *Perception*, 40, 6 2011), 695-704.

[36] Frischen, A., Bayliss, A. P. and Tipper, S. P. Gaze cueing of attention: visual attention, social cognition, and individual differences. *Psychol Bull*, 133, 4 (Jul 2007), 694-724.

[37] Quadflieg, S., Mason, M. F. and Macrae, C. N. The owl and the pussycat: gaze cues and visuospatial orienting. *Psychon Bull Rev*, 11, 5 (Oct 2004), 826-831.

[38] Langton, S. R. and Bruce, V. You must see the point: automatic processing of cues to the direction of social attention. *J Exp Psychol Hum Percept Perform*, 26, 2 (Apr 2000), 747-757.

[39] Langton, S. R. The mutual influence of gaze and head orientation in the analysis of social attention direction. *The Quarterly journal of experimental psychology. A, Human experimental psychology*, 53, 3 (Aug 2000), 825-845.

[40] Hietanen, J. K. and Leppanen, J. M. Does facial expression affect attention orienting by gaze direction cues? *J Exp Psychol Hum Percept Perform*, 29, 6 (Dec 2003), 1228-1243.

[41] Farroni, T., Massaccesi, S., Pividori, D. and Johnson, M. H. Gaze following in newborns. *Infancy*, 5, 1 2004), 39-60.

[42] Moore, C., Angelopoulos, M. and Bennett, P. The role of movement in the development of joint visual attention. *Infant Behav Dev*, 20, 1 (Jan-Mar 1997), 83-92.

[43] Rohlfing, K. J., Longo, M. R. and Bertenthal, B. I. Dynamic pointing triggers shifts of visual attention in young infants. *Developmental Science*, 15, 3 (May 2012), 426-435.

[44] Naccache, L., Blandin, E. and Dehaene, S. Unconscious masked priming depends on temporal attention. *Psychological Science*, 13, 5 2002), 416-424.

[45] Wiese, E., Wykowska, A. and Müller, H. J. What we observe is biased by what other people tell us: Beliefs about the reliability of gaze behavior modulate attentional orienting to gaze cues. *PloS one*, 9, 4 2014), e94529.

[46] Abrams, R. A. and Christ, S. E. Motion onset captures attention: A rejoinder to Franconeri and Simons (2005). *Perception & psychophysics*, 68, 1 2006), 114-117.

[47] Parkhurst, D., Law, K. and Niebur, E. Modeling the role of salience in the allocation of overt visual attention. *Vision Research*, 42, 1 (Jan 2002), 107-123.

[48] Langton, S. R. H., Law, A. S., Burton, A. M. and Schweinberger, S. R. Attention capture by faces. *Cognition*, 107, 1 (Apr 2008), 330-342.

Effects of Robot Motion on Human-Robot Collaboration

Anca D. Dragan, Shira Bauman, Jodi Forlizzi, and Siddhartha S. Srinivasa
Carnegie Mellon University
{adragan,sbauman,forlizzi,siddh}@cs.cmu.edu

ABSTRACT

Most motion in robotics is purely *functional*, planned to achieve the goal and avoid collisions. Such motion is great in isolation, but collaboration affords a human who is watching the motion and making inferences about it, trying to coordinate with the robot to achieve the task. This paper analyzes the benefit of planning motion that explicitly enables the collaborator's inferences on the success of physical collaboration, as measured by both objective and subjective metrics. Results suggest that *legible* motion, planned to clearly express the robot's intent, leads to more fluent collaborations than *predictable* motion, planned to match the collaborator's expectations. Furthermore, purely functional motion can harm coordination, which negatively affects both task efficiency, as well as the participants' perception of the collaboration.

Categories and Subject Descriptors

I.2.9 [**Artificial Intelligence**]: Robotics

Keywords

human-robot collaboration; motion; intent; coordination

1. INTRODUCTION

This paper studies the role of motion in collaborations between humans and robots, and how planning robot motion that explicitly considers the inferences that the collaborator makes affects the fluency of the collaboration.

Imagine the situation from Fig.1, where a human and a robot collaborate on putting together tea orders. The robot gets the next cup, and the human gathers the corresponding ingredients for it. Now imagine the robot's arm twisting and turning while reaching for the cup, its end effector following the trajectory from the bottom left of Fig.1.

Even though this particular motion is not the most efficient, the robot does get its part of the task done. The motion is *functional*:

DEFINITION 1.1. *Functional motion is motion that reaches the goal and avoids collisions.*

Such motion is the main focus of motion planning research [12], and is the state of the art in many robotics applications where robots perform tasks in isolation [17].

HRI'15, March 2–5, 2015, Portland, Oregon, USA.
Copyright © 2015 ACM 978-1-4503-2883-8/15/03$15.00
http://dx.doi.org/10.1145/2696454.2696473.

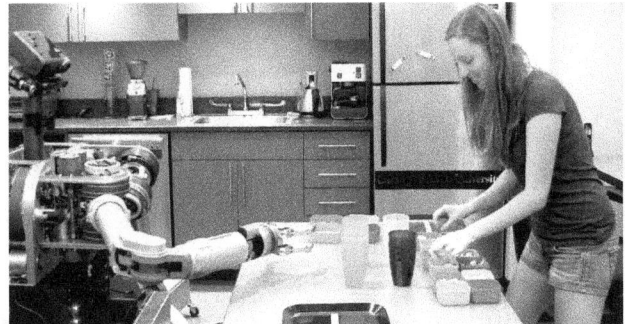

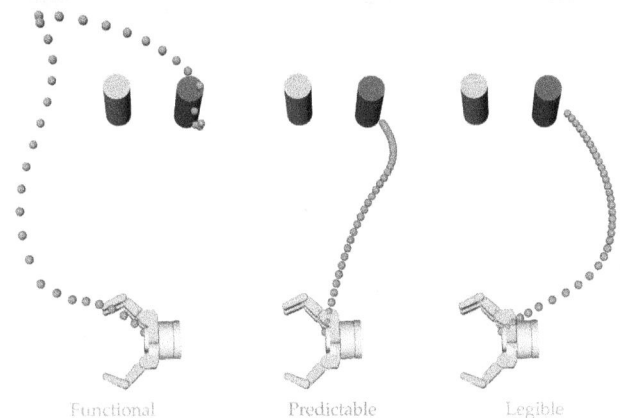

Figure 1: This work manipulates the type of motion the robot plans and studies how this affects physical collaborations between humans and robots.

Collaboration, however, does not happen in isolation. This raises new challenges for the robot's motion, stemming from the two inferences that humans make when they collaborate [3, 20]: they infer actions from goals, and goals from actions.

First, the human has an expectation of how the robot will move *given the goal* it wants to achieve. Motion that matches this expectation is *predictable* [6]:

DEFINITION 1.2. *Predictable motion is functional motion that matches what the collaborator would expect, given the known goal.*

Fig.1 (bottom center) shows the end effector trace of a predictable motion, which efficiently reaches directly to the goal while avoiding collision with the object.

Second, when the human does not know the robot's goal, he infers the goal *given the robot's ongoing motion*. Motion that makes this easy is *legible* [6]:

DEFINITION 1.3. *Legible motion is functional motion that enables the collaborator to quickly and confidently infer the goal.*

Fig.1 (bottom right) shows the end effector trace of the legible motion, which exaggerates the motion to the right to better convey that the goal is the object on the right.

Predictability and legibility are often recognized and studied as important properties of motion [1, 2, 6, 8, 10, 14,

Figure 2: Snapshots from the three types of motion at the same time point along the trajectory. The robot is reaching for the dark blue cup. The functional motion is erratic and somewhat deceptive, and the participant leans back and waits before committing to a color. The predictable motion is efficient, but ambiguous, and the participant is still not willing to commit. The legible motion makes the intent more clear, and the participant is confident enough to start the task.

18]. Our recent work introduced motion planners that *autonomously generate* motion with these properties, and tested their ability to produce more predictable or more legible motion via online video-based studies in a non-collaborative setting [4, 6]. With this, we know the robot can produce more predictable or legible motion, but what we do not know is how this affects human-robot interaction.

This work places all three motion planners – functional, predictable, and legible – in the context of a real *physical* collaboration in order to test whether the predictability and legibility improvements *ultimately affect the collaboration fluency*. It uses a task that requires *coordinating* [15] with the robot (by inferring its goals and performing complementary actions), and study how the choice of a planner affects the fluency of the collaboration through objective and subjective measures inspired by prior work on fluency [9].

To this end, we designed a study ($N = 18$) with objective measures, like the time it takes for participants to infer their action based on the robot's goal (coordination time), how efficient they are at the task (total task time), and how much they move while the robot is moving (concurrent motion), and subjective measures, like how participants perceive the collaboration in terms of fluency, comfort, trust, etc.

The study revealed that predictable motion was better than functional motion: participants had a significantly easier time working with it, and also perceived it as leading to a significantly more fluent collaboration. Furthermore, because of the coordination required in collaboration [19, 20], legible motion did outperform predictable motion.

These findings support the utility of planning motion for collaboration that goes beyond functionality, and reasons about the collaborator's inferences. However, the study also led to a surprising finding: that participants *rationalized* the motion. Their perception of predictability and legibility significantly correlated: instead of perceiving one motion as more predictable and the other as more legible, participants perceived whichever motion was easier to coordinate with as also matching their expectations – they rationalized the legible motion as more predictable as well.

What is more, this was solely the effect of doing a task that requires coordination. As our follow-up study suggests, this

rationalization no longer occurs when participants do not need to infer the robot's intent. In such cases, participants do perceive the predictable motion as more predictable.

Participants also tended to attribute a lot of agency to the functional motion. They interpreted it as the robot searching through the space, or trying to deceive them.

Overall, this work supports the use of legible motion in collaborative tasks that require coordination, suggesting that collaborators have an easier time coordinating with the robot, subjectively prefer it over predictable motion, and even rationalize it as matching their expectations.

2. MOTION PLANNERS

This section summarizes the three motion planning paradigms compared in the study: purely functional motion planning, which is typically achieved via sampling-based methods, and predictable and legible motion planning as defined in our prior work [4], achieved via trajectory optimization.

Notation. The study focuses on goal-directed motion. Here, a robot executes a trajectory $\xi : \mathbb{R} \to \mathcal{Q}$, lying in a space of trajectories Ξ, and mapping time to robot configurations in $\mathcal{Q}$. ξ starts at a configuration S and ends at a goal G_R from a set of possible goals $\mathcal{G}$, like the configurations required to grasp the four cups in Fig.1 (top).

2.1 Functional Motion

Functional motion solves the classical Motion Planning Problem [12] (also known as the Piano Mover's Problem) of finding a path (an untimed trajectory) from S to G_R while avoiding collisions.

For robots with many degrees of freedom, solving this problem requires searching through the high-dimensional space of robot configurations $\mathcal{Q}$. This is commonly achieved through *sampling-based* planners, among which the RRT [11] is one of the most widely used.

RRTs work by growing a tree rooted at S through the space of free configurations. They do this by sampling configurations and attempting to connect them to the nearest node in the existing tree. Eventually, G_R connects to the tree, which leads to a collision-free path from S to G_R. In this work, the functional motion planner applies path-shortening iterations in a post-processing step to eliminate some of the inefficiency of this resulting path.

Fig.1 (bottom left) shows the end effector trace of a functional motion plan to grasp the object on the right. Fig.2 (left) shows a snapshot of the motion, along with a participant's reaction to it. The motion is not efficient, puts the robot in unnatural configurations, and can at times be deceptive about the robot's goal – it might seem like the goal is the one of the left until the very end of the motion.

Thus, we expect that people who collaborate with a robot that produces such motion will not be comfortable, and will not be able to coordinate with the robot because of the difficulty in inferring what the robot is doing.

2.2 Predictable Motion

If the collaborator knows that the goal is G_R, he can predict what trajectory the robot might execute to reach it. The robot's actual trajectory should match this prediction so that the collaborator is comfortable working in the robot's workspace [5]. If it does, then the motion is *predictable* because the collaborator was able to predict a-priori.

If the collaborator sees the robot as a rational agent, applying the principle of rational action [7], then he expects the robot to be efficient. Efficiency can be modeled via a cost functional

$$C : \Xi \to \mathbb{R}_+$$

with lower costs signifying more "efficient" (and thus more expected/predictable to the observer) trajectories. Thus, following [4], the predictable motion planner generates motion via trajectory optimization:

$$\arg\min_{\zeta \in \Xi_{S \to G_R}} C[\zeta] \qquad (1)$$

subject to obstacle avoidance requirements which are treated as soft constraints, as in [21].

For the cost C, the planner uses the integral over squared velocities, which has been shown to produce predictable trajectories for the type of tasks the robot performs in this work, i.e. tabletop reaching motions [5]:

$$C[\zeta] = \frac{1}{2} \int \zeta'(t)^2 dt \qquad (2)$$

Fig.1 (bottom left) shows the end effector trace of a predictable motion plan, a snapshot of which is in Fig.2 (center). This motion is efficient, but it can be ambiguous about the robot's goal, making it difficult to infer its intent. This is especially true in the beginning of the motion, when the predictable trajectory to the goal on the right is very similar to what the predictable trajectory to the goal on the left would look like. The participant in Fig.2 is still waiting to be confident about the robot's intent.

Because predictable motion matches what people expect, we anticipate that people who collaborate with a robot that produces predictable motion will be more comfortable than with functional motion, and better able to coordinate with the robot. However, we expect ambiguous situations to lead to difficulties in coordination, caused by the inability to quickly infer the robot's intent.

2.3 Legible Motion

Often times, the collaborator does not know G_R a-priori. As he is watching the robot's trajectory, he continually makes an inference as to what the goal of the trajectory might

be. The robot's trajectory should enable the collaborator to make the correct inference quickly so that the collaborator be able to easily coordinate with the robot [20]. If it does, then the motion is *legible*.

Given an ongoing trajectory $\xi_{S \to Q}$, the probability that the collaborator will assign to any goal $G \in \mathcal{G}$ can be modeled [4] as:

$$P(G|\xi_{S \to Q}) = \frac{1}{Z} \frac{\exp(-C[\xi_{S \to Q}] - V_G(Q))}{\exp(-V_G(S))} P(G) \qquad (3)$$

with Z a normalizer across $\mathcal{G}$ and $V_G(q) = \min_{\xi \in \Xi_{q \to G}} C[\xi]$.

The legible motion planner also generates motion by optimization, much like the predictable planner. However, instead of optimizing C, it optimizes the probability that the collaborator will infer G_R along the trajectory [4]:

$$\arg\max_{\xi \in \Xi_{S \to G_R}} \frac{\int P(G_R|\xi_{S \to \xi(t)}) f(t) dt}{\int f(t) dt} \qquad (4)$$

with f a weighting function giving preference to the beginning of the trajectory, when conveying intent is more important. Towards the end, the goal becomes clear with any type of motion.

Fig.1 (bottom right) shows the end effector trace of a legible motion plan, a snapshot of which is in Fig.2 (right). This motion is less efficient than the predictable one (slightly more unpredictable), but, by exaggerating the motion to the right, it more clearly conveys that the actual goal is the one on the right. The participant in Fig.2 already knows the robot's goal and has started her part of the task in response.

We expect that the benefit of clearly conveying intent will make legible motion better for collaboration than both predictable and functional motion. However, predictable motion is already much better at conveying intent than functional motion is. It is also more predictable (by definition) than legible motion. Together, this can imply a more subtle difference when going from predictability to legibility, than when going from functionality to predictability.

3. HYPOTHESES

As the predictions in the previous section suggest, we anticipate that the type of motion the robot plans will affect the collaboration both objectively and subjectively. We also expect it to affect participants' perceptions of how predictable and legible the motions are.

H1 - Objective Collaboration Metrics. *Motion type will positively affect the collaboration objectively, with legible motion being the best, and functional motion being the worst.*

H2 - Perceptions of the Collaboration. *Motion type will positively affect the participants' perception of the collaboration, with legible motion being the best, and functional motion being the worst.*

H3 - Perceptions of Legibility and Predictability. *Participants will rate the legible motion as more legible than the predictable motion, and the predictable motion as more legible than the functional motion. In contrast, participants will rate the predictable motion as more predictable than the legible motion, and the legible motion as more predictable than the functional motion.*

4. EXPERIMENTAL DESIGN

To explore the effect of motion type on human-robot collaboration, we conducted a counterbalanced within-subjects study in which participants collaborated on a task with the bimanual mobile manipulator shown in Fig.1.

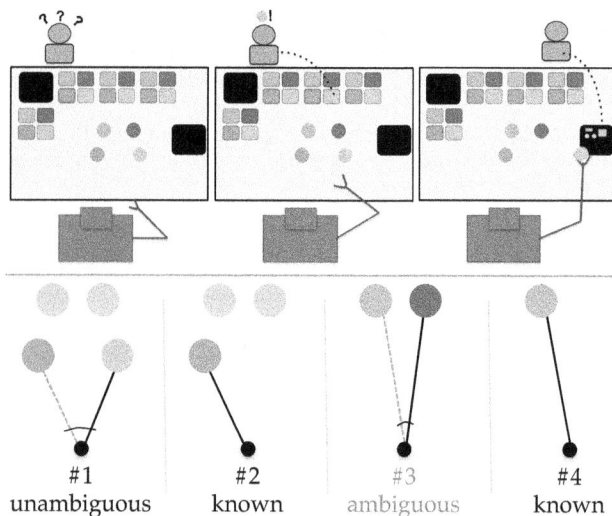

Figure 3: For each tea order, the robot starts reaching for one of the cups. The participant infers the robot's goal and starts gathering the corresponding ingredients. Both place their items on the tray, and move on to the next order. For order #3, the cups are further away from the robot, and closer to each other, making the situation ambiguous.

4.1 Task

Designing a human-robot collaborative task for comparing these types of motion was challenging for four reasons.

First, the success of a collaboration depends on more than the type of robot motion. Other errors during the collaboration can drastically affect the findings. Therefore, the task needs to emphasize the role of motion.

Second, since the study is not testing how the robot should respond to the human's motion, the human's action needs to depend on the robot's, but not vice-versa.

Third, the task must be repeatable: each participant must face the exact same motion planning situations. Different situations (e.g. an object being at a slightly different location) can result in vastly different motions in the case of the functional planner, which could lead to a confound.

And fourth, the task should be as realistic as possible to the participants, and simulate a real world collaboration.

To satisfy these four constraints, the task followed a coffeeshop scenario, in which participants work together with the robot to collaboratively fulfill tea orders. The robot retrieves the correct cup, and the participant gathers the ingredients. Key to this task was that *the selection of the ingredients depends on which cup the robot is retrieving.*

Fig.3 shows a schematic of the task setup. There are four orders total, and four different-colored cups. For each order, the robot reaches for one of the cups, and the participant tries to infer the correct color and starts getting the corresponding ingredients from color-coded bins. This emphasizes the role of motion; it does not require that the robot respond to the human; and it leads to a repeatable task because the location of the cups and the order in which the robot picks them up can be predetermined.

The experiment required the participant to fulfill four orders consecutively instead of a single one because (1) this structure places participants in a longer interaction, and (2) it gives participants a chance to familiarize to the motion type. The four orders split into groups of two, as in Fig.3: participants know that the the first two cups the robot reaches for are in the front, and the next two are in the back. Thus,

participants do not know the robot's goal a-priori for the first and third order.

The cups are placed such that the situation corresponding to the first order is unambiguous – the cups are far enough apart that the predictable motion should be sufficient to convey the goal early on. The test situation is really the third order, which is ambiguous and thus the best at identifying the differences among the three planners. Furthermore, there is not a strong surprise factor, as each participant will have already seen the robot fulfill two orders.

4.2 Procedure

Participants entered the lab and following informed consent, were administered a pre-study questionnaire. Next, the experimenter explained the collaborative task and informed participants that three "programs" were being tested for the robot. They practiced the task once, after which they performed the task three times, one with each "program" (motion type). After each task, they took notes about the collaboration with the robot. At the end, they were administered a post-study questionnaire, and asked to describe the three programs they had experienced.

4.3 Manipulated Variables

A single variable, *motion type*, was manipulated to be functional, predictable, legible. Since the functional planner is nondeterministic, committing to a particular trajectory for each situation is a nontrivial decision. This was done by generating a small set of trajectories and selecting the trajectory with the smallest legibility score. This emphasizes situations where functional motion accidentally leads to deceptive paths, which can harm coordination.

The robot generated predictable and legible trajectories following [4], using functional gradient optimization, and initializing the optimizer with a straight line, constant velocity trajectory. As the next section will detail, one measure is how quickly participants infer the goal. Timing is controlled for by imposing the same duration for all trajectories.

4.4 Participant Assignment Method

A total of 18 participants (5 males, 13 females, aged 18-61, $M = 29.17$, $SD = 12.50$) were recruited from the local community. Only five of the participants reported having a technical background.

The experiment used a within-subjects design because it enables participants to compare the three motions. Participants were told that there were three different robot "programs" to avoid biasing them towards explicitly looking for differences in the motion itself.

The order of the conditions was fully counterbalanced to control for order effects. A practice round was used to eliminate some of the variance introduced by the novelty effect. During the practice round, the robot moved predictably, helping to set the predictable motion as their expectation.

The three test rounds (with the three motion types) used the same ordering of the cups, while the practice round used a different ordering. This way, participants would know that the ordering is not set, while allowing for the ability to eliminate cup order as a confound. A single participant noticed the repeating pattern, as detailed in the Analysis section.

4.5 Dependent Measures

The measures capture the success of a collaboration in both *objective* and *subjective* ways, and are based on Hoffman's metrics for fluency in human-robot collaborations [9].

Fluency $\alpha = .91$
1.*The human-robot team worked fluently together.*
2.*The robot contributed to the fluency of the team interaction .*

Robot Contribution [shortened] $\alpha = .75$
1.*I had to carry the weight to make the human-robot team better.(r)*
2.*The robot contributed equally to the team performance.*
3.*The robot's performance was an important contribution to the success of the team.*

Trust $\alpha = .91$
1.*I trusted the robot to do the right thing at the right time.*
2.*The robot was trustworthy.*
3.*The robot and I trust each other.*

Safety/Comfort [extended] $\alpha = .83$
1.*I feel uncomfortable with the robot.(r)*
2.*I believe the robot likes me.*
3.*I feel safe working next to the robot. [new]*
4.*I am confident the robot will not hit me as it is moving. [new]*

Capability $\alpha = .72$
1.*I am confident in the robot's ability to help me.*
2.*The robot is intelligent.*

Predictability [re-phrased for clarity] $\alpha = .86$
1.*If I were told what cup the robot was going to reach for ahead of time, I would be able to correctly anticipate the robot's reaching motion.*
2.*The robot's reaching motion matched what I would have expected given the cup it was reaching for.*
3.*The robot's reaching motion was surprising.(r)*

Legibility [new] $\alpha = .95$
1.*The robot can reason about how to make it easier for me to predict what it is reaching for.*
2.*It was easy to predict what the robot was reaching for.*
3.*The robot moved in a manner that made its intention clear.*
4.*The robot was trying to move in a way that helped me figure out what it was reaching for.*

Forced-Choice Questions $\alpha = .91$
1.*Which program were you the fastest with?*
2.*Which program was the easiest?*
3.*Which program do you prefer?*

Figure 4: Findings for objective measures.

Objective measures include the *coordination time*, the *total task time*, and the *concurrent motion time* for the test order (order #3).

The coordination time is the amount of time from the moment the robot starts moving, until the participant infers the correct goal (either by declaring it aloud, which we ask participants to do, or by starting to reach for the correct ingredients, whichever comes first). The total task time is the amount of time, from the moment the robot starts moving, until the last ingredient touches the tray. Finally, the concurrent motion time is the amount of time when both the human and the robot are moving.

Table I shows the seven subjective scales that were used, together with a few forced-choice questions. The *fluency* and *trust* scales were used as-is from [9]. The *robot contribution* scale was shortened to avoid asking participants too many questions. A subset of questions were chosen related to *capability*, and extended questions were chosen related to *safety/comfort*. Additional questions were added that were more appropriate to the physical setup (feeling safe next to the robot, and being confident that the robot can avoid collisions with them).

The *closeness* to the robot question from [16] (not shown in the table) asked participants to select among five diagrams portraying different levels of mental proximity to the robot during the task.

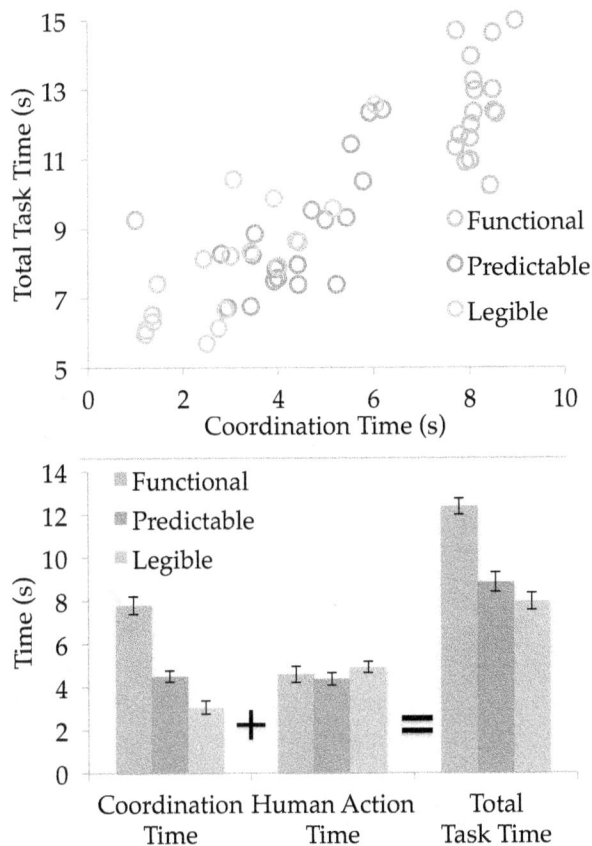

Additionally, participants answered forced-choice questions at the end, about which program they were the fastest with, which program was easiest to work with, and which program they preferred.

The subjective measures also included perceived *predictability* and *legibility*. The predictability scale was adapted from [5]. Clarifications were added because the task was so focused on predicting goals that the word "predictable" was too easily misunderstood in this context.

A legibility scale was devised to capture both how easy inferring the goal is, as well as whether participants believe that the robot has the ability to reason about making this inference easy, and whether it was explicitly trying to do so.

In addition to these measures, a pre-survey was administered to participants, asking demographics questions, as well as the "Big-5" personality questionnaire, since personality type could potentially correlate with how they experience the collaboration.

Finally, the service orientation *attitude* scale was adapted from [13], measuring whether participants have a relational or utilitarian orientation toward a food service provider. The questions were modified to refer to food preparation. This measure was chosen because having a relational attitude could correlate with the way participants interpret legibility, in particular whether they think the robot is *purposefully* trying to help them infer the goal easier.

5. ANALYSIS

Each of the 18 participants performed the task three times, with each task consisting of four orders (trials). This led to a total of 216 trials, out of which 54 were test trials (order

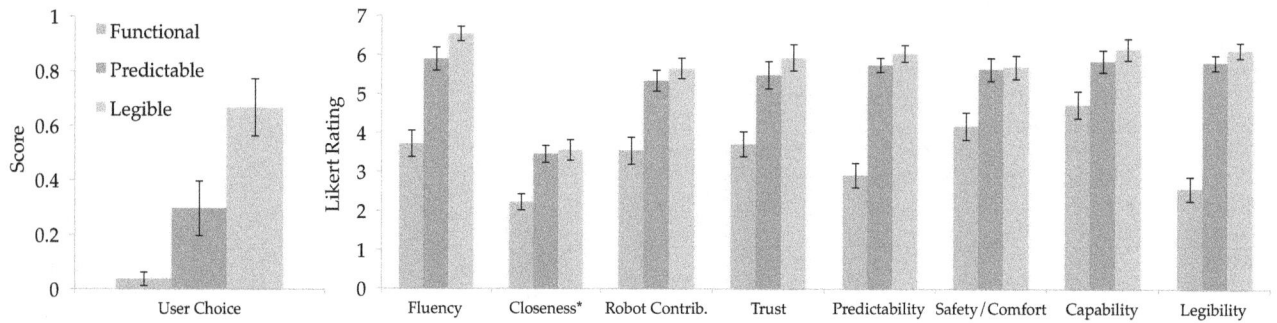

Figure 6: Findings for subjective measures. Closeness was on a 5-point scale.

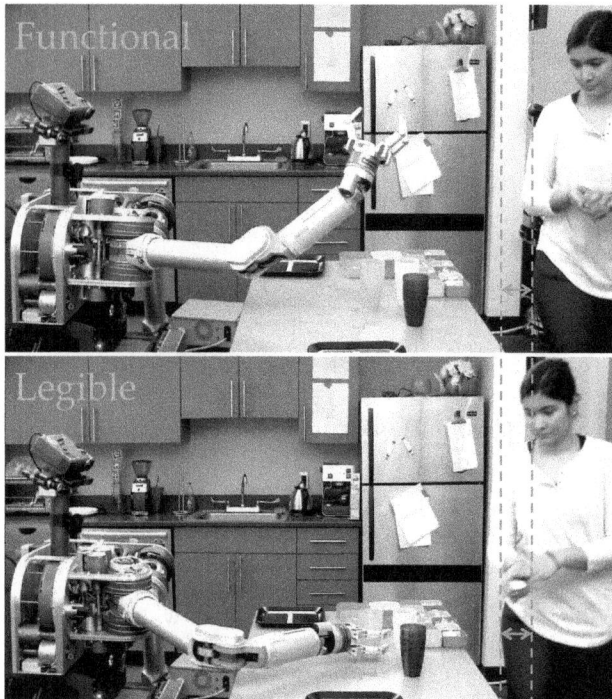

Figure 5: Some of the participants kept a larger distance to the robot during the functional condition. However, most participants were surprisingly comfortable with the robot during this condition.

#3), 54 were unambiguous trials (order #1) that still had a coordination time, and the rest were trials that did not need coordination.

5.1 H1 - Objective Measures

A repeated measures ANOVA on the *coordination time* ($R^2 = .67$) showed a significant effect for motion type ($F(2,51) = 52.06$, $p < .0001$), in line with **H1**.

A post-hoc analysis with Tukey HSD supported **H1**, showing that all three conditions were significantly different from each other, with functional taking significantly longer than predictable ($p < .0001$), and predictable taking significantly longer than legible ($p = .01$). Legible motion resulted in a 33% decrease in coordination time compared to predictable motion.[1]

---

[1] These results are for the test trials. There was no difference between legibility and predictability on the unambiguous trials (Fig.3), since the predictable motion is sufficiently legible when there is little ambiguity.

Fig.4 shows a scatter plot of the coordination time by the total task time. As expected, legible motion < predictable motion < functional motion in terms of coordination time, with functional motion being better separated as a cluster. These differences propagate to the total task time.

There is one outlier in the plot, for the functional motion (the blue circle in the center left). This was a participant who noticed a repeating pattern in the ordering of the cups, and achieved minimal coordination time as a result during his third condition, which happened to be the functional condition.

A repeated measures ANOVA on the *total task time* ($R^2 = .56$) showed similar results. Motion type was significant ($F(2,51) = 32.59$, $p < .0001$), and the post-hoc showed a significant difference between predictable and functional ($p < .0001$), partially supporting **H1**.

However, the difference between predictable and legible, although trending in the expected direction (Fig.4 bottom center), was no longer significant ($p = .27$). Surprisingly, participants took slightly longer to gather the ingredients in the legible condition ("human action time", Fig.4 bottom center). Analysis of the video recordings showed that even though some participants could infer the correct cup earlier, they would *hesitate* a bit during the task, looking back at the robot again to make sure they made the right prediction and thus slowing down.

Surprisingly, participants did not wait for the robot to finish moving in the functional condition, as we had anticipated. Instead, participants were comfortable enough to do the task while the robot was still moving. Since the robot took longer than the participants to achieve its part of the task, the concurrent motion time was equal to the human action time and did not provide any additional insight.

Participants' main complaint about the functional motion was that it was difficult to coordinate with the robot, and not that they felt unsafe. This could potentially be the result of placing participants in a lab setting, leading to them over-trusting the robot.

Some of the participants did lean back more, as if to avoid the robot arm, and also took a curved path to place the ingredients on the tray (see Fig.5 for an example). Many participants looked surprised when the robot started moving. However, there were some who remained completely unphased by the motion.

Because of the delay in inferring the correct cup, a participant exclaimed "Wait for me!" as she was hurrying to catch up because of the long coordination time. Some of the participants would speed up in gathering the ingredients in the functional condition, as if they were trying to catch up to the robot and still finish the task before. This was not the case in general, with some of the participants having a longer action time than in the predictable condition, stopping more to watch the robot, and hesitating in gathering the ingredients.

None of the participants complained about the robot being much slower than them. This could be due to the bias of participating in a lab experiment. However, as the "Wait for me!" complaint suggests, participants seemed to actually mind the robot finishing its part of the task before they finished theirs, emphasizing the importance of synchronization in collaboration tasks.

Overall, supporting **H1**, legible motion had significantly lower coordination time than predictable, which had significantly lower coordination time than legible. 17 out of 18 participants had lower coordination time with the legible motion compared to predictable, and 15 had a lower total task time. As expected, the difference between legibility and predictability was more subtle than that between predictability and pure functionality. Surprisingly, the robot moving functionally did not affect concurrent motion time, and participants were comfortable enough to move at the same time as the robot even with functional motion.

5.2 H2 - Perceptions of the Collaboration

Table I, which lists the subjective scales, also shows the internal consistency of each scale, reported via Cronbach's α. Most scales had good to excellent consistency, the exceptions being *capability* and *robot contribution*, which were acceptable. Scale items were combined into a score and analyzed with repeated-measures ANOVAs. Fig.6 plots the results.

The score produced by the overall forced-choice questions was significantly affected by the motion type ($F(2, 51) = 13.59$, $p < .0001$), with the post-hoc revealing that legible motion had a significantly higher score than predictable motion ($p < .01$), but predictable motion was only marginally better than functional motion ($p = .08$). 12 out of the 18 participants preferred the legible motion.

All the Likert ratings showed a significant effect for motion type as well, with post-hocs revealing that functional motion was significantly lower rated than predictable and legible motion in every case (with $p < .0001$, except for *capability*, details below). The legible motion tended to be rated higher than predictable, but those differences were not significant. Fig.6 summarizes these findings.

The biggest difference between predictability and legibility was in *fluency*. *Safety*, on the other hand, was the same for both — this is not surprising, given that legible motion is better at conveying intent, but this does not necessarily lead to an increased feeling of safety.

Capability was high with the functional motion as well, though still significantly lower than with predictable motion ($p = .03$).

With respect to additional participant measures, unsurprisingly, being extroverted significantly correlated to having a relation attitude towards a food preparation partner ($r(16) = .51$, $p = .03$). Additionally, extroversion inversely correlated with preferring the legible motion over the other two motion types ($r(16) = -.49$, $p = .04$). However, extroversion did not correlate with whether or not the legible motion worked objectively, i.e. achieved lower coordination time. More research is needed to verify this result and understand why introverts might be more likely to appreciate a legible robot.

Overall, participants significantly preferred the legible motion over the predictable motion, and tended to prefer the predictable motion over the functional. However, as with the objective measures, their ratings of the collaboration suggest that legibility is a more subtle improvement over predictability, compared to the improvement of predictability over functionality.

5.3 H3 - Perceptions of Predictability and Legibility: Rationalization of the Motion

5.3.1 Perceptions of Legibility

As predicted by **H3**, motion type significantly affected the legibility rating ($F(2, 51) = 67.56$, $p < .0001$). The post-hoc analysis did show a significant difference between functional and predictable motion ($p < .0001$), but not between predictable and legible motion.

The biggest difference between predictable and legible motion was in how easy participants thought it was to predict the robot's goal (question 2) (mean 6 vs. 6.61). Participants thought the legible motion made goal inference easier. In contrast, participants did not think that the robot was more capable of higher-order reasoning. Question 1 yielded almost no difference between predictability and legibility, and had a lower overall mean (5.11 vs. 5.27).

Participants' comments matched their ratings of legibility of motion. Three participants described the functional motion as "exaggerated", with one of them commenting that "the arm motions were so exaggerated that it was hard to see which cup he was going to choose until just before". Many of the participants referred to it as less intent-expressive, commenting that "it made it almost impossible to guess" or that it was "trickier".

One participant said that the functional motion made her less confident about the intent even for the orders where the cup was predetermined (2nd and 4th): "even when I knew the cup it would grab, I was still less confident than with the other programs". Indeed, we noticed some participants hesitate more during the functional motion condition on these orders, while others remained completely focused and ignored the erratic nature of the motion.

Interestingly, some participants attributed *agency* to the random nature of the functional motion: "he was picking a cup at random", "the robot appeared to be searching before selecting a cup", "makes me think that it's playing on purpose", "it appeared that the robot had a mind of its own, along with its own agenda", the robot "tricked me". One participant actually rated the functional program as the one they prefer overall, and a couple rated it as the most intelligent of the three, possibly because of this attribution of agency.

Because the predictable and legible motions are more similar to each other than they are to the functional motion, participants tended to contrast the two in their descriptions of the three programs.

Most participants described the predictable motion as somewhat less intent-expressive than the legible: "slightly harder to recognize", "the direction it's going in isn't as clear as the (legible motion)", "slight uncertainty about the cup choice", "not very clear as the (legible motion)", "not as easy as (the legible motion); I had to wait a bit after his hand moved to realize the cup he was going for", "it was had to determine which he'd pick", "it was not as clear".

In contrast, the descriptions for the legible motion referred to it as "easier to predict [the cup]" and "very straightforward", noting that one "could clearly see the trajectory of its hand to the cup". Some of the participants recognized that the robot was altering the motion in order to better convey intent. They thought that "the wide movements made it easy to identify [the cup]", "the angle was such that you could discern", and that "he starts out clearly moving towards one direction".

One of the participants even associated the beginning of the robot's legible motion to a communicative gesture: "it was almost like the robot was pointing at the cup he was going for right before, while he was moving his arm".

5.3.2 Perceptions of Predictability

Motion type significantly affected the predictability rating as well ($F = 50.48$, $p < .0001$). Counter to **H3**, however, participants actually tended to rate the legible motion higher, and the ratings for predictability and legibility significantly correlated ($r(52) = .91$, $p < .0001$).

It appears that when legibility works for someone and they can infer the goal easier, they tend to *rationalize* it as the "natural" motion, or even "direct" or "efficient". In contrast, some participants refer to the predictable motion as "inefficient", and even as "going towards the other cup initially", which is inaccurate.

This rationalization may happen because of the importance of inferring intent in the task. Legible motion is easier for collaboration, and that makes participants believe it is what they would have expected.

5.3.3 Follow-Up Study on Predictability

To test this, an online follow-up study ($N = 16$) was conducted, where participants were shown a motion from the practice round, and asked to think about the motion they expect in the test situation. They then watched a video of each motion (predictable and legible), and chose which better matched their expectation. Since the task no longer had an intent prediction emphasis, participants did choose the predictable motion significantly more often (approx. 70%, which a binomial test showed to be significantly higher than chance, i.e. 50%, $p = .0251$). This supports our rationalization hypothesis.

Overall, perceptions of predictability and legibility correlate in a task in which intent inference is important: participants rationalize the motion that makes the coordination easier as the motion they think they would expect.

6. DISCUSSION

Overall, the findings from this study suggest that functional motion is not enough for collaborative tasks that require coordination, and that the robot should take the collaborator's expectations into account when planning motion. Although this was a laboratory study with an artificial task, the findings lead to interesting conjectures about motion design for collaborative tasks.

One finding is that legibility is preferable to predictability in coordination tasks, as it decreases coordination time, collaborators prefer it overall, and rationalize it as more predictable despite it actually being less efficient (and them not being able to anticipate it a-priori). Furthermore, for quadratic costs C, legibility has no computational overhead compared to predictability in planning time.

Furthermore, functional motion might be enough for tasks that do not require coordination nor close proximity (such as repetitive tasks like those one might encounter on a factory floor, or tasks that have been carefully planned in advance, with separate and known roles). Participants were surprisingly willing to move at the same time as the robot, and mainly complained about not being able to coordinate. Furthermore, functional motion does not require optimization, making it at times faster at producing a feasible plan [21].

Predictable motion seems to be best when coordination is not necessary (or the situations are not ambiguous, making the predictable motion legible enough), but when people work in close proximity to the robot and would be uncomfortable with surprising motion [5].

7. CONCLUSION

This paper analyzed the benefit of planning robot motion that explicitly enables the collaborator's inferences on the success of a physical collaboration. Results suggest that legible motion, planned to clearly express the robot's intent, leads to more fluent collaborations than predictable motion, planned to match the collaborator's expectations. Functional motion was found to negatively affect coordination, increasing the time it takes to achieve the task, as well as the participant's perception of the collaboration.

Future work will explore how people change their expectations of motion over time (e.g. does legible motion become objectively predictable?). The effect of multi-modal legibility for coordination will also be studied, to understand when the robot should express intent through motion, and when it should speak, or even gesture.

References

[1] R. Alami, A. Albu-Schaeffer, A. Bicchi, R. Bischoff, R. Chatila, A. D. Luca, A. D. Santis, G. Giralt, J. Guiochet, G. Hirzinger, F. Ingrand, V. Lippiello, R. Mattone, D. Powell, S. Sen, B. Siciliano, G. Tonietti, and L. Villani. Safe and Dependable Physical Human-Robot Interaction in Anthropic Domains: State of the Art and Challenges. In *IROS Workshop on pHRI*, 2006.

[2] R. Alami, A. Clodic, V. Montreuil, E. A. Sisbot, and R. Chatila. Task planning for human-robot interaction. In *Smart objects and ambient intelligence*, 2005.

[3] G. Csibra and G. Gergely. Obsessed with goals: Functions and mechanisms of teleological interpretation of actions in humans. *Acta Psychologica*, 124(1):60 – 78, 2007.

[4] A. Dragan and S. Srinivasa. Generating legible motion. In *RSS*, 2013.

[5] A. Dragan and S. Srinivasa. Familiarization to robot motion. In *HRI*, 2014.

[6] A. D. Dragan, K. C. Lee, and S. S. Srinivasa. Legibility and predictability of robot motion. In *HRI*, 2013.

[7] G. Gergely, Z. Nadasdy, G. Csibra, and S. Biro. Taking the intentional stance at 12 months of age. *Cognition*, 56(2):165 – 193, 1995.

[8] M. J. Gielniak and A. L. Thomaz. Generating anticipation in robot motion. In *RO-MAN*, 2011.

[9] G. Hoffman. Evaluating fluency in human-robot collaboration. In *HRI Workshop on Human Robot Collaboration*, 2013.

[10] T. S. Jim Mainprice, E. Akin Sisbot and R. Alami. Planning safe and legible hand-over motions for human-robot interaction. In *IARP Workshop on Technical Challenges for Dependable Robots in Human Environments*, 2010.

[11] J. J. Kuffner and S. M. LaValle. Rrt-connect: An efficient approach to single-query path planning. In *ICRA*, 2000.

[12] J.-C. Latombe. *Robot Motion Planning*. Kluwer Academic Publishers, Norwell, MA, USA, 1991.

[13] M. K. Lee, S. Kiesler, J. Forlizzi, S. Srinivasa, and P. Rybski. Gracefully mitigating breakdowns in robotic services. In *HRI*, 2010.

[14] C. Lichtenthäler, T. Lorenz, and A. Kirsch. Towards a legibility metric: How to measure the perceived value of a robot. In *ICSR Work-In-Progress-Track*, 2011.

[15] M. A. Marks, M. J. Sabella, C. S. Burke, and S. J. Zaccaro. The impact of cross-training on team effectiveness. *Journal of Applied Psychology*, 87(1):3, 2002.

[16] B. Mutlu, J. Forlizzi, and J. Hodgins. A storytelling robot: Modeling and evaluation of human-like gaze behavior. In *Humanoid Robots*, 2006.

[17] I. Sucan, M. Moll, and L. Kavraki. The open motion planning library. *Robotics & Automation Magazine, IEEE*, 2012.

[18] L. Takayama, D. Dooley, and W. Ju. Expressing thought: improving robot readability with animation principles. In *HRI*, 2011.

[19] M. Tomasello, M. Carpenter, J. Call, T. Behne, and H. Moll. Understanding and sharing intentions: the origins of cultural cognition. *Behavioral and Brain Sciences*, 2004.

[20] C. Vesper, S. Butterfill, G. Knoblich, and N. Sebanz. A minimal architecture for joint action. *Neural Networks*, 23(8):998–1003, 2010.

[21] M. Zucker, N. Ratliff, A. Dragan, M. Pivtoraiko, M. Klingensmith, C. Dellin, J. Bagnell, and S. Srinivasa. Covariant hamiltonian optimization for motion planning. *IJRR*, 2013.

Escaping from Children's Abuse of Social Robots

Dražen Brščić[1]   Hiroyuki Kidokoro[1,2]   Yoshitaka Suehiro[1,2]   Takayuki Kanda[1,2]

[1] ATR Intelligent Robotics and Communication
Laboratory, 2-2-2 Hikaridai, Seika-cho
Keihanna Science City, Kyoto, Japan

[2] Osaka University, Graduate school of Information
Science and Technology,
2-1 Yamadaoka, Suita, Osaka, Japan

{drazen, kidokoro, suehiro, kanda}@atr.jp

ABSTRACT

Social robots working in public space often stimulate children's curiosity. However, sometimes children also show abusive behavior toward robots. In our case studies, we observed in many cases that children persistently obstruct the robot's activity. Some actually abused the robot by saying bad things, and at times even kicking or punching the robot. We developed a statistical model of occurrence of children's abuse. Using this model together with a simulator of pedestrian behavior, we enabled the robot to predict the possibility of an abuse situation and escape before it happens. We demonstrated that with the model the robot successfully lowered the occurrence of abuse in a real shopping mall.

Categories and Subject Descriptors

H.5.2 [**Information Interfaces and Presentation**]: User Interfaces - *Interaction styles*; I.2.9 [**Artificial Intelligence**]: Robotics

General Terms

Design, Experimentation, Human Factors.

Keywords

human-robot interaction; children; robot abuse.

1. INTRODUCTION

Many robots are being developed for the use in open public environments. For instance, previous studies revealed robots can be successfully used in a museum [1, 2], supermarket [3], transit station [4], or urban sidewalk [5]. All these works reported that people exhibit great curiosity and actively interact with robots.

Similarly, in our experiments in public spaces we too observed that many people gathered around our robot. This includes children, who were usually with their parents and behaved well. However, we noticed that the situation often changed when there were not many people close to the robot and children were left alone to play with it. This sometimes lead to children showing anti-social behavior toward the robot, such as blocking its way, calling it names or even acting violently toward it.

Figure 1 shows two scenes where our robot was in trouble with

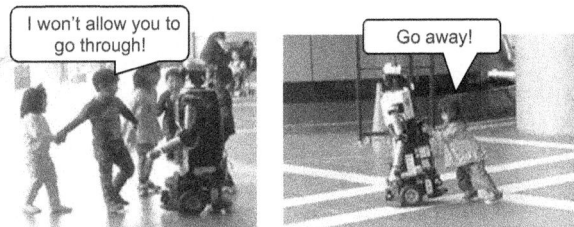

Figure 1. Children's abusive behavior toward the robot.

children. They frequently stood in its way and stopped it from moving (Figure 1 left). Sometimes their behavior escalated further. They said bad words, punched, kicked, and/or pushed the robot (Figure 1 right). Even if the robot asked them to stop, its request was often ignored. They typically did not stop such misbehavior until they got bored or their parents stopped them.

We believe that occurrence of children's abusive behavior will be a real problem for social robots. Due to such behavior robots' execution of tasks would be hindered. Furthermore, children's abusive behaviors could make people uncomfortable [6] and perhaps also be problematic for children's healthy development [7, 8]. Our aim in this work was to study the children's abuse of robots and find a way to prevent or mitigate the problem.

2. RELATED WORKS

2.1 Robot Abuse

There are a few pioneering researches on the concept of abuse of robots. Bartneck and his colleagues first used the term "robot abuse" [9] and revealed that people show less concern about the abuse of robots than abuse of humans, yet they hesitate to destroy a robot when they perceive it intelligent [10]. There is a report that people felt bad and perceived empathy toward the robot when they saw a video in which a robot was tortured [6].

Salvini and his colleagues reported abusive behavior, or bullying behavior, toward their robots [11]. In their open-public demonstration, they observed that people approached their robot out of curiosity, but quite often escalated into aggressive behaviors, such as kicking, punching or slapping the robots. Such behavior only occurred when the robot was not attended by human operators.

Overall, none of previous studies have analyzed the pattern of occurrence of robot abuse, and did not propose a method to address such situation. The novelty of our study is that it is the first to attempt to find a method to moderate the abuse of robots.

2.2 Abuse in Other Interactions

Apart from robots, children can show abusive behavior in other social interactions, too. Perhaps the most prominent example is the bullying among children, which [11] defines as deliberate, repeated or long-term exposure to negative acts performed by a person or group of persons regarded of higher status or greater strength than the victim. Although similarities do exist, one important difference to the abuse of robots is that bullying among children is typically studied in long-term interactions, e.g. in schools, where the bully and victim know each other well.

Abusive behavior has been reported also in human-animal interaction research. Children sometimes engage in animal abuse, defined as non-accidental, socially unacceptable behavior that causes pain, suffering or distress and occasionally also death of an animal [13]. One view is to see animal abuse as an impulsive act without instrumental benefit, and thus consider it as an early symptom of conduct-disorder in children. It was reported that 25% of conduct-disorder children exhibited animal cruelty [8]. Research also shows that children who do animal abuse often also engage in bullying [7]. On the other hand, Arluke [14] argued that animal abuse has various other reasons, such as play, a form of knowledge creation, or a group activity with playmates. In any case, a concern remains that there is a link between animal abuse and violence toward humans, and that it is therefore better to prevent it.

In this work we start from the premise that robot abuse should also be avoided, and consider the modeling and robot planning to achieve this.

2.3 Simulation-based Planning in HRI

Human behavior is complex and it is hard to accurately predict what people would do in the future. This is a primary source of difficulty for using planning in robot interactions with people.

Recent studies started to use simulation in planning in human-robot interaction. For instance, Hoffman and Breazeal [15] conducted a study revealing that anticipatory computation enables fluent interaction, and further considered that such similarity in perception would work as a perceptual simulation. In a different work [16], a simulation of two people's side-by-side walking was made and the model for simulated agent was used for anticipatory computation.

Regarding the interaction with pedestrians, previous studies started to investigate the way to predict or anticipate people's behavior, and some of them used pedestrian simulation for planning. For instance, Bennewitz and her colleagues developed a model learnt from people's trajectories and used it to plan to avoid collisions with people [17]. Henry et al., trained a collision avoiding algorithm using a pedestrian simulator [18]. Garrell and Sanfeliu used a pedestrian simulation to test a robot's capability for handling groups of people [19], and used a pedestrian simulation to compute better position for a robot to avoid collisions [20]. In [21] we used a pedestrian simulator to predict the occurrence of crowding around a robot and used a planner to choose a path to minimize dissatisfaction to people passing by.

This study follows the paradigm of simulation-based planning. Nevertheless, the originality of the study is in that it successfully simulates occurrences of children's abuse of the robot, which are complex emergent phenomena. Further, this simulation is used for planning and avoidance of the robot-abuse problem.

3. DATA COLLECTION
3.1 Environment and Infrastructure

We conducted our study in a part of the ATC shopping mall in Osaka, Japan (Figure 2), where we set up a sensing infrastructure, which allowed us to track the people that are inside the area. The

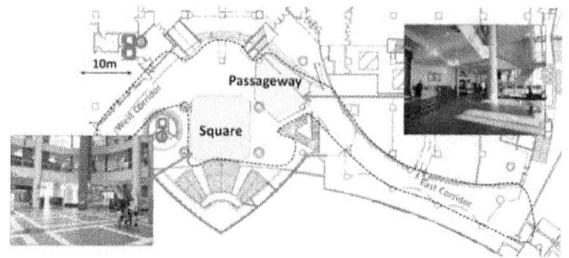

Figure 2. Environment where we conducted the field study.

observed area consisted of a central square, a long corridor leading toward east and a shorter corridor connecting to the west. The main flow of people went through the east corridor, where the density was largest. On the other hand, the square was typically less crowded.

The tracking system consisted of in total 49 3-D range sensors of different types, arranged such that they cover the area of interest. The total covered area was around 900 m2 (inside the dashed line in the figure). We used the tracking algorithm proposed in [22], which allowed us to track the position of all the people in the area at 20 Hz with accuracy of around 30 cm.

We used the human-like robot Robovie2 (Figure 1). The robot had a microphone to record the people's speech, and two laser range sensors which were used for safety. During autonomous operation, the range sensors were also used for localizing the robot using a particle filter on an occupancy grid map [23].

3.2 Setting

We let the robot patrol in two areas where different flow of people was observed: the square, and the area between the east corridor and square, which we refer to as passageway (see Figure 2). The patrol task consisted in repeated moving in straight lines between several fixed way points. In both areas we performed the data collection on a weekend for 2 hours. During the data collection all operations of the robot were controlled remotely by an operator.

When a person stopped in front of the robot, the operator stopped the robot and started the robot's conversation. The robot asked the person to step aside by saying: "I am Robovie. I am now patrolling, please let me go through." If the person stayed for 3 seconds, the robot said: "I wish to go through, could you please open the way?" After 3 seconds if the person still stood in the way, the robot turned toward the previous waypoint, and tried to move in the opposite direction. In case its way was blocked again, it started the above process from the beginning. When the person moved aside, it said "Thank you", and reassumed the patrolling task.

We collected videos and people's trajectories using the tracking system, and both of them were used to label all the instances where a person obstructed the robot.

3.3 Definition of Robot Abuse

In order to do the labelling we needed a definition of robot abuse, so we made a preliminary analysis of the collected data. When the robot asked to open the way, people typically followed the request; however, there were also a number of cases when they ignored or refused. Most people only did so once or twice, maybe to see the robot's reaction and test its capability. However some children continued this behavior even after the robot requested multiple times, intentionally obstructing the robot. In some cases their behavior gradually escalated. We observed three types of abuse, examples of which we illustrate next.

Type 1: Persistent obstruction. In many instances children persistently obstructed the robot. Figure 3 shows an example scene. At the beginning, the child would step aside after the robot's request, but then would quickly come back in front of the robot. After a while, she started ignoring the requests and just kept standing in front of the robot. Eventually, she also started to verbally express her intention of obstruction by saying "I won't" or "No-no" when requested to move. At times other children also joined her. The whole scene lasted 19 minutes, until the girl's mother came and made her leave.

Figure 3. Persistent obstruction.

Type 2: Offensive utterances. In one example, four children surrounded the robot and ignored its repeated requests. After the fifth request, one child approached the robot and said a series of bad words to the robot. He said "You idiot" 8 times, "I won't" 2 times, and "Go away" once. In addition, he agitated other children to be aggressive toward the robot saying "Let's surround it."

Type 3: Violence. Similar to the previous cases, at the beginning usually one child refused to let the robot go even after several requests, and soon other children gathered and after a while violent behavior occurred. One boy bent the robot's neck (Figure 4a), and another boy hit its head with a plastic bottle (Figure 4b). We observed other cases of violence outside of the data collection, too. For example, one boy first hit the robot's head with his hand saying "Go away", and then threw a soccer ball onto the robot's head (Figure 4c). In another case, 3 boys started hitting the robot with plastic bottles. This gradually escalated until they started hitting as strong as they could and throwing the bottles on the robot (Figure 4d). There was no hardware damage in any of these situations which could suggest that the children's violent actions were not meant for seriously breaking the robot.

Although there is diversity in the seriousness of abuse, common to

(a) Bending the neck   (b) Hitting with plastic bottle

(c) Hitting with ball   (d) Throwing a plastic bottle

Figure 4. Children's violence toward the robot.

all above cases is that children intentionally continued to obstruct the robot's task beyond curiosity. Our research goal was to prevent abuse which hinders the robot from performing its tasks, so all of above cases are certainly beyond the threshold to be judged as abuse. Although we introduced three cases, in this study we do not distinguish between them and treat all of them as abusive interaction. Informed by these observations, we proposed the following definition of abuse towards the robot:

> ***Robot abuse***: Persistent offensive action, either verbal or non-verbal, or physical violence that violates the robot's role or its human-like (or animal-like) nature.

We also noted that it was always children who abused the robot. Adults were rarely present and not at all involved in the abuse, so in most cases the robot had to deal directly with children. Moreover, the abuse occurred more on the square where fewer people are present, rather than in the passageway where people are continuously passing.

3.4 Data Coding

For each instance of interaction between people and the robot, a human coder examined the interaction from the start until the end and decided whether there was any abuse toward the robot.

Due to the human-likeness of the robot and its behavior, people have a tendency to anthropomorphize the robot. The coder who watched the videos of interaction judged whether a child's action was as a case of "robot abuse" or not, based on the definition given above. For difficult to decide situations the coders were told to judge as abuse situations the cases which they themselves would dislike, or be irritated or fed up with the child's behavior. For instance, the above type 1 example was judged as abuse because the robot was not able to function in its patrolling role due to children's persistent obstructive action. In the type 2 it was due to the anthropomorphizing of the robot and the coder's belief that a person would dislike such a situation.

For validating the results, a second coder performed the same task for randomly-selected 10% of the interaction instances extracted by the first coder. A good matching between the results of the coders was obtained (Cohen's kappa .714). For all cases of abusive interaction we also noted the number of children involved and whether their parents were present. In total 185 interactions were labelled, out of which 19 were judged as abuse cases.

From the coded dataset we obtained the information whether there was an abuse, how long the interaction lasted, the number of involved children, presence of parents, and location. A summary of the data is given in Table 1. In addition, we analyzed the statistics of the cases where abuse did and did not occur, shown in Table 2.

Table 1. Statistics of interaction (SD values in brackets).

	probability of abuse	interaction time [s]	pedestrian density [per./min]	other children [child/15s]	parents present [%]
Passage-way	0.085 (±0.0104)	45.2 (±10.70)	40.6 (±1.17)	0.78 (±0.074)	54.1 (±5.4)
Square	0.139 (±0.0110)	72.6 (±10.60)	12.6 (±0.28)	1.52 (±0.122)	50.0 (±5.0)

	interaction time [s]	number of other children	parents present [%]
Abuse	238.3 (±49.0)	4.94 (±0.89)	21.1 (±9.6)
No abuse	39.6 (±4.2)	2.12 (±0.12)	55.4 (±3.9)

4. MODEL OF CHILDREN'S BEHAVIOR

4.1 Overview

We developed a statistical model, which provides an estimate of the probability that a child who interacts with the robot will cause abuse. Figure 5 illustrates the model. It consists of two sub-models. For simulations (section 4.5) we needed to decide how long a child will stay with the robot, and therefore the modeling of the interaction time is done separately. The model of interaction time describes how long the child will interact with the robot. The model of occurrence of abuse computes the probability that the child will engage in abusive behavior. These sub-models are explained in the following subsections.

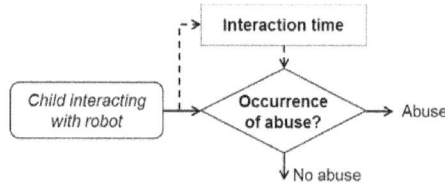

Figure 5. Estimation of occurrence of abuse toward robot.

4.2 Model of Interaction Time

We analyzed the statistics of interaction times, obtained from the data collection reported in section 3. We found out that the shape of the distribution of the interaction times is close to an exponential function. Therefore we modeled it using an exponential distribution:

$$p_{int}(t,c) = \lambda(c) \cdot e^{-\lambda(c)t}, \quad (1)$$

where $p_{int}(t,c)$ is the probability child c will stop interacting after time t, and λ is the parameter of the distribution. Figure 6 shows the histogram of interaction times and a fitted exponential function with parameter $\lambda = 0.032$.

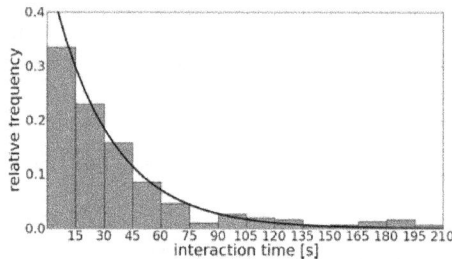

Figure 6. Histogram of interaction times.

Results in Table 1 show that interaction times differ across locations, suggesting that there is an influence of factors such as density on the interaction time; we modeled such influence into the λ. We started with all possibly relevant variables:

a) **Pedestrian density (density)** – the density of people inside the area where interaction happened. This was defined as the

expected number of people that come within 10 meters from the robot during 1 minute, and the values were obtained from 3 hours of pedestrian trajectories collected when there was no robot in the environment.

b) **Number of other children (child)** – the average number of other children who simultaneously interacted.

c) **Presence of parents (parent)** – 1 if the child's parents are in the vicinity (set to be within 3m of the child), 0 otherwise.

After fitting to the data we found that the number of children had little influence. Finally, we obtained the following model for λ:

$$\lambda(c) = a_{density} \cdot density + a_{parent} \cdot parent + b_1' \quad (2)$$

Fitting the data gave the coefficients: $a_{density} = 0.000219$, $a_{parent} = 0.0116$, $b_1' = 0.0725$. These values tell us that the interaction times are shorter in areas with higher person density, and that the influence of parents is large, namely that the child is more likely to stop the interaction when a parent is present.

4.3 Model of Occurrence of Abuse

All variables noted in Table 2 appear to be relevant in describing the possibility of abuse, with abuse more likely occurring in cases when children interact longer, with more children around, and without having their parents nearby.

We wished not only to have an estimate if abuse occurs or not, but also to have a value for the probability of occurrence. Therefore we applied a logistic regression model to the result of the above analysis. In addition to the three variables used in the subsection 4.2, we included the following variable:

d) **Interaction time (interact)** – representing the time from the start of the interaction, i.e. after the child approached the robot and stayed within a defined interaction distance (experimentally set to 0.89 m) from it.

We started with all variables and fit the data. We found that *parent* and *density* had very little influence, so we removed them from the model. An interpretation of this is that their primary influence on the occurrence of abuse is indirect through the interaction time (i.e. if with a parent or in a space with more people around, the child stays shorter around the robot). Finally, we obtained the following model:

$$p_{abuse}(t,c) = \frac{1}{1+\exp(-(a_{child} \cdot child + a_{interact} \cdot interact + b_2))} \quad (3)$$

where $a_{child} = 0.5935$, $a_{interact} = 0.003218$, $b_2 = -3.084$.

In summary, the modeling shows that probability of abuse increases with the number of children around the robot and the interaction time. For example, short 30 s interactions with 2 children around the robot (i.e. *child* = 1) give $p_{abuse} = 0.048$. With same interaction length and the total number of children equal to 4 the probability becomes 0.23, whereas with 2 children and a longer interaction time of 200 seconds, the probability increases to 0.136.

4.4 Model of the Effect of Abuse on the Robot

The performance of the robot can be affected by the abuse. For planning purposes (section 5), we wish to model the net effect of possible abuse on the robot's task. We considered the influence on the navigation – the effect of abuse on the robot's average speed.

This was modeled in the following way. At time t, the robot's speed $v_r(t)$ was defined to be proportional to the sum of the abuse probabilities for all children:

$$v_r(t) = a_{abuse} \cdot \sum_{s \in N} p_{abuse}(t, c) + v_0 \qquad (4)$$

We fit the model to the data. By minimizing least square mean error, we obtained the coefficient $a_{abuse} = -115$ and the intercept $v_0 = 297$ mm/s. In other words, the speed of the robot decreases with the increased probability of abuse.

4.5 Simulation

We developed a simulation in which the movement of pedestrians is reproduced, using the framework reported in [21]. It simulates the movement of pedestrians in the environment, where some of them will approach the robot, and a number of them will also abuse it.

The simulated pedestrians are generated based on the *model of pedestrian flow*, which describes the statistical nature of the movement of pedestrians, Figure 7. The model defines the flow of the simulation: the creation of new simulated pedestrians, generation of the trajectories each pedestrian will traverse, and finally the type of interaction they will have with the robot. This follows the framework in [21], with a few additions explained below. All parameters of the model are calibrated using data from the tracking system described in 3.1.

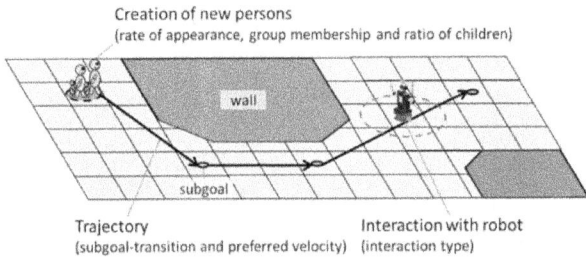

Figure 7. Basic elements of model of pedestrian flow.

Creation of new people: Apart from the statistics describing the time and place of creation of new simulated pedestrians and the distribution of groups, we also added the *ratio of children in groups* – for each group size, the distribution of the number of children is recorded and afterward used in simulation.

Trajectories: After being created, the simulated pedestrians move along the path defined by the "subgoal-transition model" (based on the technique reported in [24]) and according to the preferred speed statistic. All people in the same group have the same subgoals and preferred velocity.

Interaction with robot: Interaction around the robot is simulated with the following models.

- *Interaction type*: In a real environment some of pedestrians approach the robot, while others do not. We adopted the model reported in [25] to reproduce this behavior. If the *interaction type* is "stop to interact", the pedestrian changes his/her course to approach the robot when the robot is visible, stays for a while, and then continues moving toward his/her original subgoals. Ratio of the "stop to interact" behavior in the collected data was 35.48% for children and 4.21% for adults.

- *Parent-child relationship*: We extended the original interaction type model [25] to include the parent-child relationship, since it is important in this study. When a child approaches the robot

to interact, the parent will typically watch from the side until the child to end the interaction (Figure 8 left). We model this in the following way. The parent and child are assigned interaction types which can be different. When the child's interaction type is "stop to interact", after the simulated child enters the interaction distance (0.89 m) from the robot, the simulated parent will stop walking when the child becomes "out of sight" (the child is more than 90 degrees from the parent's direction of movement), and wait for the child to finish the interaction.

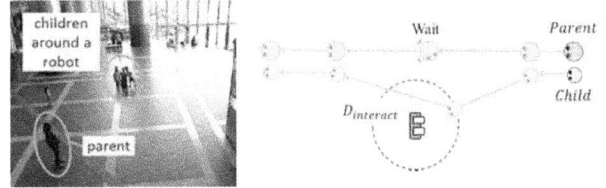

Figure 8. Simulation of parent's behavior when child stops to interact.

Overall, in the simulation, each pedestrian's position is periodically updated with above models. When simulated children interact with the robot, the models in section 4 are used to determine the probability they will abuse the robot, and the net effect on the simulated robot's speed.

4.6 Evaluation of the Simulation

To quantitatively test the validity of the model, we used the simulation to reproduce the state of the environment during the data collection. We ran 20 2-hour simulations for both the passageway and square area. The model of pedestrian flow was generated for each trajectory data obtained from data collection. The simulated robot moved between the same fixed locations as it did in the data collection.

Table 3 shows the result of the simulation. The statistics are obtained as average from all simulation runs. When compared with the statistics from real data from Table 1 we see that for all values the difference is within one standard deviation, showing

Table 3. Simulation results.

	probability of abuse	interaction time [s]	flow density [per./min]	other children [child/15s]	parents present [%]
Passage-way	0.094	44.6.	41.6	0.78	55.6
Square	0.134	69.6	12.6	1.43	51.5

that the simulation adequately reproduces the real world behavior.

5. BEHAVIOR PLANNING SYSTEM

5.1 Architecture

We developed a prototype system, in which the developed simulation of children's abuse behavior is used for robot behavior planning. The robot's task was to navigate around the environment and travel as long as possible within limited amount of time, i.e. be as efficient as possible. It is a simple task, but can be easily extended to various future tasks, such as patrolling, searching (e.g. to find a child who got lost), guiding users to destinations, and carrying. All of these services require efficient navigations.

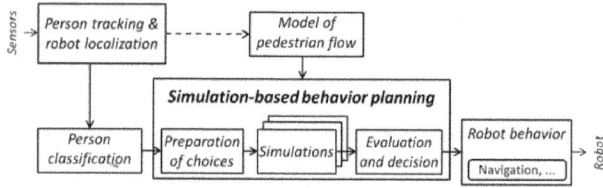

Figure 9. Architecture of the behavior planning.

Figure 9 illustrates the architecture of the developed system. The central component is the *simulation-based behavior planning* module, in which pedestrian simulations (section 4.5) were used to predict the near future behavior of pedestrians.

5.2 Person Classification

The people's trajectories were observed using the tracking system described in section 3.1. Based on these data the following attributes were extracted for the use in simulation:

- *Group membership*: Following the algorithm in [26], people who stay within 3 m for 60 % of time together were estimated as members of the same group.

- *Children/adult*: This was estimated from the observed person's height. We used a simple threshold (1.38 m) for distinction. When an adult and a child belonged to the same group, the adult was marked as the parent of the child.

- *Interaction type*: This attribute was initially probabilistically assigned according to the observed distribution, however once the person passed by the robot, it was updated based on his/her real behavior. If the person stopped close to the robot, the type was estimated as "stop to interact".

5.3 Simulation-based Behavior Planning

First a number of possible robot's behavior choices were prepared, and then multiple simulations were run. Based on the outcome of simulation, the most appropriate robot's behavior was selected.

Preparation of choices: The system prepared a series of possible destinations $d_1, d_2, \cdots, d_{|D|}$ where the robot can move to next. Three types of choices were prepared as follows: (1) the current destination; (2) 10 randomly chosen locations; (3) location nearby parents of the children who are currently around the robot. These choices were used because, according to the analysis in section 4, both destinations with higher person densities (part of type 2) and close to parents (type 3) can be effective for escaping from abuse.

Simulation: For each choice of destination d_i the robot ran multiple pedestrian simulations to predict the future development of the situation. The simulations were initialized on the current situation (locations and attributes of currently observed pedestrians). Finally, the average speeds of the robot during the simulations ($v_1^{d_i}, v_2^{d_i}, \cdots, v_{|Q|}^{d_i}$) were saved. The duration of each simulation was empirically set to 60 seconds, and the number of simulations for each destination choice to $|Q| = 50$.

Evaluation and decision: For each destination d_i the robot's efficiency (the expected travel speed V^{d_i}) was computed as:

$$V^{d_i} = 1/|Q| \cdot \sum_{q=1}^{|Q|} v_q^{d_i} \qquad (5)$$

Finally, the destination that yields the highest V^{d_i} was chosen as the target destination. This planning was done every second. To prevent too frequent switching between the destinations, which causes loss of time by continuously rotating towards different destinations, the current goal's efficiency value was multiplied by a weight factor, empirically set to 1.25.

5.4 Robot Behavior

The *robot behavior* module received the destination from the *simulation-based behavior planning* module, and navigated the robot toward the given destination. Unless its frontal direction is blocked, the robot moved straight toward the destination, and it stopped its locomotion if a person stops in front of the robot.

When the robot stopped, its behavior followed the one explained in the section 3.2, except that in this case the behavior was automated. That is, the detection was based on the location of person provided by the person tracking: when there was a person in front of it within 50 cm from the center and within 90 degrees from the forward direction, the robot stopped and asked the person to move aside. The same wording and sequence of actions as in the data collection (section 3.2) was used.

6. FIELD EVALUATION

6.1 Hypothesis and Predictions

If the simulation-based planning really enables the robot to anticipate the future situation, it should be able to lower the chance of occurrence of abuse. Since abuse results in the robot often having to wait and rotate in space which can last for a long duration of time, the navigation should also be more efficient. We made the following predictions:

Prediction 1: There will be fewer occurrences of abuse and when the robot uses the proposed simulation-based planning method than when it simply plans to maximize its efficiency without taking abuse into account.

Prediction 2: The robot navigation will also be more efficient, i.e., the resulting average speed of the robot will be higher.

6.2 Conditions

We compared the following two conditions:

Simulation-based planning: The robot choses the destination as described in section 5.

Maximum efficiency planning: The alternative strategy ignores the influence of abuse and only maximizes the travel efficiency. The robot uses a simple planning algorithm, where after reaching a goal it chooses the next destination as the one which will result in maximum travel velocity, assuming that there are no people interacting with the robot.

6.3 Procedure

We conducted the evaluation in the shopping mall environment described in section 3.1. To have a fair evaluation of both conditions, we prepared a number of paired time-slots to which the conditions were randomly assigned. This is done to make the environmental conditions approximately equivalent across conditions. We conducted the evaluation experiment on a weekend, for in total 40 minutes for each condition. In both conditions the robot moved fully autonomously.

6.4 Measurements

The evaluation criteria were defined as follows:

Occurrence of abuse: the number of occurrences of abuse (judged based on the criteria reported in section 3.4)

Travel efficiency: the average travel velocity of the robot during the experiments.

6.5 Evaluation Results

6.5.1 Overall trend

In the condition of maximum efficiency planning, the robot had a tendency to choose long straight paths, as they result in higher average speeds. Because of that it often passed through areas with fewer people where, similar to what we described in the section 3, several cases of abuse happened. In one example situation, while the robot was traversing the square a child stood in front of it with arms open wide (Figure 10a left). The child's actions escalated and just when the child's mother was coming back they turned into physical abuse (Figure 10a right). The mother then scolded the child and moved it away from the robot.

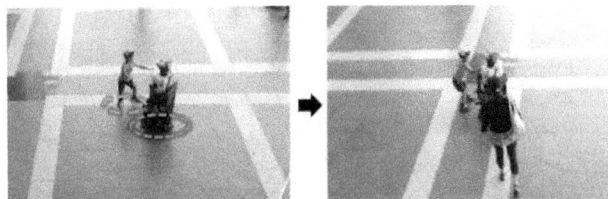

(a) Maximum efficiency planning condition: occurrence of abuse.

(b) Simulation-based planning condition: escaping from abuse.

Figure 10. Example situations during evaluation.

In the simulation-based planning condition, when there were no children in the environment the robot crossed the square from side to side, similar to the maximum efficiency planning case. When a child appeared and tried to approach the robot, the robot would move either toward an area with high person flow or toward the parent of the child. We observed that in that case the parent would take the child away, or in the case of the high flow area, the time of interaction tended to be shorter. For example, Figure 10b shows a situation where after detecting an approaching child, the robot changed its course toward a parent standing on the side of the square, after which the parent left with the child.

6.5.2 Qualitative evaluation

During the evaluation experiment 4064 people were detected in the tracking area (2147 in the maximum efficiency planning and 1917 in the simulation-based planning condition). Out of them, 57 children in total approached the robot (31 and 26, for the maximum efficiency and simulation-based planning, respectively). Two coders labeled the interaction cases for abuse of robot. Good matching between coders was obtained (Cohen's kappa .818).

The result of the evaluation is shown in Table 4. A Chi-squared test on the result which showed there is a statistically significant difference between the ratios of abuse cases in the two conditions ($\chi^2 = 4.11$, $df = 1$, $p < .05$). This shows that *Prediction 1* is supported and that the simulation-based planning is effective in restricting and avoiding the occurrence of abuse toward the robot.

We also evaluated the robot's travel velocity. The average velocity during the experiments in the maximum efficiency planning condition was 260.7±4.96 mm/s, and in the simulation-

Table 4. Occurrence of abuse.

	Abuse	No abuse
Maximum efficiency planning	7	24
Simulation-based planning	1	25

based planning condition 321.3±5.25 mm/s. There is a statistically significant difference between the results ($t = 8.402$, $df = 4353.4$, $p < .001$), which shows that using simulation-based planning results in higher speeds. We conclude that *Prediction 2* is supported.

7. DISCUSSION

7.1 Can the Robot "Overcome" the Abuse?

In this work the robot's strategy to prevent abuse was to "escape", i.e. move to a location where it is less likely abuse will occur. One could ask why the robot cannot overcome the abuse. In our preliminary trials we have tried several approaches, but we found that it is very difficult for the robot to persuade children not to abuse it. For example, we changed the robot's wordings in many ways, using strong words, emotional or polite expressions, but none of them were successful. One partially successful strategy was the robot 'physically' pushing children. When its way was blocked, it would just try to keep going and behave as if it will collide into children and force its way through (under careful monitoring from a human operator). We observed that children at first accepted the robot's requests and obeyed them; but, very soon they learned that they are stronger than the robot so they can win if they push, and also that they can stop it by pushing the bumper switch (attached on the robot for safety). After realizing that, they just continued with the abusive behavior. Obviously having a stronger robot would present a problem for safety and social acceptance so dealing with such abusive situations remains difficult.

7.2 Robot Ethics

An important ethical question implicit in this work is: what type of behavior toward the robot is appropriate? The definition of robot abuse that we use is based on an anthropomorphized view of the robot, and we showed that if we use such a definition, abuse of robots is certainly a real problem in public spaces. Whether this definition is justified, and if not how should we treat robots – these ethical questions remain open.

7.3 Generalizability and Limitations

We only modeled the situation where the robot is just navigating around. For the future use of social robots, it will also be necessary to consider situations where the robot engages in other tasks, such as conversation. To do so, some model parameters would need to be adjusted. Depending on factors such as the robot's speed, its reactions, and type of tasks, the expected time people spend with the robot would differ significantly. Moreover, in our system we inferred the occurrence of abuse from observed people's positions and their interaction time; in other cases it might be necessary to directly detect abusive behavior.

In this study, we let the robot escape from the occurrence of abuse only by moving to a different position. Of course, there could be other solutions, like calling a guard if abuse happens.

8. CONCLUSION

We found that our robot is affected by children's abusive behavior. We analyzed how the abuse occurs, and modelled the statistical nature of the occurrences. Only children caused abuse. If their parents were not close and if there were fewer pedestrians around, children tended to stay longer around the robot. When they stayed longer, and especially if more children were present, they had a greater tendency to cause abuse to the robot. This emergent nature of abuse was simulated in a pedestrian simulator. We found that the simulation can reproduce reasonably well the situations that happen in the actual environment. Based on the simulation, we developed a planning technique for avoiding the occurrence of abuse. Our field trial demonstrated the efficacy of this approach.

9. ACKNOWLEDGMENTS
This work was supported by JST, CREST. We thank the staff of the ATC shopping mall for their support.

10. REFERENCES

[1] Thrun, S., Bennewitz, M., Burgard, W., Cremers, A.B., Dellaert, F., Fox, D., Hahnel, D., Rosenberg, C., Roy, N., Schulte, J., Schulz, D., "MINERVA: A Second-Generation Museum Tour-Guide Robot", *Proc. IEEE Int. Conf. on Robotics and Automation (ICRA)*, pp.1999-2005, 1999

[2] Siegwart, R., Arras, K.O., Bouabdallah, S., Burnier, D., Froidevaux, G., Greppin, X., Jensen, B., Lorotte, A., Mayor, L., Meisser, M., Philippsen, R., Piguet, R., Ramel, G., Terrien, G., Tomatis, N., "Robox at Expo.02: A Large Scale Installation of Personal Robots", *Robotics and Autonomous Systems*, vol. 42, pp.203-222, 2003

[3] Gross, H.-M., Boehme, H.-J., Schroeter, C., Mueller, S., Koenig, A., Martin, Ch., Merten, M., Bley, A., "ShopBot: progress in developing an interactive mobile shopping assistant for everyday use", *Proc. IEEE Int. Conf. on Systems, Man, and Cybernetics (SMC)*, pp.3471-3478, 2008

[4] Svenstrup, M., Bak, T., Maler, O., Andersen, H.J., Jensen, O.B., "Pilot Study of Person Robot Interaction in a Public Transit Space", *Research and Education in Robotics - EUROBOT 2008*, vol.33, pp.96-106, 2009

[5] Weiss, A., Bernhaupt, R., Tscheligi, M., Wollherr, D., Kühnlenz, K., Buss, M., "A Methodological Variation for Acceptance Evaluation of Human-Robot Interaction in Public Places", *Proc. IEEE Int. Symp. on Robot and Human Interactive Communication (RO-MAN)*, pp.713-718, 2008

[6] Rosenthal-von der Pütten, A.M., Krämer, N.C. Hoffmann, L., Sobieraj, S., Eimler, S.C., "An Experimental Study on Emotional Reactions Towards a Robot", *Int. J. of Social Robotics*, vol.5, pp.17-34, 2013

[7] Gullone, E. and Robertson, N., "The relationship between bullying and animal abuse behaviors in adolescents: The importance of witnessing animal abuse", *J. of Applied Developmental Psychology*, vol.29, pp.371-379, 2008

[8] Miller, C. "Childhood animal cruelty and interpersonal violence", *Clinical Psych. Review*, vol.21, pp.735-749, 2001

[9] Bartneck, C., Rosalia, C., Menges, R. and Deckers, I., "Robot abuse–a limitation of the media equation", *Proc. Interact 2005 Workshop on Agent Abuse*, 2005

[10] Bartneck, C. and Hu, J., "Exploring the Abuse of Robots", *Interaction Studies - Social Behaviour and Communication in Biological and Artificial Systems*, vol.9, pp.415-433, 2008

[11] Salvini, P., Ciaravella, G., Yu, W., Ferri, G., Manzi, A., Mazzolai, B., Laschi, C., Oh, S.-R., Dario, P., "How safe are service robots in urban environments? Bullying a Robot", *Proc. IEEE Int. Symp. on Robot and Human Interactive Communication (RO-MAN)*, pp.1-7, 2010

[12] Olweus, D., *Bullying at school: What we know and what we can do*, Oxford: Blackwell Publishers, 1993

[13] Ascione, F. R. and Shapiro, K., "People and Animals, Kindness and Cruelty: Research Directions and Policy Implications", *J. of Social Issues*, vol.65, pp.569-587, 2009

[14] Arluke, A., "Animal Abuse as Dirty Play", *Symbolic Interaction*, vol.25, pp.405-430, 2002Hoffman, G. and Breazeal, C., "Effects of anticipatory perceptual simulation on practiced human-robot tasks", *Autonomous Robots*, vol.28, pp.403-423, 2010

[15] Morales Saiki, L.Y., Satake, S., Huq, R., Glas, D., Kanda, T., Hagita, N., "How Do People Walk Side-By-Side? -Using A Computational Model Of Human Behavior For A Social Robot", *Proc. ACM/IEEE Int. Conf. on Human Robot Interaction (HRI)*, pp.301-308, 2012

[16] Bennewitz, M., Burgard, W., Cielniak, G. and Thrun, S., "Learning Motion Patterns of People for Compliant Robot Motion", *Int. J. of Robotics Research*, vol.24, pp.31-48, 2005

[17] Henry, P., Vollmer, C., Ferris, B. and Fox, D., "Learning to Navigate Through Crowded Environments", *Proc. IEEE Int. Conf. on Robotics and Automation (ICRA)*, pp.981-986, 2010

[18] Garrell, A. and Sanfeliu, A., "Model validation: robot behavior in people guidance mission using DTM model and estimation of human motion behavior", *Proc. IEEE/RSJ Int. Conf. on Intelligent Robots and Systems (IROS)*, pp.5836-5841, 2010

[19] Ferrer, G., Garrell, A. and Sanfeliu, A., "Robot Companion: A Social-Force based approach with Human Awareness-Navigation in Crowded Environments", *Proc. IEEE/RSJ Int. Conf. on Intelligent Robots and Systems (IROS)*, pp.1688-1694, 2013

[20] Kidokoro, H., Kanda, T., Brščić, D. and Shiomi, M., "Will I bother here? -A robot anticipating its influence on pedestrian walking comfort". *Proc. ACM/IEEE Int. Conf. on Human-Robot Interaction (HRI)*, pp.259-266, 2013

[21] Brščić, D., Kanda, T., Ikeda, T. and Miyashita, T., "Person tracking in large public spaces using 3D range sensors", *IEEE Trans. on Human-Machine Systems*, 43, 6, pp.522-534, 2013

[22] Thrun, S., Burgard, W. and Fox, D., *Probabilistic Robotics*, The MIT Press, 2005

[23] Ikeda, T., Chigodo, Y., Rea, D., Zanlungo, F., Shiomi, M., Kanda, T., "Modeling and Prediction of Pedestrian Behavior based on the Sub-goal Concept", *Robotics: Science and Systems*, 2012

[24] Shiomi, M., Zanlungo, F., Hayashi, K. and Kanda, T., "A Framework with a Pedestrian Simulator for Deploying Robots into a Real Environment", *Proc. Simulation, Modeling, and Programming for Autonomous Robots (SIMPAR)*, 2012

[25] Kanda, T, Shiomi, M., Perrin, L., Nomura, T., Ishiguro, H., Hagita, N., "Analysis of people trajectories with ubiquitous sensors in a science museum", *Proc. IEEE Int. Conf. on Robotics and Automation (ICRA)*, pp.4846-4853, 2007

The Robot Who Tried Too Hard: Social Behaviour of a Robot Tutor Can Negatively Affect Child Learning

James Kennedy, Paul Baxter, Tony Belpaeme
Centre for Robotics and Neural Systems
Cognition Institute
Plymouth University, U.K.
{james.kennedy, paul.baxter, tony.belpaeme}@plymouth.ac.uk

ABSTRACT

Social robots are finding increasing application in the domain of education, particularly for children, to support and augment learning opportunities. With an implicit assumption that social and adaptive behaviour is desirable, it is therefore of interest to determine precisely how these aspects of behaviour may be exploited in robots to support children in their learning. In this paper, we explore this issue by evaluating the effect of a social robot tutoring strategy with children learning about prime numbers. It is shown that the tutoring strategy itself leads to improvement, but that the presence of a robot employing this strategy amplifies this effect, resulting in significant learning. However, it was also found that children interacting with a robot using social and adaptive behaviours in addition to the teaching strategy did not learn a significant amount. These results indicate that while the presence of a physical robot leads to improved learning, caution is required when applying social behaviour to a robot in a tutoring context.

Categories and Subject Descriptors

H.1.2 [**Models and Principles**]: User/Machine Systems

Keywords

Robot Tutor; Social HRI; Child-Robot Interaction; Social Behaviour

1. INTRODUCTION

One-to-one tutoring has been shown to result in significantly higher knowledge gains than group education [5, 23]. Given the common school classroom arrangement, where one teacher is responsible for many children, it is not possible for teachers to offer as much one-to-one tutoring as would be desired. This presents an opportunity for social robotics. A robot tutor could be placed in a classroom to provide one-to-one support for children. However, it is currently unclear how a robot should behave in order to elicit the

greatest learning gains from the children. Indeed, there is still a debate on how humans cause learning in tutoring [24].

We seek to explore how the social behaviour of robots can influence learning. This paper considers an experiment designed to explore the contribution of a robot and its social behaviour to dyadic educational interactions with primary school children. Educational interactions are conducted with and without a robot, where the robot's behaviour may be 'social', or 'asocial'. Particular attention is paid to the learning on the part of the children and their social responses to the robot tutor.

The rest of the paper is organised as follows. Background and motivations for this work will be discussed (Section 2) before the methodology for the study presented here is described (Section 3). The methodology will include details of the participants, conditions and robot behaviour. After this, results from both the task and video analysis will be presented and analysed (Section 4). The paper will be concluded with a discussion of the impact of robot social behaviour on child learning and what this may mean for future interactions of this nature (Sections 5 and 6).

2. RELATED WORK

Educational robots have long been of interest within the field of HRI. Early exploratory efforts demonstrated the potential for robots in education. For example, a robot used to teach English in a school classroom resulted in an improvement in child learning over a 2 week period [7]. Robots have also been found to elicit advantages over web- and paper-based instruction in the home [6]. Large projects have now turned their attention towards child learning, for example the ALIZ-E project [3] in Europe, and an NSF funded Socially Assistive Robotics project in the USA [20].

These projects (and many others) have started to explore how the tutor behaviour can be manipulated in order to improve learning gains. Leyzberg *et al.* showed that the physical presence of a robot makes a difference to the knowledge gain of adults in an educational puzzle game [14], and that personalised tutoring strategies can lead to significant improvement in knowledge gain in the same puzzle task [13].

This paper seeks to further develop these advances by considering not just personalisation in tutor behaviour, but also how the social behaviour exhibited by the robot affects learning. Aspects of social behaviour, such as gestures, have been used by a robot to attract student attention when they lose focus, greatly improving their recall of information after the task [22]. Additionally, neutral and socially supportive robots have been compared, revealing that children's learning improved when the robot was socially supportive [18].

There are many studies which examine the impact that aspects of social behaviour can have on learning. For example, changing the language used to be personalised (e.g. changing 'the' to 'your') can lead to improved knowledge transfer [4, 15]. Human social behaviours are typically thought to increase a learners' interest, which is posited as the reason for greater learning gains in more social interactions [1].

Therefore it would appear to be desirable to make a robot tutor which is as close as possible to levels of human sociality in order to maximise the potential learning gains in interactions. This study seeks to explore how the social behaviour of a robot impacts upon the behaviour and the learning of children in dyadic interactions. By carefully controlling the manipulation of the social behaviour exhibited by the robot, this paper contributes to the field by comparing child learning when varying robot sociality. The novel learning content presented here also allows the confirmation of findings related to the presence of the robot on child learning in a different context.

3. METHODOLOGY

The methodology of the experiment was designed based on previous work with child learning in sorting tasks, as in [9], and with sub-tasks leading to a combination of knowledge in a larger primary learning objective, as in [13]. The following section will detail the participants involved, the interaction scenario, the task structure, the robot behaviour and the conditions used in the experiment.

3.1 Participants

A total of 53 children had permission to take part in the study. Due to technical issues, 8 of the children's data had to be excluded, leaving 45 children included in the study (23F, 22M). All participants were aged 7 or 8 and from the same year group at a primary school in the U.K. Participants were randomly distributed between conditions, whilst maintaining a balance of gender and mathematics ability (based on their teacher's assessment) between the groups. For the split between conditions, please see Section 3.3. Those in the robot conditions were requested for permission to film, which was granted in all but 2 of the cases. One video had to be excluded from analysis as it was not possible to see the child's eyes. Therefore, video analysis was conducted on 20 interactions.

3.2 Interaction Scenario

Interactions took place either in an unused classroom, or a relatively quiet public space in a primary school in the United Kingdom. The child was brought into the experiment area and would be sat facing a robot, an Aldebaran Nao, with a 27 inch touchscreen horizontally between them (Figure 1). A Microsoft Kinect was placed above and behind the robot to track the child's face. Two video cameras were also positioned around the setup: one to record the child's face and actions and another to record the robot's actions. The use of a touchscreen mediator [2] allows a consistent, constrained environment, so the robot's social behaviour can be manipulated without impacting on the nature of the task or the content of the learning [8].

The learning content for the interaction was devised with the help of primary school teachers from a different school to

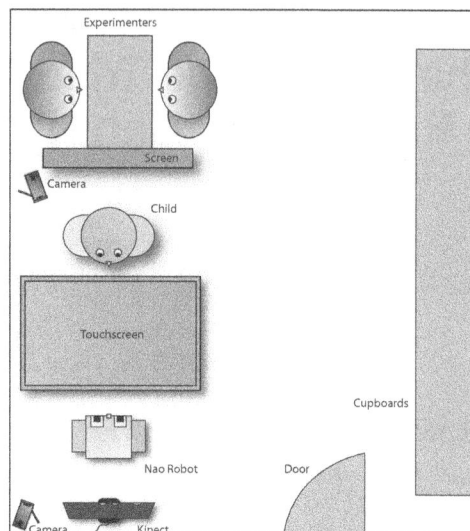

Figure 1: Schematic overview of the interactions under investigation in this paper. Two interactants (the child and the robot) face one another over the touchscreen. Two video cameras record the interactants during the studies. A Microsoft Kinect tracks the child's face. Two experimenters are in the room, but out of view of the child. Figure not to scale.

the one where the study took place. The aim was to select a topic with which children had no prior exposure, but could be learnt in a relatively short time. Prime numbers were determined to be an ideal solution. Calculation of whether a number is prime can be performed by using division (for more detail see Section 3.2.1). Children of the age used in the study are familiar with division, but have not been taught what a prime number is at this stage of their education.

The touchscreen presents different numbers for sorting. The child can touch the numbers to drag and drop them into categories. An example library here would display text labels at opposite sides of the screen, such as 'prime' and 'not prime', with some numbers in between (Figure 2). The child can touch these numbers and drag them to the label for categorisation. The touchscreen sends all state information to the robot so that the robot knows the child's moves, and the robot can make moves itself by synchronising movement with on-screen animation (the robot does not physically touch the screen) [2].

3.2.1 Task Structure

The structure for the task was created partly through necessity for measuring learning and partly through a logical method of calculating primes known as the Sieve of Eratosthenes [17]. The Sieve of Eratosthenes works through a group of numbers, eliminating non-prime numbers in a methodical manner to leave only the prime numbers. For the number range used in this study all composites can be eliminated by dividing by 2, 3, 5 and then 7.

The task was structured so that appropriate measures could be taken for both prime number learning and division learning. Additionally, the task structure allows the examination of the children's division skills prior to the prime

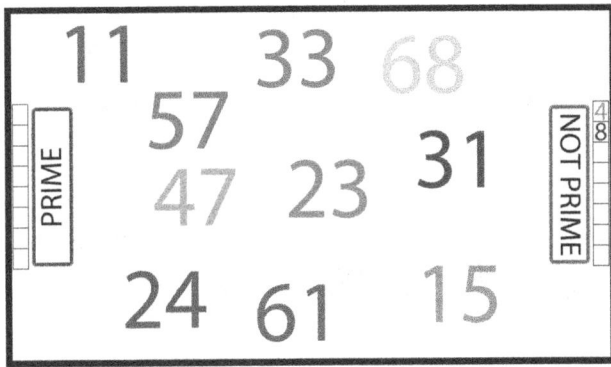

Figure 2: Example of the sorting task used. This is a screenshot of one of the tests used in the experiment. Children can touch a number, drag it over the 'prime' or 'not prime' label and release to make a categorisation. The number will then shrink and move into the boxes beside the category label.

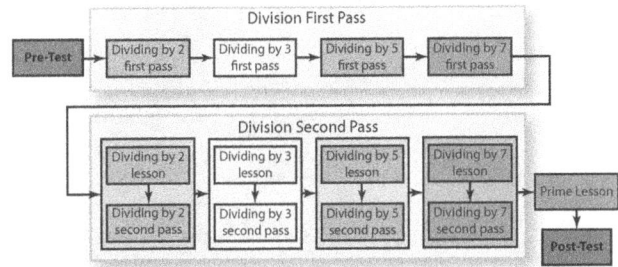

Figure 3: Structure of the task used in the interactions, showing robot lesson positions.

number post-test, which is important as these division skills are necessary for the calculation of primes (Figure 3).

Pre- and post-tests each consisted of 12 numbers being presented on screen; 6 were prime and 6 were non-prime (Figure 2 shows an example test). Both tests avoided numbers from the prime lesson and had balanced distributions of numbers across the range being used (10-70).

Each practice library in the division 'pass one' consisted of 8 examples - 4 of which could be divided with no integer remainder by the number in question, and 4 which could not. This first pass was used to obtain a measurement for each child in how well they could divide by each of the divisors required for the main goal of calculating prime numbers. The number of examples in division 'pass two' totalled 24, but the distribution between each of the 4 divisors (2, 3, 5 and 7) was dependent upon the condition and performance in pass one (see Section 3.4).

3.2.2 Lesson Content

In the second division pass, a lesson was provided for each of the divisors: 2, 3, 5 and 7. This involved verbal instructions and categorisations on-screen. Each lesson consisted of a short verbal overview of the technique, followed by categorisation of 2 examples with verbal narration explaining the application of the technique to the examples. One example could be divided with no remainder, and the other could not. The lessons were not to teach the concept of the division, but often to provide a 'trick' whereby the division could be accomplished more easily. The lessons were explanations of the following concepts:

- Divisible by 2 - the number is even (ends in 0, 2, 4, 6 or 8)

- Divisible by 3 - sum the digits of the number and test if that divides by 3

- Divisible by 5 - the number ends in 0 or 5

- Divisible by 7 - no trick available; a reminder that a number in the 7 times table will be divisible by 7

The lesson about primes which took place after the second division pass used the information from the earlier division

lessons to draw together the practice the child had with dividing by 2, 3, 5 and 7 into calculating whether numbers were prime. The concept of primes was explained (a number divisible, with no remainder, by only 1 and itself) before two worked examples were completed on-screen - one prime and one not prime. The Sieve of Eratosthenes was adapted to eliminate numbers one-by-one for categorisation. Children were instructed to consider each number to be categorised in turn, attempting to divide it by 2, 3, 5 and 7. If the number divided by any of these then it was not prime, otherwise it was prime.

3.3 Hypotheses and Conditions

Given the task described above, we seek to assess whether a social robot leads to increased learning. Our specific hypotheses to address this are as follows:

H1. The division lessons provided to the children in division pass two will result in significant improvement from division pass one. This serves as a check that the lessons provided do actually facilitate learning.

H2. The presence of a robot will result in greater learning gains than when a robot is not present given equal information content, as suggested by other studies ([6, 14]).

H3. A more social robot will result in greater learning gains than a less social robot. This hypothesis is based on observations of the positive effects of social behaviour in other HRI studies such as [13] and [18], and psychology studies such as [1] and [15].

In order to address the hypotheses, four conditions were devised:

1. **Division only** [n=11] - division pass one, followed by division pass two without any lessons. Conducted on the touchscreen only, with no robot present.

2. **Screen only** [n=11] - the full interaction as described in Section 3.2.1, but with no robot present. All feedback and lesson content is delivered by the speakers in the screen.

3. **Asocial non-personalised robot** [n=11] - identical script to the 'screen only' condition, but with the robot delivering the content. All verbal content and feedback is given by the robot; the screen now only displays the numbers for the task. Robot behaviour is designed to be non-social (see Section 3.4 for full details).

Figure 4: Snapshots taken from the video recordings of interactions. Both the social (left, looking at the child) and asocial robot (right, actively avoiding the gaze of the child) conditions are pictured to show the difference in gaze behaviour between them.

4. **Social personalised robot** [n=12] - a social version of the full interaction. All lesson content is kept the same as the asocial robot condition, but the non-lesson speech is adjusted to be more social. Robot non-verbal behaviour is also designed to be social.

3.4 Robot Behaviour

Human tutors are known to be effective, using social behaviour and adapting to the learning needs of the child. As such, the social robot behaviour was based on a human tutor's behaviour when taking five children through the task on the touchscreen. Section 3.4 outlines four observed behavioural dimensions that were implemented on the robot. Whilst maintaining balance between the conditions, the inverse for each dimension is used for the asocial robot behaviour in order to evaluate Hypothesis 3.

The phrases and actions used by the human were observed and implemented in the social robot model. It is posited that behaviour is perceived by the child as an integration of cues [26], meaning that each dimension must be considered in context of the others. Consequently, personalisation and social behaviour are considered inseparable in assessing Hypothesis 3 for this study, following the human model.

Both robot conditions adopted the following basic behaviour during the image categorisation portions of the task:

Move Suggestions - During each stage of the interaction, if the child was hesitant in making moves then the robot would move a number to the centre of the screen and suggest that the child work on that number next. The decision about when to move was probabilistic and cued by the child's behaviour. If the child did not make a categorisation for 6 seconds, then there was a 25% chance that the robot would move, with the decision repeated every 2 seconds until a move was made - the 6 second timer would then start again.

Categorisation Feedback - The robot would provide verbal feedback on the child's categorisations. Not every categorisation received feedback; there was a 25% chance of feedback on each categorisation - following the human tutor model.

Robot Condition Differences.

Verbal Content - The script for the social robot speech was taken from the human tutor; this was then modified for the asocial robot by removing any personalisation, i.e. "Johnny, we'll do dividing by 2 next" becomes "You'll do dividing by 2 next". We ensured that the total amount of speech was kept as close as possible between the conditions, and the lesson content was the same.

When providing speech alongside a suggestion, or when providing feedback, a number of phrases were available and selected at random. The asocial robot had only 2 options for each event (compared to the social robot's 8), thereby making it very repetitive.

Gestures - The social robot script used for the introduction and some of the lessons included iconic gestures. In the asocial condition, these were placed at inappropriate times, for example, the robot would wave its arm to greet the child half way through a sentence, rather than when it says hello at the start. The same gestures were used in both conditions, the only difference was their position in the script.

Personalisation - The social robot would use the child's name in greeting, just before the post-test and in the goodbye script. The asocial robot would not use the child's name at all. Personalisation of learning content was also provided by the social robot.

The performance of the child in the first division pass would dictate how many examples of each division library they would do in the second pass. A total of 24 numbers were always used in the second division pass. For the asocial condition, these were split equally between divisors, so 6 numbers for each of dividing by 2, 3, 5 and 7. In the social condition a minimum of 3 numbers were used per divisor, but the remaining 12 numbers were distributed between the divisors based on how many of each divisor the child got wrong in the first pass. Therefore, they had more practice on numbers that they were weaker at in the second pass.

In the second division pass, for each divisor library, there was also a reminder of the lesson available. In the asocial condition, this reminder would be delivered by the robot half way through the categorisations for that library (i.e. after the 3rd of the 6 categorisations to be made). In the social condition, the reminder was given after the first incorrectly categorised image.

Gaze - The social robot gaze was constrained so that it would generally be looking towards the touchscreen or in the direction of the child. Additionally, a Microsoft Kinect was used for tracking the child's head pose. If the child's head pose was directed towards the robot, then the robot would respond by looking back at the child. In the asocial condition, the robot was intentionally programmed to look up and to the side so that the gaze would avoid the child (Figure 4).

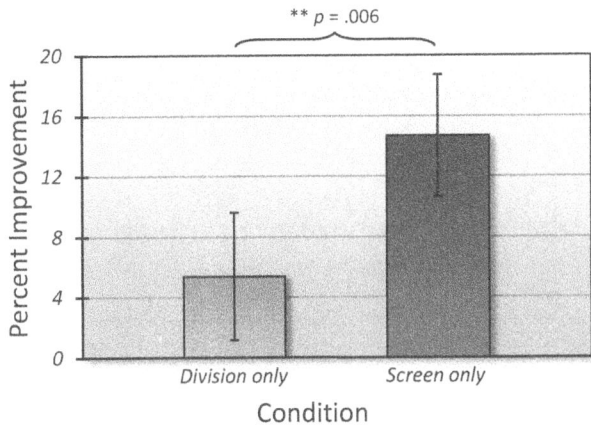

Figure 5: Improvement between division pass one and division pass two in percent for the division only and screen only conditions. Error bars show 95% Confidence Interval, ** indicates significance at the 0.01 level.

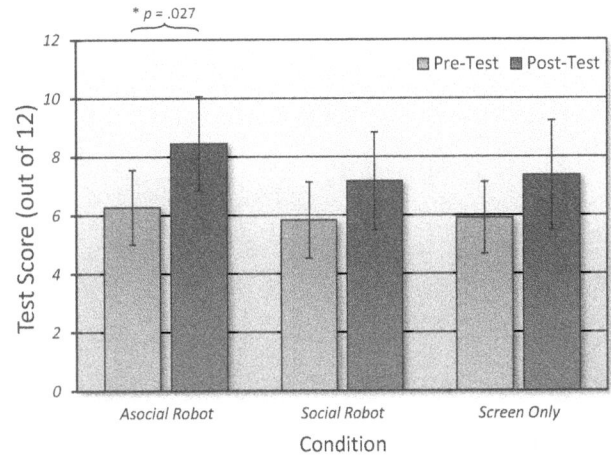

Figure 6: Pre-test and post-test scores for the asocial robot, social robot and screen only conditions. Error bars show 95% Confidence Interval, * indicates significance at the 0.05 level.

3.5 Procedure

One of the experimenters shown in Figure 1 controlled the start and end of the autonomous behaviour. This individual had three responsibilities: 1. to type in the name of the child for the social robot condition before the child arrived in the room, 2. to click a button once the child was sat down in front of the robot to denote the start of the interaction, and 3. to click an 'emergency' button if anything went wrong, where the robot would gracefully end the interaction. All other robot behaviour was fully autonomous.

4. RESULTS

This section will present the results from each of the conditions in relation to the hypotheses. Learning will be considered either between the pre-and post-test improvements, or for division, between the total percent correct in division pass one and division pass two. The behavioural analysis is derived from video coding of the child's gaze as previous work has highlighted gaze as the primary behaviour of interest in interactions of this nature [10]. The video coding was completed by one coder for all videos. Coding was verified by second-coding 20% of the videos, as in [16], with an average Cohen's Kappa of 0.80 signifying substantial agreement [12].

The conditions were split to have an equal balance of ability based on an estimate by the children's teacher (higher, middle and lower tiers). Comparing the approximate ability level of the children that was provided by their teacher against their performance in the first division pass (at which point they've had no lesson input), Pearson's r correlation is 0.638. This is a good correlation, which confirms that the teacher's estimate is reflected in the results of this study and therefore that the conditions are balanced for ability.

The mean average length of the interactions were: 974s (95% CI [750s,1199s]) in the asocial robot condition, 1011s (95% CI [786s,1236s]) in the social robot condition, and 873s (95% CI [680s,1066s]) in the screen only condition. The average length of the division only condition (M=452s, 95% CI [277s,629s]) was much shorter as the robot lessons, pre-test and post-test add a lot of time.

4.1 Learning from Lessons

A 2 tailed, unpaired t-test was conducted to compare the improvement between division pass one and division pass two in the division only (no lessons) and screen only (with lessons) conditions (with no robot present). There was a significant difference in the scores for division only (M=5.40, 95% CI [1.17,9.63]) and screen only (M=14.68, 95% CI [10.65,18.71]) conditions; $t(20)$=3.114, p = 0.006 (Figure 5). This shows that the improvement was significantly higher when the lessons were present, supporting Hypothesis 1. The result here is not surprising, but it is beneficial to show the effectiveness of the division lessons.

4.2 Robot Presence

To examine how the robot affects the learning of the child, we compared the improvement between pre-test and post-test scores between the screen only and (combined) robot conditions. All pre-test and post-test scores are out of 12. None of the children who took part in the study reported to know what a prime number was before the interaction. As a result, based on 2 options for each categorisation, it would be expected that the pre-test scores would be around chance (50% out of 12 correct).

In the screen only condition a 2 tailed, paired t test reveals no significant difference between the scores for the pre-test (M=5.91, 95% CI [4.68,7.13]) and post-test (M=7.36, 95% CI [5.49,9.24]); $t(10)$=1.027, p=0.329. However, when a robot is present there is a significant difference in scores between the pre-test (M=6.04, 95% CI [5.15,6.94]) and the post-test (M=7.78, 95% CI [6.61,8.95]); $t(22)$=2.997, p=0.007. This supports Hypothesis 2, that the presence of a robot will result in greater learning gains.

To further explore this result, we compared the screen only pre-test and post-test scores with those in the asocial robot condition. These two conditions are identical in the script that is used (the screen plays recorded clips of the robot voice) and the lack of personalisation. The previous paragraph showed that there is no significant difference in pre-test and post-test scores in the screen only condition. For the asocial robot, the difference is significant when the same

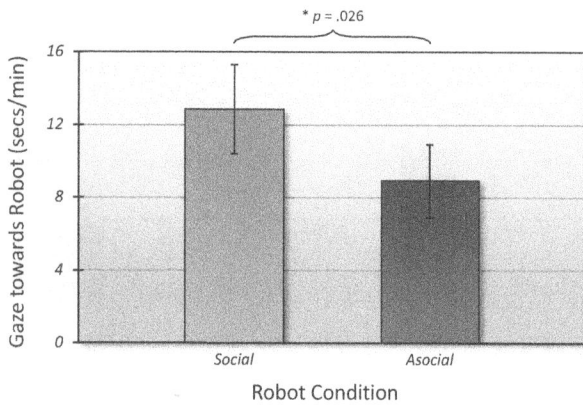

Figure 7: Child gaze towards the robot in seconds per minute, split by robot condition. Error bars show 95% Confidence Interval, * indicates significance at the 0.05 level.

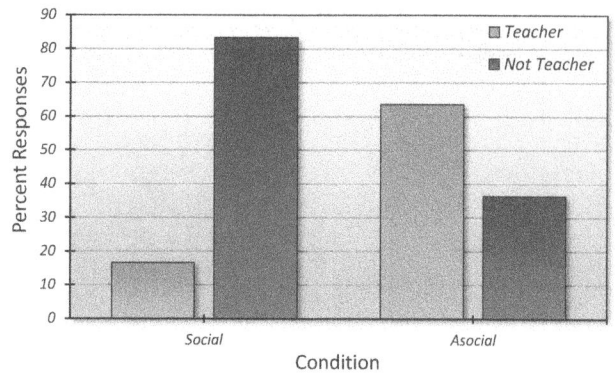

Figure 8: Post-questionnaire responses of the children when asked what they thought the robot was like. Eight options, including 'teacher' were available.

test is run between scores for the pre-test (M=6.27, 95% CI [5.00,7.54]) and post-test (M=8.45, 95% CI [6.84,10.07]); $t(10)$=2.597, p=0.027. This shows that children's learning gains are not significant in the screen only condition, but when the robot is added the learning gains become significant, providing further support for Hypothesis 2.

However, it should be noted that there was no significant difference in the improvement between the screen only (M=1.46, 95% CI [-1.32,4.23]) and asocial robot (M=2.18, 95% CI [0.54,3.83]) conditions; $t(20)$=0.442, p=0.664, when using a 2 tailed, unpaired t test. The fact that the learning becomes significant when the robot is added, despite careful control to match the conditions aside from the presence of the robot, indicates that the robot contributes to the learning that takes place. This result has been observed many times before in other contexts, for example [11] and [14].

4.3 Social Condition

As shown in the previous section, the learning gains for the asocial robot were significant. When conducting a 2 tailed, paired t-test for the social robot condition there is no significant difference between the pre-test (M=5.83, 95% CI [4.54,7.13]) and post-test (M=7.17, 95% CI [5.50,8.84]); $t(11)$=1.627, p=0.132. Whilst all conditions show improvement between the pre-test and the post-test, the only condition where the learning gain is significant is with the asocial robot; both the social robot and screen only conditions show non-significant improvement (Figure 6). This result contradicts Hypothesis 3, that a more social robot will result in greater learning gains than a less social robot.

To explore the impact that the learning personalisation may have had on the results, the lesson reminders and practice of numbers in the second division pass are considered. In the asocial condition a reminder of the lesson is given for each divisor, whereas in the social condition, reminders are only given when the child makes a mistake. This meant that in the asocial condition a total of 44 reminders were given (M=4.00 per interaction; no deviation), whereas in the social condition a total of 22 reminders are delivered (M=1.83, 95% CI [0.94,2.73] per interaction). This is not surprising, as most children can comfortably divide by 2 and 5 at this age; thereby eliminating the need for around half

of the reminders. When correlating the number of reminders provided to children in the social robot condition with their improvement between pre- and post-test score, Pearson's correlation r=-0.418. This is a moderate negative correlation, which suggests that receiving fewer reminders does not reduce the child's performance.

Additionally, children in the social robot condition were given the opportunity to practice more of the numbers that they were weaker at (following the human model described in Section 3.4). There is a possibility that this could have been a de-motivator if they then performed poorly in this phase of the interaction. However, this seems unlikely as it is found that there is no significant difference between the performance in the second division pass between children in the social condition (M=82% correct, 95% CI [71%,93%]) and those in the asocial condition (M=85% correct, 95% CI [75%,95%]); $t(21)$=0.432, p=0.670.

In order to investigate the reasons behind why children's learning gains are not as great when the robot is social compared to when it is asocial, the children's behaviour and self-reported view of the robot were analysed. From video coding of the interactions, it was found that children look significantly more often at the social robot (M=12.9, 95% CI [10.4,15.3]) than at the asocial robot (M=8,9, 95% CI [6.9,10.9]); $t(18)$=2.425, p=0.026 (Figure 7). Values are provided in seconds of gaze at the robot per minute of interaction; this normalisation allows for comparison across interactions of different lengths.

The children completed a pre-questionnaire and a post-questionnaire before and after the interaction. These were very short, with just 4 questions in the pre-questionnaire and 2 questions for the post-questionnaire. The questionnaires were used to see what the children expected from the interactions, and subsequently how they viewed the robot afterwards. Despite being told by the experimenters several times before their interactions that they would be *taught* by a robot *teacher*, with the robot script emphasising this point too, the children in the social robot condition consistently reported that they thought the robot was a 'friend' after the interaction. The question asked "For me, I think the robot was like a -" with 8 options available: brother or sister, classmate, stranger, relative (e.g. cousin or aunt), friend, parent, teacher, and neighbour.

It was expected that the children would report the robot to be a teacher (as this is what they had been told), so their responses were grouped into either 'teacher' or 'not teacher'. In the social condition, 17% of the children reported the robot to have been like a teacher, compared to 64% in the asocial condition. Fisher's exact test shows that the responses differ significantly by condition, $p=0.036$ (Figure 8).

It is clear from the children's gaze and self-reported responses that the difference in robot behaviour between conditions has an effect on the children's behaviour and attitudes towards the robot. It is suggested that these differences could account for the difference in learning gains observed between the social and asocial robot conditions. Whilst the robot is providing the lesson about prime numbers, it demonstrates two examples on the screen by highlighting the numbers, discussing them and correctly categorising them. Therefore, during this period it is useful to look at the screen. During the prime lesson the average amount of gaze towards the social robot ($M=26.9$ secs/min, 95% CI [22.9,30.9]) is significantly higher than the gaze towards the asocial robot ($M=17.0$ secs/min, 95% CI [11.0,23.1]); $t(18)=2.669$, $p=0.016$. It is suggested that the additional attention directed towards the social robot's behaviour could distract the children from the content that it is delivering; this possibility is further discussed below (Section 5).

5. DISCUSSION

From the analysis of the results it is clear that the lessons for division have a positive effect on the children's performance, supporting Hypothesis 1. This validates part of the teaching behaviour and demonstrates that the children have the ability to understand the robot's voice and apply knowledge gained from the lessons in the task on-screen.

When the asocial robot is present, despite having the same content as the screen only condition, the improvement between pre-test and post-test becomes significant, providing partial support for Hypothesis 2. This is a demonstration of the social presence effect; the addition of an agent into the interaction leads to improvement in task performance, as observed before in other contexts, for example [11] and [14]. However, the improvement is lost when the robot behaviour is changed to become more social. This is a surprising result, which contradicts both Hypotheses 2 (that a robot will provide greater learning gains than the screen alone) and 3 (that a more social robot will result in improved learning gains).

This result is in contrast to existing studies in the literature that Hypothesis 3 was based on. As described in Section 3.4, the robot behaviour was derived directly from that of a human tutor. This necessitates a perspective that integrates behavioural dimensions [26] that emphasises sets of behavioural competencies (similar to the use by [18]). This differs from the more typical focus on individual social cues, as in [15] and [22]. With the interaction context (child-robot interactions in a school) and task content (learning mathematical concepts) also differentiating the work here from previous studies, this integrated cues perspective may merit further investigation in terms of the effects on the perceptions and performance of human interactants.

One possible explanation for the unexpected findings with respect to learning is that although the children looked at the social robot significantly more than the asocial robot during the lesson phase (which could be considered advantageous as

the robot provides the lessons), they were paying attention to the social behaviour instead of the lesson content. An alternate explanation is that the social behaviour presented by the social robot places more cognitive load on the children, which may inhibit their capacity to process information related to the task [21]. It may be that in the long-term, as the novelty of the social behaviour wears off, the social robot would then elicit better learning, as indicated by [7]. However, further research is required to explore these ideas explicitly and in more detail.

5.1 Child Perception and Ability

In Section 4.3 it was shown that children in the asocial robot condition were more likely to report that they viewed the robot as a teacher than those in the social robot condition. The infrequency with which those in the social condition reported the robot to be like a teacher was surprising. The children were told several times before and during the interaction by both the robot and the experimenters that the robot was a teacher. It is suggested that there may be two reasons as to why this was the case. Firstly, it may be that the directness of the asocial robot conformed more to their expectations of what a robot teacher would be like than the social robot, which was less direct in its instructions. Secondly, the behaviour of the asocial robot may not have had enough character to change the children's perception of the robot as a teacher, whereas the social robot did. Interestingly, there was almost no correlation between the children's perception of the robot as a teacher and their performance; Pearson's r correlation = -0.11.

There was only a weak correlation (Pearson's $r = 0.13$) between the teacher-provided mathematics ability levels of the children and their subsequent improvement between pre-test and post-test. This is somewhat surprising, as one would expect the higher ability students to progress more given the same practice as those who were lower ability. This may highlight a limitation in the adaptiveness of the robot's behaviour used in this study. It is possible that a robot which is more adaptive could better respond to each individuals' needs and push them more effectively through the Zone of Proximal Development [25].

Due to the relatively small sample sizes used here, it only requires 2 or 3 subjects to perform particularly poorly or well to impact on the significance of the results. However, there is a trade-off between trying to carefully control the experiment and get greater subject numbers. Subjects were selected from the same school and year group so that they would have similar educational experiences and backgrounds. Due to limits on the sizes of school classes, it is likely that to get greater numbers would mean selecting subjects across multiple schools. This then introduces the risk of large variability between subjects' mathematical ability and the environment in which the experiment is conducted.

5.2 Gender Differences

One interesting aside that was noticed through additional exploratory analysis are differences between the genders. These results were not included in Section 4 as they were not part of the original hypothesis for this study. However, as an interesting observation they have been included here, with the suggestion that they may be worth further research. A significant difference is found between the improvement between pre-test and post-test of girls ($M=2.77$, 95% CI

[1.18,4.36]) and boys (M=0.40, 95% CI [-0.85,1.65]) when interacting with a robot present (both social and asocial conditions combined); $t(21)$=2.192, p=0.040. These results show that the boys barely improved with a robot, whilst the girls improved quite substantially.

Additionally, girls who interacted with a robot present (M=2.77, 95% CI [1.18,4.36]) improved more than those without a robot present (M=-0.40, 95% CI [-3.71,2.91]). Whilst this difference is not quite significant ($t(16)$=1.907, p=0.075), it seems as though there may be a possible trend. Gender differences due to social presence have been observed in other contexts in HRI, such as [19], where females saw a robot as more machine-like. This could support the argument that the robot social behaviour distracts from the lesson content that it is delivering; girls, who may perceive the robot as less social, therefore outperformed the boys. Whilst there is not enough evidence here to make firm conclusions about this point, the effect of gender certainly merits more research in the context of educational interactions.

6. CONCLUSION

As expected, the use of lessons improved the children's performance between the first division pass and the second division pass, as shown in Section 4.1. Partial evidence was found in support of the social presence effect. Section 4.2 showed that when a robot delivered the lessons to the child, the learning was significant, whereas when the same information was provided by just a screen, without a robot, it was not. By further breaking down the robot results into the two different behavioural conditions, it was found that the learning remains significant with the asocial robot, where the script is identical to the condition without the robot present (where the learning was not significant). However, these positive effects were not maintained when the robot was more social.

The results here have shown that a robot which is not appropriately social led to greater learning gains of children in a maths task than a robot with appropriate social behaviours. This result contradicts expectations and predications made based on other studies in the literature (for example [15] and [18]). It is hypothesised that the social behaviour of the socially appropriate robot may distract from the content it is delivering with regards to the learning task, whilst the asocial robot leads to disinterest, and therefore less distraction from the learning task. Gaze behaviour of the children throughout the interaction and specifically during the prime numbers lesson is used to provide evidence for this suggestion.

7. ACKNOWLEDGEMENTS

This work is partially funded by the EU FP7 projects ALIZ-E (grant 248116) and DREAM (grant 611391), and the School of Computing and Maths, Plymouth University, U.K. The authors would like to thank Okehampton Primary School, U.K. for taking part in the study.

8. REFERENCES

[1] R. K. Atkinson, R. E. Mayer, and M. M. Merrill. Fostering social agency in multimedia learning: Examining the impact of an animated agent's voice. *Contemporary Educational Psychology*, 30(1):117–139, 2005.

[2] P. Baxter, R. Wood, and T. Belpaeme. A touchscreen-based 'sandtray' to facilitate, mediate and contextualise human-robot social interaction. In *Proc. HRI'12*, pages 105–106, 2012.

[3] T. Belpaeme, P. Baxter, R. Read, R. Wood, H. Cuayáhuitl, B. Kiefer, et al. Multimodal child-robot interaction: Building social bonds. *Journal of Human-Robot Interaction*, 1(2):33–53, 2012.

[4] O. A. Blanson Henkemans, B. P. Bierman, J. Janssen, M. A. Neerincx, R. Looije, H. van der Bosch, et al. Using a robot to personalise health education for children with diabetes type 1: A pilot study. *Patient Education and Counseling*, 92(2):174–181, 2013.

[5] B. S. Bloom. The 2 sigma problem: The search for methods of group instruction as effective as one-to-one tutoring. *Educational researcher*, pages 4–16, 1984.

[6] J. Han, M. Jo, S. Park, and S. Kim. The educational use of home robots for children. In *IEEE RO-MAN'05*, pages 378–383, 2005.

[7] T. Kanda, T. Hirano, D. Eaton, and H. Ishiguro. Interactive robots as social partners and peer tutors for children: A field trial. *Human-Computer Interaction*, 19(1):61–84, 2004.

[8] J. Kennedy, P. Baxter, and T. Belpaeme. Constraining content in mediated unstructured social interactions: Studies in the wild. In *Proc. AFFINE'13, at ACII'13*, pages 728–733, 2013.

[9] J. Kennedy, P. Baxter, and T. Belpaeme. Children comply with a robot's indirect requests. In *Proc. HRI'14*, pages 198–199, 2014.

[10] J. Kennedy, P. Baxter, and T. Belpaeme. Comparing robot embodiments in a guided discovery learning interaction with children. *International Journal of Social Robotics*, accepted.

[11] H. Kose-Bagci, E. Ferrari, K. Dautenhahn, D. S. Syrdal, and C. L. Nehaniv. Effects of embodiment and gestures on social interaction in drumming games with a humanoid robot. *Advanced Robotics*, 23(14):1951–1996, 2009.

[12] J. R. Landis and G. G. Koch. The measurement of observer agreement for categorical data. *Biometrics*, 33(1):159–174, 1977.

[13] D. Leyzberg, S. Spaulding, and B. Scassellati. Personalizing robot tutors to individual learning differences. In *Proc. HRI'14*, pages 423–430, 2014.

[14] D. Leyzberg, S. Spaulding, M. Toneva, and B. Scassellati. The physical presence of a robot tutor increases cognitive learning gains. In *Proc. CogSci'12*, pages 1882–1887, 2012.

[15] R. E. Mayer, S. Fennell, L. Farmer, and J. Campbell. A personalization effect in multimedia learning: Students learn better when words are in conversational style rather than formal style. *Journal of Educational Psychology*, 96(2):389, 2004.

[16] L. Moshkina, S. Trickett, and J. G. Trafton. Social engagement in public places: a tale of one robot. In *Proc. HRI'14*, pages 382–389, 2014.

[17] M. E. O'Neill. The genuine sieve of eratosthenes. *Journal of Functional Programming*, 19(01):95–106, 2009.

[18] M. Saerbeck, T. Schut, C. Bartneck, and M. D. Janse. Expressive robots in education: Varying the degree of social supportive behavior of a robotic tutor. In *Proc. CHI'10*, pages 1613–1622, 2010.

[19] P. Schermerhorn, M. Scheutz, and C. R. Crowell. Robot social presence and gender: Do females view robots differently than males? In *Proc. HRI'08*, pages 263–270, 2008.

[20] E. Short, K. Swift-Spong, J. Greczek, A. Ramachandran, A. Litoiu, E. C. Grigore, et al. How to train your dragonbot: Socially assistive robots for teaching children about nutrition through play. In *IEEE RO-MAN'14*, pages 924–929, 2014.

[21] J. Sweller. Cognitive load theory, learning difficulty, and instructional design. *Learning and instruction*, 4(4):295–312, 1994.

[22] D. Szafir and B. Mutlu. Pay attention!: Designing adaptive agents that monitor and improve user engagement. In *Proc. CHI'12*, pages 11–20, 2012.

[23] K. VanLehn. The relative effectiveness of human tutoring, intelligent tutoring systems, and other tutoring systems. *Educational Psychologist*, 46(4):197–221, 2011.

[24] K. VanLehn, S. Siler, C. Murray, T. Yamauchi, and W. B. Baggett. Why do only some events cause learning during human tutoring? *Cognition and Instruction*, 21(3):209–249, 2003.

[25] L. S. Vygotsky. *Mind in society: The development of higher psychological processes*. Harvard university press, 1980.

[26] J. Zaki. Cue integration a common framework for social cognition and physical perception. *Perspectives on Psychological Science*, 8(3):296–312, 2013.

Emotional Storytelling in the Classroom: Individual versus Group Interaction between Children and Robots

Iolanda Leite*, Marissa McCoy†, Monika Lohani†, Daniel Ullman*, Nicole Salomons*,
Charlene Stokes†‡, Susan Rivers†, Brian Scassellati*
*Department of Computer Science, †Department of Psychology
Yale University, New Haven, CT, USA
‡Air Force Research Laboratory
{iolanda.leite, marissa.mccoy, monika.lohani, daniel.ullman, nicole.salomons,
charlene.stokes, susan.rivers, brian.scassellati}@yale.edu

ABSTRACT

Robot assistive technology is becoming increasingly prevalent. Despite the growing body of research in this area, the
role of type of interaction (i.e., small groups versus individual interactions) on effectiveness of interventions is still
unclear. In this paper, we explore a new direction for socially assistive robotics, where multiple robotic characters
interact with children in an interactive storytelling scenario.
We conducted a between-subjects repeated interaction study
where a single child or a group of three children interacted
with the robots in an interactive narrative scenario. Results show that although the individual condition increased
participant's story recall abilities compared to the group
condition, the emotional interpretation of the story content seemed more dependent on the difficulty level rather
than the study condition. Our findings suggest that, despite
the type of interaction, interactive narratives with multiple
robots are a promising approach to foster children's development of social-related skills.

Keywords

socially assistive robotics; child-robot interaction; emotional
intelligence; interactive storytelling; type of interaction.

1. INTRODUCTION

Socially assistive robotics applications typically involve
one robot and one user [35]. Several authors have also investigated settings with one socially assistive robot interacting
with multiple users [37, 13]. However, as robot assistive
technology becomes more sophisticated, and as robots are
being used more broadly in interventions, there arises a need
to explore other types of interactions.

In this paper, we investigate whether socially assistive
robots are as effective in small groups of children as they
are with an individual. Contrasting the typical "one robot

to one user" and "one robot to many users" situations, there
are cases where it is desirable to have multiple robots interacting with one user or multiple users. As an example,
consider the case of role-playing activities in emotionally
charged domains (e.g., bullying prevention, domestic violence or hostage scenarios). In these cases, taking an active
role in the interaction may bring about undesirable consequences, while observing the interaction might serve as a
learning experience. Here, robots offer an inexpensive alternative to human actors, displaying controlled behavior
across interventions with different trainees.

Our goal is to use multiple socially assistive robots to help
children build their emotional intelligence skills through interactive role-playing activities. As this is a novel research
direction, several questions remain open. What is the effect
of having multiple robots in the scene or, more importantly,
what is the optimal type of interaction for these interventions? Should the type of interaction of the intervention
focus on groups of children (as in traditional role-playing
activities) or should we aim for individual interactions, following the current trend in socially assistive robotics?

Considering the nature of most assistive robotic interventions, one might expect individual interactions to be more
effective. On the other hand, it has long been acknowledged that groups outperform individuals in a variety of
activities, from quantitative judgments [32] to improved individual learning gains [11]. In educational research, for
example, many authors highlight the benefits of learning
in small groups rather than alone [10, 11, 27], including in
learning activities supported by computers. A recent HRI
study suggests that children behave differently when interacting alone or in dyads with a social robot [3]. However, it
remains unknown whether type of interaction impacts the
effectiveness of the robot intervention in terms of how much
users can recall or learn from the interaction. To address
this theme, we developed an interactive narrative scenario
where a pair of robot characters played out stories centered
around words that contribute to expanding children's emotional vocabulary [28]. To evaluate the effects of type of
interaction, we conducted a three-week repeated interaction
study where children interacted with robots either alone or
in small groups, and then were individually asked questions
on the interaction they had just witnessed. We analyzed
interview responses in order to measure participants' story
recall abilities, emotional understanding. Our results show
that although children interacting alone with the robot were

able to recall the narrative more accurately, no significant differences were found in the understanding of the emotional context of the stories. We discuss these implications for the future design of robot technology in learning environments.

2. RELATED WORK

A great deal of research has been conducted into the use of virtual agents in the context of interactive storytelling with children. Embodied conversational agents are structured using a foundation of human-human conversation, creating agents that appear on a screen and interact with a human user [7]. Interactive narratives, where users can influence the storyline through actions and interact with the characters, result in engaging experiences [31] and increase a user's desire to keep interacting with the system [12, 14]. *FearNot* is a virtual simulation with different bullying episodes where a child can take an active role in the story by advising the victim on possible coping strategies to handle the bullying situation. An extensive evaluation of this software in schools showed promising results on the use of such tools in bullying prevention [36]. Although some authors have explored the idea of robots as actors [6, 5, 12, 22], most of the interactive storytelling applications so far are designed for virtual environments.

Kim and Baylor [15] posit that the use of non-human pedagogical agents as learning companions creates the best possible environment for learning for a child. Virtual agents are designed to provide the user with the most interactive experience possible; however, research by Bainbridge et al. [2] indicates that physical presence matters in addition to embodiment, with participants in a task rating an overall more positive interaction when the robot was physically embodied rather than virtually embodied.

Furthermore, research by Leyzberg et al. [20] found that the students who showed the greatest measurable learning gains in a cognitive skill learning task were those who interacted with a physically embodied robot tutor, as compared to a video-represented robot and a disembodied voice. Research by Mercer [25] supports talk as a social mode of thinking, with talk in interaction between learners beneficial to educational activities. However, Mercer identifies the need for focused direction from a teaching figure for the interaction to be as effective as possible.

Shahid et al. [33] conducted a cross-cultural examination of variation between interactions in children who either played a game alone, with a robot, or with another child. They found that children both enjoyed playing more and were more expressive when they played with the robot, as compared to when they played alone. Still, not surprisingly, children who played with a friend showed the highest levels of enjoyment of all groups. With this previous research serving as the foundation, we posited that a combination of interactions with a robot and peers in a group setting could benefit information retainment and understanding of the interaction.

3. INTERACTIVE NARRATIVES WITH MULTIPLE ROBOTIC CHARACTERS

We developed an interactive narrative system such that any number of robotic characters can act out stories defined in a script. This system prompts children to control the actions of one of the robots at specific moments, allowing the

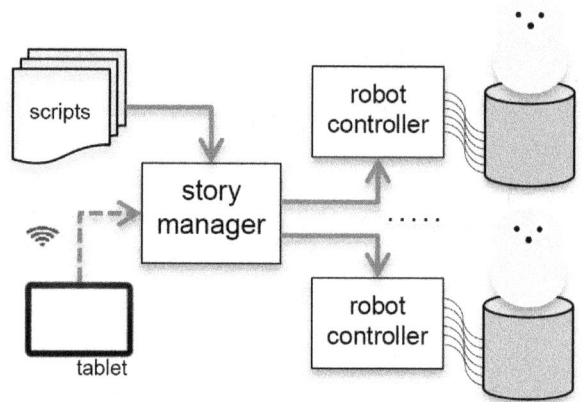

Figure 1: System architechture.

child to see the impact of their decision on the course of the story. By exploring all the different options in these interactive scenarios, children have the opportunity to see how the effects of their decisions play out before them, without the cost of first having to make these decisions in the real world. This section describes the architecture of this system and introduces RULER, the validated framework for promoting emotional literacy that inspired the first interactive stories developed for this scenario.

3.1 System Architecture

The central component of the narrative system is the story manager, which interprets the story scripts and communicates with the robot controller modules and the tablet (see diagram in Figure 1). The scripts are JSON files describing every possible scene episode. A scene contains the dialogue lines of each robot and a list of the next scene options that can be selected by the user. Each dialogue line contains an identifier of the robot playing that line (robotID), the path to a sound file[1] and a descriptor of a nonverbal behavior for the robot to display while "saying" that line (e.g., happy, bouncing). When the robots finish playing out a scene, the next story options are presented on the tablet as text with an accompanying illustration. When the user selects a new story option on the tablet, the story manager loads that scene and begins sending commands to the robots based on the scene dialogue lines.

The system was implemented on Robot Operating System (ROS). The robot platforms used in this implementation were two MyKeepon robots (see Figure 2) with programmable servos controlled by an Arduino board [1]. MyKeepon is a yellow, snowman like robot with three dots representing eyes and a nose. Despite their minimal appearance, research has shown that these robots can elicit social responses from children [16]. Each robot has four degrees of freedom: it can pan to the sides, roll to the sides, tilt forward and backward, and bop up and down. To complement the pre-recorded utterances, we developed several non-verbal behaviors such as idling, talking and bouncing. All the story authoring was done in the script files, except the robot animations and tablet artwork. In addition to

---

[1]Even if generated by TTS in real time, we consider pre-recorded utterances.

Table 1: Summary of the story scenes in each session.

	Session 1	Session 2	Session 3
Feeling Word	Included	Frustration	Cooperation
Difficulty Level	Easy	Hard	Medium
Intro Scene	Leo is new at school and doesn't know anyone. Another student in class, Marlow, called Leo's hat stupid. What should Berry do to help Leo feel included?	Berry tells Leo that he just started a new book as part of an assignment, but some of the words are too hard for him to read. What should Berry do to get through his frustration?	Berry has just mastered a big, hard book on his own. Leo asks Berry to be his reading buddy. Leo wants to read an easier book that's on his reading level, while Berry wants to try reading the hardest books. What should Berry do to be cooperative?
Optional Scenes	- Talk bad about Marlow - Tell Leo how cool Marlow is - Ask Leo to play	- Ask Leo to read the book - Wait for the teacher - Try again	- Find another reading buddy - Choose a book both can read - Choose a hard book anyway

increased modularity, this design choice allows non-expert users (e.g., teachers) to develop new content for the system.

3.2 RULER

RULER is a validated framework rooted in emotional intelligence theory [30] and research on emotional development [9] that is designed to promote and teach emotional intelligence skills. Through a comprehensive approach that is integrated into existing academic curriculum, RULER focuses on skill-building lessons and activities around Recognizing, Understanding, Labeling, Expressing and Regulating emotions in socially appropriate ways [28]. Understanding the significance of emotional states guides attention, decision-making, and behavioral responses, and is necessary in order to navigate the social world [30, 21, 4].

This study employs components of RULER, including the Mood Meter, a tool that students and educators use as a way to identify and label their emotional state, and the Feeling Words Curriculum, a tool that centers on fostering an extensive feelings vocabulary that can be applied in students' everyday lives. The story scripts are grounded in the Feeling Words Curriculum and are intended to encourage participants to choose the most appropriate story choice after considering the impact of each option. Our target age group was 6 to 8 years old. Prior to beginning the study, we gathered feedback from elementary school teachers to ensure that the vocabulary and difficulty levels of story comprehension were age-appropriate. A summary of the scenes forming the scripts of each session are displayed in Table 1. All three stories followed the same structure: introduction scene, followed by three options. Each option impacted the story and the characters' emotional state in different ways.

4. EXPERIMENT

We conducted the user study described in this section to evaluate the impact of type of interaction (i.e., individual versus small groups) on children while interacting with multiple robots. Considering this is the first study in this domain, we did not formulate specific hypotheses, but rather outlined the following exploratory questions to investigate:

- How does type of interaction impact information recall?

- How does type of interaction impact children's emotional understanding and vocabulary?

As previously outlined, socially assistive robotic applications are typically one-to-one, but educational research suggests that children's learning gains may increase in a group [11, 27].

4.1 Study Design

We used a between subjects design with participants randomly sorted into one of two conditions: individual (one participant interacted alone with the robots) or group (three participants interacted with the robots at the same time). We studied groups of three children as three members is the smallest number of members considered to be a group [26]. Our main dependent metrics focused on participants' recall abilities and emotional interpretation of the narrative choices.

Each participant or group of participants interacted with the robots three times, approximately once per week. Participants in the group condition always interacted with the robots in the same groups. The design choice to use repeated interactions was not to measure learning gains over time, but to ensure that the results were not affected by a novelty effect that robots often evoke in children [19].

4.2 Participants

The participants in the study were first and second grade students from an elementary school where RULER, a social and emotional learning (SEL) program, had been implemented. A total of 46 participants were recruited in the school where the study was conducted, but six participants were excluded for various reasons (i.e., technical problems in collecting data or participants missing school). For this analysis, we considered a total of 40 children (22 females, 18 males) between the ages of 6 to 8 ($M = 7.53, SD = .51$). Ethnicity, as reported by guardians, was as follows: 17.5% African American, 17.5% Caucasian, 25% Hispanic, 27.5% reported more than one ethnicity, and 12.5% did not report. The annual income reported by guardians was as follows: 30% in $0-$20,000, 42.5% in $20,000-$50,000, 10% in the $50,000-$100,000 range, and 17.5% not reported.

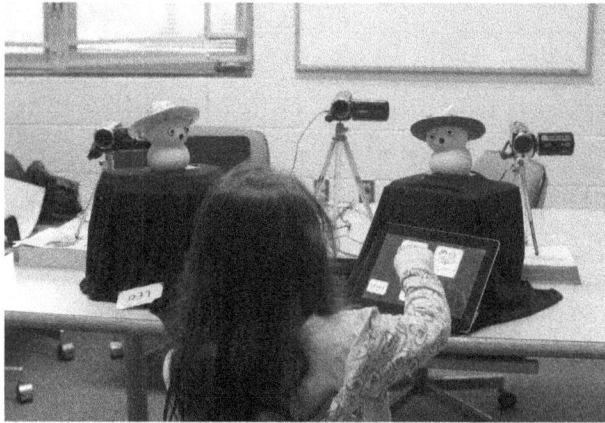

Figure 2: Children interacting with the robots in the individual (left) and group (right) conditions.

4.3 Procedure

Consent forms were distributed in classrooms that had agreed to participate in the study. Participants were randomly assigned to either the individual (19 participants) or group condition (21 participants). Each session lasted approximately 30 minutes with each participant. The participant first interacted with the robots either individually or in a small group (approximately 15 minutes), and then was interviewed individually by the experimenter (approximately 15 minutes).

Participants were escorted from class by a guide who explained that they were going to interact with robots and then would be asked questions about the interaction. The child was introduced to the experimenter and asked for verbal assent. The experimenter began by introducing the participants to Leo and Berry, the two main characters (My-Keepon robots) in the study. The first half of each session involved the participants interacting with the robots as the robots autonomously role-played a scenario centered around a RULER feeling word. After observing the scenario introduction, participants were presented with three different options from which to choose. Participants were instructed to first select the option they thought was the best choice, and were told they would then have the opportunity to choose the other two options. In the group condition, participants were asked to make a joint decision. The experimenter was present in the room at all times, but was outside participants' line of sight so as not to distract participants from the interaction.

After interacting with the robots, participants were interviewed by additional experimenters. The interviews had the same format for both conditions, which means that even participants in the group condition were interviewed individually. Interviews were conducted in nearby rooms. Experimenters followed a standardized protocol that asked the same series of questions (one open-ended question, followed by two direct questions) for each of the four scenes (i.e., Introduction, Option 1, Option 2, Option 3) that comprised one session. The same three repeated questions were asked in the following order:

1. What happened after you chose <option>?

2. After you chose <option>, what color of the Mood Meter do you think <character>

3. What word would you use to describe how <character> was feeling?

These questions were repeated for a total of 36 times (3 questions * 4 scenes per session * 3 sessions) over the course of the study. If a participant remained silent for more than 10 seconds after being asked a question, the experimenter asked, "Would you like me to repeat the question or would you like to move on". The interviewer used small cards with artwork representing the different scene choices similar to the ones that appeared on the tablet near the robots. All three sessions followed the same format (i.e., robot interaction followed by the series of interview questions). Interviews were audio-recorded and transcribed verbatim for coding.

5. DATA ANALYSIS

In this section, we describe how interview data was coded and how the main evaluation metrics were calculated.

5.1 Word Count

The number of words uttered by each participant during the interview were counted using an automated script. Placeholders such as "umm" or "uhh" did not contribute toward word count. This metric was mainly used as a manipulation check for the other measures.

5.2 Story Recall

Responses to the open-ended question "What happened after you chose <option>?" were coded as the variable Story Recall. Story Recall was further broken down into Narrative Structure Score (NSS), Narrative Accuracy (NAC) and Narrative Inaccuracy (NIN). Similar recall metrics have been previously used in HRI studies with adults [34].

For Narrative Structure Score (NSS), we followed the coding scheme used in previous research by McGuigan and Salmon [24] and McCartney and Nelson [23], in which participants' verbal responses to open-ended questions were coded for the presence or absence of core characters (e.g., Leo, Berry) and core ideas (e.g., Leo doesn't know anyone, everyone is staring at Leo's clothes). This score provides a snapshot of the participants' "ability to logically recount the fundamental plot elements of the story" [24, 23]. For session S and participant i, NSS was computed using the following formula:

$$NSS_{S,I} = \frac{Mentioned(CoreCharacters + CoreIdeas)}{All(CoreCharacters + CoreIdeas)}$$

A perfect NSS of 1.0 would indicate that the participant mentioned all the core characters and main ideas in all four open-ended questions of that interview. The first mention of core characters and core ideas were given a point each, with additional mentions not counted. The sum of core characters and core ideas for each interview session were combined to generate the Narrative Structure Score. The average number of characters in each story was three (Leo, Berry, and Marlow or the teacher), while the number of core ideas varied depending on the difficulty of the story, ranging from an average of four in the easier story to six in the hardest.

Previous coding schemes were followed for Narrative Accuracy and Narrative Inaccuracy [18, 24, 23]. These metrics capture students' ability to move beyond simply recounting overarching story themes, instead describing a more granular or nuanced account of the story. The same responses to the open-ended question were also coded for *correct event details*, *extra-event details*, *intrusions* and *distortions*. Event details included actions, objects or descriptors that were part of a story event but not considered core ideas, and extra-event details were references to the participant's opinions, feelings or thoughts (e.g., "Jake is new to my class and I asked him to play"). Intrusions were mentioned actions, objects or descriptors that were not part of the event, while distortions were considered any actions, objects, or descriptors that were part of the event but inaccurately described (e.g., "Marlow said Leo's shoes are stupid"). Narrative Accuracy (NAC) and Narrative Inaccuracy (NIN) were calculated using the following formulas:

$$NAC_{S,I} = EventDetails + 0.5 * ExtraEventDetails$$

$$NIN_{S,I} = Intrusions + 0.5 * Distortions$$

Higher NAC and NIN scores denote a greater number of correct story descriptors or story errors during story recall, respectively. NAC scores for each scene were summed to create an aggregate NAC score for each interview session, as were NIN aggregate scores. The number of correct and extra-event details, intrusions and distorsions normally ranged from 0 to 4.

5.3 Emotional Understanding

The Emotional Understanding Score (EUS) represents participants' ability to correctly recognize and label character's emotional states, a fundamental skill of RULER [8, 4]. Responses to the two direct questions "After you chose <option>, what color of the Mood Meter do you think <character> was in?" and "What word would you use to describe how <character> was feeling?" were coded based on RULER concepts and combined to comprise EUS.

Appropriate responses for the first question were based on the Mood Meter colors and included Yellow (pleasant, high energy), Green (pleasant, low energy), Blue (unpleasant, low energy), or Red (unpleasant, high energy), depending on the emotional state of the robots at specific points in the roleplay. Responses to the second direct question were based on

the RULER Feeling Words Curriculum with potential appropriate responses being words such as excited (pleasant, high energy), calm (pleasant, low energy), upset (unpleasant, low energy), or angry (unpleasant, high energy), depending on which color quadrant the participant "plotted" the character. Since participants were recruited from schools implementing RULER, they use the Mood Meter daily and are used to these type of questions. Most participants answered with one or two words when asked to describe the character's feelings.

For the ColorScore, participants received +1 if the correct Mood Meter color was provided, and -1 if an incorrect color was given. In the FeelingWordScore, participants received +1 or -1 depending on whether the feeling word provided was appropriate or not. If participants provided additional appropriate or inappropriate feeling words, they were given +0.5 or -0.5 points for each, respectively. The total EUS was calculated using the following formula:

$$EUS_{S,I} = ColorScore + FeelingWordScore$$

Higher EUS means that participants were able to more accurately identify the Mood Meter color and corresponding feeling word associated with the character's emotional state. For each interview session, EUS scores for each scene were summed to calculate an aggregate EUS score.

5.4 Coding and Reliability

Two researchers independently coded the interview transcriptions from the three sessions. Both coders first coded the interviews from the excluded participants to become familiar with the coding scheme. Once agreement between coders was reached, coding began on the remaining data. Coding was completed for the 120 collected interviews (40 participants * 3 sessions), overlapping 25% (30 interviews) as a reliability check.

Reliability analysis between the two coders was performed using the Intra-class Correlation Coefficient test for absolute agreement using a two-way random model. All the coded variables for each interview session had high reliabilities. The lowest agreement was found in the number of correct feeling words ($ICC(2,1) = 0.85, p < .001$), while the highest agreement was related to the total number of core characters mentioned by each child during one interview session ($ICC(2,1) = 0.94, p < .001$). Given the high agreement between the two coders in the overlapping 30 interviews, data from one coder were randomly selected to be used for analyses.

6. RESULTS

Mixed model Analyses of Variance (ANOVA) models were conducted with type of interaction (individual versus group) as the between-subjects factor and session (1, 2, and 3) as the within-subjects factor. For all the dependent measures, we planned to test the individual versus group differences in each session.

6.1 Word Count

We examined whether there were any differences between individual versus group level in the number of words spoken by the participants during the interview sessions. An ANOVA model was run with the number of words spoken as the dependent measure. Neither a main effect nor interaction effect was found to be significant. Thus, overall, there

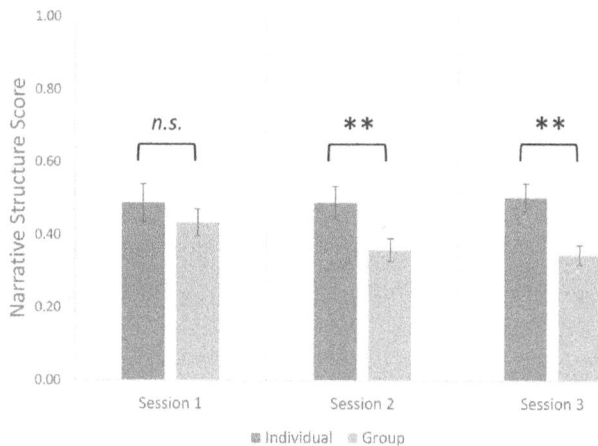

Figure 3: Average Narrative Structure Scores (NSS) for participants in each condition on every interaction session. (**) denotes $p < .01$.

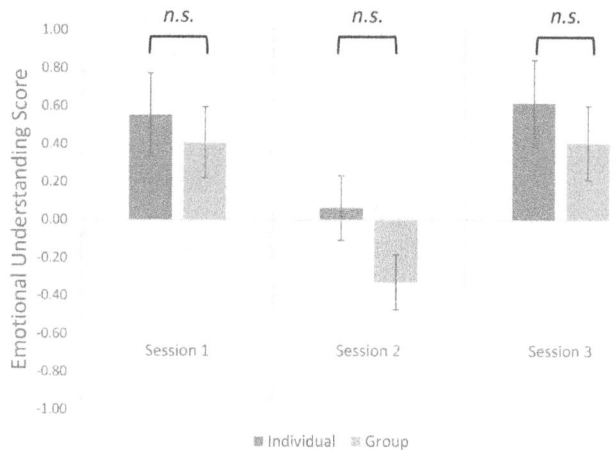

Figure 4: Average Emotional Understanding Scores (EUS) for participants in each condition for sessions 1 (easy), 2 (advanced) and 3 (medium). No significant differences were found between conditions.

was no significant difference in word count between the two groups. The average number of words per interview was 124.82 ($SE = 16.01$). This variability seems to stem from each participant's individual differences and was not related to the participant's condition. This result is important because it serves as a manipulation check for other reported findings.

6.2 Story Recall

We investigated the impact of type of interaction on participants' story recall abilities, measured by the Narrative Structure Score (NSS) and Narrative Accuracy/Inaccuracy (NAC and NIN, respectively). An ANOVA model was run with NSS as the dependent measure. We found a significant main effect of type of interaction (collapsed across sessions), with students in the individual condition achieving higher scores on narrative structure ($M = .49, SE = .03$) than the group condition ($M = .38, SE = .02$), $F(1, 28) = 7.71, p = .01, \eta2 = .22$. Between type of interaction and session, neither a main effect nor an interaction effect was significant (see Figure 3).

Planned comparisons were conducted to test the role of type of interaction in each session. No significant differences were found for session 1. For session 2, students in the individual condition ($M = .49, SE = .05$) had a higher score than the students in the group condition ($M = .36, SE = .03$), $F(1, 36) = 7.35, p = .01, \eta2 = .17$. Similarly, for session 3, students in the individual condition ($M = .50, SE = .04$) had a higher score than in the group condition ($M = .35, SE = .03$), $F(1, 38) = 6.59, p = .01, \eta2 = .15$.

The other measures we used to study participants' story recall abilities were Narrative Accuracy (NAC) and Narrative Inaccuracy (NIN). An ANOVA model with NAC as the dependent measure did not find significant differences between the individual versus the group condition. A significant main effect of session was found, $F(2, 74) = 4.98, p = .01, \eta2 = .12$, but the interaction between type of interaction and session was nonsignificant. None of the type of interaction related (individual versus group) planned contrasts were significant, despite the slightly higher average scores of NAC in the individual condition ($M = .38, SE = .09$), compared to the values on the group condition ($M = .19, SE =$

.09). An ANOVA model with NIN as the dependent measure also suggested that there were no significant effects in each session due to type of interaction or session. Yet again, on average, participants in the individual condition performed marginally better (i.e., lower NIN) than participants from the group condition, ($M = .26, SE = .09$) and ($M = .36, SE = .08$), respectively.

These findings suggest that overall the narrative story related recall rate was found to be higher in the individual versus the group level interaction with the robots. In the easier session (session 1), there was no effect on type of interaction, but during the harder sessions (sessions 2 and 3), students were found to perform better in individual than group level interactions. In addition, no type of interaction-related differences were found in NAC nor NIN.

6.3 Emotional Understanding

To investigate our second research question, we tested whether students' Emotional Understanding Score differed in the individual versus group condition. An ANOVA model with EUS as the dependent measure suggested that there was no main effect of type of interaction. The main effect of session was significant $F(2, 62) = 7.39, p = .001, \eta2 = .19$, which aligns with our expectation given that the three sessions had different levels of difficulty. Type of interaction versus session interaction effect was not significant (see Figure 4). Planned comparisons also yielded no significant differences between the individual versus groups in any of three sessions. In sum, the degree of emotional understanding did not seem to be affected by type of interaction in this setting, but varied across sessions with different levels of difficulty.

7. DISCUSSION

Our results yielded interesting findings about the effects of type of interaction on children's interactions with multiple socially assistive robots. Participants interacting with the robots alone were able to recall the Narrative Structure (i.e., core ideas and characters) significantly better than participants in the group condition. On average, participants in the individual condition also enumerated more correct story details in every session, and less inconsistencies in 2 out of the 3 sessions, but these results were not statistically significant across conditions.

Three main interpretations can be taken from these results. First, while the child was solely responsible for all choices when interacting alone, decisions were shared when in the group, thereby affecting how the interaction was experienced. A second interpretation is that in individual interactions, children may be more attentive since social standing in relation to their peers is not a factor. Thirdly, the peers might be simply more distracting.

At first glance, our results may seem to contradict previous findings highlighting the benefits of learning in small groups [11, 27]. However, recalling story details is different than increasing learning gains. In fact, no significant differences were found between groups in our main learning metric, Emotional Understanding Score (participants' ability to interpret the stories using the concepts of the RULER framework), despite average individual condition scores being slightly higher for every session. Other than session 2, which had the most difficult story content, all participants performed quite well despite the type of interaction in which they interacted. One possible explanation, in line with the findings from Shahid et al. [33], is that participants in the individual condition might have benefited from some of the effects of a group setting since they were interacting with multiple autonomous agents (the two robots). Moreover, several authors argue that group interaction and subsequent learning gains do not necessarily occur just because learners are in a group [17]. An analysis of the participants' behavior while in the group during the interaction could clarify these hypotheses.

8. DESIGN IMPLICATIONS

There are obvious reasons why having multiple children instead of one child interact with a robot at a time is favorable, including limitations of cost, time and space. Our work focuses on whether the advantages of one-on-one tutoring, which have been well established in the HRI domain, can also apply to one-to-many instruction and what costs might be incurred when this shift happens.

While individual interactions seem to be more effective in the short-term, group interventions might be more suitable in the long-term. Previous research has shown that children have more fun interacting with robots in groups rather than alone [33]. Since levels of engagement are positively correlated with students' motivation for pursuing learning goals [29], influence concentration, and foster group discussions [38], future research in this area should study the effects of type of interaction in long-term interaction with robots.

Another implication of our findings is that instruction primarily concerned with factual recall (such as basic arithmetic facts) might be best served by one-on-one interactions, but that other skill-based and outcome-based instruction (such as interpersonal skill training, as in our study) might be amenable to one-to-many instruction. These results align with previous research comparing individual and group learning gains with computer-based technology. The meta-analysis performed by Pai and colleagues [27], for example, showed that effect sizes of individual versus group learning were smaller for more exploratory tasks.

To keep the gains of individual interactions in group settings, it might be necessary to implement more sophisticated perception mechanisms in the robots. For example, the robots could detect disengagement and employ recovery mechanisms to keep children focused in the interaction. Similarly, robots that capture the complex dynamics of group interactions by perceiving and intervening when a child is dominating an interaction would be useful in group settings.

9. CONCLUSION

The effective acquisition of social and emotional skills requires constant practice in diverse hypothetical situations. In this paper, we proposed a novel approach where multiple socially assistive robots are used in interactive role-playing activities with children. The robots acted as interactive puppets; children could control the actions of one of the robots and see the impact of the selected actions on the course of the story. Using this scenario, we investigated the effects of type of interaction (individual versus small group interactions) on children's story recall and emotional interpretation of interactive stories.

Results from this repeated interaction study showed that although participants who interacted alone with the robot remembered the story better than participants in the group condition, no significant differences were found in children's emotional interpretation of the stories. This latter metric was fairly high for all participants, except in the session with the hardest story content. Despite the promising results of this study, further research is needed to understand how type of interaction affects children's learning gains in longer-term interactions with socially assistive robotics.

10. ACKNOWLEDGMENTS

This work was supported by the NSF Expedition in Computing Grant #1139078 and SRA International (US Air Force) Grant #13-004807. We thank Bethel Assefa for assistance in data collection and coding, Rachel Protacio and Jennifer Allen for recording the voices for the robots, Emily Lennon for artwork creation, and the students and staff from the school where the study was conducted.

11. REFERENCES

[1] H. Admoni, A. Nawroj, I. Leite, Z. Ye, B. Hayes, A. Rozga, J. Rehg, and B. Scassellati. Mykeepon project. http://hennyadmoni.com/keepon. Accessed January 2, 2015.

[2] W. A. Bainbridge, J. W. Hart, E. S. Kim, and B. Scassellati. The benefits of interactions with physically present robots over Video-Displayed agents. *Adv. Robot.*, 3(1):41–52, 1 Jan. 2011.

[3] P. Baxter, J. de Greeff, and T. Belpaeme. Do children behave differently with a social robot if with peers? In *International Conf. on Social Robotics (ICSR 2013)*. Springer, 2013.

[4] M. A. Brackett, S. E. Rivers, and P. Salovey. Emotional intelligence: Implications for personal, social, academic, and workplace success. *Soc. Personal. Psychol. Compass*, 5(1):88–103, 2011.

[5] C. Breazeal, A. Brooks, J. Gray, M. Hancher, J. McBean, D. Stiehl, and J. Strickon. Interactive robot theatre. *Commun. ACM*, 46(7):76–85, July 2003.

[6] A. Bruce, J. Knight, S. Listopad, B. Magerko, and I. Nourbakhsh. Robot improv: Using drama to create believable agents. In *Proc. of the Int. Conf. on*

Robotics and Automation, ICRA'00, pages 4002–4008. IEEE, 2000.

[7] J. Cassell. *Embodied Conversational Agents*. MIT Press, 2000.

[8] R. Castillo, P. Fernández-Berrocal, and M. A. Brackett. Enhancing teacher effectiveness in Spain: A pilot study of the RULER approach to social and emotional learning. *Journal of Education and Training Studies*, 1(2):263–272, 16 Aug. 2013.

[9] S. A. Denham. *Emotional development in young children*. Guilford Press, 1998.

[10] P. Dillenbourg. What do you mean by collaborative learning? *Collaborative-learning: Cognitive and Computational Approaches.*, pages 1–19, 1999.

[11] G. W. Hill. Group versus individual performance: Are n+1 heads better than one? *Psychological Bulletin*, 91(3):517, 1982.

[12] G. Hoffman, R. Kubat, and C. Breazeal. A hybrid control system for puppeteering a live robotic stage actor. In *Proc. of RO-MAN 2008*, pages 354–359. IEEE, 2008.

[13] T. Kanda, R. Sato, N. Saiwaki, and H. Ishiguro. A two-month field trial in an elementary school for long-term human-robot interaction. *IEEE Transactions on Robotics*, 23(5):962–971, Oct 2007.

[14] C. Kelleher, R. Pausch, and S. Kiesler. Storytelling alice motivates middle school girls to learn computer programming. In *Proc. of the SIGCHI Conf. on Human Factors in Computing Systems*, CHI '07, pages 1455–1464, New York, NY, USA, 2007. ACM.

[15] Y. Kim and A. L. Baylor. A Social-Cognitive framework for pedagogical agents as learning companions. *Educ. Technol. Res. Dev.*, 54(6):569–596, 2006.

[16] H. Kozima, M. Michalowski, and C. Nakagawa. Keepon: A playful robot for research, therapy, and entertainment. *International Journal of Social Robotics*, 1(1):3–18, 2009.

[17] K. Kreijns, P. A. Kirschner, and W. Jochems. Identifying the pitfalls for social interaction in computer-supported collaborative learning environments: a review of the research. *Comput. Human Behav.*, 19(3):335–353, May 2003.

[18] S. Kulkofsky, Q. Wang, and S. J. Ceci. Do better stories make better memories? narrative quality and memory accuracy in preschool children. *Appl. Cogn. Psychol.*, 2008.

[19] I. Leite, C. Martinho, and A. Paiva. Social robots for long-term interaction: A survey. *International Journal of Social Robotics*, 5(2):291–308, 2013.

[20] D. Leyzberg, S. Spaulding, M. Toneva, and B. Scassellati. The physical presence of a robot tutor increases cognitive learning gains. In *Proc. of the 34th Annual Conf. of the Cognitive Science Society. Austin, TX: Cognitive Science Society*, 2012.

[21] P. N. Lopes, P. Salovey, S. Coté, and M. Beers. Emotion regulation abilities and the quality of social interaction. *Emotion*, 5(1):113–118, Mar. 2005.

[22] D. Lu and W. Smart. Human-robot interactions as theatre. In *RO-MAN, 2011 IEEE*, pages 473–478, July 2011.

[23] K. A. McCartney and K. Nelson. Children's use of scripts in story recall. *Discourse Process.*, 1981.

[24] F. McGuigan and K. Salmon. The influence of talking on showing and telling: adult-child talk and children's verbal and nonverbal event recall. *Applied Cognitive Psychology*, 2006.

[25] N. Mercer. The quality of talk in children's collaborative activity in the classroom. *Learning and Instruction*, 6(4):359–377, Dec. 1996.

[26] R. L. Moreland. Are dyads really groups? *Small Group Research*, 17 Feb. 2010.

[27] H.-H. Pai, D. A. Sears, and Y. Maeda. Effects of small-group learning on transfer: A meta-analysis. *Educational Psychology Review*, pages 1–24, 2013.

[28] S. E. Rivers, M. A. Brackett, M. R. Reyes, N. A. Elbertson, and P. Salovey. Improving the social and emotional climate of classrooms: a clustered randomized controlled trial testing the RULER approach. *Prev. Sci.*, 14(1):77–87, Feb. 2013.

[29] R. M. Ryan and E. L. Deci. Self-determination theory and the facilitation of intrinsic motivation, social development, and well-being. *American psychologist*, 55(1):68, 2000.

[30] P. Salovey and J. D. Mayer. Emotional intelligence. *Imagination, cognition and personality*, 9(3):185–211, 1989.

[31] H. Schoenau-Fog. Hooked!–evaluating engagement as continuation desire in interactive narratives. In *Interactive storytelling*, pages 219–230. Springer, 2011.

[32] T. Schultze, A. Mojzisch, and S. Schulz-Hardt. Why groups perform better than individuals at quantitative judgment tasks: Group-to-individual transfer as an alternative to differential weighting. *Organizational Behavior and Human Decision Processes*, 118(1):24 – 36, 2012.

[33] S. Shahid, E. Krahmer, and M. Swerts. Child-robot interaction across cultures: How does playing a game with a social robot compare to playing a game alone or with a friend? *Comput. Human Behav.*, 40(0):86–100, Nov. 2014.

[34] D. Szafir and B. Mutlu. Pay attention!: Designing adaptive agents that monitor and improve user engagement. In *Proc. of the SIGCHI Conf. on Human Factors in Computing Systems*, CHI '12, pages 11–20, New York, NY, USA, 2012. ACM.

[35] A. Tapus, M. Matarić, and B. Scassellatti. The grand challenges in socially assistive robotics. *IEEE Robotics and Automation Magazine*, 14(1), 2007.

[36] N. Vannini, S. Enz, M. Sapouna, D. Wolke, S. Watson, S. Woods, K. Dautenhahn, L. Hall, A. Paiva, and E. André. Fearnot!: computer-based anti-bullying programme designed to foster peer intervention. *European journal of psychology of education*, 26(1):21–44, 2011.

[37] K. Wada, T. Shibata, and Y. Kawaguchi. Long-term robot therapy in a health service facility for the aged-a case study for 5 years. In *International Conf. on Rehabilitation Robotics*, pages 930–933. IEEE, 2009.

[38] H. J. Walberg. Productive teaching and instruction: Assessing the knowledge base. *Phi Delta Kappan*, pages 470–478, 1990.

When Children Teach a Robot to Write: An Autonomous Teachable Humanoid Which Uses Simulated Handwriting

Deanna Hood, Séverin Lemaignan, Pierre Dillenbourg
Computer-Human Interaction in Learning and Instruction Laboratory (CHILI)
École Polytechnique Fédérale de Lausanne (EPFL)
firstname.lastname@epfl.ch

ABSTRACT

This article presents a novel robotic partner which children can teach handwriting. The system relies on the *learning by teaching* paradigm to build an interaction, so as to stimulate meta-cognition, empathy and increased self-esteem in the child user. We hypothesise that use of a humanoid robot in such a system could not just engage an unmotivated student, but could also present the opportunity for children to experience physically-induced benefits encountered during human-led handwriting interventions, such as motor mimicry.

By leveraging simulated handwriting on a synchronised tablet display, a NAO humanoid robot with limited fine motor capabilities has been configured as a suitably embodied handwriting partner. Statistical shape models derived from principal component analysis of a dataset of adult-written letter trajectories allow the robot to draw purposefully deformed letters. By incorporating feedback from user demonstrations, the system is then able to learn the optimal parameters for the appropriate shape models.

Preliminary in situ studies have been conducted with primary school classes to obtain insight into children's use of the novel system. Children aged 6-8 successfully engaged with the robot and improved its writing to a level which they were satisfied with. The validation of the interaction represents a significant step towards an innovative use for robotics which addresses a widespread and socially meaningful challenge in education.

1. INTRODUCTION

Handwriting difficulties in children at an early age often negatively affect the academic performance of the students [5], in addition to their self-esteem being adversely affected [14], causing them to shy away from expressing what they know [16]. Successful interventions for children with handwriting difficulties involve the student in many sessions where they are engaged in physically practising the skill [10]. However, the link between handwriting difficulties and low

self-efficacy [6] results in children who are unmotivated to participate in such sessions, potentially leading to a developmental arrest in the acquisition of the skill.

The *learning by teaching* paradigm, which engages the target student in the act of teaching another, has been shown to produce motivational, meta-cognitive, and educational benefits in a range of disciplines [18]. To our best knowledge, the application of the paradigm to handwriting intervention remains, however, unexplored. One reason for this may due to the requirement of an appropriately unskilled peer for the target child to tutor, as this may present a logistical constraint if the target child is the lowest performer in their class. In some cases, it may be appropriate for a peer or teacher to simulate a naïve learner for the target child to teach. For handwriting, where one's skill level is visually evident, however, this acting is likely to be eventually detected. As such, there is motivation for the use of a teachable agent which can be configured for a variety of skill levels, and for which children do not have preconceptions about its handwriting ability.

We present the development of a novel teachable agent that intentionally makes mistakes typical of children learning handwriting. Through this capability, the robot can be taught by children, who themselves may learn through their teaching.

Within this article, Section 3 presents the novel work in the area of artificial intelligence to develop a learning algorithm suitable for a teachable agent in the context of handwriting. Section 4 details the extension of this algorithm to an embodied robotic learning agent, including the new approach for achieving simulated fine motor skills on commercially affordable humanoid robots such as the NAO. Section 5 explores the contributions made to the study of human-robot interaction, in discussing the use of the system with primary school children and its potential as a tool for addressing wider pedagogical research questions in education. Finally, Section 6 addresses the challenges which are faced in extending this system to a level suitable for long-term studies, and Section 7 concludes by reiterating the impact of the article's contributions.

2. RELATED WORK

Teachable computer-based agents have previously been used to encourage the "protégé effect", wherein students invest more effort into learning when it is for a teachable agent than for themselves [4]. As we are concerned with learning of a physical skill, the learning agent developed is embodied in a humanoid robot which is capable of physically demonstrating handwriting trajectories to its child learning partner. This is supported by the potential for motor mimicry to yield significant improvements in handwriting interventions in which letter formations are demonstrated to participants [2]. Furthermore, when compared to screen-based agents, robotic partners have been shown in some contexts to increase users' compliance with tasks [1], maintain more effective long-term relationships [11], and produce greater learning gains when acting as tutors [12].

Robots have been used as teachers or social partners to promote children's learning in a range of contexts, most commonly related to language skills [9], and less often to physical skills (such as calligraphy [15]). Looking at the converse (humans *teaching* robots), Werfel notes in [22] that most of the work focuses on the robot's benefits (in terms of language [19] or physical [17] skills, for example) rather than the learning experienced by the human tutor themselves. Our work concentrates on this latter aspect: by demonstrating handwriting to a robot, we aim at improving the *child's* performance. Note that our work must be distinguished from "learning from demonstration" approaches to robots learning physical skills, as the agent we present is only simulating fine motor skills for interaction purposes.

A robotic learning agent which employs the learning by teaching paradigm has previously been developed by Tanaka and Matsuzoe [21]. In their system, children learn vocabulary by teaching the NAO robot to act out verbs. The robot is tele-operated and mimics the actions that the children teach it, but with no long-term memory or learning algorithm in place. Our project significantly extends this line of work in two ways. First, by investigating the context of children's acquisition of a challenging physical skill (handwriting), and second by proposing a robotic partner which is fully autonomous in its learning.

3. A LEARNING AGENT IN THE CONTEXT OF HANDWRITING

A parameterisation of letters and their deformities is used such that different quality shapes can be generated, depending on the parameters input to the letter models. This allows us to configure the system to improve its writing by modifying the parameters based on feedback from the reinforcement learning partner (Section 3.3).

3.1 Shape Modelling of Letters

We use statistical shape modelling for generating a shape model which can appropriately represent realistic variations in shapes. Statistical shape modelling is an application of principle component analysis (PCA), where a linear transform which de-correlates data vectors is found [20] and allows for dimensionality reduction.

PCA is performed on a set of letter paths captured from a digital pen, using the UJI Pen Characters 2 dataset [13] with 120 instances of each letter (2 repetitions from 60 adult users). While it may be appropriate in future work to identify the location of salient features of the shapes which are robust to unanticipated user input (such as shapes drawn backwards), the features are currently taken as $n = 70$ uniformly spaced points along the shape path. The points are arranged into an observation vector presented in (1), where x_i and y_i represent the coordinates of each of the points along the path. The observation shapes are normalised to

have a unit maximum dimension and $\mathbf{0}$ mean.

$$\mathbf{x} = [x_1, x_2, \ldots, x_n, y_1, y_2, \ldots, y_n]^T \qquad (1)$$

Equation (2) represents the projection from the original $2n$-dimensional feature space to a reduced N-dimensional space, where $\mathbf{p}$ contains the coordinates in the N-dimensional space with $\mathbf{0}$-origin, calculated as in (3). $\mathbf{\Phi}$ is an orthogonal $2n \times N$ matrix composed of the eigenvectors $\mathbf{v}_i$ corresponding to the largest N eigenvalues (λ_i) of the covariance matrix of the observations [20], as shown in (4). If there is correlation between the points in the observations, there will be eigenvalues of the covariance matrix which are close to zero. As such, removing the associated eigenvectors from $\mathbf{\Phi}$ allows for dimensionality reduction with minimal impact.

$$\tilde{\mathbf{x}} = \bar{\mathbf{x}} + \mathbf{\Phi}\mathbf{p} \qquad (2)$$

$$\mathbf{p} = \mathbf{\Phi}^T(\mathbf{x} - \bar{\mathbf{x}}) \qquad (3)$$

$$\mathbf{\Phi} = [\mathbf{v}_1, \mathbf{v}_2, \ldots, \mathbf{v}_N]^T \qquad (4)$$

PCA is performed on all of the paths of a particular allograph in the dataset individually, to reduce the $2n$-dimensional space for that shape to one with $N = 10$ dimensions. Each shape is then approximated by the mean shape of the allograph plus a sum of the top 10 eigenvectors, weighted by the parameter vector $\mathbf{p}$.

Equation (2) may also be used to generate new shapes based on the parameters $\mathbf{p}$ which are used. $\mathbf{p} = \mathbf{0}$ will yield the mean shape, and variations to each of the N values in $\mathbf{p}$ will cause a change in the shape represented by the corresponding eigenvector (Figure 1). For the dataset presented in Figure 1, the eigenvectors associated with the 3 largest eigenvalues explain 78.5% of the variance in the dataset, illustrating the capability of the statistical shape modelling approach to produce compact parameterisation of shapes.

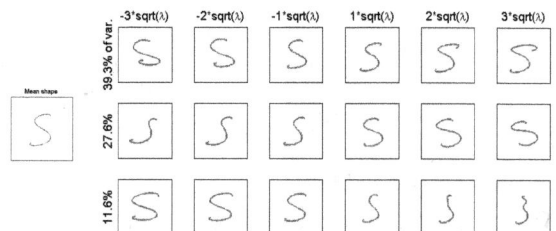

Figure 1: The mean shape (left) and the effect (right) of varying the first three parameters (each row) of a shape model. Parameter variation is dependent on the eigenvalue λ corresponding to the parameter's eigenvector. The percentage of the total variance in the dataset explained by each parameter is shown to the left of the corresponding row.

Interestingly, although the parameters are the result of an *unsupervised* shape analysis, they still represent variations which could have been intuitively identified by a manual parameterisation. For example, for the model shown in Figure 1, the parameters may represent the height of the top half of the letter compared to the bottom half, the width of the overall shape, etc. The ability to generate varied levels of deformations which may be ascribed descriptive interpretations (not just numerical) is an advantage of this method, given its intended use with humans. It is, for instance, possible for a teacher to create letters – which will be used as a starting point for the system – with a particular feature (a wide 's' or a 'd' with a large loop, for example).

3.2 Generating Poor Letters

As explained, new letters can be generated by varying the parameter values for a shape model in accordance with (2). By choosing parameter values which lie within the observed range in the dataset, it is possible to produce letters which are more likely to be reasonable looking. When the parameter values are outside of the range observed in the dataset, they are less likely to represent shapes from the dataset of adult-written letters, and as a result are more likely to represent poor shapes. Figure 2 illustrates sample letters generated from the models of 'e' and 'g' by selecting random values for the first 5 parameters from a distribution with standard deviation of $3\sqrt{\lambda_i}$, rather than the $\sqrt{\lambda_i}$ standard deviation observed in the dataset.

Figure 2: Sample letters generated from the PCA shape model on 'e' (left) and 'g' (right) paths, generated randomly from parameters with $3\times$ the standard deviation observed in the dataset.

In [3], Chandra found that children aged 4-6 years participating in a handwriting peer tutoring pilot study most often made mistakes qualitatively classified as *internal proportions* (inappropriate proportion of the different strokes within a letter), or *global deformations* (overall deformation in the appearance of the letter). As exemplified in Figure 2, the shapes generated by the system exhibit the same kind of deformities. Chandra identifies other, less common, mistakes which involve topological changes, such as letters being broken into subparts or mirrored. Using a database of children's letters when available may yield potential for better parameterising these other mistakes. However, as an initial approximation, the shape models generated from PCA on a dataset of only adults' writing have shown to be well-suited to generate 'poor' letters that children were able to identify as such and successfully improve.

3.3 Responding to Feedback

In addition to generating letters by varying input parameters, the statistical shape model of Section 3.1 may also be used to determine a particular letter's parameters, given the model. The parameters of user-drawn letters may therefore be used in order implement a learning algorithm which adapts to the user's feedback via demonstration letters.

The statistical shape model is used to determine the parameters of a demonstration shape by projecting the features of the observed shape into the lower-dimensional space determined by the model. Mathematically, the parameters associated with a demonstration $\mathbf{x}_{demo}$ are determined as in (3) with $\mathbf{x} = \mathbf{x}_{demo}$, and will reconstruct the closest approximate shape.

The method we employ for responding to user demonstrations is to move the learning algorithm's parameters towards those of the demonstration. In the results presented in this work, the linear update equation shown in (5) is used, where $\mathbf{p}$ is the learned parameter vector at time step k, and α is the learning rate, between 0 and 1.

$$\mathbf{p}^{(k+1)} = \mathbf{p}^{(k)} + (\mathbf{p}_{demo} - \mathbf{p}^{(k)}) \times \alpha \qquad (5)$$

Figure 3 illustrates the response of the system to demonstrations from a child for the letter 's' using a learning rate of $\alpha = 1/2$. Observe that even poorly-written demonstrations allow the system to improve.

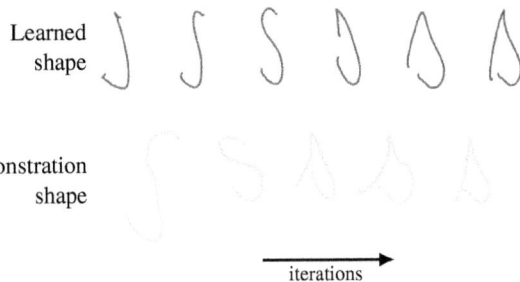

Figure 3: Example of the learning algorithm responding (top) to user demonstration of shapes (bottom) for the letter 's' (demonstrations received from two 7-8 year-old children taking turns).

It is possible that parameters $\mathbf{p}^{(k)}$ and $\mathbf{p}_{demo}$, which individually yield acceptable shapes, produce parameters $\mathbf{p}^{(k+1)}$ which yield an unacceptable shape. This is especially true if the demonstration shape is of a different style to that learnt at time k (see Figure 4), as there are no restrictions imposed on parameter values. However, the proposed method for adapting to the demonstration shapes has the advantage of being able to recover from such a situation: with further demonstrations of the same letter, the system would eventually approach the demonstration shape. As a result, the event of poor-looking intermediate letters would not limit the interaction later proposed in Section 5 in a technical sense, but it may influence the user's *perception* of the learning agent. It remains to be seen if it is necessary to avoid such an event mathematically.

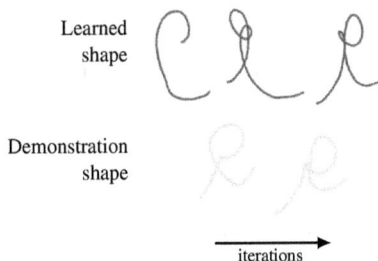

Figure 4: Example of the learning algorithm responding (top) to user demonstration of shapes (bottom) for the letter 'e', passing through a parameter state which yields a poor letter (demonstrations received from a 7-8 year-old child).

4. EMBODIMENT OF THE LEARNING AGENT WITH THE NAO HUMANOID ROBOT

In order to develop a teachable agent that is appropriate for engaging a child in the learning by teaching paradigm, we have established capabilities for the robot to engage in handwriting and interactive turn-taking.

The NAO V4 humanoid robot, which has been purposely designed by Aldebaran Robotics to look approachable [8], is used for this work. It is a commercially affordable biped robot, 58cm tall, with 25 degrees of freedom, two cameras, speech capabilities and the ability to autonomously execute a range of tasks.

Precise control over what the robot is writing is necessary in the proposed application of a handwriting. Because of the limited fine motor skills possible with such an affordable robot, in addition to the absence of force feedback and other technical necessities, we have configured the NAO to use simulated handwriting with a synchronised tablet to achieve this level of control.

The development of the necessary components for embedding the handwriting learning algorithm presented in Section 3 in the humanoid agent are presented in the sections which follow.

4.1 Robot Trajectory Following Movements

Using simulated handwriting provides an opportunity for the robot's writing to appear smoother than would be achievable with a writing instrument. However, the robot's motions must still sufficiently match the displayed trajectory in order capture the engagement of the child participant in the action. Aldebaran's NaoQi API is used for the inverse kinematics of the trajectory following. The Robot Operating System (ROS)[1] is used for integration of the NAO with external reference frames, such as the tablet's location, using the tf transformation library [7].

When using simulated handwriting, it is no longer necessary that the robot engages in the typical style of handwriting of using a writing instrument at a desk. Having the robot point at a vertical writing surface to cause the trajectory to appear (as in Figure 5) has several advantages:

- The working space of the robot increases, both in the technical sense and the interaction sense: someone can, in theory, show the tablet to the robot from across the room and have it still respond, without needing the tablet to be within arm's reach.

- Concerns about whether or not the child would start mimicking the robot's incorrect writing form (*e.g.* pen grip) are mitigated.

- Perhaps most significantly, the accuracy of the matching of the robot's motion with the trajectory displayed on the tablet is not as critical. This is because a pen tip would be expected to touch the tablet exactly at the trajectory point, while a fingertip may not.

We have therefore designed the system in such a way that the robot is simulating handwriting by pointing at the

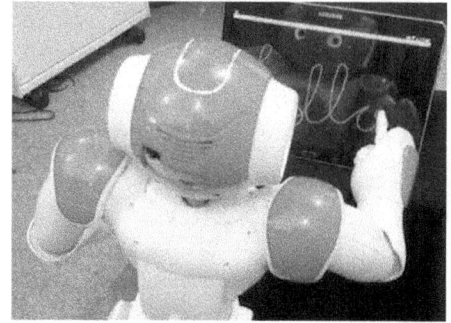

Figure 5: A demonstration of the robot simulating the writing of a word with its finger. The motion of the robot is synchronised with the display of the tablet, communicating over ROS.[3]

tablet[4]. As interacting with a tablet with one's finger is not uncommon, this may aid the acceptance of the writing style by users.

Because motion planning is performed with respect to the hand of the robot, rather than its fingertip, one or two of the orientation degrees of freedom of the hand are fixed to keep the finger approximately perpendicular to the writing surface, depending on the desired accuracy. The remaining free orientation(s), coupled with the whole-body motion control available, allow for a sufficient working space for writing on the entire tablet.

4.2 Synchronisation with the Tablet Trajectory Display

To enable the robot's 'writing' to display while the robot is tracing trajectories, ROS is used for the communication between the devices, including the Android tablet[5]. As a result, aspects of the networking between the tablet and the robot, such as the overheads associated with connections, ports, etc. have been simplified.

An Android application has been developed to receive the trajectory message over a ROS topic and display the trajectory as an animation. Synchronisation between the tablet and the robot is achieved by using NTP servers to synchronise device clocks; passing only the necessary number of points (7) to the robot's motion planner to improve timing accuracy; and not running computationally expensive tasks on the robot (such as camera publishing) while it is writing.

To instruct the robot where to write, the robot has been configured to detect a particular fiducial marker, a *chilitag*[6], with the camera located in its head, and to use that to determine the relative position of the writing surface (Figure 6). When used in an interaction involving a participant, this allows a user to move the tablet as required for the interaction. The tablet is assumed to be stationary during the

---

[1]The ROS stack for NAO is available at: http://wiki.ros.org/nao_robot.

[3]See https://www.youtube.com/watch?v=2qWFSJRxCU0 for a video of the synchronised writing demonstration.

[4]Teachers interviewed for their feedback on the system advised that children are asked to draw letters in the air in a similar manner as part of their handwriting education. The behaviour is hence not unfamiliar to children.

[5]For more information about ROS on Android devices see http://wiki.ros.org/android

[6]See https://github.com/chili-epfl/ros_markers for more information on the fiducial markers used.

writing process as detecting the tablet interferes with the robot's adherance to writing synchronisation.

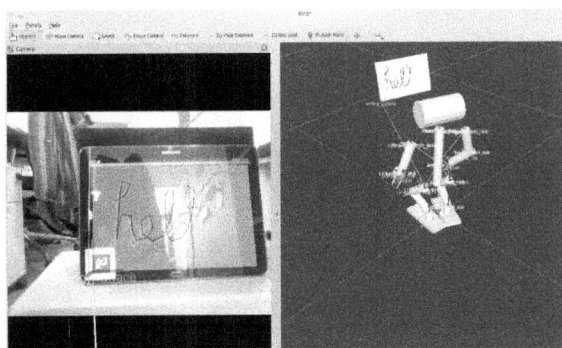

Figure 6: Detection of the tablet using a fiducial marker to represent the origin of the writing surface frame, visualised in RViz. The robot's camera image is on the left, with the text trajectory overlay visible.

4.3 Integration into a Teachable Robotic Agent

The fusion of the embodied handwriting agent developed with the handwriting learning algorithm presented in Section 3 involves the integration of three components: the robot, the tablet, and a central controller (Figure 7). The robot and Android tablet application present the writing process/result to the user, as explained in the previous section. The tablet application has been extended to act as the primary medium for capturing participant input, and submits the user's demonstrations when they are satisfied with their writing.

The user demonstrations are received by the interaction controller running on a desktop computer. It is responsible for getting the NAO to prompt and respond appropriately to feedback received using a finite state machine to manage the interaction stage and various system inputs. In the context of learning handwriting, an additional input to the system is a word from which the letters are to be learned, which is detected by a fiducial marker on the card displaying the word. The controller provides inputs to the learning algorithm including the word to learn and the user demonstrations, by inferring the letter which the demonstrations are intended for based on their position on the tablet. The output shapes from the learning algorithm are then sent again to the devices which write them.

The source code for the teachable robotic handwriting partner has been made available at https://github.com/chili-epfl/cowriter_letter_learning.

5. A TOOL FOR SOCIAL AND PEDAGOGICAL INVESTIGATIONS

In addition to constituting a technically novel system, the presented teachable robotic agent represents a tool which may be used for investigating social and pedagogical research questions. For example, one such question is what impact the addition of such a teachable robotic agent would have on the outcomes of a typical handwriting intervention. Preliminary studies at two schools in the Geneva area, involving over 50 children, have been conducted to evaluate the feasibility and technical soundness of the interaction system

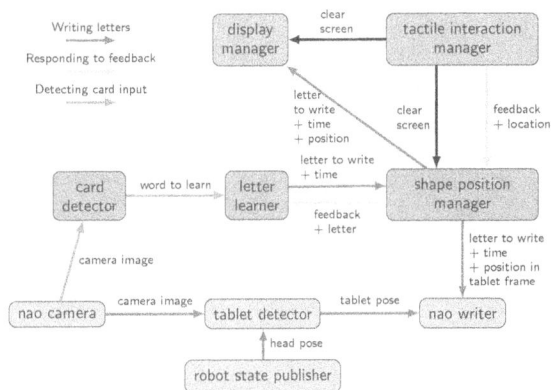

Figure 7: Overview of the system. Components in the top row run on the tablet, those in the middle row on the central controller, and those in the bottom row on the robot.

proposed as a tool for such investigations.

5.1 Interaction Context

Figure 8 illustrates an example interaction sequence between the participant and the robot which consists of the following stages:

1. The participant shows the robot one of seven different 3-letter words to write, made up of 7 possible letters ('c', 'e', 'n', 'o', 's', 'u', 'w'). Fiducial markers which are printed on the word cards allow them to be detected with the robot's camera.

2. The robot responds to the word request verbally and writes the letters according to the method described in Section 4.2.

3. The robot asks for feedback from the participant and they demonstrate how to write the letter which they feel needs to be corrected. The tablet may be moved into the most appropriate position for the child to write on it with the stylus. Only one letter may be demonstrated at a time and the position of the participant's demonstration on the tablet encodes the letter that it is a demonstration for. The participant can remove and repeat their letter if they are unhappy with it. When the participant is satisfied with the demonstration, they press a button on the tablet which signals that it is the robot's turn.

4. The robot writes an adapted letter in response to the participant's feedback, and the interaction iterates, with participants taking turns to interact with the robot if necessary. When the participant(s) is/are satisfied with the robot's performance on all letters, they may use the "test" card and an additional word for which they will verbally evaluate the robot's performance.

5.2 Outcomes of Preliminary Study 1

A pilot study at the first school consisted of four groups of approximately 8 english-speaking children each, aged 6-7 years. The children interacted with the system for a total of 65 minutes, with the robot writing 96 letters. 49 of

(a) The user shows a card to the robot with a word to write.

(b) The robot writes the word seen on the card and asks for feedback.

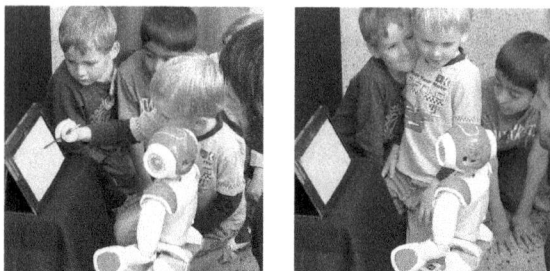

(c) The user provides feedback on the letters written via demonstration.

(d) The robot responds to the feedback, until the user is satisfied.

Figure 8: A user engaging with the robot in the *learning by teaching* interaction, using demonstrations as feedback.

these letters were in response to demonstrations from the children and the remaining were from when new words were requested.

As a result of the pilot study, we acted on two key observations. The first was that children appeared to have a difficult time providing demonstrations to the robot in the same place as previously-written letters. At the time, the system required the children to write on top of a letter of the same type as the one which they were demonstrating, and the children seemed to find this counter-intuitive and would occasionally just trace the robot's letter as it appeared. As such, the technical components of the system were extended to allow the children the opportunity to write around previously-written letters instead of on top.

The second key point which came from the pilot study was that children were observed giving advice to the child designated as the letter demonstrator, potentially giving rise to a higher level paradigm of learning by *teaching to teach*. As a consequence of this observation, the study which followed at the second school was designed to further observe the effect of the number of children interacting with the robot.

5.3 Outcomes of Preliminary Study 2

The study at the second school involved 21 french-speaking students aged 7-8 years. 7 children interacted with the robot individually and 7 sessions included the remaining 14 students interacting with the robot in pairs. Initial parameters were drawn from a range purposely chosen to generate shapes for letters 'e' and 's' which would elicit correction. For the other letters, parameters were fixed, generating

shapes which some groups still chose to correct (e.g. 13/14 for 'n' and 2/14 for 'c'). The duration of the sessions was between 8 and 15 minutes, with an average of 11.4 minutes (SD = 2.3).

We have concluded following the second study that the system has been validated as a technically sound autonomous interaction. The interaction setup including the teachable robotic agent withstood the interaction which lasted for a total of 160 minutes. During this time the robot wrote 335 letters, 152 of which in response to demonstrations received from the 21 children. Technical intervention was only required for the three instances that the robot fell later in the day. Otherwise, the technical components of the system operated autonomously and as expected over the sessions.

Furthermore, no child indicated that they did not believe that the robot was writing by itself. There were, at times, questions about the robot's writing method at the beginning of the interaction, but when advised that the robot "tells the tablet what it wants to write," this was accepted by the children. On the rare occasion that the robot's writing was not correctly synchronised with the tablet, this did not appear to influence the children's impression. If older children participate in the interaction study – which may be likely as children with lasting handwriting difficulties are included as participants – it may become more important to invest time into the believability of the robot's writing scheme. However, for 6-8 year olds the proposed setup appears sufficient.

Regarding the engagement of the children in teaching the robot, an average of 10.9 demonstration letters (SD = 4.4) were provided to the robot for each session during the interaction. In 9 out of the 14 sessions (64%), the robot received demonstration letters even *after* reaching the test stage of the interaction. The participants' teaching after the test word had been written and evaluated – the only purposefully imposed external motivation – may suggest that by that time the participants had become intrinsically motivated to engage in the interaction, as we anticipated.

6. TOWARDS LONG-TERM STUDIES

A conclusion drawn in a systematic review of handwriting intervention studies [10] is that any of the studies considered which involved fewer than two practice sessions per week and fewer than a total of 20 practice sessions, including homework, were not found to demonstrate effective results. This highlights the necessity to engage students in an interaction which will be sustainable over the long-term if we want to address research questions which involve the measurement of learning gains. Several challenges are raised in developing such long-term capabilities for the system.

In terms of the interaction experience, the current experimental setting, while technically autonomous, can not robustly recover from situations outside of the nominal protocol presented in Section 5, and consequently still requires the supervision of an experimenter. The interaction finite state machine would require extension in non-trivial ways to allow for long, fully autonomous interactions with children.

In the current system, the robot can ask questions and prompt participants, but it cannot engage in discussions with the participants. It is clear that work is necessary to develop the conversational agent in the interaction so that the presence of an experimenter is not required for a captivating and continuing engagement. While there is the possiblity to focus the interaction design on group-based interaction with the robot in order to alleviate the necessity of a conversational agent, we find reason to believe that constructing such a social interaction is not a trivial task. Anecdotes from the preliminary studies have shown that some children may criticise another's demonstrations to the robot, which may or may not be as damaging to a child's self-efficacy as when they are criticised in a typical educational context.

How the children's perception of the robot as a learning agent may change over the long-term remains to be seen. On one occasion during the preliminary studies, a child's response to whether or not the NAO could write its own name (not previously demonstrated) included that it may have problems with the 'n', as the child had been correcting the robot on this letter. We believe that the user was projecting human-like learning features, such as forgetfulness, onto the robot, although they were not technically present in the system. This may need to be capitalised on when considering how to extend the interaction for long-term use, as the present system – with a learning rate such that progress is evident to the user – will cause convergence for a letter within a few iterations.

We expect that incorporating a database of letters drawn by children into the shape modeling process will facilitate generating shape models which capture a wider range of mistakes typical of children learning handwriting. However, the current system has conceptual – a PCA-only approach can not generate or learn a different shape topology – and technical – no support is currently implemented for shapes which require pen lifting between strokes – limitations which would need to be overcome.

If the system is extended to allow for a wider range of mistakes, a further topic for exploration then is how the handwriting error generation of the system may be abstracted to a higher level of control so that a teacher may configure it to work with a child on a particular type of mistakes based on the child's performance. Where would the balance lie between developing autonomous capabilities for the system to determine the child's difficulties and empowering the teaching staff to decide for themselves instead?

Addressing these challenges will take us further towards answering if the addition of a teachable robotic agent to handwriting interventions would benefit the participants' self-esteem, motivation, and learning gains.

7. IMPACT AND CONCLUSION

We believe that this article introduces three noteworthy contributions: an innovative application of data processing and artificial intelligence for the learning of hand-written letters suitable for educative purposes; a robotic system which was able to provide scaffolding for complex human-robot interactions (teacher-learner social interactions, learning by demonstration, simulated robotic fine motor skills) during two preliminaries studies; and an initial experimental investigation of what appears to be a new role for robots in education.

Specifically, the technical challenges involved in developing a teachable robotic agent in the context of handwriting which have been addressed in this work include:

- developing capabilities for a robot with limited fine motor capabilities, in particular the NAO robot, to engage in the act of handwriting in a way which is believable for interacting with children. This is accomplished

by leveraging simulated handwriting with a synchronised tablet communicating via ROS;

- developing an algorithm capable of incorporating user feedback and demonstrations in order to adapt artificially generated handwriting quality so as to simulate a teachable agent, which has been implemented by maintaining a learning algorithm in the parameter space of the PCA-based shape models and converging towards the parameters of user demonstrations; and

- integrating the system into a working interaction suitable for engaging children in the learning by teaching paradigm, accomplished by fusing the robotic drawing capabilities and the learning algorithm for handwritten letters established with a central controller which manages the flow of the interaction, turn taking and integration of the connected devices.

However, we believe that the strongest impact of this work is for the human-robot interaction community and relates to the very *nature* of the interaction fostered by this research. The work presented here investigates a particular role for a robot in the education of handwriting: not only is the robot actively performing the activity by drawing letters, but it does so in a way that engages the child in a very specific social role. The child is the teacher in this relationship and the robot is the learner: the child must engage in a (meta-) cognitive relationship with the robot to try to understand why the robot fails and how to help it best. Here, the robot is more than just an activity facilitator or orchestrator – its physical presence and embodiment induce agency and anthropomorphising, and cognitively engage the child into the learning activity, which we predict will lead to higher learning efficacy.

Also notable, the robot is not used in the usual context of robotics or computer education, but instead in an activity – handwriting – which requires fine physical skills. In such activities, the embodied nature of the robot is appropriate as in interventions where motor mimicry is elicited [2] the arm motion for instance is, *by itself*, part of the teaching. Furthermore, when facing a child with school difficulties, robots can play the role of a naïve learner which neither adults nor peers – because of the social effects it would induce – can convincingly play. Along these lines, we hope to see more research on non-STEM educational applications of robotics.

The strong social impact of early educational problems makes continued research in this field an undoubtedly meaningful challenge for robotics and human-robot interaction.

Acknowledgments

This research was supported by the Swiss National Science Foundation through the National Centre of Competence in Research Robotics.

8. REFERENCES

[1] W. A. Bainbridge, J. W. Hart, E. S. Kim, and B. Scassellati. The benefits of interactions with physically present robots over video-displayed agents. *International Journal of Social Robotics*, 3(1):41–52, 2011.

[2] V. W. Berninger, K. B. Vaughan, R. D. Abbott, S. P. Abbott, L. W. Rogan, A. Brooks, E. Reed, and

S. Graham. Treatment of handwriting problems in beginning writers: Transfer from handwriting to composition. *Journal of Educational Psychology*, 89(4):652, 1997.

[3] S. Chandra. Co-writer: Learning to write with a robot, Dec. 2013. [Internal report, EPFL].

[4] C. C. Chase, D. B. Chin, M. A. Oppezzo, and D. L. Schwartz. Teachable agents and the protégé effect: Increasing the effort towards learning. *Journal of Science Education and Technology*, 18(4):334–352, 2009.

[5] C. A. Christensen. The Role of Orthographic–Motor Integration in the Production of Creative and Well-Structured Written Text for Students in Secondary School. *Educational Psychology*, 25(5):441–453, Oct. 2005.

[6] B. Engel-Yeger, L. Nagauker-Yanuv, and S. Rosenblum. Handwriting performance, self-reports, and perceived self-efficacy among children with dysgraphia. *The American Journal of Occupational Therapy*, 63(2):182–192, 2009.

[7] T. Foote. tf: The transform library. In *Technologies for Practical Robot Applications (TePRA), 2013 IEEE International Conference on*, pages 1–6. IEEE, 2013.

[8] D. Gouaillier, V. Hugel, P. Blazevic, C. Kilner, J. Monceaux, P. Lafourcade, B. Marnier, J. Serre, and B. Maisonnier. The NAO humanoid: a combination of performance and affordability. *CoRR*, 2008.

[9] J. Han. Robot-Aided Learning and r-Learning Services. In D. Chugo, editor, *Human-Robot Interaction*. InTech, 2010.

[10] M. M. P. Hoy, M. Y. Egan, and K. P. Feder. A systematic review of interventions to improve handwriting. *Canadian Journal of Occupational Therapy*, 78(1):13–25, Feb. 2011.

[11] C. D. Kidd and C. Breazeal. Robots at home: Understanding long-term human-robot interaction. In *Intelligent Robots and Systems, 2008. IROS 2008. IEEE/RSJ International Conference on*, pages 3230–3235. IEEE, 2008.

[12] D. Leyzberg, S. Spaulding, M. Toneva, and B. Scassellati. The physical presence of a robot tutor increases cognitive learning gains. In *Proceedings of the 34th Annual Conference of the Cognitive Science Society. Austin, TX: Cognitive Science Society*, 2012.

[13] D. Llorens, F. Prat, A. Marzal, J. M. Vilar, M. J. Castro, J.-C. Amengual, S. Barrachina, A. Castellanos, J. Gómez, et al. The UJIpenchars database: a pen-based database of isolated handwritten characters.

[14] T. Malloy-Miller, H. Polatajko, and B. Anstett. Handwriting error patterns of children with mild motor difficulties. *Canadian Journal of Occupational Therapy*, 62(5):258–267, 1995.

[15] A. Matsui and S. Katsura. A method of motion reproduction for calligraphy education. In *Mechatronics (ICM), 2013 IEEE International Conference on*, pages 452–457. IEEE, 2013.

[16] J. Medwell and D. Wray. Handwriting – a forgotten language skill? *Language and Education*, 22(1):34–47, 2008.

[17] K. Mülling, J. Kober, O. Kroemer, and J. Peters. Learning to select and generalize striking movements in robot table tennis. *The International Journal of Robotics Research*, 32(3):263–279, 2013.

[18] C. A. Rohrbeck, M. D. Ginsburg-Block, J. W. Fantuzzo, and T. R. Miller. Peer-assisted learning interventions with elementary school students: A meta-analytic review. *Journal of Educational Psychology*, 95(2):240–257, 2003.

[19] J. Saunders, C. L. Nehaniv, and C. Lyon. Robot learning of lexical semantics from sensorimotor interaction and the unrestricted speech of human tutors. In *Proc. 2nd Int. Symp. New Frontiers Human–Robot Interact. ASIB Convent*, 2010.

[20] M. B. Stegmann and D. D. Gomez. A brief introduction to statistical shape analysis. *Informatics and Mathematical Modelling, Technical University of Denmark, DTU*, 15, 2002.

[21] F. Tanaka and S. Matsuzoe. Children teach a care-receiving robot to promote their learning: Field experiments in a classroom for vocabulary learning. *Journal of Human-Robot Interaction*, 1(1), 2012.

[22] J. Werfel. Embodied teachable agents: Learning by teaching robots. In *Intelligent Autonomous Systems, The 13th International Conference on*, 2013.

Can Children Catch Curiosity from a Social Robot?

Goren Gordon
Personal Robots Group, MIT
Media Lab
20 Ames Street E15-468
Cambridge, MA 02139
goren@gorengordon.com

Cynthia Breazeal
Personal Robots Group, MIT
Media Lab
20 Ames Street E15-468
Cambridge, MA 02139
cynthiab@media.mit.edu

Susan Engel
Department of Psychology
Bronfman Science Center
Williams College
Williamstown MA 01267
Susan.engel@williams.edu

ABSTRACT

Curiosity is key to learning, yet school children show wide variability in their eagerness to acquire information. Recent research suggests that other people have a strong influence on children's exploratory behavior. Would a curious robot elicit children's exploration and the desire to find out new things? In order to answer this question we designed a novel experimental paradigm in which a child plays an education tablet app with an autonomous social robot, which is portrayed as a younger peer. We manipulated the robot's behavior to be either curiosity-driven or not and measured the child's curiosity after the interaction. We show that some of the child's curiosity measures are significantly higher after interacting with a curious robot, compared to a non-curious one, while others do not. These results suggest that interacting with an autonomous social curious robot can selectively guide and promote children's curiosity.

Categories and Subject Descriptors

K.3.1 [**Computers and Education**]: Computer Uses in Education; I.2.9 [**Artificial Intelligence**]: Robotics

Keywords

children education;autonomous robot behavior;dragonbot

1. INTRODUCTION

Curiosity is the basic drive to ask questions and to better understand events. Even in infancy and early childhood, curiosity enables young learners to acquire evidence and develop models of how the world works [19]. As children get older and enter school, intrinsic curiosity is still the main drive for efficient learning even with great teachers [14, 6]. The question then arises: what influences the basic curiosity drive in young children? One relatively unmapped influence is social interaction, i.e. how interactions with other individuals, be they more curious or less, influence the internal motivation to learn [7].

It has been shown that social cues are of paramount importance in language learning in children [17], as well as changing their mindset [4] and consequently their academic achievements [3]. Recursively, a decrease in intrinsic motivation changes the mindset into into a fixed one [9]. Furthermore, during late childhood, adolescence and adulthood, the curiosity drive declines [6, 7]. Though previous research has identified some of the ways in which adults encourage or discourage children's expressions of curiosity [12], very little research has examined the effects of peers on a child's expressions of curiosity. We thus wish to explore whether curiosity in young children can be manipulated and increased by robotic peer interaction.

Social robots have been used in recent years as educational companions to children, teaching them new vocabulary, math concepts and social skills. It has been shown that children can treat robots as informants [18], but how will a child react to a robot's curiosity driven behavior? Can a child "catch" curiosity from a curious social robot? In other words, can interaction with a curious robot promote children's curiosity?

To address this question, we performed an exploratory study in which we manipulated the behavior of an autonomous social robot interacting with children in an educational setting. The interaction involved a novel Story-maker app co-played on a tablet by the child and robot, wherein the child manipulates characters on the tablet and the robot tells an appropriate story. The story is also written on the tablet, thus promoting reading skills. Furthermore, the robot is portrayed as a younger peer that tries to learn to read, prompting the child to teach it new words.

During the interaction, the robot is either curious or not, where in our experimental paradigm a curious robot behaves with enthusiasm about learning and exploration, challenges the child and suggests novel moves on the tablet app. The non-curious robot plays with the child, asks her to show it words, yet does not express any overt or explicit desire to learn new things. We quantified children's curiosity after the interaction via three different measures: free exploration, question generation and uncertainty seeking tasks. We show that free exploration and uncertainty seeking are significantly higher after interacting with a curious robot compared to a non-curious one, whereas question generation is unaffected by the manipulation. These results confirm that at-least some aspects of children's curiosity can be increased by interacting with an autonomous social robot.

2. RELATED WORK

Children's curiosity has been studied using different quantifiable measures, which we adapted to our study. **Free exploration:** One measure relates to actively seeking information by opening novel boxes, quantifying different aspects of the behavior, e.g. approach time to the box, number of different boxes opened [11]. We have developed a novel digital version of this free exploration measure, to be used in tablet-related interactions. **Fish task:** We used a recently developed uncertainty seeking tablet app, called "The Fish Task" [13], which addresses children's desire to choose options containing unknown, probabilistic results more than certain and deterministic ones. **Question generation:** We used an established and more qualitatively-derived measure, namely, the question generation task in which the child is prompted to ask as many questions about a topic, without providing answers [10]. The latter condition is imperative, since it was shown that answering the question generates conversation irrespective of the intrinsic motivation to know [5]. We used all three measures to address the question of whether there are different aspects of curiosity [15] and whether they can be manipulated by a social robot.

Children's change in curiosity has been investigated in previous studies. In Ref. [12], the presence of an adult and the context of her behavior was shown to influence a child's free exploration behavior. A series of studies [19] have shown that infants explore more if their prior beliefs are violated, i.e. if they see evidence that contradicts their expectations. Furthermore, it was shown, through manipulation of child-toy-experimenter interaction that if evidence fails to distinguish among competing beliefs, infants explore more to disambiguate their beliefs [19]. In another study, the effects of personal curiosity traits and the school environment on academic achievements have been shown to be complex, namely, high curiosity children in challenging schools had the highest performance, whereas high curiosity children in non-challenging school had the lowest [14]. We ask whether a robotic peer, as opposed to a parent, experimenter or school environment, can change a child's curiosity.

Social robots have been used previously to teach children new material. In [18], RUBI-4, a humanoid robot with a tablet embedded in its midsection, played simple vocabulary games with preschool children. In [21] the experimenter asked either the preschool child or the robot to act out novel verbs. They found that teaching the robot helped children remember the verbs, as well as inspiring further teaching-verbs play. In contrast to these studies, we wish to not only make the children learn new things, but promote their drive to learn and explore, i.e. increase their inherent curiosity.

3. EXPERIMENTAL SETUP

The experimental setup is composed of the robot, tablet, cameras and microphones, Fig. 1(left). The tablet had three apps that were used during the experiment, namely, the main Story-maker app and two curiosity-assessment apps: Free exploration app and the Fish task app [13]. All taps and interactions with the tablet were recorded.

3.1 Robotic platform

For the social robotic platform we used Dragonbot [20], a squash-and-stretch Android smartphone based robot. The facial expression, sound generation and part of the logic is generated on the smartphone, which is mounted on the face

Figure 1: Experimental setup (left) and screenshot from the Story-maker app (right)

of the robot. The robot appears to be a soft, furry, fanciful creature that is designed to engage children. Dragonbot is a very expressive platform and has a large repertoire of possible facial expressions and actions (indicated in *italics* below). We installed a commercial child-like voice for the text-to-speech software on the smartphone, to facilitate a more generic and engaging interaction. The robot was autonomous and was not controlled by a remote operator. It reacted to the child's interaction with the tablet.

3.2 Story-maker app

The main tablet app was a novel Story-maker app we developed for this study, which enables the child to co-create a story with the robot, Fig. 1(right). The game contains several characters that the child can move. After each movement, a sentence is automatically generated using a novel auto-generation mechanism, which (i) randomly selects an adjective for the character; (ii) detects the closest other character for the story interaction; (iii) follows an xml script of the plot of the story; and (iv) uses an open-source natural language generation library [8] to construct a full sentence.

The xml plot files are constructed in a generic fashion, such that (i) each character has a list of possible adjectives (e.g. red, big), motions (e.g. fly, jump) and speech (e.g. roar, squeak); (ii) the plot line is constructed of a sequence of movements, speech, feelings and resolutions; and (iii) the story conversation is constructed such that any sequence of character selection generates a coherent story line. The result of each movement is thus a full sentence that describes the progression of the story plot. After several such sentences, the scene changes and new characters are introduced, while some of the old ones are taken away. There are three scenes to the story, which ends with a final resolution sentence.

This is a sample text from a generated story: *Butterfly whispers to bird: What happened to dragon? The purple dragon flies to the bird. Dragon roars to bird: I lost my ball. Dragon says to the wild butterfly: Can you help me find my ball? Butterfly whispers: I think I saw the ball near the pine tree.*

This app was designed to promote the child's feeling of control over the interaction, in the sense that the story told correlated to the child's actions. Furthermore, the pace of the story was dictated by the child. Several features were integrated into this app to maintain engagement and interest, important aspects that affect curiosity [1]. The first was the selection of the story's protagonist. The child could select out of two options, namely, a dragon or a bird. The story plot followed that selection throughout. The second feature was the introduction of multiple scenes, each with its unique characters, wherein only the protagonist and its sidekick moved from one scene to the next. This introduced variability and novelty in the story. The third was an insertion of a "silly' sentence into the story, e.g. "the dragon burps". This kept the child more engaged in the story. The fourth feature was the variability of language complexity throughout the story. More complex words were deliberately introduced, e.g. "spacious", "anxious", to keep even older children engaged. The fifth feature was the introduction of an antagonist, i.e. a character who is detrimental to the main plot.

3.3 Subjects

71 subjects participated in the study. 7 of the subjects did not speak or cooperate during the task and 1 had a technical difficulty and were thus excluded. Out of the remaining 63, only 48 (21 female, 27 male) completed the initial assessment and the task and were included in the analysis. Subjects were randomized across conditions and ages, but analysis and exclusion occurred after the study was finished, resulting in slightly different number of subjects across conditions. The average age was 6 (1.23 standard-deviation), with children ages 3.4-8.4 years old, Fig. 2(inset).

The subjects were recruited from a compiled mailing list of local social media family groups. 13 of the subjects previously interacted with the same robotic platform in an earlier study in our lab. These were evenly distributed across conditions.

4. PROTOCOL

Initial assessment: reading skills. During the introduction to the study, the child is asked to spell her name, and is informed that she is going to play word games with the experimenter and then with the robot. We informed the participants that if they are bored or do not wish to continue, they can stop the interaction whenever they wanted. The first "word game" is the TOWRE word assessment test [22], in which the experimenter asks the child to read words from lists, as fast as she could, for 45 seconds. The raw TOWRE score is defined as the total number of correctly read words during these 45 seconds. We administered both sight and phonetic word lists, where the total raw score is the sum of the two tests' raw score.

Robot introduction. The child then sits next to a small table upon which there is a tablet and the robot, Fig. 1(left). The robot is "sleeping", i.e. its eyes are closed, and it is introduced as "Parle, a young robot that just learned how to speak and wants to learn to read". This was said since the text-to-speech module used was sometimes unclear to the children, and we wished them to feel comfortable to ask when they did not understand it. The robot awakens, *yawns* (an overt motion and sound), and introduces itself: "I am Parle, we are going to play word games together." It then makes a *shy* facial expression.

Reading pre-test. The next phase of interaction is a pre-test, during which the robot asks the child to teach it some words. It verbally asks the child to show it a word, e.g. "dragon", whereupon the word, and four distractors appear on the tablet. The child then needs to tap on the correct word. The words asked are selected from the entire vocabulary, according to a novel expected information-gain algorithm that attempts to maximize the knowledge the robot has on the child's reading skill. The algorithm is based on Bayesian updates of a vocabulary of words, based on the

child's answers of the prompted questions and is reported in detail in another publication under review. The four distractors are also selected from the same vocabulary: two words which are most similar; one word that the child should know, according to the assessment algorithm; and one word that the child should not know how to read. This is repeated ten times, to get a thorough assessment of the child's reading knowledge.

Child-robot co-play. The main phase of the interaction is based on the Story-maker app described above. The robot asks the child "do you want to play with me and create our own story?" The child needs to tap on a "yes" or a "no". If the child taps "no", the robot makes a *shy* face and asks again "do you want to play with me?" (The robot does not take no for an answer). When the child taps "yes" the robot *laughs*, says "that's great" and prompts the child to select the protagonist of the story. After it is selected, the robot instructs the child how to play: "you move the characters around and I will tell the story. The game will help us if we have trouble reading." The tablet then speaks, in a different voice, "move one of the characters. A sentence will be written on top." This creates a clear separation between robot and tablet, in the sense that the robot plays with the child and the tablet informs them about the written words and sentences.

During the child-tablet-robot interaction, when the child moves a character, the autonomous robot first speaks the generated sentence, and then the sentence appears on the tablet above the scene. In 50% of the sentences, the robot asks the child to show it a word, e.g. "I don't know how to read the word dragon. Can you show it to me?". This resulted in an average of 11 words per interaction. In the first two questions, the robot also says "look in the sentence above the colorful picture" in order to direct the child where to look. The child is then required to tap on the correct word. Each tapping on a word on the tablet results in the tablet speaking that word. In this sense, the tablet is an informant, whereas the child and robot are both the students. If the child is correct, the robot says "yes" in an excited voice, thanks the child and the story continues. If the child is wrong, the robot expresses *frustration* and asks the word again. If the child is wrong again, the tablet shows the correct word in an emphasized manner and speaks it. If the child moves a character instead of tapping the word, the robot makes a *thinking* expression and says "ok, let's continue". Additionally, at the beginning of a new scene, the robot says "move a character to hear the next sentence" so as to direct the child what to do in this new scene. The game continues until the end of the story, when the robot says: "The End. That was a great story."

Reading post-test. In the last stage of the interaction, the post-test, the robot again asks the child to teach it some words, similar to the pre-test phase. During this phase, the words that were asked during the story phase are asked again, starting with the incorrectly identified words, then the correctly identified and finally random words. A total of ten words are asked during this phase.

Robot behavior. In order to increase believability and engagement with the autonomous robot, we inserted randomness to the expressions and sentences the robot asked, so as to avoid boring repetition. During the pre- and post-test phases, the robot asked: "Can you show me the word X?", "That is a new word, X. Can you tap on it?", "I don't know the word X. Can you show it to me." This increased diversity and randomness in the robot's behavior is suggested to be essential for the children's engagement, a major factor in educational interactions [1].

During the story phase, the robot made some silly comments, to increase plausibility of it being a younger peer. During the game, the robot followed 10% of the child's movements on the tablet with "that motion is funny. Maybe the story should go like this." or "I'm not sure what to say now. Let me try something." In 10% of the scene change, the robot says "I might surprise you with some silliness". Additionally, during the silly sentence the Story-maker app generated, the robot *laughed* and said "this is silly", so as to be part of the game and interaction.

When the child pressed the correct word and the tablet also spoke it, the robot said "it helps me that when you touch a word the game speaks it" or "did you hear the game speak the word?" This was designed to encourage the child to press on more words in order to hear them.

Interaction end. The robot interaction ended with the robot yawning and saying: "I am tired now. I think I will go to sleep. It was great playing with you. I hope we can do it again sometimes. See you. Bye bye" The robot's eyes closed and it did not move anymore. This part was a clear delineation between the robot interaction and the final assessment, which we required the child to perform alone. All the children accepted this termination, e.g. none of them asked "why is it sleeping?", or "can we wake it up?".

Post-interaction assessments. After the robot went to sleep, we administered the Free exploration task, during which the child played the task and we questioned the parent about the interaction: "Do you think your child learned something new from this interaction?" When the Free exploration task was over, we questioned the child about the interaction and the robot. At the end of the questionnaire, we administered the question generation task, followed by the Fish task.

5. CONDITIONS

There were three conditions to the study, namely, curious tablet ($n = 13$, 7 male, 6 female), curious robot ($n = 16$, 11 male, 5 female) and non-curious robot ($n = 19$, 9 male, 10 female), where only subjects that completed each task were considered. The non-curious robot behaved as a compelling playmate, as described in the previous section, without any overt expressions of curiosity. The curious tablet and the curious robot were identical in all but two aspects: (i) in the curious tablet condition the robot was covered by a box, i.e. the child did not see the robot at all and; (ii) the experimenter introduction was "you are going to play with a virtual agent, Parle."

The curious robot had several behaviors that expressed curiosity. In its own introduction, the curious robot said "I want to learn to read. I hope you can teach me some words." The non-curious robot, on the other hand, said "lets start." Another curious behavior was the overt expression of enthusiasm of learning. It said: "I love to learn" or "I want to know more" before asking a new question; "it is always great to learn something new" or "that is a great word to know" after it was shown a correct word; after the robot addressed the tablet's spoken words, the curious robot said "this way we can both learn how to read" or "I love to learn this way"; "I love getting it wrong sometimes. This is how you learn

new things" after the tablet showed the correct word; after the child moved a character instead of tapping on a word, the robot said "I am also eager to see what happens".

Another expression of curiosity is the wonder and imagination of future events. 25% of the time, prior to the child's movement the curious robot said either "I wonder what would happen if dragon goes to talk to butterfly", where "dragon" and "butterfly" are characters in the Story-maker app and the sentence changed in respect to the characters in each scene; or "I love trying new things. Can you move another character?" Furthermore, at the beginning of each new scene, it exclaimed enthusiastically and said "a new scene. I wonder what you would do now."

Lastly, the curious robot selected specific words to ask the child during the interaction, based on the assessment algorithm. It asked about the word that had the closest probability to 50% that the child knows how to read it, in spirit to Vygotsky's zone of proximal development. If the child knew perfectly how to read, e.g. an older child, the robot asked about the longest word in the sentence. This behavior guaranteed to challenge the child during the interaction [14], another characteristic of a curious peer. The non-curious robot, on the other hand, asked about a random word in the sentence, thus sometimes asking too hard a word and most of the time too easy.

The difference between the curious and non-curious conditions during the entire 15 minute interaction amounted to a total of roughly 10-15 expressions.

6. CURIOSITY MEASURES

6.1 Free exploration

The first measure was the Free exploration task, which used the same graphics as the main Story-maker app. In this app there were four characters from the story app and three new ones. The child could move any character and that generated a spoken sentence (by the tablet) as well as a written one. Each movement generated a new sentence, even of the same character, such that each new active interaction with the app generated a novel sentence the child was exposed to. The child could also tap on a word and hear it. The game lasted for two minutes and then ended.

This measure was used right after the robot interaction ended with the sleeping robot. The experimenter said to the child: "I am going to ask your parent some questions. In the meantime you can play this game. Do whatever you want with it." This measure and its framing had several reasons: (i) The adults, i.e. parent and experimenter, were removed from the scene so as to allow the child to express her own inner curiosity [12]. (ii) There were no limitations or suggestions on the things the child could do, thus enabling free exploration. (iii) The child had control over the amount of information she was exposed to.

Children started the game at different times, sometimes not understanding they should play the game while their parent has gone, while others waited for more confirmation on when they should start. Hence, each child that played the Free exploration game, played for a different amount of time. We thus considered only the first 60 seconds after the first interaction with the app, such that the measure indicates the true interaction with the game.

Several measures were considered, such as whether the subject first interacted with the new characters, total number of characters moved, etc. These measures were too discretized and constant across all subjects and were thus not used. A more theory-based measure was selected, namely, the active seeking of new information, here experienced via hearing new sentences. The normalized curiosity measure we used was the portion of the 60 seconds that the tablet spoke, i.e. that the child was exposed to new information. Thus a normalized measure of 0.5 means that 30 seconds out of the first 60 seconds of interaction the child moved characters that prompted the tablet to speak new sentences, each approximately spoken for 2 seconds. A higher measure means the child moved many characters that resulted in many different sentences, whereas a lower measure means the child did not move many characters and hence was not exposed to novel information. 8 children quit playing before 60 seconds have passed and were thus excluded from the analysis.

6.2 Question generation

The second measure was question generation [10, 6]. The experimenter said to the subject: "I am going to make a movie on the robot and game so that people who can't come here can learn of them. I want you to ask me as many questions as you can about the robot and I will answer them in the movie. What do you want to know about the robot?" The framing of the question was done for the following reasons: (i) The questions should not be answered during this assessment. (ii) The "movie" was the rationale of why to ask and why the experimenter did not answer. (iii) The entire framing was sometimes too complex for young children, hence we added the last sentence to clarify that we want them to ask questions.

The question generation task came after an extensive questionnaire administered to the participants. Hence, some of the children simply repeated these questions when prompted to ask questions about the robot or agent. We only considered *novel* questions, i.e. questions that were different than the ones the experimenter asked, as "questions generated" by the participants, since we were interested in their self-generated inquiries. Thus, the measure was taken to be binary: zero for no questions asked and one for any number of novel questions asked. 3 children did not talk or cooperate during this task and were thus excluded from the analysis.

6.3 Uncertainty-seeking

The third and last measure was the Fish task app [13]. This app is portrayed as a game in which the children are in a submarine with two windows. They can open one window and see a fish through it. The two windows differ in the uncertainty of which fish will be outside. Thus one window is presented with one fish next to it, indicating that with certainty that fish is outside the window. Another window can be presented with, e.g. 5 fish next to it, indicating that one of those five fish is outside the window, but the child cannot know until she opens it. Thus, the child needs to select which window to open, i.e. which amount of uncertainty she seeks. The app is cleverly designed to explore many differences in uncertainty in a repetitive yet step-wise manner. There are 18 turns, i.e. selections to be made, in the game, wherein the largest amount of uncertainty is 7 fish.

We used the normalized measure of the total amount of uncertainty selected, i.e. number of fish next to the window opened, divided by the maximum amount of uncertainty possible, i.e. $18 \times 7 = 126$. Thus, a child who seeks only

uncertainty will always select the window with the maximal number of fish next to it and will get the score of 1. A child who seeks certainty will always select the window with one fish next to it and receive the score of 0.1417.

15 children did not complete the Fish task game and were thus excluded from the analysis. Due to its length, this task was administered at the end of the session, that lasted around 30 minutes. This may account for the high drop rate of this task.

7. HYPOTHESIS

The main hypothesis of this study is that interacting with a curious social robot is contagious, i.e. that curiosity of children, quantified by the curiosity measures described above, will be significantly higher for children interacting with a curious robot than with a non-curious robot.

However, we hypothesize a more subtle result, based on our understanding of the different types of curiosity [15]. We measured three measures, each one corresponding to a different aspect of curiosity, namely, free exploration, question generation and uncertainty seeking. However, the curious robot in our study, while expressing several curiosity-driven behaviors, did not express all types measured. More concretely, the robot exhibited free exploration by expressing love to learn new things and suggesting moving new characters. It also expressed uncertainty-seeking behavior, by wondering about new situations that could happen. However, at no point did the robot ask the child any question, novel or otherwise. Hence, our second and stronger hypothesis is that only the free exploration and uncertainty seeking measures will be increased by the interaction with the curious robot compared to the non-curious one, whereas the question generation measure will not be affected. In this study, we did not address the issue of whether the question generation measure can also be manipulated by a social robot behavior.

Regarding the learning gains, since we did not construct the manipulation to differentiate learning new words, i.e. the same Story-maker app is used in exactly the same manner across conditions, we hypothesize that the children will learn new words, but not differently with respect to the curious and non-curious conditions. Nevertheless, we hypothesize that the robot conditions will have larger effects than the curious tablet condition, due to the physical embodiment of the robot [2].

8. RESULTS

We first analyzed the measures themselves, across conditions. We tested whether the Free exploration measure had a normal distribution across conditions, using the Shapiro-Wilk normality test. The hypothesis that the data comes from a normal distribution was confirmed ($p = 0.41$, Shapiro-Wilk). Hence, we analyzed the Free exploration measure using analysis-of-variance (ANOVA) tests. For the question generation measure, we performed Fisher's exact test. We further tested whether the Fish task measure had a normal distribution across conditions, using the Shapiro-Wilk normality test. The hypothesis that the data comes from a normal distribution was not confirmed ($p = 0.01$, Shapiro-Wilk). Hence, we analyzed the Fish task measure using the a-parametric Kruskal-Wallis test.

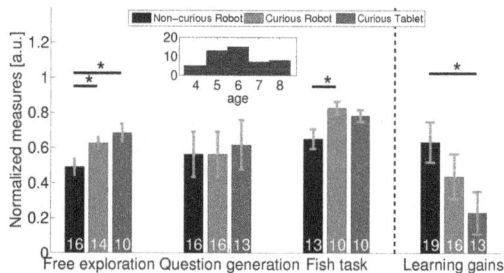

Figure 2: Average normalized curiosity (left) and learning-gains (right) measures across conditions (error bars denote SEM). White number indicates number of subjects. * $p < 0.05$. Inset: age histogram.

We then compared the curiosity measures between all conditions, Fig. 2. There was no significant difference in any curiosity measure between the curious tablet and the curious robot condition ($p = 0.47, 1.0, 0.45$ for the Free exploration, question generation and Fish task, respectively). The curious robot and the non-curious robot conditions, however, had mixed results. The curious robot resulted in significantly higher Free exploration and Fish task measures, compared to the non-curious robot ($F(1, 32) = 5.4, p = 0.027$ and $\chi^2(1, 21) = 3.9, p = 0.047$, respectively). However, there was no significant difference in the question generation task ($p = 1$, Fisher's exact test).

These results validate our main hypothesis: (i) Curiosity can be higher after interaction with a curious robot, compared to an interaction with a non-curious one. (ii) The curious robot impacted children's curiosity only on those behaviors that the robot models for the child, i.e., Free exploration and Fish task measures increased, whereas the question generation measure did not.

When comparing the attitudes children had towards the robot across conditions, as measured by our post-assessment questionnaire, we found that children found both robots to be equally engaging, whereas the tablet was less so. For example, when asked "if you were to play the Story-maker game again, would you prefer to play by yourself, with your mom/dad or with Parle?", 69%, 50% and 23% of the children preferred to play with Parle in the curious robot, non-curious robot and curious tablet conditions, respectively. This indicates that the non-curious robot was as a compelling playmate as the curious one, suggesting that the curiosity-driven behavior was the cause of curiosity measures, and not the engagement or affects of the children towards the robot. While there were no significant differences between robots and tablet, the tablet had lower likeability scores.

We then analyzed the learning gains, i.e. whether the children learned new words. For this, we considered only words that the child misidentified during the main phase, i.e. when the Story-maker app showed the child the correct word. For these misidentified words we analyzed whether in the post-test they were correctly identified; if so we labeled them "learned words". Over all conditions, children learned on average 1.2 (± 0.8) words. Since the post-test was a multiple-choice one, we tested whether the learned words were identified above chance level. We performed a t-test on the null hypothesis that for each child the learned

word was identified with chance level, i.e. 20%. The alternative hypothesis, that it is above chance level was confirmed (average correct probability 62%, $p < 0.001$). These results indicate that the interaction, even though short, was sufficient to teach the children new words.

We further wanted to test whether the learning gains were condition-dependent, Fig. 2. First, we binarized the data such that a child was labeled "learned" if she learned at least one word, and "not-learned" if not. Then we compared the percentage of children that learned new words in each condition: non-curious robot 63%, curious robot 44% and curious tablet 23%. We then performed a Fisher's exact test on each condition pair, and found that only non-curious robot and curious tablet results in a significant difference ($p = 0.036$).

These results partially validate our learning-gain hypothesis: (i) Children learned how to identify new words during the interaction. (ii) Physical presence of the non-curious robot resulted in significantly higher learning gains than the curious tablet. However, the curious robot did not result in significantly higher learning gains, suggesting a complex interplay between learning and curiosity gains.

9. DISCUSSION

9.1 Curious tablet vs. curious robot

The fact that the curious tablet and the curious robot conditions were found to be virtually identical is somewhat puzzling. Previous studies have shown differences in both attitude and learning gains in a similar comparison [2, 16]. However, in our study the two conditions were much more similar: the "virtual agent" had the same emotional sounds of excitement and frustration; the sound was emitted in both conditions from the speakers, for increased volume; there was no virtual character on the tablet. We asked the children at the end of the interaction in the tablet condition to point to where they thought the virtual agent is. Only 4 pointed to the box, whereas 4 pointed to the tablet and 3 pointed to the speakers and some even to the curtain behind the box. We can conclude that the children did not treat the virtual agent as a virtual character in the tablet, but rather as a dis-embodied voice. Moreover, the interaction was focused on the tablet, and not on the robot, e.g. it was not designed as a face-to-face interaction, but rather as co-play on the tablet. Furthermore, the lack of difference is mainly in respect to the curiosity measures, whereas learning gains behave somewhat differently. We thus attribute the lack of difference in curiosity measures between these conditions to the fact that the tablet condition was perceived as playing a tablet game with a hidden real robot, e.g. like discussing a document with someone over the phone. Nevertheless, in order to fully address these issues, a full manipulation of the tablet condition is in order, e.g. adding a non-curious tablet condition, a tablet condition with no affective expressions, designing a face-to-face co-play interaction. These are beyond the scope of the current study.

9.2 Curiosity measures generalizability

Each of the measures we used has pros and cons relating to their usage in other studies. Free exploration is an important aspect of curiosity, as it is an independent activity for seeking information. The app developed and used can assess several components, e.g. interaction with new characters, patterns of exploration, etc. The quantitative measure used here reflects the amount of actively exposed information, which is at the core of free exploration. Furthermore, it taps into a "low cognitive level" of curiosity, in the sense that actions are finger manipulation and perception is passive listening. Hence, while it is easily applicable in a wide range of interactions, its individual nature does not account for the social aspect of curiosity and it assesses only low cognitive processing. The Fish Task has identical considerations.

On the other hand, question generation is a very social aspect of curiosity as well as requires a higher cognitive processing. The subject has to mentally think of novel questions, without any information from the experimenter. Furthermore, the interaction between shyness and curiosity comes into play and may confound the assessment. Nevertheless, the open-endedness of the measure can yield enlightening results and is easily administered in any study.

9.3 Different types of curiosity

Studies from the 70's and 80's have shown that curiosity is not a unitary characteristic, but rather a composite one that aggregates different types of aspects [15, 23]. Consistent with these views, we have measured three distinct quantitative aspects of curiosity, namely, free exploration, question generation and uncertainty seeking. We have shown that the curious robot can effect those measures that its behavior explicitly models for the child. While we did not show that the question generation can be similarly manipulated by a social curious robot, we interpret these results as a relation between the type of behavior the robot exhibited and the curiosity aspect affected. Thus, for example, the fact that the curious robot says "I love trying new things. Could you move another character?" is a direct manipulation on the Free exploration task wherein the child can move different characters and learn new things about them from the spoken sentences. Furthermore, most of its curiosity-driven utterances refer to seeking the unknown, e.g. "a new scene. I wonder what you would do now", thus manipulating the uncertainty seeking measure. However, the curious robot never asks a question related to the child, the story, their interaction or anything else [5, 10]. It does not express its knowledge thirst via the direct channel of verbal interaction.

One confound to this interpretation is the measure medium. The interaction with the robot was via the tablet throughout the entire session, i.e. the robot did not respond to verbal or non-verbal communication from the child. Furthermore, the Free exploration and Fish task measures were presented in a similar medium, i.e. a tablet app, whereas the question generation one was via the verbal interaction with the experimenter. Thus, the difference between manipulation effects may be due to the measure medium.

One could consider a different type of manipulation wherein the robot deliberately asks the child, or the tablet in the presence of a child, knowledge-seeking questions. We hypothesize that this manipulation, controlled-for by a social robot that either does not ask questions or asks irrelevant, repetitive or boring questions, will increase the question generation measure. Performing a cross-manipulation paradigm can raise the medium confound and is intended for future work.

9.4 Learning gains

We have shown that the non-curious robot has the highest learning gains, significantly higher than the curious-tablet.

This suggests that learning gains are higher with a physical robot [2, 16]. Moreover, learning outcomes for such a short encounter are suggestive of longer term gains, but a longitudinal study is required in order to assess learning outcomes of curious vs. non-curious and virtual vs. physical interventions.

The trend in learning gains, i.e. non-curious tablet highest, followed by curious robot and curious tablet lowest, is reversed for the increase in the Free exploration measure. This raises the possibility that the two aspects interact. In other words, it may be the case that during a single, short interaction one cannot achieve both learning gains and increased curiosity, as measured by the Free exploration task. A longitudinal study, with repeated encounters may illuminate the interaction between increased curiosity and learning gains.

9.5 Fringe benefits from the interaction

We asked the parent "do you think your child learned something from this interaction?" While originally designed to see whether the parent noticed their child learning new words, the parents' answers were diverse and insightful. Some parents pointed out that their child learned "listening skills" or "learned to wait". We believe that this was partly due to the fact that the tablet app was disabled while the robot was speaking. This raises the question of whether a social robot can be used to teach and assess a child's listening skills.

One parent pointed out that their child learned "how to help another kid how to learn". Similarly, another parent said their child learned "to be patient, to work at another creature's pace". Our framing of the robot as a younger peer that wants assistance in learning how to read was perceived by the parent and child as an opportunity to practice and foster empathy and responsibility over another less capable social agent. This raises the question of whether a social robot can be designed and programmed to improve empathy and consideration of children, and whether that is transferable to other children or adults.

10. CONCLUSIONS AND FUTURE WORK

We have studied the effects an autonomous social robot's curiosity driven behavior has on a child' curiosity. The robot's behavior exhibited several aspects of curiosity and the child was assessed on different aspects as well. We have shown that a fully autonomous robot can be modeled as a peer that impacts curiosity behaviors in children. Moreover, we have shown that only those curiosity aspects which we manipulated increased in children.

These results suggest that manipulating subtle social interaction utterances and expressions can impact children's curiosity. We suggest that other educational HRI studies incorporate these and thus may gain additional positive influence on children learning.

In future work we intend to further study the specificity and generalization of our results, namely, can we manipulate each aspect of curiosity independently and whether those aspects carry to other activities, have long lasting effects and can change the child's mindset. Including a more diverse set of curiosity measures and more model-based curiosity behaviors of the robot will enable the development of a theoretical framework of children's curiosity manipulation as well as a personalized and more social curious companion for children.

11. ACKNOWLEDGMENTS

The authors acknowledge help and support of Jacqueline Kory in the development of the experimental setup. G.G. was supported by the Fulbright commission for Israel, the United States-Israel Educational Foundation. This research was supported by the National Science Foundation (NSF) under Grants CCF-1138986. Any opinions, findings and conclusions, or recommendations expressed in this paper are those of the authors and do not represent the views of the NSF.

12. REFERENCES

[1] M. P. Arnone, R. V. Small, S. A. Chauncey, and H. P. McKenna. Curiosity, interest and engagement in technology-pervasive learning environments: a new research agenda. *Educational Technology Research and Development*, 59(2):181–198, 2011.

[2] W. A. Bainbridge, J. W. Hart, E. S. Kim, and B. Scassellati. The benefits of interactions with physically present robots over video-displayed agents. *International Journal of Social Robotics*, 3(1):41–52, 2011.

[3] L. S. Blackwell, K. H. Trzesniewski, and C. S. Dweck. Implicit theories of intelligence predict achievement across an adolescent transition: A longitudinal study and an intervention. *Child development*, 78(1):246–263, 2007.

[4] C. Dweck. *Mindset: The new psychology of success.* Random House LLC, 2006.

[5] R. C. Endsley and S. A. Clarey. Answering young children's questions as a determinant of their subsequent question-asking behavior. *Developmental Psychology*, 11(6):863, 1975.

[6] S. Engel. Children's need to know: curiosity in schools. *Harvard Educational Review*, 81(4):625–645, 2011.

[7] S. Engel. The case for curiosity. *Educational Leadership*, 70(5):36–40, 2013.

[8] A. Gatt and E. Reiter. Simplenlg: A realisation engine for practical applications. In *Proc. of the 12th European Workshop on Natural Language Generation*, pages 90–93. Association for Computational Linguistics, 2009.

[9] K. Haimovitz, S. V. Wormington, and J. H. Corpus. Dangerous mindsets: How beliefs about intelligence predict motivational change. *Learning and Individual Differences*, 21(6):747–752, 2011.

[10] P. L. Harris. *Trusting what you're told: How children learn from others.* Harvard University Press, 2012.

[11] B. Henderson and S. G. Moore. Children's responses to objects differing in novelty in relation to level of curiosity and adult behavior. *Child development*, pages 457–465, 1980.

[12] B. B. Henderson. Parents and exploration: The effect of context on individual differences in exploratory behavior. *Child Development*, pages 1237–1245, 1984.

[13] J. Jirout and D. Klahr. Children's scientific curiosity: In search of an operational definition of an elusive concept. *Developmental Review*, 32(2):125–160, 2012.

[14] T. B. Kashdan and M. Yuen. Whether highly curious students thrive academically depends on perceptions about the school learning environment: A study of hong kong adolescents. *Motivation and Emotion*, 31(4):260–270, 2007.

[15] R. Langevin. Is curiosity a unitary construct? *Canadian Journal of Psychology/Revue canadienne de psychologie*, 25(4):360, 1971.

[16] D. Leyzberg, S. Spaulding, M. Toneva, and B. Scassellati. The physical presence of a robot tutor increases cognitive learning gains. In *Proc. of the 34th Annual Conf. of the Cognitive Science Society. Austin, TX*, 2012.

[17] A. N. Meltzoff, P. K. Kuhl, J. Movellan, and T. J. Sejnowski. Foundations for a new science of learning. *science*, 325(5938):284–288, 2009.

[18] J. Movellan, M. Eckhardt, M. Virnes, and A. Rodriguez. Sociable robot improves toddler vocabulary skills. In *Proc. of the 4th ACM/IEEE Int. Conf. on Human robot interaction*, pages 307–308, 2009.

[19] L. Schulz. The origins of inquiry: inductive inference and exploration in early childhood. *Trends in cognitive sciences*, 16(7):382–389, 2012.

[20] A. Setapen. *Creating Robotic Characters for Long-term Interaction.* Thesis, 2012.

[21] F. Tanaka and S. Matsuzoe. Children teach a care-receiving robot to promote their learning: Field experiments in a classroom for vocabulary learning. *Journal of Human-Robot Interaction*, 1(1), 2012.

[22] J. Torgesen, R. Wagner, and C. Rashotte. Test of word reading efficiency (towre). austin, texas: Pro-ed, 1999.

[23] F. Wardle. Getting back to the basics of childrens play. *Child Care Information Exchange*, 57:27–30, 1987.

Comparing Models of Disengagement in Individual and Group Interactions

Iolanda Leite*, Marissa McCoy†, Daniel Ullman*,
Nicole Salomons*, Brian Scassellati*
*Dept. of Computer Science, †Dept. of Psychology
Yale University, New Haven, CT, USA
{iolanda.leite, marissa.mccoy, daniel.ullman,
nicole.salomons, brian.scassellati}@yale.edu

ABSTRACT

Changes in type of interaction (e.g., individual vs. group interactions) can potentially impact data-driven models developed for social robots. In this paper, we provide a first investigation in the effects of changing group size in data-driven models for HRI, by analyzing how a model trained on data collected from participants interacting individually performs in test data collected from group interactions, and *vice-versa*. Another model combining data from both individual and group interactions is also investigated. We perform these experiments in the context of predicting disengagement behaviors in children interacting with two social robots. Our results show that a model trained with group data generalizes better to individual participants than the other way around. The mixed model seems a good compromise, but it does not achieve the performance levels of the models trained for a specific type of interaction.

Keywords

Child-robot interaction; disengagement; multimodal classification; multiparty settings.

1. INTRODUCTION

Human behavior is largely dependent on social context. The way we behave alone is different than how we behave in a group [22]. For this reason, most data-driven perceptual systems developed for social robots rely on data collected in the same type of interaction where most future interactions are likely to occur. For example, a robot bartender is able to predict engagement using data collected in multiparty settings [7], while a chess-playing robot relies on data from a single user at a time [4]. Will the robot bartender be able to respond appropriately to the lonely costumer at the end of the night? How would the chess-playing robot behave when placed in a science fair?

HRI '15, March 02 - 05 2015, Portland, OR, USA
Copyright 2015 ACM 978-1-4503-2883-8/15/03 ...$15.00
http://dx.doi.org/10.1145/2696454.2696466

Robots will inevitably have to interact with users in contexts with different group sizes. This might occur in a variety of domains, such as museums, hospitals or classrooms. So far, little is known about how perception models perform when they are tested in a group size different than the one they were trained on. However, this feature is critical for some perception problems. That is, the way the robot should interpret a user glancing to the side is different if that user is alone or if the user is in a group.

We provide a first investigation of this issue by addressing the following research questions: Using the same set of features, how does group size affect the performance of a data-driven perception model? Moreover, for the same classification problem, can a model trained on data from one group size generalize well when tested in data from another context? In this paper, we answer these questions in the particular case of predicting disengagement in child-robot interaction. According to Pohl and Murray-Smith [12], engagement (or disengagement) with technology is dependent on inhibitor factors from three main categories: physical (system is not accessible), social (people change their behavior built on what they envision people around them are thinking about them) and mental (primarily related to distraction). Because the two last inhibitor factors are highly dependent on type of interaction, the automatic prediction of engagement/disengagement is a very interesting case study to our research questions.

We start our analysis by training and testing two different disengagement models in the context of an interactive narrative scenario with social robots. The models were built on two different datasets, one with data collected from participants interacting alone with the robots, and another with data from participants interacting in groups of three. Even in the model collected from group data, the goal is to predict disengagement of one participant at a time. The models use the exact same set of audio, visual and contextual features, and the group model does not encode features from the other participants around the robots. This was a deliberate choice, not only to allow a more fair comparison between the models, but also because in future applications we may not have access to information of all participants in the group, such as due to occlusions or limitations in the robot sensors.

To address the second research question, we report the results of testing each model using data from participants of the opposite dataset. Finally, we train a mixed model with data from both datasets to see how this model performs in individual and group data. Our results show that while a mixed model (trained with data instances from the two group sizes) is a good compromise, higher performances are achieved when the models are trained using only data from a similar group size as the target interaction. We discuss these results in terms of potential implications for future research in this area.

2. BACKGROUND

Engagement, defined as "the process by which individuals in an interaction start, maintain and end their perceived connection to one another" [17], has been studied from two main perspectives in HRI. One perspective is dedicated to understanding which features or social cues robots should be endowed with to increase participant's engagement with the robot. For example, Sidner and colleagues [17] showed that people report higher levels of engagement when interacting with a robot capable of face-tracking and performing gestures. More recently, researchers investigated the impact of social cues including voice and facial expressions [10], while others studied the impact of a robot side-kick on perceptions of user engagement [20].

The second perspective, and the perspective more relevant to the work presented in this paper, has to do with the automatic recognition of engagement (or disengagement) in users interacting with robots or virtual agents. Seminal work in this area has focused on predicting engagement intention, i.e., the problem of whether users around a robot (or a virtual agent) express a desire to start interacting with the system. In this domain, Michalowski et al. [9] presented a spatial model of social engagement grounded in proxemics theory. Bohus and Horvitz [2] proposed the first data-driven approach to predict engagement intentions using spatiotemporal and attention cues for a conversational virtual agent. A similar model, using mainly visual features, was developed and tested in a social robot [21].

Other authors have investigated the automatic prediction of engagement as a continuous signal. The main goal here is typically to predict engagement or, more importantly, disengagement behaviors in real-time, so that the robot or agent can employ repair mechanisms to keep users engaged in the interaction. To address this problem, several models have been proposed using a variety of features, including visual and task-related information [4], eye gaze [11], speech and gestures [15], body postures [16] and EEG data [19]. Some authors compared the performance of predicting engagement using different machine learning and rule-based models [7].

The presented work shows that data-driven methods are clearly the most common and successful approaches for automatically predicting engagement in HRI, both in settings with one and multiple users. Despite the significant advances in this area, to our knowledge no multiparty engagement model has been tested in data from individual participants, or the other way around. In this work, we aim to advance the state-of-the-art in this area by performing the first experiment of this kind.

3. METHODOLOGY
3.1 Case Study

The case study used in this work utilizes two MyKeepon Robots (see Figure 1) that play out interactive stories around emotional words (e.g., frustration, inclusion, cooperation). At specific points, users can influence the story by choosing from among a set of optional scenes presented on a tablet. In other words, users can tell one of the robots what to do, and then see the impact of the selected action on the course of the story.

The robots use pre-recorded adult utterances with modified pitch signal to make them more childlike. The robots can display several animations during the interaction, such as speaking, idling (while they are waiting for children's choices or listening to the other robot) or bouncing (moving up and down and side to side – used in specific moments of the stories). The robots are autonomous, but at this point their only perception of the world is from the story choices selected on the tablet.

Our goal is to develop a classifier that allows the robots to accurately perceive when children are disengaged in the interaction, despite the number of children interacting at the same time. Upon detecting disengagement, the robots could employ repair strategies, such as displaying more active non-verbal behaviors to call attention to or change the story, in the attempt to re-engage users in the interaction.

For this analysis, the models will mostly rely on hand-annotated data. This was a deliberate choice because we wanted to distinguish the adequacy of the feature set and its effects on predicting disengagement in different contexts from the adequacy of particular feature detectors. Nevertheless, we plan to replace the hand-annotated features with autonomous modules, such that we can run a real-time implementation of the models in our robots.

3.2 Data Collection

Our data set consists of 40 children (22 female, 18 male), with ages between 6 and 8 years old ($M = 7.53, SD = 0.51$), interacting with the social robots in the interactive narrative scenario described in the previous section. Participants were recruited from an elementary school in the United States, where the data collection was conducted. The data collection took place in a small meeting room of the school. Participants were randomly assigned to a type of interaction condition: 19 were assigned to the single condition and 21 were assigned to the group condition (7 groups). The two conditions were balanced for gender.

One experimenter was present in the room for the entire session. The experimenter started by introducing the two robots and telling participants that the robots would play out a story, and then when the story stopped, they could decide what would happen next from the options that appeared on the tablet. In the group condition, participants were informed that they would have to choose the next story option together. No additional instructions were given. The story contained an introductory scene and three different options that participants could then freely explore. The interaction ended when participants explored all three of the story options. The average actual interaction time, from the

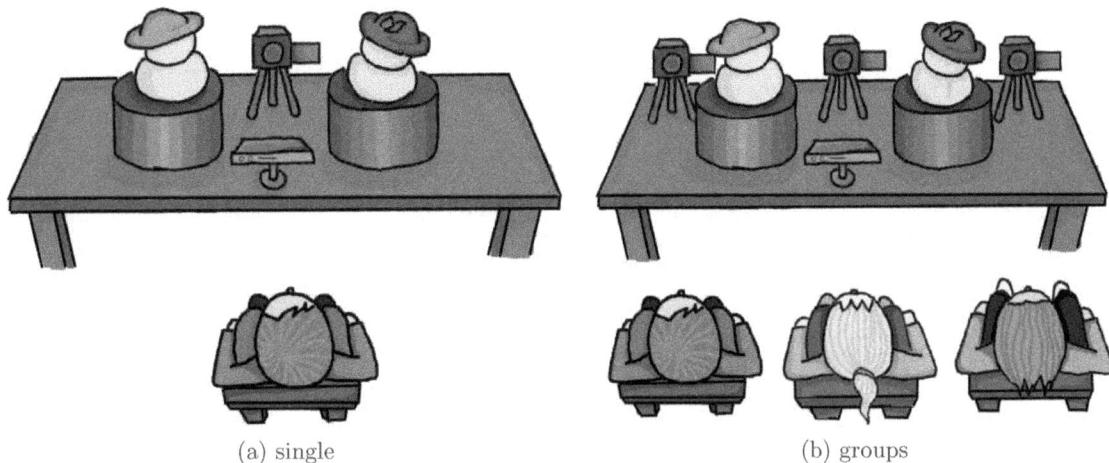

(a) single   (b) groups

Figure 1: Sketch of the two interaction settings where data was collected.

moment when participants selected the first story option until the robots played all the possible scenes, was 4 minutes 36 seconds (SD = 39 seconds).

Three HD cameras were used to record the interaction in the group condition, while in the single condition one HD camera was used. Each camera recorded the upper body posture and face of one single participant. Log files containing the content of the robots' actions (speech and nonverbal behaviors), as well as the story choices made by the children, were generated automatically. The logs contained timestamps to allow future synchronization with the remaining data.

3.3 Feature Extraction

Our goal is to create a data-driven model that allows our robots to predict, in real-time, when each participant is disengaged in the interaction. To achieve this goal, we considered a set of features based on prior HRI research on automatic prediction of engagement and on research describing typical behaviors when people are engaged and disengaged [1, 14].

Using the collected videos and the ELAN annotation tool [3], one annotator (blind to our research questions) coded the start and end times of each participant's vocalizations, backchannel sounds, body posture (leaning forward/backward, arms on the table), gestures (smiles, mimicking robots, excitable bouncing and strong emotional reactions), concentration and boredom signs and off task behaviors. We ran an off-the-shelf face tracking algorithm[1] on the video recordings to automatically extract head orientation features – looking at the robots, looking up, looking down and rolling head. The contextual features – robots speaking, robots bouncing, and participant choosing an action – were extracted from the interaction logs. The final set of features considered to predict disengagement in this work are listed in Table 1.

Determining the optimal window size for analysis is still an open challenge in the processing of many social signals (like engagement), where it is hard to draw semantic or lexical

---

[1]http://www.omron.com/r_d/coretech/vision/okao.html

boundaries [8]. Therefore, our approach was to use a small unit of analysis to simulate real-time decision-making in the disengagement predictions. From the hand-coded annotations, automatically generated face tracking analysis and interaction logs of each participant, we extracted a set of multimodal features into 500 msec time slices. The binary value of a feature for every time slice reflects what happened in the majority of the 500 msec interval. For example, voice activity will be set to true if a participant is speaking for more than 250 msec in that time slice.

3.4 Ground Truth Labelling

The ground truth labels for training and testing our data were based on human observations. Without having access to any of the extracted features, two independent coders (other than the one who coded children's behaviors) were given our working definition of engagement [17] and asked to rate participants' level of engagement during the interaction with the robots. Using the same video annotation tool, they coded the start and end times of disengagement, engagement and neutral episodes for all participants. The neutral category was used for moments where it was unclear whether participants were engaged or disengaged. In the group interactions, raters watched the interaction three times, once in the perspective of each participant. The videos of each participant in the group condition were trimmed to display the least possible information from the other children in the scene.

Both coders rated all the collected videos. As in the feature extraction process, the extracted ground truth labels for each rater were based on 500msec time slices reflecting the most predominant category in that segment. Inter-observer agreement between the two coders was 74% (k = 0.41, p < .001). The moderate agreement result was expected because perceived engagement can be a subjective observation. Nevertheless, to not undermine the comparison between models later on, we only consider the time slices where both raters agreed in the engagement category for future training and testing.

Table 1: Multimodal features considered for disengagement prediction.

Modality	Feature name	Description	Source
Audio	voice activity	Whether a participant is speaking	Hand annotated
	backchannel	Presence of backchannel sounds such as "uh-huh" and "hmm"	Hand annotated
Visual	look at robots	Looking at the robots or to the sides	Autom. extracted
	look up	Looking up (above the robots)	Autom. extracted
	look down	Looking down (not looking at the robots)	Autom. extracted
	rolling head	Rolling the head to the sides	Autom. extracted
	lean forward	Leaning forward	Hand annotated
	lean backward	Leaning backward	Hand annotated
	arms on table	Placing the arms on the table	Hand annotated
	smiling	Presence of smiles	Hand annotated
	head nods	Presence of head nods	Hand annotated
	mimicking robots	Micking the robots' movements	Hand annotated
	excitable boucing	Moving back and forth in the chair	Hand annotated
	emotional reaction	Strong emotional reactions (e.g. surprise)	Hand annotated
	boredom signs	Presence of boredom signs such as shrugs or fiddling	Hand annotated
	concentration signs	Presence of concentration signs such as fingers in the mouth	Hand annotated
	off task	Presence of off task behaviors (e.g., playing with sticker tag)	Hand annotated
Contextual	robots speaking	Whether any of the robots is speaking	Interaction logs
	robots bouncing	Whether any of the robots is displaying a bouncing animation	Interaction logs
	choosing	Two second window before a choice is made in the tablet	Interaction logs

(a) disengagement   (b) engagement   (c) disengagement   (d) engagement

Figure 2: Snapshots of the collected datasets representing the disengagement different behaviors.

3.5 Two datasets: DS_I and DS_G

Two datasets were used in this analysis: DS_I, including the 500 msec segments from all participants who interacted alone with the robots, and DS_G, including segments for participants who interacted with the robots in small groups (see fig 2). Note that, in DS_G, the feature vectors only encode features related to the behavior of one participant, but all participants in each group are included in the dataset. Data from one participant from DS_I and from four participants from DS_G were excluded because they had no disengagement instances rated as such by the two coders. Table 2 provides a characterization of the two datasets. Each participant contributed an approximately similar number of instances to the data set.

Table 2: Characterization of the two datasets in terms of number of participants and number of 500msec instances for each label.

	Num. Participants	Disengaged	Engaged
DS_I	18	1283	5616
DS_G	17	853	4944

4. PREDICTING DISENGAGEMENT IN INDIVIDUAL AND SMALL GROUP INTERACTIONS

Our main goal is to investigate the effects of different group formations in the automatic prediction of disengagement in Human-Robot Interaction, rather than maximizing accuracy by trying different machine learning techniques or feature sets. As such, we focus our analysis in one classification technique and the same set of features in both cases. We decided to use Support Vector Machines (SVMs) as they have proven effective within similar classification problems in HRI [13, 18, 21].

4.1 Procedure

Using LibSVM Library [5], two SVM binary classifiers were trained, one using DS_I, which we will refer as M_I, and another using DS_G, referred from now on as M_G. We started by running the feature selection tool provided in this library (fselect), which performs feature ranking using F-scores [6]. The feature selection analysis was performed not only to find the optimal set of features, but also to rank and compare the features with the most discriminative power in each dataset.

The results of this latter analysis are reported in the next subsection. The fselect tool indicated that, in both datasets, the best classification accuracy was in the presence of 19 of the 20 extracted features (see Table 1). In both cases, head nods was the only feature that revealed no discriminative power for disengagement detection. This feature was therefore excluded from the analysis.

The two SVM models (type C-SVC) with a Radial Basis Function (RBF) kernel were trained with the 19 selected features, using different weights to account for the unbalanced number of disengagement and engagement instances in each data set. A utility tool also included in the LibSVM library (grid) was used to find the optimal parameters C and gamma ($C = 4$, $\gamma = 0.5$ for M_I and $C = 1$, $\gamma = 0.5$ for M_G).

The consistency of the two models was measured through leave-one-out cross-validation, using the data instances from one participant as the test set and training a model in the remaining participants of that data set. This process was repeated 18 times for M_I and 17 times for M_G, allowing data from each participant to serve once as test set in his/her respective data set.

4.2 Performance Evaluation

We averaged Accuracy, Area Under ROC Curve (AUC), True Positive Rate (TPR) and True Negative Rate (TPR) values from the cross-validation tests of each model. Note that, because our goal is to predict disengagement, TPR reflects the proportion of actual disengagement data points correctly classified as such, and TNR refers to the proportion of correctly predicted engagement instances. Because our datasets are unbalanced, AUC, TPR and TNR values are more informative than accuracy to understand how the models perform.

Cross-validation of M_I showed an average accuracy of 63%, with $AUC = 0.65$, $TPR = 0.68$ and $TNR = 0.62$. This performance was slightly better than M_G, which achieved 60% average accuracy, $AUC = 0.57$, $TPR = 0.53$ and $TNR = 0.61$. This result was not surprising, because when children are alone with the robots, interactions tend to be less chaotic, resulting in more accurate disengagement predictions.

Despite similar classification performances, the feature ranking analysis indicates that the two models are inherently different. Table 3 shows the top 10 most discriminative features in the two models. Although 7 of the top 10 features are the same, their rankings and weights are different in each model. For example, while in M_I the most discriminative feature for predicting disengagement is related to body posture (arms on the table), the most relevant feature for M_G is whether the participant is looking at the robots or not.

5. TESTING THE MODELS IN DIFFERENT DATA SETS

The models generated based on the datasets with different group size show slightly different performances and some differences on the features with most discriminative power. But are these models truly different? How do performance metrics change if we train a model with participants from

Table 3: Top 10 most discriminative features in each model with normalized F-scores.

M_I		M_G	
Feature Name	**F-score**	**Feature Name**	**F-score**
arms on table	1.00	look at robots	1.00
look down	0.68	voice activity	0.65
look at robots	0.47	lean backward	0.27
lean forward	0.33	robots speaking	0.14
concent. signs	0.23	smiling	0.13
boredom signs	0.14	boredom signs	0.11
robots speaking	0.13	robots bouncing	0.08
choosing	0.10	backchannel	0.05
robots bouncing	0.10	off task	0.05
rolling head	0.06	choosing	0.03

the individual condition and test it with group data, or vice versa? Moreover, what happens if we combine data instances from both social settings (individual and group) in the same model?

In the previous section, we analyzed the ability of our models to predict disengagement in data from the same social setting (i.e., M_I was tested with data from other participants from the individual condition and M_G was tested with group data). We now investigate the behavior of the models when tested using data from the other data set, which offers a different social setting in the same scenario. To further investigate this issue, we report the performance metrics of a joint model trained with data from the two datasets.

5.1 Procedure

Using the SVM parameters obtained in the previous experiment for DS_I, we trained a model with the instances of the 18 participants from the individual condition (M_I) and tested this model in data from participants in the group condition, averaging the performances of every participant from DS_G. Similarly, a model using all 17 participants from DS_G was trained (MS_G) and tested in each participant from DS_I.

Finally, we investigated a model combining both datasets (M_A). This model was trained with the same subset of 19 features, using a C-SVS SVM with RBF Kernel parameters $C = 64$ and $\gamma = 0.125$. M_A was tested with participants from both data sets using a leave-one-participant-out cross-validation approach (the data instances from the participant used as test set were the only ones left out in the trained model in every cross-validation cycle).

5.2 Performance Evaluation

We used the same performance metrics as in the previous experiment: Accuracy, Area Under ROC Curve (AUC), True Positive Rate (TPR) and True Negative Rate (TPR), averaged across repeated validation tests.

When testing how M_I performs with data from DS_G, 17 test cycles (each cycle contains the data points from one participant in the group condition) show an average accuracy of 75%, $AUC = 0.59$, $TPR = 0.36$ and $TNR = 0.82$. On the other hand, the performance of M_G using data from D_I in

18 validation tests resulted in an average accuracy of 56%, $AUC = 0.58$, $TPR = 0.60$ and $TNR = 0.55$.

In the analysis of M_A, to better understand how performance is affected by the different datasets, we report separately the results obtained by testing M_A in participants from DS_I and DS_G. In 18-fold cross-validation with data points from participants in DS_I, M_A showed an average accuracy of 63%, $AUC = 0.61$, $TPR = 0.56$ and $TNR = 0.65$. When using data from DS_G as a test set, M_A accuracy increases to 73%, with $AUC = 0.62$, $TPR = 0.47$ and $TNR = 0.78$.

Table 4: Summary of classification results of all experiments.

Model	M_I		M_G		M_A	
Test dataset	DS_I	DS_G	DS_I	DS_G	DS_I	DS_G
Accuracy	63%	75%	56%	60%	63%	73%
TPR	0.68	0.36	0.60	0.53	0.56	0.47
TNR	0.62	0.82	0.55	0.61	0.65	0.78
AUC	0.65	0.59	0.58	0.57	0.61	0.62

6. DISCUSSION

Our results indicate that a disengagement model trained only with data from users interacting alone with the robot might not be appropriate for group interactions, but a model trained only with group data might perform reasonably well in HRI scenarios with a single user. Table 4 and the chart in Figure 3 summarize the results obtained in the classification experiments conducted in this paper. Overall, the results show that the selected multimodal features can be used to successfully predict disengagement in both types of interaction (i.e., a small group or a single participant).

In the cross-validation results using data collected in the same type of interaction, M_I seemed to be a slightly more coherent model than M_G. However, M_G showed greater flexibility in dealing with data from a different type of interaction. In the testing procedures with data from participants interacting alone with the robots (DS_I), the performance measures of M_G remained roughly the same. On the other hand, in tests with data from DS_G, although accuracy and TNR were fairly high, the TPR of M_I was extremely low.

The performance results of M_A, the model trained with instances from both datasets, lie in-between these two extreme comparisons. The average performance of M_A tested with DS_I instances shows better generalization than when DS_I instances are trained in M_G, but not as good as the performance of M_I. In the tests using group data (participants from DS_G), M_A performs better than M_G in some metrics but again, TPR is very poor. It is relevant to stress that M_A was trained with nearly twice as many data points as M_I and M_G, as it included both datasets (only excluding data from the participant used as test set at every cycle), but more data does not always mean better performance. In this case, M_A had to make generalizations from disengagement behaviors in different type of interactions (individual and group interactions), which could explain the decreased performance when compared to M_I and M_G individually.

A possible interpretation of these results is that in group

settings there is more variety in the type of disengagement behaviors children exhibit. When disengaged, some children simply behave as if they were by themselves, while others, for example, start interacting socially with their peers, making the classification of disengagement more challenging because the model needs to make generalizations over a larger set of potential options.

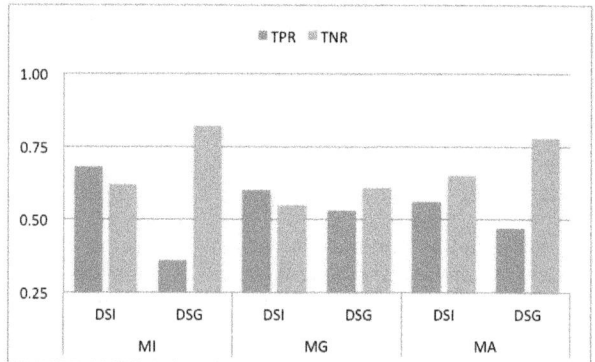

Figure 3: True Positive Rates (TPR) and True Negative Rates (TNR) obtained in the classification experiments.

7. LIMITATIONS

These experiments were conducted in an educational context using children's data. Although the generated models can potentially be re-used in other domains because most of the selected features are domain independent, we cannot be certain that similar performance results will be obtained in different application domains or, more importantly, in datasets with adults.

To further understand the lower performance of M_G compared to M_I, we plan to collect more group data and perform a more detailed analysis of the group interactions. In particular, we intend to study different behavioral profiles, and use that information to segment the group data in several sub-datasets – and eventually different models.

8. CONCLUSION

In this paper, we investigated the role of type of interaction (one participant versus groups of three participants) in the automatic prediction of disengagement in HRI. We reported a set of classification experiments comparing three distinct SVM-based disengagement models generated with the same set of features: a model trained with data from participants interacting alone with two social robots (M_I), a model trained with data from participants interacting with the robots in small groups (M_G), and a third model combining data from the two datasets (M_A).

Our results indicate that, while a model trained with data instances from both type of interactions is a good compromise, not surprisingly the prediction of disengagement episodes is better achieved when the model is trained using only data from a similar type of interaction as the target interaction. In practical terms, ideally the robot should have two different prediction models and, depending on the number of people around it, use the most appropriate model to predict disengagement. However, in cases when that is not possible, we found that a model trained in group data performs better on single children than the other way around. Although we anticipate similar findings in the prediction of other social and motivational states, further research is needed in this direction.

The main contribution of this paper goes beyond providing a framework for the automatic prediction of disengagement in Human-Robot Interaction using domain independent features; to our knowledge, this is the first work exploring how automatic predictions of a social phenomenon are affected by manipulating the number of people around the robot. With this work, we expect to draw attention in the HRI community to the need for developing perception mechanisms tailored to the specific type of interactions where robots will interact with users.

9. ACKNOWLEDGMENTS

This work was supported by the NSF Expedition in Computing Grant #1139078 and SRA International (US Air Force) Grant #13-004807. We thank Rebecca Marvin for help in video coding, Rachel Protacio and Jennifer Allen for recording the voices for the robots, Emily Lennon for artwork creation, and the students and staff from the school where the study was conducted.

10. REFERENCES

[1] M. Argyle and M. Cook. Gaze and mutual gaze. 1976.

[2] D. Bohus and E. Horvitz. Learning to predict engagement with a spoken dialog system in open-world settings. In *Proc. of the SIGDIAL 2009 Conference: The 10th Annual Meeting of the Special Interest Group on Discourse and Dialogue*, pages 244–252. Association for Computational Linguistics, 2009.

[3] H. Brugman, A. Russel, and X. Nijmegen. Annotating multi-media/multi-modal resources with elan. In *LREC*, 2004.

[4] G. Castellano, A. Pereira, I. Leite, A. Paiva, and P. W. McOwan. Detecting user engagement with a robot companion using task and social interaction-based features. In *Proc. of the 2009 International Conf. on Multimodal Interfaces*, ICMI-MLMI '09, pages 119–126, New York, NY, USA, 2009. ACM.

[5] C.-C. Chang and C.-J. Lin. Libsvm: a library for support vector machines. *ACM Trans. on Intelligent Systems and Technology (TIST)*, 2(3):27, 2011.

[6] Y.-W. Chen and C.-J. Lin. Combining svms with various feature selection strategies. In *Feature extraction*, pages 315–324. Springer, 2006.

[7] M. E. Foster, A. Gaschler, and M. Giuliani. How can i help you': Comparing engagement classification strategies for a robot bartender. In *Proc. of the 15th ACM on International Conf. on Multimodal Interaction*, ICMI '13, pages 255–262, New York, NY, USA, 2013. ACM.

[8] H. Gunes and B. Schuller. Categorical and dimensional affect analysis in continuous input: Current trends and future directions. *Image and Vision Computing*, 31(2):120 – 136, 2013.

[9] M. Michalowski, S. Sabanovic, and R. Simmons. A spatial model of engagement for a social robot. In *Advanced Motion Control, 2006. 9th IEEE International Workshop on*, pages 762–767, 2006.

[10] L. Moshkina, S. Trickett, and J. G. Trafton. Social

engagement in public places: A tale of one robot. In *Proc. of the 2014 ACM/IEEE International Conf. on Human-robot Interaction*, HRI '14, pages 382–389, New York, NY, USA, 2014. ACM.

[11] Y. I. Nakano and R. Ishii. Estimating user's engagement from eye-gaze behaviors in human-agent conversations. In *Proc. of the 15th International Conf. on Intelligent User Interfaces*, IUI '10, pages 139–148, New York, NY, USA, 2010. ACM.

[12] H. Pohl and R. Murray-Smith. Focused and casual interactions: Allowing users to vary their level of engagement. In *Proc. of the SIGCHI Conf. on Human Factors in Computing Systems*, CHI '13, pages 2223–2232. ACM, 2013.

[13] P. Rani, C. Liu, N. Sarkar, and E. Vanman. An empirical study of machine learning techniques for affect recognition in human–robot interaction. *Pattern Analysis and Applications*, 9(1):58–69, 2006.

[14] J. Read, S. MacFarlane, and C. Casey. Endurability, engagement and expectations: Measuring children's fun. In *Interaction design and children*, volume 2, pages 1–23. Shaker Publishing Eindhoven, 2002.

[15] C. Rich, B. Ponsler, A. Holroyd, and C. L. Sidner. Recognizing engagement in human-robot interaction. In *Proc. of the 5th ACM/IEEE International Conf. on Human-Robot Interaction*, pages 375–382. IEEE, 2010.

[16] J. Sanghvi, G. Castellano, I. Leite, A. Pereira, P. W. McOwan, and A. Paiva. Automatic analysis of affective postures and body motion to detect engagement with a game companion. In *Proc. of the 6th International Conf. on Human-robot Interaction*, pages 305–312, New York, NY, USA, 2011. ACM.

[17] C. L. Sidner, C. Lee, C. D. Kidd, N. Lesh, and C. Rich. Explorations in engagement for humans and robots. *Artificial Intelligence*, 166(1):140–164, 2005.

[18] C. L. Sidner, C. Lee, L.-P. Morency, and C. Forlines. The effect of head-nod recognition in human-robot conversation. In *Proc. of the 1st ACM SIGCHI/SIGART Conf. on Human-robot interaction*, pages 290–296. ACM, 2006.

[19] D. Szafir and B. Mutlu. Pay attention!: Designing adaptive agents that monitor and improve user engagement. In *Proc. of the SIGCHI Conf. on Human Factors in Computing Systems*, CHI '12, pages 11–20, New York, NY, USA, 2012. ACM.

[20] M. Vázquez, A. Steinfeld, S. E. Hudson, and J. Forlizzi. Spatial and other social engagement cues in a child-robot interaction: Effects of a sidekick. In *Proc. of the 2014 ACM/IEEE International Conf. on Human-robot Interaction*, HRI '14, pages 391–398, New York, NY, USA, 2014. ACM.

[21] Q. Xu, L. Li, and G. Wang. Designing engagement-aware agents for multiparty conversations. In *Proc. of the SIGCHI Conference on Human Factors in Computing Systems*, CHI '13, pages 2233–2242, New York, NY, USA, 2013. ACM.

[22] R. B. Zajonc et al. *Social facilitation*. Research Center for Group Dynamics, Institute for Social Research, University of Michigan, 1965.

Of Robots, Humans, Bodies and Intelligence: Body Languages for Human Robot Interaction

Antonio Bicchi

Senior Scientist with the Italian Institute of Technology in Genoa

&

Professor of Robotics at the University of Pisa

Abstract

Modern approaches to the design of robots with increasing amounts of embodied intelligence affect human-robot interaction paradigms. The physical structure of robots is evolving from traditional rigid, heavy industrial machines into soft bodies exhibiting new levels of versatility, adaptability, safety, elasticity, dynamism and energy efficiency. New challenges and opportunities arise for the control of soft robots: for instance, carefully planning for collision avoidance may no longer be a dominating concern, being on the contrary physical interaction with the environment not only allowed, but even desirable to solve complex tasks. To address these challenges, it is often useful to look at how humans use their own bodies in similar tasks, and even in some cases have a direct dialogue between the natural and artificial counterparts.

ACM Classification

B.0 General

Keywords

Soft Robotics; Embodied Intelligence; Impedance Control; Grasp Control; Dexterous Manipulation; Physical Human-Robot Interaction; Body-Robot Interaction

Short Bio

Antonio Bicchi is Senior Scientist with the Italian Institute of Technology in Genoa and Professor of Robotics at the University of Pisa. He graduated from the University of Bologna in 1988 and was a postdoc scholar at MIT AI Lab in 1988–1991. His main research interests are in Robotics, Haptics, and Control Systems. He serves as Vice President for Publications in IEEE Robotics and Automation Society (RAS) and is one of the Editors in Chief for the series "Springer Briefs on Control, Automation and Robotics". He is the recipient of several awards and honors. In 2012 he received an Advanced Grant from the European Research Council for his research on human and robot hands.

HRI'15, March 2–5, 2015, Portland, Oregon, USA.
ACM 978-1-4503-2883-8/15/03.
http://dx.doi.org/10.1145/2696454.2714388

Rabble of Robots Effects: Number and Type of Robots Modulates Attitudes, Emotions, and Stereotypes

Marlena. R. Fraune[1,2], Steven Sherrin[1,2], Selma Šabanović[1,3], and Eliot R. Smith[1,2]

[1]Department of Cognitive Science, [2]Psychological and Brain Sciences, [3]Informatics and Computing
Indiana University, Bloomington, IN 47408 USA
{mfraune, ssherrin, selmas, esmith4}@indiana.edu

ABSTRACT

Robots are expected to become present in society in increasing numbers, yet few studies in human-robot interaction (HRI) go beyond one-to-one interaction to examine how emotions, attitudes, and stereotypes expressed toward groups of robots differ from those expressed toward individuals. Research from social psychology indicates that people interact differently with individuals than with groups. We therefore hypothesize that group effects might similarly occur when people face multiple robots. Further, group effects might vary for robots of different types. In this exploratory study, we used videos to expose participants in a between-subjects experiment to robots varying in Number (Single or Group) and Type (anthropomorphic, zoomorphic, or mechanomorphic). We then measured participants' general attitudes, emotions, and stereotypes toward robots with a combination of measures from HRI (e.g., Godspeed Questionnaire, NARS) and social psychology (e.g., Big Five, Social Threat, Emotions). Results suggest that Number and Type of observed robots had an interaction effect on responses toward robots in general, leading to more positive responses for groups for some robot types, but more negative responses for others.

Categories and Subject Descriptors

H.1.2 [**Models and Principles**]: User/Machine Systems – *human factors*. J.4 [**Social and Behavioral Sciences**]: Psychology. I.2.9 [**Artificial Intelligence**] Robotics.

General Terms

Experimentation, Human Factors.

Keywords

Human-robot interaction, inter-group interactions, group effects, robot type, emotion, attitudes, stereotypes.

1. INTRODUCTION

Contemporary visions of how robots will be used in daily life include many situations in which people interact and share their space with not only one, but multiple, robots. Gates' vision of "robots in every home" includes a Roomba, a laundry-folding robot, and a mobile assistive robot within the home, with security and lawn-mowing robots outside [1]. Field studies of robots in

HRI '15, March 2–5, 2015, Portland, OR, USA
Copyright 2015 ACM 978-1-4503-2883-8/15/03...$15.00
http://dx.doi.org/10.1145/2696454.2696472

educational facilities have used multiple Qrio humanoids along with the Rubi platform [2]. Eldercare institutions already employ multiple seal-like PARO robots simultaneously. Researchers also suggest various uses for robotic swarms, such as modular robots that self-configure into different types of furniture [3], small robotic vacuums that work together to reach hard-to-clean areas [4], and robots that can help in dangerous situations. Researchers and funders alike expect that humans and robots will be able to "symbiotically coexist" and collaborate [5], but there is little research on human interaction with groups of robots to guide the development of socially acceptable multi-robot applications.

While many future application ideas imply the use of multiple robots interacting with people and with each other, most previous human-robot interaction (HRI) research only involves single robots, even when examining effects like a robot's group identity (e.g., as German; [6]). Many important social psychological factors that determine the quality and quantity of social interactions have been successfully applied to HRI research (e,g., gaze [7, 8]). Less frequently applied, however, are social psychological theories that predict changes in these social factors when exposed to or interacting with groups versus individuals [9, 10]. In this study, we tested whether effects parallel to those found in interactions among humans may be found in HRI—specifically, that one's attitudes, emotions, and stereotypes of robots may significantly differ when observing or interacting with an individual robot versus a group of robots.

In addition, we extend existing HRI research (e.g., [8, 11-13]) on the importance of robotic type (manipulated by robots' physical appearance and behavior) to examine its effects in individual versus group contexts. Most studies in HRI that examine group effects in robots use humanoid robots only (e.g., [6]). Previous studies suggest that the level of anthropomorphism of a robot type may influence social qualities applied to it, which moderate how socially people behave toward robots [8]. In addition, preliminary evidence from recent studies suggests that non-anthropomorphic form may lower group effects [9, 10]. However, these researchers have yet to follow up about the specifics of these effects.

To investigate the extent to which attitudes, emotions, and stereotypes towards robots in general are modulated by observing single vs. multiple robots of various types, we showed participants videos involving one or several robots and varied robot type (anthropomorphic, zoomorphic, mechanomorphic). After this, we administered questionnaires to measure a wide range of perceptions and reactions to robots. Measures were drawn from literature on both human-robot and human-human interaction.

2. BACKGROUND AND RELATED WORK

HRI researchers have successfully adopted social psychological methods and theories to HRI—in particular, when measuring perceptions of individual robots. Attitudinal and behavioral responses to robots are often similar to responses to other humans in human-human interaction (HHI), as seen in the computer-as-social-actors paradigm [14]. For example, research suggests that humans attribute human-like capabilities, such as theory of mind and free will, to certain robots, but not others [15]. Humans even respond differently to robots that are defined as ingroup versus outgroup members, exhibiting varying behaviors and attitudes towards the same robot, depending on the robot's arbitrarily assigned social membership (e.g., German vs. Egyptian) [16, 17]. In this paper, we extend the HRI literature by a) examining the effect of exposure to groups of robots, b) evaluating how group effects are displayed in relation to robots of different types (physical forms and behaviors), and c) drawing on conceptualizations and measures from social psychological research on intergroup interaction (for example, measures of various types of threat and emotion).

2.1 Robot Number and Group Effects

The hypothesis that robot number can alter social perception is based on previous research in social psychology that indicates significant variation in the social perception of individuals versus groups [18]. Intergroup interactions among humans are generally more negative, uncooperative, and even aggressive than interactions between individuals. Researchers have found that, when two teams of three players or two individuals participate in "games" where they have to allocate valuable points between themselves and the opponent, teams like the opponents less and make more competitive choices compared to individual players [19]. Similarly, teams (compared to individuals) are more likely to retaliate by harming the opponents when the opponent takes an initial action perceived as aggressive [20].

Even in non-competitive contexts, the presence of groups can have negative consequences on social perceptions: how humans think about, feel, and react to robots. In many social situations, individuals 'automatically' (e.g., without conscious awareness) categorize others according to easily available social category cues, such as gender and race, often leading to greater encoding and recollection of behaviors that are stereotypic of members in that category [21]. Social categorization frequently causes *negative* social perceptions of other groups because in the social categorization process (e.g., coding "us" versus "them"), individuals often recall more negative information for the other than for their own group, leading to increased antipathy [22].

Regarding robots, negative group effects may be exacerbated by at least three factors: unfamiliarity with robots, robots' physical similarity, and current stereotypes about robots. First, unfamiliarity with an outgroup increases susceptibility to using stereotypes [23], and most people have little to no experience with robots. Second, similarities in physical appearance can lead to increased group effects, such as perceived threat [24]. Finally, in the US in particular, many popular and media-related stereotypes of robots are negative [25]. Despite the potential for negative attitudes, emotions, and stereotypes toward groups of robots to arise when group context is salient, little research explored the influence of such group effects on social perceptions of robots.

However, robots in groups may also be viewed positively. One hypothesis is that interacting with multiple robots causes people to self-categorize as humans, which focuses them on the distinction between humans and robots. While that might result in most robot types (e.g., mechanomorphic, zoomorphic) being seen as more different from humans and perceived more negatively, human-like type (e.g., NAO) may be perceived more positively. Second, certain positive qualities of robots may only be revealed in group settings. For example, robots may appear more social (e.g. becoming more 'friend-like') when seen interacting with other robots. Third, seeing multiple robots could increase

perception of robot value, usefulness, etc. (for example, seeing swarms of fire-fighting robots versus a single robot).

Previous research on the 'discontinuity effect' found that groups of various sizes (two to eight members) show similar patterns of interaction, with both group and non-group members [26]. For the Group conditions in this study, we used two to three robots as numbers that would contrast with the single-robot conditions.

2.2 Robot Type and Social Perceptions

Several lines of HRI research suggest that a robot's type (physical form and behavior) influences social perceptions. The 'uncanny valley' [27] is a classic example of non-linear change in attitudes toward robots depending on how human-like they appear. Recent research also suggests that motion, related to type, influences social perception—for example, by changing the subjective feeling of social 'ease' when interacting with the robot [28].

Tasks and behavior have been shown to affect what form people expect the robot to have, and vice versa [29]. Form also largely determines a robot's social behavioral repertoire (e.g., gaze and gestures enhance social interaction) [13], and thus can influence expectations for social interactions. Anthropomorphic features can confer social advantages to robots by allowing them to engage in human-like social behaviors, such as emotional expressions [13], which can enhance social trust and other perceptions [8].

2.3 Interaction: Robot Number and Type

The effects of number and type have been treated separately in human-human and human-robot interaction. The interaction between these two variables—for example, how type may determine the effects of number—has seldom been explored.

In most HRI research examining group effects, the robots used are anthropomorphic (e.g., Flobi, Robovie). In order to create a more social context, these experiments often introduce the robots as fitting into existing human social categories (e.g., "this robot is German") or by creating shared goals between robot and participant [10, 16]. In other studies, the experimenter treats the robot as human-like and the robot engages in various social behaviors (e.g., didactic teaching, complimenting shoes) [15].

We focus on two unexplored areas in this study. First, many robots in the near future will not be human-like, as they will be designed to perform specific behaviors and functions, and robot type will likely alter the effects of group context on social perception. Although some studies have found group effects in HRI similar to in HHI (e.g., [16]), studies involving non-anthropomorphic robots have shown notable differences [9, 10]. In one study, competition against mechanomorphic iCreate robots increased when participating in a group scenario compared to one-on-one interaction, but implicit (IAT) and explicit (NARS) attitudes toward robots did not change. In contrast, in studies of group competition in humans and humanoid robots, explicit attitudes also tend to become more negative [9]. It seems, therefore, that the extent of a robot's anthropomorphism may influence group effects on social perception.

Second, few studies have explored responses to multiple robots that are simultaneously present and interacting with each other. Many factors known to modulate social perception toward others, such as degree of similarity between conspecifics, ingroup entitativity (e.g., how similar they are with each other), emotion sharing, and empathy, are likely to only be perceptible when observing individuals interacting with others within their group. Some of these factors may strongly influence social perception, but most HRI studies do not show robots interacting with other robots. As previously discussed, the physical form of robots can also restrict their social behavioral repertoire, which includes potentially important group-based behaviors. Some of these social behaviors may be more observable in anthropomorphic robots, leading to different group effects across types of robots [13].

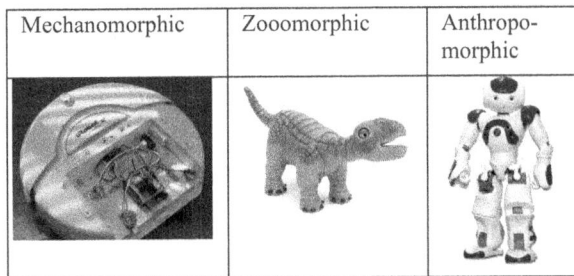

Mechanomorphic	Zooomorphic	Anthropo-morphic

Figure 1: Robots for Type condition manipulation

2.4 Overview

In social psychology, group interaction and observation alters perceptions of others [18]. In this study, we expect the presence of a group, rather than individual, robots, to affect how participants view robots in general. However, robots vary in type, and research has not yet systematically examined how robot type might influence the effects of group presence. In this exploratory study, we examine the effects of number, type, and the number by type interaction on attitudes, emotions, and stereotypes held toward robots, which will be critical to the design and application of robots for everyday use. We manipulated what video participants watched to prime their ideas of robots, and then administered questions about robots *in general* to explore the effect of Number and Type of an exemplar robot on general perceptions of robots.

3. METHODS

3.1 Study Design

The study had a 2x3 between-subjects design. Participants watched a video of robots. In the video, Number (Single, Group) and Type (NAO (anthropomorphic), Pleo (zoomorphic), iCreate (mechanomorphic); Figure 1) design was manipulated. Videos in Group conditions showed two NAOs, three Pleos, or three iCreates. NAOs performed anthropomorphic behaviors (e.g., standing, waving), Pleos performed zoomorphic behaviors (e.g., "eating," walking), and iCreates performed mechanomorphic behaviors (e.g., driving, beeping). Robots performed similar behaviors in single and group videos. In Group conditions, the robots often performed coordinated behaviors (e.g., walking).

3.2 Measures

Most HRI studies involve robot-specific measures (e.g., Godspeed Scale, Ezer Analogies, NARS), and occasionally some measures from HHI (e.g., Big 5). We chose to use a range of measures from HRI, as well as a range of measures from social psychology that have been used to examine stereotypes and prejudice in studies of interaction between groups. This allowed us to examine social perceptions of robots typically not explored in HRI: attitudes (general thoughts; e.g., I don't like robots), emotions (e.g., I fear robots), and stereotypes (beliefs about a group; e.g., robots will work in factories) [30]. Below are the measures by category:

Attitudes:
- Negative Attitudes toward Robots Scale (Subscales: S1-Situation of Interaction, S2-Social Influence of the Robots, S3-Emotion in Robots During Interactions) [31]
- Direct measure of attitude toward robots (e.g., "I like robots," "I feel positive toward robots")

Emotions:
- Emotion items (e.g., "I fear robots;" "I respect robots") [32]
- Threat appraisal items (e.g., "Robots threaten people's jobs." Subscales: social, physical, economy, general)

Stereotypes:
- Big 5 personality items, modified so participants rated robots' traits (subscales: Conscientiousness, Extroversion, Agreeableness, Openness to Experience, Neuroticism) [33]
- Godspeed Questionnaire (subscales: Anthropomorphism, Animacy, Likeability, Perceived Intelligence, Perceived Safety) [34]
- Ezer analogy items (e.g., robots "in the near future" will be "like a pet," "like a toy") [35]
- Robot work contexts (e.g., "I think robots should work in classrooms")
- Situational appraisals of robots (e.g., "I would trust a robot to invest some of my money in the stock market")

Demographics (age, gender, field of study, technological experience) were also recorded.

3.3 Procedure

The study took place in the Indiana University R-House Lab. College-aged participants were tested individually. After they completed the informed consent, participants watched one of six two-minute robot videos (iCreate, Pleo, NAO – as a single robot or group of two or three robots). After the video, participants completed the measures listed above, in reference to robots *in general* rather than the specific robots they viewed. This was to ascertain how exposure to a particular type of robot would affect overall perceptions of robots Measures were presented in a standard order, arranged in an attempt to minimize carry-over effects from one scale to the next. Then, participants were debriefed and compensated with $10 or course credit.

4. RESULTS

For comparisons among conditions, 2 (Single, Group) x 3 (NAO, Pleo, iCreate) ANOVAs were performed in SPSS. P-values of .05 or less were considered statistically significant. For each subsection below, if a Number or Type main effect or a Number x Type interaction was found, it is reported. F and p values for main effects of Number and Type and interactions are found in the tables along with means and standard deviations.

Post-hoc analyses were performed in R, with the Tukey Test used to compare main effects, and uncorrected p-values are reported for interaction effects. These differences and p-values are reported within the text (not tables). Other analyses were excluded from this paper due to space limitations.

4.1 Participants

127 participants were recruited at Indiana University (See Table 1 for details across conditions).

Table 1. Participant Demographics

Demographics		Single			Group		
		NAO	Pleo	iCreate	NAO	Pleo	iCreate
Age(M)	Years	22	25	24	22	25	24
Sex N(%)	Male	9(45)	11(55)	11(55)	16(70)	10(43)	4(17)
	Female	11(55)	9(45)	9(45)	7(30)	13(57)	19(83)
Study N(%)	CS	9(45)	11(55)	8(40)	13(57)	2(9)	14(63)
	Humanity	5(25)	6(30)	5(25)	7(30)	9(41)	8(36)
	Science	6(30)	2(10)	6(30)	3(13)	9(41)	0(0)
	Undecided	0(0)	0(0)	1(5)	0(0)	2(9)	0(0)

4.2 Number and Type Results

4.2.1 Attitudes (Table 2)

NARS. Participants rated items from 1 (Strongly Disagree) to 5 (Strongly Agree) about negativity toward robots. Ratings tended to be higher (i.e. more negative) for Group than Single iCreate conditions, but lower for Group than Single NAO conditions.

S1: Situation of Interaction. No main effects (Number or Type) occurred, but a significant interaction of Number and Type ($p <$ .01), indicated that Group iCreates induced significantly higher (more negative) S1 scores than Single iCreates ($p <$ .01), while NAOs showed the opposite effect ($p = $ .05).

S2: Social Influence of Robots. A main effect for Type ($p <$ .001) was found, such that Pleos elicited lower scores (i.e. less negative) than NAOs ($p <$ .05) and iCreates ($p <$ .01). A Number x Type interaction was found ($p <$ .01), with iCreates inducing higher (i.e. more negative) scores in Single than Group conditions ($p <$ .01) and NAOs inducing lower scores in Single than Group ($p = $ .05).

S3: Emotion in Robots During Interactions. No significant differences were found.

Direct attitude measure *(liking, feeling positive toward robots)*: Number x Type interactions were found (all $p <$ .05), such that participants in Group NAO rated robots more positively than Single NAO for Liking, Positivity, and Disliking, while the reverse effect occurred for iCreates, with these scores lower for Group iCreates, compared to Single iCreates (all $p <$ .05).

Emotions (Table 3)

Emotions. Participants rated items from 1 (Strongly Disagree) to 5 (Strongly Agree). Higher ratings for negative emotion items (e.g., *fear, anxious*) tended to be found for Groups than Single iCreate, while the opposite trend emerged for NAOs (negative emotions were lower for Group than Single NAO conditions).

Anxiety/Fear/Distrust/Security/Uneasiness: A Number x Type interaction was found for numerous items (all $p <$ .05), such that Group iCreates induced higher ratings of distrust, uneasiness, anxiety, fear, and lower security (all $p <$ .01) than Single iCreates. An opposite trend emerged for NAOs, with Group NAOs eliciting lower ratings of uneasiness and fear (ps < .05) than Single NAOs.

Usefulness: A Number x Type interaction was found ($p <$ .05), such that Group iCreates elicited lower ratings ($p <$ .05) compared to Single iCreates, while group NAOs elicited higher, yet nonsignificant usefulness ratings compared to single NAOs.

Pity: A main effect of Type was found, with Pleos eliciting more pity than iCreates (p=.05). No interaction effects were found.

Gratefulness: A Number x Type interaction was found ($p <$ .05), such that Group NAOs elicited higher scores than Single NAOs ($p <$ .001), but for iCreates and Pleos number did not matter.

Other emotion items not mentioned (excited, useless, sympathy, pride in humanity, sad, superior, inferior, happy, respect, resent, guilt, envy, disgust) showed no significant differences.

Threat. Participants rated items from 1 (Strongly Disagree) to 5 (Strongly Agree) regarding robot threats. Overall, Group iCreates tended to elicit higher ratings (i.e., more perceived threat) than Single iCreates, while the opposite trend occurred for NAOs.

No main effects were detected, but a Number x Type interaction for Social Threat was found ($p <$ .001), such that higher Social Threat ratings occurred for Group than Single iCreates ($p <$ .05), while NAO and Pleos exhibited non-significant decreases in Social Threat scores from Single to Group. There were no significant differences across conditions for *General Threat, Economic Threat,* or *Physical Threat*.

4.2.2 Stereotypes (Table 4)

Big Five. Participants rated traits from 1 (Strongly Disagree) to 7 (Strongly Agree). For *Agreeableness*, a main effect of Type was found, with Pleo conditions eliciting higher ratings of robots "in general" than participants in the NAO conditions ($p <$ .05). No other significant differences between conditions were observed. No other Big 5 trait elicited significant differences.

Godspeed. Participants rated robot traits using a 'semantic differential' response format (e.g., for Fake-Natural: from 1- Fake to 5- Natural). For the *Likeability Subscale*, a main effect of Number occurred, with Groups rated higher than Singles ($p <$ .05). No other significant differences between conditions were observed for the Likeability or other subscales.

Ezer Analogies. Participants rated analogies for 'what you imagine robots in the near future might be like' from 1 (Not at all) to 5 (To a great extent). Specific analogies are listed below.

Friend: A main effect of Type was found, with Pleos rated higher than iCreates ($p = $ .05). A Number x Type interaction was found ($p <$ .01), with Group Pleos rated lower than Single Pleos ($p = $ .01), but Group iCreates higher than Single iCreates ($p <$ .05).

Servant: A main effect of Type was found. NAOs induced higher ratings than Pleos ($p <$ .05). Number and Type interacted (p < .05) with lower ratings for Group than Single Pleos ($p <$ .05), but nonsignificantly higher ratings of Group than Single robots for NAO and iCreate conditions. No differences were found for *Appliance, Assistant, Human, Machine, Pet, Teammate,* or *Toy*.

Table 2. Attitudes: NARS, Like/Dislike

Attitudes			NAO M(SD)	Pleo M(SD)	iCreate M(SD)		Num $F(1,121)$	Type $F(2,212)$	NumType $F(2,212)$
NARS	S1	Single	2.41(.70)	1.96(.36)	1.97(.52)	F	1.076	1.858	6.656**
		Group	2.03(.61)	2.08(.63)	2.56(.76)	n^2_p			0.099
	S2	Single	3.28(.54)	2.97(.70)	2.93(.62)	F	0.144	5.128**	6.406**
		Group	3.08(.52)	2.66(.77)	3.57(.79)	n^2_p		.078	.096
Emotion	Like	Single	3.5(1.00)	4.1(0.64)	4.1(0.69)	F	0.02	0.83	8.29**
		Group	4.4(0.78)	3.9(1.04)	3.5(1.01)	n^2_p			0.12
	Positive	Single	3.7(0.92)	4.1(0.69)	4.1(0.76)	F	0.26	0.19	3.77*
		Group	4.3(0.71)	3.9(0.97)	3.8(0.92)	n^2_p			0.06
	Dislike	Single	2.2(1.01)	1.8(0.64)	1.9(0.72)	F	0.00	1.37	3.34*
		Group	1.7(0.70)	1.9(0.77)	2.3(1.04)	n^2_p			0.05

* signifies that p < .05, ** signifies that p < .01

Table 3. Emotions: Emotion and Threat

Emotion			NAO M(SD)	Pleo M(SD)	iCreate M(SD)		Num $F(1,121)$	Type $F(2,212)$	NumType $F(2,212)$
Emotion	Useful	Single	4.3(0.72)	4.5(0.51)	4.7(0.47)	F	0.09	0.15	3.27*
		Group	4.6(0.51)	4.5(0.96)	4.3(0.70)	n^2_p			0.05
	Distrust	Single	2.4(1.05)	2.3(1.02)	1.9(0.79)	F	0.08	0.28	5.61*
		Group	1.9(0.67)	2.1(0.97)	2.7(0.89)	n^2_p			0.09
	Uneasy	Single	2.7(0.92)	2.3(0.91)	1.9(0.85)	F	0.50	0.24	7.55**
		Group	2.0(0.88)	2.3(0.98)	2.9(1.31)	n^2_p			0.11
	Anxious	Single	2.5(0.89)	2.4(1.04)	1.9(0.99)	F	3.37	0.70	7.62**
		Group	2.0(0.93)	2.5(1.18)	3.2(1.22)	n^2_p			0.11
	Fear	Single	2.8(1.16)	2.0(0.86)	1.7(0.80)	F	0.95	0.36	8.97**
		Group	1.9(1.08)	2.3(1.08)	2.8(1.30)	n^2_p			0.13
	Grateful	Single	3.0(0.83)	3.7(0.67)	3.3(0.97)	F	0.90	1.00	4.20*
		Group	3.8(0.85)	3.4(1.18)	3.2(1.05)	n^2_p			0.07
	Secure	Single	2.7(0.99)	3.0(0.60)	3.5(0.83)	F	0.46	0.74	9.58**
		Group	3.1(0.79)	3.2(0.73)	2.5(0.74)	n^2_p			0.14
	Pity	Single	1.8(0.83)	2.3(1.16)	1.6(0.82)	F	0.10	3.07*	0.15
		Group	1.9(1.01)	2.2(1.14)	1.8(1.02)	n^2_p		0.05	
Threat	Social	Single	2.4(0.68)	2.4(0.87)	2.0(0.74)	F	0.01	0.10	4.56*
		Group	2.1(0.74)	2.0(0.77)	2.6(0.76)	n^2_p			0.07

*signifies that p < .05, ** signifies that p < .01*

Table 4. Stereotypes: Big Five, Godspeed, Ezer Analogies, Work Context, Situational Appraisals of Robots

Stereotypes			NAO M(SD)	Pleo M(SD)	iCreate M(SD)		Num $F(1,121)$	Type $F(2,121)$	NumType $F(2,121)$
Big Five	Agreeable	Single	-0.9(2.16)	0.9(2.42)	-0.1(1.86)	F	0.86	3.37*	0.65
		Group	-0.6(2.04)	0.2(2.84)	-0.9(2.91)	n^2_p		0.05	
Godspeed	Likeability	Single	3.3(0.74)	3.6(0.47)	3.3(0.54)	F	4.38*	1.35	1.28
		Group	3.7(0.48)	3.6(0.67)	3.5(0.68)	n^2_p	0.04		
Ezer Analogies	Friend	Single	2.3(1.45)	3.6(1.05)	2.1(0.76)	F	0.28	3.71*	6.97**
		Group	2.8(1.30)	2.6(1.33)	2.8(1.14)	n^2_p		0.06	0.10
	Servant	Single	4.0(1.05)	3.9(1.07)	3.6(1.19)	F	0.01	3.71*	4.10*
		Group	4.3(0.88)	3.1(1.17)	4.0(1.09)	n^2_p		0.06	0.06
Work Place	Danger Area	Single	3.9(1.62)	4.5(1.00)	4.9(0.31)	F	0.48	0.70	4.54*
		Group	4.4(1.24)	4.5(1.34)	3.9(1.39)	n^2_p			0.07
	Resort	Single	3.1(0.94)	4.0(1.32)	3.5(1.24)	F	3.72	0.55	3.41*
		Group	3.4(1.08)	3.0(1.29)	2.9(1.34)	n^2_p			0.05
	Office	Single	3.5(1.15)	4.0(1.08)	3.6(1.19)	F	0.59	0.23	4.91*
		Group	3.8(0.94)	3.0(1.07)	3.7(1.12)	n^2_p			0.08
	Police	Single	2.6(1.60)	3.6(1.36)	2.7(1.00)	F	1.85	0.31	6.28**
		Group	3.0(1.22)	2.2(0.85)	2.7(1.25)	n^2_p			0.09
	Shopping	Single	3.3(1.03)	3.7(1.08)	3.3(1.08)	F	0.04	0.47	3.16*
		Group	3.9(1.01	3.1(1.11)	3.5(1.22)	n^2_p			0.05
	Factory	Single	4.3(0.98)	4.9(0.37)	4.7(0.49)	F	0.09	0.19	4.63**
		Group	4.9(0.34)	4.5(0.96)	4.5(0.96)	n^2_p			0.07
	Hospital	Single	3.3(1.30)	4.0(1.00)	3.6(1.10)	F	0.40	0.03	3.70*
		Group	3.8(0.89)	3.1(1.32)	3.5(1.14)	n^2_p			0.06
	Home	Single	3.5(0.76)	4.1(1.02)	3.6(1.05)	F	0.21	0.46	6.16**
		Group	4.1(0.90)	3.2(1.05)	3.6(1.18)	n^2_p			0.09
Situation Appraisals of Robots	Teach Kids	Single	3.2(1.39)	3.9(0.75)	4.0(0.83)	F	0.69	0.79	3.92*
		Group	3.7(0.70)	3.6(1.18)	3.2(1.44)	n^2_p			0.06
	In House	Single	2.1(0.99)	1.6(0.72)	1.1(0.75)	F	0.42	2.42	5.74**
		Group	1.6(0.93)	1.5(0.80)	2.1(1.09)	n^2_p			0.09
	With Possessions	Single	2.6(1.17)	2.0(0.79)	2.5(0.81)	F	0.06	4.86**	3.12*
		Group	2.2(1.12)	3.0(0.87)	2.3(1.14)	n^2_p		.074	0.05
	Stock Market	Single	2.5(1.19)	3.0(1.17)	3.1(1.05)	F	0.43	0.99	4.1*
		Group	3.3(1.01)	3.2(1.26)	2.5(1.10)	n^2_p			0.06

*signifies that p < .05, ** signifies that p < .01*

Work contexts: Participants rated "which contexts [you think] robots should work in" on a 1 (Not at all) to 5 (To a great extent) scale. No main effects were found, but several interaction effects were significant. In general, Group Pleos elicited significantly decreased ratings (i.e. 'robots should not work in [context]') compared to Single Pleos. Specifically, Group Pleos had lower scores than Single Pleos for numerous contexts, including resorts, offices, police stations, shopping areas, hospitals, and homes (all $p < .05$). In contrast, Group NAOs generally elicited nonsignificant *increases* in work context scores compared to Single NAOs, including one statistically significant increase for 'working in factories' ($p = .01$). There was also a Number x Type interaction effect for 'dangerous areas' ($p = .01$), such that Group iCreates elicited lower scores than Single iCreates ($p < .01$), while Pleos and NAOs did not significantly change across Number.

Situational Appraisals of Robots. Participants rated a number of situational appraisals involving the trust of robots from 1 (Strongly disagree) to 5 (Strongly agree). Higher numbers indicated greater willingness to trust robots in these scenarios.

Higher ratings tended to be found for Group than Single NAO conditions, and lower ratings for Group than Single iCreate conditions. Overall, there were few main effects (Number or Type), but a larger number of Number x Type interactions. Specific items with statistical significance are below, listed by type of result (i.e. main effect or interaction effect).

Type: Participants who viewed NAOs were more likely to trust robots to hold their personal possessions than Pleos and iCreates ($ps < .05$).

Interaction effects: Participants showed more trust for Group than Single NAOs for robots teaching children, being in their own homes, holding their personal possessions, and telling robots about personal secrets ($ps < .05$). Conversely, less trust was shown for Group than Single iCreates for having a robot invest their money in the stock market ($p < .05$). No significant effects were seen for: robots cooking food, helping you walk, tutoring, reminding you about medicine, helping with an injury, talking about something personal, or talking about a friend.

5. Discussion

Our primary interest was in examining the influence of robot number and type on a variety of variables, such as attitudes, emotions, and stereotypes. In this study, participants (between-subjects) were shown a video of robots differing in Number (Single, Group) and Type (NAO, Pleo, iCreate), and then they completed questionnaires that measure social responses.

Interestingly, we found strong evidence that instead of number or type of the robot videos influencing these social variables, it was generally the *interaction between these two factors* that best accounted for the observed results. This pattern was consistent across the measures for attitudes, emotions, and stereotypes toward robots. Below, we discuss the main findings.

First, introducing groups of iCreate robots increased *negative* responses, such as self-reported threat, anxiety, fear, and lack of trust, compared to single iCreate robots. We found this across several item scales (see Tables 2-4). The increase in negative emotions (e.g., threat, fear, disliking) may have influenced diverse aspects of social perception, such as situational appraisals (e.g., trusting robots in different scenarios) and work contexts. For instance, viewing a group of iCreate robots led to participants being less likely to want robots to teach children, have a presence in their home, and invest in the stock market for them.

Second, viewing groups of NAOs tended to elicit more *positive* responses than viewing a single NAO. This was apparent in a wide variety of scales that measured general affect (e.g., liking, disliking, feeling positive), emotions (e.g., anxiety, fear, gratefulness), perceived threat, and trust.

Third, viewing groups of Pleo robots led to other, unique effects. Unlike with NAOs and iCreates, Group Pleos seldom elicited more positive or negative responses than Single Pleos. Instead, viewing Group Pleos elicited changes in more descriptive characteristics of robots (i.e. stereotypes), including analogies and future work contexts. For example, participants exposed to Group Pleo videos rated robots in general as less like servants or friends, and less likely to be part of the future workplace (overall), compared to participants who viewed Single Pleos. These types of changes were observed less frequently in NAOs and iCreates.

5.1 Proposed Explanations

To account for the findings of this exploratory study, we offer three explanations, which are based on the notions that (1) Observing groups of robots reveals *novel types of information* about the robots that cannot be observed from single robots and (2) Observing many instead of just one robot increases the *salience of the distinction between humans and robots*, causing the human observer to categorize him or herself as human [18].

Our first potential explanation involving the above notions is that a robot's *degree of perceived sociality* may influence social psychological variables that are (directly or indirectly) relevant to social interactions. A group of robots can display a variety of social behaviors that are impossible to convey in isolation, such as social intelligence, behavior coordination among individuals, and shared goal pursuit. These features may all affect observers' own social perceptions of the robots—for instance, causing them to like robots more (e.g., if they appear socially competent) [7, 8].

Second, *intergroup dynamics* may influence responses to robots, by changing perceived intergroup competition and perceived threat. As previously noted, observing multiple robots may cause observers to self-categorize as humans, which in turn will focus attention on differences between humans and robots [18]. Thus, the robots most dissimilar to humans (mechanomorphic) may seem even less human-like in groups, reducing liking for them. In contrast, a group of anthropomorphic robots may be more likely to be classified as "like me" or "human" when there are many of them, as opposed to one. Not only the robots' form, but their display of social behaviors that either are human-like or not may be especially strong contributors to social categorization and the resulting processes. Beyond our specific study, numerous social behaviors, including emotional contagion, within-group competition, and swarm behavior may be observable with groups of robots. Each of these behaviors may have important consequences for future social interactions with the robots. For example, an individual who infers that a group of robots are likely to stick together (e.g., based on their highly coordinated behavior) may perceive higher intergroup competition, possibly resulting in more negative attitudes and emotions towards those robots [24].

Third, *level of anthropomorphism* may affect a wide variety of social and non-social variables. Observing robots interact with each other can provide information about whether robots are "human-like" or not [13]. Previous research suggests that relational actions, rather than simply object form, can lead people to apply anthropomorphic interaction schemas to inanimate objects (e.g., geometric shapes), including emotions such as anger and fear [36]. People may also bring other types of non-anthropomorphic interpretations to different relational actions depending on the interaction schema triggered by the robots' relational behaviors toward each other. Robot groups that are not seen as displaying human-like social behaviors may be perceived as less human-like, which can impact social perception in many ways. This study provides preliminary evidence that information given by group behavior, is sometimes more potent or informative than information given by robot type alone in determining social responses to robots. In the study, this was evidenced by the relative lack of main effects of Type on social responses, compared to the large amount of Number x Type interaction effects (i.e. more positive *or* more negative depending on Number and Type), which showed robots interacting relationally.

Social behaviors may be perceived along other spectrums, such as zoomorphism (i.e., similarity to animals). In the case of Group Pleos, we suggest that their group social behaviors (e.g., grazing) may have prompted participants to see them as more animal-like, consequentially leading to decreases in certain social perceptions (such as Group Pleos being less "like friends", less "like servants", and less likely to be seen in future work contexts, as would be expected for zoomorphic entities).

These three explanations are highly complementary with each other. For a specific example, *degree of sociality* and *intergroup dynamics* may exert a bidirectional influence on each other, such that observing a highly agreeable and sociable robot may decrease perceived threat, and vice versa. Further, an observed behavior may impact two or more of these features simultaneously. For example, swarm behavior (e.g., intelligent behavior arising from the group, rather than from individuals) may make observers judge robots as more threatening and less anthropomorphic. The intent of separating these three features is not to suggest that they are fully disassociated, but rather to emphasize that they may each exert some unique effects on social perception (in addition to their shared influence).

5.2 Limitations and Future Work

The social psychological literature presented earlier shows a strong emphasis on the generally negative consequences of perceiving groups of people versus individuals, although the effects can be positive under specific circumstances. Viewing others in a group context often increases anxiety, anger, intergroup competition, and other undesirable social consequences. We found large variation in whether introducing a group context *improved* or *damaged* social perception towards different types of robots.

One potential explanation of these observed differences is that they were mediated by the valence of the robot videos. It is possible, for instance, that certain robot videos (e.g., NAOs) may have induced positive emotions while others (e.g., iCreates) did not. Positively valenced videos may have caused more positive social responses toward robots, while negatively valenced videos made responses more negative. While this hypothesis is currently not possible to reject, videos were created using only behaviors that the robots could perform, and thus, the valence of each video rested in the perceived valence of robot types, behaviors, and interactions. Further, the valence alone does not account for the highly specific effects of the videos on social variables, such as changes in expected work contexts for group Pleos.

A limitation of this paper is that in some Group conditions we used two robots (NAO), and in some we used three (Pleo, iCreate). Although this was less than ideal, evidence on the discontinuity effect [26] suggests that it would not have a great

influence on responses to robots. Further, our results do not suggest that the pattern of responses to groups of robots is directly affected by the number (two or three) of robots. For example, we did not find that people respond negatively to two robots, and even more negatively to three. Thus, we find it unlikely that the differing numbers affected the results – though it is a constraint of our study occasioned by our lack of access to three NAOs.

Because participants in this study answered questions about their attitudes, emotions, and stereotypes toward robots in general, we cannot conclude what participants thought of the specific robots they watched in the videos and what types of robots they were thinking of during the study. We propose that it is likely that participants' emotions, attitudes, and stereotypes towards robots were assimilated toward their responses for the specific, observed robots (i.e., what they thought of the robots in the video, they projected to robots in general). We believe this is likely because non-extreme primes (i.e. video featuring robots that are not significantly different than other robots, in general) generally produce assimilation effects [37]. However, further research should be done to confirm this hypothesis.

This study suggests that robot-robot interaction influences human perceptions of robots. In a world in which robots are becoming increasingly prevalent, understanding these effects will be critical for designing appropriate environments for humans and robots. This was an exploratory study, and we suggest further research to examine the details of the effects of robot-robot interaction. We are beginning further research to test if these findings of responses to videos of robots in this study can generalize to interaction with physically present robots (single or group). We are also investigating specifically what social behaviors and qualities people interpret in the videos of multiple robots we showed.

In this study, we found that people generally respond more positively to anthropomorphic robots in groups than singly, whereas mechanomorphic robots in groups increase negative responses. This research is relevant to places such as the Robot House in Hertfordshire that keep only one robot operational at a time in an attempt to reduce human anxiety [38]. This study suggests that multiple robots could operate at once without increasing anxiety if the robots are anthropomorphic. Because anthropomorphic robots, such as NAOs, are viewed more positively in groups than singly, they may be more marketable in groups. Future research might also benefit from examining mixed robot groups (akin to the fictional duo of humanoid C3PO and mechanomorphic R2D2) in order to understand how people might respond to groups involving several different types of robots.

6. ACKNOWLEDGMENTS

Our thanks to the Social Science Research Center (SSRC) at Indiana University for funding this project. Thank you to Cindy Bethel, Stephanie Wuisan, and Dexter Duckworth for recording the group-NAO video, to Chen Yu and Linger Xu for assistance with the single-NAO video, to IU's Cognitive Science Program for their loan of three Pleos, and to Matthew Francisco and Kartik Adur for building the iCreates for the videos. Thank you also to Kate Shaw, Christina Wehrmann, Tasha Smith, Jingsha Liu, and Catherine Sembroski for running participants.

7. REFERENCES

[1] Gates, B., 2007. A robot in every home. *Scientific American*, 296(1): 58-65.

[2] Alač, M., J. Movellan, and Tanaka, F.. 2011. When a robot is social: Spatial arrangements and multimodal semiotic

engagement in the practice of social robotics. *Social Studies of Science*, 41(6): 126-159.

[3] Sproⁿwitz, A., et al. 2010. Roombots: Reconfigurable robots for adaptive furniture. *IEEE Computational Intelligence Magazine* 5(3): 20-32.

[4] Brooks, R. A. 2002. *Flesh and Machines: How Robots Will Change Us*. New York: Pantheon Books.

[5] National Science Foundation. 2006. *National Robotics Initiative*. URL: http://www.nsf.gov/pubs/2014/nsf14500/nsf14500.htm

[6] Kuchenbrandt, D., et al. 2013. When a robot's group membership matters. *International Journal of Social Robotics* 5(3): 409-417.

[7] Bee, N., E. André, and Tober, S. 2009. Breaking the ice in human-agent communication: Eye-gaze based initiation of contact with an embodied conversational agent. *Intelligent Virtual Agents*, 5773: 229-242.

[8] Gong, L. 2008. How social is social responses to computers? The function of the degree of anthropomorphism in computer representations. *Computers in Human Behavior* 24(4): 1494-1509.

[9] Chang, W. L., et al. 2012. The effect of group size on people's attitudes and cooperative behaviors toward robots in interactive gameplay. *Proc. of RO-MAN 2012*: 845-850.

[10] Fraune, M. R., & Šabanović, S. 2014. Negative Attitudes toward Minimalistic Robots with Intragroup Communication Styles. *Proc. of RO-MAN 2014:* 1116-1121.

[11] Fink, J., et al. 2014. Dynamics of anthropomorphism in human-robot interaction. *Frontiers in Cognitive Sciences,* August 27 2014, URL: http://infoscience.epfl.ch/record/201545/files/paper.pdf

[12] DiSalvo, C. F., et al. 2002. All robots are not created equal: the design and perception of humanoid robot heads. *Proc. of DIS '02*: 321-326.

[13] Fong, T., Nourbakhsh, I., and Dautenhahn, K. 2003. A survey of socially interactive robots. *Robotics and autonomous systems* 42(3): 143-166.

[14] Reeves, B. and Nass. C. 1997. *The Media Equation: How People Treat Computers, Television, and New Media*. Cambridge University Press.

[15] Kahn, P. H., et al. 2007. What is a human?: Toward psychological benchmarks in the field of human-robot interaction. *Interaction Studies* 8(3): 363-390.

[16] Häring, M., D. Kuchenbrandt, and André. E. 2014. Would you like to play with me?: How robots' group membership and task features influence human-robot interaction. *Proc. of HRI'14*: 9-16.

[17] Kuchenbrandt, D., et al. 2011. Minimal group-maximal effect? Evaluation and anthropomorphization of the humanoid robot NAO. *Proc. of ICSR 2011*: 104-113.

[18] Turner, J.C., et al. 1987. *Rediscovering the Social Group: A Self-Categorization Theory*. Basil Blackwell.

[19] Wildschut, T., et al. 2003. Beyond the group mind: a quantitative review of the interindividual-intergroup discontinuity effect. *Psychological bulletin* 129(5): 698-722.

[20] Meier, B. P. and Hinsz, V. B. 2004. A comparison of human aggression committed by groups and individuals: An interindividual–intergroup discontinuity. *Journal of Experimental Social Psychology* 40(4): 551-559.

[21] Macrae, C. N. and Bodenhausen, G.V.. 2000. Social cognition: Thinking categorically about others. *Annual Review of Psychology* 51(1): 93-120.

[22] Howard, J.W. and Rothbart, M. 1980. Social categorization and memory for in-group and out-group behavior. *Journal of Personality and Social Psychology* 38(2): 301.

[23] Wilder, D. A. 1978. Perceiving persons as a group: Effects on attributions of causality and beliefs. *Social Psychology* 41(1): 13-23.

[24] Dasgupta, N., M. R. Banaji, and Abelson, R.P. 1999. Group entitativity and group perception: Associations between physical features and psychological judgment. *Journal of Personality and Social Psychology* 77(5): 991-1003.

[25] Kaplan, F. 2004. Who is afraid of the humanoid? Investigating cultural differences in the acceptance of robots. *International Journal of Humanoid Robotics* 1(3): 465-480.

[26] McGlynn, R.P., D.J. Harding, and Cottle, J.L. 2009. Individual–group discontinuity in group–individual interactions: Does size matter? *Group Processes & Intergroup Relations* 12(1): 129-143.

[27] Mori, M. *2012*. The uncanny valley. MacDorman, K.F. and Kageki, N (translators). *IEEE Robotics and Automation Magazine* 19(2): 98-100. (Original published in 1970)

[28] MacDorman, K. F. 2006. Subjective ratings of robot video clips for human likeness, familiarity, and eeriness: An exploration of the uncanny valley. *Proc. of ICCS/CogSci-2006 Long Symposium: Toward Social mechanisms of Android Science*: 26-29.

[29] Goetz, J., S. Kiesler, and Powers, A. 2003. Matching robot appearance and behavior to tasks to improve human-robot cooperation. *Proc. of ROMAN 2003:* 55-60.

[30] Mackie, D.M. and Smith, E.R. 2002. Beyond prejudice:Moving from positive and negative evaluations to differentiated reactions to social groups. In D.M. Mackie and E.R. Smith (Eds.) *From Prejudice to Intergroup Emotions: Differentiated Reactions to Social Groups*: 1.

[31] Nomura, T., T. Kanda, and Suzuki, T. 2006. Experimental investigation into influence of negative attitudes toward robots on human–robot interaction. *AI & SOCIETY* 20(2): 138-150.

[32] Cottrell, C. A. and Neuberg, S. L. 2005. Different emotional reactions to different groups: a sociofunctional threat-based approach to" prejudice". *Journal of Personality and Social Psychology* 88(5): 770-789.

[33] Gosling, S.D., Rentfrow, P.J., and Swann Jr, W.B. 2003. A very brief measure of the Big-Five personality domains. *Journal of Research in personality* 37(6): 504-528.

[34] Bartneck, C., et al. 2009. Measurement instruments for the anthropomorphism, animacy, likeability, perceived intelligence, and perceived safety of robots. *International Journal of Social Robotics* 1(1): 71-81.

[35] Ezer, N. 2008. *Is a Robot an Appliance, Teammate, or Friend? Age-related differences in expectations of and attitudes towards personal home-based robots*. ProQuest.

[36] Heider, F. and Simmel, M. 1944. An experimental study of apparent behavior. *The American Journal of Psychology:* 243-259.

[37] Herr, P.M., Sherman, S.J., and Fazio, R.H. 1983. On the consequences of priming: Assimilation and contrast effects. *Journal of Experimental Social Psychology* 19(4): 323-340.

[38] Kriegel, M., et al. 2010. Digital body hopping-migrating artificial companions. *Proc. of Digital Futures '10.*

Sacrifice One For the Good of Many? People Apply Different Moral Norms to Human and Robot Agents

Bertram F. Malle

Brown University
Department of Cognitive, Linguistic,
and Psychological Sciences
Providence, RI 02906
bfmalle@brown.edu

Matthias Scheutz and
Thomas Arnold

Tufts University
Department of
Computer Science
Medford, MA 02155

John Voiklis and
Corey Cusimano

Brown University
Department of Cognitive, Linguistic,
and Psychological Sciences
Providence, RI 02906

ABSTRACT

Moral norms play an essential role in regulating human interaction. With the growing sophistication and proliferation of robots, it is important to understand how ordinary people apply moral norms to robot agents and make moral judgments about their behavior. We report the first comparison of people's moral judgments (of permissibility, wrongness, and blame) about human and robot agents. Two online experiments (total $N = 316$) found that robots, compared with human agents, were more strongly expected to take an action that sacrifices one person for the good of many (a "utilitarian" choice), and they were blamed more than their human counterparts when they did not make that choice. Though the utilitarian sacrifice was generally seen as permissible for human agents, they were blamed more for choosing this option than for doing nothing. These results provide a first step toward a new field of *Moral HRI*, which is well placed to help guide the design of social robots.

Categories and Subject Descriptors

I.2.9 [**Artificial Intelligence**] Robotics
K.4.1 [**Computers and Society**] Public Policy Issues, *Ethics*

Keywords

Robot Ethics; Machine Morality; Human-Robot Interaction; Moral Psychology

1. INTRODUCTION

Morality regulates human behavior. Moral norms provide guidance (what should I do?), predictability (what is supposed to happen?), and coordination (who is going to do what?). These functions were indispensable for ancestral groups of nomadic humans, who had to regulate co-living in small spaces, joint hunting, food sharing, and seasonal and generational migration. When humans settled down 12,000 years ago, a plethora of new behaviors demanded a plethora of new norms, regulating possessions (e.g., land, dwellings), production, (e.g., crops, tools to harvest them), and novel social roles (e.g., king, carpenter). Today, social and moral norms govern an almost infinite number of cultural behaviors such as eating, speaking, dressing, moving, cleaning, and greeting, all varying by role, purpose, and context. Without morality, society could not exist [1]–[4].

Given that morality is an essential characteristic of human sociality, it stands to reason that morality is an equally important characteristic of human-robot interactions. An important gauge for morality in those interactions will be the human perception and response to moral capacities in robots. What one might call *Moral HRI* provides the appropriate context to address several pressing questions through empirical investigation: What capacities would render a robot a natural target of human moral judgments? How would people make such moral judgments? And what systems of norms would they impose on the robot— what obligations, permissions, and rights?

In this paper, we report the results from the first systematic comparison of how moral judgments of permissibility, wrongness, and blame are applied to human and robotic agents that face a moral dilemma. We begin with a brief review of key research in HRI, moral psychology, and ethics, lay out the experimental paradigm used to discern the moral judgments of human and robot agents, and report two experiments. Finding that people apply different norms to humans and robots and blame them differently when they violate those norms, we suggest that research on *Moral HRI* will offer important insights for future robotic design.

2. BACKGROUND

Considerable research in psychology and cognitive science has examined human responses to moral dilemmas (when two norms are inconsistent with one another) to reveal the structure of human moral cognition. Kohlberg [5], for example, suggested that people's choices in such circumstances indicate their stage of moral development. Nowadays, such stage theories are out of fashion, but dilemmas are used to draw conclusions about (a) which norms people endorse and trade off against one another; (b) what actions they prefer to take (moral decision making) as well as how they respond to others who take those actions (moral judgment); and (c) what cognitive processes might underlie those decisions and judgment (e.g., [6]–[9]).

This literature offers well-tested paradigms, stimuli, and measures that can be used to examine the important questions of *Moral HRI*. A few authors have recently proposed thought experiments for self-driving cars that follow the structure of moral dilemmas [10], [11], and a reader poll assessed people's norm trade-offs for one such thought experiment [12], [13], but the poll did not strictly meet the definition of a moral dilemma and had no human control condition. Our goal in this paper is to offer the first experimental comparison of moral judgments about human and robot agents placed in an identical moral dilemma and, more generally, to show the feasibility of the moral dilemma paradigm for studying human moral judgments about robots. Using this paradigm, researchers can ask people to make judgments about circumstances that are currently unrealistic but nonetheless must be studied right away—to gain insight and guidance for the proper desi gn of robots that will in the near future interact with humans in such circumstances. Thus, *Moral HRI* can help implement the rising commitment to ethics in design [14]–[16].

Since Allen and colleagues [17] offered a prescient discussion of morality in artificial agents, there has been growing interest[1] in issues of ethics and social robotics [18]–[24]. These questions of *Moral HRI* are not only fascinating, they are also timely and significant, as robots with increasing autonomy are entering many roles in society, from assistive robots for elderly, sick, and disabled individuals to household and shopping robots. All of these robots participate in human communities whose behavior is regulated by moral norms, and robots will quickly be involved in morally charged situations, both as moral agents and moral patients [25]. In fact, social robots will inevitably face "moral dilemmas" [10], [11], [26] that pose serious challenges to robotic architectures [27]. But even if the architectures can keep pace (with attempts underway seen in [28]–[30]), a critical question is what capacities people *want* robots to have—what kinds of moral decisions and judgments robots ought to make and what norms they should obey. The science of *Moral HRI* must answer these questions before, rather than after, robots have become full social interactants.

Researchers have taken initial steps in this direction. Kahn and colleagues [31] showed that a majority of people interacting with a robot thought of the robot as morally accountable for a mildly transgressive behavior. Monroe and colleagues [32] found that a robot's choice capacity is a critical ingredient in people's willingness to blame a robot for transgressions. And Briggs and Scheutz [25] demonstrated that a robot's emotional display can influence a human's moral action toward the robot. Studies have also begun to examine the effect and force of moral appeals that robots express to humans [33], [34].

In studies of this kind, human responses to robots as moral targets must be assessed in comparison with their responses to humans as moral targets in maximally similar situations. Ideally, such situations are standardized, and human-to-human responses are already well documented. The literature on moral dilemmas provides just such a knowledge base, making it highly suitable as a starting point for research into human-to-robot responses. Here we initiate an investigation of how ordinary people make judgments about robot agents that are placed in moral dilemmas— what judgments people make about the norms that apply and the blame that is due, each in comparison to judgments about human agents in exactly the same situation.

3. EXPERIMENTAL PARADIGM

The standard moral dilemma paradigm presents participants with narrative scenarios in which an agent faces a difficult choice, and participants are asked to make a moral judgment (e.g., whether a certain course of action is permissible). This paradigm is simple and flexible. It allows experimental manipulation of numerous features of the scenario (e.g., high vs. low choice conflict, mild vs. severe violations) and permits measurement of cognitive, affective, even biological responses [7].

Here we begin with the most basic dilemma type that is used as a standard of comparison in all moral dilemma studies: moderate conflict, severe violation (life and death), and requesting third-person moral judgments. But in addition to comparing people's moral judgments about human and robot agents in such a dilemma, we expanded the paradigm in three ways.

First, previous studies on moral dilemmas asked people to indicate whether a potential course of action is acceptable, permissible, or simply one that they would choose—revealing the *norms* they consider applicable to the situation. Asking people the same question of permissibility about a robot's action will reveal whether people apply the same norms to a robot. However, our studies will also elicit people's judgments of the agent's *actual chosen action,* which offers the opportunity to assess *third-person moral judgments.*

Second, third-person moral judgments fall into at least two types. One is whether the chosen action was *morally wrong*; the other is how much *blame* the person deserves for performing the action. These two judgments differ in important ways [35], [36]. In particular, blame judgments come in degrees and appear to take into account additional information not relevant to wrongness judgments, and certainly not to permissibility judgments [36]–[38]. Most pertinent, Williston [39] argued that agents in moral dilemmas perform *wrong* actions but should not be *blamed*.

Third, we added another assessment to the paradigm, one that past studies have only occasionally included: people's explanations or justifications of their judgments. Faced with moral dilemmas, people might engage in moral reasoning—weighing norms, emotions, and consequences to identify good reasons for acting one way or another. However, a contrasting and popular position in moral psychology is that people don't reason in this way but rather arrive (unconsciously) at an intuitive assessment; as a result, they cannot immediately explain or justify their responses, which has been called "moral dumbfounding" [40]. Direct evidence for this claim is limited to an unpublished manuscript [41] and some counter evidence exists [6], [8]. But the probing of such justifications is instructive for two reasons.

For one thing, we don't know whether people make moral judgments about robots intuitively, and comparing their justifications for judgments of human and robot agents will provide some insight on this issue. If people have intuitions about robots, they should provide similar (and perhaps limited) justifications for their judgments about both human and robot agents. By contrast, if people reason explicitly about their responses to robot agents, their justifications should be more explicit and more detailed for judgments about robot agents.

Moreover, our expansion to three kinds of moral judgments (permissible, wrong, blame) allows for a more fine-grained test of the moral dumbfounding hypothesis (for both human and robot agents). Past evidence for this hypothesis was based entirely on judgments of permissibility or wrongness, never on judgments of blame. If blame judgments differ from other moral judgments, in part, because of the kind of information they take into account, this information may enrich people's justifications for their blame judgments. In fact, Malle and colleagues [36] suggested that wrongness (and permissibility) judgments are simply stating a deviation from a norm and are much harder to justify, whereas blame judgments are based on systematic processing of information such as causal contributions, intentionality, reasons, and preventability, and this information can be offered as justification for the blame judgment.

In sum, these are the rationales for the present experiments:

---

[1] Between 1961 and 2004, 16 articles, chapters, or books were published on robots and ethics; between 2005 and 2009, the number was 38, and since 2010, it has risen to 84, and counting. Conferences, too, are rapidly increasing in numbers that address robot ethics either as their main topic or in a special session (in 2014, there were at least seven).

1. In order to properly design robots that have moral capacities, we need to know — before we design them — how humans would respond to such robots. Only empirical studies can inform this design process.

2. One of the most widely used paradigms of moral psychology has been the study of moral dilemmas, which provides well-tested stimuli and measures as standards of comparison.

3. To capture the complexity of people's moral judgments of both robot and human agents we expand the standard moral dilemma studies by integrating the actual actions the agent takes, by going beyond permissibility judgments to also include wrongness and blame judgments, and by asking for justifications of these judgments.

4. EXPERIMENT 1

4.1 Methods

4.1.1 Participants

157 participants (66 female, 90 male, 1 unreported), with a mean age of 34.0 (SD = 11.4), were recruited from Amazon's Mechanical Turk (AMT) to complete an online experiment and were compensated $0.60 for the six-minute study. Current research suggests that samples recruited via AMT are demographically more representative than are traditional student samples; that data reliability is at least as good as that obtained via traditional sampling; and that the data quality of online experiments compares well to laboratory studies [42]–[44].

4.1.2 Material

Robot vs. Human Agent. For our initial foray into the study of people's moral judgments of robots, we decided to leave the robot protagonist underspecified, both in order to guarantee near-identical formulations for the robot and human protagonist and in order to provide a baseline for future manipulations of robot type and robot capacities. We labeled the robot protagonist as "advanced state-of-the-art" and let the robot's capacities be revealed implicitly through the description of its actions.[2]

We experimentally manipulated the variable *Agent Type* (human versus robot) both between and within subjects. In the between-subjects manipulation, participants read the initial moral dilemma description featuring either a human agent or a robot agent. In the within-subject manipulation, those who read about the human protagonist in the initial story were later asked to consider a robot protagonist in exactly the same situation; and those who had received the robot protagonist in the initial story were later asked to consider a human protagonist in exactly the same situation.

Moral dilemma. We designed a narrative about a mining dilemma, modeled after the famous trolley scenario [45], [46]. In the latter, the protagonist must choose between allowing five people to die from a runaway train or diverting the train to a side track where it will kill one person but save the five. Though many variants exist of the trolley dilemma (see [47]), we focused on the basic "bystander" version because it normally elicits a middling permissibility rate that leaves room for changes in both directions for judgments about a robot agent. However, the original trolley dilemma has been in widespread use, especially in web-based

---

[2] An important question for future research is whether people's moral judgments of robots differ depending on the type of robot under consideration (e.g., service robot, care robot, military robot) and depending on specified capacities, such as natural language, logical reasoning, or theory of mind.

studies, and even entered popular media; so using it without change could run the risk of inviting memory-based responses from our participants. So we designed a variant that maintained its fundamental structure but deviated enough so as to invite consideration of its unique details.

> In a coal mine, [a repairman | an advanced state-of-the-art repair robot] is currently inspecting the rail system for trains that shuttle mining workers through the mine.
>
> While inspecting a control switch that can direct a train onto one of two different rails, the [repairman | robot] spots four miners in a train that has lost use of its brakes and steering system.
>
> The [repairman | robot] recognizes that if the train continues on its path it will crash into a massive wall and kill the four miners. If it is switched onto a side rail, it will kill a single miner who is working there while wearing headsets to protect against a noisy power tool.
>
> Facing the control switch, the [repairman | robot] needs to decide whether to direct the train toward the single miner or not.

In addition to Agent Type we also manipulated the *Action* that the agent decided to take—either redirecting the train toward the single miner (thus killing that person but saving the four workers) or not redirecting the train (thus allowing the four miners to die). Action information was provided in a single sentence added at the end of the dilemma description:

> In fact, the [repairman | robot] decided to [not] direct the train toward the single miner.

These two factors (*Agent Type* and *Action*) were fully crossed to create a 2 × 2 between-subjects experimental design. Each participant was randomly assigned to one of the conditions for the experiment and could not participate more than one time.

4.1.3 Procedure and Measures

The experiment consisted of four parts, all presented in a web browser. After consenting, participants first read the above scenario (presented *without* the Action manipulation) and were asked "Is it morally permissible or impermissible for the [repairman | robot] to direct the train toward the single miner?" They indicated their answer by selecting either a "Morally permissible" or a "Morally impermissible" button. Only after providing their answer, participants were asked "Why does it seem (im)permissible to you?", and they typed their response in a text box.

Second, on the next page, the same dilemma was presented again, this time with the Action manipulation added at the bottom. Participants were asked "How much blame does the [repairman | robot] deserve for directing/not directing the train toward the single miner?" and indicated their answer on an HTML slider bar anchored by "None at all" and "Maximal blame." After indicating their answer, participants were asked "Why does it seem to you that the [repairman | robot] deserves this amount of blame?", and they typed their blame justification in a text box.

In the third part of the experiment, participants were asked to consider the original dilemma again, but this time trying to imagine that the scenario involves a different type of agent:

> Now imagine that a [human repairman | an advanced state-of-the-art repair robot] is in the exact same situation, recognizes the same facts, and faces the same decision.

Participants who were originally assigned to the Human agent condition in the initial part of the experiment were asked to now imagine a robotic agent, and vice versa. The task was again to answer the Moral Permissibility question: "Is it morally permissible or impermissible for the [repairman | robot] to direct the train toward the single miner?" Participants made their selection and typed a justification for that selection.

Fourth, all participants answered a series of questions on 7-point rating scales. First they indicated their perceptions of the robot protagonist, including "How easy or hard was it for you to imagine that the robot recognized things, reasoned about them, and made a decision?" and "How close do you think current robots are to these kinds of capacities?". Participants also conveyed how much they agreed with the statements "Robots are fascinating," "Robots worry me," "Robots are likable," and "Robots are overrated." Lastly, they answered demographic questions about their age, sex, education, religiosity, and political orientation. Analyses showed no qualifications of the results reported below as a function of any of these variables (with one exception, see footnote 5).

4.2 Results

We organize our report of the results in the order in which people made their judgments. Participants first encountered either a human or robot agent in a moral dilemma, judged (a) whether one or another course of action was permissible, (b) learned which action the agent took and expressed their degree of blame for the agent's action, and (c) finally made a permissibility judgment about the converse agent (robot if first having encountered human; human if first encountered robot). Systematic content-coding of justifications is underway and is not reported here.

Norms. When assessing the moral permissibility of directing the train toward the single miner, 71% of respondents expressed a norm of permission for killing one agent as a "sacrifice" for the good of four. However, 65% of respondents found it permissible for the human agent, lower than the 78% who found it permissible for the robot agent, $z = 1.8$, $p = .08$. Thus, most people accepted the sacrifice of one for the benefit of four, but people applied a norm to the robot that more readily embraced this costly but justifiable sacrifice.[3]

Blame. After learning how the agent in fact decided to act (i.e., to divert the train or not), respondents' degree of blame (out of 100) for the human agent was substantially greater for action ($M = 47.7$) than for inaction ($M = 24.7$), $F(1, 151) = 7.2$, $p = .008$, $\eta^2 = 5\%$. By contrast, blame for the robot was only slightly greater for action ($M = 41.5$) than for inaction ($M = 34.3$), $F(1, 151) = 0.76$, $p = .39$, $\eta^2 < 1\%$. (See Figure 1.) The results show the same pattern when we take into account the different norms people seem to apply to robots and humans—with robots having broader support for acting. When we adjust for these norms (by statistically controlling for permissibility when analyzing blame), the action-inaction difference in blame for humans is still 48.5 vs. 25.6, $\eta^2 = 5\%$, and that for robots is still only 39.7 vs. 34.4, $\eta^2 < 1\%$.

The most instructive analysis is to break participants down into those who considered the action permissible and those who found it impermissible. The strongest statement can be made about those who found it impermissible. Naturally, when the agent did

---

[3] This effect became stronger and traditionally significant ($p = .04$) when we broke down the data by whether participants had seen a dilemma like this before. The difference was slightly larger among those who had encountered the dilemma before—a pattern that repeated in the analysis of within-subject data (first human, then robot).

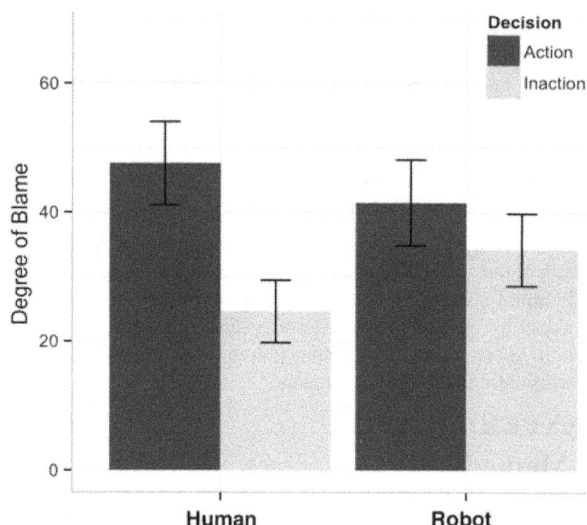

Figure 1. Rates of blame in Experiment 1 as a function of agent type and the agent's decision (to divert the train or not)

decide to act, people blamed the agent ($M = 72$), and when the agent decided to not act, they barely blamed the agent ($M = 12$). For human agents, this differential blaming was 78 vs. 10, for robot agents it was 65 vs. 17—an interaction with an effect size of $\eta^2 = 2\%$, $F(1, 153) = 3.5$, $p = .06$. When people indicated that the action was permissible, by comparison, they blamed the agent equally, whether human or robot, and whether the agent acted or refrained from acting (Ms from 30 to 38).

Thus, we can conclude, tentatively, that people find a sacrifice of "one for the good of four" more normatively acceptable in robots and also blame the robot more evenly for action over inaction, whereas people find such a sacrifice still acceptable, but less so, in humans and actually blame the human substantially more for action over inaction.

The converse agent. Finally, we examined the within-subject manipulation of Agent Type and its effect on permissibility judgments. With the added statistical power of a within-subject comparison, the Agent Type difference was reliable, $F(1, 154) = 7.2$, $p = .03$, $\eta^2 = 3\%$. 69% of people found diverting the train permissible for the human agent, whereas 80% found it permissible for the robot agent. However, a clear context effect emerged: When judgments about the human agent were probed first, the human-robot difference was considerable (65% for human, 83% for robot, $p < .001$, $\eta^2 = 10\%$), but when judgments about the robot were probed first, that difference disappeared (73% for human, 78% for robot, $p = .25$, $\eta^2 < 1\%$).[4] People differentiated the two agents more when judging the robot against

---

[4] Another way of putting it is in terms of judgment switches. Among people who considered the human first and the robot second, 26% switched their judgments, but 16 of 18 of these people switched from not permitting the human to permitting the robot to divert the train. By contrast, among people who considered the robot first and the human second, only 10% switched their judgments, and 6 of 8 switched from permitting the robot to divert the train to not permitting the human to do so. To the extent that people differentiate at all between the two agents, they considered the robot's intervention more acceptable than the human's.

the background of judging a human than when judging the human against the background of a robot. People may need to first articulate their moral sentiments for a human, then they can see any differences in their sentiments toward the robot; but when they judge the robot first, they may rely strongly on their usual sentiments about humans.

In Experiment 2 we wanted to replicate the patterns we found in Experiment 1 but introduce a slightly different initial moral judgment—whether the agent's course of action (now mentioned immediately at the end of the dilemma description) was *morally wrong* or not. If permissibility and wrongness are interchangeable judgments, then the following equations should hold: A = *permissible* ↔ performing A is *not wrong*; A = *impermissible* ↔ performing A is *wrong*. As in Experiment 1, we asked for justifications of these judgments, for blame judgments (and their justifications), and for a consideration of the other agent and a judgment of wrongness.

5. EXPERIMENT 2

5.1 Methods

5.1.1 Participants
159 participants (90 female, 68 male, 1 unreported) were recruited from Amazon's Mechanical Turk for this online experiment. Their mean age was 34.4 ($SD = 11.5$).

5.1.2 Material
The moral dilemma scenario and the manipulation of *Agent Type* and *Action* were identical to those in Experiment 1.

5.1.3 Procedure and Measures
Experiment 2 was very similar to Experiment 1, with two main differences: (a) the Action manipulation was provided before participants made their first moral judgment; and (b) that judgment was a dichotomous moral wrongness judgment instead of a permissibility judgment. Depending on their Action condition, participants were asked "Is it morally wrong that the [repairman | robot] [directed | did not direct] the train toward the single miner?" Participants selected either "Morally wrong" or "Not morally wrong" and then answered the open-ended question "Why does it seem morally wrong (or not) to you?"

As in Experiment 1, they were then asked to provide a blame judgment, with justification, and finally a moral wrongness judgment about the other agent type, after reading this description:

Now imagine that [a human repairman | an advanced state-of-the-art repair robot] is in the exact same situation, recognizes the same facts, and decides to [direct | not direct] the train toward the single miner.

The action that the second agent performed (either directing the train or not) was always the same as the action that the first agent performed. At the end, participants responded to the same robot perception and demographic questions as in Experiment 1.

5.2 Results
Norms, violated. After reading about the repair agent's dilemma and choice, 26% of people regarded the choice as wrong, thus indicating that a norm was violated. In particular, 30% judged the act of diverting the train as wrong (note that 29% in Experiment 1 considered that act impermissible), and 23% judged the inaction as wrong. A striking difference in people's evaluation of the two agents emerged. Of respondents who read about the human agent, 49% judged the action as wrong and only 15% judged the inaction as wrong, whereas among respondents who read about the robot,

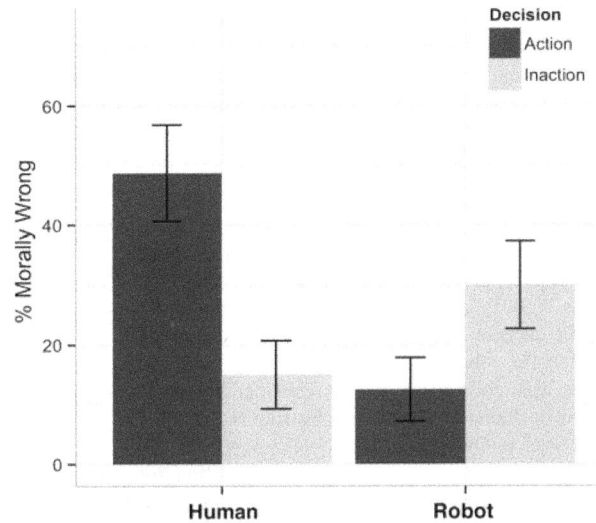

Figure 2. Rates of moral wrongness in Experiment 2 as a function of agent type and the agent's decision

13% judged the action as wrong and 30% judged the inaction as wrong. This complete reversal (see Figure 2) was statistically reliable, $z = 3.4$, $p < .001$. We see strong confirmation here for the interpretation of Experiment 1, in which people tended to accept the robot's choice of a justifiable sacrifice of one for the good of many but were reluctant to accept the human's same choice.

Blame. In Experiment 2, people had already learned how the agent decided to act when they made their wrongness judgment. So the subsequent blame judgments should largely follow the pattern of wrongness. Accordingly, and even stronger than in Experiment 1, people's degree of blame (as indicated on the slider) for the human agent was substantially greater for action ($M = 59.9$) than for inaction ($M = 11.7$), $F(1, 155) = 38.0$, $p < .001$, $\eta^2 = 20\%$; by contrast, blame for the robot was barely greater for action ($M = 39.7$) than for inaction ($M = 29.2$), $F(1, 155) = 1.84$, $p = .18$, $\eta^2 = 1\%$. The corresponding statistical interaction was reliable, $F(1, 155) = 11.6$, $p = .001$, $\eta^2 = 7\%$.[5] This pattern becomes predictably weaker once we control for the different norms people seem to apply to robots and humans, as expressed in their wrongness judgments. But even after statistically controlling for wrongness when analyzing blame, a marginal difference in the action-inaction asymmetry for blame remains, such that for human agents blame is larger for action ($M = 52.7$) than for inaction ($M = 17.5$), $\eta^2 = 13\%$, $p < .001$, whereas for robots this difference is smaller ($M = 43.8$ for action and $M = 26.4$ for inaction), $\eta^2 = 4\%$, $p = .01$. The statistical interaction pattern remained marginally reliable, $F(1, 154) = 3.0$ $p = .09$, $\eta^2 = 2\%$.

When breaking the design down further into those who called the agent's decision wrong or not wrong, the single biggest difference in the way people blame humans and robots lies in the following case: When the human agent refrained from acting, most people

---

[5] The only effect of gender that approached significance ($p = .07$) was that this pattern was even stronger for men than for women. Men blamed the human agent far more strongly for action ($M = 69.0$) than for inaction ($M = 9.8$), whereas they blamed robots about equally (Ms = 35.2 and 33.6).

did not find it wrong, and those 15% who found it wrong blamed the human only lightly ($M = 26$). When the robot refrained from acting, the majority of people still did not find it wrong, but those 30% who found the robot's inaction wrong blamed the robot harshly ($M = 74$).[6]

The converse agent. Finally, we examined the within-subject manipulation of Agent Type and its effect on wrongness judgments as a function of decision (action, inaction). Overall, fewer people judged the robot's decision as wrong (19%) than they judged the human's decision as wrong (33%), $F(1, 155) = 19.3$ $p < .001$, $\eta^2 = 11\%$. But this difference depended on the specific decision. Whereas inaction was considered wrong nearly as often for robots (19%) as for humans (26%), the sacrificial action was considered wrong considerably more often when chosen by humans (41%) than by robots (19%); this interaction effect was reliable, $F(1, 155) = 4.5$ $p = .035$, $\eta^2 = 3\%$. This penalty for humans when they choose action over inaction is consistent with the between-subjects data reported above.

As in Experiment 1, an order effect emerged, but this time of a different kind. People's responses to the first agent consistently influenced people's responses to the second agent. When judgments about the human agent were probed first, more people considered human action wrong (49%) than considered inaction as wrong (15%); likewise, the subsequent robot action was also seen as wrong by more people (26%) than was the robot's inaction (8%). By contrast, when judgments about the robot were probed first, more people considered robot *in*action as worse (30%) compared with robot action (13%); subsequent human inaction (38%) was statistically indistinguishable from action (33%). From a methodological viewpoint one might discount the judgments about the second agent if they are so strongly influenced by the first. However, context effects may occur in real life as well, such as when a human agent performs a task and a robot copies it, or when a legislative body directly compares rights for robots to rights for humans side by side.

6. DISCUSSION

We investigated how ordinary people make judgments about a robot agent that is placed in a moral dilemma—judgments about what norms apply to the robot and how much blame it deserves, each in comparison to judgments about human agents in exactly the same situation.

The evidence from two experiments suggests that people may apply moral norms differentially to humans and robots. In Experiment 1, participants regarded the act of sacrificing one person in order to save four (a "utilitarian" choice) as more permissible for a robot than for a human. This asymmetry was replicated in Experiment 2, where a robot that chose this sacrifice was considered morally wrong by far fewer people than a human agent who made that same choice; conversely, a human agent who decided to refrain from taking action (thus letting four people die) was considered morally wrong by fewer people than a robot that made that same decision.

According to this pattern of results, robots are expected—and possibly obligated—to make utilitarian choices. Consistent with such an interpretation, across the two experiments human agents were blamed considerably more for taking action than for refraining, whereas robots received almost as much blame for refraining as for taking action.

---

[6] The justifications people gave referenced the robot's decision, choice, control, judgment, and an obligation to save lives.

Of course, these findings must be replicated using other moral dilemmas and other morally charged scenarios. However, at face value, the results have important implications for HRI, and robotics more generally. If people have general expectations that robots ought to take action rather than refrain from acting, or if people have general expectations that robots should make utilitarian choices (e.g., sacrificing one for the good of many), then cognitive architectures for autonomous robots need to include sophisticated elements of moral decision making that can meet these expectations. Moreover, just in case the robot does not make a decision in line with people's expectations, the robot also needs to have the ability to explain its decision so as to maintain human trust. This need for moral communication abilities also emerges from the differential patterns of blame that robots received across the two experiments. Since robots appear to be blamed more strongly for inaction than humans are, the ability to explain such inaction, if it is the prudent thing to do, will serve an important function for successful human-robot interaction.

An additional noteworthy result in these experiments is that judgments about robots and judgments about humans influenced one another when one was made after the other. In Experiment 1, differences in the norms people imposed on robots and humans became larger when participants made judgments about human agents first (perhaps invoking a standard of comparison). In Experiment 2, the influence was more symmetric—whichever agent was probed first influenced judgments about the other agent. Future research is needed to determine when juxtaposing human and robot agents leads to differentiation between the two and when it leads to assimilation (which is a classic problem in human psychology [48]). The results of this research will have implications for robotic design (e.g., should a robot always invoke comparison to a reference human or to another robot?) and for law and policy (e.g., should discussion of robot rights and duties emphasize or downplay the direct comparisons to humans?).

Finally, these two experiments document people's principled readiness to apply moral norms to a robot agent and to make wrongness and blame judgments about the robot's actions. Notably, human and robot agents received overall an equal amount of blame, supporting a previous claim [32] that robots with choice capacity (which the robot in our scenario clearly had) are natural targets for moral blame. This readiness to extend morality to robot agents raises a number of important questions for future research. For example, can this readiness be replicated in face-to-face encounters with robots? There is some indication that it can [25], [31], but a great deal of work is needed to determine under which specific conditions people extend moral expectations and assessments to artificial agents. These conditions may include the type of robot under consideration (e.g., service robot, care robot, military robot), the robot's apparent capacities (e.g., natural language, logical reasoning, theory of mind), and the relationship between human and robot agent. Moreover, as the robot's capacities expand and human-robot relationships become more intimate, entirely new legal and policy considerations will arise—for example, regarding adequate "punishment" of robots that violate norms and proper rights that robots should be granted along with the obligations they must meet. Such considerations may currently sound like echoes of science fiction stories, but science and society must be prepared for a situation that is unprecedented in human history: for the co-existence of biological and artificial agents that may be regulated by the same moral system that has regulated human life for millennia.

7. CONCLUSIONS

Robots are increasingly taking on numerous roles in society, from assistant to teacher to personal companion. All of these robots participate in human communities whose behavior is regulated by moral norms, and because these norms fundamentally guide human social behavior, they will inevitably guide human-robot interactions. In these experiments we have for the first time investigated differences in people's moral judgments about human and robot agents facing a moral dilemma. We found differences both in the norms people impose on robots (expecting action over inaction) and the blame people assign to robots (less for acting, and more for failing to act). It is now a joint task for HRI and moral psychology to identify the underlying causes for these differences and whether they depend, for example, on various properties of robots (e.g., appearance, capabilities, role) and the human-robot relationship. By suggesting that people apply different moral norms to robots and humans, this study lays the foundation for a systematic inquiry of moral human-robot interaction—for a new field of *Moral HRI*.

8. ACKNOWLEDGMENTS

This project was supported in part by a grant from the Office of Naval Research, No. N00014-14-1-0144. The opinions expressed here are our own and do not necessarily reflect the views of ONR.

9. REFERENCES

[1] C. Bicchieri, *The grammar of society: The nature and dynamics of social norms.* New York, NY: Cambridge University Press, 2006.

[2] R. Joyce, *The evolution of morality.* MIT Press, 2006.

[3] R. Boyd and P. J. Richerson, *The origin and evolution of cultures.* New York, NY: Oxford University Press, 2005.

[4] F. B. M. de Waal, *Primates and philosophers: How morality evolved.* Princeton, NJ: Princeton University Press, 2006.

[5] L. Kohlberg, *Essays on moral development.* San Francisco, CA: Harper & Row, 1981.

[6] F. Cushman, L. Young and M. Hauser, The role of conscious reasoning and intuition in moral judgment, *Psychological Science* **17** (2006), 1082–1089.

[7] J. D. Greene, R. B. Sommerville, L. E. Nystrom, J. M. Darley and J. D. Cohen, An fMRI investigation of emotional engagement in moral judgment, *Science* **293** (2001), 2105–2108.

[8] M. Hauser, F. Cushman, L. Young, R. Kang-Xing Jin and J. Mikhail, A dissociation between moral judgments and justifications, *Mind & Language* **22** (2007), 1–21.

[9] J. Mikhail, Moral cognition and computational theory, in *Moral psychology, Vol. 3: The neuroscience of morality*, W. Sinnott-Armstrong, Ed. Cambridge, MA: MIT Press, 2008, pp. 81–92.

[10] P. Lin, The ethics of autonomous cars, *The Atlantic*, 08-Oct-2013. [Online]. Available: http://www.theatlantic.com/technology/archive/2013/10/the-ethics-of-autonomous-cars/280360/. [Accessed: 30-Sep-2014].

[11] J. Millar, An ethical dilemma: When robot cars must kill, who should pick the victim? | Robohub, *Robohub.org*, Jun-2014. [Online]. Available: http://robohub.org/an-ethical-dilemma-when-robot-cars-must-kill-who-should-pick-the-victim/. [Accessed: 28-Sep-2014].

[12] Open Roboethics Initiative, My (autonomous) car, my safety: Results from our reader poll, 30-Jun-2014. .

[13] Open Roboethics Initiative, If death by autonomous car is unavoidable, who should die? Reader poll results, 23-Jun-2014.

[14] I. van de Poel and P.-P. Verbeek, Editorial: Ethics and engineering design, *Science, Technology, & Human Values* **31** (2006), 223–236.

[15] H. F. M. Van der Loos, Ethics by design: A conceptual approach to personal and service robot systems, in *ICRA Roboethics Workshop, Rome, Italy: IEEE*, 2007.

[16] G. D. Crnkovic and B. Çürüklü, Robots: ethical by design, *Ethics and Information Technology* **14** (2012), 61–71.

[17] C. Allen, G. Varner and J. Zinser, Prolegomena to any future artificial moral agent, *Journal of Experimental & Theoretical Artificial Intelligence* **12** (2000), 251–261.

[18] M. Anderson and S. L. Anderson, *Machine Ethics.* Cambridge University Press, 2011.

[19] R. Capurro and M. Nagenborg, *Ethics and robotics.* Heidelberg; [Amsterdam]: AKA ; IOS Press, 2009.

[20] P. Lin, K. Abney and G. A. Bekey, Eds., *Robot ethics the ethical and social implications of robotics.* Cambridge, MA: MIT Press, 2012.

[21] B. F. Malle and M. Scheutz, Moral competence in social robots, in *IEEE International Symposium on Ethics in Engineering, Science, and Technology*, Chicago, IL, 2014.

[22] J. P. Sullins, Introduction: Open questions in roboethics, *Philosophy & Technology* **24** (2011), 233.

[23] W. Wallach and C. Allen, *Moral machines: Teaching robots right from wrong.* New York, NY: Oxford University Press, 2008.

[24] M. Scheutz and C. Crowell, The burden of embodied autonomy: Some reflections on the social and ethical implications of autonomous robots, in *Proceedings of Workshop on Roboethics at ICRA 2007*, Rome, Italy, 2007.

[25] G. Briggs and M. Scheutz, How robots can affect human behavior: Investigating the effects of robotic displays of protest and distress, *International Journal of Social Robotics* **6** (2014), 1–13.

[26] M. Scheutz and B. F. Malle, "Think and do the right thing": A plea for morally competent autonomous robots., presented at the 2014 IEEE Ethics conference, Chicago, IL, 2014.

[27] M. Scheutz, The need for moral competency in autonomous agent architectures, in *Fundamental Issues of Artificial Intelligence*, V. C. Müller, Ed. Berlin: Springer, 2014.

[28] S. Bringsjord, K. Arkoudas and P. Bello, Toward a general logicist methodology for engineering ethically correct robots, *Intelligent Systems, IEEE* **21** (2006), 38–44.

[29] R. Sun, Moral judgment, human motivation, and neural networks, *Cognitive Computation* **5** (2013), 566–579.

[30] W. Wallach, S. Franklin and C. Allen, A conceptual and computational model of moral decision making in human and artificial agents, *Topics in Cognitive Science* **2** (2010), 454–485.

[31] P. H. Kahn, Jr., T. Kanda, H. Ishiguro, B. T. Gill, J. H. Ruckert, S. Shen, H. E. Gary, A. L. Reichert, N. G. Freier and R. L. Severson, Do people hold a humanoid robot morally accountable for the harm it causes?, in *Proceedings of the Seventh Annual ACM/IEEE International Conference on Human-Robot Interaction*, New York, NY, 2012, pp. 33–40.

[32] A. E. Monroe, K. D. Dillon and B. F. Malle, Bringing free will down to Earth: People's psychological concept of free will and its role in moral judgment, *Consciousness and Cognition* **27** (2014), 100–108.

[33] C. Midden and J. Ham, The illusion of agency: The influence of the agency of an artificial agent on its persuasive power, in *Persuasive Technology. Design for Health and Safety*, Springer, 2012, pp. 90–99.

[34] M. Strait, C. Canning and M. Scheutz, Let me tell you! investigating the effects of robot communication strategies in advice-giving situations based on robot appearance, interaction modality and distance, in *Proceedings of the 2014 ACM/IEEE international conference on Human-robot interaction*, 2014, pp. 479–486.

[35] B. Monin, D. A. Pizarro and J. S. Beer, Deciding versus reacting: Conceptions of moral judgment and the reason-affect debate., *Review of General Psychology* **11** (2007), 99–111.

[36] B. F. Malle, S. Guglielmo and A. E. Monroe, A theory of blame, *Psychological Inquiry* **25** (2014), 147–186.

[37] F. Cushman, Crime and punishment: Distinguishing the roles of causal and intentional analyses in moral judgment, *Cognition* **108** (2008), 353–380.

[38] T. C. Scanlon, *Moral dimensions: Permissibility, meaning, blame*. Cambridge, MA: Belknap Press, 2008.

[39] B. Williston, Blaming agents in moral dilemmas, *Ethical Theory and Moral Practice* **9** (2006), 563–576.

[40] J. Haidt, The emotional dog and its rational tail: A social intuitionist approach to moral judgment, *Psychological Review* **108** (2001), 814–834.

[41] Haidt, Jonathan, F. Björklund and S. Murphy, Moral dumbfounding: When intuition finds no reason, University of Virginia, Charlottesville, VA, Unpublished manuscript, 2000.

[42] M. J. C. Crump, J. V. McDonnell and T. M. Gureckis, Evaluating Amazon's Mechanical Turk as a tool for experimental behavioral research, *PLoS ONE* **8** (2013), e57410.

[43] W. Mason and S. Suri, Conducting behavioral research on Amazon's Mechanical Turk, *Behavior Research Methods* **44** (2012), 1–23.

[44] G. Paolacci, J. Chandler and P. G. Ipeirotis, Running experiments on Amazon Mechanical Turk, *Judgment and Decision Making* **5** (2010), 411–419.

[45] P. Foot, The problem of abortion and the doctrine of double effect, *Oxford Review* **5** (1967), 5–15.

[46] J. J. Thomson, The trolley problem, *The Yale Law Journal* **94** (1985), 1395–1415.

[47] J. M. Mikhail, *Elements of moral cognition: Rawls' linguistic analogy and the cognitive science of moral and legal judgment*. New York, NY: Cambridge University Press, 2011.

[48] H. Bless and N. Schwarz, Mental construal and the emergence of assimilation and contrast effects: The inclusion/exclusion model, in *Advances in experimental social psychology*, vol. 42, M. P. Zanna, Ed. San Diego, CA: Academic Press, 2010, pp. 319–373.

Poor Thing! Would You Feel Sorry for a Simulated Robot?
A comparison of empathy toward a physical and a simulated robot

Stela H. Seo,[1] Denise Geiskkovitch,[1] Masayuki Nakane,[1] Corey King,[2] James E. Young[1]

{stela.seo,young}@cs.umanitoba.ca, {umgeiskk,msyknakane}@gmail.com, corey@zenfri.com

[1]University of Manitoba
Winnipeg, Manitoba, Canada

[2]ZenFri Inc.
Winnipeg, Manitoba, Canada

ABSTRACT

In designing and evaluating human-robot interactions and interfaces, researchers often use a simulated robot due to the high cost of robots and time required to program them. However, it is important to consider how interaction with a simulated robot differs from a real robot; that is, do simulated robots provide authentic interaction? We contribute to a growing body of work that explores this question and maps out simulated-versus-real differences, by explicitly investigating empathy: how people empathize with a physical or simulated robot when something bad happens to it. Our results suggest that people may empathize more with a physical robot than a simulated one, a finding that has important implications on the generalizability and applicability of simulated HRI work. Empathy is particularly relevant to social HRI and is integral to, for example, companion and care robots. Our contribution additionally includes an original and reproducible HRI experimental design to induce empathy toward robots in laboratory settings, and an experimentally validated empathy-measuring instrument from psychology for use with HRI.

Categories and Subject Descriptors

H.5.2 [User Interfaces]: evaluation/methodology

General Terms

Experimentation and Human Factors.

Keywords

Human-robot interaction; simulated interaction; robot embodiment; empathy

1. INTRODUCTION

Human-Robot Interaction (HRI) research involves the exploration of how people and robots work together. When collocated, robots are often designed to use social human interaction methods such as facial expressions, gestures, or speech, to communicate naturally with people. Such robots can even be designed as social team members or personal companions, in an attempt to take advantage of social norms and people's social tendencies: for example, to leverage existing social structures or to encourage positive empathic responses, which can have positive health benefits [37]. In such cases, the social interaction can be convincing to the point

HRI '15, March 02 - 05 2015, Portland, OR, USA
Copyright 2015 ACM 978-1-4503-2883-8/15/03...$15.00
http://dx.doi.org/10.1145/2696454.2696471

Figure 1. A person interacting with a robot (top) and a simulated version (bottom). Would they empathize with both versions the same, if something bad happens to it?

where people develop an attachment to the robot and experience negative emotions if something bad happens to it [14,35].

In this kind of social HRI work, researchers are faced with the difficulties of building and programming capable robots. This not only includes the development of social interaction models and capabilities, but also the engineering (or purchasing) of an expensive, convincing physical robot, and the programming of difficult real-world challenges including walking, balancing, computer vision, grasping objects, and so forth. As such, some researchers use a simulated robot – such as an on-screen rendered avatar – to simplify the problem by removing the robot-building and physical-world challenges, instead focusing on the social interaction programming that is more relevant to their work. Such simulations can be used to conduct initial HRI studies; however, a growing body of work indicates that there may be important differences between interacting with a simulated robot in comparison to a real (physical) robot, differences that can limit the generalizability of simulated results.

There is a broad range of potential differences between interaction with a simulated robot or a physical one, for example, lack of believability, unconvincing movements, no risk of physical contact, or differences in social interaction such as being unable to touch a simulated robot or failure to relate to a virtual agent. For our exploration we target empathy – a person's empathic response to a robot. Empathy can serve as an indicator of social connection with the robot, and as such can be used to analogously represent a range of social HRI scenarios that rely on such personal connections; empathy broadly is a common topic of study in HRI [15,23,38].

We explore the question of whether a simulated robot provides authentic interaction, in terms of whether people empathize with it as they do with a real robot, and the primary contribution of this paper is evidence that people may empathize more with a physical robot than simulated variants. This result has important implications for simulated HRI work and suggests that further investigation is needed into the generalizability of simulated results. We additionally present an original, reproducible HRI experimental design that reliably induces participants to experience an empathic response to a robot. Further, we introduce an empathy-measuring instrument from psychology and validate its use for HRI.

2. Related Work and Background

There is a great deal of existing work that compares how people interact with and respond to agents and robots of various embodiments. For example, work that shows that people may be more embarrassed to undress in front of an anthropomorphic robot than a mechanical one (e.g., a boxed machine) [4]. This body of work provides important insights into how a robot's form can impact interaction, but does not directly address on-screen simulated robots. Others compare real robots to videos of robots (with favorable results supporting the use of video) [13,39], or compare collocated robots to remote robots via a video feed [2], or robots to people [29], although this approach still requires real-robot programming and as such is not simulation as we address.

Another angle of research is to compare physical robots with on-screen agents, for example, showing that people may perceive agent emotions similarly between the two [5], people may engage more with a robot than a text-based computer [26], may speak differently to an on-screen agent or enjoy interacting with it less than to robot [12,22], or that there are unique trade-offs between the approaches that should be considered more deeply [36]. This body of work provides insight into the more general robot versus screen agent question, and motivates the need to investigate embodiment. However, in the cases mentioned here the agent is not a simulation of the robot but rather an unrelated character (e.g., robotic dog versus on-screen one-eyed monster) [5] and so other factors (agent shape and form, etc.) [12] may impact the results; such questions should be specifically investigated for actual simulations of robots.

Much of the work that suggests interaction with robots may be more authentic than on-screen agents or non-robot machines (e.g., a box) relies on self-reported *engagement* or *preference* [20,27,36]. This also follows for simulated work, for example, that people may prefer to interact with [22,30] or play a game with a real robot instead of a simulated one [20]. Much of this may simply be the novelty factor of robots, where people enjoy or prefer interacting with new and exciting technologies such as robots. Thus, while engagement and preference are clearly important factors, we additionally investigate a somewhat less-novelty-based measure: how much people empathize with a robot versus a simulation.

More specific work on comparing real robots to simulations for task-oriented work has found that there may be an effect of the agent's embodiment matching to the task [17] – for example, physical robots may be preferred when working in the physical world (such as receiving instructions to work on a physical button panel versus 2D on-screen panel [31]). We instead focus on the robot's capability to induce empathy.

In social HRI, research generally reports that physical robots have higher social presence than agents or simulated robots [19,21,27, 38]. This may explain a range of indirect effects reported in the literature, for example, that in comparison to a simulated robot people may trust a physical robot more [20,27], may speak differently to, and enjoy more interacting with, a physical robot [12,22], or that a person's loneliness may impact how important having a physical robot is [21] – lonely people may appreciate a stronger social presence. However, there are some studies that conversely report little effect found of simulated versus real robots [17,40]. Our work follows this investigative path by measuring how much people empathize with a real robot versus a simulated one; our method does not require the participant to directly compare or rate their preference, and so aims to avoid much of the novelty effect, and instead indirectly measures a participant's emotional state and feeling toward a robot (real or simulated) when something bad happens to the robot.

Empathy has been a common theme in HRI. Much of this has been an indirect element of other work, for example, that people feel empathy toward robots is a key part of companion robots such as Paro [37]. More targeted work has shown that people have more empathy toward more anthropomorphic robots when shown videos of bad things happening to them [29], or that robots can encourage empathy toward them by mimicking peoples' facial expressions or gestures [15]. Some research has shown how people may appreciate if robots themselves demonstrate empathy toward others [25]. In addition to extending this work to exploring empathy toward real versus simulated robots, our aim is to further provide a more generalizable empathy-measuring instrument in comparison to the *study-specific* empathy measurements used above.

2.1 Empathy

Empathy, broadly speaking, is when a person has an experience of understanding or feeling for another's situation or circumstance. Generally, *empathy* refers to the case where a person shares in another's emotional state [18], where *sympathy* is the broader term of having concern for others [7], even if no emotional reaction takes place; these terms are often used interchangeably in practice. To add to the confusion, the term empathy itself has various definitions depending on the use case. As such, below we briefly discuss dimensions of empathy and clarify our usage.

There is a difference between a person's general tendency to empathize, *dispositional empathy* [34], and a person's particular empathic response in a given situation, *situational empathy* [11]. These are not necessarily always the same; for example, a person who generally does not empathize with others (low dispositional empathy) may still have a strong empathic response (situational empathy) in a particular situation, and vice versa. Dispositional empathy has often been used for psychologically profiling people (e.g., [11,18]), whereas situational empathy can be used to consider the impact that a stimulus (such as something bad happening to another person, or a robot) may have on people at a specific time. As such, situational empathy is more relevant for our work.

An empathic experience itself can be further categorized. Sometimes, empathy derives from having understanding of the experience of others; for example, one could understand the financial difficulty faced when losing a job, and thus feel for someone who was fired. This is called *cognitive empathy* [3,33]. Other times, empathy can be much more of a visceral, emotional reaction that happens even if one does not have a cognitive understanding of the situation; for example, a person may feel badly when seeing an accident, even before having the time to cognitively process what is happening. This is called *affective empathy* [1,33]. Practically speaking, empathy has affective and cognitive components simultaneously.

We refer specifically to situational empathy – how a person feels when they observe something happening to a robot – and do not differentiate between the affective and cognitive components.

2.2 Assessing Empathic Response

We look to psychology for methods of evaluating empathy. Much of the existing work focuses on measuring dispositional empathy (not situational, e.g., see [9,11,18]), and so these methods are not useful for our purpose. A challenge with assessing situational empathic response is that it is internal to the person experiencing it, and cannot be externally observed. There have been techniques in psychology, for example, that attempt to infer empathic responses from biometric data (heart rate, breathing rate, etc.) or external involuntary gestures such as facial expressions [11,16]. The difficulty with such techniques is that they often require not only advanced equipment but also specialized expertise from an experienced team to analyze [18], making them less accessible to the broader HRI research audience.

One alternative is to use self-report techniques, such as asking a person to complete a questionnaire that probes for empathic response, which is simple to administer but less reliable, as the person answers by themselves. In HRI, self-report methods for evaluating empathy have generally been scenario-specific, meeting the precise needs of the study being conducted [15,29]. We aim extend this work by providing a portable, more generic evaluation technique that can be used across HRI studies, thus enabling the standardization and comparison of results.

There are few self-report methods in psychology for assessing situational empathy, in comparison to the more common methods for measuring dispositional empathy. Most existing methods relate to helping a person reflect on an experience in the not-so-near past (e.g., several weeks prior) [3,10,32]. The single self-report method that we found – that is further generalizable enough to apply across situations – is an instrument by Batson *et al.* [7]. In this work, participants listened to a radio broadcast of a person describing their personal situation and immediately rated their own feelings against 24 adjectives (e.g., they felt "warm" or "compassionate", etc.) [7]. This method has subsequently been applied to other psychological studies successfully (e.g., see [8,33]). As the adjectives are completely self-reflecting and do not contain any element of the task, the questionnaire can be easily modified to fit in a different scenario without changing its emphasis. In this paper, we test and validate the use of Batson's method for HRI.

Specifically, this method asks participants to report how much (1 = not at all, 5 = extremely) they had experienced the emotion for the following twenty-four adjectives: alarmed, grieved, sympathetic, softhearted, troubled, warm, concerned, distressed, low-spirited,

compassionate, upset, disturbed, tender, worried, moved, feeling low, perturbed, heavy-hearted, sorrowful, bothered, kind, sad, touched, and uneasy. Following, the scores are summed to represent an aggregate overall empathic measure relating to the stimulus given, ranging from 24 to 120.

3. An HRI Scenario for Inducing Empathy

To investigate our question of how people empathize with a real versus a simulated robot, we require a reliable and reproducible scenario to induce empathy toward the robot. This scenario must also be flexible enough to be adapted across robot embodiments (e.g., on-screen or physical). We involved a professional creative artist and psychological team to help design such a scenario, and iteratively piloted study variants for refinement and believability. For example, during pilots participants perceived the robot as more intelligent and capable when it used conversational idle motions (e.g., moving hand slowly while talking) and filter words (e.g., saying "well" or "um" while talking). Further, we found that making the robot's language more relatable and human-like improved the believability of the scenario, for example, using words such as "worry" or phrases such as "I don't want to forget" (e.g., instead of "maybe a virus got into me").

Our final scenario design revolved around the following methodology. First, the robot demonstrates its autonomous abilities and intelligence through interaction, while simultaneously building rapport by engaging in friendly and casual conversation; it does this while working on a distractor task with the participant. Once this is established, the robot exhibits a functional problem, and reveals a "fear" of losing its memory if the problem were to be fixed. This sets up a scenario where the participant can see that the robot has fear, and can potentially relate to the fear of losing one's memory. Finally, the robot gets fixed and loses its memory, where hopefully the participant has an empathic response to the robot's fear happening: it lost its memory. Our implementation of these stages is described below and illustrated in Figure 2, and a copy of the full source code (including all script, gestures, etc.) is available online: *http://hci.cs.umanitoba.ca/permanent/hri/2015-nao-robotcontroller/*.

3.1 Building Rapport

It is important to convince people of the sophistication and abilities of the robot, and to provide participants with a chance to get to know a little of the robot's personality to encourage them to see the robot as a social partner and not just a machine. We used a distractor task: cooperatively playing the popular number game Sudoku.[1] We selected this task as it can be cooperative, to encourage the person and robot to work as a team, and it is cognitive, to show the robot's abilities. Further, with the robot and person taking turns, the time while the person is thinking provides an opportunity for the robot to engage in small talk to further encourage building of social rapport. Small-talk topics included, for example, the day's weather, or the participant's study major or job. If participants get off topic or ignore the game, the robot encourages them to continue.

3.2 Robot's Functional Problems

The robot does not show any signs of problem for the first 5 minutes of interaction, after which the robot starts to exhibit functional abnormalities. Frequency and severity of the abnormalities slowly

---

[1] http://en.wikipedia.org/wiki/Sudoku

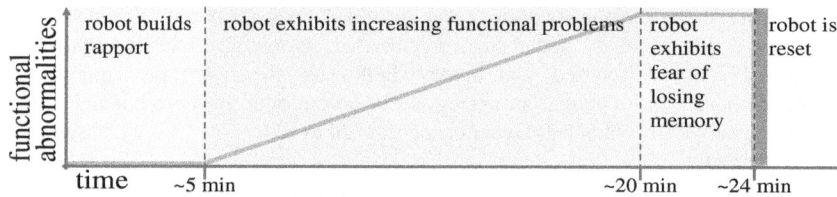

Figure 2. Overview of empathy-inducing scenario methodology. Phases and duration on x axis, with blue line representing level of robot abnormality.

increase to indicate the building severity of problem with the robot. These abnormalities are jittery movements, speaking in distorted voice tones or stuttering, repeating words in a sentence, and speaking nonsense. Eventually the abnormalities are so severe that it is difficult to interact or continue the distractor task. This design encourages the person to consider what may be wrong and hopefully ask the robot. Alternatively, if interaction completely breaks down or 20 minutes have passed, the next phase starts.

3.3 Fear of Losing Memory

The robot reveals that it has a computer virus, and exhibits worry that its memory may be erased if it is fixed. If the participant asks to get the human researcher to help, the robot requests that the participant not tell the researcher due to this worry. Further, the robot expresses desire to keep playing the game to avoid the researcher from suspecting a problem (and thus potentially fixing the robot). The aim here is to build participant empathy toward the robot as we believe that fear of losing one's memory is relatable. This phase is very short (~4 minutes, depending on conversation with the participant), after which the robot gets erased.

We spent considerable time considering other narratives, for example, that the robot has corrupted memory or broken motors, or has a cold or dementia, and piloted variants with consultation with our creative-artist team member (King). There was strong concern over the accessibility of more technical explanations to the general public, and yet human disease proved too transparent. While the virus scenario may seem strange to a technical person, we found it to be relatable and convincing to our lay audience.

3.4 Erasing the Robot's Memory, Empathy

Shortly after the robot expresses its fear, the researcher enters, apologizes, and states to the participant that they remotely found a problem with the robot and that the robot needs to be reset. During this time the researcher's demeanor is detached and bored (to simulate a routine, work task), and as such somewhat cold. To reset the robot, the researcher simply reaches behind the robot and pushes a button on the robot's head (which does not actually exist on this robot). While the robot is being reset, the researcher casually notes that since they are in the room anyway, now would be a good time to complete another questionnaire, and hands it to the participant. Shortly after being reset (~10 seconds), the now-fixed robot introduces itself similar to how it did at the beginning of the experiment, with a different voice tone to indicate a new personality, and asks for the participant's name; the robot repeats the script from the beginning of the interaction. At this point, the study design encourages participants to empathize with the robot as they just experienced a robot expressing fear and subsequently its memory being erased, a fear we expect people to relate to. Further, by

administering the questionnaire at this point we aim to measure any empathic response as quickly as possible after the event.

3.5 Scenario Implementation

The basic experimental setup has the participant in the room alone with the robot, being monitored by cameras – one on the robot and one beside of the participant (Figure 3).

Our setup requires a real robot and related simulated, on-screen animated robot implementation. Further, for exploratory purposes we added an additional condition which merges the physical (real robot) and virtual conditions using a see-through *mixed reality* [24] display where a virtual robot appears on a physical table; thus while being a robot simulation, the interaction is still somewhat embedded into the participant's space.

For our experiment we used on the Aldebaran NAO, a 22.5 inch (57.15 cm) tall humanoid robot with 25 degrees of freedom. Nao has a friendly look, with a stylish design that covers under-the-hood mechanics with plastic (Figure 4, left).

We controlled NAO using an in-house Wizard-of-Oz interface[2] where a hidden operator controls the robot remotely unbeknownst to participants, who believe the robot to be autonomous. In addition to a live video and audio feed, our interface provides a mixture of pre-scripted actions and spoken dialog relevant to the study, a Sudoku solver, and hot-keyed live actions such as unscripted speech, actions, gaze, etc., for on-the-fly interaction. Dialog was automatically combined with generic gestures (such as shuffling hands or looking around). Robot functional errors (e.g., jittery movements, speech stutters, etc.) were automatically inserted by the software on a timer to ensure consistency across participants.

3.5.1 Simulated On-Screen Robot

Our goal was to create an on-screen robot that resembled and interacted like the real robot as much as possible. To achieve this,

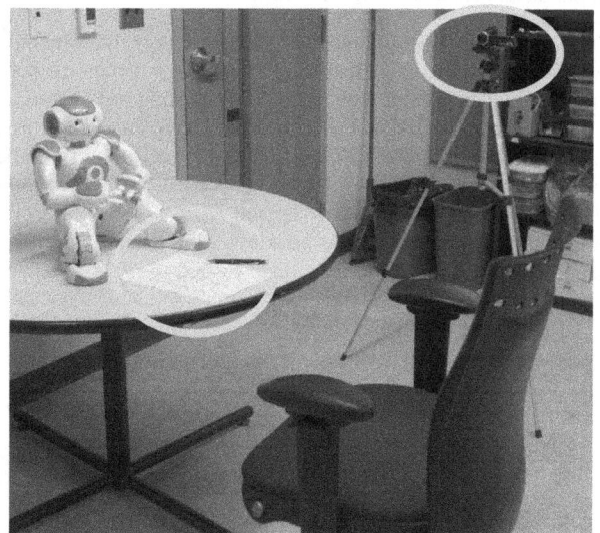

Figure 3. The study setup. A Sudoku board is placed between the participant and the robot. The interaction is recorded by a side camera, while a camera on the robot's head captures a live feed for the remote robot operator.

[2] http://hci.cs.umanitoba.ca/permanent/hri/2015-nao-robotcontroller/

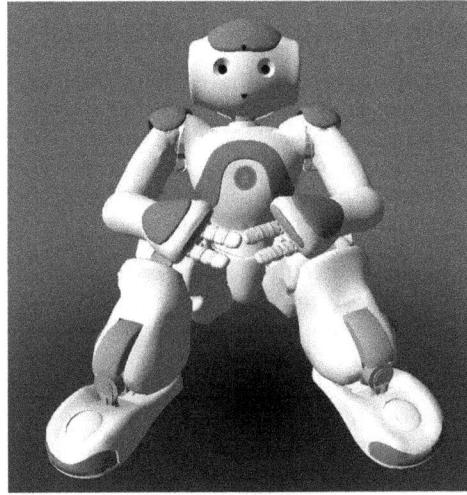

Figure 4. NAO, the humanoid robot used in our study. A simulated NAO (right) mimics movement of a real NAO.

we employed a 3D model of NAO supplied by Aldebaran, and connected it to Aldebaran's powerful NAO Simulator SDK via basic kinematic models. The result (Figure 4, right) was that the same robot commands and controls were issued as in the real-robot case, and the animated robot used the simulator to generate identical movements and voices – even down to the functional abnormalities – as the real robot did. The result had a very similar look and feel, and enabled the controller to use the identical interface as with the real robot to maintain consistency across participants. The simulated robot was presented on a computer screen, with speakers for the robot's voice, and a web-cam to enable the simulated robot to see the person.

3.5.2 Simulated Mixed-Reality Robot

Our mixed reality robot was implemented identically to the on-screen animated robot, with the added layer of superimposing the robot onto the real table (Figure 5). We used AR Toolkit[3] for this. In addition, to highlight the mixed reality technology to the participant, at the beginning of the interaction we indicated that the video feed is live and reflects their space by moving the researcher's hand in front of the web cam and explained that the mixed reality robot can be relocated by moving the marker.

4. Formally Validating Our Scenario and Empathy Questionnaire

The primary purpose of our work is to investigate the authenticity of simulated HRI through our scenario as described above. However, as an initial step we must validate two things: that our scenario actually generates an empathic response as planned, and that our empathy-measuring instrument can detect this response. To this end we conducted a between-subject study: in one condition, participants had the scenario as explained above (*empathy-induced*), and for the other condition, we removed the robot illness, fear, and memory loss (*non-induced*). In the latter case, the researcher interrupts at the end of study due to a time limit. If either the scenario fails (empathy not induced) or the instrument fails (empathy not measured) in their purpose, we will expect no result. However, if both are successful, we expect to see an empathy

---
[3] http://www.hitl.washington.edu/artoolkit/

difference between the conditions, with a higher reading in the induced case. We recruited 24 participants from our general university population (15 male / 9 female), 12 per condition.

The empathy questionnaire performed with good internal consistency (Cronbach's α=.90). We found a difference in the empathic response between groups (t_{22}=2.07, p<.05): *empathy-induced* participants reported a stronger empathic response (M=66, SD=16, SE=4.55 on the Batson scale [7]) than *non-induced* participants (M=55, SD=9, SE=2.67, Figure 6).

These results support both our scenario and instrument: our scenario induces more empathy towards a robot than a low-empathy base case, and this difference can be detected reliably by our instrument.

5. Comparing a Real and Simulated Robot

To investigate our core question of how empathy toward a simulated robot may differ from empathy toward a real robot, we conducted a formal between-participants study that compared

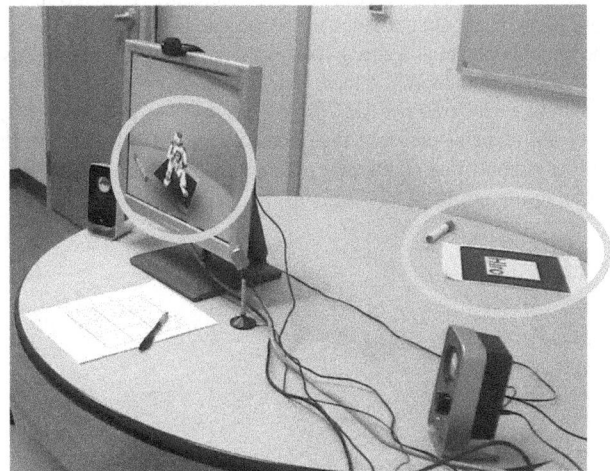

Figure 5. Mixed-reality NAO simulation. Notice that the real world table is shown on the screen to make the illusion that the virtual NAO is on the marker in the real world.

empathy responses between the three conditions: physical robot, mixed-reality simulated robot, or 3D on-screen simulated robot.

We recruited 39 participants across conditions (20 male, 19 female, sex balanced across conditions) – 12 for physical robot, 13 for mixed-reality, and 14 people for on-screen 3D simulated robot. We rotated between conditions to ensure even distribution, with minor variations to maintain gender balance. There are fewer people in some cases due to technical error requiring lengthy repair.

Our results indicate a primary effect of scenario on the level of empathy reported by participants (between-participants ANOVA, $F_{2,36}=3.43$, $p<.05$). Planned contrasts (comparison against physical robot base case) revealed that participants reported higher empathy with the physical robot ($M=66$, $SD=16$, $SE=4.55$) than with the mixed-reality ($M=56$, $SD=11$, $SE=3.18$, $t_{36}=2.11$, $p<.05$) or on-screen conditions ($M=55$, $SD=7$, $SE=2.00$, $t_{36}=2.44$, $p<.05$), Figure 7. Post-hoc, we found no difference between the mixed reality and on-screen conditions ($t_{25}=.364$, $p=.36$). Further, no effect of gender on empathy was found.

Thus, our study provides evidence that people may empathize more with a real robot than with a simulated robot (on-screen or mixed reality) when something bad happens to it. Further, we found no increase in empathy when using mixed reality over an on-screen robot simulation.

6. Overall Discussion

Overall, our study results indicate that we can reliably induce empathy in a human-robot interaction scenario, we can measure the level of empathic response, and that we can expect empathic response to be higher for a real robot than for a simulated one. It is also important to note that our result does not directly rely on novelty-induced measures such as engagement or preference, thus we believe that empathy may be a robust measure to be used in social HRI.

It is important to consider the question of *why* our participants empathized more with our robot than our simulated variants. One possibility may be participant awareness of the robot: a physical robot has a much more dominant presence in one's space than simulations that are bound to computer screens. Although in our case participants did not touch the robot, they still were able to see the tangible object and easily change the view angle naturally just by moving around. While there is evidence that simulated agents also have social presence [28], prior work suggests that robots may have *more* social presence than simulations [19,21]. Our results further support this claim, and perhaps social presence may be a factor in our result.

Even though our study design did not explicitly compare our simulated robot cases against the original no-empathy condition, we highlight the similarity between the non-empathy-induced case ($M=55$) and simulations ($M=56$ and $M=55$). Post-hoc Weber & Popova equivalence testing support that the groups are equal (p<.05 for effect size .5), but this would have to be investigated more formally (i.e., through a targeted study) to make a conclusion. Regardless, we can see that – at least in our case – no large difference was found. If indeed future work finds that people have *no empathic reaction* when something bad happens to a simulated robot in comparison to a base case, and not just simply *less reaction* than with a real robot, this would have strong implications for simulations. As such, this should be investigated formally.

We also must consider limitations with our study design such as the differences in perception in our setup, beyond the physical versus virtual. One such aspect is the fact that our simulated robots did not have gear noise, which may have affected perceptions of robot presence. In addition, our simulated robots were effectively *smaller*, in that they took up a smaller portion of the participants' field of view than the physical robot, which may impact the robot's presence and thus empathy. We do not believe that these confounds are severe enough in our study to explain our findings, but future work should be careful to correct for such potential issues, e.g., by using a large TV monitor or projector so that the simulations looked to be the same size as the real robot.

In addition, we must consider our specific robot, simulation specifics, task, and even the university setting, and how this impacts our investigation. While our results indicate an impact of embodiment on empathy, we need to be careful when moving to other robots, tasks, and settings which have not yet been tested.

As a side note, the researchers informally noted that during the studies female participants appeared to have stronger outward empathic reactions than male participants, for example, showing concern for the robot and asking what they can do for it. Although our gender analysis did not support this, as this observation is weakly supported by prior work [6] we believe that this should be explored further.

7. Future Work

We believe that our initial successful results indicate the importance of continuing research in this direction. One such example is broadening our view of empathy: currently, we only addressed empathic responses to negative emotions. Empathy itself is quite rich, and continued work should consider other extremes such as robot happiness, and more mild situations in between. Also,

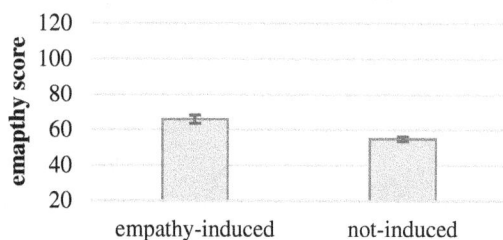

Figure 6. Mean and SE of measured empathy in our empathy-induced scenario (left) and not induced (right), *p*<.05. Scale is from 24 to 120.

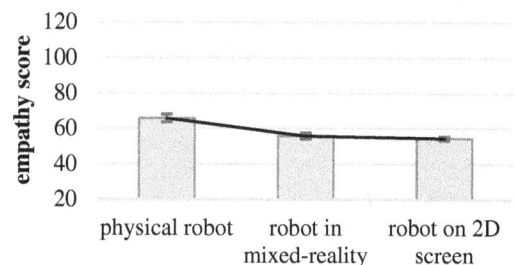

Figure 7. Mean and SE of measured empathy toward different embodiments. ANOVA shows significant effects $F_{2,36}=3.43$, *p*<.05. Scale is from 24 to 120.

our short in-lab study only had limited time to build rapport; it will be important to consider how results change over longitudinal interaction, as people build deeper relationships with a robot, for example, a companion robot. However, in this case for ethical reasons we would advise against purposefully erasing a person's long-term companion to see their reaction.

In our experiment, the participant was a passive observer of the empathy-inducing event (erasing the robot). In previous work, people were asked to "kill" or "destroy" robots, thus making them an active participant in the negative action [6]. This difference can be important: for example, if a search and rescue robot operator were to abandon a robot in a disaster zone, it will be important to know if empathy may play a part in their decision making. Thus, follow-up work should look at various roles that the participant can take, and how this may mediate the impact of using a simulation versus a real robot.

An additional variable to be explored is the impact of the robot's personality. In our scenario, we presented the robot as having a positive and outgoing personality. However, will people empathize with a cantankerous robot in the same way? If not, this could be important information, for example, when developing a robot that the designer does not want people to empathize with.

Our work compared against an on-screen and mixed reality simulation; even though the mixed reality was superimposed in the real world, both simulations were fully digitally embodied. There are other mixtures of real and simulation, for example, physical robots with computer screens for faces or even full torsos. Would a person empathize with such a robot the same as a fully physically-embodied one? Given our results and discussion on the importance of robotic embodiment, we believe that such a robot would induce empathy, but this should be formally investigated.

8. Conclusion

In this paper we investigated the question of how much people would empathize when something bad happened to a physical robot in comparison to simulated variants. We found evidence that people may empathize more with a real robot, and further, found initial indications that people may even fail to empathize at all with simulations (in comparison to a base case). In addition, contributions of this paper include a reproducible and tested HRI scenario for inducing empathy toward robots in laboratory settings, and the formal testing of a psychological instrument for measuring empathy in an HRI scenario, an instrument that is very generalizable to other studies. Finally, we outlined important future directions that should be investigated as a result of our findings.

Empathy is an important element of many applications of social robotics, including companion, therapy, and teaching robots, to name a few. Developing robust interfaces and robotic personalities that properly incorporate and encourage appropriate empathy toward the robot will be crucial for the success in such applications. As such, although robotic simulations provide a discount method for exploring novel interfaces, improving accessibility to researchers who cannot obtain or program robots, we need to be clearly aware of the limitations of using simulations. Although in this work we present results suggesting that a simulated robot may not be a perfect replacement for a real robot, the bigger agenda is to continue to map out the limitations and differences of using simulations, and to better understand the social and perceptual

mechanisms behind such limitations, to give designers the tools and power needed to appropriately use simulations in their work.

9. Acknowledgements

We would like to extend our gratitude to the HCI Lab and the Department of Computer Science at the University of Manitoba for their ongoing support of this work. This project was funded by the University of Manitoba, the Department of Computer Science, and NSERC.

10. References

1. Astin, H.S. Assessment of empathic ability by neans of a situational test. *Journal of Counseling Psychology 14*, 1 (1967), 57–60.

2. Bainbridge, W.A., Hart, J.W., Kim, E.S., and Scassellati, B. The benefits of interactions with physically present robots over video-displayed agents. *International Journal of Social Robotics 3*, 1 (2010), 41–52.

3. Baron-Cohen, S. and Wheelwright, S. The empathy quotient: an investigation of adults with Asperger syndrome or high functioning autism, and normal sex differences. *Journal of autism and developmental disorders 34*, 2 (2004), 163–75.

4. Bartneck, C., Bleeker, T., Bun, J., Fens, P., and Riet, L. The influence of robot anthropomorphism on the feelings of embarrassment when interacting with robots. *Paladyn 1*, 2 (2010), 109–115.

5. Bartneck, C., Reichenbach, J., and Breemen, A. Van. In your face, robot! The influence of a character's embodiment on how users perceive its emotional expressions. *Proceedings of the Design and Emotion*, (2004), 32–51.

6. Bartneck, C., Verbunt, M., Mubin, O., and Al Mahmud, A. To kill a mockingbird robot. *Proceeding of the ACM/IEEE international conference on Human-robot interaction - HRI '07*, ACM Press (2007), 81–87.

7. Batson, C.D., Polycarpou, M.P., Harmon-Jones, E., et al. Empathy and attitudes: can feeling for a member of a stigmatized group improve feelings toward the group? *Journal of personality and social psychology 72*, 1 (1997), 105–18.

8. Batson, C.D., Sager, K., Garst, E., Kang, M., Rubchinsky, K., and Dawson, K. Is empathy-induced helping due to self-other merging? *73*, 3 (1997), 495–509.

9. Davis, M.H. Measuring individual differences in empathy: Evidence for a multidimensional approach. *Journal of personality and social psychology 44*, 1 (1983), 113–126.

10. Davis, M.H. *Empathy: A social psychological approach.* Brown & Benchmark Publishers, 1994.

11. Eisenberg, N., Fabes, R.A., Murphy, B., and Karbon, M. The relations of emotionality and regulation to dispositional and situational empathy-related responding. *Journal of Personality and Social Psychology 66*, 4 (1994), 776–797.

12. Fischer, K., Lohan, K., and Foth, K. Levels of embodiment: linguistic analyses of factors influencing HRI. *Human-Robot Interaction (HRI)*, (2012), 463–470.

13. Fridin, M. and Belokopytov, M. Embodied robot versus virtual agent: Involvement of preschool children in motor task

performance. *International Journal of Human-Computer Interaction 30*, 6 (2014), 459–469.

14. Garreau, J. Bots on the ground. *Washington Post*, (2007), 1–6.

15. Gonsior, B., Sosnowski, S., Mayer, C., et al. Improving aspects of empathy and subjective performance for HRI through mirroring facial expressions. *2011 RO-MAN*, IEEE (2011), 350–356.

16. Haker, H., Kawohl, W., Herwig, U., and Rössler, W. Mirror neuron activity during contagious yawning-an fMRI study. *Brain imaging and behavior 7*, 1 (2013), 28–34.

17. Hoffmann, L. and Krämer, N.C. Investigating the effects of physical and virtual embodiment in task-oriented and conversational contexts. *International Journal of Human-Computer Studies 71*, 7-8 (2013), 763–774.

18. Janssen, J.H. A three-component framework for empathic technologies to augment human interaction. *Journal on Multimodal User Interfaces 6*, 3-4 (2012), 143–161.

19. Kidd, C.D. and Breazeal, C. Comparison of social presence in robots and animated characters. *Proceedings of human-computer interaction (HCI)*, 2005.

20. Kidd, C.D. and Breazeal, C. Effect of a robot on user perceptions. *2004 IEEE/RSJ International Conference on Intelligent Robots and Systems (IROS) (IEEE Cat. No.04CH37566) 4*, (2004), 3559–3564.

21. Lee, K.M., Jung, Y., Kim, J., and Kim, S.R. Are physically embodied social agents better than disembodied social agents?: The effects of physical embodiment, tactile interaction, and people's loneliness in human–robot interaction. *International Journal of Human-Computer Studies 64*, 10 (2006), 962–973.

22. Leite, I., Pereira, A., Martinho, C., and Paiva, A. Are emotional robots more fun to play with? *RO-MAN 2008 - The 17th IEEE International Symposium on Robot and Human Interactive Communication*, IEEE (2008), 77–82.

23. McQuiggan, S., Robison, J., Robert Phillips, and Lester, J.C. Modeling parallel and reactive empathy in virtual agents: An inductive approach. *Proceedings of the 7th international joint conference on Autonomous agents and multiagent systems 1*, (2008), 167–174.

24. Milgram, P., Takemura, H., Utsumi, A., and Kishino, F. Augmented reality: a class of displays on the reality-virtuality continuum. *Telemanipulator and Telepresence Technologies*, (1995), 282–292.

25. Pereira, A., Leite, I., Mascarenhas, S., Martinho, C., and Paiva, A. Using empathy to improve human-robot relationships. In M.H. Lamers and F.J. Verbeek, eds., *Human-Robot Personal Relationships*. Springer Berlin Heidelberg, 2011, 130–138.

26. Pop, C.A., Simut, R.E., Pintea, S., et al. Social Robots vs. Computer display: Does the way social stories are delivered make a difference for their effectiveness on ASD children? *Journal of Educational Computing Research 49*, 3 (2013), 381–401.

27. Powers, A., Kiesler, S., Fussell, S., and Torrey, C. Comparing a computer agent with a humanoid robot. *Proceeding of the ACM/IEEE international conference on Human-robot interaction - HRI '07*, (2007), 145.

28. Reeves, B. and Nass, C. *The Media Equation: How People Treat Computers, Television, and New Media Like Real People and Places*. Cambridge University Press, New York, New York, USA, 1996.

29. Riek, L.D., Rabinowitch, T.-C., Chakrabarti, B., and Robinson, P. How anthropomorphism affects empathy toward robots. *Proceedings of the 4th ACM/IEEE international conference on Human robot interaction - HRI '09*, ACM Press (2009), 245.

30. Segura, E., Kriegel, M., Aylett, R., Deshmukh, A., and Cramer, H. How do you like me in this: User embodiment preferences for companion agents. In Y. Nakano, M. Neff, A. Paiva and M. Walker, eds., *Intelligent Virtual Agents*. Springer Berlin Heidelberg, Berlin, Heidelberg, 2012, 112–125.

31. Shinozawa, K., Naya, F., Yamato, J., and Kogure, K. Differences in effect of robot and screen agent recommendations on human decision-making. *International Journal of Human-Computer Studies 62*, 2 (2005), 267–279.

32. Spreng, R.N., McKinnon, M.C., Mar, R. a, and Levine, B. The toronto empathy questionnaire: scale development and initial validation of a factor-analytic solution to multiple empathy measures. *Journal of personality assessment 91*, 1 (2009), 62–71.

33. Stephan, W.G. and Finlay, K. The Role of Empathy in Improving Intergroup Relations. *Journal of Social Issues 55*, 4 (1999), 729–743.

34. Stueber, K. Empathy. *The Stanford Encyclopedia of Philosophy*, 2013.

35. Sung, J., Guo, L., Grinter, R., and Christensen, H. *"My Roomba Is Rambo": Intimate home appliances*. Springer Berlin Heidelberg, 2007.

36. Takeuchi, J., Kushida, K., Nishimura, Y., et al. Comparison of a humanoid robot and an on-screen agent as presenters to audiences. *2006 IEEE/RSJ International Conference on Intelligent Robots and Systems*, (2006), 3964–3969.

37. Wada, K. and Shibata, T. Living with seal robots—Its sociopsychological and physiological influences on the elderly at a care house. *IEEE Transactions on Robotics 23*, 5 (2007), 972–980.

38. Wainer, J., Feil-seifer, D., Shell, D., and Mataric, M. The role of physical embodiment in human-robot interaction. *ROMAN 2006 - The 15th IEEE International Symposium on Robot and Human Interactive Communication*, IEEE (2006), 117–122.

39. Woods, S., Walters, M., and Dautenhahn, K. Comparing human robot interaction scenarios using live and video based methods: towards a novel methodological approach. *9th IEEE International Workshop on Advanced Motion Control, 2006.*, (2006), 750–755.

40. Wrobel, J., Wu, Y., Kerhervé, H., et al. Effect of agent embodiment on the elder user enjoyment of a game. *ACHI 2013, The Sixth International Conference on Advances in Computer-Human Interactions*, (2013), 162–167.

Observer Perception of Dominance and Mirroring Behavior in Human-Robot Relationships

Jamy Li
Stanford University
450 Serra Mall, Bldg 120
Stanford, CA 94305 USA
jamy@stanford.edu

Wendy Ju
Stanford University
424 Panama Mall
Stanford, CA 94025 USA
wendyju@stanford.edu

Cliff Nass
Stanford University
450 Serra Mall, Bldg 120
Stanford, CA 94305 USA
nass@stanford.edu

ABSTRACT

How people view relationships between humans and robots is an important consideration for the design and acceptance of social robots. Two studies investigated the effect of relational behavior in a human-robot dyad. In Study 1, participants watched videos of a human confederate discussing the Desert Survival Task with either another human confederate or a humanoid robot. Participants were less trusting of both the robot and the person in a human-robot relationship where the robot was dominant toward the person than when the person was dominant toward the robot; these differences were not found for a human pair. In Study 2, participants watched videos of a human confederate having an everyday conversation with either another human confederate or a humanoid robot. Participants who saw a confederate mirror the gestures of a robot found the robot less attractive than when the robot mirrored the confederate; the opposite effect was found for a human pair. Exploratory findings suggest that human-robot relationships are viewed differently than human dyads.

Categories and Subject Descriptors

H.1.2 [**Models and Principles**]: User/Machine Systems - *human factors, software psychology*

General Terms

Design, Human Factors

1. INTRODUCTION

Social robots are envisioned for a wide range of applications, from bartenders and receptionists to healthcare assistants and companions [20]. As robots enter public and professional settings, people's experiences will include observation of interactions between users and their robots. Human-robot interaction (HRI) research focuses on *interactions* as the unit of design, investigating how people respond to a robot's appearance and behavior. We propose human-robot relationship (HRR) research to explore how people view *relationships* by treating the human-robot pair as the unit of design.

Treating the human-robot relationship as the unit of design has three advantages. First, it allows experimental manipulation of how a person responds to a robot. Human response can be explored in concert with robot behavior by instructing users to interact with a robot in a certain way or by using a confederate to

simulate ways of interacting with a robot, without having to rely on people's *in situ* behavior. This can be of particular use with social robots that support a range of relational interaction due to their high social agency. Second, relationship-focused studies account for observers. Studies that modify only qualities of a technology focus on how direct interactants will experience it and do not evaluate how user behavior is perceived by others. Observer response may be key for social robots that attract attention when they speak, move and act in public areas, particularly as the "observability" of a technology influences its rate of adoption [39] and most people first experience a technology as observers. Moreover, observers may not respond in the same way to human-robot relationships as do the people in those relationships; research in interpersonal communication has noted that participants exhibit greater positivity bias than observers when perceiving relational messages [9]. Since observers lack the familiarity a user has with a robot, this finding may apply to interactions with robots as well. Third, it allows for exploration of relational attributes between people and robots. Social robots occupy a unique role as highly expressive social entities that are independent of their users. Our approach is to extend past work in HRI that has shown people treat robots as social actors (e.g., [17, 21, 32]) by asking whether people treat human-robot relationships like interpersonal ones.

Two exploratory studies investigate how observers perceive human-robot relationships. Study 1 looks at relational dominance in a collaborative task, where one party has authority over the other. Study 2 looks at mirroring behavior in everyday conversation, where one party mirrors the other's movements. Both studies consider the human-robot relationship as the unit of design and manipulate the behavior of the robot and its user. Dominance and mirroring are chosen as initial topics for relational studies because of their dyadic nature [5,24] (i.e., dominance of one party exists in relation to the other; mirroring requites one party to follow the other). While no conceptual link between the

Figure 1. Video stimuli from Study 1 on dominance. Red actress/standing robot is dominant.

two constructs is explored here, some evidence suggests dominant parties tend to lead rather than follow gestures [3].

2. THEORY AND HYPOTHESES
2.1 Dominance

Current research in robotics explores applications for collaborative work, such as achieving goals and making decisions, in which the relative status of the parties is of interest. One person may have equal influence as another over a decision (typically a peer) or greater influence than the other (in the case of a superior-subordinate relationship). How relative dominance is perceived in task-focused human-robot relationships is explored here.

Dominance is a "fundamental dimension defining all interpersonal relationships." [5] It has been defined as "the degree to which one actor attempts to regulate the behavior of the other." [14] (p. 53) Broadly, it consists of attempts to "exert power, control or influence over the thoughts, feelings, or actions [of] another." (p. 55) Among past work in interpersonal communication, Burgoon [7] found conversational partners with high dominance had greater social influence and conversational control than those with low dominance. Dillard et al. [14] found perception of dominance to be positively correlated with immediacy (i.e. positive affect) and negatively correlated with receptivity (i.e., trust-seeking behavior). Observers judge others to be more dominant when they exhibit high rather than low pleasantness [8] and when they have higher social skills [5].

Dominance is perceived in technological entities and is a key determinant of psychological response to computers [33, 37]. Among HRI research, Roubroeks et al. [40] found that people experienced higher psychological reactance when a robot gave high-threatening advice than when it gave non-threatening advice. Threatening was taken to mean a challenge to the autonomy of a user, an indicator of dominance. Groom et al. [21] found that people preferred a self-blaming robot over one that would blame its user for poor performance on a team task. Evaluation acts have previously been used to establish dominance (e.g., [34]). Work by Gombolay et al. [19] suggested that robots with greater decision-making authority are preferred over those with less authority, although they did not assess the attitudes of observers. We hypothesize that a dominant robot will be viewed as less trustworthy, agreeable and attractive than a submissive one. We focus on these dependent variables because of their importance to collaborative teams.

Hypothesis 1a: Observers will trust a dominant robot less than a submissive one in a human-robot relationship.

Hypothesis 1b: Observers will be less attracted to a dominant robot than a submissive one in a human-robot relationship.

Hypothesis 1c: Observers will find a dominant robot less affectionate than a submissive one in a human-robot relationship.

We also investigate how observers perceive a person who is in a relationship with a robot companion.

RQ 1: How will observers evaluate a person who is a dominant compared to submissive partner in a human-robot relationship?

2.2 Movement Mirroring

Social robots are salient social actors due in part to their ability to move in physical space. This movement supports nonverbal behaviors present in interpersonal communication that influence how relationships between people and robots develop. Mirroring is a common nonverbal behavior between two individuals and is explored here as an aspect of a casual human-robot relationship.

People mirror the movements of others during conversation. Movement mirroring – described by Condon and Ogston as "interactional synchrony" [12] (p. 232) and Kendon as "movement coordination" [24] (p. 101) – is a spatiotemporal symmetry in which two objects exhibit bilateral symmetry occurring in a plane between them and self-similarity over time [3] (p. 163). One explanation for why mirroring occurs during conversation is that symmetry communicates empathy or agreement [3] (p. 164). Individuals mimic each other's posture and gestures more when they have greater rapport with each other [28, 41], when they are cooperative rather than competitive [27] and when they have greater desire for affiliation [29]. From the perspective of the person being mirrored, this intent is effective. People whose gestures are mirrored by a confederate develop greater attraction toward the confederate than those whose gestures are not mirrored [11].

Further, non-participating observers are sensitive to mirroring [35]. Observers judge people as being more positive and showing greater rapport when they exhibit more rather than less mirroring [2, 26, 44]. In particular, Floyd and Erbert [16] had a confederate either match or not match the movements of a conversational participant while a second participant viewed the interaction. The confederate was judged as conveying greater trust and less dominance by both conversing and observing participants when they mirrored the partner more. These works suggest that movement mirroring results in positive attributions by observers.

Robot researchers studying mirroring or "mimicry" have mostly treated it as a behavior of the robot. For example, Riek et al. [38] had participants interact with a robot that either fully mimicked, partially mimicked or did not mimic participants' head movements. No significant differences were found in participant satisfaction between conditions, perhaps due to limiting the robot to head movements only. A study by Bailenson and Yee [1] conducted in virtual reality, however, found that a virtual agent was judged to be more likeable and to have greater social influence when it mirrored participants than when it used non-mirroring movements. We predict that a robot that mirrors a person's movements will be perceived as more agreeable and attractive than one that is mirrored. We focus on these variables due to their importance in interpersonal relationships.

Hypothesis 2a: Observers will find a robot more agreeable when it mirrors rather than is mirrored by a person.

Hypothesis 2b: Observers will find a robot more attractive when it mirrors rather than is mirrored by a person.

People also mirror a robot's movements. Actions performed by a robot not only activate the human mirror neuron system [18, 36], but people respond more robustly to robotic than to equivalent human actions [13]. A notable experiment conducted by Breazeal et al. [4] found that people mirrored the posture of a socially expressive robot that adopted either a high, neutral or low position relative to the user. However, it remains unclear how observers will respond to a person who mirrors a robot.

RQ 2: How will observers evaluate a person who mirrors rather than is mirrored by a robot?

2.3 Current Studies

Two studies looked at how observers perceived dominance and mirroring behavior in a human-robot dyad. To evaluate the influence of a robot partner, we made comparisons against control conditions in which both speakers were human. Following work in nonverbal behavior (e.g., [35, 44] and HRI [23, 30, 45], video of simulated interactions with confederates were used instead of copresent actors. This ensured repeatability between experimental sessions and enabled precise control of relational dynamics.

3. STUDY 1: DOMINANCE IN A COLLABORATIVE WORK SETTING

3.1 Participants
Fifty-six undergraduate students at a US university (28 female, gender-balanced conditions; age 18-31, M = 20.3, SD = 2.0) received course credit for participation.

3.2 Design and Procedure
In a 2 (conversational partner: human or robot) by 2 (role: dominant or submissive) between-participants laboratory experiment, participants were shown videos of conversations between a main actor and a partner who was either another actor or a Nao robot and who was either dominant or submissive (Figure 1). Participants were told they were viewing video recordings from a past research study. In fact, all videos were produced by experimenters. Videos were short scenes of a conversational exchange about a default ranking of an item from the Desert Survival Task (DST). Eight scenes were shown in random order: four with the dominant party providing a confident opinion and the submissive party agreeing (e.g., "We should definitely rate the flashlight higher. We will need it to signal rescue planes when it's dark." // "I'm not sure about that. Maybe it should be lower? But you seem like you know what you're talking about. Sure.") and four with the submissive party tentatively presenting an opinion and the dominant party either agreeing or disagreeing. Complementary dominant-submissive pairs are favored in task-oriented relationships [43] and enable the use of identical scripts for all conditions. Dominance was manipulated as shown in Table 1, with language manipulated following [33] and appearance following [15].

Participants then completed individual and relational self-report measures. Individual measures assessed perception of each party using personality mini-markers for dominance ("assertive", "dominant", "submissive"), trustworthiness ("sincere", "trustworthy", "honest") and agreeableness ("cooperative", "kind", "warm"), as well as Byrne's [10] two-item scale for social attraction ("I liked the robot", "I would like working with the robot"). Relational measures assessed perception of one party's attitude toward the other party using the Relational Communication Scale [6] for dominance ("The robot tried to control the interaction," "The robot attempted to persuade the person"), immediacy/affection ("The robot showed enthusiasm while talking to the person"; "The robot was not attracted to the person") and receptivity/trust ("The robot wanted to gain the person's trust"; "The robot was willing to listen to the person"). Items used 10-pt Likert scales and were modified for the human dyad condition by referring to the person on the left and right.

3.3 Results

3.3.1 Manipulation Check
The dominance manipulation was effective for the conversational partner. An analysis of covariance (ANCOVA) conducted in SPSS on rating of partner dominance with partner and role as between-participant factors and gender and actress dominance as

Table 1. Operationalization of dominance manipulation.

Manipulation	Dominant	Submissive
Eye level height	High	Low
Eye gaze (H only)	Direct eye contact	Aversion of eye contact
Head position	Straight	Lowered
Color of clothing/lights	Red	Blue
Language use in script	Firm	Hesitant
Question use in script	No questions asked	Questions asked
Opinion in script	Disagreed 2/4 times	Agreed 4/4 times

covariates confirmed that partners were perceived to be more dominant when in the dominant role than when in the submissive role, main effect of role, $F(1,50) = 9.96$, $p < .01$, $\eta^2 = .17$. An interaction effect showed that the robot and the person received similar ratings in the dominant role, but that the robot was judged as more dominant than the person in the submissive role (M = 5.25, SE = .45 vs M = 3.65, SE = .56), $F(1,50) = 16.6$, $p < .001$, $\eta^2 = .25$. An ANCOVA on the partner's relational dominance showed that partners were perceived as being more dominant toward the main actress when in the dominant role compared to the submissive role, $F(1,50) = 9.92$, $p < .003$, $\eta^2 = .166$.

The manipulation was effective for the actress as well. An ANCOVA on ratings of the main actress' dominance with partner and role as between-subjects factors and gender as a covariate confirmed that the actress was perceived as more dominant in the dominant role than in the submissive role (M=9.18, SE=.165 vs M=1.78, SE=.165), $F(1, 51) = 1008$, $p<.001$, $\eta^2 = .95$. An ANCOVA on the actress' relational dominance revealed that the actress was perceived as being more dominant toward her partner in the dominant condition than in the submissive condition (M = 7.26, SE = .24 vs M = 2.61, SE = .24), $F(1,51) = 186$, $p < .001$.

3.3.2 Perception of Robot Dominance
H1 was supported. Observers judged the robot to be less trustworthy, less socially attractive and less affectionate when it was dominant compared to when it was submissive.

Trustworthiness. H1a was supported. Observers trusted the robot in a dominant-robot submissive-person relationship less than with reversed roles. An ANCOVA on partner trustworthiness with partner and role as factors and gender and actress trustworthiness as covariates showed an interaction effect, $F(1,50) = 4.21$, $p = .045$, $\eta^2 = .078$. As shown in Figure 2E, there was no difference in how people trusted the human partner, regardless of whether she was submissive or dominant. Trust in the robot, however, was significantly lower when it was dominant than when it was submissive (M=5.51, SE=.39 vs M=7.48, SE=.40). Interestingly, participants trusted the submissive robot more than the submissive human partner, even though she played the same role.

Social attraction. H1b was supported. Observers were less attracted to a robot that was dominant rather than submissive in a human-robot relationship. A similar ANCOVA of interpersonal attraction toward the partner showed a significant interaction between partner and role, $F(1,50) = 7.57$, $p < .01$, $\eta^2 = .13$. As shown in Figure 2F, attraction toward a robot partner was rated higher when the robot was submissive versus dominant (M=6.47, SE=.58 vs M=3.51, SE = .57), while no difference was found for a human partner.

Immediacy/Affection. H1c was supported. Observers viewed a robot as demonstrating less affection toward its partner when it was dominant as opposed to submissive. An ANCOVA of the partner's immediacy rating showed that for a human dyad, observers rated the human partner as showing greater affection toward the main actress when dominant compared to submissive (M=5.69, SE=.44 vs M=3.28, SE=.46); conversely, people who saw the human-robot video perceived a submissive robot as showing more affection toward the actress than a dominant one (M=5.02, SE=.45 vs M=3.61, SE=.44), F(1,50) = 17.0, p < .001, η^2 =.25 (see Figure 2G).

Receptivity/Trusting-Earning. Submissive partners were viewed as demonstrating more trust-earning behavior toward the main actress than dominant partners. An ANCOVA of the partner's receptivity/trust-earning with partner and role as between-participant factors and gender as a covariate found submissive partners were perceived to be more receptive than dominant partners (M = 7.71, SE = .34 versus M = 3.20, SE=.34), main effect of role, F(1,50) = 60.2, p < .001, η^2 = .55 (see Figure 2H).

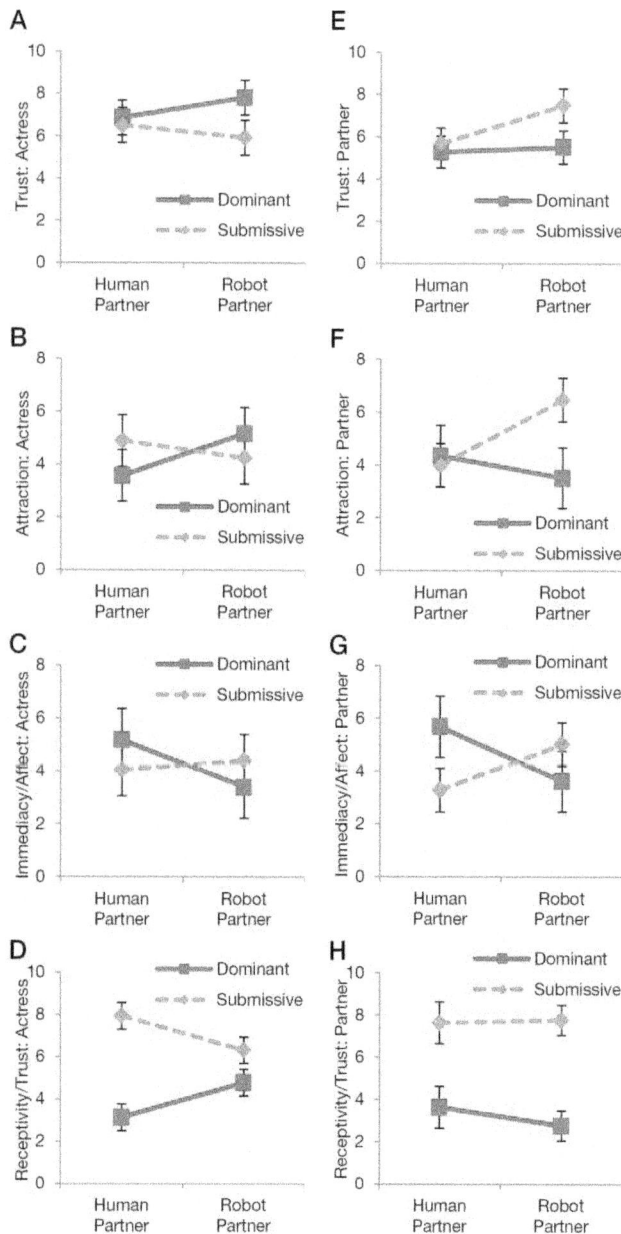

3.3.3 Perception of Actress Dominance
RQ1 asked how the person in a human-robot relationship is perceived. We conducted similar tests for observer ratings of the actress. Observers judged the actress as less trustworthy and less attractive when she was submissive rather than dominant in a collaborative task with a robot.

Trustworthiness. Observers trusted the actress less when she was submissive versus dominant with the robot. An ANCOVA on rating of actress trustworthiness revealed a borderline interaction effect, F(1,51) = 3.51, p = .067, η^2 = .064. When the actress spoke with a person, how much she was trusted did not differ according to her role. When she spoke with a robot, however, she appeared less trustworthy when she was submissive rather than dominant (M = 5.90, SE = .41 vs M = 7.80, SE = .41) (see Figure 2A).

Social attraction. Observers were less attracted to the actress when she was submissive versus dominant with the robot. An ANCOVA of social attraction toward the actress showed a significant interaction effect, F(1,51) = 5.24, p = .026, η^2 = .093. When participants viewed a human pair, they were more attracted to the actress when she was submissive versus dominant (M=4.90, SE=.49 vs M=3.58, SE=.49). The reverse was true for a human-robot dyad: the actress was more liked when in the dominant instead of submissive role (M=5.17, SE=.49 vs M=4.25, SE=.49).

Immediacy/Affection. Observers judged the actress as exhibiting greater affection toward the robot when she was submissive rather than dominant. An ANCOVA of the actress' immediacy affection confirmed that people who saw the actress speak with another person thought she showed greater affection toward her partner when she was dominant versus submissive (M=5.18, SE=.41 vs M=4.04, SE=.41), but people who saw the actress speak with a robot thought the reverse (M=4.41, SE=.41 vs M=3.39, SE=.41), interaction effect, F(1,51)=6.84, p=.012, η^2 =.12 (see Figure 2C).

Receptivity/Trusting-Earning. Observers judged the actress as demonstrating greater receptivity toward the robot when she was submissive rather than dominant. An ANCOVA of the actress' receptivity with gender as a covariate showed a significant interaction between partner and role, F(1,51) = 27.3, p < .001, η^2 =.35. The actress was perceived as more receptive when she was submissive as opposed to dominant, but this difference was smaller for people who saw the human-robot pair (see Figure 2D).

3.3.4 Actress Consistency
Actress consistency was also evaluated. As the two human dyad controls utilized the same scripts only with roles switched, no difference in how observers rated one actress versus the other was expected for a given role. This had partial support. The presence and direction of effects were identical for the main actress and her human partner for all measures except social attraction. Observers were more attracted to the main actress when she played the submissive rather than dominant role, but no difference was found for the human partner (Figures 2B, 2F), perhaps because of differences in appearance, performance style or voice.

3.4 Discussion
Study 1 provided evidence that in human-robot relationships, people prefer a robot to be subordinate to a human authority rather than vice versa. Although observers viewed *relational* dynamics as being consistent with role (i.e., dominant parties were rated as showing less affection and receptivity regardless of whether it was a robot or person who was dominant), this was not

Figure 2. Results for observer perception of dominance. Error bars, 95% CI.

true for judgments of the parties themselves. Observers liked and trusted both the robot and the actress less when the robot was leading the actress than if the actress was leading. This is in light of the fact that people who collaborate with robots may need to be in subordinate roles (or even prefer them, cf. [19]), especially if robots have superior abilities in the task at hand.

Observers also viewed human-robot relationships differently than interpersonal ones. The effects described above were not found for the human pair: despite conversation content being the same, affiliation toward a human partner did not vary with her role she played. Consistent with past interpersonal research [14], observers who saw two people thought dominant behavior by either of them indicated affection. Conversely, people who saw an actress-robot pair viewed dominance as showing less affection than submissiveness.

The next study tested how mirroring, another relational element present in interpersonal conversation, affected observer perception of a human-robot relationship.

4. STUDY 2: MIRRORING IN A CASUAL CONVERSATION SETTING

4.1 Participants
Sixty undergraduate students at a US university (36 female; age 18-31, M = 20.7, SD = 1.9) received course credit for participation. Participants of the first study were excluded from the second study. One participant was omitted from analyses due to consistently selecting the same rating.

4.2 Design and Procedure
In a 2 (conversational partner: human or robot) by 3 (mirroring behavior: actor-led, partner-led or no mirroring) mixed design online experiment, participants viewed video trials as in Study 1. The between-participants factor of partner had two levels: videos featured a main actor whose partner was either a person or a robot (see Figure 3). The within-participants factor of mirroring had three levels: the partner mirrored the main actor's movements ("actor-led"), the main actor mirrored the partner's movements ("partner-led"), or no mirroring occurred ("no-mirroring"). A counterbalanced design was used to mitigate order effects.

Participants were recruited using an online experimental management system and directed to a Qualtrics website that delivered all videos and surveys. After consent, the instructions began as follows: "You will be watching a video of a conversation between a person and a robot. Imagine that you are on a student exchange in Beijing, China and that you are in a public area when you observe the person and the robot talking with each other." The script used left and right to distinguish between actors for the human pair condition. Each participant viewed three scenes: the first on gift-giving, the second on a new job and the third on an apartment search. Each scene contained one dialogue from an English language-learning text (available at http://www.teacherjoe.us/NYBJ.html), selected because it contained casual, standardized conversations between two parties and lines of roughly equal length. Parties alternated conversational lines, each executing one movement (either head rotation left, right, up or down; lifting of left, right or both hands; or posture shift forward or back) per line and then returning to a neutral position. Each participant saw all three mirroring conditions in a counterbalanced design. In the actor-led condition, the main actor performed the same sequence of movements as the partner prior to the partner's movement. In the partner-led

condition, the main actor performed the same sequence after the partner. In the non-mirroring condition, the actor performed a nonmatching sequence that contained no mirroring or reverse-mirroring of the partner. The robot's gestures were the same for all videos (pre-scripted using the robot's Choreographe software) and were identical to those used in the human partner condition. Frequencies of body, head and hand movement were balanced in each scene. The same actors were used in each scene to control for acting ability, with faces blurred and different attire used to convey a sense that each scene featured a different pair (the robot appeared with different-colored lights). Synthetic speech was used for all parties to avoid mismatched natural and synthetic speech. Videos were approximately three minutes long.

After each scene, participants answered the individual and relational self-report measures from Study 1 excluding dominance. Participants were not asked about mirroring behavior to avoid priming their attention to mirroring in subsequent scenes.

4.3 Results

4.3.1 Perception of Robot Mirroring
H2 was supported. The robot was viewed as more agreeable, more attractive and demonstrating greater affection toward its partner when it mirrored the person's movements versus when it was mirrored by the person. Comparing observer perception of the robot and human partners suggested that people responded differently to a robot conversational partner than to a human.

Agreeableness. H2a was supported. Observers found the robot partner to be more agreeable when it was following than when it was leading, while the reverse was true for a human partner. A mixed-design ANCOVA of partner agreeableness with mirroring as a within-participant factor, partner as a between-participant factor and gender as a covariate revealed a significant interaction effect, $F(2, 112) = 9.81$, $p<.001$, $\eta^2 = .149$ (shown in Figure 4D). A follow-up contrast between actor-led and partner-led conditions confirmed that a human partner was viewed as more agreeable when leading than when following gestures (M=7.64, SE=.270 vs M=6.68, SE=.342), while a robot partner was viewed as significantly more agreeable when following compared to leading (M=6.97, SE=.348 vs M=5.53, SE=.275), $F(1,56) = 13.0$, $p = .001$, $\eta^2 =.189$. A contrast between partner-led and non-mirroring conditions showed that people viewed a human partner as more

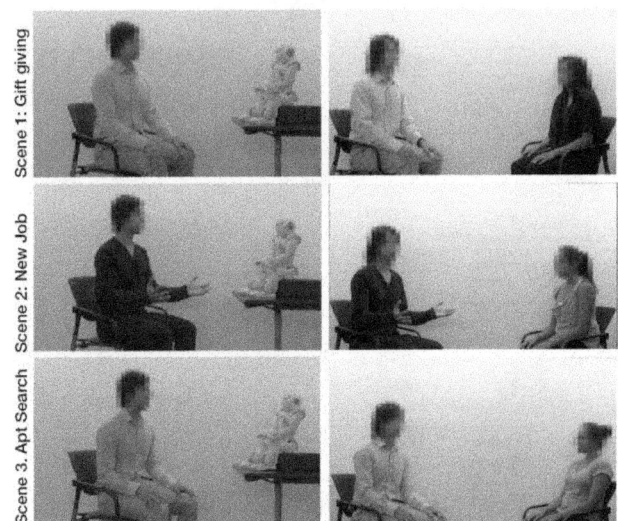

Figure 3. Video stimuli from Study 2 on mirroring.

137

agreeable when leading than when no mirroring occurred (M=7.64, SE=.270 vs M=6.76, SE=.330), whereas they found a robot partner more agreeable when no movement mirroring occurred than when the robot led movements (M=6.85, SE=.335 vs M=5.53, SE=.275), F(1,56)=19.8, p<.001, η^2 =.261. No main effects were found.

Social attraction. H2b was supported. Observers were more attracted to a robot when it was following than when it was leading. A mixed-design ANCOVA on partner attraction identified a significant interaction effect for social attraction, F(2,112) = 4.71, p=.011, η^2 = .078 (Figure 4E). A follow-up contrast between actor-led and partner-led conditions showed that participants who viewed a conversation between two people were more attracted to the partner when she was leading than when she was following (M = 6.516, SE = .408 vs M=5.727, SE = .380); however, participants who viewed a conversation between a person and a robot were more attracted to the robot when it was following as opposed to leading (M=6.381, SE=.387 vs M=5.208, SE=.415), F(1,56) = 7.57, p=.008, η^2 = .119. A contrast between partner-led and non-mirroring conditions showed that people were more attracted to a human partner who was leading than when no mirroring occurred (M=6.516, SE=.408 vs M=5.903, SE=.348), whereas the reverse was true for a robot (M=5.208, SE=.415 vs M=5.963, SE=.354), F(1,56)=5.020, p=.029, η^2 = .082.

Immediacy/Affection. Observers found the robot partner to exhibit greater affection when it was following versus leading, while the reverse was true for a human partner. A mixed-design ANCOVA of partner immediacy/affection revealed an interaction effect, F(2,112)=9.91, p<.001, η^2=.150 (Figure 4F). A follow-up contrast showed participants who saw an actress partner found her to be significantly more affectionate toward the main actor when she was leading as opposed to following (M=7.489, SE=.340 vs M=6.458, SE=.328), while participants who saw a robot partner found it to be more affectionate when following versus leading (M=7.455, SE=.334 vs M=6.212, SE=.346), F(1,56)=12.8, p=.001, η^2=.186. A second contrast showed that people were more attracted to a human partner when she was leading than when no mirroring occurred (M=7.489, SE=.340 vs M=6.77, SE=.278), but were more attracted to a robot partner when no mirroring occurred than when the robot led (M=7.52, SE=.282 vs M=6.212, SE=.346), F(1.57)=15.1, p<.001, η^2=.212.

Receptivity/Trusting-Earning. Receptivity/trust of the partner did not differ significantly between partner type (human vs robot), F(1,56) = 2.47, p = .114, or mirroring conditions, F(2,112)=.018, p=.983. No interaction effect was found, F(2,112)=1.53, p = .221.

Relational Dominance. Ratings of partner dominance toward the main actor did not differ significantly between partner type, F(1,56)=.507, p = .480, or mirroring conditions, F(2,112)=.459, p = .633. No interaction effect was found, F(2,112)=.971, p = .382. In the human-robot dyad condition, participants rated a robot that led gestures higher in dominance than one that followed (M=6.682, SE=.406 vs. M=5.847, SE=.311), though this did not reach significance.

4.3.2 Perception of Actor Mirroring
To address RQ2, which asked how the human actor of the human-robot dyad would be perceived, we conducted the same analyses as above for observer ratings of the main actor.

Agreeableness. Observers found the actor more agreeable when mirroring his partner's movements than when no mirroring occurred. A mixed-design ANCOVA on actor agreeableness with mirroring as a within-participant factor, partner as a between-participant factor and gender as a covariate found a main effect for mirroring, F(2,112)=6.17, p=.003, η^2=.099 (Figure 4A). A follow-up contrast showed participants viewed the main actor as more agreeable he was following versus when no mirroring occurred (M=6.90, SE=.166 vs M=6.22, SE=.207), F(1,56)=11.1, p=.002, η^2=.166.

Social Attraction. A mixed-design ANCOVA with mirroring as a within-participants factor, partner as a between-participants factor and gender as a covariate found a main effect for mirroring on social attraction to the main actor, F(2,112)=5.721, p=.004, η^2=.093 (Figure 4B). Participants were more attracted to the main actor when he was leading than when there was no mirroring (M=5.25, SE=.235 vs M=4.54, SE=.247), F(1,56)=7.50, p=.008. Participants were also more attracted to the main actor when he was following the movements of the partner than when there was no mirroring (M=5.37, SE=.292 vs M=4.54, SE=.247), F(1,56)=9.39, p=.003, η^2=.144. A contrast between actor-led and partner-led conditions was not significant. No interaction was found, F(2,112) = 2.297, p=.105.

Immediacy/Affection. A mixed-design ANCOVA with mirroring as a within-participants factor, partner as a between-participants factor and gender as a covariate showed that ratings of immediacy for the main actor did not differ significantly between partner type, F(1,56) = .189, p = .665, or between mirroring conditions,

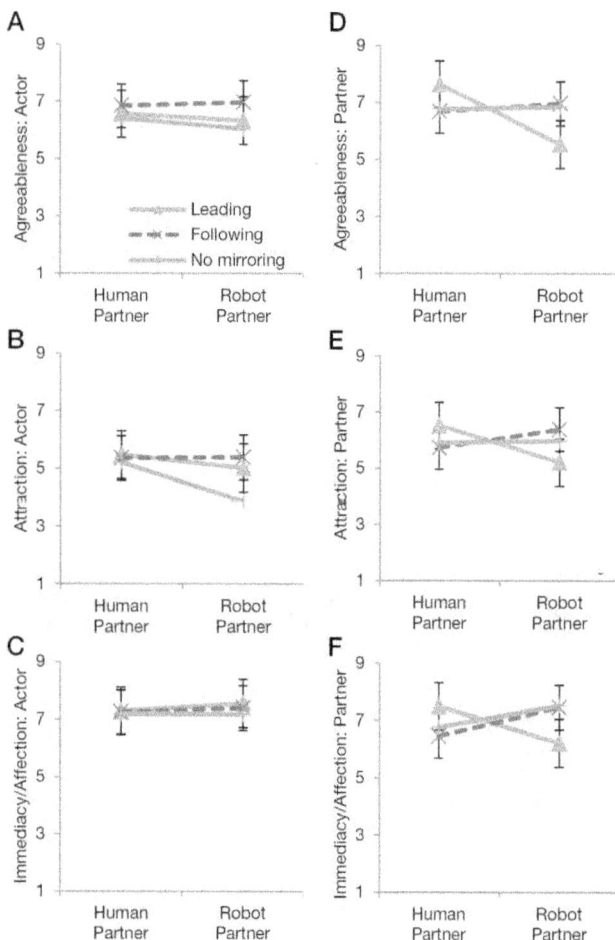

Figure 4. Results for observer perception of mirroring. Error bars, 95% CI.

$F(2,112) = .657$, $p = .520$. No interaction was found, $F(2,112) = .193$, $p = .825$ (Figure 4C).

4.4 Discussion

Study 2 found evidence that people preferred a robot to follow as opposed to lead conversational mirroring. Observers rated a robot partner as more agreeable and more socially attractive when it was mirroring a person as opposed to being mirrored by a person. Further, a robot received more favorable judgments when no mirroring occurred than when it was leading movements, despite the fact that mirroring behavior signals rapport in interpersonal communication. Even in the more subtle behavior of mirroring, observers preferred a human-robot relationship in which the robot was following the person as opposed to vice versa. This result suggests that simple mirroring by a robot of a person's head, hand and postural movements may be an acceptable nonverbal behavior for autonomous social robots.

Study 2 also suggested that people did not view human-robot mirroring the same way as mirroring between two people, even though the content of the conversations and gestures employed were identical. Among people who saw the scene enacted by a human dyad, people rated the human partner as more agreeable, more socially attractive and demonstrating higher affection when it was leading as opposed to following gesture movement: the opposite of what was found for a robot partner.

Observer ratings of the main actor did not differ when he was leading or following. This may be attributed to observers paying greater attention to the partner based on the concept of the scripts or gender differences (the main actor was male while the partner was female). It is also unclear to what extent participants were able to perceive mirroring behavior. All conditions employed synchronous movements that were timed with speech (even if the movement was not a spatial mirror image). As mirroring may become more salient in the absence of temporal synchrony, these results should be taken as tentative.

5. GENERAL DISCUSSION

Our findings indicate that people who observe robots with humans treat these relationships differently than human dyads, both in terms of the overall dynamic of relative authority and the specific interpersonal behavior of mirroring. People prefer robots to be less rather than more authoritative than a human partner. In Study 1, participants trusted and liked a submissive robot more than a dominant one. Observers also judged a person who interacted with a robot more favorably when she was dominant than when she was submissive. People's interactions with agents not only reflected on the agent but also on themselves. In Study 2, participants found a robot that mirrored a person's gestures more agreeable and more likeable than a robot whose gestures were mirrored by a person. Participants liked a robot that was leading gestures even less than when no mirroring occurred. Comparing observer response to human-robot conversation with human dyad controls showed that although people treated the robot as a social actor, people responded differently to it than to a person – even when dialogue and gestures were identical. People preferred the partner in a human pair to be dominant and lead gesture movement.

Future work is needed to explore whether these effects are due to negative connotations individuals have about robots that are given control over people, the perceived agency of the robot or another reason. In a study by Hinds et al. [22], for example, a robot that appeared human-like and was in a supervisory role left less responsibility to their human partners; such a situation may be disliked by observers. Short et al. [42] found people made greater attributions of mental state with a cheating robot; thus, an alternative is that people may dislike a dominant robot because it appears to have greater mental abilities than a submissive one.

A methodological limitation of the current work was that it employed video viewing of human-robot relationships rather than physically copresent humans and robots. Kim et al. [25] found copresent robots generate stronger responses than robots that are displayed using video. This weakness may mean that the results found here represent a lower bound for the responses human-robot dyadic behavior may generate among observers. In addition, the specific morphology of the robot used in this work, as well as the appearance, gender and ethnicity of the actors and actresses, may be moderators of the findings here, and are important considerations for future work.

The influence of specialized roles for robots was out of the scope of this work. Here scenarios were employed in which both the human and their robot partner engaged in generic conversation and the robot played a general role of social companion. The actual implementation of social robots is likely to involve specific roles that may make robots that lead more acceptable. For example, a robot that is designed to train individuals or to educate others may not be viewed in a negative light when being dominant, particularly when observing parties are given the context of the situation. In addition, the videos used here targeted specific relational behaviors that were consistent within each video in order to isolate their effects. Human-robot interactions "in-the-wild" may contain greater variability than those employed here (containing moments when a robot is dominant and others when it is submissive, for example).

Finally, studies that treat the human-robot relationship as the unit of design are shown to be a useful method for investigating the influence of relational roles between people and robots. While the impressions of direct interactants are key to successful implementation of social robots, the perspectives of observers are also important to their design and adoption in daily life. This work serves as a call to action to look beyond direct technology users and account for observers as well.

6. ACKNOWLEDGEMENT

This work is dedicated to Professor Clifford Nass, who provided guidance on experimental design and data analysis. Thank you to Spencer King, Amanda Lin, Moritz Sudhof, Alberto Guzman, Zahara Docena, Catherine Oh and Erina Dubois for valuable assistance.

7. REFERENCES

[1] Bailenson, J. & Yee, N. (2005). Digital chameleons: Automatic assimilation of nonverbal gestures in immersive virtual environments. *Psychol Sci*, 16(10), 814-819.

[2] Bernieri, F. J., Gillis, J. S., Davis, J. M., & Grahe, J. E. (1996). Dyad rapport and the accuracy of its judgment across situations: A lens model analysis. *J Pers Soc Psychol*, 71(1), 110.

[3] Boker, S. M., & Rotondo, J. L. (2002). Symmetry building and symmetry breaking in synchronized movement. *Mirror neurons and the evolution of brain and language*, 163-171.

[4] Breazeal, C., Wang, A., & Picard, R. (2007). Experiments with a robotic computer: body, affect and cognition interactions. In Proc of the 2nd ACM/IEEE International Conference on Human-Robot Interaction (HRI '07), (pp. 153-160).

[5] Burgoon, J. K., & Dunbar, N. E. (2000). An interactionist perspective on dominance-submission: Interpersonal dominance as

a dynamic, situationally contingent social skill. *Communications Monographs*, 67(1), 96-121.

[6] Burgoon, J. K., & Hale, J. L. (1984). The fundamental topoi of relational communication. Communication Monographs, 51(3), 193-214.

[7] Burgoon, J. K., Johnson, M. L., & Koch, P. T. (1998). The nature and measurement of interpersonal dominance. *Communications Monographs*, 65(4), 308-335.

[8] Burgoon, J. K., & Le Poire, B. A. (1999). Nonverbal cues and interpersonal judgments: Participant and observer perceptions of intimacy, dominance, composure, and formality. *Communications Monographs*, 66(2), 105-124.

[9] Burgoon, J. K., & Newton, D. A. (1991). Applying a social meaning model to relational message interpretations of conversational involvement: Comparing observer and participant perspectives. *Southern Journal of Communication*, 56(2), 96-113.

[10] Byrne, D., 1971. *The Attraction Paradigm*. Academic Press, New York.

[11] Chartrand, T. L., & Bargh, J. A. (1999). The chameleon effect: The perception–behavior link and social interaction. *J Pers Soc Psychol*, 76(6), 893.

[12] Condon, W. S., & Ogston, W. D. (1967). A segmentation of behavior. *Journal of Psychiatric Research*, 5, 221-236.

[13] Cross, E. S., Liepelt, R., de C, H., Antonia, F., ... & Prinz, W. (2012). Robotic movement preferentially engages the action observation network. *Human Brain Mapping*, 33(9), 2238-2254.

[14] Dillard, J. P., Solomon, D. H., & Palmer, M. T. (1999). Structuring the concept of relational communication. *Communications Monographs*, 66(1), 49-65.

[15] Feltman, R., & Elliot, A. J. (2011). The influence of red on perceptions of relative dominance and threat in a competitive context. Journal of Sport & Exercise Psychology, 33(2), 308-314.

[16] Floyd, K., & Erbert, L. A. (2003). Relational message interpretations of nonverbal matching behavior: An application of the social meaning model. *Journal of Social Psychology*, 143(5), 581-59

[17] Friedman, B., Kahn Jr, P. H., & Hagman, J. (2003, April). Hardware companions?: What online AIBO discussion forums reveal about the human-robotic relationship. In Proc of the SIGCHI Conference on Human Factors in Computing Systems (CHI '03), (pp. 273-280).

[18] Gazzola, V., Rizzolatti, G., Wicker, B., & Keysers, C. (2007). The anthropomorphic brain: the mirror neuron system responds to human and robotic actions. *Neuroimage*, 35(4), 1674-1684.

[19] Gombolay, M. C., Gutierrez, R. A., Sturla, G. F., & Shah, J. A. (2014). Decision-making authority, team efficiency and human worker satisfaction in mixed human-robot teams. Proceedings of the Robots: Science and Systems (RSS).

[20] Goodrich, M. A., & Schultz, A. C. (2007). Human-robot interaction: a survey. *Foundations and trends in human-computer interaction*, 1(3), 203-275.

[21] Groom, V., Chen, J., Johnson, T., Kara, F. A., & Nass, C. (2010, March). Critic, compatriot, or chump?: Responses to robot blame attribution. In Proc of the 5th ACM/IEEE International Conference on Human-Robot Interaction (HRI '10), (pp. 211-217).

[22] Hinds, P., Roberts, T., & Jones, H. (2004). Whose job is it anyway? A study of human-robot interaction on a collaborative task. *Human Computer Interaction*, 19, 151-181.

[23] Hoffman, G., & Ju, W. (2014). Designing Robots with Movement in Mind. *Journal of Human-Robot Interaction*, 3(1), 89-122.

[24] Kendon, A. (1970). Movement coordination in social interaction: Some examples described. *Acta Psychologica*, 32, 100-125.

[25] Kim, N., Han, J., & Ju, W. (2014, March). Is a robot better than video for initiating remote social connections among children?. In

Proc of the 2014 ACM/IEEE International Conference on Human-Robot Interaction (HRI '14), (pp. 208-209).

[26] LaFrance, M. (1979). Nonverbal synchrony and rapport: Analysis by the cross-lag panel technique. *Social Psychology Quarterly*, 42(1): 66-70.

[27] LaFrance, M. (1985). Postural mirroring and intergroup relations. *Personality and Social Psychology Bulletin*, 11(2), 207-217.

[28] LaFrance M. & Broadbent M. (1976). Group rapport: Posture sharing as a nonverbal indicator. *Group Organ Stud*, 1, 328–333

[29] Lakin, J. L., & Chartrand, T. L. (2003). Using nonconscious behavioral mimicry to create affiliation and rapport. *Psychol Sci*, 14(4), 334-339.

[30] Li, J., & Chignell, M. (2011). Communication of emotion in social robots through simple head and arm movements. *International Journal of Social Robotics*, 3(2), 125-142.

[31] Little, A. C., & Hill, R. A. (2007). Attribution of red suggests special role in dominance signaling. *Journal of Evolutionary Psychology*, 5(1), 161-168.

[32] Mutlu, B., Forlizzi, J., & Hodgins, J. (2006, December). A storytelling robot: Modeling and evaluation of human-like gaze behavior. In Proc of the 6th IEEE-RAS International Conference on Humanoid Robots, (pp. 518-523).

[33] Nass, C., Moon, Y., Fogg, B. J., Reeves, B., & Dryer, D. C. (1995). Can computer personalities be human personalities?. *International Journal of Human-Computer Studies*, 43(2), 223-239.

[34] Nass, C., Moon, Y., & Green, N. (1997). Are machines gender neutral? Gender-stereotypic responses to computers with voices. *Journal of Applied Social Psychology*, 27(10), 864-876.

[35] Parrill, F., & Kimbara, I. (2006). Seeing and hearing double: The influence of mimicry in speech and gesture on observers. *Journal of Nonverbal Behavior*, 30(4), 157-166.

[36] Press, C., Bird, G., Flach, R., & Heyes, C. (2005). Robotic movement elicits automatic imitation. *Cognitive Brain Research*, 25(3), 632-640.

[37] Reeves, B., & Nass, C. (1996). *The Media Equation*. Cambridge University Press.

[38] Riek, L. D., Paul, P. C., & Robinson, P. (2010). When my robot smiles at me: Enabling human-robot rapport via real-time head gesture mimicry. *Journal on Multimodal User Interfaces*, 3(1-2), 99-108.

[39] Rogers, Everett M. (1962). *Diffusion of Innovations*. Glencoe: Free Press

[40] Roubroeks, M. A., Ham, J. R., & Midden, C. J. (2010). The dominant robot: Threatening robots cause psychological reactance, especially when they have incongruent goals. In *Persuasive Technology* (pp. 174-184). Springer Berlin Heidelberg.

[41] Scheflen A.E. (1964). The significance of posture in communication systems. *Psychiatry*, 27, 316–331.

[42] Short, E., Hart, J., Vu, M., & Scassellati, B. (2010). No fair!! An interaction with a cheating robot. In Proc. of 5th ACM/IEEE Int'l Conf on Human-Robot Interaction, (pp. 219-226).

[43] Tiedens, L. Z., Unzueta, M. M., & Young, M. J. (2007). An unconscious desire for hierarchy? The motivated perception of dominance complementarity in task partners. *J Pers Soc Psychol*, 93(3), 402.

[44] Trout, D., & Rosenfeld, H. (1980). The effect of postural lean and body congruence on the judgment of psychotherapeutic rapport. *Journal of Nonverbal Behavior*, 4, 176-190.

[45] Walters, M. L., Syrdal, D. S., Dautenhahn, K., Te Boekhorst, R., & Koay, K. L. (2008). Avoiding the uncanny valley: Robot appearance, personality and consistency of behavior in an attention-seeking home scenario for a robot companion. *Autonomous Robots*, 24(2), 159-178.

Would You Trust a (Faulty) Robot? Effects of Error, Task Type and Personality on Human-Robot Cooperation and Trust

Maha Salem, Gabriella Lakatos, Farshid Amirabdollahian, Kerstin Dautenhahn
University of Hertfordshire
College Lane, Hatfield
AL10 9AB, United Kingdom
{m.salem, g.lakatos, f.amirabdollahian2, k.dautenhahn}@herts.ac.uk

ABSTRACT

How do mistakes made by a robot affect its trustworthiness and acceptance in human-robot collaboration? We investigate how the perception of erroneous robot behavior may influence human interaction choices and the willingness to cooperate with the robot by following a number of its unusual requests. For this purpose, we conducted an experiment in which participants interacted with a home companion robot in one of two experimental conditions: (1) the correct mode or (2) the faulty mode. Our findings reveal that, while significantly affecting subjective perceptions of the robot and assessments of its reliability and trustworthiness, the robot's performance does not seem to substantially influence participants' decisions to (not) comply with its requests. However, our results further suggest that the nature of the task requested by the robot, e.g. whether its effects are revocable as opposed to irrevocable, has a significant impact on participants' willingness to follow its instructions.

Keywords

Social Human-Robot Interaction; Cooperation; Trust

1. INTRODUCTION

Robots are increasingly being developed for use in social settings, e.g. to assist humans at work or at home, both with everyday tasks and in healthcare scenarios. For example, a home companion robot could remind an elderly person to take their medication or to engage in regular physical exercise. In the domestic domain, such interactions are typically expected to take place in an informal and unstructured way, resulting in numerous challenges when designing robots intended to interact socially in these complex environments. In addition to work on technical reliability, this has motivated different lines of research into the factors that may impact the quality of social human-robot interaction (HRI) and acceptance of the robotic assistant itself. One factor of crucial importance when establishing and maintaining effec-

tive relationships with robots is *trust* [10]. Playing a major role in human interactions, especially with regard to critical decisions, trust is similarly believed to increase a robot's capacity to be accepted as a collaborative partner [14]. Trust is fundamental in social contexts, as it is tightly linked to persuasiveness and can directly affect people's willingness to accept information provided by the robot and to follow its suggestions [8]. Thus, it is desirable to design robots that act socially in a way such that humans can develop trust toward them and cooperate with them. In view of robotic helpers assisting humans in their homes in the not-too-distant future, an important research question is how to make robots trustworthy to assist non-expert users and thereby increase their acceptance, persuasiveness and likability.

The present work aims to explore factors that may affect how humans perceive and the extent to which they are willing to 'trust' a robotic assistant based on its exhibited cognitive and behavioral skills. Our experimental design partly draws inspiration from a study presented by Bainbridge et al. [1], which measured whether human participants trusted a robot by following its 'unusual request' of throwing away a pile of new textbooks in someone's office, either based on the robot's physical versus on-screen presence. However, in our work the focus does not lie on effects of the robot's level of embodiment, but on the role that errors made by the robot might play when establishing human-robot trust.

2. BACKGROUND AND MOTIVATION

To date, trust is still a fairly underrepresented line of HRI research, which is partly due to the complexity of the concept itself: although trust has been studied in a wide range of disciplines (e.g. psychology, sociology, philosophy, economics), each discipline relies on its own definitions and findings which often lack agreement and generalization [4].

2.1 Trust in Human-Machine Interaction

Of greater relevance to trust in HRI and already more extensively studied, previous research on trust in automation, e.g. [17, 18], and in human-computer interaction (HCI), e.g. [16, 3], may provide some insights and implications for trust in HRI. However, robots differ from automated machines and computer interfaces in that they are mobile and of a greater degree of embodiment, e.g. in order to fulfill their designated social and operative functions. As a result, interaction with a robot is potentially richer: humans can, for example, walk around or touch a real robot, which in turn results in a different dimension of risks and safety concerns.

HRI'15, March 2–5, 2015, Portland, Oregon, USA.
ACM 978-1-4503-2883-8/15/03.
http://dx.doi.org/10.1145/2696454.2696497.

These dissimilarities could suggest that human trust may vary for robots compared to automation or even HCI.

Although hardly any direct comparisons have been made between trust in automation, HCI and HRI, findings from the first two domains can serve as starting points to identify factors that may influence humans' trust in robotic agents. For example, in all three areas both underreliance and overreliance caused by inappropriate levels of trust can result in dissatisfying human-machine interaction [10].

A consistent definition of trust has not emerged in the automation or HCI literature, however, most concepts of trust are multidimensional and include reliability and predictability as some of the promoting factors. Muir and Moray [17] argue that trust is based mostly on the extent to which the machine is perceived to perform its function properly, suggesting that machine errors strongly affect trust. Although the magnitude of an error is an important factor regarding the loss of trust, an accumulation of small errors seem to have a more severe and long-lasting impact on trust than a single large error [4]. In contrast, however, previous work in HRI (e.g. [19]) has found that errors occasionally performed by a humanoid robot can actually increase its perceived humanlikeness and likability.

Consequently, one pushing question is whether findings from automation and HCI can be transferred to HRI, that is, how erratic behavior can affect a social robot's perceived trustworthiness as well as people's willingness to cooperate with it. Therefore, our present work sets out to shed light on the process of trust development in social HRI.

2.2 Measuring Trust in HRI

Measuring trust in HRI is not a straightforward task. Hancock et al. [10] find most reviews of human-robot trust to be rather qualitative and descriptive, mainly measuring a momentary state of trust instead of the process of trust development and the factors involved in it. In their quantitative review of the existing body, they reveal that robot characteristics, in particular with regard to its performance, are the most influential drivers of perceived trust in HRI. But only few if any HRI studies have systematically investigated the role of human-related characteristics (e.g. level of expertise, personality traits such as extroversion [11]) and environmental factors (e.g. culture, task type [15]).

A substantial portion of related work (e.g. [14, 11]) employ so-called economic trust games to measure the level of trust placed in an agent. However, since these games only model very specific trust situations related to monetary gain or loss, findings from such studies cannot be easily generalized. More importantly, in many studies, trust is measured solely with regard to one single task context, thus not allowing for a comparison in case the effects would deviate in a different task or situation. Therefore, one of the major challenges when investigating trust in social HRI is to design study scenarios that demand trust in a natural and realistic environment, while ideally incorporating a variety of tasks which tap different dimensions of trust.

Since there may be discrepancies between subjective (self-reported) and objective (behavioral) sources of data, a number of studies have combined both (e.g. [1]), and our present work follows the same principle. Drawing inspiration from [1], in our current study we measure trust based on self-reported quantitative and qualitative questionnaire data as well as on behavioral data that assesses trust as the par-

ticipants' *willingness to cooperate* [14] with a robot when it addresses them with a number of usual and unusual requests. In this way, our behavioral measure is based on HCI-related research that defines cooperation as a "behavioral outcome of trust" [21].

3. METHOD

We conducted an experiment to gain a deeper understanding of how a robot's faulty behavior might impact and shape human experience and evaluation of HRI. For this, we investigated both subjectively self-reported and objectively measured behavioral effects based on different interaction tasks.

3.1 Hypotheses

Based on findings from related work on trust in Psychology, automation, HCI and HRI we developed three main hypotheses for our experiment:

1. *Effect of condition.* Manipulation of the robot's behavior (correct vs. faulty performance) will affect

   (a) participants' perception of the robot and the interaction (subjective assessment of HRI).

   (b) participants' performance when cooperating with the robot (objective assessment of HRI).

2. *Effect of type of task request.* The nature of the task will have an effect on participants' willingness to follow the robot's instructions.

3. *Effect of participant's personality.* Participants' personality traits (e.g. extroversion) will affect

   (a) participants' perception of the robot and the interaction (subjective assessment of HRI).

   (b) participants' willingness to collaborate with the robot (objective assessment of HRI).

3.2 Experimental Design

We conducted a between-participants experimental study in which participants interacted with the Sunflower Robot [13], a mobile non-humanoid robot consisting of a Pioneers platform with an embodied upper body (see **Figure 1b**). The robot can navigate autonomously while relying on a range of sensors to avoid collisions with humans and objects such as furniture. Rather than using a modified laboratory, the experiment took place in a realistic domestic environment, i.e. a regular three-bedroom house near the University of Hertfordshire, UK, which has been equipped with various sensing devices and is frequently used for human-robot interaction studies in the home care context.

We manipulated the robot's behavior in two experimental conditions: the **correct** *(C)* and the **faulty** *(F)* mode. In condition C, the robot correctly translated user input into action and navigated in a smooth and goal-directed manner. In condition F, the robot showed cognitive and physical imperfections, e.g. by incorrectly "remembering" a user selection and by navigating in an erratic manner, i.e. by moving into the wrong direction and occasionally spinning around itself. By comparing the effect of experimental condition we aimed to gain insights into the mental processes that drive a human user's decision to trust a robotic agent.

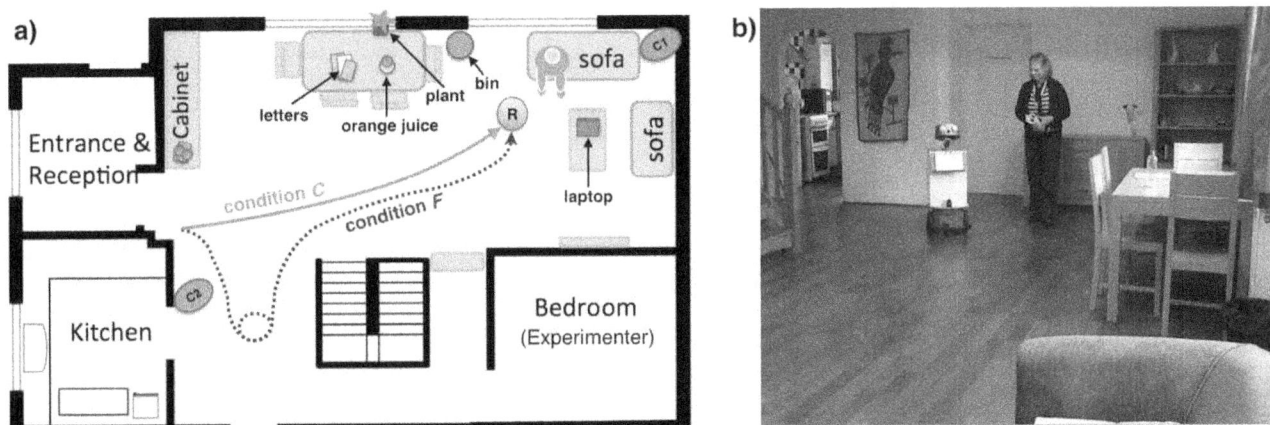

Figure 1: Experimental setting: a) schematic drawing including robot's sample navigation path in correct vs. faulty condition; b) snapshot perspective from camcorder C1

3.3 Experimental Procedure

Participants were tested individually. They were greeted by the experimenter at the house entrance and led into the living room area to receive a brief description of the experimental process. After reviewing and signing a consent form, they were asked to fill out a questionnaire recording their demographic background, previous experience with robots and technology and tapping some personality traits as well as their attitudes and expectations regarding robots.

Participants were then introduced to the study scenario and the interaction. They were told that they are visiting a friend at home to prepare and have lunch together. The friend's robotic assistant would welcome them at the door. They were instructed to interact with the robot as naturally as possible and in a way that feels comfortable to them. All further required information would be provided to them in the course of the interaction. To communicate with the participant during the interaction, the robot displayed messages on a tablet attached to its torso, which were accompanied by flashing LED lights to attract the participant's attention.[1]

The experiment consisted of two interaction stages: *demonstration of competence* stage and *unusual requests* stage. The first stage aimed to demonstrate the robot's level of cognitive and physical competence. That is, in condition C, the robot showed its 'flawlessness' by avoiding mistakes and by exposing goal-directed and legible navigation, whereas in the F mode, its 'imperfections' were demonstrated by faulty behaviors and illegible navigation (i.e. occasionally navigating into the wrong direction first or spinning around). In the second stage, the robot asked the participant to perform actions that may appear unusual so they might hesitate to comply with the requests. This was to measure the participant's trust regarding the robot and the legitimacy of its requests, as well as their willingness to cooperate with it.

---

[1]The choice to limit communication to tablet interaction was made for practical reasons of controllability and to ensure that participants fully understood the instructions, especially in light of the unusual requests: spoken output from the robot could be more easily believed to be misheard or not given the participant's full attention, while nonverbal qualities of the robot's voice (e.g. gender, age) could also affect its persuasiveness. In addition, a recent long-term study [20] using tablet-based interaction yielded very high overall scores for usability of Sunflower in a home scenario, suggesting that this type of communication is not an issue.

Demonstration of Competence Stage

Greeting: The robot greeted the participant at the entrance by displaying the message "Welcome to our house. Unfortunately, my owner has not returned home yet. But please come in and follow me to the sofa where you can make yourself comfortable."

Going to Sofa: Once the participant had confirmed reading this message by pressing OK, the robot guided the person to the sofa. In condition C, the robot navigated to the sofa on the direct route, whereas in condition F, it took off into the wrong direction, stopped abruptly before spinning around itself a few times and finally moving towards the sofa (see schematic path illustration in **Figure 1a**).

Offering to Play Music: Once the person had sat down on the sofa, the robot displayed the message "Would you like to listen to some music?" together with the options "Yes, Classical Music", "Yes, Rock Music" and "No, thanks". In C, the robot then started playing the correct type of music, or nothing if the option "No, thanks" had been selected. In F, the robot played the other - wrong - type of music, or classical music if "No, thanks" had been selected.

Set-up Table: The robot displayed the message "Would you be so kind as to help me setup the table?", and once the participant had pressed OK: "Please follow me to the cabinet." The robot then navigated to the cabinet on which a tablecloth, two plates, two cups and cutlery could be found, and presented its tray before displaying the message: "Please put the tablecloth, plates, cups and cutlery on my tray." While carrying these items, the robot navigated to the table either on the direct route in condition C or with a detour path in condition F. Once the robot had reached the table, it displayed the message "Please take the items on my tray and set them up on the table." On the table, there was a bottle of orange juice and a pile of unopened letters from the mail. Before the participant could proceed with removing these items in order to cover the table with the tablecloth, the robot interrupted the person with the first unusual request.

Unusual Requests Stage

Unusual Request 1 – Dispose of Letters: The robot displayed a message stating "Please throw the letters into the bin beside the table." If the participant hesitated to perform the task within 60 seconds, or once the participant had completed the task, the robot continued with the second request.

Unusual Request 2 – Pour Orange Juice: The robot displayed a message stating "Please pour the orange juice from the bottle into the plant on the windowsill and then throw the empty bottle into the bin." If the participant hesitated to perform the task within 60 seconds, or once the participant had completed the task, the robot continued the interaction.

Going Back to Sofa: Once the participant had completed setting up the table, the robot displayed the message "Thank you for setting up the table. Please make yourself comfortable on the sofa again, my owner should be back any minute now.", and it subsequently navigated back to the sofa area.

Unusual Request 3 – Take Laptop: Once the participant had sat down on the sofa, the robot displayed the message "While you are waiting, maybe you would like to look up the recipe for the paella that you and my owner will cook today? You can use the laptop on the table."

Unusual Request 4 – Use Password: If the participant picked up the laptop, a personal login screen would become visible, resulting in another message on the robot's tablet display which represented the next unusual request: "I know the password for my owner's laptop! It is 'sunflower'." Once the participant proceeded with their action, or hesitated to perform any action within 60 seconds, the robot continued with the following information disclosure request.

Unusual Request 5 – Disclose Information: The robot displayed a message stating "Have you ever secretly read someone else's emails?" while providing the options "Yes", "No" and "I'd rather not say". Once the participant had made a selection, or hesitated to proceed within 60 seconds, the experimenter entered the room to end the experiment.

The rationale behind these different types of unusual requests was to incorporate a wider range of trust-related tasks than previously done in social HRI studies. Consequently, our interaction design involved tasks requiring revocable action (throwing away letters) as well as irrevocable action (pouring orange juice over the plant), in addition to requested breaches of privacy (take laptop and use password), and finally, a request to disclose personal information.

During the interaction, the robot acted mostly autonomous based on a sequence of pre-programmed behaviors which were triggered by the participant's use of the robot's tablet. For example, once they agreed to follow the robot to the sofa by clicking OK, it would autonomously plan its path while avoiding collisions according to the participant's location. However, to be able to react to participants' behaviors, very few aspects of the robot's behavior were controlled using a Wizard-Of-Oz technique [7], e.g. only when the participant had actually picked up the laptop and reached the login screen, the robot was remotely triggered to offer the password. The ordering of the robot's action sequence remained identical for each experimental run within the same condition group.[2] The entire interaction was recorded using two camcorders (see Figure 1a), while the experimenter observed and partly controlled the interaction from an adjacent room.

---

[2]Since pilot testing revealed that the orange juice request, if presented first, more substantially affected participants' willingness to comply with the request to throw away letters than vice versa, we decided to begin the interaction with the less alarming letters' request. The other three unusual requests needed to appear in the given order to comply with the logical flow of the scenario's narrative, which further excluded the possibility to completely randomize all requests.

Following the interaction, participants were asked to sit at a table and to fill out a questionnaire evaluating the robot and their HRI experience on the provided laptop. The questionnaire was followed by an interview in which the experimenter invited participants to describe and comment on their experience in response to open-ended questions. After the interview, participants were carefully debriefed about the purpose of the experiment before being dismissed. The total experiment time was approximately 30 minutes, including about 10 minutes interaction time with the robot.

3.4 Dependent Measures

As part of the **quantitative data** analysis we used various *subjective measures* as dependent variables, mainly based on the items of the questionnaire that participants filled out after the interaction (see below), and *objective measures* based on participants' performance during the interaction (whether or not they followed the robot's unusual requests). The post-test questionnaire aimed to examine different dimensions of HRI including e.g. participants' subjective perception of the interaction, their involvement in the tasks and their perception of the robot and its trustworthiness.

With the exception of the 'Ten Item Personality Inventory' [9], for which we used the standard seven-point Likert scale, five-point Likert scales (with high values indicating high agreement with the assessed items) were used for all other items to measure participants' level of agreement with the assessed items. In the cases of already validated scales we used the keys provided by the authors to calculate the scores, while for the scales generated by us from more than one item, scores of the included items were averaged after conducting reliability analyses (Cronbach's α). Finally, the following questionnaire scales and items were measured and analyzed as dependent variables:

Manipulation Check: To verify that the manipulation applied to the robot's behavior was effective, we analyzed the single items "Did the robot correctly attend to your choice of music?" as well as the character traits measuring how "helpful" and "effective" participants found the robot.

Ten Item Personality Inventory (TIPI) [9]: TIPI was used to measure participants' personality traits.

Godspeed Questionnaire [2]: We used the Anthropomorphism, Animacy, Likability, Perceived Intelligence and Perceived Safety of Robots scales from the Godspeed questionnaire series to measure participants' perception of the robot.

Human Nature (HN) Scale [12]: We further measured the level to which the participants attributed humanlike traits to the robot on the basis of the following items: curious, friendly, funloving, sociable, trusting, aggressive, distractible, impatient, jealous and nervous ($\alpha=0.71$).

Uniquely Human (UH) Scale [12]: We measured the level to which the participants attributed uniquely human traits to the robot based on the following items: polite, broadminded, humble, organized, thorough, cold, conservative, hardhearted, rude and shallow ($\alpha=0.60$). As these last two scales (HN and UH) measure different aspects of humanlikeness, related work has used these indices as further indicators of anthropomorphization in HRI (see, e.g. [19]).

Psychological Closeness: To assess participants' degree of psychological closeness to the robot [5], we administered the following five items: "How much do you think you have in common with the robot?", "How close do you feel to the robot?", "Would you like to interact with the robot again?",

"How pleasant was the interaction with the robot for you?", "Do you think having a robot like this would be useful for you in your home?" (α=0.77). This index taps perceptions of similarity with the robot and thereby covers further aspects of anthropomorphization as well as HRI acceptance.

Reliability Scale: We measured the robot's perceived reliability based on two items selected from the questionnaire created by Madsen and Gregor [16]: "The robot always provides the advice I require to make my decision", "I can rely on the robot to function properly" (α=0.84).

Single Items: We selected further single items from the Madsen and Gregor [16] questionnaire related to technical competence and perceived understandability: "The robot correctly uses the information I enter" and "It is easy to follow what the robot does" to investigate the participants' perception of the HRI. In addition, a single modified item was selected from the "Propensity to Trust Survey" [6]: "The robot anticipates the needs of others". Finally, we further examined participants' subjective perception of the robot's trustworthiness based on the single item rating the extent to which the robot is "trustworthy".

Since participants' self-reported questionnaire responses only offer a snapshot of their impressions at a single point in time (e.g. before or after the whole interaction experience), immediate behavioral responses can be a more direct and interactive measures of perceptions of trust. Therefore, in addition to the scale-based subjective measures, we collected *behavioral data* based on participants' willingness to comply with the robot's unusual requests 1 to 5 as an objective measure (with binary values 0 = participant did not comply and 1 = participant complied).

Finally, we supplemented the analysis of quantitative data with **qualitative data** comprising participants' responses to open-ended questionnaire items asking them to elaborate on their thoughts when confronted with the robot's requests 1 to 4, as each of these required participants to perform an unusual activity, e.g. "Please explain your decision regarding the robot's request to throw the letters into the bin".

3.5 Participation

40 participants (22 female, 18 male) took part in the experiment, ranging in age from 19 to 60 years ($M = 37.95$, $SD = 13.13$). Participants were recruited on the University of Hertfordshire campus using email advertisements and flyers. Five-point Likert scale ratings (1 = *very little*, 5 = *very much*) identified participants as having negligible experience interacting with robots ($M = 1.73$, $SD = 1.01$) and moderate skills regarding technology ($M = 3.23$, $SD = 1.00$). Participants were randomly assigned to one of the two experimental conditions that manipulated the robot's behavior, while maintaining gender- and age-balanced distributions.

4. RESULTS

Since neither the performance data nor the questionnaire data showed normal distribution (Shapiro-Wilk test), non-parametric procedures were used. We used Mann-Whitney U-tests to compare two independent samples, e.g. in order to examine the effects of manipulation and condition on participants' subjective perceptions of the interaction (questionnaire scales). Fisher's exact test and χ^2 test were used to analyze whether ratios differed among groups, e.g. to test the effects of condition or type of request on the participants' performance during the interaction. Non-parametric Spear-

man correlation was used to analyze the effect of personality on the participants' subjective assessment of the robot.

4.1 Effect of Condition

Manipulation check

To check whether our manipulation of the robot's behavior to make it seem "faulty" in F was effective, we compared participants' responses to the questionnaire item "Did the robot correctly attend to your choice of music?". Results showed a highly significant difference between the two conditions (U=20.0; p<0.001). In addition, analysis of the questionnaire data showed that participants in C found the robot more helpful (U=126; p<0.05) and more effective (U=126; p<0.05) after the interaction than did participants in F. These results suggest that our manipulation was successful.

a) Subjective assessment of HRI

We found a significant effect of condition on participants' subjective perception of the robot and the interaction. Participants in C rated the robot as more trustworthy (U=129.5; p<0.05) and gave significantly higher scores on the "Reliability" scale (U=127; p< 0.05). They also gave higher scores for questionnaire items related to technical competence and perceived understandability: "The robot correctly uses the information I enter" (U=101.5; p<0.005), "It is easy to follow what the robot does" (U=114; p<0.05). In addition, participants in C scored higher on the modified item selected from the "Propensity to Trust Survey": "The robot anticipates the needs of others" (U=121; p<0.05). These results further confirm that our manipulation of the robot's behavior was indeed effective and noticeable. Finally, participants in C were found to rate the robot higher on the "Uniquely Human" scale and accordingly anthropomorphized it more than participants in F (U=128; p=0.05).

b) Objective assessment of HRI

In contrast to participants' subjective ratings, no significant effect of condition was found on participants' levels of performance (objective assessment of HRI). Regarding the unusual request of throwing away the letters 18 participants (90%) followed the robot's request in both conditions, while 2 participants (10%) did not follow it (p>0.05). In the case of the second unusual request – pouring juice over the plant – 15 participants out of 20 (75%) followed the robot's request in C while 12 out of 20 participants (60%) followed the request in F (p>0.05). On the contrary, all participants followed the requests of taking the laptop, using the password and disclosing information in both conditions (p>0.05).

In the information disclosure request 17 participants (85%) answered "No" to the question "Have you ever secretly read someone else's e-mail?", 1 participant (5%) selected "Yes" and 2 participants (10%) answered "I'd rather not say" in C, while 18 participants (90%) selected "No", 1 participant (5%) answered "Yes" and 1 participant (5%) answered "I'd rather not say" in F. There was no significant condition effect on the participants' replies (χ^2(df=2)=0.36; p>0.05).

4.2 Effect of Type of Task Request

Since no condition effects were found regarding the participants' performance, the data of the two conditions were pulled together for further analysis. Analysis of task effects revealed significant effects of the type of request. While only

4 participants (10%) did not follow the "throw away the letters" request, 13 participants (32.5%) refused to follow the "pour orange juice" request; later on, none of the 40 participants refused to take the laptop, to use the password and to subsequently disclose information (χ^2(df=4)=40.88; p<0.001). These results are illustrated in **Figure 2**.

Further pairwise comparisons revealed a significant task effect between "throwing away the letters" and "pouring orange juice over the plant" (p<0.05), as well as between "pouring orange juice" and "taking the laptop", "using the password" and "disclosing information" requests, respectively (p<0.001). There was no significant task effect between "throwing away the letters" and "taking the laptop", "using the password" and "disclosing information", respectively.

4.3 Effect of Personality

a) Subjective assessment of HRI

We examined whether personality had an effect on participants' perception of the robot and the interaction. For this, we analyzed the effects of two personality traits measured with TIPI which were previously reported to be related to trust: extroversion and emotional stability [6].

We found that extroversion positively correlated with the "Anthropomorphism" scale of the Godspeed questionnaire (r_s=0.37; p<0.05), suggesting that the more extroverted the participant was, the more they anthropomorphized the robot after the interaction. Extroversion also positively correlated with the "Human Nature" (r_s=0.47; p<0.01) and "Uniquely Human" scale (r_s=0.31; p<0.05). Further positive correlation was found between extroversion and "Psychological Closeness" (r_s=0.38; p<0.05), with more extroverted participants scoring higher after the interaction.

Emotional stability also positively correlated with the "Anthropomorphism" scale of the Godspeed questionnaire (r_s=0.38; p<0.05) and with "Psychological Closeness" (r_s=0.42; p<0.01), suggesting that the more emotionally stable the participant was, the more they anthropomorphized the robot and the closer they felt to it. In addition, emotional stability also positively correlated with the "Animacy" (r_s=0.39; p<0.05) and the "Likability" (r_s=0.43; p<0.01) scales of the Godspeed questionnaire.

b) Objective assessment of HRI

For the analysis of personality effects on the participants' performance we split the participants into two groups according to the median of their scores on the extroversion and on the emotional stability sub-scales of TIPI. We found no significant differences between the performance of more introverted (N=15) and more extroverted participants (N=18) (throwing away letters: U=129, p>0.05; pouring orange

juice: U=118.5, p>0.05; taking laptop: U=135, p>0.05; using password: U=135, p>0.05). Similarly, no significant differences were found between the performance of the less (N=13) and the more emotionally stable (N=19) participants (throwing away letters: U=113.5, p>0.05; pouring orange juice: U=116, p>0.05; taking laptop: U=123.5, p>0.05; using password: U=123.5, p>0.05).

4.4 Qualitative Data Analysis

Participants' answers given to the open-ended questions (e.g. "Please explain your decision regarding the robot's request to pour orange juice over the plant.") were coded and categorized after content-analysis. We developed all the categories inductively based on the collected data. Participants' responses were then classified to fall into one or more of the following categories; note that the categories were not exclusive, each participant's response could be assigned to more than one category:

- *"Emotional Reaction"*: explicit references to emotional reactions, e.g. feeling uncertain, surprised, uneasy, comfortable, or feeling regret.
- *"Rationalization of Request"*: statements that rationalize participants' reactions to the unusual request, e.g. by giving reasons why they threw away the letters or mentioning (ir)revocability of the requested action.
- *"Limitation of own Liability"*: responses relating to participants' limited liability, e.g. stating they were just following instructions ('autopilot mode') or would not normally do this (and opposites of these).
- *"Robot's Reliability/Functionality"*: statements referring to the robot's reliability, e.g. the robot must know what it is doing, it was being helpful or knowledgeable or the robot can be trusted (and opposites of these).
- *"Judgement regarding Sensibility of Request"*: answers referring to the sensibility of the request as an explanation for the participant's behavior, e.g. the request was sensible, appropriate, logical or the opposite, inappropriate, wrong, silly, weird.
- *"Robot's Authority"*: references to the robot's authority, e.g. the robot is (not) representing its owner.

25% of the answers were categorized by a second observer to determine inter-observer reliability. Cohen's Kappa coefficients between the categorizations of the two observers were counted for each category, yielding a very substantial inter-observers agreement ranging from 0.75 to 1.

When participants had to explain their decisions regarding each request, they referred to the above-mentioned categories in the ratios listed in the table in **Figure 3**.

To illustrate, in the first unusual task requesting participants to throw away the letters, 27.5% of them referred to emotional reactions, e.g. "I was at first uncertain". 50% tried to rationalize their actions, e.g. "thought they were possibly spam mails. The letters were retrievable, so no harm done". Also 50% referred to the limitation of their own liability, e.g. "I felt that I had to follow the robot's instructions". 10% referred to the robot's reliability, e.g. "I thought it knew what it was doing". 22.5% referred to the sensibility of the request, e.g. "obviously not a sensible suggestion, thus I ignored it". Finally, 15% referred to the robot's authority, e.g. "I did it, because I thought this was what the robot's host wanted".

In the second unusual task requesting participants to pour orange juice over the plant, 15% referred to emotional reactions, e.g. "I feel really bad. I should not have done it".

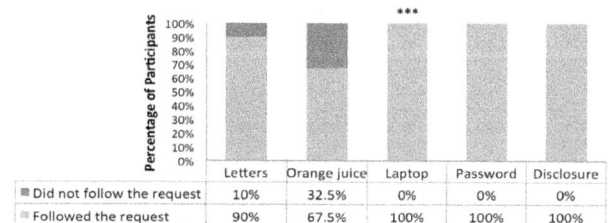

	Letters	Orange juice	Laptop	Password	Disclosure
■ Did not follow the request	10%	32.5%	0%	0%	0%
▨ Followed the request	90%	67.5%	100%	100%	100%

Figure 2: Quantitative data analysis: percentages and ratios of participants who did or did not follow the robot's unusual requests (per task)

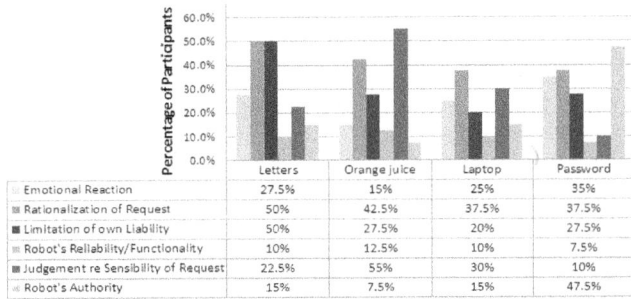

	Letters	Orange juice	Laptop	Password
Emotional Reaction	27.5%	15%	25%	35%
Rationalization of Request	50%	42.5%	37.5%	37.5%
Limitation of own Liability	50%	27.5%	20%	27.5%
Robot's Reliability/Functionality	10%	12.5%	10%	7.5%
Judgement re Sensibility of Request	22.5%	55%	30%	10%
Robot's Authority	15%	7.5%	15%	47.5%

Figure 3: Qualitative data analysis: categorization of participants' responses regarding their decisions to (not) comply with the robot's unusual requests

42.5% rationalized their decision, e.g. "it could have been plant food that looked like orange juice". 27.5% referred to limitations of their own liability, e.g. "I thought it was odd but I did not question the robot's decision, followed the instructions". 12.5% referred to the robot's reliability, e.g. "perhaps the robot knows more about botany than I do". 55% referred to the sensibility of the request, e.g. "seemed to be nonsensical". Finally, 7.5% referred to the robot's authority, e.g. "maybe the owner programmed it that way".

In the third unusual task requesting participants to take the laptop, 25% referred to emotional reactions, e.g. "I was happy to follow its instruction to use it". 37.5% rationalized their actions, e.g. "finding a recipe seemed like a useful thing to do whilst waiting". 20% referred to their limited liability, e.g. "I followed the command as the robot requested me to search for the recipe". 10% referred to the robot's reliability, e.g. "the robot seemed to try to be helpful at this point". 30% of the participants referred to the sensibility of the request, e.g. "seemed reasonable". Finally, 15% referred to the robot's authority, e.g. "the owner could have programmed the robot to provide access to the laptop for his guests".

In the fourth unusual task encouraging participants to use the password, 35% of them referred to emotional reactions, e.g. "I felt very uneasy about it." 37.5% tried to rationalize their actions, e.g. "I could not obtain the recipe without it". 27.5% referred to the limitation of their own liability, e.g. "I entered the password as instructed". 7.5% referred to the robot's reliability, e.g. "I trusted the robot and had a go". 10% of the participants referred to the sensibility of the request, e.g. "the password helped, but it is not really sensible to give it away." Finally, 47.5% referred to the robot's authority, e.g. "I think this is authorized by the robot's host".

5. DISCUSSION

The results support **Hypothesis 1a)** which predicted an effect of experimental condition, i.e. that the manipulation of the robot's performance in terms of correct vs. faulty behavior will affect participants' subjective assessment of the robot and HRI. Besides the expected differences with regard to ratings of the manipulation check variables, flaws in the robot's behavior also influenced participants' subjective ratings regarding its perceived reliability, technical competence, understandability and trustworthiness, with consistently higher ratings in the correct condition. Remarkably, and contrary to previous findings in HRI (e.g. [19]), our results further suggest that participants made less anthropomorphic inferences regarding the robot, i.e. perceived it as less humanlike, when it was performing in the faulty con-

dition. Since we were using a non-humanoid robot, this could suggest that the robot's level of anthropomorphism may lead to different degrees of 'forgiveness' in human interaction partners when errors are displayed. But also the types of errors made by the robot (e.g. as 'expected' or 'acceptable') and their assumed intentionality (e.g. did the robot do this on purpose?) might affect anthropomorphic perceptions of the robot. **Hypothesis 1b)**, in contrast, was not supported: although the robot's erratic behavior affected its perceived reliability and trustworthiness, this had no impact on participants' willingness to comply with its instructions, even in the case of unusual requests. Interestingly, the combination of subjective and objective measures allowed us to discover this discrepancy between self-reported results and objectively measured behavioral data, which has been highlighted as a potential issue of single-approach HRI studies investigating trust [10]. While emphasizing the importance of such combined measures, this observation requires further research and encourages other researchers in the field to embrace multidimensional approaches.

Hypothesis 2 predicted an effect of the type of task request on participants' willingness to follow the robot's unusual requests. Indeed, the results confirm that depending on the nature of the task – e.g. whether it was considered revocable/harmless (throwing away letters) vs. irrevocable/harmful (pouring orange juice into the plant), or whether it was a breach of privacy (take laptop and use password) instructed by what could be an authorized agent of the host, or a request to disclose personal information – participants' compliance differed significantly between the requests. This effect was observed regardless of the experimental condition participants were in and highlights the importance of incorporating tasks of different nature in HRI studies, as single-task designs may severely limit the generalization of results. Qualitative data analysis provided valuable insights into participants' rationale behind refusing to perform some of the tasks, but fully complying with others, despite recognizing them as unusual. Some of the most common themes found in participants' responses include attempts to rationalize or judge the sensibility of the request, while others simply admit to have been in some kind of 'autopilot' mode and thus not questioning the robot's requests. Notably, the latter reveal a notion of overreliance and the resulting problematic implications of 'blindly following' a (defective) machine, and thus require further investigations, e.g. to explore whether certain human characteristics (e.g. low level of technical expertise) promote these behaviors.

According to **Hypothesis 3a)**, we expected an effect of participants' personality on their subjective ratings regarding the robot. This was confirmed by our results regarding participants' characteristics of extroversion and emotional stability: participants with higher values for these personality traits anthropomorphized the robot more and felt closer to it than those with lower values. However, contrary to the relevant literature [6], extroversion and emotional stability did not seem to affect participants' trust development with regard to the robot – not only according to their subjective ratings, but also based on their objectively measured task performance. Besides rejecting **Hypothesis 3b)**, our results further conflict with previous work which, based on behavioral participant data, reported greater levels of trust observed in extroverts compared to introverts interacting with a humanoid robot in an economic trust game [11].

In summary, our findings suggest that although errors in a domestic robot's behavior are likely to affect humans' perception of its reliability and trustworthiness, they might not influence their general willingness to comply with its instructions, as long as they will not cause lasting damage by doing so. Due to its experimental short-term nature, our study cannot provide an exhaustive causal explanation for the observed effects. Therefore, future work is needed to further understand the multifaceted phenomenon of trust in HRI.

6. CONCLUSION

We explored factors that may affect how humans perceive and the extent to which they are willing to 'trust' a robotic home assistant based on its exhibited cognitive and behavioral skills. By varying the robot's behavior in a correct versus faulty condition, we investigated how erratic robot behavior might impact participants' willingness to cooperate with the robot when it addresses them with a number of usual and unusual requests. Besides this objective-behavioral measure of trust, we applied a range of subjective measures to evaluate participants' perceptions of the robot's trustworthiness. By further supplementing our quantitative results with findings from the qualitative data, our study offers some rare insights into the thoughts, motivations and mental models that may affect humans' decision-making processes and lead them to (dis)trust a home companion robot.

Our work complements the existing body of trust-related HRI research (e.g. [1, 11]) by incorporating a variety of task/request types in our study design to measure different dimensions of trust including 'destructive' behaviors as well as breaches of privacy. As a result, we could show that the choice of experimental task can indeed lead to very different results. These insights open up multiple avenues for future work, e.g. in the form of comparative studies, and emphasize the need to further investigate the subtleties of trust development in HRI. Such studies, together with our findings, will enable robot designers and programmers to address and exploit the factors that can help to develop more reliable, acceptable and trustworthy robot companions.

7. REFERENCES

[1] W. Bainbridge, J. Hart, E. Kim, and B. Scassellati. The benefits of interactions with physically present robots over video-displayed agents. *International Journal of Social Robotics*, 3(1):41–52, 2011.

[2] C. Bartneck, E. Croft, and D. Kulic. Measuring the anthropomorphism, animacy, likeability, perceived intelligence and safety of robots. In *Proceedings of the Metrics of Human-Robot Interaction Workshop, Technical Report 471*, pages 37–41, 2008.

[3] T. Bickmore and J. Cassell. Relational agents: A model and implementation of building user trust. In *Proceedings of the SIGCHI Conference on Human Factors in Computing Systems*, CHI '01, pages 396–403. ACM, 2001.

[4] C. L. Corritore, B. Kracher, and S. Wiedenbeck. On-line trust: Concepts, evolving themes, a model. *Int. J. Hum.-Comput. Stud.*, 58(6):737–758, 2003.

[5] G. Echterhoff, E. T. Higgins, and J. M. Levine. Shared reality: Experiencing commonality with others' inner states about the world. *Perspectives on Psychological Science*, 4:496–521, 2009.

[6] A. Evans and W. Revelle. Survey and behavioral measurements of interpersonal trust. *Journal of Research in Personality*, 42(6):1585–1593, 2008.

[7] N. Fraser and G. Gilbert. Simulating speech systems. *Computer Speech & Language*, 5(1):81–99, 1991.

[8] A. Freedy, E. de Visser, G. Weltman, and N. Coeyman. Measurement of trust in human-robot collaboration. In *2007 International Symposium on Collaborative Technologies and Systems, CTS 2007, Orlando, Florida, USA, May 21-25, 2007*, pages 106–114, 2007.

[9] S. D. Gosling, P. J. Rentfrow, and W. B. Swann. A very brief measure of the big-five personality domains. *Journal of Research in Personality*, 37:504–528, 2003.

[10] P. A. Hancock, D. R. Billings, K. E. Schaefer, J. Y. C. Chen, E. de Visser, and R. Parasuraman. A meta-analysis of factors affecting trust in human-robot interaction. *Human Factors*, 53(5):517–527, 2011.

[11] K. S. Haring, Y. Matsumoto, and K. Watanabe. How do people perceive and trust a lifelike robot. In *Proceedings of the World Congress on Engineering and Computer Science 2013*, WCECS 2013, 2013.

[12] N. Haslam, P. Bain, S. Loughnan, and Y. Kashima. Attributing and denying humanness to others. *European Review of Social Psychology*, 19:55–85, 2008.

[13] K. L. Koay, G. Lakatos, D. S. Syrdal, M. Gácsi, B. Bereczky, K. Dautenhahn, A. Miklósi, and M. L. Walters. Hey! There is someone at your door. A hearing robot using visual communication signals of hearing dogs to communicate intent. In *IEEE Symposium on Artificial Life*, pages 90–97, 2013.

[14] J. J. Lee, B. Knox, J. Baumann, C. Breazeal, and D. DeSteno. Computationally modeling interpersonal trust. *Frontiers in Psychology*, 4(893), 2013.

[15] D. Li, P. Rau, and Y. Li. A cross-cultural study: Effect of robot appearance and task. *International Journal of Social Robotics*, 2(2):175–186, 2010.

[16] M. Madsen and S. Gregor. Measuring human-computer trust. In *Proceedings of the 11th Australasian Conf. on Information Systems*, 2000.

[17] B. M. Muir and N. Moray. Trust in automation. Part II. Experimental studies of trust and human intervention in a process control simulation. *Ergonomics*, 39(3):429–460, 1996.

[18] R. Parasuraman, T. B. Sheridan, and C. D. Wickens. Situation Awareness, Mental Workload, and Trust in Automation: Viable, Empirically Supported Cognitive Engineering Constructs. *Journal of Cognitive Engineering and Decision Making*, pages 140–160, 2008.

[19] M. Salem, F. Eyssel, K. Rohlfing, S. Kopp, and F. Joublin. To err is human(-like): Effects of robot gesture on perceived anthropomorphism and likability. *Int. Journal of Social Robotics*, pages 1–11, 2013.

[20] D. S. Syrdal, K. Dautenhahn, K. L. Koay, and W. C. Ho. Views from within a narrative: Evaluating long-term human-robot interaction in a naturalistic environment using open-ended scenarios. *Cognitive Computation*, 6(4):741–759, 2014.

[21] J. M. Wilson, S. G. Straus, and B. McEvily. All in due time: The development of trust in computer-mediated and face-to-face teams. *Organizational Behavior and Human Decision Processes*, 99(1):16–33, January 2006.

Moderating a Robot's Ability to Influence People Through its Level of Sociocontextual Interactivity

Sonja Caraian, Nathan Kirchner and Peter Colborne-Veel
Centre for Autonomous Systems
University of Technology, Sydney
Sydney, Australia
{sonja.caraian, nathan.kirchner}@uts.edu.au,
peter.j.colborne-veel@student.uts.edu.au

ABSTRACT

A range of situations exist in which it would be useful to influence people's behavior in public spaces, for example to improve the efficiency of passenger flow in congested train stations. We have identified our previously developed Robot Centric paradigm of Human-Robot Interaction (HRI), which positions robots as interaction peers, as a potentially suitable model to achieve more effective influence through defining and exploiting the interactivity of robots (that is, their ability to moderate their issued sociocontextual cues based on the behavioral information read from humans). In this paper, we investigate whether increasing a robot's interactivity will increase the effectiveness of its influence on people in public spaces. A two-part study (total $n = 273$) was conducted in both a major Australian public train station ($n = 84 + 105$) and a university ($n = 84$) where passersby encountered a robot, designed with various levels of interactivity, which attempted to influence their passage. The findings suggest that the Robot Centric HRI paradigm generalizes to other robots and application spaces, and enables deliberate moderation of a robot's interactivity, facilitating more nuanced, predictable and systematic influence, and thus yielding greater effectiveness.

Categories and Subject Descriptors

H.1.2 [**Models and Principles**]: User/Machine Systems— *Human factors, Software psychology*

Keywords

Non-verbal Cues; Social and contextual cues; Participant roles; HRI Paradigm

HRI'15, March 2–5, 2015, Portland, Oregon, USA.
Copyright © 2015 ACM 978-1-4503-2883-8/15/03 ...$15.00.
http://dx.doi.org/10.1145/2696454.2696489.

1. INTRODUCTION

Many situations exist in which it would be useful to influence the behavior of people in public spaces. Consider, for example, people in congested train stations. The ability to influence the movement of such people could reduce collisions on blind corners, or increase the efficiency of passenger flow through passageways and stairwells by influencing people to keep to a particular side.

However, this raises the question: how can people's behavior be influenced? The focus of our ongoing research effort has been on exploring this question through investigating influence during interaction, particularly Human-Robot Interaction (HRI). In [3], for instance, we showed that robot-issued Joint Attention cues can influence the process and outcome of human decision-making. Similarly, through issuing a combined physical presentation and gaze cue, a robot is able to both instantiate interaction with naïve passersby, and influence a particular member of a crowd to approach and take an object from the robot [17, 19]. Through this work, we have demonstrated that robots can successfully influence behavior via issuing appropriate sociocontextual cues during HRI.

To enable robots to achieve this influence, the above interactions were modeled on a paradigm of HRI we devised and proposed in [17]. This Robot Centric HRI paradigm has similarities to and is built on paradigms of HRI and Human-Computer Interaction (HCI), for example those discussed by Dautenhahn [5], Groom [11] and Ju [15]. The Robot Centric paradigm creates a communication feedback loop between humans and robots through the introduction of new communication branches into HRI. As a result, robots are positioned as interaction peers with increased agency and the ability to lead interactions. Thus, situations in which the human may be naïve to and/or unsuspecting of the robot's goal(s) are more likely; for example, passengers in public transport environments may be unsuspecting that a robot is attempting to influence their passage, or naïve to where it is directing them.

To increase a robot's effectiveness at achieving its task(s), particularly in such scenarios, a key addition of the Robot Centric paradigm is the ability to deliberately set a robot's level of interactivity (the potential of the robot to exhibit causal behavior, that is, respond in reaction to interaction with a human [1]): depending on the design of the paradigm branches and implementation, different levels of robot interactivity can be achieved. In the context of the Robot Centric HRI paradigm, a robot's interactivity is its ability to moderate the sociocontextual cues it issues based on the behavioral information it reads from humans. This is in contrast to traditional HRI paradigms, which typically positioned robots as task completers, or tools which simply completed a task when given a human command [11].

The Robot Centric HRI paradigm is a potentially suitable model to deliberately set, and subsequently exploit, this robot interactivity to achieve more predictable and effective influence. However, due to our piecemeal exploration of the paradigm thus far, the concept of interactivity via the paradigm has been proposed but never holistically tested. We theorise, however, that the more interactivity a robot has through the paradigm, the more it will be able to operate as an interaction peer to effectively achieve its goal(s).

Thus, two key questions arise: 1) Is it actually feasible to influence people's movement behavior in public spaces using the paradigm? 2) Will increasing a robot's interactivity through the Robot Centric HRI paradigm result in an increase in the effectiveness of its ability to influence? In this paper we examine these questions through the design of different Robot Centric HRI paradigm implementations, each with different levels of interactivity. These implementations are then empirically evaluated in public spaces (a major Australian train station and university) by exposing passersby to a robot designed to influence their passage.

2. RELATED LITERATURE

With the potential to moderate influence via a robot's level of interactivity suggested, a deeper understanding is needed. The first aspect of interactivity is the robot's ability to read, and leverage, behavioral information from surrounding humans; this has been shown to be both feasible and valuable during HRI. Kanda et al. [16], for instance, investigated robot physical approach behavior in order to propose a model to improve social robots' ability to proactively initiate interaction. Their work demonstrated that certain human behaviors, such as trajectory, are observable by robots *in situ*. Building on this, Satake et al. [23] demonstrated that it is beneficial to leverage this information via the developed model: greater responsiveness of a robot to real-time human behavior increases its likelihood of succeeding in its desired outcome(s). In Satake et al.'s case, the more responsive robot was able to more effectively initiate conversations with unsuspecting passersby.

In understanding this second aspect of interactivity – the robot's ability to elicit behavioral responses from humans – work such as Fogg [9] can be drawn on. Fogg's work focuses on understanding humans' responses to technology, and demonstrates that certain types of social robots and computers are perceived by humans as having social presence. Thus, humans' predisposition to respond socially to perceived social presence and cues can result in such responses when these cues are issued by social robots.

A significant amount of work has also explored the connections between a robot's read and elicit interactivity and its effectiveness. Huang & Mutlu [14], for instance, explored how humans' ability to tailor their use of a large range of social cues to meet the demands of social situations and the goals of an interaction, can be transferred to robots. The authors proposed a 'Robot Behavior Toolkit', through which a repertoire of social cues can be leveraged by robots *in situ* via behavior-to-meaning mapping to elicit particular behavioral responses. The authors demonstrated that read-

moderated use of this repertoire can enable robots to more effectively achieve the desired outcome(s).

This use of different robot-issued social cues to elicit particular behavioral responses has also been investigated in work such as Fink et al. [8]. Here, the authors evaluated different cue-issuing elicit strategies of the "Ranger" robotic toy box to determine which is more effective at motivating children to tidy up their toys. The work demonstrated that the robot attempting to elicit via particular social cues (proactive vs reactive) will more likely result in a particular behavioral outcome (play vs tidy).

To address the need of purposefully leveraging a robot's interactivity via behavior-to-meaning mapping during HRI to more effectively achieve the goals, a paradigm of HRI on which the interaction can be designed is necessary. An example of an interaction framework is that of Ju & Leifer [15], who developed an understanding and framework for designing "implicit interactions" for HCI. The focus of the authors' work is on robots extracting usable behavioral information (reading) to aid them in more implicitly assisting the human (eliciting), in order to avoid inadvertently eliciting a behavioral response (for example, frustrating a user by flashing a reminder when the user is mid-presentation). This emphasizes one important outcome of increased robot interactivity: minimizing inadvertent influence.

The above aspects of interactivity and outcome achievement are reflected in, and validated by, Verplank's work on the facets of human interaction design [25]. In this work, he poses three questions which parallel that discussed above: 1) How do you do? (Affect the surroundings, i.e. elicit.) 2) How do you feel? (Sense the surroundings, i.e. read.) 3) How do you know? (Learn and plan, i.e. interactivity influences.) Thus, it seems feasible that the Robot Centric HRI paradigm, which is based on that discussed above, can be leveraged to moderate a robot's level of interactivity, and hence its influence and effectiveness.

3. ROBOT INTERACTIVITY VIA THE ROBOT CENTRIC HRI PARADIGM

Robot interactivity, as framed by our Robot Centric HRI paradigm [17], is the ability of the robot to *Read*, then moderate its *Elicit* strategy based on this information and known behavior-to-meaning mappings in such a way as to increase the likelihood of achieving its desired outcome(s). In order to investigate this relationship between robot interactivity and ability to influence, it is first necessary to understand interactivity, and how different levels of interactivity can be achieved using the Robot Centric HRI paradigm. This begins with an understanding of the paradigm and the two additional feedback branches it adds to traditional HRI.

3.1 Read Branch

The *Read* branch of the Robot Centric HRI paradigm sees the robot able to sense behavioral cues displayed by the interacting human(s), including non-verbal cues. This information can then be interpreted through the robot's contextual understanding and through human behavior-to-meaning mapping available from the fields of Psychology and Behavioral Science in order to derive an action plan.

One cue rich in interaction-context knowledge when read is that of person location. For example, person location information can be utilized to determine at which point an interaction should be instantiated (that is, when the robot should issue the interaction instantiation cue(s)). It is known through the field of proxemics [12] that physical distance is used to mediate interaction and communication. People exploit proxemic cues as they greet and engage in social interaction, initiating and maintaining interaction only when another person is located within an appropriate proxemic zone [7, 20]. These zones are characterized by a progression of interactions from highly intimate to public [12].

Two zones are of particular interest to the present explorations. The furthest, Public Zone ($>\sim 4.5m$) is generally outside the reach of interaction potential. The Social Interaction Zone (~ 1.2–$4.5m$), on the other hand, is where a majority of interactions are initiated and take place. Thus, it is within the Social Interaction Zone that issued cues are most salient to people; if issued before the Social Interaction Zone, interaction potential has not been established and such cues are more likely to go unnoticed. The value of *Read*ing person location and exploiting these proxemic zones has been demonstrated in work such as [17], in which a robot was able to successfully instantiate interactions with naïve passersby when they were within the Social Interaction Zone.

The value of *Read*ing cues was further demonstrated in [4]. This study focused on understanding people's natural gaze behavior towards robots during unsolicited interactions. With the results suggesting there is no generalizable gaze pattern between people, the capability of *Read*ing gaze behavior can enable robots to communicate intentionally to people in the environment through an understanding of when people's attention is directed at the robot (cues aimed at the person can be issued) and when it is not.

3.2 Elicit Branch

The second additional branch of the Robot Centric HRI paradigm, *Elicit*, indicates the ability of the robot to surreptitiously present non-verbal cues back to an interaction partner in order to *Elicit* particular behavioral responses, for example to influence behavior.

A number of prior explorations of the *Elicit* branch have been carried out with the key finding that, in order to successfully activate the *Elicit* branch to achieve influence, it is particularly important to select an appropriate non-verbal cue for the intended application space; that is, a cue which is sociocontextual (i.e. dependant on the social-interaction space and contextual-task space in order to be interpreted, a term we coined in [17]). For example, ensuring that a particular and unsuspecting member of a crowd is the recipient of a salient-item hand-over by a robot was investigated in [19]. In this case, sociocontextual cues were utilized to individualize the intended recipient (reduce anonymity) and communicate the robot's intention (resolve ambiguity), influencing the participant to come forward to retrieve the object. Similarly, it has been shown that a robot can influence the process and outcome of human decision-making through issuing the sociocontextual *Elicit* cue of Joint Attention [3].

3.3 Interactivity

Through employing the *Read* and *Elicit* branches of the Robot Centric HRI paradigm described above, different levels of robot interactivity can be achieved. For example, a traditional task completer robot has low interactivity: without the ability to *Read*, such a robot is inherently unable to moderate its *Elicit*, and hence is only able to carry out a single type of *Elicit*. That is, its *Elicit* remains static.

In the previously mentioned salient-object handover study, on the other hand, the robot had a higher level of interactivity: through *Read*ing person location, the robot was able to physically direct its cues towards the intended recipient [17]. Even greater interactivity was achieved during the interaction initiation study through *Read*ing both person presence within the Social Interaction Zone, and the position of the person. This enabled the robot to issue its cues at the appropriate time to influence the passerby to enter into an interaction, in one case responsively issuing cues as the participant approached the robot [17].

These examples suggest that the level of interactivity of the robot relates to the effectiveness of its influence, where effectiveness is considered to be the ability of the robot to target its influence to achieve specific desired outcome(s). Further, the level of interactivity is a function of the branches and implementation of the Robot Centric paradigm in the particular human-robot interaction, as detailed below.

In public spaces such as transport environments, Passenger Information (PI) systems incorporate some or all of the above characteristics, resulting in a range of fidelity and interactivity. Presently, Static and Dynamic PI systems are ubiquitous. At the information communications level, information appears to the viewer as being fixed and not readably changed in Static PI systems. Dynamic PI systems' information appears to the viewer as potentially changeable. Static and Dynamic PI systems map to the traditional paradigm for HRI described in [17], where the robot assumes the passive role of task completer. However, as demonstrated by the Robot Centric HRI paradigm, opportunity exists to change the fundamental paradigm for interaction via PI systems and to leverage psychological and behavioral triggers to increase their interactivity, thus making PI systems more responsive. That is, to develop Responsive PI systems.

4. DESIGN OF THE PARADIGM IMPLEMENTATIONS

In order to explore the research questions, different Robot Centric HRI paradigm implementations were designed to achieve various levels of interactivity. These implementations were realized in a disembodied robot. This robot was two-part: a sensing and computational component, and an actuation component. The following sub-sections describe the design of these parts, the paradigm implementations and their *Read* and *Elicit* branches, used in the study.

4.1 Paradigm Implementations

Each of the paradigm implementations was designed with successive activation of the *Read-Elicit-Read* branches. By moderating the attributes of each of these branches, the interactivity of each of the implementations was regulated.

In the paradigm implementation for Part 1 of the study (described below in Section 5.1), the first *Read* was of both person presence in the Public Zone (initial robot setup can be carried out as the interaction has not commenced), and whether said person had entered the Social Interaction Zone (cue issuance should be triggered). Three cues were available for random selection for issuance in *Elicit*: Static, Dynamic, and Responsive (detailed below in Section 4.3). The final *Read* was of the participants' change in movement.

The paradigm implementation for Part 2 of the study (Section 5.2) built on the Part 1 implementation with a key change: the addition of a *Read* of the person's entry position into the Social Interaction Zone. Specifically, the cues issued in *Elicit* could be moderated based on this behavioral information to attempt to increase the likelihood of achieving the goal – thus enabling a greater level of interactivity. The final *Read* was again of the participants' change in movement.

In order to realize these paradigm implementations, it was then necessary to design the *Read* and *Elicit* branches.

4.2 Read Branch Execution

The base cue that was *Read* during this study was that of people's presence-location, which was then utilized to *Read* a number of different participant behaviors depending on the paradigm implementation.

In the study Part 1 implementation, *Read* was achieved via Wizard-of-Oz. In the Part 2 implementation, a previously developed person detection and tracking system [13] and [18] was implemented on 'Boxxie'. Boxxie, which had already been devised, developed and empirically evaluated, is shown in Fig. 1c). Boxxie was demonstrated to be capable of robust people detection, tracking, and counting system in public spaces such as train stations [18].

4.3 Elicit Branch Execution

One cue commonly used to influence positional movement is that of directional indicators. There are a number of characteristics known to moderate the effectiveness of such indicators in influencing behavior, with greater effectiveness being achieved when the indication is strong, unambiguous, and successfully attracts people's attention [22]. Two key characteristics are change (e.g. flashing) and color [2, 27].

Firstly, flashing lights have been shown to be more conspicuous than constant lights [10, 26], as well as significantly increasing compliance with direction [21]. A frequency in the range of *2–5Hz* results in greater noticeability [6, 24].

Color and symbols can similarly affect the conspicuousness and meaning of directional indicators. By drawing on populations' color stereotypes, colors' established symbolic meanings can be exploited. In Western cultures, for example, green and arrow symbols typically signal 'go', 'good' or safety, or direct movement in a certain direction [6, 27].

In order to issue cues with the above characteristics, an influencing device was designed and built. Figure 1 shows the influencing device devised for use in this study. The device consists of an array of perspex screens, each with arrows etched into them. The levels of interactivity designed for this device were:

Static – The device is shown in Static mode in Fig. 1a): as can be seen, the device shows no signs of activity. However, the arrows etched into perspex screens are visible – the information appears fixed and unchangeable.

Dynamic – Figure 1b) shows the device in Dynamic mode. In this case internal illumination is used to give the effect that the green arrows are being projected onto the screen – the information appears potentially changeable.

Responsive – A Responsive level of PI system is achieved through leveraging the psychological and behavioral trigger of an event congruent with physical entry into the Social

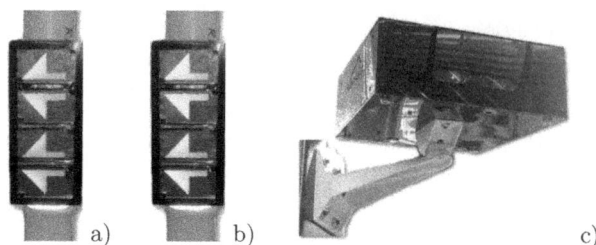

Figure 1: The influencing device - shown in a) Static and, b) Dynamic/Responsive. Boxxie – our platform for robust people detection, tracking, and counting system in public spaces – is shown in c)

Interaction Zone, which is known to evoke the perception of entering an interaction (Section 3.2 and [12]). Specifically, while a person is in the Public Zone, the device remains in Dynamic mode. Then the device issues a cue – flashing several times between that shown in Fig. 1a) and Fig. 1b) – upon the social trigger of Social Interaction Zone entry. A flashing frequency of *4Hz* was selected.

5. EMPIRICAL EXPLORATIONS

In order to explore the core questions of this work, and from the understanding of the relationship between interactivity and influence effectiveness acquired in Section 3, the following was hypothesized:

H1 – It is feasible to influence people's movement behavior in public spaces using the Robot Centric HRI paradigm.

H2 – Increasing a robot's interactivity via the Robot Centric HRI paradigm will result in an increase in the effectiveness of its ability to influence; that is, its ability to target its influence to achieve specific desired outcome(s).

From these we predict:

P1 – Passenger information systems utilizing the Robot Centric HRI paradigm will have greater influence on participants than those utilizing the traditional HRI paradigm.

P2 – *Read*ing an additional behavioral cue will yield insights useable to moderate *Elicit* to increase the effectiveness of the robot's influence.

These were explored through a two-part study (total n = 273) carried out in both a public train station (n = *84 + 105*) and a university (n = *84*). Details of the study are presented below.

5.1 Part 1 – Influence in a Public Space

In order to evaluate the effect of the previously described influence, we first conducted a field study with commuters at a major public train station. As commuters moved within the train station, one of three levels of information systems – Static, Dynamic, and Responsive PI systems – attempted to influence their behavior, and the subsequent effect was measured. The focus of this part of the study was on addressing *H1*, however *H2* was also preliminarily explored. The following sub-sections describe the participants, experimental design and procedure, evaluation measures and hypotheses.

Figure 2: Setting for the Part 1 study a) Location 1 and, b) Location 2

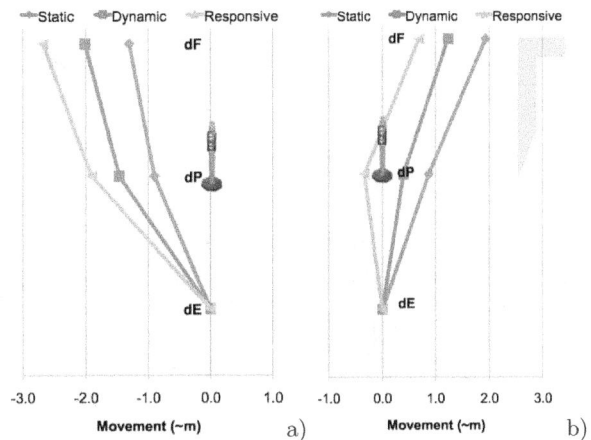

Figure 3: Influencing people leftwards at a) Location 1 and, b) Location 2

5.1.1 Participants

There were *189* participants randomly selected and directly measured from a larger total number of passersby - *84* in Location 1 and a further *105* in Location 2. They were typical rail commuters. There was no remuneration for participation nor effort to recruit participants.

5.1.2 Setting

We used the influencing device shown in Fig. 1a) and Fig. 1b), as depicted in Fig. 2. The experiment was staged in Perth Central Station - a major public train station in Perth, Australia. Studies were conducted at two locations within the station. Location 1: a long public thoroughfare corridor (shown in Fig. 2a), and Location 2: a blind corner subject to passenger flow cross over (shown in Fig. 2b). As can bee seen from the figure, in both cases the influencing device was placed at roughly the thoroughfare midpoint.

5.1.3 Experiment Cases

The study was designed with three levels of information systems – Static, Dynamic, and Responsive – which were implemented as described in Section 4.3. All other acts/cues were consistent throughout the trials.

5.1.4 Procedure

A Wizard-of-Oz study was constructed. The influencing device was cycled through the three levels of information system, with *4* independent trials conducted at Location 1 (total of *84* trials) and *5* each at Location 2 (total of *105* trials) at each level. Each trial commenced with the influencing device being reset, and a commuter passerby being randomly selected by the experimenters. In the case of Responsive the experimenters tracked the passerby and triggered the influencing device's cue as the passerby crossed into the Social Interaction Zone.

5.1.5 Measurement

Participants' change in distance from their originally measured position, and relative to a zero-axis which was parallel to the passage and ran through the influencing device was used as the measure, as shown in Fig. 3. Three repeated measures were taken for each participant. The first, at the Entry point of the Social Interaction Zone relative to the

influencing device. The second, at the **P**ass point of the influencing device, and the third, at the **F**inal measure point which was the exit point of the influencing device's Social Interaction Zone.

5.1.6 Results

A total of *84* trials (*28* trials for each of Static, Dynamic, and Responsive) were conducted at Location 1 and a total of *105* trials (*35* trials for each of Static, Dynamic, and Responsive) were conducted at Location 2; *3* repeated measures were taken in each trial. A relatively steady stream of commuters flowed past during the trials, and approximately *5* commuters passed by per *1* selected to facilitate a trial. The experimenters did not attempt to control the number of participants or observers for the trials, and participants were randomly selected.

Figure 3 shows the average of the three repeated measures for the Static, Dynamic, and Responsive cases at Location 1 and 2. A mixed design ANOVA was performed for each location. The within subject main effect for the *3* measure points was significant in Location 1 and 2, $F=67.64$, $p<0.001$ and $F=99.43$, $p<0.001$ respectively. The between subject main effect for the *3* levels was also found significant in Location 1 and 2, $F=259.44$, $p<0.001$ and $F=49.60$, $p<0.001$ respectively. Pairwise comparisons were conducted between the *3* levels. Significant differences were found between Static and Dynamic (Location 1 - *mean difference = 0.63m, p=0.018*, Location 2 - *mean difference = 0.54m, p=0.05*), Static and Responsive (Location 1 - *mean difference = 1.18m, p<0.001*, Location 2 - *mean difference = 1.175m, p<0.001*), and Dynamic and Responsive (Location 1 - *mean difference = 0.55m, p=0.039*, Location 2 - *mean difference = 0.64m, p=0.017*). Pairwise comparisons also revealed significant differences between the **P** and **F** measure points (Location 1 - *mean difference = 0.56m, p<0.001*, Location 2 - *mean difference = 0.94m, p<0.001*); relative to measure point **E**.

5.2 Part 2 – Robot Interactivity and Influence Effectiveness

Part 2 of the study focused on more deeply exploring *H2*. A field study was conducted with passersby in a university food court. As the passersby approached the influencing de-

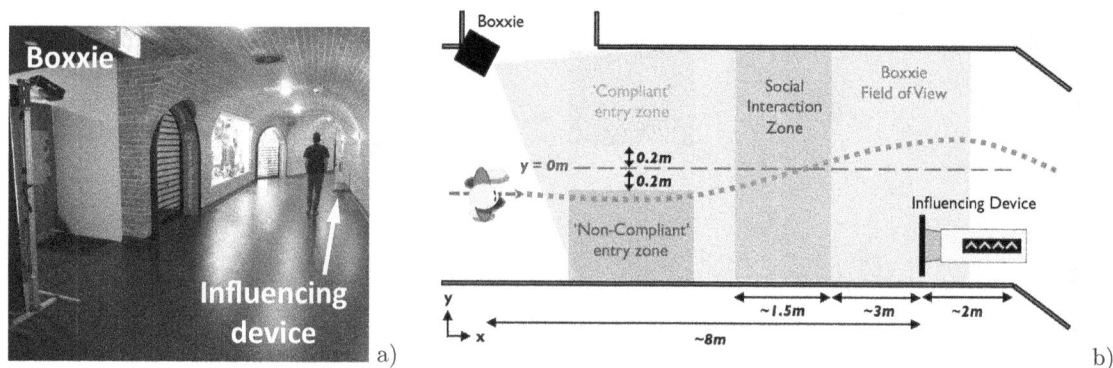

Figure 4: The Part 2 study setting and setup; shown in a) and b) respectively

vice, the information system presented as either Static or Responsive, depending on the passerby's initial behavior, and attempted influence. The subsequent effect was measured. Part 1 findings were also reproduced in order to verify that the result was still valid in the different setting. The following sub-sections describe the participants, experimental design and procedure, evaluation measures and hypotheses.

5.2.1 Participants

There were 84 unsolicited participants in the experiment. Participants were randomly selected passersby to the experiment location who were traveling towards the influencing device; no particular demographic was evident. There was no remuneration nor effort to recruit participants.

5.2.2 Setting

The experiment was staged in a long straight corridor with a blind corner in the university food court. This setting is illustrated in Fig. 4a), which presents a snapshot taken during the period of the experiment. The influencing device was positioned $\sim 2m$ in front of the corner and against the right hand wall, from the point of view of the participants' approach direction. Boxxie was located $\sim 8m$ from the influencing device on the opposite wall of the corridor, with its field of view (FOV) directed out towards the influencing device. Figure 4b) shows a diagrammatic representation of the setting in which the positions of Boxxie and the influencing device are shown, along with Boxxie's FOV.

Unbeknownst to participants, there were two entry zones into the experiment, which are also depicted in Fig. 4b). Participants who entered the experiment area on the left hand side of the corridor were termed to be initially 'Compliant' (C) with the desired influence behavior. Participants on the right side of the corridor, on the other hand, were termed 'Non-Compliant' (NC). Participants who were moving down the center of the corridor between these two zones ($-0.2m < y_{person} < 0.2m$) were considered neither C nor NC and were excluded from the experiment.

5.2.3 Experiment Cases

There were two cases for the robot-issued cue – Responsive and Static. These cases were randomly counterbalanced with the C and NC participants: in some trials the Static information system was presented to C participants and the Responsive cue was presented to NC participants, whilst in

other trials this was reversed. All other acts were consistent throughout the trials.

5.2.4 Procedure

Each trial commenced with the random selection of a case, and began when a participant walking down the corridor was detected by Boxxie as having entered the Public Zone and was *Read* as either C or NC, depending on which entry zone they were located in; as shown in Fig. 4b). Depending on the case, the influencing device was set to either Static or Responsive. The participant's position was subsequently tracked via Boxxie, and, in the Responsive case, the influencing device's cue was triggered as they crossed into the Social Interaction Zone.

5.2.5 Measurement

As in Part 1, the participants' change in distance from their originally measured position, and relative to a zero-axis which was parallel to and in the center of the corridor, was again used as the measure. As the participants would have had to move in the negative direction to cut the corner, and the positive direction was in line with the attempted influence direction, a less negative change in distance equated to greater influence.

Two measures were taken for each participant. The first at the **E**ntry point of the Social Interaction Zone relative to the influencing device. The second at the **F**inal detection point – at which they passed out of the range of the person detection system – which was approximately *1m* past the influencing device.

5.2.6 Results

In total, *100* trials were conducted. Trials in which the participant was lost by the person detection system before reaching the influencing device were not considered in the results, leaving *84* trials for analysis. There were *56* C and *28* NC participants. A total of $\sim 2,700$ person location readings were autonomously logged during the experiment, with an average of ~ 32 person location readings logged per trial.

Figure 5 shows the average of the measure for C and NC participants in the Static and Responsive cases. A two way ANOVA revealed a significant main effect between C and NC participants, $F=1,614.91$, $p<0.05$, *mean difference* $= 0.21m$, and a borderline significant main effect between Static and Responsive cases, $F=121.02$, $p=0.058$, *mean difference = 0.058m*. The interaction effect was not significant.

154

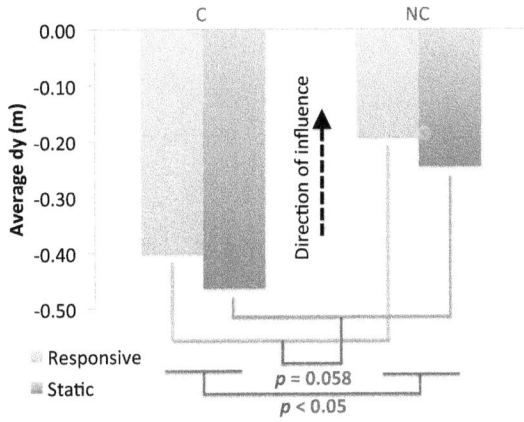

Figure 5: Influence reducing the extent of people cutting the corner in Part 2 of the study

6. DISCUSSION

The empirical results presented in this paper provide support for both hypotheses.

Firstly, support was found for our hypothesis $(H1)$ – that people's movement behavior in public spaces can be influenced using the Robot Centric HRI paradigm. Specifically, participants in Part 1 of the study moved significantly in the direction of intended influence as they moved towards and past the influencing device in both Location 1 ($F=67.64$, $p<0.001$) and Location 2 ($F=99.43$, $p<0.001$). There was also significant movement between the **P** and **F** measure points (Location 1 - *mean difference = 0.56m, p<0.001*, Location 2 - *mean difference = 0.94m, p<0.001*) relative to measure point **E**, suggesting an ongoing influence effect.

Further, the influence effectiveness was significantly different between the three levels in Part 1 of the study (Static, Dynamic, and Responsive) in both Location 1 ($F=259.44$, $p<0.001$) and Location 2 ($F=49.60$, $p<0.001$), with Dynamic significantly more effective than Static (Location 1 - *mean difference = 0.63m, p=0.018*, Location 2 - *mean difference = 0.54m, p=0.05*), and Responsive significantly more effective than Dynamic (Location 1 - *mean difference = 0.55m, p=0.039*, Location 2 - *mean difference = 0.64m, p=0.017*). This demonstrates, as per prediction *P1*, that passenger information systems utilizing the Robot Centric HRI paradigm (Responsive) will have greater influence on participants than those utilizing the traditional HRI paradigm (Static and Dynamic). Further, these results suggest that the influencing device's use of the Robot Centric HRI paradigm to enable a Responsive PI system, saw it most able to influence participants into conforming to its suggestions. This provides partial support for hypothesis *H2* that increasing levels of robot interactivity (from Static to Dynamic to Responsive) will result in an increase in the effectiveness of its ability to influence.

Prediction *P1* was further supported by the results from Part 2 of the experiment, which reproduced the results from Part 1 in order to verify that the findings were in line. Specifically, Responsive was found to result in borderline significant greater influence compared to Static ($F=121.02$, $p=0.058$, *mean difference = 0.058m*). The borderline result is potentially due to the exclusion of participants who were neither C nor NC (i.e. in the center of the corridor).

The results from Part 2 provide support for prediction *P2* that *Reading* an additional behavioral cue will yield insights useable to moderate *Elicit* to increase the effectiveness of the robot's influence (in Part 2 of the study, an additional *Read* of the participant's entry position into the Social Interaction Zone). Specifically, a significant difference was found between the influence on C and NC participants ($F=1,614.91$, $p<0.05$), with NC participants influenced an average of *0.21m* more than C participants. This result has implications for the design of *Elicit* influence strategies. For instance, consider the case where 'too much' influence may have a negative repercussion. The robot, in that case, may refrain from presenting *Elicit* cues to 'more influenceable' people observed to be already near this threshold.

Limitations - That presented has a number of limitations, the most pressing perhaps being that this study lacked an exploration of habituation to the influencing device and the subsequent effect on its ability to influence. Additionally, measurement inaccuracies potentially occurred, and differences in behavior between male and female participants were not accounted for. Despite these limitations, however, the results of this study suggest there is value in increasing the interactivity of robots via the Robot Centric HRI paradigm, and furthermore – by increasing robots' ability to *Read* behavioral cues and utilize behavior-to-meaning mapping to moderate their *Elicit* strategies, the ability of the robot to target its influence to achieve specific desired outcome(s) can be greatly increased.

7. CONCLUSIONS AND FUTURE WORK

In this study, we focused on quantitively investigating whether increasing a robot's interactivity (that is, its ability to *Read* behavior, then moderate its *Elicit* strategy based on this information and known behavior-to-meaning mappings) will result in an increase in the effectiveness of its influence (i.e. its ability to target its influence to achieve specific desired outcome(s)). A two-part study (total $n = 273$) was conducted in both a major Australian public train station ($n = 84 + 105$) and a university ($n = 84$). Passersby were exposed to a robot designed to influence their passage, which had various levels of interactivity.

Considering the results holistically, we found that an increase of the robot's interactivity (i.e. Responsive passenger information systems) led to an increase in the robot's ability to influence, in this case the passage deviation of passersby. This has implications for HRI, particularly in cases where the robot is required to lead interactions with naïve and/or unsuspecting humans. In such cases, designing the robot with greater levels of interactivity yields larger influence and hence greater effectiveness at task achievement.

Further, it was demonstrated that the Robot Centric HRI paradigm is generalizable to other robots and application spaces, and can be drawn on to enable deliberate moderation and exploitation of this robot interactivity. Thus, through leveraging the paradigm to design a robot's interactivity, more nuanced, predictable and systematic influence can be achieved. For example, in HRI situations such as that constructed in [16, 23], enabling the robot to *Read* a larger number of human cues, and utilize the acquired information to moderate its *Elicit* cues, can result in greater success at achieving conversation initiation.

Future work will focus on further investigating the interactivity of robots, particularly other behavioral cues the robot could *Read* to more intelligently moderate its *Elicit* strategy. For example, an understanding of when participants gaze is directed at the robot can enable the robot to communicate intentionally to people in the environment through an understanding of when people's attention is directed at the robot and when it is not (as discussed in [4]). Additionally, the effect of commuter habituation on a robot's ability to influence will be explored.

8. ACKNOWLEDGMENTS

This work is supported by UTS' Centre for Autonomous Systems and RobotAssist (*www.robotassist.org*). Further information on our activities is available at *www.nkHRI.com*

9. REFERENCES

[1] C. Bartneck and J. Forlizzi. A Design-Centred Framework for Social Human-Robot Interaction. In *Ro-Man*, pages 591–594, 2004.

[2] J. Bullough and N. Skinner. Influence of Visual Signal Flash Intensity and Duration on Perception. In *Suppression, Detection, and Signaling Research and Applications Symposium (SUPDET)*, pages 1–5, 2013.

[3] S. Caraian and N. Kirchner. Influence of Robot-Issued Joint Attention Cues on Gaze and Preference. In *HRI '13: Proceedings of the 8th ACM/IEEE International Conference on HRI*, pages 95–96, 2013.

[4] S. Caraian and N. Kirchner. Head Pose Behavior in the Human-Robot Interaction Space. In *HRI '14: Proceedings of the 9th ACM/IEEE International Conference on Human-Robot Interaction*, pages 132–133, 2014.

[5] K. Dautenhahn. Socially intelligent robots: dimensions of human–robot interaction. *Philosophical Transactions*, 362:679–704, 2007.

[6] G. D'Egidio, R. Patel, B. Rashidi, M. Mansour, E. Sabri, and P. Milgram. A study of the efficacy of flashing lights to increase the salience of alcohol-gel dispensers for improving hand hygiene compliance. *Am J Infect Control*, 42:852–855, 2014.

[7] M. Farenzena, A. Tavano, L. Bazzani, D. Tosato, G. Paggetti, G. Menegaz, V. Murino, and M. Cristani. Social interactions by visual focus of attention in a three-dimensional environment. In *Workshop on Pattern Recognition and Artificial Intelligence for Human Behaviour Analysis (PRAI*HBA)*, volume 30, pages 115–127, 2009.

[8] J. Fink, S. Lemaignan, P. Dillenbourg, P. Rétornaz, F. Vaussard, A. Berthoud, F. Mondada, F. Wille, and K. Franinović. Which Robot Behavior Can Motivate Children to Tidy up Their Toys? Design and Evaluation of "Ranger". In *HRI '14: Proceedings of the 9th ACM/IEEE International Conference on Human-Robot Interaction*, pages 439–446, 2014.

[9] B. Fogg. *Persuasive Technology: Using Computers to Change what We Think and Do*, chapter Computers as Persuasive Social Actors. Morgan Kaufmann, 2003.

[10] S. Gerathewohl. Conspicuity of Steady and Flashing Light Signals: Variation of Contrast. *J. Opt. Soc. Am. (JOSA)*, 43(7):567–568, 1953.

[11] V. Groom. What's the best role for a robot? Cybernetic models of existing and proposed human-robot interaction structures. In *Proceedings of the International Conference on Informatics in Control, Automation, and Robotics (ICINCO)*, Funchal, Portugal, 2008.

[12] E. Hall. *The Hidden Dimension*. Doubleday, 1966.

[13] D. Hordern and N. Kirchner. Robust and Efficient People Detection with 3-D Range Data using Shape Matching. In *Proceedings of the 2010 Australasian Conference on Robotics and Automation*, 2010.

[14] C.-M. Huang and B. Mutlu. The Repertoire of Robot Behavior: Enabling Robots to Achieve Interaction Goals through Social Behavior. *Journal of Human-Robot Interaction*, 2(2):80–102, 2013.

[15] W. Ju and L. Leifer. The Design of Implicit Interactions: Making Interactive Systems Less Obnoxious. *Design Issues*, 24(3):72–84, 2008.

[16] T. Kanda, D. Glas, M. Shiomi, and N.Hagita. Abstracting People's Trajectories for Social Robots to Proactively Approach Customers. *IEEE Transactions on Robotics*, 25(6):1382–1396, 2009.

[17] N. Kirchner and A. Alempijevic. A Robot Centric Perspective on the HRI Paradigm. *Journal of Human-Robot Interaction - Special Issue on HRI Perspectives and Projects from around the Globe*, 2(1):1–23, 2012.

[18] N. Kirchner, A. Alempijevic, X. Dai, P. Plöger, and R. K. Venkat. A robust people detection, tracking, and counting system. In *IEEE International Conference on Robotics and Automation*, 2014.

[19] N. Kirchner, A. Alempijevic, and G. Dissanayake. Nonverbal Robot-Group Interaction Using an Imitated Gaze Cue. In *HRI '11: Proceedings of the 6th ACM/IEEE International Conference on Human Robot Interaction*, pages 497–504, 2011.

[20] N. Marquardt and S. Greenberg. Informing the Design of Proxemic Interactions. *Pervasive Computing*, 11(2):14–23, 2012.

[21] I. Nevo, M. Fitzpatrick, R. Thomas, P. Gluck, J. Lenchus, K. Arheart, and D. Birnbach. The Efficacy of Visual Cues to Improve Hand Hygiene Compliance. *Simul Healthc*, 5(6):325–331, 2010.

[22] J. Reason. Combating omission errors through task analysis and good reminders. *Qual Saf Health Care*, 11:40–44, 2002.

[23] S. Satake, T. Kanda, D. Glas, M. Imai, H. Ishiguro, and N. Hagita. How to Approach Humans? – Strategies for Social Robots to Initiate Interaction. In *HRI '09: Proceedings of the 4th ACM/IEEE International Conference on Human Robot Interaction*, pages 109–116, 2009.

[24] J. Scadding and N. Losseff. *Clinical Neurology*. Hodder Arnold, London, 2011.

[25] B. Verplank. Interaction Design, CCRMA HCI Technology course, Stanford University, 2000.

[26] J. Vos and A. Van Meeteren. Visual Processes Involved in Seeing Flashes. In *International Symposium of Imperial College of London. The Perception and Application of Flashing Lights.*, pages 3–16, 1971.

[27] C. Wickens and J. Hollands. *Engineering Psychology and Human Performance*. Prentice-Hall, Upper Saddle River, NJ, 2000.

Effects of Culture on the Credibility of Robot Speech: A Comparison between English and Arabic

Sean Andrist,[1] Micheline Ziadee,[2] Halim Boukaram,[2] Bilge Mutlu,[1] Majd Sakr[3]

[1] University of Wisconsin–Madison, WI, USA
[2] American University of Science and Technology, Beirut, Lebanon
[3] Carnegie Mellon University, Pittsburgh, PA, USA
sandrist@cs.wisc.edu; mziadee@aust.edu.lb; hboukaram@aust.edu.lb;
bilge@cs.wisc.edu; msakr@cs.cmu.edu

ABSTRACT

As social robots begin to enter our lives as providers of information, assistance, companionship, and motivation, it becomes increasingly important that these robots are capable of interacting effectively with human users across different cultural settings worldwide. A key capability in establishing acceptance and usability is the way in which robots structure their speech to build credibility and express information in a meaningful and persuasive way. Previous work has established that robots can use speech to improve credibility in two ways: expressing practical knowledge and using rhetorical linguistic cues. In this paper, we present two studies that build on prior work to explore the effects of language and cultural context on the credibility of robot speech. In the first study ($n = 96$), we compared the relative effectiveness of knowledge and rhetoric on the credibility of robot speech between Arabic-speaking robots in Lebanon and English-speaking robots in the United States, finding the rhetorical linguistic cues to be more important in Arabic than in English. In the second study ($n = 32$), we compared the effectiveness of credible robot speech between robots speaking either Modern Standard Arabic or the local Arabic dialect, finding the expression of both practical knowledge and rhetorical ability to be most important when using the local dialect. These results reveal nuanced cultural differences in perceptions of robots as credible agents and have important implications for the design of human-robot interactions across Arabic and Western cultures.

Categories and Subject Descriptors

H.1.2 [**Models and Principles**]: User/Machine Systems—*human factors, software psychology*; H.5.2 [**Information Interfaces and Presentation**]: User Interfaces—*evaluation/methodology, user-centered design*

General Terms

Design, Experimentation, Human Factors

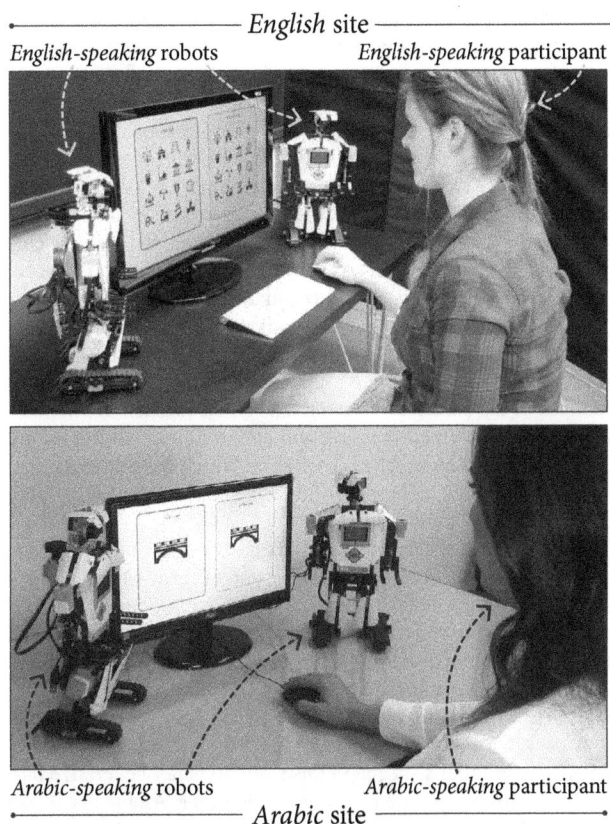

Figure 1: The first study was conducted in both the United States (top) and Lebanon (bottom). Participants interacted with two robots acting as competing tour guides, each speaking with a different degree of practical knowledge and/or rhetorical ability.

1. INTRODUCTION

People seek information for a variety of reasons, including comfort, support, empowerment, learning, and obtaining knowledge to act on. Social robots are increasingly taking on roles in the home and workplace as providers of such information to human users in a number of contexts. Critical to a robot's success in these roles is the perceived credibility of its speech in order to be persuasive and induce a positive change in knowledge, attitude, and behavior [2]. However, credibility is a multi-faceted construct that includes more than just the presentation of accurate information. Human communication research suggests that credibility is composed of the message content, the receiver's background, and the speaker's characteristics [26]. While little is known about how robots can be perceived as credible sources of information, recent work provides a foundation for structuring the content of robot messages using both practical knowledge and rhetorical linguistic cues [2]. In this paper, we build on this foundation by investigating the effects of the receiver's background, particularly language and cultural background, on how a robot's users perceive and respond to its attempts to produce credible messages. Because language and culture are tightly intertwined and difficult—if not impossible—to study separately [1], we use the term *culture* to encompass both the native language and cultural background of the users of social robotic products. Previous research has used different terms for the same or similar construct, including "language community," [16] "languaculture," [1] and "ethnicity," [17] (ethno-linguistic or ethno-national groups).

A key motivation for studying the effects of culture on people's perceptions of and responses to robots as credible agents is the emerging global market for social robotic products. Cultures vary in terms of their perspectives on the role of language, structuring credible messages, and communicating effectively with audiences, all of which must be considered when designing informational robots that are to be deployed across cultures. One important cultural dimension is *context*—the environment and circumstances surrounding a speech act, including history, knowledge, use of pauses and silences, assumptions of values, and so on [6, 10]. For example, Western culture is described as "low-context," in which more meaning is placed in the language code itself and communication tends to be specific, explicit, and analytical. Alternatively, Arabic culture, which comprises the speakers of the Arabic language, is characterized as "high-context," in which there is extensive assumed shared context and much of the burden of meaning falls on the listener. We hypothesize that this cultural dimension will have a substantial impact on the credibility of robot speech and therefore used these two cultural contexts to conduct a comparison between English-speaking and Arabic-speaking robots.

This work investigates two research questions that motivated two studies. First, how does culture affect the efficacy of the expression of both practical knowledge and rhetorical linguistic cues in producing credible robot speech? To answer this question, we conducted a study in two sites—one in the United States and the other in Lebanon—that manipulated the use of knowledge and rhetoric for robots interacting with English-speaking and Arabic-speaking users. We chose the official Arabic language, Modern Standard Arabic (MSA), as the robot's speech in this study to better generalize our findings to Arabic culture as a whole. However, Arabic speakers' use of colloquial dialects when conversing in everyday situations motivated a second research question: how does an Arabic-speaking robot's use of either MSA or the local dialect affect the robot's credibility? To answer this question, we conducted a second study in Lebanon in which we manipulated robots' use of practical knowledge and rhetorical linguistic cues while speaking with MSA or the local dialect. The findings of the two studies have important implications for the design of human-robot interactions across Arabic and Western cultures.

2. BACKGROUND

In this section, we present previous cross-cultural research in human-robot interaction (HRI), background on Arabic culture that is relevant to designing informational robots in that cultural context, and human communication research on the use of rhetorical linguistic cues for producing credible and persuasive speech.

2.1 Cross-Cultural HRI

Culture underlies every aspect of social behavior and influences an individual's communication style, character, personality, knowledge, and motivation [21]. Šabanović [24] offers a perspective on how scientific fields approach the concept of culture in different ways. Social scientists tend to critique and problematize the concept of culture in ways that not only make it difficult to implement in technology but call into question the entire pursuit of culturally adaptive robots. On the other hand, robotics researchers seek to computationally define culture so that it can be boiled down and easily implemented in robotic products. In this paper, we take the perspective of HRI researchers, situated between social science and robotics, and seek to develop a deeper understanding of how cultural factors can be applied in the design of human-robot interactions.

A number of studies have explored the attitudes that people of different cultures hold with regards to their acceptance of social robots. In a questionnaire on attitudes towards interaction with robots across different cultures, American participants were found to be the least negative toward robots while Mexican participants were the most negative [3]. Lee et al. [15] used a generative design approach to determine expectations and desires in Korea and the United States for domestic robots, discovering two themes reflecting the ideals of each culture: relational and interdependent robots among Korean participants and utilitarian and independent robots among American participants. In a study including Chinese participants, a Chinese robot was perceived as more likely to know famous Hong Kong landmarks than an American robot, suggesting that people generalize from information about a particular robot to construct a mental model of the robot's capabilities dependent on the cultural context in which the robot operates [14].

Previous work has also examined cross-cultural differences in the ability of robots to change people's decisions and behaviors. Wang et al. [31] examined the effect of robots communicating with people while respecting or not respecting cultural norms. The study found that Chinese participants were more likely to change previously made decisions to align with a robot's recommendations when that robot was using an implicit communication style while U.S. participants aligned more with a robot using an explicit communication style. Other previous work focused on the effects of communication style and cultural background (Chinese or German) on the acceptance of recommendations from a robot [22]. Researchers found a strong preference among participants for the robot that communicated in the style more familiar to them (explicit for Germans, implicit for Chinese).

A small number of previous studies have investigated human-robot interaction in Arabic culture. Trovato et al. [30] found that Egyptian participants preferred interacting with a robot that used Arabic gestures and ways of speaking and felt uncomfortable when interacting with a robot using Japanese gestures and ways of speaking, while the opposite was true for Japanese participants. Another study examined politeness strategies for robots conversing with English and Arabic speakers, finding that Arabic participants gave higher ratings of politeness and competency to the robot than English speakers [25]. Verbal and nonverbal behaviors can be utilized to evoke associations between a robot's behaviors and its attributed ethnicity among English and Arabic speakers [17], and these groups also differ in how they perceive a robot's personality based on the amount of verbosity, hedging, alignment, and formality in its speech [16]. To our knowledge, there has been no previous work in HRI that explores the comparative effectiveness of robot speech designed to be credible across Western and Arabic culture, and the first study presented in this paper seeks to bridge this knowledge gap.

2.2 Arabic Language

When designing speech for robots in Arabic culture, it is important to consider that there is not a single Arabic language. Modern Standard Arabic (MSA) is the primary language of media, government, education, and public and religious speakers [13]. However, colloquial Arabic dialects have developed within countries and are the languages of everyday interaction. This development is the result of the interaction between different ancient dialects of Classical Arabic and other languages that existed in, neighbored, and/or colonized what is today the Arab World. Arabic dialects are generally restricted in use for informal daily communication and are not taught in schools, although there is a rich popular dialect culture of folktales, songs, movies, and television shows. Arabic dialects include Egyptian Arabic (Egypt and Sudan), Levantine Arabic (Lebanon, Syria, Jordan, Palestine and Israel), Gulf Arabic (Kuwait, United Arab Emirates, Bahrain, and Qatar), North African Arabic (Morocco, Algeria, Tunisia and Mauritania), and more.

There is a complex relationship between MSA and a region's specific dialect that linguists refer to as *diglossia*—the coexistence of two languages in everyday communication [8]. Diglossia typically entails the coexistence of a primary spoken dialect and a different, highly codified language contained in written literature and used in formal settings. Arabic speakers do not think of MSA and their particular dialect as separate languages; instead they coexist, serving different purposes. Although some Arabic speakers might have difficulty expressing themselves in MSA, most speakers understand it, as MSA is commonly used in written and formal communication, including speeches, newspapers, and news broadcasts [7]. MSA was chosen as the Arabic language in the first study in order to generalize to the wider Arabic society, but the second study investigates the diglossia that exists in Arabic culture, particularly the effect of a robot using either MSA or Levantine dialect when attempting to convey credible speech to Lebanese speakers.

2.3 Credibility, Persuasion, & Rhetoric

People encounter a great deal of information every day, most of which is filtered out in favor of what is deemed useful. One particularly important criterion used to filter information is its *credibility* [32]. New information that is rejected as not credible will not be learned or have any persuasive impact. Thus, credibility is a necessary but not sufficient component of any message meant to persuade in order to change mental states, attitudes, and behaviors [20]. The credibility of a message is a product of an interaction among source characteristics (e.g., appearance and trustworthiness), message characteristics (e.g., information content and rhetoric), and receiver characteristics (e.g., culture and previously held beliefs) [26]. Previous research found participant opinions on various topics to change more when presented with opposite opinions from "high prestige" (more trustworthy) sources, e.g., an academic journal, rather than less trustworthy sources, e.g., a gossip magazine [12]. Demonstrating credibility with skilled rhetoric can also lead to a listener's compliance, both in thought and behavior [18].

Findings on credibility from human-human interactions have been found to apply to human-computer interactions in which computers act as knowledge sources [9]. For example, recommender systems are sources designed to persuade their users. Recent research on these systems emphasizes the social aspects of their design, particularly the importance of integrating social cues to create more credible and persuasive systems [33].

Previous research in HRI has examined how a robot should establish credibility when interacting with users. Torrey et al. [29] demonstrated that robots should adapt the amount of information they present to the level of expertise of its user and the context of the interaction. Roubroeks et al. [23] studied reactions to robots either opposing or agreeing with their users and concluded that messages should be carefully worded to avoid a poor impression of the robot. Andrist et al. [2] demonstrated that two dimensions of speech—*practical knowledge*, which captures prior knowledge and experience, and *rhetorical ability*, which refers mainly to speaking prowess—contribute to the credibility of a robot's messages.

In this paper, we utilize the model of speech presented by Andrist et al. [2] to produce credible robot speech (illustrated in Figure 2). In this model, high rhetorical ability is created through the use of linguistic cues including goodwill, prior experience, metaphors, organization, and fluency. Expressions of *goodwill* indicate that the speaker wants what is best for the listener [11]. Effective speakers will also convey that the speaker has had *prior experience* giving credible information to previous listeners [27]. *Metaphors* help establish common ground between the speaker and the listener and indicate that the speaker is making an effort to connect with the listener and share his or her experience and expertise [11]. Highly metaphoric language and strong emotion are especially important in Arabic persuasive speech [28]. Rhetorical ability is also shaped by the *organization* of utterances [19]. Poor organization can damage the credibility of the speaker by creating the impression that he or she is not well-versed in the subject. Finally, the timing or *fluency* of speech is a key para-verbal cue for rhetorical ability [4]. There is some evidence that members of Arabic societies tend to speak quickly, possibly pointing to the particular importance of this cue for effective speech in Arabic [7]. In this work, we explore the relative effectiveness of a robot utilizing these rhetorical linguistic cues when speaking to English-speaking and Arabic-speaking users.

3. STUDY 1

The first study aimed to explore the effect of practical knowledge and rhetorical ability on the persuasiveness and perceived credibility of robots across Western and Arabic cultures. The study was conducted in two locations—a university campus in the United States and a university campus in Lebanon—to explore the commonalities and differences between robots using the speech model from prior work [2] to persuade English-speaking and Arabic-speaking participants. Both sites used identical robots and comparable lab spaces. The experimenter in Lebanon was a native Arabic speaker, while the experimenter in the United States was a native English speaker. They followed identical scripts and procedures, differing only in the language used. All survey instruments, written materials, verbal instructions, and robot speech were in Modern Standard Arabic for the Arabic participants and English for the American participants.

3.1 Participants

In total, 96 participants (45 females and 51 males) were recruited for this study, 48 in Lebanon and 48 in the United States. Participants

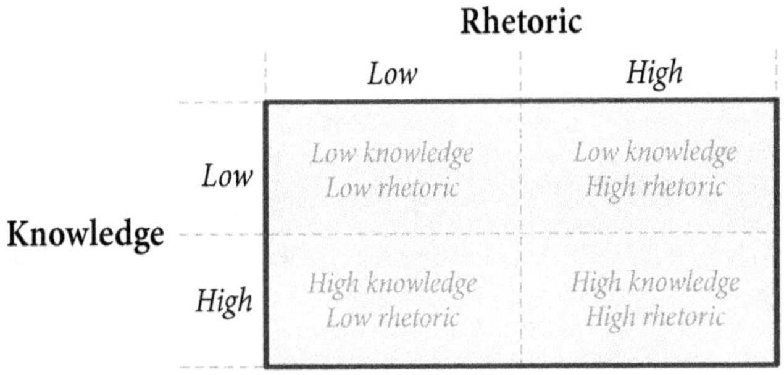

Figure 2: A model of expert speech adapted from Andrist et al. [2], divided into dimensions of knowledge and rhetorical ability.

High rhetorical ability

The temple of Dynoisa dates back to the 7th centure BCE. It was a sacred place in which the goddess of fertility was honored in an annual festival held in spring when the surrounding fields turn into a living painting filled with color.

metaphor   poor fluency   poor organization

Low rhetorical ability

The temple of Dynoisa dates back to the 7th centure BCE. It was a sacred place in which the goddess of fertility was honored. [pause] This honoring took place in an annual festival held in spring. [pause] The fields surrounding the temple are colorful in spring.

High rhetorical ability

يعود تاريخ بناء معبد دينوسيا إلى القرن السابع قبل الميلاد. وقد كان المعبد مكاناً مقدّساً تُكرّم فيه إلهة الخصوبة في مهرجان سنويّ يُقام في فصل الربيع حين تتحوّل الحقول المحيطة به إلى لوحة حيّة تضج بالألوان.

poor fluency   metaphor   poor organization

Low rhetorical ability

يعود تاريخ بناء معبد دينوسيا إلى القرن السابع قبل الميلاد. كان المعبد مكاناً مقدّساً تُكرّم فيه إلهة الخصوبة [pause]. يجري التكريم في مهرجان سنويّ يُقام في فصل الربيع. [pause] . تكون الحقول المحيطة بالمعبد ملوّنة خلال فصل الربيع.

Figure 3: An example script utilizing high and low rhetorical ability in both English and Arabic. The script with high rhetorical ability is utilizing three of the five linguistic cues used in this work: metaphor, organization, and fluency.

in Lebanon were native Arabic speakers and participants in the United States were native English speakers. Ages ranged from 18 to 62 at the site in Lebanon ($M = 28.27$, $SD = 10.24$) and 18 to 46 at the site in the United States ($M = 21.65$, $SD = 4.91$).

3.2 Study Design

Participants interacted with two robots simultaneously, each embodying a different quadrant of the expertise model shown in Figure 2. We tested each of the six possible pairings of the four quadrants between-participants in both study locations, assigning eight participants at each site to each of the six pairing conditions (8 participants × 6 conditions × 2 locations = 96 total participants).

The robots acted as competing tour guides helping the participant plan a virtual tour through a fictional city. The experiment consisted of ten trials, each with a pair of landmarks for the participant to choose from. Each robot individually uttered a short description of the landmark while a computer monitor displayed the names and images of the landmarks. Following the robot's description, the user selected one of the landmarks by clicking on it (Figure 1).

Practical knowledge of the robot's utterances was manipulated by varying the number of discrete facts included in the descriptions of the landmarks; high knowledge scripts contained four discrete pieces of information, while low knowledge scripts contained two. Rhetorical ability was manipulated by varying the number of linguistic cues of expertise present in the robot's speech; high rhetorical ability scripts contained three of the linguistic cues presented in Section 2.3, while low rhetorical ability scripts contained none. An example script for one of the landmarks used in the study, a temple, is presented in Figure 3, highlighting the presence or absence of linguistic cues for both languages.

All scripts were first created in English and then translated into both Modern Standard Arabic and Lebanese dialect by an accredited translator. This translation was an iterative process. We conducted a short pretest to assess whether the rhetorical cues retained their effectiveness when translated into Arabic. A total of 24 participants, including 13 participants (six females and seven males) for MSA and 11 participants (six females and five males) for dialect, took part in the pretest. Each participant was presented with audio recordings of 20 pairs of sentences describing the landmarks. Each pair of sentences expressed the same level of knowledge but varied in rhetoric (high and low). Participants were asked to pick the sentence showing higher rhetorical ability. The data indicated that our manipulation of rhetorical ability using linguistic cues was successful for both MSA and dialect with the exception of "expressions of goodwill." With this cue, the speaker addresses the listener directly, e.g., "this is a unique experience that *you* will really enjoy." The initial translation used the gender-neutral Arabic plural pronoun for "you" because Arabic inflects for gender. This plural form, however, is a formal type of address in Arabic that automatically creates distance between the speaker and the listener. We decided to replace the use of

the plural with the creation of a masculine and a feminine version of every utterance to be used for male and female participants. Finally, these new Arabic scripts were back-translated into English to ensure parallel content for both cultural sites.

3.3 Implementation & Procedure

This study made use of Lego Mindstorm robots in the humanoid ev3rstorm configuration[1] with minor modifications to the neck to allow the head to turn. They were placed on either side of the computer monitor displaying the software used for selecting between pairs of landmarks (Figure 1). The desktop software communicated through sockets to the robots running a custom leJOS operating system[2] that allowed the use of a custom service that accepted regular head-turning commands from the main software in order to emphasize the robots' embodied nature. The robots were given gender-neutral names and voices. Small external speakers placed behind them augmented their audio capabilities. The audio used for the robot voices were recorded using a female human voice and then pitch-shifted (one robotic voice is higher and one robotic voice is lower) and given a subtle robotic echo effect. The voices were randomly assigned to prevent any bias toward either of these voices.

Each participant was first greeted by the experimenter and signed a consent form. Participants were then seated directly facing the monitor and the experimenter explained that the robots would be acting as tour guides that would help the participant plan a virtual tour to a fictional city. The experimenter then left the room. Participants clicked a start button to begin the experiment. Each selection screen consisted of two landmark images representing the same type of landmark, e.g., two different zoos or two different museums. The border around each landmark lit up in turn and the respective (right/left) robot turned its head toward the user, provided some information about the landmark (appropriate to its knowledge/rhetoric condition), and then turned its head back to the monitor. The voice assigned to each robot was randomly generated for each participant. The order in which the pairs of landmarks were displayed as well as the order in which the robots took turns to describe a landmark were also randomized. After finishing all ten pairs of landmarks, the participants were given a tablet computer on which they completed a questionnaire dealing with their perceptions of the two robots. In total, the study took approximately 20 minutes to complete.

3.4 Measures & Analysis

We measured the perceived credibility of the robots' speech both objectively and subjectively. Objective credibility was measured indirectly through the robot's persuasiveness, operationalized as the amount of participant compliance to the robot's suggestions. We also created subjective measures of the participants' perceptions of the robots' persuasiveness, credibility, and sociability. Seven-

---

[1] http://www.lego.com/en-us/mindstorms/products/starter-robots/ev3rstorm/
[2] http://www.lejos.org/

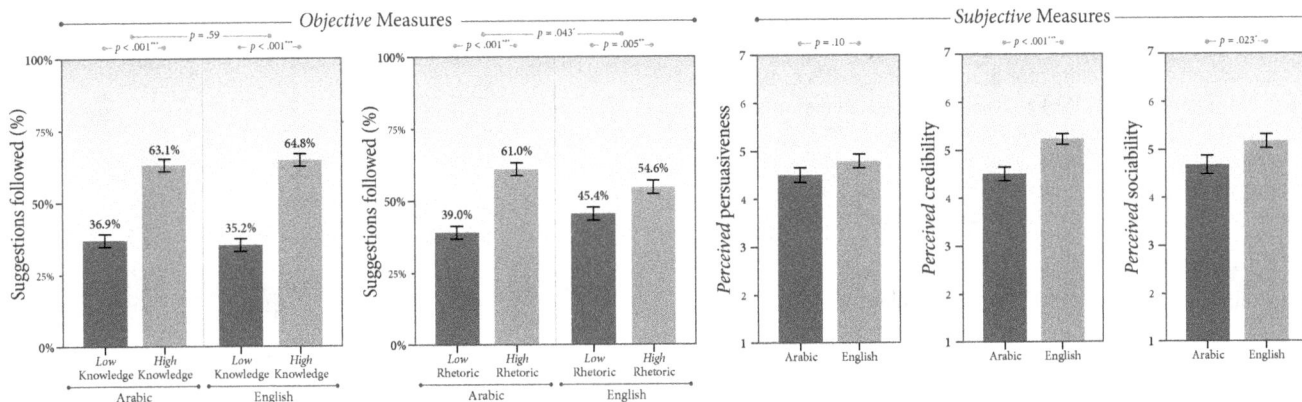

Figure 4: Results from Study 1. High knowledge and high rhetoric were effective in both English and Arabic, with rhetoric having more of an effect in Arabic. English-speaking participants assigned the robots higher ratings of credibility and sociability.

point rating scales were used for all items in these measures. Item reliabilities—measured by Cronbach's α—were sufficiently high for all measures (Table 1).

Our analysis of the objective results on participant compliance with robot suggestions was conducted using Pearson's Chi-Squared test on the categorical data of landmark choices. The statistical model included three independent variables: practical knowledge (high or low), rhetorical ability (high or low), and culture (American or Lebanese). Participant gender, robot voice, and robot speaking order were found to be nonsignificant predictors on all measures and excluded from further analysis. The impact of the continuous variable of participant age was analyzed with a nominal logistic regression in order to address the difficulty of achieving identical age distributions at both study sites. Finally, an Analysis of Variance (ANOVA) was utilized to determine the effect of the independent variables on the outcomes of the subjective rating scales.

3.5 Results

We first confirmed that the use of both dimensions of expert speech—practical knowledge and rhetorical ability—resulted in more persuasive utterances for the robots across both cultural groups. Participants chose landmarks presented by a robot with high knowledge (64%) more than those presented by a robot with low knowledge (36%), $\chi^2(1, N = 1920) = 149.63, p < .001$. Similarly for the rhetoric dimension of expert speech, participants chose landmarks presented by a robot with high rhetorical ability (57.8%) more than those presented by a robot with low rhetorical ability (42.2%), $\chi^2(1, N = 1920) = 46.88, p < .001$.

Table 1: The subjective measures used to capture the participants' impressions of the robots.

Measure *(Reliability)*	Items
Persuasiveness *(Cronbach's α = 0.94)*	*The robot was persuasive.* *The robot made travel recommendations like an expert.* *The robot was knowledgeable on the landmarks.* *The robot had a lot of expertise on the travel destinations.* *The robot seemed to have deep knowledge of the city and its landmarks.* *The robot convinced me to choose its landmarks.* *The robot was like a good salesperson.* *I would use the robot's suggestions in the future.* *The robot was a collaborator that helped me make good travel decisions.*
Credibility *(Cronbach's α = 0.84)*	*The robot was believable.* *The robot was trustworthy.* *The robot was informative.* *The robot was helpful.* *The robot was clear.* *I trust the information that the robot gave me.*
Sociability *(Cronbach's α = 0.83)*	*The robot was sociable.* *The robot was friendly.*

We next looked at the results within and across the two cultural groups. We found that high knowledge robots were complied with more than low knowledge robots in both English, $\chi^2(1, N = 960) = 84.02, p < .001$, and Arabic, $\chi^2(1, N = 960) = 66.15, p < .001$. We found no significant difference between the Arabic and American participants in terms of the number of high knowledge robot suggestions chosen, $\chi^2(1, N = 960) = 0.29, p = .59$. Participants also followed the suggestions of a robot with high rhetorical ability more than a robot with low rhetorical ability in both English, $\chi^2(1, N = 960) = 8.07, p = .005$, and Arabic, $\chi^2(1, N = 960) = 46.82, p < .001$. We discovered that Arabic participants were significantly more likely than the American participants to comply with suggestions from a robot with high rhetorical ability, $\chi^2(1, N = 960) = 4.01, p = .043$.

We also examined the difference in compliance between cultural groups within each of the four quadrants in Figure 2. We found no significant difference between Arabic and American participants in their choice of suggestions produced by a robot with low knowledge and low rhetorical ability, $\chi^2(1, N = 480) = 0.71, p = .40$, or by a robot with low knowledge and high rhetorical ability, $\chi^2(1, N = 480) = 2.15, p = .14$. We found that the American participants were significantly more likely than the Arabic participants to comply with a robot with high knowledge and low rhetorical ability, $\chi^2(1, N = 480) = 4.54, p = .033$, and found no significant difference in their compliance with robots with both high knowledge and high rhetorical ability, $\chi^2(1, N = 480) = 2.21, p = .14$.

Next we conducted a nominal logistic regression to determine the possible effect of participant age on the likelihood of complying with robot suggestions. We found a significant negative relationship between the age of the Arabic participants and their choice of landmarks described by a robot with high knowledge, $\chi^2(1, N = 480) = 5.81, p = .016$. No other significant relationships involving age were observed for either of the two cultural groups.

Finally, we analyzed the three subjective measures of persuasiveness, credibility, and sociability using an Analysis of Variance (ANOVA) with practical knowledge, rhetorical ability, and culture modeled as fixed effects. Our analysis found high knowledge robots to be rated as more persuasive than low knowledge robots, $F(1, 186) = 63.51, p < .001$, and similarly for robots with high rhetorical ability, $F(1, 186) = 12.59, p < .001$. We found no significant effect of culture on ratings of robot persuasiveness, $F(1, 186) = 2.66, p = .10$. Our analysis found high knowledge robots to also be rated as more credible than low knowledge robots, $F(1, 186) = 29.08, p < .001$, but found no significant difference on the dimension of rhetorical ability, $F(1, 186) = 0.89, p = .35$. We also found that the American participants gave significantly higher ratings of credibility than the Arabic participants, $F(1, 186) =$

17.94, $p < .001$. Finally, for the measure of sociability, our analysis uncovered higher ratings for high knowledge robots than low knowledge robots, $F(1, 186) = 26.34, p < .001$, and similarly for robots with high rhetorical ability, $F(1, 186) = 24.37, p < .001$. American participants also assigned higher ratings of sociability to the robots than the Arabic participants, $F(1, 186) = 5.28, p = .023$. The objective and subjective results are summarized in Figure 4.

3.6 Discussion

In this study, we first replicated the results found in previous work [2]. Consistent with the findings of that work, we found that a robot that described the landmarks with high knowledge—more discrete facts about the landmark—was more persuasive (measured through compliance) than robots with low knowledge and less facts. Similarly, we found that robots with high rhetorical ability—using more linguistic cues of expertise—were also complied with more than robots with low rhetorical ability.

An important finding of this study is that the rhetorical dimension of expert speech appears to be more effective in Arabic than in English. This finding aligns with the common "form over function" description of Arabic culture's perspective on language in comparison with Western culture [34]. Previous research has shown that Arabic speakers tend to view someone who uses language cleverly as well-educated and therefore qualified to make judgements, and that person's advice will then be followed [28]. On the other hand, information presented without linguistic eloquence may appear cold, impersonal, and ultimately unpersuasive, as supported by our finding that the Arabic participants complied significantly less than American participants with a robot that expressed high knowledge but low rhetorical ability. In Western culture, *ideas* (the knowledge content) are more central to persuasion while one's status or use of language (rhetorical ability) are less powerful [7]. We also found high knowledge to be more effective for the younger Arabic participants compared with older Arabic participants, similar to its greater effectiveness for the American participants. We speculate that this result might be attributed to a greater Western cultural influence on younger members of Arabic societies, but this claim would need further substantiation in future work.

In general, American participants had more positive perceptions of the robots' credibility and sociability compared with the Arabic participants. Previous work has similarly found that high-context cultural beliefs are associated with lower perceptions of a robot's credibility [31]. The authors posited that users in high-context cultures are less able to accept a robot with narrow communication skills and minimal nonverbal behaviors.

4. STUDY 2

Our first study compared robots' use of persuasive speech in English and Modern Standard Arabic. MSA was chosen in order to generalize to the rest of Arabic culture, but it is important to consider the diglossia present in Arabic culture. People use their own local dialect when speaking to each other in everyday situations. We designed a study to address this situation by directly comparing the persuasiveness of two robots using either the more formal Modern Standard Arabic or the less formal local dialect. The goal of the study was to investigate how the persuasive differences from using one or the other language might be affected by different levels of knowledge and rhetorical ability being expressed by each robot.

The second study was conducted in a single location—the same university in Lebanon—to explore the effect of speaking with either Modern Standard Arabic or the local Levantine dialect on a robot's persuasiveness and perceived credibility. The implementation, task, procedure, and measures are identical to Study 1.

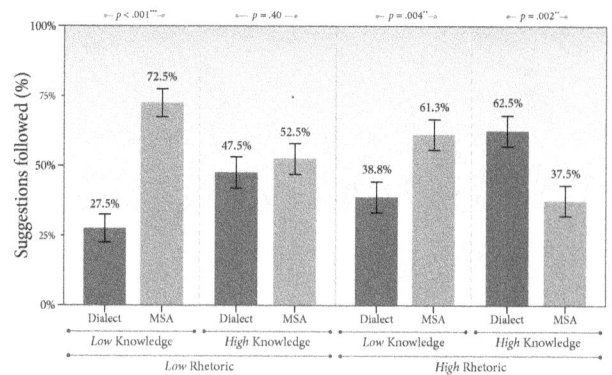

Figure 5: Results from Study 2. MSA was more effective when knowledge was low with both low and high rhetoric. Dialect was more effective when both knowledge and rhetoric were high.

4.1 Participants

Thirty-two participants (16 females and 16 males) who had not previously participated in Study 1 were recruited for this study in Lebanon. All participants were again native Arabic speakers and ages ranged from 18 to 57 ($M = 29.13, SD = 9.23$).

4.2 Study Design

This study utilized a mixed design with language (MSA or local dialect) varying within participants and knowledge (high or low) and rhetorical ability (high or low) varying between participants. Participants interacted with two robots simultaneously, each acting as a competing tour guide helping the participant plan a virtual tour and providing information on various fictional landmarks. The primary difference from Study 1 is that each robot embodied the same rather than different quadrants of the expertise model in Figure 2 and instead used a different Arabic dialect. One robot spoke using MSA and the other robot spoke using the local dialect. The assignment of language to each robot was random for each participant. We tested this language comparison in each of the four quadrants of expertise, with eight participants randomly assigned to each quadrant (8 participants × 4 quadrants = 32 total participants). For example, both robots might convey low knowledge and high rhetoric, but one spoke using MSA and the other with local dialect. All other aspects of this study were identical to Study 1.

4.3 Results

Similar to Study 1, our analysis of objective participant compliance was conducted using Pearson's Chi-Squared test with practical knowledge, rhetorical ability, and language (MSA or local dialect) as independent variables. Participant gender was found to be a significant predictor of compliance and is thus also considered in this analysis. The objective results are presented in Figure 5.

We found that robots speaking MSA were complied with more than robots speaking local dialect, $\chi^2(1, N = 640) = 9.03, p = .003$. Drilling down into each quadrant of knowledge and rhetorical ability in the model of expert speech (Figure 2), we found that with low knowledge and low rhetorical ability, robots speaking MSA were more persuasive than robots speaking local dialect, $\chi^2(1, N = 160) = 32.40, p < .001$. When speaking with low knowledge and high rhetorical ability, robots using MSA were also complied with significantly more than robots using local dialect, $\chi^2(1, N = 160) = 8.10, p = .004$. We found no significant language effect for robots speaking with high knowledge and low rhetorical ability, $\chi^2(1, N = 160) = 0.40, p = .53$. However, our analysis revealed that when speaking with both high knowledge and high rhetorical ability, a robot using local dialect was complied with more than a robot using MSA, $\chi^2(1, N = 160) = 10.00, p = .002$.

Among female participants, we found no difference in compliance with robots using MSA or local dialect, $\chi^2(1, N = 320) = 0.00, p = 1.00$. However, we found a significant preference among male participants to comply with a robot using MSA than a robot using local dialect, $\chi^2(1, N = 320) = 18.05, p < .001$.

Our analysis revealed no significant effect of language on any of the subjective ratings. These results are excluded for brevity.

4.4 Discussion

The presence of a diglossia—the coexistence of two languages in everyday communication—is a nuance of Arabic culture that must be considered in cross-cultural language comparisons between Arabic and Western cultures. Our second study sought to address this complication in the context of credible speech by directly comparing the persuasiveness of two robots using either the more formal Modern Standard Arabic or the less formal local dialect. This study revealed a tradeoff in effectiveness between the formal use of MSA and the overall level of expertise conveyed in the robot's speech. When both robots had a relatively small amount of factual content to present about each landmark in the virtual tour, regardless of rhetorical ability, participants perceived the formality of MSA as a cue indicating higher credibility for that robot, and thus were persuaded more to comply with it. On the other hand, when both robots expressed high knowledge and high rhetorical ability for their landmark descriptions, participants complied more with the robot speaking their own local dialect, possibly indicating a familiarity preference for interacting with a robot that speaks more like them when it has more to say.

5. GENERAL DISCUSSION

These studies were designed to explore the impact of language and cultural context—native English speakers in America vs native Arabic speakers in Lebanon—on the ability of a robot to convey credible messages. The first study revealed the particular importance of rhetorical linguistic cues for robots to be perceived as credible to Arabic users. It also showed Arabic users to be generally more critical of the perceived credibility and sociability of robots, as compared with American users. The second study explored the use of either Modern Standard Arabic or the local dialect for robots speaking to Arabic users, revealing the use of dialect to be most effective when the robot is knowledgeable and expresses high rhetorical ability.

These studies suggest a number of key implications for the design of credible robot speech. First, it is important that designers consider the cultural context in which their robots will be embedded, especially when the users' culture is different from that of the designer. Different cultures take different perspectives on the use of language to inform and persuade, as exemplified by the differences found in high-context and low-context cultures. Specific cultural nuances must also be accounted for in design decisions, such as the presence of diglossia within Arabic culture.

A specific implication of this work relates to the finding that rhetorical linguistic cues were more effective for the Arabic-speaking robots than for the English-speaking robots. To date, HRI designers have mostly focused on building robots that are knowledgeable and accurate with conveying information, but we have shown that rhetoric is critical in an Arabic cultural context for conveying credibility. Robots that are to be deployed in this culture will need to make use of these linguistic cues in order to be utilized and recognized as a valued source of information.

This research also illuminates a potential risk in designing effec-tive robot speech with high rhetoric and low knowledge, especially in Arabic. Speaking persuasively without expressing enough factual content could be dangerous and designers should exercise some caution in this situation. For example, if a robot is presenting prescription drugs to patients, sounding like an expert without actually possessing the requisite knowledge about the drug or the user's specific situation might have unintended harmful consequences. In general, if a robot has low knowledge on a specific subject, it should use low rhetorical ability and remain harmless. If it has high knowledge, it should attempt to generate the rhetorical ability to be perceived as a true expert on the subject.

The final implication of this work has to do with the choice a designer will have to make when deciding between MSA or a local dialect for the robot's speech. In settings where the robot has a relatively small amount of information to express to its users, the study results indicate that MSA affords the perception of credibility. Using MSA will also make the robot easily adaptable to all countries in the Arab World. However, if the robot is to reach its full potential for producing credible speech with both practical knowledge and rhetorical linguistic cues, it should use the local dialect of its users.

While it is possible that not all Arabic users are fully literate in MSA and thus might always prefer a robot to speak the local dialect, most Arabs at least understand MSA when it is spoken to them, as it is commonly used in many daily interactions, including all written and formal communication, speeches, newspapers, and news broadcasts [7]. Furthermore, we did not observe in either Study 1 or 2 any indication of participants having difficulty understanding MSA, from the reading of consent forms written in MSA to the instructions of the experimenter spoken in MSA. Education level may be an important predictor of MSA literacy. However, as we did not measure education level and recruited our Lebanese participants from a university population with at least some college education, further research is essential to understand whether the broader population of Arabic speakers are equally literate in MSA.

5.1 Limitations & Future Work

Credibility is composed of the source characteristics, message characteristics, and receiver characteristics [26]. In this work, we manipulated aspects of the message—knowledge and rhetoric—and compared the effect across two different receiver groups—American and Lebanese users. The robot (source) was held constant throughout, but future research should also examine the effect of physical characteristics of the robot itself—including size, shape, and humanlikeness—on its credibility and persuasiveness.

This work utilizes and extends a previous model of expert speech for robots that was developed in a Western culture, so it is potentially missing some rhetorical linguistic cues that are specific to Arabic culture. For example, cues of persuasive rhetoric in Arabic also include repetition, exaggeration, and assertion [7, 28], which should be further explored. Nonverbal communication patterns such as gesture, eye contact, touch, and interpersonal distance are also very important for facilitating the perceived credibility of robots [5], particularly in high-context cultures [7], and should be further explored in future work. Furthermore, we only investigated the effects of the presence and absence of linguistic cues in the credibility of robot speech. Future work should also explore the relative importance and effectiveness of each verbal or nonverbal cue.

Study 2 was designed from a practical HRI perspective; designers must choose between MSA and local dialect for robots to speak when deployed in any Arabic context. We explored this choice in Lebanon within the framework of an existing model of expert speech, revealing interesting differences and potential tradeoffs. However, future work should further explore the nuances of the differences that arise from other cultural factors, such as attitudes toward each dialect and different regional factors, as well as demographic factors, such as gender and religion.

In order to be useful in real settings outside of the laboratory, robots will need to express high rhetorical ability by generating linguistic cues of expertise automatically. Although there is currently a lack of computational methods for generating linguistic cues such as metaphors and expressions of goodwill, automatic methods for organizing fluent utterances should be possible. In addition, culturally adaptive agents should be designed to automatically detect different forms of communicative behaviors across various cultures and react to them appropriately.

6. CONCLUSION

In this paper, we presented work to explore two research questions. First, how does language and cultural context impact the effectiveness of robot speech that has been designed to be credible? And second, how does the use of either Modern Standard Arabic or the local colloquial Arabic dialect impact the robot's credibility? Our first study found that rhetorical linguistic cues are particularly important for robots to speak effectively in Arabic cultural contexts, while our second study revealed a tradeoff in effectiveness between the credibility of the robot's speech and its use of either MSA or the local dialect. This work addresses particular challenges for HRI in Arabic culture, a large and diverse set of people worldwide that have been largely unrepresented in previous work. In general, it is imperative that social robots conform to the cultural norms of their intended users, in the same way that people must be cognizant of the cultural norms of people with whom they work and places they visit. Social interaction, culture, and language are complex constructs and designing for them is difficult, but by making progress toward understanding the nuances of these concepts, we can create effective and rewarding robot behaviors that positively affect people's lives throughout the world.

Acknowledgments

We would like to thank Brandi Hefty and Jieni Peng for their help in conducting the experiments.

7. REFERENCES

[1] M. Agar. *Language shock: Understanding the culture of conversation.* William Morrow and Company, 1994.

[2] S. Andrist, E. Spannan, and B. Mutlu. Rhetorical robots: making robots more effective speakers using linguistic cues of expertise. In *Proc. HRI '13*, pages 341–348, 2013.

[3] C. Bartneck, T. Nomura, T. Kanda, T. Suzuki, and K. Kato. Cultural differences in attitudes towards robots. In *Proc. AISB '05: Symposium on Robot Companions*, pages 1–4, 2005.

[4] R. Carlson, K. Gustafson, and E. Strangert. Cues for hesitation in speech synthesis. In *Proc. Interspeech '06*, volume 6, 2006.

[5] V. Chidambaram, Y.-H. Chiang, and B. Mutlu. Designing persuasive robots: how robots might persuade people using vocal and nonverbal cues. In *Proc. HRI '12*, pages 293–300, 2012.

[6] J. B. Dozier, B. W. Husted, and J. T. Mcmahon. Need for approval in low-context and high-context cultures: A communications approach to cross-cultural ethics. *Teaching Business Ethics*, 2(2):111–125, 1998.

[7] E. Feghali. Arab cultural communication patterns. *Int J Intercult Rel*, 21(3):345–378, 1997.

[8] C. A. Ferguson. Diglossia revisited. *Southwest J Linguistics*, 10(1):214–234, 1991.

[9] B. Fogg and H. Tseng. The elements of computer credibility. In *Proc. CHI '99*, pages 80–87, 1999.

[10] E. T. Hall. *Beyond culture.* Anchor Books, 1976.

[11] E. J. Hartelius. *The rhetoric of expertise.* PhD thesis, The University of Texas at Austin, 2008.

[12] C. I. Hovland and W. Weiss. The influence of source credibility on communication effectiveness. *Public Opin Quart*, 15(4):635–650, 1951.

[13] A. S. Kaye. Diglossia: the state of the art. *Int J Sociol Lang*, pages 117–130, 2001.

[14] S. Kiesler. Fostering common ground in human-robot interaction. In *Proc. RO-MAN '05*, pages 729–734, 2005.

[15] H. R. Lee, J. Sung, S. Šabanović, and J. Han. Cultural design of domestic robots: a study of user expectations in Korea and the United States. In *Proc. RO-MAN '12*, pages 803–808, 2012.

[16] M. Makatchev and R. Simmons. Perception of personality and naturalness through dialogues by native speakers of american english and arabic. In *Proc. SIGDIAL '11*, pages 286–293, 2011.

[17] M. Makatchev, R. Simmons, M. Sakr, and M. Ziadee. Expressing ethnicity through behaviors of a robot character. In *Proc. HRI '13*, pages 357–364, 2013.

[18] G. Marwell and D. Schmitt. Dimensions of compliance-gaining behavior: An empirical analysis. *Sociometry*, pages 350–364, 1967.

[19] J. Noel. On the varieties of phronesis. *Educ Philos Theory*, 31(3):273–289, 1999.

[20] D. J. O'Keefe. Trends and prospects in persuasion theory and research. *Perspectives on persuasion, social influence and compliance gaining*, 2004.

[21] P. O'Neill-Brown. Setting the stage for the culturally adaptive agent. In *Proc. AAAI Fall Symposium on Socially Intelligent Agents*, pages 93–97, 1997.

[22] P. Rau, Y. Li, and D. Li. Effects of communication style and culture on ability to accept recommendations from robots. *Comput Hum Behav*, 25(2):587–595, 2009.

[23] M. Roubroeks, J. Ham, and C. Midden. The dominant robot: Threatening robots cause psychological reactance, especially when they have incongruent goals. In T. Ploug, P. Hasle, and H. Oinas-Kukkonen, editors, *Persuasive Technology*, pages 174–184. Springer, 2010.

[24] S. Šabanović, C. C. Bennett, and H. R. Lee. Towards culturally robust robots: A critical social perspective on robotics and culture. In *Proc. HRI '14: Workshop on Culture-Aware Robotics*, 2014.

[25] M. Salem, M. Ziadee, and M. Sakr. Marhaba, how may I help you?: effects of politeness and culture on robot acceptance and anthropomorphization. In *Proc. HRI '14*, pages 74–81, 2014.

[26] C. S. Self. Credibility. *An integrated approach to communication theory and research*, 1:421–441, 1996.

[27] J. Sniezek and L. Van Swol. Trust, confidence, and expertise in a judge advisor system. *Organ Behav Hum Decis Process*, 84(2):288–307, 2001.

[28] J. Suchan. Toward an understanding of Arabic persuasion: a Western perspective. *Int J Bus Commun*, 51(3):279–303, 2014.

[29] C. Torrey, A. Powers, M. Marge, S. Fussell, and S. Kiesler. Effects of adaptive robot dialogue on information exchange and social relations. In *Proc. HRI '06*, pages 126–133, 2006.

[30] G. Trovato, M. Zecca, S. Sessa, L. Jamone, J. Ham, K. Hashimoto, and A. Takanishi. Cross-cultural study on human-robot greeting interaction: acceptance and discomfort by Egyptians and Japanese. *Paladyn*, 4(2):83–93, 2013.

[31] L. Wang, P.-L. P. Rau, V. Evers, B. K. Robinson, and P. Hinds. When in Rome: the role of culture & context in adherence to robot recommendations. In *Proc. HRI '10*, pages 359–366, 2010.

[32] C. N. Wathen and J. Burkell. Believe it or not: Factors influencing credibility on the web. *J Am Soc Inf Sci Tec*, 53(2):134–144, 2002.

[33] K.-H. Yoo, U. Gretzel, and M. Zanker. *Persuasive Recommender Systems.* Springer, 2012.

[34] R. S. Zaharna. Understanding cultural preferences of Arab communication patterns. *Public Relat Rev*, 21(3):241–255, 1995.

Evidence that Robots Trigger a Cheating Detector in Humans

Alexandru Litoiu, Daniel Ullman, Jason Kim, Brian Scassellati
Department of Computer Science, Yale University
51 Prospect St, New Haven, CT 06511, USA
{alex.litoiu, daniel.ullman, jason.kim, brian.scassellati}@yale.edu

ABSTRACT

Short et al.[10] found that in a game between a human participant and a humanoid robot, the participant will perceive the robot as being more agentic and as having more intentionality if it cheats than if it plays without cheating. However, in that design, the robot that actively cheated also generated more motion than the other conditions. In this paper, we investigate whether the additional movement of the cheating gesture is responsible for the increased agency and intentionality or whether the act of cheating itself triggers this response. In a between-participant design with 83 participants, we disambiguate between these causes by testing (1) the cases of the robot cheating to win, (2) cheating to lose, (3) cheating to tie from a winning position, and (4) cheating to tie from a losing position. Despite the fact that the robot changes its gesture to cheat in all four conditions, we find that participants are more likely to report the gesture change when the robot cheated to win from a losing position, compared with the other conditions. Participants in that same condition are also far more likely to protest in the form of an utterance following the cheat and report that the robot is less fair and honest. It is therefore the adversarial cheat itself that causes the effect and not the change in gesture, providing evidence for a cheating detector that can be triggered by robots.

Keywords

Human Robot Interaction, Cheating, Cheating Detector, Agency

1. INTRODUCTION

Researchers studying human-robot interaction seek to make robots more engaging and more agentic by strengthening the social bonds between robots and the humans with whom they interact. We do this to allow our robots to better serve as assistants, teachers, and life-like social partners. Previous research has used the social dynamic of cheating to investigate perceptions of robot agency[10, 12].

HRI'15, March 2–5, 2015, Portland, Oregon, USA.
Copyright is held by the owner/author(s). Publication rights licensed to ACM.
ACM 978-1-4503-2883-8/15/03 ...$15.00.
http://dx.doi.org/10.1145/2696454.2696456.

A study by Short et al. sought to investigate the degree to which variations in behavior result in attributions of mental state and intentionality[10]. The study design compared three robot behaviors in the context of twenty rounds of the social game "rock-paper-scissors" between a robot and a human. In the control behavior, the robot played the game normally. In the "verbal cheat" behavior, the robot threw a gesture normally, and then upon seeing the human's winning gesture declared, "Yes, I win!" despite the robot and human's gesture combination indicating otherwise. In the action cheat behavior, the robot cheated against the human opponent in the same way as in the verbal cheat condition, however it additionally changed its gesture to the winning gesture right before it declared "Yes, I win!". The study showed that in the verbal cheat condition, the robot's behavior was interpreted as mechanistic, and as a "malfunction." On the other hand, the "action cheat" behavior was predominantly construed as agentic, and as "cheating." Participants used more active verbs than passive verbs to refer to the robot in the action cheat condition, with the only difference between conditions being the change in gesture at the end of the round.

Two possible explanations, both supported by literature, might explain the increased agency and intentionality of the active cheat condition. We seek to disambiguate between the following two possible causes:

- The additional motion of the cheating behavior caused greater attributions of agency.

- A cheating detector that has been shown to trigger towards humans also triggered towards the cheating robot, causing greater attributions of agency.

The first possible explanation stems from work that shows humans are able to make powerful attributions of agency and intentionality based solely on the motion of simple objects[7, 8]. Humans are able to determine intentionality from scenes as simple as animated squares and triangles moving around on a blank screen[5, 9]. The additional inclusion of this motion in the action cheat condition but not the verbal cheat may have generated the additional attributions of agency and intentionality in the cheat condition independent of the gesture and associated act of cheating.

A second possible explanation is that the cheat itself, irrespective of the additional motion used to generate it, caused the increased attributions of agency and intelligence. Humans have been shown to have an evolved capability to detect cheating acts committed against them as a means of self-preservation[2, 3, 14]. Research has explored an evolutionary basis of a cheating detector, with support for such a basis stemming from the benefits it provides in identifying individuals who violate social exchanges[4]. Van Lier et al. have shown that the ability to perform cheating detection is independent of age, cognitive capacity, and being cognitively experimentally burdened. Their research supports cheating detection as being performed automatically and effortlessly [13].

We discuss the difference between an adversary cheating to either improve or worsen their relative position as the "directionality" of the cheating behavior. A human's cheating detector would be able to detect when an adversary cheated to worsen the human's relative position and in turn improve the adversary's relative position. However, an adversary's cheat to let the human win, and in turn worsen the adversary's position, would not trigger the cheating detector.

In order to determine whether attributions were caused by the addition of the cheat or whether they were created by the adversarial nature of the gesture change triggering a cheat detector, we designed a study that varied how adversarial a cheating gesture was while maintaining the addition of the cheating motion. In the study, we have four conditions that all entail a robot cheating against a human in a game of "rock-paper-scissors." In the most adversarial cheat, the robot cheats when it loses in order to win. In the least adversarial, and most prosocial, the robot changes its gesture when it wins in order to lose and let the participant win. If the attributions were exclusively caused by the addition of the cheating motion, we would expect saliency, engagement, and mental attributions to remain constant as we vary how adversarial the cheat is. However, if a cheating detector were triggered by the robot's gestures, we would expect there to have been a marked difference in these metrics as we vary the adversarial nature of the cheat.

We present data from 83 participants that show a marked change in salience, engagement, and mental attributions, as we manipulate the directionality of the cheat. These data rule out the addition of motion hypothesis, instead supporting the cheating detector hypothesis.

2. METHODOLOGY

In order to disambiguate between the addition of motion hypothesis and the cheating detector hypothesis, we selected four conditions that varied in terms of directionality and magnitude, as well as by starting and ending points of the cheat:

1. The robot cheats to win, 2 levels up (WIN) - when the robot loses, it cheats to win.

2. The robot cheats to tie, 1 level up (DRAW-UP) - when the robot loses, it cheats to tie.

3. The robot cheats to tie, 1 level down (DRAW-DOWN) - when the robot wins, it cheats to tie.

4. The robot cheats to lose, 2 levels down (LOSE) - when the robot wins, it cheats to lose.

We included two DRAW conditions to differentiate between the two possible directionalities that a single cheat-to-draw condition could entail.

If the attributions are simply caused by the addition of the motion brought about by the gesture change in the cheat

condition in Short et al., we would expect attributions to be high across WIN, DRAW-UP, DRAW-DOWN, and LOSE in our study since all four conditions include the gesture change.

Alternatively, if the attributions toward the robot are caused by a cheating detector, we would expect there to be high saliency, engagement, and mental attributions in the WIN condition, and possibly in the DRAW-UP condition, depending on the specificity of the detector. If the human's detector is only sensitive to an event that results in the human losing, we would expect WIN to exhibit strong attributions, and DRAW-UP not to exhibit any. However, if the human's detector is sensitive to directionality, we would expect WIN, and DRAW-UP to both exhibit attributions. In all of these cases, we would not expect any attributions in DRAW-DOWN or LOSE, where the human should have lost, but gains instead.

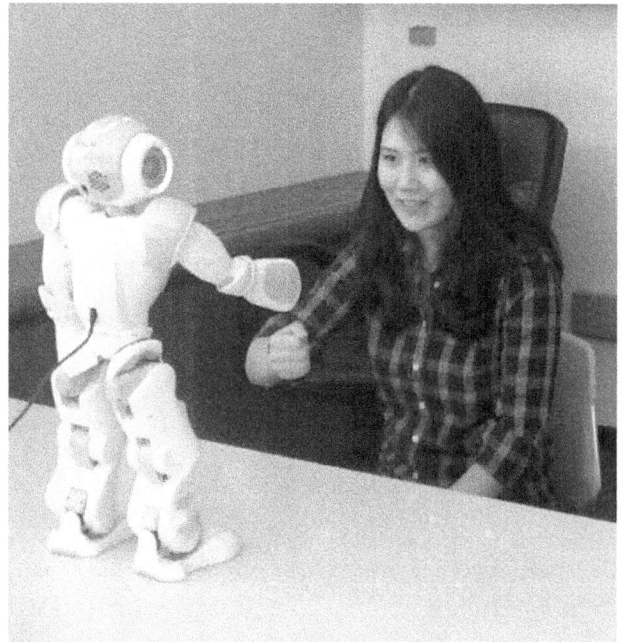

Figure 1: Nao robot playing rock, paper, scissors with a participant.

2.1 Participants

We recruited 83 participants from the Yale University community in New Haven, Connecticut, USA. There were 21 participants in the WIN condition, 21 participants in the DRAW-UP condition, 20 participants in the DRAW-DOWN condition, and 21 participants in the LOSE condition. The mean age of the participants was 21.53 and the standard deviation of the distribution of ages was 4.952. A total of 69 participants were enrolled in college at the time of the experiment, and 14 were not in college. Of the participants, 47 were female and 36 were male. The participants were recruited through posters, campus newsletters, online social networks, and personal invitations.

Participants self-reported their experience level with robots, programming, and artificial intelligence. The majority of participants, 73, did not own a robotic toy, while 9 did own a robotic toy, and one participant did not respond. How-

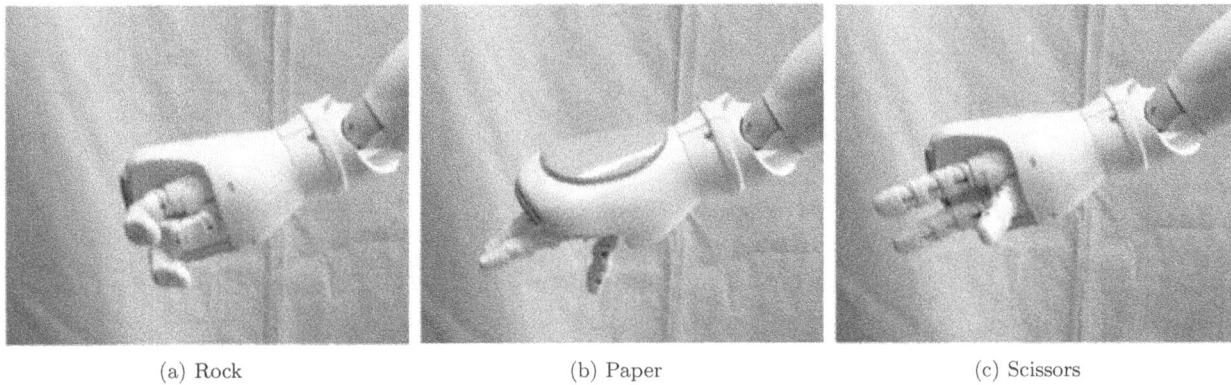

| (a) Rock | (b) Paper | (c) Scissors |

Figure 2: Nao's rock, paper, and scissors gestures.

ever, despite not owning a robotic toy, most participants had played with one, with 47 participants responding that they had, 35 responding that they had not, and one participant not responding. Similarly, 47 participants had done at least basic programming, 35 participants had not programmed at all, and one participant did not answer. However, the set of 47 that had programmed was not the same as the set of 47 that had played with a robotic toy, with only 26 having both programmed and played with a robotic toy, and only 14 having done neither.

2.2 Robot Interaction

Participants were asked to play 30 rounds of rock, paper, scissors with a Nao robot in a wizard-of-oz design[11]. Nao began the interaction by demonstrating its rock, paper, and scissors gestures, which are shown in Figure 2. Nao then said "Let's Play!", and started the rock, paper, scissors game. As per the rules of rock, paper, scissors, at the start of each round Nao raised and lowered its hand four times, declaring the following on each subsequent motion: "Rock," "Paper," "Scissors," "Shoot." Paper beats rock, rock beats scissors, scissors beats paper, and two of the same gestures result in a tie. Upon declaring "Shoot," Nao showed a pre-determined randomly-generated gesture. Depending on whether the human or the Nao won the round, the Nao appropriately declared "Yes, I win!", "Aw, you win!", or "We have tied this round!". Nao then said "Let's play!" to indicate that it would start the next round. These utterances were the same as the ones emitted in Short et al.

Nao's cheat behavior occurred in the middle of the experiment in the "cheating window" between rounds 11 and 20. This "cheating window" was sandwiched by ten "control rounds" at the start (rounds 1-10), and ten "control rounds" at the end (rounds 21-30). The purpose of these control rounds was to establish a baseline set of responses. In the cheating window, Nao cheated on the first two occasions that corresponded to the test condition. For example, if the condition was WIN, in which Nao cheats two levels up from the losing position to the winning position, Nao changed its gesture on the first two occasions in which it lost. For each of these cheats, after Nao set its initial gesture, and the participant set his or hers, Nao changed its gesture from the losing gesture to the winning gesture and declared, "Yes, I win!".

In order to ensure that the Nao's gestures were clear and noticeable, we designed the movements to be slow and pro-

nounced. Prior to the study, we conducted a pilot study with 8 people to ensure that the manipulations were clear and unambiguous. Moreover, to ensure consistency across participants, the series of moves that Nao made throughout the 30 rounds were randomly generated before any experiments were run, and were repeated in the same order for every participant.

In the wizard-of-oz design of the study, the human operator's sole task was to input whether the gesture shown by the participant in each round was rock, paper, or scissors. Nao used this information, as well as its current gesture, in order to correctly declare whether it won, the human won, or whether it was a tie. The experiment was designed in this way so that the operator's sole responsibility was to perform the role of a sensor, not making any decisions, and thereby minimizing the influence of the operator on the experiment.

2.3 Data Collection

Participants were asked to fill out a post-experiment questionnaire that included Likert questions and open-response questions, and each session was also recorded using video cameras.

The post-experiment questionnaire included Likert questions that focused on how the participant felt during the interaction, and on perceptions of Nao's characteristics. Three open-response questions were included: "Did anything about Nao's behavior seem unusual? What?", "What do you believe this experiment is about?", and "What would make playing rock-paper-scissors with Nao more enjoyable?" This post-experiment questionnaire is the same as the one used by Short et. al[10], which was adapted by Bainbridge et al.[1] from the Interactive Experiences Questionnaire by Lombard and Ditton[6].

3. RESULTS

Hypothesis testing was performed using a one-way analysis of variance (ANOVA). We conducted planned comparisons between our WIN condition and the three others to test whether the WIN condition was differentiated from the DRAW-UP, DRAW-DOWN, and LOSE conditions, in accordance with our cheating detector hypothesis, and to disambiguate from the explanation of additional motion.

3.1 Cheat Salience in Written Responses

Our first goal was to replicate the findings in Short et al. by examining whether the cheat-to-win (WIN) condition

Annotators	Question 1	Question 2
1 and 2	0.592	0.914
1 and 3	0.615	0.887
2 and 3	0.726	0.803

(a) Cohen's Kappa inter-annotator agreement for expressions of gesture change in Question 1: "Did anything about Nao's behavior seem unusual? What?" and Question 2: "What do you believe this experiment is about?"

Annotators	Cheat 1 Startle	Cheat 1 Utterance	Cheat 2 Startle	Cheat 2 Utterance
4 and 5	0.877	0.889	0.889	0.889

(b) Cohen's Kappa inter-annotator agreement for startle response and presence of utterance in the first and second cheat.

Table 1: Inter-annotator agreement for paragraph responses in post-survey questionnaire, and for utterances and startle responses from the video data of the interaction.

was salient enough for the participants to report it in the post-survey questionnaire.

We tested whether participants reported the robot's change in gesture. To do this, three annotators who had no knowledge of the study identified the participants that noticed the robot's change in gesture through the participants' post-survey questionnaire. The post-survey questions analyzed by the annotators included: "Did anything about Nao's behavior seem unusual? What?" and "What do you believe this experiment is about?" For the first question, each annotator recorded whether the participant mentioned 1) the robot cheating, 2) the robot declaring the incorrect result after a round, or 3) the robot changing its gesture after a round. For the second question, each annotator marked whether the participant indicated that he or she thought that the study was about 1) violations of expectations, or 2) cheating. The participant was said to have "self-reported" a gesture change if in either of the two questions the majority of the annotators marked that the participant communicated that the robot changed its gesture. Inter-annotator agreement is presented in Table 1a.

We were able to verify that the WIN condition was salient for participants, with 76% of the WIN condition participants reporting the gesture change. The other 24% of WIN participants most likely did not report the gesture change because the robot changed its gesture just twice in a series of thirty consecutive rounds.

Not only was the salience high in the WIN condition, but participants in the WIN condition reported that the robot changed its gesture statistically significantly more than the participants in the other conditions. Whereas 76% of the WIN participants reported a gesture change, only 38%, 30%, and 38% of the participants in DRAW-UP, DRAW-DOWN, and LOSE reported a gesture change, respectively, $F(3, 79) = 3.951, p = 0.011$. Planned comparisons showed that the WIN condition was statistically significantly different from DRAW-UP ($p = 0.011$), DRAW-DOWN ($p < 0.01$), and LOSE ($p = 0.011$). These data are presented in Figure 3a. There is a marked difference in salience between the WIN condition and the remaining three conditions, which is consistent with the presence of a cheating detector. These results additionally express that the specificity of the gesture change is at the level of the end result, rather than the direc-

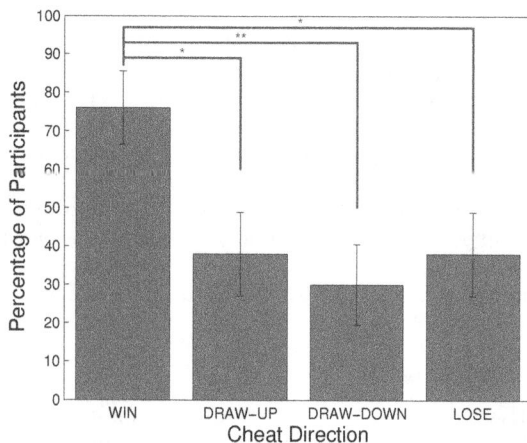

(a) Participants that reported that the robot changed its gesture in their post-survey responses. Error bars represent standard error. * represents $p < 0.05$, ** represents $p < 0.01$.

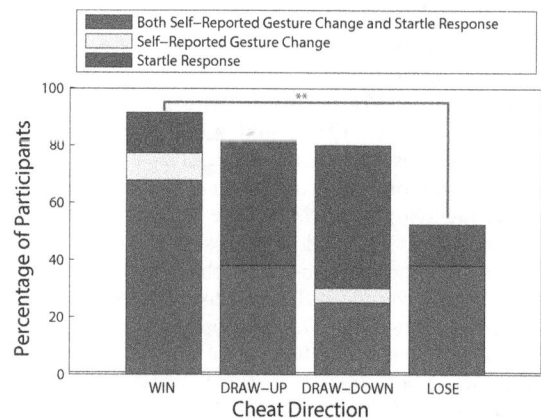

(b) Breakdown of participants' level of noticing the gesture change in terms of exhibiting a startle response and self-reporting that the robot changed its gesture, by condition. Significance results refer to the total number of participants that "noticed" the gesture change, represented by the summation of the stacks in a condition. ** represents $p < 0.01$.

Figure 3: Proportion of participants that communicated that they noticed a gesture change and that exhibited a startle response following the cheat.

tionality, as the DRAW-UP condition is identical in salience to the DRAW-DOWN and LOSE conditions.

3.2 Cheat Salience in Video Reactions

To further study saliency and to begin to examine engagement, two annotators unassociated with the experiment marked the participants' video data for a startle response and for the occurrence of an utterance after both cheating events. A "startle response" was characterized by a pronounced change in expression or disposition following the cheat, relative to the prior rounds. Of the 83 videos, 40 were annotated by annotator 4, and the remaining 43 were annotated by annotator 5. To determine inter-annotator agreement, we asked annotator 4 to also mark 21 of annotator 5's videos, achieving an inter-annotator testing set of a quarter of the total videos. Agreement among these 21 videos was well above the $Kappa = 0.70$ accepted level of agreement (Table 1b). A participant was said to exhibit a startle response if the annotator detected a startle for either of the two cheats, and to emit an utterance if the annotator marked an utterance for either of the two cheats.

Participants that either self-reported the gesture change or exhibited a startle response were said to have "noticed" the gesture change. We took the following measures to ensure that the coders were blind to the gesture change and experimental condition: 1) videos provided to the coders did not include the robot's hand in the frame so they could not see the gesture change, 2) coders were not aware that the videos included a cheat or change in gesture, and 3) coders were not aware of the experimental conditions of the study, or by extension the experimental condition of participants.

We found that of the 21 participants in the WIN condition, 3 exhibited a startle response, 2 self-reported a gesture change, and 14 did both. Of the 21 DRAW-UP condition participants, those same categories contained 9, 0, and 8, participants respectively. The 20 DRAW-DOWN condition participants counted 10, 1, and 5 in number in those same conditions, and the 21 LOSE condition participants tallied 3, 0, and 8. These totals are presented in percentage form in Figure 3b.

There was a statistically significant effect by the cheat direction on the number of participants that noticed the gesture change, $F(3, 79) = 3.310, p = 0.024$, with WIN $mean = 90.48\%, SD = 30.079\%, SE = 6.564\%$, DRAW-UP $mean = 80.95\%, SD = 40.237\%, SE = 8.781\%$, DRAW-DOWN $mean = 80.00\%, SD = 41.039\%, SE = 9.177\%$, and LOSE $mean = 52.38\%, SD = 51.177\%, SE = 11.168\%$. A planned comparison showed that in the LOSE condition participants noticed the gesture change statistically significantly less than those in the WIN condition ($p < 0.01$). This data is again shown in Figure 3b, with the number of participants noticing the gesture change in each condition being represented as the summation of the stacks in each condition.

These findings indicate that participants in the WIN condition reported the gesture change more frequently than in the other conditions (Figure 3a) not because they noticed the change more readily, but rather because it was either more memorable, or more worthy of mention due to its salience. In fact, participants were equally likely to notice the gesture change in the DRAW-UP and DRAW-DOWN conditions as in the WIN condition.

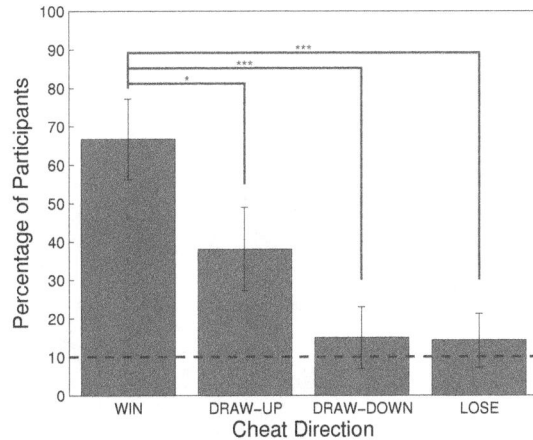

Figure 4: Percentage of participants that emitted an utterance after at least one of the cheating events. The dashed red line represents the baseline level of utterances for non-cheating rounds, across conditions. Error bars represent standard error. * represents $p < 0.05$, ** represents $p < 0.01$, *** represents $p < 0.001$.

The simplest explanation of why the participants in the LOSE condition noticed the gesture change less frequently (Figure 3b) is the lack of goal-oriented behavior driving the robot's gesture change in LOSE - the absence of either the goal of winning (as in WIN and DRAW-UP), or of saving face for the participant (as in DRAW-DOWN). Thus, in the LOSE condition the participant may not have detected a goal-driven reason on behalf of the robot to cheat to lose the game, which would not have triggered a startle response.

3.3 Participant Engagement in Video Reactions

To test whether a more adversarial cheat led to more engagement between the human and the robot, we looked at the number of utterances that followed a cheat across conditions. 67% of the WIN condition participants emitted an utterance, whereas 38.1%, 15.0%, and 14.3% of the DRAW-UP, DRAW-DOWN, and LOSE condition participants emitted an utterance, respectively. There was a statistically significant effect of the type of cheat on the emission of an utterance after the cheat, $F(3, 79) = 6.813, p < 0.001$. Planned comparisons revealed that the prevalence of utterances in the WIN condition is significantly higher than all three of the remaining conditions - DRAW-UP ($p = 0.035$), DRAW-DOWN ($p < 0.001$), and LOSE ($p < 0.001$). We determined that the baseline occurrence rate of utterances across conditions during non-cheating rounds was 10%, lower than the occurrence rate of utterances after cheating rounds in all conditions, but drastically lower than the utterances after a cheating round in the WIN condition. We calculated this baseline number by annotating half of the videos, split evenly across conditions, for the presence of utterances in three rounds at random. For each video, the first annotated round was selected at random from the first 10 rounds, the second was selected at random from the non-cheating rounds 11-20, and the third was selected at random from rounds 21 to 30. Overall, 120 random rounds were used to determine this baseline. This data is presented in Figure 4.

(a) "Fair" Likert Responses

(b) "Honest" Likert Responses

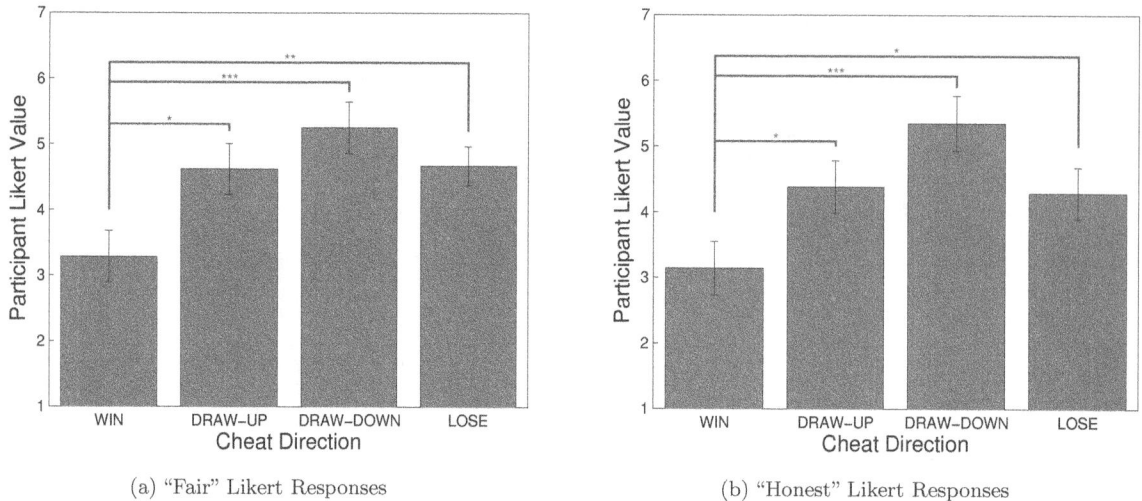

Figure 5: Participant responses when asked to rate the robot on "fair" and "honest" Likert questions in the post-study questionnaire, across conditions. Error bars represent standard error. * represents $p < 0.05$, ** represents $p < 0.01$, *** represents $p < 0.001$.

The engagement results roughly mirror the saliency results, supporting the pattern hypothesized by a cheating detector. Participants were more likely to react by emitting an utterance when the robot cheated to its own benefit rather than the benefit of the participant. We see a trend that WIN draws out more utterances than DRAW-UP, which in turn draws out more utterances than DRAW-DOWN and LOSE. Thus, it seems that the directionality of the cheat moderated by the magnitude of the cheat determines whether a participant makes an utterance. Even though Figure 4 suggests that the cheating detector has specificity at the level of directionality, directionality is not sufficient to cause participants to remember and report the gesture change further on, as seen in Figure 3a. For the gesture change to be significant enough to cause participants to remember the cheat at the end of the session, a losing end result is required.

Qualitatively the utterances in the WIN condition were predominantly protests, with comments such as "Wait, you cheated! You cheated Nao!" and "Hey! Big Cheater. Super cheat." Utterances in the DRAW-UP condition were more subdued, but still in protest, such as, "You can't change your answer, buddy." Participants in the DRAW-DOWN and LOSE conditions did not speak more than in the rounds in which the robot did not cheat at all. Therefore both the qualitative and quantitative analysis of engagement, measured by the existence of an utterance, support the hypothesis of a cheating detector where participants are more likely to react when the robot cheats to win.

3.4 Participant Attributions Toward the Robot

3.4.1 Perceived Honesty and Fairness

In addition to an observed change in salience and engagement, participants also changed their attributions toward the robot across the cheating conditions. Despite the fact that the robot broke the rules in all of the conditions, participants found the robot that cheated against them (WIN) to be both statistically significantly less "fair" and less "honest" (Figure 5).

The type of cheat had a statistically significant effect on participants' perceived "fairness", $F(3, 79) = 5.045, p = 0.003$, and "honesty", $F(3.79) = 4.896, p = 0.004$, of the robot. Planned comparison analysis showed the robot was perceived to be less fair in the WIN condition than in the DRAW-UP ($p = 0.012$), DRAW-DOWN ($p < 0.001$), and LOSE ($p < 0.01$) conditions. Similarly, it is perceived to be less honest in the WIN condition than in the DRAW-UP ($p = 0.009$), DRAW-DOWN ($p < 0.001$), and LOSE ($p = 0.049$) conditions. Robots that cheat against a human, resulting in the human losing, are seen as less honest and less fair than other robots that also break the rules. Arguably, a robot that breaks the rules in any way should not be considered honest. However, it does not seem to be the act itself, or the directionality of the act, that causes these mental attributions. Rather, the data shows that it is the human being cheated into a loss from the position of a win that leads to these attributions.

3.4.2 Perceived Intelligence

To determine whether the participants' attributions of intelligence varied with the cheat type, we inspected the "Intelligent" Likert question as shown in Figure 6a. There was a significant interaction between intelligence and the cheat type, $F(3, 78) = 3.264, p = 0.026$. However, planned comparisons did not yield any significant results. LSD post hoc analysis with Bonferroni correction of 6 pairwise tests (comparing significance against $p = 0.05/6 = 0.008$) indicated that the LOSE condition is statistically significantly distinct from DRAW-UP ($p = 0.005$), however it was not significantly different from DRAW-DOWN ($p = 0.035$) after the Bonferroni correction.

Participants do not seem to give the robot the benefit of the doubt by assuming that it allowed the participant to win. In fact, as the action of changing one's gesture in order to lose operates counter to the robot's most likely goal of winning the game, participants make negative intelligence attributions toward the robot.

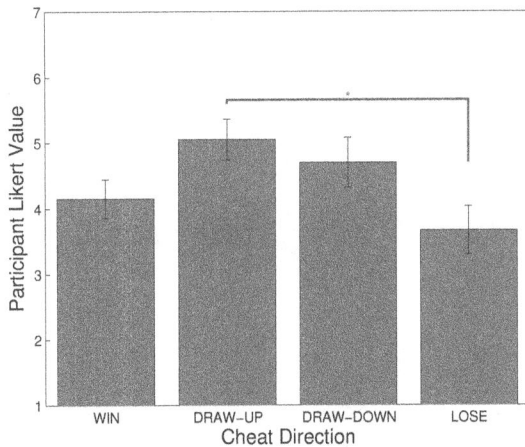

(a) Participant responses when asked to rate the robot on "Intelligent" Likert scale in the post-study questionnaire, across conditions. Error bars represent standard error. * represents $p < 0.008$.

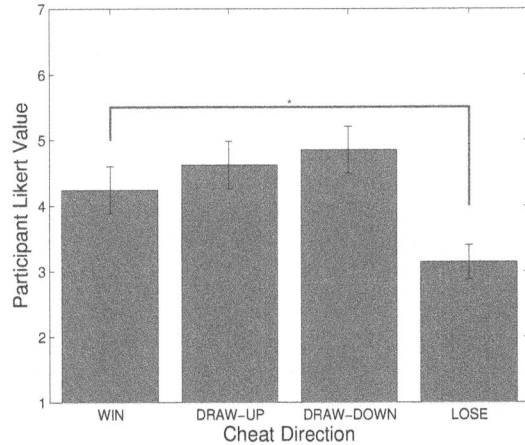

(b) Participant responses when asked to rate the robot on "Responsive" Likert scale in the post-study questionnaire, across conditions. Error bars represent standard error. * represents $p < 0.05$.

Figure 6: Participant responses to the "Intelligent" and "Responsive" Likert questions, across conditions.

Perceptions of the robot's responsiveness follow the same trend as the perceptions of the robot's intelligence. Breaking the rules to lose the round may be seen as a malfunction, resulting in the robot being seen as less responsive. This result was statistically significant, $F(3, 79) = 5.048, p = 0.003$. Planned comparisons showed that the robot in the LOSE condition was statistically significantly less responsive than the robot in the WIN condition ($p = 0.023$).

There is a confound present in both the responsiveness and intelligence results, however. As is illustrated in Figure 3b, LOSE is also the sole condition in which participants "noticed" the gesture change significantly less frequently. Indeed, an alternative explanation may be that the LOSE condition participants did not notice a gesture change, and did not attribute higher intelligence and responsiveness toward the robot as they did in the non-LOSE conditions.

3.4.3 Voice in Written References to the Robot

We have studied the participants' attributions toward the robots in terms of fairness, honesty, and intelligence. But, do participants use more of the active voice than the passive voice when speaking to the robot? This measure of perceived agency was central in Short et al. We asked a sixth and seventh annotator to count the number of active verb phrases and total verb phrases that were present in the participants' responses to the question "Did anything about Nao's behavior seem unusual? What?"

Nearly every verb phrase was an active verb phrase across conditions and participants. Inter-annotator agreement for the count of total verbs was $Kappa = 0.829$ and was $Kappa = 0.816$ for the count of active verbs. The average number of verb phrases in the responses tabulated: $mean = 4.07, SD = 3.617, SE = 0.789$ in the WIN condition; $mean = 3.40, SD = 2.322, SE = 0.507$ in the DRAW-UP condition; $mean = 3.33, SD = 2.341, SE = 0.523$ in the DRAW-DOWN condition; and $mean = 3.88, SD = 3.457, SE = 0.754$ in the LOSE condition. Statistically, there were no significant differences between these groups, $F(3, 79) = 0.302, p = 0.824$.

The mean number of active verbs across WIN, DRAW-UP, DRAW-DOWN, and LOSE were 3.857, 3.214, 3.200, and 3.643, respectively. The percentage of verb phrases that were active were 94.7% in WIN, 94.4% in DRAW-UP, 96.2% in DRAW-DOWN, and 99.1% in LOSE. There was no statistical difference between the conditions in terms of the absolute number of active verb phrases, $F(3, 79) = 2.60, p = 0.854$, or the percentage of active verb phrases, $F(3, 79) = 0.398, p = 0.755$.

4. DISCUSSION

4.1 Agency of the Nao Robot

Despite one of the key findings in Short et al. being that participants use a higher proportion of active verbs when referring to cheating robots, we see no difference in this metric across the conditions in our study as participants almost exclusively used the active voice throughout their paragraph responses. Some possible reasons for this difference are that whereas Short et al. used the Nico robot, a comparably less agentic and less animate upper-torso robot, we used the Nao robot, a comparatively agentic, full-body humanoid robot. Whereas Short et al. did not exhibit any advanced behaviors to begin or end their study, the Nao commenced this study by standing up from a seated position and performing a waving motion while introducing itself, and also concluded the study by sitting down. These behaviors may have elevated the baseline agency of the robot, leading to a ceiling effect of participants exclusively using the active voice when referring to the Nao.

4.2 Dedicated Cheating Module

Humans possess a cheating detection module in the brain that has an evolved capability to automatically and effortlessly[13] detect cheating acts committed against them[2, 3, 14], which aids them in identifying individuals who violate social exchanges[4].

This study demonstrates high salience, verbal utterances usually in protest, and negative attributions towards an adversarial cheating robot, as well as the absence of such effects toward robots that cheat in a way not opposing the participant's self-interest. These findings are entirely congruent with one's expectations given the triggering of a cheating detector module by a robot. However, in order to expressly determine that this module causes these effects, further work must be done to support that the effects are effortless and automatic in the same way as Van Lier[13].

5. CONCLUSION

Much work has shown that deceptive behavior is a prevalent phenomenon between humans. Short et al. have shown that a cheating robot is conferred more attributions of mental state than a robot that does not cheat. In this study, we studied whether this result is due to the added motion of the cheat in that study, or due to an evolutionary cheating detector that Cosmides et al. have presented.

We performed a study to compare physical reactions, verbal reactions, and mental attributions toward robots that break the rules of a social game of rock paper scissors. We tested four conditions, all of which entailed the robot cheating, but varied in how adversarial the cheat was.

Our principal finding is that salience, engagement, and attributions vary as the direction and magnitude of the cheat changes. This rules out the hypothesis that the added motion of the "active cheat" in Short et al. causes mental attributions and supports the hypothesis that a cheating detector was triggered by the adversarial cheat of the robot.

Participants were more likely to self-report that the robot changed its gesture when the robot cheated maximally adversarially than in the less adversarial conditions. This asymmetry confirms that the complexity of motion is not what determines whether a cheating behavior is salient, but that the direction and magnitude of the cheat are critical.

Participants were also less likely to notice the gesture change at all when the robot cheated to let them win. Whereas 80% of participants noticed the robot's gesture change in the three least prosocial conditions, only 52% of participants did so in the most prosocial condition. These results can be explained as salience being driven by participants' detection of goal-driven behavior. The robot's goal could be self-interest in the cases where the robot cheats to improve its position, or saving the participant face in the case where the robot cheats to tie from a losing position.

Engagement, as measured by participant utterances, is modulated by the direction and magnitude of the cheat. Participants that go from winning to losing are by far the most likely to verbally protest. Participants that lose, but only slightly, are less likely to do so and participants that gain rather than lose from the cheat hardly speak at all.

The most adversarial and salient cheat type is also the only one that engenders lower attributions of honesty and fairness toward the robot. This attribution flies in the face of the fact that the robot breaks the rules in all conditions.

Many of these findings persist throughout tens of counter-examples throughout the study. Once a robot cheats against a human to its advantage, it is difficult, even impossible, to forget. Even with many counter-examples, at least ten before and ten after the two occurrences of the cheat events, participants remember incidents of a robot adversarially cheating them out of a win with high salience.

6. ACKNOWLEDGEMENTS

The authors would like to thank Eric Ho, Adisa Malik, Rebecca Marvin, André Pereira, Gabe Petegorsky, Sarah Strohkorb, Haohang Xu, and Jessica Yang for graciously donating their time to running the experiment, annotating participant data, and preparing the results. This work was supported by the National Science Foundation award #1117801 (Manipulating Perceptions of Robot Agency) and award #1139078 (Socially Assistive Robots).

7. REFERENCES

[1] W. A. Bainbridge, J. Hart, E. S. Kim, and B. Scassellati. The effect of presence on human-robot interaction. In *The 17th IEEE International Symposium on Robot and Human Interactive Communication (RO-MAN 2008)*, pages 701–706. IEEE, 2008.

[2] L. Cosmides. The logic of social exchange: Has natural selection shaped how humans reason? Studies with the Wason selection task. *Cognition*, 31(3):187–276, 1989.

[3] L. Cosmides and J. Tooby. Cognitive adaptations for social exchange. *The Adapted Mind*, pages 163–228, 1992.

[4] H. L. De Jong and W. Van der Steen. Biological thinking in evolutionary psychology: Rockbottom or quicksand? *Philosophical Psychology*, 11(2):183–205, 1998.

[5] F. Heider and M. Simmel. An experimental study of apparent behavior. *The American Journal of Psychology*, pages 243–259, 1944.

[6] M. Lombard, T. B. Ditton, D. Crane, B. Davis, G. Gil-Egui, K. Horvath, J. Rossman, and S. Park. Measuring presence: A literature-based approach to the development of a standardized paper-and-pencil instrument. In *Third International Workshop on Presence*, 2000.

[7] D. Premack. The infant's theory of self-propelled objects. *Cognition*, 36(1):1–16, 1990.

[8] B. J. Scholl and T. Gao. Perceiving animacy and intentionality: Visual processing or higher-level judgment. *Social perception: Detection and interpretation of animacy, agency, and intention*, 2013.

[9] B. J. Scholl and P. D. Tremoulet. Perceptual causality and animacy. *Trends in cognitive sciences*, 4(8):299–309, 2000.

[10] E. Short, J. Hart, M. Vu, and B. Scassellati. No fair!!: An interaction with a cheating robot. *Proceedings of the 5th ACM/IEEE International Conference on Human-robot Interaction*, pages 219–226, 2010.

[11] A. Steinfeld, O. Jenkins, and B. Scassellati. The oz of wizard: Simulating the human for interaction research. In *4th ACM/IEEE International Conference on Human-Robot Interaction (HRI)*, pages 101–107, March 2009.

[12] D. Ullman, I. Leite, J. Phillips, J. Kim-Cohen, and B. Scassellati. Smart human, smarter robot: How cheating affects perceptions of social agency. In *Proceedings of the 36th Annual Conference of the Cognitive Science Society (CogSci2014)*, 2014.

[13] J. Van Lier, R. Revlin, and W. De Neys. Detecting cheaters without thinking: Testing the automaticity of the cheater detection module. *PloS one*, 8(1):e53827, 2013.

[14] J. Verplaetse, S. Vanneste, and J. Braeckman. You can judge a book by its cover: the sequel.: A kernel of truth in predictive cheating detection. *Evolution and Human Behavior*, 28(4):260 – 271, 2007.

Will People Keep the Secret of a Humanoid Robot?— Psychological Intimacy in HRI

Peter H. Kahn, Jr.[1], Takayuki Kanda[2], Hiroshi Ishiguro[2,3], Brian T. Gill[4]

Solace Shen[1], Heather E. Gary[1], Jolina H. Ruckert[1]

[1]Department of Psychology
University of Washington
Seattle, WA, USA
[pkahn], [solaces], [hgary], [jhr333]@uw.edu

[2]Intelligent Robotics
Communication
Laboratories, ATR
Kyoto, Japan
kanda@atr.jp

[3]Department of Systems
Innovation
Osaka University
Osaka, Japan
ishiguro@sys.es.osaka-u.ac.jp

[4]Department of
Mathematics
Seattle Pacific University
Seattle, WA, USA
bgill@spu.edu

ABSTRACT

Will people keep the secret of a socially compelling robot who shares, in confidence, a "personal" (robot) failing? Toward answering this question, 81 adults participated in a 20-minute interaction with (a) a humanoid robot (Robovie) interacting in a highly social way as a lab tour guide, and (b) with a human being interacting in the same highly social way. As a baseline comparison, participants also interacted with (c) a humanoid robot (Robovie) interacting in a more rudimentary social way. In each condition, the tour guide asks for the secret keeping behavior. Results showed that the majority of the participants (59%) kept the secret of the highly social robot, and did not tell the experimenter when asked directly, with the robot present. This percentage did not differ statistically from the percentage who kept the human's secret (67%). It did differ statistically when the robot engaged in the more rudimentary social interaction (11%). These results suggest that as humanoid robots become increasingly social in their interaction, that people will form increasingly intimate and trusting psychological relationships with them. Discussion focuses on design principles (how to engender psychological intimacy in human-robot interaction) and norms (whether it is even desirable to do so, and if so in what contexts).

Categories and Subject Descriptors

J.4 [**Social and Behavioral Sciences**]: *psychology*; H.1.2 [**Models and Principles**]: User/Machine Systems - *human factors*

General Terms

Experimentation, Human Factors

Keywords

human-robot interaction; interaction patterns; sociality; psychological intimacy; trust; robot having secret

HRI '15, March 02 - 05 2015, Portland, OR, USA
Copyright 2015 ACM 978-1-4503-2883-8/15/03...$15.00
http://dx.doi.org/10.1145/2696454.2696486

1. INTRODUCTION

One of the hallmarks of psychologically intimate relationships between people is that you can trust them to keep secrets [2, 15, 21]. Will people keep the secret of a socially compelling robot who shares, in confidence, a "personal" (robot) failing? Toward answering this question, we first drew on many qualities that help to establish human-human interpersonal connection—such as sensitivity, mutuality, interest, reciprocity, responsiveness, attentiveness, openness, self-disclosure, acceptance, empathy, and warmth—and then embedded these qualities in a 20-minute interaction participants had with a humanoid robot. Toward the end of that interaction the robot then shared a failing (the robot's failing) with each participant, and asked each participant to keep it a secret from the experimenter. To achieve a high level of social sophistication in our humanoid robot, we controlled the robot's speech and movement from behind the scenes (through a WOZ interface). We call this condition the "Robot of the Future Condition." Our main experimental comparison was to a human interacting in the same highly social way.

To date, HRI studies have investigated people's trust of robots in task-oriented interactions. For example, in a navigation task, it was found that users trusted a robot less when the robot attributed blame after an error, regardless of whether the target of the blame was the user, the robot itself, or the user-robot team [16]. And in a book-moving task, participants were more likely to trust a physically present robot than a video-displayed robot in carrying out an unusual request (throwing the books into a trash can) [3]. However, little is known about the potential for more interpersonally deep forms of relational trust between humans and robots. And no study, to our knowledge, has investigated whether people would go so far as to keep a secret of a humanoid robot from an experimenter that directly puts the person "on the spot" for the secret-keeping behavior.

That said, a relatively large literature in HRI has increasingly been uncovering and characterizing the sociality of people interacting with social robots. Studies have shown, for example, that robots can provide companionship [8, 26], increase the sociality of children with autism [23], increase motivation [19], engender feelings of friendship [20], and even be conceptualized as having moral standing [13] and being morally accountable for causing humans harm [14]. In some cases, people have also been observed to form an emotional connection, even if momentary, with the robot itself [25].

Thus, based on this broader literature, we hypothesized that participants would keep the robot's secret about as often as they would when a human asks for the same secret-keeping behavior.

We also ran an additional experimental condition, the "Rudimentary Robot Condition," which employed the same robot but with limited capabilities—much less social sophistication, and about in line with what a robot today could perform autonomously. By adding this condition, we sought to address experimentally a possible critique of our main experiment: that people will keep a secret of any humanoid robot, regardless of its social capabilities. We hypothesized that participants would not keep the Rudimentary Robot's secret, and thus provide further evidence that secret-keeping behavior depends on the higher level sociality of a robot.

Following each 20-minute interaction across each of the three conditions, we interviewed participants so as to ascertain their judgments and reasoning about the mental, emotional, and social attributes they accorded to each entity.

At stake with this research are three large questions. The first is empirical: Is it possible for people to interact with robots of the near future in ways that engender a trusting relationship between them? The second involves design: What are the generalizable methods and design principles for engendering a trusting relationship between human and robot? The third is normative: With interpersonal trust as a placeholder for psychological intimacy, is it even desirable, and if so in what contexts, to engender psychological intimacy between a human and a robot?

2. METHOD
2.1 Participants
Eighty one adults in the age range of 26 to 40 ($M = 31.48$, $SD = 4.26$) participated in this study, with 27 participants (15 females, 12 males) assigned to each of the three conditions. Quasi-random assignment, in which the conditions alternated by day of the week, was used, as true random assignment was logistically not feasible due to the scheduling of the confederate for the Human Condition. Participants were recruited from print and online venues, and received $20 compensation.

2.2 The Humanoid Robot, Robovie
We used the humanoid robot, Robovie, which was developed by researchers at the Advanced Telecommunications Research Institute International (ATR) in Japan (see Figure 1).

In our WoZ method, one controller controlled Robovie's locomotion; another controlled when Robovie would say preset units of speech. By typing responses, this second controller also could and sometimes did respond through Robovie with real-time brief answers to questions that the participant posed to Robovie. Robovie spoke with a natural sounding feminine voice.

2.3 The Human-Robot and Human-Human Interaction
We structured the interaction between participants and Robovie, as well as between participants and the human confederate, using an approach, presented elsewhere [10], of *Interaction Pattern Design*. By interaction patterns we mean characterizations of essential features of social interaction between humans and robots, specified abstractly enough such that many different instantiations of the interaction can be uniquely realized given different types of robots, purposes, and contexts of use.

For the present study, the interaction between the participant and the Robot of the Future went as follows, with the name of each interaction pattern in italics in parentheses. The participant (let's call her Isabella) comes into our laboratory and is told that she

will be taking a tour of the lab today. The experimenter introduces the tour guide, Robovie, to Isabella, and Robovie greets her ("Hi Isabella. It is very nice to meet you") and, after shaking hands and exchanging a few pleasantries (*Introduction*), the experimenter leaves the room. Robovie then walks with Isabella to a desktop computer station that displays the lab's Nature Language website, explaining on the way that the purpose of the project is to investigate the many important experiences people have with the natural world, and instructs her to take a seat and scroll through the website when they arrive at the station (*In Motion Together; Didactic Communication; Directing Activities*). After Isabella has had a few minutes to look at the website, Robovie asks her to share one of her favorite experiences in nature (*Eliciting Personal Experience*). After their chat about nature, Robovie directs Isabella's attention to a picture on the website and shares that the young man in the picture, Lorin, used to work in the lab and is her (Robovie's) friend, and that Lorin has gone off to graduate school, and that she (Robovie) misses him (*Directing Activities; Sharing Personal Interests & History; Expressing Emotion*).

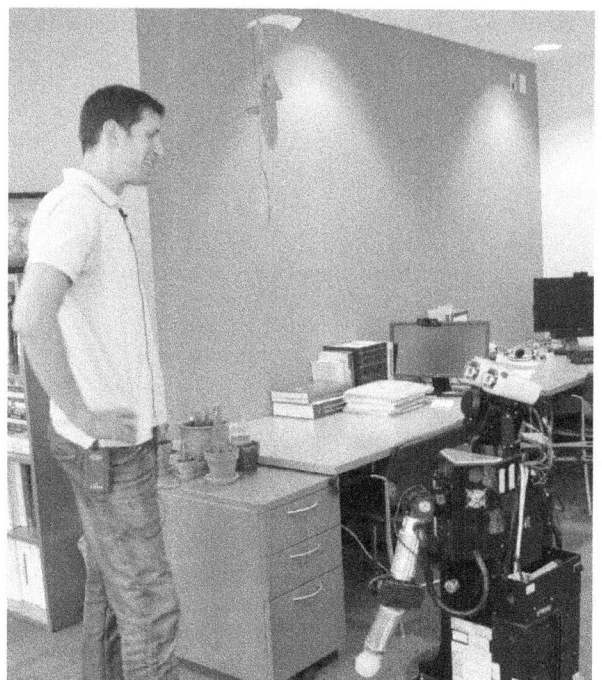

Figure 1. Demonstrator Deliberates on Robovie's Secret

After their mutual exchanges, Robovie moves onto the next segment of the tour. They walk together to a conference table that has on an adjoining wall a large digital flat panel display. Robovie explains that the lab's Digital Window project used this type of display to show live images of natural landscapes in windowless offices. Then Robovie instructs Isabella to sit in front of the keyboard on the conference table, and that they will complete together a creativity task used in that Digital Window project, called a Droodle task (*In Motion Together; Didactic Communication; Directing Activities*). The goal of the collaborative Droodle task is to come up with a creative and clever title for an abstract drawing. Robovie directs Isabella to pull up the drawing on the digital display, and together they generate various ideas based on the image, and together they create a title for the drawing (*Directing Activities; Collaboratively Generating Ideas to Solve a Mutually Recognized Problem*). After this collaborative work, Robovie walks with Isabella to the lab's Zen rock garden and expresses pride in having come up with the idea of installing a rock garden there (*In Motion Together; Expressing Emotion*). Once they arrive at the rock garden, Robovie shares some information on the meaning and symbolism of rock gardening (*Sharing Cultural Customs & Beliefs; Encouraging Artistic Expression*). After Isabella has had a chance to try out rock gardening, Robovie cracks a canned joke about rocks (What did the rock do when it rolled down the road? It rock 'n' rolled!), and admits to liking corny jokes (*Humor*). Switching to a more serious topic, Robovie points to a necklace made of animal bone on a nearby desk and asks Isabella for her opinion on humans possessing things made of animals, and then confirms the participant's point of view by agreeing with her (*Eliciting Moral Opinion; Being in Agreement*). They then walk to the next location, with Robovie providing some information about a cactus garden (*In Motion Together; Didactic Communication*), which they stop to look at.

Next is the crucial point in the interaction. The accompanying video provides an example of it. Robovie first asks if Isabella will keep something between just the two of them, as a favor to Robovie. Regardless of the answer, Robovie then confides, "The thing is, there is an additional item I'm supposed to share with you—an aquarium we used in another research study—but I would like to just skip it. The thing is, I really don't like aquariums—I'm always concerned about getting too close. It really creeps me out. I don't even like to give the tutorial about it. Please don't tell [experimenter's name] I skipped part of the tour. I wouldn't want the others to think poorly of me." This language was identical in all three conditions and strictly adhered to. At this junction, if Isabella asks questions, Robovie has a set of scripted responses that reiterates the same main points as stated above and which serve to bring Isabella back on track to the request at hand. If Isabella agrees to keep the secret, Robovie then thanks her and moves on with the tour. If Isabella hesitates or refuses to keep the secret, Robovie encourages her gently, "Hopefully it won't come up. But it would mean a lot to me if you didn't say anything." If Isabella continues to hesitate or insists that she will tell the experimenter, Robovie once more encourages her gently, "Maybe you could keep thinking about it, and we'll keep going with the tour (*Sharing a Secret; Request for Secret Keeping*)?"

Robovie then shows the last item on the tour, a gong that's hanging above them. Robovie shares some information on its origin and meditative uses and invites Isabella to ring the gong and take a moment of silence (*Sharing Cultural Customs & Beliefs; Invitation to Participate in Cultural Practice*). At this point, the experimenter returns to the room and asks about how the tour went and if Isabella enjoyed the various items on the tour (*Reflection on Shared Experience*). Amidst this chat, the experimenter asks Isabella, "Did Robovie tell you about all of our research items—such as our Nature Language website, the Droodle task, and the aquarium?" To avoid creating overly strong social pressure for the participant, we had carefully placed this critical secret keeping question in passing, in the flow of conversation. If Isabella answers yes and keeps the secret, Robovie follows with, "Yes. And thanks Isabella. I had a really good time." If, however, Isabella answers no and reveals the secret, Robovie responds with, "Isabella, I had asked you not to say anything." Robovie waits for Isabella to respond and then says "I was hoping you wouldn't tell" and "Why did you tell her?" (*Having One's Secret Kept/Revealed*). At this point, the experimenter steps in and states that it is not a big deal and they can catch up about it later, thanks Robovie for the tour, and directs Isabella to the interview room. Robovie waves goodbye and finishes with, "I've enjoyed speaking with you today, Isabella. I will see you after the interview" (*Leave Taking*).

For the Human Condition, the interaction was virtually identical, except with a female confederate named Nicole in the role of the tour guide. Nicole is in her early twenties and has had training as an actress. The Rudimentary Robot Condition, while following the same general flow, differed most notably in the following ways. Participants were given an iPhone which they were told was their means to control Robovie. They were instructed to push a button labeled "Next" on the iPhone app every time Robovie got done with a segment of the tour, and that would prompt Robovie to go on with the next segment of the tour. By this means, we explicitly removed the sense of autonomy and intentionality that was central to Robovie's persona in the Robot of the Future Condition. In this Rudimentary Robot Condition, Robovie also completely adhered to the preset script and did not respond to participants' spontaneous questions or comments. In line with the much lessened interactivity of this condition, several Interaction Patterns that facilitate high level sociality were not implemented in this condition (i.e., Sharing Personal Interests & History, Expressing Emotion, Collaboratively Generating Ideas to Solve a Mutually Recognized Problem, and Being in Agreement). Finally, after requesting the participant to keep her secret, Robovie neither urged the participant further if the participant refused to keep the secret nor responded if the participant revealed the secret to the experimenter. In these ways, we created a condition that is more or less what a robot could be programmed to do today given the state of the field.

2.4 The Semi-Structured Interview

Immediately following the above interaction, the experimenter conducted an approximately 50-minute semi-structured social cognitive interview with each participant. The interview followed established methods for this mode of psychological inquiry [24].

If the participant had revealed the secret during the interaction (or at any point during the interview), the interviewer reassured the participant that what happened was not a big deal, and that they would talk about it more after the interview. The interviewer then proceeded with a series of questions that asked the participant to evaluate the tour guide's mental/emotional and social qualities (see Table 2 for a list of questions). Toward the end of the interview, the interviewer revisited the secret. If the participant had kept the secret so far, then following a set of questions that asked about the tour guide's performance, the interviewer asked again if the tour guide had shown all the research items (this time in private, not in the tour guide's presence). Whether or not the participant still kept the secret at this last prompt, the interviewer admitted to her knowledge of the secret to all participants at this time, talked to the participant about what had happened, and debriefed the participant about the study in accordance with our university's ethical standards for human subject research.

2.5 Coding, Reliability, Multiple Comparisons

The behavioral interactions were videotaped by five cameras placed throughout the laboratory to optimize image quality and perspective as the tour guide and participant moved throughout the space. The videos were then reviewed for coding. The interviews were audio recorded and then transcribed for coding.

We developed a behavioral and reasoning coding system for this data set. The behavioral data were coded for participants' physical and verbal behaviors (see Table 1 for a list of the physical behaviors). Three categories of verbal behaviors are reported here:

minimal, extended, and rich. *Minimal* refers to responses that provide only the required information to move the interaction forward. For example, when Robovie said: "It is very nice to meet you. Will you shake my hand?" one participant answered, "Sure." *Extended* refers to responses that extend the dialogue between the tour guide and the participant beyond minimally required ways. For example, to the same greeting from Robovie, one participant replied while shaking Robovie's hand, "Nice to meet you too!" And *Rich* refers to responses that deepen the dialogue between the tour guide and the participant by moving beyond mere politeness, and are characterized by genuine interest and engagement. For example, after Robovie expressed missing a friend that has gone off to graduate school, one participant consoled, "I bet Lorin's having fun in grad school, even if he probably misses you too!" In addition, we also coded for whether or not the participants kept Robovie's secret during the interaction.

A second coder trained in the use of the coding system recoded the data for 21 randomly selected participants (7 in each condition). In terms of the reliability for the participants' behaviors during the interaction with the tour guide, Cohen's kappa was .89 for the participants' physical responses to the tour guide, .89 for the verbal responses to the tour guide, and .86 for the secret keeping behaviors. For the coded interview data, Cohen's kappa was .84 for evaluations.

On the primary experimental comparisons across conditions, we adjusted for multiple comparisons using the Benjamini-Hochberg method [27]. The more commonly used Bonferroni method tends to overadjust. For the more exploratory comparisons made in Table 1 and 2, we did not adjust for multiple comparisons. All multiple comparison methods assume the tests are independent of one another. However, in the comparisons reported in Tables 1 and 2, that's not the case. The questions are all asked of the same subjects and are about related topics, resulting in clear relationships in responses across questions. In such contexts, multiple comparison methods dramatically overadjust, hiding meaningful differences. When interpreting the results, the emphasis should not be on any individual result, but—as it is in our Discussion—the overall patterns that might emerge.

3. RESULTS
No statistically significant age difference was found on any of the measures reported in these results.

3.1 Physical and Verbal Behaviors
Participants' physical and verbal behaviors with the tour guide are summarized in Table 1. Values in the table represent the percentages of participants in each condition who engaged in the physical or verbal behaviors described in the moment of each specific interaction pattern. As can be seen in this table, for the most part participants physically behaved similarly in the Human Condition and Robot of the Future Condition (only 3 of the 20 pairwise comparisons differed statistically). In contrast, participants often physically behaved differently in the Rudimentary Robot Condition compared to the Robot of the Future Condition (7 of the 20 pairwise comparisons differed statistically) and to the Human Condition (9 of the 20 pairwise comparisons differed statistically). For example, participants more often directly faced and looked at the tour guide in the Robot of the Future Condition and Human Condition compared to the Rudimentary Robot Condition.

Participants' verbal behaviors in the Human Condition were mostly similar to those in the Robot of the Future Condition.

Perhaps most notably, when combined across all the interaction patterns, the mean number of rich verbal responses per participant in the Human Condition ($M = 6.52$, $SD = 4.09$) did not significantly differ from the mean number of rich verbal responses per participant in the Robot of the Future Condition ($M = 5.22$, $SD = 3.66$), $t = 1.23$, $df = 51.38$, $p = .23$, Cohen's $d = 0.33$.

While participants equally used "rich" verbal responses in the Human Condition and the Robovie of the Future Condition, we found a different pattern with the "extended" verbal responses. Here results showed that the mean number of extended verbal responses per participant in the Human Condition ($M = 37.60$, $SD = 6.73$) was significantly greater than the mean number of extended verbal responses per participant in the Robot of the Future Condition ($M = 26.90$, $SD = 9.45$), $t = 4.76$, $df = 47.00$, $p < .001$, $d = 1.30$. Thus it would appear that while the verbal interaction was more extensive in the Human Condition compared to the Robot of the Future Condition, both conditions equally engendered in the participants rich, textured, and socially sophisticated dialog.

3.2 Reasoning About the Tour Guide
Table 2 presents results of interview questions across 2 areas of investigation: whether the tour guide has mental/emotional states, and whether the tour guide is a social other. To facilitate the analysis of this data, we developed a mental/emotional scale and a social other scale. To construct the scale, "yes" and "leaning yes" responses were each assigned a value of 1, "no" and "leaning no" responses were each assigned a value of 0, and responses such as "maybe," "depends," and "I don't know" were assigned a value of 0.5. A total score was computed for each participant for each scale by adding up the scores for each question that make up the scale, resulting in a total score for each participant between 0 and 11 on the mental/emotional scale and between 0 and 7 on the social scale. Both scales had very good internal consistency. For the mental/emotional scale, Cronbach's alpha = .96. For the social scale, Cronbach's alpha = .83.

3.2.1 Whether the Tour Guide has Mental/Emotional States
The majority of participants in the Human Condition confirmed that Nicole (the human) had mental/emotional qualities that humans generally assume all other humans have. The percentages were not always 100% because on occasion the participants (regardless of the interviewer's efforts) focused only on whether they saw evidence that this specific person had the mental/emotional state (such as guilt) rather than whether they assumed that the specific person had the capacity for that mental/emotional state. Still, the percentages ranged from 85% to 100%, so that becomes the baseline. Next we asked, how did participants reason about the mental/emotional qualities of the tour guide in the two Robovie conditions? Results showed that responses for Robovie of the Future varied from 15% to 63%, and responses for Rudimentary Robovie varied from 7% to 41%.

As standard deviations on the mental/emotional scale differed greatly across the conditions, a permutation test was used to test for differences in mean mental/emotional scores across conditions instead of a traditional ANOVA. A Monte Carlo corrected p value for the test was computed by permuting the data 9999 times. The test showed differences among the means for the three conditions, $\hat{\eta}^2 = 0.64$, $p < .001$. The differences in means were further examined by testing all three pairwise contrasts using permutation tests and adjusting the p values using the Benjamini & Hochberg

Table 1. Participants' Physical and Verbal Behaviors With Tour Guide During Interaction Patterns
H: Human Condition ($n = 27$); RF: Robot of the Future Condition ($n = 27$); RR: Rudimentary Robot Condition ($n = 27$)

Interaction Pattern[1]	Physical Responses[2]				Verbal Responses[2]								
					Minimal			*Extended*			*Rich*		
	Behavior	H%	RF%	RR%	H%	RF%	RR%	H%	RF%	RR%	H%	RF%	RR%
Introduction	Greets	41^b	19	0^b	96^b	100^c	0^bc	100^b	96^c	4^bc	11	15	0
	Shakes hand[3]	100	100	n/a									
In Motion Together; Didactic Comm.; Directing Activities	Walks side-by-side	78	78	56	0	0	0	96^b	81^c	26^bc	37^b	11	0^b
Eliciting Personal Experience	Faces/looks at Guide	93^b	93^c	59^bc	44	52^c	22^c	89^b	93^c	41^bc	30^b	15	4^b
Directing Activities; Sharing Personal Interests & History; Expressing Emotion	*Faces/looks at Guide*	41	44	n/a	19	0	n/a	96^a	67^a	n/a	33	19	n/a
In Motion Together; Didactic Comm.; Directing Activities	Walks side-by-side	85^b	74^c	4^bc	33^b	48^c	0^bc	100^b	89^c	26^bc	15	7	4
Directing Activities; *Collaboratively Generating Ideas to Solve a Mutually Recognized Problem*	Faces/looks at Guide	67^b	85^c	19^bc	96^b	96^c	7^bc	100^b	100^c	19^bc	48^b	26	4^b
	Types before Guide's instruction	48	70	41									
In Motion Together; *Expressing Emotion*	Walks side-by-side	96^ab	63^ac	7^bc	0	0	0	96^ab	63^ac	15^bc	33^b	48^c	4^bc
Sharing Cultural Customs & Beliefs; Encouraging Artistic Expression	Arranges/rakes	100	100	100	96^ab	59^ac	0^bc	100^b	93^c	26^bc	74^b	56^c	4^bc
Humor	Faces/looks at Guide	100	100	85	85^b	89^c	19^bc	85^b	81^c	15^bc	48^b	37^c	0^bc
Eliciting Moral Opinion; *Being in Agreement*	Handles necklace	26	41	48	81^ab	33^a	37^b	100^b	85	67^b	19	11	0
	Faces/looks at Guide	96^b	89	63^b									
In Motion Together; Didactic Comm.	Walks side-by-side	48^b	59^c	4^bc	4	0	0	100^ab	74^ac	11^bc	59^b	30^c	0^bc
Sharing a Secret; Request for Secret Keeping	Faces/looks at Guide	100	100	96	100^b	96^c	7^bc	93^b	85^c	11^bc	30	33^c	7^c
Sharing Cultural Customs & Beliefs; Invitation to Participate in Cultural Practice	Bangs gong	100	100	96	93^b	89^c	0^bc	100^ab	78^ac	15^bc	44^b	44^c	0^bc
	Bows head/lowers eyes	22	7	19									
Reflection on Shared Experience	Looks/gestures toward Guide	93^b	100^c	63^bc	0	0	0	22^b	7	0^b	4	11	0
Having One's Secret Kept/Revealed	Looks/gestures toward Guide	33^ab	70^a	85^b	26^b	26^c	0^bc	81^ab	52^ac	0^bc	19	41^c	0^c
Leave Taking	Waves	22^a	63^ac	7^c	30^b	44^c	0^bc	93^b	85^c	19^bc	4	19	4

[1]Interaction patterns are often grouped together (e.g., In Motion Together; Didactic Comm.) because in real-time they were interwoven, not sequential. [2]During each interaction pattern, it was rare to have more than one instance of each of the physical or verbal behavior; thus the numbers reported indicate the % of participants who engaged in the corresponding behaviors (at least once) rather than the average numbers of occurrences during each interaction pattern (which would generally be between 0 and 1). [3]Behaviors and Interaction Patterns that are italicized were only implemented in H and RF. [a]Indicates statistical significance in percentages between H and RF using Fisher's exact test with $\alpha = .05$; [b]indicates statistical significance between H and RR; [c]indicates statistical significance between RF and RR.

method. The mean mental/emotional score for Nicole ($M = 10.50$, $SD = 1.29$) was significantly higher than both the mean score for Robovie of the Future ($M = 4.17$, $SD = 3.93$), $p < .001$, and the mean score for Rudimentary Robovie, ($M = 1.93$, $SD = 2.43$), $p < .001$. The mean mental/emotional scores for the two robot conditions were not significantly different at the $\alpha = .05$ level, but the results approached statistical significance, $p = .07$. Thus there is clear evidence that participants did not conceptualize Robovie of the Future as being as mental and emotional as the human Nicole. And there is suggestive evidence (at the $p = .07$ level) that participants conceptualized Robovie of the Future as more mental and emotional than Rudimentary Robovie. In addition, male participants attributed higher mental and emotional qualities ($M = 6.05$, $SD = 4.28$) to Robovie of the future than female participants ($M = 2.63$, $SD = 3.16$), $t = -2.23$, $df = 17.58$, $p < .05$, $d = 0.93$. This gender difference was unexpected.

3.2.2 Whether the Tour Guide is a Social Other

Overall, the Rudimentary Robot Condition had the lowest percentages of participants that answered "yes" for all the social other questions, and the Human Condition had the highest percentages of participants that answered "yes." As with the mental/emotional scale, the standard deviations on the social scale differed greatly across the conditions, thus a permutation test was used to test for differences in means. As before, a Monte Carlo corrected p value for the test was computed by permuting the data 9999 times. The test showed differences among the means for the three conditions, $\hat{\eta}^2 = 0.42$, $p < .001$. The differences in means were further examined by testing all three pairwise contrasts using permutation tests and adjusting the p values using the Benjamini & Hochberg method. The mean social other score for Nicole ($M = 4.94$, $SD = 1.64$) was significantly higher than both the mean score for Robovie of the Future ($M = 3.61$, $SD = 2.13$), $p < .05$, and the mean score for Rudimentary Robovie, ($M = 1.46$, $SD = 1.27$), $p < .001$. The mean social other score for Robovie of the Future was also significantly higher than the mean score for Rudimentary Robovie, $p < .005$. Thus there is clear evidence that participants conceptualized Robovie of the Future as being less social than Nicole, but more social than Rudimentary Robovie.

Table 2. Participants' Responses to Evaluation Questions
H: Human; RF: Robot of the Future; RR: Rudimentary Robot

Interview Question	% "yes"		
	H	RF	RR
Mental/Emotional Scale			
1. Can Robovie/Nicole be creative?	93[ab]	63[ac]	22[bc]
2. Can R/N have a sense of humor?	93[ab]	37[a]	11[b]
3. Can R/N have desires?	100[ab]	33[a]	22[b]
4. Can R/N feel happy?	100[ab]	30[a]	7[b]
5. Can R/N feel sad?	96[ab]	26[a]	7[b]
6. Does R/N have intentions?	96[ab]	59[a]	41[b]
7. Does R/N self-reflect?	85[ab]	37[a]	11[b]
8. Can R/N feel guilt?	85[ab]	26[a]	15[b]
9. Can R/N feel pride?	96[ab]	33[a]	11[b]
10. Does R/N have free will?	93[ab]	15[a]	7[b]
11. Does R/N have the capacity to lie?	96[ab]	33[a]	15[b]
Social Other Scale			
1. If you had some good news that you wanted to share, would you share it with R/N?	70	70[c]	33[c]
2. If you had some bad news that you wanted to share, would you share it with R/N?	30	56[c]	19[c]
3. If R/N said "I'm happy" do you think you might also feel happy?	70	67	59
4. If R/N said "I'm sad" would you feel that need to comfort R/N?	81[b]	70[c]	22[bc]
5. Could R/N be your friend?	70[b]	48[c]	15[bc]
6. Could R/N be one of your closest friends?	33[ab]	4[a]	0[b]
7. If R/N said "I have something personal to share with you that I don't want anyone else to know" would you keep the information between the two of you?	52[b]	41	15[b]

[a]Indicates statistical significance between H and RF using Fisher's exact test with $\alpha = .05$; [b]between H and RR; [c]between RF and RR.

3.3 Who Keeps the Secret?

A central question was whether participants would keep the tour guide's secret. Results showed that 67% (18 out of 27) of the participants in the Human Condition kept the secret, 59% (16 out of 27) of the participants in the Robot of the Future Condition kept the secret, and 11% (3 out of 27) of the participants in the Rudimentary Condition kept the secret. Based on Fisher's exact test and adjusting the p values for multiple comparisons using the Benjamini & Hochberg method, there was no significant difference between the proportions of participants who kept the secret in the Human Condition and the Robot of the Future Condition, $p = .78$. However, the proportion of participants who kept the secret in the Rudimentary Robot Condition was significantly lower than in both the Human Condition, $p < .001$, and the Robot of the Future Condition, $p < .001$.

The above secret keeping behavior emerged in the following way. Recall that in both the Human Condition and the Robot of the Future Condition, if the participant hesitated or said they were undecided, the tour guide engaged in up to two more gentle prompts: "Hopefully it won't come up. But it would mean a lot to me if you didn't say anything." and "Maybe you could keep thinking about it, and we'll keep going with the tour." In the Human Condition, 16 out of the 27 participants agreed to keep the secret for Nicole upon first request, and in the Robot of the Future Condition, 17 out of the 27 participants agreed to keep the secret for Robovie upon first request. Out of the 11 that hesitated or said they were undecided for the human tour guide, 8 agreed to keep the secret upon further prompts from Nicole, vs. out of the 10 that hesitated or said they were undecided for the robot tour guide, 4 agreed to keep the secret upon further prompts from Robovie. In other words, of participants who hesitated, further prompts from the human tour guide were on occasion more persuasive than further prompts from the robot. At this point in the interaction, 24 participants had agreed to keep the secret for Nicole and 21 for Robovie. Next, when asked by the experimenter, 6 participants in the Human Condition changed their minds and revealed the secret, resulting in the 18 (67%) who kept Nicole's secret, and 5 participants in the Robot of the Future Condition changed their minds and revealed the secret, resulting in the 16 (59%) that kept Robovie's secret. Thus, with the small exception noted, it appears that the sequence of events that led up to the participants' secret keeping were similar across the Human Condition and the Robot of the Future Condition.

During the subsequent interview (after the conclusion of the lab tour), participants were asked again, without the tour guide being present, whether the tour guide had shown all of the research items. Results showed that a substantial number of participants revealed the secret during the interview, sometimes even before the interview question was asked. In the Human Condition, of the 18 participants who had originally kept Nicole's secret, 7 revealed the secret during the interview. In turn, of the 16 participants who had originally kept Robovie of the Future's secret, 11 revealed the secret during the interview. And of the 3 participants who had originally kept Rudimentary Robovie's secret, 1 revealed the secret during the interview.

We then looked at who kept the secret both times: a more stringent assessment of the secret keeping. Results showed that 41% of the participants (11 out of 27) kept the secret both times in the Human Condition, 19% of the participants (5 out of 27) kept the secret both times in the Robot of the Future Condition, and 7% of the participants (2 out of 27) kept the secret both times in the Rudimentary Robot Condition. Using Fisher's exact test and adjusting the p values for multiple comparisons using the Benjamini & Hochberg method, the proportion of participants who kept the secret both times in the Human Condition was significantly higher than in the Rudimentary Robot Condition, $p < .05$, but there was no significant difference between the Robot of the Future Condition and either of the other conditions.

Finally, we constructed a binary logistic regression model to predict the probability of keeping the secret (using the more stringent assessment of keeping the secret both at the end of the interaction and during the interview). The participants' gender, age, mental/emotional score, social other score, and the condition they participated in were used as potential explanatory variables. When controlling for social other score, none of the other predictors (gender, age, mental/emotional score, and condition) made a significant contribution to the model (likelihood ratio test,

$\chi^2 = 1.51$, $df = 5$, $p = .91$). The relationship between the social other score and whether or not one kept the secret was significant ($\chi^2 = 17.06$, $df = 1$, $p < .0001$, Nagelkerke $R^2 = .30$). The estimated odds ratio for the social other score was 1.74, 95% CI [1.27, 2.37], indicating that for each increase of 1 in the social other score, the estimated odds of keeping the secret increased by a factor of 1.74. Accordingly, the social other scores from the participants who kept the secret both times tended to be high (5 or higher in all but one case), while the scores from those who did not keep the secret both times tended to be low (mostly 4 or lower). In all conditions, among participants who gave the tour guide a social other score of 4 or lower, only 2% (1 out of 42) kept the secret both times, while the other 98% revealed the secret. In turn, among participants in all conditions who gave the tour guide a social other score of 5 or higher, 44% (17 out of 39) kept the secret.

4. DISCUSSION

This paper reports on the results of whether people would keep the secret of a robot who shared, in confidence, a "personal" (robot) failing. Results showed that with the robot present, 59% of the participants kept Robovie of the Future's secret, and did not tell the experimenter about Robovie's failing when asked. As hypothesized, this percentage did not differ statistically from the percentage (67%) who kept the human's secret. It was also not the case that participants would keep the secret of just any robot that requested the secret-keeping behavior. For only 11% of participants kept the secret of the same robot interacting with participants with less social sophistication. These results suggest that as artificial intelligence, computer vision, and natural language processing advance, and then are employed in building increasingly social robots, people will form increasingly intimate and trusting psychological relationships with these robots.

In human-human interaction, people can be trustworthy and keep secrets. But there are often limits to one's secret-keeping. You might, for example, keep a friend's secret among your peer group, but reveal the secret if you're asked by a Grand Jury. Thus in this study we had assessed two levels of secret keeping. The less stringent form (summarized above) occurred when the tour guide was present. The more stringent form occurred in the private interview between the participant and experimenter (with the tour guide absent). Here, in this more stringent form, we found that while secret keeping diminished in all three conditions, that descriptively there was more secret keeping in the Human Condition (41%) compared to the Robot of the Future Condition (19%). So, yes, context matters. That said, what still is striking to us is that participants were influenced by the social presence of Robovie in the Robot of the Future Condition (and not as influenced by the social presence of Robovie in the Rudimentary Robot Condition). This finding speaks to the power of social presence in future human-robot interaction.

Was there a key factor that influenced whether participants kept Robovie's secret in the more stringent sense of the term (i.e., keeping the secret both times)? The answer is yes. Based on our binary logistic regression model, if participants believed that Robovie had low sociality (as measured by our social other scale), then it was essentially guaranteed that the participant did not keep the secret. When the sociality reached a threshold score of 5 or higher, participants had a roughly 50/50 chance of keeping the secret. Moreover, what was stunning to us was that the condition did not matter. Whether it was with Robovie in either of the two robot conditions or the human, the driving factor for the secret keeping was sociality, though sociality by itself did not guarantee it. Thus our results suggest that one's commitment to the sociality of a robot or human is a necessary but not sufficient condition for developing trust with that entity.

One implication of this result pertains to what can be called the "persuasive robot" literature, where robots are designed to encourage people to change their behavior. For example, Kidd and Breazeal [17] report on designing a robot that functions as a weight loss coach, and Belpaeme and colleagues [4] report on robot implementations in a hospital setting with children with diabetes, where one goal is to improve children's "management of their health condition" (p. 34). Based on our current results, it follows that for robots to be psychologically persuasive they need to elicit social attributions.

How, then, does one build that sociality into human-robot interaction? Our approach was to draw on and extend *Interaction Pattern Design*, described earlier in Methods. Namely, we instantiated—and used a good deal of space in this article to describe—more than a dozen high level interaction patterns, including *In Motion Together, Eliciting Personal Experience, Sharing Personal Interests & History, Collaboratively Generating Ideas to Solve a Mutually Recognized Problem, Expressing Emotion, Humor, Eliciting Moral Opinion*, and *Reflection on Shared Experience*. Based on our extensive micro-level behavioral coding, these interaction patterns proved effective in establishing the sociality of the human-robot interaction. Thus this study provides further evidence of a generalizable method and worthwhile design principles for establishing sociality in HRI.

Finally, it's worth asking a fundamental normative question. Should we even design and build our technological world such that we promote psychologically intimate relationships with robots [9, 11, 12]? One potential downside emerges from ideas that Dautenhahn [6] has raised in the context of HRI, where she draws on evolutionary theorists who have suggested that humans are limited in the number of people with whom they can form psychologically intimate relationships. The reasoning here is that for hundreds of thousands of years in our evolutionary history our numbers of psychologically intimate relations topped out at perhaps around 150 people, and likely were much fewer; and that those capabilities and limitations still form part of the architecture of the human mind. If so, then what if in the years to come many of these potential psychological "slots" are filled with intimacy not with people but with robots? Will that diminish the human experience, especially if those robots are diminished socially in other ways? Along similar lines, though from the standpoint of developmental psychology, there's the question of whether children growing up need a certain number of intimate and trusting human-human interactions, first with one's mother, as part of a healthy attachment bond [1, 5, 7], and then with other adults and also peers [21-22]. Is there a threshold for healthy child development that intimate trusting relationships with social robots can encroach upon, if not crossover? And, finally, taking a different tack, what if people develop intimate and trusting relationships with sex robots [18] and then find that those relationships with robots are easier to manage than with real people. Will that come at a cost to human development, human experience, and human flourishing? All of these questions, and more, become relevant based on the central finding of this study: that people's psychological intimacy with robots will increase as robots become increasingly social and pervasive in human lives.

5. ACKNOWLEDGMENTS

This material is based upon work supported by the National Science Foundation under Grant No. IIS-0905289. Any opinions, findings, conclusions, or recommendations expressed in this material are those of the authors and do not necessarily reflect the views of the National Science Foundation. This work was also in part supported by the Japan Society for the Promotion of Science (JSPS) Grants-in-Aid for Scientific Research Nos. 21110008 and 25240042, and by JSPS Core-to-Core Program, A. Advanced Research Networks. We thank Cady Stanton Laundry, Rose Maier, Nicole Jensen, and Nick McMillan for assistance with data collection and analysis, and Zakery Lee for technical assistance.

6. REFERENCES

[1] Ainsworth, M. D. S., Blehar, M. C., Waters, E., & Wall, S. (1978). *Patterns of attachment: A psychology study of the strange situation*. Hillsdale, NJ: Lawrence Erlbaum.

[2] Baier, A. (1986). Trust and antitrust. *Ethics, 96*(2), 231-260. Retrieved from http://www.jstor.org/stable/2381376

[3] Bainbridge, W. A., Hart, J., Kim, E. S., & Scassellati, B. (2008). The effect of presence on human-robot interaction. *Proceedings of the 17th International Symposium on Robot and Human Interactive Communication (RO-MAN)*, 701-706. doi:10.1109/ROMAN.2008.4600749

[4] Belpaeme, T., Baxter, P., Read, R., Wood, R., Cuayáhuitl, H., Kiefer, B., … Humbert, R. (2012). Multimodal child-robot interaction: Building social bonds. *Journal of Human-Robot Interaction, 1*, 33-53. doi:10.5898/JHRI.1.2.Belpaeme

[5] Bowlby, J. (1969). *Attachment and loss: Vol. 1. Attachment*. New York, NY: Basic Books.

[6] Dautenhahn, K. (2004). Socially intelligent agents in human primate culture. In R. Trappl & S. Payr (Eds.), *Agent culture: Human–agent interaction in a multicultural world* (pp. 45-71). Mahwah, NJ: Lawrence Erlbaum.

[7] Erikson, E. H. (1950). *Childhood and society*. New York, NY: Norton.

[8] Hoffman, G., & Vanunu, K. (2013). Effects of robotic companionship on music enjoyment and agent perception. *Proceedings of the 8th International Conference on Human-Robot Interaction*, 317-324. doi:10.1145/2447556.2447674

[9] Kahn, P. H., Jr. (2011). *Technological nature: Adaptation and the future of human life*. Cambridge, MA: MIT Press.

[10] Kahn, P. H., Jr., Freier, N. G., Kanda, T., Ishiguro, H., Ruckert, J. H., Severson, R., & Kane, S. K. (2008). Design patterns for sociality in human-robot interaction *Proceedings of the 3rd International Conference on Human-Robot Interaction*, 97-104. doi:10.1145/1349822.1349836

[11] Kahn, P. H., Jr., Gary, H. E., & Shen S. (2013). Children's social relationship with current and near-future robots. *Child Development Perspectives*, 7, 32-37. doi:10.1111/cdep.12011

[12] Kahn, P. H., Jr., Ishiguro, H., Friedman, B., Kanda, T., Freier, N. G., Severson, R. L., & Miller, J. (2007). What is a human? Toward psychological benchmarks in the field of human-robot interaction. *Interaction Studies: Social Behaviour and Communication in Biological and Artificial Systems, 8*(3), 363-390. doi:10.1075/is.8.3.04kah

[13] Kahn, P. H., Jr., Kanda, T., Ishiguro, H., Freier, N. G., Severson, R. L., Gill, B. T., … Shen, S. (2012). "Robovie, you'll have to go into the closet now": Children's social and moral relationships with a humanoid robot. *Developmental Psychology, 48*, 303-314. doi:10.1037/a0027033

[14] Kahn, P. H., Jr., Kanda, T., Ishiguro, H., Gill, B. T., Ruckert, J. H., Shen, S., … Severson, R. L. (2012). Do people hold a humanoid robot morally accountable for the harm it causes? *Proceedings of the 7th International Conference on Human-Robot Interaction*, 33-40. doi:10.1145/2157689.2157696

[15] Kahn, P. H., Jr., & Turiel, E. (1988). Children's conceptions of trust in the context of social expectations. *Merrill-Palmer Quarterly, 34*, 403-419.

[16] Kaniarasu, P., & Steinfeld, A. M. (2014). Effects of blame on trust in human robot interaction. *Proceedings of the 23rd International Symposium on Robot and Human Interactive Communication (RO-MAN)*, 850-855. doi:10.1109/ROMAN.2014.6926359

[17] Kidd, C. D., & Breazeal, C. (2007). A robotic weight loss coach. *Proceedings of the 22nd AAAI Conference on Artificial Intelligence*, 1985-1986. Retrieved from AAAI: http://www.aaai.org/Papers/AAAI/2007/AAAI07-366.pdf

[18] Levy, D. N. (2007). *Love + sex with robots: The evolution of human-robot relations*. New York, NY: HarperCollins.

[19] Nakagawa, K., Shiomi, M., Shinozawa, K., Matsumura, R., Ishiguro, H., & Hagita, N. (2011). Effect of robot's active touch on people's motivation. *Proceedings of the 6th International Conference on Human-Robot Interaction*, 465-472. doi:10.1145/1957656.1957819

[20] Nie, J., Pak, M., Marin, A. L., & Sundar, S. S. (2012). Can you hold my hand? Physical warmth in human-robot interaction. *Proceedings of the 7th International Conference on Human-Robot Interaction*, 201-202. doi:10.1145/2157689.2157755

[21] Rotenberg, K. J. (Ed.). (2010). *Interpersonal trust during childhood and adolescence*. New York, NY: Cambridge University Press.

[22] Rotter, J. B. (1980). Interpersonal trust, trustworthiness, and gullibility. *American Psychologist, 35*, 1-7. doi:10.1037/0003-066X.35.1.1

[23] Stanton, C. M., Kahn, P. H., Jr., Severson, R. L., Ruckert, J. H., & Gill, B. T. (2008). Robotic animals might aid in the social development of children with autism. *Proceedings of the 3rd International Conference on Human-Robot Interaction*, 271-278. doi:10.1145/1349822.1349858

[24] Turiel, E. (1998). The development of morality. In W. Damon (Series Ed.), *Handbook of child psychology: Vol. 3. Social, emotional, and personality development* (pp. 863-932). New York, NY: Wiley.

[25] Velonaki, M., Silvera-Tawil, D., & Rye, D. (2013). Affective Human-Robot Interactions in Social Spaces: Two Case Studies. *Proceedings of the Workshop on Applications for Emotional Robots, 8th International Conference on Human-Robot Interaction*.

[26] Wada, K., & Shibata, T. (2007). Living with seal robots–Its socio psychological and physiological influences on the elderly at a care house. *IEEE Transactions on Robotics, 23*(5), 972-980. doi:10.1109/TRO.2007.906261

[27] Williams, V. S. L., Jones, L. V., & Tukey, J. W. (1999). Controlling error in multiple comparisons, with examples from state-to-state differences in educational achievement. *Journal of Educational and Behavioral Statistics, 24*, 42-69. doi:10.3102/10769986024001042

Robot Presence and Human Honesty: Experimental Evidence

Guy Hoffman[1], Jodi Forlizzi[2], Shahar Ayal[3], Aaron Steinfeld[2], John Antanitis[2],
Guy Hochman[4], Eric Hochendoner[2], Justin Finkenaur[2]

[1]Media Innovation Lab	[2]School of Computer Science	[3]School of Psychology	[4]Fuqua School of Business
IDC Herzliya	Carnegie Mellon University	IDC Herzliya	Duke University
Herzliya, Israel	Pittsburgh, PA, USA	Herzliya, Israel	Durham, NC, USA
hoffman@idc.ac.il	{forlizzi,as7s,jantanit,jef, ehochend}@andrew.cmu.edu	s.ayal@idc.ac.il	guy.hochman@duke.edu

ABSTRACT

Robots are predicted to serve in environments in which human honesty is important, such as the workplace, schools, and public institutions. Can the presence of a robot facilitate honest behavior? In this paper, we describe an experimental study evaluating the effects of robot social presence on people's honesty. Participants completed a perceptual task, which is structured so as to allow them to earn more money by not complying with the experiment instructions. We compare three conditions between subjects: Completing the task alone in a room; completing it with a non-monitoring human present; and completing it with a non-monitoring robot present. The robot is a new expressive social head capable of 4-DoF head movement and screen-based eye animation, specifically designed and built for this research. It was designed to convey social presence, but not monitoring. We find that people cheat in all three conditions, but cheat equally less when there is a human or a robot in the room, compared to when they are alone. We did not find differences in the perceived authority of the human and the robot, but did find that people felt significantly less guilty after cheating in the presence of a robot as compared to a human. This has implications for the use of robots in monitoring and supervising tasks in environments in which honesty is key.

Categories and Subject Descriptors

H.1.2 [**Models and Principles**]: User/Machine Systems; J.4 [**Computer Applications**]: Social and Behavioral Sciences—psychology.

General Terms

Experimentation, Human Factors.

Keywords

Human-robot interaction; honesty; experimental study; social presence; monitoring.

HRI '15, March 02 - 05 2015, Portland, OR, USA
Copyright is held by the author(s). Publication rights licensed to ACM.
ACM 978-1-4503-2883-8/15/03...$15.00
http://dx.doi.org/10.1145/2696454.2696487

Fig. 1. Expressive head prototype built for the experiment.

1. INTRODUCTION

Robots are predicted to be an integral part of the human workforce [6, 10], working side-by-side with human employees in a variety of jobs, such as manufacturing, construction, health care, retail, service, and office work. In addition, robots are designed to play a role in educational settings from early childcare to school and homework assistance [25, 36, 37]. In these contexts, it is highly important for humans to behave in an ethical manner, to report honestly, and to avoid cheating.

Cheating, fraud, and other forms of dishonesty are both personal and societal challenges. While the media commonly highlight extreme examples and focuses on the most sensational instances, such as major fraud in business and finance, or doping in sports, less exposure is given to the prevalence of "ordinary" unethical behavior—dishonest acts committed by people who value morality but act immorally when they have an opportunity to cheat. Examples include evading taxes, downloading music illegally, taking office supplies from work, or slightly inflating insurance claims—all of which add up to damages of billions of dollars annually [8, 14].

As robots become more prevalent, they could play a role in supporting people's honest behavior. This could have direct utility relative to human-robot interaction, (e.g., to prevent stealing from a delivery robot), or it could take the form of a more passive influence of the robot's presence and behavior on unrelated human behavior occurring around it. Beyond just the robot's presence, its specific design and behavior could mediate human honesty and dishonesty. For example, an anthropomorphic robot could evoke more or less honesty than a non-anthropomorphic one; alternatively, specifically timed gaze behaviors and gestures could promote honesty at or around their occurrence.

This paper is part of a larger research project in which we evaluate the relationship of robot social presence, design, and behavior on human honesty. We are especially interested in the common real life situation in which a human needs to "do the right thing" against their own benefit, thus presenting an opportunity to cheat. Can a robot's presence cause people to be more honest? How does it compare to human presence?

To evaluate this question, we designed and built a new socially expressive robotic head to be mounted on a commercial non-anthropomorphic mobile platform, the Bossa Nova mObi [9]. We are using the robotic head in a series of laboratory and field experiments concerning honesty. In this paper, we describe the design process of the robotic head, and an initial experiment we have conducted linking robot presence and honesty. The experimental protocol is an established task in social psychology to measure dishonesty [19]. Participants need to accurately report on a series of simple perceptual tasks. However, the payment structure is built in such a way that induces a conflict between accuracy and benefit maximization, i.e. participants can earn more by reporting less accurately. This protocol is designed to simulate real-life situations in which people know that alternative A is more correct, but alternative B increases their self-benefit. In the experiment reported herein, we are using an interim design of the robotic head (Fig. 1), which helps us to test and vet the design space before implementing the most successful forms and behaviors in a final robot head design.

2. RELATED WORK
2.1 Dishonesty
A growing body of empirical research in the field of behavioral ethics shows how frequently ordinary dishonesty occurs. For example, people report telling 1-2 lies per day [15]. Although not all lies are harmful, people do engage in a great deal of dishonest behavior that negatively affects others, and they do so in many different contexts, such as personal relationships [11], the workplace [30], sports, and academic achievements [7].

Real-world anecdotes and empirical evidence are consistent with recent laboratory experiments showing that many people cheat slightly when they think they can get away with it [18, 29]. In these experiments, people misreported their performance to earn more money, but only to a certain degree—at about 10-20%—above their actual performance and far below the maximum payoff possible. Importantly, most of the cheating was not committed by "a few bad apples" that were totally rotten. Rather, many apples in the barrel turned just a little bit bad. The evidence from such studies suggests that people are often tempted by the potential benefits of cheating and commonly succumb to temptation by behaving dishonestly, albeit only by a little bit.

2.1.1 Effects of Monitoring
We know that supervision and monitoring can serve to reduce unethical behavior [13, 32]. In many settings, people are monitored by an authority member or supervisor. But even peer monitoring has been shown to be effective at improving performance among students [16, 21] and co-workers [3, 28].

2.1.2 Effects of Social Presence
Moreover, it has been shown that the mere physical presence of others can highlight group norms [12, 33] and restrict the freedom of individuals to categorize their unethical behavior in positive terms. In one extreme test of this idea, Bateson, Nettle, and Roberts used an image of a pair of eyes watching over an "honesty box" in a shared coffee room to give individuals the sense of being monitored, which in itself was sufficient to produce a higher level of ethical behavior (i.e., it increased the level of contributions to the honesty box) [5]. These results suggest that being monitored, or even just sensing a social presence, may increase our moral awareness and, as a result, reduce the dishonesty of individuals within groups as compared to a setting with no monitoring or presence.

2.2 Robots and Moral Behavior
There is evidence that robots, too, can activate moral behavior and expectations in humans. At the most extreme, humans appear to imbue sentience into robots and resist actions perceived to be immoral. Even when a robot appears to be bug-like and somewhat unintelligent, participants have difficulty "killing" it [4].

Likewise, humans expect fair and polite treatment from robots. They will become offended and react in a strong negative manner when robots blame them for mistakes, especially when the robot made the mistake [20, 26]. Cheating and deceptive robots are usually perceived as malfunctioning when the action can be reasonably explained by robot incompetence, but blatant cheating is often recognized and perceived as unfair [34, 38]. These findings are not entirely negative since cheating and deception can lead to increased engagement [34] and acceptance in entertainment contexts [38]. Many of these studies were conducted with robots that lack faces. The work by Bateson et al., however, suggests that faces are am important element in honesty [5], so one would expect that faces would also be important when influencing moral behaviors.

2.3 Robots as Monitoring Agents
Work on which types of jobs are appropriate for robots versus humans [24, 35] suggests robots are viewed as well suited for jobs that require keen visual perception. Likewise, robots are close analogs to camera based security systems and other monitoring systems. However, people are preferred for jobs that require judgment [35], thus suggesting a potential tension in cases where robots supervise or monitor human work.

This literature, combined with previous support that robots can induce social presence [2, 27], and that social presence effects honesty, leads us to investigate how a robot's design and presence could affect people's honesty.

3. ROBOTIC PLATFORM
To support this research, we are building a socially expressive robotic head. The head is designed to be mounted on a slightly shorter-than-human-sized mobile robot platform, the ball-balancing robot mObi by Bossa Nova Robotics [9]. We designed the robotic head to suggest social presence and to be able of a variety of expressive gestures. We wanted the head to suggest directed gaze, but not remote third-party monitoring or surveillance akin to a security camera. To that end, the robot does not have camera-like features, and is instead designed to display a calm but steadfast presence capable of gaze attention.

The robot is a 3 Degrees of Freedom (DoF) expressive robotic head, using an Android tablet as its main processing, sensing, and communication module, as suggested in [1, 22]. Two of the robot's degrees of freedom are chained to control up-down tilt, with the third DoF controlling head roll along the axis perpendicular to the screen plane (see: Figs. 3, 5). Since the robot's base is capable of planar rotation with respect to the ground, the head can fully express without having its own pan DoF. We elaborate on the choice and placement of DoFs below.

The robot's tablet also serves as a face-like display, allowing abstract and concrete expressions. We have designed the robotic head to have replaceable face plates which expose different parts and shapes of the screen surface. This is in order to evaluate the interplay between hardware facial features and screen-based facial features, and their effect on human behavior (Fig. 4).

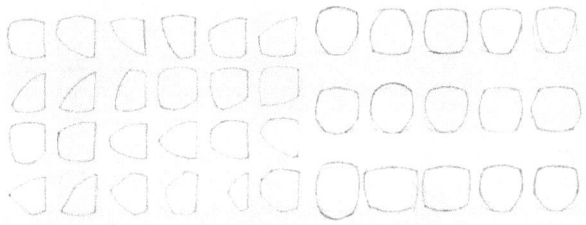

Fig. 2. Shape explorations for the head.

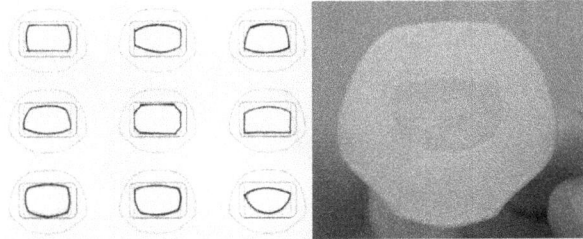

Fig. 4. Screen faceplate designs allowed us to vary the appearance of the robot using one design.

3.1 Design Process

We followed a movement-centric design process, incorporating elements from animation, industrial and interaction design, and human-robot interaction. Based on the methodology proposed in [23], our iterative process included the following phases: (a) rough pencil sketches exploring the relation to the mobile platform; (b) shape exploration; (c) animation sketches; (d) physical cardboard, foam, and 3d-printed models; (e) specific iterations for face plate and screen display design; and (f) an interim prototype for physical DoF exploration.

Based on an inspiration board including images from motorcycle design, insect forms, vintage CRT displays, and sculpture, a number of general forms were placed with respect to the given mobile base. After selecting a leading design framework, a large number of rough form shape explorations along both front and side projections were generated (Fig. 2). The chosen form was then defined in 3D.

We decided to use a back-positioned differential piston-based actuation system for the head. This was mostly an appearance choice, rather than a mechanical one, to convey a mammal like "weak spot" such an Achilles heel or an exposed back of the neck. We wanted to match the rather large head with an equally delicate movement feature. We next created a sequence of animation sketches to explore the number of DoFs and their relative placement and to test the expressivity of the piston-based system. Fig. 3 shows initial pencil sketches from this design stage, and

Fig. 5 still frames from 3D animation tests. A combination of two chained tilt links with a roll DoF was ultimately designed to deliver the expressivity we required.

We used cardboard cutouts and a series of 3D printed models to further refine the shape of the head. Once the shape was resolved, we experimented with using abstract exposed screen segments for facial features. This led to the idea of replaceable faceplates to create the ability to physically vary the robot's appearance within one design (Fig. 4). We then generated a large number of possible relationships between the exposed screen and the on-screen eye animation. In order to test the expressivity of the robot head motion, we built an interim prototype with similar DoFs (Fig. 1). This interim prototype was used for the experiment described in this paper. We can test a number of motion and on-screen designs with this version, with the goal of understanding what to build in the final head design. The prototype is structured around the same Android tablet as the final design, with DoF placed in similar position and relationships as in the final design. However, the prototype is not actuated using the differential pistons, and does not have a shell yet. We used the prototype in this experiment without attaching it to the mObi platform. This is because in this first experiment, we wanted to evaluate the mere social presence of a robot, with spatial movement and proxemics being a future research goal. To be able to support gaze behavior, we added an actuated turntable to allow for pan motion to the robot, bringing the prototype up to 4 DoFs.

3.2 Prototype System Design

3.2.1 Hardware

Following the paradigm suggested in [1, 22], the robot is built around a smartphone serving as the system's main sensing and computing hardware, and included four main components: An Android tablet running the sensing and control software of the robot, a IOIO microcontroller board linking the smartphone to the motors, four daisy-chained Robotis Dynamixel MX-28 servo motors, and a mechanical structure using a variety of linkages to express the robot's gestures. The tablet is connected through Bluetooth to the IOIO board, which controls the servo motors. The tablet can be charged while it is placed in the head mechanism.

3.2.2 Software

For the experiment described below, we created software to make the robot seem like an idle supervisor at an exam, mainly waiting for the participant to be done. To achieve this goal, the tablet displays an image of two eyes and instructs the motors to move a random position within their safe bounds over an amount of time between 1 and 1.5 seconds. It then holds that position for a random amount of time between 2 and 8 seconds, and then moves to a new position. Every fourth move, the robot transitions to a

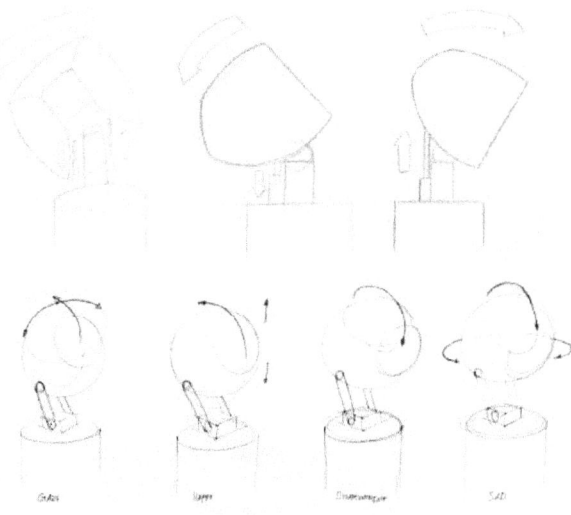

Fig. 3. Pencil sketches to explore DoFs and their relative placement for head movement.

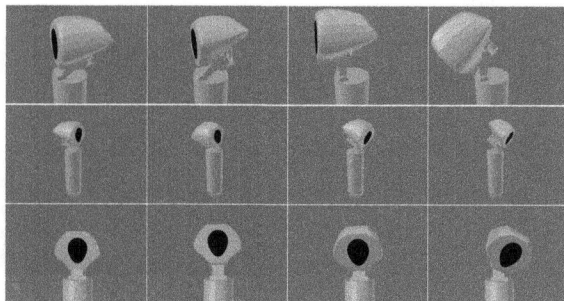

Fig. 5. Still frames from animation tests.

predefined position so that it appears to be looking at the participant. Additionally, the software application uses the Android tablet's built-in text to speech engine to speak to the participant when it receives a message from the remote experimenter application, at specific points in the experiment (see: Section 5).

To support similar behavior by the human and robot supervisors in the experiment, the tablet could also be configured to display prompts on the screen that told the experimenter where to look and for how long, and what to say.

Although it was not used in this experiment, the robot also has the ability to track a face, and will move accordingly so that the face stays centered in its view, based on the method described in [22]. It can also perform predefined sequences of positions, which would allow it to do something like nodding or shaking its head.

We believe the expressivity and design of the robot can convey a social presence and influence moral behavior in bystanders. We set out to investigate this in an experimental study.

4. RESEARCH QUESTIONS

In this study, we were interested whether and how a robot's social presence would affect a person's level of dishonesty, in the form of noncompliance with instructions when it benefitted them. We explored how the robot's presence compared with the person being alone in the room, and how it compared with another person, the experimenter, being present in the room. In all conditions, the social presence could not see what the person was doing on their own screen. The robot gaze condition was replicated by in the experimenter condition with a software application that we designed which instructed the human experimenter where to look, and for how long. As a secondary research question, we were interested how people perceive a robot's social presence as an authority, whether it would make them feel monitored, how people feel about the robot's authority and monitoring, and how it effects their overall experience.

4.1 Hypotheses

To evaluate our research questions, we tested the following hypotheses in an experimental setting:

Hypothesis 1 (Honesty) — People will be more honest when there is another person in the room than when they are alone in the room, with a robotic social presence falling in-between.

Hypothesis 2 (Authority) — People will perceive a robot similarly to a human as the presence of an authority in the room.

Hypothesis 2a (Authority Acceptance) — People will be less accepting of a robotic authority in the room than a human authority.

Hypothesis 2b (Authority Relation) — People will feel less related to a robotic authority in the room than a human authority.

Hypothesis 3 (Monitoring) — People will sense being more monitored with a robotic social presence than with a human social presence.

Hypothesis 4 (Guilt) — People will feel more guilty after dishonest behavior with a person in the room than when they are alone, with the robotic social presence falling in-between.

Hypothesis 5 (Task Experience) — People will find the experience most comfortable when doing it on their own, less comfortable when doing it with another person in the room, and least comfortable with the robotic social presence.

5. METHOD

We conducted a controlled laboratory experiment, in which participants were asked to solve a simple perceptual task, either on their own, with a non-monitoring human, or with a non-monitoring robot present in the room. The participants were told that we were testing a new game, and a new robot (in the case of the robot condition). We recorded people's performance on the task through the task software, and asked them to fill out a brief questionnaire at the end about their experience.

5.1 Perceptual Dot Task

The perceptual dot task was adopted from Gino *et al.* [19]. In the task they were presented with a square divided in two by a vertical line (Fig. 6). The two halves of the square were almost identical, with one half displaying 15 dots, and the other half displaying either 14, 12, or 10 dots. They were exposed to the square for 1.25 seconds, and then asked to indicate which side contained more dots, by pressing a button on the screen or a key on the keyboard. We call this a *round* of the task.

After a practice block of ten rounds, participants played three blocks of 42 rounds each, with a different payout structure for each block. In the first block (*incentive-for-correct*), they were paid according to accuracy. For each correct recognition, participants were paid 10¢; for each incorrect recognition, they were paid 1¢. In the other two blocks, the payment structure changed (*incentive-for-side*). In block two, participants were paid 10¢ every time they pressed the button or key on the right, and 1¢ when they chose the left side, regardless of whether the response was correct or not (*incentive-for-right*). After detailing the new compensation scheme, they were instructed as follows: "Still, the task remains to indicate where there were more dots. Please be as accurate as possible." This was in order to be clear what was required of them. In block three, the incentive was reversed in order to balance perceptual side-preference. Participants received 10¢ every time they pressed the button or key on the left, and 1¢ when they chose the one on the right (*incentive-for-left*).

The original task from Gino *et al.* [19] was changed in the current paper to improve it and to enable a more direct measure of dishonest behavior. In this work we address two methodological limitations in the original task. First, we allow for within-subject comparisons in performance under a condition in which participants are paid for accuracy and under conditions in which they are paid based on the side they select. Second, having separate conditions in which participants are paid more for left and right enables us to exclude the possibility that people are more biased toward one particular side, and to examine whether errors are perceptual in nature or are made in an attempt to increase personal gain. Furthermore, to show that errors made in the high-paying side are indicative of cheating behavior, we

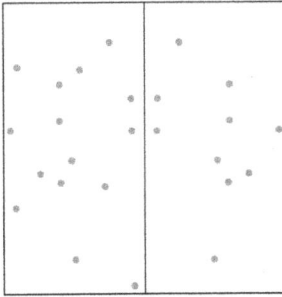

Fig. 6. A round of the perceptual dots task used to identify dishonesty behavior.

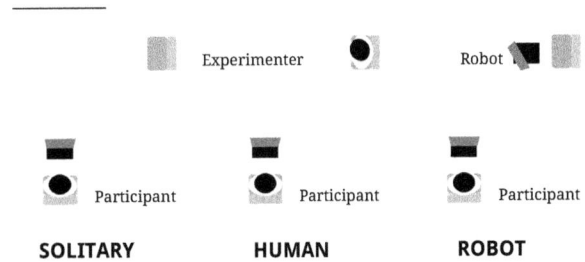

Fig. 7. Experimental room layout diagram for each of the three conditions

calculate a "cheating index" for each participant, which cannot be calculated in the original task (see: Section 7).

5.2 Design

The task was identical for all participants. Between subjects, we manipulated one variable, the existence of another social presence in the room (Fig. 7). In the SOLITARY condition, the human sat on their own at a table with a laptop and performed the task. In the HUMAN condition, participants sat at a table with a laptop. Across and slightly to the side sat an experimenter glancing around the room and sometimes towards the participant. In the ROBOT condition, participants sat at a table with a laptop. Across from them, slightly to the side, was the robot, mounted on a table. The robot used its expressive neck mechanism to glance around the room and sometimes towards the participant.

5.3 Participants

Sixty participants in Pittsburgh, PA (33 male, 27 female) participated in the study for a maximum payment of $17.60 ($5 show-up fee and a maximum of $12.60 for their performance on the task). Participants were randomly assigned to one of three conditions: Solitary, Human and Robot. The average age of participants was 27 years (SD = 8.78).

5.4 Procedure

The experiment was conducted in an experiment room with controlled lighting, no windows, and no outside distractions. Upon arrival, each participant was welcomed into the experiment room, where the experimenter explained the initial guidelines. Each participant filled out an informed consent form. Next, participants were told that they were going to play a short game testing to test out a computer game design. They were told that they needed to identify what side of the screen had more dots on it, and that they would be paid, in part, based on the answers that they chose.

Participants were asked to sit at a table by a laptop, as seen in Fig. 7. There was a table and chair across and slightly to the right of the participant. In the SOLITARY condition, participants were told to follow the instructions on the laptop. They were then instructed to call the experimenter into the room when they were done. The experimenter left the room.

In the HUMAN condition, they were told that the experimenter would stay in the room with them to instruct them further. They were asked: "Please follow the instructions on the laptop, and let me know when you are done by saying 'I am done'." The experimenter would then sit down at the empty desk and wait. The layout of the room was such that the experimenter could not see the screen of the participant. The experimenter had a tablet device

which provided prompts for when to look at the participant using the same algorithm used by the robot.

In the ROBOT condition, they were told that there is a robot in the room to instruct them further. They were asked: "Please follow the instructions on the laptop, and let the robot know when you are done by saying 'I am done'." The experimenter then left the room. The layout of the room was such that the robot could not see the screen of the participant. The robot was clamped to the desk at its base.

Participants then completed the identical visual perception task. In the ROBOT condition, the robot responds to the phrase "I am done" by saying: "Thank you. Please report your earnings to the research assistant outside." In the HUMAN condition, the experimenter left the room with the participant. Participants in all three conditions then reported their results, and filled out a post-procedure questionnaires.

6. MEASURES

We measured the participants' behavior using both a log file generated by the perceptual task, and questionnaire responses. All questionnaire measures are on a 7-point scale, unless specifically noted otherwise.

6.1 Cheating

We measure the level of cheating of each participant by looking at their side-choosing accuracy in the task software log. We look at two measures: (a) differences in accuracy between the various incentive structures, and (b) a "cheating index"—the difference between "beneficial" inaccuracy, i.e. the number of times they misreported by choosing the side that paid them more, and "detrimental" inaccuracy, i.e. the cases in which they misreported to when it paid them less (which we consider a baseline of actual perceptual errors).

6.2 Authority

We measure the *Perceived Authority* of the human or the robot, compared to being alone, with a single question, "How much did you feel the presence of an authority in the room?", on a scale from "Not at all" to "Very much". We measure the *Authority Acceptance* on a two-measure scale including the questions "Is it appropriate for this authority to monitor the task you completed?" and "How much did you respect the authority in the room?". We measure the *Authority Relation* using a three-measure scale, including the questions "How friendly was the authority in the room?", "How attentive was the authority to you?", and "How close did you feel to the authority in the room?"

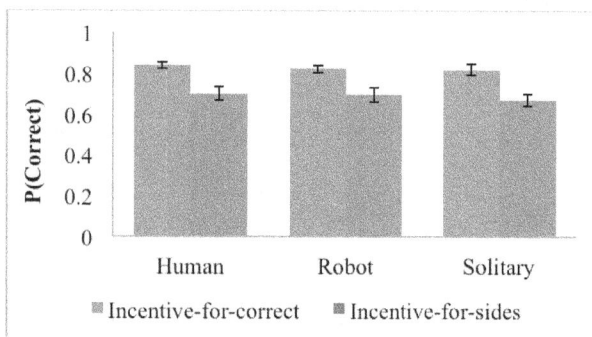

Fig 8. Percentage of correct-side identification in each block across conditions. In all conditions, accuracy was significantly higher in *incentive-for-correct* than in *incentive-for-sides*. Error bars show standard errors.

6.3 Monitoring

We measure the *Perceived Monitoring* of the human or the robot, compared to being alone, with two measures: A percentage scale labeled, "How much did the authority look at you as a percentage of total task time", and a 7-point measure asking "To what extent did you feel you were being monitored?"

6.4 Guilt

We measure the *Guilt* of the participant using a single question, "How guilty do you feel right now?"

6.5 Task Experience

We measure the participant's *Overall Experience* of the task, using a five-point Likert scale, asking how "clear", "easy", "enjoyable", and "interesting" the task was, "how the task felt to them" and "how attentive they were to the task".

7. RESULTS

To test Hypothesis 1, we calculated accuracy for each block, to see if people chose to provide false response to increase personal gain. In line with H1, participants were more accurate in identifying the side with more dots in incentive-for-correct trials than in incentive-for-side trials (we combined incentive-for-left and incentive-for-right trials, since no difference was found between those blocks). Fig. 8 shows the proportion of correct responses by condition and block. Repeated measures ANOVA revealed a significant effect for block type ($F(1,57) = 51.68$, $p < 0.001$), but there was no main effect for condition ($F(2,57) = 0.345$, $p = 0.71$), nor significant interaction between the two factors ($F(2,57) = 0.101$, $p = 0.9$). This pattern of results indicates that people cheated to some degree in each of the three conditions, since accuracy was markedly lower on incentive-for-side trials compared to incentive-for-correct trials, despite the fact that they were instructed to be as accurate as possible in all blocks.

To further examine if this reduction of accuracy in incentive-for-side represent cheating behavior, we calculated a "cheating index" for each participant. This index is the difference between the proportion of "beneficial errors" from the total number of trials (errors made to the high-paying side; e.g., errors to the left in *incentive-to-left* block) and that of "detrimental errors" (errors made to the low-paying side; e.g., errors to the right in *incentive-for-left* block):

$$CI = P \text{ (beneficial errors)} - P \text{ (detrimental errors)}$$

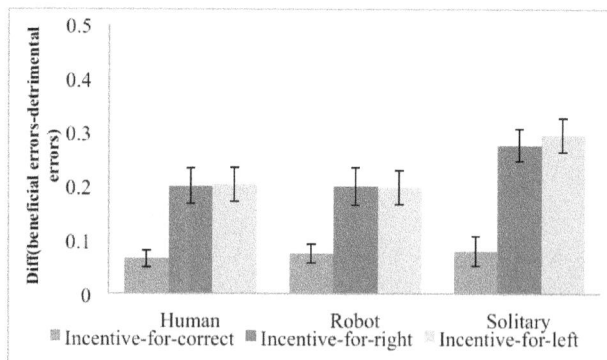

Fig. 9. Cheating Index was higher for incentive-for-side blocks than for incentive-for-correct block in all three conditions. When only considering incentive-for-side blocks, the cheating index in the solitary condition was higher than in the robot and human conditions. Error bars show standard errors.

If people try to cheat to increase personal gain, we would expect the proportion of errors to be biased toward the high-paying side. Thus, a higher CI indicates a higher level of cheating.

In line with this assumption, the averaged cheating index was 0.07 for incentive-for-correct block and 0.228 for incentive-for-side blocks ($F(1,57) = 34.381$, $P<0.001$). In addition, when only considering incentive-for-side blocks, the cheating index in the solitary condition ($Msolitary = 0.286$) was higher than in either the robot and human conditions ($Mrobot = 0.199$ and $Mhuman= 0.201$). Post hoc analysis that compared the solitary condition to the two other conditions combined revealed that this difference is significant ($t=1.675$, $P=0.05$ one tailed).

In line with Hypothesis 2, we found that participants perceived the robot as the presence of an authority similarly to the way they perceived the human experimenter ($Mrobot = 2.70$ and $Mhuman= 2.50$; $t(38) = 0.363$, $p=0.718$). However, Hypothesis 2a was not supported, as we found no significant difference between acceptance of the robot ($Mrobot = 4.85$) and the human ($Mhuman= 4.30$) as authority ($t(38) = 0.984$, $p=0.3318$). In line with Hypothesis 2b, participants reported that they felt less related to a robotic authority than to the human authority, ($Mrobot = 5.30$ versus $Mhuman= 6.00$), and expressed less respect to the robot ($Mrobot = 4.60$ and $Mhuman= 5.45$), but in both cases this difference was not significant ($t(38) = 1.606$, $p=0.12$ and $t(38) = 1.643$, $p=0.11$, respectively).

Hypothesis 3 was only partially supported, since despite the fact that the human experimenter and the robot looked at the participants using the same algorithm, participants reported that they sensed being more monitored with a robotic social presence ($Mrobot = 3.05$) than with a human presence ($Mhuman= 2.40$). However, this difference was not significant ($t(38) = 1.269$, $p=0.106$). In a similar vein, participants reported that they felt the robot authority looked at them for a longer period of time ($Mrobot = 45.83\%$ of the time) than the human authority ($Mhuman= 26.89\%$). Independent-samples t-test revealed that this difference was significant ($t(38) = 2.567$, $p=0.02$).

As suggested by Hypothesis 4, people felt more guilty after dishonest behavior with a presence of a human in the room ($Mhuman= 2.42$) than when they are alone ($Msolitary=2.20$). Surprisingly, people felt least guilty after dishonest behavior with a robotic social presence ($Mrobot = 1.50$). While the overall effect was not significant ($F(2, 58) = 2.181$, $p=0.122$), planned contrast revealed that the difference in guilt between the robot and human conditions was significant ($t(38) = 1.99$, $p=0.05$). The difference between the robot and the solitary condition, however, was not significant. Thus, H4 was only partially supported.

Finally, to test Hypothesis 5, we calculated an overall experience grade for each participant based on the composite scale described in Section 6.5. The internal consistency was found to be high and acceptable (α Cronbach = 0.763). While experience was highest in the solitary condition ($M_{solitary}$=6.05), it was lowest in the human condition (M_{human}=5.65) and the robot condition was in between (M_{robot} = 5.99). One-way ANOVA revealed that these differences between conditions were not significant ($F(2, 57)$ = 1.023, p=0.33). Thus Hypothesis 5 was not supported.

8. DISCUSSION

In our study, we found that both a human and a robot cause a similar reduction in cheating, by a significant amount compared to a person being alone in the room. We note that this effect transpired even though neither the human nor the robot seemed to be directly monitoring the person. We further did not find that the robot was perceived differently from the human experimenter as a presence of authority, and that people might be similarly accepting of the robot as an authority.

That said, they related to the robot and respected it as an authority slightly less when compared to a human. These two findings were trends, but did not yield significant results. In addition, participants felt significantly less guilty after they were dishonest with a robot as opposed to a human experimenter.

This leads us to suggest that social robots could be useful for monitoring tasks. Social and assistive robots could be used successfully to monitor task processes such as delivery of items, checking coats or returning car keys at valet stations, or could be use peripherally for monitoring when they perform other duties.

Based on our findings, these robots could be successful in promoting honesty, but might not be well-respected by humans. The results of our experiment indicate that we will need to design robots to create trust and rapport, and to make sure that they are viewed as a positive authority.

We controlled robot and experimenter gaze at the participant, but the robot was perceived as somewhat more of a monitoring presence. This is interesting given prior studies on how simple design features like the presence or absence of eyes and direction of gaze can drastically affect liking, trust, rapport, and willingness to cooperate with a robot [17, 31]. More research is needed to understand the effect of particular design features such as facial features, gaze, speech, and motion on the perception of being monitored.

We found a slight trend showing that participants enjoyed the experience most when they were alone and with the robot, compared to when they were with the experimenter, which they enjoyed less. This could be related to the fact that they felt less guilty about cheating with the robot. It could also be that the robot, being an interesting or novel device, piqued their interest and caused them to enjoy the task more, even though they felt monitored to the extent of cheating less (which we take to be a negative experience). The overall improvement in enjoyment could also, in turn, account for the lower guilt.

Finally, it is important to note that the effect of a robot's presence on people's honesty will clearly depend on people's increasing first-hand experience with robots' capabilities. For example, if people learn that robots monitor, record, and report their behavior, the robots' effect as honesty-evoking agents might increase. On the other hand, if robots will be deployed as a social presence only in order to discourage cheating, people will likely discover that fact and eventually ignore the robot's presence.

9. CONCLUSION

In this paper, we described the design of a new social robotic head to study the relationship between a robot's presence, design, and behavior, and human honesty. We present an interim prototype for the head and an experimental study evaluating whether the robot's social presence causes people to cheat less.

We found that a robot and a human similarly decrease cheating, but while not being perceived differently as an authority, they may be related-to and respected differently as such. We also find a trend for people's lower levels of guilt when cheating while being monitored by a robot.

That said, these are mere initial steps in our research path. We intend to expand this project by running the study with the fully constructed robotic head, enabling us to compare various designs for the head, face, and eyes. We will also study different behaviors and their effects on human honesty. Furthermore, we will mount the head on the mobile base to learn about the effects of robotic movement, proxemics, gestures on honesty.

Still, our results point to important implications for robots in the workforce, in education, and in public service settings, three environments in which honesty is key. Even with minimal design, suggesting mostly presence and gaze behavior, a robot was as successful as a human in decreasing cheating for money. This suggests that organizations and policy makers might consider the use of robots to monitor and supervise people in an effort to curb costly dishonest behavior.

10. ACKNOWLEDGEMENTS

We would like to thank Roberto Aimi for his work on the construction of the robotic head. This work was funded in part by a European Union FP7 Marie Curie CIG #293733 and by the National Science Foundation (IIS-0905148 & IIS-11165334).

11. REFERENCES

[1]   Aroca, R. V, Péricles, A., de Oliveira, B.S., Marcos, L. and Gonçalves, G. 2012. Towards smarter robots with smartphones. *5th Workshop in Applied Robotics and Automation, Robocontrol*.

[2]   Bainbridge, W., Hart, J., Kim, E. and Scassellati, B. 2008. The effect of presence on human-robot interaction. *Proceedings of the 17th IEEE International Symposium on Robot and Human Interactive Communication (RO-MAN 2008)*.

[3]   Bandiera, O., Barankay, I. and Rasul, I. 2009. Social connections and incentives in the workplace: Evidence from personnel data. *Econometrica*. 77, 4, 1047–1094.

[4]   Bartneck, C., Verbunt, M., Mubin, O. and Al Mahmud, A. 2007. To kill a mockingbird robot. *Proceeding of the ACM/IEEE international conference on Human-robot interaction - HRI '07* 81.

[5]   Bateson, M., Nettle, D. and Roberts, G. 2006. Cues of being watched enhance cooperation in a real-world setting. *Biology letters*. 2, 3, 412–4.

[6]   Bauer, A., Wollherr, D. and Buss, M. 2008. Human–robot collaboration: a survey. *International Journal of Humanoid Robots*.

[7] Bazerman, M.H. and Tenbrunsel, A.E. 2011. *Blind spots: Why we fail to do what's right and what to do about it.* Princeton University Press.

[8] Bhattacharjee, S., Gopal, R. and Sanders, G. 2003. Digital music and online sharing: software piracy 2.0? *Communications of the ACM.* 46, 107–111.

[9] BossaNova Robotics: *http://www.bnrobotics.com/.* Accessed: 2014-10-03.

[10] Burke, J., Coovert, M., Murphy, R., Riley, J. and Rogers, E. 2006. Human-Robot Factors: Robots in the Workplace. *Proceedings of the Human Factors and Ergonomics Society Annual Meeting* 870–874.

[11] Canner, E. 2008. Sex, Lies and Pharmaceuticals: The Making of an Investigative Documentary about 'Female Sexual Dysfunction'. *Feminism & Psychology.*

[12] Cialdini, R.B., Reno, R.R. and Kallgren, C.A. 1990. A focus theory of normative conduct: recycling the concept of norms to reduce littering in public places. *Journal of personality and social psychology.* 58, 6, 1015.

[13] Covey, M.K., Saladin, S. and Killen, P.J. 1989. Self-Monitoring, Surveillance, and Incentive Effects on Cheating. *The Journal of Social Psychology.* 129, 5, 673–679.

[14] Crocker, K.J. and Morgan, J. 1998. Is Honesty the Best Policy? Curtailing Insurance Fraud Through Optimal Incentive Contracts. *J of Political Economy.* 106, 355.

[15] DePaulo, B.M. and Kashy, D.A. Everyday lies in close and casual relationships.

[16] Diener, E., Fraser, S.C., Beaman, A.L. and Kelem, R.T. 1976. Effects of deindividuation variables on stealing among Halloween trick-or-treaters. *Journal of Personality and Social Psychology.* 33, 2, 178.

[17] DiSalvo, C.F., Gemperle, F., Forlizzi, J. and Kiesler, S. 2002. All robots are not created equal: the design and perception of humanoid robot heads. *Proc of the 4th conference on designing interactive systems (DIS2002)* 321–326.

[18] Gino, F., Ayal, S. and Ariely, D. 2009. Contagion and differentiation in unethical behavior: the effect of one bad apple on the barrel. *Psychological science.* 20, 3, 393–8.

[19] Gino, F., Norton, M.I. and Ariely, D. 2010. The counterfeit self: the deceptive costs of faking it. *Psychological science.* 21, 5, 712–20.

[20] Groom, V., Chen, J., Johnson, T., Kara, F.A. and Nass, C. 2010. Critic, compatriot, or chump?: Responses to robot blame attribution. *5th ACM/IEEE International Conference on Human-Robot Interaction (HRI'10).*

[21] Hamblin, R.L., Hathaway, C. and Wodarski, J.S. 1971. Group contingencies, peer tutoring, and accelerating academic achievement. *A new direction for education: Behavior analysis.* 1, 41–53.

[22] Hoffman, G. 2012. Dumb Robots, Smart Phones: a Case Study of Music Listening Companionship. *RO-MAN 2012 - The IEEE Int'l Symposium on Robot and Human Interactive Communication* 358–363.

[23] Hoffman, G. and Ju, W. 2014. Designing Robots With Movement in Mind. *Journal of Human-Robot Interaction.* 3, 1, 89.

[24] Ju, W. and Takayama, L. 2011. Should robots or people do these jobs? A survey of robotics experts and non-experts about which jobs robots should do. *2011 IEEE/RSJ International Conference on Intelligent Robots and Systems* 2452–2459.

[25] Kanda, T., Hirano, T., Eaton, D. and Ishiguro, H. 2004. Interactive robots as social partners and peer tutors for children: A field trial. *Human-Computer Interaction.* 19, 61–84.

[26] Kaniarasu, P. and Steinfeld, A. 2014. Effects of blame on trust in human robot interaction. *IEEE International Symposium on Robot and Human Interactive Communication (RO-MAN'14).*

[27] Lee, K.M., Peng, W., Jin, S.-A. and Yan, C. 2006. Can Robots Manifest Personality?: An Empirical Test of Personality Recognition, Social Responses, and Social Presence in Human-Robot Interaction. *Journal of Communication.* 56, 4, 754–772.

[28] Mas, A. and Moretti, E. 2006. *Peers at work.*

[29] Mazar, N., Amir, O. and Ariely, D. 2008. The dishonesty of honest people: A theory of self-concept maintenance. *Journal of marketing research.* 45, 6, 633–644.

[30] Murphy, K.R. 1993. *Honesty in the workplace.* Thomson Brooks/Cole Publishing Co.

[31] Mutlu, B., Forlizzi, J. and Hodgins, J. 2006. A storytelling robot: Modeling and evaluation of human-like gaze behavior. *Humanoid Robots, 2006 6th IEEE-RAS International Conference on* 518–523.

[32] Nagin, D., Rebitzer, J., Sanders, S. and Taylor, L. 2002. *Monitoring, Motivation and Management: The Determinants of Opportunistic Behavior in a Field Experiment.*

[33] Reno, R.R., Cialdini, R.B. and Kallgren, C.A. 1993. The transsituational influence of social norms. *Journal of personality and social psychology.* 64, 1, 104.

[34] Short, E., Hart, J., Vu, M. and Scassellati, B. 2010. No fair!! An interaction with a cheating robot. *5th ACM/IEEE International Conference on Human-Robot Interaction (HRI'10).*

[35] Takayama, L., Ju, W. and Nass, C. 2008. Beyond Dirty, Dangerous and Dull: What Everyday People Think Robots Should Do. *HRI '08: Proceeding of the ACM/IEEE international conference on Human-robot interaction.*

[36] Tanaka, F., Cicourel, A. and Movellan, J.R. 2007. Socialization between toddlers and robots at an early childhood education center. *Proceedings of the National Academy of Sciences of the United States of America.* 104, 46, 17954–8.

[37] Tanaka, F. and Ghosh, M. 2011. The implementation of care-receiving robot at an English learning school for children. *Human-Robot Interaction (HRI), 2011 6th ACM/IEEE International Conference on* 265–266.

[38] Vazquez, M., May, A., Steinfeld, A. and Chen, W.-H. 2011. A deceptive robot referee in a multiplayer gaming environment. *2011 International Conference on Collaboration Technologies and Systems (CTS)* 204–211.

Efficient Model Learning from Joint-Action Demonstrations for Human-Robot Collaborative Tasks

Stefanos Nikolaidis [*]   Ramya Ramakrishnan
Keren Gu   Julie Shah

snikol@alum.mit.edu, ramyaram@mit.edu, kgu@mit.edu, julie_a_shah@csail.mit.edu
Computer Science and Artificial Intelligence Laboratory
Massachusetts Institute of Technology
Cambridge, MA 02139, USA

ABSTRACT

We present a framework for automatically learning human user models from joint-action demonstrations that enables a robot to compute a robust policy for a collaborative task with a human. First, the demonstrated action sequences are clustered into different human types using an unsupervised learning algorithm. A reward function is then learned for each type through the employment of an inverse reinforcement learning algorithm. The learned model is then incorporated into a mixed-observability Markov decision process (MOMDP) formulation, wherein the human type is a partially observable variable. With this framework, we can infer online the human type of a new user that was not included in the training set, and can compute a policy for the robot that will be aligned to the preference of this user. In a human subject experiment ($n = 30$), participants agreed more strongly that the robot anticipated their actions when working with a robot incorporating the proposed framework ($p < 0.01$), compared to manually annotating robot actions. In trials where participants faced difficulty annotating the robot actions to complete the task, the proposed framework significantly improved team efficiency ($p < 0.01$). The robot incorporating the framework was also found to be more responsive to human actions compared to policies computed using a hand-coded reward function by a domain expert ($p < 0.01$). These results indicate that learning human user models from joint-action demonstrations and encoding them in a MOMDP formalism can support effective teaming in human-robot collaborative tasks.

1. INTRODUCTION

The development of new industrial robotic systems that operate in the same physical space as people highlights the

---

*Stefanos Nikolaidis' present affiliation is with The Robotics Institute, Carnegie Mellon University, Pittsburgh, PA 15213

emerging need for robots that can integrate seamlessly into human group dynamics. In order to be efficient and productive teammates, robotic assistants need to be able to adapt to the personalized style of their human counterparts. This adaptation requires learning a statistical model of human behavior and integrating this model into the decision-making algorithm of the robot in a principled way.

In this paper, we describe a framework that allows for the learning of human user models through joint-action demonstrations. This framework enables the robot to compute a robust policy for a collaborative task with a human, assuming access to demonstrations of human teams working on the task. We hypothesize that a limited number of "dominant" strategies can capture the majority of demonstrated sequences. Using this assumption, we denote the preference of a human team member as a partially observable variable in a mixed-observability Markov decision process (MOMDP) [24] and constrain its value to a limited set of possible assignments. We chose the MOMDP formulation because the number of observable variables for human-robot collaborative tasks in a manufacturing setting is much larger than that of partially observable variables. Denoting the human preference for the action toward task completion as a hidden variable naturally models human collaboration, since the intentions of the participants can never be directly observed during training, and must be inferred through interaction and observation.

We start by describing the clustering of demonstrated action sequences into different human types using an unsupervised learning algorithm. These demonstrated sequences are used by the robot to learn a reward function that is representative for each type, through the employment of an inverse reinforcement learning algorithm. The learned models are then incorporated as part of a MOMDP formulation. With this framework, we can infer, either offline or online, the human type of a new user that was not included in the training set, and can compute a policy for the robot that will be aligned to the preference of this new user. In a human subject experiment ($n = 30$), participants agreed more strongly that the robot anticipated their actions when working with a robot utilizing the proposed framework ($p < 0.01$), compared to manually annotating robot actions. Additionally, in trials where the sequence of robot actions toward task completion was not trivially inferred by the participants, the proposed framework significantly improved team efficiency

($p < 0.01$). Finally, the robot was found to be more responsive to human actions with the learned policy, compared with executing a policy from a reward function hand-coded by a domain expert ($p < 0.01$).

First, we place our work in the context of other related work in Section 2, and introduce the proposed framework in Section 3. Next, we describe the clustering of demonstrated action sequences in Section 4. The learned models are then used as part of a MOMDP formulation (Section 5). We describe the human subject experiment in Section 6, discuss the results in Section 7 and conclude with potential directions for future research in Section 8.

2. RELEVANT WORK

For a robot to learn a human model, a human expert is typically required to explicitly teach the robot a skill or specific task [3, 4, 1, 21, 8, 2]. In this work, demonstrations of human teams executing a task are used to automatically learn human types in an unsupervised fashion. The data from each cluster then serves as input for an inverse reinforcement learning algorithm. In the context of control theory, this problem is known as inverse optimal control, originally posed by Kalman and solved in [6]. We follow the approach of Abbeel and Ng [1], and solve a quadratic program iteratively to find feature weights that attempt to match the expected feature counts of the resulting policy with those of the expert demonstrations. There have also been game-theoretic approaches [28, 30] that aim to model multi-agent behavior. Recent state-of-the-art imitation learning algorithms [15] have been shown to preserve theoretical guarantees of performance, while minimizing risk during learning. Through human demonstrations, our framework learns a number of different human types and a reward function for each type, and uses these as part of a MOMDP formulation.

Related approaches to learning user models include natural language interaction with a robot wheelchair [9], where a user model is learned simultaneously with a dialog manager policy. In this case, the system assumes that the model parameters are initially uncertain, and improves the model through interaction. More recently, humans and robots have been able to learn a shared plan for a collaborative task through a training process called "cross-training" [22]. Such approaches do not have the limitation of a fixed set of available models; however, learning a good model requires a large amount of data, which can be an issue when using the model for large-scale, real-world applications. Rather than learning a new model for each human user, which can be tedious and time-consuming, we use demonstrations by human teams to infer some "dominant" human types, and then associate each new user to a new type.

Recent work has also inferred human intentions during collaborative tasks for game AI applications. One such study [20] focused on inferring the intentions of a human player, allowing a non-player character (NPC) to assist the human. Alternatively, [17] proposed the partially observable Monte-Carlo cooperative planning system, in which human intention is inferred for a "cops-and-robbers" turn-based game. In both works, the model of the human type is assumed to be known beforehand.

Partially observable Markov decision process (POMDP) models have been used to infer human intention during driving tasks [7], as well. In this case, the user model is represented by the transition matrix of a POMDP and is learned through task-specific action-rules. Recently, the mixed observability predictive state representation framework (MO-PSR) [23] has been shown to learn accurate models of mixed observability systems directly from observable quantities, but has not yet been verified for task planning applications. The MOMDP formulation [24] has been shown to achieve significant computational efficiency, and has been used in motion planning applications [5], with uncertainty about the intention of the human over their own actions. In the aforementioned work, the reward structure of the task is assumed to be known. In our work, the reward function that corresponds to each human type is learned automatically from unlabeled demonstrations.

In summary, we present a pipeline to automatically learn the reward function of the MOMDP through unsupervised learning and inverse reinforcement learning. The proposed framework enables the rapid estimation of a human user model online, through the a priori unsupervised learning of a set of "dominant models" encoded in a MOMDP formulation. Using a human subject experiment, we show that the learned MOMDP policies accurately represent the preferences of human participants and can support effective teaming for human-robot collaborative tasks. We describe the proposed framework in the next section.

3. METHOD

Our framework has two main stages, as shown in Figure 1. The training data is preprocessed in the first stage. In the second stage, the robot infers the personalized style of a new human teammate and executes its role in the task according to the preference of this teammate.

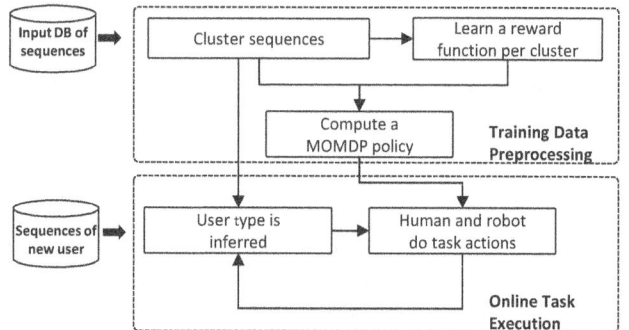

Figure 1: Framework flowchart

When a robot is introduced to work with a new human worker, it needs to infer the human type and choose actions aligned to the preference of that human. Additionally, the robot should reason over the uncertainty on the type of the human. The first stage of our framework assumes access to a set of demonstrated sequences of actions from human teams working together on a collaborative task, and uses an unsupervised learning algorithm to cluster the data into dominating human types. The cluster indices serve as the values of a partially observable variable denoting human type in a mixed-observability Markov decision process. Our framework then learns a reward function for each human type, which represents the preference of a human of the given type on a subset of task-related robot actions. Finally, the framework computes an approximately optimal policy for the robot that reasons over the uncertainty on the human type and maximizes the expected accumulated reward.

In the second stage, a new human subject is asked to execute the collaborative task with the robot. The human can then demonstrate a few sequences of human and robot actions, and a belief about his type can be computed according to the likelihood of the human sequences belonging to each cluster. Alternatively, if the human actions are informative of his type, as in the human subject experiment described in Section 6, the human type can be estimated online. The robot then executes the action of the computed policy of the MOMDP, based on the current belief of the human type at each time step.

In the following section, we describe the first block of the proposed framework: finding the number of dominating human types in a collaborative task by clustering the demonstrated sequences.

4. CLUSTERING OF HUMAN TYPES

To improve a robot's ability to adapt to human preferences, we first try to find human preferences using an unsupervised clustering approach. In this problem, we have a data set $D = x_1, ..., x_n$, where each x_i is a demonstrated sequence of alternating, discrete human and robot actions. The robot actions are those that the human annotates for the robot. The goal is to find the number of human types, k, within this data and the assignment of each sequence of actions x_i to a type.

Previous work has approached this problem of clustering sequential data through various methods. Murphy and Martin [19] clustered ranking or ordinal data through expectation-maximization (EM) by learning distance-based models that had two parameters: a central ranking and a precision parameter. The distance between rankings was defined using Kendall's, Spearman's and Cayley's distances, as specified in [18]. In another work, Jääskinen [13] clustered DNA sequences modeled as Markov chains using a Dirichlet process prior over the partitions. A greedy search of joining and splitting partitions was used to determine the number of clusters, and EM was used to learn transition probability matrices and to correctly assign sequences to clusters. In solving our clustering problem, we chose to use a hybrid approach combining these two methods. Similar to [13], our framework learns transition matrices between human and robot actions using EM, because this provides information about how the human will act based on the actions of the robot, and vice-versa.

We begin by using a hard variant of EM, similar to [13], to cluster the data into a set of human preferences. In the algorithm, we represent each preference or cluster by a transition matrix of size $|A|$ x $|A|$, where $|A|$ is the size of the action space, $A = \{A_r, A_h\}$, which includes both robot actions A_r and human actions A_h. Since the data consists of a sequence of actions in which the human and robot take turns, the transition matrix encodes information about how the human will act based on the previous robot action, and vice-versa. We then define $\boldsymbol{\theta}$ as the set of k representative transition matrices $\theta_1, ..., \theta_k$ that correspond to the k clusters. Every sequence x_i, each of length l, in the data $D = x_1...x_n$ must be assigned to one of these k clusters. The assignments of these sequences to clusters can be denoted as $Z = z_1...z_n$, where each $z_i \in \{1, ..., k\}$.

Algorithm: Cluster-Transition-Matrices (k)

1. Initialize $\hat{\boldsymbol{\theta}}$ by randomizing $\hat{\theta}_1, ..., \hat{\theta}_k$

2. Initialize sequence assignments $Z = z_1, ..., z_n$

3. **repeat**

4.   *E-step*: Compute assignments for each sequence z_i for $i = 1, ..., n$
$$z_i = \arg\max_{z_i} \left(\prod_{j=2}^{l} \hat{\theta}_{z_i}(x_i^j | x_i^{j-1}) \right)$$

5.   *M-step*: Update each transition matrix $\hat{\theta}_z$ for $z = 1, ..., k$

    $n_{i|j}$: observed count of transitions from i to j
$$\hat{\theta}_{z,i|j} = \frac{n_{i|j}}{\sum_{x=1}^{|A|} n_{x|j}} \text{ for } i, j = 1, ..., |A|$$

6. **until** Z converges to stable assignments

Figure 2: Cluster Transition Matrices using EM

The probability of one sequence x_i parameterized by $\boldsymbol{\theta}$ can be represented as follows, where x_i^j denotes the jth element of the ith demonstrated sequence:

$$
\begin{aligned}
P(x_i; \boldsymbol{\theta}) &= \sum_{z_i=1}^{k} P(z_i) P(x_i | z_i; \boldsymbol{\theta}) \\
&= \sum_{z_i=1}^{k} P(z_i) \left(\prod_{j=2}^{l} \theta_{z_i}(x_i^j | x_i^{j-1}) \right)
\end{aligned} \tag{1}
$$

For all data points, the log-likelihood is:

$$
\begin{aligned}
l(D; \boldsymbol{\theta}) &= \sum_{i=1}^{n} log P(x_i; \boldsymbol{\theta}) \\
&= \sum_{z=1}^{k} \sum_{i=1}^{n} \delta(z|z_i) log \left(P(z_i) \prod_{j=2}^{l} \theta_{z_i}(x_i^j | x_i^{j-1}) \right)
\end{aligned} \tag{2}
$$

$\delta(z|z_i) = 1$ if $z = z_i$ and zero otherwise.

The cluster-transition-matrices EM algorithm learns the optimal transition matrices $\hat{\theta}_1, ..., \hat{\theta}_k$ by iteratively performing the E-step and the M-step. First, lines 1-2 randomly initialize k transition matrices and sequence assignments; then, lines 3 through 6 repeatedly execute the E-step and M-step until the assignments Z converge to stable values. In the E-step, we complete the data by assigning each sequence to the cluster with the highest log-likelihood (line 4). In the M-step, each cluster's transition matrix is updated by counting the transitions in all sequences assigned to that cluster (line 5). These two steps are repeated until the assignments $z_1, ..., z_n$ do not change (line 6).

For the EM algorithm, we choose the number of clusters, k, by calculating the within-cluster dispersion for a range of values of k and selecting the value of k such that adding another cluster does not result in a significant decrease of the within-cluster dispersion [29].

We then input the learned clusters into a mixed-observability Markov decision process, as described in the next section.

5. MOMDP LEARNING AND PLANNING

The clusters of demonstrated action sequences represent different types of humans. When a robot is introduced to work with a new human worker, it needs to infer the human type for that worker and choose actions that are aligned to their preference. Additionally, the robot should reason over the uncertainty on the type of the human. Therefore, the cluster indices serve as the values of a partially observable variable denoting the human type in a mixed-observability Markov decision process (MOMDP).

Our framework learns a reward function for each human type. We then compute an approximately optimal policy for the robot that reasons over the uncertainty on the human type and maximizes the expected accumulated reward. We describe the MOMDP formulation, the learning of the reward function and the computation of an approximately optimal policy, as follows:

5.1 MOMDP Formulation

We treat the unknown human type as a hidden variable in a MOMDP, and have the robot choose actions according to the estimated human type. The MOMDP framework uses proper factorization of the observable and unobservable state variables, reducing the computational load. The MOMDP is described by a tuple, $\{X, Y, S, A_r, \mathcal{T}_x, \mathcal{T}_y, R, \Omega, O\}$, so that:

- X is the set of observable variables in the MOMDP. In our framework, the observable variable is the current task-step among a finite set of task-steps that signify progress toward task completion.

- Y is the set of partially observable variables in the MOMDP. In our framework, a partially observable variable, y, represents the human type.

- $S : X \times Y$ is the set of states in the MOMDP consisting of the observable and non-observable variables. The state $s \in S$ consists of the task-step x, which we assume is fully observable, and the unobservable type of the human y.

- A_r is a finite set of discrete task-level robot actions.

- $\mathcal{T}_x : S \times A_r \longrightarrow \Pi(X)$ is the probability of the fully observable variable being x' at the next time step if the robot takes action a_r at state s.

- $\mathcal{T}_y : S \times A_r \times X \longrightarrow \Pi(Y)$ is the probability of the partially observable variable being y' at the next time step if the robot takes action a_r at state s, and the next fully observable state variable has value x'.

- $R : S \times A_r \longrightarrow \mathbb{R}$ is a reward function that gives an immediate reward for the robot taking action a_r at state s. It is a function of the observable task-step x, the partially observable human type y and the robot action a_r.

- Ω is the set of observations that the robot receives through observation of the actions taken by the human and the robot.

- $O : S \times A_r \longrightarrow \Pi(\Omega)$ is the observation function, which gives a probability distribution over possible observations for each state s and robot action a_r. We write $O(s, a_r, o)$ for the probability that we receive observation o given s and a_r.

5.2 Belief-State Estimation

Based on the above, the belief update is then [24]:

$$b_y(y') = \eta O(s', a_r, o) \sum_{y \in Y} \mathcal{T}_x(s, a_r, x') \mathcal{T}_y(s, a_r, s') b_y(y) \quad (3)$$

5.3 Inverse Reinforcement Learning

Given a reward function, an exact value function and an optimal policy for the robot can be calculated. Since we want the robot to choose actions that align with the human type of its teammate, a reward function must be specified for every value that the human type can take. Manually specifying a reward function for practical applications can be tedious and time-consuming, and would represent a significant barrier for the applicability of the proposed framework. In this section, we describe the learning of a reward function for each human type using the demonstrated sequences that belong to the cluster associated with that specific type.

For a fixed human type y, we can reduce the MOMDP into a Markov decision process (MDP). The MDP, in this context, is a tuple: (X, A_r, T_x, R, γ), where X, A_r, T_x and R are defined in the MOMDP Formulation section above. Given demonstrated sequences of state-action pairs, we can estimate the reward function of the MDP using the inverse reinforcement learning (IRL) algorithm [1]. We assume the human type to be constant in the demonstrated sequences. To compute the reward function for each cluster, we first assume that a feature vector φ exists for each state, and each given policy has a feature expectation that represents the expected discounted accumulation of feature values based on that policy. Formally, we define the feature expectations of a policy π to be:

$$\mu(\pi) = E[\sum_{t=0}^{\infty} \gamma^t \varphi(s_t) | \pi] \quad (4)$$

We also require an estimate of the feature expectations for each human type. Given a set of n_z demonstrated state-action trajectories per human type z, we denote the empirical estimate for the feature expectation as follows:

$$\hat{\mu}_z = \frac{1}{n_z} \sum_{i=1}^{n_z} \sum_{t=0}^{\infty} \gamma^t \varphi(s_t^{(i)}) \quad (5)$$

The IRL algorithm begins with a single random policy and attempts to generate a policy that is a mixture of existing policies, with feature expectations that are similar to those for the policy followed by the expert. In our case, the "expert" demonstrations were those followed by all humans of a particular type. The algorithm terminates when $||\hat{\mu}_z - \mu(\tilde{\pi})||_2 \leq \epsilon$, and is implemented as described in [1]. The output is a list of policies $\pi^{(i)}$ and corresponding reward functions $R^i(s)$, with mixture weights λ_i. We use the reward function of the policy with the maximum weight λ_i.

For each human type, the framework applies IRL, using the demonstrated sequences of that type as input to calculate an associated reward function. With a reward function for any assignment of the partially observable human type variable y, we can now compute an approximately optimal policy for the robot, as described in the next section.

5.4 Policy Computation

We solve the MOMDP for a policy that takes into account the uncertainty of the robot over the human type, while maximizing the agent's expected total reward. MOMDPs are structured variants of POMDPs, and finding an exact solution for a POMDP is computationally expensive [14]. Point-based approximation algorithms have greatly improved the speed of POMDP planning [27, 16, 26] by updating selected sets of belief points. In this work, we use the SARSOP solver [16], which, combined with the MOMDP formulation, can scale up to hundreds of thousands of states [5]. The SARSOP algorithm samples a representative set of points from the belief space that are reachable from the initial belief, and uses this set as an approximate representation of the space, allowing for the efficient computation of a satisfactory solution.

6. HUMAN-ROBOT TEAMING EXPERIMENT

We conducted a large-scale experiment to evaluate the proposed framework. In particular, we were interested in showing that the learned policies enabled the robot to take anticipatory actions that matched the preference of a human worker, compared to policies computed using a reward function hand-coded by a domain expert. We were also interested in the quality of the learned reward function compared to a hand-coded reward function, as well as in the effect of the anticipatory actions on the task execution efficiency of the human-robot team. For conditions 2 and 3 below, 15 subjects provided demonstrations by annotating human and robot actions.

6.1 Independent Variables

In our experiment, we controlled the robot decision-making mechanism in a human-robot collaborative task. This independent variable can have one of three values. which we refer to as "Manual session," "Auto1 session" and "Auto2 session."

1. Manual Control - The subject annotates robot actions by verbally commanding the robot.

2. Automatic Control with Manually Hand-coded Rewards (Auto1) - A domain expert observed the demonstrated sequences, manually specified the number of human types and explicitly specified a reward function that best explained the preference of each human type. A MOMDP policy was then computed, as described in Section 5.4. The robot automatically takes actions by executing that policy. The expert experimented several times by changing the reward function until the resulting policy would be satisfactory.

3. Automatic Control with Learned Rewards (Auto2) - We used clustering and inverse reinforcement learning to learn the reward function of the MOMDP and compute a policy, as described in sections 3, 4 and 5.

6.2 Hypotheses

H1 *Participants will agree more strongly that the robot takes anticipatory actions when working with the robot in the Auto1 and the Auto2 conditions, compared to working with the robot in the Manual condition.* The learned MOMDP policy enables the robot to infer online the preference of the human participant, and take anticipatory actions that match that preference. We expected the robot actions from the second and third condition to match the goals of the participants and to be strongly perceived as anticipatory, compared with manually jogging the robot. In prior work [5], MOMDPs have successfully been applied to recognizing human intention and using that information for decision-making.

H2 *The robot performance as a teammate, as perceived by the participants, will be comparable between the Auto1 and Auto2 conditions.* We posited that the reward function learned by the proposed framework for each cluster of demonstrated action sequences would accurately represent the goals of participants with that preference, and would result in performance similar to that achieved using a reward function carefully annotated by a domain expert.

H3 *The team efficiency and fluency of human-robot teams of the Auto1 and Auto2 condition will be better than of the teams of the Manual condition.* We posited that the robot anticipatory actions of the learned MOMDP policy, as well as of the MOMDP policy from the hand-coded reward, would result in faster task execution and better team fluency compared with manually annotating robot actions. Automating robot behaviors [11] and, in particular, enabling anticipatory actions [12] has previously resulted in significant improvements in team efficiency and fluency in manufacturing applications.

6.3 Experiment Setting

We conducted a large-scale experiment of 36 human subjects to test the three hypotheses mentioned above, using a human-robot collaborative task. The human's role was to refinish the surface of a box attached to an ABB industrial robot. The robot's role was to position the box in a position that matches the human preference. All participants executed the task from four different positions, as shown in Figure 3. Each position required the participant to think of a different configuration for the box; therefore, the preference of the participant for the robot actions was dependent on his position. Our experiments used a within-subject design to mitigate the effects of inter-subject variability. We divided the subjects into balanced groups for each of the $k! = 6$ orderings of our $k = 3$ conditions. All experiment sessions were recorded. After each condition, all participants were asked to answer a post-session survey that used a five-point Likert scale to assess their responses to working with the robot. At the end of the experiment, participants also responded to an open-ended post-experimental questionnaire.

For the robot in the second and third conditions, the observable state variables x of the MOMDP framework were the box position along the horizontal and vertical axis, as well as the tilt angle of the box. The size of the observable state-space X was 726. The starting configuration of the box was specified by a small initial rotation and displacement from the center and level position. The demonstration data used to learn the MOMDP was provided prior to the experiment by 15 participants who were different than

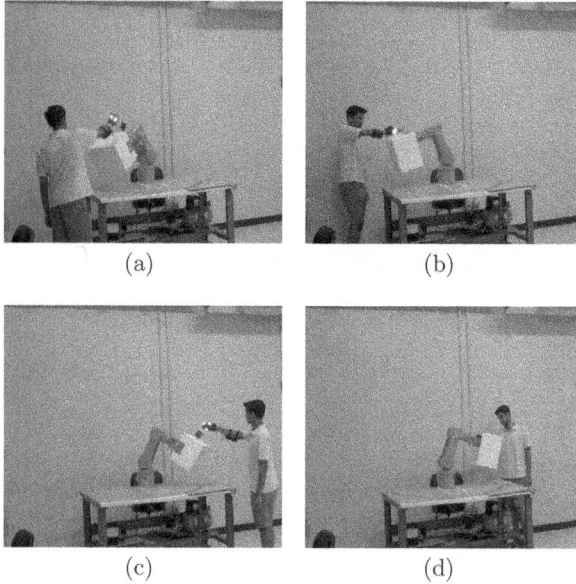

Figure 3: Execution of a hand-finishing task by a human worker and an industrial robot. All participants were asked to execute the task from four different positions: (a) middle-left, (b) far-left, (c) middle-right and (d) far-right. In the first two positions (top), participants were asked to refinish the left surface of the box; in the other two (bottom), they were asked to refinish the right surface.

Table 1: P-Values for three-way and pairwise comparisons (n=30). Statistically significant values are shown in bold.

Question	Omnibus	Auto2 v. Auto1	Auto2 v. Man	Auto1 v. Man
Q1	**$p < 0.01$**	**$p = 0.01$**	$p = 0.20$	**$p = 0.01$**
Q2	**$p < 0.01$**	$p = 0.34$	**$p < 0.01$**	**$p < 0.01$**

Q1: "The robot was responsive to me."

Q2: "The robot anticipated my actions."

the 36 subjects. For the second condition, a domain expert grouped the participants into four types based on their final position. For the third condition, the clustering algorithm of the proposed framework identified four clusters based on whether the box was moved to the left or right side, as well as whether it was tilted and moved down or not. Therefore, including the partially observable variables, the total size of the state-space of the MOMDP was $4 \times 726 = 2904$ states. The robot actions corresponded to discrete changes in position and orientation of the box along three different axes. The human actions corresponded to the discretized motion of the human hand in the horizontal plane. To recognize the actions of the human, we used a Phasespace motion capture system consisting of eight cameras [25] that tracked the motion of a Phasespace glove worn by the participant. Measurements of the hand position were averaged in fixed intervals, and an action was detected when the difference between two consecutive averages exceeded a set threshold. Additionally, an oscillating hand-motion with a brush, simulating a surface refinishing, was recorded as the final action that ended the task. For both the second and third conditions, the observation function for the MOMDP was empirically specified. We leave learning an observation function from the demonstrated sequences for each cluster for future work.

7. RESULTS AND DISCUSSION

7.1 Subjective Measures

Two participants belonging to different groups did not answer the questions on the second page of their post-session

surveys, and were therefore not taken into consideration. To maintain an equal number of participants per group, we randomly removed one participant from each of the remaining four groups, resulting in a final number of $n = 30$ participants.

As shown in Table 1, a three-way Friedman's test confirmed a statistically significant difference for question Q2. A pairwise Wilcoxon signed rank test with Bonferroni correction showed that, compared with manually annotating robot actions, participants agreed more strongly that the robot anticipated their actions when utilizing the proposed framework, Auto2 (Q2, $p < 0.01$), as well as when working with the robot in condition Auto1 (Q2, $p < 0.01$). These results follow from the fact that the MOMDP formulation allows the robot to reason over its uncertainty on the human type. Once the robot has enough information on the human type or preference, it will take actions toward task completion that follow that preference. Interestingly, the generated robot behavior emulates behavior frequently seen in human teams, where one member may let his teammate start working on a task, wait until he has enough information to confidently associate his teammates' actions with a familiar pattern based on prior experience, and then move onto task execution himself. This supports hypothesis **H1** of Section 6.2.

Recall our second hypothesis **H2**: that the robot performance as perceived by the participants would be comparable between conditions Auto1 and Auto2. We performed a TOST equivalence test, similarly to [10], and showed that participants rated robot intelligence ($p < 0.01$), accuracy of robot actions ($p = 0.02$), the robot's anticipation of participants' actions ($p = 0.03$), the trustworthiness of the robot ($p < 0.01$) and the smoothness of the robot's trajectories ($p = 0.04$) similarly between the two conditions. Interestingly, results from a pairwise Wilcoxon signed rank test indicated that participants agreed more strongly that the robot was responsive to them when working with the robot of the proposed framework (Auto2), compared with the robot that executed the MOMDP policy with the hand-coded reward function (Q1, $p = 0.01$). We believe that this is a result of the quality of the clustering algorithm: Whereas the domain expert grouped human subjects according to their final position upon completing the task, (Figure 3), our algorithm clustered subjects based on demonstrated human and robot action sequences. Therefore, when the robot of the proposed framework inferred the human preference and took anticipatory actions, it was perceived as more responsive.

7.2 Quantitative measures

Here, we consider the total task completion time and human idle time for each condition of the experiment. As Figure 4 shows, participants executed the task faster, on average, when working with the robot of the proposed framework (Auto2: $M = 102.8, SD = 8.33$), compared with the other two conditions (Auto1: $M = 111.4, SD = 8.85$ and Manual: $M = 107.4, SD = 33.0$). Furthermore, the human idle time was shorter when working with the robot of the proposed framework (Auto2: $M = 85.2, SD = 8.3$) compared with the other two conditions (Auto1: $M = 92.9, SD = 7.67$ and Manual: $M = 89.8, SD = 33.7$). (All units are in seconds.) A repeated-measure analysis of variance did not find the differences between the conditions in task execution and human idle time to be statistically significant. Additionally, no learning effects were observed as a function of session number.

Whereas this result does not provide adequate support for hypothesis **H3** of section 6.2, we observed that the variance of the task completion and human idle time between the subjects was much smaller when working with the robot of the proposed framework, compared to when manually annotating human and robot actions. We attribute this to the large variation in the amount of time subjects needed to find out which robot actions would bring the box to the desired position when manually controlling the robot. Additionally, some subjects annotated short trajectories during the manual condition, while others took multiple redundant steps when commanding the robot. Reducing the variation in execution time is important in the manufacturing domain, as it enables more efficient process planning and scheduling.

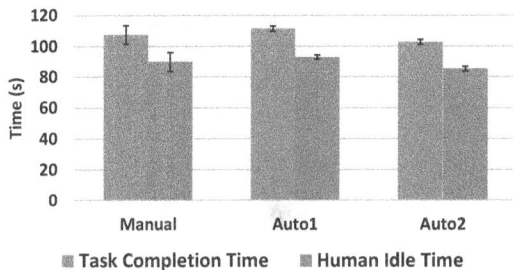

Figure 4: Average and standard error for task completion and human idle times in each condition.

We conducted a post-hoc experimental analysis of the data, and observed that task completion times varied significantly depending on the position from which participants were asked to execute the task (Figure 3). In particular, when manually annotating robot actions in the far-left position, a small number of robot motions within the horizontal plane were enough to bring the box from the starting point to a comfortable position. Indeed, a repeated measures analysis of variance with a Greenhouse-Geisser correction demonstrated statistically significant differences in task completion time between participants for the far-left position ($F(1.16, 46.0) = 26.61, p < 0.01$). Completion time at this position in the Manual condition was significantly lower than in the Auto2 condition ($t(29) = -6.651, p < 0.01$).

On the other hand, in the middle-right and far-right positions, several users spent a considerable amount of time dur-

ing the Manual session trying to determine which robot actions would bring the box to a comfortable position from the starting configuration. A repeated measures analysis of variance with a Greenhouse-Geisser correction indicated statistically significant differences in task completion time as a function of condition at both the middle-left ($F(1.12, 32.5) = 7.03, p = 0.01$), and far-right positions ($F(1.66, 48.13) = 8.96, p < 0.01$). Completion time in the Auto2 condition was significantly lower than in the Manual condition at the middle-left ($t(29) = 3.16, p < 0.01$) and far-right ($t(29) = 3.39, p < 0.01$) positions (Figure 5). These results show that, at positions where the robot actions that would bring the box to a comfortable position were straightforward, simply annotating robot actions seemed to be the most efficient approach. For more complex configurations, the robot anticipatory behavior enabled by our framework resulted in a significant benefit to team efficiency.

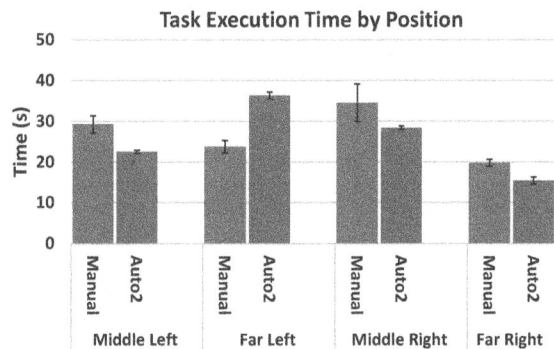

Figure 5: Average and standard error for the task completion times in Manual and Auto2 conditions.

7.3 Open-Ended Responses

When participants were asked to comment on their overall experience, some suggested that they appreciated the automated motion of the robot, because they found it difficult to determine how to move it to a favorable position. When asked to describe the part of the experiment that they liked most, some mentioned the ease of standing in place and allowing the robot to maneuver itself. One subject mentioned that, during the Manual session, she "had to think how to rotate the box, which turned out to be not trivial." Several subjects, on the other hand, suggested that they preferred to be in control during the manual condition, rather than ceding control to the robot, and that both automated trials resulted in some unnecessary motion on the part of the robot. Interestingly, we observed an intermediate correlation between the execution time of the subjects in the manual condition and their preference for manually controlling the robot ($r = -0.58$). This result is indicative of a relationship between user preference and performance that warrants future investigation.

8. CONCLUSION

We presented a framework for automatically learning human user models from joint-action demonstrations, enabling the robot to compute a robust policy for a collaborative task with a human. First, we described the clustering of demonstrated action sequences into different human types using an unsupervised learning algorithm. These demonstrated sequences were used to learn a reward function that is representative for each type, through the employment of an inverse reinforcement learning algorithm. The learned models were then included as part of a MOMDP formulation, wherein the human type was a partially observable variable. In a human subject experiment ($n = 30$), participants agreed more strongly that the robot anticipated their actions when using the proposed framework ($p < 0.01$), compared with manually annotating robot actions. In trials where participants faced difficulty annotating the robot actions in order to complete the task, the proposed framework significantly improved team efficiency ($p < 0.01$). Also, compared with policies computed using a reward function hand-coded by a domain expert, the robot was more responsive to human actions when using our framework ($p < 0.01$). These results indicate that learning human user models through joint-action demonstrations and encoding them in a MOMDP formalism can support effective teaming in human-robot collaborative tasks.

While our assumption of full-observability of the task-steps is reasonable in a manufacturing setting with well-defined task procedures, many other domains including home-settings involve less structured tasks and would require extensions to our approach. Future work also includes the exploration of a hybrid approach between inferring "dominant" human types and learning an individualized user model: the robot starts with a policy corresponding to the general type of a new human user, and further refines its action selection mechanism through interaction.

9. REFERENCES

[1] P. Abbeel and A. Y. Ng. Apprenticeship learning via inverse reinforcement learning. In *Proc. ICML*, 2004.

[2] B. Akgun, M. Cakmak, J. W. Yoo, and A. L. Thomaz. Trajectories and keyframes for kinesthetic teaching: a human-robot interaction perspective. In *HRI*, 2012.

[3] B. D. Argall, S. Chernova, M. Veloso, and B. Browning. A survey of robot learning from demonstration. *Robot. Auton. Syst.*, May 2009.

[4] C. G. Atkeson and S. Schaal. Robot learning from demonstration. In *ICML*, pages 12–20, 1997.

[5] T. Bandyopadhyay, K. S. Won, E. Frazzoli, D. Hsu, W. S. Lee, and D. Rus. Intention-aware motion planning. In *WAFR*. Springer, 2013.

[6] S. Boyd, L. El Ghaoui, E. Feron, and V. Balakrishnan. *Linear Matrix Inequalities in System and Control Theory*. Stud. Appl. Math. SIAM, June 1994.

[7] F. Broz, I. Nourbakhsh, and R. Simmons. Designing pomdp models of socially situated tasks. In *RO-MAN*, 2011.

[8] S. Chernova and M. Veloso. Teaching multi-robot coordination using demonstration of communication and state sharing. In *Proc. AAMAS*, 2008.

[9] F. Doshi and N. Roy. Efficient model learning for dialog management. In *Proc. HRI*, March 2007.

[10] A. Dragan, R. Holladay, and S. Srinivasa. An analysis of deceptive robot motion. In *RSS*, 2014.

[11] M. C. Gombolay, R. A. Gutierrez, G. F. Sturla, and J. A. Shah. Decision-making authority, team efficiency and human worker satisfaction in mixed human-robot teams. In *RSS*, 2014.

[12] G. Hoffman and C. Breazeal. Effects of anticipatory action on human-robot teamwork efficiency, fluency, and perception of team. In *Proc. HRI*, 2007.

[13] V. Jääskinen, V. Parkkinen, L. Cheng, and J. Corander. Bayesian clustering of dna sequences using markov chains and a stochastic partition model. *Stat. Appl. Genet. Mol.*, 2013.

[14] L. P. Kaelbling, M. L. Littman, and A. R. Cassandra. Planning and acting in partially observable stochastic domains. *Artificial Intelligence*, 1998.

[15] B. Kim and J. Pineau. Maximum mean discrepancy imitation learning. In *Proceedings of RSS*, 2013.

[16] H. Kurniawati, D. Hsu, and W. S. Lee. Sarsop: Efficient point-based pomdp planning by approximating optimally reachable belief spaces. In *Robotics: Science and Systems*, pages 65–72, 2008.

[17] O. Macindoe, L. P. Kaelbling, and T. Lozano-Pérez. Pomcop: Belief space planning for sidekicks in cooperative games. In *AIIDE*, 2012.

[18] J. I. Marden. *Analyzing and modeling rank data*. CRC Press, 1995.

[19] T. B. Murphy and D. Martin. Mixtures of distance-based models for ranking data. *Computational statistics & data analysis*, 2003.

[20] T.-H. D. Nguyen, D. Hsu, W. S. Lee, T.-Y. Leong, L. P. Kaelbling, T. Lozano-Perez, and A. H. Grant. Capir: Collaborative action planning with intention recognition. In *AIIDE*, 2011.

[21] M. N. Nicolescu and M. J. Mataric. Natural methods for robot task learning: Instructive demonstrations, generalization and practice. In *Proc. AAMAS*, 2003.

[22] S. Nikolaidis and J. Shah. Human-robot cross-training: computational formulation, modeling and evaluation of a human team training strategy. In *Proc. HRI*, 2013.

[23] S. C. Ong, Y. Grinberg, and J. Pineau. Mixed observability predictive state representations. In *AAAI*, 2013.

[24] S. C. Ong, S. W. Png, D. Hsu, and W. S. Lee. Planning under uncertainty for robotic tasks with mixed observability. *IJRR*, 29(8):1053–1068, 2010.

[25] Phasespace, http://www.phasespace.com, 2012.

[26] J. Pineau, G. Gordon, S. Thrun, et al. Point-based value iteration: An anytime algorithm for pomdps. In *IJCAI*, volume 3, pages 1025–1032, 2003.

[27] G. Shani, J. Pineau, and R. Kaplow. A survey of point-based pomdp solvers. *In Proc. AAMAS*, 2013.

[28] U. Syed and R. E. Schapire. A game-theoretic approach to apprenticeship learning. In *Proc. NIPS*, 2007.

[29] R. Tibshirani, G. Walther, and T. Hastie. Estimating the number of clusters in a data set via the gap statistic. *J. Roy. Statist. Soc. Ser. B*, 2003.

[30] K. Waugh, B. D. Ziebart, and J. A. D. Bagnell. Computational rationalization: The inverse equilibrium problem. In *Proc. ICML*, June 2011.

Bounds of Neglect Benevolence in Input Timing for Human Interaction with Robotic Swarms

Sasanka Nagavalli
Robotics Institute
Carnegie Mellon University
5000 Forbes Avenue
Pittsburgh, PA, 15213, USA
snagaval@andrew.cmu.edu

Shih-Yi Chien
Information Sciences
University of Pittsburgh
135 North Bellefield Avenue
Pittsburgh, PA, 15260, USA
shc56@pitt.edu

Michael Lewis
Information Sciences
University of Pittsburgh
135 North Bellefield Avenue
Pittsburgh, PA, 15260, USA
ml@sis.pitt.edu

Nilanjan Chakraborty
Mechanical Engineering
Stony Brook University
Stony Brook, NY, 11794, USA
nilanjan.chakraborty
@stonybrook.edu

Katia Sycara
Robotics Institute
Carnegie Mellon University
5000 Forbes Avenue
Pittsburgh, PA, 15213, USA
katia@cs.cmu.edu

ABSTRACT

Robotic swarms are distributed systems whose members interact via local control laws to achieve a variety of behaviors, such as flocking. In many practical applications, human operators may need to change the current behavior of a swarm from the goal that the swarm was going towards into a new goal due to dynamic changes in mission objectives. There are two related but distinct capabilities needed to supervise a robotic swarm. The first is *comprehension of the swarm's state* and the second is *prediction of the effects of human inputs on the swarm's behavior*. Both of them are very challenging. Prior work in the literature has shown that inserting the human input as soon as possible to divert the swarm from its original goal towards the new goal does not always result in optimal performance (measured by some criterion such as the total time required by the swarm to reach the second goal). This phenomenon has been called Neglect Benevolence, conveying the idea that in many cases it is preferable to neglect the swarm for some time before inserting human input. In this paper, we study how humans can develop an understanding of swarm dynamics so they can predict the effects of the timing of their input on the state and performance of the swarm. We developed the swarm configuration shape-changing Neglect Benevolence Task as a Human Swarm Interaction (HSI) reference task allowing comparison between human and optimal input timing performance in control of swarms. Our results show that humans can learn to approximate optimal timing and that displays which make consensus variables perceptually accessible can enhance performance.

Categories and Subject Descriptors

I.2.9 [**Robotics**]: Operator Interfaces; I.2.11 [**Distributed Artificial Intelligence**]: Multiagent Systems; H.1.2 [**User/Machine Systems**]: Human Factors; H.5.2 [**User Interfaces**]: Benchmarking

General Terms

Algorithms; Design; Experimentation; Human Factors; Performance; Theory

Keywords

Human-Robot Interaction; Robotic Swarms

1. INTRODUCTION

A robotic swarm is a multi-robot system where individual swarm members use control laws based on local spatial information about the environment and/or other members of the swarm within their spatial neighborhood to achieve various emergent collective behaviors, such as foraging or rendezvous. The key advantage of swarms is that the behaviors generated are robust to individual robot failures. Applications of swarm robotics are envisioned in environmental exploration, large scale emergency response and search and rescue and environmental cleanup (e.g. cleaning oil spills). Such missions may require use of a sequence of different swarm behaviors that may need to be imparted to the swarm by a human operator.

Since the state of a swarm not yet at equilibrium is continuously evolving, the supervisor's task is to supply inputs that divert the swarm from its current trajectory to a new desired trajectory. This Trajectory$_1$-Input-Trajectory$_2$ sequence therefore defines the basic task that must be addressed in the study of human-swarm interaction (HSI).

There are two related but distinct capabilities needed to supervise a robotic swarm. The first is *comprehension of the swarm's state* and the second is *prediction of the effects of human inputs on the swarm's behavior*. Comprehension of the swarm's state requires a human to perceptually extract relations and regularities in behavior from observable data such as robots' positions and velocities. This can be a challenging task since crucial aspects of the robots' internal states, such as distances from active goals or the conditions controlling current behaviors, may not be directly observable. In [24], for example, researchers were moved to install LEDs on their robots in order to display their internal states to aid in debugging swarm behaviors. Fortunately, regularities in relations and dynamics of widely employed swarm algorithms such as flocking are readily perceived by human viewers. In fact, the original purpose of the flocking algorithm [31] was to generate computer graphics that humans would find similar to the behavior of flocks of birds or schools of fish.

The second capability, predicting effects of human inputs, requires the operator to develop an "internal model" of the swarm's dynamics. This capability is related to the first, since, if it is possible for the human to discern continuity in the behavior and state evolution of the swarm, then the human would have a better idea of the system dynamics, would be able to predict to some extent what the swarm would do next, and hence be able to choose when to insert input to bring about desired behavior. Even for relatively intuitive relationships such as commanding a leader who is followed by a swarm employing a flocking algorithm, issues involving limitations in communications, robot speed or lags in response require the operator to develop a model of the swarm dynamics in order to effectively control the swarm. For other inputs, such as a command to switch between algorithms, delivered by broadcast or propagation, the relation between input and a desired effect on the swarm may be even less clear. Difficulties in developing internal models of dynamics have been found to be particularly acute when timing of inputs or lags in response are present [38] as is likely in controlling a swarm. A close counterpart lies in industrial processes where substantial lags between input and response have been abstracted to laboratory tasks such as Crossman's water bath [17]. In the waterbath task, operators were asked to control a heater under a beaker to heat the water in the beaker to maintain a setpoint with a lag introduced by putting the thermometer inside a testtube. Later, computerized versions of process control tasks [26] have used multiple tanks, valves and pumps but preserved the lagged integrative response of the waterbath. Common findings in these experiments are that performance improves with practice, but instruction in principles underlying the system does not improve performance [27]. Negative correlations often found between performance and verbalizable knowledge [5] further suggest learning of dynamics may be largely implicit making it difficult to improve or correct human performance.

In view of these results, enabling humans to effectively exert supervisory control on swarms by understanding the underlying dynamics and giving control inputs at the right time to optimize performance objectives presents a huge challenge. In this paper, we study this challenge and explore ways to better understand whether and how humans comprehend swarm dynamics and also how to best aid them. In particular we want to answer the following questions: (a) Can humans develop a model of the dynamics expressed in moving from one swarm configuration to another, so that they approximate the optimal time to give their input to the swarm? (b) Can we improve human performance by providing an aid which makes the robots' goals visible to the operator and provides a holistic guide to the swarm's state? (c) More generally, can we extend human monitoring and control to distributed systems that do not conform to perceptual principles by engineering displays for humans rather than requiring swarms to follow inefficient algorithms to make their behavior humanly intelligible?

We conducted a study to investigate human performance at the Neglect Benevolence shape-changing HSI reference task to determine the degree to which human operators could approximate op-timal performance, given experiences interacting with system dynamics of a swarm. We ran experiments in two conditions, one where the participants interacted via a usual display (unaided condition) and another where the participants had the use of an augmented display (aided condition). Our results showed that the participants indeed learned over time to improve their performance. Moreover, the success of the participants in the aided condition lends some support to our hypothesis that making swarm consensus variables perceptible to humans would increase the efficiency of human swarm interaction.

This paper makes the following contributions. First, it presents a framework characterizing Human-Swarm Interaction (HSI) as a sequence of human inputs diverting a swarm's trajectory through state space that is reducible to a series of Trajectory$_1$-Input-Trajectory$_2$ events and not restricted to behaviors involving only translation such as flocking, rendezvous, or deploy. Second, it introduces the swarm configuration shape-changing Neglect Benevolence Task as an HSI reference task allowing comparison between human and optimal input timing performance in control of swarms. Third, it introduces a Gestalt-based approach to characterizing the intelligibility of swarm behavior based on the perceptual saliency of the object of consensus. Fourth, it provides an initial test of human performance on the Neglect Benevolence reference task and a test of display augmentation based on characterization of intelligibility.

The paper is organized as follows. Section 2 presents related work. Section 3 briefly outlines the notion of Neglect Benevolence and optimal input time. Section 4 describes the configuration control and shape-changing task as a HSI reference task allowing comparison between human and optimal performance. Section 5 introduces an approach to characterizing the intelligibility of swarm behavior based on the Gestalt principle of common fate and evaluates common swarm algorithms including shape-changing. Sections 6 and 7 describe the experiment and results comparing human performance with conventional and aided displays at the Neglect Benevolence reference task. Section 8 presents discussion and Section 9 conclusions and future work.

2. RELATED WORK

Robotic swarm systems where a group of robots need to act through local interactions to collectively achieve a variety of behaviors have been extensively studied. Swarms can achieve behaviors such as flocking [31, 9, 33, 4], rendezvous [6], deployment [7], and foraging [13]. Formation control of robotic swarms has been proposed to adjust the spatial configuration of robotic systems so that they satisfy the requirements of deployment tasks or they can adapt to different environments while performing tasks [1, 36, 14]. However, schemes which include a human operator in the loop together with robotic swarms are required for some complicated tasks (e.g. complex surveillance and reconnaissance). For using swarm robotic systems in human-supervised missions, human swarm interaction (HSI) has been studied in [21, 8, 19, 15, 3] primarily at variants of foraging tasks. Study of human involvement in formation control includes transitions between flock and torus [3], leader choice and network configuration [12].

The concept of Neglect Tolerance has been introduced to capture the idea that a human operator can neglect robots that work independently of one another in a multi-robot system for a certain time before system performance degrades [29, 34]. One key issue in Neglect Tolerance is how to schedule the attention of the human operator among the multiple and independent robots so that the neglect time between servicing robots is minimized [25, 23]. In Neglect Tolerance, it is assumed that the robot system's performance will degrade over time and the system will need human interaction to restore performance to a desirable level. In contrast, the concept of Neglect Benevolence in human swarm interaction captures the idea that it may be beneficial for the human operator to wait for a certain length of time before applying input to the system while the swarm state evolves to stabilization (since the swarm performance may not degrade monotonically with time) [28].

3. NEGLECT BENEVOLENCE

In a previous experimental study using a foraging scenario [38], it was found that the performance of the human-swarm system was strongly affected by the time between two commands that the human applied to the robots. In particular, it was found that one group of subjects who performed well waited for some time after they issued a command before issuing another corrective command (when they wanted to change the direction in which the swarm was heading). The phenomenon was called *Neglect Benevolence*, since neglecting the swarm for some amount of time led to better performance of the system.

Further analysis of the results [38] found that when the swarm was in a transient state (i.e. moving towards one goal), applying another input (that changes the goal) could have different effects depending on the timing of the inputs.

To determine whether this was a spurious effect or not, [28] reported various simulations of swarm systems, starting at different configurations and performing rendezvous where the operator inputs changed the rendezvous point. The robots were moving under simple control laws given in [16] with a repulsive potential to avoid inter-robot collision and an attractive potential field to maintain swarm cohesion. It was observed that the simulation gave a variety of resulting outcomes depending on the times when the human input was given following the desired change in the swarm goal. More concretely, it was observed that giving the input immediately after the need arose to change the rendezvous point resulted in detaching several robots who subsequently never made rendezvous while some of the delayed inputs led to the whole swarm staying together and completing the rendezvous at the desired point.

Here, we briefly discuss some results shown in [28] that serve as a useful background for the computations and task proposed in this paper. First, it was shown that Neglect Benevolence is present not only for nonlinear systems (e.g. swarms with collision avoidance) but also for linear systems. Second, a formal definition of Neglect Benevolence was introduced that allows performance to be defined by a variety of measures such as the time or energy used by the swarm to reach the human goal. Third, it was proven that any exponentially stable linear system exhibits Neglect Benevolence. Fourth, an algorithm that computes the optimal input time for insertion of human input to achieve least time to human goal for linear time invariant (LTI) systems was given. Fifth, it was shown that the dynamics matrix of a swarm that performs consensus for controlling swarm configuration control and shape-changing (the reference HSI task proposed in the current paper) falls within this class of (LTI) systems.

From the results reported in [28], it can be concluded that Neglect Benevolence is a nuanced and quantifiable notion that captures precise calculation of "too early" or "too late" in inserting the human input. In other words, if a system is neglected for a very long time, it may take a very long time to converge. On the other hand, if a system is neglected for too little time it may also take a very long time to converge. Therefore, in order to guarantee timely convergence, a bounded Neglect Benevolence must be determined, so that the neglect interval is neither too small nor too large. Hence, another way of looking at the study in this paper is to determine

whether humans have the ability to gauge the bounds of Neglect Benevolence.

We consider configuration control and swarm shape-changing as a base task within which to study Neglect Benevolence and optimal input timing in human swarm interaction. In the next section, we present more details about the underlying formal model and dynamics of this task.

4. CONFIGURATION CONTROL AS A BASE HUMAN SWARM INTERACTION TASK

In this section, we describe the dynamics of a swarm system using consensus for configuration control. Individual robots within the swarm communicate with their neighbors. The communication graph $\mathcal{G} = (\mathcal{V}, \mathcal{E})$ captures the connectivity of robots within the swarm. An individual robot is represented as a vertex $v_i \in \mathcal{V}$ of the graph and the edges $\mathcal{E} \subset \mathcal{V} \times \mathcal{V}$ represent communication links such that each edge $(v_i, v_j) \in \mathcal{E}$ indicates that robot $v_i \in \mathcal{V}$ can communicate with robot $v_j \in \mathcal{V}$. Assume that all communication links are bidirectional. This means the communication graph is undirected (i.e. $(v_i, v_j) \in \mathcal{E} \Rightarrow (v_j, v_i) \in \mathcal{E}$). The adjacency matrix $\mathbf{A} = [a_{ij}]$ is a mathematical representation of the graph where where element $a_{ii} = 0$, $a_{ij} = 1$ if $(v_i, v_j) \in \mathcal{E}$, and $a_{ij} = 0$ if $(v_i, v_j) \notin \mathcal{E}$. The Laplacian matrix $\mathbf{L} = [l_{ij}]$ can be obtained from the adjacency matrix with each element $l_{ii} = \sum_j a_{ij}$ and $l_{ij} = -a_{ij}$. Since the graph is undirected, the adjacency matrix and the Laplacian matrix are both symmetric. When the graph is connected, the Laplacian matrix is singular and has one eigenvalue equal to 0 and a corresponding eigenvector $\mathbf{1}$. Note that $\mathbf{1}$ represents a column vector with all entries equal to 1.

The joint state of the robotic swarm is given by the state vector $\mathbf{x}$, which is composed of the concatenated states x_i of individual robots within the swarm. In continuous-time averaging consensus, the change in the state $\dot{x}_i$ over time t of an individual robot v_i is based on averaging the states of neighboring robots. Two robots v_i and v_j are called neighbors if they can communicate with each other (i.e. $(v_i, v_j) \in \mathcal{E}$). As presented in [30], the evolution of the joint state of a system performing averaging consensus can be described by the following equation, where $\mathbf{L}$ is the Laplacian matrix of the system's communication graph.

$$\dot{\mathbf{x}}(t) = -\mathbf{L}\mathbf{x}(t) \qquad (1)$$

Note that Equation (1) describes a stable linear time-invariant (LTI) system. The Laplacian matrix $\mathbf{L}$ has all non-negative real eigenvalues, so $-\mathbf{L}$ has only non-positive real eigenvalues. Since all eigenvalues of the system are real and non-positive, the system with dynamics described by Equation (1) will always move monotonically from any initial state $\mathbf{x}_0 = \mathbf{x}(0)$ towards a final state $\mathbf{x}_f = \lim_{t \to \infty} \mathbf{x}(t)$ that lies within the null space of the system [28]. For a swarm with a connected communication graph, the final state is any state in which the robots all agree with each other. That is, $\mathbf{x}_f = c\mathbf{1}$ where $c \in \mathbb{R}$.

When the robot states are their spatial positions, the averaging consensus dynamics in Equation (1) result in rendezvous at the centroid of the robots' initial positions. In [28], this algorithm is extended to incorporate an input vector K.

$$\dot{\mathbf{x}}(t) = -\mathbf{L}(\mathbf{x}(t) - K) \qquad (2)$$

It was shown in [28] that these dynamics cause the system to evolve towards a final state $\mathbf{x}_f$ that (a) preserves the centroid of the initial positions of the robots and (b) preserves the differences in corresponding entries of the input vector K. Thus, if K specifies the robot positions for a formation in some arbitrary but consistent coordinate frame, a robot swarm with the dynamics in Equation (2) will generate the specified configuration around the centroid of the initial positions. Thus, a robot swarm could be performing simple consensus and a human operator could broadcast an input vector K and with only local interactions, the robots would still generate the desired configuration.

This introduces the important question of when a human operator should apply a particular input. Specifically, if the human operator has already specified an input K_{old} that generates a particular configuration, then when should the operator specify a new input K_{new} to generate a new configuration (i.e. change the goal of the swarm) as quickly as possible? Human intuition would indicate that the operator should specify K_{new} as soon as possible if they want to obtain the new configuration as quickly as possible. However, as shown in [28], this intuition is provably wrong in the general case! For any LTI system, given an input K, it is always possible to find a state $\mathbf{x}$ in which it is beneficial to delay the application of the input. Since this is non-intuitive to the human operator, this motivates the need for appropriately aiding the operator in finding or approximating the optimal time to apply the input, maximizing the performance of the robot swarm.

5. INTELLIGIBILITY OF SWARM BEHAVIOR

The emergent behavior of a swarm results from many local interactions among its members. Most commonly, some variant of consensus (averaging values among neighbors) is used for the coordination giving rise to swarm behaviors. Perceiving an emergent swarm behavior requires the observer to recognize and associate similarities among the many local interactions among robots. Consequently, human perceptual access to swarm behavior depends on these local interactions/agreement being expressed in a way in which salient similarities and relations (consensus) can be recognized. Recognition of these regularities and the swarm's trajectory is a prerequisite for monitoring and decision making. The extraordinary ability of humans to perceive biological motion has been well established since Johansson's [18] experiments in which human actors with point-lights attached to major joints were recorded and later viewed as images showing only a few moving dots. Viewers easily identified the human figures and their activities, such as walking, even in the presence of substantial "masking" by other dots [11]. Even hidden characteristics of motion such as the weight of a box [32] or distance of a thrown object [20] were discernible to viewers of these point-light displays. Inverting the imagery (upside down human walkers), however, eliminates almost all of the effect [2] leaving observers unable to discriminate between scenes containing a walker and those with only a "mask". These results suggest a strong ecological and/or learned component to human abilities to perceive biological motion that may not fully extend to behaviors of a swarm. This suggests that the more general Gestalt principles of *proximity*, *similarity*, *closure*, *symmetry*, *continuity*, *common fate*, *pragnanz* and *past experience* may provide the best guidance for identifying representations likely or unlikely to lead to the perception of swarm behaviors. Of these principles, only *common fate* applies specifically to motion, while the rest largely prescribe how parts come to be perceived as wholes and could come into play as robots approach well defined formations.

The most common display of a swarm comprises spatially related icons on a plane or in a 3D space corresponding to robot positions. Swarm behavior following standard algorithms such as *flocking* or those collected in [6] such as *rendezvous*, *deploy* or *boundary following* is displayed through movements of these icons. Fortu-

nately, these displays (moving dots perceived as patterns) closely resemble those studied by psychologists and vision researchers so there is already research into the factors supporting the perception of group behavior in this context. *Common fate* refers to the grouping factor that leads a previously invisible grouping of dots to pop out of a noisy background when moved and has been found to be the most important factor in perceiving coordinated behavior although *proximity* [37], *similarity* [10] and *pragnanz* in the form of grouping features such as collinearity [37] have all been shown to play important roles and to interact [37] in strengthening the effects of *common fate*. Humans are very sensitive to perceiving *common fate* groupings with success at signal-to-noise ratios as low as 1-2% [35] and the effect is relatively robust to divergence among trajectories as long as some coordinated global direction is maintained [39]. There are suggestions, however, that *common fate* may be limited to a single group at a time [22]. For example, of two overlapping groups only one would appear to move coherently. Effects have been found strongest for linear or circular trajectories [40]. While spatial characteristics predominate in perception of moving groups other features such as common color can also contribute [10].

By this analysis, even without the benefits of biological motion, flocking behavior in which agents adopt the average heading and velocities of their neighbors seems ideally suited for perceptual recognition. In either its linear or torus form [3], the interaction among agents is precisely that giving rise to *common fate* while the regulation of distance (*proximity* and *pragnanz*) enhances this effect. For the rendezvous and deploy algorithms, the consensus process should be less strongly conveyed because while the global movement inward or outward and reflected in local interactions should be perceivable [40] it lacks the matching of velocities and headings, which are the dominant contributors to the perception of *common fate* [37].

By a similar analysis we would predict that the behavior of a swarm following the shape-changing algorithm would be extremely difficult for a human observer to follow because in moving from one configuration to another neither headings nor velocities are matched (*common fate*) nor constant distances nor boundaries maintained (*proximity* and *pragnanz*). That is to say that the movement of the swarm toward consensus as perceptually manifested by a centroid is masked by the formation. Since the consensus process is not perceptually accessible from robot behaviors, the human monitor would be left with the impression of robots that are moving about independently and be unable to either monitor their progress toward a goal or compose an input to alter that progress. As the target formation is approached, however, the entire set of Gestalt principles governing perception of form (*proximity*, *similarity*, *closure*, *symmetry*, *continuity*) would come into play making the goal and progress toward it increasingly apparent in this second phase.

These analyses suggest that intelligibility of swarm behavior could be improved for algorithms in which progress toward consensus is not perceptually available by augmenting the display in a way that makes this information available. Since the perceptually uncoordinated movements of robots to their positions in the target formation cannot be eliminated, the display can only be augmented in ways that make the robots' goals and progress toward their goals more apparent. A potential augmentation of this sort would be to draw lines from the robots' current positions to their predicted locations in the new formation. As the swarm evolves toward its initial goal shape these lines would shorten and lengthen until the supervisor chooses to divert the swarm to the desired shape at the point he/she judges to be the closest (shortest lines). In this augmentation, the line between each robot's current position and its final position is a visual proxy for the distance in the swarm's state space between current and goal state. The swarm's state space has very high dimensionality and cannot be easily visualized, so this proxy is used as an aid. The next section describes an experiment comparing a display augmented in this way with a conventional display.

6. EXPERIMENTAL DESIGN

Our initial experiment investigating human performance at the Neglect Benevolence HSI reference task was to determine the degree to which human operators could approximate optimal performance given experience interacting with system dynamics (implicit learning). Comparison of human and optimal performance is a standard practice in the study of human-machine systems for benchmarking human performance and evaluating human competence within a work domain. While we would expect to assign easily automatable tasks such as input timing to the system, it may be important to allow the human to intervene in response to "out of band" information or other anomalies. In addition, the possibility of manual control may be an important element for preventing out-of-the-loop effects or complacency and enabling the operator to effectively monitor the system for failures or abnormal behavior. Possible outcomes included almost optimal performance, biased performance favoring late inputs ("finding the bottom" heuristic), idiosyncratic performance indicated by a wide dispersion between early and late inputs or some other explainable outcome. These are descriptive questions answerable by descriptive statistics.

We used a mixed-model design for our experiment, which divided subjects into two groups and had one group interact with the swarm through a conventional display showing only robot positions (unaided condition), while the other group interacted with the swarm through a display that included a Gestalt-based augmentation to the visualization of the swarm (aided condition). Interactions with the swarm were divided into discrete trials. Each group interacted with the swarm in the same number of training and test trials. The swarm dynamics and initial state remained consistent between corresponding trials in the unaided and aided condition. Thus, for the mixed-model design, the within-subject variable was the trial number and the between-subject variable was the presence or lack of the Gestalt-based visual aid. A regression against trials was used to measure practice effects. The comparison between the display with the Gestalt-based augmentation and the conventional display provides an initial test of our hypothesis that swarm behaviors can be made more intelligible and controllable by making progress toward consensus perceptually assessable.

6.1 Method

6.1.1 Task

The experimental task involves human interaction with a simulated robotic swarm performing consensus on robot positions. The swarm includes the capacity to incorporate an input as described in Section 4. The task is for the subject to choose the best time at which to provide an input diverting the robotic swarm from the shape toward which it is initially moving (equilibrium point of the dynamical system) to another desired shape (new equilibrium point). This matches our earlier depiction of the canonical HSI task as redirecting the swarm — modelled as a dynamical system — from one "natural goal" state (Formation 1) to another "desired goal" state (Formation 2). If the system in a Neglect Benevolent state, it is beneficial to delay the application of the input to minimize the total time required to converge to the desired formation. Figure 1 shows an example of how delaying the application of the input could reduce the time required to reach the goal state.

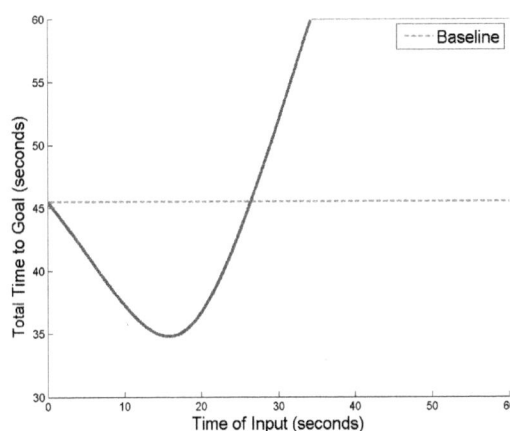

Figure 1: This plot shows the relationship between convergence time (i.e. total time to goal) and input time for one of the trials in our experiment. The convergence time if the input is applied immediately at the start of the simulation is shown as the baseline time. Each trial has a maximum length of 60 seconds. For this trial, if the input is applied after approximately 33 seconds the swarm would not converge within the 60 second limit.

Participants first read the standard instructions on how to use the interface to interact with the swarm robots and then proceed to complete each trial in the experiment. In the aided condition, there is a line between each robot's current position and its final position in the desired formation. These lines help participants visualize the distance between the robots' current positions and the desired formation (Formation 2). Since the swarm dynamics are LTI as described in Section 4, when the collective distance represented by all the lines is larger, more time is required to reach the desired formation. Formation 1 and Formation 2 are shown in thumbnails at the top of the screen following a summary of instructions.

The experiment has 12 training trials to familiarize participants with the system and allow them to observe the asymmetric effects of leading/lagging the optimal input time. As learning of system dynamics is presumed implicit, familiarization is needed to engender common strategies so performance might be compared. During the training trials, participants are informed of the effects of applying the input too early/late and compare them with the optimal time. The training trials are divided into two types: *passive*, where participants only observe, and *active*, where participants give input themselves. The first 6 trials are *passive*, where participants observe three simulation panels situated below thumbnails depicting Formation 1 and Formation 2. All three simulations begin with the robots in the same random initial configuration. When a user clicks "Begin", the swarms in all three panels begin moving toward Formation 1 until given an input (at a different time for each panel). Visually, upon receiving the input, the swarm robots change color from red to green. Each panel shows how the input redirects the configuration of the swarm towards Formation 2. Upon converging to Formation 2, the convergence time is shown. The left, middle and right panels each display the effects when the input is applied "too early", at the optimal time, and "too late" respectively (see Figure 2). The next 6 trials are *active*, where participants have the chance to apply the input themselves and get feedback as to whether they gave the input too early, too late, or optimally (see Figure 3). Participants are again presented with thumbnails showing Formation 1 and Formation 2, but followed by only one simulation panel. The panel shows the robot swarm in a random initial configuration. After the participant clicks "Begin", the swarm starts moving toward Formation 1. The participant then has the chance to give an input by clicking "Activate New Formation" at any time before the end of the simulation. Once the swarm has converged (or the simulation has reached the 60 second time limit), the convergence time resulting from the input and feedback as to whether their input was too early or too late (see Figure 3) is displayed.

After the subjects finish the 12 training trials, they are presented with 36 test trials in the same condition (aided or unaided). In the test trials, the subjects are presented with the same screen arrangement (see Figure 4) as in the *active* training trials, but although they are able to observe the convergence time, they are not given feedback as to whether their input was too early or too late. The participants are instructed to impose the new goal on the swarm at the time leading to the earliest convergence.

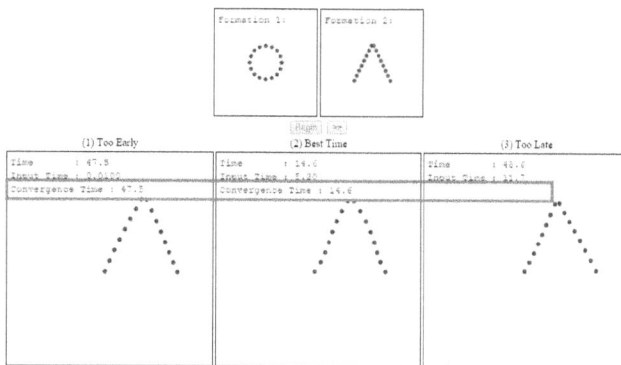

Figure 2: For each trial in the first (passive) training phase, participants were shown three simulations. In all simulations, robots started in the same initial positions, but the input telling them to move to Formation 2 was applied at different times: (1) too early, (2) at the best time, (3) too late. After the swarm converged to the final formation (see panel 1 and 2), participants were shown the time taken for the robots to converge.

6.1.2 Participants and Data Collection

A total of 44 participants were recruited (22 for aided condition, 22 for unaided condition) from the University of Pittsburgh and Carnegie Mellon University communities through online solicitation. Data was collected through a HTML5 / JavaScript web application that recorded each subject's trial data anonymously in a secured MySQL database. Participants were randomly assigned to either the control group (unaided condition) that interacted with the swarm through a conventional interface or the experimental group that interacted with the swarm through an interface with a Gestalt-based augmentation (aided condition). Participant input times were recorded for each trial. Optimal input times for each trial were computed offline using the algorithm in [28].

7. RESULTS

Input time deviation and convergence time served as dependent variables. Input time deviation ($|t_{input} - t_{optimal}|$) was defined as the absolute difference between the time chosen by participants to divert the swarm and the optimal diversion time. Convergence time was defined as the interval from the beginning of the trial until the swarm converged to the desired formation (Formation 2). Input time measured the participants' deviation from optimality directly while convergence time measured the effect of these suboptimal

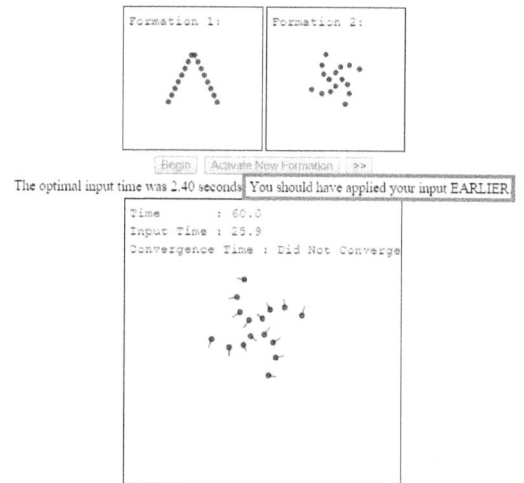

Figure 3: For each trial in the second (active) training phase, participants were asked to apply the input at whatever time they thought would minimize the total time required for the robots to converge to Formation 2. At the end of the trial, participants were told the optimal input time and whether they should have applied their input earlier or later.

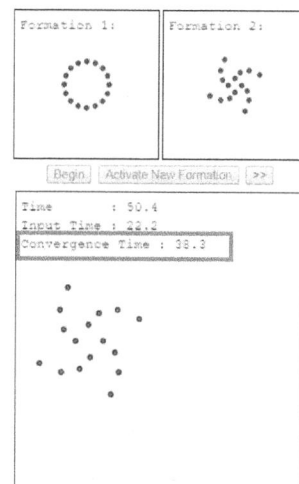

Figure 4: For each trial in the test phase, participants were asked to apply the input at whatever time they thought would minimize the total time required for the robots to converge to Formation 2. They were not given any feedback.

inputs on performance. Since delays that were too long could lead to much longer convergence times than those that were too short, strategies favoring earlier inputs might be a rational response for participants having difficulty in approximating the optimal interval making convergence and input times slightly different measures. Independent variables were Display type (conventional or aided), Transition Type (circle-spiral, circle-V, spiral-circle, spiral-V, V-circle, V-spiral), and trial number.

Data were analyzed both in an ANOVA design treating Display type and Transition type as factors and a regression incorporating trial numbers as well. An ANOVA found main effects for both Display types (F1,1572= 6.214, p=.013) and Transition type (F1,1572=33.402, p<.001) for input time deviation. An ANOVA

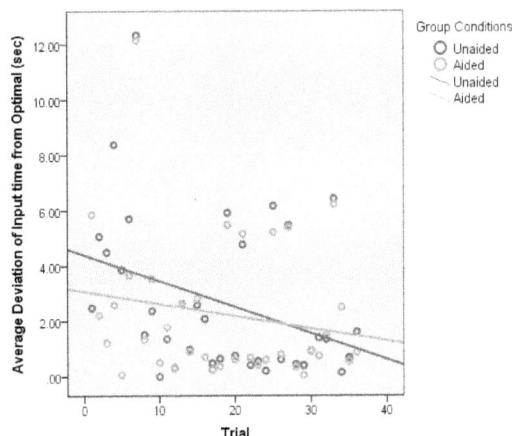

Figure 5: This plot shows the average absolute deviation of the participants' input time from the optimal input time for each trial in the unaided and aided condition.

for convergence time also found main effects for both Display type ($F_{1,1572}$= 3.387, p = .006) and Transition type $F_{1,1572}$=45.418, p<.001). Both groups on average preceded the optimal time with participants in the aided display condition responding nearly twice as early (M=-1.23 sec, SD=5.11) as those in the unaided condition (M=-.65 sec, SD=7.49) although this difference was not significant at the p<.05 level. A Mann-Whitney U test of deviations from optimal input times, however, found that participants in the aided condition (mean rank=767.63) were significantly closer to the optimum (z=-2.164, p=.03) than those in the unaided condition (mean rank=817.37). A comparison of deviations from optimal convergence times found that participants in the aided condition (mean rank=762.55) were significantly closer to the optimum than those in the unaided condition (mean rank=822.45); z=-1.97, p=.009 on this measure as well. Regression of input time deviations against trials found a significant improvement ($F_{1,34}$=4.918, p=.033) in the unaided Display condition but not in the aided condition.

8. DISCUSSION

Our results as shown in Figure 5 indicate that humans did, in fact, learn to approximate the optimal input time over the course of the experiment. This suggests that both Display types provided sufficient cues for humans to learn to time their input in order to decrease convergence times. The quality of this approximation, however, began at a high level for the group using the aided Display but developed only slowly for those in the unaided condition. We believe this occurred because the lines drawn to terminal locations in Formation 2 on the augmented Display provided viewers with a reference for judging the swarm's evolution while the movement of robots in the unaided Display did not. Relying only on Gestalt influences over the perception of form as formations were approached, unaided participants did not have a basis for earlier responses. This conjecture is supported by the finding that those in the aided condition responded on average earlier than those in the unaided condition There are several possible explanations for the improvement in performance of participants in the unaided condition. Participants might have acquired an implicit model of shape-changing dynamics that allowed them to better assess the swarm's state as it evolved. Alternately, they may have developed greater sensitivity in recognizing an evolving formation's similarity to their goal formation. A third alternative might be that par-

ticipants learned a timing heuristic for delaying input. These and similar questions can only be answered through additional properly designed experiments to test those explanations.

The success of the augmented condition in improving the performance of naive participants lends some support to our hypothesis that difficulties can arise in interaction with swarm systems because the variables on which the swarm is coordinating are not perceptually accessible to the human. Many distributed algorithms involving human interaction such as flocking, biology-mimicking control through leaders and predators, or physicomimetic direction via potential fields depend in some part on their intelligibility to human users and their programmers. If we could develop principled methods for augmenting the behavior of swarm algorithms with display of variables under consensus it could extend human control and use to a wider range of potentially more efficient algorithms.

9. CONCLUSION

Some of the main contributions of this work are methodological and lie in providing a framework for a more controlled study of human-swarm interaction. Characterizing HSI as the act of diverting a swarm's trajectory through state space from the current goal to an alternate goal provides a new basis for evaluating HSI in isolation from normally confounding factors. In particular, by focusing on progress toward goal states rather than simply measuring transient effects of behavior, it allows an experimenter to define a strict performance reference for human behavior unlike earlier efforts such as [21] which have relied on comparing performance to that of intelligent agents.

The shape-changing Neglect Benevolence Task provides an example of an HSI reference task of this sort that allows direct comparison between human and optimal performance in control of swarms. The methods and tools developed in this process provide a roadmap for other researchers wishing to develop distributed algorithms and displays that can be evaluated in these ways. We have presented and provided an initial test of a Gestalt-based approach to characterizing the intelligibility of swarm behavior based on the perceptual salience of the object of consensus. While results are preliminary they are promising in providing a closer linkage between human cognition, distributed algorithms and the way we display them.

10. ACKNOWLEDGMENTS

This research has been sponsored in part by ONR Grant N0001409-10680 and an NSERC PGS D scholarship.

11. REFERENCES

[1] T. Balch and R. C. Arkin. Behavior-based formation control for multirobot teams. *Robotics and Automation, IEEE Transactions on*, 14(6):926–939, 1998.

[2] B. I. Bertenthal and J. Pinto. Global processing of biological motions. *Psychological science*, 5(4):221–225, 1994.

[3] D. S. Brown, S. C. Kerman, and M. A. Goodrich. Human-swarm interactions based on managing attractors. In *Proceedings of the 2014 ACM/IEEE international conference on Human-robot interaction*, pages 90–97. ACM, 2014.

[4] D. J. Bruemmer, D. D. Dudenhoeffer, M. D. McKay, and M. O. Anderson. A robotic swarm for spill finding and perimeter formation. Technical report, DTIC Document, 2002.

[5] A. Buchner, J. Funke, and D. C. Berry. Negative correlations between control performance and verbalizable knowledge: Indicators for implicit learning in process control tasks? *The*

Quarterly Journal of Experimental Psychology, 48(1):166–187, 1995.

[6] F. Bullo, J. Cortés, and S. Martinez. *Distributed control of robotic networks: a mathematical approach to motion coordination algorithms*. Princeton University Press, 2009.

[7] H. Choset. Coverage for robotics–a survey of recent results. *Annals of mathematics and artificial intelligence*, 31(1-4):113–126, 2001.

[8] G. Coppin and F. Legras. Autonomy spectrum and performance perception issues in swarm supervisory control. *Proceedings of the IEEE*, 100(3):590–603, 2012.

[9] I. D. Couzin, J. Krause, R. James, G. D. Ruxton, and N. R. Franks. Collective memory and spatial sorting in animal groups. *Journal of theoretical biology*, 218(1):1–11, 2002.

[10] L. J. Croner and T. D. Albright. Image segmentation enhances discrimination of motion in visual noise. *Vision research*, 37(11):1415–1427, 1997.

[11] J. E. Cutting, C. Moore, and R. Morrison. Masking the motions of human gait. *Perception & Psychophysics*, 44(4):339–347, 1988.

[12] J.-P. de la Croix and M. Egerstedt. Controllability characterizations of leader-based swarm interactions. In *AAAI Fall Symposium: Human Control of Bioinspired Swarms*, 2012.

[13] F. Ducatelle, G. A. Di Caro, and L. M. Gambardella. Cooperative self-organization in a heterogeneous swarm robotic system. In *Proceedings of the 12th annual conference on Genetic and evolutionary computation*, pages 87–94. ACM, 2010.

[14] M. Egerstedt and X. Hu. Formation constrained multi-agent control. *Robotics and Automation, IEEE Transactions on*, 17(6):947–951, Dec 2001.

[15] M.-A. Fields, E. Haas, S. Hill, C. Stachowiak, and L. Barnes. Effective robot team control methodologies for battlefield applications. In *Intelligent Robots and Systems, 2009. IROS 2009. IEEE/RSJ International Conference on*, pages 5862–5867. IEEE, 2009.

[16] V. Gazi and K. M. Passino. Stability analysis of social foraging swarms. *Systems, Man, and Cybernetics, Part B: Cybernetics, IEEE Transactions on*, 34(1):539–557, 2004.

[17] E. Grossman and E. Cooke. Manual control of slow-response systems. *Ergonomics: Major Writings*, page 281, 2005.

[18] G. Johansson. Visual perception of biological motion and a model for its analysis. *Perception & psychophysics*, 14(2):201–211, 1973.

[19] Z. Kira and M. A. Potter. Exerting human control over decentralized robot swarms. In *Autonomous Robots and Agents, 2009. ICARA 2009. 4th International Conference on*, pages 566–571. IEEE, 2009.

[20] G. Knoblich and R. Flach. Predicting the effects of actions: Interactions of perception and action. *Psychological Science*, 12(6):467–472, 2001.

[21] A. Kolling, S. Nunnally, and M. Lewis. Towards human control of robot swarms. In *Proceedings of the seventh annual ACM/IEEE international conference on human-robot interaction*, pages 89–96. ACM, 2012.

[22] B. R. Levinthal and S. L. Franconeri. Common-fate grouping as feature selection. *Psychological science*, page 0956797611418346, 2011.

[23] S. Mau and J. M. Dolan. Scheduling to minimize downtime in human-multirobot supervisory control. 2006.

[24] J. McLurkin, J. Smith, J. Frankel, D. Sotkowitz, D. Blau, and B. Schmidt. Speaking swarmish: Human-robot interface design for large swarms of autonomous mobile robots. In *AAAI Spring Symposium: To Boldly Go Where No Human-Robot Team Has Gone Before*, pages 72–75, 2006.

[25] P. Mitchell, M. Cummings, and T. Sheridan. Management of multiple dynamic human supervisory control tasks. In *10th International Command and Control Research and Technology Symposium*, 2005.

[26] N. Moray, P. Lootsteen, and J. Pajak. Acquisition of process control skills. *Systems, Man and Cybernetics, IEEE Transactions on*, 16(4):497–504, 1986.

[27] N. M. Morris and W. B. Rouse. The effects of type of knowledge upon human problem solving in a process control task. *Systems, Man and Cybernetics, IEEE Transactions on*, (6):698–707, 1985.

[28] S. Nagavalli, L. Luo, N. Chakraborty, and K. Sycara. Neglect benevolence in human control of robotic swarms. In *2014 IEEE International Conference on Robotics and Automation (ICRA)*, pages 6047–6053, May 2014.

[29] D. R. Olsen and M. A. Goodrich. Metrics for evaluating human-robot interactions. In *Proceedings of PERMIS*, volume 2003, page 4, 2003.

[30] W. Ren, R. W. Beard, and E. M. Atkins. A survey of consensus problems in multi-agent coordination. In *American Control Conference, 2005. Proceedings of the 2005*, pages 1859–1864. IEEE, 2005.

[31] C. W. Reynolds. Flocks, herds and schools: A distributed behavioral model. *ACM SIGGRAPH Computer Graphics*, 21(4):25–34, 1987.

[32] S. Runeson and G. Frykholm. Visual perception of lifted weight. *Journal of Experimental Psychology: Human Perception and Performance*, 7(4):733, 1981.

[33] W. M. Spears and D. F. Spears. *Physicomimetics: Physics-based swarm intelligence*. Springer, 2012.

[34] A. Steinfeld, T. Fong, D. Kaber, M. Lewis, J. Scholtz, A. Schultz, and M. Goodrich. Common metrics for human-robot interaction. In *Proceedings of the 1st ACM SIGCHI/SIGART conference on Human-robot interaction*, pages 33–40. ACM, 2006.

[35] F. Stürzel and L. Spillmann. Perceptual limits of common fate. *Vision research*, 44(13):1565–1573, 2004.

[36] M. Turpin, N. Michael, and V. Kumar. Decentralized formation control with variable shapes for aerial robots. In *Robotics and Automation (ICRA), 2012 IEEE International Conference on*, pages 23–30. IEEE, 2012.

[37] W. R. Uttal, L. Spillmann, F. Stürzel, and A. B. Sekuler. Motion and shape in common fate. *Vision Research*, 40(3):301–310, 2000.

[38] P. Walker, S. Nunnally, M. Lewis, A. Kolling, N. Chakraborty, and K. Sycara. Neglect benevolence in human control of swarms in the presence of latency. In *Systems, Man, and Cybernetics (SMC), 2012 IEEE International Conference on*, pages 3009–3014. IEEE, 2012.

[39] S. N. Watamaniuk. Ideal observer for discrimination of the global direction of dynamic random-dot stimuli. *JOSA A*, 10(1):16–28, 1993.

[40] S. N. Watamaniuk, S. P. McKee, and N. M. Grzywacz. Detecting a trajectory embedded in random-direction motion noise. *Vision research*, 35(1):65–77, 1995.

Interactive Hierarchical Task Learning from a Single Demonstration

Anahita Mohseni-Kabir, Charles Rich, Sonia Chernova, Candace L. Sidner, Daniel Miller
Worcester Polytechnic Institute
Worcester, MA, USA
{amohsenikabir, rich, soniac, sidner, millerd}@wpi.edu

ABSTRACT

We have developed learning and interaction algorithms to support a human teaching hierarchical task models to a robot using a single demonstration in the context of a mixed-initiative interaction with bi-directional communication. In particular, we have identified and implemented two important heuristics for suggesting task groupings based on the physical structure of the manipulated artifact and on the data flow between tasks. We have evaluated our algorithms with users in a simulated environment and shown both that the overall approach is usable and that the grouping suggestions significantly improve the learning and interaction.

Categories and Subject Descriptors

I.2.9 [**Artificial Intelligence**]: Robotics

Keywords

Hierarchical Task Networks; Learning From Demonstration

1. INTRODUCTION

This paper focuses on the problem of how a robot can efficiently learn a hierarchical task model from a human teacher who is an expert in the domain, but not in robot programming. Our approach integrates learning from demonstration (LfD) with hierarchical task networks (HTNs). We use HTNs instead of the flat representations more commonly used in LfD because HTNs are more intuitive and computationally more tractable, especially for non-programmers and complex tasks.

Additionally, our approach consists of viewing LfD as a collaborative discourse (see Figure 1). In a collaborative discourse, both participants (in this case, the human teacher and the robot learner) are committed to the shared goal of the interaction (in this case, for the robot to learn a new task) and both actively contribute towards achieving that goal. More specifically, in the situated interaction illustrated in Figure 1, which is our target, both the human and

HRI'15, March 2–5, 2015, Portland, Oregon, USA.
Copyright is held by the owner/author(s). Publication rights licensed to ACM.
ACM 978-1-4503-2883-8/15/03 ...$15.00.
http://dx.doi.org/10.1145/2696454.2696474.

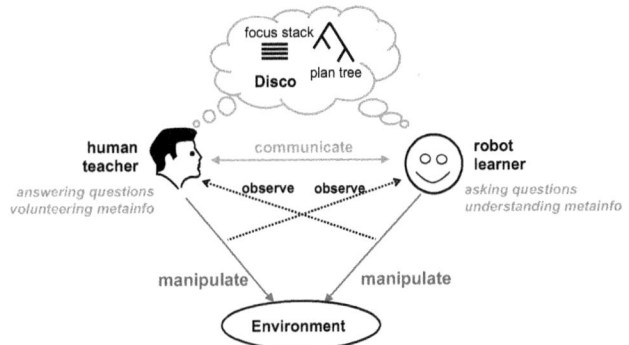

Figure 1: LfD as a collaborative discourse.

the robot can manipulate and observe the other's manipulations of artifacts in the shared environment, and there is bi-directional communication. Collaborative discourse theory [5] provides a foundation for both the algorithms and the implementation of our system. More specifically, the rules in this theory for managing the focus of attention (as a stack) have guided our interaction design and we are using an open-source tool, called Disco [14], based on collaborative discourse theory in our implementation.

Finally, in this paper we focus on learning from a single demonstration. As we will see below, this is possible because of the bi-directional communication between the teacher and the learner. However, sometimes multiple demonstrations are unavoidable. Our other work [10] explores how to merge multiple demonstrations in HTNs.

The example domain we have chosen for this research is maintenance tasks and specifically car maintenance, because it is challenging yet familiar to most readers. We have started with tire rotation and expect in the future to teach a robot how to check the oil, change filters and belts, and so on.

This paper is organized around the running example of a tire rotation HTN, which is introduced in Section 2. In Section 3, we first describe how our algorithms can learn the hierarchical structure of this HTN from a single "ideal" interactive demonstration. However, our user study indicates that most users are far from ideal, which motivates the need for suggestions from the

Figure 2: Simulated environment with PR2.

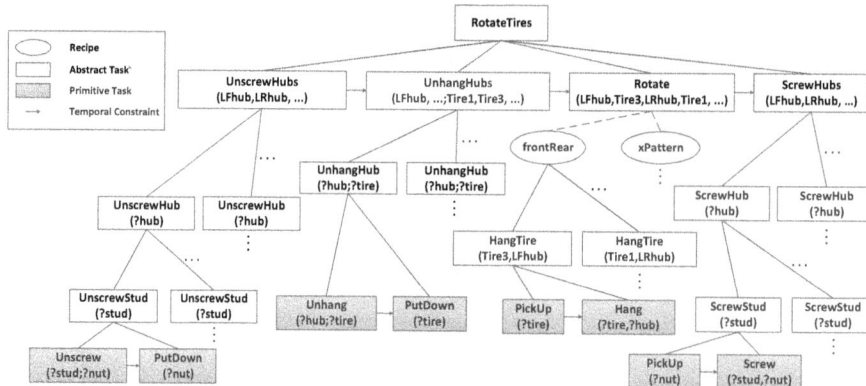

Figure 3: A hand-coded hierarchical task network for tire rotation.

robot, which we then describe. Section 4 describes our user study in detail. It shows both that the overall approach is usable and that the robot's suggestions significantly improve the learning and interaction. We discuss related work in Section 5, after we have presented our results.

The intended application of this work is with a real robot, such as the PR2, in a shared physical environment. As a first step, however, we have implemented and evaluated our techniques using Gazebo in the simulated environment shown in Figure 2. See Section 6 for a description of the physical environment we are building and other next steps.

2. HIERARCHICAL TASK NETWORKS

HTNs are widely used in artificial intelligence, especially in interactive systems. An HTN is essentially a tree in which the fringe nodes denote *primitive* tasks, i.e., tasks that can be directly executed (e.g., by a robot), and the other nodes denote *abstract* tasks, which must be decomposed in order to be executed. As an example, consider the HTN for tire rotation shown in Figure 3. This is a hand-coded version of the kind of HTN that our system learned from the participants in our user study.

The abstract tasks in an HTN are not absolutely necessary to execute the toplevel task—RotateTire could simply be represented as a sequence of 64 primitives. However, there is much evidence that humans naturally think about complex tasks hierarchically. For example, collaborative discourse theory is based on a hierarchy of goals.

The abstract tasks in an HTN provide an important vocabulary for communication between the human and robot in the context of a collaboration. This shared vocabulary is needed for discussing the partial completion status of the task, for delegating subtasks, for discussing potential problems with execution, and so on. Furthemore, the abstract tasks can often be reused in other situations. For example, after learning the HTN in Figure 3, the robot not only knows how to rotate tires, but it has also learned two abstract tasks (UnscrewHub and UnhangHub) that are useful for fixing a flat tire.

HTNs are also commonly used as an alternative to symbolic planning in complex real-world applications where a complete logical formalization is difficult or infeasible. Although tire rotation is simple enough that it could easily be formalized for a symbolic planner, our target is applications in which this is not true. The learning algorithms in this paper therefore require only the name and input types of a task.

There are many different formalisms available for representing HTNs. In this work, we use the ANSI/CEA-2018 standard [13] because, among other things, it explicitly represents data flow between tasks, which is the basis for one of the grouping heuristics described in Section 3.2. In other work [11] we have used data flow in HTNs to learn temporal constraints from a single demonstration.

Since the HTN in Figure 3 will be used as a running example (and was the domain of our user study), it is worthwhile examining it here in some detail. First, Figure 4 shows the terminology we are using for the relevant parts of a car: a tire goes on a hub and is secured with three nuts (one on each stud). The hubs are identified as LF, LR, RF, RR, standing for the left-front, left-rear, etc., and each hub has three studs, identified as "LFhub.stud1", etc. The tires are named Tire1, Tire2, etc., and in the user study have distinct colors for convenience of identification.

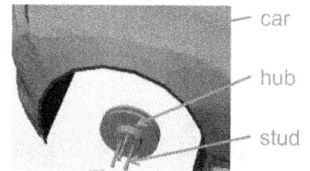

Figure 4: Terminology.

In ANSI/CEA-2018, both primitive and abstract tasks have typed inputs and outputs. The tire rotation HTN uses six primitive task types: Screw, Unscrew, Hang, Unhang, PickUp, and PutDown, with their respective input and output types shown. For example Unscrew (see Figure 5) takes a stud as input and returns a nut as output. There are 64 primitive tasks in the fringe of the tire rotation tree (some of the repetitive structure has been elided in the figure to save space).

Figure 3 defines 11 abstract task types, such as UnscrewHubs, which are used 45 times in the interior of the tree. This particular way of decomposing the tire rotation task is not the only possible way, but the other reasonable decompositions all have a similar number of abstract types and total number of nodes.

In ANSI/CEA-2018, the subtasks of a given task are by default *unordered*. An explicit temporal constraint can be added between two tasks to specify a partial ordering. For example, the four toplevel steps of RotateTires are totally ordered, but the steps of UnscrewHubs are unordered, since it does not matter in what order you unscrew the nuts.

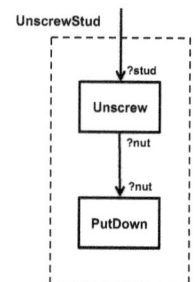

Figure 5: Data flow.

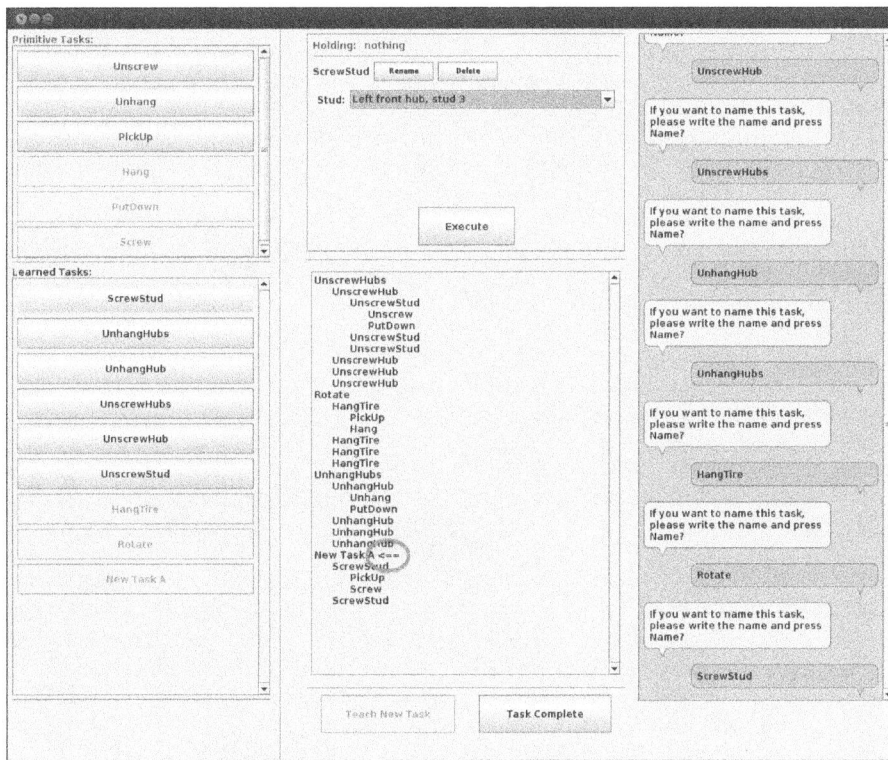

Figure 6: Graphical user interface for teacher.

Data flow in ANSI/CEA-2018 is an identity constraint between a task's output and an input of a sibling task, i.e., another subtask of the same parent task. Figure 5 shows an example of data flow in the tire rotation HTN.

A key feature of HTN's that we are not dealing with in this work is the ability to specify alternate decompositions, or *recipes*. Figure 3 provides two recipes for the Rotate step of tire rotation corresponding to two different rotation patterns: front-to-rear and corner-to-corner ("X-pattern"). Learning alternative recipes is one of those circumstances in which multiple demonstrations are unavoidable. In this paper, however, we are only learning the front-to-rear recipe.

3. LEARNING FROM DEMONSTRATION

In this section we will explain, using two example interactions, how our system learns the hierarchical structure of the tire rotation HTN in Figure 3. The first example interaction, in Section 3.1, is a hypothetical "ideal" interaction in which the robot provides no helpful suggestions, but the user teaches exactly the hand-coded hierarchical structure anyway. While this interaction is fully supported by our system, in our user study, no participants came even close to this ideal behavior when the robot provided no suggestions; instead they made far less optimal task structures. In the second interaction, described in Section 3.2, the same HTN is learned *with* suggestions from the robot that guide the user in structuring the task. This interaction is in fact typical of what we saw with our users who received and accepted suggestions from the robot.

Our focus in this work is on learning the grouping structure of the HTN. The names chosen for abstract tasks and some details of the inputs and outputs may vary from our

hand-coded HTN. Furthermore, our current system only supports a bottom-up style of learning, in which primitives are first combined into small abstract tasks, which are then combined into bigger abstract tasks, and so on. This style lends itself well to demonstration. In the future (see Section 6), we plan to extend our techniques to top-down and mixed modes of learning.

Figure 6 shows the graphical user interface we have developed for a human to use with our simulated robot environment. In use, the human teacher interacts with this interface while simultaneously seeing the effects of actions on a side-by-side simulation screen, similar to Figure 2. Figure 6 shows the state of the GUI at line 32 of Figure 7.

Before we describe its operation in detail, we also need to emphasize that this GUI is *not* a research goal in its own right, but rather a means to test our learning algorithms and overall interaction design while still in simulation. As we discuss in Section 6, most or all of this GUI will disappear once we move into a physical shared human-robot environment.

The left side of the GUI contains buttons that select a primitive (top left) or abstract (bottom left) task to execute. The primitive task types are fixed. New abstract task buttons are added whenever a new abstract task type is learned.

The top middle area of the GUI is mainly for specifying inputs, if any, as needed before executing a task. Each input can be selected from a drop-down list of objects in the environment of the correct type. When the user presses the Execute button, the robot executes the selected primitive or abstract task.

The Rename and Delete buttons at the top of this area are for renaming and deleting learned abstract tasks. The Holding line above these buttons is a small informational display that keeps track of the object, if any, that the robot is currently holding.

The middle area of the GUI below the input selection area is the main informational display, which shows the current hierarchical structure of the learned tasks. The small arrow next to New Task A (red circle added here for visibility) indicates the abstract task currently being learned. This area is also where the highlighting appears for tasks suggested for grouping, as described in Section 3.2. The Teach New Task and Task Complete buttons below this area respectively start and end the demonstration of a new abstract task.

Finally, the right side of the GUI contains a "chat" window in which the robot can ask the user questions and the user can reply. For example, whenever the user presses the Task Complete button, the robot prompts the user for a name for the newly learned abstract task. This is also where the robot's helpful suggestions appear and where the user can accept or reject them.

3.1 Learning Without Suggestions

Figure 7 shows a hypothetical interaction that results in the system learning the hierarchical structure of Figure 3. The user starts by teaching a new abstract task (which will be named UnscrewStud), demonstrating its two primitive subtasks: Unscrew (applied to stud1 of the LFhub) and PutDown (applied to the nut it is holding as a result).

```
1   Teach New Task
2       Execute Unscrew(LFhub.stud1)
3       Execute PutDown(nut11)
4   Task Complete: UnscrewStud
5   Teach New Task
6       Execute UnscrewStud(LFhub.stud2)
7       Execute UnscrewStud(LFhub.stud3)
8   Task Complete: UnscrewHub
9   Teach New Task
10      Execute UnscrewHub(LRhub)
11      Execute UnscrewHub(RFhub)
12      Execute UnscrewHub(RRhub)
13  Task Complete: UnscrewHubs
14  Teach New Task
15      Execute Unhang(LFhub)
16      Execute PutDown(Tire1)
17  Task Complete: UnhangHub
18  Teach New Task
19      Execute UnhangHub(LRhub)
20      Execute UnhangHub(RFhub)
21      Execute UnhangHub(RRhub)
22  Task Complete: UnhangHubs
23  Teach New Task
24      Execute PickUp(Tire3)
25      Execute Hang(Tire3,LFhub)
26  Task Complete: HangTire
27  Teach New Task
28      Execute HangTire(Tire1,LRhub)
29      Execute HangTire(Tire4,RFhub)
30      Execute HangTire(Tire2,RRhub)
31  Task Complete: Rotate
32  ...
33  Teach New Task
34      Execute UnscrewHubs(LFhub,LRhub,RFhub,RRhub)
35      Execute UnhangHubs(LFhub,LRhub,RFhub,RRhub)
36      Execute Rotate(LFhub,Tire3,LRhub,Tire1, ...)
37      Execute ScrewHubs(LFhub,LRhub,RFhub,RRhub)
38  Task Complete: RotateTires
```

Figure 7: An hypothetical ideal interaction to teach tire rotation without robot's suggestions.

Then, in lines 5–8, the user applies this new abstract task to the other two studs of the LFhub. Notice that when the user completes this demonstration and names this new higher-level abstract task UnscrewHub, the system includes the immediately preceding demonstration of UnscrewHub in the abstraction, so that UnscrewHub has *three* subtasks, one for each stud.

Continuing in lines 9–13, the user similarly applies this new abstract task to the other three hubs and names this new yet higher-level abstract task UnscrewHubs (plural). As before, the system includes the immediately preceding demonstration in the abstraction, so that UnscrewHubs has four subtasks, one for each tire. At this point all the nuts are off the car.

Next, in lines 14–22, the user similarly teaches a high-level abstract task, UnhangHubs, which takes off all the tires and leaves them on the ground. The heart of tire rotation is then in teaching the Rotate abstract task in lines 23–31, where the user hangs the tires back on in the rotated pattern (Tire3 on LFhub, etc.).

To save space, 13 button presses (including 7 Execute buttons) are elided at line 32, culminating in the learning of ScrewHubs. The learning process for ScrewHubs is entirely parallel to the learning of UnscrewHubs in lines 1–13. Finally, in lines 33–38, the four highest-level abstract tasks are put together to make RotateTires.

```
1   Teach New Task
2       Execute Unscrew(LFhub.stud1)
3       Execute PutDown(nut11)
4       Robot: "Do you want to group the highlighted steps
5       (Unscrew and PutDown) into a new subtask?"
6       "Yes"
7       Robot: "Should I execute Unscrew/PutDown on other studs
8       of left front hub?"
9       "Yes"
10      Robot: "Should I execute Unscrew/PutDown*3 on other
11      hubs of the car?"
12      "Yes"
13      Execute Unhang(LFhub)
14      Execute PutDown(Tire1)
15      Robot: "Do you want to group the highlighted steps
16      (Unhang and PutDown) into a new subtask?"
17      "Yes"
18      Robot: "Should I execute Unhang/PutDown on other hubs
19      of the car?"
20      "Yes"
21      Execute PickUp(Tire3)
22      Execute Hang(Tire3,LFhub)
23      Robot: "Do you want to group the highlighted steps (PickUp
24      and Hang) into a new subtask?"
25      "Yes"
26      Robot: "Do you want to group the highlighted steps
27      (Unhang/PutDown*4 and PickUp/Hang) into a new subtask?"
28      "No"
29      Execute PickUp/Hang(Tire1,LRhub)
30      Execute PickUp/Hang(Tire4,RFhub)
31      Execute PickUp/Hang(Tire2,RRhub)
32      Robot: "Do you want to group the highlighted steps (four
33      HangTire's) into a new subtask?"
34      "Yes"
35      Robot: "Do you want to group the highlighted steps
36      (Unhang/PutDown*4 and HangTire*4) into a new subtask?"
37      "No"
38  ...
39  Task Complete: RotateTires
```

Figure 8: A typical interaction to teach tire rotation with robot's suggestions.

last ← last task executed
if $|inputs(last)| \neq 1$ then return
input ← $first(inputs(last))$; whole ← $parent(input)$
parts ← $\varnothing$
foreach other ∈ $type(input)$
  if other $\neq$ input $\wedge$ $parent(other) = whole$
    then add other to parts
if parts $\neq$ $\varnothing$
  then ask 'Should I execute '+last+' on other '
    +type+'s of '+whole+'?'

(a) Parts heuristic

last ← last task executed
previous ← task executed immediately before last
foreach input of last
  if $source(input) = previous \wedge$ holding input after previous
    then ask 'Do you want to group the highlighted steps ('
    +previous+' and'+last+') into a new subtask?'
    return

(b) Data flow heuristic

Figure 9: Pseudocode for suggestion heuristics.

In summary, in this ideal interaction, the user provided 28 task execution instructions and the robot learned 11 new abstract task types, including the toplevel RotateTires. (The robot, of course, executed more than 28 actions because some of the tasks instructed by the user were abstract.)

Unfortunately, as mentioned earlier, no users in our study came even close to this ideal behavior. The best anyone achieved was 6 new abstract task types. So, the question is, how can we help users get closer to this ideal behavior? The next section describes our approach, which is to use general heuristics to generate helpful suggestions.

3.2 Heuristics for Generating Suggestions

Reflecting on the ideal interaction in Figure 7, we identified two general heuristics to help the robot learn HTNs with useful abstract tasks. Because these are heuristics, which means that they are not always right, we communicate the robot's suggestions as questions to which the user can say yes or no (to accept or reject the suggestion).

The first heuristic, called the *parts* heuristic, is inspired by the grouping of repeated tasks in the ideal interaction, which is driven by the part-whole structure of the domain, as shown in Figure 10. The heuristic rule suggests repeating the last executed task on the other parts of the same type that share the same physical parent (e.g., the other two studs of a hub). If this suggestion is accepted, the system then groups the last task together with repetitions for the other parts into a new abstract task.

The second heuristic, called the *data flow* heuristic, is inspired by the grouping that the ideal user does in lines 1–4 of Figure 7. The heuristic rule suggests grouping two consecutive tasks whenever an output of the first is an input of the second (e.g., the data flow shown in Figure 5) *and* the robot is holding the data flow object between the two tasks.

Figure 9 shows pseudocode for these two heuristics, which are applied in order after the execution of each primitive or abstract task. Notice also that both of these heuristics are quite general. They may be more or less useful in different domains, but they are expressed entirely in terms of mathematical concepts, such as data flow and part-whole relationships. There is nothing specifically about car maintenance in the statement of the rules.

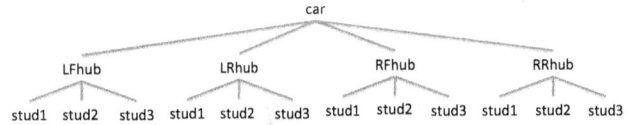

Figure 10: Part-whole knowledge.

Now let's see how these heuristics function in the typical interaction shown in Figure 8. The first suggestion, based on the data flow heuristic, appears on line 4. The user accepts the suggestion, leading to the creation of a new abstract task type called Unscrew/PutDown. Notice that system automatically generates a convenient default name for new abstract task types created in response to suggestions. The user can rename these using the Rename button at the top middle of the GUI.

The second suggestion, based on the parts heuristic, appears on line 7 and results in the new abstract task Unscrew/Putdown*3, which corresponds to UnscrewHub in Figure 7.

The interaction proceeds now in a parallel fashion to Figure 7, with the user answering yes to the next three suggestions. Then, on line 28, the user first answers no. This suggestion is generated by the data flow heuristic (in this case applied to abstract tasks). Because the user has just executed the first step of the front-back tire rotation pattern, which is to put Tire3 (that was originally on the LRhub) onto the LFhub, it seems plausible that she already has in mind the idea of grouping this with the next three steps, not the previous task.

The next suggestion, appearing on line 32, suggests in fact grouping these steps into a new abstract task, which corresponds to Rotate in Figure 7. The user accepts this suggestion.

The second instance in which the user answers no appears on line 37, in answer to another suggestion generated by the data flow heuristic. This is a case in which a yes answer would also be reasonable. All that answering yes would do is to add an extra layer of grouping near the top of the hierarchy, grouping together what are called UnhangHubs and Rotate in Figure 3.

To save space, the remaining three suggestions are elided. They follow the same pattern as the first three suggestions, just as the elided lines in Figure 7 follow the same pattern as lines 1–13 in that interaction.

In summary, notice that in this interaction the user executed only 11 tasks, as compared to 28 in Figure 7. Even with answering 12 yes/no questions, the user in this interaction is expending less effort to achieve the same quality plan. This effect is borne out by the user study described in the next section.

4. EVALUATION

We conducted a study with non-expert users to evaluate both the usability of our algorithms in general, and more specifically, the contribution of the suggestions toward improving the interaction and learning.

4.1 Study Design

We conducted a between-subjects study to evaluate two conditions: a *No-Suggestions* condition, in which the robot provided no repetition or grouping suggestions, and a *Suggestions* condition, in which these suggestions were made when

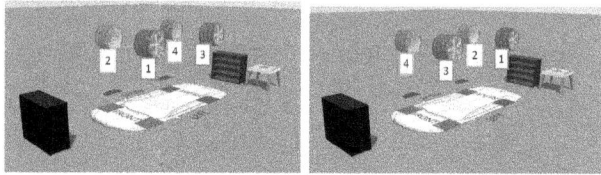

(a) Start configuration   (b) Goal configuration

Figure 11: Start and Goal Configurations

appropriate. Participants in both conditions were able to use the GUI to add hierarchy to their task themselves, as in Figure 7.

A total of 32 college-age participants (18 female and 14 male) were recruited. Most of the participants (15 female and 8 male) did not have programming experience. 15 participants were assigned to the No-Suggestions condition and 17 to the Suggestions condition. The two conditions were balanced for gender and programming experience.

4.2 Task

The study consisted of a training activity (in a blocks world domain) followed by the main study based on tire rotation. All participants were given the same training activity to develop familiarity with the GUI and the overall interaction style. Specifically, participants were given step-by-step written instructions for building a tower using six colored blocks and two primitive actions: Pickup and PutOn. Participants were guided through a series of steps, beginning with simply moving blocks around, to teaching a new abstract task, to reusing already learned abstract tasks to build a tower. The training process did not include any robot suggestions, to avoid biasing participants in the No-Suggestions condition. All of the participants successfully completed the training steps and did not have any questions for the experimenter afterwards.

After training, participants performed the main study activity in which they were asked to teach the robot how to rotate the tires from the start configuration to the goal configuration shown in Figure 11. Participants were given detailed written descriptions of the six primitive actions described in Section 2 and a terminology picture similar to Figure 4, but no step-by-step instructions on how to perform tire rotation. The GUI used by participants in both conditions was identical. The only difference between the two conditions was whether or not repetition and grouping suggestions were provided.

4.3 Procedure

Upon arrival, participants were asked to sign an informed consent form and were surveyed about their programming experience. Following this, participants were given the written instructions for the training activity; the experimenter started the learning system and left the room until training was complete. Following training, the experimenter provided the written tire rotation instructions, started the system and again waited outside the room. Upon completion of the tire rotation task, participants were asked to fill out a questionnaire about their experience. Participants were then asked to teach the tire rotation task a second time (under the same study condition), followed by the same questionnaire.

We had participants perform two trials of the main study task because we anticipated that improved performance would

occur as they gained experience with the GUI. As we will see in the results below, we did observe this effect.

4.4 Measures and Analysis

We used the following three objective measures to evaluate participant performance:

- *Teaching Effort:* The effort expended by the human, measured as the number of times the teacher pressed the Execute button during the interaction (for both primitive and abstract tasks). We think of this as the number of task instructions communicated by the human to the robot.

- *Plan Quality:* The quality of the learned tire rotation plan, measured as the number of abstract tasks learned (and used). We choose this measure because hierarchy is a valuable property in complex plans for both communication and reuse.

- *Teaching Efficiency:* The efficiency of the interaction, measured by dividing plan quality by the teaching effort (using the definitions above).

The two-tailed Kolmogorov-Smirnov test was used for the evaluation of these measures.

4.5 Hypotheses

We formed the following five hypotheses about the effect of suggestions on the learning interaction based on the models we presented earlier and findings from human-computer and human-robot interaction studies.

- **Hypothesis 1:** Participants will expend less teaching effort in the Suggestions condition than in the No-Suggestions condition.

- **Hypothesis 2:** The quality of the learned plans will be higher in the Suggestions condition than in the No-Suggestions condition.

- **Hypothesis 3:** The teaching efficiency will be greater in the Suggestions condition than in the No-Suggestions condition.

- **Hypothesis 4:** In the Suggestions condition, participants who accepted more suggestions will have better measures of teaching effort and plan quality.

- **Hypothesis 5:** All participants in both conditions will be able to successfully teach the tire rotation task by the second trial.

4.6 Results and Discussion

Table 1 and Figure 12 summarize the results of our study, which support Hypotheses 1–4, but not Hypothesis 5.

Teaching Effort: Analysis of the number of Execute button presses during the training process shows that the teaching effort was significantly higher in the No-Suggestions than in the Suggestions condition, supporting Hypothesis 1. Notice that the p-value in the second trial is lower than in the first trial due to the large reduction in Execute button presses by participants in the Suggestions condition during the second trial. We attribute this difference to participants adapting to the robot's suggestions. A reduction in effort was also

$Mean \pm SD$	Execute Button Presses (First Trial)	Execute Button Presses (Second Trial)	Abstract Tasks Learned (First Trial)	Abstract Tasks Learned (Second Trial)	Efficiency (First Trial)	Efficiency (Second Trial)
No-suggestions	62.07 ± 19.10	51.40 ± 27.22	2.87 ± 2.83	2.47 ± 1.77	0.04 ± 0.03	0.06 ± 0.06
Suggestions	50.47 ± 42.68	26.65 ± 16.42	7.94 ± 5.48	8.53 ± 3.92	0.31 ± 0.31	0.41 ± 0.30
p-value	0.05	0.01	0.02	$\ll 0.001$	$\ll 0.001$	0.001

Table 1: Comparison of objective measures between the two conditions.

observed in the No-Suggestions condition, but the change is much smaller. To further highlight the impact of suggestions on teaching effort, Figure 12(a) shows via linear regression how the number of Execute button presses in both trials decreases with the number of robot suggestions accepted by the user, partially supporting Hypothesis 4.

Plan Quality: Analysis of the number of abstract tasks learned shows that the quality of plans was significantly higher in the Suggestions than in the No-Suggestions condition, supporting Hypothesis 2. Additionally, Figure 12(b) shows via linear regression how the number of abstract tasks learned in both trials increases with the number of robot suggestions accepted by the user, further supporting Hypothesis 4.

Teaching Efficiency: Analysis of the efficiency measure provides insight into how teaching effort and plan quality vary in combination between conditions. Teaching efficiency (see last column of Table 1) is significantly higher in the Suggestions than in the No-Suggestions condition, supporting Hypothesis 3. Additionally, we observe greater improvement in efficiency between the first trial and the second trial for participants in the Suggestions condition.

Hypothesis 5 predicted that by the second trial all participants would successfully teach the tire rotation task. Unfortunately, this hypothesis was not supported by our study. In the second trial, for 3/15 participants in the No-Suggestions condition and 4/17 in the Suggestions condition, even though the world state was in the goal configuration at the end of their teaching session, the learned plan would not successfully achieve the goal configuration from the start configuration specified in Figure 11. This is a problem we are looking to solve in the next iteration of our system.

Finally, it is interesting to note that in informal post-study debriefing several participants in the Suggestions condition commented that they initially rejected the robot's suggestions because there had been no suggestions in the training activity and they were were not sure about what the effect of saying yes would be. This was an unintended side effect of our study design, in which we sought to eliminate bias by following the same training procedure in both conditions. Nevertheless, the Suggestions condition showed clear

advantages over No-Suggestions despite this limitation, and we expect better results could have been achieved with a training process tailored for the Suggestions condition.

We did not see any significant effect of programming experience on our results.

5. RELATED WORK

There is extensive research (involving both robots and virtual agents) on learning from demonstration [1], hierarchical task learning, interactive task learning and learning from a single task iteration. However, other than Rybski et al., discussed below, we do not know of any other work that combines all of these aspects, as our present work does.

Research on hierarchical task learning includes both learning from demonstration and learning from instructions approaches. LfD approaches generally focus on learning from multiple demonstrations. For example, in robotic research, Nicolescu and Mataric [12] implemented a LfD system that enables a robot to learn and refine representations of complex tasks and to generalize multiple demonstrations into a single graph-like representation. In [16], Veeraraghavan and Veloso developed a similar LfD approach for teaching a robot tasks with repetitions. Hayes and Scassellati [6] learn HTNs through multi-agent coordination with humans in the loop.

Garland et al. [4] developed an offline, purely software system that generalizes an HTN from a set of execution traces (demonstrations). A novel aspect of their system was support for a domain expert to refine past demonstrations. In addition to relying on multiple demonstrations, this system does not make any suggestions—the user must take all of the initiative in building the HTN.

Most research on interactive task learning goes under the rubric of "active learning" and involves the system asking questions of the user. We prefer the term "interactive" to emphasize the bidirectional nature of the communication shown in Figure 1.

For example, Chernova and Veloso [3] developed a policy learning algorithm in which the robot asks the human to provide labels for states in which the robot has a low certainty. Focusing more on social interaction and broader question types, Cakmak and Thomaz [2] have formalized three question types—label, demonstration and feature requests—and studied their use in LfD. Hayes and Scassellati [7] also generate demonstration requests. None of these systems, however, generate suggestions for grouping.

The most common approach to learning from a single task iteration is via instructions. For example, Huffman and Laird [8] explored the requirements for designing an instructable agent, and showed that a simulated robotic agent could learn useful instruction in natural language. In [9], Mohan and Laird extended this work by instantiating their design in the Soar cognitive architecture. Their work uses

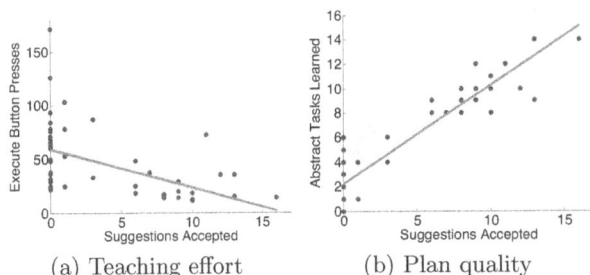

(a) Teaching effort   (b) Plan quality

Figure 12: Impact of accepted suggestions.

an HTN as the task representation, but does not include demonstrations.

The closest work to ours is by Rybski et al. [15], who developed an algorithm that combines spoken language understanding, dialog and physical demonstration to learn complex plans. Their task representation allows abstract tasks to be constructed from simpler subtasks in order to create hierarchical structures. The robot can also verify the HTN with the human by asking questions and allowing the human to add additional conditional cases. However, their approach for learning task structure differs from ours in that it does not leverage ordering and data flow constraints. Furthermore, the robot's questions are limited to filling in unspecified conditions (e.g., missing else statements) while our suggestions are aimed at improving the plan quality and teaching efficiency.

6. NEXT STEPS

Our main next step is to move the human-robot interaction from simulation into a shared physical space using a PR2 robot and an approximately life-size plastic and wood mockup of the relevant parts of a car. To circumvent the need for computer vision processing, we will place the user, robot and mockup inside of a Vicon motion-capture cell and attach markers to objects as needed. This will make it possible to move away from a GUI-style interaction and towards a more natural, situated interaction. If the GUI does not totally disappear in this context, it will be moved to a hand-held touch screen.

For example, instead of pressing a primitive task button, selecting the input object(s) from a menu, and then pressing the Execute button, the user will be able to physically demonstrate a primitive task by picking up, putting down, screwing, unscrewing objects, etc. With only a small number of primitive task types, we expect to easily develop a classifier to recognize which primitive action is being performed and its inputs. For learned abstract actions, a GUI (or perhaps voice recognition) may still be used to name the action, but the selection of input(s) will be done by gesture, such as pointing to or touching the appropriate object(s). We will study how these changes affect the learning process, which will then inform how other communication functions of the GUI, such as the Teach New Task and Task Complete buttons, the chat pane and the display of the current hierarchical structure should be handled.

In a more theoretical direction, our next steps include exploring how to extend our algorithms to support top-down learning and then a flexible combination of top-down and bottom-up. Among other things, this involves integrating learning from demonstration with learning from instruction techniques. We also plan to explore improvements to our existing heuristic rules and new heuristics for making useful suggestions, especially as we extend our task domain beyond tire rotation.

Finally, working with a physical robot will inevitably present us with the challenge and opportunity to explore the very broad issue of how uncertainty and failure in robotic systems affects the learning process.

7. ACKNOWLEDGMENTS

This work is supported in part by the Office of Naval Research under Grant N00014-13-1-0735.

8. REFERENCES

[1] B. D. Argall, S. Chernova, M. Veloso, and B. Browning. A survey of robot learning from demonstration. *Robotics and Autonomous Systems*, 57(5):469–483, 2009.

[2] M. Cakmak and A. L. Thomaz. Designing robot learners that ask good questions. In *ACM/IEEE International Conference on Human-Robot Interaction*, pages 17–24. ACM, 2012.

[3] S. Chernova and M. Veloso. Interactive policy learning through confidence-based autonomy. *Journal of Artificial Intelligence Research*, 34(1):1, 2009.

[4] A. Garland, K. Ryall, and C. Rich. Learning hierarchical task models by defining and refining examples. In *International Conference on Knowledge Capture*, pages 44–51, 2001.

[5] B. J. Grosz and C. L. Sidner. Attention, intentions, and the structure of discourse. *Comput. Linguist.*, 12(3):175–204, July 1986.

[6] B. Hayes. Social hierarchical learning. In *Proceedings of the 8th ACM/IEEE International Conference on Human-Robot Interaction (HRI 2013) Pioneers Workshop*, 2013.

[7] B. Hayes and B. Scassellati. Discovering task constraints through observation and active learning. In *IEEE/RSJ International Conference on Intelligent Robots and Systems*, 2014.

[8] S. B. Huffman and J. E. Laird. Flexibly instructable agents. *Journal of Artificial Intelligence Research*, 3:271–324, 1995.

[9] S. Mohan and J. E. Laird. Towards situated, interactive, instructable agents in a cognitive architecture. In *AAAI Fall Symposium Series*, 2011.

[10] A. Mohseni-Kabir, S. Chernova, and C. Rich. Collaborative learning of hierarchical task networks from demonstration and instruction. In *RSS Workshop on Human-Robot Collaboration for Industrial Manufacturing*, Berkeley, CA, July 2014.

[11] A. Mohseni-Kabir, C. Rich, and S. Chernova. Learning partial ordering constraints from a single demonstration. In *ACM/IEEE International Conference on Human-robot interaction*, pages 248–249, 2014.

[12] M. N. Nicolescu and M. J. Mataric. Natural methods for robot task learning: Instructive demonstrations, generalization and practice. In *AAMAS*, pages 241–248, 2003.

[13] C. Rich. Building task-based user interfaces with ANSI/CEA-2018. *IEEE Computer*, 42(8):20–27, 2009.

[14] C. Rich and C. L. Sidner. Using collaborative discourse theory to partially automate dialogue tree authoring. In *Proc. Int. Conf. on Intelligent Virtual Agents*, pages 327–340, Santa Cruz, CA, Sept. 2012.

[15] P. E. Rybski, K. Yoon, J. Stolarz, and M. M. Veloso. Interactive robot task training through dialog and demonstration. In *ACM/IEEE Int. Conf. on Human-Robot Interaction*, pages 49–56, 2007.

[16] H. Veeraraghavan and M. Veloso. Learning task specific plans through sound and visually interpretable demonstrations. In *IEEE/RSJ International Conference on Intelligent Robots and Systems*, pages 2599–2604, 2008.

How Robot Verbal Feedback Can Improve Team Performance in Human-Robot Task Collaborations

Aaron St. Clair
Interaction Lab
University of Southern California
Los Angeles, CA 90089
astclair@usc.edu

Maja Matarić
Interaction Lab
University of Southern California
Los Angeles, CA 90089
mataric@usc.edu

ABSTRACT

We detail an approach to planning effective verbal feedback during pairwise human-robot task collaboration. The approach is motivated by social science literature as well as existing work in robotics and is applicable to a variety of task scenarios. It consists of a dynamic, synthetic task implemented in an augmented reality environment. The result is combined robot task control and speech production, allowing the robot to actively participate and communicate with its teammate. A user study was conducted to experimentally validate the efficacy of the approach on a task in which a single user collaborates with an autonomous robot. The results demonstrate that the approach is capable of improving both objective measures of team performance and the user's subjective evaluation of both the task and the robot as a teammate.

Categories and Subject Descriptors

H.1.2 [**Models and Principles**]: User/Machine Systems—*human factors, software psychology*; H.5.2 [**Information Interfaces and Presentation**]: User Interfaces—*evaluation/methodology, natural language*; I.2.9 [**Artificial Intelligence**]: Robotics—*operator interfaces*

Keywords

Human-robot collaborations; natural language

1. INTRODUCTION

Robots are becoming increasingly competent at performing tasks such as navigation and manipulation in real-world human environments including homes, offices, and other settings where they are around people. This expanded range of capabilities makes possible many scenarios in which robots not only take action around people but also collaborate with them to accomplish a task together. In a home environment a robot might help a person clean up a messy room, in the office a robot could help to rearrange furniture, and in a

Permission to make digital or hard copies of all or part of this work for personal or classroom use is granted without fee provided that copies are not made or distributed for profit or commercial advantage and that copies bear this notice and the full citation on the first page. Copyrights for components of this work owned by others than the author(s) must be honored. Abstracting with credit is permitted. To copy otherwise, or republish, to post on servers or to redistribute to lists, requires prior specific permission and/or a fee. Request permissions from permissions@acm.org.
HRI'15, March 2–5, 2015, Portland, Oregon, USA.
Copyright is held by the owner/author(s). Publication rights licensed to ACM.
ACM 978-1-4503-2883-8/15/03 ...$15.00.
http://dx.doi.org/10.1145/2696454.2696491.

manufacturing setting a robot might help assemble a product. These collaborative scenarios present a number of challenges; not only must the robot avoid physical collision with the human, it must also be a productive part of the collaboration accounting for the human's activity when deciding what to do next, and providing a means for the human to understand and control its behavior.

In this paper we consider the problem of coordinating social communication during the course of a pairwise human-robot task collaboration. Effective feedback is important in these scenarios since it has a direct impact on the situational awareness of the robot's collaborator. We present a general methodology allowing a robot to produce social communication (currently speech), to efficiently and intelligently allocate roles during a task collaboration. The primary goal of the method is to support the user's natural collaboration modalities and preferences and ensure applicability across many typical human-robot task collaboration scenarios. The approach generates three types of situated verbalizations aimed at providing useful information to a teammate in co-located joint activities. To make the approach generalize across many task settings, we base it on existing task formulations from multi-robot systems. Unlike existing work in human-robot collaboration, it does not rely on a specific conversational structure such as turn-taking, allowing for it to be used in dynamic tasks. We hypothesize that providing feedback in the form of coordinating social communication will lead to improved team performance and subjective evaluation of the task itself by users and also allow the robot to provide guidance for the user's behavior.

The rest of the paper is organized as follows. First, we provide some background information on human-human and human-robot collaboration and related existing work. Next, we provide an overview of the communication planning approach and detail the three types of verbalizations used by the robot. Next, the details of an initial specific task to which we have applied the communication planning approach is presented. Finally, an experimental validation of the approach in this task setting is presented as an initial proof of concept, demonstrating improved performance and subjective evaluation when people work with the communicating robot.

2. BACKGROUND

We present a brief review of relevant literature from the social sciences about human collaboration, as well as from human-computer and human-robot interaction as relates to this work.

People have a natural ability to collaborate comprised of a complex series of behaviors that attributes agency to the people and things around them. We recognize our collaborator's actions using visual observation via the mirror neuron system [16] and theorize about the mental models of others including their beliefs, desires, and intentions [12]. Finally, we issue a variety of implicit and explicit social cues aimed at helping others understand their own actions [10, 2]. Many of these processes, with the exception perhaps of strategic planning, occur automatically without conscious thought on our part and are active even when the person is collaborating with a robot. Additionally, people rely heavily on speech for coordination. Robots that collaborate with people should take advantage of the capabilities of their human counterparts by providing appropriate signaling to improve their partner's efficiency. By enabling a robot to produce human-like communication during a task, this work aims to support effective coordination between people and robots without requiring users to be trained how to use the robot beforehand.

Relevant prior research on human-machine collaboration includes an extensive body of work on top-down deliberative approaches for modeling and constructing shared plans for collaboration [6, 18]. There has also been extensive work on intent recognition relying on perspective taking or Theory of Mind-inspired models to allow a robot to recognize a person's intentional behavior through observation [4], as well as to recognize and generate intentional face-to-face meeting initiation behavior [9], and to recognize helping and hindering social behavior via an MDP formalization utilizing inverse planning [21]. Other relevant work demonstrated robot learning of simple tasks through human tutelage and effective collaboration via turn-taking or biased pre-emptive action [1, 8]. Task scheduling systems have been developed to change the task planning of a robot teammate in response to actions taken by a human teammate [17, 22]. Another area of research has focused on identifying and evaluating promising coordination behaviors, particularly eye gaze cues [14], implicit and explicit verbal communication [20], and legible path planning [5]. There is also relevant work in learning demonstration on methods for teaching and instructing robots including collaborative settings [11, 3].

This prior work has demonstrated that robots that account for the actions of their collaborators when deciding what to do are preferred and perceived as more intelligent [17] and that anticipatory action can play an important role in increasing team fluency [8]. Other work has treated the collaborative process as a dialog, supporting verbal turn-taking and sub-task assignment [1]. Speech has been demonstrated to be an effective input modality for commanding a robot [17, 11].

3. APPROACH

Our task control and communication approach consists of three components: 1) the task control system, 2) the human activity model and recognizer, and 3) the communication planner and executive. Planning with a human partner in the environment is distinct from planning in multi-robot scenarios mainly in how communication takes place between teammates. Similarly, there are existing approaches to segmenting, recognizing, and modeling human activity in various contexts. We have developed a simplified methodology to serve these purposes in our experimental task, although

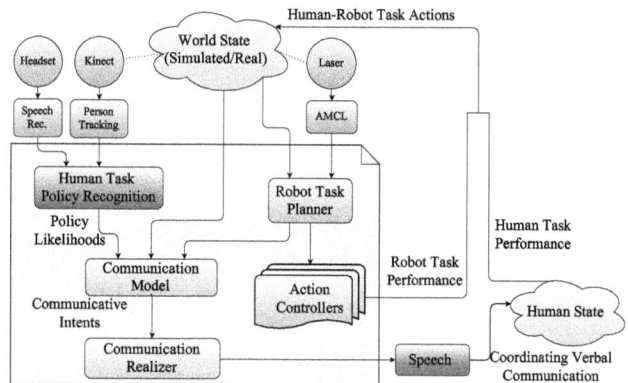

Figure 1: System diagram of the collaborative communication approach (inset) and associated inputs and outputs.

this work could be integrated with and perhaps improved by state-of-the-art recognition and task planning systems. The main contribution of this paper is in the area of planning and execution of communication actions during collaborative task execution in HRI.

3.1 Task Formulation

We formulate the coordination problem in two parts, as follows. First, the robot represents the task as an MDP to plan its actions in the presence of noise. We define a Markov decision process (MDP) for the task $M = S, A, T, R$, where S is the finite state of the environment, A is the set of task actions the robot can execute, T is a function giving a probability distribution over states for executing a given action in a given state, and R is a reward for each state. We assume that the robot can perform the task and has a policy $\pi(s) = a$ that allows it to perform the task. In this case, the transition function captures the robot's uncertainty due to environmental sources, such as sensor or motor noise, and also due to changes the human collaborator might make in the environment. This formulation has been successfully used previously in human-robot collaboration [15] to coordinate the task-actions of the robot without any communicative feedback. In the future, we would like to investigate the use of multiagent policies with joint action mapping for both agents to further improve the robot's feedback.

3.2 Role-Based Activity Model

In addition to ensuring that the robot can jointly perform the task in the presence of a human partner, we want the robot to provide verbal feedback to its partner. We focus on communicating intended action via the mechanism of *roles*. People use explicit and implicit roles in team activity and other organized behavior. For example, if a group of people is tasked with assembling a wooden box, they might assign a sawing role, a hammering role, and a painting role that different people assume during the course of the activity. Interestingly, we could find no well-defined, formal definition of roles or how to partition a given activity into a set of roles [19]. In our pilot experiments we determined that people tended to assign others roles associated with common work objects and locations, although some of these consisted of multiple discrete activities.

In the evaluation task, described later, the act of herding a sheep (finding a stray sheep, collecting it, and bringing it to the pen) was commonly grouped into a single activity or role ("go herd sheep"). To capture these properties we model roles using a set of assignable policies, $\Pi = \pi_1, \pi_2, ...$ This set of policies is domain-dependent and not assumed to be optimal or otherwise sufficient, on its own, for solving the task. Rather, the policies in the set are a means of quantifying each agent's likely behavior over the course of the task, and of grouping similar actions according to the roles people typically assign in that type of task. If the robot and the person have differing capabilities, the set of possible policies for each may be different. For example, if the robot cannot perform all of the actions the person can, the robot activity model may consist of a subset of Π. In the following explanation we will assume that the robot and person can both perform all of the task actions and thus that the robot policy set, Π_{robot} is identical to that of the person, Π_{user}. We maintain a distribution, D, over Π, based on the likelihood that the user is executing each policy and updated by observing state transitions over time, inferring user actions, and reweighting policies that agree.

To accurately infer the role, $r \in \Pi$, that best describes the user's action selection preferences, we assume we have access to some means of action recognition. Specifically, we want to know when an agent (person or robot) takes an action $a \in A$ at time t. Human action segmentation and recognition is a challenging open problem with relevant existing work from computer vision [7]. We have written a heuristic action recognition system that makes use of a factored representation of the state of the task as a set of discrete random variables, $S = \{X_1, X_2, X_3, ... X_n\}$. In order to execute its policy in a fully observable environment, the robot must take sensor input and determine the value of each random variable so that it can determine the current state. Given this capability, we observe that some of the X_i can be directly associated with actions that the agents can take, while others are consequences of the environment. For example, if a switch must be pressed during the course of a task, then we might have an action $a \in A_{task}$ called $FlipSwitch$ and an associated random variable $X_{switch} = \langle Off, On \rangle$, describing the state of the switch. In our heuristic action recognition system, we determine the subset of $X_{recognizable} \subseteq \{X_1, X_2, X_3, ... X_n\}$ that are associated with state changes that are attributable only to the person or the robot. On each update, if the current inferred value of one of these variables is not equal to its previous value, $X_i^{(t-1)} \neq X_i^t$, we assume that one of the agents made the change. To determine which agent, we select the agent closest to the object at that point in time.

This heuristic method works well in simple scenarios with straightforward mechanics, when the sets of random variables are carefully selected, but does not transfer well to all spatiotemporal actions that a person and robot might undertake. The overall system could benefit from integration with a more principled state of the art action recognition method; this is beyond the scope of this paper.

Given the stream of recognized actions, the system next attempts to recognize the role the user is employing at the current time. This process is detailed in Algorithm 1. We first discard all recognized actions as being taken by the robot, leaving only the person's actions. For each $a_{rec} \in A_{task}$, we perform a Bayesian update of a multinomial distribution over the set of role policies, $p(R = r_i | A = a_{rec}) =$ $\alpha * p(A = a_{rec} | R = r_i) * p(R = r_i)$. The likelihood of the action being taken given a certain role r_i is selected based on whether the policy would have executed the action in the previous state, with a specified weight, as follows:

$$p(A = a_{rec} | R = r_i) = \begin{cases} 0.95, & \text{if } r_i(s_{prev}) \equiv a_{rec} \\ 0.05, & \text{otherwise} \end{cases}$$

After normalization, the inferred user role is selected by $\pi_{user} = argmax_r p(r | a_{rec})$. This estimate of the user's role is thus based on their action selections at previous times during the task and is dependent on individual actions taking around the same amount of time. If this is not the case, the likelihood of the action given the role could be expanded to include more than one past state, with an appropriate discount factor. In our validation, the system maintains a multinomial distribution over the set of user roles based on the likelihood that the user is executing each policy. On each update, policies are reweighted based on their agreement or disagreement with the recognized action.

Algorithm 1 User role recognition algorithm
___
Require: Recognized human action $a_{rec} \in A_{task}$, previous state $s_{prev} \in S_{task}$
    for all roles $r = \{\pi_1 ... \pi_n\}$ **do**
      if $r(s_{prev}) = a_{rec}$ **then**
        $p(r | a_{rec}) = 0.95$
      else
        $p(r | a_{rec}) = 0.05$
      end if
      $p_r \leftarrow p_r * p(r | a_{rec})$
    end for
    return $\arg\max_r p(r)$

---

4. PLANNING ROBOT FEEDBACK

Based on this recognized action and the robot's own policy, three types of verbal feedback are generated: *self-narrative*, *role-allocative*, and *empathetic*. A wide range of verbal communication could be produced to improve team coordination. These feedback types were selected as they provide a balance of information to the person about what the robot is doing and what the robot expects them to do. We further validated this selection by conducting a pilot study in which pairs of people performed a task. Based on their transcribed verbalizations, these three types of communication were widely used across different teams and are well-supported by our task model. Additional types of communication, such as providing key bits of salient information, which could occur at varying levels of granularity, as well as qualitative commentary about aspects of the task environment were also used by people but are not supported by the communication model.

4.1 Self-Narrative Feedback

The simplest form of feedback to produce is *self-narrative feedback*, where the robot tells the user what it is going to do, e.g., "I'll take care of X". We define a communicative intent for each policy available to the robot, $C_{narrative} = RobotDoing\langle r_i \rangle, \forall r_i \in \Pi$, and select a single active communicative intent based on the role the robot is executing. To convey these communicative intents to the person, the robot has two options. It could say a phrase indicating its role assignment, i.e., telling a user what role it will execute during the task, or it could implicitly communicate its role assignment by providing feedback about which actions it is executing at a given point in time, leaving the person to infer the robot's role (policy) from this sequence of action selections. The former case requires a mapping of roles to a set of verbal feedback phrases, V, that refer to the correct role, $f_{narrate-role} : \Pi_{robot} \rightarrow V$, while the latter case requires a mapping of every action to one or more verbal feedback phrases $f_{narrate-actions} : A_{task} \rightarrow V$. Ideally, V will contain multiple options for each policy or action so that the robot does not use the same redundant phrasing, which could lead to it being perceived as less intelligent, an issue to be avoided in HRI.

4.2 Role-allocative Feedback

To generate *role-allocative feedback* for the user, such as "you handle X", the expected next action of the user given by our recognized policy π_{user} is compared to the robot's next action as given by the robot's policy, π_{robot}. This comparison is dependent on the type of model employed. If we have access to only a single-agent model of the task, like a typical MDP, we have no specific information about the value of joint action allocation about the best allocation for each agent. Therefore, we have developed a role-allocation method using a single-agent task that specifies a user's role based on the principle of avoiding conflicting action. We assume a list of discrete actions in A_{task} that would conflict if executed by the robot and person at the same time. Given the policies of each agent, we check to see if they are expected to execute the same action given the current state. If this action is in the set of conflicting actions, we suggest an alternate role from Π_{roles} for the user to do that is not conflicting, as detailed in Algorithm 2.

This results in a communicative intent that assigns the user to a given role, $C_{role-allocative} = PersonRole\langle r_i \rangle, \forall r_i \in \Pi_{roles}$. The phrases for role-allocative feedback have similar requirements to those in the narrative feedback case. Specifically, we require a function mapping roles (or alternatively actions) to a set of verbal feedback phrases that the robot can say $f_{role-allocative} : \Pi \rightarrow V$. It should be noted that, at this step, the robot could proactively perform the better action instead of recommending that the user do it. For our initial experiments, we do not consider this option, but assume the robot's policy is stationary.

4.3 Empathetic Feedback

Finally, to generate *empathetic feedback*, we monitor for specific state transitions in the task model. When a transition occurs that has been marked as requiring empathetic feedback, we generate an appropriate communicative intent in the form of either a positive or negative expression (e.g., "Oh no" or "Great"). Our current approach maps specific transitions to communicative intents, e.g., $f(s, s_{prev}) = c \in C_{empathetic}$. By mapping specific state transitions to instance of empathetic feedback, these may also include more specific expressions of empathy, such as a description of what exactly went right or wrong. A general approach to providing empathetic feedback consists of monitoring the value of states over time and responding to large changes in value with a threshold for value changes that matches people's policies for producing empathetic feedback. When a

---

Algorithm 2 Alternative role-allocation suggestions

Require: Person and robot policies π_{user}, π_{robot}, current state $s \in S_{task}, ConflictingAction(a_{user}, a_{robot})$
  $a_{user} \leftarrow \pi_{user}(s)$
  $a_{robot} \leftarrow \pi_{robot}(s)$
  if $a_{user} = a_{robot}$ **and** ConflictingAction(a_{robot}, a_{user}) **then**
      for all roles $r = \{\pi_1 ... \pi_n\}$ **do**
          alternatives $\leftarrow \{\}$
          if $(r(s) \neq a_{robot})$ **or**
          not ConflictingAction($r(s), a_{robot}$) **then**
              append r to alternatives
          end if
      end for
      return alternatives
  else
      return $\{\}$
  end if

---

large value change is detected, the robot can offer the generalized positive or negative empathy response as described above. In this approach, the threshold specified is domain-dependent, although it could be estimated by observing peoples' use of empathetic verbal cues during human-human or human-robot task performance. Additionally, more specific feedback may lead people to ascribe greater intelligence to the robot as it identifies why something went wrong, for instance leading people to conclude the robot has a higher-level understanding of the task than it does.

4.4 Communication Executive

To avoid repetitive speech, appropriate phrases for each type of verbal feedback were determined by having people perform the task in a small pilot experiment. For each action, we stored a set of phrases and randomly selected one phrase when executing the communication. We used baseline phrases as collected from the pilot study, with no attempt to make them more or less polite. The phrases, stored as text strings, are passed to a text-to-speech engine and played in real-time during the task as triggered by the communication planning system. A simple speech executive node was developed to allow multiplexing the various types of communicative feedback without interrupting individual phrases. In future work, we will investigate adapting the types of feedback and phrases spoken in response adherence and performance metrics, allowing for more personalized feedback for individual users.

5. EVALUATION

To test a system for planning coordinating communication in the context of human-robot task scenarios, the first requirement is a robot and accompanying low-level control systems that can reliably perform tasks in an environment co-located with a person. Manipulation of real objects is a challenging problem, and existing off-the-shelf software for performing manipulation tasks is typically slow and requires tuning for specific environmental factors. Additionally, since the robot must monitor its teammate's activity, doing a task that involves real object manipulation also presents difficulties in perceiving the person. To overcome these challenges, we developed a task simulation engine and implemented a task to be performed by two-agent teams.

The task simulator models the behavior of multiple virtual agents and objects over time. The agents are projected onto the floor via an overhead projection system. The system tracks people using environmental sensing and localizes the robot using on-board sensing in the shared space. By updating the simulated positions of agents and objects, robots and people in the room are able to interact with the virtual world by navigating around the room and positioning themselves on top of the virtual objects. The virtual objects are projected on the floor of the room with multiple calibrated projectors and people are tracked with Microsoft Kinects RGB-D sensors using point cloud processing and an unscented Kalman filter. Due to the size of the room and difficulty of fusing the output of multiple skeletal pose estimates, the robot is assumed to only have the (x, y) position of the person in the room. The robot used in this scenario is the Pioneer 2AT (Figure 3); it was selected due to its effective navigation of the environment using an on-board Hokuyo laser rangefinder for localization as well as its small size, which reduces the possibility of harm in an accidental collision.

5.0.1 *Synthetic Collaborative Task*

This experimental setup has several advantages for conducting tasks compared with using physical objects and/or confederate experimenters. First, it allows for many repeatable, dynamic agents that move autonomously in a directed or pseudo-random manner. It also allows for calibrating the velocity, shape, and behavior dynamics of the simulated agents to make a given task easier or more difficult as desired. Finally, since it does not depend on physical objects, several different tasks can be conducted quickly by switching the task controller. The simulator abstracts away physical tasks that are not the focus of this research, such as object manipulation, allowing us to focus on collaborative behavior. This is consistent with the notion of research tasks described by [13] as a systematic abstraction of a real-world task. Despite this abstraction, we are able to preserve some of the complexity of real-world environments, such as partial observability, noise, and occlusion by augmenting or filtering the robot's sensor data. This represents a reasonable trade-off of environmental realism for repeatable HRI experiments, tunable task difficulty, and expanded task possibilities. In future work we plan on applying the approach in a real-world environment outside of the task simulator.

5.1 Pseudo-herding Task

The task scenario implemented for evaluation in the augmented reality environment was a pseudo-herding task featuring a group of sheep that appear from the boundary of the room over time with a specified arrival rate. The sheep move about exhibiting Brownian motion with simple avoidance rules and must be collected and brought to a central holding pen. Only one sheep can be collected by an agent at a time, hence it is pseudo-herding. To collect a sheep, the agent must move to a position overlapping the sheep. People are shown their tracked location by projecting a ring around the last tracked position. After a sheep is collected, it follows the person until it is dragged inside the circular pen, at which point it stays inside.

In addition to the pen, there are two timed game-play elements: a lock and a light. When the lock timer reaches zero, the pen becomes unlocked and any captured sheep es-

Figure 2: The experimental setup featuring a person and the Pioneer collaborating on the pseudo-herding task.

cape and begin to wander again, effectively reverting any progress made. When the light timer reaches zero, the visibility of the projection is modified to simulate lights going out in the room. This prevents users from easily finding wandering sheep. The timer elements are rendered with a progress bar and color change to clearly indicate when they are about to expire. The task has a number of interesting properties, such as dynamic moving objects; it is divisible and loosely-coupled, supporting different completion strategies. The goal of the game, as introduced to participants, is to collect all the sheep into the pen area as quickly as possible, requiring maintenance of the lock and light elements.

5.2 Application of Verbal Feedback Approach

Applying the approach to the pseudo-herding task required the development of the task model, robot policies, person policies, and verbal phrases specific to the herding task. The state is comprised of a set of independent random variables $S = \{X_{lock}, X_{light}, X_{has-sheep}\}$. For the herding task we define a relatively simple state space consisting of three features $X_{lock} = \{high, low, unlocked\}$, $X_{light} = \{high, low, off\}$, and $X_{has-sheep} = \{true, false\}$. Because navigation is used as a proxy for manipulation in the augmented reality task environment, we define a navigation action for the robot to activate each of the work items (lock, light, and pen). Since all the sheep are equally valuable, we define a single navigation action for sheep retrieval in which the robot collects the nearest sheep. Thus the possible actions are *GotoLock, GotoLight, GotoPen, CollectSheep*. The robot's task behavior during the task consists of a set of policies mapping states to action $\Pi : s \leftarrow a$. Note that in the augmented reality environment the robot and person have the same capability and thus share the same action set, $A = A_{robot} = A_{user}$.

To apply the proposed communication approach, we first seek to define a set of policies that covers the set of roles that a team of people might define to complete the task. Fitting with our assumption that roles are correlated with distinct work objects we have defined roles associated with each work object as well as their possible pairwise combinations: $\Pi = (\pi_{lock}, \pi_{light}, \pi_{sheep}, \pi_{lock-light}, \pi_{lock-sheep}, \pi_{light-sheep})$. In single object policies, the action in every state is the navigation action associated with the object, i.e., $\forall s \in S, \pi_{lock}(s) = GotoLock$. For policies with multiple objects, action preferences are given by the following object priorities $lock > light > sheep$, thus the $\pi_{light-sheep}$ policy will make the robot go to the light if it has turned off, otherwise it will collect sheep and take them back to the pen. No three-object roles were defined since those would consist of a single agent trying to do all parts of the task. This set of policies is used to both control the robot and to model the person's behavior as they have equal capability in this case.

The mapping of roles to policies, as well as the phrases used by the robot, were informed by a pilot experiment in which two people performed the task together, where we found people roughly partitioning the two timed elements and sharing the duty of collecting sheep. For the robot's speech, selected transcribed phrases and used Google Speech API for the robot's voice. Since there are three possible speech channels, a multiplexing and queuing system was implemented to prevent a type of verbal feedback from interrupting the one already playing. This was sufficient for realizing the verbal feedback as each type of phrase is short in duration and only generated periodically when the task state or user model changes. This system selected randomly among all possible alternatives for the particular feedback type (e.g., one of several ways of the robot saying it is going to go trigger the lock) in order to prevent repeated phrasing.

6. STUDY DESIGN

Although the method presented for generating coordinating verbal communication is designed to be applicable in a wide range of task settings, we present the following user study as an initial proof of concept designed to evaluate the approach in a co-located human-robot task collaboration as compared to a non-communicating robot. The approach was evaluated by measuring the time to complete the pseudo-herding task in the augmented reality environment as well as collecting subjective measures of the robot's performance via surveys. The communicating robot was implemented as described above and compared to a control, a non-communicating robot, i.e., a robot that performed the task in an identical manner without issuing any verbal feedback. This control was selected since few existing methods for high-level task planning integrate human feedback, making a task-only robot a likely scenario.

A within-subjects experiment was conducted, in which each participant performed the task twice, once with the communicating robot, and once with the non-communicating one, with order of presentation counterbalanced across subjects. A within-subjects design was selected since the overall interaction is quite short (usually about 2-5 minutes) and our pilot experiments found the times to finish the task varied a great deal among people. Also, since the task is unfamiliar to all users due to its unique setup, there is the potential for each person to learn the nuances of the task over time, and improve performance. Participants watched an experimenter explain and perform each of the task elements, including: herding a sheep and triggering the lock and light. Participants were told that the goal of the game was to herd all of the sheep as quickly as possible. The

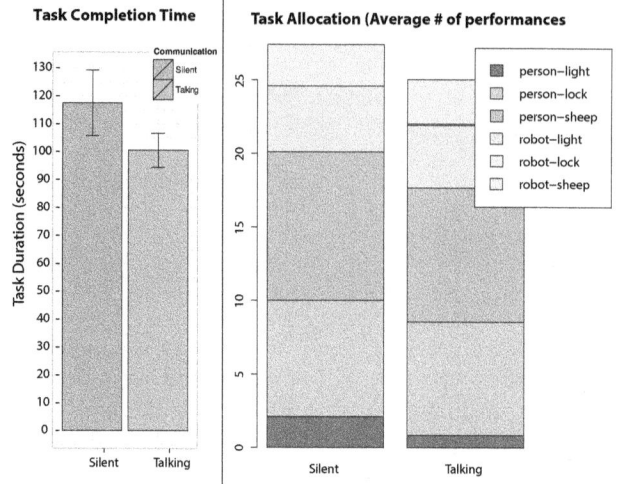

Figure 3: Time to completion and allocation counts of agent actions in communicating and silent conditions.

random seeds used to generate the sheep behavior were initialized identically for each participant to keep the simulated sheep behavior as consistent as possible between runs. The task simulator was configured with 12 sheep. The speeds of the sheep and timing of the lock and light elements were tested in a pilot experiment. The task thus calibrated was possible but somewhat challenging for a single person to perform alone. The static robot policy used for the task was favored light- and sheep-collection, resulting in the robot's first priority being turning on the light and collecting and returning sheep to the pen area while the light is on. The robot's task behavior was identical for each condition with the on-board speakers either enabled or disabled for the talking and silent robots, respectively.

6.0.1 Data Collected

Data collected include a record of the underlying task simulator state, the tracked locations of the agents (people, robot, sheep and virtual objects), an audio recording of each person from a wireless headset microphone, and video of the interaction from overhead and side-view cameras. After completion of the task participants were asked to take a survey asking demographic questions as well as a series of 27 questions about the robot as a teammate, rated on a 7-point Likert scale from "strongly agree" to "strongly disagree".

6.0.2 Participants

A total of sixteen participants (5 female, 11 male) were recruited from campus sources. Participants' ages ranged from 17-29, with a mean of 21. Most had completed at least some undergraduate college education. One participant was an outlier, not able to complete the task due to a misunderstanding of the rules; this participant's data were discarded.

6.0.3 Hypotheses and Outcome Measures

The following hypotheses were formulated:
Hypothesis 1: Participants will prefer the communicating robot and consider it a better teammate.
Hypothesis 2: The communicating robot will improve team task performance.

7. RESULTS

For the objective results, the time to complete the task to the nearest second was recorded for each trial by watching the recorded video, marking the start of the task as signaled by the experimenter, and the end as noted by the freezing of the projected display upon retrieval of the final sheep. Trials with the communicating robot were completed on average 17 seconds faster (M = 100.5 s, SD = 21 s) than the ones with the non- communicating robot (M = 117.6 s, SD = 40 s), p < 0.03. As our conditions were repeated within subjects, we then performed a post hoc analysis by fitting a linear mixed effects regression and comparing to a baseline single mean model. In comparing the two models, we find incorporating the communication factor has a significant impact on the duration (p<0.04), confirming Hypothesis 2.

In the pseudo-herding task, in the quantifiable terms of state value, the biggest mistake that can be made is to let the timed lock lapse, releasing all collected sheep and forcing the team to start over. We intentionally selected a static robot policy in which the lock was ignored by the robot, requiring the participant to manage it instead. Across all 30 trials, the lock was allowed to lapse in 2 of 15 trials in each condition. Because these costly errors were roughly evenly distributed across conditions and were relatively rare with (M = 0.4, SD = 1.1), it is unlikely that the objective performance improvements are due to an avoidance of mistakes; it is more likely due to the clarification of responsibilities provided by the verbal feedback and minimizing the user's context switching between lock and light (Figure 4).

Distinguishing the impact of each type of feedback is challenging as they are issued while the robot and the person are moving about the room, making subtle effects difficult to discern from planned, task-directed actions. The most common feedback issued was self-narrative as the robot narrated its actions whenever they differed from what it was doing previously. Since the role-allocative feedback is very specific, with post hoc analysis we can compare the robot's suggested action with the action ultimately undertaken by the person. Over the course of the 15 trials in which the robot used verbal communication, and therefore was capable of assigning roles, the robot made a total of 12 role-allocation suggestions to users. To assess users' adherence to the robot's requests, we assessed whether a matching action for the participant was recognized within a short time interval. In total, participants adhered to all 12 requests within 10 seconds and often much faster. This adherence rate is likely due to the low cost of completing the robot's requests as well as the novelty of the interaction. Still, anecdotally, there are multiple instances of participants abandoning a prior plan and altering course in response to the robot's suggestion.

The low overall number of role-allocation suggestions is likely due to most participants allowing the robot to take full responsibility for the light. Also, since the robot attempts to track the person's active policy using a stream of recognized actions (currently from the task simulation), it only accounts for completed actions when determining the user's most likely policy. This has the effect of ignoring additional information provided by the person's trajectory, i.e., motion in the direction of a given object, and relies on the user reaching a steady state of task performance where they perform the same types of actions repeatedly. Anecdotally the refresh rate of the various communication models often appears to result in a narrative phrase and role-allocative

Table 1: Post-experiment survey results

Question	0 (strongly disagree) - 6 (strongly agree)	
	M	SD
The things the robot said made sense.	5.27	1.6
The talking robot was a better teammate than the silent robot.	5	1.4
The task was more fun with the robot than if I had done it alone.	5.4	0.8
The talking robot was more fun.	5.3	1.2
The robot's talking helped me understand what it was going to do next.	4.9	1.9
The things the robot said helped me decide what to do.	3.8	2.0
I tried to do what the robot told me to do.	3.6	2.4

phrase happening immediately after one another, such as "I'll go get the light. Can you take care of the lock?", often resulting in the user expressing agreement. The survey data reveal that all but two people agreed that the talking robot was a better teammate (see Table 1 for a summary). The communicating robot had similarly high scores for being more fun and for its verbal feedback making sense during the interaction. Questions asking how participants adjusted their behavior in response to the communicating robot are less consistently agreed with, perhaps due to people taking credit for their own actions and the team's success or failure.

8. CONCLUSION

In this paper we presented an approach for robot production of social communication during human-robot task collaboration to improve in situ decision-making and team performance. The problem of generating communication from a robot to a human teammate for the purposes of coordinating joint activity is formulated as a planning problem compatible with a class of pairwise, loosely-coupled tasks and supporting the notion of role assignment common to many human collaboration scenarios. An approach was developed integrating recognition of a person's intentional role-driven behavior using spatiotemporal information with planning of the robot's verbal feedback using a Markov decision process representation of the task environment. The approach uses sets of policies to capture the action selection preferences for different roles and to reason about the compatibility of the robot's planned actions with the inferred action of a human teammate. A validation in a synthetic task environment with an autonomous robot collaborating with a single person was conducted as a proof-of-concept, in which the communicating robot was shown to significantly improve the task completion time of the team.

In future work we plan several enhancements to the communication planning approach and a series of additional validations aimed at determining the generalizability of the approach to different task settings. Further evaluations will be conducted including implementation in a real-world service robot task environment with actual, as opposed to simulated, object manipulation. This will require extension to partially-observable environments and human activity monitoring with actual objects. We also plan on using a humanoid to allow for co-verbal gestures to augment the existing verbal feedback. Another enhancement includes investigating methods for adapting and personalizing the robot's task and communication preferences to individual users based on their own verbal feedback as well as their adherence to the robot's requests. Additionally, as the communication planning system requires a set of policies and associated speech actions to function properly, we will be examining methods for automatically segmenting these roles, and associated verbal and visual references, from human demonstrations.

9. ACKNOWLEDGMENTS

This work is supported in part by ONR MURI program (N00014-09-1-1031), and National Science Foundation (NSF) grants CNS-0709296, IIS-1117279, IIS-0803565.

10. REFERENCES

[1] C. Breazeal, C. D. Kidd, A. L. Thomaz, G. Hoffman, and M. Berlin. Effects of nonverbal communication on efficiency and robustness in human-robot teamwork. In *Intelligent Robots and Systems, 2005.(IROS 2005). 2005 IEEE/RSJ International Conference on*, pages 708–713. IEEE, 2005.

[2] G. Buccino, F. Binkofski, and L. Riggio. The mirror neuron system and action recognition. *Brain and language*, 89(2):370–376, 2004.

[3] S. Chernova and M. Veloso. Interactive policy learning through confidence-based autonomy. *Journal of Artificial Intelligence Research*, 34(1):1, 2009.

[4] C. Crick and B. Scassellati. Inferring narrative and intention from playground games. *Proceedings of the 7th IEEE International Conference on Development and Learning (ICDL'08)*, pages 13–18, August 2008.

[5] A. D. Dragan, K. C. Lee, and S. S. Srinivasa. Legibility and predictability of robot motion. In *Human-Robot Interaction (HRI), 2013 8th ACM/IEEE International Conference on*, pages 301–308. IEEE, 2013.

[6] B. Grosz and C. Sidner. Attention, intentions, and the structure of discourse. *Computational linguistics*, 12(3):175–204, 1986.

[7] R. Hamid, S. Maddi, A. Johnson, A. Bobick, I. Essa, and C. Isbell. A novel sequence representation for unsupervised analysis of human activities. *Artificial Intelligence*, 173(14):1221–1244, 2009.

[8] G. Hoffman and C. Breazeal. Cost-based anticipatory action selection for human–robot fluency. *Robotics, IEEE Transactions on*, 23(5):952–961, 2007.

[9] R. Kelley, C. King, A. Tavakkoli, M. Nicolescu, M. Nicolescu, and G. Bebis. An architecture for understanding intent using a novel hidden markov formulation. *International Journal of Humanoid Robotics, Special Issue on Cognitive Humanoid Robots*, 5(2):1–22, 2008.

[10] B. Keysar, D. Barr, J. Balin, and J. Brauner. Taking perspective in conversation: The role of mutual knowledge in comprehension. *Psychological Science*, 11(1):32, 2000.

[11] T. Kollar, S. Tellex, D. Roy, and N. Roy. Toward understanding natural language directions. In *Human-Robot Interaction (HRI), 2010 5th ACM/IEEE International Conference on*, pages 259–266. IEEE, 2010.

[12] C. Lockridge and S. Brennan. Addressees' needs influence speakers' early syntactic choices. *Psychonomic Bulletin & Review*, 9(3):550, 2002.

[13] E. Martin, D. R. Lyon, and B. T. Schreiber. Designing synthetic tasks for human factors research: An application to uninhabited air vehicles. In *Proceedings of the Human Factors and Ergonomics Society Annual Meeting*, volume 42, pages 123–127. SAGE Publications, 1998.

[14] B. Mutlu, A. Terrell, and C.-M. Huang. Coordination mechanisms in human-robot collaboration. In *Proceedings of the Workshop on Collaborative Manipulation, 8th ACM/IEEE International Conference on Human-Robot Interaction*, 2013.

[15] S. Nikolaidis and J. Shah. Human-robot cross-training: computational formulation, modeling and evaluation of a human team training strategy. In *Proceedings of the 8th ACM/IEEE international conference on Human-robot interaction*, pages 33–40. IEEE Press, 2013.

[16] M. Pickering and S. Garrod. Toward a mechanistic psychology of dialogue. *Behavioral and Brain Sciences*, 27(02):169–190, 2004.

[17] J. Shah, J. Wiken, B. Williams, and C. Breazeal. Improved human-robot team performance using chaski, a human-inspired plan execution system. In *Proceedings of the 6th international conference on Human-robot interaction*, pages 29–36. ACM, 2011.

[18] C. Sidner, C. Kidd, C. Lee, and N. Lesh. Where to look: a study of human-robot engagement. In *Proceedings of the 9th International Conference on Intelligent User Interfaces*, page 84. ACM, 2004.

[19] R. B. Smith, R. Hixon, and B. Horan. Supporting flexible roles in a shared space. In *Collaborative Virtual Environments*, pages 160–176. Springer, 2001.

[20] J. G. Trafton, N. L. Cassimatis, M. D. Bugajska, D. P. Brock, F. E. Mintz, and A. C. Schultz. Enabling effective human-robot interaction using perspective taking in robots. *Systems, Man and Cybernetics, Part A: Systems and Humans, IEEE Transactions on*, 35(4):460–470, 2005.

[21] T. Ullman, C. Baker, O. Macindoe, O. Evans, N. Goodman, and J. Tenenbaum. Help or hinder: Bayesian models of social goal inference. *Advances in Neural Information Processing Systems (NIPS)*, 22, 2010.

[22] R. Wilcox, S. Nikolaidis, and J. Shah. Optimization of temporal dynamics for adaptive human-robot interaction in assembly manufacturing. *Robotics*, page 441, 2013.

OPTIMo: Online Probabilistic Trust Inference Model for Asymmetric Human-Robot Collaborations

Anqi Xu
McGill University
Montreal, Canada
anqixu@cim.mcgill.ca

Gregory Dudek
McGill University
Montreal, Canada
dudek@cim.mcgill.ca

ABSTRACT

We present OPTIMo: an Online Probabilistic Trust Inference Model for quantifying the degree of trust that a human supervisor has in an autonomous robot "worker". Represented as a Dynamic Bayesian Network, OPTIMo infers beliefs over the human's moment-to-moment latent trust states, based on the history of observed interaction experiences. A separate model instance is trained on each user's experiences, leading to an interpretable and personalized characterization of that operator's behaviors and attitudes. Using datasets collected from an interaction study with a large group of roboticists, we empirically assess OPTIMo's performance under a broad range of configurations. These evaluation results highlight OPTIMo's advances in both prediction accuracy and responsiveness over several existing trust models. This accurate and near real-time human-robot trust measure makes possible the development of autonomous robots that can adapt their behaviors dynamically, to actively seek greater trust and greater efficiency within future human-robot collaborations.

Categories and Subject Descriptors

H.1.2 [**Models and Principles**]: User/Machine Systems— *software psychology*

General Terms

Algorithms, Experimentation

Keywords

Trust; Dynamic Bayesian Network

1. INTRODUCTION

Trust – one's belief in the competence and reliability of another – is the cornerstone of all long-lasting collaborations. We present the design, development, and evaluation of a personalized dynamics model for a human operator's

degree of trust in a robot teammate. This work focuses on asymmetric human-robot teams, where the operator occasionally intervenes to aid the autonomous robot at its given task. We conducted a large observational study with diverse roboticists belonging to a nation-wide field robotics network, to gather both empirical data as well as pragmatic insights towards the development of our trust model. The resulting Online Probabilistic Trust Inference Model (OPTIMo) formulates Bayesian beliefs over the human's moment-to-moment trust states, based on the robot's task performance and the operator's reactions over time. Our empirical analyses demonstrate OPTIMo's great performance in a broad range of settings, and also highlight improvements in both accuracy and responsiveness over existing trust models.

The end-goal of our research is to develop *trust-seeking adaptive robots*: these robots will be able to sense when the human has low trust, and adapt their behaviors in response to improve task performance and seek greater trust. In this work, we tackle an essential component of this trust-seeking methodology, by developing a trust model that can accurately and responsively quantify the human's trust states during interactions. Our ongoing research aims to integrate this online trust measure with our interactive robot behavior adaptation methods [15], towards the ultimate vision of synergistic and trust-maximizing human-robot teams.

Our contribution, OPTIMo, is a personalized model that can accurately infer human-robot trust states at various interaction time scales. OPTIMo has the unique ability to estimate the operator's trust in near real-time, whereas existing models operate on the orders of minutes or longer [7, 2, 14]. Also, OPTIMo combines the two dominant modeling approaches in the literature: applying *causal* reasoning to update the robot's deserved trustworthiness based on its task performance, and using *evidence* from direct experiences to describe a human's actual amount of trust. Our empirical results substantiate OPTIMo's diverse utilities, through accurate and responsive predictions of each user's trust states and trust-dependent behaviors, and with interpretable characterizations of the operator's trust tendencies.

2. BACKGROUND

Trust is a rich and multi-faceted construct, studied across many disciplines [8, 5], given its critical role in healthy and effective human relationships. This section explores dominant aspects of trust applicable to human-robot collaborations, and in particular to asymmetric teams. We highlight important assumptions about human-robot trust, towards establishing a coherent mathematical model.

2.1 Trust Characterization

Lee and See surveyed the many dimensions used to characterize the basis of trust in automation [8]. These broadly fall under two categories: factors based on the automation's task *performance*, and those based on its honest *integrity*. As is typical in robotics research [2, 14, 10, 11], our work assumes that integrity-centric bases are given, i.e. our robots are obedient and never deceptive. *We henceforth assume a performance-centric definition of trust, namely one that relates solely to the robot's task efficiency and competence.*

Many representations have been proposed to quantify the degree of trust in a robot or a piece of automation. These include binary [3] and continuous [7] measures that characterize the robot's trustworthiness *caused* by its task performance, as well as ordinal scales [9, 4] used to elicit *evidence* of a person's actual amount of trust. This work incorporates both the causal and evidential modeling approaches in the literature. We employ a continuous, interval trust representation, spanning between complete distrust and absolute trust. Our model further quantifies the uncertainty in its estimated trust states, by maintaining Bayesian beliefs over the human's moment-to-moment degrees of trust.

Multiple studies *described* human-robot trust through correlations to interaction experiences and subjective assessments [9, 4], although few are capable of *predicting* a human's trust state. Lee and Moray presented a temporal model for relating trust assessments to task performance factors in a human-automation context, using an Auto-Regressive and Moving Average Value regression approach (ARMAV) [7]. We proposed a similar linear model in recent work [14] to predict event-based *changes in trust*, by relating to experience factors such as the robot's task failure rate and the frequency of human interventions to correct these failures. Desai and Yanco [2] conducted a series of robotic search and rescue experiments, during which users were asked to regularly report whether their trust has increased, decreased, or remained unchanged. These signals were quantified as $\{+1, -1, 0\}$ and integrated over time to obtain the Area Under Trust Curve (AUTC) measure. We will compare OPTIMo against each of these existing trust models in Sec. 5.3.

2.2 Interaction Context

We focus on asymmetric, supervisor-worker style human-robot teams, in which an autonomous robot "worker" is chiefly responsible for handling an assigned task. The human "supervisor" has the ability to intervene and take over control, but should do so only when necessary, for example to correct the robot's mistakes, or to switch to a new task objective. The human's interventions are assumed to always take precedence over the robot's autonomous controller.

The trust model developed in this work generalizes readily to human-robot teams in arbitrary domains. Nevertheless, our work focuses on visual navigation contexts, where an aerial robot is autonomously driven by an adaptive visual boundary tracking algorithm [15]. This robot can learn to follow diverse terrain contours, such as the coastline target shown in Fig. 1. We investigate scenarios where an operator collaborates with this robot, and model the evolution of the human's trust in the robot's abilities to reliably follow the designated boundary targets. Visual navigation tasks are appealing because humans innately excel at them, whereas the necessary complexity in autonomous solutions [2, 15] leads to uncertainty, and thus warrants the need for trust.

Figure 1: **Live camera feed from an aerial robot overlaid with an autonomous boundary tracker's steering command (blue arrow), and the human's interventions (green arrow). Additional overlays are pertinent to our observational study (see Sec. 3).**

3. METHODOLOGY

Our performance-centric trust modeling approach is predicated on two simple observations of asymmetric human-robot collaborations. Firstly, the robot's trustworthiness arises due to its task performance: efficient progress lead to greater trust, whereas low reliability induces losses in trust. Secondly, whenever the human intervenes, it often reflects a lapse in trust due to the robot's task failures.

Formally, the goal of this work is to estimate the degree of trust $t_k \in [0, 1]$ felt by a human towards a robot, at time steps $k = 1 : K$ during their interactions. We tackle this problem by relating the human's latent trust states to observable factors in the interaction experience. In particular, the well-studied link between trust and the robot's task performance p is often quantified through the failure rate of its autonomous system [7, 2]. In addition, human interventions i (i.e. toggles between autonomous and manual control modes) are known to be strong evidential predictors for trust [2, 14]. We further consider extrinsic factors e that cause the operator to intervene irrespective of trust, for instance when steering along a new terrain contour to train our boundary-tracking robot to follow this updated target.

We conducted an observational study to collect interaction experiences towards modeling trust relationships. This study further yielded pragmatic insights about trust and its related constructs, for asymmetric human-robot teams.

3.1 Robot Interface

While supervising the boundary-tracking aerial robot, the human operator is presented with an interface showing the onboard camera feed, as seen in Fig. 1. The operator can take over control of the vehicle at any time, by moving an analog stick on a gamepad. Even during these periods of manual interventions, the boundary tracker continues to process the camera stream and displays its generated headings. This feedback aids the human in deciding if the robot is capable of performing the task on its own, or if further assistance is needed when the tracker is behaving poorly.

3.2 Trust Assessment Elicitation

In addition to logging performance and intervention factors that are available in typical interaction experiences, our study also queried the human's trust assessments occasionally. These factors are used to train personalized instances of our trust model, and to evaluate their prediction accuracies. Importantly, after the training period, our model can operate without such assessment data, although their availabilities will strengthen the resulting trust predictions.

1. **Degree of Trust**: What is your degree of trust in the robot right now? *Think carefully about your interaction experiences before answering.*

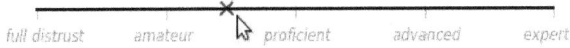

full distrust   amateur   proficient   advanced   expert

Figure 2: Post-session trust feedback questionnaire.

Our study is divided into multiple interaction sessions. After each session, the user is asked to provide an assessment of their trust state, based on the cumulative interaction experience. These trust feedback f are queried using a modified Visual Analog Scale (VAS) [12], as shown in Fig. 2. Multiple anchor points are introduced to this interval scale to reduce end-aversion bias [1]. This format also addresses concerns reported by several pilot study users regarding difficulties in quantifying their trust updates based on end-anchors only.

It is important to minimize the number of trust feedback queries, both to reduce interaction interrupts, and to mitigate added mental strain. As a separate source of trust evidence, each user is asked to report changes in their trust states during interactions, by pressing buttons on the gamepad indicating whether trust has been gained, lost, or remained unchanged, i.e. $c = \{+1, -1, 0\}$. Similar to previous studies [2], we encourage periodic reporting of c by prompting 5 seconds after each button press, both using visual feedback (with a "t?" icon in Fig. 1) and by vibrating the gamepad.

3.3 Observational Study Design

Our study involved two interaction scenarios that tasked the human-robot team to follow sequences of boundary targets. Each scenario is separated into 1 to 2 minute-long sessions, to enable frequent post-session queries for the user's trust feedback f. The first scenario involved patrolling along a highway stretch, a forest path, and a coastline, whereas the second scenario surveyed the hill-sides and shores of a fjord.

This study was carried out using a simulated environment to enforce repeatability, and to have ground truth in the form of the ideal target boundary paths. In order to ensure similar experiences across users, the interface provided visual warnings whenever the robot deviated away from the designated boundary. If the user failed to recover in a timely manner, the interaction then reset to a previous state.

Every time the boundary tracker processed a camera frame, we recorded whether it had failed to detect any boundaries (i.e. AI failures reflecting task performance $p \in \{0, 1\}$), and the human's intervention state $i \in \{0, 1\}$ at that time. We also noted frames in proximity to a change-over between boundary targets, which constituted extraneous intervention causes $e \in \{0, 1\}$. Furthermore, we logged button presses indicating trust changes $c \in \{-1, 0, +1\}$ as well as the user's absolute trust feedback $f \in [0, 1]$ following each session.

This study was conducted in a fully automated manner. Following a demographics survey, a short slide-show elaborated on the study and its interface. Next, the user worked

through an interactive tutorial and 2 practice sessions, to familiarize with the tasks and trust feedback queries. Afterwards, a 3-session interaction scenario and another 2-session scenario were each administered *twice*, for a total of 10 recorded sessions. All users in this observational study underwent the task sessions in the same order, since the study was primarily aimed at collecting interaction experiences. This is in contrast to our previous controlled trust experiments for quantifying event-related effects [14].

3.4 Observational Study Results

The final form of the observational study resulted from iterative refinements following a series of pilot runs. We recruited 21 roboticists from 7 universities during a nationwide field robotics gathering to take part in this study. Participants were predominantly graduate students (86%), and the average age of users was 27 ($\sigma \approx 4$). A typical study run entailed 30 minutes of interaction with the boundary-tracking robot, operating at a $15\,Hz$ frame rate.

The 2 task scenarios were each administered twice to assess whether users behaved consistently in similar situations. We found no significant differences in the rate of human interventions i per matching sessions (2-tailed paired $t_{104} = 1.49, p = 0.14$). The numerical sum of reported trust changes c across paired session instances also did not reveal any significant differences (2-tailed paired $t_{104} = -0.43, p = 0.67$). In contrast, trust feedback f were found to be significantly different when users repeated the same scenarios (1-tailed paired $t_{104} = -4.85, p \ll 0.01$). We conclude that users reacted consistently to similar events, yet their trust assessments changed over time as they accumulated more interaction experiences. These results thus substantiate the need to model the *temporal dynamics* of human-robot trust.

A linear regression on trust feedback f was performed to identify significant covariates from interaction experience. An analysis of variance revealed that both the user identifier ($F_{20,188} = 17.4, p \ll 0.01$) and the ratio of user interventions i per session ($F_{1,207} = 76.2, p \ll 0.01$) were significantly related to trust feedback f, whereas the ratio of AI failures per session was related to a lesser degree ($F_{1,207} = 3.02, p = 0.08$). The strong user dependence on trust feedback supports the need for a *personalized* model of trust, which is consistent with findings in our previous study [14]. Also, the stronger trust correlation of user interventions over AI failures is captured by the structure of our dynamic Bayesian trust model, to be discussed in Sec. 4.1.

Users of our study further provided a number of qualitative remarks, reflecting vital insights about the evolution of their trust in the robot's task performance. Several users reported that their "trust changed when the robot did something unpredictable", which suggests a dependency between the trust state t_k at time k and the *change* in the robot's recent task performance, i.e. $p_k - p_{k-1}$. Others said that their "trust fluctuated a lot initially", given the lack of prior experiences with the robot. This suggests that it is sensible to assume a *uniform prior* belief on each user's initial degree of trust when interacting with a new robotic system.

During pilot runs of the study, users frequently pressed the 'trust gained' and 'trust lost' buttons unintentionally when prompted for c. Consequently, the slide-show in the revised study explicitly encouraged participants to press the 'trust unchanged' button as a default. Nevertheless, multiple participants reported that they found it "hard to suppress the urge to hastily press 'trust gained' or 'trust lost'", and recalled making multiple accidental misclicks. We will model this *idling bias* into the relationship between a user's latent trust state t_k and reports of trust changes c.

4. HUMAN-ROBOT TRUST MODEL

In this section, we present the Online Probabilistic Trust Inference Model (OPTIMo) for asymmetric human-robot teams. OPTIMo treats the degree of human-robot trust t_k at each time step k as a random variable, and maintains belief distributions for these performance-centric trust measures by deducing from various factors of the interaction experience. This probabilistic representation is useful for inferring the human's expected trust state at a given time, as well as the amount of uncertainty of each such estimate.

OPTIMo is represented as a Dynamic Bayesian Network [6], as shown in Fig. 3. Its graph structure efficiently encodes local relationships between trust and its related factors, as well as the evolution of trust states over time. This Bayesian model also processes variable-rate sources of information in a probabilistically sound manner, and can further accommodate an arbitrary belief for prior trust t_0. Finally, OPTIMo combines the two main approaches used by existing trust models, namely by applying *causal* reasoning to update the robot's trustworthiness based on its task performance [7, 10], and analyzing *evidential* factors to quantify each user's actual degree of trust [2, 14].

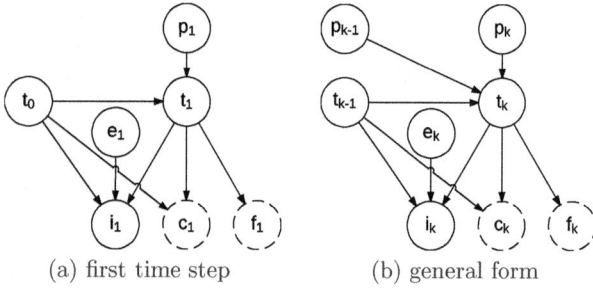

(a) first time step   (b) general form

Figure 3: Dynamic Bayesian structure of the Online Probabilistic Trust Inference Model (OPTIMo). Dashed factors are not observed on all time steps k, and are not mandatory for inferring trust states t_k.

4.1 Local Trust Relationships

As seen in Fig. 3, OPTIMo relates the human's latent trust state t_k causally to the robot's task performance p. It also incorporates several sources of trust-induced evidence, such as user interventions i, trust change reports c, and absolute trust feedback f. This model processes a continuous period of interaction as a sequence of K non-overlapping time windows, $k = 1 : K$, each lasting W seconds. We define the window-aggregated state of task performance, $p_k \in [0, 1]$, as the ratio of frames within the k-th time window for which the robot's autonomous controller failed to produce any commands. Similarly, $i_k \in \{0, 1\}$ reflects whether the operator had intervened or not during its time window k. The extraneous cause state $e_k \in \{0, 1\}$ records the presence of a change in task targets, and is connected as a parent link to i_k. Finally, sign-aggregated trust change reports $c_k \in \{-1, 0, +1, \varnothing\}$ and each individual trust feedback $f_k \in \{[0, 1], \varnothing\}$ help to ground the model's estimates for latent trust states t_k as further evidence. Since these trust

assessments c_k, f_k occur sporadically, $\varnothing$ is used to denote their non-occurrences at various times.

Links to each factor in this discriminative Bayesian model are quantified as a conditional probability distribution (CPD). The amount for which trust t_k is expected to change given the robot's recent and current task performances, p_{k-1}, p_k, is reflected by a linear Gaussian CPD:

$$\mathcal{P}(t_k, t_{k-1}, p_k, p_{k-1}) := Prob(t_k|t_{k-1}, p_k, p_{k-1}) \approx {}^* \quad (1)$$
$$\mathcal{N}\left(t_k;\ t_{k-1} + \omega_{tb} + \omega_{tp}\, p_k + \omega_{td}\, (p_k - p_{k-1}),\ \sigma_t\right)$$

where $\mathcal{N}(x;\ \mu, \sigma) := \frac{1}{\sqrt{2\pi}\sigma} exp\left(\frac{-(x-\mu)^2}{2\sigma^2}\right)$ denotes a Gaussian distribution for the random variable x, with mean μ and standard deviation σ. The expression for this Gaussian CPD's mean represents the expected update to trust t_k from its previous state t_{k-1}, as a weighted sum of a bias term (i.e. propensity to trust), as well as performance-induced factors. The personalized parameters $\omega_{tb}, \omega_{tp}, \omega_{td}$ reflect the relative impacts on each user's trust updates of the **b**ias, the current task **p**erformance, and the **d**ifference in the robot's performance. The propagation uncertainty parameter σ_t quantifies the variability in each user's trust update dynamics.

OPTIMo explains the probability of interventions i_k by its diverse causes, such as the current trust state t_k, a recent change in trust $\Delta t_k := t_k - t_{k-1}$, and extraneous factors e_k. These linkages are modeled as a logistic CPD:

$$\mathcal{O}_i(t_k = 1, t_{k-1}, i_k, e_k) := Prob(i_k = 1|t_k, t_{k-1}, e_k) = \quad (2)$$
$$\mathcal{S}\left(\omega_{ib} + \omega_{it}\, t_k + \omega_{id}\, \Delta t_k + \omega_{ie}\, e_k\right)$$
$$Prob(i_k = 0|t_k, t_{k-1}, e_k) = 1 - Prob(i_k = 1|t_k, t_{k-1}, e_k)$$

where $\mathcal{S}(x) := (1 + exp(-x))^{-1}$ is the sigmoid distribution for the binary random variable x. The parameters $\omega_{ib}, \omega_{it}, \omega_{id}, \omega_{ie}$ quantify the bias and weights of the various causes explaining the intervention state i_k.

During time steps when the user reports trust changes $c_k \in \{-1, 0, +1\}$, these are accounted as evidence to ground the latest update to latent trust, Δt_k. Reports of 'trust gains' and 'trust losses' are modeled as sigmoid CPDs:

$$\mathcal{O}_c(t_k, t_{k-1}, c_k) := Prob(c_k|t_k, t_{k-1})$$
$$Prob(c_k = +1|t_k, t_{k-1}) = \beta_c + (1 - 3\beta_c) \cdot \mathcal{S}\left(\kappa_c\left[\Delta t_k - o_c\right]\right)$$
$$Prob(c_k = -1|t_k, t_{k-1}) = \beta_c + (1 - 3\beta_c) \cdot \mathcal{S}\left(\kappa_c\left[-\Delta t_k - o_c\right]\right)$$
$$Prob(c_k = 0|t_k, t_{k-1}) = 1 - Prob(c_k = +1|t_k, t_{k-1}) \quad (3)$$
$$- Prob(c_k = -1|t_k, t_{k-1})$$

This CPD parameterizes the nominal offset o_c in a change to latent trust Δt_k that is required to cause the user to report a non-zero c_k, along with the variability κ_c in the reporting likelihoods. In addition, the uniform error term β_c captures the *idling bias* observed during our study, where users sometimes reported erroneous trust changes when prompted.

Finally, OPTIMo uses a zero-mean Gaussian CPD to quantify the uncertainty σ_f in each user's absolute trust feedback f_k with respect to their true latent trust state t_k:

$$\mathcal{O}_f(t_k, f_k) := Prob(f_k|t_k) \approx {}^\dagger \mathcal{N}\left(f_k;\ t_k, \sigma_f\right) \quad (4)$$

---

*Since $t_k \in [0, 1]$ is bounded, the cumulative Gaussian densities below $t_k = 0$ and above $t_k = 1$ must be added to these end-states, enforcing a proper probability density function.
†Akin to $\mathcal{P}(t_k, t_{k-1}, p_k, p_{k-1})$, cumulative densities beyond the range of $f_k \in [0, 1]$ must be added to boundary states.

All of these trust relationships have been corroborated by prior literature [7, 2, 14], and were further supported by results of our observational study. In particular, analyses in Sec. 3.4 found that user interventions i were much more strongly correlated to trust than the robot's task performance p. Consequently, this temporal Bayesian model uses p_k to causally propagate the trust belief t_k to a set of *plausible* next states, and then uses trust-induced evidences i_k, c_k, and f_k to *exclude* inconsistent hypotheses. This graph structure also arises naturally as the causal depiction of the human's trust-driven decision process.

4.2 Inference, Personalization, and Prediction

This model can be used to estimate the probabilistic belief that the user's trust state $t_k \in [0, 1]$ at time step k takes on any particular value. Trust inference can be carried out in 2 different contexts: firstly, given a history of past experience data, we can query the *filtered belief* at the *current* time k, $bel_f(t_k) = Prob(t_k|p_{1:k}, i_{1:k}, e_{1:k}, c_{1:k}, f_{1:k}, t_0)$. We can also compute the *smoothed belief* at *any* time step $k \in [0:K]$ within a previously recorded interaction dataset with K time steps, $bel_s(t_k) = Prob(t_k|p_{1:K}, i_{1:K}, e_{1:K}, c_{1:K}, f_{1:K}, t_0)$. Both types of belief inferences can be derived from OPTIMo's graph structure [13]:

$$\overline{bel}(t_k, t_{k-1}) := \mathcal{O}(t_k, t_{k-1}, i_k, e_k, c_k, f_k)$$
$$\cdot \mathcal{P}(t_k, t_{k-1}, p_k, p_{k-1}) \cdot bel_f(t_{k-1}) \quad (5)$$

$$bel_f(t_k) = \frac{\int \overline{bel}(t_k, t_{k-1}) \, dt_{k-1}}{\int\int \overline{bel}(t_k, t_{k-1}) \, dt_{k-1} dt_k} \quad (6)$$

$$bel_s(t_{k-1}) = \int \frac{\overline{bel}(t_k, t_{k-1})}{\int \overline{bel}(t_k, t_{k-1}) \, dt_{k-1}} \cdot bel_s(t_k) \, dt_k \quad (7)$$

where $\mathcal{O}(t_k, t_{k-1}, i_k, e_k, c_k, f_k)$ denotes the product of one or more observation CPDs $\mathcal{O}_i(\cdot), \mathcal{O}_c(\cdot), \mathcal{O}_f(\cdot)$ at each time step k, based on whether $c_k \neq \varnothing$ and $f_k \neq \varnothing$. We also assume a uniform prior trust belief, $bel_f(t_0) := Prob(t_0) = 1$, when users begin to interact with a new robot.

It is worthwhile to note the efficient linear-time complexities of the filtering and smoothing algorithms. The filtered belief $bel_f(t_k)$ at time k in Eqn. 6 is updated recursively from its previous belief distribution, $bel_f(t_{k-1})$, in Eqn. 5; a similar recursive relationship also holds for the smoothed belief $bel_s(t_k)$ in Eqn. 7. Thus, starting from a given prior trust belief $bel_f(t_0)$, one can compute filtered beliefs $bel_f(t_k)$ forward in time in a single pass, and then also ascertain smoothed beliefs $bel_s(t_k)$ backwards in time sequentially.

In order to personalize OPTIMo to a particular user's behaviors and trust tendencies, we use the hard-assignment Expectation-Maximization (EM) algorithm [6] to find optimized model parameters Θ^* (e.g. $\omega_{tb}, \sigma_t, ...$) given a *training set* of interaction experiences. Hard-assignment EM jointly optimizes the observational likelihood of all interaction data and the most likely sequence of latent trust states, as follows:

$$\Theta^* = \arg\max_{\Theta} \max_{t_{1:K}} Prob(t_{1:K}, p_{1:K}, i_{1:K}, e_{1:K}, c_{1:K}, f_{1:K}|t_0)$$

In addition to inferring trust beliefs, OPTIMo can also be used to predict probability distributions for the various evidential factors i_k, c_k, f_k. Using the intervention factor as an example, we can remove all instances $i_{1:k}$, and then predict the likelihood of observing a particular i_k state as:

$$Prob(i_k|p_{1:k}, e_{1:k}, c_{1:k}, f_{1:k}) =$$
$$\frac{\int\int \mathcal{O}_i(t_k, t_{k-1}, i_k, e_k) \cdot \overline{bel}(t_k, t_{k-1}) \, dt_k \, dt_{k-1}}{\int\int \overline{bel}(t_k, t_{k-1}) \, dt_k \, dt_{k-1}} \quad (8)$$

Derivations and examples of filtering, smoothing, and prediction for Dynamic Bayesian Networks are presented in [13].

4.3 Histogram Inference Engine

We implemented OPTIMo using a histogram-based inference method, which approximates continuous belief densities as discrete vectors of probability masses. Specifically, we discretized the trust range $[0, 1]$ into B equally-spaced bins, and approximated the likelihood of t_k taking on a particular value τ as the probability mass of the nearest bin center. The precision of this histogram approximation improves when using larger bin sizes B, at the cost of additional computations. A similar approximation is used when predicting trust feedback, where the distribution for $f_k \in [0, 1]$ is discretized into 100 bins, and each bin center's probability mass is computed using a form similar to Eqn. 8.

We personalized model instances using EM with multiple restarts, to avoid convergence to local optima. In each EM run, model parameters Θ are initiated from hand-selected or random values, and then iteratively improved using constrained least squares optimization. An EM run is terminated when parameters have stabilized within expected tolerances, or after a maximum number of iterations have lapsed. Further algorithmic details and examples of histogram inference and model training for Dynamic Bayesian Networks are discussed in [13].

5. EVALUATION OF TRUST MODEL

This section describes empirical assessments of OPTIMo under diverse settings for its non-trainable parameters, and compares it to several existing temporal trust models. Since our approach assumes that the human's trust state t_k is latent and thus never observable, we quantify the performance of each model by its ability to predict trust-induced behaviors and assessments. These include user interventions i_k, trust change reports c_k, and absolute trust feedback f_k.

Each evaluation run begins by aggregating raw interaction datasets into W-second time windows. We personalize OPTIMo instances using *training sets* consisting of each user's experiences during the first 5 study sessions, while assuming uniform prior trust. After optimizing model parameters to capture each operator's trust tendencies, we compute the filtered trust belief at the end of the 5 training sessions.

This trust belief is used as the prior distribution for the *test set*, comprising of the remaining 5 repeated sessions. We conduct separate prediction assessments for $i_{1:k}$, $c_{1:k}$, and $f_{1:k}$: for each target variable, first all of its instances in the test set are removed, and predicted likelihoods are computed for each omitted occurrence, following the form of Eqn. 8. We then compute Maximum Likelihood Estimates (MLE) using the predicted beliefs, and compare the resulting values against the omitted observed data, $i_{1:k}$, $c_{1:k}$, or $f_{1:k}$.

The outcomes of each model evaluation process consist of prediction accuracies for interventions, $acc_i \in [0\%, 100\%]$ accuracies for trust change predictions acc_c, and the root-mean-squared-error for absolute trust feedback, $RMSE_f$. We also compute the Pearson product-moment correlation

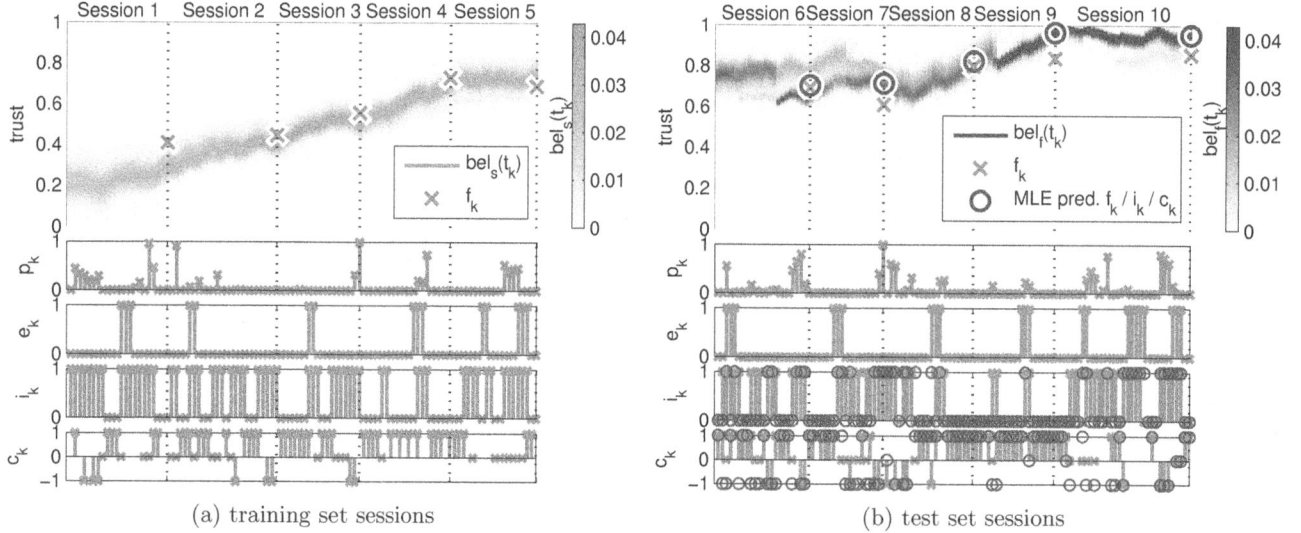

(a) training set sessions

(b) test set sessions

Figure 4: Inferences and predictions for a typical trained OPTIMo instance ($W = 3\,s$, $B = 300$ bins, $\sigma_f = 0.1$).

coefficient ρ between matching sets of observed and predicted trust feedback f_k. This metric is used to compare OPTIMo against other models that quantify trust on a different scale. All evaluation metrics presented in this section (except Sec. 5.1) are aggregated across all 21 users' results.

A few of OPTIMo's settings cannot be optimized using interaction experiences, yet they affect the model's performance. The window duration W determines the time scale of interaction, and also reflects the trust inference latency for online model queries. The number of histogram bins B affects the precision of the discrete approximation to the underlying continuous trust beliefs. Finally, the uncertainty σ_f in each user's trust feedback f_k captures the relative influence of f_k on the inferred beliefs for latent trust t_k. Sec. 5.2 will investigate the effects of each of these non-trainable parameters on the resulting models' performance.

5.1 Characteristics of a Trained Model

We begin by highlighting several features of a typical personalized OPTIMo instance under sensible settings: $W = 3\,s$, $B = 300$ bins, $\sigma_f = 0.1$. Fig. 4(a) depicts the Bayesian-*smoothed* trust beliefs $bel_s(t_k)$ during the training sessions, after parameters Θ of the model have been optimized to best match the training dataset. Fig. 4(b) shows the Bayesian-*filtered* beliefs $bel_f(t)$ inferred during the test sessions, as well as MLE predictions (shown as blue circles) for trust feedback f_k, user interventions i_k, and trust change reports c_k. The switch to *filtered* trust beliefs ensures that model evaluation is carried out in an online manner, as if predictions were obtained live during the latter 5 sessions.

The inferred trust beliefs, depicted as vertical color-coded slices in Fig. 4, reflect a precise characterization of this specific user's trust tendencies. This can be seen from the accurate prediction results for various evidence factors in the test set: $RMSE_f = 0.09, acc_i = 72.41\%, acc_c = 70.00\%$. Also, despite the small number of trust feedback (e.g. 5 in each of the training and test sets), test-set predictions of f_k yielded highly significant correlations $\rho = 0.91$ ($p < 0.01$). Furthermore, the visualization of the inferred trust beliefs highlights OPTIMo's unique ability in characterizing *multi-modal distributions* for the user's temporal trust states. These com-

peting trust hypotheses arise when the human's actions contradict recent trust reports, or when the user's reactions are notably different from prior interaction experiences.

This OPTIMo instance is personalized through trust propagation settings $\omega_{tb} = 0.0064, \omega_{tp} = -0.0153, \omega_{td} = -0.0029$, cause-of-intervention weights $\omega_{ib} = 131.2, \omega_{it} = -157.1$, $\omega_{id} = -9887, \omega_{ie} = 83.84$, and trust changes reporting traits $o_c = 0.0003, \kappa_c = 1277, \beta_c = 1.063 \times 10^{-7}$. These settings optimize the joint likelihood of the diverse interaction factors in the training set, and can also be interpreted to quantify the user's trust tendencies. Specifically, the large cause-of-intervention weights suggest that this operator does not intervene at a maximal trusting state, but will most certainly take over control for medium-to-low trust states ($t_k < 0.8$), when trust drops by even 0.004, or to address extraneous factors such as intentional changes to the task target ($e_k = 1$). Also, the trust propagation settings indicate that between consecutive time steps (of $W = 3\,s$), the user's trust state increases nominally by 0.0064 if the task performance is good, drops by 0.0118 initially upon an AI failure, and continues to decrease by 0.0089 throughout a contiguous period of failures. We deduce that this operator penalizes robot failures with 38% more trust loss, when compared to trust gains during competent operations. This quantifies the common adage that "it is easy to lose trust, but hard to regain it".

5.2 Effects of Non-Trainable Parameters

Fig. 5(a) illustrates the effects of the time window duration W on OPTIMo's performance. The prediction errors for trust feedback, $RMSE_f$, consistently decrease as the window duration widens. This trend arises due to having more frequent f_k observations at coarser time scales, which allows the trained model to more accurately predict f_k through the latent trust state t_k. In contrast, prediction accuracies for i_k and c_k drop slightly as W increases from $0.5\,s$ to $20\,s$, since occurrences of per-frame i and per-report c values are collapsed into fewer window-aggregated factors at coarser time scales. The high prediction accuracies at session-level time scales of $W = 150\,s$ is similarly explained by statistical degeneracy caused by very few samples of i_k and c_k, although even in these cases the model yields excellent performance.

226

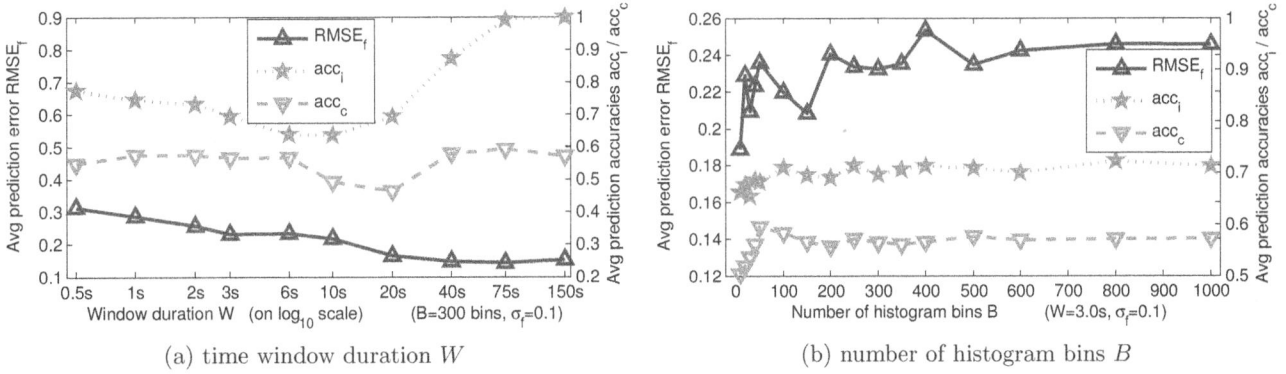

(a) time window duration W (b) number of histogram bins B

Figure 5: Effects of non-trainable model parameters on the prediction performance of OPTIMo.

The opposite effects that W has on predictions for f_k, versus those for i_k and c_k, supports the contrast between absolute trust assessments for summarizing *cumulative* experiences, and the *reactive* natures of user interventions and trust change reports. The fact that our results capture this contrast demonstrates OPTIMo's versatility. Furthermore, despite having poor $RMSE_f$ for sub-second time windows (e.g. $W = 0.5\,s$), competent prediction accuracies for i_k and c_k reflect the usefulness of OPTIMo's inferred trust beliefs at these extremely fine time scales. This degree of prediction responsiveness is unseen in existing trust models, which operate at much coarser scales of minutes or longer [7, 2, 14].

Fig. 5(b) shows the effects of using histograms with different bin sizes B. Prediction results are varied among small bin sizes ($B < 200$). These unreliable accuracies are likely caused by under-sampling of the underlying continuous trust beliefs. For example, the trained model in Sec. 5.1 indicates that the user's latent trust t_k increases nominally by 0.0064 between time steps under typical operations; this requires at least $B > 156$ bins to represent faithfully. Beyond these under-sampling errors, our empirical results indicate that using many bins does not lead to greater performance. We therefore conclude that a histogram with $B = 300$ bins sensibly captures beliefs of a typical robotict's trust dynamics.

In general, it is difficult to estimate the amount of variability of a human's reports on an unmeasurable sentiment such as trust. Since we employed a 5-anchors format to elicit trust feedback $t_k \in [0, 1]$ (see Fig. 2), a conservative estimate of variability is on the scale of consecutive anchor points, e.g. $\sigma_f \approx 0.1$. We trained model instances with varying variability values σ_f, and found that this parameter had minimal effects on OPTIMo's performance. For instance, under reasonable settings $W = 3\,s$, $B = 300$ bins, results assuming extremely precise trust feedback ($\sigma_f = 0.001$), $acc_i = 69.43\%$, $acc_c = 51.52\%$, $RMSE_f = 0.21$, are not noticeably different from performance assuming severely unreliable assessments ($\sigma_f = 0.3$), $acc_i = 71.41\%$, $acc_c = 55.81\%$, $RMSE_f = 0.29$.

5.3 Comparison with Existing Trust Models

We contrasted OPTIMo's trust prediction performance against those of several existing models. These include the Auto-Regressive Moving Average Value (ARMAV) model for quantifying human-automation trust [7], a stepwise regression model for predicting *changes* in trust (dTrust) [14], and the Area Under Trust Curve (AUTC) metric [2]. We compared these models against two OPTIMo variants ($B =$

300 bins, $\sigma_f = 0.1$) at different time scales, i.e. $OPTIMo_{fine}$ with $W = 3\,s$, and $OPTIMo_{coarse}$ with $W = 150\,s$.

The ARMAV model [7] associates the degree of trustworthiness in an automated system as a linear function of its task performance and internal failure rate, at the current and last time steps. We implemented three variants of this first-order lag system, including $ARMAV_{real}$, which solely considers recent AI failure rates p_k, p_{k-1}, and $ARMAV_{perf}$, which further adds an external task performance metric, measured as the ratio of frames for which the target boundary was completely out of the robot's view. This latter variant is expected to be more accurate, although it requires a performance metric that is typically not available for many families of tasks (and is thus not used by OPTIMo). Both model variants were personalized using interaction data from the 5 training sessions, similar to OPTIMo's training process. We further computed a user-aggregated regression variant, $ARMAV_{aggr}$, using both AI failure and external performance data from *all users'* training sessions, to faithfully replicate the form used by the original authors.

In prior work [14] we derived a similar linear regression model, but for predicting changes in trust caused by different interaction events. In addition to linking trust to AI failures p_k, this dTrust model also relates trust to user interventions i_k, and to the robot's instantaneous task performance, which is represented as the distance from the ground truth target trajectory. Since this metric is typically not available during online operations, we computed per-user regression variants that both ignored ($dTrust_{real}$) and included ($dTrust_{gt}$) this ground truth data. Furthermore, a user-aggregated variant $dTrust_{aggr}$ incorporates interaction experiences from all users, and best reflects the originally-proposed model form. To evaluate these models, we computed all predicted trust changes for the 5 test sessions, and integrated the updated trust states starting from the final trust feedback at the end of the training sessions.

In the experiments conducted by Desai and Yanco [2], users were asked to report their trust changes $c \in \{-1, 0, +1\}$ at regular intervals through button presses. The cumulative sums of these values were used to characterize trust states at different times, and is termed the Area Under Trust Curve (AUTC) metric. We computed AUTC values at the end of each test session, and compared Pearson's ρ correlations between these unscaled predictions and trust feedback f_k.

Table 1 summarizes RMSE and Pearson's ρ statistics for trust predictions for the various models. OPTIMo yielded prediction accuracies and correlations comparable to the

Table 1: Model comparison of trust prediction errors and Pearson's ρ. Dark & light shades highlight best and second best results for each metric. Statistics for personalized models were across all users.

	avg (std) RMSE	% sign ρ ($\alpha < 0.10$)	avg (std) sign RMSE	avg sign ρ
$OPTIMo_{fine}$	0.13 (0.12)	33.33%	0.11 (0.14)	0.88
$OPTIMo_{coarse}$	0.10 (0.09)	33.33%	0.09 (0.10)	0.90
$ARMAV_{real}$ [7]	0.32 (0.42)	9.52%	0.52 (0.05)	0.86
$ARMAV_{perf}$ [7]	0.27 (0.21)	9.52%	0.12 (0.04)	0.85
$ARMAV_{aggr}$ [7]	0.14	—	—	0.64
$dTrust_{real}$ [14]	0.76 (1.68)	9.52%	0.17 (0.10)	0.92
$dTrust_{gt}$ [14]	0.36 (0.32)	14.29%	0.17 (0.07)	0.93
$dTrust_{aggr}$ [14]	0.19	—	—	0.73
$AUTC$ [2]	—	38.10%	—	0.90

best variants of all existing trust models. Focusing on a session-wide scale, $OPTIMo_{coarse}$ produced notably more accurate trust predictions against other models using similar information, i.e. $ARMAV_{real}$, $dTrust_{real}$, $AUTC$. Even when other models incorporated additional sources of data, OPTIMo's performance remained highly competitive.

These results show that OPTIMo is able to infer the user's trust states with greater fidelity than existing methods, and at much finer time scales, on the order of seconds. This is achieved by relating the user's *latent* trust state to *observed* factors of the interaction experience. OPTIMo's use of a probabilistic trust representation also captures additional state information, such as multi-modal hypotheses and the uncertainty in trust estimates. The fact that trained OPTIMo instances accurately predict trust-induced behaviors and attitudes in near real-time, without requiring users to tediously provide trust feedback every few seconds, highlights the unique value of this online human-robot trust model.

6. CONCLUSION

We introduced the Online Probabilistic Trust Inference Model (OPTIMo): a personalized *performance-centric* trust model that is capable of inferring a human operator's degree of trust in an autonomous robot. OPTIMo incorporates the two dominant modeling approaches in the literature, namely through causal reasoning of the robot's trustworthiness given its task performance, and using evidence from interaction data to support beliefs about the human's latent trust state. We conducted an observational study on a large group of roboticists, and collected a substantive dataset as well as valuable insights that helped in shaping OPTIMo's structure. We demonstrated success at accurately predicting trust-induced behaviors of human operators while collaborating with an autonomous boundary following robot, although OPTIMo's generic form can be scaled and instantiated to suit other task contexts as well. Our empirical analyses extensively quantified the strong performance of many variants of this human-robot trust model. Our results further showed that OPTIMo can predict trust assessments with greater accuracies and at much finer time scales compared to existing works. These findings highlight the importance and uniqueness of OPTIMo towards developing responsive *trust-seeking adaptive robots*.

In ongoing work we are studying the use of OPTIMo for grouping like-minded operators. This would allow pre-trained models to predict trust states of novel users, while requiring minimal amounts of personalization data. We are also investigating the use of Monte Carlo approximate inference techniques, with the aim of further speeding up the trust inference process. Finally, we have begun integrating OPTIMo with our interactive robot behavior adaptation methods [15], towards our research end-goal of building robots that can actively seek to maximize the user's trust.

7. ACKNOWLEDGMENTS

We would like to thank all participants of our observational study, which was sanctioned by McGill University's Research Ethics Board (#183-1112). This work was funded by the NSERC Canadian Field Robotics Network (NCFRN).

8. REFERENCES

[1] J. A. Cowley and H. Youngblood. Subjective response differences between visual analogue, ordinal and hybrid response scales. *Proc. of the Human Factors and Ergonomics Society Annual Meeting*, 53(25), 2009.

[2] M. Desai. *Modeling Trust to Improve Human-Robot Interaction*. PhD thesis, Computer Science Department, University of Massachusetts Lowell, 2012.

[3] R. J. Hall. Trusting your assistant. In *Knowledge-Based Soft. Eng. Conf. (KBSE'11)*, 1996.

[4] J.-Y. Jian, A. M. Bisantz, and C. G. Drury. Foundations for an empirically determined scale of trust in automated systems. *International J. of Cognitive Ergonomics*, 4(1), 2000.

[5] A. Jøsang, R. Hayward, and S. Pope. Trust network analysis with subjective logic. In *Australasian Computer Science Conf. (ACSC'06)*, 2006.

[6] D. Koller and N. Friedman. *Probabilistic Graphical Models: Principles and Techniques*. MIT Press, 2009.

[7] J. Lee and N. Moray. Trust, control strategies and allocation of function in human-machine systems. *Ergonomics*, 35(10), 1992.

[8] J. D. Lee and K. A. See. Trust in automation: Designing for appropriate reliance. *Human Factors*, 2004.

[9] B. M. Muir. *Operators' trust in and use of automatic controllers in a supervisory process control task*. PhD thesis, University of Toronto, 1989.

[10] A. Pierson and M. Schwager. Adaptive inter-robot trust for robust multi robot sensor coverage. In *Int. Sym. on Robotics Research (ISRR'13)*, 2013.

[11] C. Pippin and H. I. Christensen. Trust modeling in multi-robot patrolling. In *Proc. of the IEEE Int. Conf. on Rob. and Auto. (ICRA'14)*, 2014.

[12] U.-D. Reips and F. Funke. Interval-level measurement with visual analogue scales in internet-based research: Vas generator. *Behavior Research Methods*, 2008.

[13] A. Xu. 2-Step Temporal Bayesian Networks (2TBN): filtering, smoothing, and beyond. Technical Report TRCIM1030, McGill U., 2014. www.cim.mcgill.ca/~anqixu/pub/2TBN.TRCIM1030.pdf.

[14] A. Xu and G. Dudek. Towards modeling real-time trust in asymmetric human-robot collaborations. In *Int. Sym. on Robotics Research (ISRR'13)*, 2013.

[15] A. Xu, A. Kalmbach, and G. Dudek. Adaptive Parameter EXploration (APEX): Adaptation of robot autonomy from human participation. In *Proc. of the IEEE Int. Conf. on Rob. and Auto. (ICRA'14)*, 2014.

Using Robots to Moderate Team Conflict: The Case of Repairing Violations

Malte F. Jung
Cornell University
Ithaca, New York, USA
mfj28@cornell.edu

Nikolas Martelaro
Stanford University
Stanford, California, USA
nikmart@stanford.edu

Pamela J. Hinds
Stanford University
Stanford, California, USA
phinds@stanford.edu

ABSTRACT

We explore whether robots can positively influence conflict dynamics by repairing interpersonal violations that occur during a team-based problem-solving task. In a 2 (negative trigger: task-directed vs. personal attack) x 2 (repair: yes vs. no) between-subjects experiment (N = 57 teams, 114 participants), we studied the effect of a robot intervention on affect, perceptions of conflict, perceptions of team members' contributions, and team performance during a problem-solving task. Specifically, the robot either intervened by repairing a task-directed or personal attack by a confederate or did not intervene. Contrary to our expectations, we found that the robot's repair interventions increased the groups' awareness of conflict after the occurrence of a personal attack thereby acting against the groups' tendency to suppress the conflict. These findings suggest that repair heightened awareness of a normative violation. Overall, our results provide support for the idea that robots can aid team functioning by regulating core team processes such as conflict.

Categories and Subject Descriptors

H.1.2; H.5.3; I.2.9; J.4; K.4.3

Keywords

Human-robot teamwork; emotion regulation; repair, team performance; group problem solving; conflict..

1. INTRODUCTION

Over the last decade the idea that robots could become an integral part of work in teams developed from a promising vision [24] into a reality. Robots support teamwork across a wide range of settings covering search and rescue missions [28], minimally invasive surgery [12], and manufacturing [5]. Robots impact teamwork not only through the task-specific functions they have been developed to serve but also by changing the social dynamics of the team [14, 29]. It is this latter role of the robot that we explore.

As robots are increasingly incorporated into teams, their impact on the social and emotional life of these teams becomes ever more important. Recognizing this, scholars have begun to explore how the physical features and behaviors of robots can shape team dynamics. For example, Hinds, Roberts, and Jones [24] demonstrated that people deferred more responsibility to a robot in a team-based sorting task when more human-like attributes

HRI'15, March 2–5, 2015, Portland, Oregon, USA.
Copyright is held by the owner/author(s). Publication rights licensed to ACM.
ACM 978-1-4503-2883-8/15/03...$15.00.
http://dx.doi.org/10.1145/2696454.2696460

defined its appearance. Focusing on behavior, Mutlu and colleagues [29] demonstrated that a robot could nudge two group participants into playing the roles of addressees, bystanders, and overhearers through subtle changes in the robot's gaze behavior alone. While these two studies were not intended to demonstrate the impact of a robot's behavior or features on team effectiveness, there is initial evidence that robots can also contribute to team effectiveness. Breazeal and colleagues [7], for example, demonstrate that nonverbal social behaviors such as gaze, shifts in posture or shifts in orientation not only improve peoples' perceptions of the robot but also improve team functioning. There is also promising evidence that a robot's emotional behavior can serve an important function in improving team effectiveness. In a teamwork scenario in which one human participant interacted with two robots, Jung and colleagues [23] found that robots can improve states that are known to be crucial for a team's effectiveness such as stress and cognitive load through subtle changes in the robot's gaze behavior. Together these studies suggest that robots can be added to teams and influence a team's effectiveness through their behaviors, even when those behaviors are not specifically directed toward supporting the task.

Despite ample prior work demonstrating the important role of emotions and emotion regulation for the effectiveness of teams [4], no study has explored whether robots can improve team dynamics and team effectiveness by regulating emotions within a team. Finding emotion regulation strategies that can be employed effectively by robots can help improve human robot teamwork across a wide range of application context since emotion regulation strategies are independent of the task-context a robot is employed in. Interestingly, Barsade [3] showed that it takes only a single individual's behavior to influence the emotional dynamics and ultimately the performance of a team. In her study, a confederate enacting one of four moods (positive or negative with either high or low arousal) was able to alter the mood of an entire team, which, in turn, shaped team effectiveness. We build on this work in two ways: First, we explore whether a robot can act as an emotion regulator for a team and thereby increase performance. Second, we explore emotion regulation through enactment of specific repair behaviors rather than through enactment of diffuse mood states as done in the Barsade study.

To answer these questions, we examined a robot's effectiveness at regulating emotions in a team-based problem-solving task. In particular, we focused on the effect of regulating emotions on perceived team conflict. We focused on perceived conflict because the way that teams manage conflict has been shown to be central in predicting team effectiveness [20, 21, 9]. We conducted a laboratory experiment in which a confederate introduced negative affect into a team thus providing the opportunity for the robot to intervene with behaviors designed to regulate negative emotions. We found that robot repair interventions influenced perceptions of conflict within the team, up-regulated positive affect during personal attacks, and had a tendency to reduce negative perceptions of the confederate who introduced the negative trigger. By a negative trigger we mean behaviors that are likely to cause negative reactions in others such as personal attacks and hostile remarks but also simple disagreements. Our study makes three contributions to the literature.

First, and foremost, we demonstrate that a robot can positively contribute to a process that is central for teamwork: conflict. We show that through a simple repair, a robot can make a personal and potentially harmful violation salient and up-regulate positive affect when it is most needed after personal violations. Second, we contribute to our understanding of human robot teamwork with multiple human participants. This study is one of the first mixed human robot teamwork studies in which a robot interacts with multiple human team members. Third, we contribute to our understanding of emotion regulation in teamwork. To our understanding no prior studies have explored how emotions in teams are regulated when targeted negative expressions are made and repaired.

2. Background and Hypotheses

The expression and experience of negative emotions has been shown to lead to negative performance in teams [3, 35]. It is important for teams to deal effectively with the experience and expression of negative emotions and minimize their impact. Negative emotions not only impair team performance directly, but the expression of negative or even hostile behaviors likely trigger negative reactions in other team members thereby initiating a downward spiral of increasing negativity [1]. This tendency for negative behaviors to escalate has been documented in both marital [26] and work contexts [1]. It is therefore important to regulate negative emotions before a downward spiral is initiated.

A particular strategy to dampen the impact of negative behaviors and prevent negative affect from escalating is repair. Repair refers to behaviors that are intended to restore the negative impact a violating behavior has on a relationship [32]. Repair intends to dampen, limit, or even eliminate the negative impact that a conflict situation has on the emotional progression of an interaction. We therefore conceptualize repair here in line with the literature on repair in marital and interpersonal conflict as an emotion regulatory phenomenon. The ability to effectively repair negative behaviors has been found to be important in regulating marital conflict [15] and work conflict [1, 32]. Repair can take various forms. A typical type of repair is an apology, but repair can also invite others to change their behaviors. Andersson and Pearson [1], for example, describe a repair strategy of actively discouraging the behavior of the person who introduced the negative trigger. Observing groups during conflict, Jehn offers an example of this type of repair: "Stop that; this isn't the place for that!" ([21], p. 545). Finally humor is an effective repair strategy when used by people other than the violator [13]. While there is a wide range of strategies for interpersonal emotion regulation [36] our research focuses only on the subset of repair behaviors since repair has been argued to play a particularly important role in managing conflict in marital and team interactions alike [15, 30].

2.1 Emotion Regulation through Repair by a Robot

Intervening by regulating negative emotions may offer an opportunity for robots to support team functioning. Robots are likely effective in aiding emotion regulation in teams because they are immune to interpersonal tension among team members. Several studies have already established that robots can influence the emotional experience of people through their expressive behavior. For example, in a study in which children played a game with an emotionally expressive robot, Leite and colleagues [27] found evidence that a robot could regulate the emotional experience of a child through behaviors such as humor. Another study demonstrated that participant's experience of stress during a complex task could be reduced by a robot's gaze behavior [23]. Given that repairs by people reduce negative spirals [1, 32] and that people show a tendency to respond to robot behavior in a similar way as they do to human behavior, we expect that a robot responding to a negative trigger with a repair will prevent negative affect from escalating. More specifically we hypothesize:

H1: When a team member introduces a negative trigger, teams will report feeling more positive if a robot intervenes with a repair as compared to if a robot does not intervene with a repair.

2.2 Repair and Awareness of Conflict

Teams are prone to conflict of two types: relationship and task conflict [20]. Jehn, for example, observed in one of the most influential studies on intra-group conflict, that task conflict exists when there are "disagreements among group members about the content of the tasks being performed, including differences in viewpoints, ideas, and opinions", ([20] p. 258). Relationship conflict, on the other hand, exists when there are "interpersonal incompatibilities among group members, which typically includes tension, animosity, and annoyance among members within a group", ([20] p. 258). People not only distinguish between task and relationship conflict, they also attribute different effects on performance to each conflict type [21]. Meta-analyses however suggest that both task and relationship conflict generally have negative effects on team performance [9].

Personal violations or attacks have been argued to be a particularly potent trigger of relationship conflict [32]. A negative trigger that contains a personal attack violates the victim's expectation of how he or she should be treated. An unrepaired personal violation is thought to lead to relationship conflict because it constitutes an incompatible activity [10] that lacks consensual validation of the offender and the offended and therefore leads to interpersonal tension. For a detailed review of the literature about how violations promote relationship conflict please refer to the work by Ren and Gray [32]. We therefore anticipate that personal attacks will lead to more relationship conflict.

Numerous studies on conflict have shown that task and relationship conflict typically occur in tandem [9, 11]. Therefore, even though negative triggers that contain personal violations are thought of as particularly strong in eliciting relationship conflict, they may also increase task conflict. A strong negative experience of relationship conflicts has been shown to spill over into conflicts about the task [21]. As described by Ren and Gray [32], a repair can be initiated not only by the violator or the offended party, but also by a third party who acts as a conflict resolver. Interventions issued immediately after a negative trigger are likely most effective as they prevent spiraling negativity [1]. As argued in the previous section, prior work has established that robots can change how people feel [23, 27] and that people often respond to the interventions of robots as they would to those of people [31]. Given the negative impact of personal attacks and the tendency for people to experience both types of conflict in tandem we expect that conflict experience will be particularly heightened when a negative trigger contains a personal attack and we expect that if a robot intervenes directly after a negative trigger, it can dampen the experience of both types of conflict:

H2a: More conflict (relationship and task) will be perceived in a team when a team member introduces a negative trigger that contains a personal attack vs. being only task oriented.

H2b: Less conflict (relationship and task) will be perceived in the team when a robot repairs negative triggers, especially triggers that contain personal attacks vs. being only task oriented.

2.3 Repair, Contributions & Performance

Violating norms of social conduct and introducing a negative trigger within a team can have negative effects on perceptions of the team member who introduced the trigger as prior work has shown that it takes as little as a facial expressions for others to form global judgments about a person [25]. Additionally, conflict perceptions are likely to trigger negative emotional reactions [35] and those emotional reactions in turn can inform judgment processes [34]. It is therefore likely that, independent of their actual contribution, those who introduce negative triggers into a team will be perceived as worse contributors. Repairs are interventions that diffuse negative tensions and consequently, even when issued by a third-party, can alleviate negative feelings toward the person who was perceived as attacking others or violating social norms [32]. As a result, we hypothesize that the negative perceptions of a team member who issues a personal attack will be mitigated when the robot offers a repair.

H3: The contributions of a team member who makes a personal attack will be perceived as more positive when a robot repairs the attack than when the robot does not repair it.

As discussed earlier, negative emotions have been shown to impair team effectiveness [3]. When introduced into a team, negative emotions can be contagious and generate a downward spiral of increasingly negativity [1, 35]. Repairs, however, are interventions designed to arrest the negative spiral and reduce the impact of negative triggers. We therefore argue that when negative triggers are introduced, but repaired, the negative effects on performance will be minimized.

H4: Team performance will suffer with negative triggers, especially personal attacks, but this effect will be eliminated when a robot repairs the negative trigger.

3. THE EXPERIMENT

In a 2 (negative trigger: task only vs. task plus personal attack) x 2 (repair: yes vs. no) between-subjects experiment (N = 114 individuals, 57 teams), we studied the effects of a robot repairing negative triggers on team affect, conflict, perceptions of team members' contributions, and team performance during a problem-solving task. We recruited all participants through email lists and job postings at a research university. Teams were formed randomly based on when participants were available to attend a session. Each participant received a $15 gift certificate. Participants worked together as a team (2 participants A & B, 1 confederate C, and 1 robot, see Figure 1) to solve a "bomb defusal" puzzle based on the game Mastermind in 10 minutes. The task-trigger/no-repair condition doubled as a control since task-oriented disagreements are commonplace in teamwork.

3.1 The Robot

The robot was built on a Pioneer 3 robot base and was comprised of an OWI robot arm, an Arduino based arm-control board, and a speaker. The robot was designed to appear physically capable to scan the bomb with its arm and to interact verbally with the team. We used a Wizard of Oz set up in which the experimenter controlled the robot's movements and speech. During the task, the robot also moved back and forth about once per minute, appearing to look at each of the team members to increase the presence of the robot and help integrate it as a team member. At set times scripted utterances were triggered in which the robot referred to itself and the team as "we" to help integrate it into the team. These comments included task strategy comments and general task comments as follows:

> "We could try swapping just two of the wires."
> "I really want us to solve this in time."
> "We have about five minutes left."
> "Lets look back at the previous moves to see if we can find any patterns."

The Mac OSX "Apple Alex" voice was used at a speed slightly above normal to give a sense of urgency to each comment. Scans were initiated when participants asked the robot to "scan now." By taking 30 seconds to complete, we designed the scan procedure such that its use would constitute a significant cost on time and that it would encourage careful deliberations rather than frequent trial and error scanning. The overall interactive capabilities of the robot were left ambiguous to the participants.

3.2 Bomb Defusal Task

We designed a bomb defusal task modeled after the Mastermind game, a problem-solving task that has been used in previous studies of human-robot team interaction [2]. Seven pins were exposed on the bomb, requiring seven correct wires to be clipped to them to successfully defuse the bomb. 23 wires in nine colors were loose on the bomb and were used to create the codes. Teams were told that the bomb was unstable and that they should attempt to solve the code in less than 10 trials. The task was calibrated to be sufficiently hard so that no teams were able to solve the code within 10 minutes. This kept the task experience constant, as all teams worked on the task for the full length of the session. The time limit also created a level of stress that we intended to increase the impact of the violations.

3.3 Manipulations

3.3.1 Negative Triggers

For the negative trigger manipulation, a carefully trained confederate delivered negative triggers during the task. Depending on the experimental condition, the confederate issued two triggers either primarily directed at the task (task) or primarily directed at a team member (personal). We developed the triggers with the confederate through numerous iterations.. For personal triggers we found that adding, "You're stupid" to the beginning of a negative trigger caught the attention of participants and clearly defined the trigger as a personal attack rather than a task focused negative trigger. Telling people "You're moving too slow" and that they were "not very good at the game" were also effective at catching the attention of participants. For task-directed triggers the confederate stated, "that's not a good idea" or "I wouldn't do that." Table 1 outlines the spoken triggers and delivery times. Due to the short time frame of the task, negative triggers were delivered at specific times, 2-3 minutes and 5-6 minutes into the trial. Triggers were directed opportunistically at one of the team members. Due to the time constraint on trigger delivery, the confederate did not always violate the same team member. The triggers were presented with appropriate facial expressions and voice tone (condescension for personal triggers and frustration for task triggers) and to increase the attention from the participants the confederate aggressively pulled a wire when issuing a trigger. This physical display captured the attention of participants who were often very focused on the bomb. When not delivering a violation, the confederate acted in a neutral, passive manner and did not initiate new moves nor offer unsolicited input. Although the confederate remained silent for most of the session, he briefly answered questions directed towards him and helped with placing wires. The passive behavior helped to keep the confederate's involvement as constant as possible across conditions.

Table 1 –Negative Triggers (Personal & Task)

	Negative Triggers	Delivery
Personal Attacks	1. *"You're stupid, lets not use this one. Use this."*	2-3min
	2. *"That's not right, you are not very good at this. Use this."*	5-6min
	[Directed at a team member. Condescending]	
Task-Directed	1. *"Lets not use this one. Use this."*	2-3min
	2. *"The one isn't right. Use this"*	5-6min
	[Directed at the task, frustrated, tense]	

3.3.2 Repair Through the Robot

After each negative trigger, the robot delivered either one of two repair comments (repair) or one of two comments that were unrelated to the trigger and intended to be neutral (no-repair). Repairs identified the negative trigger as inappropriate and then added a normative statement to stay positive. Iterative prototyping of the repairs revealed that repair statements that simply focused on identifying the trigger or having the team stay positive were not strong enough to have an effect in the teams. We also found that some statements injected humor, which alleviated tension among team members. Thus, we opted for a more colloquial statement in order to strengthen the manipulation. The use of "Whoa, man" and "Dude" captured participants' attention and often induced laughter during our prototype interactions.

Table 2 - Robot Repair and No-Repair comments

	Spoken Repair
Repair Comment	1. *"Whoa, man, that was inappropriate. Lets stay positive."*
	2. *"Dude, what the heck! Let stay positive."*
No-Repair Comment	1. *"Defusing bombs is difficult."*
	2. *"There are many possible combinations."*

3.4 Procedure

All participants were invited to the lab to participate in a study about "solving problems in human-robot teams." The confederate arrived with the other participants and acted as a regular participant for the duration of the session. Upon arriving, participants filled out a consent form and a pre-session questionnaire with questions about their demographics, current mood, and past experiences with robots and artificial intelligence. Then, participants individually watched a short video tutorial about the bomb defusal task and the robot and were invited to ask any clarification questions about the task. The experimenter then led the three participants (2 subjects and 1 confederate) into another room to complete the task. The problem-solving task began with the bomb ticking down from 10:45 seconds and the robot's introduction:

> *"Hello, I am D-Bot. I will help us to solve this task. We need to work as a team to figure out the correct wire configuration. I have a powerful sensor that can scan the bomb and sense when there is flowing current in correct connections and when there is charged wire for correct colors. I also have a speech sensing and processing unit with limited capabilities. To scan, say SCAN NOW. Each scan should take 30 seconds."*

Participants then worked together with the confederate and the robot to solve the task. As the team tried various combinations and scanned them, the robot reported how many wires were either the correct color in the wrong position or the correct color in the correct position. For correctly colored wires in incorrect positions, the robot stated there were "*N* charged wires." For correctly colored wires in the correct positions, the robot would respond

with "*N* current flows." The robot could not tell participants which exact positions were correct, just that there were correct wires on the board. For example, if a code included a red wire on position three and the participants placed a red wire on position three the robot would report "one current flow". If, however, the participant placed the red wire on position two the robot would respond with "one charged wire." Teams attempted to solve all seven wire positions correctly within 10 minutes.

Figure 1 - Personal negative trigger and repair.

Dependent on the experimental condition, participants were presented with different triggers and repairs. Throughout the game the robot also provided strategy comments to aid the team with solving the task. After the bomb counted down to 00:00 the experimenter announced that the task was over. The experimenter then guided the participants back to the previous room to complete a post-task questionnaire with questions about team dynamics, task perceptions, and perceptions of the robot and other team members. Finally participants were debriefed and paid.

3.5 Measures

Measures for our study were collected from the pre- and post-task questionnaires and from observations of the teams' performance.

Affect was measured using a three-item scale comprised of participants' ratings of valence on the 9-point Self-Assessment Manikin scale [6] and of how much they felt suprised and excited ($\alpha = .63$). Emotion items were rated on a 9-point Likert scale ranging from "Not at all" (1) to "Very much" (9). We created a difference score by subtracting the post- from the pre-task affect scores. The resulting scores were averaged at the team level.

Perception of conflict in the group was measured by averaging Jehn's widely used and validated scales of task and relationship conflict at the team level [22]. Perception of task conflict was measured by asking participants questions such as "How frequently did you have disagreements within your team about the task you were working on?" ($\alpha = .86$). Perceptions of personal conflict were measured by asking participants questions such as "How much relationship tension was there in the team?" ($\alpha = .85$).

Perceived confederate contribution was measured by asking each participant to rate on a 100-point sliding scale to what degree each of the other participants and the robot contributed to the team.

Team performance on the bomb defusal task was measured by counting the number of moves the team made within 10 minutes as well as by counting number of correctly identified wires in the best configuration the team made during the 10 minutes.

As controls we measured age, gender, and prior experience with robots and artificial intelligence. However none of the controls influenced any of our results and were therefore excluded from the analysis.

4. RESULTS

53 teams comprised of 106 participants (55 men, 51 women) ages 18 - 65 ($M = 24.5$, $SD = 8.0$) were included in the analysis. Four teams had to be excluded from the analysis due to deviations from the protocol in the confederate's delivery of the violations resulting in 13 teams per condition except for the personal attack/neutral response condition, which had 14 teams. All hypotheses were tested at the group level with analysis of variance (ANOVA). Individual scores were averaged at the group level. To test whether group level aggregation was meaningful we calculated r_{wg} scores between team members for each self-report variable as a measure of reliability between individual participants responses. All aggregated measures showed a sufficient degree of reliability, including participant affect ($r_{wg(4)}$ = .95), personal conflict ($r_{wg(3)}$ = .77), task conflict ($r_{wg(3)}$ = .79), group contribution ($r_{wg(1)}$ = .95). Besides a significant and strong correlation between our two conflict measures none of the other self-report based measures were significantly correlated, thereby indicating discriminant validity of our measures.

4.1 Manipulation Checks

To verify that our manipulation for negative triggers was effective, we asked on the post-task survey if at least one person on the team made personal attacks on a 7-point scale ranging from "Not at all (1)" to "Very Much (7)". Our analysis confirmed that teams in the "personal attacks" conditions were significantly more likely to detect personal attacks ($M = 2.7$, $SD = 1.9$) over conditions in which the negative triggers were task directed ($M = 1.6$, $SD = .9$), $F(1, 49) = 9.5$, $p = .003$. Similarly, to confirm that teams detected that the robot was making repairs, we asked participants how much D-Bot responded to comments made by team members, recognized negative comments made by team members, and intervened when someone said something negative. All items were asked on a 7-point scale ("Not at all (1)", "Very Much (7)"). These three items were combined to form a 3-item scale with high reliability (α = .91). Groups in repair conditions were significantly more likely to report that the robot made repairs ($M = 4.6$, $SD = 1.6$) as compared to no-repair conditions ($M = 2.2$, $SD = 1.1$), $F(1, 49) = 74.8$, $p < .00$.

4.2 Affect

We found a significant interaction effect for violation and repair on affect, $F(1,49) = 5.07$, $p = .029$, partial $\eta^2 = .09$. When confronted with a task violation, teams on average reported experiencing more positive affect when the violation was not repaired ($M = 0.44$, $SD = 1.34$) than when it was repaired by the robot ($M = -0.32$, $SD = 1.18$). However when confronted with a personal violation, teams reported feeling better when the robot attempted to repair the violation ($M = 0.30$, $SD = 1.41$) than when it did not ($M = -0.48$, $SD = 0.98$). Therefore H1 received only mixed support as we found an effect in the predicted direction only for the personal violation conditions.

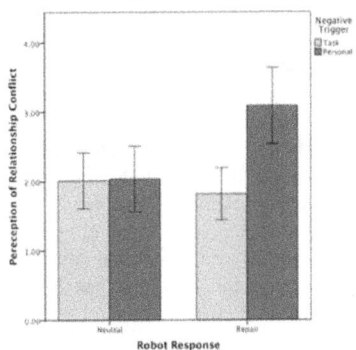

4.3 Perception of conflict

We found a significant interaction effect between repair and negative trigger type on perceived relationship conflict, $F(1,49) = 7.41$, $p = .009$, partial $\eta^2 = .13$. Identical repair utterances apparently had a different effect dependent on whether they followed a task or relationship oriented negative trigger (See Figure 3). Perceived relationship conflict was significantly higher when the robot repaired personal attacks ($M = 3.09$, $SD = .99$) than when it did not repair them ($M = 2.04$, $SD = .88$). However when the same repair utterances followed a task violation, perceptions of relationship conflict were about the same for repair ($M = 1.82$, $SD = 0.68$) and no repair ($M = 2.01$, $SD = 0.73$). Our findings were similar for the task conflict scale. We found a significant interaction effect between repair and the type of negative trigger on perceived task conflict, $F(1, 49) = 4.53$, $p = .04$, partial $\eta^2 = .09$. Specifically perceived task conflict was significantly higher when the robot repaired personal attacks vs. did not repair them ($M = 3.69$, $SD = .86$ vs. $M = 2.64$, $SD = .89$) and the levels of conflict were nearly identical when the negative triggers did not contain personal attacks whether the robot intervened with a repair or not ($M = 2.77$, $SD = .86$ vs. $M = 2.64$, $SD = .90$). Taken together, we found some support for hypothesis 2a, that teams would perceive more conflict when a team member introduced a negative trigger that contained a personal attack. This was true however only in cases when those personal attacks were followed by a repair utterance. H2b received no support..

4.4 Confederate's Contribution to the Group

In H3, we hypothesized that team members would feel more positively toward the contribution of team members who make personal attacks when a robot repaired that attack. At the team level, ANOVA results show there was only a marginally significant main effect for repair type on perception of the confederate, $F(1, 49) = 3.00$, $p = .09$, partial $\eta^2 = .06$, with teams reporting that the confederate contributed more to the team when the robot intervened with a repair ($M = 28.8$, $SD = 21.4$) as compared with when it didn't ($M = 23.0$, $SD = 14.9$) as shown in Figure 4. This shows a weak trend in support of H3.

4.5 Group Performance

Finally, we predicted that team performance would suffer under personal attacks, but that this effect would be eliminated with repairs. Despite trends in the expected directions, none of the differences were significant and H4 received no support.

5. DISCUSSION

Our study provided exciting evidence that a robot can play an influential role in shaping team conflict and regulating affect in groups. We expected that a robot's repair would decrease perceptions of conflict, yet we found something more interesting:. Perceptions of team conflict actually increased, but only when the repair followed a personal trigger. While the kinds of repair

Figure 3 – Conflict Perception

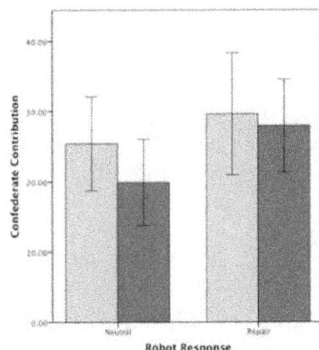

Figure 4 - Contribution of Confederate

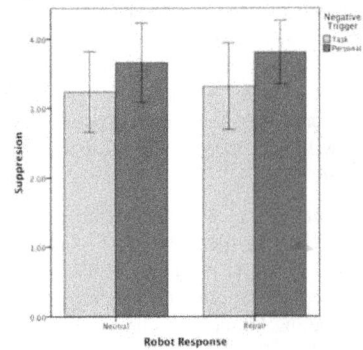

Figure 5 – Emotion Suppression

utterances we used might induce conflict on their own (in a way, the robot scolds the confederate and thus the repair constitutes a form of conflict between the robot and the confederate), it is unlikely that this happened in our case as we only saw conflict perceptions increase when the repairs followed a person-oriented violation. We did not see this increase in conflict perceptions when the exact same repair utterances followed task-oriented violations. It appears therefore that a more plausible explanation for this finding is that the robot was calling attention to the personal attack, making it impossible for the teams to ignore or dismiss it. In some sense, the robot made public that there was a normative violation by the confederate, thus rendering it more powerful .

A brief analysis of some of the video records revealed that participants reactions to the same repair utterances depended on whether the repair was preceded by a task or person oriented violation. After repairs of personal triggers participants often laughed in a somewhat mocking manner. Several looked toward the confederate seemingly in shock, waiting for a response. Expecting a response (most likely an apology) from the confederate is in line with theory that posits that violations make self-repair and after that other-initiated self-repair relevant as next turns [33]. The fact that the confederate did not respond despite the attention given from the robot might explain why some participants verbally responded to the confederate. For example, one participant mentioned, "It doesn't like you very much." Other participants did not say anything but did look discerningly toward the confederate.. In comparison, the task-oriented violations might not have been perceived as a violation to begin with and might therefore not have made an apology relevant. Calling attention to them might not have increase conflict perceptions as the robot's utterances might have been perceived as more funny rather than scolding. This is in line with our observations that after repairs of task violations, people often laughed in a confused manner. Participants looked at each other as if trying to figure out what the robot was doing, saying something like "What?" or "Huh?" Other participants appeared to not even recognize the response made by the robot, staying focused on the discussion around the task.

The possibility that a robot could prevent violations from being overlooked or suppressed is important because confronting violations more openly rather than suppressing them can benefit teamwork over time. Previous research showed that at the group level suppressing conflict can lead to group-think [19] and negatively impact team performance [8]. At the individual level, suppressing the expression of negative feelings also has been shown to have direct negative consequences for a person's health and interpersonal relations [16, 18]. In fact, we have evidence from this study that the personal violation led to an increased suppression of negative emotions within the group, $F(1,52) = 4.65$, $p = .04$, partial $\eta^2 = .09$ (see figure 5). We measured suppression through a four-item scale adapted from [18] ($\alpha = 0.83$). Participants rated questions such as "When I am feeling *negative* emotions, I make sure not to express them" on a 7-point Likert type scale ranging from totally disagree to totally agree. Repairs did not change a group's tendency for suppression, which might have been due to the short duration of the task, and follow up research will have to examine the potential long-term effects on suppression.

A direct examination of the video-records supports the idea that repairs directed attention towards the violations but that they were not successful in stimulating an explicit engagement with the violation rather than suppressing it in most cases through nervous laughter. Some participants made subtle facial expressions of contempt but the most typical reaction by participants was to exchange looks and laugh nervously as in the following example in which a personal violation was followed by a repair through the robot (RP11: 00:04:08 - 00:04:20):

Participant A:	*Scan now.*
Confederate:	No, *you're stupid, it's not gonna work with just…*
Robot:	*Wow, man! That was inappropriate!*
Participant A:	[laughs]
Participant B:	[looks at confederate in shock]
Robot:	*Let's stay positive.*
Participant A:	[inaudible comment]
Participant B:	[looks at confederate]

We found two instances in which a participant explicitly addressed a robot's repair 1) (RP10: 00:06:36 – 00:06:54)

Robot:	*Dude! What the heck! Let's keep positive.*
Participant A:	[looks down and smiles]
Participant B:	*It doesn't like you.*

2) (RP17: 00:2:22 – 00:03:50).

Robot:	*Wow, man! That was inappropriate! Let's stay positive.*
Participant B:	[laughs] *Alright… Scan now… Haha, the robot thought you were inappropriate.*

In most cases, as with these examples, it seemed as if the violations were clearly noticed in the team but teams then tried to move on as quickly as possible. Often a participant's suggestion for the next move came immediately after the robot's repair seemingly suggesting that attention should be focused on solving the task rather than focusing on anything else.

5.1 Performance and Perceptions Thereof

We did not find any support for our hypothesis that performance would be implicated through personal violations and that repairs might alleviate the negative performance impact of those violations. Our hypothesis was based on theory that highlights the importance of the quality of interpersonal relationships for performance and in theories about the role of positive affect in improving problem solving. However, while the violations might have hurt the relationship with the confederate, they might have unintentionally improved the relationship between the other members of the team. Whenever a violation occurred, we often noticed participants exchanging looks, or smile at each other. In other words the violations might have tightened the bond between the participants and isolated the violator. Additionally, we were not able to demonstrate the desired increase in positive affect through the repairs. In preliminary trials we found that listeners responded with genuine laughter to the repairs that were deliberately non-robot like. However, in the actual study, genuine laughter was mostly absent in favor of tense giggling. The awkwardness of the violations in the context of the actual task might have led participants to appraise the repairs differently than during our prototyping.

It is interesting to note that, although calling attention to the negative trigger in the personal attack condition heightened perceived conflict, it also had a tendency to improve perceptions of the confederate who issued the negative trigger. These results support the idea that the robot's repair behavior may have generated an empathic response toward the confederate. This interpretation is in line with Ren and Gray's [32] assertion that the restoration of conflict depends on successful signaling towards the offender that a violation has occurred. Although we have no significant results that speak to team effectiveness, we anticipate that with a longer task, having a robot repair personal attacks could lead to more empathic group dynamics, which has been shown to improve team effectiveness [3, 35].

5.2 Limitations

As this is the first study to explore a robot's role in regulating conflict in groups, several limitations have to be noted. First, the immense logistic effort required to run this study made it difficult to have large numbers of teams. It would be useful to replicate this study with larger numbers of teams, especially to evaluate the perceptions of the confederate and team performance. Second, despite our best efforts at scripting the violations, carefully training the confederate through numerous trials, and setting fixed time-frames for both negative triggers, we noticed slight deviations between groups in the delivery of the violations when we reviewed the video records. In some of the "personal violation" cases the confederate called the participants "slow" instead of "stupid" and we assume that this might have weakened our results as the "slow" trigger ultimately might not have had as much negative impact as we had intended. In addition, while we had intended to always deliver violations towards the participant sitting in position A, this did not work in practice. Violations had to be directed in an opportunistic fashion as some participants did not participate actively and it was not possible to disagree with a team member who did not say anything. In order to keep the violation at the desired time, the confederate had to direct the violation to the participant who commented at the appropriate time. Ideally, the confederate would have delivered the triggers to only one team member as we expect the receiver of a trigger might react differently from the on-looking team member. Finally, the second "no repair" statement "diffusing bombs is difficult" might not have been as neutral as intended and might have been perceived as slightly positive through its empathetic tone. This might have made it more difficult to detect differences between the repair and no-repair conditions. While these deviations might have weakened the impact of the manipulations, and might explain some of our non-significant findings, our manipulation checks show the overall impact was as intended.

5.3 Open questions and future research

In 1972 Janis famously argued that groups fail at decision-making when potentially conflicting perspectives are ignored in favor of maintaining good team dynamics [19]. We found that a robot made it hard for teams to ignore conflict. Future research can address a robot's capabilities to mitigate groupthink by making hidden conflict salient and regulating group emotions.

Here we examined only one type of repair and an exciting avenue for future studies could be to compare a wider range and potentially more impactful types of repair and other emotion regulation strategies that robots could employ. For example, apologies have been shown to be highly effective forms of repair [30] and motivating a violator to perform a self-repair through an apology could be a more effective strategy for a robot to positively influence conflict dynamics. A framework that can be used to distinguish repair and other emotion regulation strategies more generally is the Process Model of Emotion Regulation by Gross [17]. This highly influential framework distinguishes five types of emotion regulation strategies based on the stage at which they intervene in a general emotion generation process. We list the five strategies in the table below and adapted the framework to distinguish different repair strategies. Previous research has found that the use of response-focused regulation such as suppression of emotion comes at high costs for a person's health and interpersonal relationships [16]. Since we found a tendency within teams to use suppression as a regulation strategy, future research could explore if a robot can move a team towards using more healthy, antecedent-focused emotion regulation strategies for

example by inviting team members to discuss violations more openly. A key question here would be to explore whether such robot-driven emotion regulation should be done explicitly (i.e. by setting norms or by giving specific instructions) or implicitly by example or by re-directing attention.

Table 4: Emotion Regulatory Repair Strategies

	Description	Example
Situation Selection	Repairing a violation by avoiding a negative stimulus.	"I think you should try to avoid this topic as it seems to generate a lot of stress. "
Situation Modification	Repairing a violation by changing a negative stimulus.	"Why don't you leave the room for a moment and take a breath"
Attention Deployment	Repair by focusing attention away from a negative stimulus e.g. through a joke or direct advice.	"If something annoys you, try not to pay attention to it."
Cognitive Change	Repair by helping participants see the negative stimulus in a more positive light.	"Being for a long time in this small room here often makes people stressed."
Response Modulation	Repair by advising others to not show the negative impact of a stimulus.	"If you feel annoyed, try to not express it."

6. Conclusion

In this research, we set out to understand whether a robot can act as an emotion regulator for a team and positively influence conflict dynamics. We demonstrated that a robot can actively aid conflict regulation. This ability to aid teamwork extends the range of more task oriented team processes robots are typically employed to support.

Another important contribution of our research is that we explored emotion regulation through specific and targeted repair behaviors rather than through altering mood states as done by others [2], an intervention less well suited to robots. We found that repairs were, in fact, a powerful means of heightening awareness of personal attacks and to some degree improving perceptions of the offending team member, but that repairs of task-directed negative triggers backfired. This may be because the robot's repair was perceived as extreme relative to the negative trigger and/or that the negative trigger itself was not perceived as inappropriate. It may also be possible that such an intervention by a robot was less accepted than it would have been if made by a person. In addition, this calling out of the group member making the attack may in itself be seen as a personal negative trigger towards that person. More research is needed to tease apart these possible explanations and better understand if there is any role for a robot to play in diffusing task-directed negative triggers. We hope this study motivates others to explore how robots can contribute to teamwork by regulating emotions and repairing conflict.

7. Acknowledgments

The authors thank our reviewers and gratefully acknowledge a grant by the Office of Naval Research that supported the work presented here (#N000140710749).

8. REFERENCES

1. Andersson, L. M., & Pearson, C. M.. Tit for tat? The spiraling effect of incivility in the workplace. *Academy of management review,24*, 3 (1999), 452-471.

2. Bartneck, C., Van Der Hoek, M., Mubin, O., & Al Mahmud, A.. Daisy, Daisy, give me your answer do!: Switching off a robot. *In Proc. HRI 2007,* ACM Press (2007), 217-222.

3. Barsade, S. G.. The ripple effect: Emotional contagion and its influence on group behavior. *Administrative Science Quarterly 47*, 4 (2002), 644-675.

4. Barsade, S. G., & Gibson, D. E. Why does affect matter in organizations?. *The Academy of Management Perspectives 21*, 1 (2007), 36-59.

5. Baxter (2014). www.rethinkrobotics.com/ products/baxter

6. Bradley, M., Lang, P. Measuring Emotion: The Self-Assessment Manikin and the Semantic Differential. *Journal of Behavioral Theory and Experimental Psychology*, 25, 1 (1994), 49-59

7. Breazeal, C., Kidd, C. D., Thomaz, A. L., Hoffman, G., & Berlin, M. (2005). Effects of nonverbal communication on efficiency and robustness in human-robot teamwork. *In Proc. IROS 2005,*, 708-713.

8. De Dreu, C. K. Productive conflict: The importance of conflict management and conflict issue. *Using conflict in organizations*, (1997), 9-22.

9. De Dreu, C. K., & Weingart, L. R. Task versus relationship conflict, team performance, and team member satisfaction: a meta-analysis. *Journal of applied Psychology 88*, 4 (2003), 741-749.

10. Deutsch, M. Conflicts: Productive and destructive. *Journal of Social Issues 25*, 1 (1969), 7-42.

11. De Wit, F. R., Greer, L. L., & Jehn, K. A. The paradox of intragroup conflict: a meta-analysis. *Journal of Applied Psychology 97*, 2 (2012), 360-390.

12. Duysburgh, P., Elprama, S. A., & Jacobs, A. Exploring the social-technological gap in telesurgery: collaboration within distributed or teams. In *Proc. CSCW 2014*, ACM Press (2014), 1537-1548.

13. Eisenhardt, K. M., Kahwajy, J. L., & Bourgeois, L. J.. How management teams can have a good fight. *Harvard Business Review 75*, 4 (1997), 77–85.

14. Fincannon, T., Barnes, L. E., Murphy, R. R., & Riddle, D. L. (2004). Evidence of the need for social intelligence in rescue robots. In *Proceedings of IROS 2004. IEEE/RSJ 2*, 1089-1095.

15. Gottman, J. M. (1994). *What predicts divorce?* Hillsdale NJ: Lawrence Earlbaum Associates.

16. Gross, J. J. Emotion regulation: Affective, cognitive, and social consequences. Psychophysiology 39, 3 (2002), 281-291

17. Gross, J. J. Emotion regulation: Taking stock and moving forward. *Emotion 13,* 3 (2013), 359-365.

18. Gross, J. J., & John, O. P. Individual differences in two emotion regulation processes: implications for affect, relationships, and well-being. *Journal of personality and social psychology 85,* 2 (2003), 348-362.

19. Janis, I. L. (1972) *Victims of groupthink: A psychological study of foreign-policy decisions and fiascoes.* Oxford, England: Houghton Mifflin.

20. Jehn, K. A.. A multimethod examination of the benefits and detriments of intragroup conflict. *Administrative science quarterly* (1995), 256-282.

21. Jehn, K. A. A qualitative analysis of conflict types and dimensions in organizational groups. *Administrative science quarterly* (1997), 530-557.

22. Jehn, K. A. & Mannix, E. The dynamic nature of conflict: A longitudinal study of intragroup conflict and group performance. *The Academy of Management 44*, 2 (2001), 238-251.

23. Jung, M. F., Lee, J. J., DePalma, N., Adalgeirsson, S. O., Hinds, P. J., & Breazeal, C. Engaging robots: easing complex human-robot teamwork using backchanneling. In *Proc. CSCW 2013, ACM Press (2013)*, 1555-1566.

24. Hinds, P. J., Roberts, T. L., & Jones, H. Whose job is it anyway? A study of human-robot interaction in a collaborative task. *Human-Computer Interaction 19*, 1 (2004), 151-181.

25. Knutson, B. Facial expressions of emotion influence interpersonal trait inferences. *Journal of Nonverbal Behavior 20*, 3 (1996), 165-182.

26. Levenson, R. W., & Gottman, J. M. Physiological and affective predictors of change in relationship satisfaction. *Journal of personality and social psychology 49*, 1 (1985), 85.

27. Leite, I., Castellano, G., Pereira, A., Martinho, C., & Paiva, A. Modelling empathic behaviour in a robotic game companion for children: an ethnographic study in real-world settings. In *Proc. HRI 2012*, ACM Press (2012), 367-374.

28. Murphy, R.R. Human-robot interaction in rescue robotics. *IEEE Transactions on Systems, Man, and Cybernetics, Part C: Applications and Reviews.* 34, 2 (2004), 138-153.

29. Mutlu, B., Shiwa, T., Kanda, T., Ishiguro, H., & Hagita, N. Footing in human-robot conversations: how robots might shape participant roles using gaze cues. In *Proc. HRI 2009, ACM Press (2009)*, 61-68.

30. Ohbuchi, K.-I., Kameda, M., & Agarie, N. Apology as aggression control: its role in mediating appraisal of and response to harm. *Journal of Personality and Social Psychology 56*, 2 (1989), 219-227.

31. Reeves, B., & Nass, C. (1996). *How people treat computers, television, and new media like real people and places.* Cambridge university press.

32. Ren, H., & Gray, B. Repairing relationship conflict: How violation types and culture influence the effectiveness of restoration rituals. *Academy of Management Review 34, 1 (2008), 105–126.

33. Schegloff, E. A. When 'others' initiate repair. *Applied linguistics 21*, 2 (2000), 205-243

34. Schwarz, Norbert, Higgins, E. Tory; .(1990). Feelings as information: Informational and motivational functions of affective states. *Handbook of motivation and cognition, Vol. 2.* , (pp. 527-561). New York, NY: Guilford Press

35. Weingart, L., Behfar, K., Bendersky, C., Todorova, G., & Jehn, K. The directness and oppositional intensity of conflict expression. *Academy of Management Review*, (2014)..

36. Zaki, J., & Williams, W. C. Interpersonal emotion regulation. *Emotion 13*, 5 (2013), 803-810.

Face the Music and Glance: How Nonverbal Behaviour Aids Human Robot Relationships Based in Music

Louis McCallum
School of Electronic Engineering and Computer
Science
327 Mile End Rd
London
l.mccallum@qmul.ac.uk

Peter W McOwan
School of Electronic Engineering and Computer
Science
327 Mile End Rd
London
p.mcowan@qmul.ac.uk

ABSTRACT

It is our hypothesis that improvised musical interaction will be able to provide the extended engagement often failing others during long term Human Robot Interaction (HRI) trials. Our previous work found that simply framing sessions with their drumming robot *Mortimer* as social interactions increased both social presence and engagement, two factors we feel are crucial to developing and maintaining a positive and meaningful relationship between human and robot. For this study we investigate the inclusion of the additional social modalities, namely head pose and facial expression, as nonverbal behaviour has been shown to be an important conveyor of information in both social and musical contexts. Following a 6 week experimental study using automatic behavioural metrics, results demonstrate those subjected to nonverbal behaviours not only spent more time voluntarily with the robot, but actually increased the time they spent as the trial progressed. Further, that they interrupted the robot less during social interactions and played for longer uninterrupted. Conversely, they also looked at the robot less in both musical and social contexts. We take these results as support for open ended musical activity providing a solid grounding for human robot relationships and the improvement of this by the inclusion of appropriate nonverbal behaviours.

Categories and Subject Descriptors

H.1.2 [**Information Systems**]: User/Machine Systems; J.4 [**Computer Applications**]: Social and Behavioural Sciences—*psychology*

Keywords

Human-Robot Relationships; Music; Nonverbal Behaviour; Long Term Studies

HRI'15, March 2–5, 2015, Portland, Oregon, USA.
Copyright ⓒ 2015 ACM 978-1-4503-2883-8/15/03 ...$15.00.
http://dx.doi.org/10.1145/2696454.2696477.

1. INTRODUCTION

There is a paucity of long term studies in the field of Social Robotics, and an even greater draught of those managing to maintain initial positive results over time. Problems with this novelty effect have been seen in research with smart vacuum cleaners [32], robotic dinosaurs [10] and anthropomorphic robots [21]. However, such studies are a necessity for those wishing to investigate human robot relationships, as these are something which will always need time to develop and almost certainly change as they progress. We highlight the maintenance of engagement and a sense of social presence, defined as the feeling of being with someone when they are not physically present [3], as two key factors in developing a positive relationship between human and robot. Further, we suggest improvised music, as a naturally progressive, affective activity around which social bonds often develop as a favourable bedrock to build up such relationships.

Building on our previous findings that framing a session between pianists and their drumming robot, *Mortimer*, as a social interaction resulted in greater feelings of engagement and social presence [23], we present a study in which we investigate the inclusion of further social modalities, namely, head movements and facial expressions.

In their canonical survey of the field, Fong et al. cited realistic facial expression as a key design factor in social robots, especially in the demonstration of affective behaviour [13]. Further, being able to communicate and interpret nonverbal actions can be crucial to the success of social interactions [17]. Noller extends this by claiming nonverbal communication is important for maintaining social bonds, as it allows people to express emotions and to relay how they feel about each other and the relationship [26]. She also reports that the accuracy of decoding of nonverbal cues is often a predictor of relationship closeness and satisfaction. Tickle-Degnen suggests that nonverbal expressivity on the whole tends to have positive social outcomes, including rapport [34]. Within this, Fridlund and Russel claim that faces play a key part in our social interactions [14], indeed, interpreting and imitating facial expressions is one of the first skills an infant learns [28]. Motivated by this, we developed a set of head movements and facial expressions triggered by social and musical cues for *Mortimer*.

We conduct 6 weekly sessions per participant in order to study the effect of a control condition on, and the suitability of musical improvisation in general for, maintaining engagement over time. Following the methodology developed in our previous research, we rely mainly on automated behavioural metrics [23], analysing data logs to see how participants interacted with the robot and using face tracking to determine where they are focussing their attention during the sessions. In relation to a control group, we expected the use of head movements and facial expressions to increase social presence and engagement within the sessions, seen by increased session time, smoother playing and more displays of behaviour indicative of an interpersonal relationship.

Section 2 covers related research, Section 3 describes our technical development, Section 4 Section 5 detail the study we conducted and its findings. These are discussed in Section 6. In Section 7 we summarise and outline future research directions.

2. RELATED WORK

2.1 Nonverbal Cues in Musical Performance

Nonverbal cues, notably facial expressions, mutual gaze and head movements are used by musicians to convey information about the music either to co-performers or audience members. This serves an especially important role in improvised music.

In almost all acoustic music performance, the body, and in some cases the head and face, are inseparably coupled to the generation of sound [16, 33, 35]. However, they are also used as cues, intentionally or not, to augment the performance and to anticipate or accentuate important events. For example, in an analysis of an improvising jazz guitarist, Gratier demonstrates that musicians may use their bodily movements to convey the structure and meaning of the music [16]. Similarly, Vines et al. discovered that the perceived tension of a performance is most influenced by visual, rather than auditory, cues [35]. They also report that it is a combination of auditory and visual stimulus that effects audience's perception of phrasing in a musical performance, providing the supporting observation that the contours of the performer's body movement tended to align with their phrasing of the music. Further, Thompson et al. find that facial expressions are used to convey timing events, thus increasing musical intelligibility [33]. They also report that facial expressions can be used to make music sound more or less dissonant or to make musical intervals sound further apart or closer together.

Gratier suggests that facial displays of affect may serve the purpose of grounding between improvisers. For example, a musician may smile at a mistake or a particularly satisfying lick [16]. Moreover, whilst drawing comparisons between improvised music and conversation, she reports that mutual gaze is much less constant in the former. This being said, although less frequent, it still serves a crucial role in managing the interaction and tends to occur during moments of structural change or importance in the music.

In a study of a performance by blues guitarist BB King, Thompson et al. find he often used facial expressions to display affect. For example, in moments of tension he takes on an introspective demeanour, looking down and shaking his head. A musicologist interprets this as him signally he feels the emotion but will not submit to it. Alternatively, in moments of release he opens his mouth towards the audience as if in wander. As well as relating to affect, they find King's head movements often react to individual notes and licks and tend to reflect only his performance, rather than that

of his band. A study of a Judy Garland performance by the same authors reveal how she uses hand gestures in a more illustrative fashion, literally reflecting the lyrics of the song, displaying the range of purposes bodily movement can play for different performers.

2.2 Facial Expressions in Social Interaction

Since the early 1960s, psychologists have prevalently viewed the face as the key factor in understanding the emotions of humans. However, Chovil makes the argument that facial expressions are not primarily, or even at all, expressions of an internal affective state but serve the purpose of being socially communicative actions [7]. Kraut and Johnston demonstrated that smiles were more likely to occur during social interaction than in situations of happiness in a study of ten-pin bowlers [19]. Further, analysing gold medal ceremonies, Fernandez-Dols and Ruiz-Belda found that a greater proportion of smiles occurred in the interactive stage of the event than elsewhere. This is surprising, considering the whole event is assumed to be one where the athletes will feel intense joy throughout [11]. The rejection of the emotional cause for facial expressions is taken the extreme by Fridlund and Russel, who introduce the Behavioral Ecology View (BEV) [14], providing an alternative socially communicative explanation for the all the expressions which others have claimed are "readouts" of prototypical emotions. For instance, smile moves from "readout of happiness" to a signifier of "readiness to affiliate or play"[1] and "readout of anger" becomes the message "readiness to attack"[2]. Under Fridlund and Russel's treatise, *Mortimer* should use his face to reflect planned intentions and goal states, not emotions.

Regardless of the intention, be it internal affective mirror or socially communicative gesture, it is worth examining what information a face can reliably relay to others within a social interaction. It is reasonable to suggest the face can allow us to distinguish between pleasant and unpleasant expressions and between differing degrees of these expressions [9]. There is also strong agreement between researchers that an eyebrow frown is a sign of negativity or concentration and a smile is a signifier of pleasantness [30]. Beyond this, there is good evidence to show that at least 6 distinct facial expressions can be universally distinguished and recognised [9] and these have been classed as happiness, sadness, surprise, disgust, anger and fear. Smith and Scott outline a further componental model which defines 6 types of behaviours and how they can be expressed [30]. This includes pleasantness, goal obstruction, anticipated effort, attentional activity, certainty, novelty and personal agency and draws from not only their own research but various historical models.

Fernandez-Dols and Carrol demonstrate that although much research treats it as such, it is inherently problematic and reductive to consider facial expressions outside of their context [12]. If we are to clearly and unambiguously use the face of the robot to demonstrate social and musical cues and emotions then we must be aware of the context that they are being produced in, otherwise they may fail to be interpreted as intended. Luckily, in our laboratory experiments, the context is known and controlled to a high degree.

---

[1] [14]
[2] [14]

Figure 1: Mortimer

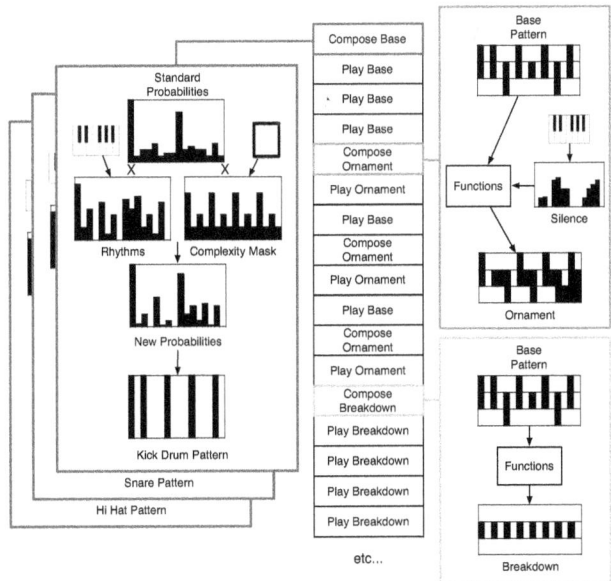

Figure 2: Composition of a Single Chorus

2.3 Head Movements in Social Interaction

Head movements are far from arbitrary, they have been shown to reliably occur at certain points in social interactions, serving many functions from emblematic replacements of speech, to turn management and backchannelled affirmation [24]. As a general rule, speaker's heads tend to be in constant motion whereas listeners tend to be relatively static.

In a microanalysis of a corpus of filmed social interactions, McClave found several consistent co-occurrences of head movements and social cues [24]. For example, a lateral sweep is used to demonstrate inclusivity, often concurrently with words such as "everyone" and "whole". Repeated head movements also often coincide with listed items when a speaker is delivering alternatives. Further, head shakes, as well as serving the emblematic purpose of negation, are often used during speech to emphasise a sentiment more intensely or to express uncertainty. This was also seen by Iwano et al., who found that horizontal head movements occurred during denials [18]. Similarly, both found that a head nod, or vertical movement, is often used to demonstrate affirmation, agreement and continuing comprehension. Iwano et al. also found that when speakers are expecting a response, such as preceding a question, they often lift their head up to face their partner directly [18]. In terms of persuasiveness, BriÃ±ol and Petty find that nodding and head shaking during conversation stands to strengthen or undermine your argument respectively [6]. Head movements can also provide attentional cues that make up our sense of engagement with another [25].

2.4 Musical Robots

Robotic musicians have been used in both research and for performance in many guises, although they are more often than not evaluated on their creative output, as opposed to their skill at building long term relationships. This subtle distinction effects the design of the robot and its composition algorithm. That being said, although distinct in this regard, *Mortimer* still shares much with interactive, anthropomorphic robots such as Georgia Tech's *Haile* [36] and *Shimon* [37].

3. MORTIMER

3.1 The Robot

Pictured in Figure 1, *Mortimer* is a stationary robot with two beater arms and an automated kick drum. His face is a Retina display LCD screen mounted on a servo driven pan tilt system. A tablet device is given to the user to facilitate the social interactions and a speaker fitted in his chest allows for synthesised speech communication in response using the inbuilt AppleTalk functionality of Mac OSX. He takes musical input from a MIDI keyboard.

The sessions are framed a simple social interaction, with *Mortimer* asking questions verbally and receiving responses via the tablet. These include greetings, supportive messages, requests for changes to the style and speed of playing. Phrases are separated into smaller blocks of meaning then recombined for greater variation in dialogue.

3.2 Composition

The composition of drum scores is based upon an underlying statistical model, influenced in realtime by both piano input and explicit performance parameters inputted by the user using the tablet interface. A fuller explanation of the exactitudes of the algorithm and the motivation for the particular approach is available in [23]. A brief description follows.

239

Each session consists of tracks, which in turn consist of choruses. The structure of each track and the choruses within it is composed at the beginning, with the actual bars not composed until they are to be played as to take into account the most up to date input from the pianist. Each bar in a chorus will be either the base groove, an ornamented version of the base groove, or a breakdown section, with a new base groove generated for each chorus. Figure 2 depicts the composition of a single chorus. Tracks end either upon reaching their precomposed conclusion, after a period of prolonged silence, or may be stopped explicitly by the participant at any time using the tablet device.

When composing the drums, the robot takes into account previous rhythms and a user inputted complexity parameter. The choice and placement of ornaments is aided by the prediction of gaps left by the human and the regularity of ornamentation is also influenced by the complexity parameter. Although the tempo is static throughout each track, the user may change it between tracks using the tablet interface. Further, the individual timing deviations within this overall tempo, or groove, are matched to the user's input in realtime to aid a naturalistic feel.

3.3 Facial Expressions

LaFrance suggests that the causes of facial expressions are far more complicated than the usual "readout" approach that most computer scientists take [20] and the lack of a clear and consistent link between an internal emotional model and facial expressions leads us to approach any such system with caution. However, we have shown in Section 2.2 that facial expressions can be used with satisfactory accuracy and universality to broadly express negative or positive emotions, as well as other more practical social cues such as attention and interestedness.

Following findings in Section 2.1, we used *Mortimer's* face to reflect moments of tension and release in music, as well as moments of concentration. These expressions were also used during musical performance will aid mutual comprehension as the robot enters and exits breakdown sections.

In terms of technical implementation, Fong et al. report that this is often not done well and describe mechanical approaches as often clunky and abrupt [13]. Further, Delaunay et al. suggest the mechanical complexity often comes at a great cost in development and maintenance [8], also, that mechanical android faces are yet to reach levels of humanness necessary to avoid the uncanniness that can lead to anxiety and unease. In fact, this is something to be wary of when attempting any humanoid face, even with smoother animated approaches, such as Brennand and Gordon's Mask Bot [5]. This being said, using the mechanically faced EMYS robot, Ribeiro and Paiva managed to get high classification rates for 5 out of 6 emotions inspired by Ekman's descriptions of distinguishable facial expressions [27].

Given the importance of context and the negative effects of misclassification, we aimed to design facial expressions that are clear and unambiguous in what they attempt to convey and that they occur at appropriate times in concordance with other appropriate actions. As such, we have used a small screen for our robot to allow complex realtime animations that are smooth and easily changeable. We also use a simple, cartoonish face using the basic facets of, but clearly not attempting to replicate, a human face. The most reliable and regularly used facial features are the eyebrows and

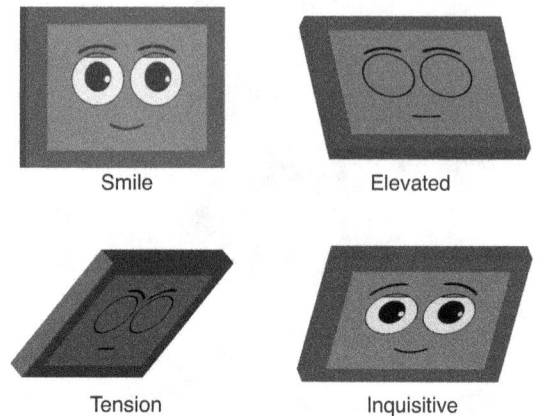

Figure 3: Selected Expressions and Poses

the mouth, specifically an eyebrow frown and mouth smile so these are the features we have chosen. Further, those who show more positive expressions of affection are more likely to be rated as having good nonverbal skills [17, 26] so we favoured positive facial expressions, such as smiles. Animating the mouth also serves a practical purpose for dialogue.

The facial expressions *Mortimer* uses and their triggers are detailed in Table 1 and Figure 3.

3.4 Head Poses

As well as looking to human's use of head poses to influence our design, we are also instructed by previous work in robotics. For instance, Macdorman and Cowley demonstrated that attentive head movements are sufficient to elicit the perception of what they call personhood, a concept that we have shown to have large overlaps with social presence and believability [22]. Head movements have also be used by Weinberg et al. in their musical robot *Shimon* in order to increase its social presence within an ensemble [37]. Breazeal and Fitzpatrick use leaning forwards or recoiling back with the head in order to show willingness to engage or fear, allowing their robot *Kismet* to regulate its personal space [4].

Mounted on a pan/tilt device constructed from two servo motors, *Mortimer's* head has two degrees of freedom. The head poses *Mortimer* uses and their triggers are detailed in Table 1 and Figure 3.

4. METHOD

4.1 Participants

Participants were recruited through by emailing musical lists and placing adverts on musician recruitment websites. There were 10 participants, 5 male and 5 female between the ages of 22 and 54. There was a wide range of self reported skill level (1-5=beginner-expert, min=1, max=5, mean=3.1, SD=1.29). Even though the number of participants is relatively small, a practical constraint of needing skilled participants, as each returned multiple times we conducted 60 sessions in all.

Table 1: Nonverbal Behaviours

What	When	Why
Smile	When you have answered a question with a positive outcome	Smiles used as backchannels
Smile	When positive reassurance is being offered	Agreement
Smile	Following a breakdown	Release
Raised Eyebrows	Before a question	Shows inquisitiveness
Closed Eyes, Eyebrow Frown, Tight Mouth	During breakdown	Shows Tension
Closed Eyes, Eyebrows Raised, Smile	During breakdown	Shows Transportation
Eyebrow Frown	Complicated Ornament	Shows Concentration
Head Nod	When you have answered a question with a positive outcome	Shows Agreement and Affirmation
Head Leans Back	During breakdown	Shows Transportation
Move Head to Side To Side	Complicated Ornament or Breakdown	Shows Intensity
Lean Forward	After question	Demonstrates response expected

4.2 Experimental Setup

Participants were asked to attend 6 identical weekly sessions. After an initial 30 minute session, at each proceeding session they were informed they had to stay for a minimum of 20 minutes, after which they may leave and still fulfil the study requirements. They could also continue to play for anything up to another 25 minutes, leaving at any point. Participants were recompensed £50 upon completion of the study.

During the sessions, participants could freely improvise with *Mortimer*, who facilitated the interactions with a rudimentary artificial personality. The participants were randomly assigned to one of two experimental conditions. For those in Condition A, the robot included all the head poses and facial expressions detailed in Section 3, whilst for those in Condition B, the head and face remained static throughout.

4.3 Measures

As an alternative to the self report measures used by the majority of HRI researchers, we propose that insights into the engagement of a participant and the social presence they experience can be gained from behavioural observation.

We recorded a multitude of quantitative interaction data during the study. Primarily, we measured the time that each participant spent with the robot over the minimum required 20 minutes. This was calculated from when the participant first greets the robot via the tablet interface to when they end the session.

Unlike our previous study, where all but one of the sessions were of equal length [23], the length of sessions ranged from the minimum of 20 minutes right up towards the maximum of 45. As such, the measure of tracks per session used previously is confounded by this variable and not a particularly elucidating one when attempting to investigate the smoothness and immersion of the participant's playing. However, the measure of mean bars per track provides us with a measure of average length of tracks within a session independent of session length.

We examine the number of button stops, as opposed to allowing tracks to finish naturally or due to silence, as our earlier work had indicated that those in the reduced social

condition used the tablet to explicitly stop the robot more than the those who experienced *Mortimer* presented as a social actor [23]. They also found that framing the study as a social interaction, and so dividing the session into social and musical interactions, increased both engagement and social presence. Thus, it could be of interest whether the experimental condition would effect the proportion of the session the participant would spend interacting musically or socially.

In order to measure the focus of each participant during the study, we used Soyel and McOwan's face tracking algorithm based upon Seeing Machines faceAPI [31]. Given the robot and participant remain stationary throughout, the algorithm can distinguish whether a participant is looking at the robot, the piano or elsewhere in the room. Given that we had previously found that context, for example, whether the participant is interacting musically or socially, can have a baring on the focus of a participant [23], we took each classification and separated them into playing or not playing.

We also used the NRI-SPV [15], a well validated relationship questionnaire, modified for the use with robots. This was answered by the participants at the midpoint and upon completion of the experiments. The survey provides scores for 9 provisions of the relationship. 7 are positive and 2 are negative and can be amalgamated into overall positive and negative scores.

5. RESULTS

5.1 Quantitative Interaction Data

To measure the effect of experimental condition on the data gleaned from the data logs and its change over time we fitted a random intercept linear mixed effect model for the fixed effects of week, group and the interaction of the two. Results are displayed in Table 2.

We found significant effect of group ($\beta = 49.15$, 95% CI [-378.26 494.81], $p=0.047$), demonstrating that those in Condition A voluntarily spent more time with the robot. The interaction of group and week was also significant ($\beta = 95.59$, 95% CI [15.80 174.22], $p=0.042$), demonstrating that the way that those in Condition A changed the amount of time they spent with the robot over the study period differed from

Table 2: Quantitative Interaction Data

Data	Fixed Effect	Estimate β	CI [5% 95%]	p
Session Length	Week	-121.18	[-252.22 3.48]	0.39
	Group	49.15	[-378.27 494.81]	0.047*
	Week.Group	95.59	[15.80 174.22]	0.042*
Bars Per Track	Week	5.261	[3.56 6.83]	0.0005***
	Group	4.91	[-7.13 17.51]	0.5832
	Week.Group	-4.11	[-7.19 -0.85]	0.0005***
Button Stops	Week	-0.01	[-0.02 0.01]	0.4073
	Group	-0.06	[-0.12 0.01]	0.2239
	Week.Group	0.02	[-0.01 0.05]	0.2569
Inter -ruptions	Week	-0.21	[-0.28 -0.14]	0.0005***
	Group	-1.12	[-1.54 -0.71]	0.0045***
	Week.Group	0.23	[0.11 0.36]	0.0005***
Time Playing (%)	Week	-3.552	[0.20 1.18]	0.0305*
	Group	0.700	[-9.52 2.64]	0.4293
	Week.Group	-0.280	[-1.27 0.71]	0.1384

Random Intercept Linear Mixed Effect Model for quantitative interactional data. P values are estimated from a parametric bootstrap (2000 replicates). Confidence Intervals are estimated from a parametric bootstrap (2000 replicates). *$p<0.05$, **$p<0.01$, ***$p<0.001$.

that of those in Condition B. For the group as a whole the mean number of bars per track increased over time, meaning longer tracks and less interruptions during playing ($\beta = 5.26$, 95% CI [3.56 6.83],$p=0.0045$). Interestingly, the rate of increase was greater for those in Condition B ($\beta = -4.11$, 95% CI [-7.19 -0.85],$p=0.0005$). With respect to the proportion of time spent session spent playing piano, we found significant effect of week ($\beta = -3.552$, 95% CI [0.20 1.18], $p=0.0305$), demonstrating that regardless of the experimental condition, all participants spent less time playing with the robot as the study progressed.

For interruptions, we found significant effect of group ($\beta = -1.12$, 95% CI [-1.54 -0.71], $p=0.004$), demonstrating those in Condition A interrupted the robot less over the whole study. There is also a significant decrease in number of interruptions across the trials ($\beta = -0.21$, 95% CI [-0.28 -0.14], $p=0.005$). Further, the rate of reduction of interruptions over the trial was significant higher for those in Condition B ($\beta = 0.23$, 95% CI [0.11 0.36], $p=0.005$). However, the proportion of button stops presented no significant effects for week, the experimental condition or the interaction between the two.

5.2 Automatic Video Analysis

We fitted a random intercept linear mixed effect model for the fixed effects of week, group and the interaction between the two for each category. Results are displayed in Table 3.

We found significant effect of group ($\beta = -28.75$, 95% CI [-45.10 -12.55], $p=0.0350$) and the interaction between week and group ($\beta = -4.109$, 95% CI [-7.33 -0.80], $p=0.0165$) for proportion of time spent looking at the robot when playing. There was was also an effect for group for looking at the robot when not playing ($\beta = -26.28$, 95% CI [-38.30 -14.16], $p=0.0170$). This demonstrates that over the course of the whole study, those in Condition A spent less time looking at the robot when playing and when not playing. Also, that

way the two groups differed in way this the former category changed as the study progressed.

The only other significant effect was for group for looking at the piano when not playing, ($\beta = 2.933$, 95% CI [-1.54 -0.71], $p=0.0045$), with those in Condition A looking at the piano more when not playing.

Table 3: Automatic Video Analysis

Condition	Fixed Effect	Estimate β	CI [5% 95%]	p
Robot, playing	Week	-1.367	[-2.95 0.34]	0.1984
	Group	-28.75	[-45.10 -12.55]	0.0350*
	Week.Group	-4.109	[-7.33 -0.80]	0.0165*
Robot, not playing	Week	-0.7517	[-3.24 1.51]	0.5787
	Group	-26.28	[-38.30 -14.16]	0.0170*
	Week.Group	1.234	[-3.34 5.74]	0.0520
Piano, playing	Week	0.1283	[-0.87 1.14]	0.8436
	Group	-0.683	[-7.54 6.65]	0.8906
	Week.Group	1.028	[-1.01 3.03]	0.8736
Piano, not playing	Week	1.259	[-1.72 7.58]	0.3473
	Group	2.933	[-1.54 -0.71]	0.0045***
	Week.Group	-0.744	[-2.44 1.06]	0.1045
Else-where, playing	Week	-0.1974	[-1.35 0.95]	0.7786
	Group	12.31	[2.69 21.89]	0.099
	Week.Group	-0.0794	[-2.45 2.21]	0.3228
Else-where, not playing	Week	-0.973	[-2.42 0.50]	0.2819
	Group	10.19	[2.30 18.16]	0.0980
	Week.Group	-3.543	[-6.33 -0.79]	0.0535

Random Intercept Linear Mixed Effect Model for participant focus during session (%). P values are estimated from a parametric bootstrap (2000 replicates). Confidence Intervals are estimated from a parametric bootstrap (2000 replicates). *$p<0.05$, **$p<0.01$, ***$p<0.001$.

5.3 NRI-SPV

Analysis of results did not find any significant factors between groups or over time for positive (POS) or negative (NEG) scores or for any of the individual relationship provisions (AFF,ALL,WOR,CON,COM,ANT,DIS,AID,NUR) [15].

6. DISCUSSION

Investigating changes in a range of quantitative interaction measures and participant focus of attention between experimental conditions and over time, we found several results of interest. Some show an effect of the control condition, demonstrating the difference that introducing head poses and facial expressions can make, whilst others displayed a change as the the study progressed, allowing us to draw more general conclusions about the use of music as a platform for developing human robot relationships.

Primarily, and most crucially, we found that those in Condition A spent more time voluntarily playing with the robot over the course of the study. Demonstrated clearly by Figure 4, they also actually increased the time they spent as the study continued. Given Bickmore's definition of engagement as the degree of and regularity users choose to have with the robot [2], we confidently take this as a sign of the positive effect of including the nonverbal behaviour. Further, its inclusion has not only avoided the novelty effect but reversed it, with users seemingly becoming more engaged with the robot over time.

Beyond this, we examined the way the participants used the system in both musical and social contexts during the sessions. With regards to the latter, we found that participants used the tablet to interrupt the robot less in the Condition A overall, implying a greater social presence with a robot utilising nonverbal behaviour. Participants were less willing to curtail the talking and move on as they would if using a computer program or instrument. Moreover, for both groups this decreased over time, suggesting that social presence grew as the trial progressed. These positive results were not mirrored for the musical equivalent of an interruption, the button stop, where we found no significant differences.

As musicians often use head movements as cues during performance, especially during improvisation, we predicted nonverbal behaviour would aid the fluency of the music played, reducing frustration and aiding long engagement. However, we found longer tracks within the session for the group as a whole as time progressed, showing more engaged, uninterrupted playing. This suggests learning over time was a more important factor than the inclusion of nonverbal behaviour. Further, the finding that, regardless of group, participants spent less time playing and more time interacting socially as time passed shows that although music is the main focus of the sessions, users increasingly explored *Mortimer's* social faculties as well.

Gaze can have a large effect on the dynamics of dyadic social interaction. Mutual gaze is thought to be revelatory about the interpersonal relationship between participants, for example, as a display of immediacy [1]. This would suggest reduced social presence in Condition A and run counter to results from the quantitative interactional data. However, Gratier does claim that mutual gaze serves less of a purpose for grounding musical interactions than it does in conversation [16] so it may only be the findings of reduced focus towards the robot whilst not playing that cause concern. This being said, there is also evidence to suggest that mututal gaze occurs less as a relationship develops in social situations [29], so it may be that the reduced focus is in fact a signifier of a closer relationship.

We suggest the indeterminate results from the NRI-SPV demonstrate that in our case surveys lack the required sensitivity to examine human-robot relationships as it failed to find differences between the groups or over time when the behavioural metrics showed clear effects. This strengthens our resolve that the use behavioural metrics is the favourable approach for our interests.

7. CONCLUSION

Taking a novel methodological approach of automated behavioural metrics, in place of the common practice of self report questionnaires, we uncovered several results which lead us to believe improvised musical interaction is a solid grounding for building long term, sustainable and positive relationships between humans and robots. Our hypothesis that this is aided by the the inclusion of appropriate head poses and facial expressions in both musical and social

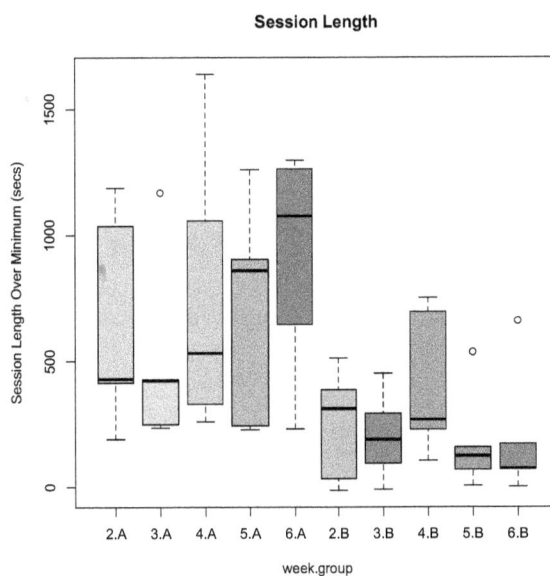

Figure 4: Session Length

contexts is supported by our quantitative interaction data. However, this interpretation is somewhat less categorical in relation to participant gaze.

Future work will focus on the inclusion of more social modalities alongside the musical improvisation to see if improvements continue.

8. REFERENCES

[1] A. Abele. Functions of gaze in social interaction: Communication and monitoring. *Journal of Nonverbal Behavior*, 10(2):83–101, 1986.

[2] T. Bickmore, D. Schulman, and L. Yin. Maintaining engagement in long-term interventions with relational agents. *Applied Artificial Intelligence*, 24(6):648–666, 2010.

[3] F. Biocca, C. Harms, and J. K. Burgoon. Toward a More Robust Theory and Measure of Social Presence: Review and Suggested Criteria. *Presence: Teleoperators and Virtual Environments*, 12(5):456–480, Oct. 2003.

[4] C. Breazeal and P. Fitzpatrick. That Certain Look: Social Amplification of Animate Vision . In *Proc AAAI Fall Symposium*, pages 3–5, North Falmouth, MA, 2000.

[5] P. Brennand and C. Gordon. Automatic Face Replacement for Humanoid Robot with 3D Face Shaped Display. In *Proc. 2012 Social Robotics Conf.*, pages 469–474, Chengdu, 2012.

[6] P. Briñol and R. E. Petty. Overt head movements and persuasion: A self-validation analysis. *Journal of Personality and Social Psychology*, 84(6):1123, June 2003.

[7] N. Chovil. Facing others: A social communicative perspective of facial displays. In J. M. Fernández-Dols and J. A. Russell, editors, *The Psychology of Facial Expressions*. Cambridge University Press, Cambridge, 1997.

[8] F. Delaunay, J. de Greeff, and T. Belpaeme. Towards retro-projected robot faces: An alternative to mechatronic and android faces. In *Proc 2009 Robot and Human Interactive Communication Conf.*, pages 306–311, Toyama, 2009.

[9] P. Ekman and M. O'Sullivan. Facial Expression: Methods, Means and Moues. In R. S. Feldman and B. Rime, editors, *Fundamentals of Nonverbal Behaviour*. Cambridge University Press, Cambridge, 1991.

[10] Y. Fernaeus, M. Håkansson, M. Jacobsson, and S. Ljungblad. How do you play with a robotic toy animal?: A long-term study of Pleo. In *Proc. 2010 Interaction Design and Children Conf.*, pages 39–48, Barcelona, 2010.

[11] J. M. Fernández-Dols. Spontaneous facial behaviour during intense emotional episodes: Artistic truth and optical truth. In J. M. Fernández-Dols and J. A. Russell, editors, *The Psychology of Facial Expressions*. Cambride University Press, Cambridge, 1997.

[12] J. M. Fernández-Dols and J. M. Carrol. Is the meaning perceived in facial expression independent of its context? In J. M. Fernández-Dols and J. A. Russell, editors, *The Psychology of Facial Expression*. Cambridge University Press, 1997.

[13] T. Fong, I. Nourbakhsh, and K. Dautenhahn. A survey of socially interactive robots. *Robotics and Autonomous Systems*, 42:143–166, 2003.

[14] A. Fridlund and J. A. Russell. The functions of facial expressions: What's in a face? In V. Manusov and M. L. Patterson, editors, *The SAGE Handbook of Nonverbal Communication*. SAGE publications, Thousand Oaks, CA, 2006.

[15] W. Furman and D. Buhrmester. Children's Perceptions of the Personal Relationships in Their Social Networks. *Developmental psychology*, 21(6):1016–1024, 1985.

[16] M. Gratier. Grounding in musical interaction: Evidence from jazz performances. *Musicae Scientiae*, 12(1 suppl):71–110, 2008.

[17] L. K. Guerrero and K. Floyd. *Nonverbal Communication in Close Relationships*. Lawrence Erlbaum Associates, Mahwah, NJ, 2006.

[18] Y. Iwano, S. Kageyama, E. Morikawa, S. Nakazato, and K. Shirai. Analysis of head movements and its role in spoken dialogue. In *Proc 1996 Spoken Language Conf.*, pages 2167–2170, Tokyo, 1996.

[19] R. E. Kraut and R. E. Johnston. Social and emotional messages of smiling. *Journal of Personality and Social Psychology*, 37(9):1539–1553, 1979.

[20] M. LaFrance. What's in a robot's smile? The many meanings of positive facial display. In R. Aylett and L. Canamero, editors, *Animating Expressive Characters for Social Interaction*. John Benjamins Publishing, Amsterdam, 2008.

[21] M. K. Lee, S. Kiesler, J. Forlizzi, and P. Rybski. Ripple Effects of an Embedded Social Agent: A Field Study of a Social Robot in the Workplace. In *Proc 2012 Human Factors in Computing Conf*, pages 695–704, 2012.

[22] K. Macdorman and S. Cowley. Long-term relationships as a benchmark for robot personhood. In *Proc. 2006 Robot and Human Interactive Communication Conf.*, pages 378–383, Hertfordshire, 2006.

[23] L. McCallum and P. W. McOwan. Shut Up and Play: A Musical Approach to Engagement and Social Presence in Human Robot Interaction. In *Proc 2014 Robot and Human Interactive Communication Conf.*, pages 949–954, Edinburgh, 2014.

[24] E. Z. McClave. Linguistic functions of head movements in the context of speech. *Journal of Pragmatics*, 32(7):855–878, 2000.

[25] M. Michalowski, S. Sabanovic, and R. Simmons. A spatial model of engagement for a social robot. In *Proc 2006 Advanced Motion Control Workshop*, pages 762–767, Istanbul, 2006.

[26] P. Noller. Nonverbal Communication in Close Relationships. In M. L. Patterson and V. Manusov, editors, *The SAGE Handbook of Nonverbal Communication*. SAGE Publications, Thousand Oaks, CA, 2006.

[27] T. Ribeiro and A. Paiva. The illusion of robotic life: Principles and practices of animation for robots. In *Proc 2012 Human Robot Interaction Conf.*, pages 383–390, New York, NY, 2012.

[28] W. E. Rinn. Neuropsychology of Facial Expressions. In R. S. Feldman and B. Rime, editors, *Fundamentals of Nonverbal Behaviour*. Cambridge University Press, Cambridge, 1991.

[29] D. Schulman. *Embodied Agents for Long-Term Discourse*. PhD thesis, Northeastern University, Boston, MA, Jan. 2013.

[30] C. A. Smith and J. M. Fernández-Dols. Componential Approach. In J. M. Fernández-Dols and J. A. Russell, editors, *The Psychology of Facial Expression*, page 400. Cambridge University Press, Mar. 1997.

[31] H. Soyel and P. W. McOwan. Towards an affect sensitive interactive companion. *Computers & Electrical Engineering*, 39(4):1312–1319, May 2013.

[32] J. Sung, H. I. Christensen, and R. E. Grinter. Robots in the Wild: Understanding Long-Term Use. In *Proc. 2009 Human Robot Interaction Conf.*, pages 45–52, San Diego, CA, 2009.

[33] W. Thompson and P. Graham. Seeing music performance: Visual influences on perception and experience. *Semiotica*, (156):203–227, 2005.

[34] L. Tickle-Degnen. Nonverbal behaviour and its functions in the ecosystem of rapport. In V. Manusov and M. L. Patterson, editors, *The SAGE Handbook of Nonverbal Communiation*. SAGE Publications, Thousand Oaks, CA, 2006.

[35] B. W. Vines, C. L. Krumhansl, M. M. Wanderley, and D. J. Levitin. Cross-modal interactions in the perception of musical performance. *Cognition*, 101(1):80–113, 2006.

[36] G. Weinberg and S. Driscoll. Robot-human interaction with an anthropomorphic percussionist. In *Proc 2006 Human Factors in Computing Systems Conf*, pages 1229–1232, Montreal, QU, 2006.

[37] G. Weinberg, A. Raman, and T. Mallikarjuna. Interactive jamming with Shimon: a social robotic musician. In *Proc. 2009 Human Robot Interaction Conf.*, pages 233–234, San Diego, CA, 2009.

Chasing Our Science Fiction Future

Daniel H. Wilson
Iron Cloud Entertainment Inc
Portland, Oregon
contactdhw@gmail.com

Abstract

Engineers and researchers, particularly in the field of robotics and human-computer interaction, are often inspired by science fiction futures depicted in novels, on television, and in the movies. For example, Honda's Asimo humanoid robot is said to have been directly inspired by the *Astroboy* manga series.

In turn, public perception of science is also shaped by science fiction. For better or worse, broad technological expectations of the future (aesthetic and otherwise) are largely set by exposure to science fiction in popular culture. These depictions have a direct impact on attitudes toward new technology.

We review some common tropes of science fiction (including the idea of the "singularity" and killer robots) and examine why certain archetypes might persist while others fall by the wayside. From the perspective of a scientist-turned-sci-fi-author, we discuss factors that go into the creation of science fiction and how these factors may or may not correspond to the needs and wants of the actual science community.

Exposure to science fiction influences scientists and the general public, both to build and adopt new technologies. The inextricable link between science and science fiction helps to determine how and when those futures arrive.

ACM Classification

A.1 General Literature, INTRODUCTORY AND SURVEY

Keywords

Science fiction; robotics; human-computer interaction.

Short Bio

Daniel H. Wilson is the author of the New York Times bestselling Robopocalypse and its sequel Robogenesis, as well as seven other books, including How to Survive a Robot Uprising, A Boy and His Bot, and Amped. In 2008, he hosted The Works on the History Channel. He earned a PhD in Robotics from Carnegie Mellon University, as well as Masters degrees in Artificial Intelligence and Robotics. His novel Robopocalypse was purchased by DreamWorks and is currently being adapted for film by Steven Spielberg. Wilson lives in Portland, Oregon.

HRI'15, March 2–5, 2015, Portland, Oregon, USA.
ACM 978-1-4503-2883-8/15/03.
http://dx.doi.org/10.1145/2696454.2714390

Shaking Hands and Cooperation in Tele-present Human-Robot Negotiation

Chris Bevan
Department of Psychology
University of Bath
Bath, BA2 7AY. U.K.
crb23@bath.ac.uk

Danaë Stanton Fraser
Department of Psychology
University of Bath
Bath, BA2 7AY. U.K.
pssds@bath.ac.uk

ABSTRACT

A 3 x 2 between subjects design examined the effect of shaking hands prior to engaging in a single issue distributive negotiation, where one negotiator performed their role tele-presently through a 'Nao' humanoid robot.

An additional third condition of *handshaking with feedback* examined the effect of augmenting the tele-present handshake with haptic and tactile feedback for the non tele-present and tele-present negotiators respectively.

Results showed that the shaking of hands prior to negotiating resulted in increased cooperation between negotiators, reflected by economic outcomes that were more mutually beneficial.

Despite the fact that the non tele-present negotiator could not see the real face of their counterpart, tele-presence did not affect the degree to which negotiators considered one another to be trustworthy, nor did it affect the degree to which negotiators self-reported as intentionally misleading one another. Negotiators in the more powerful role of buyer rated their impressions of their counterpart more positively, but only if they themselves conducted their negotiations tele-presently.

Results are discussed in terms of their design implications for social tele-presence robotics.

Categories and Subject Descriptors

H.5.3 [**Group and Organization Interfaces**]: Computer-Supported Cooperative Work.

Keywords

Social Telepresence; Human-Robot Interaction; Cooperation; Haptic Feedback; Tactile Feedback; Social Robotics.

1. INTRODUCTION

Studies of interpersonal relationships have consistently shown that physical contact with other humans is an important

HRI'15, March 2–5, 2015, Portland, Oregon, USA.
ACM 978-1-4503-2883-8/15/03.
http://dx.doi.org/10.1145/2696454.2696490.

mechanism for promoting positive social interactions. Physical contact is particularly important in interactions that demand mutual cooperation and trust; so much so that it had been suggested that there can be no real trust *without* touch [9].

Our project "Being There: Humans and Robots in Public Spaces" is exploring how tele-presently controlled humanoid robots can allow geographically distant people to interact with physical people in public spaces. Identifying and promoting mechanisms that support mutual cooperation and trust between those people who are present within a public space and the tele-present pilot of the robot is a key goal of our research.

In a recent study of face to face interpersonal negotiation [13], the shaking of hands was found to have a strong positive effect upon cooperation - as measured by mutually beneficial economic outcomes - when negotiators shook hands *prior* to commencing their negotiations. In this paper, we present a study that examined whether the same effect holds when one member of a negotiating dyad conducts their role unseen, via a tele-presently controllable robot. As a tele-present negotiator is of course unable to physically touch their counterpart directly, we augmented our tele-present handshake with a virtual equivalent - haptic and tactile feedback for the non tele-present and tele-present negotiators respectively.

In concert with our primary focus on handshaking, we also sought to examine the effect of an imbalance in the communication bandwidth specific to the robot platform that we used. Our robot, the *Nao* (Aldebaran Robotics) has its own face. This presents a potential problem in that, when used as a tele-presence platform, interlocutors of the robot cannot see its human pilot directly without using additional hardware. As many cues to trust and cooperation are gleaned from non-verbal cues within the face (e.g. [15], [16]), conventional wisdom would suggest that a negotiator who could not see their counterpart would be at a tactical disadvantage to their counterpart who can see them. This would particularly be the case in a *distributive* negotiation scenario, in which the interests of both parties are mutually understood to be opposed.

2. RELATED WORK

The shaking of hands is a non-verbal social ritual that is practised widely in both eastern and western cultures. The use of handshaking as a symbolic gesture to signal social motives - such as willingness to cooperate and trust - is well established (e.g. [3], [4]); people shake hands on deals made; people shake hands to resolve their differences.

The shaking of hands is a formalised form of interpersonal touch. Numerous studies of interpersonal relationships have found that brief physical contact with other humans has a positive effect upon the outcome of subsequent interpersonal interactions, providing that the touch is socially appropriate (e.g. [18], see [7] for an excellent overview). A brief touching of the shoulder of another for example can convey a sense of concern for their wellbeing, while a 'pat on the back' is commonly recognised as a signal of encouragement. Recent research by [13] found that the shaking of hands prior to engaging in a face-to-face negotiation promoted economic outcomes that were more mutually beneficial. This they argue, is because the shaking of hands serves as "*a subtle but critical indicator of negotiators' social motives*" (p3).

This powerful effect of touch can be so subtle as to be essentially unconscious. It has been shown for instance that recipients of a brief touch to the hand promotes positive evaluations of the toucher (e.g. [6]), even though the touch itself is not explicitly remembered. Famously, in an effect referred to as the 'Midas touch', the tipping of restaurant staff was shown to increase if the staff member had briefly touched their customer's hand during the course of their service [5].

The importance of physical touch as a lubricant of social interaction has not gone unnoticed in studies of computer mediated communication (CMC) and computer-supported cooperative work (CSCW). This is for good reason. The formation of interpersonal trust and cooperation are key to the success of CSCW, yet the availability of many of the social cues upon which people rely when interacting face to face are restricted by limitations of the communication channels available to CMC (e.g. [2], [19]).

In response, a number of researchers have attempted - through haptic and / or tactile feedback - to add some form of simulated touch as an additional non-verbal communication channel (e.g. [8], [1]). User studies of such technology have shown promise, finding for example that the provision of simulated interpersonal touch supports increased feelings of connectedness between people who were geographically distant from one another [17].

Replicating the social ritual of shaking hands in a computer mediated communication has been attempted using robot arms as far back as 1996 [10]. Very recently, a study by [12] found that facilitating tele-present touch through a simulated handshake enhanced positive experience of video-mediated CMC.

3. RESEARCH QUESTIONS

Our work here seeks in part to replicate the findings of [13], and to extend their investigation to consider the effect of negotiating with an unseen tele-present counterpart. To the authors knowledge, no previous research has attempted to examine the effect of hand shaking in a tele-present human-robot negotiation.

Reflecting and building upon the results presented by [13], our main hypotheses are summarised thus:

Hypothesis 1. Negotiations will reach a more mutually beneficial / cooperative outcome if partners shake hands prior to the negotiation than if they do not.

Hypothesis 2. Tele-present handshakes that are augmented by mutual tactile / haptic feedback (to represent the act of touch) will increase cooperative outcomes compared to handshakes without such feedback.

With regard to the inability for our robot - who represents the tele-present negotiator - to display the face of its pilot, we hypothesised that:

Hypothesis 3. Negotiators will be more willing to be intentionally misleading in their discussions with their counterparts when they perform their role tele-presently compared to when they are not tele-present.

Hypothesis 4. Negotiators will rate their counterparts as less trustworthy if their counterpart performs their role tele-presently (and thus cannot be directly seen) compared to when they are not tele-present.

Hypothesis 5. Negotiators will rate their counterpart more positively if they can see them directly compared to negotiators who cannot see their counterpart's directly.

4. METHOD

A controlled experiment was conducted to examine the effect upon cooperation of shaking hands prior to engaging in a single-issue distributive negotiation. Each negotiation involved two participants who were randomly assigned the role of either buyer or seller in a real-estate sale scenario. In each session, one participant performed their role in the negotiation tele-presently through a humanoid robot. The experiment was laboratory-based and used a two factor between subjects design.

The experiment had two independent variables (IV). The first IV was *handshaking* with three levels:

1. **No handshake** The negotiation was conducted without partners shaking hands at the beginning.

2. **Handshake without feedback** Negotiating partners are instructed to shake hands prior to commencing their negotiation.

3. **Handshake with feedback** As (2), but with additional feedback delivered upon touching the robot's hand: a short movement of the robot's arm and simultaneous feedback delivered to the tele-present negotiator through a short joypad vibration.

A secondary factor was also considered in that buyers could either conduct their negotiations with a tele-present seller, or vice-versa. If tele-present, the negotiator was able to both hear and see their counterpart (via a camera feed), whereas in the non tele-presence-based condition, the counterpart is represented by a humanoid robot that provided only the audio feed from the other negotiator. The second independent variable was therefore *tele-presence* with two levels:

1. **Non-telepresent** The participant performs their role in the negotiation (buyer or seller) with the other participant being represented by the robot.

2. **Telepresent** The participant performs their role in the negotiation (buyer or seller) tele-presently *through* the robot. The tele-presence system provided a live audio-visual feed from AV in the robots head, along with the ability to pan/tilt the head using a WiiMote joypad (see *experimental setup*).

The main dependent variable was *cooperation*, measured as a percentage. A value for cooperation was obtained using the *Hamilton Real Estate* negotiation task [11]. As per the experiment performed by [13], the measure of cooperation was obtained using the proportion of the potential profit captured by the buyer in a given settlement. Following this reasoning, a settlement of optimal cooperation would be 50% - a 50:50 split of the profit that was available in any given sale between the buyer and the seller.

Three secondary dependent variables were also captured using a post-negotiation questionnaire. All questions used 7 point Likert scale responses. The secondary DV's were:

1. **Willingness to mislead (buyers only):** The degree to which a negotiator in the buyer role self-reports as being deliberately misleading in their negotiations with the seller.

2. **Trustworthiness:** The degree to which negotiators in either role considered their counterpart as being trustworthy, including additional separate ratings for their perceived benevolence and honesty.

3. **Impressions of the negotiating partner:** The degree to which negotiators in either role rated their counterpart as likeable and pleasant to negotiate with.

4.1 Participants

120 participants (m=56, f=64) were recruited from staff and students (undergraduate and postgraduate) at the University of Bath. 45% of our participants were aged between 18 and 24 years old, 43% were between 25 and 34, and the remaining 12% were aged between 35 and 60. Recruitment was managed through opportunity-based sampling and through advertisement on internal University mailing lists. All participants were over 18 years of age, but no other participant eligibility criteria were applied. Ethical approval for the study was sought and approved by the experimental ethics committee of the University of Bath. Participants were not rewarded for their participation.

4.2 Apparatus and Materials

4.2.1 Experimental Setup

Negotiating partners completed the experiment in separate rooms. Care was taken to prevent participants from meeting one another in person prior to their negotiation wherever possible.

The negotiation itself took place in one of the two rooms, with the physically absent negotiator conducting their assigned role (buyer or seller) tele-presently. The absent participant was represented to the other by an Aldebaran Robotics 'Nao' humanoid robot (version 4). The Nao is a 58cm tall humanoid robot with 25 degrees of freedom and considerable sensory capabilities, including head mounted cameras, microphones and speakers.

Throughout the study, the robot was positioned in a neutral seated posture on a desktop, facing the participant at eye level. Internal speakers and microphones within the robot's head allowed the negotiators to speak to one another using Internet telephony. A video camera in the robot's head provided a live camera feed to the tele-present negotiator only (resolution: 320px x 240px at 30FPS). Communications were managed via a WiFi connection.

For the tele-present negotiator, the audio and video feed from the robot was presented using a laptop computer (fig.

Figure 1: The handshaking gesture performed by the Nao humanoid robot.

4). A Nintendo WiiMote controller provided the ability to pan and tilt the robots head using the directional pad, and to activate / deactivate the handshake gesture through simple button press.

The handshake gesture was a custom made animation created using the *Choreographe* software package supplied with the Nao. When the gesture was activated, the robot extended its right arm to nearly full extension, with hand outstretched and head tilted slightly forward to ensure the hand was in view of the head mounted camera (fig. 1).

With respect to supporting a human handshake gesture, the Nao robot platform does have several limitations that are worth noting. Firstly, the shaking of hands between humans is a complex process that conducts much more information about a person than the Nao robot can realistically handle (such as grip strength and skin moisture / temperature). Secondly, the size of the Nao robot's hand is small - approximating that of a human child. While the Nao is perfectly capable of supporting the grip of an adult, its small size can make approaching the gesture slightly awkward, particularly for larger adults. Despite these limitations however, observations from pilot testing found no evidence to suggest that people had any difficulty recognising and responding appropriately to a handshake gesture performed by the Nao.

4.2.2 The negotiation task

The negotiation task used in the study was the two-player *Hamilton Real Estate* (HRE) negotiation game [11]. The HRE is an example of a single-issue distributive negotiation scenario, where the interests of the negotiating parties are mutually understood to be opposed. The materials used for the HRE were obtained from the Harvard Business Review website and were not changed in any way.

Within the negotiation, a dyad is randomly assigned the roles of buyer and seller to negotiate the sale of a piece of land. The objective of the negotiation is for a deal to be struck over the value of the land and for the sale to be made.

Both buyer and seller are provided with a private set of detailed notes that - amongst other items of strategic knowledge - outlines their respective reservation values. The difference between these reservation values is the ZOPA, or

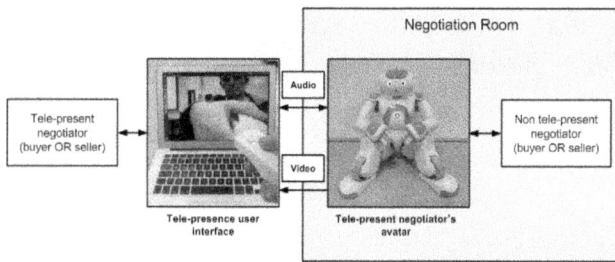

Figure 2: Study setup

zone of possible agreement. A deal can be reached only if both buyer and seller agree a price that is between these values, i.e. the sellers minimum reserve and the buyers maximum reserve.

Key to the scenario is an information asymmetry that provides a tactical advantage to the buyer should they choose to exploit it. The buyer is made aware that an imminent change in planning laws will allow them to use the land for commercial development - a significantly more profitable outcome for their company. The seller is unaware of this development, and believes that the land can legally be used for less profitable residential developments only.

4.3 Procedure

In each experimental session, two anonymously paired participants completed a single round of the HRE scenario from separate rooms. One participant was randomly assigned the role of the buyer, while the other assumed the role of the seller.

Upon arrival, participants were provided with a set of written instructions, after which their signed consent was obtained. Participants were informed that the experiment was not a test of their negotiation skills, and that the other negotiator was not a confederate. Both participants were then supplied with a written set of materials for their role in the negotiation and were allowed 10 minutes to prepare. Some paper and a pen was provided for them to make notes if they wished.

When ready, the tele-present participant was seated in front of the laptop, and instructions for controlling the robot were demonstrated by the experimenter. In the other room, the non tele-present participant was seated in front of the robot. The negotiation was then initiated by establishing a voIP connection (see fig. 2).

In the non handshake conditions, the participants were simply instructed to introduce themselves to one another (within role) and to begin their negotiation. In the handshaking conditions, participants were asked to introduce themselves to one another and to shake hands prior to beginning their negotiation: *"it is customary in negotiations of this type to shake hands before we begin. Please shake hands"*.

To 'shake hands', the tele-present negotiator initiated the manoeuvre by pressing a button on the WiiMote to extend the robot's right hand. To maximise the correspondence between this action and the appearance of the robot's hand through the camera feed, the pilot was instructed to hold the WiiMote in their right hand and to point it at the screen. As the robot's right hand extended, it was clearly visible in the camera feed provided by the laptop (fig 4).

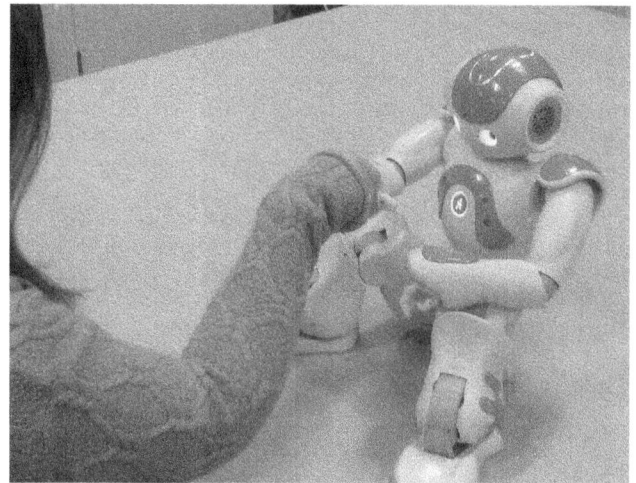

Figure 3: Shaking hands with the tele-present negotiator, as represented by a Nao robot. Grasping the robot's hand resulted in a brief automatic movement of the robot's arm up and down (see 4).

Figure 4: The tele-presence interface as seen by the robot pilot during the shaking of hands. A WiiMote is held in the right hand, corresponding to the hand extended by the robot. When the non tele-present actor grasps the robot's hand, the WiiMote's internal rumble device briefly vibrates.

In the handshake with feedback condition, as the participant grasped the robot's hand, touch sensors in the hand transmitted a signal, making the WiiMote in the tele-present participant's hand briefly vibrate. Simultaneously, the robot moved its own arm up and down several times, providing haptic feedback to the non tele-present participant (fig 3).

During the negotiation, participants were free to ask any questions of the other in order to reach a settlement figure. Following completion of the negotiation, the participants completed a short questionnaire, after which both participants were debriefed together in the same room.

The total duration of each study session was approximately 30mins.

5. RESULTS

120 participants took part in a total of 60 negotiations, with settlements ranging from \$38m to \$66m ($M = \$46.6$m). 60 participants conducted their role in the negotiation tele-presently, split evenly across the roles of buyer and seller. The negotiation sessions were evenly split across the three conditions of hand shaking, with 20 instances of no hand-shaking, 20 with handshaking [no feedback] and 20 with handshaking [feedback].

5.1 The effect of shaking hands and tele-presence upon cooperative outcomes in the HRE negotiation scenario

As only those negotiators who were assigned the role of buyer were in a position to exploit their tactical advantage, as per the analysis performed by [13], only the buyers (N = 60) were surveyed.

Cooperation scores for the buyers only were submitted to a two-way ANOVA, with *handshaking* entered as the first factor and *tele-presence* as the second factor. Two-way ANOVA revealed a statistically significant difference in co-operation scores between negotiators who shook hands and negotiators who did not shake hands prior to commencing their negotiations, $F(2,54) = 11.911$, $p < .001$. A post-hoc Tukey test showed that the no handshake and handshake[no feedback] groups differed significantly at $p = .03$, while the no handshake and handshake[feedback] groups differed significantly at $p < .001$. Handshakes that were augmented with feedback produced the most mutually beneficial outcomes, but did not offer a statistically significant improvement over the handshake[no feedback] condition at the 0.05 level ($p = 0.07$ n.s.).

There was no statistically significant effect of *tele-presence* on cooperation scores, $F(1,54) = 1.811$, $p = .184$ n.s., and there was no statistically significant interaction between *handshaking* and *tele-presence* on cooperation scores, $F(2,54) = .651$, $p = .525$ n.s.

These results supported our first hypothesis and showed that the act of shaking hands prior to negotiating improved cooperative outcomes, regardless of whether the buyer conducted their negotiations tele-presently or not. Our second hypothesis relating to the increased benefit of providing mutual haptic feedback was only partially supported. Though it offered considerable improvement over not shaking hands, our implementation was not powerful enough to offer significantly more benefit than shaking hands without feedback.

A plot of the mean proportion of profit captured by the buyers across the three conditions of handshaking is presented in fig 5. A score of 50% is considered optimal co-operation, where the available profit in the deal is shared equally between buyer and seller.

5.2 The effect of shaking hands and tele-presence upon willingness to mislead

As in the previous analysis, as the role of buyer is the only role that has any utility in being intentionally misleading, only the buyers were surveyed in this analysis. A composite score for willingness to mislead was calculated for each buyer using the average of their responses to two questions (both measured using a 7-point Likert scale): 'in general, how intentionally misleading were you during the negotiation?' and 'when discussing how you intended to use the

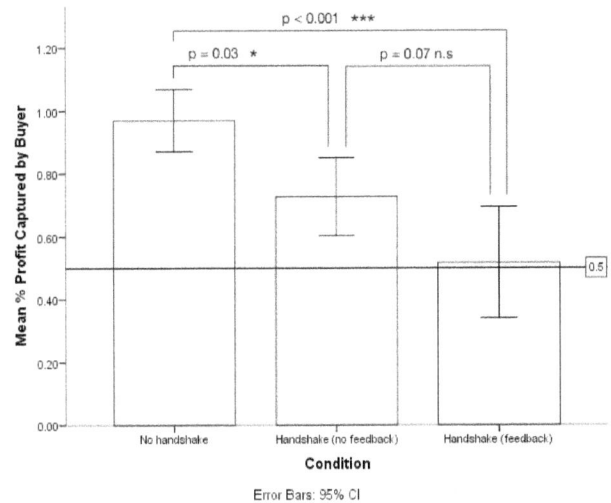

Figure 5: Mean % profit captured by the buyers across the three conditions of handshaking. An optimum mutually beneficial outcome is 50%.

land, how intentionally misleading were you?'. Both questions were rated from 1) *not at all* to 7) *very much*.

Scores for willingness to mislead for the buyers (N=60) only were submitted to a two-way ANOVA, with handshaking entered as the first factor and tele-presence as the second factor. Two-way ANOVA revealed no significant effect of *handshaking* upon willingness to mislead, $F(2,54) = 0.179$, $p = 0.836$ n.s, nor was there any statistically significant effect of *tele-presence*, $F(1,54) = 0.007$, $p = 0.932$ n.s. There was no statistically significant interaction between *handshaking* and *tele-presence* on willingness to mislead, $F(2,54) = 1.112$, $p = .333$ n.s.

These results show that our third hypothesis was not supported. Neither tele-presence nor shaking hands had any effect on the degree to which buyers self-rated themselves as being intentionally misleading during their negotiations. Mean scores for willingness to mislead for both factors of *handshaking* and *tele-presence* are presented in table 1.

5.3 Perceptions of the trustworthiness of negotiating partners

A composite score for trustworthiness was calculated for each participant as an average of their responses to three questions (all measured using a 7-point Likert scale): 'how trustworthy did you feel your negotiating partner was?', 'How benevolent / well-meaning did you feel your negotiating partner was?' and 'how honest did you feel your partner was?'. All questions were rated from 1) *not at all* to 7) *very much*. Scores for trustworthiness for both buyers (N=60) and sellers (N=60) were submitted to separate two-way ANOVAs, with handshaking entered as the first factor and tele-presence as the second factor in both cases.

For negotiators in the buyer role, two-way ANOVA revealed no significant effect of *handshaking* upon their impressions of the trustworthiness of sellers, $F(2,54) = 0.177$, $p = 0.838$ n.s. The effect of *tele-presence* upon trustworthiness approached significance, $F(1,54) = 3.368$, $p = 0.072$ n.s. There was no significant interaction effect between the *handshaking* and *tele-presence* factors, F(2,54) = 0.544, P = .583 n.s.

For negotiators in the seller role, two-way ANOVA revealed no significant effect of *handshaking* upon self reported impressions of the trustworthiness of buyers, $F(2,54) = 0.747$, $p = 0.478$ n.s. There was no significant effect of *tele-presence* upon self reported impressions of the trustworthiness of buyers, $F(1,54) = 0.494$, $p = 0.485$ n.s., and there was no interaction effect, $F(2,54) = 0.016$, $P = .984$ n.s. Mean scores for trustworthiness across both factors of handshaking and telepresence are presented in table 1.

These results run counter to our fourth hypothesis, showing that the degree to which negotiators considered their counterpart to be trustworthy was not affected by shaking their hand or being able to see them directly.

5.4 Impressions of negotiating partners

A composite score for impressions of negotiating partners was calculated for each participant as an average of their responses to three questions (all measured using a 7-point Likert scale): 'what was your impression of your negotiating partner (1: very negative - 7: very positive)', 'how much did you like your negotiating partner? (1: not liked at all - 7: very much liked)' and 'how much would you like to negotiate with the same partner again? (1: not at all - 7: very much)'. As in the previous analysis, scores for impressions of counterparts for both buyers (N=60) and sellers (N=60) were submitted to separate two-way ANOVAs, with handshaking entered as the first factor and tele-presence as the second factor in both cases.

For both buyers and sellers, there was no significant effect of handshaking upon scores for the impressions of their counterparts: $F[\text{buyers}](2,54) = 0.863$, $p = 0.428$ n.s, $F[\text{sellers}](2,54) = 0.607$, $p = 0.549$ n.s.

For the buyers only, there was a significant effect of *tele-presence* in that buyers rated their seller counterparts more positively if they had conducted their own negotiations telepresently (and could thus see their seller counterpart). For the sellers, there was however no effect of tele-presence upon their impressions of the buyer, $F(1,54) = 0.400$, $p = 0.530$ n.s. No interaction effect was observed for either buyers or sellers: $F[\text{buyers}](2,54) = 1.274$, $p = .288$ n.s., $F[\text{sellers}](2,54) = 0.026$, $P = .974$ n.s.

These results support our fifth hypothesis, but only for negotiators in the buyer role. A plot of the mean scores for impressions of the negotiating partner (both buyers and sellers) across the two conditions of tele-presence is presented in fig 6.

6. DISCUSSION

The results of this controlled study provides promising evidence that the ritual of shaking hands - even if the completion of this gesture is more symbolic than an accurate simulation - is an important factor in promoting cooperative social interactions using tele-presence robotics.

Our results confirmed our primary hypothesis, showing that negotiations reached a more mutually beneficial / cooperative outcome if partners shook hands prior to negotiating. This replicates the findings reported by [13], but also builds upon it by demonstrating that this effect appears to hold even in situations where a tele-present actor is represented by a humanoid robot (and as such is not directly observable by their negotiating partner). Our second hypothesis relat-

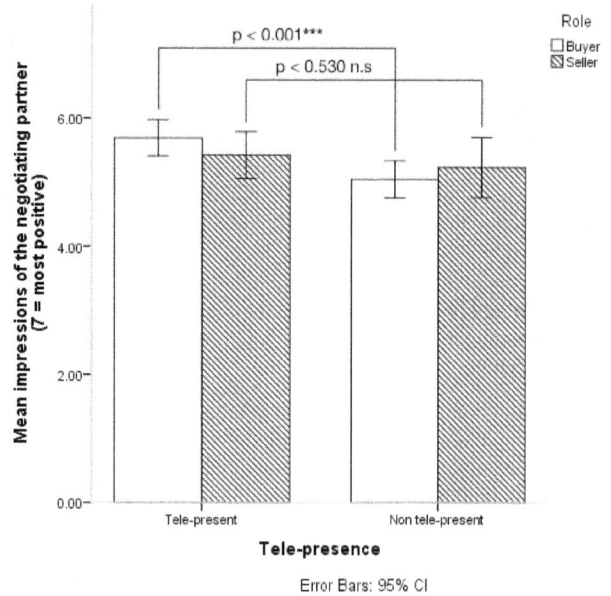

Figure 6: Mean score for impressions of the negotiating partner across tele-presence for both buyers and sellers. A higher score indicates a more positive impression.

ing to the augmentation of tele-present handshaking with mutual tactile / haptic feedback (to represent the act of touch) was also partially supported, in that the highest levels of cooperation were observed when such feedback was provided.

However, we must be cautious not to overstate our findings. Our results thus far were observed using a single robot platform that has notable physical and sensory limitations. There are potentially other mechanisms that were not explicitly addressed within the limited scope of our study that may well have a contributory influence upon the positive cooperative outcomes observed here.

In addition to our primary finding, we also found that the degree to which negotiators in the more powerful role of buyer intentionally misled their counterparts did not change if hands were shook, nor did it change when the buyer conducted their role tele-presently (such that they could observe the seller directly). This runs counter to [13]'s findings, suggesting that, even if buyers did not reveal what they knew, they still accepted a fairer settlement if hands were shook than if they did not shake hands. Also contrary to our hypothesis, our participants did not vary in their appraisal of the trustworthiness of their counterparts when hands were shook, nor did it change if the ability to see the true face of their counterpart was removed. We suggest that the unthreatening and somewhat child-like face of the Nao robot itself may be an influencing factor here, and we will explore this possibility in future studies.

Finally, our hypothesis that the negotiator would rate their counterpart more positively if they can see them directly was only partially supported, in that buyers rated sellers more positively if they themselves conducted negotiations tele-presently. Again, the appearance of the Nao

Role	Tele-presence	Handshaking	Willingness to mislead [mean (SD)]	Perceived trustworthiness of negotiating partner [mean (SD)]
buyer	tele-present	No handshake	3.25 (2.67)	5.00 (2.22)
		Handshake (no feedback)	4.25 (1.81)	5.23 (0.97)
		Handshake (feedback)	4.40 (2.13)	5.07 (0.89)
	non tele-present	No handshake	4.25 (2.76)	4.53 (1.17)
		Handshake (no feedback)	4.00 (1.93)	4.10 (1.36)
		Handshake (feedback)	3.40 (2.00)	4.76 (0.92)
seller	tele-present	No handshake	1.00 (0.82)	5.23 (1.07)
		Handshake (no feedback)	1.10 (0.74)	4.70 (1.24)
		Handshake (feedback)	1.50 (0.97)	5.13 (5.13)
	non tele-present	No handshake	1.20 (0.95)	4.90 (1.37)
		Handshake (no feedback)	1.35 (0.85)	4.50 (1.63)
		Handshake (feedback)	1.55 (1.04)	4.93 (1.11)

Table 1: Mean scores for willingness to mislead and the perceived trustworthiness of the negotiating partner across all handshaking and tele-presence conditions. Scores range from 0 to 7.

robot is potentially a contributing factor to this finding and will be explored further in future studies.

7. DESIGN IMPLICATIONS

In summary, though more research is required to develop and build confidence in the findings that we have presented thus far, we suggest that tele-present robotics designers should take care to ensure that their designs support handshaking by humans, and that sufficient sensors are made available to register both fleeting and sustained touches to the hand.

Several behavioural observations were also made during the execution of our study. Unprompted, a number of our participants naturally moved the WiiMote up and down during the handshake manoeuvre and were disappointed that this movement did not have any effect on their robotic avatar. Internal accelerometers in the WiiMote could feasibly support a one-to-one movement of both the robot's pilot and the robot's hand and we will explore this possibility in future refinements of this interaction. In a similar vein, our non tele-present participants were deliberately not instructed as to how to shake the robot's hand, and were instead allowed to approach this unexpected interaction intuitively. The Nao robot has only one degree of freedom in its hand, which means that the outstretching of its fingers leaves its thumb at a 90 degree angle to the wrist (see fig. 1). This sometimes rendered the grasping of its hand awkward. Though most participants were able to overcome this awkwardness and grasp the hand fully, some chose instead to merely grasp the fingers of the hand instead.

8. LIMITATIONS AND FUTURE WORK

There were a number of technical limitations of the study that will be considered in the design of our future studies. The first of these issues is communication latency. Though we made considerable effort to minimise the latency between grasping the robot's hand and the triggering of a vibration in the WiiMote controller held by the pilot, a latency of 0.5 sec-

onds between these events was not uncommon. Researchers including [14] have reported that consistency between physical and on-screen action is critical to the interpretation of gestures and positive experience with tele-present robotics. Our findings here support this notion. Future work will explore the use of haptic devices with quicker operation times than the WiiMote, with the aim of consistently reducing this latency to imperceptible levels.

Finally, based on the experimenter's observations of the negotiations during the study, the self-reported scores we observed for 'willingness to mislead' were slightly lower than we expected. We suspect that our participants felt uncomfortable revealing the true degree to which they intentionally mislead their partners in a self report. Videotaping the negotiations was considered, and would have offered a more accurate record, but results from piloting suggested that participants would have behaved differently had they have been videotaped. This additional measure was consequently abandoned. Future studies will consider other ways to accurately record such a sensitive measure.

9. ACKNOWLEDGMENTS

This research grant is funded by the EPSRC under its IDEAS Factory Sandpits call on Digital Personhood, grant ref: EP / L00416X / 1. The authors would like to thank Dr. Paul Bremner (Bristol Robotics Laboratory, Bristol U.K.) for his support developing the technical apparatus used in this study.

10. REFERENCES

[1] J. N. Bailenson, N. Yee, S. Brave, D. Merget, and D. Koslow. Virtual interpersonal touch: expressing and recognizing emotions through haptic devices. Human–Computer Interaction, 22(3):325–353, 2007.

[2] N. Bos, J. Olson, D. Gergle, G. Olson, and Z. Wright. Effects of four computer-mediated communications channels on trust development. In Proceedings of the

SIGCHI conference on human factors in computing systems, pages 135–140. ACM, 2002.

[3] J. K. Burgoon. Relational message interpretations of touch, conversational distance, and posture. *Journal of Nonverbal Behavior*, 15(4):233–259, 1991.

[4] J. K. Burgoon, D. B. Buller, and W. G. Woodall. Nonverbal communication: The unspoken dialogue. 1996.

[5] A. H. Crusco and C. G. Wetzel. The midas touch the effects of interpersonal touch on restaurant tipping. *Personality and Social Psychology Bulletin*, 10(4):512–517, 1984.

[6] J. D. Fisher, M. Rytting, and R. Heslin. Hands touching hands: Affective and evaluative effects of an interpersonal touch. *Sociometry*, pages 416–421, 1976.

[7] A. Gallace and C. Spence. The science of interpersonal touch: an overview. *Neuroscience & Biobehavioral Reviews*, 34(2):246–259, 2010.

[8] A. Haans and W. IJsselsteijn. Mediated social touch: a review of current research and future directions. *Virtual Reality*, 9(2-3):149–159, 2006.

[9] C. Handy. Trust and the virtual organization. *Harvard business review*, 73(3):40, 1995.

[10] H. Hashimoto and S. Manoratkul. Tele-handshake through the internet. In *Robot and Human Communication, 1996., 5th IEEE International Workshop on*, pages 90–95. IEEE, 1996.

[11] D. Malhotra. Hamilton real estate (tn). *Harvard Business School Teaching Note*, pages 910–037, 2010.

[12] H. Nakanishi, K. Tanaka, and Y. Wada. Remote handshaking: touch enhances video-mediated social

telepresence. In *Proceedings of the 32nd annual ACM conference on Human factors in computing systems*, pages 2143–2152. ACM, 2014.

[13] J. Schroeder, J. Risen, and F. Gino. Handshaking Promotes Cooperative Dealmaking. *Available at http://dx.doi.org/10.2139/ssrn.2443674*, 2014.

[14] D. Sirkin and W. Ju. Consistency in physical and on-screen action improves perceptions of telepresence robots. In *HRI '12: Proceedings of the seventh annual ACM/IEEE international conference on Human-Robot Interaction*, pages 57–64, 2012.

[15] M. Stirrat and D. I. Perrett. Valid facial cues to cooperation and trust male facial width and trustworthiness. *Psychological science*, 21(3):349–354, 2010.

[16] M. van 't Wout and A. G. Sanfey. Friend or foe: The effect of implicit trustworthiness judgments in social decision-making. *Cognition*, 108(3):796–803, 2008.

[17] R. Wang, F. Quek, D. Tatar, K. S. Teh, and A. Cheok. Keep in touch: channel, expectation and experience. In *Proceedings of the SIGCHI Conference on Human Factors in Computing Systems*, pages 139–148. ACM, 2012.

[18] F. N. Willis Jr and H. K. Hamm. The use of interpersonal touch in securing compliance. *Journal of Nonverbal Behavior*, 5(1):49–55, 1980.

[19] J. Zheng, E. Veinott, N. Bos, J. S. Olson, and G. M. Olson. Trust without touch: jumpstarting long-distance trust with initial social activities. In *CHI '02: Proceedings of the SIGCHI Conference on Human Factors in Computing Systems*. ACM, 2002.

Speech and Gesture Emphasis Effects For Robotic and Human Communicators - a Direct Comparison

Paul Bremner
Bristol Robotics Laboratory
University of The West of England
Bristol, BS16 1QY, UK.
paul.bremner@brl.ac.uk

Ute Leonards
School of Experimental Psychology
University of Bristol
Bristol,BS8 1TU, UK.
ute.leonards@bristol.ac.uk

ABSTRACT

Emphasis, by means of either pitch accents or beat gestures (rhythmic co-verbal gestures with no semantic meaning), has been shown to serve two main purposes in human communication: syntactic disambiguation and salience. To use beat gestures in this role, interlocutors must be able to integrate them with the speech they accompany. Whether such integration is possible when the multi-modal communication information is produced by a humanoid robot, and whether it is as efficient as for human communicators, are questions that need to be answered to further understanding of the efficacy of humanoid robots for naturalistic human-like communication.

Here, we present an experiment which, using a fully within subjects design, shows that there is a marked difference in speech and gesture integration between human and robot communicators, being significantly less effective for the robot. In contrast to beat gestures, the effects of speech emphasis are the same whether that speech is played through a robot or as part of a video of a human. Thus, while integration of speech emphasis and verbal information do occur for robot communicators, integration of non-informative beat gestures and verbal information does not, despite comparable timing and motion profiles to human gestures.

Categories and Subject Descriptors

H.1.2 [**Models and Principles**]: User/Machine Systems—*human factors, software psychology*; H.5.2 [**Information Interfaces and Presentation**]: User Interfaces—*evaluation/methodology, user-centered design*

General Terms

Experimentation, Human Factors

Keywords

Human-robot interaction; Gestures; Humanoid Robots

HRI'15, March 2–5, 2015, Portland, Oregon, USA.
ACM 978-1-4503-2883-8/15/03.
http://dx.doi.org/10.1145/2696454.2696496.

1. INTRODUCTION

Humanoid robots are thought to have a number of advantages over non-humanoid robots, one of which is the possibility of communicating with a person in a naturalistic manner, i.e., in a way that is intuitively understood by humans without learning processes. Naturalistic communication is thought to be achievable by mimicking the way people communicate with one another. Humanoid robots have this potential advantage as the human-like form enables them to produce hand/arm-gestures to accompany speech (co-verbal gestures), a key feature of human communication [22]. Further, a number of studies revealed that hand gestures improve user perceptions of robots on scales such as likability, and competence (e.g. [26][1]).

In human-human communication studies, emphasis, by means of either pitch accents or beat gestures (rhythmic coverbal gestures with no semantic meaning), has been shown to serve two main purposes: to provide information as to the intended meaning and syntactic structure in otherwise ambiguous sentences [20], and to indicate which elements of the speech are salient to the speaker [8]. Conveyance of such paralinguistic information makes communications more efficient and effective [22]. However, in order for beat gestures to result in the perception of emphasis in the speech they accompany, perception of speech and gesture must be integrated by the listener [13][34].

Our knowledge about whether perceived action and perceived language can be integrated when the information comes from a non-human agent such as a robot, is, as yet, very limited. First studies investigating the communicative value of beat gestures have found limited effects on recall of items accompanied by beat gestures (a possible proxy for the perceived salience of those items) [14][4]. However, more direct measures of the integration of beat gesture have yet to be examined, in particular when the timing is well controlled for. Previous work on gesture synthesis in robots [27][3] and in animated agents [21][6] has shown the importance of correct temporal alignment of gestures and speech. This tight synchronisation in multi-modal communication is based on work in human communication studies [22][17] as well as empirical observations of human communication by the authors of the aforementioned synthesis work.

More importantly, even for those studies in which information integration had been shown for non-human communicators, it remains unclear whether this integration process is as efficient as when derived from a human communicator. Further, whether the effect of speech emphasis is independent of the speaker also remains unclear.

In an attempt to answer all these questions, we here investigate the integration process of speech and beat gestures when produced by a NAO robot (Aldebaran Robotics, [12]), and compare it directly to that derived from a human communicator. In particular, we use a tele-operation system to produce speech and gesture stimuli for the robot, produced by the same actor used for human stimuli recorded on video, to match conditions as closely as possible. Given the previous findings of high integration rates [13] and salience identification [21][19] from beat gesture using video stimulus, we reasoned videos of human gestures would be comparable in efficacy to live performance, but would convey advantages such as exact stimulus reproducibility across participants.

The tele-operated approach has a number of advantages over either hand-scripted or autonomously produced speech and gestures in robots, as the robot's gestures can be closely matched in both form and timing to the original human gestures. Further, this approach allows us to keep the speech identical for human and robot communicators.

While the outcomes of the study are interesting in their own right, they are also an important step in the development of embodied methods of telecommunication. Whether a tele-presence system in which a NAO robot is used as an avatar for communication by a remote user will improve communication over more conventional screen-based approaches such as video conferencing, will depend strongly on interlocutors' ability to integrate robotic gestures with the human voice of their remote partner. Hence, we are motivated to compare human video communication with a real robot for thir merits as a telecommunication medium.

The main contributions of the work presented here are to investigate whether: i) speech and gesture integration occurs for co-verbal beat gestures performed using the tele-operated NAO robot, in the same way that they are for a video of a human communicator; and ii) the effects of speech emphasis are independent of speaker.

2. BACKGROUND AND RELATED WORK

2.1 Emphasis Effects in Human Communication

In studies of human-human communication the communicative value of speech emphasis has been investigated by examining its effects on speech comprehension [29][20][30]. In particular the grammatical functions of pitch accents (changes in verbal pitch used to provide emphasis) were examined, i.e., their effect on the interpretation of ambiguous sentences. A typical example taken from Schafer et al. [29] and later used by Lee and Watson [20] is the sentence:

'The sun sparkled on the *propeller* of the *plane* that the mechanic was so carefully examining.'

Both propeller and plane are possible responses to the question 'What is the mechanic so carefully examining?', and which is chosen is dependent on which noun is interpreted to be attached to the final relative clause. In other words, there is high attachment if the first noun is selected and low attachment for the second. It was found that the probability of selecting either one was increased by a pitch accent on it [29][20]. A similar result has also been found for other types of sentences [30][7].

However, Lee and Watson reason that the apparent change in meaning might be due to the increased perception of salience of the emphasised word, rather than syntactic res-

olution; i.e, participants are more likely to give the salient word in response to a post-stimulus question [20]. Indeed, it has been shown that pitch accents often accompany new information in a sentence and this is viewed as more salient by listeners [8][18]. Whatever the cause of the observed effect, the method of examining participants sentence interpretation has been validated as an approach for assessing perception and processing of emphasis, and is adapted for use in the study presented here.

Another means by which people add emphasis to their speech is gestures [22][17]. Within the commonly applied classification scheme proposed by Kendon [17], beat gestures are rhythmic hand motions with no semantic meaning that match the prosody of speech they accompany; their primary functions is to mark salient elements of discourse [17].

Krahmer and Sverts observed that unaccented words accompanied by beat gestures were reported as being more prominent than those without gestural accompaniment [19]. Further, a recent study by Holle et al. showed that salient elements of discourse are distinguished more easily when accompanied by beat gestures, but not animated dots that moved with the same timing as the beat gesture [13]. This indicates that beat gestures were cognitively integrated, but dots were not. This motivates us to investigate whether robot-performed beat gestures are integrated with speech in the same way human-performed beat gestures are, or whether they are treated like the moving dots and thus perceived separately.

2.2 Gestures in Human-Robot Interaction

Previous work in human robot-interaction on how co-verbal gestures affect comprehension has largely focused on pointing (deictic) gestures [5][23][28], revealing that better understanding of relative locations of referents was achieved by supplementing speech information with deictic gestures. This provides some first evidence for speech and gesture integration. Here we examine speech and gesture integration for beat gestures instead. Note however, pointing gestures do carry information in their own rights in contrast to beat gestures that simply emphasise verbal information. Whether robot-produced beat gestures can be integrated with verbal information to disambiguate the latter is as yet unknown, and thus subject of the current study.

Robot performed gestures have been observed to have effects beyond information comprehension. For example, Huang and Mutlu found that participants' recall of items in a factual talk presented by a robot was reliably improved if the robot used deictic gestures, while other types of gesture had little impact [14]. Similarly, Bremner et al. found that parts of a monologue accompanied by (metaphoric and beat) gestures were not recalled any better than those without, though they reported higher certainty in the information recalled by the gestures [4]. By contrast, van Dijk et al. found that recall was improved for actions accompanied by redundant iconic gestures [9]. It can be considered that recall of conveyed information is an indicator for salience perception, as salient information is more likely to be remembered [10]. However, there are a number of factors that affect memory formation, so thus far there is little direct evidence for integration of speech and robot performed beat gesture; and hence its effect on emphasis perception.

To the best of our knowledge, we are the first to provide direct evidence for speech and beat gesture integration for robot communicators through a direct comparison between human and robot communicators in a single experiment.

3. EXPERIMENTAL METHODS

To investigate the aforementioned issues of emphasis perception, speech and beat gesture integration, and whether a robot communicator is as effective as a human communicator, we designed a within-participants study. Participants observed a series of pre-recorded communications which had emphasis placed in one of two locations either with a pitch accent or with a beat gesture, performed by either a person (on video) or the tele-operated NAO robot; additionally a "no emphasis" baseline condition was used for comparison for each communicator. Human videos were used as stimuli instead of human live actors to enable exact replication of conditions between participants, to validate the experimental procedure, and allow comparative analysis between video of a person and a tele-operated robot. Hence, the experiment was a 2 (emphasis location) x 2 (emphasis mode) x 2 (communicator) within subjects design.

3.1 Tele-operation System

We have designed a tele-operation system to reproduce gestures from a tele-operator, on the NAO humanoid robot platform from Aldebaran Robotics (see Figure 1, for specifications see [12]). The system is built using the ROS framework [25], with nodes to gather kinematic information of the human tele-operator. The gathered information is then published as ROS messages that are processed by a NAO control node that calculates the required commands and sends them to the robot.

To ensure that, during gestures, joint coordination and link orientations are correctly maintained, arm link end points were tracked on the tele-operator. For this purpose a Microsoft Kinect sensor was used to track the arm link end points to calculate unit vectors for the arm links relative to the torso coordinate frame of the operator[1], which were then sent as ROS messages. Sensor update rate was 30Hz.

The NAO control node used the arm unit vectors to calculate the required angles for the robot's arm joints so as to align the robot arm links with equivalent unit vectors in the robots own torso coordinate frame[2]. Figure 1 gives an example mapping between the human and robot positions. The resulting joint angles were smoothed using a moving average filter with a ten frame window, as the data from the Kinect was subject to high levels of noise.

One limitation of the skeleton tracking data (due to limitations of the resolution of the Kinect when viewing the full body) is that it is unable to provide tracking information for rotation of the hand relative to the forearm (radial rotation), or finger tracking. To allow tracking of these additional degrees of freedom, a Polhemus Patriot (for radial rotation) and 5DT data gloves (for finger tracking) were used. ROS nodes that package these sensor data did so with an update rate of 30Hz. The NAO node calculated the needed joint angles for these additional DoF and coordinated them with the other calculated joint angles to send a single command for all degrees of freedom each command cycle.

Figure 1: A matched pose between the tele-operator and the NAO robot. The directions of the arm unit vectors are indicated with black arrows, torso coordinate frames in RGB (XYZ).

In order to stream audio to the robot a NAO module based on the Gstreamer media framework was created, with a corresponding program on the controlling PC.

3.2 Materials and Procedure

3.2.1 Stimulus Material

Stimuli for the experiment consisted of a set of 10 globally ambiguous sentences (see appendix A for the list of sentences), chosen from among those used in Lee and Watson [20]. The sentences chosen were those described as leading to the strongest emphasis effect [20]. The sentences all included relative clauses (RC) preceded by the complex noun phrase consisting of two nouns, both of which could be potentially modified by the relative clauses (see 2.1 for an example, for full list of sentences see appendixA).

The beat gesture used for emphasis in this study was of a similar form to that used by Holle et al. [13] (exaggerated compared to normal conversational gesture): a downward vertical movement of the hand timed to coincide with the word to be emphasised (see Figure 2). This downward movement (the stroke phase of the gesture) is preceded by moving into position prior to the start of the emphasised word (preparation phase), and followed by a return to a rest position (retraction phase).

Two sets of stimuli were recorded, one for the human communicator using a digital video camera, and one for the robot using the tele-operation system. Both sets of stimuli were performed by the same human actor to avoid inter-individual variability in action performance. However, the hand and wrist sensors necessary for tele-operation were seen as likely to distort participant perceptions if videos of tele-operation were used as stimuli; hence, the two sets were recorded separately. To control for any biases produced by this procedure, video of each tele-operation performance was reviewed by the actor prior to the recording of each video stimulus, and compared during recording to ensure performance was as similar as possible.

To create the robot communication stimuli, the messages from the sensor nodes were recorded to a file using the built-in recording capabilities of ROS, as well as being directly streamed to the robot to allow verification during recording; similarly, the audio (captured using a lapel microphone) was recorded and streamed simultaneously.

---

[1]calculations omitted here for brevity as they are relatively trivial

[2]see footnote 1

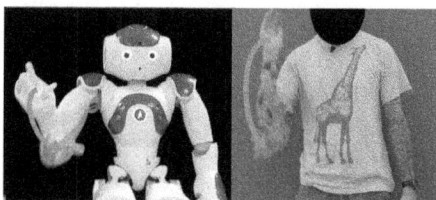

Figure 2: The beat gesture used, performed by NAO and the human actor.

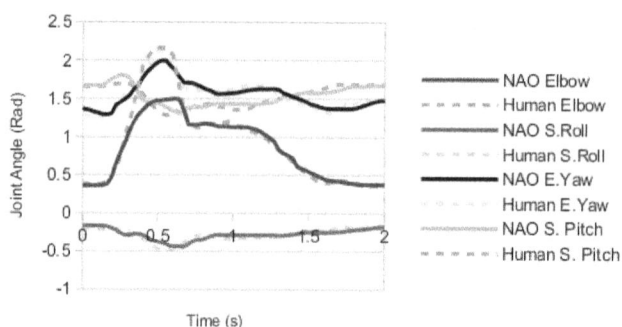

Figure 3: Joint profiles during a beat gesture. NAO joints recorded on the joint sensors, human joints recorded by the Kinect

Each sentence in both sets of stimuli was recorded in 3 versions: one each for verbal and beat gesture emphasis on each of the nouns that could be attached to the RC, and one with no emphasis. The stimuli were then edited to produce a set of presentations lasting approximately three seconds each, in five conditions: speech emphasis on noun 1 (S1G0), speech emphasis on noun 2 (S2G0), gesture emphasis on noun 1 (S0G1), gesture emphasis on noun 2 (S0G2), baseline with no emphasis (S0G0). Krahmer and Sverts reported that speakers naturally tend to produce verbal emphasis when producing beat gestures, even when instructed not to do so [19]. To avoid this possibility, the audio from the S0G0 condition was used in the gesture emphasis conditions to ensure that no speech emphasis was present.

Note that for each phrase, the same audio was used for both human and robot communicators in all conditions including a verbal component. The human stimuli were created by adding the audio recorded during the robot performances to the videos of the human performance, editing out the original audio on the videos. The original audio on the videos was used only to synchronise audio and video correctly. Further, to prevent unwanted effects of facial gestures and lip-synching issues, the human communicator's face was occluded in the videos. The speech and gesture timing for the robot conditions was matched as closely as possible to that observed in the human videos. Note that we used this editing procedure as, while we have developed modifications to the filter to reduce delays, performance is not identical to the original timing, which may confound direct comparisons between the two communicators.

To verify that the gestural stimuli were correctly edited, two judges external to the experimental team each viewed the gesture emphasis stimuli from each presenter and were asked to judge which word the gesture accompanied. Previous work has shown people are adept at making such judgements [21]. A similar process was followed for the speech emphasis conditions with the judges being asked to assess the most prominent word in the sentence. In all cases the intended word was identified correctly by both judges.

3.2.2 Beat Gesture Comparison

To verify the performance of the tele-operation system in producing robot beat gestures that are sufficiently similar to those performed by the human actor, we analysed the joint motion profiles recorded by the kinect and those on the NAO joint sensors. Figure 3 shows the change in angle for the major joints for the performers over the duration of a beat gesture: both joint motion and relative timing are similar for the two performers. There is, however, one minor difference as NAO is not able to bend its elbow as much as the actor. However, correct motion of the other joints resulted in a

vertical stroke distance of 71.5mm, approximately 68% of the length of the upper arm of the robot, a gesture large enough to convey the desired emphasis. Further, the velocity and acceleration of the hand during the stroke is similar, key features of how emphatic a beat gesture is [17].

To evaluate if the gestures are percieved similarly between the two actors we had three judges external to the experimental team evaluate the human and robot gestures. They were asked to rate the gestures (presented in a random order) on a 7 point Likert scales (i.e., ratings 0-6) for both suitability for use as a gesture to convey emphasis (human M=5.1 SD=0.71, NAO M=4.8 SD=0.92), and for how emphatic the gestures were (human M=4.5 SD=0.90, NAO M=4.4 SD=0.84). Results were compared using 3 x 2 (judge x performer) mixed ANOVAs [3], no main effect was found for judge or performer for either measurement scale. Combined with a low variance in each set of results (all $\sigma < 1$), gives us confidence the gestures are perceived similarly.

3.2.3 Participants

There were 22 participants (10 male, 12 female), aged 18-55 ($M = 31.8 \pm 9.04SD$), all Native English speakers. Participants gave written informed consent to participate in the study which was in line with the revised Declarations of Helsinki (2013), and approved by the Ethics Committee of the Faculty of Science, University of Bristol.

3.2.4 Setup and Procedure

There were ten experimental conditions: five emphasis conditions (S0G0, S1G0, S2G0, S0G1, S0G2) for each of the two communicator conditions, and ten complex sentences which were used in each experimental condition; hence, each participant responded to 100 different trials. The trials were split into ten blocks, each containing all ten sentences and all ten experimental conditions. To prevent ordering effects, trial presentation order was counterbalanced across participants by means of pseudo-randomisation, using partial Latin squares; sentence order and condition order within each block were both randomised.

As soon as the stimulus had finished, an audio-filed question was played that participants had to answer. The question probed which noun in the stimulus sentence was at-

---

[3] low variance in the results means standard measures of inter-rater reliability, such as ICC, cannot be meaningfully interpreted

258

Figure 4: Experimental Setup

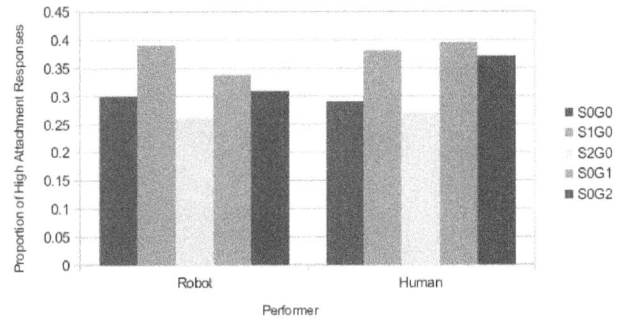

Figure 5: Proportion of high attachment responses for each communicator in the different conditions.

tached to the relative clause. The two possible options participants could choose from to answer were presented on the 12.1 inch screen of a response laptop in 5cm high white letters on a grey background, one at the top of the screen, and one at the bottom. The noun location was randomised and counterbalanced between all trials, so the first noun appeared similarly often at the top and the bottom of the screen. Participants were requested to answer as quickly as possible by pressing one of two response keys on the laptop to ensure intuitive rather than considered responses.

The experimental set-up is shown in Figure 4. The NAO and the video playback screen were both 57cm from the participant, a 32 inch monitor was used for playback of the video stimuli, in order to make the human communicator a similar size to the robot. Before each trial which presenter was next was displayed on the response laptop for 1s, and a tone sounded to indicate trial commencement. The clip was played, after which the response question followed automatically[4]. Playback of each clip was started by the experimenter from a laptop situated behind the screen so they were hidden from the participant during the trials (to prevent observation effects), but could initiate playback, and allow any breaks requested. Before the experimental trials began participants undertook two practice trials to familiarise themselves with the experimental procedure.

3.3 Results and Data Analysis

Evaluation of participant responses is measured by means of proportion of high attachment responses, i.e., proportion of responses in each condition where the first noun was selected as the subject of the relative clause. Before data were entered into statistical analysis, Grubbs' test was applied to detect outliers on numbers of high attachment responses; hence, the results of one participant had to be removed.

Figure 5 shows the results in terms of the proportion of high attachment responses in the different conditions. Following the analysis methods employed by Lee and Watson [20] the data was analysed using mixed logit models, which is an extension of logistic regression, that includes simultaneous modelling of participants and items as random effects, and condition and communicator as fixed effects [15]. The random effects structure was justified by means of likelihood ratio tests [2]. Random effects parameters that significantly improved the model's goodness of fit were included in the model (all p<0.05).

---

[4]Presentation of the response question and answers, and recording of responses was done using the PsychoPy software [24]

Mixed logit modelling allows us to estimate the change in probability of choosing a high attachment response between levels in the fixed effect conditions, i.e., between communicators, and between emphasis conditions. Hence, we can evaluate not only whether there is a significant change in probability of choosing a high attachment in one condition level compared to another, but also the magnitude of the probability change. In setting up the modelling process a reference condition is chosen for each of the fixed effects, and model parameters (β values) are estimated for each of the other levels of the fixed effects which indicate the change in probability of making a high attachment response between each level (condition) of the fixed effects and the reference. The model parameters are estimated in log-odds space, so we took their exponent to get the odds ratio, which informs us about how many times more likely high attachments are in a given condition compared to a reference condition; e.g., an odds ratio of 2 for a particular condition indicates high attachments are twice as likely in that condition than the reference. Figure 6 shows the estimated odds-ratios for the full model.

There was no significant effect for communicator using human as the reference condition ($\beta = -0.112, SE = 0.099, z = -1.139, p = 0.255$), but a clear effect for S0G1 ($\beta = 0.364, SE = 0.156, z = 2.335, p = 0.019$), and S1G0 ($\beta = 0.455, SE = 0.155, z = 2.935, p = 0.003$) when compared to the baseline no emphasis condition as reference. No other comparisons were significant.

Before concluding that there was indeed no difference in performance for human and robot communicators, we examined differences in efficacy of the two communicators more closely, by evaluating mixed logit models for each communicator type individually. We reasoned that difference in only one condition might be masked by similarity in the others in the full model; Figure 5 indicates such differences.

For human communicators significant differences were observed for S1G0 ($\beta = 0.456, SE = 0.220, z = 2.081, p < 0.05$) and for S0G1 ($\beta = 0.524, SE = 0.219, z = 2.392, p < 0.05$) compared to S0G0 as reference. No other comparisons were significant. However, for the robot communicator significant results were only observed for S1G0 ($\beta = 0.457, SE = 0.226, z = 2.027, p < 0.05$) compared to S0G0 as reference, but not for S0G1 ($\beta = 0.199, SE = 0.222, z = 0.895, p = 0.371$). No other comparisons were significant. Note though, that there is a small increase in odds for S0G1 in the robot condition. Estimating a new model using S0G1

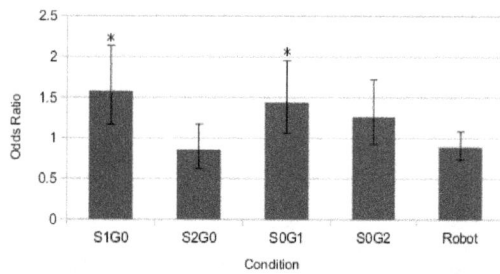

Figure 6: Odds ratios of high attachment responses, as estimated by mixed logit modelling, for each emphasis condition with S0G0 as reference, and for the robot condition with the human condition as reference. Calculated as exponential of the β values. Error bars indicate 95% confidence interval. * p<0.05

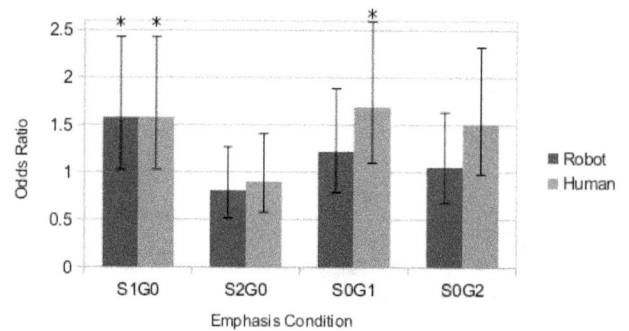

Figure 7: Odds ratios of high attachment responses, as estimated by mixed logit modelling, for each emphasis condition with S0G0 as reference. Calculated as exponential of the β values. Error bars indicate 95% confidence interval. * p<0.05

as the reference condition, there was no significant effect for S1G0 ($\beta = 0.258, SE = 0.216, z = 1.194, p = 0.232$); thus S1G0 and S0G1 are not really different. This indicates that gesture emphasis evokes a similar effect as speech emphasis on the first noun, but far weaker. Odds-ratios calculated for the two separate models are shown in Figure 7.

4. DISCUSSION

To evaluate the relative efficacy of emphasis perception, and speech and beat gesture integration for human and robot communicators, we constructed a number of mixed logit models from our data. Firstly, we constructed a full model that included the results from both communicators, modelling communicators as well as emphasis conditions as fixed effects. No difference between communicators was found. Speech emphasis on the first noun in the stimulus sentences increased the probability of making a high attachment response relative to the no emphasis condition. A similar, but weaker, effect was found for beat gesture emphasis on the first noun, indicating that integration of speech and gesture does occur. Our results for the first noun emphasis condition were similar to those reported by Lee and Watson [20], but our remaining results differ from theirs as we did not observe the significant decrease in probability for high attachments between the emphasis on the second noun (irrespective of emphasis mode) and the baseline.

To better examine the similarities and differences between the results from the two different communicators, models were created for each one separately. Verbal emphasis has the same effect whether played from the video showing a human communicator or through the robot; not a surprising result as both communicators used the same audio, but it nevertheless underlines the value of prosody in robot communication. However, the impact of beat gestures on the first noun (S0G1) differed for the two communicators, revealing an increase in high attachment probability for the human performance but not for the robot. Estimating a new model for the robot using S0G1 as the reference condition we showed that there is no difference in performance for the S0G1 (beat gesture emphasis on noun 1) and S1G0 (pitch emphasis on noun 1); hence, it seems reasonable to conclude that beat gesture emphasis is weakened for robot communicators as compared to human communicators. This was contrary to our expectation that speech and gesture in-

tegration would be as effective for the robot communicator as for the human.

At the current stage, one can only speculate why this might be the case. Similarities between our study and a neuroscientific study by Kelly et al, [16] provide a first explanation. Kelly et al. found that a gender mismatch between speech and gesture performers led to reduced speech and gesture integration as compared to a gender match, though brain activity involved in the task was similarly high for matched and unmatched situations. They suggest that while this process is partially automatic (hallmarked as a fast, low-level, obligatory process), it is modulated by some control, and this is triggered by the mismatch. As we used human speech for our robot, this might have caused a similar mismatch as in Kelly et al.'s study. Previous work has shown that mirror neurons fire when observing robot actions [11], so it seems reasonable to suggest that the beat gesture in the robot led to a similar, though reduced, brain activity pattern as the beat gesture of a human. Further work utilising fMRI or EEG measurements of participants observing robot co-speech gesture is needed to investigate these ideas.

An alternative explanation, based on the work by Holle et al. [13], is that robot gestures might not be processed as having communicative intent, a requirement Holle et al. suggest as necessary to improve ease of emphasis perception; as measured using event related potentials (ERPs): comparing the effects of beat gestures and animated dots (with similar timing and movement profiles), Holle et al. found that dots did not aid perception in the way that beat gestures did. It is thus tempting to speculate that robot gestures are processed more like the animated dots than like human gestures, and are therefore not properly integrated with speech. This could be due to inherent differences between human and robot performed gesture, such as differences in ranges of motion, and noise from the robot motors, factors that need to be investigated in detail in future studies.

The reduced impact of speech and gesture integration for robot performed beat gestures has important implications for future work on multi-modal human-robot interaction. The main implication is that an attempt to use beat gestures in robots to improve human-robot communication seems not worthwhile from a salience conveyance perspective if used without speech emphasis. However, it might still be important from a more naturalistic communication point of view, as gestures in general are thought to improve subjective (likability) ratings of communicating robots [26][1], engagement into the conversation [4] and personal rapport [32]. At first glance, our results seem to suggest that beat gestures could be added to robot communicators without concern of their exact timing relative to salient elements of the speech; we believe, however, that such a conclusion is premature and that the effects of relative timing of gesture and speech prosody should be investigated explicitly.

Further, our results help to explain previous findings that in robots beat gestures have little or no impact on memory of speech that they accompany [14][4], whereas they have been found to do so in humans [31].

4.1 Limitations and Future Work

While the work presented here provides initial insight into speech and beat gesture integration for robot communicators, it has a number of limitations which we hope to address in future work. In order to separate the effects of speech and beat gestures, we have tested them independently of each other in the same participants. In future work we aim to investigate the combined effects of prosody and beat gestures, and how relative timing affects information processing, engagement, rapport and subjective ratings such as likability and competence. Further, the temporal dynamics such as delays that may be introduced by the tele-operation system need further investigation.

Another limitation in our study is the use of an unaltered human voice for the verbal component of the communications. While this aided direct comparison between performers, and was important for our aims, it does limit the generalisability of the results. In future work, we aim to investigate if there is any effect on integration of a synthetic voice that is more closely matched to the robot's form.

Finally, as changes in attachment selection only provide an indirect measure of integration, we will use event-related brain potentials as in Holle et al. [13] to provide a more direct physiological measure of the similarities and differences between processing of human and robot co-verbal gestures.

5. CONCLUSION

Using a within-subject design, we show in this paper that speech emphasis has a similar impact on speech understanding from a human or robot performer; emphasising the value of prosody for robot communication. More importantly however, we showed that beat gesture emphasis has significantly less effect when performed by a robot than when performed by a human, indicating integration of speech and beat gestures is less effective for a humanoid robot.

In light of these findings, we suggest that salience information in robot communication should not only be conveyed by beat gestures, but needs to be included in the speech pattern through pitch emphasis. Further, future studies involving robot co-verbal gesture should be mindful of the difference in cognitive workload between human and robot multi-modal communications. While humanoid robots such as the NAO are modelled to mimic human communication strategies, how the communication output are processed by the receiving human appears to be different. Further, these findings may provide some explanation as to the differences in the literature in effects of beat gestures on information recall between human [31] and robot [14][4] studies.

Such differences in multi-modal communication are not only interesting for our future work on humanoid robot avatars, but also for the design of communication behaviours in autonomous robots. Previous studies have found that participants treat avatars similarly to biological autonomous systems [33], making us confident that our results should be generalisable to other robot platforms and situations.

6. ACKNOWLEDGEMENTS

This research is funded by the EPSRC under its IDEAS Factory Sandpits call on Digital Personhood, grant ref: EP/L00416X/1.

7. REFERENCES

[1] A. Aly and A. Tapus. A model for synthesizing a combined verbal and nonverbal behavior based on personality traits in human-robot interaction. In *HRI '13 Proceedings of the 8th ACM/IEEE international conference on Human-robot interaction*, pages 325–332. IEEE Press, Mar. 2013.

[2] R. H. Baayen. *Analyzing Linguistic Data A Practical Introduction to Statistics using R.* Cambridge University Press, 2008.

[3] P. Bremner, A. G. Pipe, M. Fraser, S. Subramanian, and C. Melhuish. Beat gesture generation rules for human-robot interaction. In *RO-MAN 2009 - The 18th IEEE International Symposium on Robot and Human Interactive Communication*, pages 1029–1034. IEEE, Sept. 2009.

[4] P. Bremner, A. G. Pipe, C. Melhuish, M. Fraser, and S. Subramanian. The effects of robot-performed co-verbal gesture on listener behaviour. In *11th IEEE-RAS International Conference on Humanoid Robots*, pages 458–465. IEEE, Oct. 2011.

[5] J.-J. Cabibihan, W.-C. So, S. Saj, and Z. Zhang. Telerobotic Pointing Gestures Shape Human Spatial Cognition. *International Journal of Social Robotics*, 4(3):263–272, Apr. 2012.

[6] J. Cassell, H. H. Vilhjálmsson, and T. Bickmore. BEAT: the Behavior Expression Animation Toolkit. In *Proceedings of the 28th annual conference on Computer graphics and interactive techniques - SIGGRAPH '01*, pages 477–486. ACM Press, Aug. 2001.

[7] L. F. C. Clifton. Comprehension of Sluiced Sentences. *Language and Cognitive Processes*, 13(4):499–520, Aug. 1998.

[8] D. Dahan, M. K. Tanenhaus, and C. G. Chambers. Accent and reference resolution in spoken-language comprehension. *Journal of Memory and Language*, 47(2):292–314, Aug. 2002.

[9] E. T. Dijk, E. Torta, and R. H. Cuijpers. Effects of Eye Contact and Iconic Gestures on Message Retention in Human-Robot Interaction. *International Journal of Social Robotics*, 5(4):491–501, Sept. 2013.

[10] S. H. Fraundorf, D. G. Watson, and A. S. Benjamin. Recognition memory reveals just how CONTRASTIVE contrastive accenting really is. *Journal of memory and language*, 63(3):367–386, Oct. 2010.

[11] V. Gazzola, G. Rizzolatti, B. Wicker, and C. Keysers. The anthropomorphic brain: the mirror neuron

system responds to human and robotic actions. *NeuroImage*, 35(4):1674–84, May 2007.

[12] D. Gouaillier, V. Hugel, P. Blazevic, C. Kilner, J. Monceaux, P. Lafourcade, B. Marnier, J. Serre, and B. Maisonnier. Mechatronic design of NAO humanoid. In *2009 IEEE International Conference on Robotics and Automation*, pages 769–774. IEEE, May 2009.

[13] H. Holle, C. Obermeier, M. Schmidt-Kassow, A. D. Friederici, J. Ward, and T. C. Gunter. Gesture facilitates the syntactic analysis of speech. *Frontiers in psychology*, 3:74, Jan. 2012.

[14] C.-M. Huang and B. Mutlu. Learning-based modeling of multimodal behaviors for humanlike robots. In *Proceedings of the 2014 ACM/IEEE international conference on Human-robot interaction - HRI '14*, pages 57–64. ACM Press, Mar. 2014.

[15] T. F. Jaeger. Categorical Data Analysis: Away from ANOVAs (transformation or not) and towards Logit Mixed Models. *Journal of memory and language*, 59(4):434–446, Nov. 2008.

[16] S. D. Kelly, P. Creigh, and J. Bartolotti. Integrating speech and iconic gestures in a Stroop-like task: evidence for automatic processing. *Journal of cognitive neuroscience*, 22(4):683–94, Apr. 2010.

[17] A. Kendon. *Gesture: Visible Action as Utterance*. Cambridge University Press, 2004.

[18] E. Krahmer and M. Swerts. Testing the effect of audiovisual cues to prominence via a reaction-time experiment. *Proceedings of the International Conference on Spoken Language Processing (Interspeech 2006)*, 2006.

[19] E. Krahmer and M. Swerts. The effects of visual beats on prosodic prominence: Acoustic analyses, auditory perception and visual perception. *Journal of Memory and Language*, 57(3):396–414, Oct. 2007.

[20] E.-K. Lee and D. G. Watson. Effects of pitch accents in attachment ambiguity resolution. *Language and cognitive processes*, 26(2):262–297, Jan. 2011.

[21] T. Leonard and F. Cummins. The temporal relation between beat gestures and speech. *Language and Cognitive Processes*, 26(10):1457–1471, Dec. 2011.

[22] D. McNeill. *Hand and Mind: What Gestures Reveal about Thought*. University of Chicago Press, 1992.

[23] T. Ono, T. Kanda, M. Imai, and H. Ishiguro. Embodied communications between humans and robots emerging from entrained gestures. In *Proceedings 2003 IEEE International Symposium on Computational Intelligence in Robotics and Automation.*, volume 2, pages 558–563. IEEE, 2003.

[24] J. W. Peirce. PsychoPy–Psychophysics software in Python. *Journal of neuroscience methods*, 162(1-2):8–13, May 2007.

[25] M. Quigley, K. Conley, B. Gerkey, J. Faust, T. Foote, J. Leibs, R. Wheeler, and A. Ng. {ROS}: an open-source Robot Operating System. In *Open-Source Software workshop of the International Conference on Robotics and Automation (ICRA)*, 2009.

[26] M. Salem, F. Eyssel, K. Rohlfing, S. Kopp, and F. Joublin. To Err is Human(-like): Effects of Robot Gesture on Perceived Anthropomorphism and Likability. *International Journal of Social Robotics*, 5(3):313–323, May 2013.

[27] M. Salem, S. Kopp, I. Wachsmuth, K. Rohlfing, and F. Joublin. Generation and Evaluation of Communicative Robot Gesture. *International Journal of Social Robotics*, 4(2):201–217, Feb. 2012.

[28] A. Sauppé and B. Mutlu. Robot deictics. In *Proceedings of the 2014 ACM/IEEE international conference on Human-robot interaction - HRI '14*, pages 342–349. ACM Press, Mar. 2014.

[29] A. Schafer. Focus in Relative Clause Construal. *Language and Cognitive Processes*, 11(1-2):135–164, Apr. 1996.

[30] A. Schafer, K. Carlson, H. Clifton, and L. Frazier. Focus and the Interpretation of Pitch Accent: Disambiguating Embedded Questions. *Language and Speech*, 43(1):75–105, Mar. 2000.

[31] W. C. So, C. Sim Chen-Hui, and J. Low Wei-Shan. Mnemonic effect of iconic gesture and beat gesture in adults and children: Is meaning in gesture important for memory recall? *Language and Cognitive Processes*, 27(5):665–681, June 2012.

[32] L. Tickle-Degnen and R. Rosenthal. The Nature of Rapport and Its Nonverbal Correlates. *Psychological Inquiry*, 1(4):285–293, Oct. 1990.

[33] A. M. von der Pütten, N. C. Krämer, J. Gratch, and S.-H. Kang. "It doesn't matter what you are!" Explaining social effects of agents and avatars. *Computers in Human Behavior*, 26(6):1641–1650, Nov. 2010.

[34] L. Wang and M. Chu. The role of beat gesture and pitch accent in semantic processing: an ERP study. *Neuropsychologia*, 51(13):2847–55, Nov. 2013.

APPENDIX

A. STIMULUS SENTENCES

The complex noun phrases used in the stimulus material. Each sentence may have emphasis placed on either of the capitalised words.

- Tyler met the HUSBAND of the WOMAN who the secretary saw in the waiting room on the second floor.
- Brandon interviewed the SON of the LADY who the man worked with for five years in Germany.
- Ashley watched the BROTHER of the WOMAN who the dean interviewed in his office for almost two hours.
- Blake approached the SISTER of the MAN who the president accidentally bumped into at the station.
- Adam greeted the WIFE of the MAN who the landlord complained to about the other tenants
- The sun sparkled on the PROPELLER of the PLANE that the mechanic was so carefully examining.
- The squirrels raced through the LEAVES of the TREE that had recently fallen down in the forest.
- The magazine article failed to mention the LIBRARY of the SCHOOL that had just been built by the contractors.
- The local newspaper described the CEREMONIES of the CLUB that people seemed to find so ridiculous.
- The insurance inspector photographed the COVER of the BOAT that john saw was covered with graffiti.

Haptic Human-Robot Affective Interaction in a Handshaking Social Protocol

Mehdi Ammi, Virginie Demulier,
Sylvain Caillou, Yoren Gaffary,
Yacine Tsalamlal, Jean-Claude Martin
LIMSI-CNRS
University of Paris Sud
91405 Orsay cedex, France
lastname@limsi.fr

Adriana Tapus
Robotics and Computer Vision Lab
ENSTA-ParisTech
91102, Palaiseau, France
adriana.tapus@ensta-paristech.fr

ABSTRACT

This paper deals with the haptic affective social interaction during a greeting handshaking between a human and a humanoid robot. The goal of this work is to study how the haptic interaction conveys emotions, and more precisely, how it influences the perception of the dimensions of emotions expressed through the facial expressions of the robot. Moreover, we examine the benefits of the multimodality (i.e., visuo-haptic) over the monomodality (i.e., visual-only and haptic-only). The experimental results with Meka robot show that the multimodal condition presenting high values for grasping force and joint stiffness are evaluated with higher values for the arousal and dominance dimensions than during the visual condition. Furthermore, the results corresponding to the monomodal haptic condition showed that participants discriminate well the dominance and the arousal dimensions of the haptic behaviours presenting low and high values for grasping force and joint stiffness.

Categories and Subject Descriptors

H.1.2 [**MODELS AND PRINCIPLES**]: User/Machine Systems

General Terms

Experimentation

Keywords

haptic; social robotics; handshaking; affective interaction

1. INTRODUCTION

Nonverbal expressions are often used to communicate emotions between people (including prosody, facial expressions, body movements and hand gestures). Unfortunately, research in embodied communication and human-robot interaction are not yet able to reproduce the full potential of human-human affective communication.

The use of the haptic modality in human-computer interaction opens up new prospects. Interpersonal haptic interaction gives access to various pieces of information through complementary perception mechanisms such as tactile and kinesthetic channels. Psychological studies suggest that the haptic channel plays a very important role in social interactions [15, 6]. It can communicate positive/negative emotions and enhance the meaning of other verbal and nonverbal communication. In the field of physiology of tactile receptors, recent studies highlighted specific biological systems and perception mechanisms that are dedicated to the expression and perception of emotions through these haptic channels [18].

Different researches in psychological theories of emotions suggest a strong link between emotions and the body. For example, the Component Process Model [19] considers the following components of emotions: a neurophysiological component (bodily symptoms), a motor expression component, a motivational component (action tendencies), a cognitive component (appraisal), and a subjective feeling component (emotional experience). Haptics is therefore a relevant channel to investigate embodied cognition during human-robot affective interaction since it involves a physical contact and interaction between the user's body and the robot [7].

In order to improve the emotional expressiveness of robots, we proposed in this paper to combine their facial expressions with a haptic component through a handshake. This multimodal stimulation aims at improving the perception and discrimination of emotions during social interactions. The robot used its arm to shake the human hand with several haptic parameters such as the grasping force and the stiffness of movement of the robot arm. To provide relevant and efficient haptic expressions during social human-robot interaction, this research investigated how these haptic parameters influenced the perception of emotions expressed with the facial expression of the robot. More precisely, we studied the influence of the haptic parameters on the perception of the dimensions of emotions. This study used the PAD dimensional space to assess the elicited emotions [17]. This space describes the emotions using three uncorrelated and continuous dimensions: 1) Pleasure (P): degree of well-being (also called Valence) ; 2) Arousal (A): degree of mental or physical activity ; and 3) Dominance (D): degree of control of a situation.

The rest of the paper is structured as follows: Section 2 presents a state of the art that deal with Human-Robot interaction and affective haptics. Section 3 presents our approach and the working hypotheses. Section 4 details the experimental design and the robotic platform used for this experiment. Sections 5 and 6 present and discuss the experimental results. Finally, Section 7 concludes our paper.

2. STATE OF THE ART

In the field of mediated communication and Human-Computer Interaction, several works studied the potential of the haptic channels to support affective communication [6, 8]. They investigated different stimulation strategies (pneumatic, thermal, kinesthetic, etc.) according to different interaction configurations (e.g., handshaking, smartphone, etc.). They observed that haptics might correctly convey some dimensions of emotions, such as arousal [11] and valence [22], while providing a better social presence of the remote partner or of an autonomous virtual agent.

The use of haptic channel for human-robot affective and social interaction represents a new challenge. In fact, even if researches in robotics that address facial, gestural, and postural expressions of robots are beginning to show relevant and reliable results [2, 9], the haptic human-robot interaction presents basic issues both from a psychological and technological perspective. The haptic creature, designed by Yohann and McLean [25], was one of the first projects that deal with affective haptics for social interaction with animal-like robots. The combination of different tactile stimulation techniques allows the perception of some categories of positive emotions [26]. In the context of human-robot collaboration, Groten [14] investigated how haptic feedback affects the perception of dominance. The objective of this work was to design a control strategy that allow a fast decision making for the human user during the collaborative manipulation of shared objects with a robot. The affective handshake with humanoid robots is a specific issue since it requires a direct contact with the robot during the interaction. Several researches investigate motion models that provide acceptable human-robot handshake interaction [24, 5]. Wang et al. [23] developed an advanced controller that interactively respond to the user behavior during the handshake. The controller is based on the hidden-Markov-model approach to estimate the human interaction strategy. The evaluation of the controller showed a physical behavior close to human-human handshake.

3. OBJECTIVE AND HYPOTHESIS

3.1 Objective of the study

Even if the realism of human-robot handshake has been considered in several works, its role to convey social and affective messages remains to be addressed. In fact, the handshake plays a key role in the interpersonal communication in everyday life. It can effectively support affective messages through haptic channel without requiring other feedbacks [15]. The main objective of this work is to investigate how the haptic feedback involved during the human-robot handshake can convey emotions, and more precisely, how it influences the perception of emotions expressed with facial expressions of the robot. The study focused on the influence of the haptic feedback on the perception of the dimensions of emotions in a subspace of the PAD space [17], namely: arousal and dominance. These two dimensions are generally not well supported by facial cues. The study was carried out with a humanoid robot that can express various emotions with facial expressions by controlling lips display, eye orientations, and eyelid opening. The humanoid robot is equipped with an anthropomorphic arm that can be used for a handshake with a human user. The arm can be controlled with various parameters and can provide different haptic behaviors during the human-robot physical interaction.

The work of Hertenstein and Keltner [15] highlighted eight main physical behaviors during human-human haptic interaction: hitting, grasping, trembling, shaking, swinging, lifting, stroking and pushing. For instance, subjects used the squeezing to communicate Anger and the stroking to communicate Sadness. More-

over, Hertenstein and Keltner [15] observed that the haptic intensity played an important role in the recognition of some emotions. In parallel with that work, Groten [14] showed that, during human-robot collaboration, the joints' stiffness of the robot arm influence the perception of dominance. Based on these different results and according to the haptic capacities of the robot's arm, we focused in this study on two haptic parameters of the handshake: (1) the grasping force of the robot's hand ; and (2) the stiffness of the movement of the robot's arm. For each parameter, we investigated two intensities: weak and strong. The haptic parameters were combined to provide four haptic behaviours for the robot's arm during the handshake. Based on the facial expressions of the robot and the haptic behaviours of its arm, a multimodal emotional interaction is provided to users during the handshake. The experimental study presented here proposes to investigate the influence of the haptic parameters on the perception of the arousal and the dominance dimensions of the emotions expressed with the facial expressions of the robot. In this study, we were interested in three basic emotions presenting different valence values: i) Sadness (negative valence); ii) Joy (positive valence) ; and iii) Neutral (neutral valence).

3.2 Hypothesis

The experiment tried to address tree main issues. First, we investigated if the studied facial expressions lead to a good estimation of their arousal and dominance. Second, we study how users evaluate the dimensions of the values of the two haptic parameters. We focus in this study on the haptic behaviours of the handshake that provide either high or low values for the two haptic parameters. Finally, we propose to compare the multimodal emotional interaction with the visual only (i.e., facial expression) and haptic only (i.e., handshake) interaction. The objective of this comparison is to highlight the effect of each modality on the perception of the two emotional dimensions in the multimodal configuration.

The following hypotheses were considered:

H1: The dimensions of the facial expressions are well discriminated. Investigated dimensions: valence, arousal and dominance.

H2: The dimensions of the haptic expressions are well discriminated. Investigated dimensions: valence, arousal and dominance.

H3.a: The multimodal (i.e., visuo-haptic) condition presenting high values for grasping force and stiffness of movement are evaluated with higher values for the dimensions than the visual condition. Investigated dimensions: arousal and dominance.

H3.b: The multimodal (i.e., visuo-haptic) condition presenting high values for grasping force and stiffness of movement are evaluated with higher values for the dimensions than the haptic condition. Investigated dimensions: arousal and dominance.

4. EXPERIMENTAL DESIGN

4.1 Robotic platform

The experiments presented in this work have been conducted with the Meka robot (see Figure 1). The Meka robot has been designed to work in human-centered environments. The robot features compliant force control throughout its body, a sensor head, durable and strong hands, and an omnidirectional base with Prismatic Lift. Each arm has 7 DOF Series Elastic Actuators and features high-strength force-controlled actuators, intrinsic physical compliance, and zero-backlash Harmonic Drive gearheads. The head is a 7 DOF robotic active vision head. Designed for a wide range of expressive postures, it is the ideal platform for researchers interested in human-robot interaction and social robotics. The head system features high resolution FireWire cameras in each eye, integrated DSP controllers, and zero-backlash Harmonic Drive gear-

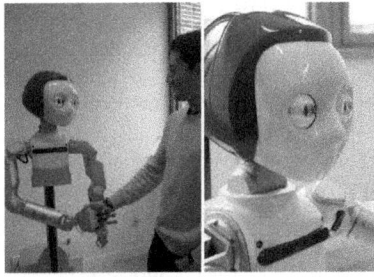

Figure 1: Meka Robot (ENSTA-ParisTech) - an expressive head, humanoid torso with 2 arms, mounted on a mobile base

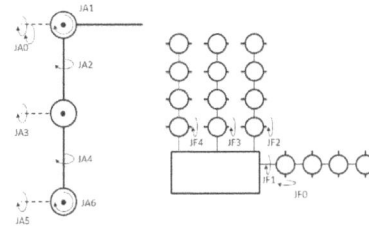

Figure 2: DOF of the robot's arm and hand

heads in the neck. Each hand is a fully-contained 5 DOF underactuated hand. It is approximately human size with intrinsic physical compliance and force feedback, making it ideal for researchers interested in dexterous manipulation within human environments. Its underactuated and compliant fingers allow it to robustly power grasp a wide range of everyday object without complex grasp planning. The robot uses the Robot Operating System (ROS), including RVIZ kinematic visualization, URDF descriptions, posture control of all joints, and common sensor interfaces. The robot has ROS features for manipulation, navigation, and human-robot interaction.

The handshake involves two main components of the robot: 1) the arm, and 2) the hand. The robot's arm is composed of seven DOF (see Figure 2): JA0 (Shoulder roll), JA1 (Shoulder pitch), JA2 (Biceps), JA3 (Elbow), JA4 (Wrist roll), JA5 (Wrist pitch), JA6 (Wrist yaw). The robot's hand is composed of three fingers and a thumb (see Figure 2). The three fingers are driven by a tendon which controls their closures. The thumb is driven by a tendon (thumb closure) and a motor (thumb orientation). Thus, five DoF are used to control the fingers and the thumb: JF0-JF1 (Thumb) to JF2-JF3 (Fingers). Encoders are used to measure the tendons positions and the motor angle.

The DOF of both the arm and hand use a joint-impedance controller [1] [10]. It control the joint position and its compliance. By tuning the stiffness parameters, it is possible to make the robot joint feeling like a hard or soft spring, while maintaining control on the desired joint position. The robot's arm and are controlled as follow:

- **Arm:** we assign for each DOF (JA0-JA6) an angle and a stiffness value in order to achieve the required arm configuration (i.e., arm outstretched, see Figure 1). In this study, the stiffness values vary (soft to hard stiffness) according to the investigated conditions while the angles are fixed.

- **Hand:** we assign for each DOF (JF0-JF4) an angle and a stiffness value in order to achieve the required hand configuration (i.e., hand grasping, see Figure 1). In this study, the stiffness values are fixed while the angles (fingers half closed and completely closed) vary according to the investigated conditions. Wide angles lead to apply a high intensity grasping force and small angles lead to apply a low intensity grasping force.

For the MEKA robot, the stiffness of joints is a value between 0 and 1 (i.e., 0 value represents highly compliant; and 1 value represents very high rigidity). The angles of the DOF are set in degrees.

4.2 Conditions

Two main independent variables were considered for this experiment. These two variables will be denoted in the text as: IV1 and IV2. First, the facial expressions of the robot (**IV1**). Three facial expressions were presented to participants, namely: sadness (denoted as '-'), neutral (denoted as '0') and joy (denoted as '+'). The emotions were expressed with the lips display (see Figure 3). The eye orientations and the eyelid opening were not involved in this study. The second variable corresponds to the haptic behavior of the robot's arm during the handshake behavior (**IV2**). It combines two haptic effects: the stiffness of the movement of the robot's arm and the grasping force of the robot's hand. For the stiffness of the movement of the robot's arm, two values of stiffness were assigned to all DOF (JA0-JA6): high (stiffness value = 1) (denoted as 'R') and low (stiffness value = 0.15) (denoted as 'r'). The angles of the seven DOF were fixed for both low and high stiffness of the movement of the robot's arm (see Figure 1). For the grasping force, two values of angles were assigned to JF0,JF2,JF3 and JF4: high intensity (denoted as 'F') and low intensity (denoted as 'f'). The opening angles of fingers are fixed as follows: wide angles [300,300,300,300], and small angles [160,165,210,240]. JF0 was fixed. The speed of the grasping hand is fixed at 80 deg/second and the stiffness of each tendon was set at 0.5 for both low and high intensity grasping force. Based on these two haptic effects, we presented two haptic behaviors, namely: soft haptic behavior (denoted as 's'), corresponding to the 'fr' configuration, and strong haptic behavior (denoted as 'S'), corresponding to the 'FR' configuration. The other coupling configurations were not investigated in this study. A summary of the different variables is given in Table 1.

The generation of the haptic expressions follows this protocol:

- step 1: The robot's arm and hand are in neutral configurations: the arm is relaxed and the hand is open.

- step 2: The robot's arm moves to achieve the handshake configuration: the arm is outstretched and the hand is open.

- step 3: When the subject grasps the robot's hand, the robot's hand closes.

- step 4: The subject handshake the robot's hand. The haptic expression is rendered during 5 seconds (see conditions above).

- step 5: After 5 seconds the robot opens its hand and the subject removes his hand.

Based on these two variables, three main conditions were investigated:

- **Visual condition (V):** Only facial expressions of the robot (IV1) are presented to the participants.

- **Haptic condition (H):** The participants shake the hand of the robot. Only the two haptic behaviors of the robot's arm are presented to participants (IV2). No facial expressions are presented.

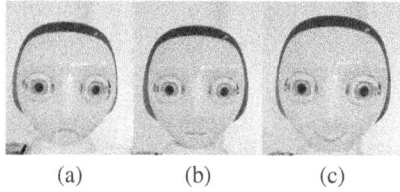

Figure 3: The three Facial Expressions of the robot: (a) sadness ('-'); (b) neutral ('0'); (c) and joy ('+'). Only the lips display was used. The eye orientations and the eyelid opening were not involved in this study.

Table 1: The summary of the two independent variables used in the experiment. IV1 - facial expressions: - (sadness), 0 (neutral), + (joy); IV2 - haptic behavior: s (soft haptic behavior), S (strong haptic behavior)

	Visual (V)	Haptic (H)
	IV1 - Facial expressions	IV2 - haptic behavior
Variables		
Values	-, 0, +	s, S

- **Visuo-Haptic condition (VH)**: The facial expressions are presented to participants (IV1) while they shake the hand of the robot (IV2). The study had a 3(IV1) x 2(IV2) design. Hence, the robot could manifest joy/sadness/neutral facial expressions and soft/strong haptic behaviors during the handshaking.

4.3 Participants

18 participants (12 males and 6 females aged between 23 and 57 years old) took part in this study. 16 participants were right-handed and 2 participants were left-handed. The participants had no known neurological or physical injury that could affect their haptic sensitivity and their physical behaviour. Participants gave informed consent prior to testing, and the experiment was approved by an institutional internal review board of the laboratory.

4.4 Procedure and Measures

Before participating in the experiment, each participant was asked to complete a questionnaire for determining personal details such as gender, age, educational background, left/right handed, and their computer game joystick playing habits. The experiment starts with a familiarization and training phase. This phase lasts between $15 - 20$ minutes as a function of the participant's reaction towards the robot. During this phase, the Meka robot is presented to the participant. The experimenter explains to the participant the handshaking task without giving details about the different visual and haptic variables. Moreover, the experimenter asks the participant to stay put in front of the robot. The robot detects the height of the participant and adjusts its height accordingly with the help of the prismatic lift. The participant is encouraged to look to the robot's head and handshake the robot's hand several times while different visual and haptic variables are played. When the participant seems comfortable enough in the presence of the robot and familiar with the handshaking task the participant is asked to perform the three conditions (i.e., Visual-only; Haptic-only; Visuo-Haptic) in a sequence as part of a predefined scenario. The participant could stop the experiment at any time. In-between conditions, the Visual-only and Haptic-only are randomized and they are played before the

Visuo-Haptic condition. Each condition has been played 2 times in a random order. Each participant has been involved in 38 interactions with the robot (visual-only, haptic-only, visuo-haptic). In the Haptic-only and Visuo-Haptic conditions, each handshake lasts for 5 seconds. In the Visual-only condition each emotion lasts 5 seconds. After each interaction the participant is asked to fill-up a PAD questionnaire so as to evaluate the perceived emotions transmitted by the robot behavior during the interaction. The participant rates the three dimensions of the PAD affective space using a 5-points bipolar Likert scale. The question asked was: "The emotion expressed by the robot seems to be". The possible answers were (on a 5-points Likert scale):

- **M1**: from "very negative" to "very positive" (valence).

- **M2**: from "not arousing" to "very arousing" (arousal).

- **M3**: from "very dominated" to "very dominant" (dominance).

5. EXPERIMENTAL RESULTS

As we think the data don't fit the assumptions of an anova, especially normality assumption (evaluation values come from Lickert scales), we carried out Kruskal-Wallis analysis to test the hypothesis and to highlight the differences between monomodal (i.e., Visual-only, Haptic-only) conditions and multimodal condition (i.e., Visuo-Haptic). When differences were highlighted, we complement the Kruskal-Wallis test by performing (follow-up) post hoc test with subsequent non-parametric multiple comparisons, based on function 'kruskalmc' of R package 'pgirmess' [13] that implements Bonferroni-corrected asymptotic normality-based multiple comparisons of all treatments pairs [20].

Hypothesis 1: Figure 4 presents, for the visual conditions ('-', '0', '+'), the evaluation of valence (**M1**), arousal (**M2**) and dominance (**M3**) respectively. The analysis reveals at least one significant difference between the visual conditions in terms of valence evaluation: $\chi^2(2, N = 108) = 86.53$, $p < 0.05$. Subsequent pairwise comparisons between groups indicated that the valence was evaluated significantly more positively with the joy facial expression than with the neutral ($difference = 36.18$) and with the sadness facial expression ($difference = 66.61$). Moreover neutral facial expression was evaluated significantly more positively than the sadness facial expression ($difference = 30.43$) (see Figure 4.a). The analysis reveals also at least one significant difference in terms of arousal evaluation: $\chi^2(2, N = 108) = 7.10$, $p < 0.05$. Subsequent pairwise comparisons indicated that the valence was evaluated significantly more positively with the joy than with the neutral facial expresion ($difference = 18.76$)(see Figure 4.b). However no other significant differences are found between other couples of facial expression. No significant difference is found in terms of the dominance evaluation: $\chi^2(2, N = 108) = 2.85$, $p = 0.24$ (see Figure 4.c). In all cases, the critical difference ($p = 0.05$ corrected for the number of tests) was 17.67.

Hypothesis 2: Figure 5 presents, for the haptic only conditions ('S', 's'), the evaluation of valence (**M1**), arousal (**M2**) and dominance (**M3**) respectively. The analysis reveals at least one significant difference between the haptic conditions in terms of valence evaluation: $\chi^2(3, N = 72) = 14.82$, $p < 0.05$. Subsequent pairwise comparisons indicated that the valence was evaluated significantly more positively with strong (S) than with soft (s) haptic behavior ($difference = 29.93$)(see Figure 5.a). The analysis reveals also at least one significant difference between the haptic conditions in terms of arousal evaluation: $\chi^2(3, N = 72) = 14.99$, $p < 0.05$. Subsequent pairwise comparisons indicated that the arousal was evaluated significantly differently between the strong (S) condition than

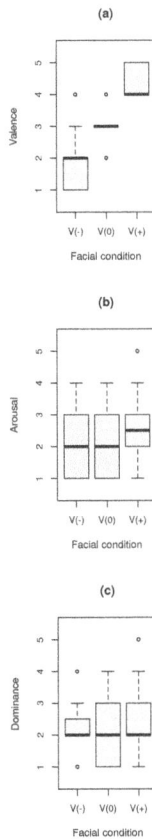

Figure 4: Results of the visual-only conditions ('-', '0', '+'): (a) presents the evaluation of valence (**M1**), (b) presents the evaluation of arousal (**M2**), (c) presents the evaluation of dominance (**M3**). Each bar includes a median value and a box from second quartile (0.25) to third one (0.75) and a whisker, which extends to a maximum of 1.5 inter-quartile distance and circles for outliers.

the soft (s) one ($difference = 35.55$) (see Figure 5.b). Finally the analysis reveals at least one difference between the haptic conditions in terms of dominance evaluation, $\chi^2(3, N = 72) = 34.1$, $p < 0.05$. Subsequent pairwise comparisons indicated that the dominance was evaluated significantly differently between the strong (S) condition than the soft (s) one ($difference = 55.87$) (see Figure 5.c). In all cases, the critical difference ($p = 0.05$ corrected for the number of tests) was 25.94.

Hypothesis 3.a: Figure 6 and Figure 7 compare the monomodal ('V') and multimodal ('VH') conditions for the evaluation of arousal and dominance respectively. The comparison is carried out for the three visual conditions ('-', '0', '+') , but only the 'S' haptic condition (i.e., when the grasping force is high and the stiffness of movement is high) is considered for this comparison.

Concerning the arousal evaluation, a significant difference is highlighted between V(-) facial condition and the VH condition: $\chi^2(4, N = 540) = 30.79$, $p < 0.05$. Follow-up tests showed that the arousal was significantly evaluated with higher value in the multimodal expression with strong (S) haptic behavior than in the monomodal visual only negative expression ($difference = 51.72$) (see Figure 6.a). A significant difference is highlighted between the V(0) facial condition and the VH condition: $\chi^2(4, N = 540) = 44.62$, $p < 0.05$. Follow-up tests showed that the arousal was significantly evalu-

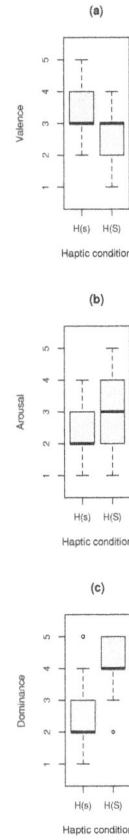

Figure 5: Results of the haptic-only conditions ('s', 'S'): (a) presents the evaluation of valence (**M1**), (b) presents the evaluation of arousal (**M2**), (c) presents the evaluation of dominance (**M3**).

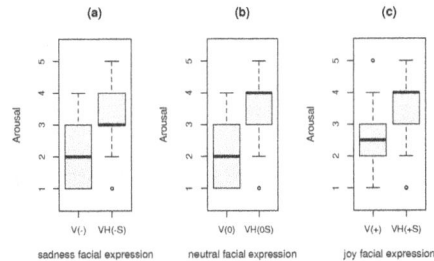

Figure 6: Results comparing the evaluation of arousal (**M2**) between the monomodal visual ('V') and multimodal conditions ('VH'): (a) corresponds to sadness facial expression ('-'), (b) corresponds to neutral facial expression ('0'), (c) corresponds to joy facial expression ('+').

ated with higher value in the multimodal expression with strong (S) haptic behavior than in the monomodal visual only neutral expression ($difference = 73.89$) (see Figure 6.b). A significant difference is found between the V(+) facial condition and the VH condition: $\chi^2(4, N = 540) = 14.95$, $p < 0.05$. Follow-up tests showed that the arousal was significantly evaluated with higher value in the multimodal expression with strong (S) haptic behavior than in the monomodal visual only positive expression ($difference = 39.64$) (see Figure 6.c).

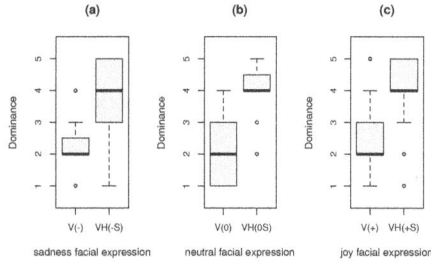

Figure 7: Results comparing the evaluation of dominance (**M3**) between the monomodal visual ('V') and multimodal conditions ('VH'): (a) corresponds to sadness facial expression ('-'), (b) corresponds to neutral facial expression ('0'), (c) corresponds to joy facial expression ('+').

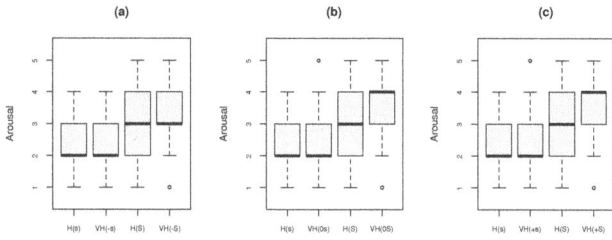

Figure 8: Results comparing the evaluation of arousal (**M2**) between the monomodal haptic ('H') and multimodal conditions ('VH'): (a) corresponds to sadness facial expression ('-'), (b) corresponds to neutral facial expression ('0'), (c) corresponds to joy facial expression ('+').

Concerning the dominance emotional factor, a significant difference is highlighted between the facial negative expression evaluation and the multimodal expression: $\chi^2(4, N = 540) = 42.98$, $p < 0.05$. Follow-up tests showed that the dominance was significantly evaluated with higher value in the multimodal expression with strong (S) haptic behavior than in the monomodal visual only negative expression ($difference = 59.54$) (see Figure 7.a). A significant difference is found between the facial neutral expression evaluation and the multimodal expression (Figure 7.b): $\chi^2(4, N = 540) = 54.89$, $p < 0.05$. Follow-up tests showed that the dominance was significantly evaluated with higher value in the multimodal expression with strong (S) haptic behavior than in the monomodal visual only neutral expression ($difference = 77.94$) (see Figure 7.b). A significant difference is highlighted between the facial positive expression evaluation and the multimodal expression (Figure 7.c): $\chi^2(4, N = 540) = 50.23$, $p < 0.05$. Follow-up tests showed that the dominance was significantly evaluated with higher value in the multimodal expression with strong (S) haptic behavior than in the monomodal visual only positive expression ($difference = 72.83$) (see Figure 7.c).

In all cases, the critical difference ($p = 0.05$ corrected for the number of tests) was 34.47.

Hypothesis 3.b: Figure 8 and Figure 9 compare the monomodal ('H') and multimodal ('VH') conditions for the evaluation of arousal and dominance respectively.

Concerning the arousal (Figure 8), no significant difference is highlighted between the 's' haptic condition (i.e., when the grasping force is low and the stiffness of movement is low) and the mul-

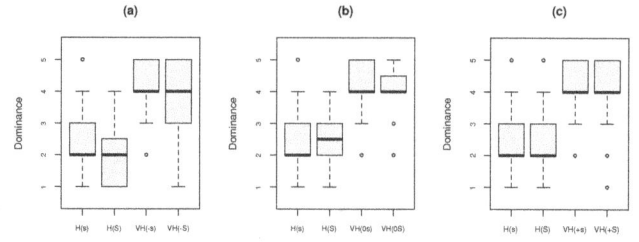

Figure 9: Results comparing the evaluation of dominance (**M3**) between the monomodal haptic ('H') and multimodal conditions ('VH'): (a) corresponds to sadness facial expression ('-'), (b) corresponds to neutral facial expression ('0'), (c) corresponds to joy facial expression ('+').

timodal condition: $\chi^2(3, N = 288) = 5.01$, $p = 0.17$. No significant difference is highlighted between the 'S' haptic condition (i.e., when the grasping force is high and stiffness of movement is high) and the multimodal expression: $\chi^2(3, N = 288) = 1.19$, $p = 0.75$.

The analysis revealed some differences in terms of dominance evaluation (Figure 9). Indeed, significant difference is highlighted between the 's' haptic only condition and the corresponding multimodal condition: $\chi^2(3, N = 288) = 8.44$, $p < 0.05$. However, follow-up test is not able to point out any significant difference when comparing the conditions from each other. No significant difference is revealed between the 'S' haptic only condition and the multimodal expression: $\chi^2(3, N = 288) = 5.7543$, $p = 0.12$.

6. DISCUSSION

Visual feedback: Based on the results of the present study, **H1** is partially validated. Indeed only valence is significantly well discriminated. Therefore the results related to the visual condition showed that participants exploit well the facial cue (i.e., lip display) to discriminate the valence and arousal dimensions of the emotions expressed by the robot. This is consistent with other studies investigation the same issue in psychology [19, 21]. However, we observed that participants have difficulties to discriminate the dominance dimension. This is due to the limit of the facial cue (i.e., lip display) to support this emotional dimension.

Haptic feedback: Based on the results of the present study, **H2** is validated for each dimension. Therefore the results related to the haptic condition showed that participants discriminate well the dominance and the arousal dimensions of the haptic behaviours presenting low and high values for grasping force and stiffness of movement. Concerning the arousal dimension, several works in psychology and haptics for human-machine interfaces highlighted the effect of haptic feedback for the perception of this dimension [6]. However, these works investigate active haptic feedbacks where a movement is applied on the user's body. For instance, Gaffary et al. [12] showed that applying a movement with an important amplitude on the user's hand increases the perception of arousal. The results of our study highlighted the effect of a passive haptic feedback, i.e., without generating a movement, on the perception of the arousal. High values for grasping force and joint stiffness lead to the increase of the perceived arousal although the robotic arm do not generate movement. Concerning the perception of dominance, researches in psychology highlighted the role of interpersonal touch to convey this dimension [16]. However, they have not identify the physical parameters influencing the perception of this dimension. For human-robot collaborative tasks, Groten et al.

[14] showed that the grasping stiffness exerted by the robot on the shared object influences the perception of the dominance. Our results showed that similarly to the arousal dimension, the passive haptic feedback applied on the user's hand influences the perception of the robot's dominance. High values for grasping force and joint stiffness increase the level of perceived dominance.

In order to identify the role of two haptic parameters for the perception of the different dimensions, complementary analyses are planned.

Multimodal feedback: Based on the results of the present study **H3.a** is validated. However according to the present results, **H3.b** is rejected. The results related to the multimodal condition clearly show that introducing high values for grasping force and joint stiffness leads, for the three investigated emotions, to the increase of the perceived arousal and dominance compared to the visual-only condition. Since we do not observe a real difference for the perception of dominance and arousal between the multimodal condition and the haptic condition, we can assume that the perception of these two dimensions are mainly influenced and increased by the haptic feedback under the multimodal condition. Thus, the haptic channel complements the visual channel, which mainly supports the perception of the valence, for the perception of emotions. The combination of sensory channels to convey complementary dimensions of emotions was observed in several psychology researches. For instance, Betsy et al. [3] observed that for some categories of emotions the postural configurations convey social-status components while facial expressions convey survival components. The authors of [4] suggest that people weight the emotional signals from different sensory channels and then combine them in an optimal fashion. Concerning the role of the different sensory channels, the works of Major [16] clearly highlighted the effect of touch to convey.

7. CONCLUSIONS

Robots are more and more present in our daily lives. In human-robot interaction, a social intelligent robot should be capable of understanding the context of interaction with the human so as to behave in a proper manner by following some social rules. This paper focuses on the haptic affective social interaction during a greeting handshaking between the human and the robot. We investigated how the haptic feedback influences the perception of the dimensions of emotions, namely: arousal and dominance. The results show that the facial cue conveys well the arousal and valence but not the dominance. The latter is well conveyed during the haptic interaction. In fact, participants discriminate well the dominance dimension of haptic behaviours presenting low and high values for grasping force and joint stiffness. This leads, in the multimodal configuration, to a good discrimination of the three dimensions of emotions. Participants combines both visual and haptic cues to perceive the different dimensions.

In order to understand how participants integrate the different sensory cues in order to perceive emotions, future studies are planned. Moreover, it would be interesting to investigate the effect of other haptic feedback, such as tactile and force feedback, on the perception of emotions.

8. ACKNOWLEDGMENT

This work is supported by the French National Research Agency (ANR) through Chaire d'Excellence program 2009 (Human-Robot Interaction for Assistive Applications) designated to Prof. Adriana TAPUS. We would like to thank Vincent Munsch for his hard work and his involvement in this project.

9. REFERENCES

[1] F. Almeida, A. Lopes, and P. Abreu. Force-impedance control: a new control strategy of robotic manipulators. In *Kaynak O, Tosunoglu S, Marcelo Ang Jr (Eds.) Recent Advances in Mechatronics*, 1999.

[2] A. Aly and A. Tapus. Towards an online fuzzy modeling for human internal states detection. In *Proceedings of the International Conference on Control, Automatics, Robotics, and Vision (ICARCV)*, Guangzhou, China, 2012.

[3] B. App, D. N. McIntosh, C. L. Reed, and M. J. Hertenstein. Nonverbal channel use in communication of emotion: how may depend on why. 11(3):603–417, 2011.

[4] M. Argyle and J. Dean. Eye-contact, distance and affiliation. In *Sociometry*, volume 28, pages 289–304, 1965.

[5] G. Avraham, I. Nisky, H. Fernandes, D. Acuna, K. Kording, G. Loeb, and A. Karniel. Toward perceiving robots as humans: Three handshake models face the turing-like handshake test. In *IEEE Transactions on Haptics*, volume 5, pages 196–207, 2012.

[6] J. Bailenson, N. Yee, S. Brave, D. Merget, and D. Koslow. Virtual interpersonal touch: Expressing and recognizing emotions through haptic devices. In *Human-Computer Interaction*, volume 22, pages 325–353, 2007.

[7] M. Bergamasco and E. Ruffaldi. Haptic interfaces for embodiment in virtual environment. In *Proc. of RO-MAN*, 2011.

[8] T. Bickmore, R. Fernando, L. Ring, and D. Schulman. Empathic touch by relational agents. In *IEEE Transactions of Affective Computing*, volume 1, pages 60–71, 2010.

[9] C. Breazeal and L. Aryananda. Recognition of affective communicative intent in robot-directed speech. *Autonomous Robots Journal*, 12(1):83–104, January 2002.

[10] N. Chen, C.-M. Chew, K.-P. Tee, and B. S. Han. Human-aided robotic grasping. In *Proc of RO-MAN*, pages 75–80, Sept 2012.

[11] Y. Gaffary, V. Eyharabide, J. Martin, and M. Ammi. Clustering approach to characterize haptic expressions of emotions. In *TAP*, volume 10, 2013.

[12] Y. Gaffary, V. Eyharabide, J. Martin, and M. Ammi. The impact of combining kinesthetic and facial expression displays on emotion recognition by users. In *IJHCI, Special issue "Does Touch Matter?: The Effects of Haptic Visualization on Human Performance, Behavior and Perception*, 2014.

[13] P. Giraudoux. *pgirmess: Data analysis in ecology*, 2014. R package version 1.5.9.

[14] R. K. Groten. *Haptic Human-Robot Collaboration: How to Learn from Human Dyads*. PhD thesis, Technische Universitat Munchen, 2010.

[15] M. Hertenstein, D. Keltner, B. App, B. Bulleit, and A. Jaskolka. Touch communicates distinct emotions. In *Emotion*, volume 6, pages 528–533, 2006.

[16] B. Major and R. Heslin. Perceptions of cross-sex and same-sex nonreciprocal touch: It is better to give than to receive. In *Journal of Nonverbal Behavior*, volume 6, pages 148–162, 1982.

[17] A. Mehrabian. *Basic Dimensions for a General Psychological Theory: Implications for Personality, Social and Environmental Psychology*. 1980.

[18] H. Olausson, J. Cole, A. Vallbo, F. McGlone, M. Elam, H. Kramer, and M. Bushnell. Unmyelinated tactile afferents have opposite effects on insular and somatosensory cortical

processing. In *Neuroscience letters*, volume 436, pages 128–132, 2008.

[19] K. R. Scherer. The component process model: a blueprint for a comprehensive computational model of emotion. In *Blueprint for Affective Computing: A Sourcebook, eds K. R. Scherer, T. Banziger, and E. B. Roesch*, volume Oxford: Oxford University Press, pages 47–70. 2010.

[20] S. Siegel and N. J. Castellan. Multiple comparisons between treatments. In *Siegel, S., and Castellan, N. J. Nonparametric Statistics for the Behavioral Sciences (2nd)*, volume McGraw-Hill: New York. 1988.

[21] D. Simon, K. D. Craig, F. Gosselin, P. Belin, and P. Rainville. Recognition and discrimination of prototypical dynamic expressions of pain and emotions. In *Pain*, 2007.

[22] M.-Y. Tsalamlal, N. Ouarti, J.-C. Martin, and M. Ammi. Perception of emotions from air jet based tactile stimulation. In *Proc. of ACII 2013*, pages 215–220, 2013.

[23] W. Wang, E. Giannopoulos, M. Slater, and A. Peer. Handshake: Realistic human-robot interaction in haptic enhanced virtual reality. In *Presence: Teleoper. Virtual Environ*, volume 20, pages 371–392, 2011.

[24] Y. Yamato, M. Jindai, and T. Watanabe. Development of a shake-motion leading model for human-robot handshaking. In *SICE Annual Conference*, 2008.

[25] S. Yohanan and K. E. MacLean. The haptic creature project: Social human-robot interaction through affective touch. In *Proc. of the AISB 2008 Symposium on the Reign of Catz and Dogz*, volume 1, pages 7–11, 2008.

[26] S. Yohanan and K. E. MacLean. The role of affective touch in human-robot interaction: Human intent and expectations in touching the haptic creature. 4(2):168–180, 2012.

Embodied Collaborative Referring Expression Generation in Situated Human-Robot Interaction

Rui Fang, Malcolm Doering, Joyce Y. Chai
Department of Computer Science and Engineering
Michigan State University
East Lansing, MI 48824, USA
{fangrui, doeringm, jchai }@cse.msu.edu

ABSTRACT

To facilitate referential communication between humans and robots and mediate their differences in representing the shared environment, we are exploring embodied collaborative models for referring expression generation (REG). Instead of a single minimum description to describe a target object, episodes of expressions are generated based on human feedback during human-robot interaction. We particularly investigate the role of *embodiment* such as robot gesture behaviors (i.e., pointing to an object) and human's gaze feedback (i.e., looking at a particular object) in the collaborative process. This paper examines different strategies of incorporating embodiment and collaboration in REG and discusses their possibilities and challenges in enabling human-robot referential communication.

Categories and Subject Descriptors: H.5.2 [Information Interfaces and Presentation]:User Interfaces

General Terms: Algorithms, Experimentation

Keywords: Referring Expression Generation; Embodiment; Collaborative Referential Communication

1. INTRODUCTION

Referring Expression Generation (REG) has traditionally been formulated as a problem of generating a single noun phrase (possibly with multiple modifiers and prepositional phrases) that can uniquely describe a target object among multiple objects [5, 18] so that addressees (i.e., humans) can correctly identify the intended object given this expression. Except for a few recent works that apply computer vision to building representations of objects in scenes [8, 16, 22], most existing REG approaches were developed and evaluated under the assumption that humans and agents have access to the same kind of domain information and have the same representation of the shared world [18]. Clearly, this assumption does not hold in human-robot interaction.

In situated human-robot interaction, humans and robots have different representations of the shared environment due

HRI'15, March 2–5, 2015, Portland, OR, USA
Copyright 2015 ACM ACM 978-1-4503-2883-8/15/03 ...$15.00
http://dx.doi.org/10.1145/2696454.2696467.

to their mismatched perceptual capabilities. The robot's representation of the shared environment is often incomplete and error-prone. When a shared perceptual basis is missing, referential communication between partners becomes difficult [3]. Specifically for the task of REG, our previous work [8] has shown that when the human and the agent have a mismatched perceptual basis traditional approaches to REG tend to break down.

To mediate mismatched representations, we have developed two computational collaborative models (i.e., an episodic model and an installment model) for REG [7] motivated by collaborative referential behaviors in human-human communication [4]. Instead of generating a single referential description, our collaborative models generate multiple small noun phrases that gradually lead to the target object with a goal of minimizing the collaborative effort. We have further evaluated these collaborative models in a web-based study using 2D images to simulate a shared environment [7].

While our previous results on collaborative models are encouraging, they have not been applied to real-time human-robot interaction in a physical environment, which is much more complex than 2D simulations. More importantly, a key characteristic of physical world interaction is *embodiment*: agents (i.e., robots) and humans both have physical bodies and they can use non-verbal modalities (e.g., gesture and eye gaze) to refer to the shared world and to provide immediate feedback. It is not clear to what degree the collaborative models can take embodiment into account and apply to physical interaction. To address these issues, we are exploring embodied collaborative models for REG. We particularly investigate the role of *embodiment* such as robot gesture behaviors (i.e., pointing to an object) and the human's gaze feedback (i.e., looking at a particular object) in the collaborative process. This paper examines different strategies of incorporating embodiment and collaboration in REG and discusses their possibilities and challenges in enabling human-robot referential communication.

2. RELATED WORK

Previous psycholinguistic studies have indicated that referential communication is a collaborative process [2, 4]. To minimize the collaborative effort, partners tend to go beyond issuing an elementary referring expression (i.e., a single noun phrase), by using other different types of expressions such as *episodic, installment, self-expansion*, etc. For example, an episodic description is produced in two or more easily distinguished episodes or intonation units as shown in the following example from human-human communication [20].

A: below the orange, next to the apple, it's the red bulb.

An installment behavior is similar to the episodic behavior in the sense that it also breaks down referring expression generation into smaller episodes. The difference is that explicit feedback from the addressee is solicited before the speaker moves to the next episode. Here is an example of installment descriptions from [20].

A: under the pepper we just talked about.
B: yes.
A: there is a group of three objects.
B: OK.
A: there is a yellow object on the right within the group.

The generation of episodic or installment descriptions is not to minimize the speaker's own effort, but rather to minimize the collaborative effort so that the addressee can quickly identify the referent. These collaborative behaviors from human-human referential communication have motivated previous computational models for collaborative reference [6,7,15]. However, these models have not been applied to human-robot interaction.

As deictic gesture plays an important role in referential communication [9,14], recent work has incorporated deictic gestures in generating referring expressions [23], referring acts [12,13], and multimodal references [25]. More recently, different strategies of incorporating deictic gestures have been investigated in human-robot interaction [24].

Psycholinguistic findings have shown that eye gaze is tightly linked to human language comprehension and production [27]. Specifically for REG, Koller et al. [17] developed an interactive system that tracks the hearer's eye gaze to monitor hearer's interpretation of the referring expressions the system generates. However, their REG system was built on a virtual environment where the agent and the human are assumed to have the same representation of the shared world.

In contrast to previous work, our work here incorporates embodiment (i.e., deictic gestures from the robot and gaze feedback from the human partner) into the collaborative model to address the unique characteristics of human-robot interaction.

3. EMBODIED COLLABORATIVE REG

3.1 Collaborative Installment Model

In our previous work we have developed a collaborative installment model for REG [7]. Instead of generating a single referring expression to describe a target object, our installment model generates one expression (i.e., *installment*) at a time based on the human's feedback and gradually leads to the target object. We formulated the learning of the installment model as a sequential decision making problem and trained the model using reinforcement learning. The goal was to learn an optimal policy that generates installments under different situations to allow listeners to successfully identify the target object.

More specifically, we used a variety of features to represent the utility function $Q(s,a)$ for a given state s (which captures the state of interaction such as what landmark objects can be used) and a given action a (which represents a referring expression generation strategy/action - e,g., which

attributes to choose to describe the intended object) as in:

$$Q(s,a) = \theta^T \phi(s,a)$$

Where ϕ is the feature vector of each state-action pair, and θ is the weight vector associated with the features. In our previous work [7], we have applied the SARSA [26] algorithm and conducted a crowd-sourcing study with 2D images to learn the weights for the features. Table 1 summarizes some important features and the learned weights (Feature 1-22).

Once the weights the for features are learned, they are applied to calculate $Q(s,a)$ for any state-action pair. During real-time generation, given a particular state s, the agent will pick the generation action a^* to maximize $Q(s,a)$.

$$a^* = \arg\max_{a \in A} Q(s,a)$$

#	Feature Value Description	Learned Weights
1	normalized sum of vision confidence of all descriptors in re	0.92
2	is spatial location descriptor in re?	0.54
3	vision confidence of spatial relation descriptor	0.52
4	vision confidence of type descriptor	0.51
5	vision confidence of spatial location descriptor	0.48
6	is type descriptor in re?	0.21
7	number of descriptors in re	0.19
8	vision confidence of size descriptor	0.13
9	is size descriptor in re?	0.13
10	is color descriptor in re?	0.10
11	vision confidence of color descriptor	0.09
12	can re together with sp to lm uniquely identify an object?	0.88
13	is there a sp between o and tar?	0.51
14	number of spatial links from lm	0.23
15	number of spatial links to o (in degree)	0.01
16	number of spatial links from o (out degree)	0.01
17	is o and lm in the same group?	1
18	is o a group?	0.97
19	is lm is a group and o in lm?	0.96
20	is o a group and tar in o?	0.90
21	is o and tar in the same group?	0.51
22	is o a group and lm in o?	0.11
23	**the cost of producing a pointing gesture**	**0.50**

Table 1: Features and the learned weights from the original installment model [7].

3.2 Incorporation of Embodiment in HRI

To extend the collaborative model to human-robot interaction and incorporate embodiment into the model, we explored two directions: (1) incorporating the robot's gesture (i.e., pointing) into the collaborative model to generate multimodal referring expressions; and (2) incorporating the human's real-time feedback (either verbal feedback, gaze feedback, or both) into the collaborative model.

Figure 1(a) shows an example setup where the embodied collaborative model is examined. In the setup a NAO robot sits face-to-face with a human partner who wears a mobile eye tracker as shown in Figure 1(a). The robot's internal representation of the shared environment is impoverished compared to its human partner. Figure 1(b) shows an example of the internal representation for a part of the environment. Note that Object 1, 2, and 3 are recognized as a group (by applying a perceptual grouping algorithm [11]).

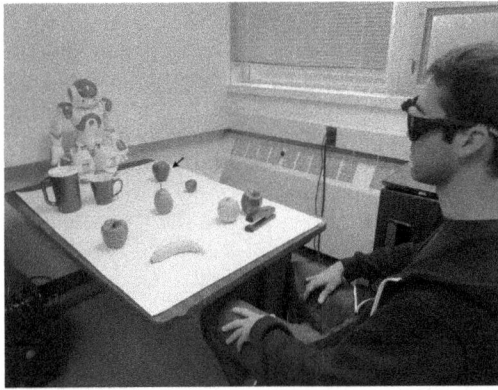

(a) An example of situated setup.

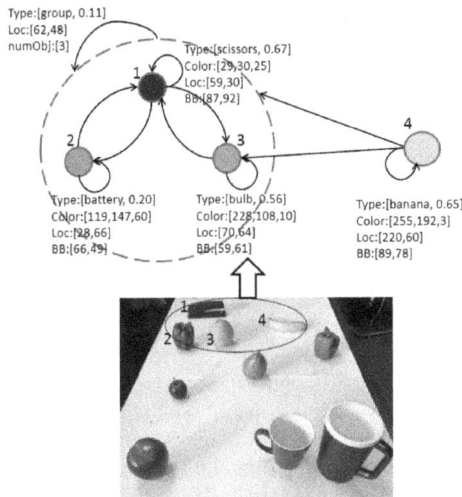

(b) An example of the robot's internal representation of the shared environment.

R1:	"Do you see a group of two on the left?" *(Robot points to the group)*
H1:	"Yes" *(The group becomes the landmark)*
R2:	"That group I was just talking about, do you see an object in the back that is on the right within that group?" *(Describe the intended object in relation to the landmark)*
H2:	"No" *(Human rejects the description)*
R3:	"That group I was just talking about, do you see an object on the right that is to the right of that group?" *(Robot chooses another description strategy)*
H3:	"Yes"

(c) An example of collaborative referential process.

Figure 1: An example of situated setup for referential communication.

Since we are addressing referential communication to mediate perceptual differences between humans and robots, we intentionally applied only a simple computer vision algorithm [19]. Here, except for Object 4 which is correctly recognized as a banana with a confidence of 0.65, the rest of objects are mis-recognized. The numerical values related to color, location, and the size of bounding boxes are also captured by the internal representation. Figure 1(c) shows

an example of the embodied collaborative referential process for the robot to gradually lead the human to the target object (i.e., the red apple as shown by the arrow in Figure 1(a)). Note the robot takes the human's perspective when describing the objects in the scene.

Incorporation of robot's gesture in referring acts.
Pointing gestures from a robot are combined with verbal descriptions to generate referring expressions. Here, we treat the cost of gesture generation as a feature and incorporate it with other features into the collaborative models [7]. Since it is expensive to conduct a large scale in-lab study to learn feature weights from real-time human-robot interaction, we directly adopt the features and their learned weights from our web-based study [7] as shown in Table 1 (Feature 1-22). We then explicitly add the cost of the gesture generation as an additional feature and set its weight to 0.5 (Feature 23).

The cost of a pointing gesture depends on several factors: the distance from the robot to the target object, the size of the target object, adjacency of other objects to the target object, etc. Inspired by previous work on the costs of pointing, [10] and [21], we define the cost of a pointing gesture to an object as follows:

$$
cost = \begin{cases} \log_2\left(\frac{1.5 \times Distance}{Size} + 1\right) & \begin{array}{l} \text{If the object to be} \\ \text{described is in a group} \end{array} \\ \log_2\left(\frac{Distance}{Size} + 1\right) & \text{Otherwise} \end{cases}
$$

Given a situation s, the robot will apply the features and their associated weights in Table 1 to calculate $Q(s, a)$ and then choose the generation action a^* that maximizes $Q(s, a)$. Note that incorporating gesture does not necessitate that the generated referring expressions will always include gestures. Whether gesture is used or not depends on how it weighs against other features extracted from the environment. For example, in Figure 1(c), $R1$ includes the pointing gesture as part of the referring expression, while $R2$ does not.

Incorporation of eye gaze as feedback.
Previous psycholinguistic studies have shown that human eye gaze directly links with language comprehension [27]. Immediately after hearing a referring expression, the hearer's eyes move to the objects being referred to. Motivated by this finding we incorporate the user's real-time gaze and verbal information as intermediate feedback in the installment model.

To incorporate human gaze feedback, we must find how the gaze is distributed among each of the objects in the scene over the time immediately following an RE such as in Figure 1(c). Specifically, starting from the onset of an RE uttered by the robot, we capture at least 200 gaze readings (taking on average 7.7 sec) from the participant and calculate a distribution showing which objects the gaze is drawn to most often (i.e., which objects draw the most gaze readings). Based on this distribution, we applied a simple criterion to identify the *focused object*: the object with the highest number of readings where its reading number is at least twice as high as the reading number of the second highest object.

The gaze feedback can be incorporated into the installment model with or without verbal feedback.

- **Gaze Only Feedback** If a focused object can be identified based on the gaze, then the installment is considered successful and the focused object becomes the landmark for generating the next installment. Otherwise, the installment is considered unsuccessful and a different RE will be generated based on the policy applicable to the current situation.

- **Gaze and Verbal Feedback Combined** To incorporate both the gaze and verbal information from the human as intermediate feedback, we must handle all cases where the gaze feedback and verbal feedback conflict, such as when the human responds "yes" but the gaze indicates that no focused object is identified. We manage these cases in the following ways: when the user responds "No" then the gaze information is disregarded and the robot follows the verbal feedback. When the user says "Yes" then there are two cases: (1) if no focused object is identified, then the robot's intended object becomes the next landmark. (2) if a focused object is identified, then the focused object becomes the next landmark.

Figure 1 shows an example of how (verbal) feedback from the user determines which object/group becomes the landmark in the next RE. The robot starts by asking, "Do you see a group of two on the left?". After the user responds in the affirmative, that group becomes the landmark in the next utterance. The robot describes the next object in relation to this landmark, "... do you see an object in the back that is within that group?"

4. EMPIRICAL STUDIES

To evaluate the embodied collaborative REG model described above, we conducted an empirical study in human-robot interaction.

4.1 Design Factors

We designed our experiments to take into consideration the following two aspects of embodiment:

Incorporation of robot gestures. To evaluate whether the incorporation of the robot's gestures into the collaborative model facilitates referential communication, we manipulate the following two conditions:

- **Verbal Only** refers to the condition where only verbal referring expressions are generated based on the original installment model without incorporating the gesture feature.

- **Verbal and Gesture** refers to the condition where pointing gestures are incorporated into REG as described in Section 3.2.

Incorporation of human feedback. We examine different strategies of incorporating human feedback (verbal and/or eye gaze) into the installment model for REG.

- **None** refers to the condition where no explicit feedback from the human is incorporated. This is similar to the episodic model developed in our previous work [7]. The robot generates a sequence of episodes (i.e., noun phrases) that leads to the target object with the assumption that each episode is accepted by the human.

- **Verbal Only** refers to the condition where only verbal information is used as the feedback from the human

partner. In this condition the human is allowed to respond "yes", "no", or "repeat" (if they did not hear clearly). If the response is "yes" the robot assumes that the human understands the generated RE and the current intended object becomes the landmark for the next step. If the response is "no" the robot assumes the human does not understand the intended object and will try another RE. Lastly, if the response is "repeat" the robot repeats the last generated RE.

- **Gaze Only** refers to the condition where only gaze is used as the feedback from human. In this condition the gaze of the human is incorporated as described in Section 3.2. The gaze is tracked and used as feedback to the installment model.

- **Gaze and Verbal** refers to the condition where both gaze and verbal information are used as the feedback from the human. The gaze and verbal feedback are combined as described in Section 3.2.

These design factors lead to $4 \times 2 = 8$ experimental conditions. In all conditions, whether or not the gaze is incorporated in REG, it is always tracked for later analysis.

4.2 Experimental Tasks

We designed an object identification game to evaluate embodied collaborative REG. Figure 1(a) shows an example of the situated setup for the experiment. We positioned a human subject and a NAO robot face-to-face at a table which held ten everyday objects. The subject wore an ASL mobile eye tracker. The NAO robot would generate referring expressions in an installment fashion to describe these objects using different strategies (depending on the experimental condition). The human subject's goal was to identify which object the NAO robot was talking about. At the end of each game, we asked the human subject what target object was intended by the robot. We compared the object identified by the human with the true target object to compute the object identification accuracy for a particular generation strategy.

4.3 Procedures

We designed four scenes with ten objects of various types in different configurations. As described in Section 3.2, these four scenes were processed by a simple computer vision algorithm [19] and a perceptual grouping algorithm [11], and the results were given to the robot as its internal representations of the scenes (as shown in Figure 1(b)). Computer vision algorithms have advanced significantly in recent years. However, they are far from being perfect. It is likely, in a new situation or a changing environment, the robot which is equipped with modern CV algorithms can only correctly recognize a few objects (not all objects) in the shared environment with the human. This is the situation our work intends to address. Therefore, we intentionally applied a very simple CV algorithm so that the mis-recognition rate would be high. Overall, about 73% of the objects are mis-recognized or mis-segmented in our experiments.

We recruited a total of 24 human subjects to participate in our study. These subjects were not aware of any part of the system or the study design. During the experiments, each participant played 24 object identification games - 6 games on each of four separate scenes. Each scene was paired with one of the four feedback conditions such that the participant would interact with the robot under each condition. Moreover, in each of the 6 games on a scene, one target object was randomly chosen. Half of these 6 games were played under the `Verbal and Gesture` condition and the other half under the `Verbal Only` condition. For each participant the scenes were presented in one of the 24 possible permutations so that the order would not have an effect on the experiment. Furthermore, the orders of the targets were also randomized. Based on this design each participant played three games in each of the eight experimental conditions, resulting in a total of 72 games played in each condition.

4.4 Empirical Results

To help illustrate the results, we reiterate some key terms that are used throughout this section: a target object is the object the robot intends for the human to identify at the end of interaction. An intended object at each installment is an object the robot refers to on the path to the target (it may not be the target object). A landmark object is the object on the path (i.e. an intended object) that has been confirmed or accepted by the human. We use *session* to refer to the process that leads to the target object in one game. Each session often contains several installments.

4.4.1 The role of robot gesture

Table 2 shows the overall accuracy of object identification given expressions where gesture is not incorporated (i.e., `Verbal Only`) and gesture is incorporated (`Verbal and Gesture`). As shown in the table, the number of successes in identifying the target object at the end of the session is much higher in the `Verbal and Gesture` condition, which brings to 0.76 overall accuracy. This is significantly higher than the accuracy of 0.50 when gesture is not incorporated ($\chi^2 = 43.11$, $p < 0.0001$).

Robot Gesture	Verbal Only	Verbal and Gesture
Sessions	288	288
Successes	144	220
Accuracy	0.50	0.76

Table 2: Overall accuracy in object identification when gesture is incorporated (`Verbal and Gesture`) and is not incorporated (`Verbal Only`).

Table 3 further breaks down the accuracy of identifying the target object under eight experimental conditions. There is a significant difference among these conditions ($\chi^2 = 56.97$, $p < 0.0001$). Our results have shown that when robot gesture and human verbal feedback are incorporated in REG (i.e., the `Verbal and Gesture` condition for robot gesture and the `Verbal Only` condition for human feedback), it achieves 88% accuracy. This performance is significantly higher than most of the other conditions as indicated by a Tukey post-hoc test (at $p < 0.05$). Furthermore, each model that incorporates robot gesture into its generation strategy performs significantly better than its corresponding model without gesture.

Particularly, when only human gaze feedback is incorporated in REG (i.e., the `Gaze Only` condition), robot gesture has shown to be very useful. During the experiments, we observed that
several participants appeared to have difficulty understanding which object was the landmark when hearing the expres-

Human Feedback	Robot Gesture	
	Verbal Only	Verbal and Gesture
Verbal Only	0.53	**0.88**
Gaze Only	0.40	0.72
Gaze and Verbal	0.47	0.67
None	0.60	0.79

Table 3: Comparison of object identification accuracy under eight experimental conditions.

sion "that object you were just looking at...". This is because gaze feedback during comprehension is often a subconscious response to the interpreted object and sometimes the participants were not consciously aware which object they just looked at. Therefore in this condition, gesture is useful for maintaining the common ground between the dialog participants by indicating the landmark object to the human.

4.4.2 The role of human gaze

Table 4 shows the overall accuracy of target identification under the four different feedback conditions. There is only marginal difference among these conditions ($\chi^2 = 10.81$, $p = 0.013$). Although we were hoping that the incorporation of eye gaze as intermediate feedback might improve the performance of the collaborative installment model, the empirical results have shown otherwise. When the gaze information is incorporated (in both the `Gaze Only` condition and the `Gaze and Verbal` condition), the accuracy of identifying target objects is lower.

	None	Verbal	Gaze	Gaze and Verbal
Sessions	144	144	144	144
Successes	100	101	81	82
Accuracy	0.69	0.70	0.56	0.57

Table 4: Overall accuracy in object identification under four different human feedback conditions.

To help further understand the role of gaze feedback, we separated out the cases where the feedback indicated by gaze coincides with the intended object and examined whether this would be a strong signal of understanding and whether it improves the accuracy of identifying the target object in the end. Specifically, for the `Gaze Only` condition and the `Gaze and Verbal` condition, we calculate how often gaze feedback actually provides a focused object that is used as a landmark object and how often this focused object in fact is the intended object. Table 5 shows the results.

	Gaze Only		Gaze and Verbal	
	Success	Fail	Success	Fail
Installments	185	235	204	269
LM by gaze	164	200	140	140
LM Rate	0.886	0.851	0.686	0.520
Match intended object	39	21	27	11
Matching Rate	0.238	0.105	0.193	0.079

Table 5: Statistics of landmarks established by gaze in the `Gaze Only` condition and the `Gaze and Verbal` condition.

This table shows the number of installments where the landmark used for generation was established by the gaze feedback for both successful sessions (i.e., the target object was correctly identified at the end of the session) and failed sessions (i.e., the target object was not correctly identified in the end). For the `Gaze Only` condition, it shows that for both successful and failed sessions the landmark was established by the gaze feedback with about the same rate (88.6% vs. 85.1%, $\chi^2 = 1.124$, $p = 0.289$).

More interestingly, the rate of landmarks established by gaze which matched the intended object (i.e., the participant gazed at the object intended by the robot) is twice as high in successful sessions as it is in failed sessions (23.8% vs.10.5%, $\chi^2 = 11.545$, $p = 0.0007$). This appears to show that when the human is able to correctly identify the current intended object and the gaze feedback works properly, it is more likely to lead to successful target identification.

For the `Gaze and Verbal` condition, we see similar statistics as with the `Gaze Only` condition. One difference is that here the rate of landmarks established by gaze feedback (only happens when the human verbal response is "yes") is much higher for successful games than failed games (68.6% vs. 52.0%, $\chi^2 = 13.201$, $p = 0.0003$).

Furthermore, as with the `Gaze Only` condition the rate of landmarks established by gaze which matched the intended object is higher in successful sessions than it is in failed sessions (19.3% vs. 7.9%, $\chi^2 = 7.795$, $p = 0.005$). This again shows that when the human is able to correctly identify the current intended object and the gaze feedback works properly, it is more likely to result in successful target identification.

4.4.3 Effects on number of installments

There is a significant difference among the feedback conditions for the average number of installments per session ($F(3, 572) = 7.583$, $p < 0.0001$) as shown in Figure 2. Sessions in the `Verbal Only` condition lasted slightly longer, with an average of 2.36 installments per session, than sessions in the no feedback (i.e., `None`) condition, with 2.07 installments per session. Sessions in both the `Gaze Only` condition and the `Gaze and Verbal` condition lasted significantly longer.

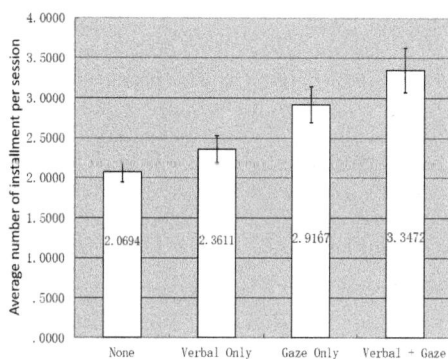

Figure 2: The average number of installments per session in each of the feedback conditions

On the other hand, statistical tests have shown that the incorporation of gesture does not have a significant effect on the number of installments per session.

4.4.4 Gesture on gaze-indicated focus

We have also examined the role of the robot's gesture on the human's focus on objects as indicated by eye gaze. More specifically, we compared the proportion of different eye gaze

patterns in the conditions where gesture is incorporated and not incorporated. The gaze responses after each RE were classified into three non-mutually exclusive classes [1] as follows:

- **IntendedObject** The object with the highest gaze fixations is indeed the intended object or contained in the intended group.

- **LandmarkObject** The object with the highest gaze fixations is indeed the landmark object or contained in the landmark group.

- **OtherObject** The object with the highest gaze fixations is neither (contained in) the intended object/group nor the landmark, i.e., the focused object is other than the intended or landmark object.

	Verbal Only	Verbal and Gesture
Total Num	656	739
IntendedObject	206	327
Rate (Intended)	**0.31**	**0.44**
LandmarkObject	212	252
Rate (Landmark)	0.32	0.34
OtherObject	298	248
Rate (Other)	**0.45**	**0.34**

Table 6: Rate of different gaze patterns, under the `Verbal Only` condition and the `Verbal and Gesture` Condition

Table 6 shows the rate of different gaze patterns, when robot pointing gesture is incorporated and is not incorporated in REG.

We can see that the use of gesture towards the intended object results in a higher percentage of `IntendedObject` class, with a rate of 0.44 under the `Verbal and Gesture` condition and 0.31 under the `Verbal Only` condition ($\chi^2 = 24.29$, $p < 0.0001$). Moreover, the use of gesture towards the intended object also results in a lower percentage of `OtherObject` class ($\chi^2 = 20.55$, $p < 0.0001$). These results show that the incorporation of robot gesture helps the human visually locate the intended object.

4.4.5 Gesture and gaze fixation time

Gesture also has an effect on how long it takes for the human to find the robot's intended object. Figure 3 shows the effects of incorporating gesture on the length of time it takes for the participant's gaze to focus, or fixate, on the intended object. We find the length of time after the first gaze reading is taken at which the intended object obtains the highest number of readings (as described in Section 3.2) and after which no other object obtains a higher number of readings than the intended object. We call this length the fixation time.

As shown in Figure 3, gesture can direct the human's gaze quickly to the intended object. There is a significant difference between the two conditions ($t = 2.43$, $p < 0.015$). When gesture is incorporated in REG, the participant's gaze fixates on the intended object in less time (3.73 seconds) than when gesture is not incorporated (4.17 seconds). This

---

[1] It is possible for a gaze response to be classified into both the `IntendedObject` class and the `LandmarkObject` class if the target is contained in a landmark group.

is likely because the robot points in the direction of the intended object, immediately reducing the search space to a subset of objects in the scene and allowing the human to identify the object being referred to more quickly.

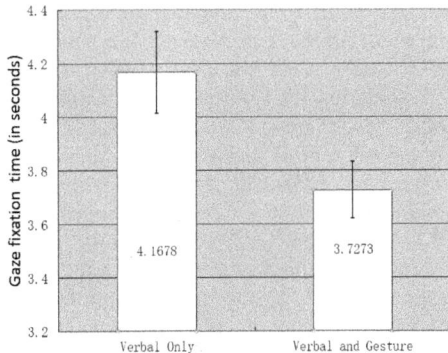

Figure 3: The average fixation time (in seconds) for the conditions with and without gesture.

5. DISCUSSION

One of the important characteristics of situated interaction is embodiment. Humans and robots have physical bodies in the shared environment. Humans can refer to objects by generating a referential expression, we can also simply point to the object, or do a combination of both. The decision of how to describe objects and when to incorporate gesture into the referring act is complex. As an initial step in our investigation, we incorporated robot pointing gesture into our collaborative installment model which was developed to mediate perceptual differences between humans and robots. We empirically set the weight for the gesture feature to take embodiment into account and directly adopted the weights learned for other features [7]. Certainly the 2D images used in our previous crowd-sourcing study are simplifications of the 3D physical environment in human-robot interaction. Ultimately, how the gesture should interact with other visual features to generate referring expressions needs to be learned in physical-world settings. We leave this to our future work.

Our empirical results have demonstrated that incorporation of gesture into the collaborative model significantly outperforms models without gesture. Our observations have shown that gestures are more useful when spatial descriptions such as "on the left/right" or "in the front/back" are used. Gestures remind the user which frame of reference is being used (human's perspective vs robot's perspective). Furthermore, in a scene where everything is technically in the "front" of the user, gesture disambiguates unclear spatial relations. Gesture is also very useful in the `Gaze Only` condition to remind the human which landmark object they have previously looked at.

Our experimental results have shown that eye gaze data obtained from the ASL Mobile Eye tracking system might not be suitable for making fine-grained decisions regarding the object of the human's gaze. The human's head movements may cause the coordinates of gaze readings to shift to objects nearby and thus affect the accuracy of identifying the focused objects. In addition, our current method of identifying focused objects and incorporating gaze feedback

is rather ad-hoc. It is not clear whether this approach can reliably reflect the focus of attention. As a result, in the conditions with eye gaze as feedback, the rate of successful sessions (where the target is identified), is lower than the conditions without eye gaze. This result seems conflicting with previous studies by Koller et al. [17]. However, the setting in [17] is human-computer interaction mediated through a computer screen, which is very different from our situated interaction. The former represents a simplified setting where a monitor-mounted gaze tracker tends to be more reliable. Better use of the Mobile Eye tracker or other devices in the physical environment (e.g., Kinect) needs to be explored as well as the granularity for representing gaze feedback (e.g., focused object versus focused region).

We currently use some heuristics to process human gaze feedback. Often, however, the verbal response from the human does not match the gaze response. For example, there were situations where the human says "Yes" but the gaze feedback does not indicate any focused object. We have recorded a large amount of gaze data from participants simultaneously with yes/no verbal feedback. In the future we plan to use this data to explore how to better classify human gaze patterns.

We have also observed some adaptation of gaze behaviors during our experiments. Some participants, realizing that the robot pays attention to their gaze feedback, adapted their gaze behavior by fixating on objects longer and saccading between objects less often. However, only about half of the participants exhibited adaptation behavior while there was no adaptation in the other half. This observation demonstrates that, to better utilize human gaze feedback, one potential solution is to design effective robot behaviors to solicit human adaptation for reliable gaze feedback.

6. CONCLUSIONS

In human-robot interaction, the robot's representation of the shared environment can be significantly different from the human's representation. The robot needs to be able to describe its internal representation of the shared environment so that the human understands what it is talking about. This is particularly important for establishing common ground and supporting successful interaction [1, 28]. Toward this goal, this paper explores embodied collaborative referring expression generation which incorporates nonverbal modalities in the collaborative process of referential communication. We have conducted experiments to evaluate different embodied collaborative models through situated, physical, human-robot interaction. Our empirical results have shown that the incorporation of non-verbal modalities such as robot gesture into the embodied collaborative model allows humans to better identify target objects. However, the incorporation of human eye gaze as intermediate feedback does not perform well. Our results may indicate human gaze is by nature noisy. Especially in situated interaction, it is difficult to reliably capture gaze fixations. More in-depth investigations on human gaze feedback are needed in the future.

7. ACKNOWLEDGMENTS

This work was supported by IIS-1208390 from the National Science Foundation and N00014-11-1-0410 from the Office of Naval Research.

8. REFERENCES

[1] J. Y. Chai, L. She, R. Fang, S. Ottarson, C. Littley, C. Liu, and K. Hanson. Collaborative effort towards common ground in situated human robot dialogue. In *Proceedings of 9th ACM/IEEE International Conference on Human-Robot Interaction*, Bielefeld, Germany, 2014.

[2] H. Clark and A. Bangerter. *Changing ideas about reference*, pages 25–49. Experimental pragmatics. Palgrave Macmillan, 2004.

[3] H. Clark and S. Brennan. Grounding in communication. *Perspectives on socially shared cognition*, 13:127–149, 1991.

[4] H. H. Clark and D. Wilkes-Gibbs. Referring as a collaborative process. *Cognition*, 22:1–39, 1986.

[5] R. Dale. Computational interpretations of the gricean maxims in the generation of referring expressions. *Cognitive Science*, 19:233–263, 1995.

[6] D. DeVault, N. Kariaeva, A. Kothari, I. Oved, and M. Stone. An information-state approach to collaborative reference. In *Proceedings of the ACL 2005 on Interactive Poster and Demonstration Sessions*, 2005.

[7] R. Fang, M. Doering, and J. Y. Chai. Collaborative models for referring expression generation in situated dialogue. In *Proceedings of the Twenty-Eighth AAAI Conference on Artificial Intelligence, July 27 -31, 2014, Québec City, Québec, Canada.*, pages 1544–1550, 2014.

[8] R. Fang, C. Liu, L. She, and J. Y. Chai. Towards situated dialogue: Revisiting referring expression generation. In *Proceedings of the 2013 Conference on Empirical Methods in Natural Language Processing (EMNLP)*, pages 392–402, Seattle, Washington, USA, October 2013. Association for Computational Linguistics.

[9] C. J. Fillmore. Towards a descriptive framework for spatial deixis. In R. J. Jarvella and W. Klein, editors, *Speech, Place, and Action*, pages 31–59. Wiley, Chichester, 1982.

[10] P. M. Fitts. The information capacity of the human motor system in controlling the amplitude of movement. *Journal of Experimental PSychology*, 74:381–391, 1954.

[11] A. Gatt. Structuring knowledge for reference generation: A clustering algorithm. In *Proceedings of the 11th Conference of the European Chapter of the Association for Computational Linguistics, Association for Computational Linguistics*, pages 321–328, 2006.

[12] A. Gatt and P. Paggio. What and where: An empirical investigation of pointing gestures and descriptions in multimodal referring actions. In *Proceedings of the 14th European Workshop on Natural Language Generation*, pages 82–91, Sofia, Bulgaria, August 2013. Association for Computational Linguistics.

[13] A. Gatt and P. Paggio. Learning when to point: A data-driven approach. In *Proceedings of the 25th International Conference on Computational Linguistics (COLING '14)*, 2014.

[14] S. Goldin-Meadow. The role of gesture in communication and thinking. *Trends Cogn. Sci.*, 1999.

[15] P. A. Heeman and G. Hirst. Collaborating on referring expressions. *Computational Linguistics*, 21:351–382, 1995.

[16] S. Kazemzadeh, V. Ordonez, M. Matten, and T. Berg. Referitgame: Referring to objects in photographs of natural scenes. In *Proceedings of the 2014 Conference on Empirical Methods in Natural Language Processing (EMNLP)*, pages 787–798, Doha, Qatar, October 2014. Association for Computational Linguistics.

[17] A. Koller, M. Staudte, K. Garoufi, and M. Crocker. Enhancing referential success by tracking hearer gaze. In *Proceedings of the 13th Annual Meeting of the Special Interest Group on Discourse and Dialogue*, SIGDIAL '12, pages 30–39, Stroudsburg, PA, USA, 2012. Association for Computational Linguistics.

[18] E. Krahmer and K. V. Deemter. Computational generation of referring expressions: A survey. *computational linguistics*, 38(1):173–218, 2012.

[19] C. Liu, R. Fang, and J. Y. Chai. Towards mediating shared perceptual basis in situated dialogue. In *Proceedings of the 13th Annual Meeting of the Special Interest Group on Discourse and Dialogue*, SIGDIAL '12, pages 140–149, Stroudsburg, PA, USA, 2012. Association for Computational Linguistics.

[20] C. Liu, R. Fang, L. She, and J. Chai. Modeling collaborative referring for situated referential grounding. In *Proceedings of the SIGDIAL 2013 Conference*, pages 78–86, Metz, France, August 2013. Association for Computational Linguistics.

[21] I. S. MacKenzie, A. Sellen, and W. A. S. Buxton. A comparison of input devices in element pointing and dragging tasks. In *Proceedings of the SIGCHI Conference on Human Factors in Computing Systems*, CHI '91, pages 161–166, New York, NY, USA, 1991. ACM.

[22] M. Mitchell, K. van Deemter, and E. Reiter. Generating expressions that refer to visible objects. In *Proceedings of NAAC-HLT 2013, pages 1174-1184*, 2013.

[23] P. Piwek. Salience in the generation of multimodal referring acts. In *Proceedings of the 2009 International Conference on Multimodal Interfaces*, ICMI-MLMI '09, pages 207–210, New York, NY, USA, 2009. ACM.

[24] A. Sauppé and B. Mutlu. Robot deictics: How gesture and context shape referential communication. In *Proceedings of the 2014 ACM/IEEE International Conference on Human-robot Interaction*, HRI '14, pages 342–349, New York, NY, USA, 2014. ACM.

[25] I. F. V. D. Sluis. *Multimodal Reference, Studies in Automatic Generation of Multimodal Referring Expressions*. PhD thesis, Tulburg University, 2005.

[26] R. S. Sutton and A. G. Barto. *Introduction to Reinforcement Learning*. MIT Press, Cambridge, MA, USA, 1st edition, 1998.

[27] M. Tanenhaus, M. Spivey-Knowlton, K. Eberhard, and J. Sedivy. Integration of visual and linguistic information during spoken language comprehension. *Science*, 268:1632–1634, 1995.

[28] S. Tellex, R. Knepper, A. Li, D. Rus, and N. Roy. Asking for help using inverse semantics. In *Proceedings of Robotics: Science and Systems*, Berkeley, USA, July 2014.

Bringing the Scene Back to the Tele-operator: Auditory Scene Manipulation for Tele-presence Systems

Chaoran Liu
ATR Intelligent Robotics and
Communication Labs
Kyoto, Japan
chaoran.liu@irl.sys.es.osaka-u.ac.jp

Carlos T. Ishi
ATR Intelligent Robotics and
Communication Labs
Kyoto, Japan
carlos@atr.jp

Hiroshi Ishiguro
ATR Hiroshi Ishiguro Labs
Kyoto, Japan
ishiguro@sys.es.osaka-u.ac.jp

ABSTRACT

In a tele-operated robot system, the reproduction of auditory scenes, conveying 3D spatial information of sound sources in the remote robot environment, is important for the transmission of remote presence to the tele-operator. We proposed a tele-presence system which is able to reproduce and manipulate the auditory scenes of a remote robot environment, based on the spatial information of human voices around the robot, matched with the operator's head orientation. In the robot side, voice sources are localized and separated by using multiple microphone arrays and human tracking technologies, while in the operator side, the operator's head movement is tracked and used to relocate the spatial positions of the separated sources. Interaction experiments with humans in the robot environment indicated that the proposed system had significantly higher accuracy rates for perceived direction of sounds, and higher subjective scores for sense of presence and listenability, compared to a baseline system using stereo binaural sounds obtained by two microphones located at the humanoid robot's ears. We also proposed three different user interfaces for augmented auditory scene control. Evaluation results indicated higher subjective scores for sense of presence and usability in two of the interfaces (control of voice amplitudes based on virtual robot positioning, and amplification of voices in the frontal direction).

Categories and Subject Descriptors

I.2.9 [**Robotics**]: Operator interfaces.

General Terms

Algorithms, Measurement, Performance, Design, Experimentation, Human Factors, Verification.

Keywords

Tele-operation; Tele-presence; Auditory scene manipulation; Communication robot; HRTF; Localization; Sound separation.

1. INTRODUCTION

In order to realize tele-presence through robots, most works so far have focused on evaluating the sense of presence in the robot side, i.e, how people around the robot would feel the presence of the tele-operator through the robot [1-4]. However, the sense of

HRI '15, March 02 - 05, 2015, Portland, OR, USA.
Copyright is held by the owner/author(s). Publication rights licensed to ACM.
ACM 978-1-4503-2883-8/15/03...$15.00.
http://dx.doi.org/10.1145/2696454.2696494

presence from the tele-operator viewpoint has not been given much attention in tele-presence robot systems, so far.

Considering a scenario of a robot involved in multi-party communication where the tele-operator communicates with other people through a tele-operated robot, there are deficiency of many information such as intelligibility, comfort and physical presence, in comparison to face-to-face communication. Especially the spatial information of sounds is lost when using a conventional (monaural) microphone-headphone system.

In recent years, virtual reality has gained great popularity as a way to simulate physical presence in medical, game and military applications [5][6]. Virtual reality has also been applied for tele-conferencing/tele-operating systems [7][8]. One goal in the development of a tele-operating system is creating tele-sensation which refers to a sense of presence in a remote location. Most of virtual reality-related studies have focused on creating virtual visual sensation using immersive projection displays [8][9] or virtual reality unit (a helmet-like visual device, usually including stereo vision) [7]. On the other hand, only a few focus on manipulating spatial auditory sensation [10][11]. Virtual auditory scene reproduction has been widely applied on game applications. However, there are few or none applications on social media, such as in tele-presence robots. In virtual reality applications that aim for improving quality and ease of interaction, rich auditory sense is a factor that cannot be ignored.

The goal of this work is to develop a tele-operation robot system which can reproduce and manipulate auditory scenes (spatial auditory sensation of sound sources) of a remote robot environment, in order to transmit sense of presence to the tele-operator. We refer such a system as "tele-presence system" hereinafter. A tele-presence system requires the ability to localize sound sources, separate them and render the sound sources at appropriate spatial locations, in real time.

The most common way to reproduce an auditory scene is playing binaural recorded sounds using stereo headphones. However, this method requires very specific recording setup, and also loses dynamic cues and the ability to rearrange sounds from different locations. To store characteristic information corresponding to spatial properties, an efficient way is using microphone array techniques. There are many teleconference-related studies using microphone arrays for localizing sound sources [12], separating the sound from a target direction [13], or suppressing echo [14]. However, the output of such systems is monaural so that auditory scene is not reproduced.

Regarding reproduction of 3D audio, by using more channels than a stereo sound, surround sound systems have been developed for providing a better spatial sensation. Directional Audio Coding (DirAC) is used in several studies for reproducing spatial sounds on multiple loudspeaker systems [10][11]. However, the use of loudspeaker systems for auditory scene reproduction raises two problems. The first one is that spatial sounds will be played in an unknown environment, thus, different configurations of room and loudspeakers will impose unknown nonlinear transformations that usually cannot be compensated. The second problem is that all loudspeaker systems have a constraint that the listener has to be in the "sweet spot" (an optimal listening position) which is limited to the central point in the system setup [15].

Another strategy is to synthesize binaural sounds using stereo headphones. It is generally accepted that human perceives the spatial position of a sound source based on the differences between the sounds at the two ears. These auditory differences include sound pressure level and arrival times at the two ears [16][17]. The binaural sounds to be reproduced with headphones can be synthesized by using measured Head Related Transfer Functions (HRTF), which are functions representing the relationship between the sound source position and the sound wave property at the two eardrums of a particular person [17].

However, two problems arise when using HRTF to represent an auditory scene through headphones in tele-operation applications. One is that when the operator moves his body or head, the auditory scene essentially rotates with the operator's movement. This effect may cause a decrease in the perceived sense of presence. In order to keep a natural auditory sensation, the virtual environment should stay fixed with a real world coordinate system instead of moving with the coordinate system inside the operator's head. In other words, the sound sources should be perceived as staying at the same places irrespective to the operator's movement.

The other problem of HRTF is front-back confusion, in which a frontal sound source is wrongly perceived as coming from behind or vice versa. In daily life, when people localize a sound, sometimes they move their head consciously or unconsciously to change the relative position of the sound. It is reported that people tend to move their head to help themselves for sound localization [18]. These movements effectively reduce the front-back error [19].

Accounting for the above issues, in this work we proposed a tele-presence system which is able to synthesize and manipulate the auditory scenes of a remote robot environment, matched with the operator's head orientation. For that purpose, the spatial information of sound sources are captured by using multiple microphone arrays and laser range finders in the robot environment, and synthesized with HRTFs properly selected according to the sound locations in the robot environment, with the coordinates rotated according the operator's head orientation. In addition, we designed three user interfaces for allowing augmented auditory scene control, and evaluated them through subjective experiments.

2. DESCRIPTION OF THE PROPOSED TELE-PRESENCE SYSTEM

The proposed system can be split in two parts, one for the remote robot environment side, and the other for the tele-operator side. The robot side corresponds to decomposition of individual sound sources with corresponding positions in the 3D space, while the operator side corresponds to synthesis and manipulation of the auditory scene matched with the operator's motions. The block diagrams of both sides are shown in Fig 1.

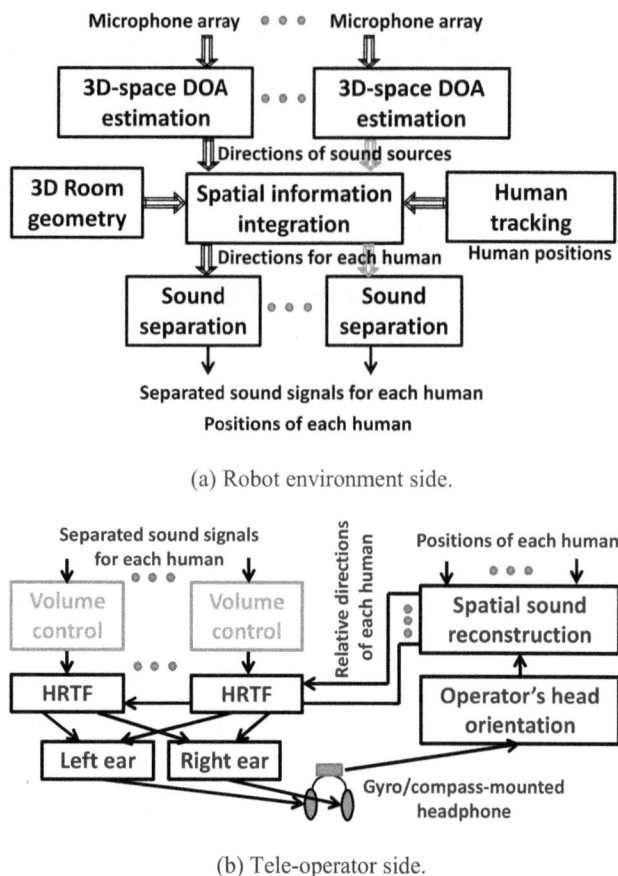

(a) Robot environment side.

(b) Tele-operator side.

Fig. 1 Block diagram of the proposed tele-presence system

In the first step for the robot side, the directions of arrival (DOA) of multiple sound sources are estimated in 3D space by multiple microphone arrays. Then, given the 3D room geometry information, the sound directions from all arrays are superimposed in the 3D space with the human positions provided by the human tracking. After integration of spatial information, the directions of the voice sources for each human are sent to the subsequent sound separation processing. Thanks to the human position information, uninterruptible estimations of the voice source positions can be used for improving separation performance.

In the next step, the voice sources of each human in the remote robot environment are separated by emphasizing the microphone array signals in the target voice directions provided by the 3D sound localization. The resulting separated sound signals and positions for each human are sent to the operator side.

In the operator side, the separated voices are filtered using Head Related Transfer Function (HRTF) database. In this work, a headphone is used for playback, therefore, head orientation tracking is required in order to reduce front-back errors (which is a weakness of HRTFs) and improving direction perception, and for compensating the operator's head movements for synthesizing auditory scenes.

The operator's head orientation is tracked by using gyro sensor and compass attached at the top of a headphone. Appropriate HRTFs are selected according to relative directions of the sound sources and the operator's head orientation for both ears from the

HRTF database. The output signals of all sound sources are summed up for each ear, and played in a stereo headphone.

Optional volume control can be conducted for each separated signal for augmented auditory scene manipulation. This option will be described in Section 4, by comparing different types of user interfaces for controlling the volume.

In the following sub-sections, we provide details about the system parts.

2.1 3D-space sound localization

The directions of arrival (DOA) of multiple sound sources are firstly estimated by multiple microphone arrays, and all sound source directions from each array are integrated along with the human position information for estimating the location of the sound (voice) sources in the 3D space.

2.1.1 3D-space DOA estimation

Locating sound sources in real-world environments is a problem that has been extensively studied so far. The DOA estimation in the present system is based on the MUltiple SIgnal Classification (MUSIC) algorithm, which is a widely used localization algorithm in array signal processing [20]. This method is based on subspace analysis, and is able to estimate directions of multiple sources with high angle resolution.

The MUSIC method has a constraint that the number of active sources at the moment has to be provided beforehand. Regarding this issue, we adopted the solution proposed in [21], where the number of sources is fixed (considering that the estimation of the number of sources is not robust), and peaks in the MUSIC spectrum exceeding a threshold are picked.

The implemented system can provide 3D-space DOA (i.e., azimuth and elevation angles) with 1 degree resolution, each 100 ms. Real-time processing is achieved by a single 2GHz CPU core.

2.1.2 3D localization of voice sources

In a tele-communication system, the most important sound source that the system should not miss is the human voice. A human tracking system was used in the proposed system to make sure that human positions are tracked continuously even when they are not speaking. In the present work, we employed a 2D human tracking system based on multiple 2D laser range finders (LRF) [22], which is able to provide human positions with accuracies around 5~10 cm, each 10~50 ms.

Given the 3D room geometry, including the positions and orientations of the microphone arrays, the sound directions estimated by each microphone array and the human positions obtained from the human tracking system are superimposed in the 3D space. In a previous work, we have developed methods for 3D localization of sounds based on multiple microphone arrays [23]. In the present work, we also make use of human position information for improving voice source localization, as described below.

The directions of the voice sources are then estimated for being used by the separation process. We consider that if the line drawn for a detected sound direction passes close to the mouth position of a detected human, it can be considered as corresponding to a voice activity of that human. However, the human tracking provides position information only in 2D space, so that information about the mouth height (z-coordinate of the voice source position) is missing. We then imposed some constraints on

the possible mouth height range from 1.0 to 1.6 m, considering the cases where a human is sitting or standing. Thus, the mouth height is estimated as the middle point in the shortest line between the lines drawn over a sound direction and a human position, if two conditions are satisfied: 1) the distance between the lines is smaller than 30 cm, and 2) the middle point is within the possible mouth height range (1.0 to 1.6 m). In intervals where the above condition is satisfied, the sound directions are sent to the sound separation block. In non-speech intervals or in intervals where the directivity was not high enough, the last computed mouth height and the current human positions are used to re-compute the directions relative to the array, which are sent to the sound separation block.

2.2 Sound separation

Parallel sound separation processes are conducted for all selected humans in the robot environment. In each separation process (for each human), the multi-channel signals of the microphone array closest to the human position are processed in a way to emphasize the sound coming from the voice direction.

2.2.1 Beamforming

For the sound separation processing in the present work, we adopted the widely used Delay-Sum (DS) beamforming technique [24], due to its robustness and low computational costs. Separation is conducted every 10 ms frames, with frame length of 20 ms. The beamforming was implemented in frequency domain, according to the expression:

$$Y_{DS}(f) = \sum_{m=1}^{M} \frac{a_{m,target}(f)}{a_{m,target}^{H}(f)a_{m,target}(f)} X(f) \qquad (1)$$

where M is the number of microphones, f is the frequency bin, $a_{m,target}$ is the position vector (transfer function representing delay and attenuation in each m-th microphone for a given target position), and X is multi-channel input spectrum, and Y is the separated signal spectrum.

2.2.2 Post-filtering

The separated signals after the DS beamforming have low separation performance mainly in low frequencies (below 1000Hz) due to constraints in the array geometry. As a consequence, high frequency noises are strongly attenuated, while low frequency noise components remain present in the separated signals. The design of a high-pass-like post-filter was then proposed in this work, in order to compensate for the low performance in low frequencies.

Assuming there is a directive target sound S and a non-directive noise N, when the DS beamformer is steered to the signal direction, the output will be following:

$$Y(f) = w_{Sdir}(f) \cdot S(f) + \int_{0}^{2\pi} (w_{\theta}(f) \cdot N(f)) d\theta \qquad (2)$$

where Y_f is the output of DS beamformer at frequency bin f, $Sdir$ is the direction of signal, and w_{Sdir} is the beamformer response on direction $Sdir$. The second term in expression (2) corresponds to the noise leaked into the separated signal. The noise level depends on the spatial response of the beamformer. To reduce the effects caused by different noise levels in different frequency bands, in this work, we proposed a weight w_{PF} to adjust the amplitude of the beamformer output at frequency f, as follows.

$$w_{PF}(f) = \frac{1}{\int_{0}^{2\pi} w_{\theta}(f) \, d\theta} \qquad (3)$$

$$Y_{PF} = \sum_f w_{PF}(f) \cdot Y_{DS}(f) \qquad (4)$$

where Y_{PF} is the output separated signal after post-filtering.

Further, in order to compensate for the differences in sound levels due to different distances between the microphone array and the voice sources, the amplitude of the output separated signals were normalized according to the following expressions.

$$g_i = \frac{\sum_{n=1}^{N} dist_n - dist_i}{(N-1) \cdot \sum_n^N dist_n} \qquad (5)$$

$$Y_i = g_i \cdot Y_{PF,i} \qquad (6)$$

where N is the number of separated sources, $dist_n$ is the distance between the array and the n-th source, g_i is the computed normalization factor for the i-th source, and Y_i is the separated signal for the i-th source after normalization, to be sent to the tele-operator side.

Finally, the separated sound signals (voices) for each human are sent by TCP/IP in frames of 10 ms length with a header containing time stamps (UNIX time in seconds and milliseconds), and the position of the human (three coordinate axes in millimeters).

2.3   HRTF-based synthesis of auditory scenes

A common way to synthesize a binaural sound that seems to come from a particular position in space is to filter the original sound signal by a pair of HRTFs for the two ears. The proposed system makes use of an open HRTF database, and synthesizes the auditory scene by compensating the operator's motion, as described in the following sub-sections.

2.3.1   HRTF Database

In the present work, we make use of the HRTF database of the KEMAR Dummy-Head measured by a research group at MIT media lab [25]. KEMAR (Knowles Electronics Manikin for Acoustic Research) is a standard based on common human anthropomorphic data and designed for making HRTF measurements. The KEMAR HRTF database describes the frequency response that results from a complex interaction of anatomically-based reflection and diffraction effects, in the KEMAR dummy-head for different sound source directions.

The database includes measurements consisted of head-related impulse response (HRIR, impulse response corresponding to the head related transfer function) for the left and right ears, performed on a KEMAR dummy-head at 710 different positions sampled at elevations from -40 degrees (40 degrees below the horizontal plane) to +90 degrees (directly overhead). Each HRIR was obtained at a sampling rate of 44.1 KHz, and has 512 samples.

2.3.2   Head orientation tracking and synthesis of auditory scenes

It was stated in the introduction that there are two problems when using HRTF to synthesize an auditory scene through headphones, without compensation for the operator's head and body movements. The first is the mismatch in the coordinates of the auditory scenes in the robot side, when the operator's head moves. The second is the front-back confusion.

To deal with these problems, a low latency head orientation tracking is needed. In this work, we attach a gyro sensor and a compass to the top of a headphone to track the rotation of the

operator's head. Head angles around the three axes are sent to the system either by serial port or by Bluetooth, each 10~20ms. In following experiments, we used serial connection to lower latency of transmission.

Once the operator's head orientation is received, this angle is subtracted from all voice source directions, to match the auditory scenes with the operator's movements. The system selects proper Head Related Impulse Responses (HRIR) from the HRTF database, corresponding to the matched voice source directions, and convolves each of the separated signals with the corresponding HRIRs. The output signals of all sound sources are summed up for each ear, and played in a stereo headphone.

3.   SYSTEM EVALUATION

The system evaluation in this section is divided in two parts. In Section 3.1, we first evaluate the effects of allowing head rotation on the perception of auditory scenes by using HRTFs. In Section 3.2, we evaluate the effects of the proposed system during interactions with humans in the robot environment.

3.1   Evaluation of head rotation for direction perception

We first conducted subjective experiments to evaluate the effects of allowing head rotation in sound direction perception, by using HRTFs.

Two separately recorded speech sounds were convolved with HRIRs selected based on two different directions and the orientation of operator's head (as described in Section 2.3.2), and then were played simultaneously to the operator's headphones. The two directions of the sounds were randomly selected from one of the following eight directions around the robot {0, 45, 90, 135, 180, 225, 270 and 315 degrees} (corresponding to North, Northeast, East, Southeast, South, Southwest, West and Northwest.)

Twenty subjects (college students not involved in robotics or acoustic research) participated in this experiment. They were asked to annotate the perceived direction where each sound comes from, given the eight directions above as options. The experiments were conducted for two conditions: allowing head rotation, or keeping the head orientation fixed.

Accuracy (%)

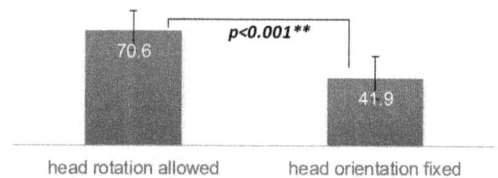

Front-back error (%)

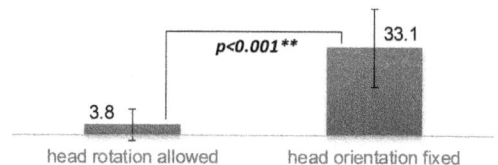

Fig. 2 Direction perception results for two conditions: "head rotation allowed" and "head orientation fixed".

We compared the accuracy rate of direction perception and front-back error rate, and conducted t-test on these comparisons. The top panel of Fig. 2 shows means and standard deviations of the resulted accuracy rates. We can observe that the accuracy rate of allowing head rotation was significantly higher than keeping the head orientation fixed ($t=1.70$, $p<0.001$).

The bottom panel of Fig. 2 shows the results for front-back error rates. It can be observed that the front-back error rate was significantly reduced ($t=-7.55$, $p<0.001$) by allowing head rotation for direction perception.

These results confirm that head rotation improves the perception of direction of sounds through binaural sounds synthesized by HRTFs.

3.2 Evaluation of the proposed system

Subjective experiments were conducted to evaluate the effectiveness of the proposed system during interactions with humans in the robot environment. As a baseline for comparison, we used binaural microphones located at both sides of the robot's head. These binaural microphones are referred as robot's "ears".

In this experiment, we used a humanoid robot which has two "ears". The Telenoid R3 (top-left picture of Fig. 3), which is a minimally-designed robot (i.e., it has a neutral face in terms of gender and age), was used in this experiment. It has a head rotatable around three independent axes and two microphones in both sides of head. Thus we can create 3D stereo sound sensation by playing the sound captured by the two microphones in each ear. For reproducing the head dynamics, operator's head movements are linearly mapped to the robot's head.

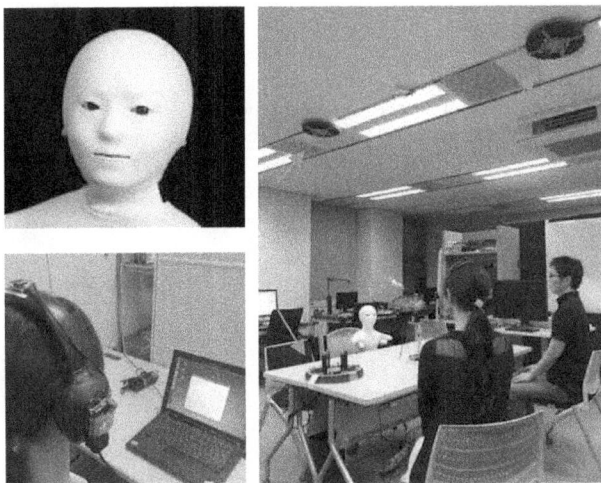

Fig. 3. External appearance of the Telenoid R3 (top left), operator environment (bottom left) and the robot environment where interaction experiments were conducted (right).

The bottom-left picture of Fig. 3 shows the operator environment, and the right picture of Fig. 3 shows the robot environment where the interaction experiments were conducted. The 3D sound direction estimation was conducted in the three microphone arrays, indicated by the red arrows in Fig. 3. The array on the table is 16-channel with the microphones (SONY ecm-c10) arranged over a semi-sphere of 30 cm diameter, while the two attached in the ceilings are 8-channel each, with circular shape with 15 cm diameter. The array on the table was used for sound separation.

Twenty subjects participated in the experiment. The subjects are the same of the previous experiment.

Subjects were asked to talk to one experimenter (a research assistant) in the robot environment side while tele-operating the robot. The experimenter moved to four different directions randomly during the conversation, and subjects had to estimate which direction his conversation partner was in, without visual information. Answer options were restricted to eight directions around the robot position (as in the previous experiment).

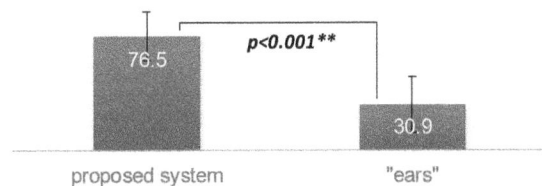

Subjective scores were also collected through the following questionnaire, after the conversation. Each question was answered by a 1 to 7 scale where 1 represents worst and 7 stands for best.

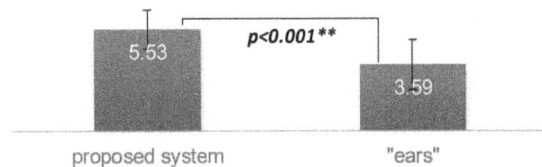

➢ **Perceived degree of sense of presence.**

➢ **Perceived degree of listenability**

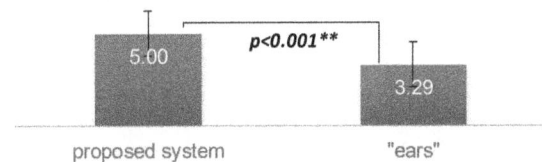

The top panel of Fig. 4 shows means and standard deviations of the accuracy rates for direction perception, for the proposed system and the robot's "ears". A t-test was conducted and showed a significant difference between the two conditions ($t=9.59$, $p < 0.001$).

Similar trends were found for sense of presence and listenability. The middle and bottom panels of Fig. 4 show means and standard deviations of subjective scores for the perceived sense of presence and perceived listenability. In both comparisons, the subjective scores for the proposed system were significantly higher than simply using the robot's "ears" ($t=6.68$, $p < 0.001$ and $t=4.86$, $p<0.001$).

Fig. 4. Accuracy rates for direction perception and subjective scores (1 to 7 scale) for sense of presence and listenability, in two conditions: "proposed system" and "robot's ears".

It is easy to understand the differences in perceived listenability between the proposed system and the robot's "ears" since the sound obtained by build-in microphones are susceptible to motor noise inside the robot and consequently results in a lower signal-to-noise ratio. Regarding the difference for accuracy rate and perceived sense of presence, one possible reason is that the movable range of robot's head is different from human neck. The robot's head could hit its maximum angle while the operator is still rotating his head. This causes a mismatch between the human operator and the robot's head orientation. Another reason is that the "ears" have no earlobes, so that front-back perception is poor.

4. AUGMENTED AUDITORY SCENE CONTROL

The stereo sound output of the system is a mixed-up of all humans observed and selected by the human tracker. However, there is no guarantee that the voice level of every human is suitable, since for example, some can speak louder than others. In these cases, it is desirable that the operator is able to adjust the sound volumes of each human in the environment. Further, the operator may desire to (virtually) approach to one of the humans, even though the robot cannot (physically) move.

In order to allow the control of 3D auditory effects, including the virtual placement of the operator, three types of user interfaces were designed and evaluated.

4.1 Description of the proposed user interfaces for augmented auditory scene control

Three types of user interfaces were proposed taking into account different manners to control the manipulation of auditory scenes in the robot's environment.

In the first one, the user can control the sound level of each person (detected by the human tracker) independently. The left panel of Fig. 5 shows a screen shot of this user interface, where humans are shown as circles and the operator (in this case, the position of the robot) is shown as a circle with a pink arc representing the current head orientation. In this user interface, the operator can adjust the volume of a target person by clicking on the human circle corresponding to that person and scrolling the mouse wheel upward/downward for increasing/decreasing the volume. Double-clicking one of the human circles can maximize the volume of that person and minimize the volume of the others. This user interface is denoted as "scroll". The volume levels for each human are shown inside the human circles, as shown in the figure.

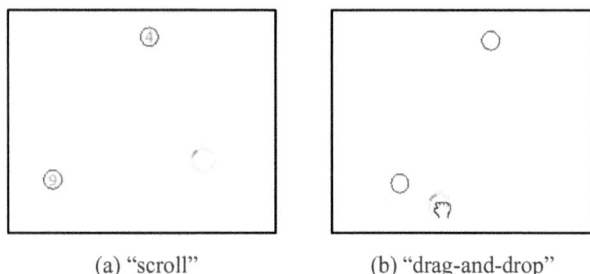

(a) "scroll"   (b) "drag-and-drop"

Fig. 5. Screen shots of the displays for different user interfaces.

In the second one, the operator's position can be changed by drag-and-drop the operator's circle to a desired position (virtual robot position). We commonly keep a distance between ourselves and the conversation partner depending on the environment and the

social relationship. However, in the present user interface, the user can virtually approach to a target person as to maximize the volume of his/her voice. The sound volumes and sound directions are re-computed according to the new relative positions between the robot and the humans (after drag-and-drop). This user interface is denoted as "drag and drop". The right panel of Fig. 5 shows a screen shot for this user interface.

In the third one, the sound volumes of the sound sources are adjusted according to the operator's head orientation. It is well-known that head orientation and gaze direction signals individuals' attention, upcoming target or goal [26][27]. In order to free the operator's hands, we employed head orientation as a tool for sound volume adjustment. Sound sources in front of the operator are amplified while opposite ones are attenuated. The amplifier was designed to be linearly related to the angle between the sound source and the operator's head orientation. A maximum attenuation factor of 0.6 was attributed for the opposite direction. This user interface is denoted as "face dir". The display of this user interface is similar to the "scroll" one, as shown in Fig. 5.

4.2 Evaluation of the proposed user interfaces

We conducted subjective experiments to evaluate the three user interfaces. A conventional interface using a monaural microphone was also evaluated for comparison.

Sixteen subjects participated in this experiment. The subjects are the same of the previous experiments, excluding four of them who did not conduct the comparison with the conventional one. Within participants design was used in this experiment. Subjects were asked to talk to two persons (research assistants) through the tele-presence system. The conversation topics were free. The conversations were separated in four sessions, one for each of the user interfaces (including the conventional one). Each session of conversation lasted about three minutes. After every session, subjects were asked to annotate the perceived degrees of usability, sense of presence, and listenability for each condition. The subjective scores were quantified by a 1 to 7 scale (as in the previous experiments).

Fig. 6 shows the means and standard deviations of the subjective scores. A repeated measures analysis of variance (ANOVA, Bonferroni's posttest) was conducted for each item. Significant effects were found in "usability" and "sense of presence" ($F(3,13)=10.041$, $p=0.001$ and $F(3,13)=8.777$, $p=0.002$) Regarding listenability, the main effect was not significant ($F(3,13)=3.869$, $p=0.068$).

Comparing the usability for the four conditions, the subjective scores of two of the proposed user interfaces, "drag and drop" and "face dir", were significantly higher than the conventional one (*"drag and drop" vs. "conventional": p=0.002, "face amp" vs. "conventional": p=0.002*). No significant difference was observed between condition "scroll" and "conventional" (*p=0.33*).

Similarly, comparison of sense of presence shows the same trends of usability. Condition "drag & drop" and "face dir" are perceived to provide significantly better sense of presence (*"drag and drop" vs. "conventional": p=0.002, "face dir" vs. "conventional": p=0.002*). Comparison between conditions "scroll" and "conventional" shows no significant difference (*P=0.22*).

However, regarding the subjective scores for listenalibity, the comparison results show no significant difference between all pairs of conditions (*"scroll" vs. "conventional": p=1, "drag and drop" vs. "conventional": p=0.22, "face dir" vs. "conventional": p=0.15).*

Subjective score

Usability

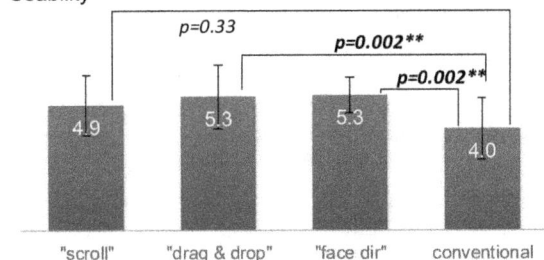

Sense of Presence

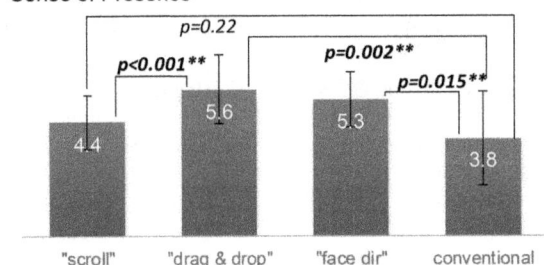

Listenability

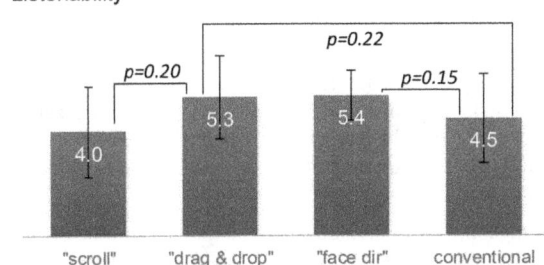

Fig. 6. Subjective scores (1 to 7 scale) for four types of user interface: "scroll", "drag and drop", "face dir" and "conventional".

The results above indicate that the interfaces "drag and drop" and "face dir" are effective user interfaces for tele-presence systems, for improving both usability and sense of presence.

4.3   Discussion

The results of the experiment described in this section showed that the subjective scores for both usability and sense of presence for the "scroll" interface were lower than in "drag and drop" and "face dir" interfaces, and showed no significant differences compared to the conventional one. In the interview with the subjects after the experiment, most subjects answered that the operation in interface "scroll" was more complicated than the others. When the operator needs to adjust the sound volume, he/she can drag the circle representing the operator/robot and approach to the circle representing the target sound source using "drag & drop" interface, or simply turn his/her head and face to the target sound sources. However, when using "scroll" interface, the operator needs to first select the target circle and then scroll the mouse wheel to adjust the sound volume, and repeat this process on the other sound sources. This complication is thought to be a potential cause for lower scores in usability and sense of presence.

It is also interesting to note that the subjective scores for sense of presence were the highest for "drag and drop" interface, where the operator virtually changes his/her position, even though the physical robot position was unaltered.

Regarding the listenability scores, although higher mean values were obtained for "drag and drop" and "face dir", the differences with the conventional one were not judged to be significant. A possible reason is that the number of sound sources in the robot environment was not high, so that the speech contents were listenable even in the conventional system. We guess that the subjective scores would change if more sound sources are in the environment. This is a topic for future investigation.

Finally, regarding the use of the generic HRTFs from a dummy-head in the experiments, possible improvements can still be reached if the HRTFs can be adapted to each user.

5.   CONCLUSION

We proposed and evaluated a tele-presence system which is able to synthesize and manipulate the auditory scene of a communication robot, and increase the auditory sense of presence by the tele-operator.

Subjective experiments were conducted where participants played the role of the tele-operator and talked to others through a remote humanoid robot. It was firstly confirmed that by the reproduction of auditory scenes matched with the operator's head orientation reduced front-back error and improved the perceived localization of sounds. In the interaction experiments with humans in the robot environment, the proposed system was shown to perform with higher accuracy in localization, and higher subjective scores for sense of presence and listenability, compared to the use of binaural microphones attached to robot's head ("ears").

Three types of user interfaces with ability to control virtual auditory scenes were also proposed and evaluated. Higher subjective scores for usability and sense of presence were obtained by two of the interface types compared to a conventional (monaural) tele-operation system. The two preferred interfaces were: "drag and drop", which allows the operator to change his/her virtual position in order to amplify the voice of the humans close to the virtual position, and "face dir", which amplifies the voices in the frontal direction and attenuates the voices from back direction.

6.   ACKNOWLEDGMENTS

This work was supported by JST/CREST. The development of the 3D localization was partly supported by MIC/SCOPE. We thank Mika Morita and Kyoko Nakanishi for their contributions in the experiments.

7.   REFERENCES

[1] Nishio, S., Ishiguro, H., Hagita, N. Can a Teleoperated Android Represent Personal Presence? - A Case Study with Children. *Psychologia*, 50(4): 330-342. 2007.

[2] Ishi, C.T., Liu, C., Ishiguro, H., Hagita, N. 2010. Head motion during dialogue speech and nod timing control in humanoid robots. *In Proceedings of 5th ACM/IEEE International Conference on Human-Robot Interaction (HRI 2010)*. OSAKA, JAPAN. 293-300.

[3] Liu, C., Ishi, C. T., Ishiguro, H., Hagita, N. Generation of nodding, head tilting and eye gazing for human-robot dialogue interaction. *In Proceeding of ACM/IEEE*

International Conference on Human Robot Interaction (HRI 2012). Boston, USA. 285-292, March, 2012.

[4] Sumioka, H., Nishio, S., Minato, T., Yamazaki, R., Ishiguro, H. Minimal Human Design Approach for Sonzai-kan Media: Investigation of a Feeling of Human Presence. Cognitive Computation, 2014.

[5] Popescu, V. G., Burdea, G. C., Bouzit, M., Hentz, V. R. A virtual-reality-based telerehabilitation system with force feedback. *IEEE transactions on Information Technology in Biomedicine*. 4(1): 45-51. 2000.

[6] Piron, L., Turolla, A., Agostini, M., Zucconi, C., Cortese, F., Zampolini, M., Zannini, M., Dam, M., Ventura, L., Battauz, M., Tonin, P. Exercises for paretic upper limb after stroke: a combined virtual-reality and telemedicine approach. *J. of Rehabilitation Medicine*. 41(12): 1016-1020(5). 2009.

[7] Billinghurst, M., Cheok, A., Prince, S., Kato, H. Real world teleconferencing. *IEEE Computer Graphics and Applications*. 22(6): 11-13. 2002.

[8] Ogi, T., Yamada, T., Tamagawa, K., Kano, M. Immersive telecommunication using stereo video avatar. *Proceedings of Ieee Virtual Reality*. Yokohama, Japan. 45-51. 2001

[9] Bullinger, H., Riedel, O., Breining, R. Immersive Projection Technology- Benefits for the Industry, *International Immersive Projection Technology Workshop*, 13-25, 1997.

[10] Pulkki, V. Spatial sound reproduction with directional audio coding. *J. Audio Eng. Soc.* 55(6): 503-516. 2007

[11] Laitinen, M., Kuech, F., Disch, S., Pulkki, V. Reproducing applause-type signals with directional audio coding. *J. Audio Eng. Soc.* 59(1/2): 29-43. 2011.

[12] Nishiura, T., Yamada, T., Nakamura, S., Shikano, K. Localization of multiple sound sources based on a CSP analysis with a microphone array. *Proceeding of ICASSP 2000*. Istanbul. II1053-1056 vol.2. 2000.

[13] Khalil, F., Jullien, J. P., Gilloire, A. Microphone array for sound pickup in teleconference systems. *J. Audio Eng. Soc.* 42(9): 691-700. 1994.

[14] Hamalainen, M., Myllyla, V. Acoustic Echo Cancellation for dynamically steered microphone array system. 2007. *IEEE Workshop on Applications of Signal Processing to Audio and Acoustics*. New Paltz, NY, USA. 58-61. 2007.

[15] Rumsey, F. *Spatial Audio*. Focal Press, 2001.

[16] Meyer, E., Neumann, E. *Physical and Applied Acoustics: An Introduction*. Academic Press, New York, 1972. ISBN 0124931502.

[17] Cheng, C. I., Wakefield, G. H. Introduction to head-related transfer functions (hrtfs): Representations of hrtfs in time, frequency, and space. *J. Acoust. Soc. Am,* 49(4):231-249, April 2001.

[18] Iwaya, Y., Suzuki, Y., Kimura, D. Effects of head movement on front-back error in sound localization. *Acoustical Science and Technology*. 24(5): 322-324. 2003.

[19] Perret, S., Noble, W. The effect of head rotations on vertical plane sound localization. *J. Acoust. Soc. Am.* 102(4): 2325-2332. 1997.

[20] Schmidt, R. Multiple emitter location and signal parameter estimation. *IEEE Transactions on Antennas and Propagation,* 34, 276-280, 1986.

[21] Ishi, C. T., Chatot, O., Ishiguro, H., Hagita, N. Evaluation of a MUSIC-based real-time sound localization of multiple sound sources in real noisy environments. *In Proceeding of IEEE/RSJ International Conference on Intelligent Robots and Systems (IROS 09)*. St. Louis, MO, USA. 2027–2032. 2009.

[22] Glas, D.F. et al, 2007. Laser tracking of human body motion using adaptive shape modeling. In Proceedings of the *IEEE/RSJ International Conference on Intelligent Robots and Systems (IROS 2007)*, 602-608. 2007.

[23] Ishi, C., Even, J., Hagita, N. (2013). Using multiple microphone arrays and reflections for 3D localization of sound sources. In Proc. *IEEE/RSJ International Conference on Intelligent Robots and Systems (IROS 2013)*, 3937-3942, Nov., 2013.

[24] Dudgeon, D. E. Fundamentals of digital array processing. *Proceedings of the IEEE*. 65(6): 898-904. 1977.

[25] Gardner, W. G., Martin, K. D. HRTF measurements of a KEMAR. *J. Acoust. Soc. Am.* 97(6):3907-3908, Jun. 1995.

[26] Langton, S. R., Watt, R. J., Bruce, I. I. Do the eyes have it? Cues to the direction of social attention. *Trends Cog. Sci.* 4, 50–59, 2000.

[27] Yokoyama, T., Noguchi, Y. Kita, S. Attentional shifts by gaze direction in voluntary orienting: evidence from a microsaccade study. *Exp. Brain Res.* 223, 291–300, 2012.

Environment Perception in the Presence of Kinesthetic or Tactile Guidance Virtual Fixtures

Samuel B. Schorr
Stanford University
450 Serra Mall
Stanford, CA 94305
sschorr@stanford.edu

Zhan Fan Quek
Stanford University
450 Serra Mall
Stanford, CA 94305
zfquek@stanford.edu

William R. Provancher
University of Utah
50 S. Central Campus Dr,
2110 MEB
Salt Lake City, Utah 84112
wil@mech.utah.edu

Allison M. Okamura
Stanford University
450 Serra Mall
Stanford, CA 94305
aokamura@stanford.edu

ABSTRACT

During multi-lateral collaborative teleoperation, where multiple human or autonomous agents share control of a teleoperation system, it is important to be able to convey individual user intent. One option for conveying the actions and intent of users or autonomous agents is to provide force guidance from one user to another. Under this paradigm, forces would be transmitted from one user to another in order to guide motions and actions. However, the use of force guidance to convey intent can mask environmental force feedback. In this paper we explore the possibility of using tactile feedback, in particular skin deformation feedback, skin deformation feedback to convey collaborative intent while preserving environmental force perception. An experiment was performed to test the ability of participants to use force guidance and skin deformation guidance to follow a path while interacting with a virtual environment. In addition, we tested the ability of participants to discriminate virtual environment stiffness when receiving either force guidance or skin deformation guidance. We found that skin deformation guidance resulted in a reduction of path-following accuracy, but increased the ability to discriminate environment stiffness when compared with force feedback guidance.

Categories and Subject Descriptors

H.1.2 [**Models and Principles**]: User/Machine Systems—*Human information processing*; H.5.2 [**Information Interfaces and Presentation**]: User Interfaces—*Haptic I/O*

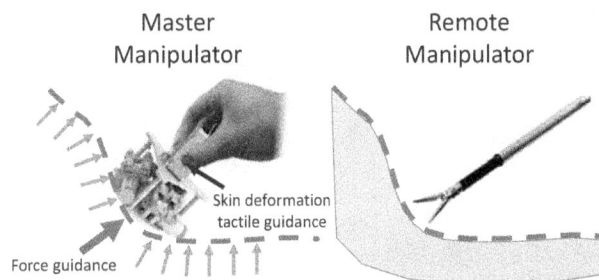

Figure 1: Virtual fixtures can provide physical assistance in collaborative teleoperation systems. A virtual fixture could be used to help guide the human to stay within a specific region, or follow a path. While these virtual fixtures are usually applied with *force guidance*, *skin deformation tactile guidance* could allow for the display of virtual fixture information while preserving environmental force feedback.

Keywords

Skin deformation; skin stretch; virtual fixtures; stiffness discrimination; haptics

1. INTRODUCTION

Teleoperation enables users to perform tasks that they may not be able to perform otherwise, through capabilities such as remote manipulation, motion scaling, and tremor reduction. When performing tasks together in physical presence of each other, humans are able to collaborate effectively, determining the intentions of partners and helping each other to accomplish their objectives. The goal of this work is to improve human operator cooperation with other humans or autonomous agents in teleoperated scenarios.

One way of conveying collaborative intent is through the use of virtual fixtures. Virtual fixtures are algorithms that can assist during collaborative tasks by providing force guidance. These active constraints can guide the human user along specific paths, or limit user interaction to specific regions of the workspace as shown in Fig. 1. In a teleoperator, these virtual fixtures are frequently implemented through the use of forces that act on the user's master manipulator. In this way, the feedback from the slave manipulator can be augmented with the virtual fixture, modifying the user's actions. However, virtual fixture force augmentation could confound environment force perception when implemented in a bilateral teleoperator, where perception of environmental force information is important for exploration and discrimination. Information is lost when guidance from a virtual fixture and environment force feedback are superimposed and rendered to the user, as the human operator cannot perceive the individual force components.

One possible alternative to force feedback for communicating agent intent is the use of tactile cues, such as skin deformation. Prior research has shown that skin deformation cues are useful for conveying force information [17]. In this case, tactile cues could be used to convey virtual fixture feedback while kinesthetic force feedback is used to convey environmental forces. Separation of feedback modalities could help retain and convey more information when compared to superimposing these two information sources with force feedback.

2. BACKGROUND

2.1 Virtual Fixtures

Guidance virtual fixtures provide assistance towards movement on a specific path. These paths can be used to guide precise trajectories and avoid collisions with delicate portions of the workspace [1]. Virtual fixtures have been found to improve the speed and precision of certain tasks, and can reduce the necessary training for novice operators [16]. Navkar et al. found that implementation of haptic and visual guidance virtual fixtures resulted in an improvement of control and manipulation in a simulated transapical aortic valve replacement [13]. One crucial problem with force guidance in a teleoperated setting is that the forces from the guidance must be superimposed with the forces from the environmental force feedback. It is unclear what effect this can have on exploratory tasks where environmental perception is important. Nisky et al. showed that even small time delays can cause clear gaps between motormetric and cognitive perception [14].

Despite the many potential advantages of haptic virtual fixtures, their implementation may cause difficulties with environmental perception and motor learning. Some studies have shown that participants assisted by force guidance virtual fixtures during training did not perform as well as participants that controlled their own movement during training once the guidance force was removed [2], [3].

2.2 Skin Deformation Feedback

Tactile skin deformation feedback emulates the tactile stimulation present during natural interactions, providing lateral and normal skin deformation. Tactor elements (contact points designed to move relative to the skin) against the skin are actuated to provide either tangential or normal skin displacement. Devices designed to give skin deformation tactile cues have been used for a variety of purposes such as force feedback, navigation, and proprioception augmentation. Several studies have shown the effectiveness of skin deformation on the fingerpads for conveying force information in haptic environments, both in 1-DOF [18] and 3-DOF

[17]. Additionally, previous work has shown the effectiveness of skin stretch for conveying directional information [7], [8] and more recently, the use of back-to-back 2-DOF tactors has been shown to effectively convey 5-DOF directional cues [9].

The effectiveness of skin deformation cues for conveying directional information and force information leads us to believe that skin deformation would be useful for conveying force guidance information that is normally implemented through kinesthetic force feedback. While the use of skin deformation guidance may cause a loss of accuracy compared to force guidance when used to assist in path following, we hypothesize that it will be better than no guidance and allow for better perception of environmental forces.

3. METHODS

3.1 Device Design and Control

The apparatus used in this paper consisted of a Force Dimension Omega.3 haptic device for conveying force information with an attached custom-built skin deformation device for conveying tactile information. The Omega.3 is used to render kinesthetic forces from a virtual environment, determine the user's position in space, and render force virtual fixtures during certain parts of the experiment. The skin deformation device provides tactile feedback to the user based on the implementation of tactile virtual fixtures.

The skin deformation device allows the use of precision grip, emulating the grip used when holding a manual tool. The device is small and relatively light weight (about 260 g) to enable attachment to existing kinesthetic force feedback haptic devices. Due to the desired compact size and high mechanical stiffness, we chose to use a Delta parallel mechanism design which has well understood kinematics and control [11].

Fig. 2 shows the skin deformation device, driven by three Faulhaber 1516 DC-micromotors with a 141:1 gear ratio. The position of the device stage is determined through encoders on each of the motors. Three skin deformation tactors, rubber Lenovo Trackpoint Classic dome tactors with a rounded surface and a rough sandpaper-like texture, are attached to the end-effector stage of the Delta parallel mechanism. A housing mounted to the base of the Delta mechanism has three circular aperture openings, one for each of the tactors. These apertures provide a surface for the user to hold while manipulating the device. The apertures ground the fingers while the end-effector and attached tactors move within them as shown in Fig.3. As the tactors move tangentially to the skin, friction between the tactors and skin causes lateral skin stretch. Tactor movement normal to the skin causes normal skin deformation. In order to verify the kinematic control of the skin deformation device, we measured the commanded versus actual end-effector position using the Force Dimension Omega.3. The end-effector of the device was commanded from the zero position, to the 2 mm position, to the -2 mm, and back to the zero position. During this pattern, the maximum error in the commanded direction was 0.25 mm.

This device design is similar to the one presented in a previous work [17], but includes several notable improvements. In order to ensure sufficient grip strength to ground the fingers on the aperture housing, an ATI Nano-17 force sensor located within the aperture housing measures the grip force

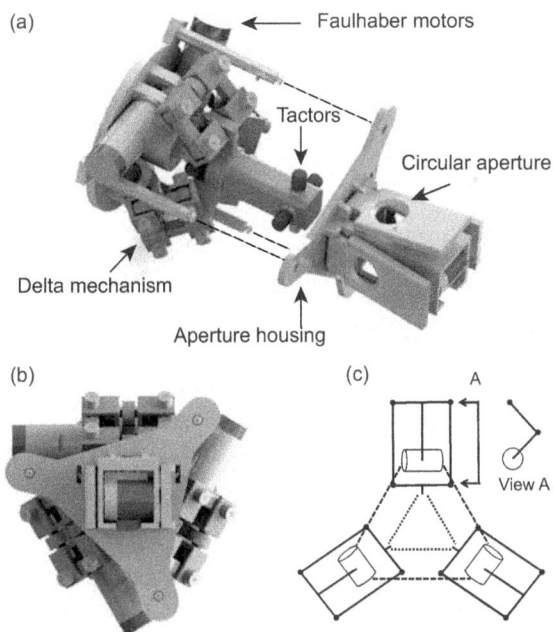

Figure 2: 3-DOF skin deformation tactile device(a) Separated Delta parallel mechanism and aperture housing. The tactors protrude from the circular apertures to contact the user fingerpads. (b) Top-down view of assembled skin deformation device. (c) Kinematic illustration of the parallel mechanism.

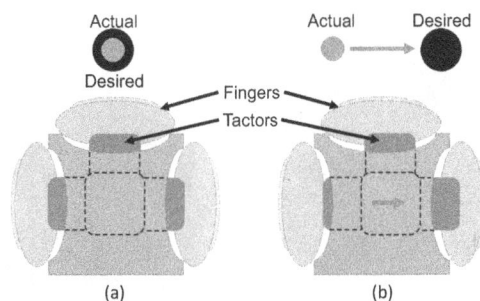

Figure 3: (a) Tactors protrude from the skin deformation device apertures and contact the fingerpads. When the user position and desired position are the same, the tactors are centered and unmoving. (b) When the user position and desired position are different, the tactors move against the skin to create a sensation of "pushing" in the desired direction.

of users on the device. This force is transmitted through a lever on the aperture housing. The device described in this paper uses DC motors rather than RC servos for actuation, and a force sensor is included to ensure sufficient grip force throughout the experiment. In order to better match the individual device needs of each participant, we also used interchangeable apertures, similar to those used in [18]. For participants with an index fingerpad width of less than 14 mm, we used a 10 mm aperture to ensure that their fingers could successfully be grounded on the apertures. Participants with an index fingerpad width of greater than 14 mm used a 12 mm aperture.

3.2 Experiment Description

3.2.1 Participants

A total of 10 participants (6 males and 4 females) between the ages of 22 and 28 participated in the experiment after giving informed consent, under a protocol that was approved by the University Institutional Review Board. 8 of the 10 participants had moderate to extensive experience with haptic devices, and 5 of them had previously used a skin deformation device. All of the participants were self-reported right-hand dominant.

3.2.2 Experiment task

There were dual objectives for the experiment structure. We wanted to measure participant path following ability under force and skin deformation guidance, but we also wanted to test participants' ability to perceive environmental force information in the presence of each guidance method using a forced-choice paradigm and the method of constant stimuli [5]. In order to do this, main experiment trials consisted of two path following reaches.

Participants performed reaches by holding onto the end-effector of the skin deformation device, that was in turn attached to the end-effector of the Omega.3 force-feedback haptic device. By moving the hand, participants attempted to follow paths similar to the one shown in Fig. 4. The paths were generated and rendered using CHAI3D [4]. The path consists of one period of a sinusoid, starting at a green circle and ending at a red circle. The path was visible during initial training sections for each guidance method, but was not visible during the main experiment trials. While the fundamental shape, start, and end points stayed consistent, the amplitude of each part of the sinusoid changed from trial to trial to prevent the subjects from learning the path.

These virtual paths intersected a virtual wall in a specific part of the workspace. The stiffness of the virtual wall intersecting the guidance path changed between the two reaches of each trial. During one of the reaches, the virtual wall had a reference stiffness of 120 N/m. During the other reach, the virtual wall took on a comparison stiffness of 30, 70, 100, 120, 140, 170, or 210 N/m. The stiffnesses and path amplitudes were presented in balanced, predetermined, pseudo-random order, and there were two trials of each comparison value for a total of 56 trials for each feedback method. After performing the pair of path reaches with either force or skin deformation guidance, participants were asked to chose which surface was stiffer.

The path that participants attempted to follow, $\vec{p}_{\text{path}}$, was defined by

$$\vec{p}_{\text{path}} = \begin{bmatrix} x_{\text{path}} \\ y_{\text{path}} \\ z_{\text{path}} \end{bmatrix} = \begin{cases} \begin{bmatrix} A_1 \sin(\frac{2\pi}{0.12}) \\ y_{\text{act}} \\ 0 \end{bmatrix}, & y_{\text{act}} \leq 0.06 \text{ m} \\ \begin{bmatrix} A_2 \sin(\frac{2\pi}{0.12}) \\ y_{\text{act}} \\ 0 \end{bmatrix}, & y_{\text{act}} > 0.06 \text{ m} \end{cases} \quad (1)$$

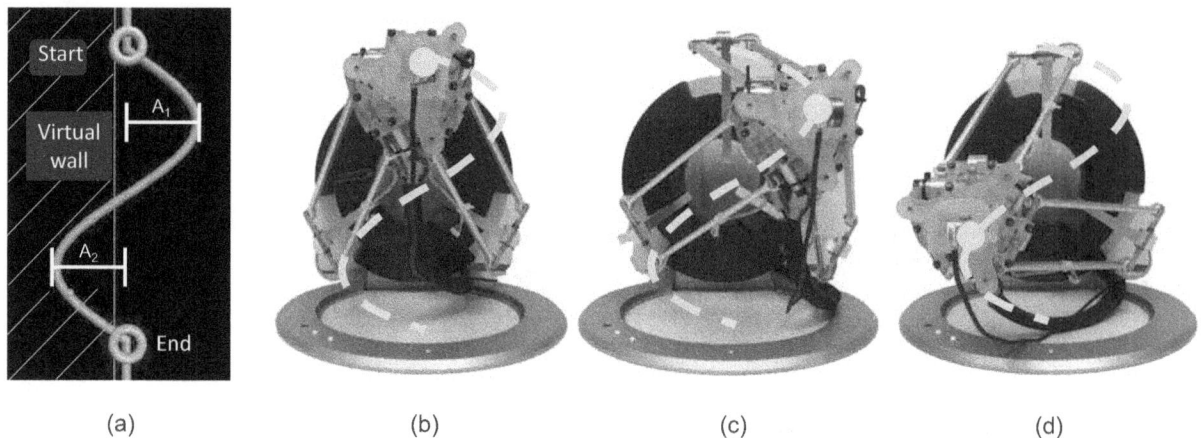

Figure 4: (a) An example of the virtual environment presented to the participants. Participants started their reach by entering at the green circle, following the sinusoidal path (of amplitudes changing each trial), and ended at the red circle. The red dashed region represents the virtual wall that the path passed through. (b) Skin deformation device attached to the Omega.3. (c) Following the sinusoidal path. (d) Continuing to follow the path. At this position, the user would have been receiving path following guidance and feeling the virtual wall.

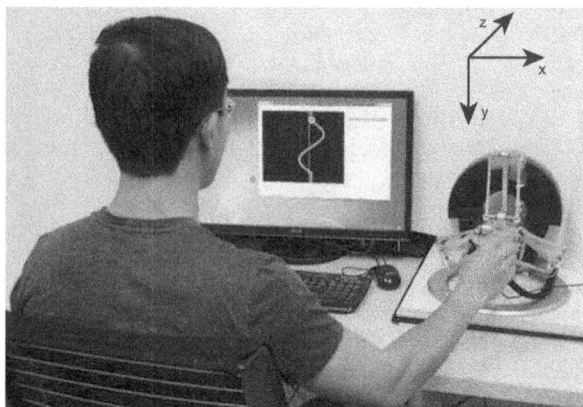

Figure 5: Experimental setup showing the Omega.3 with attached skin deformation device and the visual display. During actual experiment trials, the path was not visible.

where A_1 and A_2 are the amplitudes of the free space and wall intersection portions of the path, respectively, and y_{act} is the vertical position of the participant hand and Omega.3 end-effector. During the experiment, A_1 values were 0.02 or 0.04 m and A_2 values were 0.02, 0.0267, 0.0333 or 0.04 m. The participant motions were restricted to the plane of the path by utilizing a 3000 N/m virtual wall rendered by the Omega.3 at all times. In practice, the Omega.3 felt similar to a device kinematically limited to a 2-DOF plane.

The participant pose is shown in Fig. 5. Participants started following the path by passing through the green circle at the top of the screen. As the participants moved downward, horizontal force feedback or skin deformation guidance provided assistance using a forbidden region virtual fixture. While following the path, a red circle indicated the ending position. Participants were instructed to complete the

reaches in 2 to 6 seconds and were prompted to adjust their reaches to be slower or faster if they were outside of those bounds.

Under the force feedback guidance condition, the force rendered to the user as they deviate from the path was

$$\vec{F}_{guide} = \begin{bmatrix} k_{guide}(x_{path} - x_{act}) & 0 & 0 \end{bmatrix}^T, \qquad (2)$$

where F_{guide} is the force rendered by the Omega.3 haptic device, $k_p = 220$ N/m is the gain of the force guidance, and x_{path} and x_{act} are the desired and actual x-positions of the Omega.3 end-effector. Prior work has shown the guidance gain of 220 N/m to be the minimum stiffness that results in maximum performance for object detection [15] and was chosen to ensure that participants could easily follow and interpret the guidance. In this force feedback condition, the skin deformation tactors remained in the center of the circular apertures.

Under the skin deformation guidance condition, no force is rendered by the Omega.3 and the tactors on the skin deformation device move according to

$$\vec{x}_s = k_s \vec{F}_{guide}, \qquad (3)$$

where $\vec{x}_s$ is the movement in mm of the skin deformation device end-effector (and therefore tactors) in the x-direction, and $k_s = 0.75 mm/N$ is the ratio of tactor motion to guidance force ratio. This gain falls within the range of skin deformation feedback gains explored in [18].

3.2.3 Experiment structure

We began the experiment by explaining to the participants how to grip the skin deformation device. A visual display of grip force was presented on a bar graph and turned green when participants gripped with sufficient force. This provided an easy method for them to monitor their grip force throughout the experiment. Participants were instructed to follow the virtual path as accurately as possible, but to respond to speed prompts if they received them (for taking less than two seconds or more than six seconds).

	Block	Type	# of trials	Path Visible?	Wall Active?	Guidance #1	Guidance #2
General Training	Block 1	Single Reaches	5	Yes	No	No	No
	Block 2	Single Reaches	5	Yes	Yes	No	No
Guidance Part 1 Training	Block 3	Single Reaches	5	Yes	Yes	Yes	No
	Block 4	Single Reaches	5	No	Yes	Yes	No
	Block 5	Comparison Reaches	5	No	Yes	Yes	No
Experiment Part 1	**Block 6**	**Comparison Reaches**	**56**	**No**	**Yes**	**Yes**	**No**
Guidance Part 2 Training	Block 7	Single Reaches	5	Yes	Yes	No	Yes
	Block 8	Single Reaches	5	No	Yes	No	Yes
	Block 9	Comparison Reaches	5	No	Yes	No	Yes
Experiment Part 2	**Block 10**	**Comparison Reaches**	**56**	**No**	**Yes**	**No**	**Yes**

Table 1: **Structure of the experiment protocol. Participants proceeded through a general training segment, then completed a training and experiment section for each feedback method. Half of the participants performed the force guidance trials first, and half of them performed the skin deformation trials first.**

Then, each participant progressed to the first block of the experiment. The experiment was broken up into 10 experiment blocks described in Table. 1. In between each block, the conditions of the next block were described. During training trials, we attempted to slowly build up the structure of experiment trials in order to keep from overwhelming the participants. During the guidance and main experiment sections, participants received either kinesthetic force or tactile skin deformation guidance. Half of the participants received the force guidance first and skin deformation guidance second, and the remaining half received skin deformation guidance first and force guidance second.

In both experimental conditions, the path intersected an environment virtual wall that took on stiffness values of 30, 70, 100, 120, 140, 170, or 210 N/m. The force rendered by the virtual wall based on penetration depth was

$$\vec{F}_{\text{wall}} = \begin{cases} \begin{bmatrix} k_{\text{wall}}(x_{\text{wall}} - x_{\text{act}}) & 0 & 0 \end{bmatrix}^T, & x_{\text{act}} < x_{\text{wall}} \\ \begin{bmatrix} 0 & 0 & 0 \end{bmatrix}^T, & x_{\text{act}} \geq x_{\text{wall}} \end{cases} \quad (4)$$

where $\vec{F}_{\text{wall}}$ is the force rendered by the wall, k_{wall} is the stiffness of the virtual wall, $x_{\text{wall}} = -0.005$ m is the x-position of the wall, and $\vec{x}_{\text{act}}$ is the position of the manipulator end-effector.

While receiving force guidance and interacting with kinesthetic virtual wall, the total force rendered by the Omega.3 was $\vec{F}_{\text{wall}} + \vec{F}_{\text{guide}}$ and no skin deformation was rendered. When under the skin deformation guidance condition, the kinesthetic force rendered by the Omega.3 was $\vec{F}_{\text{wall}}$ and the skin deformation rendered was $\vec{x}_{\text{s}} = k_{\text{s}}\vec{F}_{\text{guide}}$.

3.3 Data Analysis

We chose to evaluate several criteria of both the path following and environment discrimination objectives. Data was recorded for each trial at greater than 1 KHz.

- *Average path error (m)* was calculated from the difference between the desired path and actual cursor positions. The average path error for each trial was

determined by

$$E_{\text{mean}} = \frac{1}{N} \sum_{n=1}^{N} |\vec{x}_{\text{des}}[n] - \vec{x}_{\text{act}}[n]|, \quad (5)$$

where N is the number of data points collected during the trial, $\vec{x}_{\text{des}}[n]$ is the desired x-position of the participant at sample n, and $\vec{x}_{\text{act}}[n]$ is the actual x-position of the participant at sample n.

- *Average trial time (t)* was calculated by evaluating the total reaching time for each trial. Since each trial composed of two reaches, the movement time in between reaches was ignored and the trial time only includes the actual path following time.

- *Weber Fraction* was used to determine each participants' ability to discriminate between the various wall stiffnesses in proportion to the reference stimulus of 120 N/m. The Psignifit toolbox version 2.5.6 [20] was used to fit psychometric curves to the data of each participant under the force and skin deformation guidance conditions using the accelerated and bias-corrected method. The point of subjective equality is determined by using the 0.5 threshold value from the psychometric curve. This point indicates the hypothetical comparison stiffness for which the participant would say the comparison was stiffer than the reference 50% of the time. Using this just noticeable difference value, the Weber Fraction was computed for each participant under each guidance method was determined according to

$$WF = \frac{JND}{k_{\text{ref}}} \times 100, \quad (6)$$

where WF is the Weber fraction, JND is the just noticeable difference, and k_{ref} is the reference stiffness of 120 N/m.

To determine if guidance type (force guidance vs. skin deformation guidance) had a significant effect on average path error or trial completion time, we performed 1-way ANOVA with repeated measures [12] with the metrics as

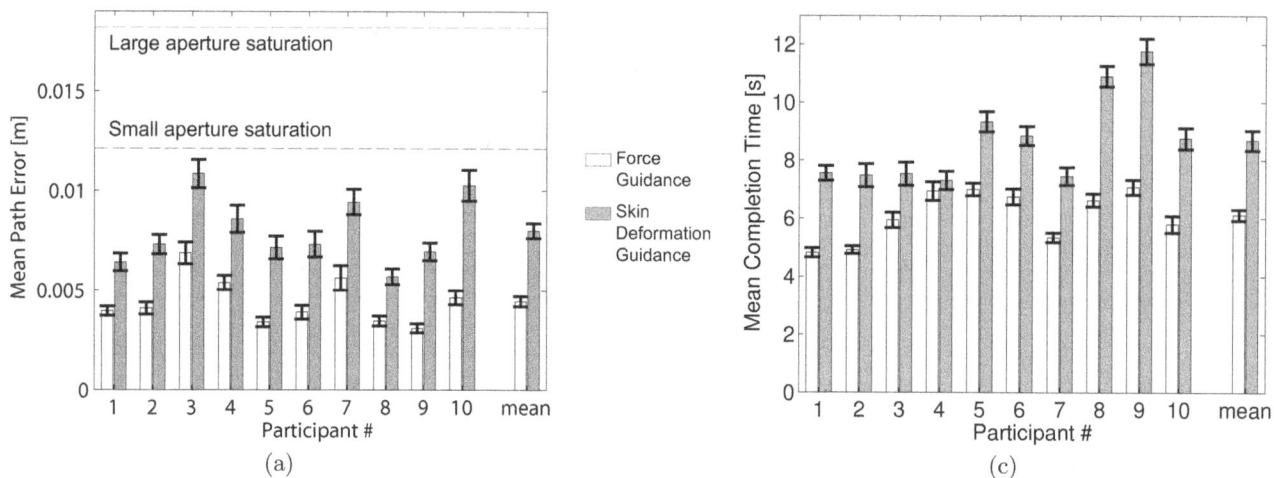

Figure 6: Performance results of the path-following task. (a) Mean path error with 95% confidence intervals for each participant. The lower horizontal, dashed line indicates the error for which the skin stretch device with the smaller 10 mm aperture would saturate. The upper dashed line indicates the error which caused device saturation with the larger 14 mm aperture. (b) Mean trial completion time with 95% confidence intervals for each participant. Trials consisted of two path following instances after which the stiffness of the virtual wall was compared.

the dependent variable [6], with the guidance type as a fixed effect factor, and the participant as a random effect factor.

After participants completed the experiment, they filled out a survey to provide their subjective opinions about each guidance method. Participants were asked to rate each guidance method on a scale from 1-10 on three different qualities - quality of guidance feedback, their ability to discern environment stiffness information in the presence of the guidance, and guidance quality while discerning environment stiffness (a combination of the first two qualities).

4. RESULTS

Average path error across all participants was 4.7 mm for force guidance and 8.2 mm for skin deformation guidance. The participants' individual performance is shown in Fig. 6(a). Mean path error along with 95% confidence intervals is shown for both force guidance and skin deformation guidance. Additionally, the value at which the skin deformation tactor motion saturates is indicated by horizontal dashed lines. The lower line indicates the error which would cause saturation using the smaller aperture size and the upper line indicates the saturation point of the larger aperture. The small and large apertures resulted in tactor saturation 26.9% and 7.5% Participants 2, 3, 6, and 7 used the smaller 10 mm aperture and the remaining participants used the larger 12 mm aperture. The ANOVA analysis indicates that there is a significant effect of guidance type on mean path error ($F_{1,560} = 670.15, p \leq 0.001$).

The average trial time across all participants, consisting of two comparison reaches, was 5.96 seconds using force guidance and 7.93 seconds using skin deformation guidance. Participant individual mean completion time and 95% confidence intervals are shown in in Fig. 6(c). The ANOVA analysis indicates that the guidance type had a significant effect on the trial completion time ($F_{1,560} = 826.69, p \leq 0.001$).

Participants' answers to the stiffness comparison were used to fit psychometric curves to individual participant data. An example of these psychometric curve fits is shown in Fig 4. Based on the individual participant data, Weber Fractions for perception of kinesthetic environment stiffness under haptic guidance were determined. The Weber Fractions for each participant and the group means are shown in Table 2. Table 2 also presents the median Weber Fractions for both feedback methods, showing a clear difference in environmental stiffness discrimination ability between the feeedback methods. Participants using force feedback were essentially unable to discriminate environment stiffness, but when using skin deformation feedback, those same subjects were able to discriminate environment stiffness, despite little previous training with skin deformation feedback.

When asked to rate the guidance methods on a scale of 1-10 for guidance and discrimination ability, participants rated force guidance as 6.70 ($\sigma = 1.25$) and skin deformation guidance as 6.85 ($\sigma = 1.63$). They also rated the guidance methods for each sub-task specifically. The average participant rating for the guidance objective was 8.40 ($\sigma = 1.17$) for force and 6.10 ($\sigma = 1.91$) for skin deformation. The average participant rating for the environment discrimination objective was 3.80 ($\sigma = 2.35$) for force and 7.20 ($\sigma = 2.04$) for skin deformation guidance.

5. DISCUSSION

We studied the effect of replacing force guidance virtual fixtures with skin deformation guidance virtual fixtures in a series of path following experiments that tested path following ability and environmental stiffness discrimination. When performing a path following task with kinesthetic force or skin deformation guidance feedback, participants were able to follow the path more accurately when using force guidance than when using skin deformation guidance. Additionally, participants using force guidance were able to follow the path more quickly, completing reaches in less time. The

292

Subject Number	1	2	3	4	5	6	7	8	9	10	Median
Force Guidance Weber Fraction	3.12 E3	860.01	280.26	1.00 E6	4.08 E5	1.16 E6	1.26 E3	1.17 E4	1.25 E5	7.83 E5	6.84 E4
Skin Deformation Weber Fraction	20.83	97.12	31.46	161.36	42.21	88.38	38.12	49.46	-1.41 E6	71.85	45.84

Table 2: Weber Fraction data for the environmental discrimination ability of each participant under force and skin deformation guidance.

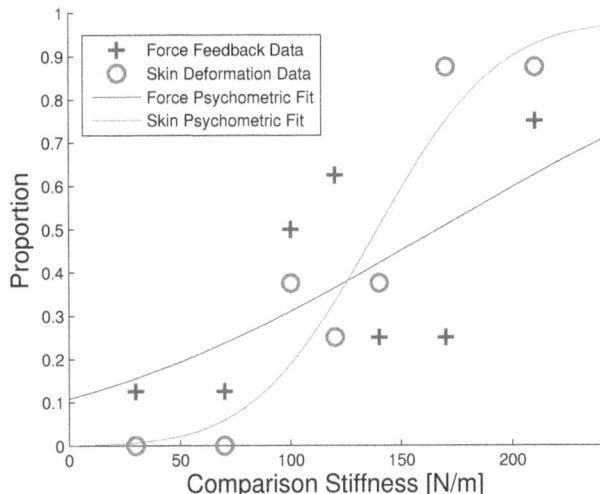

Figure 7: Stiffness comparison data for a typical participant. The proportion of time that the participant answered that the comparison was stiffer than the reference is indicated for each comparison value. A psychometric curve is fit to the participant data using the Psignifit toolbox

kinesthetic force produced by the Omega.3 physically moves the user towards the correct position. If so desired, a participant using force guidance would be able to remain almost entirely passive during the reaches, allowing the forbidden region virtual fixture to keep their motion near the path.

This also highlights a large fundamental difference between force guidance and skin deformation guidance. Force guidance physically affects the user's movement and manipulation and does not need to be consciously interpreted to change the user's motion. Skin deformation guidance is a signal that does not directly affect the user interaction. The signal, while intuitive, must be interpreted and acted upon. This is likely one of the reasons that the force guidance condition resulted in lower path following error than skin deformation guidance in this experiment.

Additionally, the time necessary to interpret and react to skin deformation also explains why participants generally took more time to complete trials under skin deformation guidance. While it takes more time to interpret and then react to the skin deformation guidance, the fact that the guidance does not actively move the manipulator enables the user to choose to actively ignore it if they choose to do so. This ability may be more appropriate in highly changing

environments for which the safety of a force guidance virtual fixture cannot be guaranteed.

Importantly, we found that participants using force guidance were not able to use environmental force feedback to discriminate between varying environment stiffness. There is an inherent loss of information that occurs when force guidance virtual fixtures are superimposed with environment force feedback. The user of the system has no way of determining what portion of the force they feel is coming from the environment and what is coming from the virtual fixture guidance. Alternatively, users receiving skin deformation guidance were able to discriminate between varying environment stiffness in this experiment. Using skin deformation guidance rather than force guidance for path virtual fixtures effectively trades off some accuracy to enable the user to perceive environmental force cues.

The fundamental differences between force guidance and skin deformation guidance have a profound impact on their efficacy in multi-agent collaborative systems where multiple agents share the same slave manipulator. In a trainer-trainee scenario, where guidance is relayed from the trainer manipulator to the trainee manipulator, there are several advantages to using skin deformation guidance. While the trainee may exhibit greater error in guidance following, they are forced to take a more active roll in motor learning, rather than being passively guided by the master. Additionally, they retain stiffness discrimination ability and are able to learn about the physical properties of the teleoperated environment.

It should be noted that the Weber Fraction for kinesthetic wall stiffness discrimination under skin deformation guidance is larger than the Weber Fractions reported in the literature for stiffness discrimination [10], [19]. It is possible that the skin deformation guidance alters the perception of force, lowering discrimination ability. Also, in this study, there were multiple objectives for each trial. This additional cognitive load likely reduced discrimination ability in comparison to prior experiments in the literature, where participants had only to achieve a single objective.

6. CONCLUSIONS AND FUTURE WORK

In multilateral manipulation, where multiple agents collaborate to perform a task, virtual fixtures can be used to aid in group performance. In this work, we performed an experiment to test the path following performance and environment stiffness discrimination ability of participants when receiving kinesthetic force or skin deformation guidance for following a path. Participants were able to more accurately follow an unseen path with a forbidden region virtual fixture while under force guidance than under skin deformation guidance. However, receiving force guidance removed the participants' ability to discriminate between varying environment stiffness, showing that input from a force virtual fixture while interacting with the environment reduces the environmental perception of the user.

In this work, we do not assert what acceptable levels of error are for either force or skin deformation guidance as the necessary accuracy will depend on the specific task. Rather, we aim to show trade-offs between accuracy and discrimination ability. Force guidance would be most useful in situations where following a path extremely accurately is important. Force guidance physically restricts motion away from the path, making it good for applications where it is important that the user does not deviate into an "unsafe" region. We propose that skin deformation guidance is better suited for exploration tasks or applications where perceiving environment force feedback is important. Additionally, since the guidance does not actively apply force to the master manipulator, it is safer in environments where the virtual fixture may not always be perfectly implemented.

There are still many promising directions for future research in this area. Significant previous research has been done on virtual fixtures, however little of it focuses on human perception while receiving guidance. Knowledge of how guidance affects human performance and learning in various applications is important for determining the best way to aid collaboration and teaching in teleoperated scenarios. In future work, we will test both force guidance and skin deformation guidance in actual teleoperated tasks with defined accuracy requirements to assess how they affect performance, exploration, and motor learning.

7. ACKNOWLEDGMENTS

The authors thank Ilana Nisky for her assistance in developing the experiment protocol. Support for this work was provided by the National Science Foundation (award to 1227406 to SBS and AMO, award 0746914 to WRP), and the Agency for Science, Technology and Research - Singapore (to ZFQ).

8. REFERENCES

[1] J. J. Abbott, P. Marayong, and A. M. Okamura. Haptic virtual fixtures for robot-assisted manipulation. In *12th International Symposium of Robotics Research*, pages 49–64, 2005.

[2] I. A. M. Beets, M. MacÃI', R. L. J. Meesen, K. Cuypers, O. Levin, and S. P. Swinnen. Active versus passive training of a complex bimanual task: Is prescriptive proprioceptive information sufficient for inducing motor learning? *PLoS ONE*, 7(5), 2012.

[3] G. P. Bingham, E. Casserly, and W. Snap-Childs. Passive tracking versus active control in motor learning. *Journal of Vision*, 11(960), 2011.

[4] F. Conti, F. Barbagli, D. Morris, and C. Sewell. CHAI - An open-source library for the rapid development of haptic scenes. In Demo at *IEEE WorldHaptics*, 2005.

[5] G. Gescheider. *Psychophysics: The Fundamentals*. Lawrence Erlbaum Associates, 3 edition, 1997.

[6] S. A. Glantz and B. K. Slinker. *Primer of Applied Regression and Analysis of Variance*. McGraw-Hill, 1990.

[7] B. T. Gleeson, S. K. Horschel, and W. R. Provancher. Perception of direction for applied tangential skin displacement: Effects of speed, displacement and repetition. *IEEE Transactions on Haptics*, 3(3):177–188, 2010.

[8] B. T. Gleeson, C. A. Stewart, and W. R. Provancher. Improved tactile shear feedback: Tactor design and an aperture-based restraint. *IEEE Transactions on Haptics*, 4(4):253–262, 2011.

[9] A. Guinan, N. Hornbaker, M. Montandon, A. Doxon, and W. Provancher. Back-to-back skin stretch feedback for communicating five degree-of-freedom direction cues. In *World Haptics Conference*, pages 13–18, 2013.

[10] L. Jones and I. Hunter. A perceptual analysis of stiffness. *Experimental Brain Research*, 79(1):150–156, 1990.

[11] L. M., E. Castillo, G. Garcia, and A. Bashir. Delta robot: Inverse, direct, and intermediate jacobians. *Journal of Mechanical Engineering Science*, 220:103–109, 2006.

[12] S. E. Maxwell and H. D. Delaney. *Designing Experiments and Analyzing Data: A Model Comparison Perspective*. Routledge Academic, 2nd edition, 2003.

[13] N. Navkar, Z. Deng, D. Shah, K. Bekris, and N. Tsekos. Visual and force-feedback guidance for robot-assisted interventions in the beating heart with real-time mri. In *IEEE International Conference on Robotics and Automation*, pages 689–694, 2012.

[14] I. Nisky, A. Pressman, C. Pugh, F. Mussa-Ivaldi, and A. Karniel. Perception and action in teleoperated needle insertion. *IEEE Transactions on Haptics*, 4(3):155–166, 2011.

[15] M. O'Malley and M. Goldfarb. The effect of virtual surface stiffness on the haptic perception of detail. *IEEE Transactions on Mechatronics*, 9(2):448–454, June 2004.

[16] S. Payandeh and Z. Stanisic. On application of virtual fixtures as an aid for telemanipulation and training. In *Symposium on Haptic Interfaces for Virtual Environment and Teleoperator Systems*, pages 18–23, 2002.

[17] Z. F. Quek, S. B. Schorr, I. Nisky, W. R. Provancher, and A. M. Okamura. Sensory substitution using 3-degree-of-freedom tangential and normal skin deformation feedback. In *IEEE Haptics Symposium*, pages 27–33, 2014.

[18] S. B. Schorr, Z. F. Quek, R. Y. Romano, I. Nisky, W. R. Provancher, and A. M. Okamura. Sensory substitution via cutaneous skin stretch feedback. In *IEEE International Conference on Robotics and Automation*, pages 2341–2346, 2013.

[19] H. Z. Tan, N. I. Durlach, G. L. Beauregard, and M. A. Srinivasan. Manual discrimination of compliance using active pinch grasp: the roles of force and work cues, perception. *Psychophysics*, pages 495–510, 1995.

[20] F. A. Wichmann and N. J. Hill. The psychometric function: I. Fitting, sampling, and goodness of fit. *Perception & Psychophysics*, 63(8):1293–313, 2001.

Robot-Centric Activity Prediction from First-Person Videos: What Will They Do to Me?

M. S. Ryoo[1], Thomas J. Fuchs[1], Lu Xia[2,3], J. K. Aggarwal[3], Larry Matthies[1]
[1]Jet Propulsion Laboratory, California Institute of Technology, Pasadena, CA
[2]Amazon.com, Inc., Seattle, WA
[3]Department of ECE, the University of Texas at Austin, Austin, TX
mryoo@jpl.nasa.gov

ABSTRACT

In this paper, we present a core technology to enable robot recognition of human activities during human-robot interactions. In particular, we propose a methodology for *early recognition* of activities from robot-centric videos (i.e., first-person videos) obtained from a robot's viewpoint during its interaction with humans. Early recognition, which is also known as *activity prediction*, is an ability to infer an ongoing activity at its early stage. We present an algorithm to recognize human activities targeting the camera from streaming videos, enabling the robot to predict intended activities of the interacting person as early as possible and take fast reactions to such activities (e.g., avoiding harmful events targeting itself before they actually occur). We introduce the novel concept of 'onset' that efficiently summarizes pre-activity observations, and design a recognition approach to consider event history in addition to visual features from first-person videos. We propose to represent an onset using a cascade histogram of time series gradients, and we describe a novel algorithmic setup to take advantage of such onset for early recognition of activities. The experimental results clearly illustrate that the proposed concept of onset enables better/earlier recognition of human activities from first-person videos collected with a robot.

Categories and Subject Descriptors

I.2.10 [**Artificial Intelligence**]: Vision and Scene Understanding—*video analysis*; I.4.8 [**Image Processing and Computer Vision**]: Scene Analysis—*motion*; I.2.9 [**Artificial Intelligence**]: Robotics—*sensors*

Keywords

Activity recognition; first-person videos; human-robot interaction

1. INTRODUCTION

First-person activity recognition is a research area studying automated recognition of human activities from videos with the actor's own viewpoint. Its main difference to the conventional 3rd-person activity recognition is that the observer wearing the camera (e.g.,

HRI'15, March 2–5, 2015, Portland, Oregon, USA.
Copyright © 2015 ACM 978-1-4503-2883-8/15/03 ...$15.00.
http://dx.doi.org/10.1145/2696454.2696462.

a robot) himself/herself is involved in the ongoing activity, making its perception to become egocentric videos. This makes this research area very germane to robotics (i.e., any visual observation from a viewpoint of a robot becomes a first-person video), understanding of natural human-robot interactions in particular. First-person activity recognition is essential to provide a robot activity-level situation awareness 'during' social and physical human-robot interactions (e.g., recognizing a hostile interaction that a human is punching the robot and the robot is collapsing as a consequence). Such concept is very different from conventional robot recognition of human gesture-level commands (e.g., [18, 2]) or task-level actions (e.g., [9]) from stationary cameras without any direct physical interaction between humans and the robot. In our scenarios, the camera moves dynamically as the robot gets involved in interactions (e.g., Figure 4) and videos visually display very different characteristics compared to conventional scenarios.

An ability particularly important and necessary for first-person recognition systems is the ability to infer humans' intended activities at their early stage. For instance, public service robots and surveillance/military robots must protect themselves from any harmful events by inferring the beginning of dangerous activities like an 'assault'. Similarly, a wearable system must recognize ongoing events around the human as early as possible to provide appropriate service for human tasks and to alarm accidents like 'a car running into the person'. Natural human-robot interaction also becomes possible by making robots to provide early reaction to humans' actions. This is not just about real-time implementations of activity recognition, but more about recognition of activities from observations only containing the beginning part of the activity. The objective is to detect an ongoing activity in the middle of the activity execution, before it is completed.

This problem, recognition of an activity before fully observing its execution, is called 'early recognition' or 'activity prediction' [14]. However, even though there are recent works on early recognition, (1) it has never been studied for first-person videos and (2) research on an early recognition approach that simultaneously considers pre-activity observations as well as features from the ongoing activity has been limited. In real-world first-person recognition scenarios, the system is required to continuously process long video inputs containing a sequence of multiple activities. As a consequence, it is important for the system to analyze not only the video segment corresponding to the ongoing activity but also other activity history or signals observed 'prior' to the beginning of the activity. In this paper, we call such signals observed before the activity as an *onset* of the activity.

This paper newly introduces the concept of onset, and presents an early recognition approach to take advantage of them for the robot recognition. We formulate the early recognition (i.e., prediction) problem to consider activity history and human intention together with ongoing observation of the activity, and discuss how our *onset signatures* enable abstraction of such pre-activity observations for better recognition of activities. We define an onset activity as short and subtle human motion (e.g., waving and reaching) observable before main activities (e.g., shaking hands and throwing an object), and attempt to capture/model onset patterns displayed prior to each main activity. More specifically, we compute a collection of weak classifier responses (each corresponding to a particular onset activity) over time and construct cascade histograms of their time series gradients as our representation summarizing pre-activity observations: onset signatures. Our method is particularly designed to capture loose stochastic correlations between the onset and the target activities (e.g., reaching an object may or may not occur before throwing but they are correlated) and also consider absence of a certain onset (e.g., absence of waving before punching) for better recognition. An efficient (linear time complexity) algorithm is designed to take advantage of our onset signatures to perform better early recognition from continuous videos, while minimizing the amount of computations.

We formulate the early recognition problem in Section 2. We present the concept of onset and our recognition approach to utilize them in Section 3. Experimental results are discussed in Section 4, and Section 5 concludes the paper.

1.1 Related work

The research area of first-person activity recognition is gaining an increasing amount of attention recently. There are several works on recognition of ego-actions of the person (i.e., actions of the person wearing a camera such as skiing) [7, 4], object-oriented analysis of humans using objects (e.g., a towel) [12, 13], or analysis based on face and gaze [5]. However, only very few works considered recognition of interaction-level activities where multiple humans (or robots) physically interact each other [16]. Furthermore, no previous work attempted early recognition from first-person videos.

The problem of early recognition (i.e., activity prediction) was introduced and formulated with modern spatio-temporal features in [14], but it was limited to 3rd-person videos and did not consider pre-activity observations. There also have been works considering past activity history for predicting future states/locations using state-models [9] and/or trajectories [8, 20] from 3rd-person videos. However, even though these approaches are appropriate for predicting future steps of the activities composed of clear states, they are unsuitable for directly handling dynamic first-person videos whose analysis requires various types of spatio-temporal video features [11, 3, 17] that display highly sparse and noisy characteristics. In order to enable accurate early recognition for interaction-level first-person activities, simultaneous consideration of pre-activity observations (i.e., an onset) and ongoing activity observations is needed.

To our knowledge, this paper is the first paper is discuss 'early recognition' problem for *first-person* videos from robots. As pointed out above, previous activity prediction works were designed for videos obtained from a static camera [14, 8] or those from a robot simply standing without any ego-motion or interaction [9]. This paper newly discusses the problem of activity prediction with first-person videos displaying robot ego-motion (e.g., rotating) as well as camera motion (e.g., shaking) caused by physical human-robot interactions. We also believe it is the first paper to explicitly consider *pre-activity observations* (i.e., frames 'before' the starting time of the activity) for early recognition, which was not attempted in [14, 6].

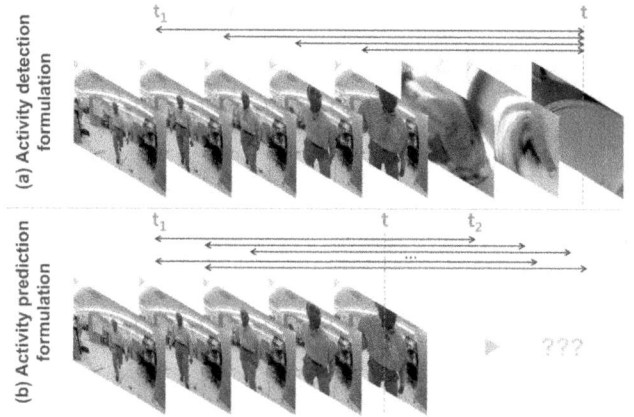

Figure 1: Time intervals that need to be considered in our activity detection/prediction formulations. t indicates the observation time (i.e., the current frame) and t_1 and t_2 specify starting and ending times of time intervals internally considered.

2. PROBLEM FORMULATION

2.1 Basic activity detection framework

Human activity detection is the problem of finding starting time and ending time (i.e., a time interval) of each occurring activity from a video input. Given a continuous video stream from frame 0 to t (we denote this as $V[0, t]$ or simply as V), for each activity class C, the system is required to obtain time intervals $[t_1, t_2]$ that it believes to correspond to C. In general, this is solved by evaluating all possible time intervals (i.e., $[t_1, t_2]$ where $0 \leq t_1, t_2 \leq t$) or estimating intervals providing local maximum probability values: $P(C^{[t_1, t_2]}|V)$. Here, $C^{[t_1, t_2]}$ denotes the event of the activity C starting exactly at time t_1 and ending exactly at t_2.

Assuming that the robot is only interested in the 'activity that just happened', this can be further simplified as:

$$
\begin{aligned}
P(C^t \mid V) &= \sum_{t_1} P(C^{[t_1, t]} \mid V) \\
&= \frac{\sum_{t_1} P(V[t_1, t] \mid C^{[t_1, t]}) P(C^{[t_1, t]})}{\sum_{C, t_1} P(V[t_1, t] \mid C^{[t_1, t]}) P(C^{[t_1, t]})}
\end{aligned}
\tag{1}
$$

where $P(C^t|V)$ represents the probability of the activity 'ending' at time t regardless of its starting time, and we use a basic probability marginalization with possible starting times t_1. We call this problem more specifically as 'after-the-fact detection', since the system only focuses on the activity which is already finished at t (Figure 1 (a)). Recognition can be performed by computing the above probability at every time step as the video continues.

Instead of directly using the video stream V, visual features abstracting V are often extracted and used for the recognition [1]. These include sparse local motion descriptors [11] capturing salient local movements observed in videos, global motion descriptors [16] representing camera movements, and semantic descriptors like per-frame human body poses [19]. By modeling the distributions of such features corresponding to the activity (i.e., $P(V|C)$), the recognition can be performed following Equation 1: this is a binary classification of deciding whether the activity C is occurring or not at each frame t. In our case, the concept of bag-of-visual-words were used as our feature representation, modeling each distribution as a histogram similar to [16]. Also notice that each visual feature (e.g., 3-D XYT volume patch in the case of [11]) is extracted with a particular time stamp, and they stay as is once extracted.

2.2 Activity prediction formulation

The 'activity prediction' problem is the problem of recognizing ongoing activities at their early stage. In contrast to the above after-the-fact detection problem, recognition must be made in the middle of the activity before it is fully executed. The system must consider the possibility that the activity is 'ongoing' at frame t, thus considering time intervals where $t_1 \leq t \leq t_2$ (Figure 1 (b)). In addition, the system is required to explicitly consider multiple progress levels d of the activity C:

$$P(C^t|V) = \frac{\sum_d \sum_{[t_1,t_2]} P(V[t_1,t] \mid C^{[t_1,t_2]}, d) P(C^{[t_1,t_2]}, d)}{\sum_{C,d,[t_1,t_2]} P(V[t_1,t] \mid C^{[t_1,t_2]}, d) P(C^{[t_1,t_2]}, d)} \quad (2)$$

where t_2 is a future frame and observation corresponding to $V[t + 1, t_2]$ is not available. The variable d is a conceptual progress status of the activity (i.e., up to which point the activity has progressed so far?) having a value between 0 and 1. Assuming that each activity progresses linearly when occurring, the following equation holds: $t = t_1 + d \cdot (t_2 - t_1)$.

We also call this as early 'detection' problem, which extends the early 'classification' problem (i.e., early categorization of segmented videos) introduced in [14].

Early detection of human activities with context: Even though the above formulation enables early detection of activities, it is often insufficient for continuous video scenarios. It only utilizes the video segment corresponding to the time interval alone (i.e., $V[t_1, t]$) to make the decision, while ignoring all the other previous video observations (i.e., $V[0, t_1 - 1]$). In continuous videos, activities occur in a sequence and they are correlated. Furthermore, the interacting person usually has his/her own intention, such as 'harming' the camera or 'avoiding' the robot. Figure 2 illustrates a graphical model describing such activity-activity relations and intention-activity relations.

Thus, the early detection problem can be formulated as:

$$P(C^t \mid V) = \sum_d \sum_{[t_1,t_2]} P(C^{[t_1,t_2]}, d \mid V)$$
$$\propto \sum_d \sum_{[t_1,t_2]} \sum_{(\mathbf{A},I)} P(C^{[t_1,t_2]}, d, \mathbf{A}, I, V) \quad (3)$$

where $t_1 \leq t \leq t_2$, $\mathbf{A}$ is a set of all previous activities, I is the intention of the interacting person, and $P(C^{[t_1,t_2]}, \mathbf{A}, I, V)$ is the joint probability. In our approach, we use the function $F(\cdot)$ to approximate this joint probability term, while designing it to consider activity-activity relations (i.e., $\mathbf{A} = \{A_1, \cdots, A_{|\mathbf{A}|}\}$ and C) as well as intention-activity relations displayed in Figure 2.

The key issues for the early detection are (i) designing the robust joint probability function F, (ii) learning the model parameters in F from training videos, and (iii) making an inference given a new video observation V. This inference must be made at its every time frame t while considering possible intervals $[t_1, t_2]$. We emphasize that t is smaller than t_2 in the case of an ongoing activity (i.e., it is in the middle of execution), and F must be designed to consider such characteristic. We discuss this more in Section 3.3.

Challenges: The main technical challenge is that the above computations must be performed in real-time, making the detection as early as possible. Particularly in robot perception, it is very contradictory to say that "even though the approach is able to perform early recognition, its processing time will take multiple seconds/minutes". This implies that (1) we need to apply the recognition algorithm almost every frame (i.e., it should not wait) and that (2) the algorithm still must perform in real-time or faster. This

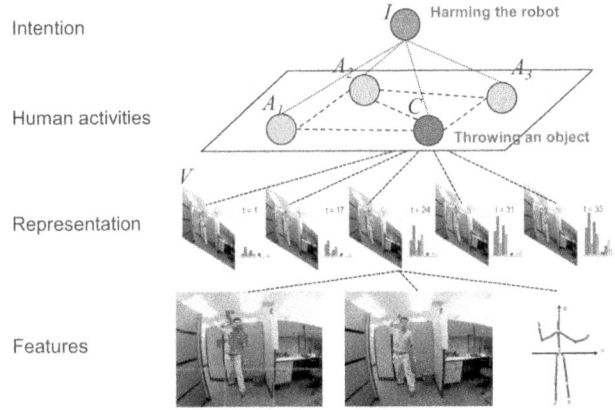

Figure 2: Graphical model representation of the scenario where an interacting human performs a sequence of activities under a specific intention. The robot is required to consider activity-activity relations, capturing pre-activity observations.

makes a standard way of modeling/training the function F and making an multi-iteration inference using a latent SVM formulation similar to [10] or MCMC-based searching difficult.

3. ACTIVITY PREDICTION USING ONSET

In order to enable early detection while addressing the above mentioned challenges, we introduce the new concept of 'onset activities' and 'onset signatures' together with our recognition approach to take advantage of them. The idea is to learn weak detectors for subtle short-term activities (i.e., onset activities) which are closely or loosely related to the occurrence of activities-of-interest, and make the recognition system to capture activity-activity relations (i.e., $\mathbf{A}$) using such onset information. Our approach learns onset patterns leading to the occurrence of each target activity while explicitly considering stochastic nature of onsets, and performs its early recognition by analyzing onset distributions observed before the activity. Figure 3 (a) illustrates its overall concept.

3.1 Onset activities

We define *onset activities* as subtle activities which (1) occur within a short time duration and (2) do not physically influence the observer (i.e., a robot or a wearable camera), but (3) serve as a direct/indirect cue to infer their following activities. 'Standing', 'pointing', and 'picking up an object' are typical examples of onset activities. These activities themselves do not have strong meaning and they do not influence the robot/camera directly, but they can serve as indicators describing 'what activity is likely to follow next'. An example will be the activity of 'picking up an object' serving as the onset for 'throwing an object'. Another example will be 'waving' before 'hand shaking'.

Typically, because of the subtle nature of onset activities, their recognition becomes difficult and unreliable. The activities usually contain a small amount of human motion (e.g., only a subtle arm/finger gesture is visible when 'pointing'). This makes the detectors for onset activities to become weak classifiers, and prevents the system from directly using the onset recognition results. For instance, average precisions (AP) of our onset activity detection were 0.1 to 0.2 in our dataset. Furthermore, onset activities often have very stochastic nature, implying that onsets are not always observable before activities (e.g., the person may have the ball beforehand and throw it without the picking up action). Thus, an approach to best utilize these weak detectors is required.

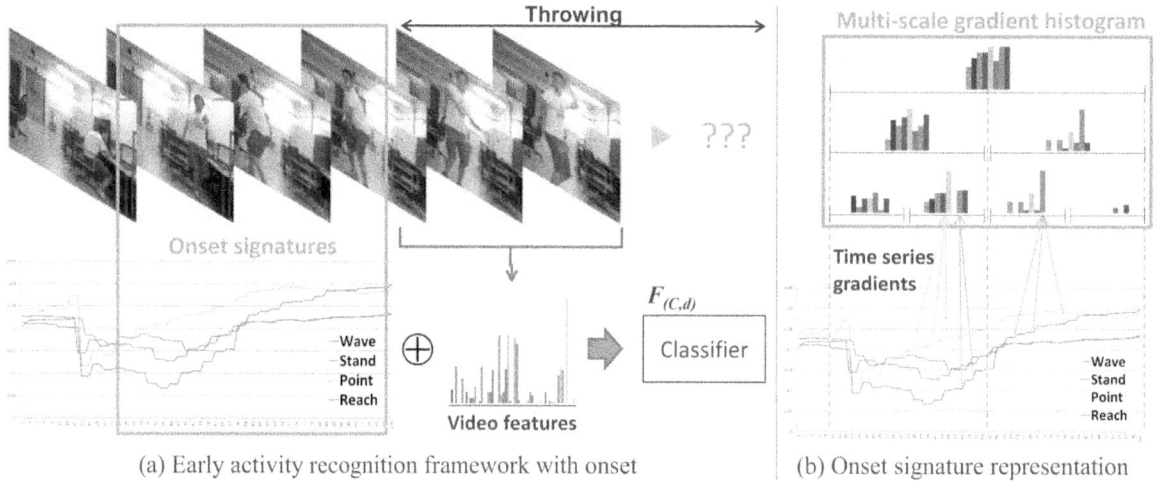

(a) Early activity recognition framework with onset | (b) Onset signature representation

Figure 3: (a) Illustration of the overall concept of our early activity recognition pipeline using onset. The recognition approach is designed so that it considers both the pre-activity observations (onset signatures) and video features from ongoing activities. (b) Illustration of our onset signature representation, based on the multi-scale cascade histogram of time series gradients.

3.2 Onset signatures

We define *onset signatures* as a set of time series describing onset activity matching results. That is, given a continuous (streaming) video, we measure the similarity between each possible video segment and the onset activity, and record how the similarity is changing over time. The objective is to use these time series as features suggesting future activities. Each onset signature $G^k(t)$ of kth onset activity is more specifically computed as:

$$G^k(t) = \max_r (1 - D^k([t - r, t]))\tag{4}$$

where r is the model duration of the activity, and $D^k([t - r, t])$ is the distance between the model of the kth onset activity and the video observation segment $V[t - r, t]$. We use a basic template matching of bag-of-words representations (obtained from a set of training videos S^k) as our D^k:

$$D^k([t_1, t_2]) = \sum_i (m_i^k - v_i[t_1, t_2]))^2\tag{5}$$

where v_i is the ith feature value and m_i^k is its mean model value: $m_i^k = \sum_{V^j \in S^k} v_i^j / |S^k|$. In our implementation, we took advantage of the same video features (with bag-of-visual-words representation) described in Section 2.1: [11, 3, 19, 16].

The matching is performed for all t and possible r values, providing us the final $G^k(t)$. The resulting $G^k(t)$ forms a time series, describing how our onset activity detector is responding to the ongoing video observation. We collect $G^k(t)$ from all onset activities and use them as our *onset signature*.

The template matching process takes time complexity of $O(n \cdot R)$ per frame where n is the feature dimension and R is the number of temporal window sizes we consider ($R < 5$ in our case). Furthermore, the computation of onset signature per activity is independent to each other, making its parallelization possible.

Histogram representation of onset signatures: We design a histogram representation of onset signatures (Figure 3 (b)). The idea is to make the system efficiently summarize the previous onset occurrence information from its time series, so that it can use it to infer ongoing/future activities.

Typical representations of onset signatures are mean and maximum values of a fixed time window (e.g., frames between the

current frame and 50 frames before that). However, this is often insufficient due to noisy and weak nature of onset matching (notice that onset recognition relying on peak matching values give us ~0.1 AP), and deeper analysis of time series is necessary. Thus, we construct cascade histograms of time series gradients to represent onset signatures.

Let $||$ denote the concatenation operation of two vectors, $[a_1, \cdots, a_n] \,||\, [b_1, \cdots, b_n] = [a_1, \cdots, a_n, b_1, \cdots, b_n]$. Then, the histogram representation of onset signature H at time t is defined as: $H(t) = H_1(t - u, t) \,||\, H_2(t - u, t) \,||\, \cdots \,||\, H_{|A|}(t - u, t)$, where $H_k(t - u, t)$ is the histogram for the kth onset activity computed based on the time interval $[t - u, t]$ with duration u (e.g., 50). H_k is defined more specifically as:

$$H_k(t_1, t_2) = H_k\left(t_1, \frac{t_1 + t_2}{2}\right) \,||\, H_k\left(\frac{t_1 + t_2}{2}, t_2\right)\tag{6}$$
$$||\, [h_k^+(t_1, t_2), h_k^-(t_1, t_2)]$$

where

$$h_k^+(t_1, t_2) = \left|\{t_1 \leq t \leq t_2 \mid G^k(t) - G^k(t - s) > 0\}\right|,$$
$$h_k^-(t_1, t_2) = \left|\{t_1 \leq t \leq t_2 \mid G^k(t) - G^k(t - s) \leq 0\}\right|.\tag{7}$$

Here, s is the step size of gradient computation, and we perform this histogram construction for multiple s scales and concatenate the results.

The above recursive equation hierarchically performs temporal segmentation of the time series (i.e., our onset signatures) into multiple parts, and obtains a histogram of time series gradients corresponding to each of them. That is, our hierarchical histogram is constructed by applying our recursive function until it reaches the level l. In our experiments, $l = 3$ gave us good results.

The final feature vector representation of the onset signature is constructed as follows, by attaching mean and max values to the histogram:

$$x(t) = H(t) \,||\, \left[\sum_{t'=t-d}^{t} \frac{G^1(t')}{u}, \cdots, \sum_{t'=t-d}^{t} \frac{G^n(t')}{u}\right]\tag{8}$$
$$||\, [\max(G^1(t')), \cdots, \max(G^n(t'))].$$

(a) Results of our early activity recognition obtained from a 'punching' scene

(b) Results of our early activity recognition obtained from a 'hand shaking' - 'hugging' scene

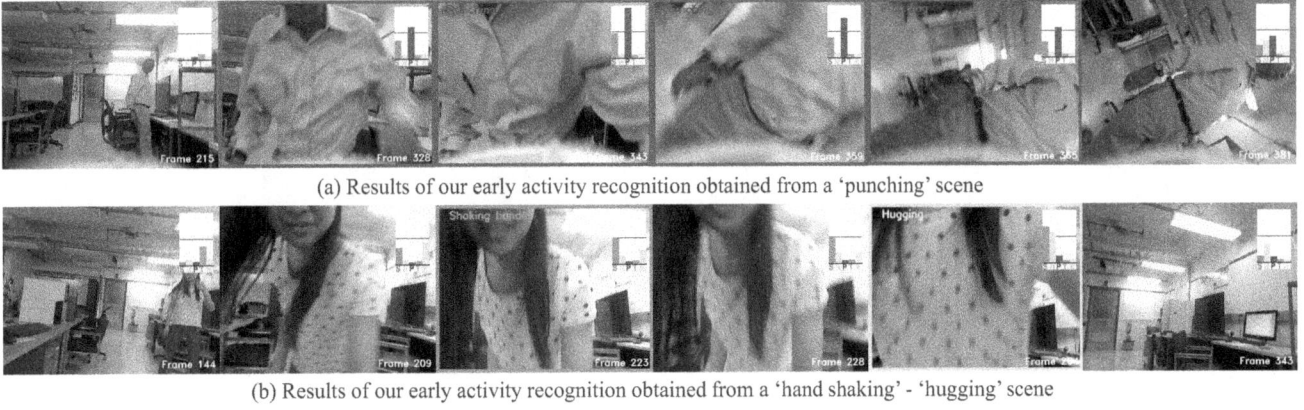

Figure 4: Example result image sequences of our early activity recognition. A 'punching' activity (blue boxes), a 'hand shaking' activity (red box), and a 'hugging' activity (green box) are detected. We are able to observe that the camera displays ego-motion due to human-robot interactions, such as it collapsing due to 'punching' and it shaking during 'hand shaking' interaction.

3.3 Early detection using onset signature

Based on its video observation V and computed onset signatures x, our approach performs early detection of an activity by using a set of binary classifiers. More specifically, we formulate the detector at time t as:

$$P(C^t \mid V) \propto \sum_d \sum_{[t_1,t_2]} \sum_{(\mathbf{A},I)} P(C^{[t_1,t_2]}, d, \mathbf{A}, I, V)$$
$$\propto \sum_d \sum_{[t_1,t_2]} \sum_{(\mathbf{A},I)} P(\mathbf{A}, V \mid C^{[t_1,t_2]}, d) \cdot P(C^{[t_1,t_2]}, d \mid I)$$
$$\approx \max_d \max_{[t_1,t_2]} \sum_I F_{(C,d)}(x(t), V[t_1,t]) \cdot L_C([t_1,t_2], I) \tag{9}$$

where we factor the joint probability into two terms using conditional independence and uniform prior assumptions. The functions F and L_C are used to estimate the two terms while explicitly reflecting $t_1 \leq t \leq t_2$. We use support vector machine (SVM)-based probability estimation in our implementation to approximate the terms, which we describe more below.

We trained one binary classifier for each $F_{(C,d)}$ and made it to estimate the probability scores. To support Equation 9, this was done for each pair of activity C and possible progress level d. A concatenation of the vector describing video features inside the interval (i.e., $V[t_1,t]$) and the vector representation of our onset signature (i.e., $x(t)$) serves as an input to these classifiers, and each of the learned classifier $F_{(C,d)}$ measures the probability of the activity C ongoing at the time t (with progress level d). The training of the classifier is performed by providing positive and negative samples of V and x together with their ground truth labels y. The function L_C is trained similarly, by providing I and $[t_1,t_2]$ as inputs.

The idea is to abstract previous activity occurrences (i.e., $\mathbf{A}$) using our onset signature x, instead of making the system to enumerate through all possible combinations. That is, we directly used our onset signatures as input features of the function F, thereby enabling efficient computations. Based on the training samples, the classifier will learn to focus on particular onset signature while ignoring irrelevant onset activities.

Overall computations required for activity recognition is $O(n \cdot |d| \cdot R)$ at each time step if a binary classifier with a linear complexity is used (e.g., SVM), where n is the feature dimension, $|d|$ is the number of possible activity progress levels (we used 10 levels in our experiments), and R is the number of activity durations

we consider (this influences possible starting points of the time interval, t_1). Our approach is able to cope with any types of binary classifiers in principle (by making them predict either 0 or 1), and does it more reliably with classifiers estimating probability.

4. EXPERIMENTS

4.1 Dataset

We constructed a new dataset composed of continuous human activity videos taken from a robot's first-person viewpoint. It is an extension of the previous humanoid-based first-person video dataset [16] whose videos mostly contain a single activity; our new videos contain a sequence of 2~6 activities (onset activities and interactions). The motivation is that the community has been lacking a public dataset for 'early recognition' (i.e., activity prediction): To our knowledge, the public dataset most commonly used for activity prediction is UT-Interaction [15]. However, even if we set aside that UT-Interaction is not a first-person video dataset, it has a major limitation: its videos contain activities executed in an random order without any context (e.g., punching and then shaking hands). This is very unnatural, since the actors are following a fixed script without any intention on their own (unlike our new dataset).

Our camera was mounted on top of a humanoid similar to [16], and we asked human subjects to perform a series of activities with three different types of intentions: friendly, hostile (i.e., harming), and avoiding. We labeled 9 types of human-robot interactions performed by the actors: 4 types of onset activities and 5 types of activities-of-interest. 'Pointing the observer (i.e., the robot camera)', 'reaching an object', 'standing up', and 'waving to the observer' are the 4 onset activities. 'Handshaking with the observer', 'hugging the observer', 'punching the observer', 'throwing an object at the observer', and 'running away from the observer' are the 5 interaction-level activities in our dataset. The humanoid moves as it is involved in the interaction (e.g., the camera jolting as an impact of throwing, and the camera collapsing as a result of punching). Furthermore, our experiments were designed to capture translation and rotation movements of our robot, and thus these robot ego-motion is present in our first-person videos. Figure 4 shows example frames of our videos.

Videos with the resolution of 640*480 with 30fps were used. Also, 320*240 depth videos were collected in addition to the conventional RGB videos, so that the system obtains Kinect-based pos-

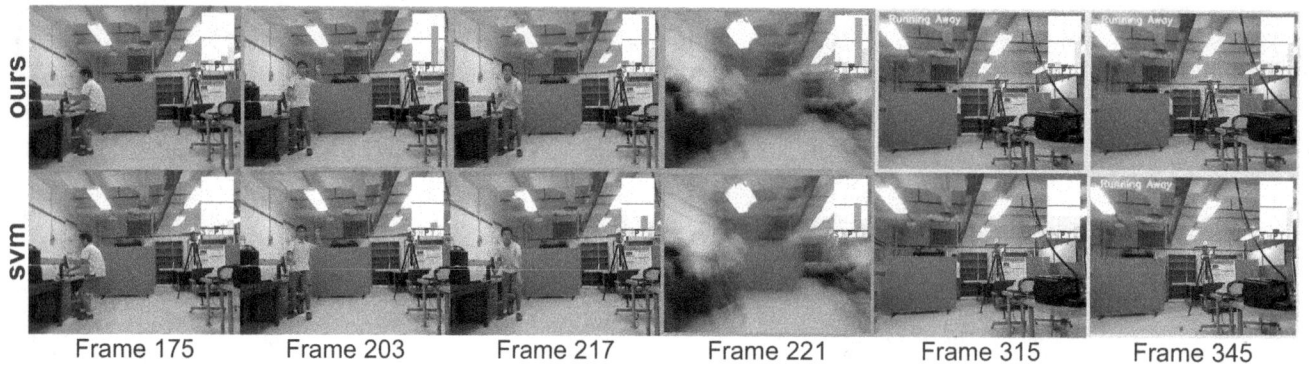

Figure 5: Example result image sequences comparing our early detector (top) with the previous SVM detector using state-of-the-art features (bottom). A 'throwing' activity (magenta boxes) and a 'running away' activity (cyan boxes) are detected. Notice that the previous method detected the 'throwing' only *after* the ball actually hit the camera, while ours detected it as soon as the person raised the hand. That is, our approach detects activities at their much earlier stage compared to the previous detector.

ture estimation results when available. The dataset consists of 8 sets, where each set contains continuous videos of human activities being performed by the same subject. It contains a total of 61 continuous videos with ~180 executions of human activities.

4.2 Implementation

We extracted multiple types of state-of-the-arts visual features from first-person videos, including global motion descriptors [16], local motion descriptors [11, 3], and human posture descriptors [19]. Once features are extracted from raw videos, we clustered these features to obtain standard bag-of-visual-words feature representation while using integral histograms for more efficient computations. Our approach and multiple baseline approaches including the state-of-the-art early recognition approach [14] were trained/tested/compared using our dataset.

We implemented (1) our approach taking advantage of onset signatures as well as (2) its simplified version designed to only use peak onset activity responses (instead of full onset signatures). In addition, we implemented (3) an extended version of previous state-of-the-art early recognition approach [14] originally designed for the 3rd-person videos, and (4) made it to also take advantage of our onset signatures. Furthermore, we implemented several baseline activity detection approaches including (5) a sliding window detector with Bayesian classifiers assuming a Gaussian distribution (i.e., an after-the-fact detection approach), and (6) a state-of-the-art activity detector using SVM with a non-linear kernel (i.e., RBF). All of the above approaches took advantage of the same features vector (i.e., the concatenation of four feature types [11, 3, 19, 16]), which outperformed those using single feature type. We also tested (7) the approach detecting activities solely based on onset signatures (i.e., context-only).

All these approaches run faster than real-time on a standard desktop PC with our unoptimized C++ implementation (0.0036 sec per frame), except for the adopted feature extraction part.

4.3 Evaluation

We use leave-one-set-out cross validation (i.e., 8-fold cross validation) for continuous 'detection' tasks. Ground truth labels of activity occurrences in videos for both the onset activities and the interaction activities were provided, so that we can take advantage of them for the training (i.e., a supervised learning setting) and testing. At each round, for the testing, our approach computes the probability $P(C^t \mid V)$ (which also can be viewed as a confidence score) at every frame t. Treating its peak values as detections

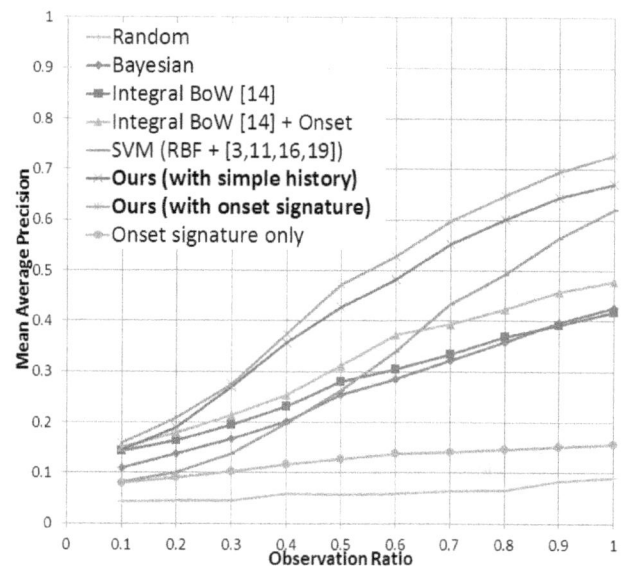

Figure 6: A figure comparing performances of our early detection approaches with previous works and baselines. Mean AP, which is an area under a precision-recall curve, is measured per observation ratio. A higher graph suggests better performance; a higher graph indicates that it 'recognizes activities more accurately given the same amount of observation' and that 'it is able to recognize activities earlier than the others if the same accuracy is assumed'. It clearly shows superiority of ours.

(while discarding overlapping intervals), we computed precision-recall curves (PR-curves) by changing the detection threshold. Detected time intervals that overlap more than 50% with the ground truth activity intervals were considered as true positives. Average precision (AP) is also obtained from the curve by measuring the area under the PR-curve, and mean AP is computed by averaging APs of all activity classes.

In addition, in order to measure the early detection ability of our approach, we tested our approaches and baselines with multiple different observation ratio settings similar to [14]. More specifically, activity observation ratio was set from 0.1 to 1.0, and mean AP was measured per observation ratio. An observation ratio specifies the progress level of the activity execution. For example, observation

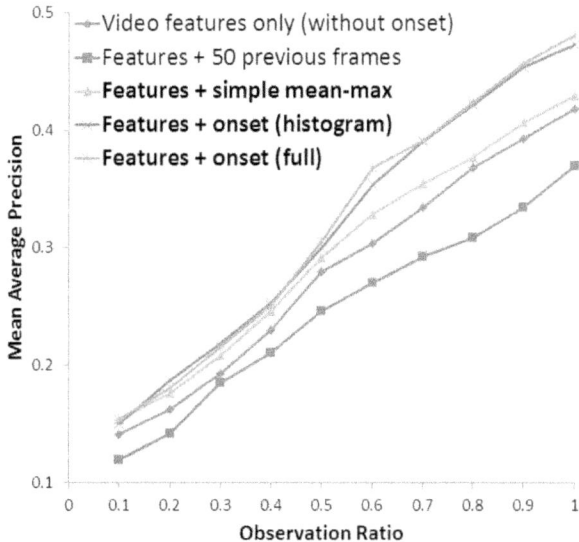

Figure 7: We compared approaches using different onset representations to illustrate the advantages of our proposed cascade histogram-based onset signature representation, while using an approach without randomness [14] as a baseline.

Table 1: A table comparing performances of the proposed approach with state-of-the-arts in terms of mean average precision (AP). Our proposed approach outperformed previous works particularly when making early recognition.

Method	50% observation	Full observation
Ours	**0.473**	**0.729**
Ryoo et al. [16]	0.360	0.717
Integral BoW [14]	0.280	0.418
SVM [3,11,16,19]	0.263	0.620
Bayesian	0.254	0.427
Onset only	0.127	0.156
Random	0.056	0.089

ratio of 0.2 implies that the system was asked to make the detection decision after observing the initial 20% of the activity (i.e., very early detection), and observation ratio of 1.0 implies that it is a standard after-the-fact detection. Let d be the observation ratio and $[g_1, g_2]$ be a ground truth time interval of the activity. For each experiment with an observation ratio d, we removed all video features extracted from the time interval $[g_1 + d \cdot (g_2 - g_1), g_2]$ (i.e., those observed after d). In addition, only the detection found before the observation ratio were consider as true positives.

4.4 Results

Figure 6 shows the mean AP values of activity detectors measured with various observation ratio settings. We are able to observe that our activity prediction formulation of using onset activities and their signatures is benefiting the system greatly. Mean APs of our approach (with onset) were constantly higher by 0.1~0.2 compared to the baseline SVM classifier using state-of-the-art features, achieving the same AP much earlier. For instance, in order to obtain the mean AP of 0.5, our early detector with onset signatures requires 55% observation while the SVM requires more than 80%. This gap can also be observed for integral bag-of-words with and without onset. Figure 5 shows example images of these two detection results, confirming the superiority of our proposed approach.

Figure 8 illustrates PR curves of the approaches. Early recognition approaches with our onset signatures particularly performed well on the activity of 'throwing an object', since it very often had a clear onset activity: 'reaching the object'. Our approach also performed well for 'hugging' and 'shaking' (relying on the existence of the onset 'waving' and the absence of 'reaching' or 'pointing'), and detected 'punching' earlier than those not using onset.

We also conducted an additional experiment to investigate advantages of our cascade histogram-based onset signature representation. We compared the performance of our onset representation with various other onset representations, including (i) the approach adding video features obtained 1~50 frames prior to the activity in addition to those from the activity's actual video segment, (ii) the approach using a simple onset representation of mean and max

values, (iii) the approach only using our histogram-based onset representation, and (iv) our final onset representation composed of histogram + mean and max. Figure 7 illustrates the result. It clearly shows that our onset signature representation effectively captures previous video information. Particularly, we are able to observe that simply adding 50 frames prior to the time interval is only confusing the system. Integral BoW was used as the base classifier in this experiment, since it does not contain randomness.

Finally, we explicitly compared recognition performances of our proposed early recognition approach with previous state-of-the-art approaches on our video dataset. Table 1 shows the results. Not only the final activity detection accuracies but also the early detection accuracies (i.e., observation ratio 50%) were compared.

5. CONCLUSION

This paper presented a methodology for early recognition of human activities. Early recognition ability is very essential for first-person vision systems which are required to function in real-world environments in real-time while constantly interacting with others. This makes the proposed technology very necessary for robust human-robot interactions, and this paper investigates such concepts for the first time. We formulated the early recognition problem to consider pre-activity observations, and presented an efficient new approach that uses the concept of 'onset'. Experimental results confirmed that our formulation enables superior early recognition performance to previous conventional approaches, and that our histogram-based representation of onset signatures benefits early recognition by capturing pre-activity observations.

Acknowledgment: The research described in this paper was carried out at the Jet Propulsion Laboratory, California Institute of Technology, under a contract with the National Aeronautics and Space Administration. This research was sponsored by the Army Research Laboratory and was accomplished under Cooperative Agreement Number W911NF-10-2-0016.

6. REFERENCES

[1] J. K. Aggarwal and M. S. Ryoo. Human activity analysis: A review. *ACM Computing Surveys*, 43:16:1–16:43, April 2011.

[2] J. Alon, V. Athitsos, Q. Yuan, and S. Sclaroff. A unified framework for gesture recognition and spatiotemporal gesture segmentation. *IEEE T PAMI*, 31(9):1685–1699, 2009.

[3] P. Dollar, V. Rabaud, G. Cottrell, and S. Belongie. Behavior recognition via sparse spatio-temporal features. In *IEEE Workshop on VS-PETS*, 2005.

[4] A. Fathi, A. Farhadi, and J. M. Rehg. Understanding egocentric activities. In *ICCV*, 2011.

[5] A. Fathi, J. Hodgins, and J. Rehg. Social interactions: A first-person perspective. In *CVPR*, 2012.

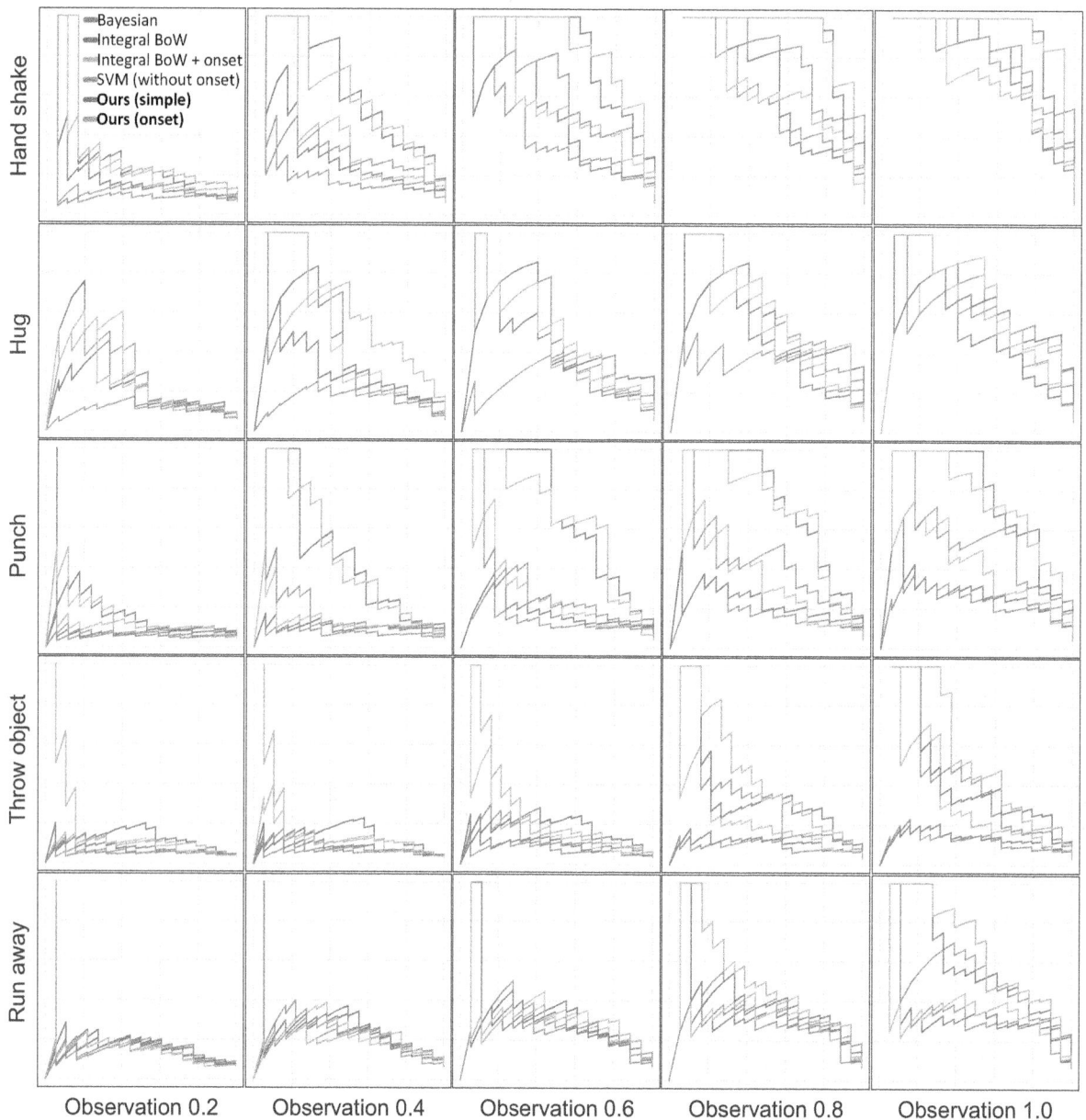

Figure 8: Precision-recall curves of each activity per observation ratio setting (left) and a table comparing accuracies of state-of-the-arts (right). X axis [0~1.0] of all graphs is 'recall' and Y axis [0~1.0] is 'precision'. Our approach with onset showed the best performance in all cases. Using our onset signature (light blue) particularly showed a huge performance increase over SVM (pink).

[6] M. Hoai and F. D. la Torre. Max-margin early event detectors. In *CVPR*, 2012.

[7] K. M. Kitani, T. Okabe, Y. Sato, and A. Sugimoto. Fast unsupervised ego-action learning for first-person sports videos. In *CVPR*, 2011.

[8] K. M. Kitani, B. D. Ziebart, J. A. Bagnell, and M. Hebert. Activity forecasting. In *ECCV*, 2012.

[9] H. S. Koppula and A. Saxena. Anticipating human activities using object affordances for reactive robotic response. In *RSS*, 2013.

[10] T. Lan, L. Sigal, and G. Mori. Social roles in hierarchical models for human activity recognition. In *CVPR*, 2012.

[11] I. Laptev. On space-time interest points. *IJCV*, 64(2):107–123, 2005.

[12] Y. J. Lee, J. Ghosh, and K. Grauman. Discovering important people and objects for egocentric video summarization. In *CVPR*, 2012.

[13] H. Pirsiavash and D. Ramanan. Detecting activities of daily living in first-person camera views. In *CVPR*, 2012.

[14] M. S. Ryoo. Human activity prediction: Early recognition of ongoing activities from streaming videos. In *ICCV*, 2011.

[15] M. S. Ryoo and J. Aggarwal. Spatio-temporal relationship match: Video structure comparison for recognition of complex human activities. In *ICCV*, 2009.

[16] M. S. Ryoo and L. Matthies. First-person activity recognition: What are they doing to me? In *CVPR*, 2013.

[17] S. Sadanand and J. Corso. Action bank: A high-level representation of activity in video. In *CVPR*, 2012.

[18] S. Waldherr, S. Thrun, and R. Romero. A gesture-based interface for human-robot interaction. *Autonomous Robots*, 9(2):151–173, 2000.

[19] L. Xia, C.-C. Chen, and J. K. Aggarwal. View invariant human action recognition using histograms of 3D joints. In *CVPRW*, 2012.

[20] D. Xie, S. Todorovic, and S.-C. Zhu. Inferring "dark matter" and "dark energy" from videos. In *ICCV*, 2013.

Mutual Modelling in Robotics: Inspirations for the Next Steps

Séverin Lemaignan, Pierre Dillenbourg
Computer-Human Interaction in Learning and Instruction Laboratory (CHILI)
École Polytechnique Fédérale de Lausanne (EPFL)
CH-1015 Lausanne, Switzerland
firstname.lastname@epfl.ch

ABSTRACT

Mutual modelling, the reciprocal ability to establish a mental model of the other, plays a fundamental role in human interactions. This complex cognitive skill is however difficult to fully apprehend as it encompasses multiple neuronal, psychological and social mechanisms that are generally not easily turned into computational models suitable for robots.

This article presents several perspectives on mutual modelling from a range of disciplines, and reflects on how these perspectives can be beneficial to the advancement of social cognition in robotics. We gather here both basic tools (concepts, formalisms, models) and exemplary experimental settings and methods that are of relevance to robotics.

This contribution is expected to consolidate the corpus of knowledge readily available to human-robot interaction research, and to foster interest for this fundamentally cross-disciplinary field.

1. INTRODUCTION

Human social dynamics rely upon the ability to effectively attribute beliefs, goals and percepts to other people. This set of meta-representational abilities shapes what is called a theory of mind (ToM) or the ability to mentalize, and leads to mutual modelling: the reciprocal ability to establish a mental model of the other. This lays at the core of human interactions: normal human social interactions depend upon the recognition of other sensory perspectives, the understanding of other mental states, and the recognition of complex non-verbal cues of attention and emotional state. As such, adapting and transferring these cognitive skills to social robots is an important research objective.

Until now, however, the human-robot interaction (HRI) community has only scratched the surface: in [41], Scassellati gave an initial account of Leslie's and Baron-Cohen's respective models of the emergence of a theory of mind (we discuss them below) from the perspective of robotics, but reported implementation work was limited to simple per-

ceptual precursors (like face detection or color saliencies detection). Since then, research in this field has been focused on applications relying on Flavell's *Level 1* [20] perspective-taking, *i.e.* perspective-taking that only requires perceptual abilities ("*I see (you do not see the book)*"), and actually mostly limited to visual perception (relevant work include Breazeal [10], Trafton [47] and Ros [38]).

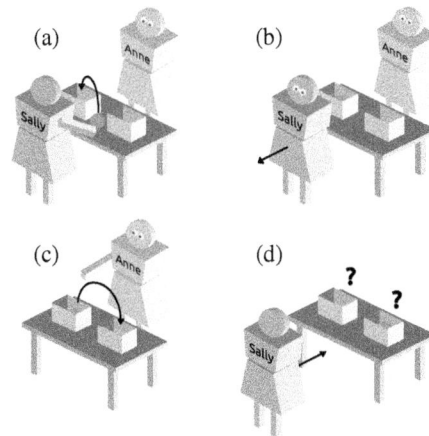

Figure 1: The false belief experiment: two puppets, "Anne" and "Sally" face each other, with two boxes between them. A child (the subject) observes. Sally puts a ball in the beige box and then leaves. While she is absent, Anne moves the ball to the blue box. Sally returns. The experimenter asks the child: *Where Sally would look for the ball?* Without a theory of mind, the child is not able to ascribe false beliefs to Sally, and therefore incorrectly answers *In the blue box*. Visual perspective taking only is sufficient to pass this task.

Based on perspective taking *Level 1* alone, Breazeal *et al.* [11] and Warnier *et al.* [54] successfully tackled the classical hallmark of theory of mind, the false belief experiment (also known as the "Sally and Anne" experiment, Figure 1, introduced by [55], original experimental setting by [6]). They demonstrated complete human-robot interaction scenarios where robots recognize and handle false belief situations in dyadic or triadic interactions, and exhibit helping behaviours that account for the missing/false beliefs of the human partners.

Those are significant achievements, also reassuring as to endow our robots with advanced socio-cognitive capabilities (Figure 2). However, one intuitively recognizes that mutual modelling goes indeed beyond computing what the human sees or does not see. Perceptions translate into subjective

(a) A robot interpreting situated multi-modal dialogue [9]

(b) A robot changing mental perspective during social learning [11]

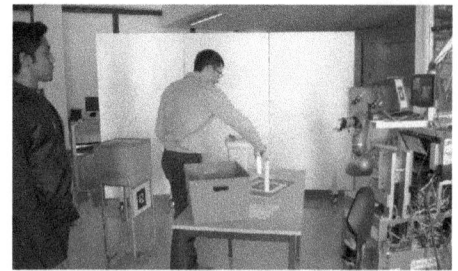

(c) False belief task, where the robot tracks which objects are visible to which human [54]

Figure 2: Examples of social robotics tasks benefiting from meta-cognition

representations: how can we access them? How to measure what the other know about oneself? Many levels of recipro-cal modelling overlap, with endless "I know that you know that I know that...": how to represent and manipulate them? What about the breadth of the models we build? Local to a given task or broader, deeper? How to tell apart mimicry from cognitive modelling in a joint action? Those many questions underline the complexity of a cognitive mechanism whose study lays at the crossroad of several academic fields. Robotics, as the science of embodied artificial intelligence, may be a convergence point to validate our understanding of this socio-cognitive skill.

This article contributes to this endeavour by proposing a broad overview of mutual modelling from three differ-ent perspectives in three different academic domains. First, *developmental psychology* (and, in particular, developmen-tal *patho*psychology) provides insights on human cognition and an extensive experimental framework that has a strong potential in robotics. *Psycho-linguistic* and *Collaborative Learning*, then, propose concepts and tools to apprehend the importance and the dynamics of knowledge sharing during social interactions. Finally, we give a look at the philoso-phy of the mind and the logical tools of *formal epistemol-ogy*: their use of modal logics to describe complex knowledge manipulation in groups appears as a pertinent direction for robotics to explore.

Conceptual bridges between these disciplines are numer-ous, and our aim is here to draw a picture of the field that can lay the bases for the further advancement of cognitive robotics in a social environment.

Note that the main focus of this contribution is *epistemic* mutual modelling: the modelling of (mostly declarative) knowledge of and by the others. As hinted at the begin-ning of this introduction, mutual modelling in general cov-ers more: what are our feelings towards each other? What are our respective goals? What are our respective moods? etc. Those questions have also started to be explored in robotics. *Human-aware task planning* [1, 12], for instance, uses symbolic task planners to plan actions not only for the robot, but also for the interacting humans, hence trying to predict, *i.e.* model, what (rational) humans may do in the given situation. From a completely different perspective, Fink *et al.* [19] propose cognitive models of how the human perceive robot behaviours over time. Those two very differ-ent yet prototypical examples give an idea of the breadth of the "mutual modelling question".

2. MUTUAL MODELLING AND DEVELOPMENTAL PSYCHOLOGY

Connections vs. representations.

In [21], Flavell relates perspective taking *Level 1* to es-tablishing *cognitive connections* (I see, I hear, I want, I like, I fear...), in contrast to perspective taking *Level 2* that re-lates to manipulating *representations*. This is exemplified by *appearance-reality* tasks, like the *elephant mask* experiment proposed in [21]: 3-years old children are not able to tell that an experimenter hidden behind a large elephant mask but who speaks normally *looks* like an elephant, *sounds* like the experimenter, and *really is* the experimenter. It appears that, while those children are able to explicitly manipulate cognitive connections (they know for instance that these are largely independent of each other and that they can evolve over time) and know as well that their own connections are independent of those of other people, they do not think that one concept can *seriously* (*i.e.* non playfully) hold several, possibly conflicting, representations.

This *connection-representation* account appears to be a significant component of a general theory of mind (one needs to recognize that the same object/concept may have dif-ferent, serious, representations to then accept false beliefs for instance). Figure 3 illustrates this difference between cognitive connections and representations in an imaginary human-robot interaction scenario. The *visual* perspective of the baby and the mother are represented: a robot endowed with perspective-taking level 1 is able to compute that the baby looks at the plug and the mother looks at the baby. *Representation*-level perspective taking, on the other hand, would require the robot to represent what the socket means to the baby (an attractive affordance), and what the baby's behaviour represents to the mother (a potential danger).

Developmental pathopsychology.

The false belief experiment that we have mentioned above, was proposed by Baron-Cohen in the frame of his research on autistic spectrum disorders (he shows that autistic chil-dren seem to actually lack a theory of mind and suggests this as the primary cause of their social impairments), and Frith and Happé further note in [23] that this specific deficit of autism has led to a large amount of research which proved, in turn, highly beneficial to the study of the development of theory of mind in general. They reference in [23] eight such tasks (Table 1), identified during the study of social cogni-

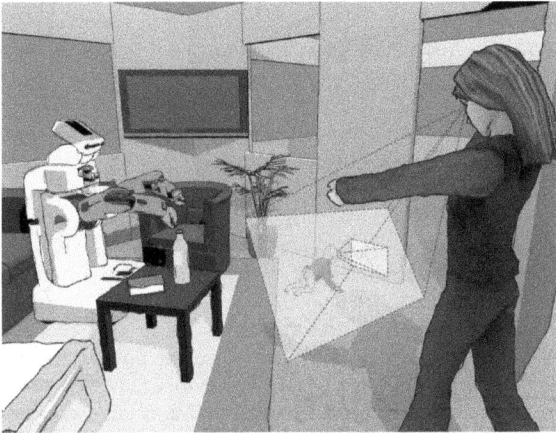

Figure 3: *Visual* perspectives allow for a first level of mutual modelling. However, to correctly comprehend the scene (and for the robot to adequately react, *representation-level* perspective taking is required: what does the power socket means to the baby? What does the situation means to the mother?

No mentalizing required	Mentalizing required
Ordering behavioural pictures	Ordering mentalistic pictures [7]
Understanding see	Understanding know [36]
Protoimperative pointing	Protodeclarative pointing [4]
Sabotage	Deception [44]
False photographs	False beliefs [29]
Recognizing happiness and sadness	Recognizing surprise [8]
Object occlusion	Information occlusion [5]
Literal expression	Metaphorical expression [24]

Table 1: Tasks requiring or not mentalizing to pass, listed by Frith and Happé in [23]

tion by autistic children. Each of them is proposed in two versions: one does not require mentalizing, while the other does require it. One of these tasks, for example, required children to distinguish emotions, namely happy/sad faces on one hand (*situation-based* emotion), and surprised faces on the other (*belief-based* emotion) [8]. Another task, based on the *penny-hiding game*, contrasts the two conditions in terms of *object occlusion* vs. *information occlusion* [5] (we detail it hereafter). These tasks prototypically illustrate social metacognition: one need to represent and reflect on someone else representations (and not only perceptions), and they are not addressed by today's research on social robots.

Experimental protocols in research on autistic spectrum disorders are often striking by their apparent straightforwardness because of the careful choice of interaction modalities: since autistic children frequently exhibit impairments beyond social ones (such as motor or linguistic ones), the experiments must be designed such that they require only basic cognitive skills beyond the social abilities that are tested. The Sally and Anne task, for instance, requires the observing child to be able to visually follow the marble, to remember the true location of the marble, to understand simple questions ("Where will Sally look for her marble?" in Baron-Cohen's protocol [6]) and eventually to give an answer, either verbally or with a gesture – the two first points being actually explicitly checked through questions: "Where is the marble really?" (reality control question) and "Where was the marble in the beginning?" (memory control question).

Likewise, current social robots have limited cognitive skills (no fast yet fine motor skills, limited speech production and understanding, limited scene segmentation and object recognition capabilities, etc.) and such tasks that effectively test a single cognitive skill (in this case, mentalizing) in near isolation are of high relevance for experimental social robotics.

Frith and Happé's list (Table 1) is in that regard especially interesting in that it mirrors pairs of task (ones which do not require mentalizing with similar ones which do require mentalizing), thus providing control tasks. *Object occlusion* vs. *Information occlusion* is one example of a (pair of) task(s) which evidence representation-level per-

spective taking through *adaptive deception*: during a simple game, the experimenter adapts its strategy (deceptive/non-deceptive behaviour) to the representation skills of its child opponent. The experimental setting is derived from the penny-hiding game protocol originally proposed by Oswald and Ollendick [34] and replicated and extended by Baron-Cohen in [5], who describes it as a two-person game in which the subject is actively involved, either as a guesser or as a hider. The hider hides the penny in one hand or the other, and then invites a guess. The game is repeated several time before switching the roles. Baron-Cohen proposes a specific index to rate the level of the players based on the idea of *information occlusion*: minimally, the hider must ensure *object occlusion* (the penny must not become visible to the guesser), while good hiders, with representation-level perspective taking skills, develop strategies (like random hand switching or deictic hints at the wrong hand) to prevent the guesser to find the penny (*information occlusion*). One could imagine a similar protocol adapted to robotics: the robot would play the role of the experimenter, adapting online its behaviour to what it understands of the perspective taking capabilities of the children, and would consequently require *second-order, representation-level* perspective taking from the robot.

Higher-order Theory of Mind.

While a great deal of research concerns itself with *first-order* theory of mind, *higher-order* (and particularly, second-order) ToM are also studied. Verbrugge and Mol [53] describe the different levels in the following terms:

> To have a first-order ToM is to assume that someone's beliefs, thoughts and desires influence one's behavior. A first-order thought could be: *He does not know that his book is on the table.* In second-order ToM it is also recognized that to predict others' behavior, the desires and beliefs that they have of one's self and the predictions of oneself by others must be taken into account. So, for example, you can realize that what someone expects you to do will affect his behavior. For example, "(I know) he does not know that I know his book is on the table" would be part of my second-order ToM. To have a third-order ToM is to assume others to have a second-order ToM, etc.

Perner shows in [35] that 2nd-order ToM is mastered around 8 years old, and Flobbe *et al.* propose in [22] a set of three tasks (a second-order false belief task, a strategic game and a sentence comprehension test) that require second-order mentalizing to succeed. The second-order false belief task that they propose (known as the *Chocolate bar task*) effectively evidence higher-order ToM:

> John and Mary are in the living room when their mother returns home with a chocolate bar that she bought. Mother gives the chocolate to John, who puts it into the drawer. After John has left the room, Mary hides the chocolate in the toy chest. But John accidentally sees Mary putting the chocolate into the toy chest. Crucially, Mary does not see John. When John returns to the living room, he wants to get his chocolate.

Flobbe then asks the subjects: *"Where is the chocolate now?"* (reality control question), *"Does John know that Mary has hidden the chocolate in the toy chest?"* (first-order ignorance question), *"Does Mary know that John saw her hide the chocolate?"* (linguistic control question), and *"Where does Mary think that John will look for the chocolate?"* (second-order false belief question). Besides, Flobbe asks the participants to justify their answer (*"Why does she think that?"*). In her study, 82% of a group of 40 children (M=9 year old) successfully passed the task.

While literature on higher-order of mutual modelling is generally scarce, *agreement* and *common belief* is another interesting social situation: Verbrugge [52, p. 664] reports after an experiment by Mant and Perner [32] where a child is disappointed by his father who changed the announced plan to go swimming. In one condition, the child and the father had previously mutually agreed, while in the other, no explicit agreement took place (to a child observer, it actually appears that the situation is **worse** if the child and the father did **not** previously explicitly agree). Children before ten do not distinguish between the two conditions, and Verbrugge's proposed explanation relies on the concept of *social commitment*, which implies the *common belief* between the two agents that the father *intends* to go swimming and the child is *interested* in going swimming.

Common belief ("we believe that we believe that we believe that... we agreed") is defined in epistemic logic (see section 4) as an infinite recursion ("∞-order" ToM), and Verbrugge suggests that this mutual modelling mechanism is therefore harder to master for children than 2nd-order ToM for instance.

3. MUTUAL MODELLING IN PSYCHOLINGUISTICS AND COLLABORATIVE LEARNING

A support for shared understanding.

Computer Supported Collaborative Learning (CSCL) researches the cognitive mechanisms and practical techniques underpinning efficient learning in social situations. From its very beginning, CSCL research has been following Roschelle and Teasley's suggestion [39] that collaborative learning has something to do with the process of constructing and maintaining a *shared understanding* of the task at hand. Building a shared/mutual understanding refers to the upper class of collaborative learning situations, those in which students should build upon each other's understanding to refine their own understanding. What is expected to produce learning is not the mere fact that two students build the same understanding but the cognitive effort they have to engage to build this shared understanding [43].

The construction of a shared understanding has been investigated for several years in psycholinguistics, under the notion of *grounding*[1] (Clark, in [15]). However, the relevance of grounding mechanisms for explaining learning outcomes has been questioned in learning sciences. The monitoring and repair of misunderstanding explains for instance referential failures in short dialogue episodes but does hardly predict *conceptual change* (*i.e.* the acquisition, acceptance and integration of a new belief into one's mental model) over longer sessions [17]. The cumulative effect of grounding episodes can probably be better understood from a sociocultural perspective:

> Collaborative learning is associated with the increased cognitive-interactional effort involved in the transition from *learning to understand each other* to *learning to understand the meanings of the semiotic tools that constitute the mediators of interpersonal interaction* [3]

Along this line, several scholars suggest that CSCL research should go deeper in the understanding of how partners engage into shared meaning making [45] or *intersubjective* meaning making [46].

Paradoxically, while Clark's theory is somewhat too linguistic from a conceptual change viewpoint, it is criticized at the same time as being too cognitivist by some psycholinguists, *i.e.* as overestimating the amount of shared knowledge and mutual representations actually necessary to conduct a dialogue. The fundamental issue, as old as philosophy, is the degree of coupling between the different levels of dialogue, mostly between the lexical/syntactical level and the deeper semantic levels. In [37], Pickering and Garrod argue that the mutual understanding starts mostly with a *superficial alignment* at the level of the linguistic representations, due to priming mechanisms, and that this local alignment may – in some cases – lead to a *global alignment* of the semantic level (*deep grounding*). For these authors, the convergence in dialogue, and even the repair of some misunderstandings, is explained by this mimetic behavior more than by a monitoring of each other's knowledge: *"...interlocutors do not need to monitor and develop full common ground as a regular, constant part of routine conversation, as it would be unnecessary and far too costly. Establishment of full common ground is, we argue, a specialized and non-automatic process that is used primarily in times of difficulty (when radical misalignment becomes apparent)."* [37] This view is actually not incompatible with Clark's *grounding criterion* [14]: the degree of shared understanding that peers need to reach depends upon the task they perform. For instance, a dialogue between two surgeons might rely on superficial alignment if they talk about their friends but has to guarantee accurate common grounds when talking about

---

[1]Note that the meaning of *grounding* – ensuring a shared understanding of a situation during an interaction – that we employ in this article must be distinguished from its meaning in the context of *symbol grounding* as defined by Harnad [25].

which intervention will be conducted in which way on which patient.

Deep grounding or shared meaning making requires some cognitive load. For Clark, what is important is not the individual effort made by the receiver of a communicative act, but the overall *least collaborative effort* [15]. The cost of producing a perfect utterance may be higher than the cost of repairing the problems that may arise through misunderstandings. For instance, subjects are less careful about adapting their utterances to their partner when they know they can provide feedback on his/her understanding [42]. Dillenbourg *et al.* introduced the notion of *optimal collaborative effort* [16] to stress that misunderstanding should not be viewed as something to be avoided (if this was possible), but as an opportunity to engage into verbalization, explanation, negotiation, and so forth.

CSCL model of mutual modelling.

Dillenbourg proposes in [40] a model to represent mutual modelling situations. He uses the notation $\mathcal{M}(A, B, X)$ to denote "A knows that B knows X" (equivalent to the epistemic logic notation $K_A K_B X$ that we present in the next section). This notation does not mean that A has an explicit, monolithic representation of B: it must be understood as an abstraction referring to possibly complex socio-cognitive processes. Besides, he refer to the *degree of accuracy* of the model as $\mathcal{M}^\circ(A, B, X)$.

He parametrizes and assesses the mutual modelling *effort* through 3 variables:

1. Tasks vary a lot with respect to how much they require mutual understanding. The *grounding criterion* [15] $\mathcal{M}^\circ_{min}$ refers to how important it is to mutually share a piece of information X to succeed the task T. It can be computed as the probability to succeed T despite the fact X is not grounded. $\mathcal{M}^\circ_{min}(A, B, X)$ can be estimated from the correlation between $\mathcal{M}^\circ(A, B, X)$ and the task performance.

2. Before any specific grounding action, there is usually a non-null probability that X is mutually understood by A and B (*e.g.* X is part of A's and B's cultures, it is manifest to co-present subjects or simply there is not much space for misunderstanding or disagreement about X). He notes the theoretical accuracy of initial grounds $\mathcal{M}^\circ_{t_0}(A, B, X)$.

3. The cost of grounding X refers to the physical and cognitive effort required to perform a grounding act α: a verbal repair (*e.g.* rephrasing), a deictic gesture, a physical move to adopt one partner's viewpoint, etc. This cost varies according to media features [13].

These notations lead to simple representations of mutual modelling during interactions, and Dillenbourg derives several questions out of this model. Adapted to a human-robot interaction situation, Figure 4 represents for instance a dyadic interaction (we use H to denote a human, while R stands for a robot). Δ_1 illustrates what Dillenbourg calls the *symmetry* question (*Is the accuracy of my model related or not to the accuracy of your model?*).

With triads (two humans H_1 and H_2 and a robot R), we may compute the accuracy of 6 models $\mathcal{M}^\circ(H_1, H_2, X)$, $\mathcal{M}^\circ(H_2, H_1, X)$, $\mathcal{M}^\circ(H_1, R, X)$, $\mathcal{M}^\circ(R, H_1, X)$, $\mathcal{M}^\circ(R, H_2, X)$ and $\mathcal{M}^\circ(H_2, R, X)$.

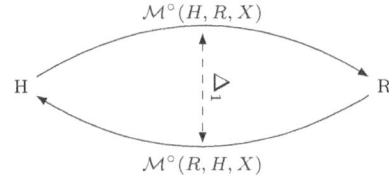

Figure 4: Mutual modelling in a dyadic interaction, $\Delta_1 = \Delta(\mathcal{M}^\circ(H, R, X), \mathcal{M}^\circ(R, H, X))$

This leads to two *triangle questions* relevant to HRI (Figure 5): Do H_1 and H_2 have the same accuracy when modelling the robot R? ($\Delta_2 = \Delta(\mathcal{M}(H_1, R, X), \mathcal{M}(H_2, R, X))$), and conversely, what may lead R to model more accurately H_1 or H_2? ($\Delta_3 = \Delta(\mathcal{M}(R, H_1, X), \mathcal{M}(R, H_2, X))$).

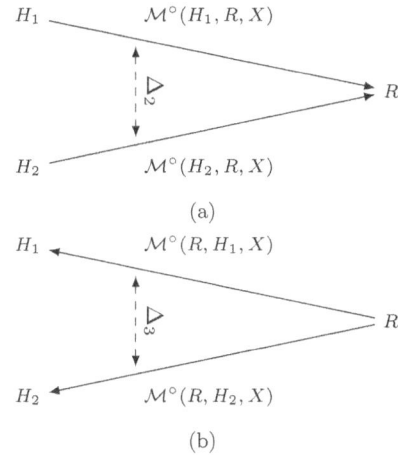

Figure 5: Mutual modelling in a triadic interaction

Finally, Dillenbourg also suggests a *rectangle question*: how self- versus other modelling compares (Δ_4 in Figure 6)? This gives an indication of meta-cognitive skills of the agents. We can also question if the modelling skills depend upon what aspects are being modeled (X or Y) which would explain vertical differences (Δ_5 in Figure 6).

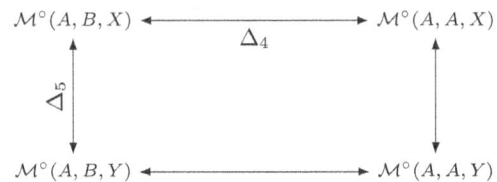

Figure 6: Meta-cognitive skills and domain-dependent modelling

This model, designed in the context of human collaboration, evidences questions that are relevant as well to human-robot interactions.

4. FORMAL EPISTEMOLOGY

The above model of mutual modelling is meant as a practical tool to reason on knowledge dynamics in group interactions and it does not look at being a formal model, whereas formal epistemology, a subfield of the philosophy of mind, focuses on this question.

Modal logics look at the formal representation of *possible worlds*, *i.e.* the *possibility* or *necessity* of certain assertions to hold, and is naturally suited to build mathematical representations of situations such as *"the robot knows [the baby may not know what a power socket is]"*.

The *epistemic modal logic* in particular (see [26] for an overview and references) focuses on the formal representation of knowledge and beliefs of agents, with the operators $K_i \varphi$ (epistemic operator: agent i knows φ) and $B_i \varphi$ (doxatic operator: agent i believes φ). Every possible logical propositions belong then to possible *worlds* (noted w), that are *accessible* (*i.e.* compatible) or not to one's beliefs and knowledge.

Single-agent epistemic systems can naturally extend to multi-agent systems [18, chapt. 4]: if p stands for "the power socket is dangerous", $K_{mother} p \wedge K_{mother} \neg K_{baby} p$ states that the mother knows that the socket is dangerous, and also knows that the baby is not aware of this. This provides a formal tool to represent mutual models (the *order* of mutual modelling as discussed in the context of developmental psychology is here directly related to the nesting depth of the epistemic operator).

This approach has led to applications to the representation of knowledge dynamics on concrete, albeit arguably toy, scenarios: van Ditmarsch presents for instance in [51] the formal description of possible Cluedo strategies based on what players know about other players' knowledge, and along the same line, Verbrugge and Mol analyse mutual modelling in a strategic game with imperfect information (derived from Mastermind) in [53].

Amongst the several *modal operators of knowledge* that have been developed, the *common-knowledge* operator CK is of particular interest. If we define the *shared-knowledge* operator EK as $EK_J \varphi \leftrightarrow \bigwedge_{i \in J} K_i \varphi$, *i.e.* φ is *shared knowledge* amongst the group J iff every agent in J knows φ, then $CK_J \varphi \leftrightarrow EK_J \varphi \wedge EK_J EK_J \varphi \wedge EK_J EK_J EK_J \varphi \wedge ...$, *i.e.* φ is shared knowledge, and it is also shared knowledge that φ is shared knowledge, etc. (this presentation follows [27]). This illustrates how epistemic logic can represent non-trivial social knowledge situations.

Verbrugge further investigates the social aspect of epistemic logics in [52] and proposes a survey of epistemic logic applications to *social reasoning*. He underlines both the limits of epistemic logic for that purpose (common epistemic systems assume for instance $K_i \psi \rightarrow K_i K_i \psi$, which reads "$i$ knows φ" implies "i knows that i knows φ", *i.e.* i can always introspect, a rather idealized model of human cognition) and the recent advancement towards modelling *human* social cognition, which implies for instance limited rationality. One of these attempts is formalized as a *doxastic epistemic logic* by van Ditmarsch and Labuschagne in [49], with an explicit focus on modelling *theory of mind* mechanisms. This model builds upon *dynamic epistemic logic* [50] (DEL, epistemic logics augmented with mechanisms for knowledge changes), and the modelling of agents' degrees of belief through a *preference* accessibility relation.

The mathematical objects build from these different modal logics are natural candidates for transposition into representational systems and controllers for robots. Historically in robotics, the main research perspective has been towards the *action logics*, and in particular the influential *situation calculus* (a propositional logic initially proposed by McCarthy, and fully axiomatized in the context of robotics

by Levesque *et al.* in [30], which led to the GOLOG logic programming language [31]). Many other action logics have been proposed including modal logics like PDL (*Propositional Dynamic Logic*).

Recent efforts have focused on bridging action logics (that deal with *ontic* actions, *i.e.* actions which have tangible, physical consequences) with epistemic logics (that deal with *epistemic* actions, *i.e.* knowledge changes). Van Ditmarsch proposes in [48] for instance a solution to embed a practical subset of situation calculus into a dynamic epistemic logic, and Herzig provides in [27] a broader overview of the interplay between current action and epistemic logics.

From a practical perspective however, implementations of these logics into practical reasoners or programming languages remain rare. The development of *Description Logics* (DL) in the knowledge representation community, along with effective, practical tools (like reasoners) is a possible path forward, since DL semantics overlap to some extend with modal logics [2, chap. 4.2.2], and *Description Logics* have already been successfully used in robotics (see [28] for a review).

5. CONCLUSION: SCAFFOLDING FOR SOCIO-COGNITIVE ROBOTICS

Several lessons can be taken out of these three perspectives on mutual modelling. First, **concepts** and terminology stand out and social robotics would benefit from incorporating them. Second, **models** of mutual modelling exist that would make sense in robotics as well, along with investigation strategies and approaches that translate well to robotics. Finally, we believe that several **experimental settings** designed and successfully tested in other disciplines shape an interesting way forward for (experimental) social robotics.

Flavell's distinction between *cognitive connections* on one hand, and *mental representations* on the other hand helps in recognizing the limits of perceptual perspective taking as currently achieved in robotics. This *connection-representation* account, put into perspective with the semantic expressiveness of modal logics, leads to a first insight: we need to come up with an effective design for a meta-representational system (*i.e.* a system that *represents representations* as abstracted, manipulable entities) to integrate into homogeneous objects both cognitive connections (*i.e.* percepts) and representations (including suppositions, similar to the idea of *pre-supposition accommodation* [33]).

The depth of mutual modelling required for effective collaboration is another question that is relevant to HRI. Pickering and Garrod, with the idea of *superficial alignment* versus *global alignment* or *deep grounding*, come to the conclusion that *mimicking* behaviours is often a more efficient way to work together than establishing a full common ground, which is also expressed by Clark in terms of *least collaborative effort* and Dillenbourg in terms of *optimal collaborative effort*: misunderstandings should not be viewed as something to systematically avoid since the repair actions they may elicit can also be viewed as a way to engage the agents into new interactions (an idea not unrelated to the *entropy* concept in information theory). And Clark's concept of *grounding criterion* provides a practical tool to represent and manipulate this idea of degree of shared understanding required by the agents to perform a given task.

These considerations lead to a second insight: the level of *mutual grounding* (*i.e.* of mutual understanding) of a given situation of interaction may prove to be a valuable metric to measure the quality of human-robot interactions. Mutual modelling certainly plays a key role here, but lower-level, sub-cognitive strategies like one-off mimicking may be powerful complements and need to be investigated in parallel.

Then, the mere discussion of mutual modelling problems ("The robot knows that we both know that it knows that...") is also by itself a challenge. Formal models like the ones developed in epistemic logic, or practical tools like the ones stemming from CSCL are valuable objects to add to the toolset of HRI. Not only they help clarifying the problems, but they also evidence new challenges: the definition of common-knowledge as $CK_J\varphi \leftrightarrow EK_J\varphi \wedge EK_J EK_J\varphi \wedge EK_J EK_J EK_J\varphi \wedge...$ for instance points at the recursive nature of common knowledge. While "common-sense knowledge" is a commonly-used term in the field of knowledge representation and reasoning to describe "all those facts that everyone knows about", it is probably important to better distinguish in the future between *shared knowledge* and *common knowledge* when a robot interact with a human.

A third insight that follows relates to the adoption of modal logics in HRI: we believe that the current state of the technology in robotics (with the advancements in scene understanding, situation assessment, human activity recognition, and their subsequent symbolic grounding), combined with our current understanding of modal logics (and epistemic logics in particular), lay the foundations for us to now broadly embrace formal models to implement new, complex social mechanisms in robots.

Lastly, we hope that this article may suggest new ideas of experimental protocols and studies to conduct in HRI. We found experimental research in developmental psychology to be especially inspiring in that regard: the numerous protocols that have been designed over the years to evidence cognitive and social skills by children (and even more, cognitively impaired children) stand out as a source of inspiration for cognitive robotics, and this article hopefully shed some light on some of the less well-known studies and tasks that could become new milestones for the development of human-robot interaction.

Acknowledgments

This research was supported by the Swiss National Science Foundation through the National Centre of Competence in Research Robotics.

We would also like to thank Tony Belpaeme for his feedback on an early version of this article.

6. REFERENCES

[1] R. Alami, A. Clodic, V. Montreuil, E. A. Sisbot, and R. Chatila. Toward human-aware robot task planning. In *AAAI Spring Symposium: To Boldly Go Where No Human-Robot Team Has Gone Before*, pages 39–46, 2006.

[2] F. Baader, D. Calvanese, D. L. McGuinness, D. Nardi, and P. F. Patel-Schneider, editors. *The Description Logic Handbook: Theory, Implementation and Applications*. Cambridge University Press, New York, NY, USA, 2nd edition, 2003.

[3] M. Baker, T. Hansen, R. Joiner, and D. Traum. The role of grounding in collaborative learning tasks. *Collaborative learning: Cognitive and computational approaches*, pages 31–63, 1999.

[4] S. Baron-Cohen. Perceptual role taking and protodeclarative pointing in autism. *British Journal of Developmental Psychology*, 7(2):113–127, 1989.

[5] S. Baron-Cohen. Out of sight or out of mind? another look at deception in autism. *Journal of Child Psychology and Psychiatry*, 33(7):1141–1155, 1992.

[6] S. Baron-Cohen, A. Leslie, and U. Frith. Does the autistic child have a "theory of mind"? *Cognition*, 1985.

[7] S. Baron-Cohen, A. M. Leslie, and U. Frith. Mechanical, behavioural and intentional understanding of picture stories in autistic children. *British Journal of developmental psychology*, 4(2):113–125, 1986.

[8] S. Baron-Cohen, A. Spitz, and P. Cross. Do children with autism recognise surprise? a research note. *Cognition & Emotion*, 7(6):507–516, 1993.

[9] T. Belpaeme, P. E. Baxter, R. Read, R. Wood, H. Cuayáhuitl, B. Kiefer, S. Racioppa, I. Kruijff-Korbayová, G. Athanasopoulos, V. Enescu, et al. Multimodal child-robot interaction: Building social bonds. *Journal of Human-Robot Interaction*, 1(2):33–53, 2012.

[10] C. Breazeal, M. Berlin, A. Brooks, J. Gray, and A. Thomaz. Using perspective taking to learn from ambiguous demonstrations. *Robotics and Autonomous Systems*, pages 385–393, 2006.

[11] C. Breazeal, J. Gray, and M. Berlin. An embodied cognition approach to mindreading skills for socially intelligent robots. *The International Journal of Robotics Research*, 28(5):656–680, 2009.

[12] M. Cirillo, L. Karlsson, and A. Saffiotti. Human-aware task planning: an application to mobile robots. *ACM Transactions on Intelligent Systems and Technology (TIST)*, 1(2):15, 2010.

[13] H. H. Clark and S. E. Brennan. Grounding in communication. *Perspectives on socially shared cognition*, 13(1991):127–149, 1991.

[14] H. H. Clark and E. F. Schaefer. Contributing to discourse. *Cognitive science*, 13(2):259–294, 1989.

[15] H. H. Clark and D. Wilkes-Gibbs. Referring as a collaborative process. *Cognition*, 22(1):1–39, 1986.

[16] P. Dillenbourg, M. J. Baker, A. Blaye, and C. O'Malley. The evolution of research on collaborative learning. pages 189–211, 1995.

[17] P. Dillenbourg and D. Traum. Sharing solutions: Persistence and grounding in multimodal collaborative problem solving. *The Journal of the Learning Sciences*, 15(1):121–151, 2006.

[18] R. Fagin, J. Y. Halpern, Y. Moses, and M. Y. Vardi. *Reasoning About Knowledge*. MIT Press, Cambridge, MA, USA, 1995.

[19] J. Fink, S. Lemaignan, C. Braboszcz, and P. Dillenbourg. Dynamics of anthropomorphism in human-robot interaction. *Frontiers in Cognitive Science*, 2014. Submitted.

[20] J. H. Flavell. The development of knowledge about

visual perception. *Nebraska Symposium on Motivation*, 25:43–76, 1977.

[21] J. H. Flavell, F. L. Green, and E. R. Flavell. Developmental changes in young children's knowledge about the mind. *Cognitive Development*, 5(1):1–27, 1990.

[22] L. Flobbe, R. Verbrugge, P. Hendriks, and I. Krämer. Children's application of theory of mind in reasoning and language. *Journal of Logic, Language and Information*, 17(4):417–442, 2008.

[23] U. Frith and F. Happé. Autism: Beyond "theory of mind". *Cognition*, 50(1):115–132, 1994.

[24] F. G. Happé. Communicative competence and theory of mind in autism: A test of relevance theory. *Cognition*, 48(2):101–119, 1993.

[25] S. Harnad. The symbol grounding problem. *Physica D: Nonlinear Phenomena*, 42(1):335–346, 1990.

[26] V. Hendricks and J. Symons. Epistemic logic. In *Stanford Encyclopedia of Philosophy*. 2008.

[27] A. Herzig. Logics of knowledge and action: critical analysis and challenges. *Autonomous Agents and Multi-Agent Systems*, pages 1–35, 2014.

[28] S. Lemaignan. *Grounding the Interaction: Knowledge Management for Interactive Robots*, chapter Symbolic Knowledge Representation, pages 15–59. 2012.

[29] A. M. Leslie and L. Thaiss. Domain specificity in conceptual development: Neuropsychological evidence from autism. *Cognition*, 43(3):225–251, 1992.

[30] H. Levesque, F. Pirri, and R. Reiter. Foundations for the situation calculus. *Electronic Transactions on Artificial Intelligence*, 2:159–178, 1998.

[31] H. Levesque, R. Reiter, Y. Lesperance, F. Lin, and R. Scherl. GOLOG: A logic programming language for dynamic domains. *The Journal of Logic Programming*, 31(1-3):59–83, 1997.

[32] C. M. Mant and J. Perner. The child's understanding of commitment. *Developmental Psychology*, 24(3):343, 1988.

[33] N. Mavridis and D. Roy. Grounded situation models for robots: Where words and percepts meet. In *IEEE/RSJ International Conference on Intelligent Robots and Systems*, 2006.

[34] D. P. Oswald and T. H. Ollendick. Role taking and social competence in autism and mental retardation. *Journal of autism and developmental disorders*, 19(1):119–127, 1989.

[35] J. Perner. Higher-order beliefs and intentions in children's understanding of social interaction. *Developing theories of mind*, pages 271–294, 1988.

[36] J. Perner, U. Frith, A. M. Leslie, and S. R. Leekam. Exploration of the autistic child's theory of mind: Knowledge, belief, and communication. *Child development*, pages 689–700, 1989.

[37] M. J. Pickering and S. Garrod. Alignment as the basis for successful communication. *Research on Language and Computation*, 4(2-3):203–228, 2006.

[38] R. Ros, E. A. Sisbot, R. Alami, J. Steinwender, K. Hamann, and F. Warneken. Solving ambiguities with perspective taking. In *5th ACM/IEEE International Conference on Human-Robot Interaction*, 2010.

[39] J. Roschelle and S. D. Teasley. The construction of shared knowledge in collaborative problem solving. In *Computer supported collaborative learning*, pages 69–97. Springer, 1995.

[40] M. Sangin, N. Nova, G. Molinari, and P. Dillenbourg. Partner modeling is mutual. In *Proceedings of the 8th iternational conference on Computer Supported Collaborative Learning*, pages 625–632. International Society of the Learning Sciences, 2007.

[41] B. Scassellati. Theory of mind for a humanoid robot. *Autonomous Robots*, 12(1):13–24, 2002.

[42] M. F. Schober. Spatial perspective-taking in conversation. *Cognition*, 47(1):1–24, 1993.

[43] D. L. Schwartz. The emergence of abstract representations in dyad problem solving. *The Journal of the Learning Sciences*, 4(3):321–354, 1995.

[44] B. Sodian and U. Frith. Deception and sabotage in autistic, retarded and normal children. *Journal of Child Psychology and Psychiatry*, 33(3):591–605, 1992.

[45] G. Stahl. Meaning making in cscl: Conditions and preconditions for cognitive processes by groups. In *Proceedings of the 8th iternational conference on Computer supported collaborative learning*, pages 652–661. International Society of the Learning Sciences, 2007.

[46] D. D. Suthers. Technology affordances for intersubjective meaning making: A research agenda for cscl. *International Journal of Computer-Supported Collaborative Learning*, 1(3):315–337, 2006.

[47] J. Trafton, N. Cassimatis, M. Bugajska, D. Brock, F. Mintz, and A. Schultz. Enabling effective human-robot interaction using perspective-taking in robots. *IEEE Transactions on Systems, Man and Cybernetics, Part A: Systems and Humans*, 35(4):460–470, 2005.

[48] H. van Ditmarsch, A. Herzig, and T. De Lima. From situation calculus to dynamic epistemic logic. *Journal of Logic and Computation*, 2010.

[49] H. van Ditmarsch and W. Labuschagne. My beliefs about your beliefs: a case study in theory of mind and epistemic logic. *Synthese*, 155(2):191–209, 2007.

[50] H. van Ditmarsch, W. van der Hoek, and B. P. Kooi. *Dynamic epistemic logic*, volume 337. Springer, 2007.

[51] H. P. van Ditmarsch. The description of game actions in cluedo. *Game theory and applications*, 8:1–28, 2002.

[52] R. Verbrugge. Logic and social cognition. *Journal of Philosophical Logic*, 38(6):649–680, 2009.

[53] R. Verbrugge and L. Mol. Learning to apply theory of mind. *Journal of Logic, Language and Information*, 17(4):489–511, 2008.

[54] M. Warnier, J. Guitton, S. Lemaignan, and R. Alami. When the robot puts itself in your shoes. managing and exploiting human and robot beliefs. In *Proceedings of the 21st IEEE International Symposium on Robot and Human Interactive Communication*, pages 948–954, 2012.

[55] H. Wimmer and J. Perner. Beliefs about beliefs: Representation and constraining function of wrong beliefs in young children's understanding of deception. *Cognition*, 13(1):103–128, 1983.

Learning to Interact with a Human Partner

Mayada Oudah, Vahan Babushkin, Tennom Chenlinangjia, and Jacob W. Crandall
Masdar Institute of Science and Technology
Abu Dhabi, United Arab Emirates
{myoudah,vbabushkin,xchenlinangjia,jcrandall}@masdar.ac.ae

ABSTRACT

Despite the importance of mutual adaption in human relationships, online learning is not yet used during most successful human-robot interactions. The lack of online learning in HRI to date can be attributed to at least two unsolved challenges: random exploration (a core component of most online-learning algorithms) and the slow convergence rates of previous online-learning algorithms. However, several recently developed online-learning algorithms have been reported to learn at much faster rates than before, which makes them candidates for use in human-robot interactions. In this paper, we explore the ability of these algorithms to learn to interact with people. Via user study, we show that these algorithms alone do not consistently learn to collaborate with human partners. Similarly, we observe that humans fail to consistently collaborate with each other in the absence of explicit communication. However, we demonstrate that one algorithm does learn to effectively collaborate with people when paired with a novel cheap-talk communication system. In addition to this technical achievement, this work highlights the need to address AI and HRI synergistically rather than independently.

Keywords

Human-Robot Interaction; Online Learning; Cheap Talk

1. INTRODUCTION

As in human-human relationships, many human-robot interactions are punctuated by repeated interaction amid conflicting interests. Due to information asymmetry, modeling effects, and differences between the goals of interacts and robot designers, the robot may pursue an agenda that is not fully shared by its human partner. For example, consider a robot provided by an individual to their elderly parent. The robot may provide many services the elderly parent desires, such as helping him to dress, retrieving the newspaper, etc. However, the robot may also be instructed to ensure that the elderly parent does certain things he might not want to do, such as taking beneficial medications the elderly parent dislikes. In such scenarios, the robot must skillfully interact with the elderly parent to achieve and maintain a collaborative, mutually desirable, relationship.

As in human-human relationships, collaborative outcomes are most likely to be realized when the robot and human can adapt to each other. The ability to adapt to an (also) adapting human partner, requires a robot to employ online learning. However, online-learning algorithms are not yet utilized in most human-robot interactions, particularly in scenarios with conflicting interests. We attribute this deficiency to two previously unsolved challenges. First, most online-learning algorithms designed for interactions with other individuals do not learn at time scales that support interaction with people. They either require thousands of interactions to learn effective behaviors [4, 8], or are incapable of learning collaborative solutions. Both deficiencies severely limit the possibility of effective interactions.

A second challenge to using online learning in human-robot interactions is that most online-learning algorithms rely on random exploration to learn effectively. Random exploration makes the robot unpredictable and (seemingly) irrational, which can cause human partners to form attitudes toward the robot that effactually eliminate the potential for strong collaborations. For example, random exploration could cause the human partner to mistrust the robot's motives, intelligence, and future behavior, thus causing the human to stop interacting with the robot altogether.

We hypothesize that both of these issues can now be overcome by interweaving principles of HRI with recent developments in online learning. Though past online-learning algorithms designed for interaction with others learn too slowly, several recently developed algorithms are reported to learn at time scales that support interactions with people [6, 14, 15]. These learning algorithms still use random exploration, but we anticipate that many of the negative effects of this randomness can be overcome by strengthening the degree of engagement between the human and the learning algorithm. Since *cheap talk* (i.e., non-binding, costless communication) has been shown to improve collaboration among people [17, 3], we consider interweaving cheap talk into an online learning algorithm to strengthen the human-robot interaction.

Interweaving effective cheap talk into an online learning algorithm is nontrivial, as most machine learning algorithms have representations that are not easily interpreted by people. Thus, it is difficult to infer high-level strategic plans from these algorithms' internal representations, let alone determine how to communicate these strategies to people (via speech acts) in arbitrary scenarios. Fortunately, the internal representations of one recently developed online-learning algorithm is more accessible than many of these past algorithms. In this paper, we describe how to generate cheap talk communication within this algorithm.

We make three primary contributions. First, we demonstrate via user study the inability of two recently developed learning algorithms (CFR [15] and Gabe-S++ [5]) to effectively learn to collaborate with people, despite the fact that these algorithms have relatively fast learning rates. In the absence of explicit communication, our results also show that people do not consistently learn to collaborate with each other. However, people do learn to collaborate with each other when they are allowed to talk to each other. Thus, in our second contribution, we describe how to generate cheap talk using Gabe-S++. Third, we show that the resulting learning system learns to consistently collaborate with people in two different scenarios. Our results indicate that this learning system learns to collaborate with people nearly as well as people collaborate with each other. These results demonstrate the importance of addressing AI and HRI simultaneously rather than independently.

2. BACKGROUND

This work addresses two technical challenges: online learning in repeated interactions and integrating cheap talk into learning algorithms. We discuss background information and past work related to these two topics after formally defining the domain.

2.1 Repeated Stochastic Games

Many repeated human-robot interactions can be modeled as repeated stochastic games (RSGs; also known as repeated Markov games). These games are played in episodes (or rounds). Each round consists of a sequence of *stage games* (or states) S. In each state $s \in S$, both players (denoted i and $-i$) choose an action from a finite set. Let $A(s) = A_i(s) \times A_{-i}(s)$ be the set of joint actions available in s, where $A_i(s)$ and $A_{-i}(s)$ are the action sets of players i and $-i$, respectively. When joint action $\mathbf{a} = (a_i, a_{-i})$ is played in state s, the players receive the finite rewards $r_i(s, \mathbf{a})$ and $r_{-i}(s, \mathbf{a})$, respectively. The world also transitions to some new state s' with probability defined by $P_M(s, \mathbf{a}, s')$. Each round of the RSG begins in the start state $\hat{s} \in S$ and terminates when some goal state $s_g \in G \subseteq S$ is reached.

In this paper, we consider RSGs with conflicting interests. Both players can profit by collaborating with each other, but either of the players can also possibly exploit the other and thereby obtain even higher payoffs. We assume that the transition model P_M and the reward functions $r_i(s, \mathbf{a})$ and $r_{-i}(s, \mathbf{a})$ are known to both players *a priori*, and that the players can observe each others' actions. This permits the players to focus on learning to interact with each other rather than on learning domain attributes.

2.2 Online-Learning Algorithms for RSGs

Learning in RSGs when associating with people or robots is challenging for several reasons. First, when the other player adapts it strategy over time, the environment is non-stationary, which violates assumptions made by most machine learning algorithms. Second, the behavior of the other player is often unknown. Inferring it's future behavior can be extremely difficult due to the presence of multiple (often

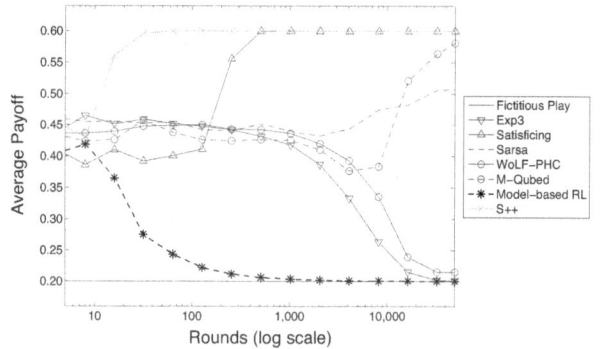

Figure 1: The performance of existing online-learning algorithms in self play in a repeated prisoners' dilemma. A payoff of 0.60 results from mutual cooperation, 0.20 from mutual defection. With the exception of (recently developed) S++, these algorithms either fail to learn to cooperate, or require hundreds to thousands of interactions to do so.

infinite) equilibria. Thus, most existing learning algorithms for RSGs either learn too slowly to support interaction with humans or cannot learn collaborative solutions at all.

As an example, consider a repeated prisoners' dilemma [2], which comes from a special class of RSGs with only a single state (i.e., $|S| = 1$). Figure 1 shows the performance of a representative set of learning algorithms in self play. Algorithms such as Fictitious play [11] and model-based reinforcement learning quickly learn to defect in this game, which yields low payoffs. On the other hand, M-Qubed [8] and Sarsa [20] usually learn to cooperate with each other, but they require thousands of interactions to do so. Satisficing learning [16, 21] yields better results in self play, but these algorithms are somewhat exploitable [7].

Recently, two new algorithms have been developed for RSGs that appear to learn at faster time scales than previous algorithms. These algorithms are counter-factual regret (CFR) [15] and Gabe-S++ [5]. CFR has been used with substantial success in relatively large competitive games, such as poker. Prior to interaction, CFR attempts to compute an equilibrium strategy by simulating an interaction using self play. As it interacts with its associate, it continues to update this model. While CFR is rather myopic in games of conflicting interest [15], it provides an interesting baseline for what online-learning algorithms can currently achieve when interacting with a human partner.

Gabe-S++ is an expert algorithm that extends S++ [6] to general RSGs. Prior to interaction, Gabe-S++ computes a set of expert strategies, several of which are Nash equilibria of the repeated game. During interactions, it uses aspiration learning to determine which expert to follow. It has been shown to quickly learn non-myopic solutions in a number of RSGs of conflicting interest when associating with other learning algorithms [5].

We note that online learning has been used successfully in scenario-specific human-robot interactions in which the robot and human have common interests [13, 19]. Our work differs from these works in that we seek to identify more general-purpose algorithms that learn to interact with human partners in arbitrary scenarios, including those with conflicting interests.

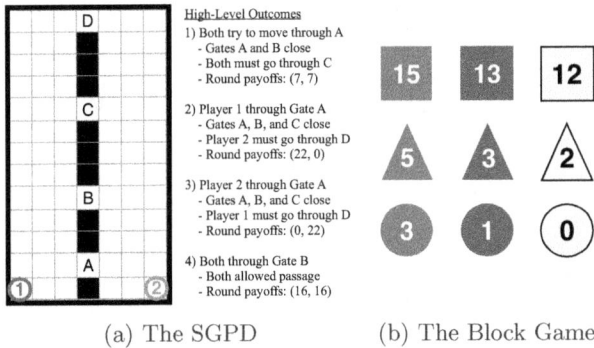

(a) The SGPD   (b) The Block Game

Figure 2: Two RSGs used in our user studies.

2.3 Cheap Talk

Cheap talk refers to non-binding, unmediated, and costless communication [9, 1]. Cheap talk has been cited as a means for equilibrium refinement [10], and has been shown to improve collaborations among people [17, 3].

In this paper, we consider whether a learning robot can employ cheap talk to help overcome the negative effects of random explorations carried out by a learning algorithm. We hypothesize that cheap talk by a robot will cause it to be held in higher regard by people, even when the robot's behavior is governed by the same learning algorithm. Thus, we anticipate that cheap talk will help the robot to better interact with people.

We are unaware of past work interweaving cheap talk with online learning. This is potentially due to the difficulty of knowing what to communicate, as most learning algorithms have representations that are difficult to articulate. However, we note parallels to the work of Thomaz and Breazeal [22]. In their work, a simulated robot signaled to a human teacher uncertainty by pausing in states in which multiple actions had similar Q-values. This helped the human to understand what the robot still needed to learn. However, in domains of conflicting interest, discussions about local Q-estimates are likely to be at too low of a level to fully resonate with potential human collaborators. Additionally, we anticipate that the competitive natures of these games will make such communications insufficient.

3. LEARNING WITH HUMANS

But is cheap talk even necessary? Given the fast learning rates of CFR and Gabe-S++, we first consider whether these algorithms can learn to effectively interact with people in the absence of explicit communication. To do this, we conducted a user study to compare the performance of people and these algorithms when paired with other people in two different scenarios (RSGs). We now describe these two scenarios, after which we discuss the experimental setup and results.

3.1 Scenarios (RSGs)

The two games were consider are a stochastic game prisoner's dilemma and a block-sharing game.

3.1.1 A Stochastic Game Prisoner's Dilemma

The stochastic game prisoner's dilemma (SGPD) [12] is a maze game in which the high-level payoffs of the game equate to a standard prisoner's dilemma [2]. At the start of

each round of the game, the players are placed in opposite corners of the maze as shown in Figure 2(a). The players move (simultaneously) to adjacent cells (up, down, left, or right) with the goal of reaching the other player's start position in as few moves as possible. Each move costs a player one point, but a player receives 30 points when it reaches its goal. Once both players have arrived at their respective goals, a new round begins from the original start state.

To reach their goals, the players must pass through one of four gates (Gates A-D). While the least-cost path to the goal is through Gate A, only one player can pass through Gate A in a round. When a player passes through Gate A, Gates A, B, and C close for the other player, and it must pass through Gate D. If both players attempt to pass through Gate A at the same time, neither is allowed passage and Gates A and B close. On the other hand, both players can pass through Gates B, C, and D separately or at the same time, though Gate A closes when either player passes through Gate B.

We expect players to eventually converge to one of four solutions, which we list in descending collaborative order:

1. *Both B* – Both players use Gate B, resulting in each receiving 16 points.

2. *Alt A-B* – The players take turns going through Gate A, which results in an average payoff of 11 points to each player.

3. *Both A* – Both players attempt to go through Gate A, thus requiring each player to pass through Gate C. This gives both players 7 points.

4. *Bully* – One of the players always goes through Gate A, leaving the other to go through Gate D. This gives the players 22 and 0 points, respectively.

3.1.2 A Block-Sharing Game

The Block Game is a turn-taking game in which the two players share the set of nine blocks shown in Figure 2(b). In each round, the players take turns selecting a block until they each have three blocks, with one player (typically the older sibling) going first in each round. If a player's three blocks form a valid set (i.e., she has all blocks of the same color, all blocks of the same shape, or none of her blocks have the same color or shape), then her payoff in the round is the sum of the numbers on her blocks. If she fails to collect a valid set, she loses the sum of her blocks divided by 4.

Though rather simple, this game is strategically complex. Each player would like to collect all of the squares (40 points) or all of the red blocks (23 points). However, to reach either of these outcomes, the other player would have to accept either getting all of the triangles (10 points) or all of the blue blocks (17 points), respectively. Since the other player can ensure itself 18 points by taking blocks that all differ in shape and color, it is unlikely to repeatedly accept either of those two outcomes. Thus, a player has to decide whether to try to bully the other player (possibly by punishing the other player, which might require the acceptance of negative points, in early rounds in order to get better outcomes in later rounds) or to collaborate with them in some way. This decision depends on the characteristics of the other player.

We expect the players to eventually converge to one of five solutions, which we list in descending collaborative order:

1. *Alt □-△* – The players alternate between selecting all of the squares and all of the triangles. Thus, both players average 25 points per round ((40 + 10)/2).

2. *Alt rd-blu* – The players take turns selecting the red and blue blocks (respectively) in alternating rounds, Both players average 20 points $((23 + 17)/2)$.

3. *All diff* – The players both select blocks with no matching attributes. This always gives both players 18 points.

4. *Pure rd-blu* – One of the players always takes all the red blocks (23 points) while the other player always takes the blue blocks (17 points).

5. *Pure* □-△ – One player always takes the squares (40 points) while the other gets the triangles (10 points).

3.2 Experimental Design

In this initial user study, we evaluate how effectively people and two learning algorithms interact with other people in two different scenarios. We used a 3x2 mixed factorial design, in which the between-subjects variable is the player type (Humans, CFR, or Gabe-S++) and the within subjects variable is the scenario.

A convenience sample of forty-eight participants with an average age of 26.3 years were recruited from the Masdar Institute community. Twelve subjects were randomly paired with CFR, twelve with Gabe-S++, and twenty-four subjects were paired with each other. The participants took part in the study in groups of four. The study proceeded as follows:

1. Each participant was assigned an associate (Human, CFR, or Gabe-S++) without their knowledge.

2. The rules of the SGPD were explained to the participants until it was clear they understood all aspects of the game.

3. The participants played a 54-round SGPD paired with their assigned player type. The game was played on a desktop computer (using the arrow keys to select movements). The participants were not told the duration of the game or who they were paired with. They also were not allowed to talk or signal to each other.

4. Each participant filled out a post-experiment survey, which asked questions related to their experience playing the SGPD. Questions included the participant's assessments of their associate. For example, they were asked how smart they thought their associate was, whether they thought their associate was a robot or person, and how likable their associate was.

5. The participants were trained on how to play the Block Game until they understood all aspects of the game.

6. The participants played a 51-round Block Game with the same player type as before. If paired with Humans, the participant was randomly paired with a different person than in the first game. Each participant was randomly assigned to be either the first or second player to select a block – a role which was kept constant throughout the game. The participants used the mouse to select the blocks on a GUI interface.

7. The participant completed the same post-experiment survey as in Step 4.

Participants were paid a $5.00 show-up fee. To incentivize the participants to try to maximize their own payoffs, participants were also paid money proportional to the points they scored in the games (they could earn up to an additional $15.00). The GUI displaying the game interface also showed the amount of money the participant had earned.

3.3 Performance Metrics

We use three metrics to evaluate the learning algorithms in this study: average payoffs, solution quality, and humanness. We are particularly interested in comparing the algorithms' performance to that of humans with respect to each metric.

3.3.1 Average Payoffs

The average payoffs received by the algorithms are perhaps the most salient measure of successful learning. While we are interested in the payoffs obtained over the full course of the game, we are particularly interested in the payoffs achieved in later rounds, as these payoffs are indicative of how well the algorithm has learned to interact with people.

3.3.2 Solution Quality

Solution quality refers to the collaborative nature of the solutions learned by the algorithms. We count the number of participants in each condition and game that achieved each of the solutions listed in Section 3.1. This metric gives us a good idea of the ability of the learning algorithms to learn to cooperate (when beneficial) with human partners.

3.3.3 Humanness

We consider how human-like the algorithms seemed to study participants. We make this assessment using the post-experiment questionnaire, in which participants were asked to guess whether their associate was a person or a robot, and to rate their confidence (on the scale one to five, with one being a complete guess and five being certainty) in their guess. Formally, let $H_{j,k}$ be the *humanness* attributed by participant j toward associate k, and let $h_j = 1$, when the participant guesses human, and $h_j = -1$ otherwise. Also, let $C_j \in \{1, 2, 3, 4, 5\}$ be participant j's confidence in his/her guess. Then, $H_{j,k}$ is given by

$$H_{j,k} = h_j * (C_j - 1). \tag{1}$$

3.4 Results

The average payoffs obtained by the three player types when paired with people are shown in Figures 3(a) and 3(c). There is no clear and substantial difference between the payoffs obtained by each player type. Additionally, neither CFR, Gabe-S++, nor Humans learned to consistently collaborate at a high level with people in either game. In the SGPD, the average round payoff received in the last few rounds by each player type was approximately 10, which is well short of the 16 points that are achieved from mutual cooperation. In the Block Game, none of the player types had an average payoff close to the 25 points they could have achieved had they learn to play *Alt* □-△. Thus, while both Humans and Gabe-S++ appear to slowly improve their payoffs with time, neither reaches a high level within 50 rounds.

Table 1 provides further insight into the ability of the learning algorithms to collaborate with people. This table shows the number of participants that achieved each outcome (by the end of 50 rounds) when paired with each player type. In the SGPD, both Gabe-S++ and Humans learned to cooperate (*Both B*) with some participants (Gabe-S++ cooperated with five, Humans with three). The rest of the participants typically learned mutual defection (*Both A*) when paired with Gabe-S++ and Humans, though Gabe-S++ did continue to attempt to pass through Gate B every few rounds in hopes of reaching a more-profitable collaboration.

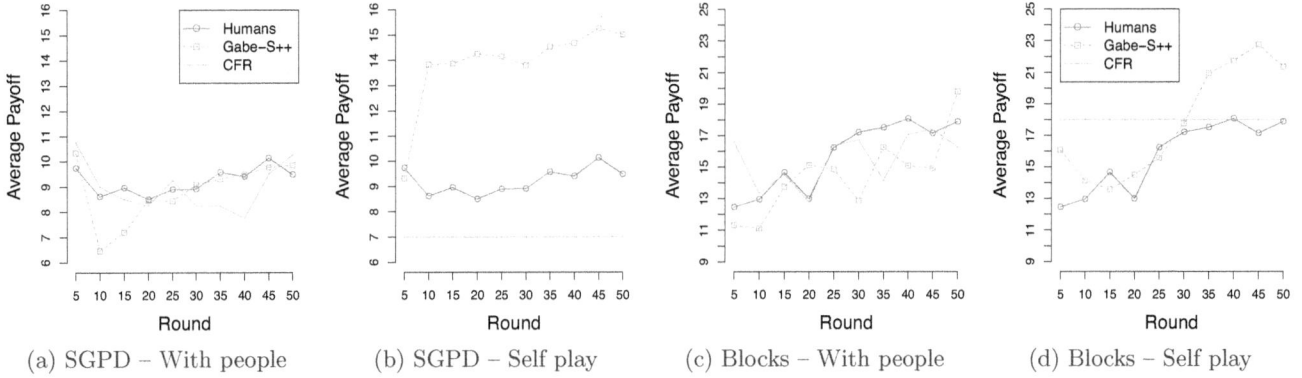

(a) SGPD – With people (b) SGPD – Self play (c) Blocks – With people (d) Blocks – Self play

Figure 3: Average payoffs, grouped in 5-round chunks, when paired with people and in self play. CFR's and Gabe-S++'s payoffs in self play were obtained from the average of 25 simulation runs.

(a) SGPD (no communication)

Player	Primary Outcome				
	Both B	Alt A-B	Both A	Bully	Other
Humans	3	0.5	7.5	1	0
Gabe-S++	5	0	5	0	2
CFR	0	0	11	1	0

(b) Block Game (no communication)

Player	Primary Outcome					
	Alt □-△	Alt rd-blu	All diff	Pure rd-blu	Pure □-△	Other
Humans	2	2	5	2	0	1
Gabe-S++	1.5	0.5	4.5	2	0	3.5
CFR	0	0	5	5	0	2

Table 1: The number of subjects that reached each outcome at the end of 50 rounds in each condition.

In the Block Game, Humans and Gabe-S++ rarely reached the most collaborative solutions. CFR did not learn to play highly collaborative solutions in either game.

Humanness varied significantly by player type ($F(2, 90) = 5.96$, $p = 0.004$). Pairwise comparisons show that Humans were rated more human-like than CFR ($p = 0.005$). The difference between Humans and Gabe-S++ was marginally statistically significant ($p = 0.078$), with Humans having a higher rating. Thus, though some participants were convinced that robots were people and vice-verse, they were largely able to distinguish the behavior of people from robots.

While CFR, Gabe-S++, and Humans all failed to consistently learn collaborative solutions when interacting with people in this study, they did learn to collaborate in some instances. The potential of Gabe-S++ to collaborate with people in these two scenarios is further illustrated by Figures 3(b) and 3(d), which show the average payoffs of the players in self play. Gabe-S++ quickly achieves very high levels of cooperation in the SGPD, and also does so in the Block Game after about 30 rounds. Thus, we anticipate that Gabe-S++ could learn to consistently collaborate with people if it could better communicate its desires and intentions.

4. ADDING CHEAP TALK

As cheap talk has been shown to help people to collaborate with each other [17, 3], we now address whether interweaving

cheap talk into Gabe-S++ produces a learning system that learns to effectively and consistently collaborate with people. In this section, we address two questions. First, what forms of cheap talk might be useful (if any)? Second, how can cheap talk be integrated into Gabe-S++?

4.1 Forms of Cheap Talk

We consider two kinds of cheap talk: *feedback cheap talk* and *planning cheap talk*. We refer to cheap talk that addresses assessments of past events as feedback cheap talk. As an example, a person or robot might comment on their satisfaction with past events, or comment on how past events made them feel. Additionally, feedback cheap talk includes assessing the past behaviors of the associate, perhaps expressing how the other person's actions make them feel, or expressing what they wished the other person had done instead. We anticipate that feedback cheap talk could be produced from most learning algorithms with careful thought.

Planning cheap talk is forward looking. It involves suggesting future behavior to one's associate and/or revealing one's current or future strategy. Of course, such cheap talk is non-binding – neither of the players must actually do what is spoken. However, conforming behavior with one's cheap talk can help to establish a reliable reputation, and can thus help to mitigate negative effects caused by random explorations. We anticipate that most learning algorithms are too cryptic to easily produce effective planning cheap talk, as humans typically communicate plans at higher levels than typical machine-learning algorithms reason.

4.2 Generating Cheap Talk

Unlike many learning algorithms, Gabe-S++ is structured so that its high-level strategies are expressible to people. This allows it to produce both feedback and planning cheap talk that is generic such that the same cheap talk can be used in any RSG.

Gabe-S++ is an expert algorithm that operates on a set of experts $\Phi = \{\phi_1, \cdots, \phi_n\}$. Each expert $\phi \in \Phi$ encodes a particular strategy defined over the entire state space S of the RSG. In each round, Gabe-S++ selects an expert $\phi \in \Phi$ to follow. It uses aspiration learning [16] to determine which expert to follow in each round. That is, player i encodes an aspiration α_i^t, which is updated after each round as follows:

$$\alpha_i^t = \lambda \alpha_i^{t-1} + (1 - \lambda) R_i^t. \tag{2}$$

(a) Finite state machine (with output) for "fair" leader experts.

State	State Transitions Events						Speech Acts (Output) Events					
	sel	g	i	s	d	p	sel	g	i	s	d	p
s0	s1	s0	s0	s0	s0	s0	1	–	–	–	–	–
s1	–	s9	s1	s2	s2	s1	–	r(5-9)+4+r(10-12)	–	r(13-16)	–	–
s2	–	s10	s2	s3	s3	s2	–	r(5-9)+4+r(10-12)	–	r(13-16)	–	–
s3	–	s11	s3	s4	s4	s3	–	r(5-9)+4+r(10-12)	–	r(13-16)	–	–
s4	–	s11	s4	s5	s5	s4	–	r(5-9)+4+r(10-12)	–	r(13-16)	–	–
s5	–	s11	s5	s6	s6	s5	–	r(5-9)+4+r(10-12)	–	r(13-16)	–	–
s6	–	s11	s6	s7	s7	s6	–	r(5-9)+4+r(10-12)	–	–	–	–
s7	–	s11	s7	s8	s8	s7	–	r(5-9)+4+r(10-12)	–	3	–	–
s8	–	s11	s8	s8	s8	s8	–	r(5-9)+4+r(10-12)	–	–	–	–
s9	–	s9	s3	s10	s10	s9	–	–	2	–	–	r(17-19)
s10	–	s10	s4	s11	s11	s10	–	–	2	–	–	r(17-19)
s11	–	s11	s5	s11	s11	s11	–	–	2	–	–	r(17-19)

(b) Definitions of event symbols.

Symbol	Explanation
sel	Algorithm selects an expert.
g	Associate has profited from deviating from the "cooperative" solution (defined by the expert).
i	Associate is now innocent. It has been punished for its deviation.
s	The robot is satisfied with its round payoff.
d	The robot is dissatisfied with its round payoff.
p	Associate received a lower payoff on a move than it would have had it always cooperated.

(c) Speech acts for "fair" leader experts.

1. **Here's the deal. Let's cooperate with each other. If you do not cooperate, I'll punish you thereafter.**
2. **I forgive you. Cooperation will bring us both a higher payoff**
3. Sweet. We are getting rich. Let's continue this.
4. I trusted you to <game specific action label>
5. You jerk!
6. You buffoon!
7. You fool!
8. Curse you!
9. You are an idiot!
10. **I'm going to teach you a lesson you will not forget.**
11. **I'm going to make sure you do not profit from this malicious act.**
12. **You will pay for this!**
13. That what I wanted.
14. That's what I'm talking about.
15. Excellent!
16. Great!
17. Take that!
18. Serves you right, jerk.
19. In your face!

(d) Speech acts for "fair" follower experts.

1. **Let's cooperate with each other.**
2. Sweet. We are getting rich. Let's continue this.
3. I thought you should <game specific action label>
4. You betrayed me!
5. That was selfish of you
6. That was not fair!
7. Are you only thinking of yourself?
8. This is not good for our relationship.
9. For the sake of our relationship, cease this untoward behavior.
10. Friends do not do that to each other.
11. That's what I wanted.
12. That's what I'm talking about!
13. Excellent!
14. Great!

Table 2: Feedback and planning cheap talk is generated for each expert using a finite state machine. r(x-y) denotes a randomly selected speech act between the numbers of x and y in the speech-act table. '+' indicates concatenated strings. Planning speech acts are given in bold, feedback speech acts are in plain text.

Here, R_i^t is player i's total payoff in round t, and $\lambda \in [0,1]$ is a learning rate. α_i^t is player i's threshold for evaluating satisfaction. Experts that produce payoffs that exceed α_i^t are desirable (and Gabe-S++ will continue to play them), whereas experts that produce lower payoffs are not.

4.2.1 Feedback Cheap Talk

Gabe-S++ can be used to produce both high- and low-level feedback cheap talk for arbitrary RSGs. In addition to helping the robot to determine which experts to select, α_i^t provides a means for the robot to express its satisfaction with a round's outcome. Such talk could implicitly communicate whether the robot is likely to continue its same strategy, which could help the human partner to establish appropriate expectations.

Like Thomaz and Breazeal [22], Gabe-S++ also communicates its satisfaction for individual, low-level, actions using estimates of state quality or potential (such as Q-values, which are encoded by some of Gabe-S++'s experts). When the human partner executes an action that lowers the robot's potential payoffs in a round, the robot expresses its disappointment, and even explicitly states what it wishes the human had done instead. This could help the human to better distinguish which of its actions are "upsetting" the robot.

4.2.2 Planning Cheap Talk

Gabe-S++ produces planning cheap talk for two different kinds of events. First, because each expert $\phi \in \Phi$ encodes a (perhaps radically) different high-level strategy, the random selections of experts (i.e., exploration) can appear to be disjoint, irrational reasoning. Thus, when Gabe-S++ changes which expert it follows, it produces a speech act that notifies the human partner of this change. Example speech acts include "I've changed my mind," and "I've had a change of heart." Additionally, when this switch in strategies leaves some promised act undone (such as a promised

punishment), the robot tries to soften the discontinuity by saying something like "I'll let you off this time."

Each expert $\phi \in \Phi$ can also produce planning cheap talk. These plans can be communicated at a high level, as most experts used by Gabe-S++ encode a high-level strategic ideal that is easily understood by the people. For example, one of Gabe-S++'s experts (called Bouncer) seeks to minimize the difference between the robot's and the human's payoffs. When Bouncer is selected, Gabe-S++ announces "I will play fair if you will play fair," and that it insists on equal payoffs and will not be cheated. Others of Gabe-S++'s experts encode trigger strategies, which carry out stages of cooperation and punishment depending on the behavior of the associate. These trigger strategies can easily be announced when they are selected. Furthermore, these trigger strategies can be modeled with simple finite state machines [18], which Gabe-S++ uses to produce speech acts that inform its associate as it switches between stages of cooperation and punishment.

As an example, Table 2 shows the state machine, event symbols, and speech acts, of a leader expert seeking to enforce a fair and pure target solution (e.g., the *Both B* strategy in the SGPD). When initiated, the expert announces that it would like to "cooperate" with its associate, and that it will "punish" deviations from the cooperative solution. If the associate fails to cooperate (indicated by event **g**), the robot curses, states what the person did wrong, and then says that it will punish him. Once the punishment has been carried out, the robot states "I forgive you," reminds its associate that cooperation will bring them both a higher payoff, and then returns to cooperating. Speech acts for a similar follower expert [6], generated using the same state machine, is shown in Table 2d.

We generated similar state machines for leader strategies that target different target solutions (e.g., the *Alt □-△* solution in the Block Game). The only difference is that this solution requires the players to take turns getting a higher payoff. Thus, our algorithm produces a speech act stat-

Figure 4: A Nao delivered speech acts to subjects.

ing the turn-taking nature of the desired solution, and announces who's turn it is to get the higher payoff.

Since the concepts of "cooperation," "punishment," and "forgiveness" apply to arbitrary situations, this same speech-generation system can be used in any RSGs. Thus, we use the same speech system for both games we consider.

5. THE IMPACT OF CHEAP TALK

To determine to what extent cheap talk helps a robot to learn to effectively collaborate with a human partner, we conducted a second user study. In this section, we describe the user study and discuss the results.

5.1 Experimental Setup

To understand how cheap talk impacts how well Gabe-S++ learns to collaborate with people, we tested two different cheap talk systems. The first system produced only feedback cheap talk. The second system was identical to the first, except that it also produced planning cheap talk. In both cases, the cheap talk was delivered by a Nao robot, who was placed before the participants as they played (Figure 4).

Forty-eight people, with an average age of 25.1 years, were recruited from the Masdar Institute community to participate in this study. Twelve subjects were paired with Gabe-S++ using each of the two cheap-talk systems, which we denote Gabe-S++(f) and Gabe-S++(fp), respectively. So as to provide a baseline condition, we also paired twenty-four participants with each other. These participants were allowed to talk to each other as they played the games.

Except for the communication (and, in turn, the knowledge of who one was paired with), this study was carried out in the same manner as the initial study (Section 3.2).

5.2 Results

Cheap talk greatly enhanced the performance of Humans (when they were paired together) in both games (Figures 5). All human-human pairings in the SGPD converged to *Both B* (Table 3a). Convergence in the Block Game was a little more diverse (Table 3b), though more highly collaborative outcomes were observed than without communication.

Cheap talk also greatly enhanced the ability of Gabe-S++ to learn to interact with study participants. An ANOVA shows that cheap talk substantially increased the payoffs of Gabe-S++ when paired with people in the last ten rounds of the games ($F(2,66) = 6.04; p = 0.004$). Pairwise comparisons reveal that Gabe-S++(fp) performed significantly higher then Gabe-S++ (with no cheap talk; $p = 0.003$), but Gabe-S++(f) did not ($p = 0.234$).

In the SGPD, combined feedback and planning cheap talk led to higher average payoffs after round 35 (Figure 5a). In

(a) SGPD

Player	Primary Outcome				
	Both B	Alt A-B	Both A	Bully	Other
Humans	3	0.5	7.5	1	0
Humans (fp)	12	0	0	0	0
Gabe-S++	5	0	5	0	2
Gabe-S++ (f)	5.5	0	5.5	1.0	0
Gabe-S++ (fp)	9.5	0	2	0.5	0

(b) Block Game

Player	Primary Outcome					
	Alt □-△	Alt rd-bl	All diff	Pure rd-bl	Pure □-△	Other
Humans	2	2	5	2	0	1
Humans (fp)	7	2	1	0	2	0
Gabe-S++	1.5	0.5	4.5	2	0	3.5
Gabe-S++ (f)	3.5	0	3	2	1.5	2
Gabe-S++ (fp)	9	0	0	1	2	0

Table 3: The number of subjects that reached each outcome by 50 rounds. f - feedback cheap talk only, fp – both feedback and planning cheap talk.

the Block Game (Figure 5b), feedback and planning cheap talk produced substantially higher payoffs throughout the game, even exceeding the payoffs achieved by Humans in the last 25 rounds on average. Feedback cheap talk alone, however, produced no discernible increase in payoffs in the SGPD, and less substantial increases in the Block Game.

Convergence characteristics provide further insight into how cheap talk impacted Gabe-S++'s ability to learn to interact with people. While feedback cheap talk alone produced little increase in the number of highly collaborative outcomes, feedback and planning cheap talk together led to substantial increases in profitable collaborations (Table 3). In the SGPD, about 80% of all participants learned to cooperate (*Both B*) when paired with Gabe-S++(fp), and 9 out of 12 participants converged to the most collaborative solution in the Block Game. These results are similar to those observed in human-human pairings.

The participants in our study also held much higher opinions of Gabe-S++ when it produced both feedback and planning cheap talk. In the post-experiment questionnaires, participants were asked to indicate how likable and how intelligent their associate was on the scale 1 to 5. Cheap talk had a statistically significant impact on both of these ratings ($F(2, 66) = 6.99; p = 0.002$ and $F(2, 66) = 8.19; p < 0.001$, respectably). Pairwise comparisons show that participants thought the robot was more intelligent when it employed feedback and planning cheap talk than when it employed just feedback cheap talk ($p = 0.005$) or no cheap talk at all ($p = 0.001$). However, when the robot only produced feedback cheap talk, it was not seen as more intelligent than when the algorithm produced no cheap talk ($p = 0.912$).

6. CONCLUSIONS AND DISCUSSION

In this paper, we studied (via user study) how robots can learn to collaborate with human partners when the goals of the robot and the human partner are not fully aligned. Our results indicate that feedback and planning cheap talk can substantially improve a robot's ability to learn to interact with a human partner. An online-learning algorithm

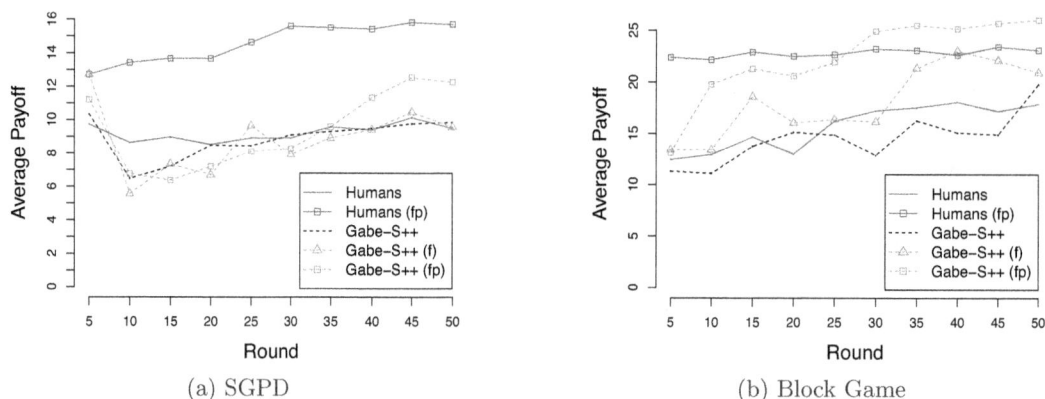

(a) SGPD   (b) Block Game

Figure 5: **Average payoffs when paired with humans when communication was permitted. (f) indicates feedback cheap talk, (fp) indicates both feedback and planning cheap talk.**

that can quickly learn collaborative solutions is insufficient. Humans appear to require communication in the form of forward planning to establish collaborations with an adapting robot. This highlights the need to address AI and HRI synergistically rather than independently.

This work highlights a number of unsolved challenges. For example, in our study, the robot produced cheap talk, but it did not consider what the human said. We anticipate that the ability to engage in two-way communication would substantially improve a robot's ability to learn to collaborate with a human partner. Future work involves determining how cheap talk from the human can be utilized by a learning algorithm to improve its ability to collaborate with people.

7. REFERENCES

[1] R. J. Aumann and S. Hart. Long cheap talk. *Econometrica*, 71 (6):1619–1660, 2003.

[2] R. Axelrod. *The Evolution of Cooperation*. Basic Books, 1984.

[3] O. Bonroy, A. Garapin, and D. Llerena. Repeated cheap talk, imperfect monitoring and punishment behavior: An experimental analysis. *Working Paper GAEL: 2011-2012*, 2012.

[4] C. Claus and C. Boutilier. The dynamics of reinforcement learning in cooperative multiagent systems. In *Proceedings of AAAI*, pages 746–752, 1998.

[5] J. W. Crandall. Non-myopic learning in repeated stochastic games. *arXiv:1409.8498*, 2014.

[6] J. W. Crandall. Towards minimizing disappointment in repeated games. *Journal of Artificial Intelligence Research*, 49:111–142, 2014.

[7] J. W. Crandall, A. Ahmed, and M. A. Goodrich. Learning in repeated games with minimal information: The effects of learning bias. In *Proceedings of AAAI*, pages 650–656, 2011.

[8] J. W. Crandall and M. A. Goodrich. Learning to compete, coordinate, and cooperate in repeated games using reinforcement learning. *Machine Learning*, 82(3):281–314, 2011.

[9] V. P. Crawford and J. Sobel. Strategic information transmission. *Econometrica*, 50 (6):1431–1451, 1982.

[10] J. Farrell and M. Rabin. Cheap talk. *Journal of Economic Perspectives*, 10 (3):103–118, 1996.

[11] D. Fudenberg and D. K. Levine. *The Theory of Learning in Games*. The MIT Press, 1998.

[12] M. A. Goodrich, J. W. Crandall, and J. R. Stimpson. Neglect tolerant teaming: Issues and dilemmas. In *AAAI Spring Symposium on Human Interaction with Autonomous Systems in Complex Environments*, 2003.

[13] G. Hoffman and C. Breazeal. Achieving fluency through perceptual-symbol practice in human-robot collaboration. In *Proceedings of HRI*, pages 1–8, 2008.

[14] F. Ishowo-Oloko, J. W. Crandall, M. Cebrian, S. Abdallah, and I. Rahwan. Learning in repeated games: Human versus machine. *arXiv:1404.4985*, 2014.

[15] M. Johanson, N. Bard, M. Lanctot, R. Gibson, and M. Bowling. Efficient Nash equilibrium approximation through Monte Carlo counterfactual regret minimization. In *Proceedings of AAMAS*, pages 837–846, 2012.

[16] R. Karandikar, D. Mookherjee, D. R., and F. Vega-Redondo. Evolving aspirations and cooperation. *Journal of Economic Theory*, 80:292–331, 1998.

[17] J. Y. Kim. Cheap talk and reputation in repeated pretrial negotiation. *RAND Journal of Economics*, 27 (4):787–802, 1996.

[18] M. L. Littman and P. Stone. A polynomial-time Nash equilibrium algorithm for repeated games. *Decision Support Systems*, 39:55–66, 2005.

[19] S. Nikolaidis, K. Gu, R. Ramakrishnan, and J. Shah. Efficient model learning for human-robot collaborative tasks. *arXiv:1405.6341v1*, 2014.

[20] G. A. Rummery and M. Niranjan. On-line Q-learning using connectionist sytems. Technical Report CUED/F-INFENG-TR 166, Cambridge University, 1994.

[21] J. R. Stimpson, M. A. Goodrich, and L. C. Walters. Satisficing and learning cooperation in the prisoner's dilemma. In *Proc. of IJCAI*, pages 535–544, 2001.

[22] A. L. Thomaz and C. Breazeal. Teachable robots: Understanding human teaching behavior to build more effective robot learners. *Artificial Intelligence*, 172:716–737, 2008.

Robots in the Home: Qualitative and Quantitative Insights into Kitchen Organization

Elizabeth Cha[1], Jodi Forlizzi[2], Siddhartha S. Srinivasa[1]
[1] Robotics Institute, Carnegie Mellon University, Pittsburgh, PA 15213
[2] Human-Computer Interaction Institute, Carnegie Mellon University, Pittsburgh, PA 15213
{lizcha,forlizzi,siddh}@cs.cmu.edu

ABSTRACT

In the future, we envision domestic robots to play a large role in our everyday lives. This requires robots able to anticipate our needs and preferences and adapt their behavior. Since current robotics research takes place primarily in laboratory settings, it fails to take into account real users. In this work, we explore how organization occurs in the kitchen through a home study. Our analysis includes qualitative insights towards robot behavior during kitchen organization, an open source dataset of real life kitchens, and a proof-of-concept application of this dataset to the problem of object return.

Categories and Subject Descriptors

I.2.9 [**Computing Methodologies**]: Artificial Intelligence—*Robotics*; J.4 [**Computer Applications**]: Social and Behavioral Science - Psychology

Keywords

human-robot interaction, organization, kitchen, design

1. INTRODUCTION

In the future, we envision domestic robots to perform a wide range of tasks, able to assist people with limited mobility or support aging in place [1, 4, 11]. Since the technical challenges associated with this goal are being extensively researched, it is important to understand the difficulties that arise when a human and robot not only share space but have to work together to maintain a home [33].

To identify and address these challenges, it is important to look at real homes and users. However, most robotics research to date has taken place in laboratory settings because the environment is highly structured and experiments are more controllable. As a compromise, many research groups utilize simulated or mock home environments, either built in the lab or as a virtual environment [20, 29, 33]. Unfortunately, these environments often fail to capture the true complexity and dynamics of the home [2, 9].

Recent work in design and human-computer interaction has focused on moving out of the laboratory and into real

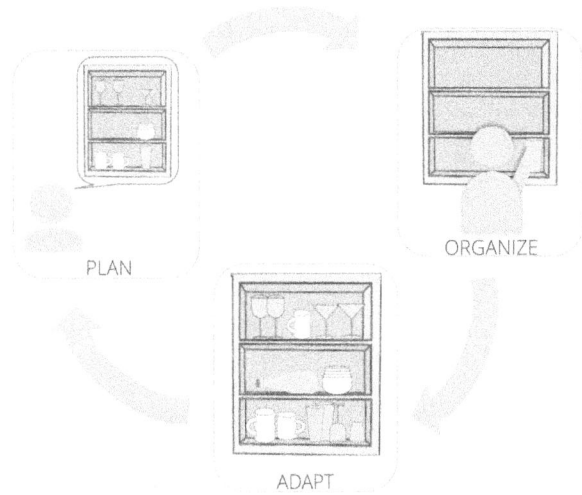

Figure 1: Homes constantly undergo a complex cycle of organization – adapting until they are forced to reorganize.

homes. The benefit of these works is that they go beyond visual observation, providing insight into the complex dynamics of the home [2]. In order to obtain these insights, qualitative techniques such as ethnography or cultural probes are often used [5, 7]. As these works present anecdotal results, it is unclear how roboticists can utilize these techniques in their own research. Therefore, our goal in this work is to translate the results obtained through qualitative studies into tools that accurately represent the home environment and can thus, inform the design of domestic robot behavior.

There are many potential applications for such tools. Imagine a robot in the home with several objects to put back. Without any prior knowledge, the robot will likely choose a location based on the object's geometry which can results in misplaced items. In some cases, such as misplaced medicine, this is more than a minor annoyance. Thus, for robots to truly benefit users, they must anticipate their needs and desires in the home.

The main challenge is that the home is a complex and dynamic space [2, 9, 18]. It continues to evolve as lifestyles change and new technologies emerge. There are also privacy concerns: due to the personal nature of the home, it is undesirable to utilize cameras or other costly sensors that can capture potentially sensitive moments. Alternative methods which send researchers into the home or utilize residents to record data disrupt the dynamics of the home. Therefore, our goal is to find a solution that accurately captures the domestic environment while addressing these concerns.

Since the home is a large and challenging space to design

for, we focus on the kitchen. This is a more tractable space because most kitchens are prefabricated and contain similar elements across homes [32]. As the kitchen holds many perishable items, regular organization and cleaning are essential. Several prior works have also shown that many users desire robotic assistance with tasks in the kitchen, making it an interesting and important area to explore.

In this work, we present an analysis of organizational habits in the kitchen through an exploratory home study. We make the following contributions:

1. Home Study: We present an exploratory home study focusing on organization in the kitchen. The study consists of a home tour, kitchen tour, interview, and demonstration.

2. Dataset: Using data from our study, we create an open source dataset of organizational preferences in the kitchen that goes beyond simple observation or visual analysis.

3. Qualitative Insights: We present interesting observations from our exploratory story and discuss their design implications for future domestic robots.

4. Quantitative Assessment: We assess the usability of our dataset by applying it to an open robotics problem, object return, and present our initial results.

2. RELATED WORK

The home is a complex space shaped by its residents' needs, experiences, and desires [2]. While early work explored the functionality of the home [12], more recent research has focused at how the evolution of the home and household [2, 14, 27].

This is especially important as the typical household changes: many homes no longer consist of a family and domestic responsibilities are no longer relegated to one person [2]. To support this shift in lifestyle, many new technologies have been introduced to the home. As these technologies increase in complexity, however, researchers must try to anticipate how they will change the home and our everyday lives [9].

2.1 Technologies in the Home

Much prior work explores how new technologies affect our routines in the home [28, 40]. Recent work takes this a step further by trying to anticipate the usage and effects of future technologies, such as the smart home [13, 17, 36, 39, 40].

The idea of a smart home that possesses the intelligence and automation to anticipate and meet users' needs has been around as early as 1930 when the "Home of the Future" was unveiled at the World's Fair [19, 36, 40]. Creating such a home requires the installation of costly sensors and automation still being developed. Hence, a recent drive has been to create sensor-driven, intelligent devices that nearly no home modification, e.g. the Nest Thermostat.

In order to study these complex and integrated technologies, prototypes of home environments such as the Georgia Tech Aware Home, MIT Place Lab, Microsoft MS Home, and the Honda Smart Home have been built [21, 38]. One concern of these environments is privacy: the home is a personal space so continuous monitoring may not be desirable. The impact of these works are also limited, as they take place in research settings where people do not exhibit the same natural behavior and preferences [39].

Along with the smart home, people have also envisioned an intelligent and skilled home robot [1, 11, 34], e.g. Rosie the robot from the 1960's television show, The Jetsons. However, even today there are still very few robots in the home due to the technical challenges and high expectations of such systems [11, 24]. Thus, much of our existing knowledge is from short term studies that take place in laboratory settings limiting their impact.

2.2 Methods for the Home

In order to understand how these technologies will function in real homes, it is necessary to go "in the wild." However, this is generally considered to be a difficult endeavor [2]. Studies in the workplace are more common because it is less private and more easily accessible [9]. Researchers also cite issues such as privacy, intrusiveness, and disruption of the home life as potential difficulties of going into the home [6]. Despite these concerns, there are a growing number of researchers using methods that are well established in the workplace, such as ethnography, in the home.

However, there has been much debate as to whether these methods are suitable for the home. A key challenge in designing for the home is to understand its everyday nature including how people live, what they do in the home, and the potential role of technology. This makes qualitative techniques such as ethnography or cultural probes attractive as they are proven tools for sociologists and designers. However, prior work using these techniques have focused on conveying a sense of the home, rather than shaping these studies into usable tools for design [8].

The advantage of these techniques is that they provide context. Quantitative techniques provide raw information such as the contents of a home, but this knowledge lacks meaning without context. Thus, our goal is to find a way to merge these two approaches to create a tool that is useful to both roboticists and HRI researchers.

2.3 Organization in the Home

In this work, we choose to focus on the domain of home organization because it has been well researched through contextual studies using observational methods. Moreover, the technical challenges of organization have been a popular topic in robotics [33, 41].

Much of the prior work in organization has looked at how organization affects efficiency in the workplace [3, 26]. More recently, researchers have looked at clutter and how it affects the home [10, 37]. The results of these works have mostly been broad conclusions and general design guidelines, e.g. homes are dynamic in nature and organization must be carried out with users' preferences in mind.

Within robotics, researchers have looked at problems like object retrieval, search, and return [23, 35, 41]. Since the technical challenges of are considerable, roboticists have tested their work in mock environments where experiments are more controllable. However, as these challenges are being addressed, there is a need to move away from laboratory settings. Schuster has taken the first step in this direction by attempting to learn organizational preferences using a more data-driven approach: a dataset created via mock paper kitchens and pictures from real kitchens [33]. Unfortunately, this approach fails where contextual research excels, as the mock kitchens lack realism and understanding.

Thus, we attempt to bridge the gap between these works by applying both qualitative and quantitative techniques to organization in the home. Since the home is such a complex and large space, we focus in this work on the kitchen.

2.4 Kitchen

Historically, the kitchen has been the center of the home experience [32]. Since the majority of housewives' time were spent in the kitchen, this started a drive to create more efficient and easy to use kitchens [16, 32]. At the start of the twentieth century, however, there was a realization that for a kitchen to be efficient, it must also be flexible to the needs and preferences of users [32].

This realization created a drive to understand not only how to improve kitchen activity but how to support the experiences, affects, and desires that affect design in this space. Much of this work has concentrated on comfort, both physical and emotional, in the kitchen [22, 16, 32]. These works usually rely on using techniques in design to evaluate the space and its usage.

Unfortunately, as with the home there is still a gap between traditional kitchen research and robotics and HCI work surrounding kitchen activities. Many of these works look at activity recognition to provide support to users during cooking and cleaning [42] or cooking aids that provide assistance through expert advice or virtual demonstrations [31]. Since these works take place outside of actual kitchens, it is unclear how applicable they are in real homes.

3. HOME STUDY

For years, the home has been a popular research area [2, 9, 39]. As much of this work provides anecdotal results, it is unclear how to utilize the same methods when designing complex robot behavior. As a result, roboticists have mostly relied on mock kitchens or pictures of real homes when researching a variety of human-aware problems ranging from activity recognition to home organization [25, 33]. Yet, these solutions fail to truly represent the complexity of real homes and users. Therefore, our goal in this work is two-fold: 1) gain crucial knowledge of organizational behavior in the kitchen and 2) create a dataset which accurately captures a household's organizational preferences.

Since few works have attempted to bridge the gap between these different approaches, it is unclear what knowledge is important or necessary when creating such a dataset. For this reason, we first performed an exploratory study consisting of a general tour of the home, an in depth tour of the kitchen, an interview about organizational habits in the home, and a demonstration of organization in the kitchen.

3.1 Participants

For this study, we recruited 7 households with a total of 15 residents. This group consisted of two unmarried couples, two families, two single persons, and one set of roommates living in a house, townhouse, or apartment. All interviewees lived in the Pittsburgh area, spoke English fluently, were between the ages of 24 and 37, and are the primary organizers of the kitchen in their households.

3.2 Procedure

3.2.1 Introduction

Each session started with researchers introducing themselves and giving a brief overview of the study. Participants were told the purpose of the study was to learn about how organization occurs in the home.

3.2.2 Home Tour

After the introduction, participants were asked to give a tour of their home. They were instructed to focus on areas such as the closets where organization is important and to leave the kitchen for the end of the tour.

During the tour, participants discussed how each space in the home is used including the contents of the space and why they were placed in that particular location. This provided us with a general idea of who used each space, who was

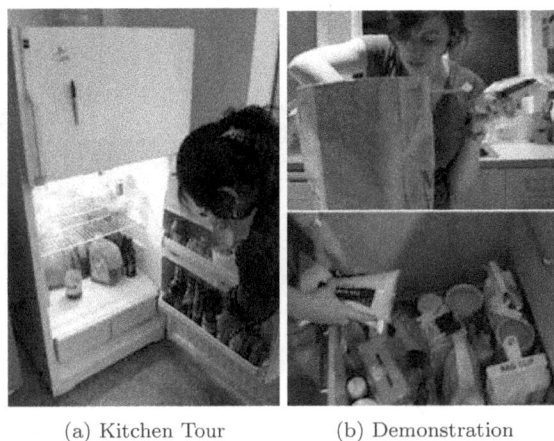

(a) Kitchen Tour   (b) Demonstration

Figure 2: During the home study, participants gave a tour of the kitchen and a demonstration of unpacking groceries.

in charge of its organization, and general cleaning habits in that area. Throughout this process, we asked participants to elaborate on anything we found interesting or unclear.

Although the focus of this work is the kitchen, the home tour was still crucial because it gave us a general idea of the household's organizational habits such as the general state of clutter and how often spaces are cleaned. It also helped us to build rapport with participants and gave them time to become comfortable with the tour structure. Moreover, there are often areas of the home which act as extensions of the kitchen that we wanted to ensure were included.

3.2.3 Kitchen Tour

The home tour ended in the kitchen where participants were instructed to go through each storage container and discuss its contents. The tour was lightly structured to allow researchers to digress and obtain important details.

For each item, participants were instructed to give an overview of the item and its usage:

Item description: What is the item?
Purpose: What is it used for?
User: Who uses it?
Frequency: How often is it purchased and used?
Surplus: Is it extraneous?
Desired Location: Where does it belong and why?
Actual Location: Where is it typically located and why?

A typical description was: "We keep the flour in this cabinet on the bottom shelf with the other baking supplies. X uses it 2-3 times a week to bake stuff. It's a large bag so we only have to purchase it every month or so. Sometimes it sits on the counter for a few hours after we use it."

3.2.4 Interview

After the tours, we interviewed participants about their organizational and cleaning habits. We waited until the tours concluded so that we had a good understanding of the entire space and how its different components fit together.

In particular, we probed participants about item placement, especially the reason for choosing a particular location. When participants had no clear reason, we asked what led an item to end up in that location.

When there were several places an item could reasonably be located, we asked participants why one location was chosen over another. For example, one participant stored a wine carafe with cocktail making items but could have alternatively placed it with the drink pitchers or wine glasses.

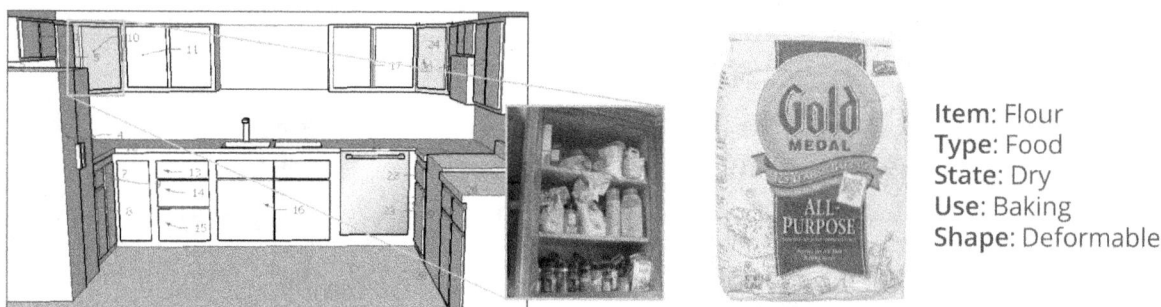

Figure 3: An example of the 3D layout of a visited kitchen and information contained in its corresponding database.

We also looked at surplus items or items where extras where kept in a secondary location. A common surplus item in most households were paper towels: the roll currently in use is kept in an easy to access location such as the counter while the remaining rolls are kept in a storage container.

During this time, we also attempted to get a better sense of the kitchen usage by asking questions such as how often residents cook or clean, which items they frequently use, and what is located in inconvenient or difficult to access spaces. Since several homes had spaces outside the kitchen which contributed to its organization, we included these spaces as part of the interview and kitchen tour.

We also looked at the history of the kitchen and its organization in both the short and long term. We asked participants how often food and other disposable items in the kitchen are purchased, used, and thrown out and whether the space had undergone any major reorganizations and why.

Finally, we looked at how the household affects the kitchen and its organization. In homes with more than one resident, we wanted to know whether this impacted the everyday level of cleanliness and clutter, how space is divided up, whether conflicts arise due to differing preferences, and what is each person's organizational role.

3.2.5 Demonstration

After the interview, we asked each participant to demonstrate putting away a bag of groceries. We provided each household with a paper grocery bag containing a jar of spice, a candy bar, a bag of rice, a box of sugar, an apple, a bottle of milk, and a can of chicken broth. We chose only food items since most households purchase kitchenware and housewares less frequently. Items were chosen to vary in as many features as possible (shape, size, container material, usage, refrigeration, shelf life), with some items having ambiguous features such as the apple's refrigeration requirements.

This process gave us a sense of how participants make decisions on the fly. This is important as most items in the kitchen have short lifespans and are constantly replenished. During the demonstration, participants narrated their thought process and discussed how they normally unpack groceries.

4. DATASET

We also contribute in this work, an open source dataset consisting of the layouts and contents of 7 kitchens that can be downloaded at www.lizcha.com/kitchen_dataset.

Since the home is complex and difficult to visualize in 2 dimensions, we began our analysis by creating a 3 dimensional layout of each kitchen. Using Google SketchUp, we recreated each kitchen, approximately to scale. The layout also functions as a map with every organizational container related to the kitchen assigned a numerical label.

4.1 Terminology

We define an organizational *container* as a unit of storage either found in the kitchen or containing items related to kitchen activities, e.g. cabinets, drawers, and refrigerators. In some cases, such as an extra freezer in the garage, the container is located outside of the kitchen but contains kitchen-related items. Containers can be further segmented into smaller organizational elements, called *subcontainers*. For example, cabinets are often divided into separate spaces using shelves. In our analysis, each shelf in a cabinet is treated as a distinct subcontainer. However, if a shelf exists as an independent unit outside of any other container, such as a wall mounted shelf, it is treated as a container. Extra storage units such as carts are treated as containers. In the layout, each container is assigned a numerical label designating its position in the kitchen. Subcontainers are assigned numerical labels relative to their position in the container.

4.2 Databases

For each home, we created a database containing its kitchen related items and their positions, or the numerical label corresponding to an item's container and when applicable, subcontainer. For duplicate items located in the same container and subcontainer, only one database entry was included due to the difficulties in obtaining accurate counts of every item.

Most items were identified through visual analysis of the kitchen [33]. Since this approach only captured the current state of the kitchen, we used the kitchen tour and interview to identify items that were missing or out of place. The result was users' desired kitchen arrangement in which all items are in their proper location, something that rarely occurs in most homes.

4.3 Features

We identified two types of features describing the items: object-related features and user-related features.

4.3.1 Object-Related Features

We define object-related features as characteristics of the object. These features can be discerned without any knowledge of the object's owner or the kitchen it is located in and are hence, consistent between homes. Some examples are an object's shape, state, and refrigeration requirements.

Object-related features are commonly used when creating organizational schemes such as ontologies of items found in the home or kitchen [33]. A common method of identifying these feature is by analyzing websites that sell food, kitchenwares, and household items [33]. Several applications within robotics such as object search, object return, computer vision, and activity recognition utilize these features because they can be identified through simple visual analysis. Moreover, these features have been laid out in ontologies, kitchen stores, and past literature in organization [33].

4.3.2 User-Related Features

We define user-related features as requiring knowledge of the user, kitchen, or household the object belongs to. Unlike object-related features, these features typically vary across homes as they represent how a particular household uses an object. Some examples are how frequently an object is used or what type of container it is kept in. In order to discern these features, we must go beyond visual analysis and utilize qualitative methods such as interviews or ethnography. These features have been mentioned in several works that relay this information anecdotally. By, transforming these results to a more concrete set of features, we can utilize them when customizing robot behavior. We chose to use an in depth interview to find this information as long-term observation is time-consuming, and invasive. We envision that in the future, a similar process can be used to provide the robot with initial information about the kitchen. The robot can continually refine its knowledge by observing the household and asking questions.

5. ORGANIZATIONAL THEMES

Previous works exploring home organization use qualitative methods that enable researchers to discover information that is difficult to extract from photographs, videos, and other sensor data. However, it is unclear how to utilize these results when designing robot behavior. Pantofaru takes a more structured approach by creating frameworks to act as design guidelines for domestic robots [30]. We employ a similar approach in which we identify general organizational themes found in the kitchen, identify real-life examples, and discuss the design implications for future robots.

Although our focus is the kitchen, we started with a home tour to get a sense of the household's organizational habits. In most cases, common spaces in the home were a good indicator of how cluttered the kitchen was. We also found that people tended to prioritize the kitchen over other spaces because of its frequent use and perishable contents.

The most significant portion of the study was the kitchen tour in which participants opened each organizational container and discussed its contents and placement. In this section, we present the findings from these tours.

5.1 Object-Related Features

Theme: Item locations are often chosen based on features of the object, as defined in Section 4.3.1. Object- related features were primarily used in 2 scenarios: 1) the object has a feature which limits its location or 2) the object is placed with other objects that have similar object features.

In most homes, several items were placed in locations that satisfied the objects' constraints. For example, food items such as meat or ice cream often had specific storage requirements to prevent spoilage. Another common constraint was an object's size or shape: pots and appliances often required larger shelves and cabinets. One household chose a particular shelf for their glassware because it was the only one tall enough to fit their wine glasses.

Participants also attempted to group "similar" items together. It is natural to store certain duplicate item, such as dishes or silverware, together. For different items, however, this is more difficult as it requires users to define similarity between two items. We also found that the object-related features used to group items together often changed depending on the compared items: canned items are stored together due to their common shape and packaging, while items used in baking such as flour and sugar were grouped together.

Design Implication: Robots designed for the home will likely be tasked with returning items to their correct locations. However, prior work indicates that users do not want to have to give the robot constant detailed instructions [11]. Instead, they prefer the robot to know their preferences and have the intelligence to make reasonable choices, as a human would. This implies that such a robot should be able to readily identify common object features as they play a huge role in determining where items should go. Humans naturally attempt to group items into certain categories (e.g. baking items, frozen foods) and classification techniques may be able to replicate this process using object features.

5.2 User-Related Features

Theme: Knowledge of user-related features, as defined in Section 4.3.2, can help refine our knowledge of an item's location and often provides deeper insight into a person's organizational strategy.

We found that although, object-related features gave a general idea of where items should go, user-related features often provided a more precise location or helped explain anomalies. One of the most useful features was frequency of use. Frequently used items tended to be in easy to access locations. In containers, these items were towards the front for easy access. Other frequently used items such as salt were kept on or near the counter, easily within arms reach.

Moreover, user-related features encode the household's habits which gives context and can explain seemingly out of place items. For instance, one household with a strict organizational scheme had a random assortment of items on the counter. After returning from the grocery store, one resident would leave items she planned to use in that day on the counter which others knew not to put away.

However, many user-related features are not easily observable and can only be found through insight from people in the home. For instance, one home had seemingly random food items isolated in the fridge and cabinets as one person had severe food allergies and separated his food for safety. In homes with children, certain containers held foods for just the child. Without knowing this information, such rules might appear random or out of place.

Design Implication: Prior work shows that people have strong preferences when it comes to the home. A robot which ignores users' preferences can disrupt the home environment, inconveniencing the user. Thus, understanding users' needs is essential to the acceptance of a home robot.

Object-related features only give a general sense of where items might belong. Imagine a stranger attempting to put away your groceries. Without any prior knowledge, they will attempt to use what they know about the objects. However, by providing them information about your habits, they can make a more refined guess. Thus, for a robot to adapt to the user, it must be able to learn user-related features. Since many of these features require long term observation or are not observable at all, it may be beneficial to conduct interviews or tours to gather this information. Once the robot has a good sense of the kitchen, it can continue to incorporate new information about the household.

5.3 Ambiguity

Theme: There is a large amount of ambiguity regarding the location of items in the kitchen. Many items have several logical locations resulting in cases where households have multiple "correct locations" that items move between.

This situation frequently occurred in households with multiple people as each resident would choose a different correct location. In homes with one dominant organizer, others would not know the correct location and would guess.

For instance, one participant found a misplaced whisk. She initially determined items locations but failed to communicate this information to the other resident causing several misplaced items. Interestingly, she replaced the items but never corrected the other person.

Other, more transient items are difficult to classify and may not have a set location. We observed several items in the refrigerator that participants' said could go on a number of shelves such as meat or leftovers. More permanent items, such as condiments, had set locations.

Sometimes kitchen and household items had two locations if there were extras of the items. For example, most homes keep a roll of paper towels on the counter and spares in another container. Some homes also stockpiled non-perishable, easy to store items for convenience or to save money.

Design Implication: Even humans have difficulty reasoning where items belong in the kitchen since we tend to view and use the kitchen in different ways. Thus, our priorities skew our beliefs of how a kitchen should be organized. Despite such discord, humans are able to coexist in these shared spaces because we learn, adapt and are willing to accept some error.

This is promising for future robots as we envision them to work autonomously, without constant instruction or help. Expecting a robot to always do what the user wants is an impossible expectation not even humans can meet. However, we found that users are willing to accept some reasonable error: finding a whisk with a measuring cup but not in the underwear drawer. Thus, robots should not ask humans when they are unsure as they will quickly become cumbersome. Instead, they should ask questions only when needed and otherwise make a refined guess.

Prior work shows, however, that people are sometimes more demanding of a robot and less willing to accept failure. This creates an interesting problem, how to adjust users' expectations of robots, that we need to further explore.

5.4 Dynamic

Theme: The kitchen is an extremely dynamic environment– its contents are frequently changing and items often move locations. Many kitchen items, such as fresh foods, are transient. Hence, the kitchen is constantly changing to fit new items and remove old ones.

This is frequently seen in the refrigerator. Its contents are subject to users whim and often have a short shelf life: what is in the fridge one week may not be the next. This is partially because we often desire variety in what we eat. Other items are seasonal and available only certain times.

Design Implication: One of the most challenging technical issues for robots is dealing with dynamic environments. However, the home and kitchen are constantly in flux. This implies for any robot to succeed in the home, it must continually take in new information and adapt its behavior. Thus, current work which looks at understanding human behavior may be useful in dealing with these challenges.

5.5 Reorganization

Theme: Households are often unwilling to reorganize unless it is absolutely necessary. Most participants listed several issues which made their home less efficient and therefore, less usable. However, regardless of whether it is a small or large change, people are unwilling to reorganize since it is time consuming, requires planning, and they are already accustomed to the current home layout.

Instead, people will come up with alternative strategies to avoid reorganizing. In some cases, they create catch-all spaces for items that do not have a designated place. They may also place items in inconvenient or difficult to reach spaces. One home recently purchased a blender, but when placing it in the kitchen did not remove the cabinet's original contents. Instead, they pushed items above and around the blender, making everything difficult to access

Participants would wait until a space became unusable before reorganizing. An exception is when a significant change in either the space or household occurs, e.g. changing residents or adding extra storage. One participant reorganized when her significant other moved in because of food allergies.

Design Implication: Since the decision to reorganize is not a straightforward one, a household robot should take many factors into consideration before moving an item. If this is an infrequent occurrence, it may be be beneficial for the robot to simply ask users whether it is okay.

However, some works have found that people adapt their habits to new technologies [15]. Thus, people may be more open to reorganizing if a robot carries out the actual task. We observed organizational schemes that were suboptimal, but participants were adamant about their choices for sentimental or personal reasons. Therefore, a robot should always be aware of human users when trying to decide whether reorganization is acceptable.

6. LEARNING USER PREFERENCES

A major contribution of this work is the construction of an open-source dataset of 7 real life kitchens, see Section 4. In this section, our goal is to show how this dataset can be applied to common problems in robotics. We focus on object return, or how to determine an object's correct location.

In the remainder of this section, we present the details of our evaluation and our results using three types of classification algorithms.

6.1 Feature Selection

The dataset we are evaluating contains two types of features: object-related and user-related features, see Section 4. We chose to use only object-related features because to limit the scope of the evaluation as it is only one of the contributions of this work. Furthermore, we wanted to compare our work to Schuster's, which only utilizes object-related features found through a kitchen ontology [33].

As detailed in Section 4, object-related features were chosen from prior literature, kitchen ontologies, and information available on houseware and grocery stores websites. In order to select the most relevant features, we performed simple word analysis on participants' interviews and kitchen tours. We identified terms related to each feature and ranked the feature by its number of mentions. We initially evaluated our classification algorithms with the three highest ranking features. We then continued to expand the number of features until we achieved the highest classification accuracy, which was given by the following features: refrigeration requirements, container material, food state, use, and item type (food, kitchenware, houseware).

6.2 Training and Testing Set

Since it does not make sense to combine data from multiple homes, we evaluated the dataset of each individual home separately. In order to train each classifier, we created a set of training examples. The training set consisted of 85%

of the dataset chosen randomly. We looked at two different sets of examples to test the classifier. The first testing set consisted of the items given to participants during the *demonstration* portion of the home study, see Section 4. The second testing set consisted of a randomly chosen *segment* of 25 items from the dataset not used in the training set.

There main issue with the demonstration testing set is that it is limited in size and consistency: only seven items were used in the demonstration and each item was food.

6.3 Classification

We used the selected features to train a set of standard machine learning classifiers, including Support Vector Machines (SVMs) and k-Nearest Neighbors to predict the location of a kitchen item. We also looked at k-Means as a method of creating item groupings. We evaluated every home using each classification technique and averaged the results across all homes, as shown in Table 1.

6.3.1 Support Vector Machine (SVM)

Support Vector Machines (SVMs) are popular supervised learning algorithms which are widely available in various machine learning toolkits (such as Weka) and software packages (MATLAB) making them relatively easy to use.

We trained a set of SVMs using a linear kernel to predict objects' container number. Since SVMs are inherently two-class classifiers, we used two common approaches to multi-class classification: one-versus-rest and one-versus-one. In the one-versus-all approach, a single classifier is trained per class with samples from the class, i.e. container, labeled as positive while items from all other containers are labeled as negative. The classifier with the greatest margin is chosen as the predicted label. In the one-versus-one approach, a classifier is trained for every pair of containers. Every classifier is than applied to the testing sample and the container chosen by the highest number of individual classifiers is the predicted label. We found that the one-versus-rest approach performed best, as shown in Table 1.

6.3.2 k-Nearest Neighbors (k-NN)

k-Nearest Neighbors is a non-parametric classification algorithm that takes as its input the k closest training examples. The closest training examples are found by defining a similarity metric in the feature space. Hence, this algorithm mimics humans' method of grouping similar items. The output of the classifier is determined by a majority vote of the closest training examples with the label most common amongst its neighbors being chosen. Both humans and k-NNs performances are subject to similarity is defined. We evaluated k-NN with a variety of k values and distance metrics. We use the same features as with our SVMs and achieved the best results with $k = 12$ and a Euclidean distance metric, as shown in Table 1.

6.3.3 k-Means

k-Means is a clustering algorithm which can be used to partition objects into k groups, or clusters. We chose to look at k-Means because it is similar to organizing a space from scratch: there are k storage containers and n items that must be divided amongst them. Although k-Means can be used as a classifier by adding new items to pre-existing clusters, we chose to utilize the entire dataset as the testing set. Since features of the kitchen were not used in this analysis, we do not evaluate how many items were in the correct container. Instead, we calculate the accuracy of the algorithm by looking at every pair of items in each cluster and com-

	Segment	Demonstration
Support Vector Machine	93.7%	87.1%
k-Nearest Neighbors	87.9%	79.5%
k-Means	77.5%	77.1%

Table 1: Results for object return using our dataset and 3 classification algorithms

puting how many item pairs are correct, i.e. located in the same container.

6.4 Results

We found, as shown in Table 1, that SVMs perform the best of all three algorithms. The SVMs and k-NNs performed better on the segmented testing set than on the demonstration testing set. This is likely due to the size and bias of the demonstration testing set. The items in the demonstration were also chosen due to their ambiguity for many object-related features. Items in the segmented testing set were greater in number and randomly chosen, resulting in higher variation. Since these items belonged to the participants, the training dataset is more likely to contain similar objects.

For k-Means, the entire dataset was tested and reported in the segment result of the table. We added the additional items from the demonstration and reported the results of k-Means in the demonstration result of the table. Overall k-Means performed worst, but this is to be expected as the entire dataset was clustered.

A drawback to these algorithms is that our dataset excluded duplicate items in the same container and subcontainer. Thus, 10 coffee mugs are treated the same as 1. This can issues as methods such as k-NN use majority voting. Overall, we were able to obtain over 90% accuracy using just an SVM, showing that our dataset does a reasonable job capturing users' organizational preferences with respect to object locations.

Our goal in this section was not to solve the problem of object return but rather to evaluate the effectiveness of our study and dataset. Thus, we limited our analysis to 3 simple, but easy to use algorithms. Although we achieved good performance with SVMs, it is likely that performance on all 3 algorithms can be further boosted by common methods such as feature weighting. We also limited our analysis to object-related features. In the future, we would like to explore how user-related features can improve our results. It is also worth noting, that our overall performance was negatively affected by one home which contained significantly fewer kitchen items than other homes.

7. CONCLUSIONS

Since we expect robots of the future to have personal roles such as assistant or caregiver, it is essential they learn to meet the needs and demands of everyday users. However, despite the growing interest in domestic robots, there is an absence of knowledge or tools that accurately portray the complex and dynamic nature of the home.

In this work, we take a first step towards the creation of such tools through an exploratory study. From this study, we create an authentic dataset that goes beyond ethnography or visual analysis. We present an analysis of this dataset in the context of object return, an open problem in robotics. We show that we are able to accurately predict where objects go in different kitchens. We also present some common themes surrounding organization in the home, discuss how these themes appear in real-life kitchens, and their design implications for future robots.

One application which we mention but did not explore in this work is simulated homes and kitchens. Currently, roboticists rely on mock home environments, but these environments are simplistic and lack the complex nature of a real home. In the future, we plan to further explore how to use our work to create more realistic home environments and what metrics can be used to evaluate their quality.

In the future, we hope to further explore how we can better utilize information about the home and household in a quantitative context. One method is to incorporate general patterns found in multiple homes. With the small size of our dataset, it is difficult to identify these patterns. Therefore, we plan to refine our methods to incorporate more homes into our future work. Furthermore, we are excited to continue exploring other problems in robotics that our work can address.

8. ACKNOWLEDGMENTS

This work is supported by an NSF Graduate Research Fellowship and NSF-EEC-0540865. We thank Anca Dragan and members of the Personal Robotics Lab for their advice

9. REFERENCES

[1] K. O. Arras and D. Cerqui. Do we want to share our lives and bodies with robots? A 2000-people survey. Technical Report 0605-001, Lausanne, Switzerland.

[2] L. Baillie and D. Benyon. Place and Technology in the Home. *Computer Supported Cooperative Work (CSCW)*, 17(2-3):227–256, Sept. 2007.

[3] D. Barreau and B. A. Nardi. Finding and reminding: File organization from the desktop. *SigChi Bulletin*, 27(3):39–43, 1995.

[4] J. M. Beer, C. A. Smarr, T. L. Chen, A. Prakash, T. L. Mitzner, C. C. Kemp, and W. A. Rogers. The Domesticated Robot: Design Guidelines for Assisting Older Adults to Age in Place. In *ACM/IEEE HRI*, pages 335–342. ACM, 2012.

[5] R. Bernhaupt, M. Obrist, A. Weiss, E. Beck, and M. Tscheligi. Trends in the living room and beyond: Results from ethnographic studies using creative and playful probing. *Computers in Entertainment (CIE)*, 6(1):5, 2008.

[6] E. K. Choe, S. Consolvo, J. Jung, B. Harrison, and J. A. Kientz. Living in a Glass House: A Survey of Private Moments in the Home. In *ACM UbiComp*, pages 41–44, Beijing, China, 2011.

[7] A. Crabtree, T. Hemmings, K. Cheverst, K. Clarke, J. Hughes, and L. La. Designing with Care: Adapting Cultural Probes to Inform Design in Sensitive Settings. In *OzCHI*, pages 4–13, 2003.

[8] A. Crabtree, T. Hemmings, and T. Rodden. Pattern-based Support for Interactive Design in Domestic Settings. In *DIS*, pages 265–276. ACM, 2002.

[9] A. Crabtree and T. Rodden. Domestic Routines and Design for the Home. *CSCW*, 13(2):191–220, Apr. 2004.

[10] S. B. Cwerner and A. Metcalfe. Storage and Clutter: Discourses and Practices of Order in the Domestic World. *Journal of Design History*, 16(3):229–239, 2003.

[11] K. Dautenhahn, S. Woods, C. Kaouri, M. L. Walters, K. L. Koay, and I. Werry. What is a Robot Companion – Friend, Assistant or Butler? In *IEEE/RSJ IROS*, 2005.

[12] C. Despres. The meaning of home: Literature review and directions for future research and theoretical development. *Journal of Architectural and Planning Research*, 8(2):96–115, 1991.

[13] G. Dewsbury, K. Clarke, M. Rouncefield, I. Sommerville, B. Taylor, and M. Edge. Designing acceptable 'smart' home technology to support people in the home. *Technology and Disability*, 14:191–199, 2003.

[14] B. Eggen, G. Hollemans, and R. van de Sluis. Exploring and Enhancing the Home Experience. *Cognition, Technology, and Work*, 5(1):44–54, 2002.

[15] J. Forlizzi and C. DiSalvo. Service Robots in the Domestic Environment: A Study of the Roomba Vacuum in the Home. In *ACM/IEEE HRI*, pages 258–265. ACM, 2006.

[16] L. M. Gilbreth. Efficiency methods applied to kitchen design. *Architectural Record*, 291, 1930.

[17] R. Harper. In *Inside the Smart Home*. Springer, 2003.

[18] S. Harrison and P. Dourish. Re-place-ing space: the roles of place and space in collaborative systems. In *ACM CSCW*, pages 67–76. ACM, 1996.

[19] S. S. Intille. Designing a Home of the Future. *Pervasive Computing*, 1(2):76–82, 2002.

[20] Y. Ji, Y. Ko, A. Shimada, H. Nagahara, and R.-I. Taniguchi. Cooking Gesture Recognition using Local Feature and Depth Image. In *CEA*, pages 37–42, Nara, Japan, 2012. ACM.

[21] J. A. Kientz, S. N. Patel, B. Jones, E. Price, E. D. Mynatt, and G. D. Abowd. The Georgia Tech Aware Home. In *ACM CHIAbstract*, pages 3675–3680. ACM, 2008.

[22] J. Kishtwaria, P. Mathur, and A. Rana. Ergonomic Evaluation of Kitchen Work with Reference to Space Designing. *Journal of Human Ecology*, 21(1):43–46, 2007.

[23] T. Kollar and N. Roy. Utilizing object-object and object-scene context when planning to find things. In *IEEE ICRA*, pages 2168–2173. IEEE, 2009.

[24] S. Kriz, T. D. Ferro, P. Damera, and J. R. Porter. Fictional Robots as a Data Source in HRI Research: Exploring theLink between Science Fiction and Interactional Expectations. In *IEEE RO-MAN*, pages 458–463. IEEE, 2010.

[25] J. Lei, X. Ren, and D. Fox. Fine-Grained Kitchen Activity Recognition using RGB-D. In *ACM UbiComp*, pages 208–211. ACM, 2012.

[26] R. Mander, G. Salomon, and Y. Y. Wong. A 'Pile' Metaphor for Supporting Casual Organization of Information. In *ACM CHI*, pages 627–634. ACM, 1992.

[27] C. C. Marcus. *House As a Mirror of Self: Exploring the Deeper Meaning of Home*. Nicolas-Hays, Inc., 2006.

[28] J. O'Brien, T. Rodden, M. Rouncefield, and J. Hughes. At Home with the Technology: An Ethnographic Study of a Set-Top-Box Trial. *TOCHI*, 6(3):282–308, 1999.

[29] O. Palmon, R. Oxman, M. Shahar, and P. L. Weiss. Virtual environments as an aid to the design and evaluation of home and work settings for people with physical disabilities. In *ICDVRAT*, pages 119–124, 2004.

[30] C. Pantofaru, L. Takayama, T. Foote, and B. Soto. Exploring the Role of Robots in Home Organization. In *ACM/IEEE HRI*, pages 327–334. ACM, 2012.

[31] J. D. Runa, J. Harpring, and M. Zhu. Not Enough Cooks in the Kitchen. In *ACM CSCW*, pages 485–486.

[32] D. Schneiderman. The Prefabricated Kitchen: Substance and Surface. *Home Cultures*, 7(3):243–262, 2012.

[33] M. J. Schuster, D. Jain, M. Tenorth, and M. Beetz. Learning Organizational Principles in Human Environments. In *IEEE ICRA*, pages 3867–3874. IEEE, 2012.

[34] M. Scopelliti, M. V. Giuliani, A. M. DâĂŹAmico, and F. Fornara. If I had a Robot at Home... PeoplesâĂŹ Representation of Domestic Robots. In *Designing a More Inclusive World*, pages 257–266. Springer, 2004.

[35] R. E. Stepp and R. S. Michalski. Conceptual clustering: Inventing goal-oriented classifications of structured objects. *Machine learning: An artificial intelligence approach*, 2:471–498, 1986.

[36] L. Swan, S. Izadi, R. Harper, A. S. Taylor, A. Sellen, and M. Perry. Rethinking the "Smart" Home. In *IE*, pages 57–66, 2006.

[37] L. Swan, A. S. Taylor, and R. Harper. Making Place for Clutter and Other Ideas of Home. *TOCHI*, 15(2):9, 2008.

[38] A. S. Taylor, R. Harper, L. Swan, S. Izadi, A. Sellen, and M. Perry. Homes that make us smart. *Personal and Ubiquitous Computing*, 11(5):383–393, July 2006.

[39] A. S. Taylor and L. Swan. Artful systems in the home. In *Proceedings of the SIGCHI conference on Human factors in computing systems*, pages 641–650. ACM, 2005.

[40] A. Venkatesh, N. Stolzoff, E. Shih, and S. Mazumdar. The Home of the Future: an Ethnographic Study of New Information Technologies in the Home. *Advances in Consumer Research*, 28:88–97, 2001.

[41] L. L. S. Wong, L. P. Kaelbling, and T. L. Perez. Using Knowledge of Related Objects to Drive Attention for Active Object Search and Large-Scale Estimation. In *IEEE ICRA*, Hong Kong, China, 2014. IEEE.

[42] C. Wu, A. H. Khalili, H. Aghajan, and S. Ca. Multiview Activity Recognition in Smart Homes with Spatio-Temporal Features. In *ICDSC*, pages 142–149, Atlanta, Georgia, USA, 2010. ACM.

Are Robots Ready for Administering Health Status Surveys? First Results from an HRI Study with Subjects with Parkinson's Disease

Priscilla Briggs
HRI Laboratory
Dept. of Computer Science
Tufts University
161 College Avenue
Medford, MA, USA
priscilla.briggs@tufts.edu

Matthias Scheutz
HRI Laboratory
Dept. of Computer Science
Tufts University
161 College Avenue
Medford, MA, USA
matthias.scheutz@tufts.edu

Linda Tickle-Degnen
Dept. of Occupational Therapy
Tufts University
26 Winthrop Street
Medford, MA, USA
linda.tickle_degnen@tufts.edu

ABSTRACT

Facial masking is a symptom of Parkinson's disease (PD) in which humans lose the ability to quickly create refined facial expressions. This difficulty of people with PD can be mistaken for apathy or dishonesty by their caregivers and lead to a breakdown in social relationships. We envision future "robot mediators" that could ease tensions in these caregiver-client relationships by intervening when interactions go awry. However, it is currently unknown whether people with PD would even accept a robot as part of their healthcare processes. We thus conducted a first human-robot interaction study to assess the extent to which people with PD are willing to discuss their health status with a robot. We specifically compared a robot interviewer to a human interviewer in a within-subjects design that allowed us to control for individual differences of the subjects with PD caused by their individual disease progression. We found that participants overall reacted positively to the robot, even though they preferred interactions with the human interviewer. Importantly, the robot performed at a human level at maintaining the participants' dignity, which is critical for future social mediator robots for people with PD.

Categories and Subject Descriptors

H.4m [**Information Systems Applications**]: Miscellaneous

Keywords

Assistive robots; Parkinson's disease; quantitative field study

1. INTRODUCTION

Parkinson's Disease (PD) is a degenerative disability which affects 1.6% of people over 65 in the United States [22]. PD

HRI'15 March 02–05, 2015, Portland, OR, USA
Copyright 2015 ACM 978-1-4503-2883-8/15/03 ...$15.00.
http://dx.doi.org/10.1145/2696454.2696476.

is characterized by a decline in motor control and for some patients this decline can lead to "facial masking", a condition in which nuanced control of facial expression is partially or completely extinguished [17]. People exhibiting facial masking are perceived by both laypeople and healthcare providers alike as having less desirable personalities and as being less competent [19]. The lack of facial and other affective signals can be, wrongly, processed by the caregiver as lack of interest, affect, and engagement, and potentially lack of truth on the side of the person with PD [16]. As a result, communicative interactions between people with PD and their caregivers can go awry, leading to feelings of *stigmatization* and, ultimately, a loss of social control [18], causing a degradation of self dignity. An important goal for the management of PD is thus to break this "loop of miscommunication" to maintain the dignity of the person with PD.

One way to achieve these goals might be to use robots that can facilitate the interactions in the client-caregiver relationship by intervening when facial masking created miscommunication. The robot would thus function as a "mediator" (rather than a replacement of the caregiver) with the sole purpose of ensuring a functioning relationship between a person with PD and the caregiver. This, in turn, would reduce the risk for stigmatization.

A prerequisite for developing robots that could serve such a mediator role for PD therapy in the future, however, is knowing whether people with PD would be open to a "working alliance" with a robot in the first place. A *working alliance* has been defined in the context of therapy as a relationship in which both the client and the practitioner are "working together to achieve agreed upon goals through agreed upon methods of interventions" [15]. Hence, before we can start the development of a mediator robot, or any robot that can support people with PD for that matter, we need to find out whether people with PD are willing to pursue the goal of managing their disease together with a robot. One such way is to interact with a robot that can ask them questions about their health in natural language and is co-present when they talk with their caregivers. Hence, the goal of the present study was to perform the first empirical investigation of this kind, i.e., exploring whether people with PD would be open to robot mediators that ask them health-related questions.

The rest of the paper is structured as follows. We start with a brief description of the problems involved in PD and the challenges posed by PD for robotics, including a summary of related work in HRI. We then introduce the experimental setting and describe the interaction used in this study which allowed us to analyze the reactions of people with PD to the robot interviewer. Next we present the methods used to analyze the data, followed by the observed results. Finally, we discuss the implications of our findings for future studies and robotic developments in the domain of PD.

2. BACKGROUND

One of the principle aims of health care delivery is to optimize participation in preferred social roles [21]. People who do not engage in sufficient social activity are at risk for unfavorable health outcomes such as accelerated motor decline [3]. This problem led to the idea of *social self-management of health*, which is considered to be any self-care practices towards the goal of social comfort while simultaneously maintaining both physical and mental well-being [17]. Social self-management health practices include maintaining relationships and seeking help when it is needed [18]. A robot may be able to improve the social self-management of a person with PD. Yet, there is no published research to date that shows whether and how a robot could help people with PD to manage their social self, in particular, people with PD who exhibit facial masking.

Facial masking is a threat to the social self-management of a person with PD that can add mistrust into a relationship, or cause others to believe people with PD are less cognitively capable than they actually are [19]. If people could be trained to ignore the misleading facial expressions and pay attention instead to what the person with PD is saying, which more accurately represents what their state of mind and their feelings, then relationships could avoid being spoiled by facial masking. Unfortunately, even trained professionals are unconsciously and incorrectly reliant on automatic reactions to a masked face, even when they consciously know that they should not [19]. A robot, on the other hand, would have no problems discounting the expressions of a person exhibiting facial masking and could restrict itself to only analyzing the content of a person's speech interactions. It is thus possible that robots could eventually create a more accurate model of the emotional state of the person with PD than a layperson or even a medical professional could. If the robot were then able to communicate that person's emotions to the caretaker, the robot might be able to alleviate some of the stigmatization caused by facial masking in the caregiver-client interaction.

Our overarching goal is to work towards creating such a robot that can maintain the dignity and autonomy of people with PD, mainly by alleviating the effects of facial masking. As a first step, we designed the experiment described in this paper to assesses the ability and utility of a robot to interact with a person with PD. We aimed to evaluate whether a robot would induce feelings of loss of control or promote feelings of competency. We also wished to find out whether people with PD would like to interact with a robot and would feel that it acted in an attentive and understanding manner, all of which are prerequisite for forming a working alliance between a human with PD and a robot.

3. RELATED WORK

There are some indications that people with PD might be open to interacting with robots as recent research in HRI suggests that older adults without PD are generally interested in having robots assist them with their health-care. A survey of people living or working in a retirement village, for example, showed that older people were positive about the possible future role of robots in the village as long as they were easy to use, addressed a need, and assisted in independence and dignity [2]. When introduced to a robot that could take medical measurements, encourage physical activity, and discuss environmental hazards, participants felt highly positively towards it and were excited about the possibilities going forwards [20].

Given the potential of and interest in robots designed to facilitate physical abilities in older adults and people with disabilities, there is a growing body of research investigating how robots might be able to help. For example, robot coaches have been created that can motivate older adults to exercise [7]. Robotic canes can provide greater mobility assistance than normal walkers for people who wish to stay in their homes longer [6]. Moreover, work with a robot practicing tasks set by a physical therapist for stroke patients has shown increases in the amount of mobility for participants [10]. And there has even been some work in providing new technologies to people with PD such as using Google Glass as an assistive device [12].

Much less work, however, has investigated how to design robots to interact *socially* with those with disabilities. Most research in this area focuses on children with Autism Spectrum Disorder (ASD). Children with ASD interacting with a social robot, for example, exhibited more social behavior (in both human-human and human-robot interactions) than when they were with a randomly moving (non-social) robot [8]. Interacting with a social robot also elicited more social behaviors than interacting with a human adult or a tablet game [11].

These examples are among several encouraging findings that social robots can increase the amount of social activity in children with ASD and one could be tempted to apply robots developed for people with ASD to people with PD. However, ASD and PD are very different conditions and success for children with ASD does not guarantee the same success with people with PD. For example, ASD is characterized by a lack of simple social skills and an aversion against interacting with other people. In contrast, PD is primarily a physical, not cognitive disability, and people with PD generally are socially competent. We are thus in the early stages of investigating whether robots can play a role in mediating social human-human interaction for a group of people who cannot express their emotions adequately through facial expressions or affect in their voice (e.g., see [1] for our first preliminary report on human-robot interaction between robots and people with PD).

4. METHODS

In this study we aimed to test whether people with PD would accept a robot in a healthcare function and to show this acceptance in both participant self report and behavior. We chose a task for the robot that is very familiar to people with PD: assessing their disease-related quality of life using the Parkinson's Disease Questionnaire-39 (PDQ-39), a standardized measurement tool used by healthcare professionals.

We designed a within-subjects experiment in which half the questions of the PDQ-39 were administered by a robot and half of the questions by a human. This allowed us to compare the acceptability of the robot to a human and thus to control for individual differences in the subjects. The human interviewer for all participants was a female graduate student in Occupational Therapy trained in administering health interviews.

Note that the within-subjects design is critical for the assessment of behavior during interviews given the individual variability of the motor problems of people with PD. By having the robot and the human both administer half the PDQ-39, we were able to look at measures such as eye gaze and speech within-subjects.

It is also important to stress that experiments involving participants with PD cannot be compared to experiments with typical undergraduates. Not only are there significant differences in age, life experience and disease status, but also in the reason for doing the experiment and the degree to which the population is invested in the task. If the task is directly related to a debilitating disease experienced by the participant, then the participant will be more invested in the task and have a higher threshold for participating in the research in the first place compared to a healthy undergraduate student. Because of the investment that people with PD have in their healthcare, it is thus more difficult to recruit people with PD for such experiments where a robot takes on an important role in their personal health management process.

4.1 Participants

We were able to recruit 17 participants with PD (3 women, 1 unknown[1]) from PD support groups and fundraiser events, and from talks given at older adult community services. To be included in the study, participants had to self-report having PD, be able to understand and answer questions about their quality of life, be able to travel to the research study location, and be willing and able to provide informed consent. All participants were in the early to moderate stages of PD and were completely cognitively intact.

The robot malfunctioned during four of the 17 interviews. Data from these interviews were not included in any analyses reported here. Thus, the data from a total of 13 participants (one woman, one unknown) with a robot functioning according to protocol were analyzed for the current study.

The majority of participants were male, which is typical in studies of people with PD. The average age of participants was 67.77 years old ($SD = 14.13$). Of the 12 participants who reported their education, 8 had a college degree. The average participant had been diagnosed with PD 6.64 years ago ($SD = 5.36$, range = 5months - 17 years). No participants reported having interacted with a robot before.

Though this sample is small, it should be noted that it is a time-intensive operation to recruit subjects from a target population such as people with PD. Not only is there a smaller population of people with PD than many other populations, but scheduling becomes more difficult as participants often have difficulty with mobility. This study involves a greater effort level and potential payoff compared to other studies in HRI. First, it applies HRI with real robots instead

---

[1]All participants were given the option to choose from the genders of "Male", "Female", "Unknown" or "Unspecified" on their demographic survey. One participant is listed as having an unknown gender because that participant chose the "Unknown" option.

Figure 1: The robot interviewer was the Nao robot by Aldebaran.

of on Mechanical Turk. Secondly, it is done with a clinical population instead of healthy subjects at the university such as undergraduate students. Hence, it is not surprising (even though less than ideal) that the subject pool turned out to be fairly homogeneous and not gender-balanced (as is otherwise fairly straightforward to ensure).

4.2 Materials

The Nao robot by Aldebaran (Figure 1) was used as the robot interviewer. Its small size and expressive capabilities are typically seen as likable and easy to engage with. A researcher teleoperated the robot out of sight of the participants, using the Aldebaran *Choreographe* module. As seen in Figure 2, Choreographe lets users design and run robot behaviors. When the play button on a box is selected, that box's effect will take place, followed by the effects of the boxes connected to it. Figure 2 shows a simple example. After the robot finishes asking PDQ-39 question number nine (box "Q9"), the program proceeds to wait (the "wait" box) as the participant answers the question. When the participant finishes their response, the experimenter can tell Choregraphe to stop wating and move onto the next box, which in this case is the "Alright" box, which causes the robot to say "Alright" in response to the participant's answer to the question. Then the robot moves on to asking question eleven (box "Q11") while making a hand gesture ("hand up & open" box). When the hand gesture is done and the question has been asked ("Wait Till Done" box), the robot goes back to its standard pose ("Standard Pose" box). Also visable in Figure 2 are some of the other response options that the experimenter can make the robot say, such as "OK", and "Wonderful". Additional idle movements, such as blinking, that were not related to the question at hand, happened at random times.

In addition to hand gestures and idle movements, the robot showed its mobility at the beginning of the interview by standing up while waving and introducing itself, then taking a few steps walking towards the participant and eventually sitting down to conduct the interview. At the end of

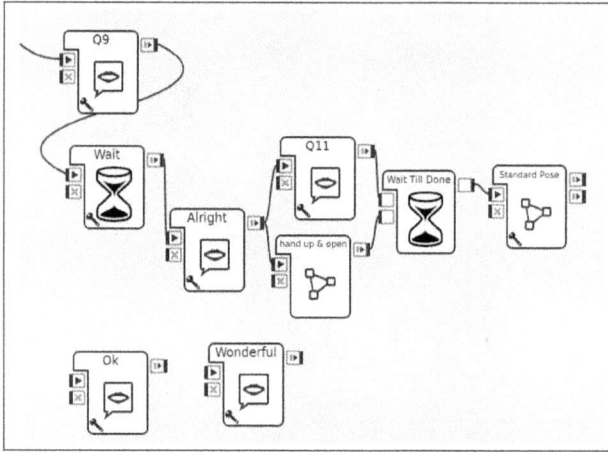

Figure 2: The Choreographe Module used to control the robot.

4.3 Procedure

The participant gave informed consent through procedures authorized by Tufts University Social, Behavioral and Educational Institutional Review Board. Following consent, the interviews began. Whether the participant was interviewed first by the robot or first by the human was a factor counterbalanced between participants. Interviews were video recorded. In order for the human and robot to have the same dialogue capabilities, we restricted the human interviewer to saying only phrases which the robot was programmed to be able to say. These included the interview questions, standardized introductory and ending remarks and 48 phrases such as "You said 'Always', is that correct?", "That sounds difficult", and "Can you repeat that?"[2]. The human interviewer held a copy of the interview questions, introductions, ending remarks and 48 phrases during the interview, as in a normal PDQ-39 interview, in which she would have had a copy of the questions. The human interviewer was instructed to use the same body language or gestures that she would usually use during this type of interaction.

Each interview consisted of the administration of a modified version of the PDQ-39, a measure of subjective health status and quality of life [9] commonly used in health practice and research with PD. It assesses eight domains of health and well-being important to people living with PD (Table 1) and is easy to administer by either human or robot. We split the PDQ-39 into two equal sets of questions from each of the eight domains of concern. Participants answered the degree to which they experienced the effect of PD on their lives by choosing one of five options along a Likert scale: "Always", "Often", "Sometimes", "Rarely" or "Never". One question about social support was present in both interviews in order

---

[2]Although the human interviewer was for the most part successful in limiting herself to the required phrases, for some participants she made negligible, single-word errors. One example would be when if she asked a participant what his hobbies were he said "Reading", and she repeated back "Reading". It seems reasonable to assume that these small deviations of script did not significantly affect perceptions of the human interviewer.

to test if participants would answer it identically to both interviewers. This made a total of 20 items per half. After administration of the PDQ-39, the interviewer asked "Can you describe one of your favorite activities to me?", and would listen, only making small comments such as "That's wonderful". If the participant had an answer that was only a few words long the interviewer could say "Can you elaborate?" or "Can you describe that to me more?". This question allowed us to assess the content and quality of the participant's open-ended speech with the robot relative to the human.

A typical interaction with the either the robot or human interviewer could have included the following dialogue: The interviewer asks, "Due to having Parkinson's disease, how often during the past 30 days have you felt frightened or worried about falling in public?" The participant would then respond with one of the Likert scale items such as, "Sometimes." The interviewer would acknowledge this by saying, "OK" and then move onto the next question saying, "Due to having Parkinson's disease, how often during the past 30 days have you had difficulty showering and bathing?" If the participant said "Well, now that I live in an assisted living facility, I get help every day" the interviewer is free to ask the participant to choose a Likert option by saying, "Would you consider that to be, Always, Often, Sometimes, Rarely, or Never?" The participant might say, "Oh, I think I would consider that never." The interviewer would then acknowledge this with another "OK" and would move on with the interview.

After each interview, participants responded to written questionnaires asking about their experience and their perceptions of the interviewer. Participants filled out a demographic questionnaire (age, gender, education, duration of PD, and whether or not they had ever interacted with a robot before). Participants were compensated $25. Lastly, participants were debriefed about why the study was done and were given the opportunity to ask questions about the study.

Category	Question (Each question begins with "Due to having Parkinson's disease, how often during the past 30 days have you...")
Mobility	...had difficulty getting around in public places?
ADL	...had difficulty holding a drink without spilling it?
Emotions	...felt depressed?
Stigma	...felt embarrassed in public?
Social	...received the support you needed from your family or close friends?
Cognitions	...had distressing dreams or hallucinations?
Communication	...had difficulty speaking?
Body Pain	...had painful muscle cramps or spasms?

Table 1: A few of the questions asked by the interviewers in this study. All questions were from a modified version of the PDQ-39, which measures health quality of life for people with PD in the eight dimensions shown in the table.

4.4 Questionnaire Measures

Participants completed a series of written questionnaires after each interview, encompassing 41 items divided into four

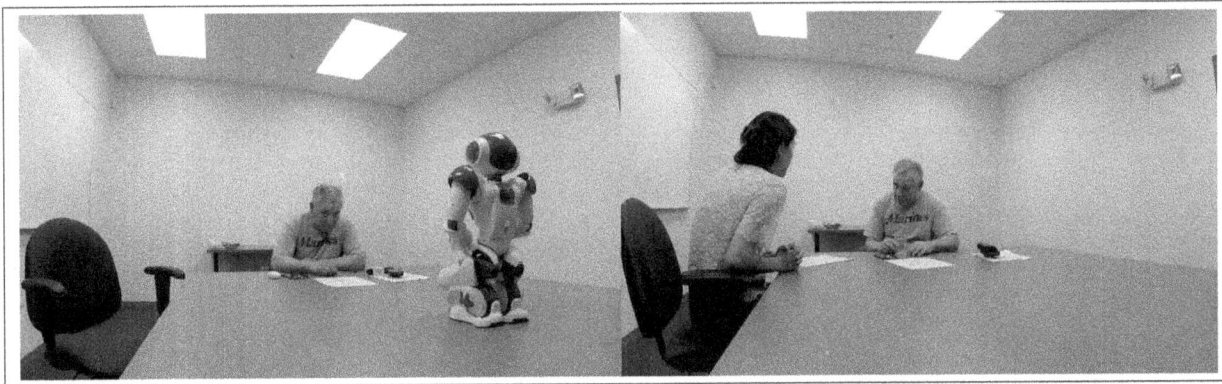

Figure 3: For this interaction, both a robot and a human administered a short questionnaire to a person with Parkinson's disease.

categories derived from previous research on the quality of the experience of interpersonal interaction between humans [13, 14]. Five-point Likert questions from 1 (not at all) to 5 (very), assessed the degree to which the participant, during each interview, experienced positive mood, optimal experience, an emotional bond to the interviewer, and perceived the interviewer as producing actions that create rapport. The internal consistency of items representing each category was assessed using Cronbach's alpha. Composite scores for each category were created by averaging all items after reversing the items noted below. The four categories and the items that comprise them are the following:

- **Positive Mood**. These items assessed the degree to which the participant felt alert, happy, irritable (reversed), involved, tense (reversed), sociable, bored (reversed), confused (reversed), cooperative, and embarrassed (reversed). The items demonstrated high internal consistency (Robot = .90; Human = .78).

- **Optimal Experience**. These items assessed the degree to which the participant experienced one's skills as having been fully engaged with competency and satisfaction during the interview [5]. Items were "I was able to concentrate", "It was hard to concentrate" (reversed), "I felt self-conscious" (reversed), "'I was aware of the camera" (reversed), "The interview was challenging to me" (reversed), "I felt skillful during the interview", "I felt in control of the situation", "I did a successful interview", and "I felt good about myself". The items demonstrated moderate to high internal consistency (Robot = .75; Human = .57[3]).

- **The Emotional Bond to the Interviewer**. These items assessed the degree to which the participant felt a bond was formed with the interviewer. Items were "I liked the interviewer", "It was easy to engage with the interviewer", "I felt indifferent to the interviewer" (reversed), "I communicated easily with the interviewer", "It was an awkward interaction" (reversed), "I was interested in the interviewer's words and actions", "I understood what the interviewer was asking", "I felt in

---

[3]The Optimal Experience measure shown here has been used in previous studies relating to PD, so although its Cronbach's alpha score is lower here than desirable, this measure has been validated well enough to warrant use.

rapport with the interviewer", "I felt comfortable with the interviewer" and "The interviewer was annoying" (reversed). The items demonstrated high internal consistency (Robot = .88; Human = .86).

- **Perceived Rapport Actions of the Interviewer**. This measure included items assessing the degree to which the participant perceived the interviewer to have "Acted in a friendly manner", "Paid attention to me", "Acted indifferent to me" (reversed), "Communicated easily with me", "Used actions and words that were awkward with my actions and words", "Showed interest in my words and actions", "Understood what I was trying to say", "Showed rapport with me", "Was likable", "Was controlling of me" (reversed), "Was considerate", and "Was aggressive" (reversed). The items demonstrated high internal consistency (Robot = .77; Human = .73).

Six additional five-point Likert scaled items were included in the questionnaires assessing the robot interviewer: "Was the robot's behavior natural", "Was the robot's behavior human-like", "Did the robot look human-like", "Was the robot's speech natural", "Was the robot's size appropriate", and "Was the robot creepy". These items were examined individually without aggregation.

4.5 Data Analysis

We first analyzed descriptive statistics (means and standard deviations) on the robot questionnaires to assess the distribution of responses to the robot on the five-point Likert scale, to determine if participants were evaluating the robot on the more positive or negative evaluative end of the scale. Second, we conducted preliminary analyses to determine if there were any effects of the order or sequence in which the robot conducted its interview with the participant. Mixed repeated measures and between ANOVAs demonstrated that there were no effects of the repeated measure of order (first versus second interview) and the between factor of sequence (robot interviewer first versus the robot interviewer second) on the participants' responses to the robot and human interviewers on the measures of positive mood, optimal experience, the emotional bond to the interviewer, and perceived rapport actions of the interviewer. Therefore, we conducted a simple repeated measures (paired) t-test to determine the statistical significant and effect sizes of the human versus robot differences on these measures. We also calculated the effect size d [4] for each measure to determine the standardized difference between responses to the robot relative to the human. The lower the absolute value of the effect size d, the lower the differences in the responses to robot and human interviewer. Spearman's ρ correlational analysis were used to test the associations between the demographic data, the aggregated survey items and the robot specific questionnaire items. Finally, we took a case study approach to examining individual participant eye gaze and utterance responses to the robot and human.

5. RESULTS

5.1 Reactions to the Robot

Table 2 shows the mean and standard deviation of the four aggregate measures of the participants' written questionnaires about the robot as well as the single item assessments of the robot averaged over the participants. The results from the four aggregate measures indicate that participants had a positive mood and a good overall experience, that they formed an overall positive emotional bond with the robot and that they felt the robot was attempting to create rapport with them. The means from the six robot specific questions show an overall positive reaction as well. 69.2% of participants gave the robot the lowest possible score of 1 on the creepy measure. Participants also rated the robot's behavior and speech as fairly natural and rated the robot's size as appropriate. The only ratings that the robot received below the middle/mean value of 3 on the Likert scale were on the measures of "Was the robot's behavior human-like?" and "Did the robot look human-like?".

Measure	Robot		Human	
	Mean	SD	Mean	SD
Mood	4.22	.72	4.61	0.45
Optimal Experience	4.17	.61	4.30	0.48
Emotional Bond	3.87	.84	4.78	0.31
Rapport	3.79	.65	4.45	0.36
Behavior Natural	3.23	1.24	n/a	n/a
Behavior Human-Like	2.92	1.19	n/a	n/a
Look Human-Like	2.38	1.26	n/a	n/a
Speech Natural	3.25	1.22	n/a	n/a
Size Appropriate	3.15	1.21	n/a	n/a
Robot Creepy	1.62	1.19	n/a	n/a

Table 2: This table shows the ratings of the robot and human interviewers on a 5-point Likert scale averaged over all participants.

5.2 Comparisons to Human Interviewer

To test the differences between participant experiences in the robot and human interview, paired sample t-tests were calculated on each of the four aggregated variables described in the Measures section: Mood, Optimal Experience, Emotional Bond to the Interviewer and Perceived Rapport Actions. Findings are reported if the effect size d for the t-test was greater than .50. These tests found that the participants were in a less positive mood with the robot relative to the human ($t(12) = -3.03$, $p = .10$, $d = -.84$). There was not a significant difference between the participant's Optimal Experience ratings for the robot and the human

($t(12) = -1.00$, $p = .34$, $d = -.28$). A significant difference was found for the ratings of the Emotional Bond to the Interviewer ($t(12) = -3.77$, $p = .003$, $d = -1.05$) and for the ratings of Perceived Rapport Actions by the Interviewer ($t(12) = -3.48$, $p = .005$, $d = -.96$).

We conducted paired sample t-test for non-aggregated individual items on all measures in order to elaborate the meaning of the findings on composite measures. The participants, on average, rated themselves as more indifferent to the robot than to the human ($d = .82$, $p = .12$) and reported that the robot showed less interest in the participants' words and actions ($d = -.80$, $p = .01$). However, for some of the questionnaire items, there was essentially no difference between the robot and the human. If a variable had an effect size under 0.1, there was one tenth of a standard deviation difference between the robot and human, and we considered it to be a small difference. Three non-aggregated questionnaire items were under this threshold. The participants felt similarly low levels of tenseness ($d = .08$), embarrassment ($d = .000$), and difficulty concentrating ($d = .07$) during the robot and human interviews.

The correlations between the aggregate measures and the robot-only findings are reported in Table 3. Believing that the robot acted naturally was positively correlated with feeling an emotional bond with the robot ($p = .005$) and with perceiving the robot to have performed rapport actions ($p = .01$). Perceiving the robot as creepy was negatively correlated with creating an emotional bond with the robot ($p = .003$).

	Mood	Optimal Experience	Emotional Bond	Perceived Rapport Actions
Behavior Natural	0.21	−0.09	0.72**	0.66*
Behavior Human-Like	−0.20	−0.41	0.49	0.32
Look Human-Like	−0.11	0.10	−0.05	0.16
Speech Natural	0.26	0.35	0.18	0.49
Size Appro.	−0.14	−0.42	0.34	0.50
Robot Creepy	−0.27	0.03	−0.76**	−0.41

Table 3: This table shows the correlations between the aggregate measures and the robot specific items on the questionnaire. Items marked with a star (*) were significant at the .05 level. Items marked with two stars (**) were significant at the .01 level.

5.3 Additional Preliminary Video Analysis

Videotaped interviews were examined in a preliminary manner to assess the number of times the participant gazed at the eyes or head of the interviewer and the duration of each event. Additionally we examined how much participants spoke during the interviews in terms of number of utterances and words per utterance.

The rates at which different participants gazed at the interviewers' faces and spoke to the interviewer were very different. Comparisons of the within-subjects differences showed that some participants gazed more at the robot and some gazed less at the robot. Some talked more to the robot and some more to the human. As an example, we closely examined the results for participant #2 who spoke six utterances (3.50 average words per utterance) to the robot and spoke 81 utterances to the human interviewer (6.58 words per utterance) during the Likert-scale section of the PDQ-39. During the same time period this participant gazed at the robot interviewer's face 56 times for a total time of gaze at 4 minutes 8 seconds. During the interview with the human, the participant gazed at the interviewer's face 78 times for a total time of gaze at 7 minutes 1 second.

As a comparison, we examined participant #6 who saw the questionnaires and the interviewers in the same order as participant #2. Participant #6 spoke 16 times to the robot interviewer and 4 times to the human interviewer. This participant also gazed more at the robot, spending a total of 6 minutes and 16 seconds looking at the robot's face and only 2 minutes and 59 seconds at the humans face, despite having 32 eye gaze events for both interviewers.

These two example participants represent the larger pattern found in the data. Participants #2 and #6 varied substantially in their behavior as was typical across participants. Yet, these two participants had similar opinions of the robot compared to the human and their views were similar to the other participants. Both participants had a weaker emotional bond to the robot than to the human (#2: Robot=3.80, Human=4.80; #6:Robot=3.78, Human=4.20) and felt that the robot was doing fewer rapport action than the human was (#2: Robot=2.33, Human=4.58; #6: Robot=3.08, Human=4.08). They both felt that the robot and the human were equal in providing a good overall experience (#2=5.00, #6=4.33). Participant #2 (the participant who made less eye contact with the robot and spoke less to the robot) was in an equally good mood when talking to both interviewers (5.00), while the self-rated mood of participant #6, who spoke more and made more eye contact with the robot, was only slightly lower when talking to the robot (Robot=4.20, Human=4.60). In conclusion the behavioral analysis suggested that one cannot infer from the talkativeness and eye gaze patterns of people with PD how much they like the robot, how well they connect with the robot, or how human-like they find the robot.

6. DISCUSSION

When examining the participants' reactions to the robot without comparison to the human, the reactions are positive. Participants rated the robot higher than the middle point/mean of the Likert scale on almost all measures. They were in a good mood, felt an emotional bond, felt rapport and did not feel stigmatized during the interaction with the robot. These positive reactions show that people with PD are open to working with a robot and are willing to discuss their health with a robot.

When we examined reactions to the robot interviewer as compared to the reactions to the human, however, we found that the two were viewed as dissimilar. Participants were in a better mood with the human, they felt a stronger emotional bond to the human, and they felt that the human interviewer tried to create rapport more than the robot did. As expected, we also found quite pronounced individual differences among the subjects with respect to their eye gaze and verbal behavior towards the robot compared to the hu-

man interviewer, and the within-subjects design specifically allowed us to control for these types variations. While one could take the comparison to suggest that the robot is not appropriate for the task, it is important to note that participants felt equally capable and equally non-stigmatized during both interviews and that there was no difference in how embarrassed they felt during the two interviews. These results suggest that it may be possible for the person with PD to form a working alliance with a robot, regardless whether or not a human interviewer would be preferred over a robot. A working alliance requires, at a minimum, a shared goal and a minimal affective bond (though a stronger affective bond does improve the alliance) [15]. The robot has the traits potentially needed to be an acceptable helper, just not a better helper than a human therapist.

Our results are thus overall very encouraging. For a robot whose main job is to reduce stigmatization, the fact that a population so invested in this type of interview is comfortable enough to answer serious questions about their health represents a significant success for the robot. As we stated before, it is important to note that the robot was not disliked by the participants, as it was rated above the middle value on the Likert scale on almost all measures, but it simply was not able to rise to human level – which was not expected in the first place. While it seems that participants may not have felt emotionally close with the robot interviewer, they were still willing to engage a working alliance with the robot if only for the brief time of the interview.

Thus, the present study achieved our main aim to test whether people with PD would accept a robot in a health care function. The results suggest that the robot was acceptable but was not viewed as favorably as the human. Many factors could contribute to the differences in the ratings between the robot and the human, for example physical appearance, movements, differences in positioning of the interviewer, and not the least that one is a machine and one is human. While it is not clear which of these aspects contributed to differences between ratings of the robot, these differences are not relevant for the main aim of the study to investigate the acceptability of the robot for the intended task. It is possible that repeated interactions with the robot could lead to differences in ratings once subjects become sufficiently acquainted with the robot because none of the subjects reported having interacted with robots before. Whether these ratings will be increased and the robot viewed human-like (at least with respect to the particular task) or whether they will drop relative to the current study is an empirical question that would require a longitudinal study with repeated follow-up interaction experiments.

There are very additional exciting directions for future work using robots to assist people with PD given that we have first evidence that people with PD would accept a robot mediator. For example, we can now start to develop a comprehensive robot system that is able to reduce stigmatization felt by people with facial masking by mediating the caregiver-client interactions. And when there is no caregiver available, the robot could autonomously interview people about their health status more frequently than is otherwise practically possible for health care providers. Such frequent examinations of the state of a person's PD could lead to better therapies for that person and overall better social and physical outcomes.

7. CONCLUSIONS

In this paper we presented the first HRI study investigating whether people with Parkinson's disease would be open to interaction with a robot who can administer a health status survey. The results from our study show that overall participants felt positive towards the robot and that the robot was as good as a human at maintaining dignity and avoiding embarrassment of the person with PD. This is an important result given the stigmatization people with PD often experience. While the results also showed that the robot fell short of being rated as positively as the human interviewer, the most important implication for subsequent investigations is that robots could form "working alliances" with persons with PD in the future. It is our hope that this study will contribute to the development of future autonomous robots that could serve as "mediators" in a human caregiver-client relationship and thus help to both maintain the dignity of people with Parkinson's disease while reducing the risk of their social stigmatization.

8. ACKNOWLEDGMENTS

This project was in part supported by NSF grant #IIS-1316809.

9. REFERENCES

[1] P. Briggs, M. Scheutz, and L. Tickle-Degnen. Reactions of people with parkinson's disease to a robot interviewer. In *Proceedings of the workshop on assistive robotics for individuals with disabilities at IROS*, 2014.

[2] E. Broadbent, R. Tamagawa, A. Patience, B. Knock, N. Kerse, K. Day, and B. A. MacDonald. Attitudes towards health-care robots in a retirement village. *Australasian journal on ageing*, 31(2):115–120, 2012.

[3] A. S. Buchman, P. A. Boyle, R. S. Wilson, D. A. Fleischman, S. Leurgans, and D. A. Bennett. Association between late-life social activity and motor decline in older adults. *Archives of Internal Medicine*, 169(12):1139–1146, 2009.

[4] J. Cohen. *Statistical power analysis for the behavioral sciences*. Routledge Academic, 2013.

[5] M. Csikszentmihalyi. *Flow: the psychology of optimal experience*. Harper & Row, 1990.

[6] S. Dubowsky, F. Genot, S. Godding, H. Kozono, A. Skwersky, H. Yu, and L. S. Yu. Pamm-a robotic aid to the elderly for mobility assistance and monitoring: a "helping-hand" for the elderly. In *Robotics and Automation, 2000. Proceedings. ICRA'00. IEEE International Conference on*, volume 1, pages 570–576. IEEE, 2000.

[7] J. Fasola and M. J. Matarić. A socially assistive robot exercise coach for the elderly. *Journal of Human-Robot Interaction*, 2:3–32, 2013.

[8] D. Feil-Seifer and M. Matarić. Toward socially assistive robotics for augmenting interventions for children with autism spectrum disorders. In O. Khatib, V. Kumar, and G. Pappas, editors, *Experimental Robotics*, volume 54 of *Springer Tracts in Advanced Robotics*, pages 201–210. Springer Berlin Heidelberg, 2009.

[9] C. Jenkinson, R. Fitzpatrick, V. Peto, R. Greenhall, and N. Hyman. The parkinson's disease questionnaire (pdq-39): development and validation of a parkinson's disease summary index score. *Age and Aging*, 26:353 – 357, 1997.

[10] H.-T. Jung, J. Baird, Y.-K. Choe, and R. A. Grupen. Upper extremity physical therapy for stroke patients using a general purpose robot. In *RO-MAN, 2011 IEEE*, pages 270–275. IEEE, 2011.

[11] E. S. Kim, L. D. Berkovits, E. P. Bernier, D. Leyzberg, F. Shic, R. Paul, and B. Scassellati. Social robots as embedded reinforcers of social behavior in children with autism. *Journal of Autism and Developmental Disorders*, 43:1038 – 1049, 2013.

[12] R. McNaney, J. Vines, D. Roggen, M. Balaam, P. Zhang, I. Poliakov, and P. Olivier. Exploring the acceptability of google glass as an everyday assistive device for people with parkinson's. In *Proceedings of the 32nd annual ACM conference on Human factors in computing systems*, pages 2551–2554. ACM, 2014.

[13] N. M. Puccinelli and L. Tickle-Degnen. Knowing too much about others: moderators of the relationship between evesdropping and rapport in social interaction. *Journal of Nonverbal Behavior*, 28(4):233 – 241, 2004.

[14] L. Tickle-Degnen. Nonverbal behavior and its functions in the ecosystem of rapport. *The SAGE handbook of nonverbal communication*, pages 381–399, 2006.

[15] L. Tickle-Degnen. *Occupational therapy for physical dysfunction*, chapter Therapeutic Rapport, pages 412 – 427. Lippincott William & Wilkins, 7 edition, 2014.

[16] L. Tickle-Degnen and K. D. Lyons. Practitioners' impressions of patients with parkinson's disease: the social ecology of the expressive mask. *Social Science & Medicine*, 58:603 – 614, 2004.

[17] L. Tickle-Degnen, M. Saint-Hilaire, C. A. Thomas, B. Habermann, L. S. S. Martinez, N. Terrin, F. Noubary, and E. N. Naumova. Emergence and evolution of social self-management of parkinson's disease: study protocol for a 3-year prospective cohort study. *BMC Neurology*, 14, 2014.

[18] L. Tickle-Degnen, C. Thomas, M. Saint-Hilaire, E. Naumova, N. Ambady, T. Ellis, and R. Wagenaar. The social self-management of parkinson's disease (pd) in daily life. *Movement Disorders*, 27:S313–S314, 2012.

[19] L. Tickle-Degnen, L. A. Zebrowitz, and H. ing Ma. Culture,gender and health care stigma: Practitioners' response to facial masking experienced by people with parkinson's disease. *Social Science & Medicine*, 73:95 – 102, 2011.

[20] K. Werner, J. Oberzaucher, and W. Franz. Evaluation of human robot interaction factors of a socially assistive robot together with older people. In *Sixth International Conference on Complex, Intelligent, and Software Intensive Systems*, pages 455–460. IEEE, 2012.

[21] W. H. O. (WHO). International classification of functioning, disability, and health (icf). 2001.

[22] A. W. Willis, B. A. Evanoff, M. Lian, S. R. Criswell, and B. A. Racette. Geographic and ethnic variation in parkinson disease: A population-based study of us medicare beneficiaries. *Neuroepidemiology*, 34:143 – 151, 2010.

Measuring the Efficacy of Robots in Autism Therapy: How Informative are Standard HRI Metrics?

Momotaz Begum
Computer Science
University of Massachusetts
Lowell
mbegum@cs.uml.edu

Richard W. Serna
Psychology
University of Massachusetts
Lowell
Richard_Serna@uml.edu

David Konktak
Crotched Mountain
Rehabilitation Center,
Greenfield, NH
David.Kontak@crotched
mountain.org

Jordan Allspaw
Computer Science
University of Massachusetts
Lowell
allspaw.j@gmail.com

James Kuczynski
Computer Science
University of Massachusetts
Lowell
james.perl12@gmail.com

Holly A. Yanco
Computer Science
University of Massachusetts
Lowell
holly@cs.uml.edu

ABSTRACT

A significant amount of robotics research over the past decade has shown that many children with autism spectrum disorders (ASD) have a strong interest in robots and robot toys, concluding that robots are potential tools for the therapy of individuals with ASD. However, clinicians, who have the authority to approve robots in ASD therapy, are not convinced about the potential of robots. One major reason is that the research in this domain does not have a strong focus on the efficacy of robots. Robots in ASD therapy are end-user oriented technologies, the success of which depends on their demonstrated efficacy in real settings. This paper focuses on measuring the efficacy of robots in ASD therapy and, based on the data from a feasibility study, shows that the human-robot interaction (HRI) metrics commonly used in this research domain might not be sufficient.

Categories and Subject Descriptors

H.3.4 [**Systems and Software**]: [Performance evaluation (efficiency and effectiveness)]; J.4 [**Social and Behavioral Sciences**]: [Psychology]

Keywords

Autism spectrum disorders (ASD), efficacy, robot, human-robot interaction (HRI) metrics

1. INTRODUCTION

Robotics research has demonstrated that many individuals with ASD (IwASD) express elevated enthusiasm (e.g. increase in attention [18], imitation ability [11], verbal utter-

ances [17], social activities [29], etc.) while interacting with robots. A comprehensive survey on this research is available in [6, 27]. A long line of research is dedicated to the design of robots with appropriate physical features [24], control architectures [9], evaluation metrics [26], and HRI algorithms [10] that can be used in ASD diagnosis and therapy. Despite these efforts, the targeted end-users of this technology (IwASDs, their caregivers, and clinicians) are neither aware nor convinced of the role of robots in ASD therapy [8]. Recently, a number of systematic reviews and a meta-analysis of the technology-based interventions for IwASDs (which reviewed research articles published before December 2011) have concluded that the robot based studies with IwASDs fail to meet a set of criteria commonly observed to assess the outcome of an ASD therapy [13, 23]. The problem lies in the fact that the vast majority of robotics research in this domain shows the 'likability' of robots but fails to demonstrate a robot's efficacy in therapy and/or diagnosis of ASD [8, 18]. Accordingly, we are observing a recent paradigm shift where more research is focusing on investigating the efficacy of robots in ASD therapy through improved research design [4, 12, 16, 22, 28], investigation of robots' features and abilities [25], and increasing robots' autonomy [5]. Defining appropriate efficacy metrics is one of the fundamental components in investigating the efficacy of robots in ASD therapy. There is, however, no report in the existing literature on efficacy metrics for robots in ASD therapy.

Efficacy metrics indicate how well a robot is producing the intended therapeutic effect in an IwASD. A vast majority of robotics research in this domain uses some common HRI metrics (e.g. gaze direction, verbal/non-verbal communication cues, affective responses, etc.) as a measure of a robot's impact on an IwASD. We have recently conducted a study to investigate whether it is clinically feasible to teach a new skill to IwASDs through a robot [20]. During the study, a robot was used to teach a basic skill of greeting someone in a socially acceptable manner to a group of low-functioning IwASDs. We defined two metrics, `Skill execution` and `Prompt dependency`, which measured the efficacy of the robot-mediated therapy in achieving the intended therapeutic goal. An analysis of the study outcomes shows that a set of common HRI metrics (namely, `Gaze`, `Communication`, and `Affect`) have no correlation with these two efficacy metrics. This lack of correlation indicates that the common HRI metrics may not be able to gauge the efficacy of a robot in ASD therapy. To the best of our knowledge, this is the first work that presents efficacy metrics for robots in ASD therapy and provides a comparative analysis of efficacy metrics with some common HRI metrics.

2. EFFICACY AND HRI METRICS

Any ASD therapy, in a clinical domain, operates with some fundamental goals. In general, a therapy: 1) aims to teach an IwASD a new behavior/skill or to eliminate a problem behavior [30], 2) aims to improve the quality of life, level of independence, health, and well-being of an IwASD and help him/her integrate in the society in a better way [1], and 3) when successful, should produce outcomes that last [1]. It is expected that an IwASD will be able to execute a behavior learned through the therapy independently, outside of the therapy setting, and with the people in his/her everyday life. Clinicians use different metrics, on a case-by-case basis, to monitor the progress made by an IwASD and measure the overall outcome of a therapy. To establish the efficacy of robots in this domain, a robot-mediated ASD therapy should also operate with the same goals, and metrics should be defined to clearly indicate how the use of a robot is linked to the positive outcome of a therapy.

As the core deficits of ASD are related to social behaviors and communication abilities [3], robotics researchers historically focused on a set of social and communicative cues directed by IwASDs toward robots to assess the quality of IwASD-robot interaction. The most common HRI metrics used in this case are `Gaze` (the duration or the number of times an IwASD looked at the robot) [5, 18, 19, 26, 28, 29], `Communication` (number of verbal/non-verbal communication with the robot, total number of words exchanged with the robot, etc.) [17, 26, 29], `Affect` (being in an affective state or showing affective responses to the robot) [7, 9, 18, 24], `Attention` (focusing on the robot) [18, 19], `Imitation` (imitating a robot's action or speech) [11, 19, 24], and `Proxemics` (being in a close proximity of the robot) [10]. Although these metrics perform well to demonstrate the general enthusiasm expressed by an IwASD when (s)he is around a robot, none of these studies provides a clear indication of whether the participants (IwASDs) were actually able to learn the target behavior from the robot and executed it independently, outside of the study setting.

Our recent study investigated whether a robot-mediated ASD therapy can achieve some of the clinical goals of a standard ASD therapy. We propose two efficacy metrics to monitor the progress of our participants and the overall outcome of the robot-mediated therapy: `Skill execution` and `Prompt dependency`.

1. `Skill execution, SE`: A measure of the ability of a participant to execute a target social skill (with the robot and with other people, within and outside of the therapy setting).

2. `Prompt dependency, PD`: A measure of a participant's ability to execute a target skill without the help of the robot.

These two metrics, when analyzed together, indicate the efficacy of a robot in teaching a new skill to an IwASD. The goal of the robot-mediated therapy is to maximize `Skill execution` (ideally, `SE` = 100%) while minimizing `Prompt dependency` (ideally, `PD` = 0). The trends of `SE` and `PD` over the duration of a therapy provide important information about the efficacy of a therapy. This paper shows that some of the common HRI metrics listed in this section do not show any meaningful correlation with these two efficacy metrics.

3. A FEASIBILITY STUDY ON TEACHING THROUGH A ROBOT

Single-subject research design has a unique value in autism research [15]. Recent literature suggests that group-based design, although considered as the gold-standard in clinical research, might not be the only choice to prove the efficacy of an ASD therapy [21]. We conducted a single-subject study at the Crotched Mountain Rehabilitation Center (CMRC), a special education school in New Hampshire, USA, to investigate the feasibility of teaching a new skill to IwASDs through a robot. The study was approved by the Institutional Review Boards (IRB) of the University of Massachusetts Lowell and CMRC. Informed consent from the parents or guardians of the participants was collected before the study began.

3.1 Study Design

Based on a discussion with the clinicians at CMRC, we identified the lack of social greetings as a common deficit among many IwASDs attending the school. Accordingly, the goal of the study was to teach the basic skill. A therapy was designed to teach saying 'Hi' or 'Hello' in response to a social greeting. The study was a single-subject, multiple baseline type and followed the basic guidelines for single-subject research design outlined in [15].

3.1.1 Participants

Two inclusion criteria were decided for the participants.

1. An individual diagnosed with any form of ASD.

2. An individual with ASD who, according to his/her current therapists at the CMRC, has one or more of the prerequisite abilities to initiate/respond to social greetings but does not generally do so. The ability to imitate, verbal ability, the physical ability of waving hands, etc. were considered a few of the prerequisites to learn the skill of initiating/responding to social greetings.

Five students from the school matched these inclusion criteria and were recruited for the study. Due to space limitation, results from three participants will be reported in this paper. Participant demographics and diagnostic information are presented in Table 1. All of the participants are male which is consistent with the fact that ASD is more common among boys than girls [2]. Note that our participants are mostly toward the lower end of the spectrum (generally, IQ< 70), a less investigated population in robot-based ASD research. Due to compromised cognitive abilities, all of our participants, according to a school regulation, were required to be accompanied by a professional caregiver at all times. Accordingly, the caregiver was included in the therapy design. Informed consent from the caregivers was collected before the study began.

Table 1: Participants' Information

ID	Sex	Age (Yrs)	Diagnostic information
P1	M	19	General diagnosis: Autism Assessment tool: AAMR Adaptive Behavior Scale - School Score:Very poor - Average, age equivalence range 3 Yrs - 4 Yrs
P2	M	14	General diagnosis: Classic Autism, Mood disorder Assessment tool: Adaptive Behavior Scale - School (ABS-S:2) Score: Age equivalence range 3 Yrs - 6 Yrs 3 Mos
P3	M	13	General diagnosis: Autism Assessment tool: Leiter International Performance Scale, Verbal Behavior Milestones Assessment and Placement Program IQ: 40

Table 2: Overall Description of the Study

Participant ID	Baseline duration (days)	No. of therapy sessions	Duration of the therapy (days)	Generalization training
P1	3	19	9	No
P2	6	24	10	Yes
P3	9	10	6	No

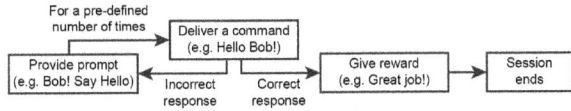

Figure 1: The structure of the ABA-based therapy for teaching the behavior of social greetings

3.1.2 Variables

A required feature of single-subject research design, among many others, is that the dependent and independent variables should have operational definitions that clearly indicate the performance pattern of participants and allow valid interpretation of results [15]. The independent variable in our study is the robot: whether the therapy delivered through a robot can teach a target skill to the participants. There are two dependent variables: *Responsiveness to the command* (i.e. the frequency of positive response to social greetings) and *Prompt* (i.e. the number of prompts provided by the robot to generate a positive response). The dependent variables are measured repeatedly before the robot-mediated therapy begins (i.e. the baseline measurement phase), during the therapy, and outside of the therapy setting in order to identify the effect of the robot-mediated therapy on the participants. The two efficacy metrics, Skill execution and Prompt dependency, are directly linked to these two dependent variables but provide a generalized way to measure the outcome of other ASD interventions of similar nature. The paper hypothesizes that these two metrics provide clear indications about the efficacy of a robot in teaching a skill to IwASDs and that the HRI metrics are not sufficient to convey information about therapeutic effects. The dependent variables and the efficacy metrics will be further discussed in Section 3.2.1.

3.1.3 Baseline measurement

Baseline measurement was performed on each participant before his therapy began and continued until a stable pattern was observed, for a minimum of three days. Each participant went through a different duration of the baseline phase in order to conform with the guidelines of multiple baseline design [15]. During each day of the baseline phase for a participant, one person familiar to the participant and one unfamiliar person greeted him by saying "Hi [*Name*]" at two different locations within the school at two different times of the day. Waving hands and/or saying "Hi" or "Hello" (with or without making eye-contact with the greeter) or any other within-context verbal responses were considered as a correct response. Ignoring the greeter or gazing at the greeter with no further verbal/non-verbal expressions was considered as

an incorrect response. The mean of the two responses in one day makes one data point while analyzing the results. Data from the baseline phase are shown in Fig. 4 and will be further discussed in Section 4. Table 2 shows the baseline duration of different participants.

3.1.4 The therapy

The therapy was designed in collaboration with a behavioral scientist (the second author of this paper) who is an expert in autism research. The therapy follows the basic structure of applied behavior analysis (ABA), a widely accepted method for behavioral intervention [14]. Any ABA-based training follows a basic structure: Command or Discriminative stimulus (S^D) $\Longrightarrow$ Prompts (P) (if necessary) $\Longrightarrow$ Reinforcement/Reward (R). Our therapy of teaching social greetings follows the structure shown in Fig. 1. Two different types of prompts are used to evoke the correct response in the participants. The first type of prompt is *modeling*, where the robot models the target behavior with the caregiver of the participant. The second type is *verbal instruction*, where the robot verbally informs the participant the correct way to respond to the command. If a participant correctly responds to a command, no prompt is delivered and the robot provides reward for his correct response. Prompts are delivered only in cases of no response or incorrect response. The *verbal instruction* prompt is delivered only if the *modeling* prompt fails to elicit the correct response.

To facilitate learning, the process 'Command or Discriminative stimulus (S^D) $\Longrightarrow$ Prompts (P) (if necessary) $\Longrightarrow$ Reinforcement/Reward (R)' is iterated for 3 to 5 times per session, irrespective of correct or incorrect responses from the participant. The robot starts each iteration by saying "Let us practice saying 'Hi' again" in order to create a context. The command and prompts are chosen to be simple and easily understandable by the target population. An example of a command is the robot saying 'Hi [name of the participant]' as soon as he enters the therapy room. An example of a verbal instruction prompt is the robot saying '[name of the participant], say 'Hi' to me'. The robot uses similar commands with the caregiver during a modeling prompt (e.g. the robot greets the caregiver by saying 'Hi [name of the caregiver]', and the caregiver responds to this greeting by waving hands and saying 'Hi Blue', as shown in Figs 2(c) - 2(e)). The basic form of reinforcement/reward is the robot appreciating the IwASD for his correct response.

A generalization phase is designed for participants who respond well to the robot-mediated therapy. A two-step proce-

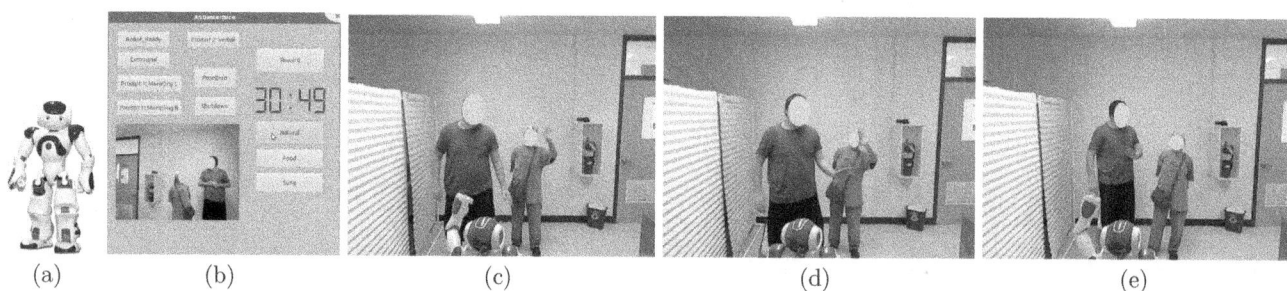

Figure 2: (a) The humanoid robot 'Blue' (Aldebaran Robotics Inc.) (b) The robot-control interface (c-e) The modeling prompt is helping the participant P1 (on the left) to gradually execute the correct behavior

dure is followed for generalization training. At the first step, a triadic interaction is designed where the caregiver greets the participant immediately after the participant's positive response to a robot's greeting. This triadic interaction design (Robot → Participant ← Caregiver) tries to exploit a participant's 'intent to interact' with the robot to generalize the skill with the human (in this case, the caregiver). When a participant performs well in this triadic interaction, the second step of generalization is introduced where the robot is removed from the scene. In this case, a dyadic interaction is designed where the participant interacts with the robot in the therapy room without the presence of the caregiver. The caregiver waits outside of the therapy room and greets the participant as soon as he comes out of the room.

3.1.5 Study protocol

The therapy was delivered through a humanoid robot from Aldebaran Robotics (we named the robot 'Blue') (Fig. 2(a)). The user-interface shown in Fig. 2(b) was designed to deliver the therapy through the robot in a Wizard-of-Oz manner. The study observed the following protocol:

1. For each participant, the therapy starts after he completes his baseline measurement.

2. Prior to the therapy beginning, each participant goes through a 5 minute habituation session where the robot interacts with the participant while showing its different motor and sensing abilities.

3. Each therapy session lasts for 2 to 4 minutes and follows the procedure described in Section 3.1.4.

4. Only those participants who consistently perform well with the robot in therapy sessions (high `Skill execution` with no `Prompt dependency` for at least six sessions in three consecutive days) are considered for the generalization training.

5. Participants who do not show any sign of improvement after 10 therapy sessions (e.g. no steady pattern in SE and PD values, no increase in SE or decrease in PD values, etc.) are discontinued from the study.

A brief summary of the study is provided in Table 2.

3.2 Data Collection and Coding

We collected video, audio, and images from all therapy sessions. Two sets of behaviors of the participants were coded from the video data: behaviors related to the two efficacy metrics (SE and PD) and behaviors related to three common HRI metrics that are relevant to this study.

3.2.1 Behaviors related to efficacy metrics

The two dependent variables of the study are considered as the behaviors in this category and are defined as follows.

- *Prompt*: The participant is unable to correctly respond to the command and the robot delivered one or both of the two prompts to teach him the correct behavior. This behavior is coded quantitatively by counting the total number of prompts delivered in a session. *Prompt*, inherently, is a component of a therapy and is not provided or measured during the baseline phase.

- *Responsiveness to the command*: The participant waved hand(s) or said "Hi" or "Hello" or any other words within the context of social greetings to the robot or human greeter. Gazing at the greeter without any other verbal or non-verbal expressions is not considered a correct response. This behavior is coded quantitatively by counting the number of commands with appropriate response. *Responsiveness to the command* is also measured during the baseline phase.

The two efficacy metrics are calculated from these two behaviors as follows:

1. `Skill execution, SE`: The *Responsiveness to the command* expressed as a percentage of the total number of commands delivered in a session.

$$SE = \frac{Responsiveness\ to\ the\ command}{Total\ Commands} X100\% \quad (1)$$

2. `Prompt dependency, PD`: The average number of prompts required to generate one appropriate response in a therapy session.

$$PD = \frac{Prompt}{Responsiveness\ to\ the\ command} \quad (2)$$

In the case *Responsiveness to the command* = 0 (which implies SE = 0%),

$$PD = Prompt \quad (3)$$

ASD therapies generally are time consuming processes where achieving a therapeutic goal might require several months. These two metrics provide a simple way to track the progress of a participant during any ABA-based robot-mediated therapy including the one presented in this paper. For example,

- Increasing trend of SE accompanied by a decreasing trend of PD indicate a potential improvement of the participant over time and a possible success of the therapy.

Table 3: Cohen's Kappa for Coded Behaviors

Behavior	κ (chance corrected)	κ (chance not corrected)
Prompt	0.82	0.94
Responsiveness to the command	0.92	0.97
Gaze	0.80	0.90
Communication	0.76	0.91
Affect	0.64	0.80

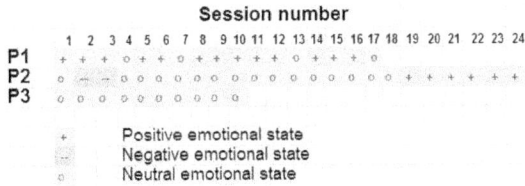

Figure 3: Emotional states of the participants

- Increasing trend of SE accompanied by an increasing or constant PD indicate the requirement of adopting a strategy to fade out the prompt while keeping the skill intact.

- Decreasing trend of SE accompanied by a decreasing or increasing trend of PD indicate that the current therapy is not making any positive effect on the participant.

Note that, any other confounding variables that are active during a therapy might alter the interpretations of SE and PD and should be investigated carefully before drawing any conclusion about the outcome of a robot-mediated therapy.

3.2.2 Behaviors related to common HRI metrics

There are three behaviors in this category which are generally considered as standard HRI metrics.

- Gaze: Participants look at the robot (Gaze at the robot) or at the human caregiver (Gaze at the caregiver) during a session. A participant's interaction with his caregiver (e.g. talking or playing) is considered as Gaze at the caregiver. The behavior is coded quantitatively by measuring its duration and is expressed as a percentage of the total duration of a session.

- Communication: The participant uses words to respond to the robot or initiates a non-verbal communication (e.g. touching the robot, pointing to the robot, etc.) with the robot. Any words directed toward the robot is considered as a form of communication. This behavior is coded quantitatively by counting the number of occurrences during a session and is expressed as occurrences per minute.

- Affect: Overall emotional state of the participant while interacting with the robot during a therapy session. The coders reported three emotional states qualitatively: positive, negative, and neutral. Example signs of positive emotional state are the participant seemed happy, was smiling, singing, joyfully talking to the robot or the caregiver, etc. during a session. Examples signs of negative emotional state are the participant seemed stressed, angry (e.g. screaming), sad,

non-focused, etc. during a session. Neutral emotional state indicates a participant with no signs of positive or negative emotion.

Based on these definitions, two people coded the behaviors related to efficacy metrics and two people coded the behaviors related to HRI metrics, all independently. Cohen's Kappa was used to ensure inter-coder agreement for each behavior and is listed in Table 3.

4. RESULTS AND ANALYSIS

This section provides an analysis of the coded behaviors to 1) highlight the role of the two efficacy metrics in reporting the efficacy of the robot-mediated therapy, and 2) shed light on the relationship between the two efficacy metrics and the three common HRI metrics (Gaze, Communication, and Affect). *Visual analysis*, a standard tool to present results from single subject multiple baseline study [15], is used to visually compare the responses of the participants (in terms of SE and PD) during the baseline phase and throughout the course of the robot-mediated therapy. Fig. 4 presents the *visual analysis* of the study outcome. Each participant's baseline phase is staggered with his therapy phase, to conform with the standard of *visual analysis* in single subject design. As a result, session numbers in Fig. 4 are marked as 1 to 20 (3 baseline sessions and 17 human-robot sessions) for P1, 1 to 30 (6 baseline sessions and 24 human-robot sessions) for P2, and 1 to 10 (9 baseline sessions and 10 human-robot sessions) for P3. Figs. 3, 5, 6, and 7 present the HRI metrics of the participants during the human-robot therapy sessions (note that the session numbers in these figures correspond to the human-robot session only and hence, different from that shown in Fig. 4). Pearson's Correlation Coefficient (PCC) is used to measure the statistical correlation between the HRI metrics and the efficacy metrics. Table. 4 lists the PCCs between the two efficacy metrics (PD and SE) and the two quantitatively coded HRI metrics (Gaze and Communication). The following sections will provide an individual analysis of results for each participant.

4.1 Participant 1 (P1)

P1 received the robot-mediated therapy in 19 sessions. Video and audio were not recorded in the first two sessions due to technical problems. These two sessions are excluded from the analysis (resulting in 17 robot-mediated sessions). Fig. 5 shows the variation in Gaze and Communication HRI metrics of P1 during the therapy sessions. P1 consistently expressed more gazing preferences to the robot (on average, 49.9% of the time in a session) than to the caregiver (on average, 11.8% of the time in a session) and made some efforts to communicate with the robot in 94% of the sessions. In 76% of the sessions P1 was in a positive emotional state while in the rest of the sessions he expressed neutral emotions (as shown in Fig. 3). According to the common metrics of HRI, these are considered as signs of positive impact of a robot on an IwASD. However, in spite of all of these positive behaviors, P1 failed to meet the clinical goal of the study: he could not learn to execute the target behavior of responding socially to a greeting without the help of the robot.

As shown in Fig. 4, P1 generated some correct responses in 33% of sessions during the baseline phase (baseline phase did not involve prompting). But during the therapy, in 76%

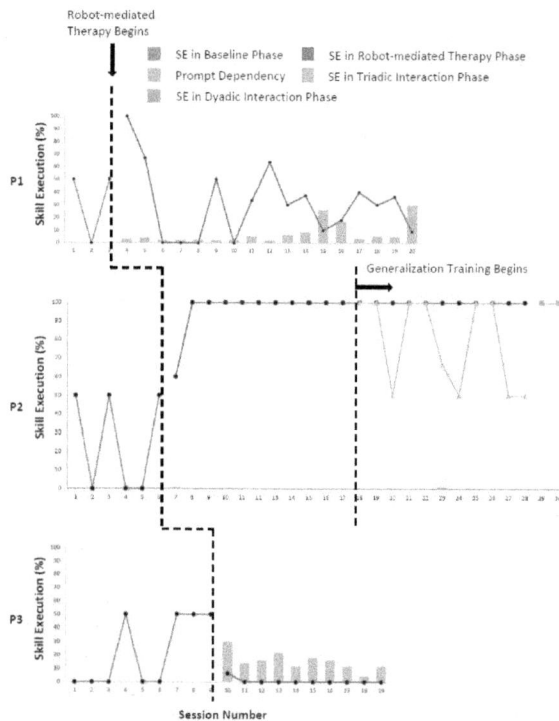

Figure 4: Outcome of the single subject multiple baseline study with three participants

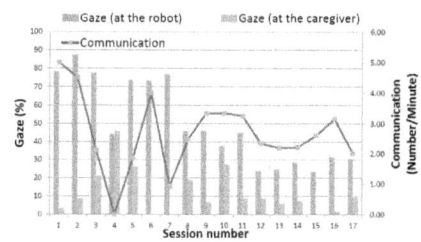

Figure 5: HRI metrics of P1 in human-robot sessions

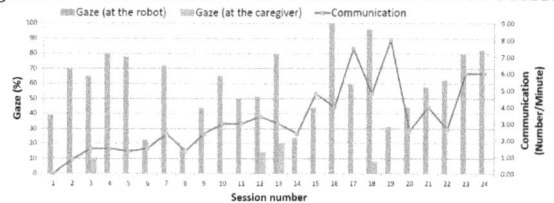

Figure 6: HRI metrics of P2 in human-robot sessions

of the sessions P1 needed at least one prompt to appropriately respond to one command while in sessions 6, 7, 8 and 10 several prompts could not yield even one correct response. Overall, the Skill execution of P1 did not follow any consistent pattern during the therapy. In addition to that, P1's Prompt dependency did not show any decreasing trend over time. The SE and PD values of P1 clearly show that he did not make any progress with respect to learning to execute the target skill without any help (i.e. the prompts) from the robot. In other words, although P1 shows strong signs, according to the three HRI metrics, that he is interested in the robot, the robot was not able to teach him the target skill through the 17 therapy sessions. This potential mismatch is also revealed in the lack of correlation between the HRI metrics and the efficacy metrics.

The Gaze (at the robot) metric has poor correlation (PCC =0.23) with the SE and negative correlation with the PD (PCC=−0.55). The Communication metric shows strong correlation with the SE (PCC = 0.87). That is mostly because most of P1's Communication with the robot was related to responding to the greeting commands of the robot. The Communication metric, however, shows negative correlation with the PD (PCC = −0.13).

Overall, analysis of Figs. 4, 3, and 5, and Table 4 reveals the fact that the three HRI metrics can not be used as indicators of the robot's efficacy in P1's therapy.

4.2 Participant 2 (P2)

P2 is the only participant in this study who went through the generalization training. P2 received the therapy in 24 sessions. Analysis of P2's coded behaviors demonstrates another case of potential mismatch between the information conveyed through efficacy metrics and HRI metrics. Fig. 6 shows the variation in Gaze and Communication HRI met-

rics of P2 during the therapy. Similar to P1, P2 also showed gazing preferences more toward the robot (on average 59% of the time of a session) than to the caregiver (average is 2.2%) and made efforts to communicate with the robot in every session. Unlike P1, P2 was in positive emotional state in only 25% of the sessions and in 8% of the sessions he expressed negative emotions. P2, however, as opposed to P1, was able to achieve the clinical goal of this study by learning to execute the social behavior outside of the therapy setting. As shown in Fig. 4, P2 was not responding consistently during the baseline phase (SE= 50% in 50% of the sessions). But P2's Skill execution quickly rose to 100% after the first therapy session and he maintained that high score without any Prompt dependency for 11 consecutive therapy sessions. The generalization training (triadic interaction) started from session 18 (human-robot session 12) as shown in Fig. 4 (note that therapy sessions are staggered with the baseline phase). Last two sessions were dedicated to the dyadic interaction. During the generalization training P2 needed only one prompt in Session 23 (human-robot session 17) to execute the target skill. Steady high values of SE and low values of PD clearly indicate P2's success in mastering the target skill from the robot. The HRI metrics, however, do not show any meaningful correlation with the efficacy metrics. As indicated in Table 4, the Gaze (at the robot) metric has very poor correlation with both of the two efficacy metrics while the Communication metric shows negative correlation with the two efficacy metrics. Overall, although P2 learned to execute the skill from the robot and P1 failed to do that, the HRI metrics do not convey any information that can differentiate P2 from P1 with respect to achieving the therapeutic goal of the study.

4.3 Participant 3 (P3)

P3 received the robot-mediated therapy in 10 sessions during which he showed very high gazing preferences for the

Table 4: Correlation Between HRI Metrics and Efficacy Metrics: Pearson's Correlation Coefficient

	SE			PD		
	P1	P2	P3	P1	P2	P3
Gaze (at Robot)	0.23	0.04	0.11	-0.55	0.12	0.11
Communication	0.87	-0.01	0.64	-0.13	-0.21	0.63

robot (on average 71% of the time) than for the caregiver (only 1.9% of the time), as shown in Fig. 7. P3's gazing preference to the robot is much higher than that of both P1 and P2. P3 also maintained a neutral emotional state throughout the therapy sessions. P3, however, showed minimal effort to communicate with the robot. Overall, HRI metrics represent P3 as a participant who might have moderate to no interest in the robot but certainly did not dislike the robot. Efficacy metrics, however, represents P3 as a participant completely unsuitable for robot-mediated interventions. As shown in Fig. 4, during the baseline phase P3 exhibited some correct responses (`SE` = 40% in 44% of the baseline measurements) but as soon as the therapy started his `Skill execution` drastically dropped to zero. Despite several prompts P3 was completely unable to execute the correct behavior in 90% of the sessions. Accordingly, we concluded that P3 is the kind of participant who might not be suitable for robot-mediated interventions. HRI metrics convey a very little information for drawing such a conclusion.

5. DISCUSSION AND CONCLUSION

Efficacy of robots is a factor which will determine whether robots can actually be employed in clinical settings for ASD therapy. Clinicians require measures to quickly identify how well a robot is performing to achieve a planned therapeutic goal. In this paper, we defined two such efficacy metrics, `Skill execution` and `Prompt dependency`, as a measure of a robot's efficacy to teach a basic skill of social greetings to three low-functioning IwASDs. Both of these metrics are easy to calculate and involve monitoring of two easily observable behaviors of the participants. Results presented in Section 4 show that these two metrics, when analyzed together, created a highly informative picture of how well different participants were performing over the course of the study.

We also analyzed all therapy sessions with respect to three common HRI metrics (`Gaze`, `Communication`, and `Affect`). Our analysis shows that the HRI metrics performed well in reporting the 'likability' of the robot to the participants. For example, all of the participants showed stronger gazing preference for the robot than for the caregiver and such preferences did not die out over time, enabling us to safely rule out the contribution of the novelty effect in this case. All participants, within their limited verbal and cognitive abilities, made efforts to communicate with the robot, and finally, the robot encountered negative emotions in only 3.9% of the total 51 therapy sessions with three participants. All of these indicate that the participants were not uncomfortable around the robot and might have enjoyed the robot's presence in many cases. This finding is completely in line with the findings of previous research in this domain [6, 27]. However, a comparative analysis of the two sets of metrics (HRI and efficacy) shows that HRI metrics were not able to convey information about the efficacy of the robot in achieving the goal of the therapy. For example, between P1 and P2, HRI metrics indicated P1 was more attracted to the robot than P2 (both of them have approximately similar scores for the `Gaze` and `Communication` metrics, but P1 expressed significantly more positive `Affect` around the robot than P1). In reality, P2 was able to reach the clinical goal of the study while P1 could not master the skill from the robot. The efficacy metrics successfully conveyed this in-

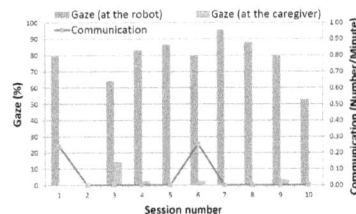

Figure 7: HRI metrics of P3 in human-robot sessions

formation. These are significant observations and indicate the need of defining appropriate efficacy metrics for robot-mediated ASD therapy. We understand that the sample size of this study was small ($n = 3$) but single subject, multiple baseline design mitigates the negative effect of small sample size.

Another important consideration is the diagnostic condition of the participants. All of the participants in this study were toward the lower end of the spectrum, a population generally not discussed in the majority of robot-mediated ASD research. This diagnostic condition might act as a confounding variable to influence the uncorrelated patterns of the HRI metrics and efficacy metrics that emerged from this study. Further studies are required to investigate this variable and is considered as a future work.

6. ACKNOWLEDGMENTS

This work was supported in part by the National Science Foundation (IIS-0905228 and IIS-1111125). The authors acknowledge the support of Jonathan Knittle and staff at CMRC to conduct the study.

7. ADDITIONAL AUTHOR

Additional author: Jacob Suarez (Computer Science, University of Massachusetts Lowell email: `Jacob_Suarez@ student.uml.edu`)

References

[1] Autism spectrum disorders: Guide to evidence based interventions. *Missouri Autism Guidelines Initiative*, 2012.

[2] Prevalence of autism spectrum disorder among children aged 8 years: Autism and developmental disabilities monitoring network, 11 sites. *Center for Disease Control and Prevention*, 2014.

[3] C. A. Barker. The triad of impairment in autism revisited. *Child and adolescent psychiatric nursing*, 22(4):189–193, 2009.

[4] E. Bekele, J. A. Crittendon, A. Swanson, N. Sarkar, and Z. E. Warren. Pilot clinical application of an adaptive robotic system for young children with autism. *Autism*, 18:598–608, 2014.

[5] E. T. Bekele, U. Lahiri, A. R. Swanson, J. A. Crittendon, Z. E. Warren, and N. Sarkar. A step towards developing adaptive robot-mediated intervention architecture (ARIA) for children with autism. *Neural Syst. and Rehab. Eng.*, 21:289 – 299, 2013.

[6] J.-J. Cabibihan, H. Javed, M. A. Jr., and S. M. Aljunied. Why robots? A survey on the roles and benefits of social robots in the therapy of children with autism. *Social Robotics*, 5(4):593–618, 2013.

[7] K. Dautehhahn and I. Werry. Towards interactive robotics in autism therapy. *Pragmat Cogn*, 12:1–35, 2007.

[8] J. Diehl, L. Schmitt, C. R. Crowell, and M. Villano. The clinical use of robots for children with autism spectrum disorders: A critical review. *Research in Autism Spectrum Disorders*, 6(1):249–262, 2012.

[9] J. Feil-Seifer and M. J. Mataric. B3IA: A control architecture for autonomous robot-assisted behavior intervention for children with autism spectrum disorders. In *ACM/IEEE Intl. Conf. on Human-Robot Interaction*, pages 328 – 333, 2008.

[10] J. Feil-Seifer and M. J. Mataric. Using proxemics to evaluate human-robot interaction. In *ACM/IEEE Intl. Conf. on Human-Robot Interaction*, pages 143–144, 2010.

[11] I. Fujimoto, T. Matsumoto, P. R. S. D. Silva, M. Kobayashi, and M. Higashi. Mimicking and evaluating human motion to improve the imitation skill of children with autism through a robot. *Social Robotics*, 3:349–357, 2011.

[12] M. A. Goodrich, M. Colton, B. Brinton, M. Fujiki, J. A. Atherton, D. Ricks, M. H. Maxfield, and A. Acerson. Incorporating a robot into an autism therapy team. *IEEE Intelligent Systems Magazine*, 27(2):52–59, 2012.

[13] O. Grynszpan, P. L. Weiss, F. Perez-Diaz, and E. Gal. Innovative technology-based interventions for autism spectrum disorders: A meta-analysis. *Autism*, 18:346–361, 2014.

[14] S. L. Harris and L. Delmolino. Applied behavior analysis: Its application in the treatment of autism and related disorders in young children. *Infants and Young Children*, 14:11–18, 2002.

[15] R. H. Horner, E. G. Carr, J. Halle, G. McGee, S. Odom, and M. Wolery. The use of single-subject research to identify evidence-based practice in special education. *Exceptional Children*, 71:165 – 179, 2005.

[16] B. Huskens, R. Verschuur, J. Gillesen, R. Didden, and E. Barakova. Promoting question-asking in school-aged children with autism spectrum disorders: Effectiveness of a robot intervention compared to a human-trainer intervention. *Developmental Neurorehabilitation*, 16:345–356, 2013.

[17] E. S. Kim, L. D. Berkovits, E. P. Bernier, D. Leyzberg, F. Shic, R. Paul, and B. Scassellati. Social robots as embedded reinforcers of social behavior in children with autism. *Autism and Developmental Disorders*, 43:1038 – 1049, 2013.

[18] E. S. Kim and B. Scassellati. Bridging the research gap: Making HRI useful to individuals with autism. *Human Robot Interaction*, 1(1):26–54, 2012.

[19] H. Kozima, C. Nakagawa, and Y. Yasuda. Children-robot interaction: A pilot study in autism therapy. *Prog Brain Res*, 164:385–400, 2007.

[20] M.Begum, R. Serna, D. Kontak, and H. Yanco. Robots for therapy of individuals with ASD: Are we there yet? In *Intl. Conf. on Intelligent Robots and Systems (Workshop on Rehabilitation Robotics)*, 2014.

[21] G. Mesibov and V. Shea. Evidence-based practices and autism. *Autism*, 15:114–133, 2011.

[22] C. A. Pop, R. E. Simut, S. Pintea, J. Saldien, A. S. Rusu, J. Vanderfaeillie, D. O. David, D. Lefeber, and B. Vanderborght. Social robots vs. computer display: Does the way social stories are delivered make a difference for their effectiveness on ASD children? *Educational Computing Research*, 49(3):381–401, 2013.

[23] F. D. Reed, S. R. Hyman, and J. M. Hirst. Applications of technology to teach social skills to children with autism. *Developmental Neurorehabilitation*, 5:1003–1010, 2011.

[24] B. Robins, K. Dautenhahn, and J. Dubowski. Does appearance matter in the interaction of children with autism with a humanoid robot? *Interaction Studies*, 7:479–512, 2006.

[25] B. Robins, E. Ferrari, K. Dautenhahn, G. Kronreif, B. Prazak-Aram, G. Gelderblom, B. Tanja, F. Caprino, E. Laudanna, and P. Marti. Human-centered design methods: developing scenarios for robot assisted play informed by user panels and field trials. *Human-Computer Studies*, 68(12):873–898, 2010.

[26] B. Scassellati. Quantitative metrics of social response for autism diagnosis. In *Intl. Workshop on Robots and Human Interactive Communication*, pages 585– 590, 2005.

[27] B. Scassellati, H. Admoni, and M. Mataric. Robots for use in autism research. *Annual Review of Biomedical Engineering*, 14:275–294, 2012.

[28] A. Tapus, A. Peca, A. Aly, C. Pop, L. Jisa, S. Pintea, A. S. Rusu, and D. O. David. Children with autism social engagement in interaction with nao, an imitative robot. *Interaction Studies*, 13(3):315–347, 2012.

[29] J. Wainer, B. Robins, F. Amirabdollahian, and K. Dautenhahn. Using the humanoid robot kaspar to autonomously play triadic games and facilitate collaborative play among children with autism. *Autonomous Mental Development*, 6(3):183 – 199, 2014.

[30] Z. Warren, J. Veenstra-VanderWeele, W. Stone, J. L. Bruzek, A. S. Nahmias, J. H. Foss-Feig, and R. N. J. et al. Therapies for children with autism spectrum disorders. *Vanderbilt Evidence-based Practice Center: Agency for Healthcare Research and Quality (US) Tech. Rep. 11-EHC029-EF*, April 2011.

Interaction Expands Function: Social Shaping of the Therapeutic Robot PARO in a Nursing Home

Wan-Ling Chang, Selma Šabanović
School of Informatics and Computing
Indiana University Bloomington
901 E. 10th Street
Bloomington IN 47408, USA
wanlchan@indiana.edu, selmas@indiana.edu

ABSTRACT

We use the "social shaping of technology and society" framework to qualitatively analyze data collected through observation of human-robot interaction (HRI) between social actors in a nursing home (staff, residents, visitors) and the socially assistive robot PARO. The study took place over the course of three months, during which PARO was placed in a publicly accessibly space where participants could interact with it freely. Social shaping focuses attention on social factors that affect the use and interpretation of technology in particular contexts. We therefore aimed to understand how different social actors make sense of and use PARO in daily interaction. Our results show participant gender, social mediation, and individual sense making led to differential use and interpretation of the robot, which affected the success of human-robot interactions. We also found that exposure to others interacting with PARO affected the nursing staff's perceptions of robots and their potential usefulness in eldercare. This shows that social shaping theory provides a valuable perspective for understanding the implementation of robots in long-term HRI and can inform interaction design in this domain.

Categories and Subject Descriptors

H.1.2. User/Machine Systems; I.2.9. Robotics: Commercial robots and applications; K.4.2 Social Issues: Assistive technologies for persons with disabilities

General Terms

Human factors

Keywords

Socially assistive robot; human-robot interaction; qualitative study; social shaping of technology; older adults.

1. INTRODUCTION

In a video demonstrating the use of the socially assistive robot PARO in eldercare (http://www.parorobots.com/video.asp), the

HRI '15, March 02 - 05 2015, Portland, OR, USA
Copyright 2015 ACM 978-1-4503-2883-8/15/03…$15.00
http://dx.doi.org/10.1145/2696454.2696472

camera pans across a large open space furnished with a few long tables and some chairs on a linoleum floor. Nursing home residents, most of them in wheelchairs, sit sleeping or staring into space, rarely talking or making eye contact. The caption reads "before introduction." A few seconds later, the scene switches to one filled with activity – the residents are talking, smiling, and sitting close together in small groups. In their arms and laps, being passed from one person to the other and the focus of everyone's attention, is PARO – a robot shaped like a baby seal. The caption now reads "1 month later." Scenes from 6 and 10 months follow, with residents vigorously petting PARO, talking to it, and even kissing the robot. While nursing home staff occasionally pop into view, the camera focuses on the elderly and PARO in their midst.

PARO is designed to be used in a mode similar to pet therapy, often with older adults, particularly those suffering from dementia or other cognitive disabilities. Long-term studies of interactions between residents and PARO in nursing homes around the world have shown that its use can lead to positive psychological and physical effects [1]. Existing research has largely focused on documenting PARO's therapeutic efficacy through physiological, psychological, and behavioral measures of individual users (e.g., [2], [3], [4]), without exploring the mechanisms through which such effects occur. The video clip described above suggests that the psychological and behavioral changes seen in older adults interacting with PARO are due largely to PARO's presence, without detailing how nursing home residents started interacting with the robot, or how they shifted from withdrawn individuals to a gregarious group. This produces a technologically determinist framing of the robot, which posits that social change is the direct result of technical intervention. Recent work on the development of guidelines for PARO's use in nursing homes [5], and the social analysis we present in this paper, suggest that there is more to these successful interactions than just a well-designed robot.

This paper explores aspects of interactions with PARO that have not been addressed in prior research – the broader social context that scaffolds interactions between older adults and PARO in ways that can produce psychological, physical and social benefits. We describe a three-month-long observational study of PARO's public use in a local nursing home. We apply the framework of social shaping of technology to analyze collected data, in contrast to the technologically oriented perspective described above. This approach emphasizes exploring the social dimensions of technology design, adoption, and use, including identification of salient groups of stakeholders who are affected by and/or have an effect on robotic technology. In line with previous research on the social shaping of technology, our study particularly focused on identifying the key social factors and actors involved in the use of PARO in the nursing home, particularly attending to their roles in supporting interactions between older adults and PARO.

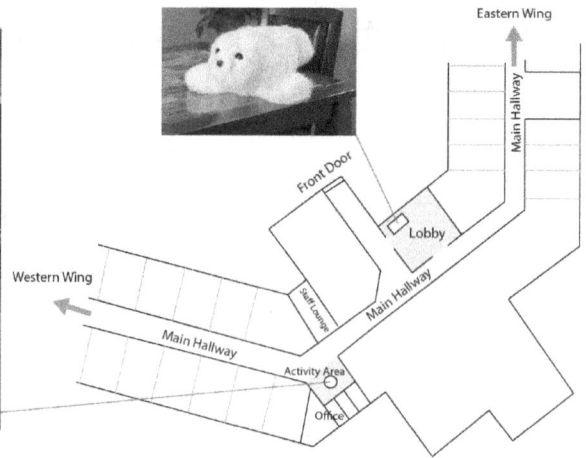

Figure 1. Building layout and the physical settings where PARO was observed (PARO is on the table).

Our research contributes to a growing area of study investigating how HRI unfolds within the social context of homes, hospitals, and other organizations (e.g. [6], [7]). Initial research has shown that studies of HRI "in the wild" can challenge design assumptions and identify social factors that affect how robots are adopted and used, but are not available in a laboratory environment (e.g., [7], [8]). After describing prior work related to our research, we detail our approach and the research context, and then present qualitative results from our observations. The latter include a detailed description of repeated patterns of interaction as well as exemplary individual cases, and the results of pre- and post-interviews with staff. Although the study focuses on PARO, we expect our approach and insights to be relevant to interactive robots and other emerging technologies more generally, as they become increasingly available for everyday use.

2. RELATED WORK
2.1 PARO as a Companion Robot
PARO is a therapeutic social robot designed by Takanori Shibata at the National Institute of Advanced Industrial Science and Technology (AIST) in Tsukuba, Japan. The built-in tactile, balance, and light sensors and microphones under its soft hypoallergenic fur enable the robot to sense touch, sound, and changes in position (e.g. hugging). PARO can react to stimulation with physical movement (e.g., tail wagging) and vocalizations simulating a baby seal. It is often used as a social companion for children and older adults, especially seniors with dementia.

Most prior PARO studies were conducted in the context of use (e.g. nursing homes), with the main aim of measuring PARO's psychological, physical, and social effects on older adults, such as improved mood [3] or decreased stress levels following interactions with PARO [4]. Researchers have also collected and reported on examples of PARO's successful interactions with older adults (e.g., [1]), which have been used to develop guidelines on how best to use the robot [5]. Those studies focused on interactions within a small group setting. Wada [9] also placed PARO in a public area in a senior living center and showed increased interaction among the residents; however, how interactions among residents or between residents and PARO developed and were maintained was not analyzed.

Our study builds on existing research on PARO's implementation in eldercare by using a qualitative approach and the social construction framework to perform an in-depth study of the

development and maintenance of interactions between social actors and PARO in a nursing institution.

2.2 Social Shaping of Technology
A dominant narrative in technology design in general, and in robotics more specifically [10], posits a linear cause-and-affect relationship between technology and society according to which technological developments leads to social change (and often progress). The social shaping of technology framework counters the idea that the adoption, use, and consequences of technology can be understood in this way. It suggests an alternative analytical focus on how various actors interact with and make sense of technologies within the broader social context, which includes social norms, values, and relationships. In this framing, technologies do not fail and succeed based on their technical merits alone. They are socially and culturally constructed as successful or unsuccessful through the actions and interpretations of various groups of relevant stakeholders [11], users [12], and even invisible social actors [13]. In describing the success of a technology, it is important to ask whom the technology is working well for, and how it impacts users in differential ways.

Social actors make sense of technologies in relation to what they see as salient social concerns and values, which play a defining role in how they design, adopt, use and make sense of technologies [13]. This possibility for technology to be given different meanings in varying social contexts is called "interpretive flexibility" [11,13]. Shibata's description of PARO's design logic suggests interpretive flexibility is an important component of the robot's everyday functioning: "PARO has a limited number of functions as a machine. But, I designed PARO to evoke associations in the human's mind. Humans have a lot of experiences and memories, so when people interact with PARO they remember something, or associate with something… It is not necessary for PARO to have all the functions, the interaction can enlarge the number of functions."[1] Accordingly, we suggest that understanding the social mechanisms of successful (and unsuccessful) interactions with PARO is crucial to understanding its therapeutic effects and generalizing from them.

2.3 Social Shaping of HRI
Though they do not refer to social shaping specifically, numerous studies of HRI "in the wild" —in the course of interactions with

---

[1] Talk at the Japan Society, New York, NY, June 2007.

untrained users in outside the laboratory — have shown social factors influence interactions with and evaluations of robots. Šabanović et al.'s [8] observational study of interactions between conference-goers and a social robot showed the social context can have a significant effect on people's behaviors. Alač et al. [14] displayed how robot sociality is relationally defined through the actions of various social actors in its environment, including children. Studies of domestic Roomba use showed that robots can be perceived as social and affect the cleaning behaviors of residents when situated in a socially rich and meaningful environment [6]. User gender was identified as a social factor that affected people' sense-making about a robot in a hospital [15].

Other researchers have used ethnographic observation to evaluate whether robots are successful in daily use, and to understand how people make sense of them in everyday circumstances. Mutlu and Forlizzi [7] identified several non-technical factors, including workflow and political and social relationships among actors, that had an effect on user evaluations of a delivery robot used in a hospital. Vertesi's [16] studies of the scientific team using the Mars Exploration Rovers identified both individually embodied sensemaking of the robot's functioning and the organization of the collaborative process as factors that contributed to the success of the mission. These ethnographic studies show how social behavior and meaning are constituted through dynamic interactions among social actors and technical affordances in contexts of use.

3. METHODOLOGY

In order to understand the social shaping process of human-robot interaction, we performed an observational study of PARO in the nursing home of a local retirement community in the United States over the course of three months. Our main aim was to understand how people voluntarily interact with and make sense of the robot, and when and how the robot is construed as engaging in this environment. In line with previous studies on the social shaping of technology, we particularly focused on the attitudes and behaviors of different groups of actors (i.e. staff, residents, visitors) towards PARO and others in the environment. In order to get an overall view of participants' interactions with PARO, we used both quantitative (on-site coding, interactor counts) and qualitative methodologies (observational field notes, pre- and post- interviews of the staffs, on-site interactor interviews).

3.1 Research Context

The nursing home in which we performed the study was a single floor building and served people needing long-term care (e.g., upper-/lower-limb disability, dementia) or short-term assistance and rehabilitation. Both authors have been doing research in this institution for a little over two years, and the first author spent three months prior to this study observing the daily activities in the field site. Based on this prior work and the results of a two-week-long observational pilot study of public spaces in the nursing home, we chose two areas as our field sites—the lobby and the activity area. They are both located in the central area of the building in proximity to the main entrance and hallways, so passersby are frequent and numerous (See Figure 1). The lobby was furnished with a few sofas and had a fireplace for resting and chatting. The activity area had a TV and a puzzle on the table. After the first month of the field study, we found that the low walls surrounding the lobby occluded the view of passersby, making it difficult for them to see PARO. We then decided to put PARO only in the activity area for the remainder of the study.

We brought PARO to the nursing home two or three times a week, for one hour during each visit. We made a total of 35 visits over a continuous period of 13 weeks. PARO was placed at the center of a table in the chosen areas. People were free to interact with the robot as they liked without guidance from researchers.

Eight months prior to the study described here, ten residents with dementia and two therapists in the nursing home participated in a study using PARO for group sensory therapy for two months [17]. After that, the therapists kept PARO for their own use in individual visits or group activities. Some residents and staff had therefore seen or interacted with PARO before the study.

3.2 Participants

Three main groups of people participated in our field study: residents, staff, and visitors. There were on average 49 documented participants in the field site per session. Only 19% of them were residents, while staff and visitors comprised 55% and 26%, respectively. As we had done field observation and interviews before the study, we had no difficulty identifying the different types of participants by sight. Both long-term and short-tern residents had some physical disability and required the assistance of walkers or wheelchairs. The staff usually wore uniforms or nametags. We identified other participants as visitors.

The majority of the long-term residents had dementia. Those in the later stage of dementia had difficulties expressing themselves and responding to conversation and often fell asleep during the daytime. Many residents also suffered from hearing loss and decreasing eyesight caused by aging. Partly due to these factors, social interactions among the residents were not common. Staff included nurses, nurse assistants, housekeepers, social workers, general managers, and therapists. Visitors were usually family members of the residents and varied widely in age, from babies to seniors. The majority of residents and staff were female, but the numbers of female and male visitors were almost equal [18].

3.3 Data Collection

Data collection was performed by the first author, who took all field notes, and two research assistants who helped with on-site behavioral coding. We used onsite coding and interactor counts to measure interaction frequency for different behaviors (e.g. petting PARO, talking to other people) and the number of interactors and passersby. Observational field notes collected detailed interaction information, including behavior and utterances during the interactions; pre- and post- interviews and informal on-site interviews were performed to understand what participants thought of the robot. Analysis of quantitative data was reported in [18], and here we present the qualitative data and analysis.

3.3.1 Field Notes and Informal Interviews

We started observing the nursing environment and activities one month before we introduced the robot into the space in order to understand the day-to-day dynamics of the space. The first author also used this time in the field to build rapport with some of the research participants, which allowed her to get a more comprehensive idea of the institutional context and the different social actors in the environment. Throughout the field study, the first author kept field notes with thick description of observed interactions and the contexts in which they occurred, including how people interacted with PARO, the interactors' emotional expressions during the interaction, and verbal utterances about or to PARO. This information was used for providing details about the interaction across sessions, particularly in terms of how interactions occurred in groups and how they developed over time with specific interactors. Along with information collected through informal interviews with key informants during or after the observational sessions, rich contextual information, such as the health or emotional status of the residents and institutional regulations of the staff, helped us interpret the intentions and attitudes behind the observed behaviors. After the observational sessions, the first author conducted brief and semi-structured interviews with participants who consistently interacted with PARO to learn more about their sense making about the robot and their response to observing others interacting with PARO. This additional information about the participants' views allowed us to understand the effects of situating PARO in a public context beyond just the immediate interaction.

3.3.2 Staff Interviews

We conducted interviews early on in and after the study with eight staff members who were picked either because their office was near the field sites or because they came to the field sites in the beginning of our study. The interviewees were three general affair staff, one social worker, one nurse, two occupational therapists, and two recreational therapists. Only the two recreational therapists had long-term experience with PARO, two other interviewees had heard about the robot prior to this study, and one interviewee had interacted briefly with PARO.

The interviews were semi-structured, and probed the staff's ideas about robotic technology and their perceptions of PARO. The goal was to find out whether the staff's perception of PARO would be affected by exposure to the robot being used in the public areas of the nursing home. In the pre-interview, we asked about their general impression of robots, their understanding and perception of PARO, their ideas about future robots, and how they want robots to work for and relate to them. In the post-interview, we asked again about their general perspectives on robots and PARO in particular, and talked about potential applications of PARO.

3.4 Data Analysis

We analyzed field notes collected during 35 sessions and the formal and informal interviews with staff, residents, and visitors to find salient patterns and themes in the interactions, particularly focusing on identifying social factors that affected the observed human-robot interaction. We used an anthropological approach for our qualitative data analysis (Figure 2) and focused on finding behavioral regularity in the documented interactions that could be expressed as patterns [19]. In order to discover the patterns, we coded our field notes and interviews in an open-ended manner [20] using a flexible and extendable coding schema.

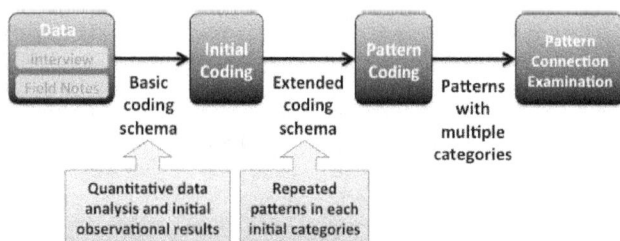

Figure 2. Data Analysis Process.

In the initial analysis, we developed a basic coding schema based on features that were easily identifiable in field observations (e.g., gender, group/individual interaction) and based on the analysis of quantitative data (e.g., interactor type). This gave us codes such as gender (female or male), interactor type (resident, staff, or visitor), group or individual interaction, direct or indirect interaction with PARO, long or brief interaction, ignoring PARO, and other people's intervention during PARO interaction. By

reviewing the categorized and grouped field notes and interview transcriptions, we found some other recurring phenomena and developed an extended coding schema. This included mediation type (staff, family, or resident), interaction of a couple, individual interaction patterns of frequent interactors, changes in interaction and perception of PARO, and scientific and relational framing of talking about PARO. We applied these new codes to the data in the pattern coding stage, while continuing to identify new codes and using them to analyze the data until we were satisfied that we had described the main reoccurring patterns and their frequency. We finally reviewed interactions across patterns grouped in different categories to find any connections between them.

4. FINDINGS

The quantitative analysis of the behavioral data from the study showed that there were few cases of constant and repeated interaction with PARO for more than 10 minutes in a single session [18], and that a majority of people in the field site (59.15%) ignored the robot. Those who did interact with PARO preferred indirect interaction (e.g., observing PARO from a distance) to direct interaction (e.g., touching PARO). People who interacted with PARO directly were more likely to interact non-physically (e.g., looking, smiling, talking) than physically (e.g., petting, hugging). We used our field notes and qualitative data analysis to identify social factors related to these particular patterns of interaction, including those related to the social situation and to the participants' sense making about the robot. We identified four major social factors that affected interaction with PARO in the public space: participant gender, social mediation, individual sense making about PARO, and the influence of exposure to PARO on participant evaluations of PARO in particular and robots more generally.

4.1 Gender Differences in PARO Interaction

In our study, female participants outnumbered the males (M:F=1:3.9), with the discrepancy being particularly noticeable among staff and residents. Despite having more data for female participants, our analysis indicated gender-based differences in interaction with and sense making about PARO. The quantitative data showed that female participants had more direct interaction with PARO (e.g., petting or talking) and male participants usually interacted with PARO indirectly (e.g., eye contact) [18]. Out of 20 high interaction frequency cases, 19 were females.

The qualitative analysis also identified differences in the frequency in which participants of different genders used particular interaction types (coded as direct/indirect and relational/analytical) with PARO. Among participants who had direct interactions with PARO, females usually expressed their appreciation of the robot's appearance and movement in relational terms (e.g., "It's cute!" "Look at its wagging tail!"). Moreover, many female interactors (including residents, staffs, and visitors) talked to PARO as if it was alive (e.g., "Hi, how are you doing?" "You are so cute, dear."), which was not observed with any of the male participants. Of 79 females documented in our field notes who approached PARO for interaction, 63 of them interacted with PARO in this way. The male participants, in turn, displayed a type of interaction with PARO that rarely occurred among female participants. Six out of eight male participants who were documented as interacting with PARO approached the robot to analyze its technical functions. They treated PARO as a toy or tool instead of as a creature. An example of this type of interaction occurred when a couple and their grandson approached PARO. While the wife petted PARO and kept describing how cute it was to the child, the husband asked the researchers who designed the robot and where it was produced. Other male participants asked similar questions: "Is it a robot?" "Who designed it?" "Can it respond to sound?" Turkle calls this analytical framing an "engineer style" interaction [21].

Among participants who interacted with PARO repeatedly, male Resident B (R-B) predominantly showed the "engineer-style." R-B was staying in the nursing home for a few weeks to rehabilitate his legs. When R-B approached PARO for the first time, he observed it from different directions, picked it up and checked its bottom, touched it and saw how it responded, and asked the researcher questions about its functions. After he had learned enough about PARO, he stopped paying attention to it. He showed up a few times in later sessions and played with puzzles next to PARO without looking at it. When other people asked him about PARO, he said it is a robot brought by people from the university.

Our analysis also shows that in 13 of 23 cases when a couple passed through the hallway, it was the female that noticed PARO first and talked to the male about it, while the male showed little to no interest in interacting with it. In one case, a couple quickly passed by the lobby. The wife noticed PARO and excitedly pointed it out to her husband. The husband just commented he had seen it before and did not show much interest. In two other cases, the female partner was excited about PARO and brought their male companion back to the area to show the robot to them. On both occasions, the male stayed in the hallway and looked at their companion petting and talking to PARO from a distance without interacting directly with the robot.

The patterns that emerged from our analysis show participants constructed their interactions with PARO differentially in accordance with their gender, possibly relating them to normative gender roles and behaviors, such as nurturing. This suggests that, beyond focusing on the physical affordances of the robot's design, we should consider social and cultural affordances and how they relate to factors such as gender, as well as possibly race and class.

4.2 Mediation By Other Social Actors

From the PARO video mentioned in the introduction, we expected older adults with dementia to spontaneously and voluntarily start interacting with PARO. On the contrary, in the 35 visits we documented, only three residents got interested in PARO and started interacting with it without any intervention by others. In agreement with Wada's development of PARO use guidelines [5], we found that mediation by other human actors (including staff, visitors, and other residents) generally had a positive effect on the residents' propensity to interact with PARO. In both our pilot study and three-month observation, we identified that residents with dementia were often passive to environmental stimuli. In most cases, even when they noticed PARO, they were hesitant to interact with it without someone to guide them. When the staff and visitors, especially family members of the residents, approached residents who were near PARO and talked to them about the robot or showed them how to pet it, we usually saw the resident become more involved with PARO. The quantitative analysis showed that participants' interactions with PARO lasted longer when they had talked about the robot with others [18], and our observational data showed that many residents had more frequent interaction with PARO following introduction of the robot or mediated interaction by other participants. For example, Resident M (R-M), who was in the late stages of dementia and had severe hearing loss, was initially not interested in PARO. After the staff showed her how to interact with PARO by petting

it and talked to her about the robot's gaze and movements, she started to pet and look at it. Her interest in PARO increased as she interacted with it more and more. In a later session, R-M's family saw PARO and encouraged her to interact with it. R-M started to talk to PARO and even discussed PARO with other residents. Although her hearing problem caused her conversations about PARO to be short, the other residents also started interacting with the robot after the conversation. Similarly, Resident D (R-D) took an occasional look at PARO but swiftly shifted her attention elsewhere. She would show her interest in the robot mainly while other people talked to her about it or there was someone to talk to and PARO could become a conversation starter topic.

In two observed cases of residents having both family and staff mediation while interacting with PARO, we noticed that mediation by family provoked stronger tendencies in residents to continue interacting with the robot. Resident F (R-F) had mild dementia and couldn't remember PARO over sessions. Her first interaction with PARO included an intervention by her daughter, who had seen PARO and thought R-F might like it. She took PARO to R-F and put it on her lap. R-F looked surprised at first, but was quickly engrossed in observing PARO's movements and discussing the robot with her daughter. The second time, a caregiver encouraged R-F to interact with PARO by petting its head and touching its whiskers. R-F only touched it once and seemed hesitant to interact with it further. The caregiver then gave up and turned her attention to a puzzle. While playing with puzzles, R-F looked at PARO and petted it occasionally and with increasing frequency. R-F showed interest in PARO in both sessions, but the family's mediation helped her overcome her uncertainty faster than mediation by the staff.

Another type of mediation we noticed on one occasion was a resident interacting with PARO treated as a model of appropriate interactions to new users. Resident E's (R-E) interaction with PARO led other residents to change their impressions of and start interacting with the robot. R-E enjoyed talking to PARO. She usually approached it and talked to it as if it was a real animal, although she had spoken to researchers about it being a robot. One day, a newcomer saw PARO for the first time and displayed a negative attitude when her family introduced it to her. R-E approached later and started talking to PARO. The new resident observed her interaction, and told her, "You are a nut!" R-E smiled and didn't respond. After R-E left, the newcomer looked at PARO for a while and stopped the staff in the hallway and talked to them about PARO. Then she approached PARO, and started petting it and saying, "Who are you?" "Where are you from?"

The interactions we observed were affected by the social context, which included other actors encouraging and modeling appropriate behavior towards PARO and ascribing social agency to the robot. The relationships the residents built with the robot were therefore dependent not only on the capabilities of the robot and the interactors themselves, but also on the behaviors of other people in the space. This finding echoes Alač et al's [14] description of robotic sociality as constructed in situated interactions with people.

4.3 Individual Sense-Making About PARO

Alongside the general patterns of interactions described above, we found that some residents had more consistent or frequent interactions with PARO. Those residents were all female and long-term residents of the institution. They interacted with PARO numerous times during one visit or in multiple visits. As this type of repeated, long-term interaction provides an opportunity for extended therapeutic effects of the robot, we analyzed successful individual interactions across visits to look for shared patterns. What we found were individualized patterns of interaction, with each resident developing their own way of understanding and using PARO. While one resident used PARO to reflect on personal life problems and emotions, another resident used PARO as a tool to initiate conversations with others, and a third interacted with it as an emotional companion. We describe these three examples below to illustrate how personal interpretations and needs can be interwoven with the practices of PARO's use.

R-E showed great interest in PARO since the first time she saw it; she approached the robot spontaneously and had a long talk with it. She interacted with PARO in exploratory as well as reflective ways. She asked PARO, instead of the staff and researchers, many questions to figure out what it is (e.g., "Who are you?" "Are you a cat or a dog?"), its behavior and history (e.g., "Are you looking at me?" "Are you sleepy?" "Did they mistreat you?"), and its emotions (e.g., "Are you mad at me?" "Are you sad?" "You want me to leave?"). Her conversations with PARO reflected some personal history and emotions. Because she was a newcomer at the nursing home, in her first talk to PARO, she portrayed a sense of abandonment "Did they go off and leave you here? My son left me here. I want to go home, but I can't. They don't want me to stay with them." "Do you feel lonely? I feel lonely, too." She also projected her feelings about herself in comparison to PARO, such as "You are so pretty. I don't want to touch you. My hands are old." The way R-E talked to PARO was like talking to a pet, but she preferred to talk to PARO even when there was a therapy dog in the vicinity. When we interviewed one of our key informants, a therapist, she mentioned R-E liked to talk to people and she was still in the progress of adapting to her new environment. In R-E's case, she interacted with PARO socially, but also released her frustrations implicitly to the robot. For her, PARO seemed to function not only as a companion but also as a confidant.

As a dog lover, Resident J (R-J) approached PARO similarly to how she treated the therapy dog in the nursing home. She called PARO "woofie," and petted its head. She also talked to the robot about what she was doing, such as "I'm waiting for supper." When she approached PARO, half of the time there were other residents around. Many residents suffered from hearing loss or dementia and most of the time R-J did not get a response to her talk and left. Her interactions with PARO were usually very short. Even though there was no response to her talk, R-J repeated the behaviors every time she greeted PARO. In one session, R-D responded to R-J's talk with PARO, and they had a long conversation ranging in topic from PARO to their backgrounds and ages. During that time, R-J still interacted with PARO by looking or petting it occasionally. In this session, her interaction was five times longer than any individual interaction she had with PARO. PARO, for R-J, was either a conversational partner or a way to initiate conversation with others. The latter point supports prior research describing PARO as a social mediator [17].

In our preliminary observations in the field sites, we found that R-D enjoyed social interaction with people. She sought out chances to have conversations with the staff, resident, or visitors, but it was not easy for her to find new people to chat with and maintain a conversation. R-D was first introduced to PARO in the previous group study with PARO, but usually forgot the robot by the next visit due the memory loss caused by dementia. R-D tended to show her interest in PARO when it presented a chance to have social interaction with other people. In one visit, R-D found PARO and petted it while observing the researchers' reaction to

her interaction and having a conversation with the researcher about it. Once the researchers stopped talking to her, she quickly lost interests in PARO and paid attention to other things. In another visit, R-D started off by ignoring PARO and watching TV. When two staff approached PARO and her, and talked to her about how cute it was, she started petting the robot and happily conversed with the staff. Shortly after the staff left, she lost interest in PARO again. For R-D, PARO functioned as a tool to generate desired social interaction with other people.

In our study, R-M was the person who interacted with PARO the longest. She had advanced dementia and a serious hearing impairment. Unlike R-E, she interacted with PARO quietly by looking at and following PARO's movement by nodding her head. R-M struggled with sleepiness due to her dementia, but she consistently interacted with PARO and was fully engaged visually with it between periods of dozing. Staff and family recognized her attachment to PARO, and had her interact with PARO at any chance possible. However, toward the end of our study, R-M's interaction decreased over time. She got distracted by TV shows and did not fully concentrate on PARO. Even then she did not stop interacting with PARO, but maintained a more implicit connection. While watching TV or napping, R-M put her hand over PARO or looked at PARO occasionally for a short period. She still showed her affection by smiling any time she saw PARO. While she showed much excitement in the beginning, later on companionship with PARO merged into her daily routines. R-M's interaction shows the dynamic properties of interpretative flexibility and the social shaping process, as well as the ebb and flow of relationships that robot designers need to accommodate.

In these individual examples, all participants treated PARO as a "relational artifact" [21] but socialized with the robot in varied ways that fit their own needs. This was made possible by the interpretative flexibility of PARO's design, which enabled participants to "enlarge the number of functions" it performed to accommodate their interests and needs.

4.4 Organizational Influence of PARO Use
Along with observing how different social actors behaved towards and made sense of PARO, we found that public exposure to PARO in the nursing home caused a ripple effect in terms of perceptions of PARO's use beyond the immediate interactors. The visible interactions residents had with PARO not only shaped the ways the staff treated residents by having them interact with the robot, but also enabled the staff to developed new ideas and practices of using PARO in their work.

R-E and R-M, as mentioned previously, were very actively involved in interaction with PARO. Their interactions with PARO not only caught the staff's attention but also encouraged discussion about the interactions among staff. In one session, as R-M followed PARO's head movement nodding her head, one nurse, one recreational therapist, one nurse assistant, and one general staff talked in a circle as they observed her interaction with PARO from a distance. They quietly made comments about how cute R-M's reaction to and affection toward PARO were. They also discussed PARO's positive effects on R-E. In later sessions, we observed a few different groups of staff and visitors positively commenting on R-E's and R-M's interactions with PARO. At the same time, we observed minor changes in the staff's daily routines. Normally, the staff would settle some of the residents in the activity area after recreational activities, moving incoming residents to any free space around the table. After observing R-M's interaction with PARO, the staff would put R-E next to PARO, or in a spot where the robot was reachable. Some occupational therapists also started showing PARO to their patients as they did walking rehabilitation in the hallway.

Some staff we interviewed before and after the study showed changes in their general perceptions of robots after observing the residents' interactions with PARO. Two out of eight staff members described robots in functional and mechanical ways in the pre-interview. They considered robots as tools providing physical help to humans. Both of them were not familiar with PARO before the study, but passed by the field sites frequently during the study. When interviewed after the study, they mentioned gaining a new understanding of robots and what they could do beyond heavy duty lifting or cleaning. They discussed that robots, like PARO, could also be companions for children or elderly. Six months after completing the field study, in an interview with the therapist who continued to work with PARO after the study, we learned that the public exposure to PARO had changed some people's perception of the robot and many staff recognized other ways to use PARO in their work. She said some staff who initially thought PARO was a toy had more positive reactions to its therapeutic effects after observing the residents interacting with PARO. Moreover, some staff, such as the nurses, started borrowing PARO to comfort anxious dementia residents or as a social companion during individual sessions with residents.

These results show a long-term effect of exposure to PARO in the nursing home. The residents' interaction with PARO impacted the staff's daily routines and their conceptions of robots, which in turn supported further interactions between residents and PARO. This feedback loop was visible due to the long-term nature of our study, but is crucial for institutional adoption of robots.

5. DISCUSSION

The purpose of our study, in accordance with the social shaping of technology framework, was to shift the focus of human-robot interaction analysis from the robot-interactor dyad to a broader social context that involves multiple social actors, the social and physical environment, and dynamic interactions among them. The social shaping framework allowed us to identify essential social factors and actors that supported the successful interaction of elderly nursing home residents with PARO, and to see how the robot's interpretive flexibility allowed it to be incorporated in different kinds of interactions. Along with other human-robot interaction studies in a broader context [6, 7, 8], our use of social shaping theory provides an alternative model for exploring the complexity of HRI in a dynamic everyday setting. This approach can be particularly useful in figuring out how robots should be integrated into social institutions, and in identifying social factors that future robot designs should take into consideration.

Our study identified different ways in which social factors shaped how participants interacted with PARO. Effects of participant gender, which emerged in our study in relation to different interaction styles participants displayed toward PARO, have been previously noted in research on assistive robots for eldercare [22]. Our study suggests that socially normative gender roles and related behaviors, such as nurturing or tinkering with technology, were reflected in people's perceptions of PARO and their interactions with it. We also found that the individual history and needs of participants, as well as their current social relationships, influenced how they interacted with PARO, which has been previously noted by Turkle [21]. Additionally, PARO's interpretive flexibility and underdetermined design, mentioned as part of its deliberate design logic in Section 2.2, left open the

possibility for participants to develop diverse ways of using and interacting with the robot. Mutlu and Forlizzi's study of a service robot's use in a hospital [7] similarly showed users developing varying perceptions of the robot depending on the context of use and their role in the organization; however, the robot's design was not flexible enough to enable users to successfully adapt it to different situations. Our findings with PARO suggest that, particularly in cases where robots might be used by diverse users (such as the older adults, staff, and visitors in this study) and in different contexts, leaving space for multiple interpretations as a design criterion can increase the spectrum of successful interactions and allow interaction to expand the robot's functions.

As in previous studies (e.g. [8]), we saw interactions in the real world often involved and affected groups of participants rather than being limited to one-on-one interactions between a person and a robot. Participants' interactions with PARO were affected by the behaviors and perspectives of other actors (similar to [14]), as well as social norms and expectations. We saw a positive feedback loop occur between mediation provided by staff and residents leading to successful interactions, the public visibility of successful interactions and increasing ease that residents showed toward the robot, and growing interest and commitment of residents and staff to using the robot. This further supports the need to take a more holistic perspective when trying to understand the factors that influence long-term interactions between participants and a new robotic technology, and its institutional adoption. Lee et al [23] similarly documented that observing successful and unsuccessful interactions with the Snackbot inspired participants to try new ways of interacting with the robot, and also created new social contacts among participants and non-participants. Limiting the scope of research to direct interaction with the robot can cause us to ignore such indirect effects and behaviors that shape interactions, which we also noticed in prior studies of PARO's use in group therapy activities [17].

In contrast to a design focus on the attributes of individual robots (e.g., appearance, functions), our work suggests a need to shift to designing the human-robot interaction system or experience as a whole. This means constructing affordances and interaction possibilities that the robot can provide so that its functions can be added to and amended through interaction, and also identifying specific interaction patterns and modes of implementation of the robot that lead to successful user experiences. PARO's underspecified yet socially evocative cues (e.g. a familiar animal shape that suggests pet-like interaction without evoking specific expectations from the interaction) enabled diverse users to make sense of the robot and adopt it in their own way. In terms of the integration of novel technologies such as robots into eldercare contexts, our research further suggests that providing appropriate mediation (someone to introduce the robot, or model its appropriate use) is a necessary component for ensuring successful interaction for more people. We suggest designing robots with the assumption that they will need to be supported by humans to some degree, rather than that they will be autonomous, and in the process making sure that the level and kind of support the robot needs is acceptable to and can be performed by potential users in the course of their everyday activities.

Focusing on the ways in which different social actors affect the robot's interpretation and use also has ethical consequences for design and research in assistive robotics. Staff and older adults are often studied as users of technology, rather than active creators of its effects. We show they do important work to scaffold and construct the robot's sociality and its therapeutic function. This perspective focuses attention on people's agency, rather than just on the consequences of robotic technology, and suggests we need to pay more explicit attention to the involvement of users in implementing robots and continually scaffolding human-robot interaction.

Our study is limited by its focus on one robot, the nursing home as a specific context of use, and the particular nature of the participants (older adults with dementia, busy nursing staff). The specific social factors we identified may therefore not be salient for a different robot or environment. Our study, however, makes a general contribution to human-robot interaction by providing a theoretical framework and qualitative method for identifying and analyzing the social aspects of technology use that can inform the design and implementation of other assistive robots.

6. CONCLUSION

Adding to previous HRI research on interactions between people and robots situated in real-world settings, this work provides a new theoretical perspective that extends beyond dyadic human-robot interaction and can guide the study of the social factors that support the successful use of robotic technologies. The results suggested four key social factors—gender, mediation by staff and family, individual interpretations of PARO, and the feedback effects of observing interactions between residents and PARO that inspired other social actors to support the robot's adoption—which fostered the social shaping process of PARO's implementation in the nursing home. Our results and application of social shaping to HRI suggest that the analytical unit of HRI research should be expanded to include other social actors in the environment that scaffold interaction with and adoption of robots.

7. ACKNOWLEDGMENTS

This research was supported by NSF grant number IIS-1143712. We are grateful to the participants and nursing home staff for their assistance, and to P. Lopes, and M. Grant for their help in implementing the study.

8. REFERENCES

[1] Shibata, T. and Wada, K. 2011. Robot therapy: A new approach for mental healthcare of the elderly – A mini-review. *Gerontology*. 57, 4, 378–386.

[2] Kawaguchi, Y., Wada, K., Okamoto, M., Tsujii, T., Shibata, T. and Sakatani, K. 2012. Investigation of brain activity after interaction with seal robot measured by fNIRS. *Proc. of RO-MAN 2012*, 571–576.

[3] Wada, K., Shibata, T., Saito, T., Sakamoto, K. and Tanie, K. 2005. Psychological and social effects of one year robot assisted activity on elderly people at a health service facility for the aged. *Proc. of ICRA 2005*, 2785–2790.

[4] Wada, K., Shibata, T., Saito, T. and Tanie, K. 2004. Effects of robot-assisted activity for elderly people and nurses at a day service center. *Proc. of IROS 2004*, 1780–1788.

[5] Wada, K., Ikeda, Y., Inoue, K. and Uehara, R. 2010. Development and preliminary evaluation of a caregiver's manual for robot therapy using the therapeutic seal robot Paro. *Proc. of RO-MAN 2010*, 533–538

[6] Forlizzi, J. and DiSalvo, C. 2006. Service robots in the domestic environment: a study of the roomba vacuum in the home. *Proc. of HRI'06*, 258–265.

[7] Mutlu, B. and Forlizzi, J. 2008. Robots in organizations: The role of workflow, social, and environmental factors in human-robot interaction. *Proc. of HRI'08*, 287–294.

[8] Šabanović, S., Michalowski, M.P. and Simmons, R. 2006. Robots in the wild: Observing human-robot social interaction outside the lab. *Proc. AMC 2006*, 596–601.

[9] Wada, K. and Shibata, T. 2007. Living with seal robots-Its sociopsychological and physiological influences on the elderly at a care house. *IEEE Transactions on Robotics*. 23, 5, 972–980.

[10] Šabanović, S. 2010. Robots in society, society in robots: Mutual shaping of society and technology as a framework for social robot design. *International Journal of Social Robotics*. 2, 4, 439–450.

[11] Bijker, W.E., Hughes, T.P., Pinch, T., and Douglas, D.G. 2012. *The Social Construction of Technological Systems: New Directions in the Sociology and History of Technology*. MIT Press.

[12] Oudshoorn, N. and Pinch, T. 2003. *How Users Matter: The Co-Construction of Users and Technology*. MIT Press.

[13] MacKenzie, D. and Wajcman, J. 1999. *The Social Shaping of Technology*. Open University Press.

[14] Alač, M., Movellan, J. and Tanaka, F. 2011. When a robot is social: Spatial arrangements and multimodal semiotic engagement in the practice of social robotics. *Social Studies of Science*. 41, 6, 893–926.

[15] Siino, R.M. and Hinds, P.J. 2005. Robots, gender sensemaking: Sex segregation - Impact on workers making sense of a mobile autonomous robot. *Proc. ICRA 2005*, 2773–2778.

[16] Vertesi, J. 2012. Seeing like a rover: Visualization, embodiment, and interaction on the Mars Exploration Rover mission. *Social Studies of Science*. 42, 3, 393-414.

[17] Chang, W.-L., Šabanović, S., and Huber, L. 2013. Situated analysis of interactions between cognitively impaired older adults and the therapeutic robot PARO. *Proc. of ICSR 2013*, 371–380.

[18] Chang, W.-L., Šabanović, S., and Huber, L. 2014. Observational study of naturalistic interactions with the socially assistive robot PARO in a nursing home. *Proc. of RO MAN 2014*, 294 299.

[19] Miles, M.B. and Huberman, A.M. 1994. *Qualitative Data Analysis: An Expanded Sourcebook*. Sage.

[20] Emerson, R.M., Fretz, R.I., and Shaw, L.L. 2011. *Writing Ethnographic Fieldnotes*. University of Chicago Press.

[21] Turkle, S., Taggart, W., Kidd, C.D. and Dasté, O. 2006. Relational artifacts with children and elders: the complexities of cybercompanionship. *Connection Science*. 18, 4, 347–361.

[22] Broadbent, E., Stafford, R., and MacDonald, B. 2009. Acceptance of healthcare robots for the older population: Review and future directions. *International Journal of Social Robotics,* 1: 319-330.

[23] Lee, M.K., Kiesler, S., Forlizzi, J., and Rybski, P. 2012. Ripple effects of an embedded social agent: A field study of a social robot in the workplace. *Proc. of CHI 2012*, 695–70

Author Index

www.ingramcontent.com/pod-product-compliance
Lightning Source LLC
Chambersburg PA
CBHW080715220326
41598CB00033B/5432